AutoCAD 13 Instructor

James A. Leach
University of Louisville

IRWIN
GRAPHICS
SERIES

IRWIN

Chicago • Bogotá • Boston • Buenos Aires • Caracas
London • Madrid • Mexico City • Sydney • Toronto

Dedication

"You can accomplish anything
you make up your mind to. . ."

Norman G. Leach
to whom this book is dedicated

© Richard D. Irwin, a Times Mirror Higher Education Group, Inc. company, 1996

Irwin Book Team

Publisher:	*Tom Casson*
Senior sponsoring editor:	*Elizabeth A. Jones*
Marketing manager:	*Brian Kibby*
Project editor:	*Beth Cigler*
Production supervisor:	*Pat Frederickson*
Manager, prepress:	*Kim Meriwether*
Cover image:	*Autodesk, Inc.*
Compositor:	*Interactive Composition Corporation*
Printer:	*Malloy Lithographing, Inc.*

Times Mirror
Higher Education Group

Library of Congress Cataloging-in-Publication Data

```
Leach, James A.
  AutoCAD 13 instructor / James A. Leach
    p.   cm. -- (Irwin graphics series)
  Includes index.
  ISBN 0-256-19445-9
  1. Computer graphics.  2. AutoCAD (Computer file)  I. Title
II. Series
  T365.L38263  1996                          95-45018
  620'.0042'028555369--dc20
```

Printed in the United States of America
1 2 3 4 5 6 7 8 9 0 ML 1 0 9 8 7 6 5

The Irwin Graphics Series

Providing you with the highest quality textbooks that meet your changing needs requires feedback, improvement, and revision. The team of authors and Richard D. Irwin Publishers are committed to this effort. We invite you to become part of our team by offering your wishes, suggestions, and comments for future editions and new products and texts.

Please mail or fax your comments to: Jim Leach
c/o Richard D. Irwin Publishers
1333 Burr Ridge Parkway
Burr Ridge, IL 60521
fax 708-789-6946

TITLES IN THE IRWIN GRAPHICS SERIES INCLUDE:

Engineering Graphics Communication by Bertoline, Wiebe, Miller, and Nasman, 1995

Technical Graphics Communication by Bertoline, Wiebe, Miller, and Nasman, 1995

Fundamentals of Graphics Communication by Bertoline, Wiebe, Miller, and Nasman, 1996

Problems for Engineering Graphics Communication and Technical Graphics Communication, Workbook #1, 1995

Problems for Engineering Graphics Communication and Technical Graphics Communication, Workbook #2, 1995

Problems for Engineering Graphics Communication and Technical Graphics Communication, Workbook #3, 1995

AutoCAD Instructor Release 12 by James A. Leach, 1995

AutoCAD Companion Release 12 by James A. Leach, 1995

AutoCAD 13 Instructor by James A. Leach, 1996

AutoCAD 13 Companion by James A. Leach, 1996

CADKEY Companion by John Cherng, 1995

Hands-On CADKEY by Timothy Sexton, 1995

Engineering Design and Visualization Workbook by Dennis Stevenson, 1995

Preface

AutoCAD 13 Instructor is written to instruct you in the full range of AutoCAD Release 13 features. The best possible means are used to communicate the concepts, commands, and applications in a printed format. Because the subject of this book is graphical, illustrations (totaling over 1200 for the book) are used whenever possible to communicate an idea. The objective is to provide a printed medium for you to learn AutoCAD, even in the case that you have no other help. This book is your AutoCAD instructor.

AutoCAD 13 Instructor is presented in a pedagogical format by delivering the fundamental concepts first, then moving toward the more advanced and specialized features of AutoCAD. The book begins with small pieces of information explained in a simple form and then builds on that experience to deliver more complex ideas, requiring a synthesis of earlier concepts. The chapter exercises follow the same progression, beginning with a simple tutorial approach and ending with more challenging problems requiring a synthesis of earlier exercises.

AutoCAD 13 Instructor teaches you both the DOS and Windows versions of AutoCAD Release 13. Although most of the commands operate similarly in the DOS and the Windows versions, differences in accessing or using the commands are explained.

AutoCAD 13 Instructor is helpful if you are already an AutoCAD user but upgrading from a previous release to Release 13. All new Release 13 commands, concepts, features, and variables are denoted by a "R13" vertical bar on the edges of the pages. In this way, the book provides a useful reference to all AutoCAD topics, but allows you to easily locate the new Release 13 features.

AutoCAD 13 Instructor is a useful reference guide to AutoCAD. A complete index gives an alphabetical listing of all AutoCAD commands, command options, system variables, and concepts discussed. Every command is explained in simple terms and given with a "Command Table" listing the possible methods of invoking the command.

AutoCAD 13 Instructor is for both professionals and students in the fields of engineering, architecture, design, construction, manufacturing, and any other field that has a use for AutoCAD. Applications and examples from many fields are given throughout the text. The applications and examples are not intended to have an inclination towards a particular field. Instead, applications to a particular field are used when they best explain an idea or use of a command.

AutoCAD 13 Instructor serves as a companion to other application-specific books. Whether your application is engineering, architecture, design, construction, or manufacturing, *AutoCAD 13 Instructor* discusses the AutoCAD concepts and commands you need to generate CAD drawings or 3D models for your application. *AutoCAD 13 Instructor* provides a link between AutoCAD commands and engineering graphics concepts by including **CAD References** for *Engineering Graphics Communication* and *Technical Graphics Communication* by Bertoline, et al.

I predict you will have a positive experience learning AutoCAD. Although learning AutoCAD is not a trivial endeavor, you will have fun learning this exciting technology. In fact, I predict that more than once in your learning experience you will say to yourself, "Cool!" (or something to that effect).

James A. Leach

ABOUT THE AUTHOR

James A. Leach (B.I.D., M.Ed.) is an associate professor of engineering graphics at the University of Louisville. He began teaching AutoCAD at Auburn University early in 1984 using Version 1.4, the first version of AutoCAD to operate on IBM personal computers. Jim is currently the director and primary instructor at the AutoCAD Training Center (ATC) at the University of Louisville, one of the first fifteen centers to be authorized by Autodesk, having been established in 1985.

Jim has published numerous journal and magazine articles, workbooks, and textbooks about AutoCAD and engineering graphics instruction. He has designed facilities and written AutoCAD- related course materials for Auburn University, University of Louisville, the ATC at the University of Louisville, and several two-year and community colleges. Jim is the author of four AutoCAD books published by Irwin.

CONTRIBUTING AUTHORS

Dr. Patrick McCuistion is an assistant professor of Industrial Technology at Ohio University. Dr. McCuistion taught three years at Texas A&M University and previously worked in various engineering design, drafting, and checking positions at several manufacturing industries. He has provided instruction in geometric dimensioning and tolerancing to many industry, military, and educational institutions, as well as prepared several articles and presentations on the topic. Dr. McCuistion is an active member in several ANSI subcommittees, including Y14.5 Dimensioning and Tolerancing, Y14.3 Multiview and Section View Drawings, Y14.35 Revisions, Y14.36 Surface Texture, and B89.3.6 Functional Gages. Dr. McCuistion contributed the material on geometric dimensioning and tolerancing for *AutoCAD 13 Instructor*.

Michael E. Beall is the owner of Computer Aided Management and Planning in Shelbyville, Kentucky. Michael offers contract services and professional training on AutoCAD as well as CAP and CAP.Spex from Sweets Group, a division of McGraw-Hill. He is the co-author of *AutoCAD Release 13 for Beginners* from New Riders Publishing and the *AutoCAD Release 13 for the Professional: Level I* courseware for New Riders to be certified for use at Autodesk Authorized Training Centers. Michael has been presenting CAD training seminars to architects and engineers since 1982 and is currently an instructor at the University of Louisville ATC. He received a Bachelor of Architecture degree from the University of Cincinnati. Michael Beall assisted with several topics in *AutoCAD 13 Instructor*, including the geometric calculator, slides and scripts, layer filters, toolbar customization, and point filters.

Steven H. Baldock is an engineer at a consulting firm in Louisville and operates a CAD consulting firm, Infinity Computer Enterprises (ICE). Steve also teaches five courses at the University of Louisville AutoCAD Training Center. He has eight years experience using AutoCAD in architectural, civil, and structural design applications. Steve has degrees in engineering, computer science, and mathematics. Steve is also a contributing author for *AutoCAD 13 Companion* by James A. Leach. Contact Steve at 102661.1706@COMPUSERVE.COM. Steve Baldock prepared material for *AutoCAD 13 Instructor* for the sections on xrefs, groups, text, multiline drawing and editing, and dimensioning. Steve also created several hundred figures for *AutoCAD 13 Instructor*.

ACKNOWLEDGMENTS

I want to thank all of the contributing authors for their assistance in writing *AutoCAD 13 Instructor*. Without their help, this text could not have been as application-specific nor could it have been completed in the short time frame. I especially want to thank Steven H. Baldock for his valuable input and hard work on this book.

I am very grateful to Gary Bertoline for his foresight in conceiving the Irwin Graphics Series and for including my efforts in it.

I would like to give thanks to the excellent group at Richard D. Irwin, Inc. who gave their talents and support during this project, especially Betsy Jones, Kelley Butcher, Beth Cigler, and Brian Kibby. My experience with Irwin continues to be positive and productive.

Barry Bergin of Interactive Composition Corporation and Karen Collins and Bryan Chamberlain of The Cobb Group deserve much credit for the layout and design of *AutoCAD 13 Instructor*. They were instrumental in fulfilling my objective of providing the most direct and readable format for conveying concepts.

I also acknowledge: my colleague and friend, Robert A. Matthews, for his support in all the important things; Charles Grantham of Contemporary Publishing Company of Raleigh, Inc., for generosity and consultation; and Speed Scientific School Dean's Office for support and encouragement.

Thanks again to my wife, Donna, for the many hours of copy editing required to produce this and the other texts.

TRADEMARK AND COPYRIGHT ACKNOWLEDGMENTS

The object used in the Wireframe Modeling Tutorial, Chapter 36 appears courtesy of James H. Earle, *Graphics for Engineers, Third Edition*, (pg. 120) ©1992 by Addison-Wesley Publishing Company, Inc. Reprinted by permission of the publisher.

The following drawings used for Chapter Exercises appear courtesy of James A. Leach, *Problems in Engineering Graphics Fundamentals*, *Series A* and *Series B*, ©1984 and 1985 by Contemporary Publishing Company of Raleigh, Inc.: Gasket A, Gasket B, Pulley, Holder, Angle Brace, Saddle, V-Block, Bar Guide, Cam Shaft, Bearing, Cylinder, Support Bracket, Corner Brace, and Adjustable Mount. Reprinted or redrawn by permission of the publisher.

ASE, ADI, AME, ADS, ACAD, DXF, Autodesk, AutoCAD, AutoCAD Designer, AutoVision, AutoSurf, AutoCAD Training Center, and AutoLISP are registered trademarks of Autodesk, Inc. All AutoCAD sample drawings appearing throughout the text are reprinted courtesy of Autodesk, Inc. Windows, Notepad, MS-DOS, and MS-DOS Edit are registered trademarks of Microsoft Corporation. WordPerfect is a registered trademark of WordPerfect Corporation. Norton Editor is a registered trademark of S. Reifel & Company. City Blueprint, Country Blueprint, EuroRoman, EuroRoman-oblique, PanRoman, SuperFrench, Romantic, Romantic-bold, Sans Serif, Sans Serif-bold, Sans Serif-oblique, Sans Serif-BoldOblique, Technic Technic-light, and Technic-bold are Type 1 fonts, copyright 1992 P. B. Payne.

LEGEND

The following special treatment of characters and fonts in the textual content is intended to assist you in translating the meaning of words or sentences in the ***AutoCAD Companion***.

<u>Underline</u>	Emphasis of a word or an idea.
Helvetica font	An AutoCAD prompt appearing on the <u>screen</u> at the command line.
Italic (Upper and Lower)	An AutoCAD command, option, menu, or dialogue box name.
UPPER CASE	A file name.
UPPER CASE ITALIC	An AutoCAD system variable or a drawing aid (*OSNAP*, *SNAP*, *GRID*, *ORTHO*, and *COORDS*).

Anything in **Bold** represents user input:

`Bold`	What you should <u>type</u> or press on the keyboard.
`Bold Italic`	An AutoCAD <u>command</u> that you should type or <u>menu item</u> that you should select.
`BOLD UPPER CASE`	A <u>file name</u> that you should type.
`BOLD UPPER CASE ITALIC`	A <u>system variable</u> that you should type.
`PICK`	Move the cursor to the indicated position on the screen and press the <u>select</u> button (button #1).

Table of Contents

Introduction

WHAT IS CAD?

CAD is an acronym for Computer-Aided Design or Computer-Aided Drafting. CAD allows you to accomplish design and drafting activities using a computer. A CAD software package, such as AutoCAD, enables you to create designs and generate drawings to document those designs.

Design is a broad field involving the process of making an idea into a real product or system. The design process requires repeated refinement of an idea or ideas until a solution results—a manufactured product or constructed system. Traditionally, design involves the use of sketches, drawings, renderings, 2-dimensional and 3-dimensional models, prototypes, testing, analysis, and documentation. Drafting is generally known as the production of drawings that are used to document a design for manufacturing or construction or to archive the design.

CAD is a <u>tool</u> that can be used for design and drafting activities. CAD can be used to make "rough" idea drawings, although it is more suited to creating accurate finish drawings and renderings. CAD can be used to create a 2-dimensional or 3-dimensional computer model of the product or system for further analysis and testing by other computer programs. In addition, CAD can be used to supply manufacturing equipment such as lathes, mills, laser cutters, or rapid prototyping equipment with numerical data to manufacture a product. CAD is also used to create the 2-dimensional documentation drawings for communicating and archiving the design.

The tangible result of CAD activity is usually a drawing generated by a plotter or printer, but can be a rendering of a model or numerical data for use with another software package or manufacturing device. Regardless of the purpose for using CAD, the resulting drawing or model is stored in a CAD file. The file consists of numeric data in binary form usually saved to a magnetic device such as a diskette, hard disk, or tape.

WHY SHOULD YOU USE CAD?

Although there are other methods used for design and drafting activities, CAD offers the following advantages over other methods in many cases:

1. Accuracy

2. Productivity for repetitive operations

3. Sharing the CAD file with other software programs

Accuracy
Since CAD technology is based on computers, it offers great accuracy compared to traditional "manual" methods of drafting and design. When you draw with a CAD system, the graphical elements, such as lines, arcs, and circles, are stored in the CAD file as numeric data. CAD systems store that numeric data with great precision. For example, AutoCAD stores values with fourteen significant digits. The value 1, for example, is stored in scientific notation as the equivalent of 1.0000000000000. This precision provides you with the ability to create designs and drawings that are 100% accurate for almost every case.

Productivity for Repetitive Operations
It may be faster to create a simple "rough" drawing, such as a sketch by hand (pencil and paper), than it would by using a CAD system. However, for larger and more complex drawings, particularly those involving similar shapes or repetitive operations, CAD methods are very efficient. Any kind of shape or operation accomplished with the CAD system can be easily duplicated since it is stored in a CAD file. In

short, it may take some time to set up the first drawing and create some of the initial geometry, but any of the existing geometry or drawing setups can be easily duplicated in the current drawing or for new drawings.

Likewise, making changes to a CAD file (known as editing) is generally much faster than making changes to a traditional manual drawing. Since all the graphical elements in a CAD drawing are stored, only the affected components of the design or drawing need to be altered, and the drawing can be plotted or printed again or converted to other formats.

As CAD and the associated technology advance and software becomes more interconnected, more productive developments are available. For example, it is possible to make a change to a 3-dimensional model that automatically causes a related change in the linked 2-dimensional engineering drawing, or changing a value in a spreadsheet can automatically cause a related change in the design drawings. One of the main advantages of these technological advances is productivity.

Sharing the CAD File with Other Software Programs

Of course, CAD is not the only form of industrial activity that is making technological advances. Most industries use computer software to increase capability and productivity. Since software is written using digital information and may be written for the same or similar computer operating systems, it is possible and desirable to make software programs with the ability to share data or even interconnect, possibly appearing simultaneously on one screen.

For example, word processing programs can generate text that can be imported into a drawing file, or a drawing can be created and imported into a text file as an illustration. (This book is a result of that capability.) A drawing created with a CAD system such as AutoCAD can be exported to a finite element analysis program that can read the computer model and compute and analyze stresses. CAD files can be dynamically "linked" to spreadsheets or databases in such a way that changing a value in a spreadsheet or text in a database can automatically make the related change in the drawing, or vice versa.

Another advance in CAD technology is the automatic creation and interconnectivity of a 2-dimensional drawing and a 3-dimensional model in one CAD file. With this tool, you can design a 3-dimensional model and have the 2-dimensional drawings automatically generated. The resulting set has bi-directional associativity; that is, a change in either the 2-dimensional drawings or the 3-dimensional model is automatically updated in the other.

CAD, however, may not be the best tool for every design related activity. For example, CAD may help develop ideas, but probably won't replace the idea sketch, at least not with present technology. A 3-dimensional CAD model can save much time and expense for some analysis and testing, but cannot replace the "feel" of an actual model, at least not until virtual reality technology is developed and refined.

With everything considered, CAD offers many opportunities for increased accuracy, productivity, and interconnectivity. Considering the speed at which this technology is advancing, many more opportunities are rapidly obtainable. However, we need to start with the basics. Beginning by learning to create an AutoCAD drawing is a good start.

WHY USE AutoCAD?

CAD systems are available for a number of computer platforms: laptops, personal computers (PCs), workstations, and mainframes. AutoCAD, offered to the public in late 1982, was one of the first PC-based CAD software products. Since that time, it has grown to be the world leader in market share for

<u>all</u> CAD products. At the time of this writing, Autodesk, the manufacturer of AutoCAD, is the fifth largest software producer in the world.

Learning AutoCAD offers a number of advantages to you. Since AutoCAD is the most widely used CAD software, using it gives you the highest probability of being able to share CAD files and related data and information with others.

As a student, your learning AutoCAD, as opposed to learning another CAD software product, gives you a higher probability of using your skills in industry. Likewise, there are more employers who use AutoCAD than any other single CAD system. In addition, learning AutoCAD as a first CAD system gives you a good foundation for learning other CAD packages because many concepts and commands introduced by AutoCAD are utilized by other systems. In some cases, AutoCAD features become industry standards. The .DXF file format, for example, was introduced by Autodesk and has become an industry standard for CAD file conversion between systems.

As a professional, using AutoCAD gives you the highest possibility that you can share CAD files and related data with your colleagues, vendors, and clients. Compatibility of hardware and software is an important issue in industry. Maintaining compatible hardware and software allows you the highest probability for sharing data and information with others as well as offering you flexibility in experimenting with and utilizing the latest technological advancements. AutoCAD provides you with the greatest compatibility in the CAD domain.

This introduction is not intended as a selling point, but to remind you of the importance and potential of the task you are about to undertake. If you are a professional or a student, you have most likely already made up your mind that you want to learn to use AutoCAD as a design or drafting tool. If you have made up your mind, then you can accomplish anything. Let's begin.

Chapter 1

GETTING STARTED

Chapter Objectives

After completing this chapter you should:

1. understand how the X, Y, Z coordinate system is used to define the location of drawing elements in digital format in a CAD drawing file;

2. understand why you should create drawings full size in the actual units with CAD;

3. be able to start AutoCAD to begin drawing;

4. recognize the areas of the AutoCAD Drawing Editor and know the function of each;

5. be able to use the five methods of entering commands;

6. be able to turn on and off the *SNAP, GRID,* and *ORTHO* drawing aids;

7. know how to customize the AutoCAD for Windows screen to your preferences.

BASIC CONCEPTS

Coordinate Systems

Any location in a drawing, such as the endpoint of a line, can be described in X, Y, and Z coordinate values (Cartesian coordinates).

If a line is drawn on a sheet of paper, for example, its endpoints can be charted by giving the distance over and up from the lower left corner of the sheet (Fig. 1-1).

These distances, or values, can be expressed as X and Y coordinates; X is the horizontal distance from the lower left corner (origin) and Y is the vertical distance from that origin. In a three-dimensional coordinate system, the third dimension, Z, is measured from the origin in a direction perpendicular to the plane defined by X and Y.

Two-dimensional (2D) and three-dimensional (3D) CAD systems use coordinate values to define the location of drawing elements such as lines and circles (called <u>objects</u> in AutoCAD).

In a 2D drawing, a line is defined by the X and Y coordinate values for its two endpoints (Fig 1-2).

In a 3D drawing, a line can be created and defined by specifying X, Y, and Z coordinate values (Fig. 1-3).

Coordinate values are always expressed by the X value first and separated by a comma, then Y, then Z.

Figure 1-1

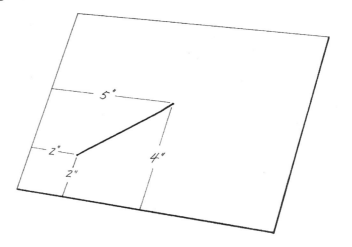

Figure 1-2

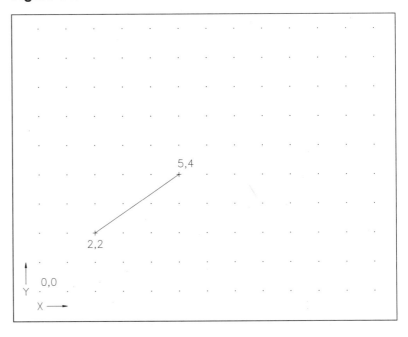

Figure 1-3

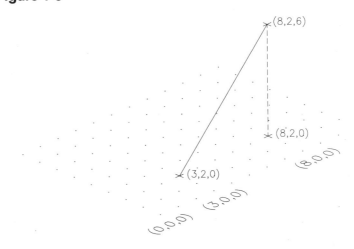

The CAD Database

A CAD (Computer-Aided Design) file, which is the electronically stored version of the drawing, keeps data in binary digital form. These digits describe coordinate values for all of the endpoints, center points, radii, vertices, etc., for all the objects composing the drawing, along with another code that describes the kinds of objects (line, circle, arc, ellipse, etc.). Figure 1-4 shows part of an AutoCAD DXF (Drawing Interchange Format) file giving numeric data defining lines and other objects. Knowing that a CAD system stores drawings by keeping coordinate data helps you understand the input that is required to create objects and how to translate the meaning of prompts on the screen.

Figure 1-4

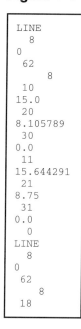

```
LINE
   8
0
  62
          8
  10
15.0
  20
8.105789
  30
0.0
  11
15.644291
  21
8.75
  31
0.0
   0
LINE
   8
0
  62
          8
  18
```

Angles in AutoCAD

Angles in AutoCAD are measured in a <u>counter-clockwise direction</u>. Angle 0 is positioned in a positive X direction, that is, horizontally from left to right. Therefore, 90 degrees is in a positive Y direction, or straight up; 180 degrees is in a negative X direction, or to the left; and 270 degrees is in a negative Y direction, or straight down (Fig. 1-5).

The position and direction of measuring angles in AutoCAD can be changed; however, the defaults listed here are used in most cases.

Figure 1-5

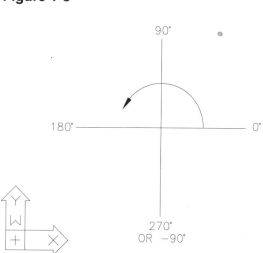

Draw True Size

When creating a drawing with pencil and paper tools, you must first determine a scale to use so the drawing will be proportional to the actual object and will fit on the sheet (Fig. 1-6). However, when creating a drawing on a CAD system, there is no fixed size drawing area. The number of drawing units that appear on the screen is variable and is assigned to fit the application.

The CAD drawing is not scaled until it is physically transferred to a fixed size sheet of paper by plotter or printer.

Figure 1-6

The rule for creating CAD drawings is that the drawing should be created <u>true size</u> using real-world units. The user specifies what units are to be used (architectural, engineering, etc.) and then specifies what size drawing area is needed (in X and Y values) to draw the necessary geometry.

Figure 1-7

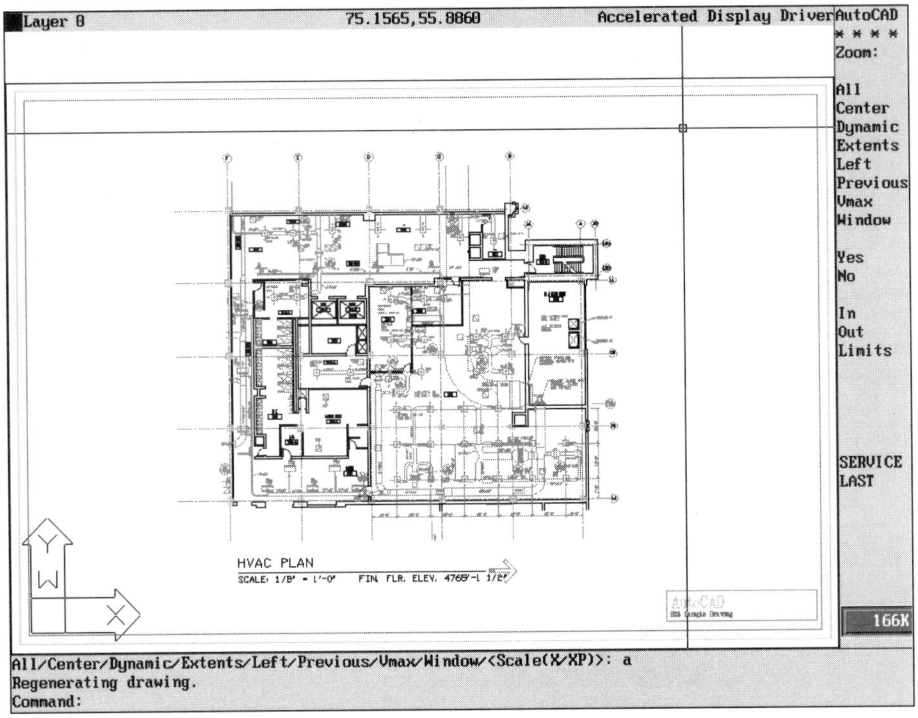

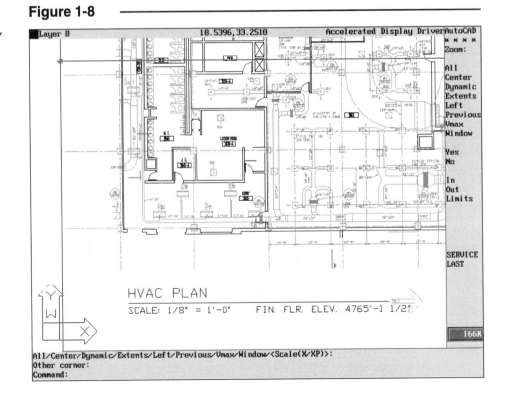

Whatever the specified size of the drawing area, it can be displayed on the screen in its entirety (Fig. 1-7) or as only a portion of the drawing area (Fig. 1-8).

Figure 1-8

Plot to Scale

As long as a drawing exists as a CAD file or is visible on the screen, it is considered a virtual, full-sized object. Only when the CAD drawing is transferred to paper by a plotter or printer is it converted (usually reduced) to a size that will fit on a sheet. A CAD drawing can be automatically scaled to fit on the sheet regardless of sheet size; however, this results in a plotted drawing that is not to an accepted scale (not to a regular proportion of the real object). Usually it is desirable to plot a drawing so that the resulting drawing is a proportion of the actual object size. The scale to enter as the plot scale (Fig. 1-9) is simply the proportion of the <u>plotted drawing</u> size to the <u>actual object</u>.

Figure 1-9

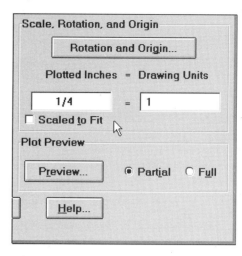

STARTING AutoCAD

Assuming that AutoCAD has been installed and configured properly for your system, you are ready to begin using AutoCAD. (See Appendix B, Installing and Configuring AutoCAD.) The steps for starting AutoCAD are different for the DOS and Windows versions.

AutoCAD for Windows

To start AutoCAD for Windows, locate the small program group icon in the Windows Program Manager titled "*AutoCAD R13*." Double-clicking on the icon (point the arrow and press the left mouse button quickly two times) will open the program group. From the AutoCAD R13 program group, double click on the *AutoCAD R13* icon (Fig. 1-10).

To exit AutoCAD, select *Exit* from the *Files* pull-down menu.

Figure 1-10

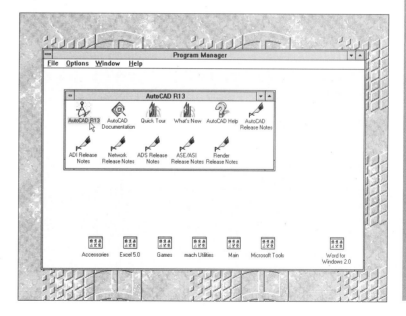

AutoCAD for DOS

1. If you don't have a menu system to start AutoCAD, go to the working directory on your hard drive before starting AutoCAD. A working directory is where drawing files and some temporary files are saved. You should <u>not</u> use the ACAD13 directory (where the AutoCAD program files are located) for your working directory. A separate working directory aids in file management and security. (See Appendix B for more information on working directories.)

    Many computer systems set up by an office or laboratory system manager have a screen menu system that appears when the computer is turned on and "boots up." If this is true for your system, making the correct selection from the menu (probably something like *AutoCAD Release 13* or *Use AutoCAD*) should set the current directory as well as start AutoCAD.

2. AutoCAD is usually started in one of three ways, depending on your system setup.

    a. Type **ACADR13**. The batch file automatically created by the AutoCAD Release 13 installation process is named ACADR13.BAT. Typing **ACADR13** runs this batch file. This batch file sets the necessary environment variables and starts AutoCAD.

    b. Type **ACAD**. This command starts ACAD.EXE, the executable program file for AutoCAD. However, <u>only</u> start AutoCAD by this method if the environment variables have previously been set by the AUTOEXEC.BAT or another batch file.

    c. Select **AutoCAD** from the screen menu native to your computer system (if one exists). In many offices and laboratories, menu systems are used to change to the working directory, to set the environment variables, and to start AutoCAD.

To exit AutoCAD, select *Exit* from the *Files* pull-down menu.

THE AutoCAD DRAWING EDITOR

After starting AutoCAD, the Drawing Editor appears on the screen and allows you to immediately begin drawing. Figure 1-11 displays the drawing editor in AutoCAD R13 for Windows.

Figure 1-11

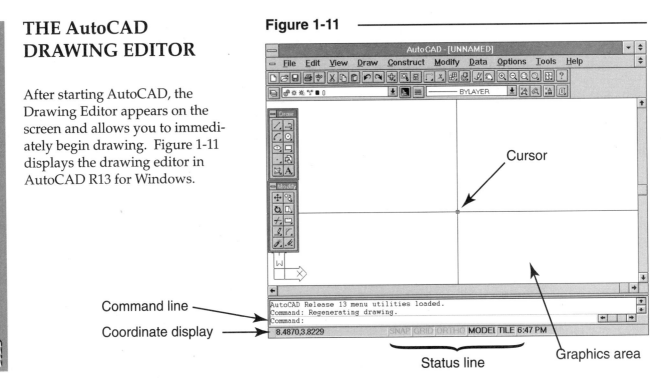

Cursor

Command line

Coordinate display

Status line

Graphics area

R13

Figure 1-12 displays the Drawing Editor for the DOS version of AutoCAD Release 13. The following sections give you the information you need to use the AutoCAD Drawing Editor to create and edit drawings.

Figure 1-12

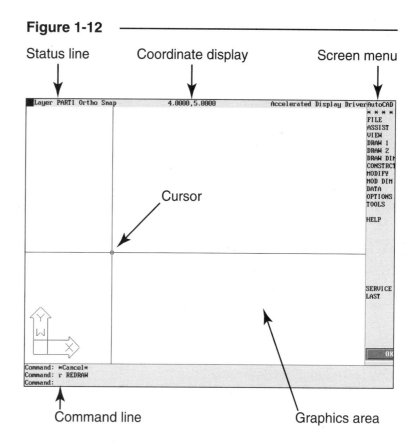

Status line   Coordinate display   Screen menu

Cursor

Command line   Graphics area

Graphics Area

The large central area of the screen is the Graphics area. It displays the lines, circles, and other objects you draw that will make up the drawing. The cursor is the intersection of the <u>crosshairs</u> (vertical and horizontal lines that follow the mouse or puck movements). The default size of the graphics area is 12 units (X or horizontal) by 9 units (Y or vertical). This usable drawing area (12 x 9) is called the drawing *Limits* and can be changed to any size to fit the application. As you move the crosshairs, you will notice the numbers in the <u>Coordinate Display</u> change (Windows—Fig. 1-11, bottom left; DOS—Fig. 1-12, top center).

Command Line

The Command Line consists of the three text lines at the bottom of the screen (by default) and is the most important area other than the drawing itself (see Figs. 1-11 and 1-12). Any command that is entered or any prompt that AutoCAD issues to you appears here. The command line is always visible and gives the current state of drawing activity. You should develop the habit of glancing at the command line while you work in AutoCAD. In the Windows version of AutoCAD R13, the command line can be set to display any number of lines and/or moved to another location (see Customizing the AutoCAD for Windows Screen).

Toolbars (Windows only)

The Windows version of AutoCAD Release 13 provides a variety of <u>tool-bars</u> (Fig. 1-13). Each toolbar contains a number of icon buttons (tools) that can be PICKed to invoke commands for drawing or editing objects (lines, arcs, circles, etc.) or for managing files and other functions. The <u>Standard Toolbar</u> is the row of icons nearest the top of the screen. The Standard Toolbar contains many standard icons used in other Windows applications (like *New, Open, Save, Print, Cut, Paste,* etc.) and other icons for AutoCAD-specific functions (like *Zoom, Pan,* and *Redraw*). The <u>Object Properties Toolbar</u>, located beneath the Standard Toolbar, is used for managing properties of objects, such as *Layers* and *Linetypes*. The <u>Draw and Modify Toolbars</u> also appear (by default) when you first use AutoCAD. As shown in Figure 1-13, the Draw and Modify Toolbars are <u>floating</u> and the Standard and Object Properties toolbars are <u>docked</u>. Many other toolbars are available and can be made to resize, float, or dock (see Customizing the AutoCAD for Windows Screen).

Figure 1-13

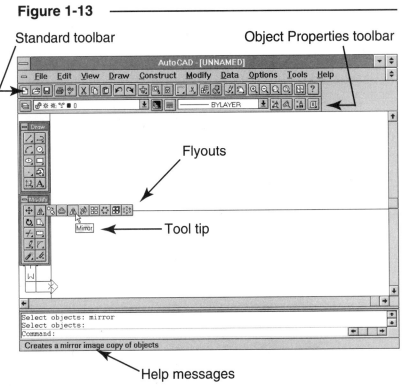

Standard toolbar

Object Properties toolbar

Flyouts

Tool tip

Help messages

If you place the pointer on an any icon and wait a second, a <u>Tool Tip</u> and a <u>Help Message</u> appear. Tool Tips pop out by the pointer and give the command name (Fig. 1-13). The Help Message appears at the bottom of the screen, giving a short description of the function. <u>Flyouts</u> are groups of related icons that pop out in a row or column when one of the group is selected. PICKing any icon that has a small black triangle in its lower right corner causes the related icons to fly out.

Pull-down Menus

The pull-down menu bar is at the top of the screen. In AutoCAD for DOS (Fig. 1-14), the menu appears only when the cursor is moved up into the top border. Selecting any of the words in the menu bar activates, or pulls down, the respective menu. Selecting a word appearing with an arrow activates a cascading menu with other options. Selecting a word with ellipsis (...) activates a dialogue box (see Dialogue Boxes). Words in the pull-down menus are not necessarily the same as the formal command names used for typing commands. Menus can be canceled by pressing Escape or PICKing in the graphics area. In AutoCAD for DOS, double-clicking on a pull-down

Figure 1-14

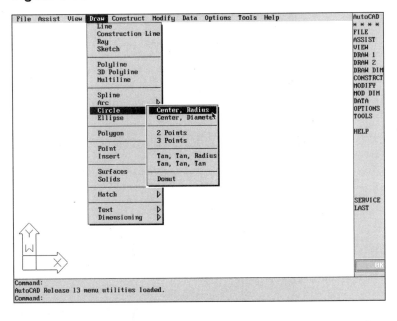

menu name (at the top menu bar) activates the last command and option used from that menu. The pull-down menus do <u>not</u> contain all of the AutoCAD commands and variables but contain the most commonly used ones.

AutoCAD for Windows ACADFULL Menu

The pull-down menu for AutoCAD for Windows shown in Figure 1-15 contains the same pull-down groups as the DOS version. This menu is activated by using the *Menu* command and selecting ACAD-FULL.MNU from the choices (in Windows only). This menu is more complete than the default Windows menu (ACAD.MNU) in that it contains the *Draw, Construct,* and *Modify* pull-down groups, like the DOS version and like all versions of Release 12. Illustrations in this book show the ACADFULL menu.

Figure 1-15

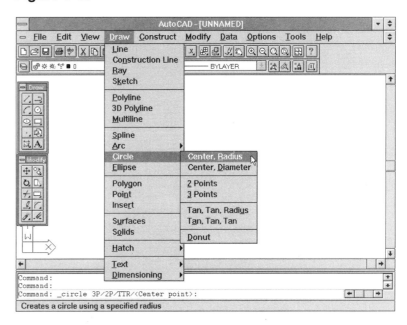

NOTE: This book uses the ACADFULL menu in all command tables and illustrations for AutoCAD for Windows. Activate the ACADFULL menu by typing *Menu*, then selecting ACADFULL.MNU from the choices.

Screen Menu

Almost all of the AutoCAD commands can be accessed through the menu system located at the right side of the screen (see Fig. 1-14). The screen menu has a tree structure; that is, other menus and commands are accessed by branching out from the root or top-level menu (Fig. 1-16). Commands (in upper and lower case followed by a colon) or menus (capital letters only) are selected by moving the cursor to the desired position until the word is highlighted and then pressing the PICK button. Words in capital letters followed by ellipsis points (...) activate dialogue boxes.

The root menu (top level) is accessed from any level of the structure by selecting the word "AutoCAD" at the top of any menu. The commands in these menus are the formal command names that can also be typed at the keyboard. If commands are invoked by typing, pull-downs, or toolbars, the screen menu automatically changes to the current command.

Figure 1-16

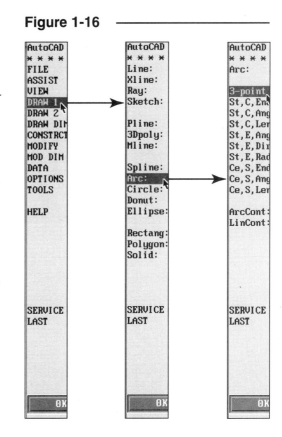

Words appearing in the screen menu follow this format:

UPPERCASE   Menu names   Selecting this activates another menu.
Upper/lower case with colon: Command   Selecting this activates the command.
Upper/lower case (no colon)   Command option   Selecting this activates a command option.

AutoCAD for Windows does <u>not</u> display the screen menu by default. It can be activated by selecting *Options* from the pull-downs, then *Preferences...*, and toggling *Screen Menu* (see Customizing the AutoCAD for Windows Screen).

Dialogue Boxes

Dialogue boxes provide an interface for controlling complex commands or a group of related commands. Depending on the command, the dialogue boxes allow you to select among multiple options and sometimes give a preview of the effect of selections. The *Layer Control* dialogue box (Fig. 1-17) gives complete control of layer colors, linetypes, and visibility.

Dialogue boxes are accessible through the pull-down and screen menus by selecting items followed by <u>ellipsis points</u> (...). Dialogue boxes can also be invoked by typing or selecting one of several commands beginning with "*DD*." For example, *DDLMODES* is the call for the *Layer Control* dialogue box.

Figure 1-17

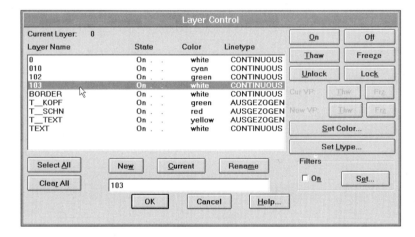

The basic element or smallest component of a dialogue box is called a <u>tile</u>. Several types of tiles and the resulting actions of tile selection are listed below.

Button	Resembles a push button and triggers some type of action
Edit box	Allows typing or editing of a single line of text
Image tile	A button that displays a graphical image
List box	A list of text strings from which one or more can be selected
Pop-down list	A text string that pops open to display a list of selections
Radio button	A group of buttons, only one of which can be turned on at a time
Check box	A check box for turning a feature on or off (displays an "X" when on)

In AutoCAD for DOS, the *Dlgcolor* command allows you to customize the colors for your dialogue boxes. The changes made with this command can be saved (in the ACAD.CFG file) so that the next drawing session on that particular computer will display the same color combination.

AutoCAD for Windows users can change dialogue box border colors (for all applications) with the Windows Control Panel. The AutoCAD screen colors can also be customized (see Customizing the AutoCAD for Windows Screen, this chapter).

New dialogue boxes can be created and customized. Programming the configuration of tiles and resulting action of tile selection requires use of Dialogue Control Language (DCL) to configure the tiles and AutoLISP programs to control the action of tile selection.

Status Line

The Status Line is a set of informative words or symbols that gives the status of the drawing aids. The AutoCAD for Windows Status Line appears at the very bottom of the screen (Fig. 1-11) and the DOS version Status line is at the upper left corner of the screen (Fig. 1-12). The operation of the Status Line is somewhat different in the Windows and DOS versions.

Windows: *SNAP, GRID, ORTHO, MODEL, TILE*
These drawing aids can be toggled on or off by double-clicking on the desired word or by using Function keys. The function of each of these words is explained in this and following chapters.
DOS: *Layer NAME, SNAP, ORTHO, P*
The current layer name and color are always displayed. *SNAP* and *ORTHO* appear when these functions are toggled on by using the F7 and F8 keys, commands, or dialogue boxes. The letter P appears when paper space is activated.

Coordinate Display (*COORDS*)

The Coordinate Display is located in the lower left corner of the Windows screen (Fig. 1-18) and at the top of the DOS screen (Fig. 1-12). The Coordinate Display (*COORDS*) displays the current position of the cursor in one of two possible formats explained below. This display can be very helpful when you draw because it can give the X and Y coordinate position of the cursor or give the cursor's distance and angle from the last point established. The format of *COORDS* is controlled by toggling the **F6** key or double-clicking on the numbers (Windows). *COORDS* can also be toggled off.

Figure 1-18 ───────────────

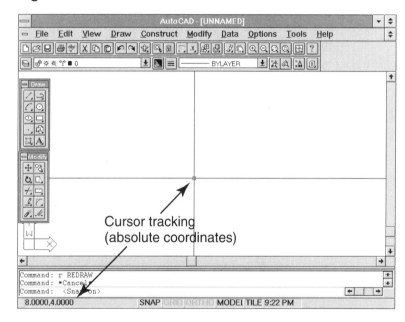

Cursor tracking
(absolute coordinates)

Cursor tracking
When *COORDS* is in this position, the values display the current location of the cursor in absolute (X and Y) coordinates (Fig. 1-18).

Relative polar display
This display is only possible if a draw or edit command is in use. The values give the distance and angle of the "rubberband" line from the last point established (Fig. 1-19).

Figure 1-19 ───────────────

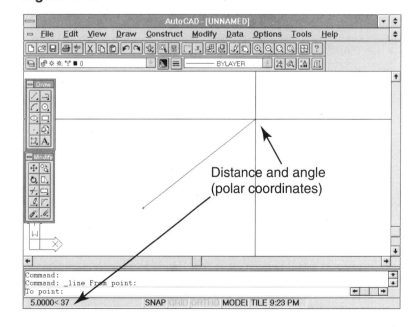

Distance and angle
(polar coordinates)

Digitizing Tablet Menu

If you have a digitizing tablet, the AutoCAD commands are available by making the desired selection from the AutoCAD digitizing table menu (Fig. 1-20). The open area located slightly to the right of center is called the Screen Pointing area. Locating the digitizing puck there makes the crosshairs appear on the screen. Locating the puck at any other location allows you to select a command. The icons on the tablet menu are identical to the toolbar icons. Similar to the format of the toolbars, commands are located in groups such as Draw, Edit, Zoom, Dimension, etc. The tablet menu has the columns numbered along the top and the rows lettered along the left side. The location of each command by column and row is given in this book. For example, the *Line* command can be found at *10,J*.

Figure 1-20

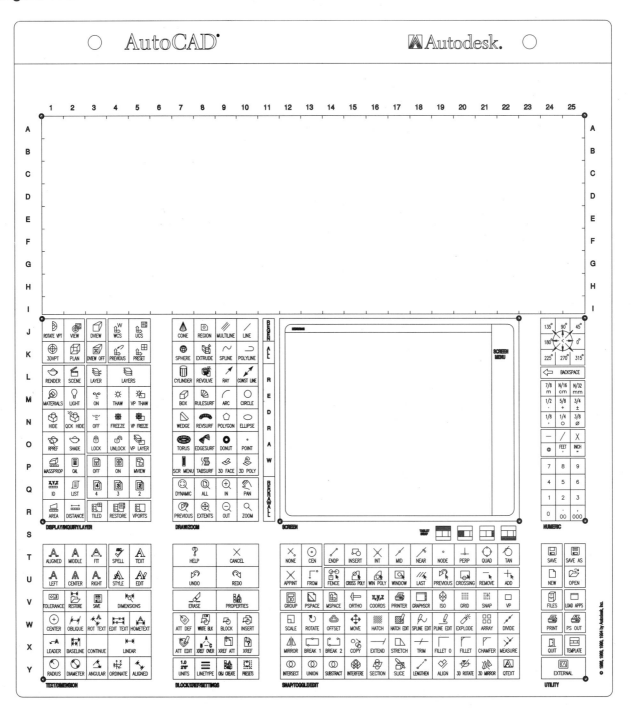

COMMAND ENTRY

Methods for Entering Commands

There are five possible methods for entering commands in AutoCAD, depending on your version (Windows or DOS) and availability of a digitizing tablet. Generally, <u>any one</u> of the five methods can be used to invoke a particular command.

1. **Toolbars** (Windows)   Select the command or dialogue box by PICKing an icon (tool) from a toolbar.
2. **Pull-down menu**   Select the command or dialogue box from a pull-down menu.
3. **Screen menu**   Select the command or dialogue box from the screen menu.
4. **Keyboard**   Type the command name, command alias, or accelerator keys at the keyboard.*
5. **Tablet menu**   Select the command from the digitizing tablet menu (if available).

*A command alias is a one- or two-letter shortcut. Accelerator keys use CTRL+ another key and are used in AutoCAD for Windows for utility operations. The command aliases and accelerator keys are given in the Command Tables (see below).

All five methods of entering commands accomplish the same goals; however, one method may offer a slightly different option or advantage to another, depending on the command used. A few considerations are listed below.

- Commands invoked by any method automatically change the screen menu to display the same command.
- Typing commands requires that no other commands are currently in use; therefore, the **Escape** key should be used to cancel active commands before typing.
- Pull-downs are easily visible but do <u>not</u> contain all of the commands.
- The screen menus contain almost <u>all</u> AutoCAD commands; however, locating a particular command in the menu structure may take a few seconds.

All menus, including the digitizing tablet, can be customized by editing the ACAD.MNU file, and command aliases can be added to the ACAD.PGP file so that command entry can be designed to your preference (see Chapter 42, Customization).

Using the "Command Tables" in This Book to Locate a Particular Command

Command tables, like the one below, are used throughout this book to show the possible methods for entering a particular command. The table shows the icon used in the Windows toolbars and digitizing tablet, gives the selections to make for the pull-down and screen menus, gives the correct spelling for entering commands and command aliases at the keyboard, and gives the command location (column, row) on the digitizing tablet menu. This example uses the *Copy* command.

COPY

PULL-DOWN MENU	SCREEN MENU	TYPE IN	TABLET MENU
Construct *Copy*	*CONSTRUCT* *Copy:*	*COPY* *or CP*	*15,X*

Mouse and Digitizing Puck Buttons

Depending on the type of mouse or digitizing puck used for cursor control, a different number of buttons are available. In any case, the buttons perform the following tasks:

#1 (left mouse)	**PICK**	Used to select commands or point to locations on screen.
#2 (right mouse)	**Enter**	Performs the same action as the Enter or Return key on the keyboard (except when entering text in a drawing).
#3	*OSNAP*	Activates the cursor *OSNAP* menu.
#4	**Cancel**	Cancels a command.

Function Keys

There are several function keys that are usable with AutoCAD. They offer a quick method of turning on or off (toggling) drawing aids.

F1 (Windows)	*Help*	Opens a help window providing written explanations on commands and variables.
F1 (DOS)	*FLIPSCREEN*	Activates a text window showing the previous command line activity (command history).
F2 (Windows)	*FLIPSCREEN*	Activates the Windows internal text editor showing the command history.
F6	*COORDS*	Toggles the coordinate display between cursor tracking mode and off. If used transparently (during a command in operation), displays a polar coordinate format.
F7	*GRID*	Turns the *GRID On* or *Off* (see Drawing Aids).
F8	*ORTHO*	Turns *ORTHO On* or *Off* (see Drawing Aids).
F9	*SNAP*	Turns the *SNAP On* or *Off* (see Drawing Aids).
F10 (Windows)	*STATUS*	Turns the Status Line *On* or *Off*.
F10 (DOS)	*TABLET*	Turns the *TABLETMODE On* or *Off*. If *TABLETMODE* is *On*, the tablet can be used to digitize an existing paper drawing into AutoCAD.

Special Key Functions

Escape	The Escape key cancels a command, menu, or dialogue box or interrupts processing of plotting or hatching.
Spacebar	In AutoCAD, the space bar performs the same action as the Enter key or #2 button. Only when you are entering text into a drawing does the space bar create a space.
Enter	If Enter, Spacebar, or #2 button is pressed when no command is in use (the open Command: prompt is visible), the last command used is invoked again.

Drawing Aids

This section gives a brief introduction to AutoCAD's Drawing Aids. For a full explanation of the related commands and options, see Chapter 6.

SNAP (F9 or Ctrl+B)

SNAP is a function that forces the cursor to "snap" to a regular interval (1 unit by default), which aids in drawing geometry accurate to equal interval lengths. The *Snap* command or *Drawing Aids...* dialogue box allows you to specify any value for the *SNAP* interval. In Figure 1-21, the *SNAP* is set to .125 (note the values in the coordinate display).

GRID (F7 or Ctrl+G)

A drawing aid called *GRID* can be used to give a visual reference of units of length. The *GRID* default value is 1 unit. The *Grid* command or *Drawing Aids...* dialogue box allows you to change the interval to any value. The *GRID* is not part of the geometry and is not plotted. Figure 1-21 displays a *GRID* of 1.0.

SNAP and *GRID* are independent functions—they can be turned *On* or *Off* independently. However, you can force the *GRID* to have the same interval as *SNAP* by entering a *GRID* value of 0 or you can use a proportion of *SNAP* by entering a *GRID* value followed by an X.

ORTHO (F8 or Ctrl+L in Windows, Ctrl+O in DOS)

If *ORTHO* is *On*, lines are forced to an orthogonal alignment (horizontal or vertical) when drawing (Fig. 1-22). *ORTHO* is often helpful since so many drawings are composed mainly of horizontal and vertical lines. *ORTHO* can only be turned *On* or *Off*.

Figure 1-21

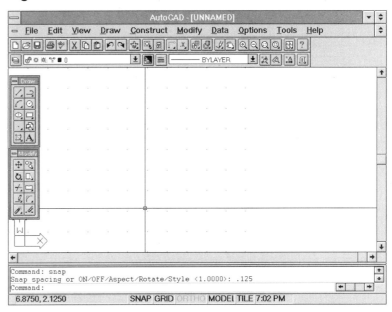

Figure 1-22

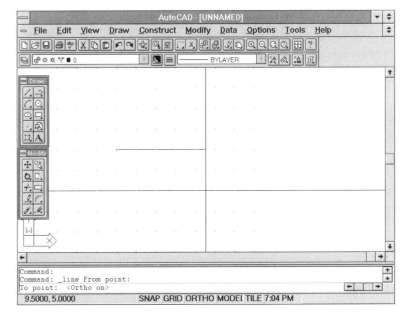

Command Entry Methods Practice
Start AutoCAD. Invoke the *Line* command using each of the command entry methods.

1. Type the command

STEPS	COMMAND PROMPT	PERFORM ACTION	COMMENTS
1.		press **Escape** if another command is in use	
2.	Command:	type *Line* and press **Enter**	
3.	From point:	**PICK** any point	a "rubberband" line appears
4.	to point:	**PICK** any point	another "rubberband" line appears
5.	to point:	press **Enter**	to complete command

2. Type the command alias

STEPS	COMMAND PROMPT	PERFORM ACTION	COMMENTS
1.		press **Escape** if another command is in use	
2.	Command:	type *L* and press **Enter**	
3.	From point:	**PICK** any point	a "rubberband" line appears
4.	to point:	**PICK** any point	another "rubberband" line appears
5.	to point:	press **Enter**	to complete command

3. Pull-down menu

STEPS	COMMAND PROMPT	PERFORM ACTION	COMMENTS
1.	Command:	select the *Draw* menu from the menu bar on top	menu pops down (use the ACADFULL menu file in Windows)
2.	Command:	select *Line*	menu disappears
3.	line From point:	**PICK** any point	a "rubberband" line appears
4.	to point:	**PICK** any point	another "rubberband" line appears
5.	to point:	press **Enter**	to complete command

4. Screen menu (if available on your setup)

STEPS	COMMAND PROMPT	PERFORM ACTION	COMMENTS
1.	Command:	select **AutoCAD** from screen menu on the side	only if menu is not at root level
2.	Command:	select *DRAW 1* from the root screen menu	menu changes to DRAW 1
3.	Command:	select *Line:*	
4.	Line From point:	**PICK** any point	a "rubberband" line appears
5.	to point:	**PICK** any point	another "rubberband" line appears
6.	to point:	press **Enter**	to complete command

5. Toolbars (if using AutoCAD for Windows)

STEPS	COMMAND PROMPT	PERFORM ACTION	COMMENTS
1.	Command:	select the *Line* icon from the *Draw* toolbar	the *Line* tool should be located near the top left of the toolbar, possibly on a flyout
2.	line From point:	**PICK** any point	a "rubberband" line appears
3.	to point:	**PICK** any point	another "rubberband" line appears
4.	to point:	press **Enter**	to complete command

6. Digitizing tablet menu (if available)

STEPS	COMMAND PROMPT	PERFORM ACTION	COMMENTS
1.	Command:	select *LINE*	at **10,J**
2.	line From point:	**PICK** any point	a "rubberband" line appears
3.	to point:	**PICK** any point	another "rubberband" line appears
4.	to point:	press **Enter**	to complete command

When you are finished practicing, use the *Files* pull-down menu and select *Exit* to exit AutoCAD. You do not have to "Save Changes."

CUSTOMIZING THE AutoCAD FOR WINDOWS SCREEN

Toolbars

By default, the Object Properties and Standard toolbars are docked and the Draw and Modify toolbars are floating (see Fig. 1-22). A floating toolbar can be easily moved to any location on the screen if it obstructs an important area of a drawing. Placing the pointer in the title background allows you to move the toolbar by holding down the left button and dragging it to a new location (Fig. 1-23). Floating toolbars can also be resized by placing the pointer on the narrow border until a two-way arrow appears, then dragging left, right, up, or down (Fig 1-24).

Figure 1-23 ———   **Figure 1-24** —

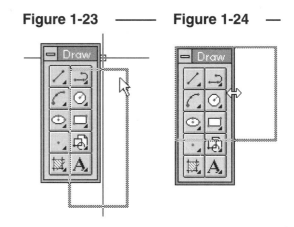

A floating toolbar can be docked against any border (right, left, top, bottom) by dragging it to the desired location (Fig. 1-25). Several toolbars can be stacked in a docked position. By the same method, docked toolbars can be dragged back onto the graphics area. The Object Properties and Standard toolbars can be moved onto the graphics area or docked on another border, although it is wise to keep these toolbars in their standard position. The Object Properties toolbar will only display its full options when located in a horizontal position.

Figure 1-25 —————————

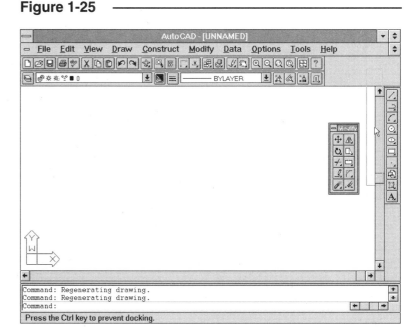

Holding down the **Ctrl** key while dragging a toolbar near a border of the drawing window prevents the toolbar from docking. This feature enables you to float a toolbar anywhere on the screen.

There are many toolbars available, each with a group of related commands for specialized functions. For example, when you are ready to dimension a drawing, you can activate the Dimensioning toolbar for efficiency. Selecting the *Tools* pull-down menu, then *Toolbars>*, displays the list of possible selections (Fig. 1-26). Making a selection activates that toolbar. You may instead type in the *Toolbars* command to enter a selection. Toolbars can be removed from the screen by clicking once on the minus (-) symbol in the upper left corner of the toolbar.

New toolbars can be created and existing toolbars can be customized. Typically, you would create toolbars to include groups of related commands that you use most frequently or need for special activities. See Customizing Toolbars in Chapter 42.

Figure 1-26

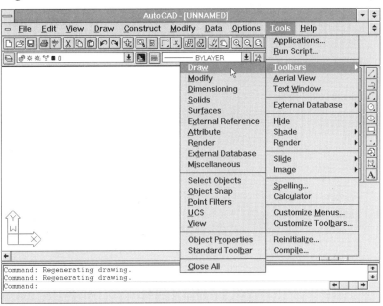

Command Line

The command line, normally located near the bottom of the screen, can be resized to display more or fewer lines of text. Moving the pointer to the border between the graphics screen and the command line until two-way arrows appear allows you to slide the border up or down (Fig. 1-27). A <u>minimum of two lines</u> of text is recommended. The command line text window can also be moved to any location on the screen by pointing to the border, holding down the left button, and dragging to the new position.

Figure 1-27

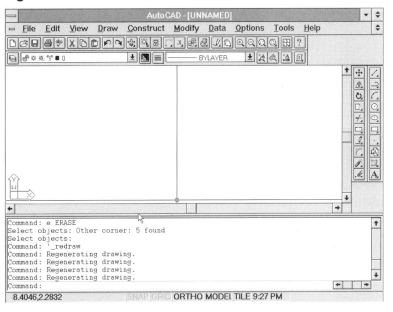

Preferences

Fonts, colors, and other features of the AutoCAD for Windows drawing editor can be customized to your liking by using the *Preferences* command. Using the command by typing in *Preferences* or by selecting from the *Options* pull-down menu activates the dialogue box shown in Figure 1-28. The Screen Menu can also be activated through this dialogue box.

Figure 1-28

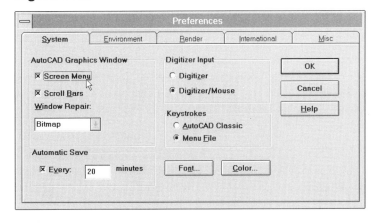

Selecting the *Color...* tile provides a dialogue box for customizing the screen colors (Fig. 1-29).

All changes made to the Windows screen by any of the options discussed in this section are automatically saved for the next drawing session. The changes are saved in the ACAD.INI file. However, if you are working in a school laboratory, it is likely that the computer systems are set up to present the same screen defaults each time you start AutoCAD.

Figure 1-29 ───────────────────

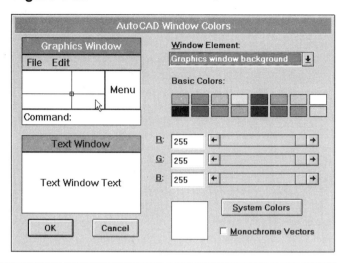

CHAPTER EXERCISES

1. **Starting and Exiting AutoCAD**

    Start AutoCAD by whatever method is used on your computer system. Draw a *Line*. Exit AutoCAD by selecting the *Exit* option from the *Files* pull-down menu. PICK the *Discard Changes* tile. Repeat these steps until you are confident with the procedure.

2. **Using Drawing Aids**

    Start AutoCAD. Turn on and off each of the following modes.

    SNAP, GRID, ORTHO

3. **Understanding Coordinates**

    Begin drawing a *Line* by PICKing a "From point:". Toggle *COORDS* to display each of the three formats. PICK several other points at the "to point:" prompt. Pay particular attention to the coordinate values displayed for each point and visualize the relationship between that point and coordinate 0,0 (absolute value) or the last point established (relative polar value). Finish the command by pressing Enter.

4. **Using *FLIPSCREEN***

    Use *FLIPSCREEN* (**F1** for DOS, **F2** for Windows) to toggle between the text screen or window and the graphics screen.

5. **Drawing with Drawing Aids**

    Draw four *Lines* using each Drawing Aid: *GRID, SNAP, ORTHO*. Toggle *On* and *Off* each of the drawing aids one at a time for each set of four *Lines*. Next, draw *Lines* using combinations of the Drawing Aids, particularly *GRID + SNAP* and *GRID + SNAP + ORTHO*.

Chapter 2
WORKING WITH FILES

Chapter Objectives

After completing this chapter you should be able to:

1. name drawing files;

2. use file-related dialogue boxes;

3. create *New* drawings;

4. *Open* existing drawings;

5. *Save* drawings to disk;

6. *Import* and *Export* drawings and related data in a variety of formats.

7. *Exit AutoCAD*;

8. use the *Files* command to list, copy, rename, and delete files.

AutoCAD DRAWING FILES

Naming Drawing Files

What is a drawing file? A CAD drawing file is the electronically stored data form of a drawing. The computer's hard disk is the principal magnetic storage device used for saving and restoring CAD drawing files. Diskettes are used to transport files from one computer to another, as in the case of transferring CAD files among clients, consultants, or vendors in industry. The AutoCAD commands used for saving drawings to, and restoring drawings from, files are explained in this chapter.

An AutoCAD drawing file has a name that you assign and a file extension of ".DWG." An example of an AutoCAD drawing file is:

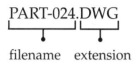

PART-024.DWG

filename   extension

The file name you assign must be compliant with the DOS filename conventions; that is, it can only have a <u>maximum</u> of eight alphanumeric characters. Characters such as _ - $ # ( ) ^ can be used in names, but no spaces or other characters are allowed. AutoCAD automatically appends the extension of .DWG to all AutoCAD-created drawing files.

Beginning and Saving an AutoCAD Drawing

When you start AutoCAD, the drawing editor appears and allows you to begin drawing even before using any file commands. If you choose, you can assign a name for the drawing when you begin with the *New* command. As you draw, you should develop the habit of saving the drawing periodically (about every 15 or 20 minutes) using *Save*. *Save* stores the drawing in its most current state to disk.

The typical drawing session would involve using *New* to assign a name for the drawing at the start or using *Open* to open an existing drawing. *Save* would be used periodically, and *Exit* would be used for the final save and to end the session.

Accessing File Commands

Proper use of the file-related commands covered in this chapter allows you to manage your AutoCAD drawing files in a safe and efficient manner. Although the file-related commands can be invoked by any of several methods, they are easily accessible via the first pull-down menu option, *File* (Fig. 2-1). Most of the selections from this pull-down menu invoke dialogue boxes for selection or specification of file names.

File commands and related dialogue boxes are also available from the *File* screen menu. File commands can

Figure 2-1

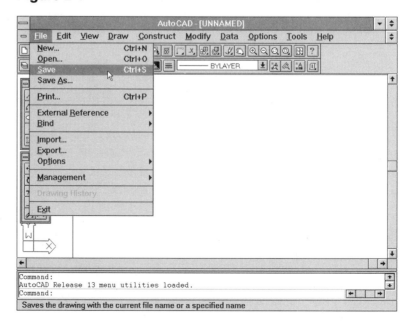

also be typed at the keyboard or selected from the digitizing menu. AutoCAD for Windows has icon buttons on the Standard toolbar for *New*, *Open*, and *Save*.

File Dialogue Box Functions

There are many dialogue boxes appearing in AutoCAD that help you manage files. All of these dialogue boxes operate in the same manner. A few guidelines will help you to use them. The *Save Drawing As* dialogue box for Windows (Fig. 2-2) and for DOS (Fig. 2-3) are used as examples.

Figure 2-2

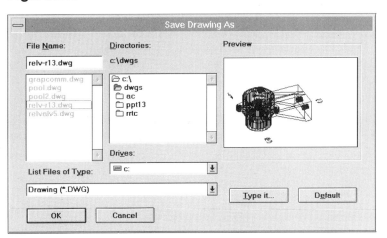

- The top of the box gives the title describing the action to be performed. It is <u>very important</u> to glance at the title before acting, especially when saving or deleting files.
- The desired file can be selected by PICKing it, then PICKing *OK*. Double-clicking on the selection accomplishes the same action. File names can also be typed at the command line by selecting the *Type it* tile.
- Every file name has an extension (three letters following the period) called the <u>type</u> or <u>pattern</u>. In AutoCAD for Windows (Fig. 2-2), file types can be selected from the *List Files of Type* section of the dialogue boxes, while in the DOS version (Fig. 2-3) the top edit box gives the *Pattern*. In either case, the file extension can be selected or changed by entering the desired file extension.

Figure 2-3

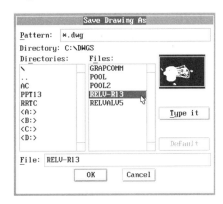

- The current drive and directory are also listed. Other directories can be selected by double-clicking the choice under *Directories:*. In the DOS version, PICKing the double dots (..) activates the parent directory (one level up).
- Scroll bars with up and down arrows appear at the right of the *Directory* and/or *File* list if the list is longer than one page. PICKing the arrows pages up and down slowly or sliding the button causes paging at any rate.
- As an alternative, the file name (and path) can be typed in the edit box labeled *File* or *File Name*. Make sure the blinking cursor appears in the box (move the cursor and PICK) before typing.

AutoCAD FILE COMMANDS

NEW

PULL-DOWN MENU	SCREEN MENU	TYPE IN	TABLET MENU
File *New...*	*FILE* *New:*	*NEW or* *Ctrl+N (Win)*	*24,U*

The *New* command should be used to assign a name to the drawing before beginning to draw or to use a specific prototype (Fig. 2-4). A prototype drawing is one that is used as a template, or starting point. The default prototype drawing supplied with AutoCAD is named ACAD.DWG, but other default drawings can be created and retained as the default. Keep in mind that you can draw immediately on entering the Drawing Editor and specify a name at a later time when saving. It is not required that the drawing be named until it is saved.

The *Prototype* option allows you to start a new drawing by using an <u>existing</u> drawing as a starting point, like a template or prototype.

Selecting the *Prototype* tile invokes a dialogue box (Fig. 2-5) which shows all .DWG files in the directory where the default prototype is kept. Other directories can be selected from the *Directories:* list. Thus, any .DWG file can be used as a prototype.

A prototype drawing can have the initial drawing setup steps already completed so you don't have to repeat the same steps every time you start a new drawing. A copy of the selected drawing is loaded into the Drawing Editor and used as a starting point. The original drawing on disk is not affected.

Figure 2-4 ——————————————

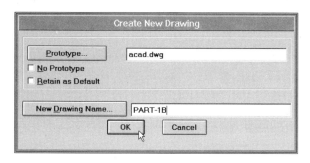

Figure 2-5 ——————————————

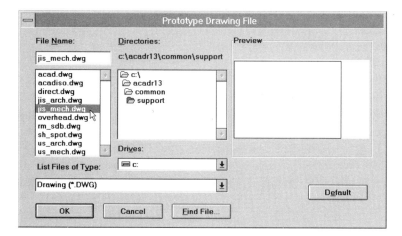

OPEN

PULL-DOWN MENU	SCREEN MENU	TYPE IN	TABLET MENU
File *Open...*	*FILE* *Open:*	*OPEN or* *Ctrl+O (Win)*	*25,U*

This command is intended for selecting an existing drawing or a partially completed drawing that you want to load and continue drawing.

The *Select File* dialogue box allows selection of any drawing in the current directory or selection of another directory to list. The file name of the drawing to be loaded can also be typed in the file edit box.

The *Preview* feature is helpful for selecting a drawing from the list by displaying a small bitmap image of any drawing saved in Release 13 format. The *Makepreview* command (must be

Figure 2-6 ——————————————

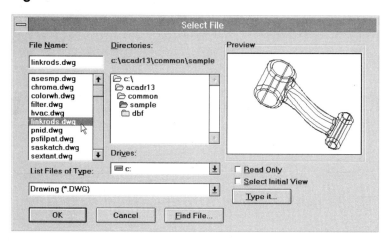

typed) creates a bitmap image (separate .BMP file) of Release 12 or earlier drawings if you want to use them with Release 13 but keep them in Release 12 format.

If you are using AutoCAD for Windows, PICKing the *Find File...* tile in the *Select File* dialogue box (Fig. 2-6) invokes the *Browse/Search* dialogue box (Fig. 2-7). This box displays a small bitmap image of all drawings in the search directory. You can open a drawing by double-clicking on its image.

The *Search* page of the *Browse/Search* dialogue box enables you to search for files meeting specific criteria that you specify (Fig. 2-8). You can enter file names (including wildcards) in the *Search Pattern* box, and the desired file extension can be selected from the *File Types* pop-down list. The *Date Filter* helps you search for files by the date that the files were last saved. Any drive or path can be selected using the *Search Location* cluster.

After specifying the search criteria, select the *Search* tile. All file names meeting the criteria appear in the image tiles on the left of the dialogue box. AutoCAD Release 13 .DWG files appear with a bitmap image by the name. Files can be opened by double-clicking on the name or image tile, or by selecting either and PICKing *Open*.

Figure 2-7

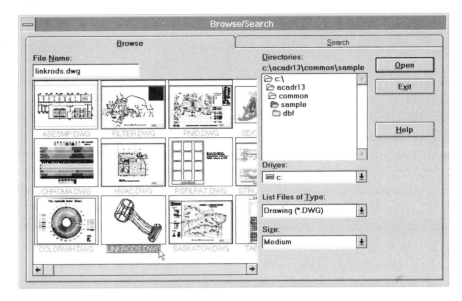

Figure 2-8

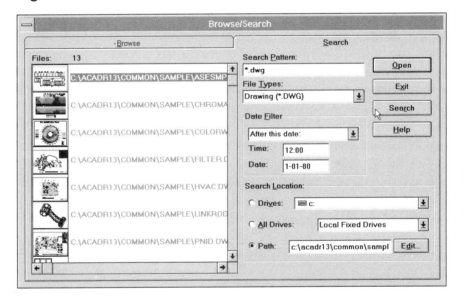

SAVE

PULL-DOWN MENU	SCREEN MENU	TYPE IN	TABLET MENU
File *Save*	*FILE* *Save:*	*SAVE or* *Ctrl+S (Win)*	*24,T*

The *Save* command is intended to be used periodically during a drawing session (every 15 to 20 minutes is recommended). When *Save* is selected from the menus, the current version of the drawing is saved to disk without interruption to the drawing session. The first time an unnamed drawing is saved, the *Save Drawing As* dialogue box (Figs. 2-2 and 2-3) appears, which prompts you for a drawing name. Typically, however, the drawing already has an assigned name, in which case *Save* actually performs a *Qsave* (quick save).

Typing *Save* always produces the *Save Drawing As* dialogue box. You can enter a new name and/or path to save the drawing or press Enter to keep the same name and path.

NOTE: Changing the name and/or path with *Save* resets the current drawing name and/or path. Therefore, you should not use *Save* to save the drawing to a diskette in A: or B: drive. See the next NOTE.

SAVEAS

PULL-DOWN MENU	SCREEN MENU	TYPE IN	TABLET MENU
File *Save As...*	*File* *SaveAs:*	*SAVEAS*	*25,T*

The *Saveas* command fulfills two functions: assigns a new file name for the current drawing and saves the drawing file to disk under the new name. If a name has previously been assigned, *Saveas* allows you to save the current drawing under a different name; but, beware, *Saveas* sets the current drawing name to the last one entered. This dialogue box is shown in Figures 2-2 and 2-3.

A typical scenario follows. A design engineer wants to make two similar but slightly different design drawings. During construction of the first drawing, the engineer periodically saves under the name "DESIGN1" using *Save*. The first drawing is then completed and *Saved*. Instead of starting a *New* drawing, *Saveas* is used to save the current drawing under the name "DESIGN2." *Saveas* also resets the current drawing name to "DESIGN2." The designer then has two separate but identical drawing files on disk which can be further edited to complete the specialized differences. The engineer continues to work on the current drawing "DESIGN2."

NOTE: If you want to save the drawing to a diskette in A: or B: drive, do not use *Saveas*. Since *Saveas* resets the drawing name and path to whatever is entered in the *Save Drawing As* dialogue box, entering A:NAME would set A: as the current drive. This could cause problems because the temporary files that AutoCAD uses would also be written to A: instead of to the hard drive. Instead, you should save the drawing to the hard drive (usually C:), then close the drawing (by using *Open, New,* or *Exit*). Next, use DOS commands or the Windows File Manager to copy the drawing file to A:.

SAVEASR12

DOS PULL-DOWN	WIN PULL-DOWN	SCREEN MENU	TYPE IN	TABLET MENU
File *Export* *Release 12 DWG...*	*File* *Save R12 DWG*	*FILE* *EXPORT* *SaveR12:*	*SAVEASR12*	---

The *Saveasr12* command saves the current drawing in Release 12 format. The Release 13 drawing can then be opened and edited in Release 12. The original Release 13 drawing is saved to a .BAK (backup) file with the same name.

Because Release 13 has new objects that do not exist in Release 12, some information is lost when the "downward" conversion is made. The new Release 13 objects are *Leader, Xline, Ray, Ellipse, Tolerance, Mline,* OLE objects, *Xref overlay, Mtext, Spline,* and all 3D solids. When possible, the new objects are converted to the closest Release 12 matching entity. However, with some new objects, information cannot be converted and is lost.

EXIT

PULL-DOWN MENU	SCREEN MENU	TYPE IN	TABLET MENU
File *Exit*	*FILE* *Exit:*	*EXIT*	---

This is the simplest method to use when you want to exit AutoCAD. This option invokes a dialogue box requiring you to *Save Changes..., Discard Changes,* or *Cancel Command* (Fig. 2-9). Depending on your selection, AutoCAD actually uses *End, Quit,* or *Cancel.* The *Quit* command could optionally be typed to accomplish the same action as using *Exit.*

Figure 2-9

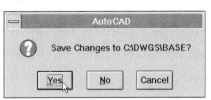

QSAVE

PULL-DOWN MENU	SCREEN MENU	TYPE IN	TABLET MENU
---	---	*QSAVE*	---

Qsave (quick save) must be typed. *Qsave* saves the drawing under the previously assigned file name. No dialogue boxes appear, nor are any other inputs required. This is the same as using *Save* (from the menus), assuming the drawing name has been assigned. However, if the drawing has not been named when *Qsave* is invoked, the *Save Drawing As* dialogue box appears.

QUIT

PULL-DOWN MENU	SCREEN MENU	TYPE IN	TABLET MENU
---	---	*QUIT*	24,X

The *Quit* command accomplishes the same action as *Exit*. *Quit* discontinues (exits) the AutoCAD session and produces the dialogue box shown in Figure 2-9. If the drawing was just *Saved*, the dialogue box does not appear before exiting AutoCAD.

END

PULL-DOWN MENU	SCREEN MENU	TYPE IN	TABLET MENU
---	---	*END*	---

The *End* command ends the AutoCAD session and saves the drawing under the assigned name. If no name has been assigned, the *Save Drawing As* dialogue box appears. Using *End* has the same effect as selecting *Exit*, then *Yes* to "Save Changes."

RECOVER

PULL-DOWN MENU	SCREEN MENU	TYPE IN	TABLET MENU
File *Management >* *Recover...*	*FILE* *MANAGE* *Recover:*	*RECOVER*	---

This option is used only in the case that *Open* does not operate on a particular drawing because of damage to the file. Damage to a drawing file can occur from improper exiting of AutoCAD (such as power failure) or from damage to a diskette. *Recover* can usually <u>reassemble</u> the file to a usable state and load the drawing. The *Recover* dialogue box operates like the *Open Drawing* dialogue box.

FILES

PULL-DOWN MENU	SCREEN MENU	TYPE IN	TABLET MENU
File Management > Utilities	*FILE MANAGE Files:*	*FILES*	*24,V*

A group of file utility commands are available for managing files. Each of the options shown in Figure 2-10 invokes a dialogue box (described below).

Figure 2-10

List Files...

This option invokes the *File List* dialogue box (Fig. 2-11). Files can only be listed and cannot be opened, saved, or have any other action performed. Any file type (other than .DWG) can be listed by entering the desired three-character extension in the edit box. Any drive or directory can be selected for listing by double-clicking on the choice.

Figure 2-11

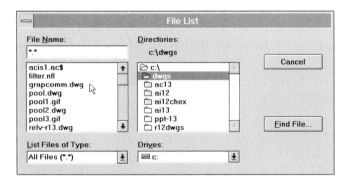

Copy Files...

This option allows you to copy the selected file to another drive or directory. Two dialogue boxes appear in sequence. The desired file to copy is selected from the *Source File* box (Fig. 2-12). The *Destination File* box (not shown) is used to select the new directory or drive to copy to. Do not PICK an existing file name from the list in the *Destination File* dialogue box unless you want the selected file to be overwritten (a warning message appears if you do).

Figure 2-12

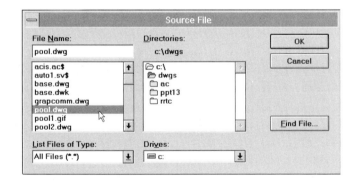

Rename Files...

This operation also has a two dialogue box sequence like the *Copy Files* option. Select the desired file from the *Old File Name* dialogue box. Type the new name in the edit box of the *New File Name* dialogue box. Make sure that the destination drive and directory are set as desired.

Do not *Rename* any files ending with .AC$ or .DWK. They are temporary files that are needed by AutoCAD and are deleted automatically when you exit AutoCAD properly (using *Exit, Quit,* or *End*).

Delete Files...
Select the file to delete from the *File(s) to Delete*
dialogue box. <u>Do not delete</u> any files with .AC$
extensions. They are temporary files that are
needed by AutoCAD and are deleted automatically when you exit AutoCAD properly (using
Exit, Quit, or *End*) (Fig 2-13).

Figure 2-13

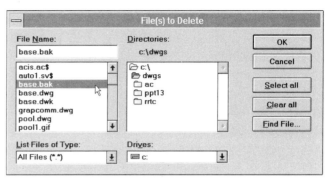

Unlock Files...
The *Unlock Files* option deletes "orphan" .DWK
files. While an AutoCAD drawing is in use, a
.DWK file is produced to prevent other users
(on a network) from accessing the same drawing. The .DWK file is automatically deleted when the
drawing is closed properly. Exiting AutoCAD improperly (power failure, etc.) causes the "orphan"
.DWK file to be left on disk. Use the *Unlock Files* option to delete the .DWK file and to allow opening the
"parent" drawing.

IMPORT

PULL-DOWN MENU	SCREEN MENU	TYPE IN	TABLET MENU
File	*FILE*	*IMPORT*	---
Import...	*IMPORT*		

The *Import* command enables you to
bring files other than AutoCAD DWG
files into the current drawing. Using
this command produces the *Import File*
dialogue box. The *List Files of Type*
pop-down list displays the file formats
that you can import (Fig. 2-14).

Figure 2-14

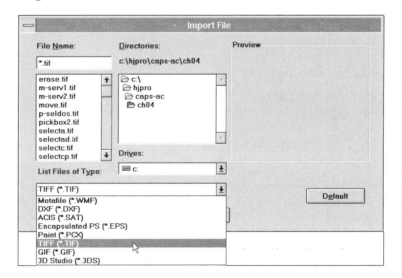

The file types that AutoCAD Release 13 accepts are:

.WMF	Windows Meta File	(Windows vector format file)
.DXF	Drawing Interchange File	(AutoCAD drawing ASCII file format)
.SAT	ACIS file	(AutoCAD solid model file format)
.EPS	Encapsulated PostScript	(raster format file)
.PCX	MicroSoft Paint file	(raster format file)
.TIF	Tagged Image File Format	(raster format file)
.GIF	Graphic Interchange Format	(raster format file)
.3DS	3D Studio	(Autodesk 3D Studio model file)

The result of importing the file depends on the type of file. A .WMF file is converted to an AutoCAD
Block. A .DXF file is converted to the AutoCAD drawing format. For some raster files, AutoCAD will
convert the pixels to AutoCAD objects.

R13

EXPORT

PULL-DOWN MENU	SCREEN MENU	TYPE IN	TABLET MENU
File *Export...*	*FILE* *EXPORT*	*EXPORT*	---

The *Export* command writes the current drawing (or selected objects in the current drawing) to disk in the file format that you specify (Fig. 2-15).

Figure 2-15

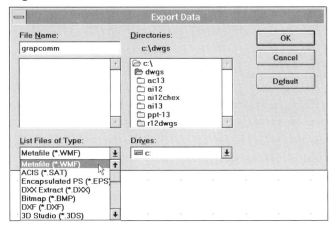

The file types that can be created are:

.WMF	Windows Meta File	(Windows vector format file)
.SAT	ACIS file	(AutoCAD solid model file format)
.EPS	Encapsulated PostScript	(raster format file)
.DXX	Drawing Extract File	(AutoCAD attribute extract file)
.BMP	Bitmap file	(raster format file)
.DXF	Drawing Interchange File	(AutoCAD drawing ASCII file format)
.3DS	3D Studio	(Autodesk 3D Studio model file)

SAVETIME

PULL-DOWN MENU	SCREEN MENU	TYPE IN	TABLET MENU
Options *Auto Save Time*	*OPTIONS* *SaveTim:*	*SAVETIME*	---

SAVETIME is a variable that controls AutoCAD's automatic save feature. AutoCAD automatically saves the current drawing for you at time intervals that you specify. The default time interval is 120 (minutes)! If you want to use this feature effectively, change the value to about 15 or 20 (minutes). A value of 0 disables this feature.

When automatic saving occurs, the current drawing is always saved in the current directory under the name AUTO.SV$. The current drawing name is not overwritten. If you want to save the drawing under the assigned name, *Save* or *Qsave* must be used, or *Saveas* should be used to save under a new name.

SHELL

PULL-DOWN MENU	SCREEN MENU	TYPE IN	TABLET MENU
---	---	*SHELL*	25,Y

If you like to use DOS commands for file management, you can temporarily exit AutoCAD and type commands at the DOS prompt by using *Shell*. *Shell* automatically switches to the text mode while AutoCAD runs "in the background." The OS command: prompt appears and allows one operating system command before switching back to the AutoCAD command prompt. If you choose to use more than one DOS command, press **Enter** <u>twice</u> after entering *Shell*. A message appears instructing you to type **Exit** to return to AutoCAD.

Shell is very handy at times, but also very dangerous. You can perform most DOS operations like copying, deleting, or renaming files while using *Shell*. However, it is very important to remember that AutoCAD is running while you are "shelled out." You cannot turn off your computer during *Shell* because AutoCAD is still running. Two >> symbols appearing at the DOS prompt (for example, C:\ACADR13\DWG>>) remind you that you must type **Exit** and return to AutoCAD.

AutoCAD keeps several temporary files open while in operation. These files are only "cleaned up" if you return to AutoCAD and exit AutoCAD properly. The results of turning off the computer system while "shelled out" are that the current drawing is lost and several opened temporary files are left on disk. Do not delete any lock files (ending with *.--k extensions) or unrecognizable files (ending with *.$AC, *.$A, or *.SWR) while using *Shell*. Do not try to start AutoCAD by typing **ACADR13**. Do not use the DOS command **chkdsk/f** or **scandisk** while using *Shell*. You can use other DOS commands, but make sure that you eventually type **Exit** to return to AutoCAD.

AutoCAD Backup Files

When a drawing is saved, AutoCAD creates a file with a .DWG extension. For example, if you name the drawing PART1, using *Save* creates a file named PART1.DWG. The next time you save, AutoCAD makes a new PART1.DWG and renames the old version to PART1.BAK. One .BAK (backup) file is always kept automatically by AutoCAD (see the highlighted file name in Figure 2-13).

You cannot *Open* a .BAK file. It must be renamed to a .DWG file. Remember that you already have a .DWG file by the same name, so rename the extension and the filename. For example, PART1.BAK could be renamed to PART1OLD.DWG. Use the *Rename* option of *File Utilities* to rename the file if needed. Alternatively, you could use *Shell* and use the DOS **ren** command to rename the file.

The .BAK files can also be deleted without affecting the .DWG files. The .BAK files accumulate after time, so you should periodically delete the unneeded ones to conserve disk space.

CHAPTER EXERCISES

1. **Determine what the default directory is for saving files on your computer system**

   It should have a name like "C:\ACAD13\DWG" or "D:\ ACAD\FILES." The default (current) directory is used to keep AutoCAD drawing files that you create. (HINT: Use the *Saveas* command. The current directory name appears at the top of the *Saveas* dialogue box.)

2. *Save* **and name a drawing file**

   Start AutoCAD. Draw 2 vertical *Lines*. Select *Save* from the *Files* pull-down. (The *Saveas* dialogue box appears since a name has not yet been assigned.) Name the drawing "**CH2VERT**."

3. **Using** *Qsave*

   Draw 2 more vertical *Lines*. Select *Save* from the menu. (Notice that the *Qsave* command appears at the command line since the drawing has already been named.)

4. **Start a *New* drawing**

   Invoke *New* from the *Files* pull-down. Enter "**CH2HORZ**" as the name for the drawing. Draw 2 horizontal *Lines*. Use *Save*. (Notice *Qsave* is actually used.) Draw 2 more horizontal *Lines*, but <u>do not</u> *Save*. Continue to exercise 5.

5. ***Open* an existing drawing**

   Use *Open* to open **CH2VERT**. Notice that AutoCAD first forces you to select *Yes* or *No* to "Save Changes?" to your current drawing. PICK *Yes* to save the changes. Open CH2VERT.

6. **Using *Saveas***

   Draw 2 inclined (angled) *Lines* in the CH2VERT drawing. Invoke *Saveas* to save the drawing under a new name. Enter "**CH2IN**" as the new name. (Notice the current drawing name is reset to the new name.) Draw 2 more inclined *Lines* and *Save.*

7. ***Open* an AutoCAD sample drawing**

   Open a drawing named **LINKRODS** usually located in the C:\ACADR13\COMMON\SAMPLE directory. Use the *Directories* section of the dialogue box to change drive and directory if necessary. Do <u>not</u> *Save* the sample drawing after viewing it. Practice the *Open* command by looking at other sample drawings in the SAMPLE directory.

8. *List Files*

   Type the *Files* command and select *List Files...* to list the drawings in the directory where your drawings are saved. Check for CH2VERT, CH2HORZ and CH2IN.

9. *Rename* **a drawing**

   Type *Files* again and use the *Rename File...* option. Change the name of CH2IN.DWG to **CH2INCL.DWG**.

Chapter 3

DRAW COMMAND BASICS

Chapter Objectives

After completing this chapter you should be able to:

1. recognize drawing objects;

2. draw *Lines* <u>interactively</u>;

3. use *SNAP*, *GRID*, and *ORTHO* while drawing *Lines* and *Circles* interactively;

4. create *Lines* by specifying <u>absolute</u> coordinates;

5. create *Lines* by specifying <u>relative rectangular</u> coordinates;

6. create *Lines* by specifying <u>relative polar</u> coordinates;

7. create *Circles* by each of the four coordinate entry methods.

AutoCAD OBJECTS

The smallest component of a drawing in AutoCAD is called an <u>object</u> (sometimes referred to as an entity). An example of an object is a *Line*, an *Arc*, or a *Circle*. A rectangle created with the *Line* command would contain four objects.

Draw commands <u>create</u> objects. The draw command names are the same as the object names.

Simple objects are *Point*, *Line*, *Arc*, and *Circle*.

Complex objects are shapes such as *Ellipse, Polygon, Polyline, Spline,* and *Donut*, which are created with one command. Even though they appear to have several segments, they are <u>treated</u> by AutoCAD as one object.

It is not always apparent whether a shape is composed of one or more objects. However, if you pick an object with the "pickbox," an object is "highlighted," or shown in a broken line pattern (Fig. 3-3). This highlighting reveals whether the shape is composed of one or several objects.

Figure 3-1

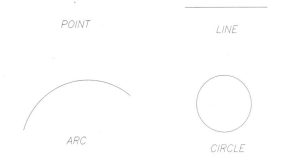

Figure 3-2

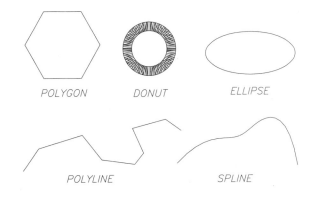

Figure 3-3

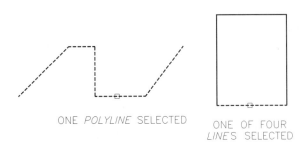

LOCATING THE DRAW COMMANDS

To invoke Draw commands, any of the five command entry methods can be used depending on your computer setup.

1. **Toolbars** (Windows)   Select the icon from the Draw toolbar.
2. **Pull-down menu**   Select the command from the *Draw* pull-down menu.
3. **Screen menu**   Select the command from the *Draw* screen menu.
4. **Keyboard**   Type the command name, command alias, or accelerator keys at the keyboard (a command alias is a one- or two-letter shortcut).
5. **Tablet menu**   Select the icon from the digitizing tablet menu (if available).

For example, a draw command can be activated by PICKing its icon button from the Draw toolbar (Fig 3-4). Related commands or options are located in groups (flyouts). The figure shows how all of the options for the *Circle* command fly out when the "top" button is PICKed.

The *Draw* pull-down menu can also be used to select draw commands (Fig. 3-5). Options for a command are found on cascading menus. The options for drawing a *Circle* shown here are the same options as indicated by the icon buttons in the previous figure.

Figure 3-4 ───────────

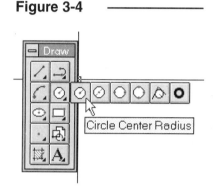

Figure 3-5 ─────────────────────────

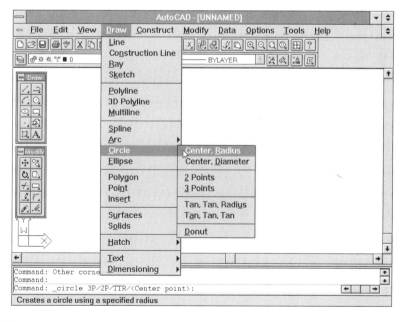

Figure 3-6

NOTE: Use the ACADFULL menu in Windows.

Additionally, the Screen menu can be used to select draw commands. Three menus contain all the draw commands: *DRAW1, DRAW2,* and *DRAWDIM* (Fig. 3-6).

THE FOUR COORDINATE ENTRY METHODS

All drawing commands prompt you to specify points, or locations, in the drawing. For example, the *Line* command prompts you to give the "From point:" and "to point:", expecting you to specify locations for the first and second endpoints of the line. After you specify those points, AutoCAD stores the specified coordinate values to define the line. A 2-dimensional line in AutoCAD is defined and stored in the database as two sets of X and Y values, one for each endpoint.

There are four ways to specify coordinates; that is, there are four ways to tell AutoCAD the location of points when you draw objects.

1.	**Interactive method**	**PICK**	Use the cursor to select points on the screen.
2.	**Absolute coordinates**	**X,Y**	Type explicit X and Y values relative to the origin at 0,0.
3.	**Relative rectangular coordinates**	**@X,Y**	Type explicit X and Y values relative to the last point (@ means "last point").
4.	**Relative polar coordinates**	**@dist<angle**	Type a distance value and angle value relative to the last point (< means "angle of").

DRAWING *LINES* USING THE FOUR COORDINATE ENTRY METHODS

The *Line* command can be activated by any one of the methods shown in the command table below.

LINE

PULL-DOWN MENU	SCREEN MENU	TYPE IN	TABLET MENU
Draw *Line*	*DRAW1* *Line:*	*LINE or L*	*10, J*

Drawing Horizontal Lines

1. Draw a horizontal *Line* of 2 units length starting at point 2,2. Use the <u>interactive</u> method. See Figure 3-7.

STEPS	COMMAND PROMPT	PERFORM ACTION	COMMENTS
1.		turn on *GRID* (**F7**)	Grid appears
2.		turn on *SNAP* (**F9**)	"Snap" appears on Status Line
3.	Command:	select or type *Line*	use any method
4.	From point:	**PICK** location **2,2**	watch *COORDS*
5.	to point:	**PICK** location **4,2**	watch *COORDS*
6.	to point:	press **Enter**	completes command

The preceding steps produce a *Line* as shown.

Figure 3-7

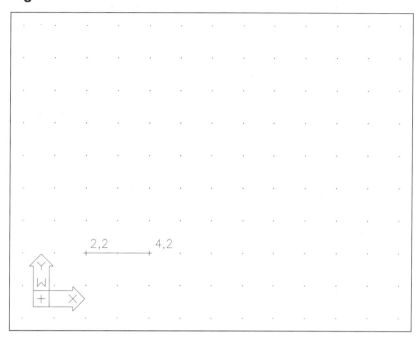

2. Draw a horizontal *Line* of 2 units length starting at point 2,3 using <u>absolute coordinates</u>.

STEPS	COMMAND PROMPT	PERFORM ACTION	COMMENTS
1.	Command:	select *Line*	use any method
2.	From point:	type **2,3** and press **Enter**	"blip" should appear
3.	to point:	type **4,3** and press **Enter**	a *Line* should appear
4.	to point:	press **Enter**	completes command

The above procedure produces the new *Line* above the first *Line* as shown.

Figure 3-8

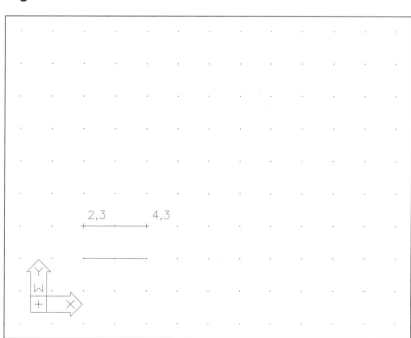

3. Draw a horizontal *Line* of 2 units length starting at point 2,4 using <u>relative rectangular coordinates</u>.

STEPS	COMMAND PROMPT	PERFORM ACTION	COMMENTS
1.	Command:	select *Line*	use any method
2.	From point:	type **2,4** and press **Enter**	"blip" should appear
3.	to point:	type **@2,0** and press **Enter**	@ means "last point"
4.	to point:	press **Enter**	completes command

The new *Line* appears above the previous two as shown here.

Figure 3-9

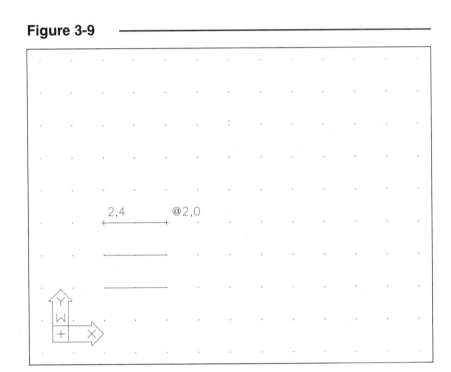

4. Draw a horizontal *Line* of 2 units length starting at point 2,5 using <u>relative polar coordinates</u>.

STEPS	COMMAND PROMPT	PERFORM ACTION	COMMENTS
1.	Command:	select *Line*	use any method
2.	From point:	type **2,5** and press **Enter**	"blip" should appear
3.	to point:	type **@2<0** and press **Enter**	@ means "last point" < means "angle of"
4.	to point:	press **Enter**	completes command

The new horizontal *Line* appears above the other three. See Figure 3-10.

One of these methods may be more favorable than another in a particular situation. The interactive method is fast and easy, assuming that O*SNAP* is used (see Chapter 7) or that *SNAP* and *GRID* are used and set to appropriate values. *SNAP* and *GRID* are used successfully for small drawings where objects have regular interval lengths.

Figure 3-10

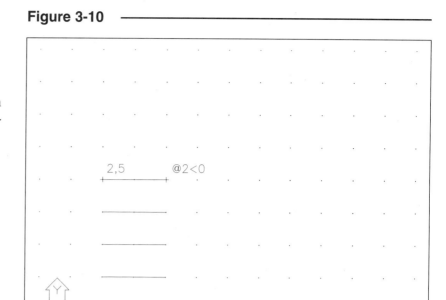

Drawing Vertical Lines

Below are listed the steps in drawing vertical lines using each of the four methods of coordinate entry. The following completed problems should look like those in Figure 3-11.

Figure 3-11

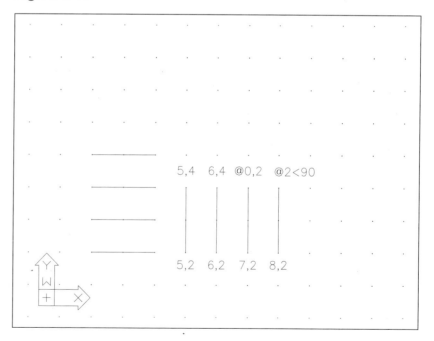

1.   Draw a vertical *Line* of 2 units length starting at point 5,2 using the <u>interactive</u> method.

STEPS	COMMAND PROMPT	PERFORM ACTION	COMMENTS
1.		turn on *GRID* (**F7**)	Grid appears
2.		turn on *SNAP* (**F9**)	"Snap" appears on Status Line
3.	Command:	select or type *Line*	use any method
4.	From point:	**PICK** location **5,2**	watch *COORDS*
5.	to point:	**PICK** location **5,4**	watch *COORDS*
6.	to point:	press **Enter**	completes command

2.   Draw a vertical *Line* of 2 units length starting at point 6,2 using <u>absolute coordinates</u>.

STEPS	COMMAND PROMPT	PERFORM ACTION	COMMENTS
1.	Command:	select *Line*	use any method
2.	From point:	type **6,2** and press **Enter**	a "blip" should appear
3.	to point:	type **6,4** and press **Enter**	a *Line* should appear
4.	to point:	press **Enter**	completes command

3.   Draw a vertical *Line* of 2 units length starting at point 7,2 using <u>relative rectangular coordinates</u>.

STEPS	COMMAND PROMPT	PERFORM ACTION	COMMENTS
1.	Command:	select *Line*	use any method
2.	From point:	type **7,2** and press **Enter**	a "blip" should appear
3.	to point:	type **@0,2** and press **Enter**	@ means "last point"
4.	to point:	press **Enter**	completes command

4.   Draw a vertical *Line* of 2 units length starting at point 8,2 using <u>relative polar coordinates</u>.

STEPS	COMMAND PROMPT	PERFORM ACTION	COMMENTS
1.	Command:	select *Line*	use any method
2.	From point:	type **8,2** and press **Enter**	a "blip" should appear
3.	to point:	type **@2<90** and press **Enter**	@ means "last point" < means "angle of"
4.	to point:	press **Enter**	completes command

The method used depends on the application and the individual. The interactive method is usually fast and easy, assuming that *OSNAP* is used (see Chapter 7) or that *SNAP* and *GRID* are used and are set to appropriate values.

Drawing Inclined Lines

Following are listed the steps in drawing <u>inclined lines</u> using each of the four methods of coordinate entry. The following completed problems should look like those in Figure 3-12.

Figure 3-12

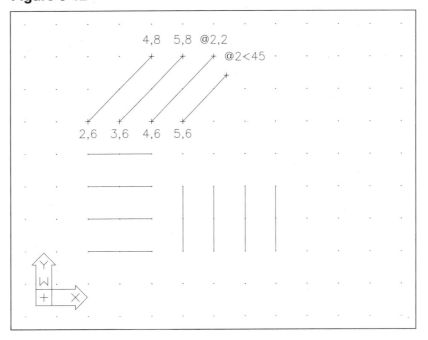

1. Draw an inclined *Line* of from 2,6 to 4,8. Use the <u>interactive</u> method.

STEPS	COMMAND PROMPT	PERFORM ACTION	COMMENTS
1.		turn on *GRID* (**F7**)	Grid appears
2.		turn on *SNAP* (**F9**)	"Snap" appears on Status Line
3.		turn off *ORTHO* (**F8**)	in order to draw inclined *Lines*
4.	Command:	select or type *Line*	use any method
5.	From point:	**PICK** location **2,6**	watch *COORDS*
6.	to point:	**PICK** location **4,8**	watch *COORDS*
7.	to point:	press **Enter**	completes command

2. Draw an inclined *Line* starting at 3,6 and ending at 5,8. Use <u>absolute coordinates</u>.

STEPS	COMMAND PROMPT	PERFORM ACTION	COMMENTS
1.	Command:	select *Line*	use any method
2.	From point:	type **3,6** and press **Enter**	a "blip" should appear
3.	to point:	type **5,8** and press **Enter**	a *Line* should appear
4.	to point:	press **Enter**	completes command

3. Draw an inclined *Line* starting at 4,6 and ending 2 units over (in a positive X direction) and 2 units up (in a positive Y direction). Use <u>relative rectangular coordinates</u>.

STEPS	COMMAND PROMPT	PERFORM ACTION	COMMENTS
1.	Command:	select *Line*	use any method
2.	From point:	type **4,6** and press **Enter**	a "blip" should appear
3.	to point:	type **@2,2** and press **Enter**	@ means "last point"
4.	to point:	press **Enter**	completes command

4. Draw an inclined *Line* of 2 units length at a 45 degree angle and starting at 5,6. Use <u>relative polar coordinates</u>.

STEPS	COMMAND PROMPT	PERFORM ACTION	COMMENTS
1.	Command:	select *Line*	use any method
2.	From point:	type **5,6** and press **Enter**	a "blip" should appear
3.	to point:	type **@2<45** and press **Enter**	@ means "last point" < means "angle of"
4.	to point:	press **Enter**	completes command

This last method, using polar values, is preferred if you are required to draw an inclined line with an exact length and angle. Notice that each of the first three methods draws an inclined line of 2.828 (2 * square root of 2) units length since the line is the hypotenuse of a right triangle.

DRAWING *CIRCLES* USING THE FOUR COMMAND ENTRY METHODS

Begin a *New* drawing to complete the *Circle* exercises. The *Circle* command can be invoked by any of the methods shown in the command table.

CIRCLE

PULL-DOWN MENU	SCREEN MENU	TYPE IN	TABLET MENU
Draw *Circle >* *Center, Radius*	*DRAW1* *Circle:* *Cen, Rad*	*CIRCLE* *or C*	*10,M*

Below are listed the steps for drawing *Circles* using the *Center, Radius* method. The circles are to be drawn using each of the four coordinate entry methods and should look like those in this figure.

Figure 3-13

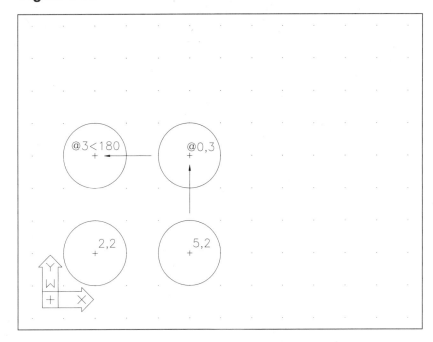

1. Draw a *Circle* of 1 unit radius with the center at point 2,2. Use the <u>interactive</u> method.

STEPS	COMMAND PROMPT	PERFORM ACTION	COMMENTS
1.		turn on *GRID* (**F7**)	Grid appears
2.		turn on *SNAP* (**F9**)	"Snap" appears on Status Line
3.		turn on *ORTHO* (**F8**)	"Ortho" appears on Status Line
4.	Command:	select or type **Circle**	use *Center, Radius* method
5.	3P/2P/TTR/<Center point>:	**PICK** location **2,2**	watch *COORDS*
6.	Diameter/<Radius>:	move 1 unit and **PICK**	watch *COORDS*

2. Draw a circle of 1 unit radius with the center at point 5,2. Use <u>absolute coordinates</u>.

STEPS	COMMAND PROMPT	PERFORM ACTION	COMMENTS
1.	Command:	select **Circle**	use *Center, Radius* method
2.	3P/2P/TTR/<Center point>:	type **5,2** and press **Enter**	a "blip" or *Circle* should appear
3.	Diameter/<Radius>:	type **1** and press **Enter**	the correct *Circle* appears

3. Draw a circle of 1 unit radius with the center 3 units above the last point (previous *Circle* center). Use <u>relative rectangular coordinates</u>.

STEPS	COMMAND PROMPT	PERFORM ACTION	COMMENTS
1.	Command:	select *Circle*	use *Center, Radius* method
2.	3P/2P/TTR/<Center point>:	type @0,3 and press **Enter**	a "blip" or *Circle* should appear
3.	Diameter/<Radius>:	type 1 and press **Enter**	the correct *Circle* appears

(If the new *Circle* is not above the last, type "ID" and enter "5,2." The entered point becomes the last point. Then try again.)

4. Draw a circle of 1 unit radius with the center 3 units to the left of the previous *Circle*. Use <u>relative polar coordinates</u>.

STEPS	COMMAND PROMPT	PERFORM ACTION	COMMENTS
1.	Command:	select *Circle*	use *Center, Radius* method
2.	3P/2P/TTR/<Center point>:	type @3<180 and press **Enter**	a "blip" or *Circle* should appear
3.	Diameter/<Radius>:	type 1 and press **Enter**	the *Circle* appears

CHAPTER EXERCISES

1. **Start a *New* drawing**

   Start a *New* drawing and assign the name "**CH3EX**." Remember to *Save* often as you complete the following exercises. The completed exercise should look like Figure 3-14.

2. **Using interactive coordinate entry**

   Draw a square with sides of 2 units length. Locate the lower left corner of the square at **2,2**. Use the *Line* command with interactive coordinate entry. (HINT: Turn on *SNAP*, *GRID*, and *ORTHO*.)

3. **Using absolute coordinates**

   Draw another square with 2 unit sides using the *Line* command. Enter absolute coordinates. Begin with the lower left corner of the square at **5,2**.

4. **Using relative rectangular coordinates**

    Draw a third square (with 2 unit sides) using the *Line* command. Enter relative rectangular coordinates. Locate the lower left corner at **8,2**.

5. **Using relative polar coordinates**

    Draw a fourth square (with 2 unit sides) beginning at a lower left corner of **2,5**. Complete the sides by drawing *Lines* with relative polar coordinates.

6. **Using relative polar coordinates**

    Draw an equilateral triangle with sides of 2 units. Locate the lower left corner at **5,5**. Use relative polar coordinates (<u>after</u> establishing the "From point:"). HINT: An equilateral triangle has interior angles of 60 degrees.

7. **Using interactive coordinate entry**

    Draw a *Circle* with a 1 unit <u>radius</u>. Locate the center at **9,6**. Use the interactive method. (Turn on *SNAP* and *GRID*.)

8. **Using relative rectangular or polar coordinates**

    Draw another *Circle* with a 2 unit <u>diameter</u>. Using relative coordinates, locate the center 3 units below the previous *Circle*.

9. *Save* **your drawing**

    Use *Save*. Compare your results with Figure 3-14. When you are finished, *Exit* AutoCAD.

Figure 3-14 ————————————————————————

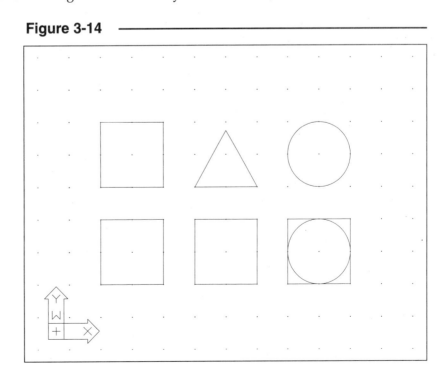

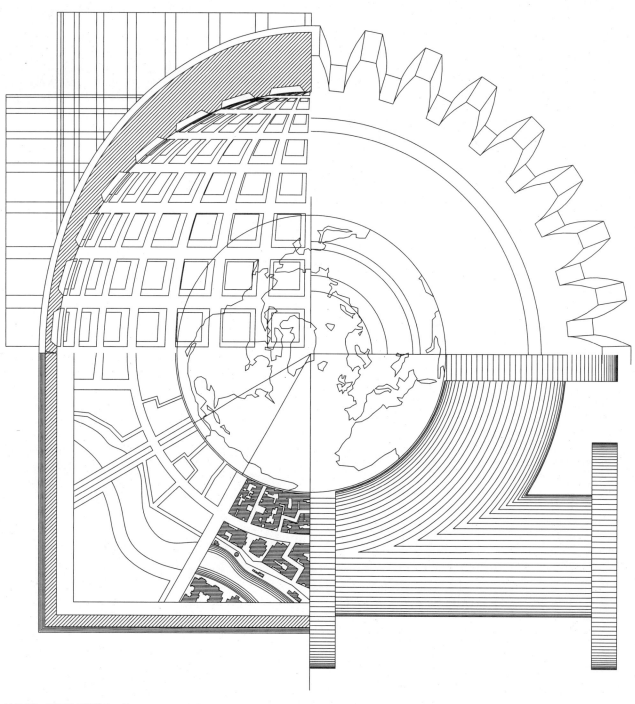

PSGLOBE.DWG Courtesy of Autodesk, Inc.

Chapter 4
SELECTION SETS

Chapter Objectives

After completing this chapter you should:

1. know that Modify and Construct commands require you to select objects;

2. be able to create a selection set using each of the specification methods;

3. be able to *Erase* objects from the drawing;

4. be able to *Move* objects from one location to another;

5. understand Noun/Verb and Verb/Noun order of command syntax.

CONSTRUCT AND MODIFY COMMAND BASICS

Draw commands create objects. <u>Construct</u> commands <u>use existing objects to create new ones</u>. An example would be to *Copy* an existing *Circle*. <u>Modify</u> commands <u>change existing objects</u>. An example would be to *Move* a *Line* or *Erase* a *Circle*.

Since all of the Construct and Modify commands use or modify <u>existing</u> objects, you must first select the objects that you want to act on. The process of selecting the objects you want to use is called building a <u>selection set</u>. For example, if you want to *Copy*, *Erase*, or *Move* several objects in the drawing, you must first select the set of objects that you want to act on.

Remember that any of the five command entry methods (depending on your setup) can be used to invoke Construct and Modify commands.

1. **Toolbars** (Windows)   Modify toolbar
2. **Pull-down menu**   *Construct* or *Modify* pull-down menu
3. **Screen menu**   *Construct* or *Modify* screen menu
4. **Keyboard**   Type the command name <u>or</u> command alias
5. **Tablet menu**   Select the command icon

All of the Construct and Modify commands will be discussed in detail later, but for now we will focus on how to build selection sets.

SELECTION SETS

No matter which of the five methods above you use to invoke a Construct or Modify command, you must specify a selection set during the command operation. There are two ways you can select objects: you can select the set of objects either (1) immediately before you invoke the command or (2) when the command prompts you to select objects. For example, examine the command syntax that would appear at the command line when the *Erase* command is used (method 2).

Figure 4-1

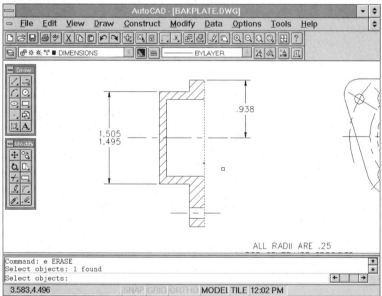

Command: **erase**
Select objects:

The "Select objects:" prompt is your cue to use any of several methods to PICK the objects to erase. As a matter of fact, every Construct and Modify command begins with the same "Select objects:" prompt (unless you selected immediately before invoking the command).

When the "Select objects:" prompt appears, the crosshairs disappear and only a small, square pickbox appears at the cursor (Fig. 4-1). You can PICK objects using only the pickbox or any of several other methods illustrated in this chapter. (Only when you PICK objects at the "Select objects:" prompt can you use all of the selection methods shown here. If you PICK immediately before the command, called Noun/Verb order, only the AUto method can be used. See Noun/Verb at the chapter end.)

When the objects have been selected, they become highlighted (displayed as a broken line), which serves as a visual indication of the current selection set. Press **Enter** to indicate that you are finished selecting and are ready to proceed with the command.

Selection Set Menus

When the "Select objects:" prompt appears, you should select objects using the pickbox or one of a variety of other methods. Any method can be used <u>independently</u> or in <u>combination</u> to achieve the desired set of objects. The pickbox is the default option which can automatically be changed to a window or crossing window by PICKing in an open area (PICKing no objects). The other methods can be selected from the screen, the tablet menu, or by typing the capitalized letters shown in the option names following.

If you are using AutoCAD for Windows, the selection set options are available on the Standard toolbar in a flyout fashion (Fig. 4-2). You can also activate a separate Select Objects toolbar so that each option is available at the top level without having to run the flyouts (Fig. 4-3).

Figure 4-2

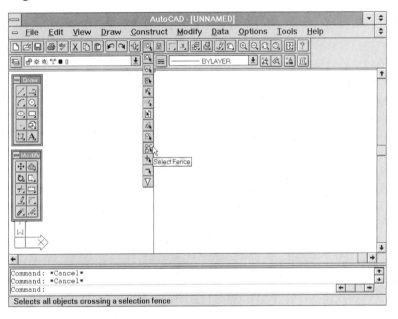

Figure 4-3

AutoCAD for DOS users may want to use the *Select Objects* section of the *Assist* pull-down menu (Fig. 4-4). The same options are in the Windows version under the *Edit* pull-down menu (ACADFULL menu).

Figure 4-4

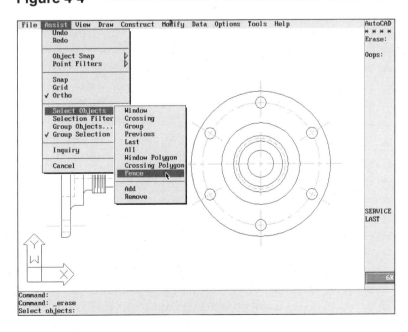

R13

Optionally, the *Service* menu can be called to access selection options. The *Service* menu is available at the bottom of any *Modify* or *Construct* screen menu.

In any version of AutoCAD you can <u>type</u> any option (shown in capital letters) at the "Select objects:" prompt to use that option. The options are also available on the digitizing tablet in the second row beneath the screen pointing area.

Figure 4-5

Selection Set Options

The options for creating selection sets (PICKing objects) are shown on this and the following pages. Two *Circles* and five *Lines* (as shown in Figure 4-6) are used for every example. In each case, the <u>circles only</u> are selected for editing. If you want to follow along and practice as you read, draw *Circles* and *Lines* in a configuration similar to this. Then use a *Modify* or *Construct* command. (Press **Escape** to cancel the command after selecting objects.)

Figure 4-6

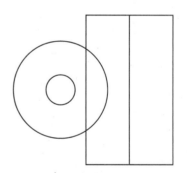

pickbox

This default option is used for selecting <u>one object</u> at a time. Locate the pickbox so that an object crosses through it and **PICK** (Fig. 4-7). You do not have to type or select anything to use this option.

Figure 4-7

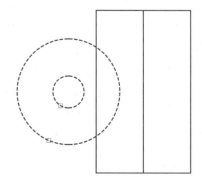

AUto
To use this option, you do not have to type or select anything from the Select Objects menu or toolbars. The pickbox must be positioned in an open area so that no objects cross through it; then **PICK** to start a window. If you drag to the <u>right</u>, a *Window* is created (Fig. 4-8). **PICK** the other corner.

Figure 4-8

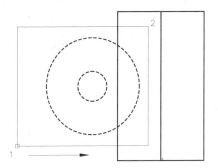

If you drag to the <u>left</u> instead, a *Crossing Window* forms (Fig. 4-9). (See Window and Crossing Window below.)

Figure 4-9

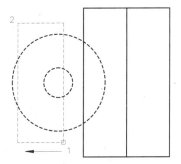

Window

 Only objects <u>completely within</u> the *Window* are selected. The *Window* is a solid linetype rectangular box. Select the first and second points (diagonal corners in either direction) as shown in Figure 4-10.

Figure 4-10

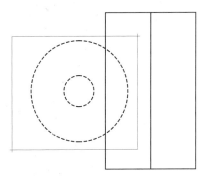

Crossing Window

 All objects <u>within and crossing through</u> the window are selected. The *Crossing Window* is displayed as a broken linetype rectangular box. Select two diagonal <u>corners</u>.

Figure 4-11

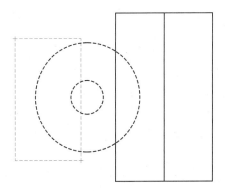

Window Polygon

 The *Window Polygon* operates like a *Window*, but the box can be <u>any</u> irregular polygonal shape (Fig. 4-12). You can pick any number of corners rather than just two as with the *Window* option.

Crossing Polygon

 The *Crossing Polygon* operates like a *Crossing Window*, but can have any number of corners like *Window Polygon* (Fig. 4-13).

Fence

 This option operates like a <u>crossing line</u>. Any objects crossing the *Fence* are selected. The *Fence* can have any number of segments (Fig. 4-14).

Last

 This option automatically finds and selects <u>only</u> the last object created.

Previous

 Previous finds and selects the <u>previous selection set</u>, i.e., whatever was selected during the previous command (except after *Erase*). This option allows you to use several editing commands on the same set of objects without having to re-specify the set.

ALL

 This option selects <u>all objects</u> in the drawing except those on *Frozen* or *Locked* layers (*Layers* are covered in Chapter 12).

Remove

 Selecting this option causes AutoCAD to <u>switch</u> to the Remove objects: mode. Any selection options used from this time on remove objects from the highlighted set (see Figure 4-15).

Add

 The *Add* option switches back to the default Select objects: mode so additional objects can be added to the selection set.

SHIFT+ #1

Holding down the **SHIFT** key and pressing the **#1** button simultaneously <u>removes</u> objects selected from the highlighted set as shown in Figure 4-15.

Figure 4-12

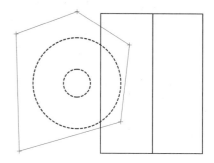

Figure 4-13

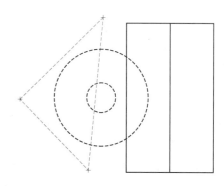

Figure 4-14

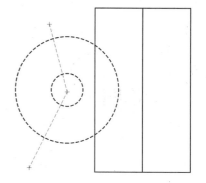

Figure 4-15

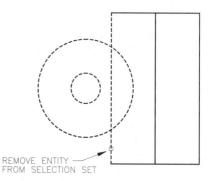

REMOVE ENTITY FROM SELECTION SET

Group

The *Group* option selects groups of objects that were previously specified using the *Group* command. Groups are selection sets to which you can assign a name (see Chapter 20).

Ctrl + #1

Holding down the **Ctrl** key and simultaneously pressing the **PICK** (#1) button will cycle through (highlight one at a time) two or more objects that may be in the pickbox. Use this method if you want to select one of two colinear lines.

SELECT

DOS PULL-DOWN	WIN PULL-DOWN	SCREEN MENU	TYPE IN	TABLET MENU
Assist *Select Objects >*	*Edit* *Select Objects >*	*EDIT* *Select:*	*SELECT*	---

The *Select* command can be used to PICK objects to be saved in the selection set buffer for subsequent use with the *Previous* option. Any of the selection methods may be used to PICK the objects.

```
Command: select
Select objects: PICK (Use any selection option.)
Select objects: Enter (Completes the selection process.)
Command:
```

The selected objects become unhighlighted when you complete the command by pressing Enter. The objects become highlighted again and are used as the selection set if you use the *Previous* selection option in the next editing command.

NOTE: The *Select* command can also be activated by making a choice from the *Select Objects* option from the pull-down menu (*Assist* in DOS, Fig. 4-4; *Edit* in Windows) or by PICKing a selection option from the icon buttons (Fig. 4-2 and 4-3). The *Select* command is activated by this method only when no command is in use. In other words, if you PICK a selection option by the above methods at the open Command: prompt, the *Select* command is invoked.

SELECTION SETS PRACTICE

NOTE: While learning and practicing with the editing commands, it is suggested that *GRIPS* be turned off. This can be accomplished by typing in **GRIPS** and setting the *GRIPS* variable to a value of **0**. The AutoCAD Release 13 default has *GRIPS* on (set to 1). *GRIPS* are covered in Chapter 23.

Using *Erase*

Erase is the simplest editing command. *Erase* removes objects from the drawing. The only action required is the selection of objects to be erased.

ERASE

PULL-DOWN MENU	SCREEN MENU	TYPE IN	TABLET MENU
Modify *Erase*	*MODIFY* *Erase:*	*ERASE* *or E*	*16,W and* *17,W*

1. Draw several *Lines* and *Circles*. Practice using the object selection options with the *Erase* command. The following sequence uses the pickbox, window, and crossing window.

STEPS	COMMAND PROMPT	PERFORM ACTION	COMMENTS
1.	Command:	type *E* and press **space bar**	*E* is the alias for *Erase*, space bar can be used like Enter
2.	Erase Select objects:	use pickbox to select one or two objects	objects are highlighted
3.	Select objects:	type *W* or use *Select Objects* menu and *Window*, then select more objects.	objects are highlighted
4.	Select objects:	type *C* or use *Select Objects* menu and *Crossing*, then select objects.	objects are highlighted
5.	Select objects:	press **Enter**	objects are erased

2. Draw several more *Lines* and *Circles*. Practice using the *Erase* command with the *AUto window* and *AUto crossing window* options as indicated below.

STEPS	COMMAND PROMPT	PERFORM ACTION	COMMENTS
1.	Command:	select the *Modify* pull-down, then *Erase*	
2.	Erase Select objects:	use pickbox to select an open area, drag *window* to the <u>right</u> to select objects	objects inside window are highlighted
3.	Select objects:	select an open area, drag *crossing window* to the <u>left</u> to select objects	objects inside and crossing through window are highlighted
4.	Select objects:	press **Enter**	objects are erased

Using *Move*

The *Move* command specifically prompts you to (1) select objects, (2) specify a "Base point," or point to move <u>from</u>, and (3) specify a "second point of displacement," or point to move <u>to</u>.

MOVE

PULL-DOWN MENU	SCREEN MENU	TYPE IN	TABLET MENU
Modify *Move*	*MODIFY* *Move:*	*MOVE* or *M*	15,W

1. Draw a *Circle* and two *Lines*. Use the *Move* command to practice selecting objects and to move one *Line* and the *Circle* as indicated in the following table.

STEPS	COMMAND PROMPT	PERFORM ACTION	COMMENTS
1.	Command:	type *M* and press **space bar**	*M* is the command alias for *Move*
2.	Move Select objects:	use pickbox to select one *Line* and the *Circle*	objects are highlighted
3.	Select objects:	press **space bar** or **Enter**	
4.	Base point or displacement:	**PICK** near the *Circle* center	base point is the handle, or where to move <u>from</u>
5.	Second point of displacement:	**PICK** near the other *Line*	second point is where to move <u>to</u>

2. Use *Move* again to move the *Circle* back to its original position. Select the *Circle* with the *Window* option.

STEPS	COMMAND PROMPT	PERFORM ACTION	COMMENTS
1.	Command:	select the *Modify* pull-down, then *Move*	
2.	Move Select objects:	type *W* and press **space bar** or use menu to select *Window*	select only the circle; object is highlighted
3.	Select objects:	press **space bar** or **Enter**	
4.	Base point or displacement:	**PICK** near the *Circle* center	base point is the handle, or where to move <u>from</u>
5.	Second point of displacement:	**PICK** near the original location	second point is where to move <u>to</u>

NOUN/VERB SYNTAX

An object is the <u>noun</u> and a command is the <u>verb</u>. Noun/Verb syntax order means to pick objects (nouns) first, then use an editing command (verb) second. If you select objects first (at the open Command: prompt) and then immediately choose a Modify or Construct command, AutoCAD recognizes the selection set and passes through the "Select Objects:" prompt to the next step in the command.

Verb/Noun means to invoke a command and then select objects within the command. For example, if the *Erase* command (verb) is invoked first, AutoCAD then issues the prompt to "Select Objects:"; therefore, objects (nouns) are PICKed second. In the previous examples, and with older versions of AutoCAD, only Verb/Noun syntax order was used.

You can use <u>either</u> order you want (Noun/Verb and Verb/Noun) and AutoCAD automatically understands. If objects are selected first, the selection set is passed to the next editing command used, but if no objects are selected first, the editing command automatically prompts you to "Select objects:".

If you use Noun/Verb order, you are limited to using only the *AUto* options for object selection (pickbox, window, and crossing window). You can only use the other options (e.g., *Crossing Polygon*, *Fence*, *Previous*, etc.) if you invoke the desired Modify or Construct command first, then select objects when the "Select objects:" prompt appears.

The *PICKFIRST* variable (a very descriptive name) enables Noun/Verb syntax. The default setting is 1 (*On*). If *PICKFIRST* is set to 0 (*Off*), Noun/Verb syntax is disabled and the selection set can only be specified <u>within</u> the editing commands (Verb/Noun).

Setting *PICKFIRST* to 1 provides two options: Noun/Verb and Verb/Noun. You can use <u>either</u> order you want. If objects are selected first, the selection set is passed to the next editing command, but if no objects are selected first, the editing command prompts you to select objects. See Chapter 20 for a complete explanation of *PICKFIRST* and advanced selection set features.

CHAPTER EXERCISES

Open drawing **CH3EX** that you created in Chapter 3 Exercises. Turn off *SNAP* (**F9**) to make object selection easier.

1. **Use the pickbox to select objects**

   Invoke the *Erase* command by any method. Select the lower left square with the pickbox (Figure 4-16, highlighted). Each *Line* must be selected individually. Press **Enter** to complete *Erase*. Then use the *Oops* command to unerase the square. (Type *Oops* or select it from the bottom of the *Modify* pull-down.)

Figure 4-16 ————————

2. **Use the *AUto* window and *Auto* crossing window**

   Invoke *Erase*. Select the center square on the bottom row with the *AUto* window and select the equilateral triangle with the *AUto* crossing window. Press **Enter** to complete the *Erase* as shown in Figure 4-17. Use *Oops* to bring back the objects.

Figure 4-17 ————————

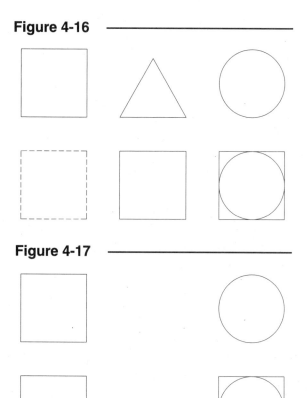

3. **Use the *Fence* selection option**

   Invoke *Erase* again. Use the *Fence* option to select all the vertical *Lines* and the *Circle* from the squares on the bottom row. Complete the *Erase* (see Figure 4-18). Use *Oops* to unerase.

Figure 4-18

4. **Use the *ALL* option and deselect**

   Use *Erase*. Select all the objects with *ALL*. Remove the four *Lines* (shown highlighted in Figure 4-19) from the selection set by pressing **Shift** while PICKing. Complete the *Erase* to leave only the four *Lines*. Finally, use *Oops*.

Figure 4-19

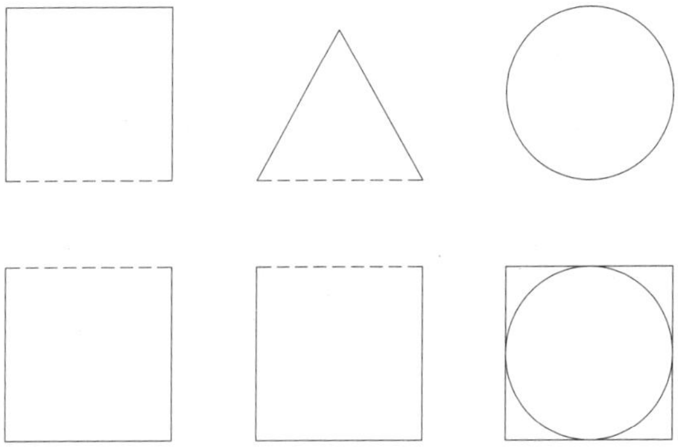

5. **Using Noun/Verb selection**

   Before invoking *Erase*, use the pickbox or *AUto* window to select the triangle. (Make sure no other commands are in use.) Then invoke *Erase*. The triangle should disappear. Retrieve the triangle with *Oops*.

6. **Using *Move* with *Wpolygon***

   Invoke the *Move* command by any method. Use the *WP* option (*Window Polygon*) to select only the *Lines* comprising the triangle. Turn on *SNAP* and PICK the lower left corner as the "Base point:". *Move* the triangle up 1 unit. (See Figure 4-20.)

Figure 4-20

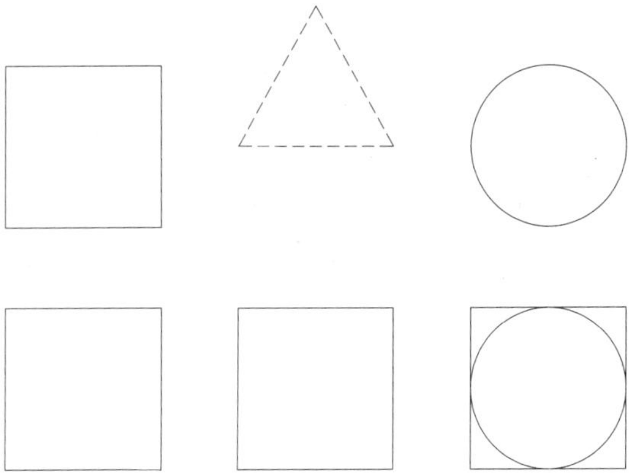

7. **Using *Previous* with *Move***

   Invoke *Move* again. At the "Select objects:" prompt, type *P* or select *Previous*. The triangle should highlight. Using the same base point, move the triangle back to its original position.

8. *Exit* AutoCAD and do not save changes.

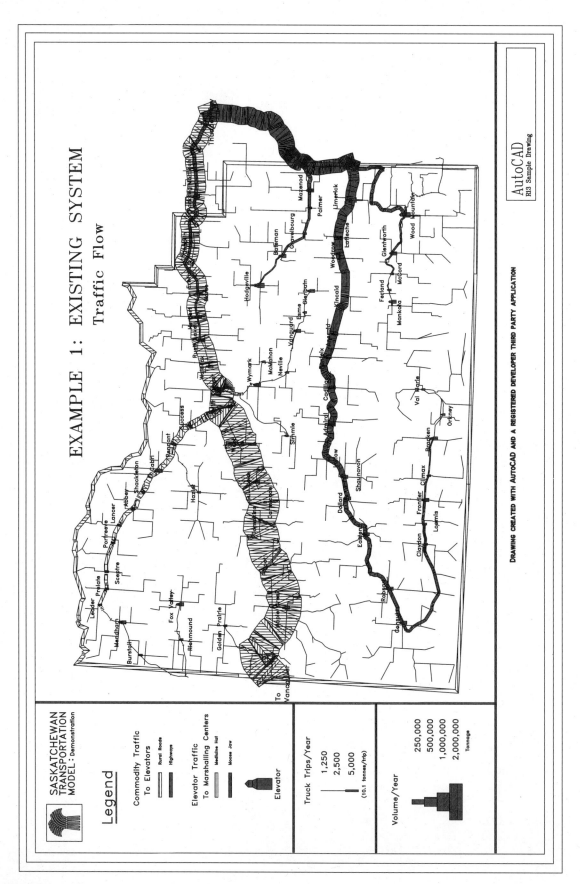

Chapter 5
HELPFUL COMMANDS

Chapter Objectives

After completing this chapter you should be able to:

1. find *Help* for any command or system variable;

2. use *Oops* to unerase objects;

3. use *U* to undo one command or use *Undo* to undo multiple commands;

4. set a *Mark* and use *Undo Back* to undo all commands until the marker is encountered;

5. *Redo* commands that were undone;

6. *Redraw* the screen;

7. regenerate the drawing with *Regen*.

BASICS

There are several commands that do not draw or edit objects in AutoCAD, but are intended to assist you in using AutoCAD. These commands are used by experienced AutoCAD users and are particularly helpful to the beginner. The commands, as a group, are not located in any one menu, but are scattered in several menus.

COMMANDS

HELP

PULL-DOWN MENU	SCREEN MENU	TYPE IN	TABLET MENU
Help	*HELP* *Help*	*HELP* *or ?*	*7,T and 8,T*

Help or *?* gives you an explanation for any AutoCAD command or system variable as well as help for using the menus and toolbars. *Help* displays a window or dialogue box which gives a variety of methods for finding the information that you need. There is even help for using help!

Help can be used two ways: (1) entered as a command at the open Command: prompt or (2) used transparently while a command is currently in use.

1. If the *Help* command is entered at an open Command: prompt (when no other commands are in use), the *Help* window appears (Fig. 5-1).

Figure 5-1 ―――――――――――――

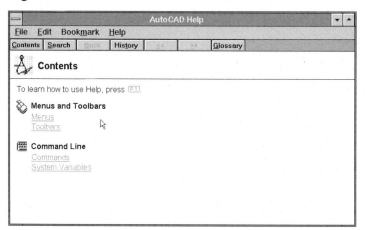

2. When *Help* is used transparently (when a command is in use), it is context-sensitive; that is, help on the current command is given automatically. For example, Figures 5-2 (Windows) and 5-3 (DOS) display the window that appears if *Help* is invoked during the *Circle* command. (If typing a transparent command, an ' [apostrophe] symbol is typed as a prefix to the command, e.g., *'HELP* or *'?*. If you PICK *Help* from the menus, it is automatically transparent.)

Figure 5-2 ―――――――――――――

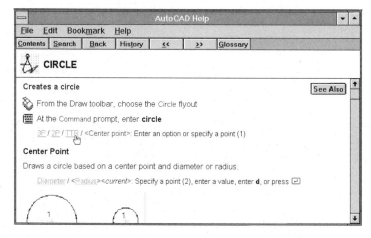

Much of the text that appears in the window can be PICKed to reveal another level of help on that item. In Windows this feature, called Hypertext, is activated by moving the pointer to a word (usually underlined and in a green color) or an icon. When the pointer changes to a small hand (Fig. 5-2), click on the item to activate the new information. In AutoCAD for DOS, selecting any words that appear in double less/greater-than symbols <<like this>> can be selected to activate information on the item (Fig. 5-3).

Figure 5-3

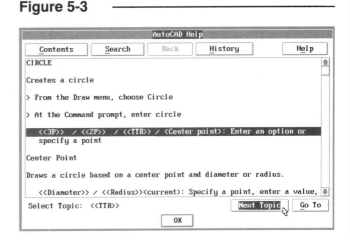

The options available on the top menu bar of the *Help* window are as follows:

Contents
Returns to the first page (Fig. 5-1).

Search
Allows you to search alphabetically for help indexed on command names, command options, and variable names.

Back
Traces your steps backward one at a time through the sequence of selections previously made.

History
Displays a list of the selections that you made in the *Help* window.

Glossary
Gives information on AutoCAD-related concepts and terms.

The *Contents* page displays the ways that you can find help. Selecting the Menus or Toolbars hypertext displays AutoCAD pull-down menus and toolbars that you can PICK to display information on the selected menu item or icon (Fig. 5-4). Selecting the Commands and System Variables hypertext allows you to search alphabetically by name.

Figure 5-4

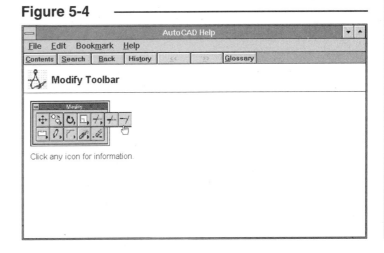

OOPS

PULL-DOWN MENU	SCREEN MENU	TYPE IN	TABLET MENU
Modify *Oops!*	*MODIFY:* *Oops:*	*OOPS*	---

The *Oops* command unerases whatever was erased with the <u>last</u> *Erase* command. *Oops* does not have to be used immediately after the *Erase*, but can be used at <u>any time after</u> the *Erase*. *Oops* is typically used after an accidental erase. However, *Erase* could be used intentionally to remove something from the screen temporarily to simplify some other action. For example, you can *Erase* a *Line* to simplify PICKing a group of other objects to *Move* or *Copy*, and then use *Oops* to restore the erased *Line*.

Oops can be used to restore the original set of objects after the *Block* or *Wblock* command is used to combine many objects into one object (explained in Chapter 21).

UNDO
and *U*

DOS PULL-DOWN	WIN PULL-DOWN	SCREEN MENU	TYPE IN	TABLET MENU
Assist *Undo*	*Edit* *Undo*	*ASSIST* *Undo*	*UNDO* *or U* *or Ctrl+Z*	*7,U and 8,U*

The *U* command undoes only the <u>last</u> command. *U* means "undo one command." If used after *Erase*, it unerases whatever was just erased. If used after *Line*, it undoes the group of lines drawn with the last *Line* command.

The *Undo* command undoes <u>multiple</u> commands in reverse chronological order. For example, you can use *Undo* and enter a value of **5** to undo the last five commands that you used. Both *U* and *Undo* do not undo inquiry commands (like *Help*), the *Plot* command, or commands that cause a write-to-disk, such as *Save*.

If you type the letter **U**, select the icon button, or select **Undo** from the pull-down menu, only the last command is undone. Typing **Undo** or selecting it from the screen menu invokes the full *Undo* command. The options are listed below.

<number>
Enter a value for the number of commands to *Undo*. This is the default option.

Mark
This option sets a marker at that stage of the drawing. The marker is intended to be used by the *Back* option for future *Undo* commands.

Back
This option causes *Undo* to go back to the last marker encountered. Markers are created by the *Mark* option. If a marker is encountered, it is removed. If no marker is encountered, beware, because *Undo* goes back to the <u>beginning of the session</u>. A warning message appears in this case.

BEgin
This option sets the first designator for a group of commands to be treated as one *Undo*.

End
End sets the second designator for the end of a group.

Auto
If *On*, *Auto* treats each command as one group; for example, several lines drawn with one *Line* command would all be undone with *U*.

Control
This option allows you to disable the *Undo* command or limit it to one undo each time it is used.

REDO

DOS PULL-DOWN	WIN PULL-DOWN	SCREEN MENU	TYPE IN	TABLET MENU
Assist *Redo*	*Edit* *Redo*	*ASSIST* *Redo*	*REDO*	*9,U and 10,U*

The *Redo* command undoes an *Undo*. *Redo* must be used as the <u>next</u> command after the *Undo*. The result of *Redo* is as if *Undo* was never used.

REDRAW

PULL-DOWN MENU	SCREEN MENU	TYPE IN	TABLET MENU
View *Redraw View or* *Redraw All*	*VIEW* *Redraw: or* *RedrwAl:*	*REDRAW* *or R*	*11,L to 11,R*

Redraw refreshes the screen by redrawing all of the objects. Redraw also erases the "blips" from the screen (the tiny crosses created from an object selection or point designation, Fig. 5-5).

The *Redraw* command should be used after *Erase.* If two *Lines* were drawn one on top of the other and then one *Erased*, a *Redraw* would be required to display the unerased *Line* again. (If desired, you can turn blips off by typing *BLIPMODE* and setting the variable to *OFF* or by using the *Drawing Aids* dialogue box from the *Options* pull-down menu.)

Redrawall is needed only when Viewports are being used (see Chapters 11, 32, and 34).

Figure 5-5 ——————————————

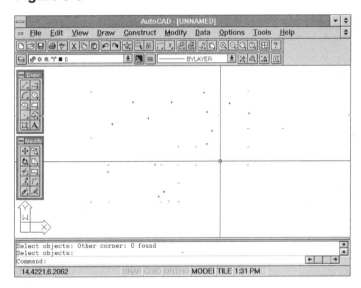

REGEN

PULL-DOWN MENU	SCREEN MENU	TYPE IN	TABLET MENU
---	*DISPLAY* *Regen: or* *Regenall:*	*REGEN*	*11,J and 11,K*

The *Regen* command reads the database and redisplays the drawing accordingly. A *Regen* is caused by some commands automatically. Occasionally the *Regen* command is required to update the drawing to display the latest changes made to some system variables. For example, if you change the form in which *Point* Objects appear (displayed as a dot, an "X," or other options), you should then *Regen* in order to display the *Points* according to the new setting. (*Points* are explained in Chapter 8.) *Regenall* is used to regenerate all viewports when several viewports are being used.

CHAPTER EXERCISES

Begin a *New* drawing. Do not assign a name. Complete the following exercises.

1. *Help*

   Use *Help* or *?* by any method to find information on the following commands. Read the text screen for each command.

   > *Line, Arc, Circle, Point*
   > *New, Open, Save, Saveas*
   > *Oops, Undo, U*

2. **Context-sensitive *Help***

   Invoke each of the commands listed below. When you see the first prompt in each command, enter *'Help* or *'?* (transparently) or select *Help* from the menus or Standard toolbar. Read the explanation for each prompt. Select a Hypertext item in each screen (underlined and in green for Windows or in double less/greater than characters <<like this>> for DOS).

   > *Line, Arc, Circle, Point*

3. ***Oops***

   Draw 3 vertical ***Lines***. ***Erase*** one line; then use ***Oops*** to restore it. Next ***Erase*** two *Lines*, each with a separate use of the *Erase* command. Use ***Oops***. Only the last *Line* is restored. ***Erase*** the remaining two *Lines*, but select both with a window. Now use ***Oops*** to restore both *Lines* (since they were *Erased* at the same time).

4. **Using delayed *Oops***

   Oops can be used at any time, not only immediately after the *Erase*. Draw several horizontal ***Lines*** near the bottom of the screen. Draw a ***Circle*** on the ***Lines***. Then ***Erase*** the *Circle*. Use ***Move***, select the *Lines* with a window, and displace the *Lines* to another location above. Now use ***Oops*** to make the *Circle* reappear.

5. ***U***

   Press the letter ***U*** (make sure no other commands are in use). The *Circle* should disappear (*U* undoes the last command--*Oops*). Do this repeatedly to *Undo* one command at a time until the *Circle* and *Lines* are in their original position (when you first created them).

6. ***Undo***

   Use the ***Undo*** command and select the ***Back*** option. Answer ***Yes*** to the warning message. This action should *Undo* everything.

   Draw a vertical ***Line***. Next, draw a square with four ***Line*** segments (all drawn in the same *Line* command). Finally, draw a second vertical ***Line***. ***Erase*** the first ***Line***.

Now <u>type</u> **Undo** and enter a value of **3**. You should have only one *Line* remaining. *Undo* reversed the following three commands:

> *Erase*   The first vertical *Line* was unerased.
> *Line*   The second vertical *Line* was removed.
> *Line*   The four *Lines* comprising the square were removed.

7. **Redo**

   Invoke **Redo** immediately after the *Undo* (from the previous exercise). The three commands are redone. *Redo* must be used immediately after *Undo*.

8. **Redraw**

   Draw a **Line**; then draw another **Line** in the same place as the first *Line* (one on top of the other). HINT: use *SNAP* and *ORTHO*. **Erase Last**. Both *Lines* seem to be *Erased*. Use **Redraw** to make the first *Line* reappear on the screen.

9. **Exit** AutoCAD and answer **No** to "Save Changes?"

DASHLINE.DWG Courtesy of Autodesk, Inc.

Chapter 6

BASIC
DRAWING SETUP

Chapter Objectives

After completing this chapter you should:

1. know the basic steps for setting up a drawing;

2. be able to specify the desired *Units*, *Angles* format, and *Precision* for the drawing;

3. be able to specify the drawing *Limits*;

4. know how to specify the *Snap* increment;

5. know how to specify the *Grid* increment.

STEPS FOR BASIC DRAWING SETUP

Assuming the general configuration (dimensions and proportions) of the geometry to be created is known, the following steps are suggested for setting up a drawing.

1. Determine and set the *Units* that are to be used.
2. Determine and set the drawing *Limits*; then *Zoom All*.
3. Set an appropriate *Snap* value.
4. Set an appropriate *Grid* value to be used.

These additional steps for drawing setup are discussed in Chapter 13, Advanced Drawing Setup.

5. Change the *LTSCALE* value based on the new *Limits*.
6. Create the desired *Layers* and assign appropriate *linetype* and *color* settings.
7. Create desired *Text Styles* (optional).
8. Create desired *Dimension Styles* (optional).
9. Create a title block and border (optional).

SETUP COMMANDS

UNITS

PULL-DOWN MENU	SCREEN MENU	TYPE IN	TABLET MENU
Data *Units...*	*DATA* *Units:*	*UNITS or* *DDUNITS*	*7, Y*

The *Units* command allows you to specify the type and precision of linear and angular units as well as the direction and orientation of angles to be used in the drawing. The current setting of *Units* determines the display of values by the coordinates display (*COORDS*) and controls the format that AutoCAD uses to display numerical values in some dialogue boxes.

You can select the *Data* pull-down or type *Ddunits* to invoke the *Units Control* dialogue box (Fig. 6-1). Type *Units* (no command alias) to produce a text screen (Fig. 6-2).

The linear and angular units options are displayed in the dialogue box format (Fig. 6-1) and in command line format (Fig. 6-2). The choices for both linear and angular *Units* are shown in the figures.

Figure 6-1

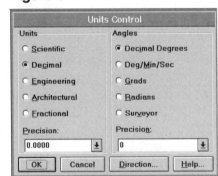

Figure 6-2

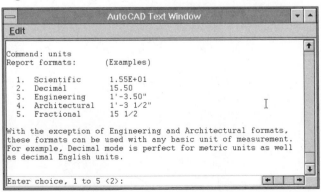

Units Format

1. *Scientific*	1.55E+01	Generic decimal units with an exponent.
2. *Decimal*	15.50	Generic decimal usually used for applications in metric or decimal inches.
3. *Engineering*	1'-3.50"	Explicit feet and decimal inches with notation, one unit equals one inch.
4. *Architectural*	1'-3 1/2"	Explicit feet and fractional inches with notation, one unit equals one inch.
5. *Fractional*	15 1/2	Generic fractional units.

Precision

When setting *Units*, you should also set the precision. *Precision* is the number of places to the right of the decimal or the denominator of the smallest fraction to display. The precision is set by making the desired selection from the *Precision* pop-up list in the *Units Control* dialogue box (Fig. 6-1) or by keying in the desired selection in command line format.

Precision controls the <u>display</u> of *COORDS* and display of values in dialogue boxes. The <u>actual precision</u> of the drawing database is always the same in AutoCAD, that is, 14 significant digits.

NOTE: Unfortunately, *Precision* also affects the display of values in the dialogue boxes. Therefore, *Precision* should always be selected as <u>at least</u> two decimal places so the dimensioning dialogue boxes display the actual values instead of rounded values.

Angles

You can specify a format other than the default (decimal degrees) for expression of angles. Format options for angular display and examples of each are shown in Figure 6-1 (dialogue box format).

The orientation of angle **0** can be changed from the default position (3 o'clock, east) to other options by selecting the *Direction* tile in the *Units Control* dialogue box. This produces the *Direction Control* dialogue box (Fig. 6-3). Alternately, the *Units* command can be typed to select these options in command line format.

Figure 6-3 ———

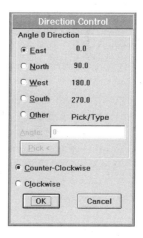

The direction of angular measurement can be changed from its default of counter-clockwise to clockwise. The direction of angular measurement affects the direction of positive and negative angles in commands such as *Array Polar*, *Rotate*, and dimension commands that measure angular values.

Keyboard Input of *Units* Values

When AutoCAD prompts for a point or a distance, you can respond by entering values at the keyboard. The values can be in <u>any format</u>—integer, decimal, fractional, or scientific, <u>regardless</u> of the format of *Units* selected.

If *Engineering* or *Architectural* units are in effect, you can type in explicit feet or inch values by using the ' (apostrophe) symbol after values representing feet and the " (quote) symbol after values representing inches. If no symbol is used, the values are understood by AutoCAD to be <u>inches</u>.

Feet and inches input <u>cannot</u> contain a blank, so a hyphen (-) should be typed between inches and fractions. For example, with *Architectural* units, key in **6'2-1/2"**, which reads "six feet two and one-half inches." The standard engineering and architectural format for dimensioning, however, places the hyphen between feet and inches (as displayed by the default setting for the *COORDS* display).

The *UNITMODE* variable set to **1** changes the display of *COORDS* to remind you of the correct format for <u>input</u> of feet and inches (with the hyphen between inches and fractions) rather than displaying the standard format for feet and inch notation (standard format, *UNITMODE* of **0**, is the default setting). If options other than *Architectural* or *Engineering* are used, values are read as generic units.

LIMITS

PULL-DOWN MENU	SCREEN MENU	TYPE IN	TABLET MENU
Data *Drawing Limits*	*DATA* *Limits:*	*LIMITS*	---

The *Limits* command allows you to set the size of the drawing area by specifying the lower left and upper right corners in X,Y coordinate values.

If you are changing the *Limits* in the default ACAD.DWG drawing, the command prompt reads as follows:

Command: **limits**
Reset Model space limits
ON/OFF/<Lower left corner> <0,0 or current values>: **X,Y** or **Enter** (Enter an X,Y value or accept the 0,0 default—normally use 0,0 as lower left corner.)
Upper right corner <12,9>: **X,Y** (Enter new values to change upper right corner to allow adequate drawing area.)

The default drawing supplied with AutoCAD (ACAD.DWG) has default *Limits* of 12 by 9, that is, 12 units in the X direction and 9 units in the Y direction (Fig. 6-4). If the *GRID* is turned on, the dots are only displayed over the *Limits*. The AutoCAD for Windows screen (default configuration) displays additional area on the right past the *Limits*, while the AutoCAD for DOS screen is closer to the same <u>proportion</u> as 12 by 9. The units are generic decimal units that can be used to represent inches, feet, millimeters, miles, or whatever is appropriate for the intended drawing. Typically, however, decimal units are used to represent inches or millimeters. If the default units are used to represent inches, the default drawing size would be 12 by 9 inches.

Figure 6-4

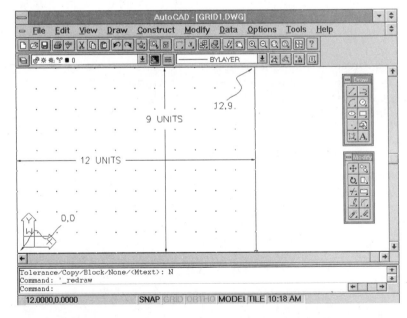

Remember that when a CAD system is used to create a drawing, the geometry should be drawn <u>full size</u> by specifying dimensions of entities in <u>real-world units</u>. A completed CAD drawing or model is virtually an exact dimensional replica of the actual object. Scaling of the drawing occurs only when plotting or printing the file to an actual fixed-size sheet of paper.

Before beginning to create an AutoCAD drawing, determine the size of the drawing area needed for the intended geometry. After setting *Units*, appropriate *Limits* should be set in order to draw the object or geometry to the <u>real-world size in the actual units</u>. There are no maximum or minimum settings for *Limits*.

The X,Y values you enter as *Limits* are understood by AutoCAD as values in the units specified by the *Units* command. For example, if you previously specified *Architectural units*, then the values entered are understood as inches unless the notation for feet (') is given (**240,180** or **20',15'** would define the same coordinate).

If you are planning to plot the drawing to scale, *Limits* should be set to a proportion of the <u>sheet size</u> you plan to plot on. For example, setting limits to 22 by 17 (2 times 11 by 8.5) would allow enough room for drawing an object about 20" by 15" and allow plotting at 1/2 size on the 11" x 8.5" sheet. Simply stated, set *Limits* to a proportion of the paper.

ON/OFF

If the *ON* option of *Limits* is used, limits checking is activated. Limits checking prevents you from drawing entities outside of the limits by issuing an outside-limits error. This is similar to drawing "off the paper." Limits checking is *OFF* by default.

Limits also defines the display area for *GRID* as well as the minimum area displayed when a *Zoom All* is used. *Zoom All* forces the full display of the *Limits*. *Zoom All* can be invoked by typing **Z** (command alias) and **A** for the *All* option.

Changing *Limits* does <u>not</u> automatically change the display. As a general rule, you should make a habit of invoking a *Zoom All* <u>immediately following</u> a change in *Limits* to display the area defined by the new limits (Fig. 6-5).

Figure 6-5

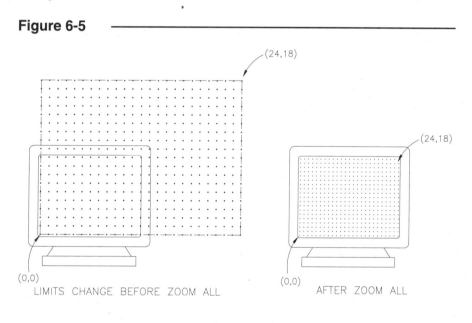

When you <u>reduce</u> *Limits* while *Grid* is ON, it is apparent that a change in *Limits* does not automatically change the display. In this case, the area covered by the grid is reduced in size as *Limits* are reduced, yet the display remains unchanged.

If you are already experimenting with drawing in different *Linetypes*, a change in *Limits* affects the display of the hidden and dashed lines. The *LTSCALE* variable controls the spacing of non-continuous lines. As a general rule, the *LTSCALE* should be <u>changed proportionally</u> with changes in *Limits*.

SNAP

PULL-DOWN MENU	SCREEN MENU	TYPE IN	TABLET MENU
Options *Drawing Aids...*	*ASSIST,* *Snap: or* *OPTIONS* *DDrmode:*	*SNAP or* *DDRMODES*	*21,V*

SNAP, when activated by pressing **F9** or double-clicking on *SNAP* in the Windows Status Line, forces the cursor position to regular increments. This function can be of assistance to you by making it faster and more accurate for creating and editing objects. The *Snap* command is used to set the value for these invisible snap increments. Since *Snap* controls the cursor position, the value of *Snap* should be set to the <u>interactive</u> accuracy desired. As a general rule, you specify the *Snap* value to be that of the <u>common</u> dimensional length expected in the drawing. For example, if the common dimensional length in the drawing is 1/2", or you intend for dimensional accuracy of the drawing to be to the nearest 1/2", the *Snap* command is used to change the snap spacing to *1/2* or *.5*. In this way the cursor always "snaps" to .5 increments. *Snap* spacing can be set to any value. The default *Snap* setting is **1**.

The *Snap* command is easily typed, displaying the options in command line format. The *Drawing Aids* dialogue box (Fig. 6-6) can be invoked by menu selection or by typing *Ddrmodes*. Enter the desired value for *Snap* in the X Spacing box and press *Enter*. The Y Spacing value automatically changes to match.

Figure 6-6 ─────────────

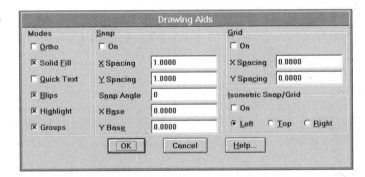

The command line format is as follows:

    Command: **snap**
    Snap spacing or ON/OFF/Aspect/Rotate/Style <1 or current value>: **(value or letter)**
    (Enter a value or option.)

ON/OFF
Selecting *ON* or *OFF* accomplishes the same action as toggling the **F9** key. Typically, *SNAP* should be *ON* for drawing and editing but turned *OFF* to make object selection easier (the cursor moves smoothly to any location with *SNAP OFF*).

Aspect
The *Aspect* option allows specification of unequal X and Y spacing for *SNAP*. This action can also be accomplished in the *Drawing Aids* dialogue box by entering different values for *X Spacing* and *Y Spacing*.

Rotate
SNAP can also be *Rotate*d about any point and set to any angle. When *SNAP* has been rotated, the *GRID*, *ORTHO*, and "cross-hairs" automatically follow this alignment. This action facilitates creating objects oriented at the specified angle, for example, creating an auxiliary view or drawing part of a floor plan at an angle. To accomplish this, use the *R* option in command line format or set *Snap Angle* and *X Base* and *Y Base* (point to rotate about) in the dialogue box.

Style
The *Style* option allows switching between a *Standard* snap pattern (the default square or rectangular) and an *Isometric* snap pattern. If using the dialogue box, toggle *Isometric Snap/Grid On*.

When the *SNAP Style* or *Rotate* angle is changed, the *GRID* automatically aligns with it.

GRID

PULL-DOWN MENU	SCREEN MENU	TYPE IN	TABLET MENU
Options *Drawing Aids*	*ASSIST* *Grid: or* *OPTIONS* *DDrmodes:*	*GRID or* *DDRMODES*	*20,V*

GRID is visible on the screen, whereas, *SNAP* is invisible. *GRID* is only a <u>visible</u> display of some regular interval. *GRID* and *SNAP* can be <u>independent</u> of each other. In other words, each can have separate spacing settings and the active state of each (*ON, OFF*) can be controlled independently. The *GRID* <u>follows</u> the *SNAP* if *SNAP* is rotated or changed to *Isometric Style*. Although the *GRID* spacing can be different than that of *SNAP*, it can also be forced to follow *SNAP* by using the *Snap* option. The default *GRID* setting is **1**.

The *GRID* <u>cannot</u> be plotted. It is <u>not</u> comprised of *Point* objects and therefore is not part of the current drawing. *GRID* is only a visual aid.

Grid can be accessed by command line format (shown below) or set via the *Drawing Aids* dialogue box (Fig. 6-6). The dialogue box is invoked by menu selection or by typing *Ddrmodes*. The dialogue box allows only *X Spacing* and *Y Spacing* input for *Grid*.

> Command: **grid**
> Grid spacing(X) or ON/OFF/Snap/Aspect <current value>: *(value or letter)*
> (Enter a value or option.)

Grid Spacing (X)
If you supply a value for the *Grid spacing*, *GRID* is displayed at that spacing regardless of *SNAP* spacing. If you key in an *X* as a suffix to the value (for example, **2X**), the *GRID* is displayed as that value <u>times</u> the *SNAP* spacing (for example, "2 times" *SNAP*).

ON/OFF
The *ON* and *OFF* options simply make the *GRID* visible or not (like toggling the **F7** key).

Snap
The *Snap* option of the *Grid* command forces the *GRID* spacing to equal that of *SNAP*, even if *SNAP* is subsequently changed.

Aspect
The *Aspect* option of *GRID* allows different X and Y spacing (causing a rectangular rather than a square *GRID*).

CHAPTER EXERCISES

1. A drawing is to be made to detail a mechanical part. The part is to be manufactured from sheet metal stock; therefore, only one view is needed. The overall dimensions are 18 by 10 inches, accurate to the nearest .125 inch. Complete the steps for drawing setup:

    A. The drawing will be automatically "scaled to fit" the paper (no standard scale).

        1. Begin a *New* drawing.
        2. *Units* should be *Decimal*. Set the *Precision* to **0.000**.
        3. Set *Limits* in order to draw full size. Make the lower left corner **0,0** and the upper right at **24,18**. This is a 4 by 3 proportion and should allow space for the part, a title block, border, and dimensions or notes.
        4. *Zoom All.* (Type **Z** for *Zoom*; then type **A** for *All.*)
        5. Set the *GRID* to **1**.
        6. Set *SNAP* to **.125**.
        7. *Save* this drawing as **CH6EX1A** (to be used again later).
            (When plotting at a later time, "Scale to Fit" can be specified.)

    B. The drawing will be plotted to scale on engineering "A" or "B" size paper (11" by 8.5" or 22" by 17").

        1. Begin a *New* drawing.
        2. *Units* should be *Decimal*. Set the *Precision* to **0.000**.
        3. Set *Limits* to the paper size (or a proportion thereof), making the lower left corner **0,0** and the upper right at **22,17**. This allows space for drawing full size and for a title block, border, and dimensions or notes.
        4. *Zoom All.* (Type **Z** for *Zoom*; then type **A** for *All.*)
        5. Set the *GRID* to **1**.
        6. Set *SNAP* to **.125**.
        7. *Save* this drawing as **CH6EX1B** (to be used again later).
            (When plotting, a scale of 1=1 can be specified to plot on 22" by 17" paper, or a scale of 1/2=1 can be specified to plot on 11" by 8.5" paper.)

2. A drawing is to be prepared for a house plan. Set up the drawing for a floor plan that is approximately 50' by 30'. Assume the drawing is to be automatically "Scaled to Fit" the sheet (no standard scale).

    A. Begin a *New* drawing.
    B. Set *Units* to *Architectural*. Set the *Precision* to **0'-0 1/4"**. Each unit equals 1 inch.
    C. Set *Limits* to **0,0** and **80',60'**. Use the **'** (apostrophe) symbol to designate feet. Otherwise, enter **0,0** and **960,720** (size in inch units is: 80x12=960 and 60x12=720).
    D. *Zoom All.* (Type **Z** for *Zoom*; then type **A** for *All.*)
    E. Set *GRID* to **24** (2 feet).
    F. Set *SNAP* to **6** (anything smaller would be hard to PICK).
    G. *Save* this drawing as **CH6EX2**.

3. A multiview drawing of a mechanical part is to be made. The part is 125mm in width, 30mm in height, and 60mm in depth. The plot is to be made on an "A4" metric sheet size (297mm x 210mm).

   A. Begin a *New* drawing.
   B. *Units* should be *Decimal*. Set the *Precision* to **0.00**.
   C. Calculate the space needed for three views. If *Limits* are set to the sheet size, there should be adequate space for the views. Make the lower left corner **0,0** and the upper right at **297,210**. (Since the *Limits* are set to the sheet size, a plot can be made later at 1=1.)
   D. *Zoom All*. (Type *Z* for *Zoom*; then type *A* for *All*.)
   E. Set the *GRID* to **10**.
   F. Set *SNAP* to **2**.
   G. *Save* this drawing as **CH6EX3** (to be used again later).

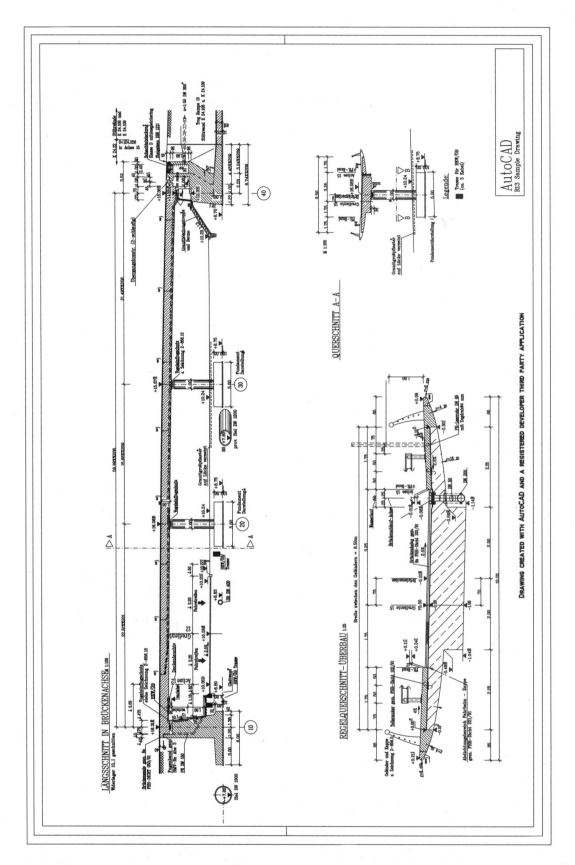

Chapter 7
OBJECT SNAP

Chapter Objectives

After completing this chapter you should:

1. understand the importance of accuracy in CAD drawings;

2. know the function of each of the *OSNAP* modes;

3. be able to invoke *OSNAP*s for single point selection;

4. be able to operate running *OSNAP* modes;

5. know that you can use *OSNAP* anytime AutoCAD prompts for a point.

CAD ACCURACY

Because CAD databases store drawings as digital information with great precision (fourteen numeric places in AutoCAD), it is possible, practical, and desirable to create drawings that are 100% accurate; that is, a CAD drawing should be created as an exact dimensional replica of the actual object. For example, lines that appear to connect should actually connect by having the exact coordinate values for the matching line endpoints. Only by employing this precision can dimensions placed in a drawing automatically display the exact intended length, or a CAD database be used to drive CNC (Computer Numerical Control) machine devices such as milling machines or lathes, or the CAD database be used for rapid prototyping devices such as Stereo Lithography Apparatus. With CAD/CAM technology (Computer-Aided Design/Computer-Aided Manufacturing), the CAD database defines the configuration and accuracy of the finished part. <u>Accuracy is critical</u>. Therefore, in no case should you create CAD drawings with only visual accuracy such as one might do when sketching using the "eyeball method."

OBJECT SNAP

AutoCAD provides a capability called Object Snap, or *OSNAP* for short, that enables you to "snap" to object endpoints, midpoints, centers, and intersections, etc. When an *OSNAP* mode (*ENDpoint, MIDpoint, CENter, INTersection,* etc.) is invoked, a box, larger than the pickbox, called an "aperture," appears at the cursor crosshairs. Selecting an object within the aperture causes AutoCAD to locate and calculate the coordinate location of the desired object feature (endpoint or midpoint, etc.).

For example, when you want to draw a *Line* and connect its endpoint to an existing *Line*, you can invoke the *Endpoint OSNAP* mode at the "to point:" prompt, then snap to the desired line end by PICKing it with the aperture (Fig. 7-1).

Figure 7-1

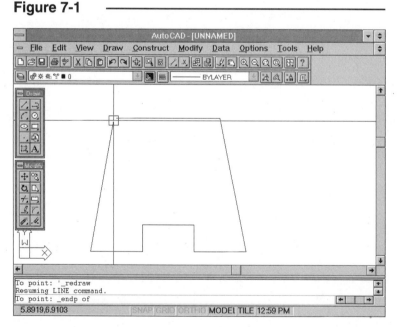

OSNAP SINGLE POINT SELECTION

DOS PULL-DOWN	WIN PULL-DOWN	SCREEN MENU	TYPE IN	TABLET MENU
Assist *Object Snap >*	*Edit* *Object Snap >*	******** (asterisks)	*(first* *three letters)*	*12,T to 22,T*

There are many methods for invoking the *OSNAP* modes, as shown in the command table. In addition to these options, a special menu called the <u>cursor menu</u> can be used. The cursor menu pops up at the <u>current location</u> of the cursor and replaces the crosshairs when invoked (Fig. 7-2). This menu is activated as follows:

2-button mouse	press **SHIFT+#2** (hold down the SHIFT key while clicking the right mouse button)
3-button mouse	press **#3**
digitizing puck	press **#3**

If you are using AutoCAD for Windows, Object Snaps are available from the Standard toolbar (Fig. 7-3) or a separate Object Snap toolbar can be activated to float or dock on the screen (Fig. 7-3, docked on the right side of the screen).

With any of these methods, *OSNAP* modes are selected <u>transparently</u> (invoked during another command operation) immediately before selecting a point when prompted. In other words, whenever you are prompted for a point (for example, the "From point:" prompt of the *Line* command), select or type an *OSNAP* option. Then PICK the desired object in the aperture. AutoCAD "snaps" to the feature of the object and uses it for the point specification. Using *OSNAP* in this way allows the *OSNAP* mode to operate only for that <u>single point selection</u>.

Figure 7-2

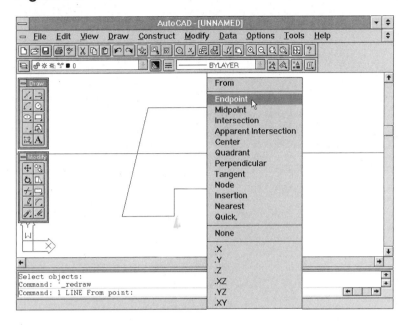

Figure 7-3

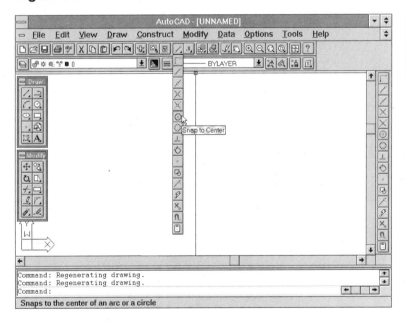

For example, when using *OSNAP* during the *Line* command, the command line reads as shown.

Command: **Line**
From Point: **ENDpoint** of (**PICK**)
to point: **ENDpoint** of (**PICK**)
to point: **Enter** (completes the command)

When you are prompted for a point ("From point:"), type or select the desired *OSNAP* mode; then **PICK** the desired object or location within the aperture. AutoCAD uses the *OSNAP* mode and "snaps" to the feature for the point specification. The aperture disappears after the single point selection.

The *OSNAP* modes can also be invoked by any of the four command input methods shown in the command table. For example, PICKing the asterisks (****) beneath the word AutoCAD on the screen menu displays the *OSNAP* selections. If you prefer typing, only the <u>first three</u> letters of the *OSNAP* mode need to be typed. For example, *CEN* invokes *CENter* and *INT* invokes *INTersection*. It is a good habit to type *ENDP* for *ENDpoint* in order to prevent accidentally invoking the *END* command (which ends the AutoCAD session).

OSNAP MODES

AutoCAD provides the following *OSNAP* modes.

CENter

This *OSNAP* option finds the center of a *Circle*, *Arc*, or *Donut*. You must PICK the *Circle* <u>object</u>, not where you think the center is.

Figure 7-4 ————————————

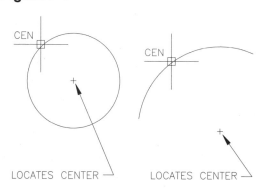

ENDpoint

The *ENDpoint* option snaps to the endpoint of a *Line*, *Pline*, *Spline*, or *Arc*. PICK the *Line* <u>near</u> the desired end.

Figure 7-5 ————————————

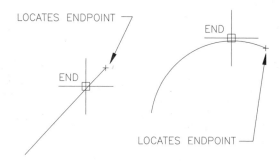

INSert

This option locates the insertion point of *Text* or a *Block*. PICK anywhere on the *Block* or line of *Text*.

Figure 7-6 ————————————

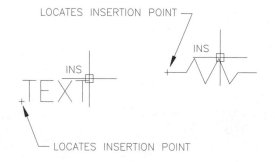

INTersection

 Using this option causes AutoCAD to calculate and snap to the intersection of any two objects. You can locate the aperture so that <u>both</u> objects pass through it, or you can PICK each object <u>individually</u>.

Figure 7-7

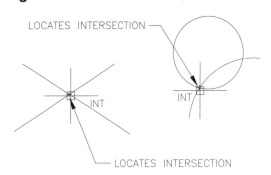

Even if the two objects that you PICK do not physically intersect, you can PICK each one individually with the *INTersection* mode and AutoCAD will find the <u>extended</u> intersection.

Figure 7-8

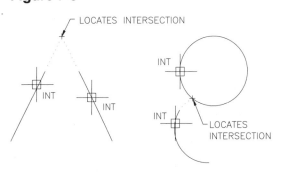

MIDpoint

 The *MIDpoint* option snaps to the point of a *Line* or *Arc* that is <u>halfway</u> between the endpoints. PICK anywhere on the object.

Figure 7-9

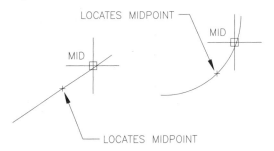

NEArest

 The *NEArest* option locates the point on an object nearest to the <u>cursor position</u>. Place the crosshair center nearest to the desired location, then PICK.

NEArest <u>cannot</u> be used effectively with *ORTHO* because *OSNAPs* override *ORTHO*. In other words, using *NEArest* to locate a "to point:" will not produce an orthogonal line if *ORTHO* is on because *OSNAPs* take priority.

Figure 7-10

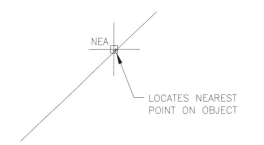

NODe

This option snaps to a *Point* object. The *Point* must be within the aperture.

Figure 7-11

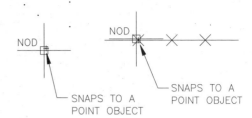

PERpendicular

Use this option to snap perpendicular to the selected object. PICK anywhere on a *Line* or straight *Pline* segment.

Figure 7-12

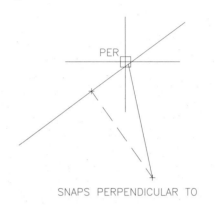

SNAPS PERPENDICULAR TO

QUAdrant

The *QUAdrant* option snaps to the 0, 90, 180, or 270 degree quadrant of a *Circle*. PICK <u>nearest</u> to the desired *QUAdrant*.

Figure 7-13

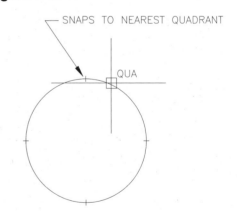

TANgent

This option calculates and snaps the object being drawn or edited to the tangent point of an *Arc* or *Circle*. PICK the *Arc* or *Circle* as near as possible to the expected *TANgent* point.

Figure 7-14

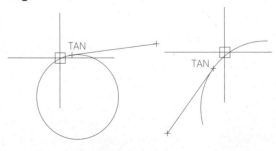

SNAPS TANGENT TO

FROm

 The *From* option is designed to let you snap to a point <u>relative</u> to another point using relative rectangular or relative polar coordinates. There are two steps: first select a "Base point:" (coordinates or another *OSNAP* may be used); then select an "Offset:" (enter relative rectangular or relative polar coordinates).

Figure 7-15

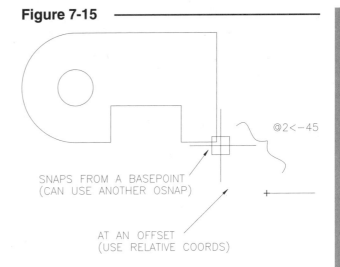

SNAPS FROM A BASEPOINT
(CAN USE ANOTHER OSNAP)

AT AN OFFSET
(USE RELATIVE COORDS)

@2<−45

APPint (apparent intersection)

 Use this option when you are working with a 3D drawing and want to snap to a point in space where two objects appear to intersect (from your viewpoint) but do not actually physically intersect.

Figure 7-16

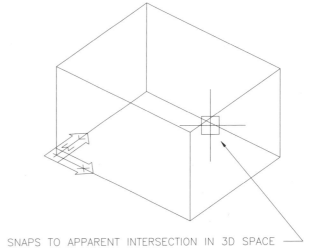

SNAPS TO APPARENT INTERSECTION IN 3D SPACE

R13

OSNAP RUNNING MODE

	PULL-DOWN MENU	SCREEN MENU	TYPE IN	TABLET MENU
	Options *Running Object Snap...*	*OPTIONS* *DDosnap:*	*OSNAP or* *DDOSNAP*	---

For other cases, such as when you have <u>several</u> *ENDpoint*s to connect, it may be desirable to turn on the *ENDpoint OSNAP* mode and leave it <u>running</u> during the multiple selections. From that time on, the aperture appears at the cursor whenever AutoCAD prompts for point selection. This is faster than continually selecting the *OSNAP* mode each time before you PICK. You can even have several *OSNAP* modes running at the same time.

Running *OSNAP*s can be turned on by these methods:

1. typing the *OSNAP* command;
2. using the *Running Object Snap* dialogue box.

For activating running *OSNAP*s (both *END*point and *INT*ersection modes) by typing, the command line reads:

> Command: **osnap**
> Object snap modes: **end,int**
> Command:

The *END*point and *INT*ersection modes remain on and the aperture appears for <u>every</u> point selection until the modes are turned off. It is critical that you <u>turn the *OSNAP* modes off</u> after you have used them for the application. Selecting points <u>not</u> associated with objects can be difficult while running *OSNAP* modes are on. Turn off the running *OSNAP* modes by using the *None* option of the *OSNAP* command as follows or by either of the other methods.

> Command: **osnap**
> Object snap modes: **none**
> Command:

Another method of activating running *OSNAP* modes is to access the *Running Object Snap* dialogue box (Fig. 7-17) from the *Options* pull-down menu, by typing *Ddosnap* or by selecting the icon button. Several modes can be running together. The *Quick* option can be used <u>only with other running *OSNAP*s</u> to find the quickest of the active options. Make sure you <u>turn off the running modes</u> when you are finished using them by selecting the *Clear All* tile. Notice that the *Aperture Size* can be adjusted through this dialogue box or through the use of the *Aperture* command.

Figure 7-17 ——————————

Quick

This option only operates in addition to other selected <u>Running</u> *OSNAP* modes. Using the *Quick* option causes AutoCAD to snap to the first snap point found.

None

This *OSNAP* option is effective only when used with <u>Running</u> *OSNAPs*. *None* can be used in two ways.

None can be used to turn off all the Running *OSNAP* modes. To do this, PICK *None* at the open command prompt (when no commands are in use) or type or select *None* in response to the "Object snap modes:" prompt of the *Osnap* command. In either case, all running modes are deactivated.

None can also be used as a single point selection override for the active Running *OSNAP* modes. If you have *OSNAP* modes running but want to deactivate them for a <u>single</u> PICK, use *None* in response to "From point:" or other point selection prompt. In other words, using *None* <u>during a draw or edit command</u> overrides any Running *OSNAPs* for that single point selection.

The current Running *OSNAP* modes are stored in the *OSMODE* variable.

Remember that keeping running *OSNAPs* going all the time can give unexpected results if you are not careful, so be sure you know whether your *OSNAPs* are the single point selection mode or running mode.

OSNAP APPLICATIONS

OSNAP can be used anytime AutoCAD prompts you for a point. This means that you can invoke an *OSNAP* mode during any draw, construct or modify command as well as during many other commands. *OSNAP* provides you with the potential to create 100% accurate drawings with AutoCAD. Take advantage of this feature whenever it will improve your drawing precision. Remember, anytime you are prompted for a point, use *OSNAP* if it can improve your accuracy.

OSNAP PRACTICE

Single Point Selection Mode

1. Turn off *SNAP* (**F9**). Draw two vertical *Line*s. Follow these steps to draw another *Line* between *ENDpoint*s.

STEPS	COMMAND PROMPT	PERFORM ACTION	COMMENTS
1.	Command:	select *Line* by any method	
2.	Line From point:	type *ENDP* and press **Enter** (or space bar)	aperture appears at crosshairs
3.	endp of:	**PICK** the endpoint of an existing *Line*	rubberband line appears
4.	to point:	type *ENDP* and press **Enter** (or space bar)	aperture appears at crosshairs
5.	endp of:	**PICK** the endpoint of the other *Line*	*Line* is created between endpoints
6.	to point:	press **Enter**	completes command

2. Draw two *Circles*. Follow these steps to draw a *Line* between the *CENters*.

STEPS	COMMAND PROMPT	PERFORM ACTION	COMMENTS
1.	Command:	select *Line* by any method	
2.	Line From point:	invoke the cursor menu (**Shift+#2**) and select *Center*	aperture appears at crosshairs
3.	center of:	**PICK** a *Circle* object	you must PICK the *Circle*, not where you think the center is
4.	to point:	invoke the cursor menu and select *Center*	aperture appears at crosshairs
5.	center of:	**PICK** the other *Circle*	*Line* is created between *Circle* centers
6.	to point:	press **Enter**	completes command

3. *Erase* the *Line* only from the previous exercise. Draw another *Line* anywhere, but <u>not</u> attached to the *Circles*. Follow the steps to *Move* the *Line* endpoint to the *Circle* center.

STEPS	COMMAND PROMPT	PERFORM ACTION	COMMENTS
1.	Command:	select *Move* by any method	
2.	Move Select objects:	**PICK** the *Line*	the *Line* becomes highlighted
3.	select objects:	press **Enter**	completes selection set
4.	Base point or displacement:	select *Endpoint* from the pull-down menu or icon button	aperture appears at crosshairs
5.	endp of	**PICK** the *Line* near an endpoint	*ENDpoint* becomes the handle for *Move*
6.	second point of displacement:	select *Center* from the pull-down menu or icon button	aperture appears at crosshairs
7.	center of:	**PICK** a *Circle* object	you must PICK the *Circle*, <u>not</u> where you think the center is

Running Mode

4. Draw several *Lines* and *Circles* at random. To draw several *Lines* to *ENDpoint*s and *TANgent* to the *Circles*, follow these steps.

STEPS	COMMAND PROMPT	PERFORM ACTION	COMMENTS
1.	Command:	type *OSNAP*	
2.	Object snap modes:	type *END,TAN* then press **Enter**	turns on the running *OSNAP* modes
3.	Command:	invoke the *Line* command	aperture appears
4.	From point:	**PICK** a *Line* <u>near</u> one endpoint	rubberband line appears connected to endpoint
5.	to point:	**PICK** an endpoint of another *Line*	a *Line* is created between endpoints
6.	to point:	**PICK** a *Circle* object	a *Line* is created *TANgent* to the *Circle*
7.	to point:	**Enter**	ends *Line* command
8.	Command:	invoke the *Line* command	use any method
9.	From point:	**PICK** a *Circle*	rubberband line does NOT appear
10.	to point:	**PICK** another *Circle*	a *Line* is created tangent to the two *Circles*
11.	to point:	**Enter**	ends *Line* command

5. The running *OSNAP* modes can also be controlled (turned off or on) by the *Running Object Snap* dialogue box. Use it to turn off the running *OSNAP* modes.

STEPS	COMMAND PROMPT	PERFORM ACTION	COMMENTS
1.	Command:	select the *Options* pull-down, then *Running Object Snap...*	dialogue box appears
2.	ddosnap	select the *Clear All* tile, then select *OK* tile	turns off the running *OSNAP* modes

CHAPTER EXERCISES

1. *Open* the **CH6EX1A** drawing and begin constructing the sheet metal part. Each unit in the drawing represents one inch.

   A. Create four *Circles*. All *Circles* have a radius of **1.685**. The *Circles*' centers are located at **5,5**, **5,13**, **19,5**, and **19,13**.

   B. Draw four *Lines*. The *Lines* should be drawn on the outside of the *Circles* by using the *QUAdrant* OSNAP mode as shown (highlighted) in Figure 7-18.

   C. Draw two *Lines* from the *CENter* of the existing *Circles* to form two diagonals as shown in Figure 7-19.

   D. At the *INTersection* of the diagonal create a *Circle* with a **3** unit radius.

Figure 7-18 ——————————————

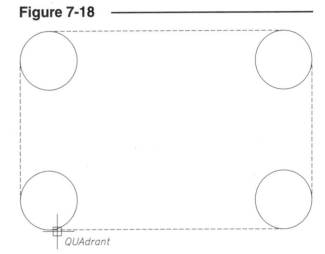

Figure 7-19 ——————————————

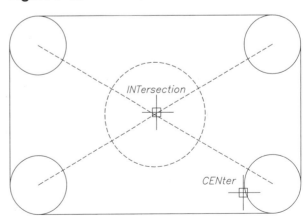

E.   Draw two *Lines*, each from the
     INTersection of the diagonals to the
     MIDpoint of the vertical *Lines* on each
     side. Finally, construct four new *Circles*
     with a radius of **.25**, each at the *CENter*
     of the existing ones.

Figure 7-20 ─────────────

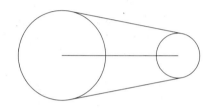

F.   *Saveas* **CH7EX1**. This drawing will be
     completed as another chapter exercise
     at a later time.

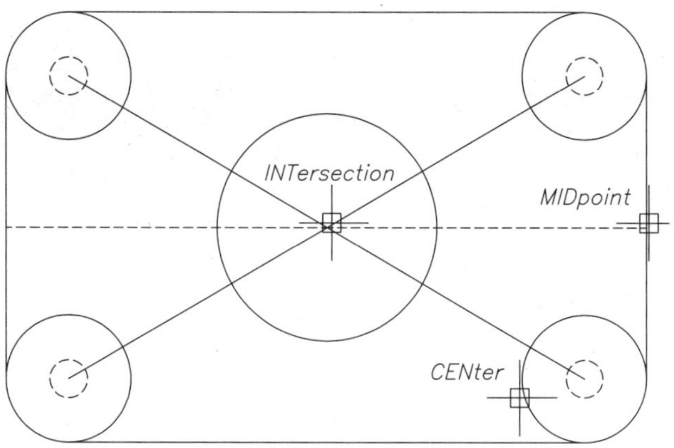

2.   A multiview drawing of a mechanical part
     is to be constructed using the CH6EX3
     drawing. All dimensions are in millime-
     ters, so each unit in your drawing equals
     one millimeter.

Figure 7-21 ─────────────

A.   *Open* **CH6EX3**. Draw a *Line* from
     60,140 to **140,140**. Create two *Circles*
     with the centers at the *ENDpoints* of the
     Line, one *Circle* having a <u>diameter</u> of **60**
     and the second *Circle* having a diameter
     of **30**. Draw two *Lines TANgent* to the
     Circles as shown in Figure 7-21. *Saveas*
     PIVOTARM.

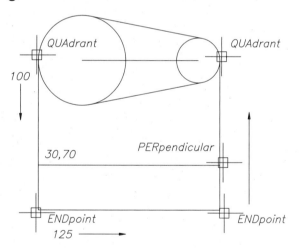

B.   Draw a vertical *Line* down from the far
     left *QUAdrant* of the *Circle* on the left.
     Specify polar coordinates to make the
     Line 100 units (**@100<270**). Draw a hori-
     zontal *Line* **125** units from the last
     ENDpoint using polar coordinates.
     Draw another *Line* between that
     ENDpoint and the *QUAdrant* of the
     Circle on the right. Finally, draw a hori-
     zontal *Line* from point **30,70** and
     PERpendicular to the vertical *Line* on
     the right.

Figure 7-22 ─────────────

C.   Draw two vertical *Lines* from the *INTersections* of the hori-
     zontal *Line* and *Circles* and *PERpendicular* to the *Line* at the
     bottom. Next, draw two *Circles* concentric to the previous
     two and with diameters of **20** and **10** as shown in Figure 7-23.

Figure 7-23 ─────────────

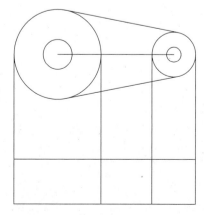

D. Draw four more vertical *Lines* as shown in Figure 7-24. Each *Line* is drawn from the new *Circles'* **QUAdrant** and **PERpendicular** to the bottom line. Next, draw a miter *Line* from the **INTersection** of the corner shown to **@150<45**. *Save* the drawing for completion at a later time as another chapter exercise.

Figure 7-24

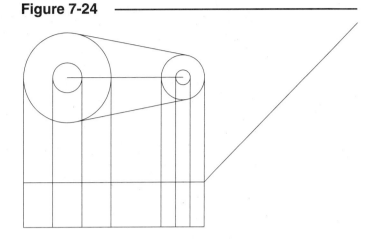

3. **Running** *OSNAP*

Create a cross-sectional view of a door header composed of two 2 x 6 wooden boards and a piece of 1/2" plywood. (The dimensions of a 2 x 6 are actually 1-1/2" x 5-3/8".)

Figure 7-25

A. Begin a *New* drawing and assign the name **HEADER**. Draw four vertical lines as shown in Figure 7-25.

B. Use the *OSNAP* command or select *Running Object Snap* from the *Options* pull-down menu and turn on the *ENDpoint* and *INTersection* modes.

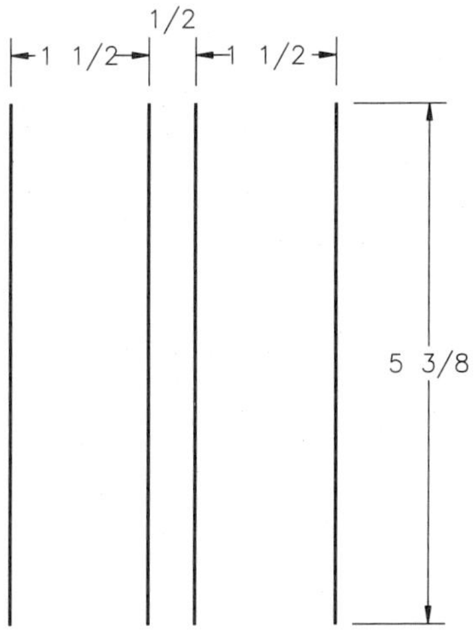

C. Draw the remaining lines as shown in Figure 7-26 to complete the header cross-section. Don't forget to turn off the running *OSNAP* modes when you are through by using the *None* option (command line format) or by selecting *Clear All* (dialogue box format). *Save* the drawing.

Figure 7-26

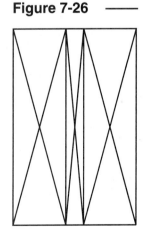

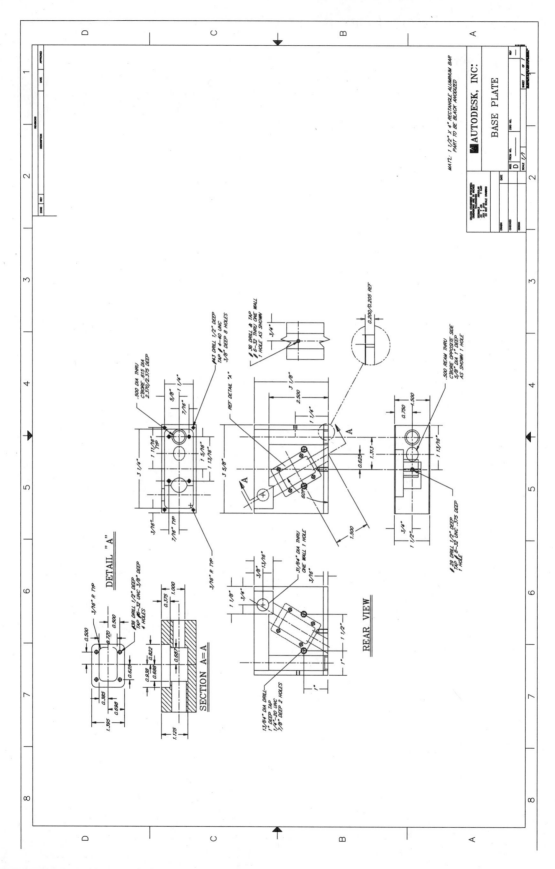

Chapter 8

DRAW COMMANDS I

Chapter Objectives

After completing this chapter you should:

1. know where to locate and how to invoke the draw commands;

2. be able to draw *Lines*;

3. be able to draw *Circles* by each of the five options;

4. be able to draw *Arcs* by each of the eleven options;

5. be able to create *Point* objects and specify the *Point Style*.

BASICS

Draw Commands—Simple and Complex

Draw commands create objects. An object is the smallest component of a drawing. The draw commands listed immediately below create simple objects and are discussed in this chapter. Simple objects <u>appear</u> as one entity.

> *Line*
> *Circle*
> *Arc*
> *Point*

Other draw commands create more complex shapes. Many of these shapes <u>appear</u> to be composed of several components, but each shape is usually <u>one</u> object. The following commands are covered in Chapter 15, Draw Commands II.

> *Pline*
> *Polygon*
> *Ellipse*
> *Donut*
> *Sketch*
> *Spline*
> *Xline (construction line)*
> *Ray*

Draw Command Access

As a review from Chapter 3, Draw Command Basics, remember that any of the five methods can be used to access the draw commands: *Draw* toolbar (Windows, Fig. 8-1), *Draw* pull-down menu (Fig. 8-2), *DRAW* screen menu, keyboard entry of the command or alias, and digitizing tablet icons. (If you are using AutoCAD for Windows, use the ACADFULL menu.)

Figure 8-1 ——————

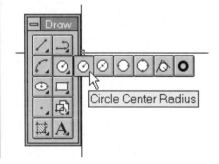

Figure 8-2 ——————

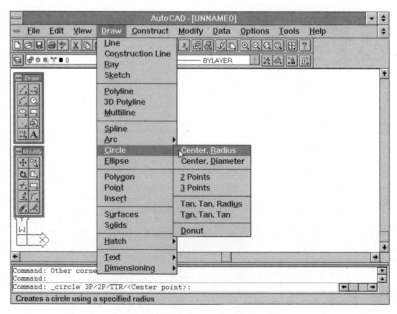

Coordinate Entry

When creating objects with draw commands, AutoCAD always prompts you to indicate points (such as end points, centers, radii, etc.) to describe the size and location of the objects to be drawn. An example you are familiar with is the *Line* command where AutoCAD prompts for the "From point:." Indication of these points, called <u>coordinate entry</u>, can be accomplished by four formats (for 2D drawings):

1.	**Interactive**	**PICK** points on screen with input device
2.	**Absolute coordinates**	**X,Y**
3.	**Relative rectangular coordinates**	**@X,Y**
4.	**Relative polar coordinates**	**@distance<angle**

Any of these methods can be used <u>whenever</u> AutoCAD prompts you to specify points. (For practice with these methods, see Chapter 3, Draw Command Basics.)

Also keep in mind that you may specify points interactively using *OSNAP* modes as discussed in Chapter 7. *OSNAP* modes can be used <u>whenever</u> AutoCAD prompts you to select points.

COMMANDS

LINE

PULL-DOWN MENU	SCREEN MENU	TYPE IN	TABLET MENU
Draw *Line*	*DRAW1* *Line:*	*LINE* *or L*	*10,J*

This is the fundamental drawing command. The *Line* command creates straight line segments; each segment is an object. One or several line segments can be drawn with the *Line* command.

> Command: **line**
> From point: **PICK** or (**coordinates**) (A point can be designated by interactively selecting with the input device or by entering coordinates. If using the input device, the *COORDS* display can be viewed to locate the current cursor position. If entering coordinates, any format is valid.)
> to point: **PICK** or (**coordinates**) (Again, device input or keyboard input can be used. If using the input device to select, *ORTHO* (**F8**) can be toggled *ON* to force vertical or horizontal lines.)
> to point: **PICK** or (**coordinates**) or **Enter** (Line segments can continually be drawn. Press Enter to complete the command.)
> Command:

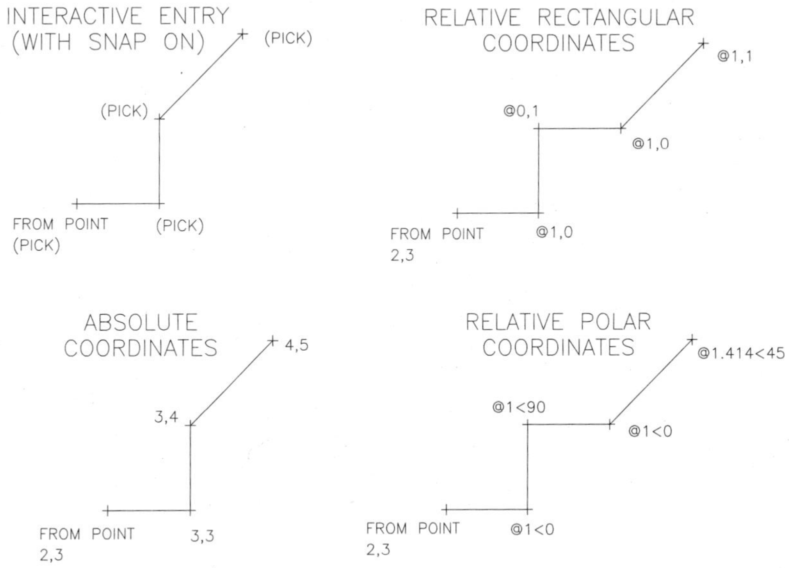

Figure 8-3 shows four examples of creating the same *Line* segments using different methods of coordinate entry.

Refer to Chapter 3, Draw Command Basics, for examples of drawing vertical, horizontal, and inclined lines using the four formats for coordinate entry.

Figure 8-3

INTERACTIVE ENTRY
(WITH SNAP ON)   + (PICK)

(PICK)

FROM POINT   (PICK)
(PICK)

RELATIVE RECTANGULAR
COORDINATES   + @1,1

@0,1

@1,0

FROM POINT   @1,0
2,3

ABSOLUTE
COORDINATES   + 4,5

3,4

FROM POINT   3,3
2,3

RELATIVE POLAR
COORDINATES   + @1.414<45

@1<90

@1<0

FROM POINT   @1<0
2,3

CIRCLE

PULL-DOWN MENU	SCREEN MENU	TYPE IN	TABLET MENU
Draw *Circle >*	*DRAW1* *Circle:*	*CIRCLE* *or C*	*10,M*

The *Circle* command creates one object. Depending on the option selected, you can provide two or three points to define a *Circle*. As with all commands, the command line prompt displays the possible options:

> Command: **circle**
> 3P/2P/TTR/<Center point>: **PICK** or (**coordinates**), (**option**). (PICKing or entering coordinates designates the center point for the circle. You can enter "*3P*," "*2P*" or "*TTR*" for another option.)

As with many other commands, when typing the command, the default and other options are displayed on the command line. The default option always appears in brackets "<option>:." The other options can be invoked by typing the indicated uppercase letter(s). Explicit *Circle* command options can be selected from the menus or icons.

The options, or methods, for drawing *Circles* are listed below. Each figure gives several possibilities for each option, with and without *OSNAPs*.

Center, Radius

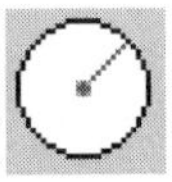

Specify a center point, then a radius. (Fig. 8-4).

Figure 8-4 ——————————————————————————————

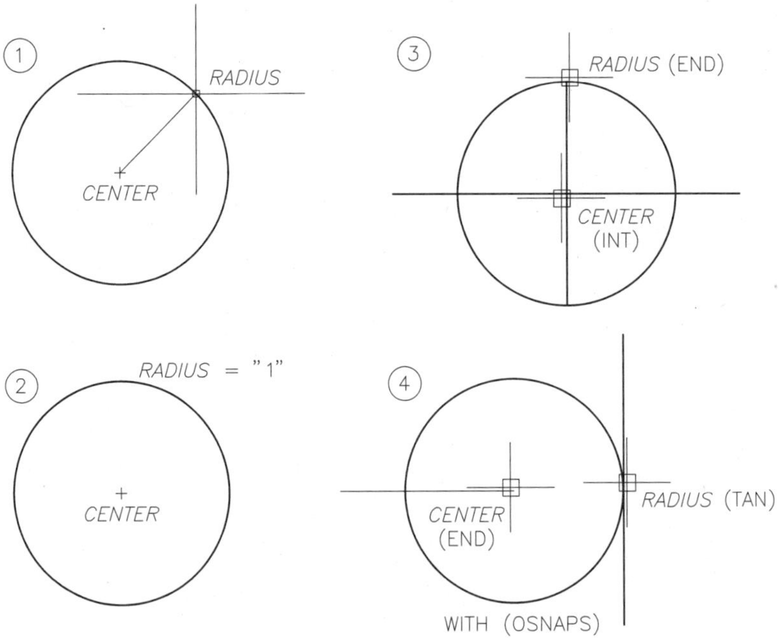

① RADIUS / CENTER

③ RADIUS (END) / CENTER (INT)

② RADIUS = "1" / + CENTER

④ CENTER (END) / RADIUS (TAN)

WITH (OSNAPS)

The *Radius* (or *Diameter*) can be specified by entering values or by indicating a length interactively (PICK two points to specify a length when prompted). As always, points can be specified by PICKing or entering coordinates. Watch *COORDS* for coordinate or distance (polar format) display. *OSNAPs* can be used for interactive point specification.

Center, Diameter

Specify the center point, then the diameter (Fig. 8-5).

Figure 8-5

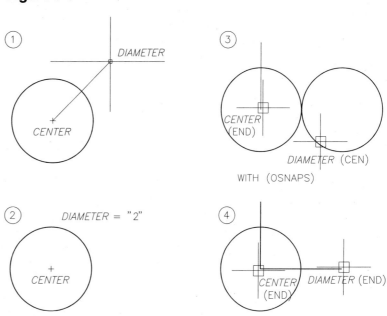

2 Points

The two points specify both the location and diameter.

Figure 8-6

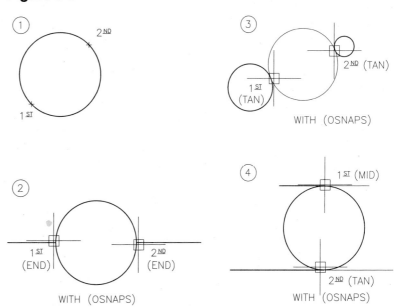

The *TANgent OSNAP*s can be used when selecting points with the *2 Point* and *3 Point* options as shown in Figures 8-6 and 8-7.

3 Points

 The *Circle* passes through all three points specified.

Figure 8-7

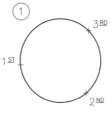

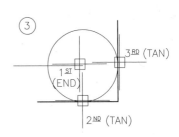

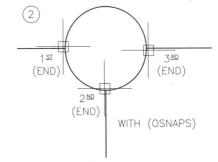

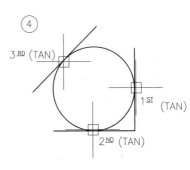

Tangent, Tangent, Radius

 Specify two objects for the *Circle* to be tangent to; then specify the radius.

Figure 8-8

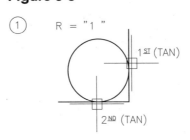

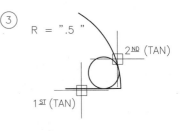

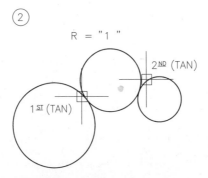

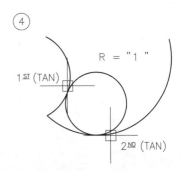

The *TTR* (Tangent, Tangent, Radius) method is extremely efficient and productive. The *OSNAP TANgent* modes are automatically invoked (the aperture is displayed on the cursor). This is the <u>only</u> draw command option that automatically calls *OSNAP*s.

ARC

PULL-DOWN MENU	SCREEN MENU	TYPE IN	TABLET MENU
Draw *Arc >*	*DRAW1* *Arc:*	*ARC* *or A*	*9,M*

An arc is part of a circle; it is a regular curve of <u>less</u> than 360 degrees. The *Arc* command in AutoCAD provides eleven options for creating arcs. An *Arc* is one object. *Arcs* are always drawn by default in a <u>counter-clockwise</u> direction. This occurrence forces you to decide in advance which points should be designated as *Start* and *End* points (for options requesting those points). The *Arc* command prompt is:

> Command: **arc**
> Center/<Start point>: **PICK** or (**coordinates**), or **C** (Interactively select or enter coordinates in any format for the start point. Type "C" to use the *Center* option instead.)

The prompts displayed by AutoCAD are different depending on which option is selected. At any time while using the command, you can select from the options listed on the command line by typing in the capitalized letter(s) for the desired option.

Alternately, to use a particular option of the *Arc* command, you can select from the pull-down menu or screen menus. These options require coordinate entry of points in <u>specific order</u>.

3Points

Specify three points through which the *Arc* passes (Fig. 8-9).

Figure 8-9

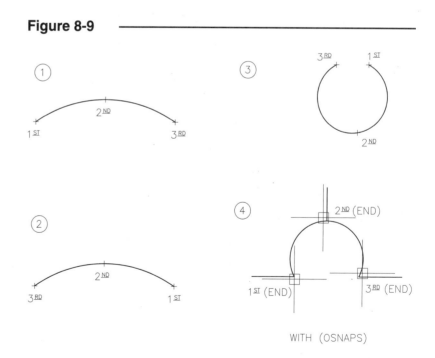

WITH (OSNAPS)

Start, Center, End

The radius is defined by the first two points that you specify (Fig. 8-10).

Figure 8-10 ───────────────────────

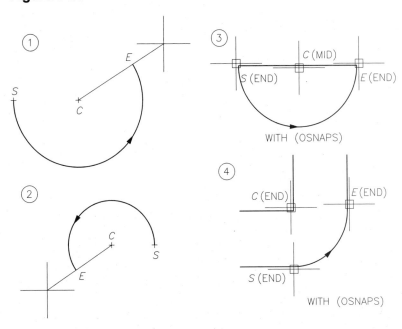

Start, Center, Angle

The angle is the <u>included</u> angle between the sides from the center to the endpoints. A <u>negative</u> angle can be entered to generate an *Arc* in a <u>clockwise</u> direction.

Figure 8-11 ───────────────────────

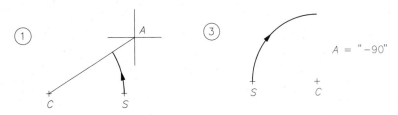

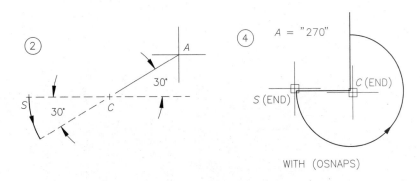

Start, Center, Length of Chord

The length of chord is between the start and the other point specified. A negative chord length can be entered to generate an *Arc* of 180+ degrees.

Figure 8-12

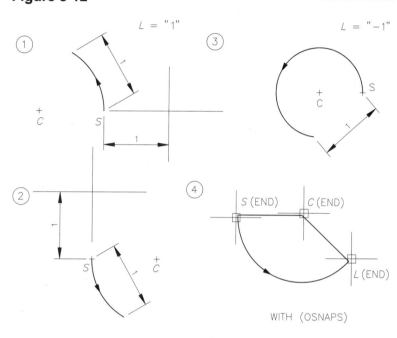

Start, End, Angle

The included angle is between the sides from the center to the endpoints. Negative angles generate clockwise *Arcs*.

Figure 8-13

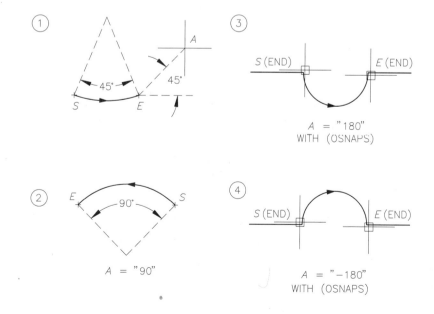

Start, End, Radius

The radius can be PICKed or entered as a value. A negative radius value generates an *Arc* of 180+ degrees.

Figure 8-14 ——————————————————————

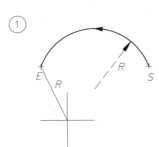

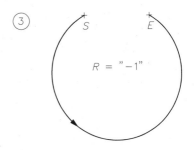

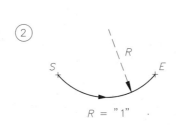

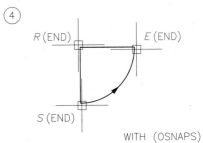

Start, End, Direction

The direction is tangent to the start point.

Figure 8-15 ——————————————————————

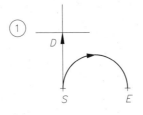

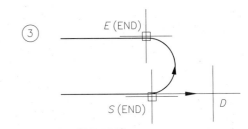

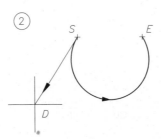

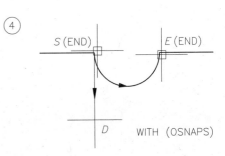

Center, Start, End

This option is like *S,C,E* but in a different order.

Figure 8-16 ————————————————————————

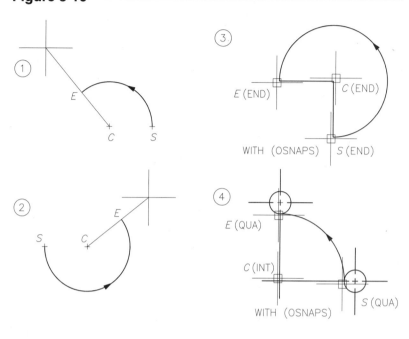

Center, Start, Angle

This option is like *S,C,A* but in a different order.

Figure 8-17 ————————————————————————

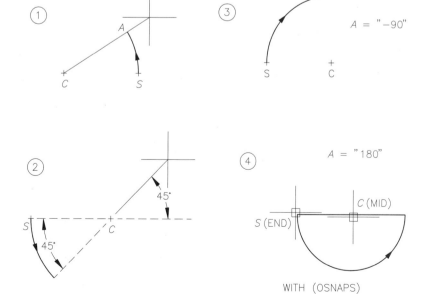

Center, Start, Length

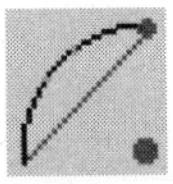

This is similar to the *S,C,L* option but in a different order.

Figure 8-18 ————————————————————————

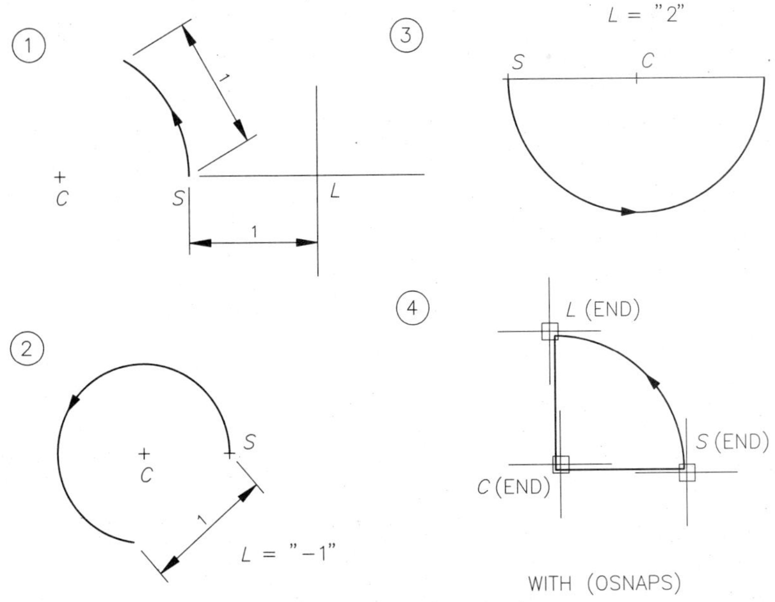

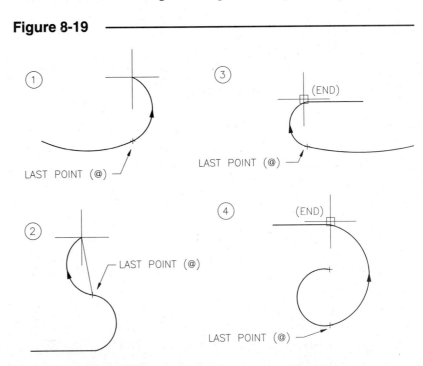

Continuous

The new *Arc* continues from and is tangent to the last point. The only other point required is the endpoint of the *Arc*. This method allows drawing *Arcs* tangent to the preceding *Line* or *Arc*.

Figure 8-19 ————————————————————————

Arcs are always created in a <u>counter-clockwise</u> direction. This fact must be taken into consideration when using any method <u>except</u> *3-Point*, *S,E,D*, and *Contin*. The direction is explicitly specified with *S,E,D* and *Contin* methods, and direction is irrelevant for *3-Point* method.

As usual, points can be specified by PICKing or entering coordinates. Watch *COORDS* to display coordinate values or distances. *OSNAPs* can be used when PICKing. The *ENDpoint, INTersection, CENter, MIDpoint,* and *QUAdrant OSNAP* options can be used with great effectiveness. The *TANgent OSNAP* option <u>cannot</u> be used effectively with most of the *Arc* options. The *Radius, Direction, Length,* and *Angle* specifications can be given by entering values or by PICKing with or without *OSNAPs.*

Use *Arcs* or *Circles?*

Although there are sufficient options for drawing *Arcs,* <u>usually it is easier to use the *Circle* command</u> followed by *Trim* to achieve the desired arc. Creating a *Circle* is generally an easier operation than using *Arc* because the counter-clockwise direction does not have to be considered. The unwanted portion of the circle can be *Trimmed* at the *INTersection* of or *TANgent* to the connecting objects using *OSNAP.* The *Fillet* command can also be used instead of the *Arc* command to add a fillet (arc) between two existing objects (see Chapter 17, Construct Commands II).

POINT

PULL-DOWN MENU	SCREEN MENU	TYPE IN	TABLET MENU
Draw *Point >* *Point*	DRAW2 *Point:*	*POINT*	*10,O*

A *Point* is an object that has no dimension; it only has location. A *Point* is specified by giving only one coordinate value or by PICKing a location on the screen.

Figure 8-20 compares *Points* to *Line* and *Circle* objects.

Figure 8-20 ——————————

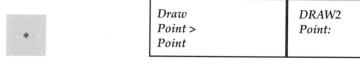

LINE

POINT OBJECTS

CIRCLE

Command: **point**
Point: **PICK** or **(coordinates)**
(Select a location for the *Point* object.)
Command:

After creating *Points,* generally the "blips" appear at the placement of these objects. Forcing a *Redraw* displays the *Points* as one-pixel dots (default display mode).

The Node OSNAP option can be used to snap to *Points. Points* are useful in construction of drawings to locate points of reference for subsequent construction or locational verification.

The *Point Style...* dialogue box (Fig. 8-21) or the *PDMODE* variable allows you to define the format for the display of *Points.* The *Point Style* dialogue box is accessed by the *Options, Display* pull-down menu, or by typing *DDPTYPE.*

Figure 8-21 ——————————

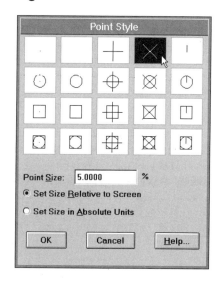

If you change the point style using this dialogue box or by typing the *PDMODE* variable, the points are not automatically displayed in the new style. You must use <u>Regen</u> to force AutoCAD to display the points in the new style.

CHAPTER EXERCISES

Create a new drawing. Use default *Limits*; set *SNAP* to **.25** and *GRID* to **1**. *Save* the drawing as **CH8EX**. For each of the following problems, *Open* **CH8EX**, complete one problem, then use *Saveas* to give the drawing a new name.

1. *Open* **CH8EX**. Create the geometry shown in Figure 8-22. Start the first *Circle* center at point **4,4.5** as shown. Do not copy the dimensions. *Saveas* **LINK**. (HINT: Locate and draw the two small *Circles* first. Use *Arc, S,C,E* or *C,S,E* for the rounded ends.)

Figure 8-22

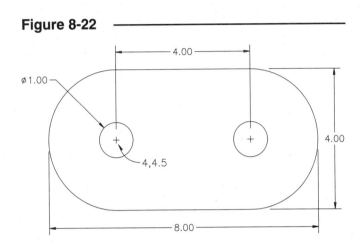

2. *Open* **CH8EX**. Create the geometry as shown in Figure 8-23. Do not copy the dimensions. Assume symmetry about the vertical axis. *Saveas* **SLOTPLAT**.

Figure 8-23

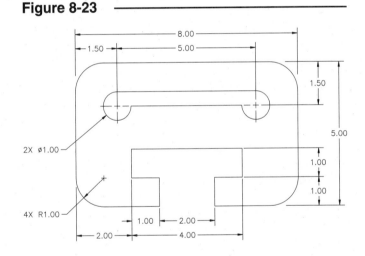

3. *Open* **CH8EX**. Create the shapes shown in Figure 8-24. Do not copy the dimensions. *Saveas* **CH8EX3**.

Draw the *Lines* at the bottom first, starting at coordinate **1,3**. Then create *Point* objects at **5,7**, **5.4,7**, **5.8,7**, etc. Change the *Point Style* to an X and *Regen*. Use the *NODe OSNAP* mode to draw the inclined *Lines*. Create the *Arc* on top with the *Start, End, Direction* option.

Figure 8-24

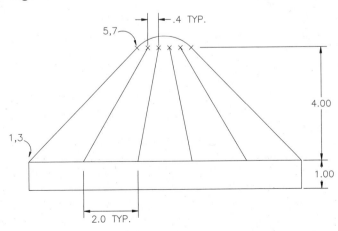

4. *Open* **CH8EX**. Create the shape shown in Figure 8-25. Draw the two horizontal *Lines* and the vertical *Line* first by specifying the endpoints as given. Then create the *Circle* and *Arcs*. *Saveas* **CH8EX4**.

   HINT: Use the *Circle 2P* method. The two upper *Arcs* can be drawn by the *Start, End, Radius* method.

Figure 8-25

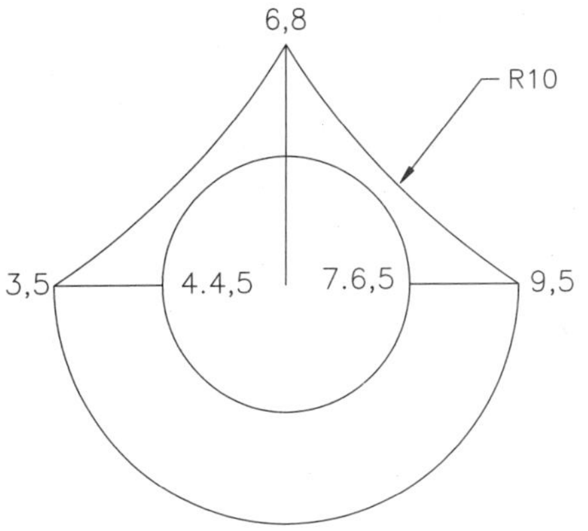

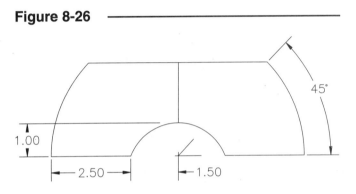

5. *Open* **CH8EX**. Draw the shape shown in Figure 8-26. Assume symmetry along a vertical axis. Start by drawing the two horizontal *Lines* at the base. Next construct the side *Arcs* by the *Start, Center, Angle* method (you can specify a negative angle). The small *Arc* can be drawn by the *3P* method. Use *OSNAPs* when needed (especially for the horizontal *Line* on top and the *Line* along the vertical axis). **Saveas CH8EX5**.

Figure 8-26

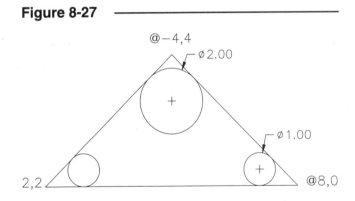

6. *Open* **CH8EX**. Complete the geometry in Figure 8-27. Use the coordinates to establish the *Lines*. Draw the *Circles* using the *Tangent, Tangent, Radius* method. **Saveas CH8EX6**.

Figure 8-27

7. A contractor plans to stake out the edge of a retaining wall located at the bottom of a hill. The following table lists coordinate values based on a survey at the site. Place *Points* at each coordinate value in order to create a set of data points. Determine the location of one *Arc* and two *Lines* representing the center line of the retaining wall edge. The center line of the retaining wall should match the data points as accurately as possible (Fig. 8-28). *Save* the drawing as **RET-WALL**.

Pt #	X	Y	
1.	60.0000	108.0000	
2.	81.5118	108.5120	
3.	101.4870	108.2560	
4.	122.2305	107.4880	
5.	141.4375	108.5120	
6.	158.1949	108.0000	
7.	192.0000	108.0000	Recommended tangency point
8.	215.3914	110.5185	
9.	242.3905	119.2603	
10.	266.5006	133.6341	
11.	285.1499	151.0284	Recommended tangency point
12.	299.5069	168.1924	
13.	314.2060	183.4111	
14.	328.3813	201.7784	
15.	343.0811	216.4723	
16.	355.6808	232.2157	
17.	370.3805	249.0087	
18.	384.0000	264.0000	

(Hint: Change the *Point Style* [i.e., *PDMODE*] to an easily visible format.)

Figure 8-28

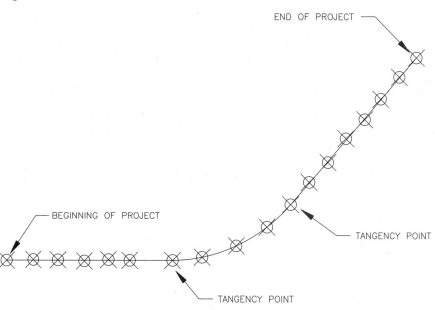

Chapter 9

MODIFY COMMANDS I

Chapter Objectives

After completing this chapter you should:

1. know where to locate and how to invoke the Modify commands;

2. be able to *Erase* objects from the drawing;

3. be able to *Move* objects from a base point to a second point of displacement;

4. know how to *Rotate* objects about a base point;

5. be able to enlarge or reduce objects with *Scale*;

6. know how to use the four *Break* options;

7. be able to *Trim* away parts of objects at cutting edges;

8. be able to *Extend* objects to selected boundary edges;

9. be able to change the length of *Lines* and *Arcs* with *Lengthen*.

BASICS

Draw commands are used to create objects, while <u>Modify</u> commands are used to <u>change</u> existing objects. Modify commands can be invoked by any one of the five command entry methods: toolbar icons, pull-down menus, screen menus, keyboard entry, and digitizing tablet menu.

The Modify toolbar is visible by default in AutoCAD for Windows (Fig. 9-1). It can be made to float in the drawing area or can be docked on any border. The toolbar contains several flyouts for related commands and options. Figure 9-1 displays flyouts for the *Break* options.

Figure 9-1 ⎯⎯⎯⎯

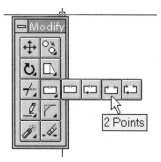

Figure 9-2 ⎯⎯⎯⎯⎯⎯⎯⎯⎯⎯

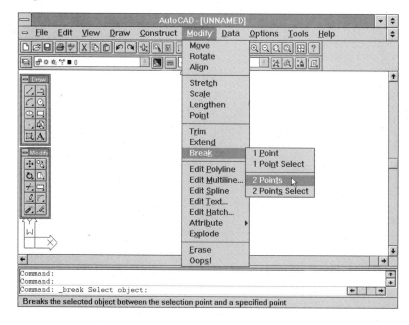

The digitizing tablet uses the same icons that are displayed for the toolbars.

The *Modify* pull-down menu (Fig. 9-2) contains commands that only <u>change</u> existing geometry. All of the Modify commands are contained in this single pull-down menu (ACADFULL menu).

Figure 9-3 ⎯⎯⎯⎯⎯

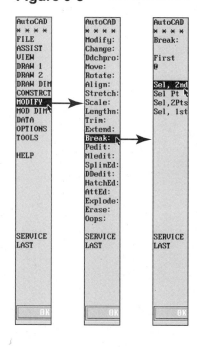

The *MODIFY* screen menu branches to the individual commands and options (Fig.9-3).

Since all Modify commands affect or use existing geometry, the first step in using any modify command is to construct a selection set (see Chapter 4). This can be done by one of two methods:

1. Invoking the desired command and then creating the selection set in response to the "Select objects:" prompt (verb/noun syntax order) using any of the select object options;

2. Selecting the desired set of objects with the pickbox or *AUto* window or crossing window <u>before</u> invoking the edit command (noun/verb syntax order).

The first method allows use of any of the selection options (*Last, All, WPolygon, Fence,* etc.), while the latter method allows <u>only</u> the use of the pickbox and *AUto* window and crossing window.

The following *Modify* commands are covered in this chapter: *Erase, Move, Rotate, Scale, Break, Trim, Extend,* and *Lengthen.* The other *Modify* commands are discussed in Chapter 16, Modify Commands II.

COMMANDS

ERASE

PULL-DOWN MENU	SCREEN MENU	TYPE IN	TABLET MENU
Modify *Erase*	*MODIFY* *Erase:*	*ERASE* *or E*	*16,W and 17,W*

The *Erase* command deletes the objects you select from the drawing. Any of the object selection methods can be used to highlight the objects to *Erase.* The only other required action is for you to press *Enter* to cause the erase to take effect.

    Command: **Erase**
    Select objects: **PICK** (Use any object selection method.)
    Select objects: **PICK** (Continue to select desired objects.)
    Select objects: **Enter** (Confirms the object selection process and causes *Erase* to take effect.)
    Command:

It is a good habit to <u>Redraw after Erasing.</u> This action clears the drawing of "blips" and redraws any objects or parts of objects that were turned to the background color during the *Erase* (Fig. 9-4).

If objects are erased accidentally, *U* can be used immediately following the mistake to undo one step, or *Oops* can be used to bring back into the drawing whatever was *Erased* the last time *Erase* was used. If only part of an object should be erased, use *Trim* or *Break.*

Figure 9-4

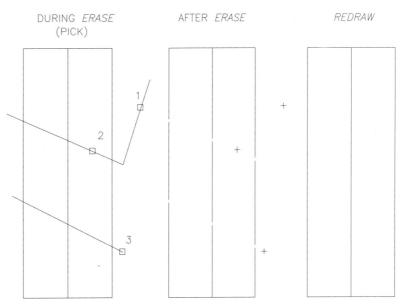

DURING *ERASE* (PICK)   AFTER *ERASE*   *REDRAW*

MOVE

PULL-DOWN MENU	SCREEN MENU	TYPE IN	TABLET MENU
Modify *Move*	*MODIFY* *Move:*	*MOVE* *or M*	*15,W*

Move allows you to relocate one or more objects from the existing position in the drawing to any other position you specify. After selecting the objects to *Move,* you must specify the "base point" and "second point of displacement." You can use any of the coordinate entry methods to specify these points as shown in Figure 9-5.

Figure 9-5

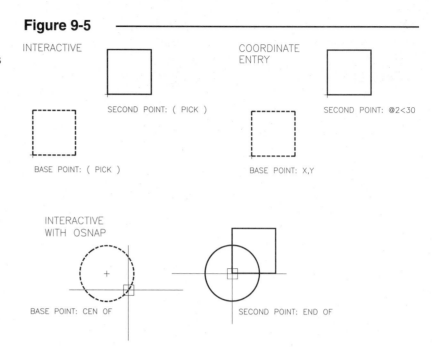

Command: **move**
Select objects: **PICK** (Use any of the object selection methods.)
Select objects: **PICK** (Continue to other desired select objects.)
Select objects: **Enter** (Press Enter to indicate selection of objects is complete.)
Base point or displacement: **PICK** or (**coordinates**) (This is the point to <u>move from</u>. Select a point to use as a "handle." An *ENDpoint* or *CENter*, etc., can be used.)
Second point of displacement: **PICK** or (**coordinates**) (This is the point to <u>move to</u>. *OSNAPs* can also be used here.)
Command:

Keep in mind that *OSNAPs* can be used when PICKing any point. It is often helpful to toggle *ORTHO ON* (**F8**) to force the *Move* in a horizontal or vertical direction.

If you know a specific distance, or a distance and an angle, that the set of objects should be moved, relative rectangular or relative polar coordinates can be used. In the following sequence, relative polar coordinates are used to move objects 2 units in a 30 degree direction (see Fig. 9-5, coordinate entry).

Command: **move**
Select objects: **PICK**
Select objects: **PICK**
Select objects: **Enter**
Base point or displacement: **X,Y (coordinates)**
Second point of displacement: **@2<30**
Command:

ROTATE

PULL-DOWN MENU	SCREEN MENU	TYPE IN	TABLET MENU
Modify *Rotate*	*MODIFY* *Rotate:*	*ROTATE*	13,W

Selected objects can be rotated to any position with this command. After selecting objects to *Rotate*, you select a "base point" (a point to rotate about) then specify an angle for rotation. AutoCAD rotates the

selected objects by the increment specified from the original position
(Fig. 9-6). For example, specifying a
value of **45** would *Rotate* the selected
objects 45 degrees counter-clockwise
from their current position; a value of
-45 would *Rotate* the objects 45
degrees in a clockwise direction.

Figure 9-6

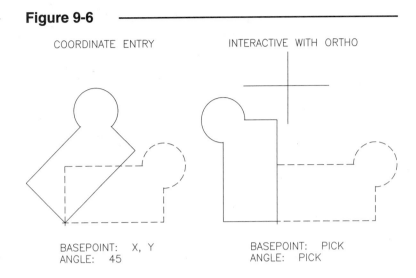

COORDINATE ENTRY

INTERACTIVE WITH ORTHO

BASEPOINT: X, Y
ANGLE: 45

BASEPOINT: PICK
ANGLE: PICK

Command: *rotate*
Select objects: **PICK** or (**coordinates**) (Select the objects to rotate.)
Select objects: **Enter** (Indicate completion of the object selection.)
Base point: **PICK** or (**coordinates**) (Select the point to rotate about.)
<Rotation angle>Reference: **PICK** or (**value**) or (**coordinates**) (Enter a value for the number of
degrees to rotate or interactively rotate the object set.)
Command:

The base point is often selected interactively with *OSNAP*s. When
specifying the angle for rotation, a value (incremental angle) can be
typed. Alternately, if you want to **PICK** an angle, *COORDS* (in the
polar format) displays the current angle of the rubberband line.
Turning on *ORTHO* forces the rotation to a 90 degree increment. The
List command can be used to report the angle of an existing *Line* or
other object (discussed in Chapter 18).

Figure 9-7

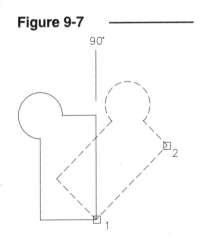

90°

2

1

REFERENCE ANGLE: PICK 1,2
NEW ANGLE: 90°

The *Reference* option can be used to specify a vector as the original
angle before rotation (Fig. 9-7). This vector can be indicated interactively (*OSNAP*s can be used) or entered as an angle using keyboard
entry. Angular values that you enter in response to the "New angle:"
prompt are understood by AutoCAD as <u>absolute</u> angles for the
Reference option only.

Command: *rotate*
Select objects: **PICK** or (**coordinates**) (Select the objects to rotate.)
Select objects: **Enter** (Indicates completion of object selection.)
Base point: **PICK** or (**coordinates**) (Select the point to rotate about.)
<Rotation angle>Reference: **R** (Indicates the *Reference* option.)
Reference angle<0>: **PICK** or (**value**) (PICK the first point of the vector.)
Second point: **PICK** (Indicates the second point defining the vector.)
New angle: **PICK** or (**value**) (Indicates the new angle value.)
Command:

SCALE

PULL-DOWN MENU	SCREEN MENU	TYPE IN	TABLET MENU
Modify Scale	MODIFY Scale:	SCALE	12,W

The *Scale* command is used to increase or decrease the size of objects in a drawing. The *Scale* command does not normally have any relation to plotting a drawing to scale.

After selecting objects to *Scale*, AutoCAD prompts you to select a "Base point:" which is the <u>stationary point</u>. You can then scale the size of the selected objects interactively or enter a scale factor. Using interactive input, you are presented with a rubberband line connected to the base point. Making the rubberband line longer or shorter than 1 unit increases or decreases the scale of the selected objects by that proportion; for example, pulling the rubberband line to two units length increases the scale by a factor of two (Fig. 9-8).

Figure 9-8

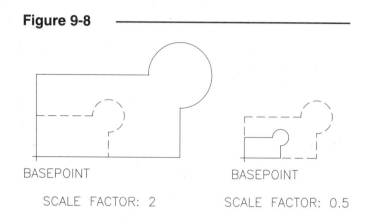

```
Command: scale
Select objects: PICK or (coordinates) (Select the objects to scale.)
Select objects: Enter (Indicates completion of the object selection.)
Base point: PICK  or (coordinates) (Select the stationary point.)
Scale factor<Reference>: PICK or (value) or (coordinates) (Enter a value for the scale factor or
interactively scale the set of objects.)
Command:
```

It may be desirable in some cases to use the **Reference** option to specify a value or two points to use as the reference length. This length can be indicated interactively (*OSNAPs* can be used) or entered as a value. This length is used for the subsequent reference length that the rubberband uses when interactively scaling. For example, if the reference distance is two, then the rubberband line must be stretched to a length greater than two to increase the scale of the selected objects.

Scale should <u>not</u> normally be used to change the scale of an entire drawing in order to plot on a specific size sheet. CAD drawings should be created <u>full size</u> in <u>actual units</u>.

BREAK

PULL-DOWN MENU	SCREEN MENU	TYPE IN	TABLET MENU
Modify Break >	MODIFY Break:	BREAK	13,X and 14,X

Break allows you to break a space in an object or break the end off an object. You can think of *Break* as a partial erase. If you choose to break a space in an object, the space is created between two points that you specify (Fig. 9-9). In this case, the *Break* creates two objects from one.

Figure 9-9

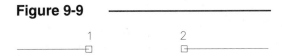

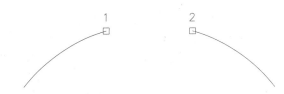

If *Break*ing a circle (Fig. 9-10), the break is in a <u>counterclockwise</u> direction from the first to the second point specified.

Figure 9-10

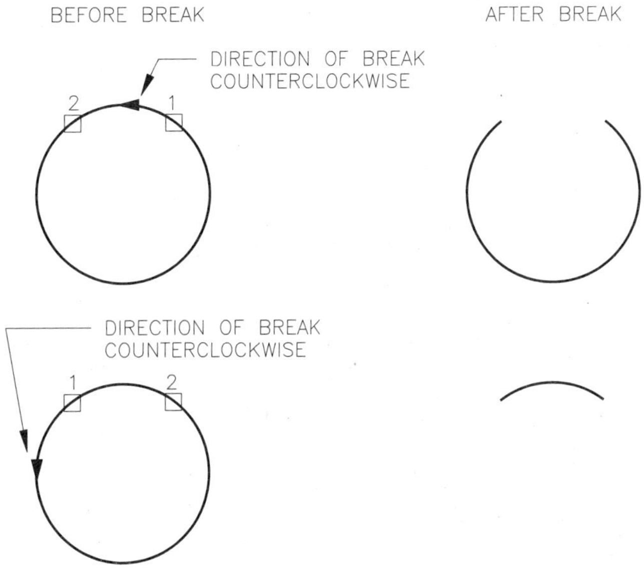

If you want to *Break* the end off a *Line* or *Arc*, the first point should be specified at the point of the break and the second point should be <u>just off the end</u> of the *Line* or *Arc* (Fig 9-11).

Figure 9-11

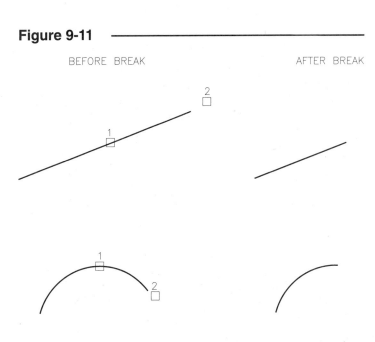

There are four options for *Break.* All four options are available in the Modify toolbar, *Modify* pull-down menu, and from the screen menus (see Figs. 9-1, 9-2, and 9-3). The digitizing tablet offers two options. If you are entering commands at the keyboard, the desired option is selected by keying the letter *F* (for *First point*) or symbol @ (for "last point"). The four options are explained next in detail.

2 Points

This method (the default if typing) has two steps: select the object to break; then select the second point of the break. The first point used to select the object is <u>also</u> the first point of the break. (See Figs. 9-9, 9-10, 9-11.)

Command: **break**
Select objects: **PICK** or (**coordinates**) (This is the first point of the break.)
Enter second point (or F for first point): **PICK** or (**coordinates**) (This is the second point of the break.)
Command:

2 Points Select

This method uses the first selection only to indicate the <u>object</u> to *Break.* You then specify the point which is the first point of the *Break,* and the next point specified is the second point of the *Break.* This option can be used with *OSNAP INTersection* to achieve the same results as *Trim.*

Selecting this option from the toolbar or the pull-down menu automatically sequences through the correct prompts (see Fig. 9-12). If you are typing the command sequence is as follows:

Figure 9-12

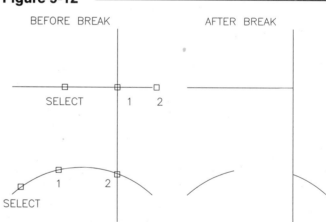

Command: **break**
Select objects: **PICK** or (**coordinates**)
(Select the object to break.)
Enter second point (or F for first point): **F**
(Indicates respecification for the first point.)
Enter first point: **PICK** or (**coordinates**)
(Select the first point of the break.)
Enter second point: **PICK** or (**coordinates**)
(This is the second point of the break.)
Command:

1 Point

This option breaks one object into two separate objects with <u>no space</u> between. You specify only <u>one</u> point with this method. When you select the object, the point indicates the object <u>and</u> the point of the break. When prompted for the second point, the @ symbol (translated as "last point") is specified. This second step is done automatically if selected from the toolbar or pull-down menu. If you are typing the command, the @ symbol ("last point") must be typed also.

Command: **break**
Select objects: **PICK** or (**coordinates**)
(This PICKs the object and specifies the first point of the break.)
Enter second point (or F for first point): **@** (Indicates the break to be at the last point.)

The resulting object should <u>appear</u> as before; however, it has been transformed into <u>two</u> objects with matching endpoints (Fig. 9-13).

Figure 9-13

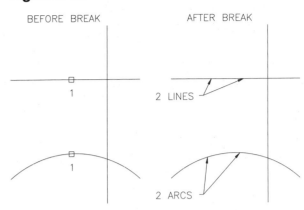

1 Point Select

This option creates a Break with <u>no</u> <u>space</u>, like the *1 Point* option; however, you can select the object you want to *Break* first and the point of the *Break* next (Fig. 9-14). If you are typing the command, the sequence is as follows.

Figure 9-14

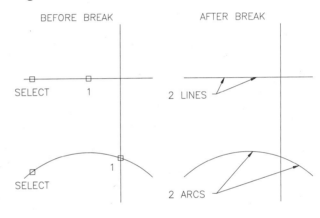

```
Command: break
Select objects: PICK or (coordinates)
(Select the object to break.)
Enter second point (or F for first point): F
(Indicates respecification for the first point.)
Enter first point: PICK or (coordinates)
(Select the first point of the break.)
Enter second point: @ (The second point of the break is the last point.)
Command:
```

TRIM

PULL-DOWN MENU	SCREEN MENU	TYPE IN	TABLET MENU
Modify *Trim*	*MODIFY* *Trim:*	*TRIM*	*18,X*

The *Trim* command allows you to trim (shorten) the end of an object back to the intersection of another object (Fig. 9-15). The middle section of an object can also be *Trimmed* between two intersecting objects. There are two steps to this command: first, PICK one or more "cutting edges" (existing objects); then PICK the object or objects to *Trim* (portion to remove). The cutting edges are highlighted after selection. Cutting edges themselves can be trimmed if they intersect other cutting edges, but lose their highlight when trimmed.

```
Command: trim
Select cutting edges: (Projmode = View,
Edgemode = No extend)
```

Figure 9-15

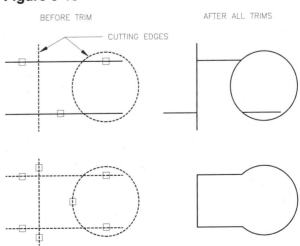

Select objects: **PICK** (Select an object to use as a cutting edge.)
Select objects: **PICK**
Select objects: **Enter**
<Select object to trim>/Project/Edge/Undo: **PICK** (Select the end of an object to trim.)
<Select object to trim>/Project/Edge/Undo: **PICK**
<Select object to trim>/Project/Edge/Undo: **Enter**
Command:

Edgemode

The *Edgemode* option can be set to *Extend* or *No extend*. In the *Extend* mode, objects that are selected as trimming edges will be <u>imaginarily extended</u> to serve as a cutting edge. In other words, lines used for trimming edges are treated as having infinite length (Fig. 9-16). The *No extend* mode only considers the actual length of the object selected as trimming edges.

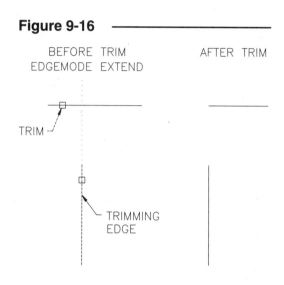

Figure 9-16

Command: **trim**
Select cutting edges: (Projmode = View, Edgemode = No extend)
Select objects: **PICK**
Select objects: **Enter**
<Select object to trim>/Project/Edge/Undo: **e**
Extend/No extend <No extend>: **e**
<Select object to trim>/Project/Edge/Undo: **PICK**
<Select object to trim>/Project/Edge/Undo: **Enter**
Command:

Projectmode

The *Projectmode* switch controls how *Trim* and *Extend* operate in 3D space. *Projectmode* affects the projection of the "cutting edge" and "boundary edge." The three options are described here.

<Select object to trim>/Project/Edge/Undo: **p**
None/Ucs/View <View>:

None

The *None* option does not project the cutting edge. This mode is used for normal 2D drawing when all objects (cutting edges and objects to trim) lie in the current drawing plane. You can use this mode to *Trim* in 3D space when all objects lie in the plane of the current UCS or in planes parallel to it, and the objects physically intersect. You can also *Trim* objects not in the UCS if the objects physically intersect, are in the same plane, and are not perpendicular to the UCS. In any case, the objects must physically intersect for trimming to occur.

Figure 9-17

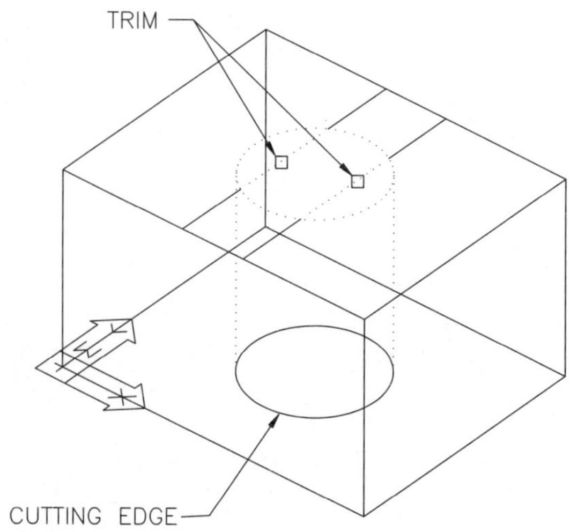

The other two options (*UCS* and *View*) allow you to trim objects that do not physically intersect in 3D space.

UCS

This option projects the cutting edge perpendicular to the UCS. Any objects crossing the "projected" cutting edge in 3D space can be trimmed. For example, selecting a *Circle* as the cutting edge creates a projected cylinder used for cutting (Fig. 9-17).

View

The *View* option allows you to trim objects that <u>appear</u> to intersect from the current viewpoint. The objects do not have to physically intersect in 3D space. The cutting edge is projected perpendicularly to the screen (parallel to the line of sight). This mode is useful for trimming "hidden edges" of a wireframe model to make the surfaces appear opaque (Fig. 9-18).

Figure 9-18

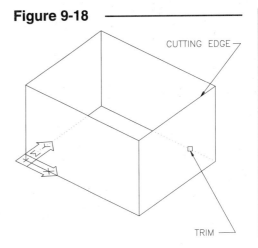

Undo
The *Undo* option allows you to undo the last *Trim* in case of an accidental trim.

Extend can be thought of as the opposite of *Trim*. Objects such as

EXTEND

PULL-DOWN MENU	SCREEN MENU	TYPE IN	TABLET MENU
Modify *Extend*	*MODIFY* *Extend:*	*EXTEND*	*16,X*

Extend can be thought of as the opposite of *Trim*. Objects such as *Lines*, *Arcs*, and *Plines* can be *Extended* until intersecting another object called a "boundary edge" (Fig. 9-19). The command first requires selection of <u>existing</u> objects to serve as "boundary edge(s)" which become highlighted; then the objects to extend are selected. Objects extend until, and only if, they eventually intersect a "boundary edge." An *Extend*ed object acquires a new endpoint at the boundary edge intersection.

Figure 9-19

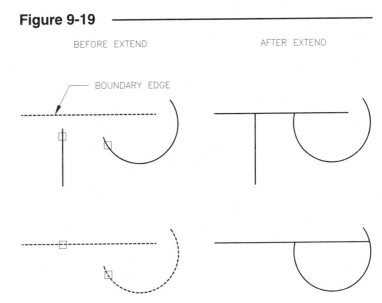

```
Command: extend
Select boundary edges: (Projmode =
View, Edgemode = No extend)
Select objects: PICK
Select objects: PICK
Select objects: Enter
<Select object to extend>/Project/Edge/Undo: PICK
(Select object to extend.)
<Select object to extend>/Project/Edge/Undo: PICK
<Select object to extend>/Project/Edge/Undo: Enter
Command:
```

Edgemode/Projectmode
The *Edgemode* and *Projectmode* switches operate identically to their function with the *Trim* command. Use *Edgemode* with the *Extend* option if you want a boundary edge object to be imaginarily extended (Fig. 9-20).

Figure 9-20

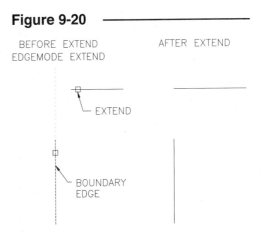

LENGTHEN

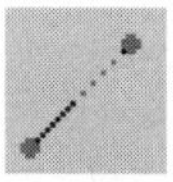

PULL-DOWN MENU	SCREEN MENU	TYPE IN	TABLET MENU
Modify *Lengthen*	*MODIFY* *Lengthen:*	*LENGTHEN*	*18,Y*

Lengthen changes the length (longer or shorter) of linear objects and arcs. No additional objects are required (as with *Trim* and *Extend*) to make the change in length. Many methods are provided as displayed in the command prompt.

Command: **lengthen**
Delta/Percent/Total/DYnamic/<Select object>:

Select object
Selecting an object causes AutoCAD to report the current length of that object. If an *Arc* is selected, the included angle is also given.

DElta
Using this option returns the prompt shown below. You can change the current length of an object (including an arc) by an increment that you specify. Entering a positive value will increase the length by that amount, while a negative value will decrease the current length. The end of the object that you select changes while the other end retains its current endpoint (Fig. 9-21).

Figure 9-21

Angle/<Enter delta length>: (**value**) or **a**

The *Angle* option allows you to change the <u>included angle</u> of an arc (the length along the curvature of the arc can be changed with the *Delta* option). You are prompted to enter a positive or negative value (degrees) to add or subtract to the current included angle, then select the end of the object to change (Fig. 9-22).

Figure 9-22

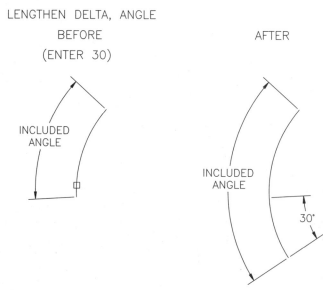

Percent

Use this option if you want to change the length by a percentage of the current total length. For arcs, the percentage applied affects the length and the included angle equally, so there is no *Angle* option. A value of greater than 100 increases the current length, and a value of less than 100 decreases the current length. Negative values are not allowed. The end of the object that you select changes.

Figure 9-23 ───────────

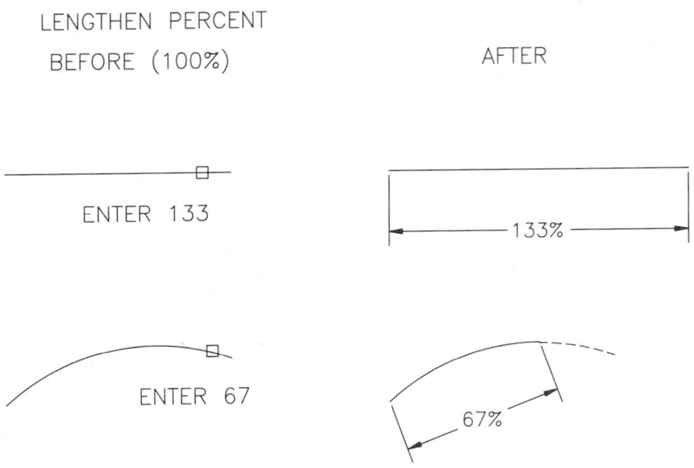

LENGTHEN PERCENT
BEFORE (100%)   AFTER

Total

This option lets you specify a value for the new total length. Simply enter the value and select the end of the object to change. The angle option is used to change the total included angle of a selected arc.

Angle/<Enter total length>: (**value**) or **a**

Figure 9-24 ───────────

LENGTHEN TOTAL
BEFORE (3 UNITS)   AFTER

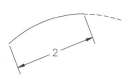

DYnamic

This option allows you to change the length of an object by dynamic dragging. Select the end of the object that you want to change. Object snaps can be used.

Figure 9-25 ───────────

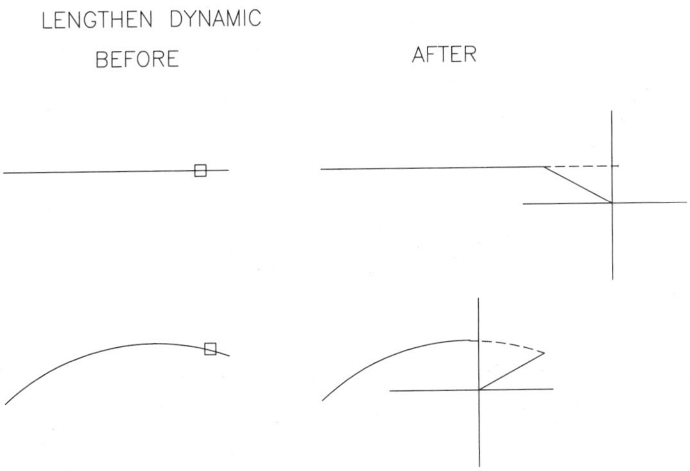

LENGTHEN DYNAMIC
BEFORE   AFTER

CHAPTER EXERCISES

1. *Move*

   Begin a **New** drawing and create the geometry in Figure 9-26 A. using *Lines* and *Circles*.
   If desired, set *SNAP* to **.25** to make drawing
   easy and accurate.

   For practice, <u>turn *SNAP OFF*</u> (**F9**). Use the
   Move command to move the *Circles* and *Lines*
   into the positions shown in illustration B.
   OSNAPs are required to *Move* the geometry
   accurately (since *SNAP* is off). Save the
   drawing as **CH9EX1**.

Figure 9-26

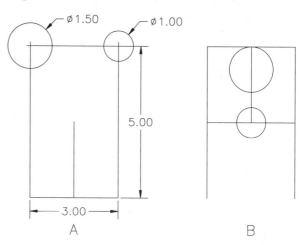

A   B

2. *Rotate*

   Begin a **New** drawing and create
   the geometry in Figure 9-27 A.

   Rotate the shape into position
   shown in step B. *Saveas* **CH9EX2B**.

   Use the *Reference* option to *Rotate*
   the box to align with the diagonal
   Line as shown in C. *Saveas* **CH9EX2C**.

Figure 9-27

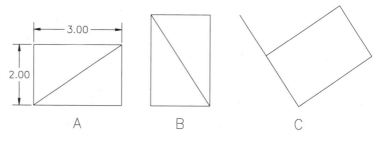

A   B   C

3. *Scale*

   Open **CH9EX2B** to again use the shape
   shown in Figure 9-28 B. *Scale* the shape by
   a factor of **1.5**.

   Open **CH9EX2C** to again use the shape
   shown in C. Use the *Reference* option of
   Scale to increase the scale of the three other
   Lines to equal the length of the original diagonal *Line* as shown. (HINT: *OSNAPs* are
   required to specify the *Reference length* and
   New length.)

Figure 9-28

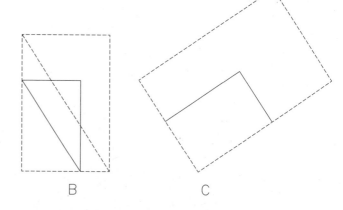

B   C

4. **Trim**

   A. Create the shape shown in Figure 9-29 A. *Saveas* **CH9EX4A**.

   B. Use *Trim* to alter the shape as shown in B. *Saveas* **CH9EX4B**.

   C. *Open* **CH9EX4A** to create the shapes shown in C and D using *Trim*. *Saveas* **CH9EX4C** and **CH9EX4D**.

5. **Extend**

   Open each of the drawings created as solutions for Figure 9-29 (**CH9EX4B**, **CH9EX4C**, and **CH9EX4D**). Use *Extend* to return each of the drawings to the original form shown in Figure 9-29 A. *Saveas* **CH9EX5B**, **CH9EX5C**, and **CH9EX5D**.

Figure 9-29

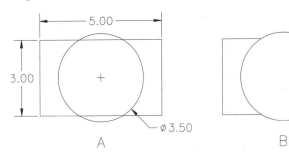

A

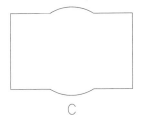

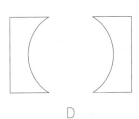

B

C

D

6. **Trim, Extend**

   A. *Open* the **PIVOTARM** drawing from the Chapter 7 Exercises. Use *Trim* to remove the upper sections of the vertical *Lines* connecting the top and front views. Compare your work to Figure 9-30.

Figure 9-30

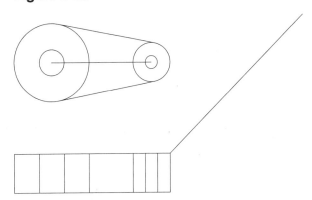

   B. Next, draw a horizontal *Line* in the front view between the *MIDpoints* of the vertical *Line* on each end of the view as shown in Figure 9-31. *Erase* the horizontal *Line* in the top view between the *Circle* centers.

Figure 9-31

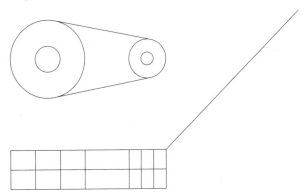

C. Draw vertical *Lines* from the *Endpoints* of the inclined *Line* (side of the object) in the top view down to the bottom *Line* in the front view as shown in Figure 9-32. Use the two vertical lines as *Cutting edges* for *Trimming* the *Line* in the middle of the front view as shown highlighted.

Figure 9-32

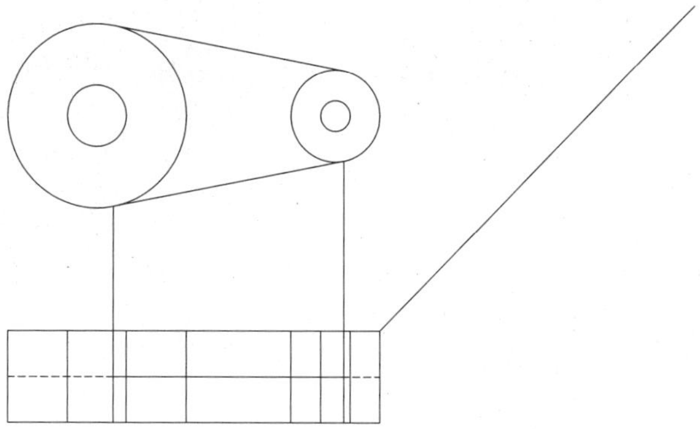

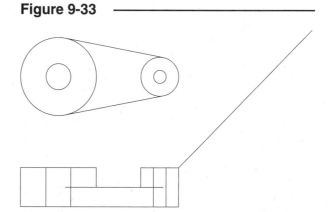

D. Finally, *Erase* the vertical lines used for *Cutting edges* and then use *Trim* to achieve the object as shown in Figure 9-33. *Save* the drawing (again as **PIVOTARM**).

Figure 9-33

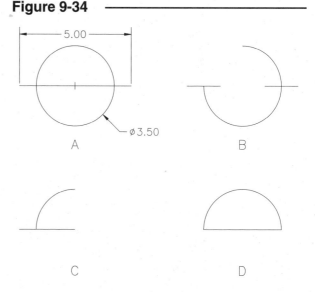

7. *Break*

A. Create the shape shown in Figure 9-34 A. *Saveas* **CH9EX7A**.

B. Use *Break* to make the two breaks as shown in B. *Saveas* **CH9EX7B**.

C. Open **CH9EX7A** each time to create the shapes shown in C and D with the *Break* command. *Saveas* **CH9EX7C** and **CH9EX7D**. (HINT: You may have to use *OSNAP*s to create the breaks at the *INTersections* or *QUAdrants* as shown.)

Figure 9-34

8. *Lengthen*

Five of your friends went to the horse races, each with $5.00 to bet. Construct a simple bar graph (similar to Figure 9-35) to illustrate how your friends' wealth compared at the beginning of the day.

Figure 9-35

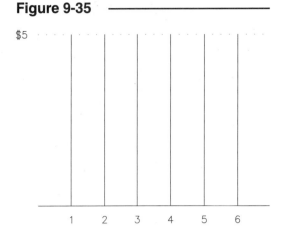

Modify the graph with *Lengthen* to report the results of their winnings and losses at the end of the day. The reports were as follows: friend 1 made $1.33 while friend 2 lost $2.40; friend 3 reported a 150% increase and friend 4 brought home 75% of the money; friend 5 ended the day with $7.80 and friend 6 came home with $5.60. Use the *Lengthen* command with the appropriate options to change the line lengths accordingly.

Who won the most? Who lost the most? Who was closest to even? Enhance the graph by adding width to the bars and other improvements as you wish (similar to Figure 9-36). *Saveas* **BET.**

Figure 9-36

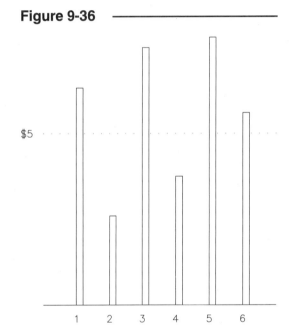

9. **GASKETA**

Begin a *New* drawing and give the name **GASKETA**. Set *Limits* to **0,0** and **8,6**. Set *SNAP* and *GRID* values appropriately. Create the Gasket as shown in Figure 9-37. Construct only the gasket shape, not the dimensions or center lines. (HINT: Locate and draw the four 1/2" diameter *Circles*, then create the concentric 1/2" radius arcs as full *Circles*, then *Trim*. Make use of *OSNAPs* and *Trim* whenever applicable.) *Save* the drawing.

Figure 9-37

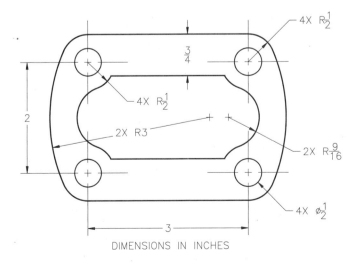

DIMENSIONS IN INCHES

10. **Chemical Process Flow Diagram**

Figure 9-38

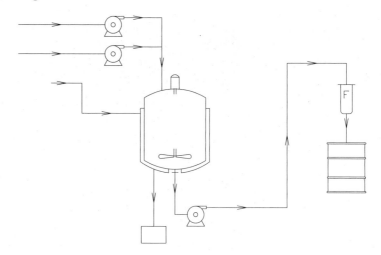

Begin a New drawing and recreate the chemical process flow diagram shown in Figure 9-38. Use *Line, Circle, Arc, Trim, Extend, Scale, Break*, and other commands you feel necessary to complete the diagram. Because this is diagrammatic and will not be used for manufacturing, dimensions are not critical, but try to construct the shapes with proportional accuracy. *Save* the drawing as **FLOWDIAG**.

Chapter 10

CONSTRUCT COMMANDS I

Chapter Objectives

After completing this chapter you should:

1. know where to locate and how to invoke the fundamental *Construct* commands;

2. be able to *Copy* objects;

3. be able to make *Mirror* images of selected objects;

4. be able to make *rectangular* and *polar Arrays* of existing objects.

BASICS

Construct commands use <u>existing</u> objects to create <u>new and similar</u> objects. For example, the *Copy* command creates a duplicate set of objects from any selected set. As with all commands, any of the five methods of command entry can be used.

The *Construct* pull-down menu is shown in Figure 10-1 (using the Windows ACADFULL menu). Both the DOS and Windows versions of AutoCAD Release 13 have identical *Construct* pull-down menu options.

Figure 10-1 ─────────────

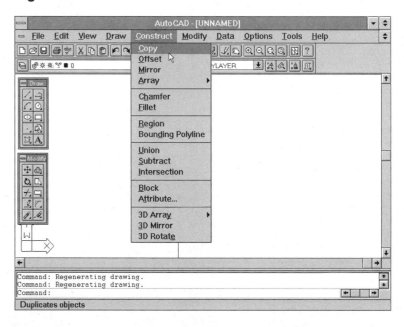

The icon buttons for Construct commands in AutoCAD for Windows are located in the Modify toolbar. Many of the Construct commands are located on one flyout (Fig. 10-2).

The *CONSTRCT* screen menu gives access to all of the Construct commands and is the same for the DOS and Windows versions of Release 13 (Fig. 10-3).

This chapter covers the following commands:

> *Copy*
> *Mirror*
> *Array*

The other Construct commands are discussed in Chapter 17, Construct Commands II.

Figure 10-2 ────────────

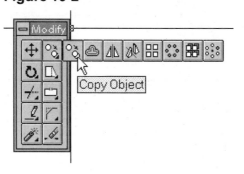

Figure 10-3 ────

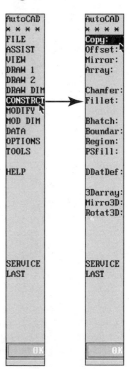

COMMANDS

COPY

PULL-DOWN MENU	SCREEN MENU	TYPE IN	TABLET MENU
Construct *Copy*	*CONSTRCT* *Copy:*	*COPY* *or CP*	15,X

Copy creates a duplicate set of the selected objects and allows placement of those copies. The *Copy* operation is like the *Move* command, except with *Copy* the original set of objects remains in its original location. You specify a "Base point:" (point to copy <u>from</u>) and a "Second point of displacement:" (point to copy <u>to</u>). See Figure 10-4.

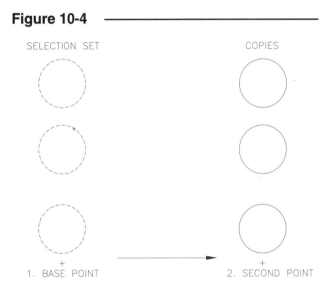

Figure 10-4 ——————————————

The command syntax for *Copy* is as follows.

    Command: ***copy***
    Select objects: **PICK** (Select objects to be copied.)
    Select objects: **Enter** (Indicates completion of the selection set.)
    <Base point or displacement>Multiple: **PICK** or (**coordinates**) (This is the point to copy <u>from</u>. Select a point, usually on the object, to use as a "handle" or reference point. *OSNAP*s can be used. Coordinates in any format can also be entered.)
    Second point of displacement: **PICK** or (**coordinates**) (This is the point to copy <u>to</u>. Select a point. *OSNAP*s can be used. Coordinates in any format can be entered.)

In many applications it is desirable to use *OSNAP* options to PICK the "Base point:" and the "Second point of displacement:" (Fig. 10-5).

Figure 10-5 ——————————————

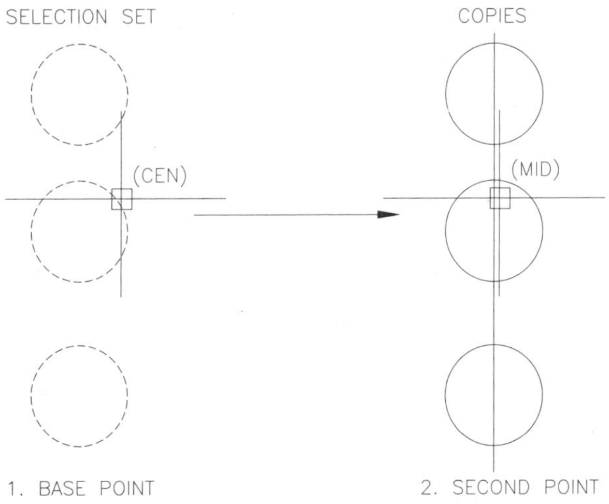

Alternately, you can PICK the "Base point:" and enter relative or polar coordinates to specify the "Second point of displacement:".

Figure 10-6

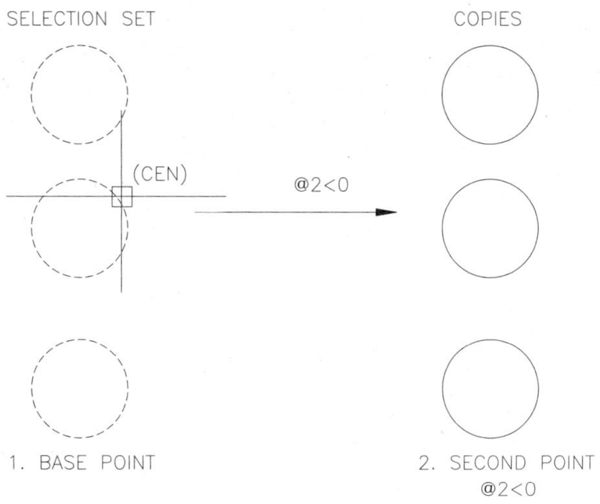

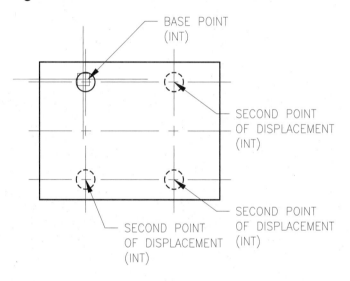

The *Copy* command has a *Multiple* option. The *Multiple* option allows creating and placing multiple copies of the selection set.

```
Command: copy
Select objects: PICK
Select objects: Enter
<Base point or displacement>/Multiple: m
Base point: PICK
Second point of displacement: PICK
Second point of displacement: PICK
Second point of displacement: Enter
Command:
```

Figure 10-7

MIRROR

PULL-DOWN MENU	SCREEN MENU	TYPE IN	TABLET MENU
Construct *Mirror*	*CONSTRCT* *Mirror:*	*MIRROR*	*12,X*

This command creates a mirror image of selected existing objects. You can retain or delete the original objects ("old objects"). After selecting objects, you create two points specifying a rubberband line, or "mirror line," about which to *Mirror*.

The length of the mirror line is
unimportant since it represents a vector or axis (Fig.
10-8).

Figure 10-8

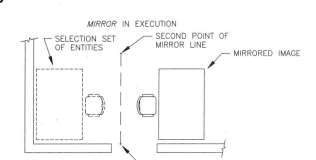

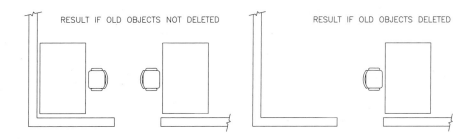

Command: *mirror*
Select objects: **PICK** (Select object or group of objects to mirror.)
Select objects: **Enter** (Press Enter to indicate completion of object selection.)
First point of mirror line: **PICK** or (**coordinates**) (Draw first endpoint of line to represent mirror axis by PICKing or entering coordinates.)
Second point of mirror line: **PICK** or (**coordinates**) (Select second point of mirror line by PICKing or entering coordinates.)
Delete old objects? <N> **Enter** or **Y** (Press Enter to yield both sets of objects or enter Y to keep only mirrored set.)

If you want to *Mirror* only in a vertical or horizontal direction, toggle *ORTHO* (**F8**) *On* before selecting the "Second point of mirror line."

Mirror can be used to draw the other half of a symmetrical object, thus saving some drawing time (Fig. 10-9).

Figure 10-9

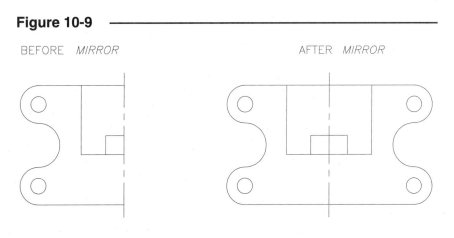

You can control whether <u>text</u> is mirrored by using the *MIRRTEXT* variable. Type *MIRRTEXT* at the command prompt and change the value to 0 if you do <u>not</u> want the text to be reflected; otherwise, the default setting of 1 mirrors text along with other selected objects (Fig. 10-10). Dimensions are <u>not</u> affected by the *MIRRTEXT* variable and therefore are not reflected (that is, if the dimensions are associative). (See Chapter 28 for details on dimensions.)

Figure 10-10

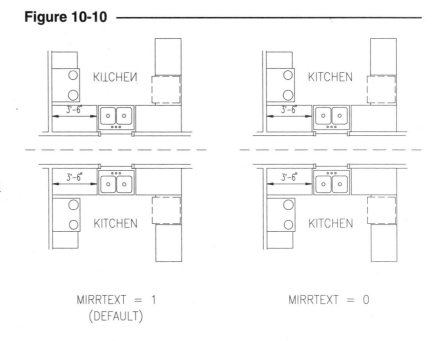

MIRRTEXT = 1
(DEFAULT)

MIRRTEXT = 0

ARRAY

PULL-DOWN MENU	SCREEN MENU	TYPE IN	TABLET MENU
Construct Array >	*CONSTRCT Array:*	*ARRAY*	*21,W*

The *Array* command creates either a *Rectangular* or a *Polar* (circular) pattern of existing objects that you select. The pattern could be created from a single object or from a group of objects. *Array* copies a duplicate set of objects for each "item" in the array.

Figure 10-11

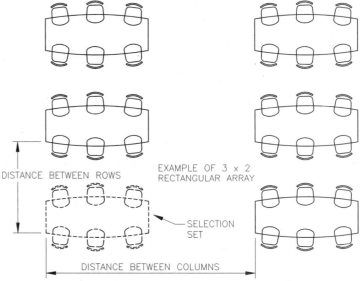

DISTANCE BETWEEN ROWS

EXAMPLE OF 3 x 2 RECTANGULAR ARRAY

SELECTION SET

DISTANCE BETWEEN COLUMNS

Rectangular Array

This option creates an *Array* of the selection set in a pattern composed of <u>rows</u> and <u>columns</u>. The command syntax for a rectangular *Array* is given next.

Command: **array**
Select objects: **PICK** (Select objects to be arrayed.)
Select objects: **Enter** (Indicates completion of object selection.)
Rectangular or Polar array (R/P) <R>: **R** (Indicates rectangular.)
Number of rows (---) <1>: **(value)** (Enter value for number of rows.)
Number of columns (|||) <1>: **(value)** (Enter value for columns.)
Unit cell or distance between rows (---): **(value)** (Enter a value for the distance from any <u>point</u> on one object to the <u>same point</u> on an object in the adjacent row. See Figure 10-11.)
Distance between columns (|||): **(value)** (Enter a value for the distance from any *point* on one object to the same point on an object in the adjacent column. See Figure 10-11.)

The *Array* is generated in a rectangular pattern with the original set of objects as the lower left "cornerstone." Negative values can be entered (distance between rows and columns) to generate and *Array* in a -X or -Y direction.

If you want to specify distances between cells <u>interactively</u>, use the *Unit cell* method (see Figure 10-12).

Unit cell or distance between rows (---): **PICK** (Pick point for first point of cell.)
Other corner: **PICK** (Pick point for other corner of cell.)

Figure 10-12 ─────────────────

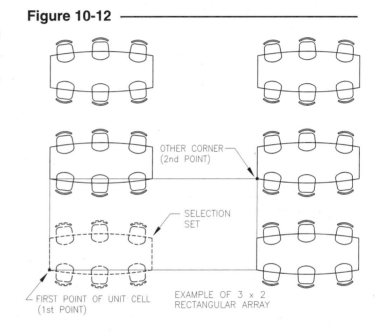

A rectangular *Array* can be created at an angle by first rotating the *SNAP* to the desired angle and then creating the *Array* as shown in Figure 10-13. See Chapter 6 for information on the *Rotate* option of the *Snap* command.

Figure 10-13 ─────────────────

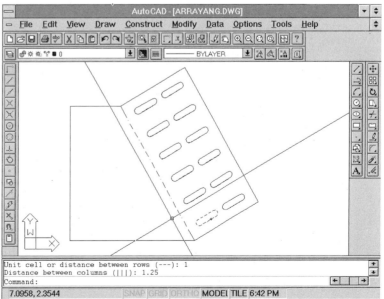

Polar Array

 This option creates a <u>circular</u> pattern of the selection set with any number of copies or "items." The number of items specified <u>includes the original</u> selection set. You also specify the center of array, angle to generate the array through, and orientation of "items."

Command: **array**
Select objects: **PICK** (Select objects to be arrayed.)
Select objects: **Enter** (Indicates object selection completed.)
Rectangular or Polar array (R/P) <R>: **P** (Indicates polar array.)
Center point of array: **PICK** (Select point for array to be generated around.)
Number of items: (**value**) (Enter value for number of copies <u>including</u> original selection set.)
Angle to fill (+=ccw, -==cw) <360>: **Enter** or (**value**) (Press Enter for full circular array; enter value for less than 360 degree array; enter negative value for clockwise generation of array.)
Rotate objects as they are copied? <Y> **Enter** or **N** (Press Enter for rotation of objects about center; N for keeping objects in original orientation.)

Figure 10-14 illustrates a *Polar Array* created by accepting the default values (360 degrees and "Rotate objects as they are copied").

Figure 10-14 ───────────────

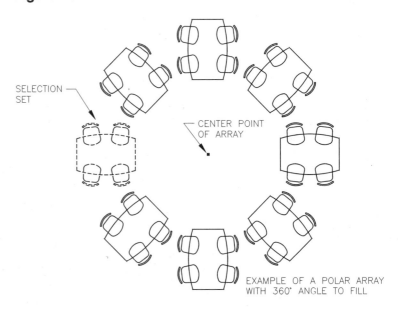

Figure 10-15 shows a *Polar Array* through 180 degrees with objects rotated.

Figure 10-15 ───────────────

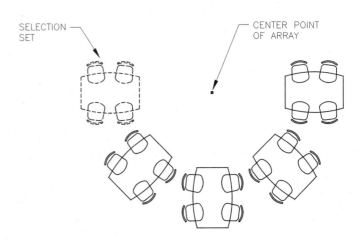

Figure 10-16 illustrates the results of answering *No* to the prompt "Rotate objects as they are rotated?" Note that the "items" remain in the same orientation (not rotated). Also notice the position of the *Array* with relation to the center point of the array.

When a *Polar Array* is created and objects are <u>not</u> rotated, the set of objects may not seem to rotate about the specified center, as shown in Figure 10-16. AutoCAD uses a single reference point for the *Array*—that of the <u>last</u> object in the selection set. If you PICK the objects one at a time (with the pickbox), the <u>last</u> one selected provides the reference point. If you use a window or other method for selection, the reference point is arbitrary. This usually creates a non-symmetrical circular *Array* about the selected center point.

Figure 10-16 ———————————————————

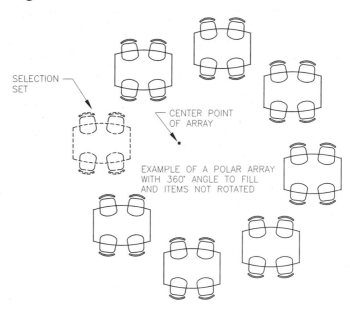

The solution is to create a *Point* object in the <u>center of the selection set</u> and select it <u>last</u>. This will generate the selection set in a circle about the assigned center. (Alternately, you can make the selection set into a *Block* and use the center of the *Block* as the *Insertion* point. See Chapter 21). This occurrence is no problem for *Polar Arrays* where the selection set is rotated.

CHAPTER EXERCISES

1. *Copy*

   Begin a *New* drawing. Set the *Limits* to **24,18**. Set *SNAP* to **.5** and *GRID* to **1**. Create the sheet metal part composed of four *Lines* and one *Circle* as shown in Figure 10-17. The lower left corner of the part is at coordinate **2,3**.

Figure 10-17 ———————————————————

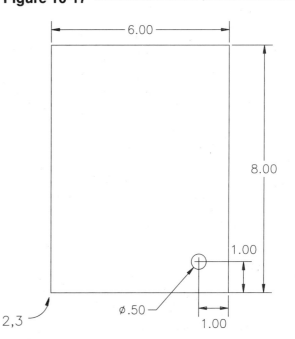

Use *Copy* to create two copies of the rectangle and hole in a side-by-side fashion as shown in Figure 10-18 Allow 2 units between the sheet metal layouts. *Saveas* **PLATES**.

A. Use *Copy* to create the additional 3 holes equally spaced near the other corners of the part as shown in Figure 10-18 A. *Save* the drawing.

B. Use *Copy Multiple* to create the hole configuration as shown in Figure 10-18 B. *Save*.

C. Use *Copy* to create the hole placements as shown in C. Each hole <u>center</u> is **2** units at **125** degrees from the previous one (use relative polar coordinates). *Save* the drawing.

Figure 10-18 ―――――――――――――――――――――――――――――――

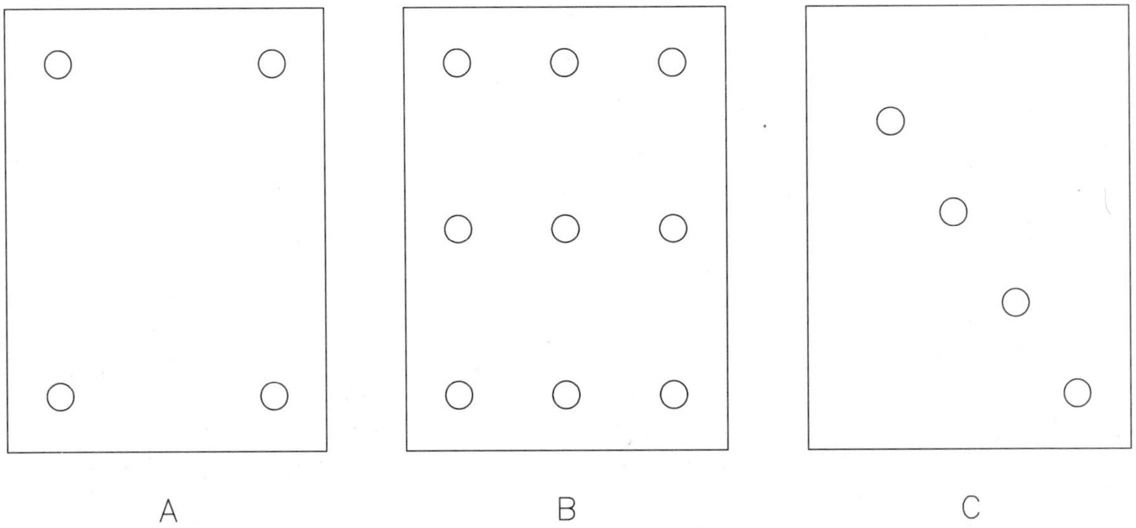

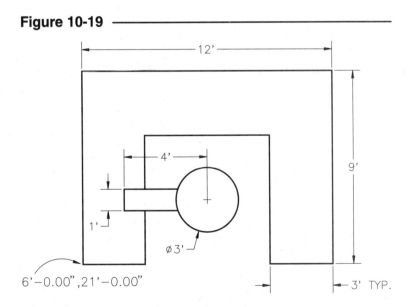

    A   B   C

2. *Mirror*

Figure 10-19 ―――――――――――――――――――――――――――

A manufacturing cell is displayed in Figure 10-19. The view is from above, showing a robot <u>centered</u> in a work station. The production line requires 4 cells. Begin by starting a *New* drawing, setting **Units** to *Engineering* and **Limits** to **40′ x 30′**. It may be helpful to set *SNAP* to **6″**. Draw one cell to the dimensions indicated. Begin at the indicated coordinates of the lower left corner of the cell. *Saveas* **MANFCELL**.

Use *Mirror* to create the other three manufacturing cells as shown in Figure 10-20. Ensure that there is sufficient space between the cells as indicated. Draw the two horizontal *Lines* representing the walkway as shown. *Save*.

Figure 10-20

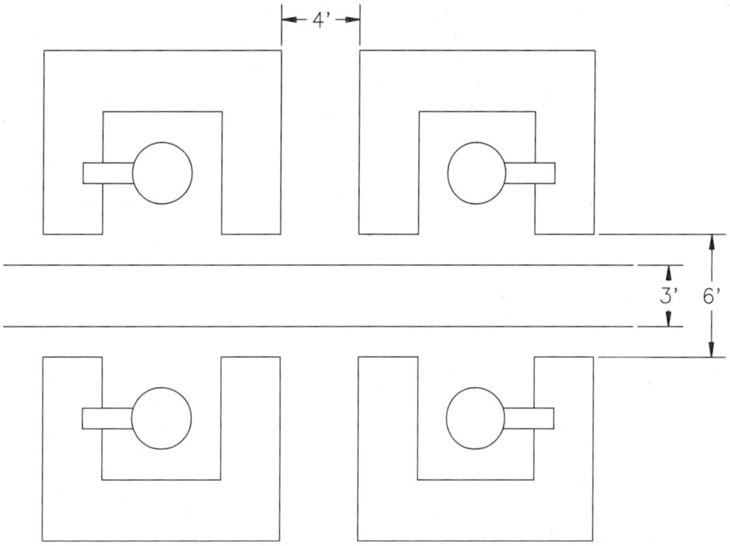

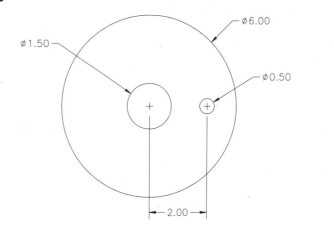

3. *Array, Polar*

Begin a *New* drawing. Create the starting geometry for a Flange Plate as shown in Figure 10-21. *Saveas* **CH10EX3**.

Figure 10-21

A. Create the *Polar Array* as shown in Figure 10-22 A. *Saveas* **CH10EX3A**.

B. *Open* **CH10EX3**. Create the *Polar Array* as shown in Figure 10-22 B. *Saveas* **CH10EX3B**. (HINT: Use a negative angle to generate the *Array* in a clockwise direction.)

Figure 10-22

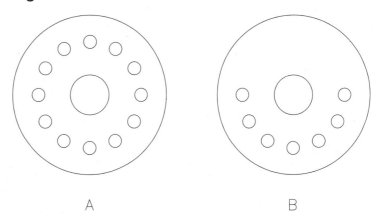

A   B

4. *Array, Rectangular*

Figure 10-23

Open a *New* drawing and assign the name **CH10EX4**. Create the *Array* of study carrels (desks) for the library as shown in Figure 10-23. The room size is 36' x 27' (set *Units* and *Limits* accordingly). Each carrel is **30"** x **42"**. Design your own chair. Draw the first carrel (highlighted) at the indicated coordinates. Create the *Rectangular Array* so that the carrels touch side-to-side and allow a 6' aisle for walking between carrels (not including chairs).

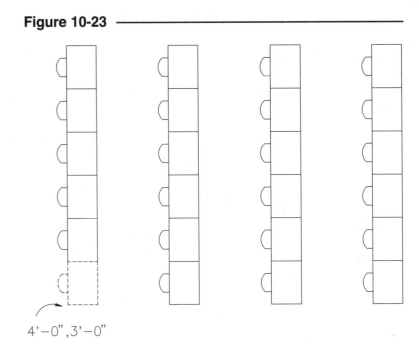

4'−0",3'−0"

5. *Array, Rectangular*

Figure 10-24

Create the bolt head with one thread as shown in Figure 10-24 A. *Array* the first thread (both crest and root lines, as indicated in B) to create the schematic thread representation. There are **10** columns with .2 units between each. Add the *Lines* around the outside to complete the fastener. *Save* as **BOLT**.

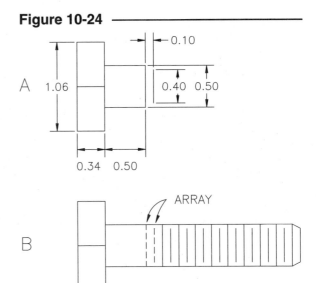

6. Create the Gasket shown in Figure 10-25. *Saveas* **GASKETB**.

Figure 10-25

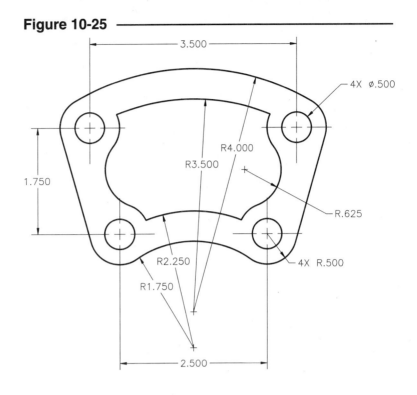

7. Create the perforated plate as shown Figure 10-26. *Save* the drawing as **PERFPLAT**.

Figure 10-26

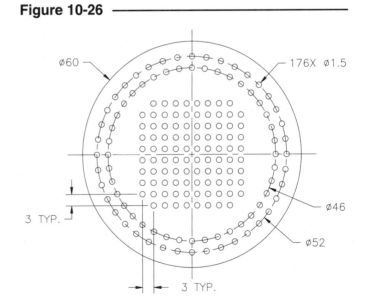

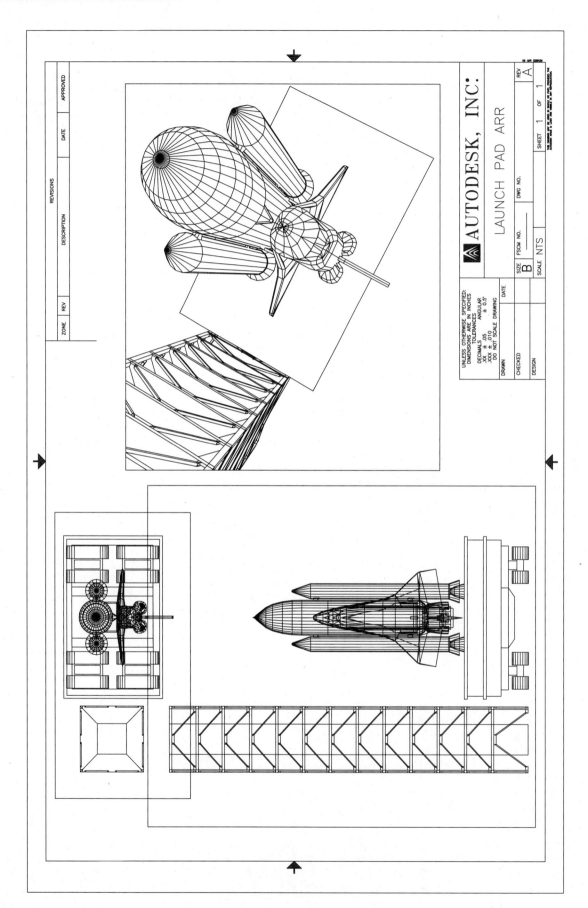

SHUTTLE.DWG Courtesy of Autodesk, Inc.

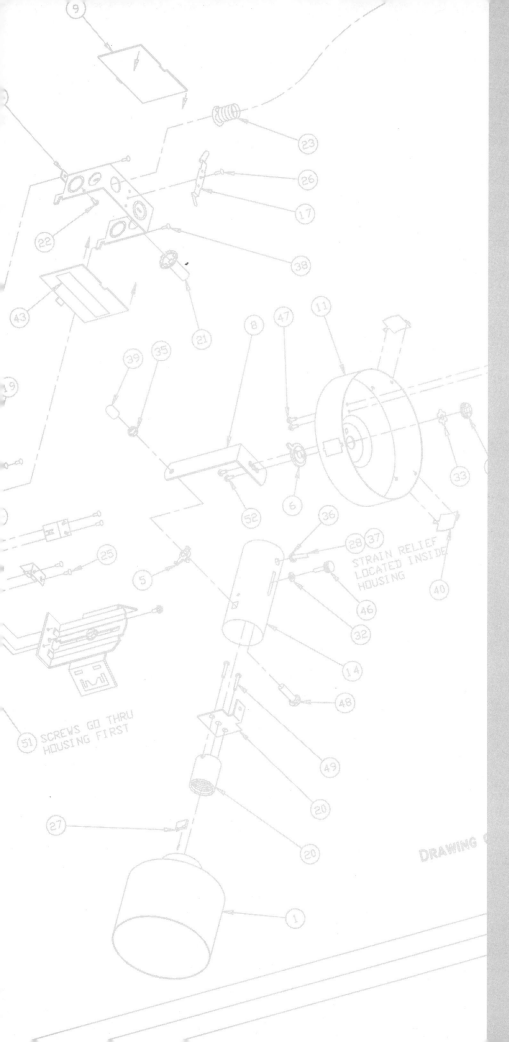

Chapter 11

VIEWING COMMANDS

Chapter Objectives

After completing this chapter you should:

1. understand the relationship between the drawing objects and the display of those objects;

2. be able to use all of the *Zoom* options to view areas of a drawing;

3. be able to *Pan* the display about your screen;

4. be able to *save* and *restore Views*;

5. know how to use *Viewres* to change the display resolution for curved shapes;

6. be able to use *Aerial View* to *Pan* and *Zoom*.

BASICS

The accepted CAD practice is to draw full size using actual units. Since the drawing is a virtual dimensional replica of the actual object, a drawing could represent a vast area (several hundred feet or even miles) or a small area (only millimeters). The drawing is created full size with the actual units, but it can be displayed at any size on the screen. Consider also that CAD systems provide for a very high degree of dimensional precision, which permits the generation of drawings with great detail and accuracy.

Combining those two CAD capabilities (great precision and drawings representing various areas), a method is needed to view different and detailed segments of the overall drawing area. In AutoCAD the commands that facilitate viewing different areas of a drawing are *Zoom, Pan,* and *View*.

The Viewing commands are found in the *View* pull-down menu (Fig. 11-1).

Figure 11-1

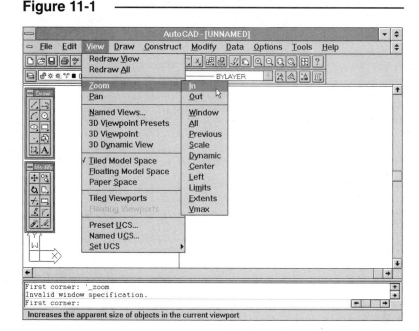

Zoom and *Pan* each have one-letter command aliases, *Z* and *P*.

COMMANDS

ZOOM

PULL-DOWN MENU	SCREEN MENU	TYPE IN	TABLET MENU
View *Zoom >*	*VIEW* *Zoom:*	*ZOOM* *or Z*	*7,Q to 10,R*

To *Zoom* <u>in</u> means to magnify a small segment of a drawing and to *Zoom* <u>out</u> means to display a larger area of the drawing. *Zooming* does <u>not</u> change the <u>size</u> of the drawing; *Zooming* only changes the area that is <u>displayed</u> on the screen. All objects in the drawing have the same dimensions before and after *Zooming*. Only your display of the objects changes.

Figure 11-2

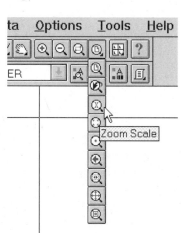

If you are using AutoCAD for Windows, you can access the *Zoom* options from the pull-down menus (Fig. 11-1) or from the Standard toolbar (Fig. 11-2). The *Zoom In, Out,* and *Window* options are on the toolbar itself, while the other *Zoom* options are selected from the flyout group.

The *Zoom* options described next can be selected by any menu. If you are typing, only the first letter is required.

Window

To *Zoom* with a *Window* is to draw a rectangular window around the desired viewing area. You PICK a first and a second corner (diagonally) to form the rectangle. The windowed area is magnified to fill the screen (Fig. 11-3). It is suggested that you draw the window with a 4 x 3 (approximate) proportion to match the screen proportion. If you type *Zoom* or *Z*, *Window* is an <u>automatic</u> option so you can begin selecting the first corner of the window after issuing the *Zoom* command <u>without</u> indicating the *Window* option as a separate step.

Figure 11-3

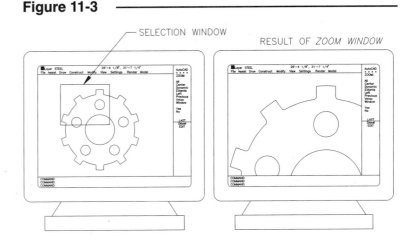

Limits

This option is <u>only available</u> from the menus or toolbar icons—it <u>cannot be typed</u> at the keyboard. This option displays all of, and only, the *Limits* of the drawing even if objects are outside of the *Limits*. *Zoom Limits* is handy to use for displaying the entire drawing area again after using *Zoom Window*.

All

This option displays <u>all of the objects</u> in the drawing <u>and all of the *Limits*</u>. In Figure 11-4, notice the effects of *Zoom All*, based on the drawing objects and the drawing *Limits*.

Extents

This option results in the largest possible display of <u>all of the objects</u>, <u>disregarding</u> the *Limits*. (*Zoom All* includes the *Limits*.) See Figure 11-4.

Figure 11-4

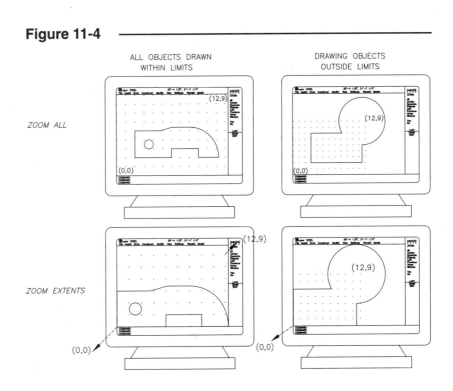

Scale (X/XP)

 This (the default) option allows you to enter a scale factor for the desired display. The value that is entered can be relative to the full view (*Limits*) or to the current display (Fig. 11-5). A value of **1**, **2**, or **.5** causes a display that is 1, 2, or .5 times the size of the *Limits*, centered on the current display. A value of **1X**, **2X**, or **.5X** yields a display 1, 2, or .5 times the size of the current display. If you are using paper space, a value of **1XP**, **2XP**, or **.5XP** yields a display scaled 1, 2, or .5 times paper space units.

Figure 11-5 ———————

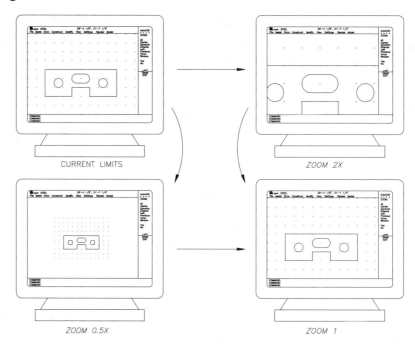

CURRENT LIMITS   ZOOM 2X

ZOOM 0.5X   ZOOM 1

In

 Zoom In magnifies the current display by a factor of 2X. Using this option is the same as entering a *Zoom Scale* of 2X.

Out

 Zoom Out makes the current display smaller by a factor of .5X. Using this option is the same as entering a *Zoom Scale* of .5X.

Center

 First, specify a location as the center of the zoomed area; then specify either a *Magnification factor* (see *Scale X/XP*), a *Height* value for the resulting display, or PICK two points forming a vertical to indicate the height for the resulting display (Fig. 11-6).

Figure 11-6 ———————

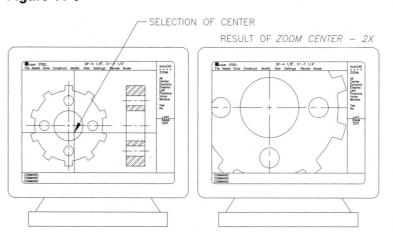

SELECTION OF CENTER

RESULT OF *ZOOM CENTER — 2X*

Left

This option is similar to the *Center* option except that you first PICK the <u>lower left</u> corner of the display window instead of the center (Fig. 11-7). The *Magnification* factor or *Height* is then specified.

Figure 11-7

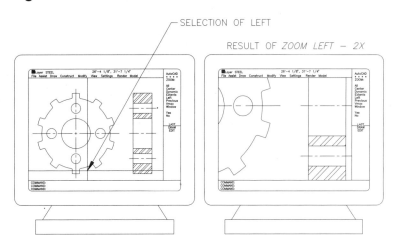

Dynamic

With this option you can change the display from one windowed area in a drawing to another without using *Zoom All* (to see the entire drawing) as an intermediate step. *Zoom Dynamic* causes the screen to display the drawing *Limits* or generated area, whichever is larger, bounded by a box. The current view or window is bounded by a green or magenta box in broken line pattern. Four red corners display the last regenerated area (called *Vmax*).

The viewbox is the box with an "X" in the center which can be moved to the desired location (Fig. 11-8). The desired location is selected by pressing **Enter** (not the PICK button as you might expect).

Figure 11-8

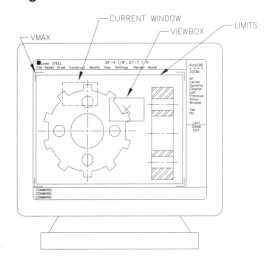

Pressing **PICK** allows you to resize the viewbox (displaying an arrow instead of the "X") to the desired size. Move the mouse or puck left and right to increase and decrease the window size. Press **PICK** again to set the size and make the "X" reappear.

When changing the display of a drawing from one windowed area to another, *Zoom Dynamic* is the fastest method because (1) a *Zoom All* is not required as an intermediate step and (2) the view box can be moved <u>while</u> AutoCAD is "redrawing" the display.

Vmax

The *Vmax* (Virtual Screen Maximum) option allows you to *Zoom* out to the maximum display without causing a regeneration. This option is helpful with large, complex drawings for achieving the maximum display without causing time-consuming regenerations.

Previous

Selecting this option automatically changes to the previous display. AutoCAD saves the previous ten displays changed by *Zoom*, *Pan*, and *View*. You can successively change back through the previous ten displays with this option.

Zoom is a <u>transparent</u> command, meaning it can be invoked while another command is in operation. You can, for example, use the *Line* command and at the "to point:" prompt *'Zoom* with a *window* to better display the area for selecting the endpoint. This transparent feature is automatically entered if *Zoom* is invoked by the screen, pull-down, or tablet menus or toolbar icons, but if typed it must be prefixed by the ' (apostrophe) symbol, e.g., "to point: *'Zoom.*" If *Zoom* has been invoked transparently, the >> symbols appear at the command prompt before the listed options as follows:

> LINE from point: **PICK**
> to point: **'zoom**
> >>Center/Dynamic/Left/Previous/Vmax/Window/<Scale (X/XP)>:

PAN

PULL-DOWN MENU	SCREEN MENU	TYPE IN	TABLET MENU
Pan >	*VIEW* *Pan:*	*PAN* *or P*	*10,Q*

The *Pan* options can be invoked by any method, including the *View* pull-down menu (Fig. 11-1) and the icon buttons accessible from the Standard toolbar (Fig. 11-9).

The *Pan* command is most useful if you want to move (pan) the display area slightly without changing the <u>size</u> of the current view window (Fig. 11-10). If *Pan* is used in this way (*Point* option), imagine "dragging" the drawing across the screen to view an area slightly out of view. The command syntax reads:

> Command: **pan**
> Pan Displacement: **PICK**
> second point: **PICK**
> Command:

The "Pan Displacement:" can be thought of as a <u>handle</u> and the "second point:" as the new location to move <u>to</u>.

Pan also allows coordinate values to be entered rather than interactively PICKing points with the cursor. The command syntax is as follows.

> Command: **pan**
> Pan Displacement: **0,-2**
> second point: **Enter**
> Command:

Entering coordinate values allows you to *Pan* to a location outside of the current display. If you use the interactive method (PICK points), you can only *Pan* within the range of whatever is visible on the screen.

Figure 11-9

Figure 11-10

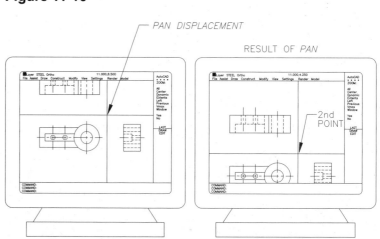

The following *Pan* options are available from the menus and toolbar icons, but <u>cannot be typed</u> at the keyboard.

Left

Automatically pans to the left, equal to about half of the current drawing area width (equal to the maximum Windows horizontal scrolling distance) (Fig. 11-11).

Right

Pans to the right—similar to but opposite of *Left* (Fig. 11-11).

Up

Automatically pans up, equal to about half of the current drawing area height (equal to the maximum Windows vertical scrolling distance) (Fig. 11-11).

Down

Pans down—similar to but opposite of *Up* (Fig. 11-11).

Figure 11-11

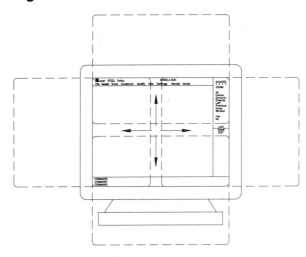

Up-Left

Automatically pans up and to the left, equal to about half of the current drawing area height and width (equal to the maximum Windows vertical and horizontal scrolling distance) (Fig. 11-12).

Up-Right

Pans up and to the right (Fig. 11-12).

Down-Left

Pans down and to the left (Fig. 11-12).

Down-Right

Pans down and to the right (Fig. 11-12).

Figure 11-12

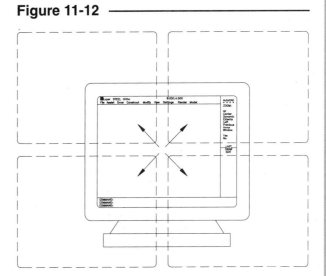

Pan, like *Zoom*, can be used as a transparent command. The transparent feature is automatically entered if *Pan* is invoked by the screen, pull-down, or tablet menus or icons. However, if you <u>type</u> *Pan* during another command operation, it must be prefixed by the ' (apostrophe) symbol.

```
Command: Line
From point: PICK
to point: 'pan
>>Displacement: PICK
>>Second point: PICK
Resuming LINE command.
To point:
```

Scroll Bars

Figure 11-13 —

If you are using AutoCAD Release 13 for Windows, you can use the horizontal and vertical scroll bars directly below and to the right of the graphics area to pan the drawing (Fig. 11-13). These scroll bars pan the drawing in one of three ways: (1) click on the arrows at the ends of the scroll bar, (2) move the thumb wheel, or (3) click inside the scroll bar. The maximum scroll distance in either direction is about half of the current display area. The scroll bars can be turned off by using the *Preferences* dialogue box from the *Options* menu (see Customizing the AutoCAD for Windows Screen, Chapter 1, and Figure 1-28).

thumbwheel

VIEW

PULL-DOWN MENU	SCREEN MENU	TYPE IN	TABLET MENU
View *Named Views...*	*VIEW* *DDVIEWS:*	*VIEW* *or DDVIEW*	*2,J*

The *View* command provides options for you to *Save* the current display window and *Restore* it at a later time. For typical applications you would first *Zoom* in to achieve a desired display, then use *View, Save* to save that display under an assigned name. Later in the drawing session, the named *View* can be *Restore*d any number of times. This method is preferred to continually *Zooming* in and out to display the same areas repeatedly. *Restoring* a named *View* requires no regeneration time. A *View* can be sent to the plotter as separate display as long as the view is named and saved. The options of the *View* command are listed below.

?   Displays the list of named views.

Delete   Deletes one or more saved views that you enter.

Restore   Displays the named view you request.

Save   Saves the current display as a *View* with a name you assign.

Window   Allows you to specify a window in the current display and save it as a named *View*.

To *Save* a *View*, first use *Zoom* or *Pan* to achieve the desired display; then invoke the *View* command and the *Save* option as follows:

```
Command: view
?/Delete/Restore/Save/Window: save
View name to save: name (Assign a descriptive name for the view.)
Command:
```

For assurance, check to see if the new *View* has been saved by displaying the list by using the *?* option. The *?* option causes a text screen to appear with the list of named (saved) views. Use *FLIPSCREEN* to return to the Drawing Editor after reading the list.

To *Restore* a named *View*, assuming a different area of the drawing is currently displayed, use the *Restore* option and supply the name of the desired *View*.

View can also be used transparently, but only if typed at the keyboard. Remember to preface the command with the ' (apostrophe) symbol, i.e., *'View*.

A feature of saving *Views* is that a named *View* can be plotted by toggling the *View* option in the *Plot Configuration* dialogue box. Plotting is discussed in detail in Chapter 14.

Typing the *View* command is generally quick and easy. Selecting *Ddview* from the pull-down or tablet menus invokes the *View Control* dialogue box (Fig. 11-14), which is helpful but requires a number of steps to operate. A word of caution when selecting from the list of named views to restore: make sure that you select (1) the desired view <u>and</u> (2) the **Restore** tile, <u>then</u> (3) the **OK** tile.

The *View Control* dialogue box provides the same options that the *View* command offers. The *New* option causes the *Define New View* dialogue box to pop up, giving access to the *Save* option (Fig. 11-15).

Figure 11-14 ——————

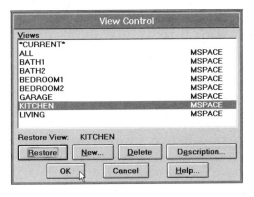

Figure 11-15 ——————

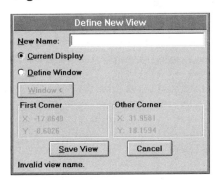

DSVIEWER

PULL-DOWN MENU	SCREEN MENU	TYPE IN	TABLET MENU
Tools *Aerial View*	---	*DSVIEWER* *or AV*	---

The Aerial Viewer is a tool for navigating in a drawing. It can be used to *Zoom* and *Pan* while in another command. The Aerial Viewer is available in both Windows and DOS versions of Release 13, but the operations are <u>not</u> identical in the two versions.

AutoCAD for Windows Aerial Viewer

Invoking the *Dsviewer* command displays the window shown in Figure 11-16. The options and operations are described next.

Figure 11-16 ——————

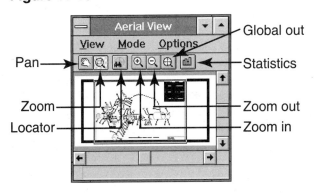

Pan

Selecting this icon or choosing *Pan* from the Aerial Viewer *View* menu sets the viewbox in the *Pan* mode. If you move the viewbox to any location <u>inside the viewer</u>, the selected area of the drawing will be displayed in the main graphics area (Fig. 11-17).

Zoom

This sets the viewer in *Zoom Window* mode. PICKing two corners <u>inside the viewer</u> causes that windowed area to be displayed <u>in the main graphics area</u> (Fig. 11-17).

Zoom In

PICKing this option causes the <u>display in the viewer</u> to be magnified 2X. This does <u>not</u> affect the display in the main graphics area.

Zoom Out

This option causes the <u>display in the viewer</u> to be reduced to .5X. This does <u>not</u> affect the display in the main graphics area.

Global

Selecting this option will resize the <u>drawing display in the viewer</u> to its maximum size.

Statistics

You can list the amount of memory used by the current display window using this option.

Locator

This option is the most unique feature of the Aerial Viewer. It allows you to dynamically move the locator window around <u>in the main graphics area,</u> while the magnified area is displayed instantaneously and dynamically inside the viewer window. This feature is especially helpful for locating small details in the drawing, like reading text (Fig. 11-18). The *Locator Magnification* can be changed by selecting from the Viewer *Options* pull-down menu (Fig. 11-19).

Figure 11-17

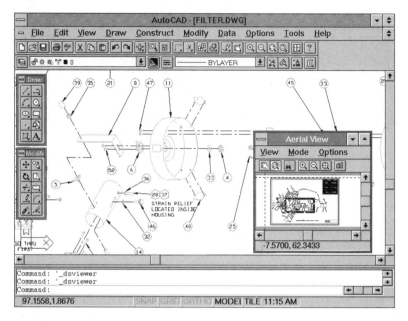

Figure 11-18

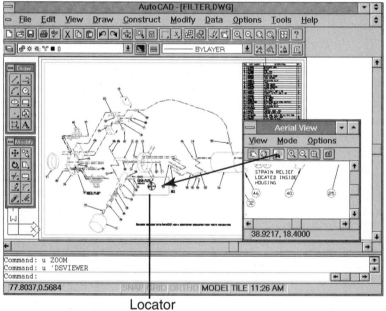

Locator

Figure 11-19

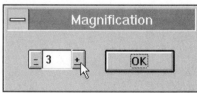

R13

To operate the *Locator*, select the *Locator* icon and, while holding down the left button, drag the *Locator* viewbox into the main graphics area (see Figure 11-18). If you want to use this feature to view some details temporarily but do not want to change the main display, drag the locator viewbox back into the viewer window and release.

AutoCAD for DOS Aerial Viewer

The Aerial Viewer for the DOS version of Release 13 has similar features to that for the Windows version. The viewer can be invoked by typing *AV* or by selecting from the *Options* pull-down menu. The *Dsviewer* command does not exist in the DOS version; the *AV* command is used instead. The AV viewer for DOS is displayed in Figure 11-20.

The options in the DOS Aerial Viewer are activated by clicking on the buttons at the top of the window.

Figure 11-20 ⎯⎯⎯⎯⎯⎯⎯⎯⎯⎯⎯⎯⎯

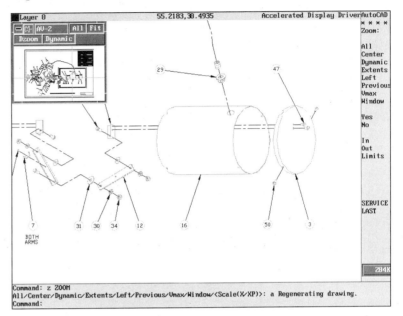

Zoom

Similar to the Windows version of Aerial Viewer, this option sets the viewbox to the *Zoom window* mode. PICKing corners in the viewer causes the selected area to display in the main graphics area.

Pan

This option is used to set the viewbox to the *Pan* mode. Moving the viewbox to any location <u>in the viewer</u> window causes the windowed area to display in the main graphics area.

Auto

Either *Zoom* or *Pan* can be used with this setting. If you PICK inside the viewbox, the viewbox can be moved (*Pan*) to another area. If you PICK outside of the viewbox, the first corner for a *Zoom window* is established.

Dzoom

Dzoom, short for Dynamic zoom, is similar to the *Dynamic* option of the *Zoom* command. That is, when you PICK, the viewbox can be resized by moving the mouse left or right (an arrow appears similar to *Zoom Dynamic*). Pressing the right mouse button (or #2 button) displays the boxed portion of the drawing in the main graphics area.

Dynamic/Static

The *Dynamic/Static* toggle is available only for the *Dzoom* or *Zoom* options. The *Dynamic* toggle is similar to the *Locator* option of the Windows Aerial Viewer. Moving the viewbox <u>inside the viewer</u> causes the windowed area to display dynamically in the main graphics area. This is <u>opposite</u> of the Windows *Locator* function in that the Windows *Locator* is moved to the main graphics area for operation while the DOS *Dzoom* viewbox moves only <u>inside the viewer</u> window. The *Static* toggle forces the main graphics display to remain static until the new *Dzoom* or *Zoom* viewbox is positioned in the Aerial Viewer.

R13

All/Fit

The portion of the drawing appearing in the Aerial viewer window can be changed quickly to show *All* of the current maximum generated area (similar to *Vmax*) or can be forced to *Fit* the entire drawing at its largest possible size within the viewer (similar to *Zoom Extents*).

Pushpin

The pushpin icon (located in the upper left corner of the DOS Aerial Viewer) can be selected (down position) to force the Aerial Viewer to remain on the screen after use. If the pushpin is in the up position, the Aerial Viewer disappears when you PICK in the main graphics area.

VIEWRES

PULL-DOWN MENU	SCREEN MENU	TYPE IN	TABLET MENU
---	OPTIONS *Viewres:*	*VIEWRES*	---

Viewres controls the resolution of curved shapes for the <u>screen display</u> only. Its purpose is to speed regeneration time by displaying curved shapes as linear approximations of curves; that is, a curved shape (such as an *Arc*, *Circle*, or *Ellipse*) appears as several short straight line segments (Fig. 11-21). The drawing database and the plotted drawing, however, always define a true curve. The range of *Viewres* is from 1-20,000 with 100 being the default. The higher the value (called circle zoom percentage),

Figure 11-21

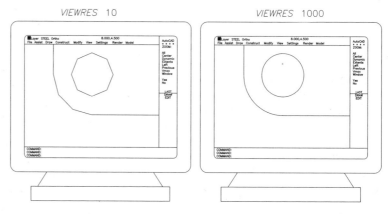

the more accurate the display of curves and the slower the regeneration time. The lower the value, the faster the regeneration time, but the more "jagged" the curves. A value of 500 to 1,000 is suggested for most applications. The command syntax is shown here.

```
Command: Viewres
Do you want fast zooms? <Y> Enter
Enter circle zoom percent (1-20000) <100>: 1000
Command:
```

If you answer *no* to *Do you want fast zooms?*, AutoCAD causes a regeneration after every *Pan*, *Zoom*, or *View* command. Otherwise, regenerations occur only when *Zoom*ing extremely far in or out.

CHAPTER EXERCISES

1. *Zoom Window, All, Previous, Center, Left*

Open the sample drawing supplied with AutoCAD called **FILTER.DWG**. It is located in the SAMPLE subdirectory. For example, if AutoCAD has been installed on your system in the C:\ACADR13 directory, you should find the sample drawings in **C:\ACADR13\ COMMON \SAMPLE**. The drawing shows an isometric exploded assembly diagram of a filter (Fig. 11- 22).

A. Use *Zoom* with the window option to examine the cylindrical part (shown as ellipses) near the center of the drawing. Select the corners of the window to display an area as shown in Figure 11-23. What is the part number of the large cylindrical piece?

B. *Zoom All*. Now *Zoom* in to the largest cylindrical part (on the right). What is the part number?

C. *Zoom Previous*. Was that faster than *Zoom All*?
Now *Zoom* in to the part nearest the bottom of the drawing. What is the part number?

D. You forgot to check the part number of the cap for the large cylinder. *Zoom Previous* until you find the display of part 16. What is the part number for the cap to part 16?

Figure 11-22 ———————————

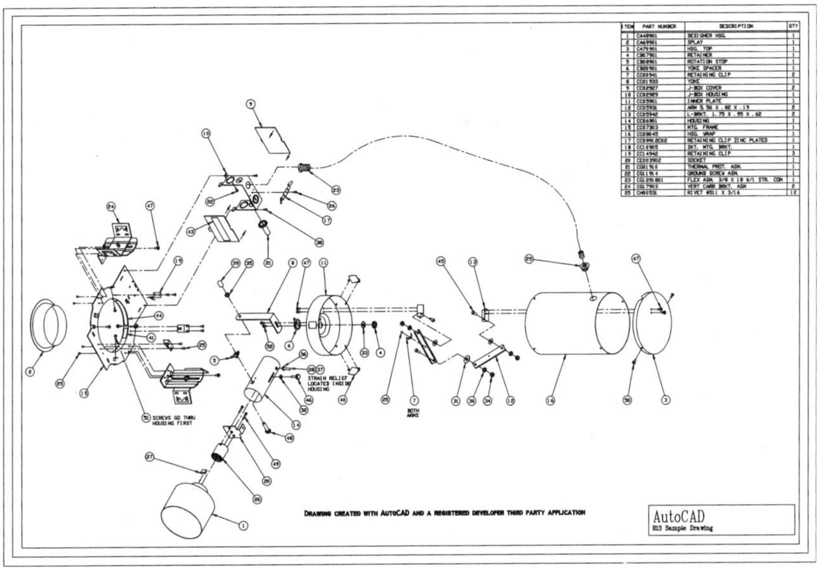

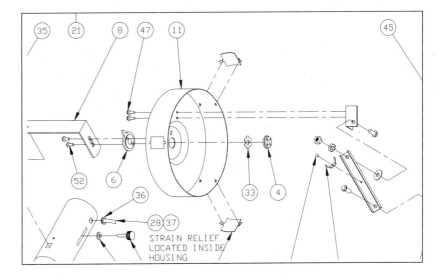

Figure 11-23 ———————————

STRAIN RELIEF
LOCATED INSIDE
HOUSING

E. **Zoom All** to achieve a display of the entire drawing. Use **Zoom Center**, **PICK** the center of the parts list (in the upper right corner), and enter a magnification factor of **3X**. You should see a display similar to that in Figure 11-24. What is the name of part 1?

Figure 11-24

ITEM	. PART NUMBER	DESCRIPTION	QTY
1	CA48901	DESIGNER HSG.	1
2	CA69901	SPLAY	1
3	CA70901	HSG. TOP	1
4	CB07901	RETAINER	1
5	CB08901	ROTATION STOP	1
6	CB20901	YOKE SPACER	1
7	CC00941	RETAINING CLIP	2
8	CC01933	YOKE	1
9	CC02927	J-BOX COVER	2
10	CC02929	J-BOX HOUSING	1
11	CC05901	INNER PLATE	1
12	CC05931	ARM 5.56 X .82 X .19	2
13	CC05942	L-BRKT. 1.75 X .95 X .62	2
14	CC06901	HOUSING	1
15	CC07303	MTG. FRAME	1
16	CC08045	HSG. WRAP	1
17	CC09912C02	RETAINING CLIP ZINC PLATED	1
18	CC10905	SKT. MTG. BRKT.	1
19	CC14942	RETAINING CLIP	3
20	CE003902	SOCKET	1
21	CG01910	THERMAL PROT. ASM.	1
22	CG11914	GROUND SCREW ASM.	1
23	CG1291801	FLEX ASM. 3/8 X 18 W/1 STR. CON	1
24	CG17903	VERT CARR BRKT. ASM	2
25	CH00531	RIVET #511 X 3/16	12

2. **View**

You are about to create some *Views* of the filter drawing. So that you don't change this drawing, use **Saveas** to save the drawing as **FILTER2**. Specify the path for your working directory (where you normally save your AutoCAD drawings, for example, C:\DWGS directory). Pick the desired drive and directory from the **Saveas** dialogue box or use the edit box to enter the path and drawing name.

A. While you are zoomed into the parts list, use the **View** command and the *Save* option to save the current view (as shown in Figure 11-24). Specify the name **PARTLIST** for the view.

B. **Zoom All** to display the entire drawing. Use **View** with the *Window* option. Name the view **HOUSING**. Specify a window around part 16 (the large cylinder). Notice that the display does not change. Use the *Window* option of **View** again to save a view of the part near the bottom of the drawing (part 1). Name the view **DESR-HSG**. *Save* the drawing.

C. Use **View, Restore** to restore the **PARTLIST**. Was a regeneration required? Now use **View** again to *Restore* **DESN-HSG** (use the *?* option to check for the correct name). Now type **DDview** to invoke the *View Control* dialogue box. *Restore* the view **HOUSING**; then *Restore* each of the other saved views.

3. **Zoom Dynamic**

A. Invoke **Zoom Dynamic**. Notice that you can move the viewbox around <u>while</u> the display is regenerating. Locate part 2 (on the far left of the drawing). Adjust the size of the viewbox to include the part and part number. *Zoom* in. What is the part number of the large component just to the right (with several holes and slots)? *Zoom* with a factor of **.5X**. Now can you see the part number?

B. Use **Zoom Dynamic** again to display the part on the very top of the drawing. What is the part number?

C. Use **Zoom Dynamic** to display the part that is most centrally located. What is the part number?

4. **Pan**

A. Use **Pan** to display the text just below the large part nearest the center. What does the text say?

B. Use **Pan** to display the text at the bottom of the drawing. What does the text say?

5. **Aerial Viewer**

Zoom All to display the entire drawing. Next, invoke the Aerial Viewer by any method. Move the Aerial Viewer to the upper right of the screen (click on the title bar, hold down the mouse button, and drag). Then use the *Locate* function (Windows) or *Dynamic* function (DOS) to locate details in the drawing. Follow the instructions immediately below for your setup.

Windows: From the Aerial Viewer pull-down menus, select *Options*, then *Locator Magnification...* and set the value to **3**. Then use the *Locate* function (drag the viewbox into the main graphics area).

DOS: In the Aerial Viewer, create a window about the size of the parts list (make sure *Auto* and *Dynamic* are toggled). Then drag the viewbox within the Aerial Viewer.

A. Find part number 31. Is it a washer, screw, or nut?

B. Find part 7. What does the note say?

C. What does the text say under part number 51?

D. Examine the parts list. What is the name of part 6?

6. *Viewres*

A. Use *Zoom All* to display the entire drawing. Then use any method to zoom in close to one of the part numbers. Notice how the circle surrounding the number appears as straight line segments. Use *Viewres* to increase the display resolution to **500**. After regenerating, the "bubble" should appear as a smooth circle.

B. Use *DDview* to invoke the *View Control* dialogue box. Select any view (other than PARTLIST) to *Restore*. Notice the shapes that previously appeared as linear approximations of ellipses and circles are now smooth.

Save the drawing. Make sure it is saved as **FILTER2**.

7. *Zoom All, Extents*

Figure 11-25 ——————————————

A. Begin a *New* drawing. Turn on the *GRID* (**F7**). Draw two *Circles*, each with a **1.5** unit *radius*. The *Circle* centers are at **3,5** and at **5,5**. See Figure 11-25.

B. Use *Zoom All*. Does the display change? Now use *Zoom Extents*. What happens? Now use *Zoom All* again. Which option <u>always</u> shows all of the *Limits*?

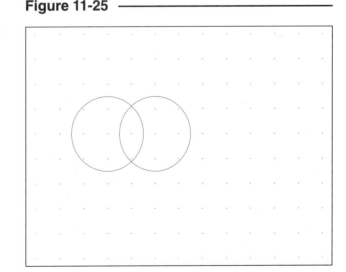

C. Draw a *Circle* with the center at **10,10** and with a *radius* of **5**. Now use *Zoom All*. Notice the GRID only appears on the area defined by the *Limits*. Can you move the crosshairs to 0,0? Now use *Zoom Extents*. What happens? Can you move the crosshairs to 0,0?

D. *Erase* the large *Circle*. Use *Zoom All*. Can you move the crosshairs to 0,0? Use *Zoom Extents*. Can you find point 0,0?

Exit AutoCAD and discard changes.

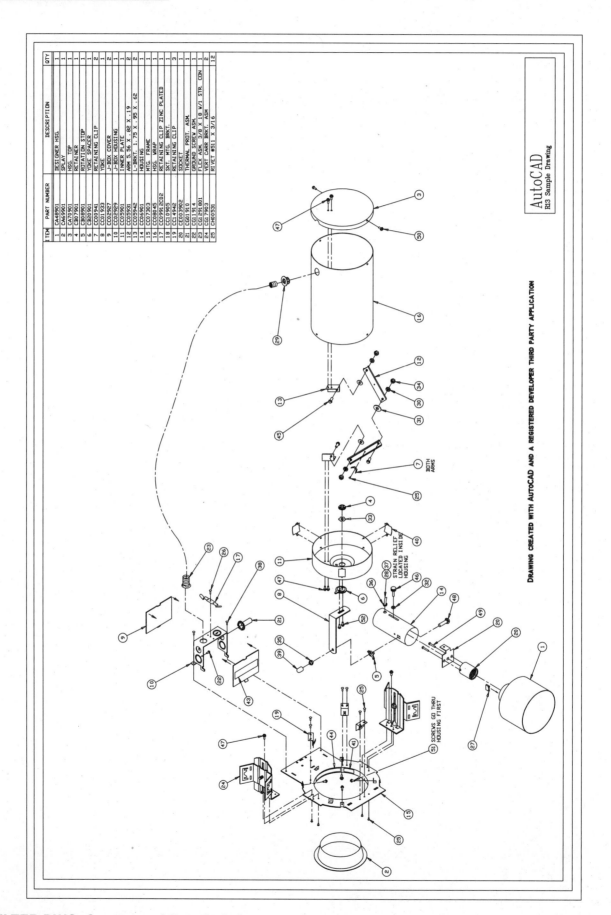

ITEM	PART NUMBER	DESCRIPTION	QTY
1	CA48901	DESIGNER HSG.	1
2	CA69901	SPLAY TOP	1
3	CB07901	HSG. TOP	1
4	CB07901	RETAINER	1
5	CB08901	ROTATION STOP	1
6	CB20901	YOKE SPACER	1
7	CC00941	RETAINING CLIP	2
8	CC01933	YOKE	1
9	CC02927	J-BOX COVER	2
10	CC02929	J-BOX HOUSING	1
11	CC05901	INNER PLATE	1
12	CC05931	ARM 5.56 X .82 X .19	2
13	CC05942	L-BRKT. 1.75 X .95 X .62	2
14	CC06901	HOUSING	1
15	CC07303	MTG. FRAME	1
16	CC08045	HSG. WRAP	1
17	CC091E202	RETAINING CLIP ZINC PLATED	1
18	CC10905	SKT. MTG. BRKT.	1
19	CC14942	RETAINING CLIP	3
20	CE003902	SOCKET	1
21	CG01910	THERMAL PROT. ASM.	1
22	CG11914	GROUND SCREW ASM.	1
23	CG1291B01	FLEX ASM. 3/8 X 18 W/1 STR. CDN	1
24	CG17903	VERT CARR BRKT. ASM	2
25	CH00531	RIVET #511 X 3/16	12

AutoCAD
RI3 Sample Drawing

DRAWING CREATED WITH AutoCAD AND A REGISTERED DEVELOPER THIRD PARTY APPLICATION

Chapter 12

LAYERS, LINETYPES, AND COLORS

Chapter Objectives

After completing this chapter you should:

1. understand the strategy of grouping related geometry with *Layers*;

2. be able to create *Layers*;

3. be able to assign *Color* and *Linetype* to *Layers*;

4. be able to assign *Color* and *Linetype* to objects;

5. be able to control a Layer's *State* (*On, Off, Freeze, Thaw, Lock, Unlock*);

6. be able to *Load Linetypes* into the drawing;

7. be able to set *LTSCALE* to adjust the scale of linetypes;

8. know that *Celtscale* can be used to set object-specific linetype scale;

9. understand that color and linetype properties can be changed with *Ddchprop* or *Ddmodify*;

10. be able to select specific layers from a long list using the *Filters* option of the *Layer Control* dialogue box.

BASICS

In a CAD drawing, layers are used to group related objects in a drawing. Objects (*Lines*, *Circles*, *Arcs*, etc.) that are created to describe one component, function, or process of a drawing are perceived as related information and, therefore, are typically drawn on one layer. A single CAD drawing is generally composed of several components and, therefore, several layers. Use of layers provides you with a method of controlling visible features of the components of a drawing. For each layer, you can control its color on the screen, the linetype it will be displayed with, and its visibility setting (on or off). Only visible layers will plot.

Layers in a CAD drawing can be compared to clear overlay sheets on a manual drawing. For example, in a CAD architectural drawing, the floor plan can be drawn on one layer, electrical layout on another, plumbing on a third layer, and HVAC (heating, ventilating, and air conditioning) on a fourth layer (Fig. 12-1). Each layer of a CAD drawing could be assigned a different color, linetype, and visibility setting similar to the way clear overlay sheets on a manual drawing can be used. Layers can be temporarily turned *OFF* or *ON* to simplify drawing and editing like overlaying or removing the clear sheets. For

Figure 12-1

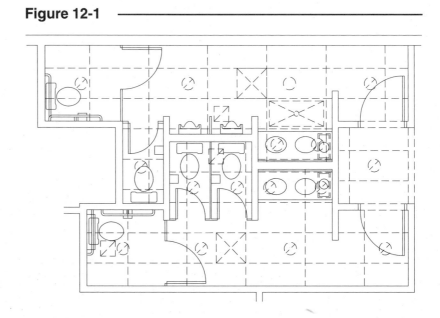

example, in the architectural CAD drawing, only the floor plan layer can be made visible while creating the electrical layout, but can later be cross-referenced with the HVAC layout by turning its layer on. Final plots can be made of specific layers for the subcontractors and one plot of all layers for the general contractor by controlling the layers' visibility before plotting.

AutoCAD allows you to create an infinite number of layers. You must assign a name to each layer when you create it. The layer names should be descriptive of the information on the layer.

There are two strategies for assigning colors and linetypes to a drawing—assign to layers or assign to objects. Usually, layers are assigned a color and a linetype so that all objects drawn on a single layer have the same color and linetype. This is called assigning color and linetype *BYLAYER*. Using the *BYLAYER* method makes it visually apparent which objects are related (on the same layer). Alternately, you can assign colors and linetypes to specific objects, overriding the layer's color and linetype setting. This method is fast and easy for small drawings and works well when layering schemes are not used. However, using this method makes it difficult to see which layers the objects are located on. It is therefore recommended that beginners use only one method for assigning colors and linetypes, then combine the two methods only after gaining some experience. Usually, the *BYLAYER* method is learned first and the object-specific color and linetype assignment method is used when layers are not needed or when complex applications are needed. The *BYBLOCK* linetype and color assignment is discussed in Chapter 21.

The colors that are assigned to layers or to objects control the pens for plotting. In the *Plot Configuration* dialogue box (see Chapter 14), *Pen Assignments* are designated based on the object's color on the screen. Each screen color can be assigned to use a separate pen for plotting so that all objects that appear in one color will be plotted with the same pen.

COMMANDS

LAYER

PULL-DOWN MENU	SCREEN MENU	TYPE IN	TABLET MENU
Data *Layers...*	*DATA* *DDlmode:*	*LAYER or LA* *or DDLMODES*	*3,L to 5,O*

The easiest way to gain complete layer control is through the *Layer Control* dialogue box (Fig. 12-2). If you are typing, *Ddlmodes* invokes the dialogue box. This dialogue box allows full control for all layers. The central area lists existing layers and their *State*, *Color*, and *Linetype*. One or more layers can be selected (highlighted) from the list in order to change the layer(s) *State* (*On*, *Off*, *Freeze*, *Thaw*, *Lock*, *Unlock*), *Color*, or *Linetype*. Changing any of the features on the right side of the box affects all highlighted layers from the list when the *OK* tile is selected.

Figure 12-2

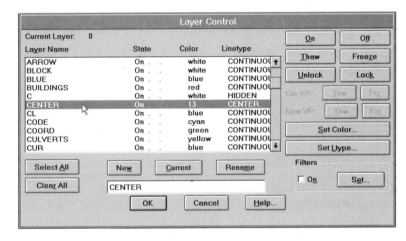

As an alternative to the dialogue box, the *Layer* command can be typed (*LA* is the command alias) in order to control layers. The command line format of *Layer* shows all of the available options.

```
Command: layer
?/Make/Set/New/ON/OFF/Color/LType/Freeze/Thaw/LOck/Unlock:
```

The options are explained below.

Current* or *Set
To *Set* a layer as the *Current* layer is to make it the active drawing layer. Any objects created with draw commands are created on the *Current* layer. You can, however, edit objects on any layer, but draw only on the current layer. Therefore, if you want to draw on the FLOORPLAN layer (for example), use the *Set* or *Current* option. If you want to draw with a certain *Color* or *Linetype*, set the layer with the desired *Color* and *Linetype* as the *Current* layer. Any layer can be made current, but only <u>one layer at a time</u> can be current.

To set the current layer with the *Layer Control* dialogue box (Fig. 12-2), select the desired layer from the list and then select the *Current* tile. Since only one layer can be current, it may be necessary to "deselect" highlighted layer names from the list until only one is highlighted. Alternately, if you are typing, use the *Set* option of the *Layer* command to make a layer the current layer.

State (On, Off, Freeze, Thaw, Lock, Unlock)

With the dialogue box, one or more layers can be selected from the layer name list. Any selections from the tiles on the right side of the box affect the highlighted layers. If you prefer typing the *Layer* command instead, activate any of the options by typing the capitalized letters of the desired option. The options are:

ON, OFF

If a layer is *ON*, it is visible. Objects on visible layers can be edited or plotted. Layers that are *OFF* are not visible. Objects on layers that are *OFF* will not plot and cannot be edited (unless the *ALL* selection option is used). It is not advisable to turn the current layer *OFF*.

Freeze, Thaw

Freeze and *Thaw* override *ON* and *OFF*. *Freeze* is a more protected state than *OFF*. Like being *OFF*, a frozen layer is not visible, nor can its objects be edited or plotted. Objects on a frozen layer cannot be accidentally *Erase*d with the *ALL* option. *Freezing* also prevents the layer from being considered when *Regen*s occur. *Freezing* unused layers speeds up computing time when working with large and complex drawings. *Thawing* reverses the *Freezing* state. Layers can be *Thawed* and also turned *OFF*. Frozen layers are not visible even though the word *ON* appears by the layer.

LOck, Unlock

Layers that are *LOck*ed are protected from being edited but are still visible and can be plotted. *LOck*ing a layer prevents its objects from being changed even though they are visible. Objects on *LOck*ed layers cannot be selected with the *ALL* option. Layers can be *LOck*ed and *OFF*.

Color and *Linetype* **Properties**

Layers have properties of *Color* and *Linetype* such that (generally) an object that is drawn on, or changed to, a specific layer assumes the layer's linetype and color. Using this scheme (*BYLAYER*) enhances your ability to see what geometry is related by layer. It is also possible, however, to assign specific color and linetype to objects which will override the layer's color and linetype (see *Linetype* and *Color* commands).

Procedures for setting one or many layers' *Color* and *Ltype* using the *Layer Control* dialogue box are similar to procedures for selecting a layer's *State*. Remember that several layers' names can be selected (highlighted) from the list for subsequent *Color* and *Ltype* setting.

Set Color

Selecting the *Set Color* tile in the *Layer Control* dialogue box causes the *Select Color* dialogue box to pop up (Fig. 12-3). The desired color can then be selected or the name or color number (called the ACI--AutoCAD Color Index) can be typed in the edit box. Alternately, the *Color* option of the *Layer* command can be typed to enter the color name or ACI number.

The actual number of colors that are available is dependent on the type of monitor and graphics controller card that are configured. For the typical VGA configuration (Video Graphics Array standard monitor and graphics controller card), 16 colors are available. SVGA (Super VGA) setups allow 256 colors in AutoCAD.

Figure 12-3

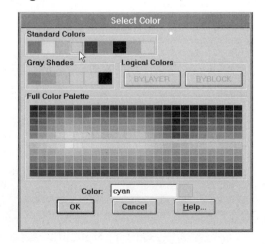

Set Ltype

To set a layer's linetype, select the *Set Ltype* tile of the *Layer Control* dialogue box, which in turn invokes the *Select Linetype* dialogue box (Fig. 12-4). Select the desired linetype from the list. Alternately, the *Ltype* option of the *Layer* command can be typed.

The default AutoCAD prototype drawing as supplied by Autodesk has only one linetype available (*Continuous*). Before you can use other linetypes in a drawing, you load the linetypes by selecting the *Load* tile or by using a default prototype drawing that has the desired linetypes already loaded.

Figure 12-4

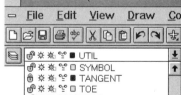

New

The *New* option allows you to make new layers. There is only one layer in the AutoCAD default drawing (ACAD.DWG) as it is provided to you "out of the box." That layer is Layer 0. Layer 0 is a part of every AutoCAD drawing because it cannot be *Purge*d, that is, erased. You can, however, change the *Ltype* and *Color* of Layer 0 from the defaults (continuous linetype and color #7 white). Layer 0 is generally used as a construction layer or for geometry not intended to be included in the final draft of the drawing. Layer 0 has special properties when creating *Blocks* (Chapter 21).

You should create layers for each group of related objects and assign appropriate layer names for that geometry. Layer names can contain up to 31 characters. There is no limit to the number of layers that can be created. To create layers with the *Layer Control* dialogue box, type a layer name (or several names separated by commas) in the edit box; then select the *New* tile. The new layer name(s) then appears in the list above with the default color (white) and linetype (continuous). Colors and linetypes should be assigned as the next step.

If you want to create layers by typing, the *New* and *Make* options of the *Layer* command can be used. *New* allows creation of one or more new layers. *Make* allows creation of one layer (at a time) and sets it as the current layer.

Filters

The *Filters* cluster of the *Layer Control* dialogue box (lower right corner, Fig. 12-2) can be used to select specific layers from a long list. See Layer Filters near the chapter's end.

AutoCAD for Windows Layer Pop-down List

The Object Properties toolbar in the Windows version of Release 13 contains a pop-down list for making layer control quick and easy (Fig. 12-5). The window normally displays the current layer name, state, and color. When you pull down the list, all the layers and their properties are displayed. Selecting any layer makes it current. Clicking on any other icon changes its state as shown below. You cannot change a layer's color or linetype, nor can you create new layers using this tool.

Figure 12-5

Unlock, Lock

Freeze, Thaw

Viewport Freeze, Thaw

Freezes or *Thaws* the layer in the current viewport if floating (paper space) viewports are in use.

On, Off

R13

LINETYPE

PULL-DOWN MENU	SCREEN MENU	TYPE IN	TABLET MENU
Data *Linetype...*	*DATA* *DDltype:*	*LINETYPE or* *DDltype*	*8,Y*

Invoking this command by the menus or by typing *Ddltype* presents the *Select Linetype* dialogue box shown in Figure 12-4. Even though this is the same dialogue box used for assigning linetypes to layers, beware!

When linetypes are selected using the *Linetype* or *Ddltype* command, they are assigned to objects—not to layers. That is, selecting a linetype by this manner causes all objects from that time on to be drawn using that linetype, regardless of the layer that they are on (unless the *BYLAYER* type is PICKed). In contrast, selecting linetypes during the *Layer* command or with the *Layer Control* dialogue box results in assignment of linetypes to layers. Remember that using both of these methods in one drawing can be very confusing until you have some experience using these methods.

To draw an object in a specific linetype, simply select it from the list and PICK the *OK* tile. That linetype stays in effect (all objects are drawn with that linetype) until another linetype is selected. If you want to use the linetypes assigned to layers, select *BYLAYER*.

Figure 12-6

BORDER
BORDER2
BORDERX2
CENTER
CENTER2
CENTERX2
CONTINUOUS
DASHDOT
DASHDOT2
DASHDOTX2
DASHED
DASHED2
DASHEDX2
DIVIDE
DIVIDE2
DIVIDEX2
DOT
DOT2
DOTX2
HIDDEN
HIDDEN2
HIDDENX2
PHANTOM
PHANTON2
PHANTOMX2
ACAD_ISO02W100
ACAD_ISO03W100
ACAD_ISO04W100
ACAD_ISO05W100
ACAD_ISO06W100
ACAD_ISO07W100
ACAD_ISO08W100
ACAD_ISO09W100
ACAD_ISO010W100
ACAD_ISO011W100
ACAD_ISO012W100
ACAD_ISO013W100
ACAD_ISO014W100
ACAD_ISO015W100

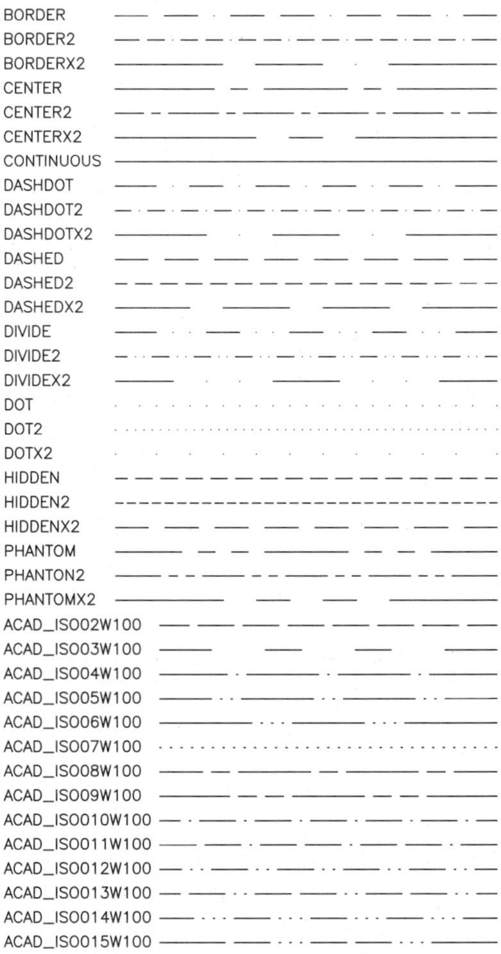

Load

The *Select Linetype* dialogue box also lets you *Load* linetypes that are not already in the drawing. Just PICK the *Load* tile to view and select from the list of available linetypes. AutoCAD supplies numerous linetypes as shown in Figure 12-6. These linetypes are loaded from the ACAD.LIN file. Complex linetypes are also available from the LTYPESHP.LIN file (Fig. 12-7).

You can also assign linetypes to objects by typing *Linetype*, yielding the following prompt:

```
Command: linetype
?/Create/Load/Set:
```

You can list (*?*), *Load*, *Set*, or *Create* linetypes with the typed form of the command. Type a question mark *(?)* to display the list of available linetypes. Type *L* to *Load* any linetypes. The *Set* option of *Linetype* accomplishes the same action as selecting from the linetypes in the dialogue box. That is, you set a specific linetype for all subsequent objects regardless of the layer's linetype setting. Use *Set* when you want an object's linetype to override its layer (*BYLAYER*) linetype.

Figure 12-7

Load or Reload Linetypes
File...
R13\COMMON\SUPPORT\LTYPESHP.lin
Available linetypes
FENCELINE1
FENCELINE2
TRACKS
BATTING
HOT_WATER_SUPPLY
GAS_LINE
ZIGZAG
—HW—HW—HW—H
—GAS—GAS—GAS—GA
Select All
Clear All
OK
Cancel
Help...

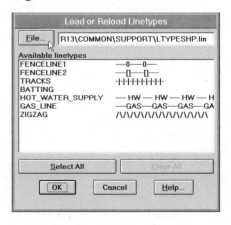

R13

You can create your own custom linetypes with the *Create* option or by using a text editor. Both simple linetypes (line, dash, and dot combinations) and complex linetypes (including text or other shapes) are possible. See Chapter 42, Customization.

The ACAD_ISO*n*W100 linetypes are intended to be used with metric drawings. In order to accommodate the relatively large linetype spacing, *Limits* should be set to metric sheet sizes.

AutoCAD for Windows Linetype Pop-down List

The Object Properties toolbar contains a pop-down list for selecting linetypes (Fig. 12-8). Although this appears to be quick and easy, you can only assign linetypes to objects by this method. Any linetype you select from this list becomes the current object linetype. If you want to select linetypes for layers, make sure this list displays the *BYLAYER* setting, then use the *Layer Control* dialogue box to select linetypes for layers.

Figure 12-8 ─────

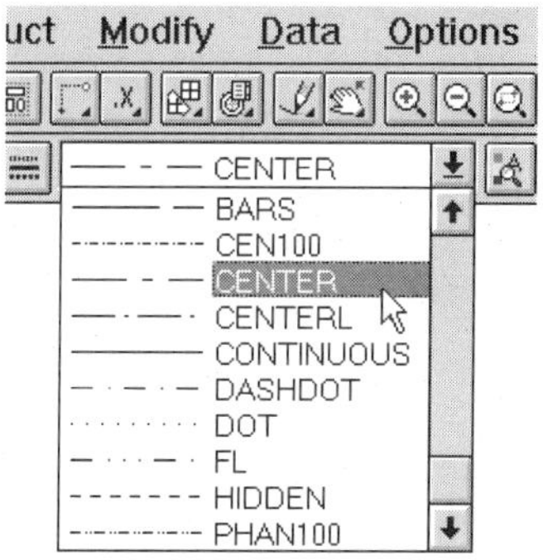

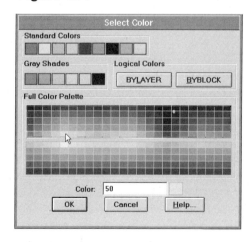

COLOR

PULL-DOWN MENU	SCREEN MENU	TYPE IN	TABLET MENU
Data *Color:*	*DATA* *Color:*	*COLOR or* *DDCOLOR*	---

Similar to linetypes, colors can be assigned to layers or to objects. Using the *Color* or *Ddcolor* command assigns a color for all newly created objects, regardless of the layer's color designation (unless the *BYLAYER* color is selected). This color setting overrides the layer color for any newly created objects so that all new objects are drawn with the specified color no matter what layer they are on. This type of color designation prohibits your ability to see which objects are on which layers by their color; however, for some applications object color setting may be desirable. Use the *Layer Control* dialogue box to set colors for layers.

Figure 12-9 ─────────

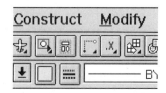

Invoking this command by the menus or by typing *Ddcolor* presents the *Select Color* dialogue box shown in Figure 12-9. This is essentially the same dialogue box used for assigning colors to layers; however, the *BYLAYER* and *BYBLOCK* tiles are accessible only when *Color* or *Ddcolor* is used. (*BYBLOCK* is discussed in Chapter 21.) When an object-specific color has been set, the Object Properties toolbar color icon displays a solid color (Fig. 12-10), whereas, when a layer-specific color is current, the icon is half color and half the "layers" symbol (see command table above). You can also use this command or dialogue box to set the color designation back to *BYLAYER* if it has been set to a specific object color. The command line format is as follows:

Figure 12-10 ─────

Command: **color**
New object color <BYLAYER>: **red** (Specify a color name or number.)
Command:

For the example, all new objects drawn will be *red* regardless of the layers' color settings until *Color* or *Ddcolor* is used again to set another color or *BYLAYER* setting.

The current color (whether *BYLAYER* or specific object color) is saved in the *CECOLOR* (Current Entity Color) variable. The current color can be set by changing the value in the *CECOLOR* variable directly at the command prompt, by using the *Color* command or by using the *Object Creation* dialogue box (see *Ddemodes* below). The *CECOLOR* variable accepts a string value (such as "red" or "bylayer") or accepts the ACI number (0 through 255).

DDEMODES

PULL-DOWN MENU	SCREEN MENU	TYPE IN	TABLET MENU
Data *Object Creation...*	*DATA* *DDemode:*	*DDEMODES*	*9,Y*

As an alternative to using the *Linetype* or *Color* commands and associated dialogue boxes, the *Object Creation Modes* dialogue box (Fig. 12-11) can be accessed. Selecting the *Color* tile produces the *Select Color* dialogue box (see Figure 12-9) and selecting the *Linetype* tile produces the *Select Linetype* dialogue box (see Figure 12-4). Keep in mind that selecting a specific color or linetype by this method causes an object-specific setting, not a *BYLAYER* setting.

Figure 12-11 —————

LTSCALE

PULL-DOWN MENU	SCREEN MENU	TYPE IN	TABLET MENU
Data *Linetype* *Linetype Scale:*	*DATA* *DDltype:* *Linetype Scale:*	*LTSCALE*	*8,Y*

Hidden, dashed, dotted, and other linetypes that have spaces are called <u>non-continuous</u> linetypes. When drawing objects that have non-continuous linetypes (either *BYLAYER* or object-specific linetype designations), the linetype's dashes or dots are automatically created and spaced. The *LTSCALE* variable (Linetype Scale) controls the length and spacing of the dashes and/or dots. The value that is specified for *LTSCALE* affects the drawing <u>globally and retroactively</u>. That is, all existing non-continuous lines in the drawing as well as new lines are affected by *LTSCALE*. You can therefore adjust the drawing's linetype scale for all lines at any time with this one command.

If you choose to make the dashes of non-continuous lines smaller and closer together, reduce *LTSCALE*; if you desire larger dashes, increase *LTSCALE*. The *Hidden* linetype is shown in Figure 12-12 at various *LTSCALE* settings. Any positive value can be specified.

Figure 12-12 ————————————————

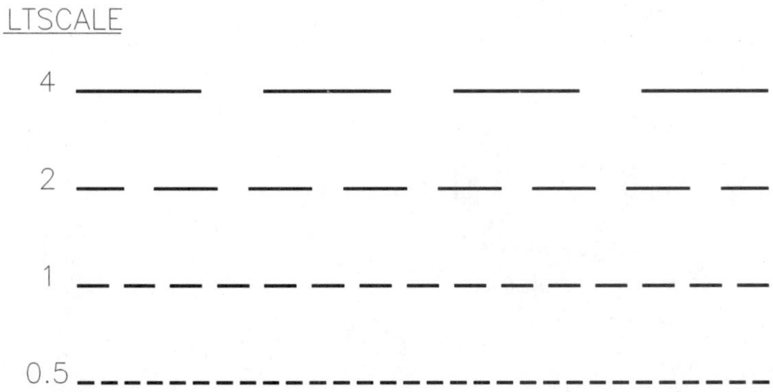

LTSCALE

4 ————   ————   ————   ————

2 —— —— —— —— —— —— ——

1 — — — — — — — — — —

0.5 – – – – – – – – – – – – – – – – – – –

LTSCALE can be set by the *Select Linetype* dialogue box (Fig. 12-13) or in command line format. The command line format is given below. <u>It is recommended that LTSCALE be set using the command line format</u> to avoid confusion. (The *Linetype Scale* option appears in five different dialogue boxes, and in three of those cases the setting actually represents the *Celtscale* value. See *CELTSCALE* below.)

LTSCALE can be used in the command line format.

> Command: **LTSCALE**
> New scale factor <1 or current value>: **(value)** (Enter any positive value.)
> Command:

Figure 12-13 ───────

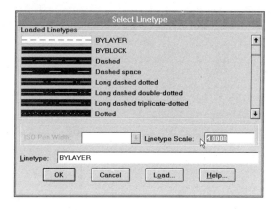

The *LTSCALE* for the default prototype drawing (ACAD.DWG) is 1. This value represents an appropriate *LTSCALE* for objects drawn within the default *Limits* of 12 x 9.

As a general rule, you should change the *LTSCALE* <u>proportionally</u> with changes in *Limits* (more specifically, inversely proportional to plot scale). For example, if you increase the drawing area defined by *Limits* by a factor of 2 (to 24 x 18) from the default (12 x 9), you also change *LTSCALE* proportionally to a value of 2. Since *LTSCALE* is retroactive, it can be changed at a later time or repeatedly adjusted to display the desired spacing of linetypes. (For more information on *LTSCALE*, see Chapter 13 and Chapter 14).

The ACAD_ISO*n*W100 linetypes are intended to be used with metric drawings. Changing *Limits* to metric sheet sizes automatically displays these linetypes with appropriate linetype spacing. For these linetypes only, *LTSCALE* is changed automatically to the value selected in the *ISO Pen Width* box. Using both ACAD_ISO*n*W100 linetypes and other linetypes in one drawing is discouraged due to the difficulty managing the two sets of linetype scales.

Even though you have some control over the size of spacing for non-continuous lines, you have almost <u>no control</u> over the <u>placement</u> of the dashes for non-continuous lines. For example, the short dashes of center lines <u>cannot</u> always be controlled to intersect at the centers of a series of circles. The spacing can only be adjusted globally (all lines in the drawing) to reach a compromise. See Chapter 24, Multiview Drawing, for further discussion and suggestions on this subject.

CELTSCALE

PULL-DOWN MENU	SCREEN MENU	TYPE IN	TABLET MENU
Data *Object Creation...*	*DATA* *Ddltype* *Linetype Scale:*	*CELTSCALE*	*9,Y*

Celtscale stands for Current Entity Linetype Scale. This setting changes the <u>object-specific linetype scale</u> <u>proportional</u> to the *LTSCALE*. The *LTSCALE* value is global and retroactive, whereas, *Celtscale* sets the linetype scale for all newly created objects. Using *Celtscale* to set an object linetype scale is similar to setting an object color and linetype in that the properties are assigned to the specific object.

For example, if you wanted all non-continuous lines (dashes and spaces) in the drawing to be two times the default size, set *LTSCALE* to 2 (*LTSCALE* is global and retroactive). If you then wanted only, say, a select two or three lines to have smaller spacing, change *Celtscale* to .5 and then draw those new lines. An even better method is to create all objects in the drawing and adjust the *LTSCALE* to the desired value, then use *Ddmodify* or *Ddchprop* to retroactively change the *Celtscale* for selected objects (see *Ddmodify* and *Ddchprop*).

To change the *Celtscale* for all new objects, use *Celtscale* in command line format or set the *LTSCALE* value in the *Object Creation Modes* dialogue box (Fig. 12-14). It is <u>highly recommended that the *Celtscale* command be typed</u> to avoid the confusion between *LTSCALE* and *Celtscale* that exists in the dialogue boxes.

Figure 12-14 ──────

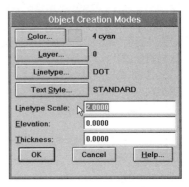

Does *Linetype Scale* Represent *LTSCALE* or *CELTSCALE*?

The *Linetype Scale* edit box appears in <u>five</u> dialogue boxes; however, it is not clear whether using these tiles affects the *LTSCALE* or the *CELTSCALE*. To help avoid this confusion, the following table is given to explain how the *Linetype Scale* tiles are related to the *LTSCALE*, *CELTSCALE*, and the selected object's linetype scale.

Dialogue Box (Command)	Displayed Setting Represents:	Changing the Setting Performs this Action	Variable Affected
Select Linetype (*DDLTYPE*)	Current *LTSCALE*	Changes global *LTSCALE*	*LTSCALE*
Layer Control (*DDLMODES*)	Current *CELTSCALE*	Disabled in Release 13 version c2	---
Object Creation Modes (*DDEMODES*)	Current *CELTSCALE*	Sets linetype scale for new lines	*CELTSCALE*
Change Properties (*DDCHPROP*)	*CELTSCALE* setting when object was created	Changes linetype scale retroactively for selected objects	---
Modify Object (*DDMODIFY*)	*CELTSCALE* setting when object was created	Changes linetype scale retroactively for selected object	---

Changing *Layer, Linetype, Color,* and Linetype Scale Properties

Figure 12-15 ──────

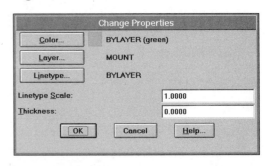

The *Change Properties* (*Ddchprop*) dialogue box shown in Figure 12-15 or *Modify* (*Ddmodify*) dialogue box can be used <u>retroactively</u> to change the properties of individual objects. Properties that can be changed are *Layer, Linetype, Color,* and object linetype scale (*Celtscale*).

For example, *Layer* could be selected to "move" objects from one layer to another. When an object is changed from one layer to another, it assumes the new layer's color and linetype, provided the object was originally created with color and linetype assigned *BYLAYER*. In other words, if an object was created with the wrong linetype or color, or on the wrong layer, it could be "moved" to the desired layer, therefore assuming the new layer's linetype and color.

These dialogue boxes can also be used to change an object's linetype or color designation retroactively. That is, if linetype and color are specifically assigned to one or a group of objects, you can change the setting to another linetype or color or change the assignment to a *BYLAYER* setting. Additionally, the linetype scale for individual existing objects (*Celtscale*) can be modified retroactively by changing the dialogue box *Linetype Scale* value. <u>Changing an individual object's linetype scale after drawing it is the preferred method.</u>

See Chapter 17, Construct Commands II, for a full explanation of *Change Properties* (*Ddchprop*) and *Modify* (*Ddmodify*).

Layer Filters

When working on drawings with a large number of layers, it is time-consuming to scroll through the list of layer names in the *Layer Control* dialogue box or in the layer pop-down list on the Object Properties toolbar (Windows). The *Set Layer Filters* dialogue box enables you to specify criteria for displaying a selected set of layers in both lists. For example, you may want to list only layer names that are *Frozen*. By using layer filters, you can shorten the layer list by filtering out the layers that do not meet this criterion.

Selecting the *Set...* tile in the lower right corner of the *Layer Control* dialogue box produces the *Set Layer Filters* dialogue box (Fig. 12-16). There are eight criteria that can be specified in the *Set Layer Filters* dialogue box. The criteria define <u>what you want to see</u> in the layer listing. When the criteria are set to *Both* or *, all layer names are displayed.

The first five criteria are in pairs, enabling you to choose one or "*Both*" of the settings. When a criteria is set to *Both*, you will see layers listed which match both items in the pair, such as layers that are *On* <u>and</u> *Off*.

Figure 12-16 ─────────────

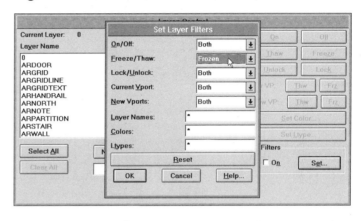

Selecting one of the pair displays only layer names meeting that condition. Selecting *Frozen* from the *Freeze/Thaw* box, for example, will cause a display of only layers that that are frozen (Fig. 12-16).

The last three criteria enable you to enter specific values. These edit boxes allow you to list only layers that match particular names, colors or linetypes. The default setting of * means that <u>all</u> layers for that criteria are displayed. As an example, if you set the *Layer Names* filter to **AR***, only those layers whose names begin with "AR" would be displayed in the layer listing (Fig. 12-17).

When a layer filter setting is enabled, the *On* box is checked in the *Filters* group of the *Layer Control* dialogue box (Fig. 12-17). If you toggle a filters setting *On* (in the check

Figure 12-17 ─────────────

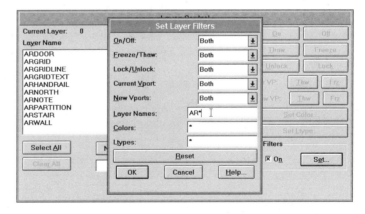

box) and exit the *Layer Control* dialogue box by PICKing *OK*, the current filters setting controls the display for subsequent uses of both the dialogue box and the Windows layer pop-down list. To temporarily override a layer filter setting and display all layer names, remove the "x" in the *On* box.

Only one layer filter configuration can be applied at a time and a configuration cannot be saved to a file.

CHAPTER EXERCISES

1. *Layer, Layer Control dialogue box, On, Off, Freeze, Thaw, Set Color*

    Open the sample drawing named **HVAC.DWG** located in the ACADR13/COMMON/SAMPLE directory. Use *Saveas* to save the drawing <u>in your working directory</u> as **HVAC2**.

    A. Invoke the *Layer* command by typing *LA*. Use the *?* option to yield the list of layers in the drawing. Notice that all the layers are *On*.

    B. Invoke the *Layer Control* dialogue box from the *Settings* pull-down menu. Turn *Off* the layer with the HVAC ductwork and dimensions (**HVACSUP**) by highlighting (PICKing) the layer and then selecting the *Off* tile. Select the *OK* tile and view the drawing. Are the dimensions and ductwork displayed?

    C. Turn *Off* layer **TEXT** using the *Layer Control* dialogue box or the (Windows) layer pop- down list on the Object Properties toolbar. This should clean up the drawing further by not displaying the detail text. Now type *Regen* and count the number of seconds it takes for the regeneration.

    D. Use the *Layer Control* dialogue box and PICK the *Select All* tile (lower left corner). Then select the *On* tile to turn the layers back on. Now select *Clear All*. Select the two layers again individually (**HVACSUP** and **TEXT**) and PICK the *Freeze* tile to freeze them. Notice the *State* column says the layers are still *On*. (*Freeze* overrides *On*.) Select *OK* to return to the drawing and view the changes. Type *Regen* and count the seconds needed for the regeneration. Is a *Regen* faster with the two layers frozen?

    E. Select the two layers again from the *Layer Control* dialogue box and *Thaw* them. Since they were already *On*, they should appear when you select the *OK* tile. PICK the *Clear All* tile to unhighlight all layers. Select the **HVACSUP** and **HVACSUPH** layers and *Set Color* of both to red. PICK the *OK* tile. If the layers don't appear, type *Regen*.

    F. *Freeze* the two layers (**HVACSUP** and **HVACSUPH**) and *Save* the drawing.

2. *Linetype, Layer Control, New, Current, Set Ltype, Set Color*

    A. Begin a *New* drawing and assign the name **CH12EX2**. Set *Limits* to **11 x 8.5**. Use the *Linetype* dialogue box to list the loaded linetypes. Are any linetypes already loaded? PICK the *Load* option and select all linetypes to load. Close the dialogue box.

    B. Use the *Layer Control* dialogue box to create 3 new layers named **OBJ, HID,** and **CEN**. Enter the names in the edit box with commas between (no spaces). Select the *New* tile to make the new layers appear in the list. Assign the following colors and linetypes to the layers using the *Set Color* and *Set Ltype* tiles.

OBJ	red	continuous
HID	yellow	hidden
CEN	green	center

    C. Make the **OBJ** layer *Current;* PICK the *OK* tile. Verify the current layer by looking at the status line or pop-down list, then draw the visible object lines only (not the dimensions) shown in Figure 12-18.

D. When you are finished drawing the visible object lines, create the necessary hidden lines by making layer **HID** the *Current* layer, then drawing *Lines*. Notice that you only specify the *Line* endpoints as usual and AutoCAD creates the dashes.

E. Next, create the center lines for the holes by making layer **CEN** the *Current* layer and drawing *Lines*. Save the drawing.

F. As a final step, create a *New* layer named **BORDER** and draw a border and title block of your design on that layer. The final drawing should appear as that in Figure 12-19. *Save* the drawing.

Figure 12-18 ————————————————

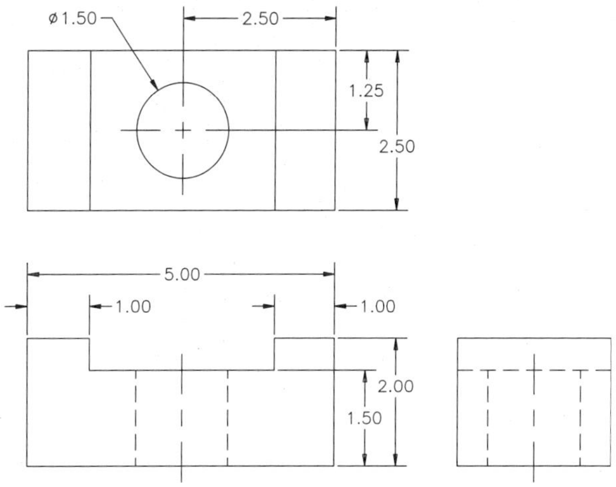

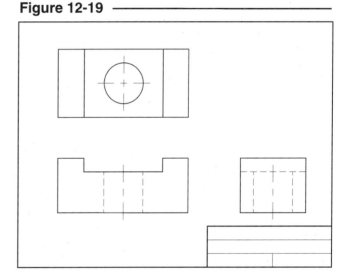

Figure 12-19 ————————————————

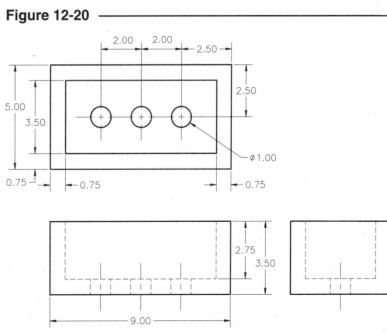

3. *LTSCALE, CELTSCALE*

A. Begin a *New* drawing and assign the name **CH12EX3**. Create the same four *New* layers that you made for the previous exercise. Set the *Limits* equal to a "C" size sheet, **22 x 17**.

B. Create the part shown in Figure 12-20. Draw on the appropriate layers to achieve the desired linetypes.

C. Notice that the *Hidden* and *Center* linetype dashes are very small. Use *LTSCALE* to adjust the scale of the non-continuous lines. Since you changed the *Limits* by a factor of slightly less than 2, try using **2** as the *LTSCALE* factor. Notice that all the lines are affected (globally) and that the new *LTSCALE* is retroactive for existing lines as well as for new

Figure 12-20 ————————————————

lines. This appears too large, however, because of the small hidden line segments, so it should be adjusted. Remember that you cannot control where the multiple <u>short</u> centerline dashes appear for one line segment. Try to reach a compromise.

D. The six short vertical hidden lines in the front view and two in the side view should be adjusted to a smaller linetype scale. Use the *Change Properties* dialogue box to retroactively adjust the individual objects' *Linetype Scale* to **0.6000**.

E. When you have the desired linetype scales, *Exit AutoCAD* and *Save Changes*. Keep in mind that the drawing size may appear differently on the screen than it will on a plot. Both the plot scale and the paper size should be considered when you set *LTSCALE*. This topic will be discussed further in Chapter 13, Advanced Drawing Setup.

4. **Using Layer Filters to Shorten a Layer Listing**

Open the sample drawing **HVAC2.DWG** that you worked on in exercise 1.

A. Use the *Layer Control* dialogue box and select the layers **ARGRID, ARGRIDLINE**, and **ARGRIDTEXT** and turn them *Off*. Choose *Clear All*; then choose the layers **ARHANDRAIL, ARPARTITION, ARSTAIR,** and **ARWALL** and *Lock* them. *Clear All* again.

B. PICK the *Set* button in the *Filters* section. This opens the *Set Layer Filters* dialogue box displaying the eight different filter criteria.

C. PICK *On* from the *On/Off* pop-down list (Fig 12-21). This filter will display only the names of layers that are currently *On*.

Figure 12-21

D. Select *Unlock* from the *Lock/Unlock* pair (Fig 12-21). This will display only names of layers that are *Unlocked*.

E. PICK the *OK* tile from the *Set Layer Filters* dialogue box. This closes the dialogue box and applies the filter configuration to the *Layer Control* layer listing. PICK the *OK* tile in the *Layer Control* dialogue box to apply the layer settings to the drawing.

G. If you are using AutoCAD for Windows, select the layer pop-down list to see that the layer filtering has been applied to this list also.

H. From the *Layer Control* dialogue box, toggle off the layer filters by removing the "x" in the *On* box. Choose the **STMETAL** layer and turn it *Off*, then toggle the filters on by checking the *On* box. Because the current filter settings will not display names of layers that are Off, the STMETAL layer name is removed from the list.

Chapter 13

ADVANCED DRAWING SETUP

Chapter Objectives

After completing this chapter you should:

1. know the steps for setting up a drawing;

2. be able to determine an appropriate *Limits* setting for the drawing;

3. be able to calculate and apply the "drawing scale factor";

4. be able to create prototype drawings;

5. know what setup steps can be considered for creating prototype drawings.

BASICS

When you begin a drawing, there are several steps that are typically performed in preparation for creating geometry, such as setting *Units*, *Limits*, and creating *Layers* with *linetypes* and *colors*. Some of these basic concepts were discussed in Chapter 6 and Chapter 12. This chapter discusses setting *Limits* for correct plotting as well as other procedures, such as layer creation and variables settings, that help prepare a drawing for geometry creation.

Most offices produce drawings that are similar in format. The similarities may be: subject of the drawing, scale, plotting size, layering schemes, dimensioning techniques, and/or text styles. <u>Prototype</u> drawings can be used to prevent having to repeatedly perform the steps for drawing setup. Prototype drawing creation and use are also discussed in this chapter.

STEPS FOR DRAWING SETUP

Assuming that you have in mind the general dimensions and proportions of the drawing you want to create, and the drawing will involve using layers, dimensions, and text, the following steps are suggested for setting up a drawing.

1. Determine and set the *Units* that are to be used.
2. Determine and set the drawing *Limits*; then *Zoom All*.
3. Set an appropriate *Snap* value to be used if helpful.
4. Set an appropriate *Grid* value.
5. Change the *LTSCALE* value based on the new *Limits*.
6. Create the desired *Layers* and assign appropriate *linetype* and *color* settings.
7. Create desired *Text Styles* (optional, discussed in Chapter 19).
8. Create desired Dimension Styles (optional, discussed in Chapter 29).
9. Create or *Insert* the desired title block and border (optional).

Each of the steps for drawing setup is explained in detail here.

1. Set *Units*

This task is accomplished by using the *Units* command or the *Units Control* dialogue box. Set the linear units and precision desired. Set angular units and precision if needed. (See Chapter 6 for details on this command.)

2. Set *Limits*

Before beginning to create an AutoCAD drawing, determine the size of the drawing area needed for the intended geometry. Using the actual *Units*, appropriate *Limits* should be set in order to draw the object or geometry to the <u>real-world size</u>. *Limits* are set with the *Limits* command by specifying the lower-left and upper-right corners. Always *Zoom All* after changing *Limits*. (See Chapter 6 for details on these operations.)

If you are planning to plot the drawing to scale, *Limits* should be set to a proportion of the sheet size you plan to plot on. For example, if the sheet size is 11" x 8.5", set *Limits* to 11 x 8.5 if you want to plot full size (1"=1"). Setting *Limits* to 22 x 17 (2 times 11 x 8.5) provides 2 times the drawing area and allows plotting at 1/2 size (1/2"=1") on the 11" x 8.5" sheet. Simply stated, set *Limits* to a <u>proportion</u> of the paper size.

Setting *Limits* to the <u>paper size</u> allows plotting at 1=1 scale. Setting *Limits* to a <u>proportion</u> of the sheet size allows plotting at the <u>reciprocal</u> of that proportion. For example, setting *Limits* to 2 times an 11" x 8.5" sheet allows you to plot 1/2 size on that sheet. (Standard paper sizes are given on page 184.)

Drawing Scale Factor

The <u>proportion</u> of the *Limits* to the <u>plotting sheet size</u> is the "drawing scale factor." This factor can be used as a general scale factor for other size-related drawing variables such as *LTSCALE*, *DIMSCALE* (dimensioning scale), and *Hatch* pattern scales.

All size-related AutoCAD drawing variables are set to 1 by default. This means that all variables (such as *LTSCALE*) that control sizing and spacing of objects are set for creating a drawing on a 12 x 9 sheet plotted full size. When *Limits* are changed from the sheet size, the size-related variables should also be changed proportionally. For example, if the default *Limits* (12 x 9) are changed by a factor of 2 (to 24 x 18), then 2 becomes the "drawing scale factor." Then, as a general rule, the values of variables such as *LTSCALE*, *DIMSCALE*, and other scales would be multiplied by a factor of 2 (Fig. 13-1).

Figure 13-1

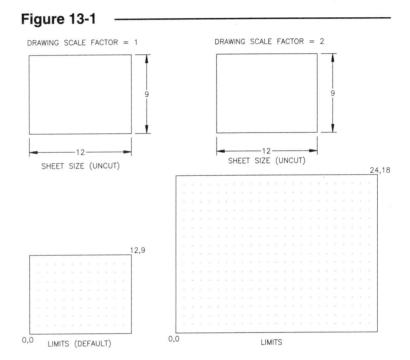

Limits should be set to a proportion of the paper size used for plotting. In many cases, "cut" paper sizes are used based on the 11" x 8.5" module. Assume you plan to plot on an 11" x 8.5" sheet. Changing the *Limits* (based on the paper size) by some multiplier makes that value the drawing scale factor. The <u>reciprocal</u> of the drawing scale factor is the scale for plotting on that sheet (Fig. 13-2).

Since Drawing Scale Factor is the proportion of *Limits* to the sheet size, you can use this formula:

$$DSF = \frac{Limits}{sheet\ size}$$

Because plot scale is the reciprocal of the drawing scale factor:

$$Plot\ Scale = \frac{1}{DSF}$$

Figure 13-2

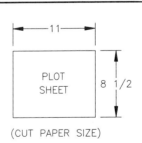

(CUT PAPER SIZE)

LIMITS	SCALE FACTOR	PLOT SCALE	
11 x 8.5	1	1=1	(FULL SIZE)
22 x 17	2	1=2	(HALF SIZE)
44 x 34	4	1=4	(1/4 SIZE)
110 x 85	10	1=10	(1/10 SIZE)

The term "drawing scale factor" is not a variable or command that can be found in AutoCAD or its official documentation. This concept has been developed by AutoCAD users and teachers to describe the factor that is used to associate the variables in an AutoCAD drawing related to keeping geometry proportional and plotting drawings to a particular size.

3. Set *Snap*

Use the *Snap* command or *Drawing Aids* dialogue box to set an appropriate *Snap* value if it is useful. The value of *Snap* is dependent on the <u>interactive</u> drawing accuracy that is desired.

In some drawings where the *Limits* are relatively small and the dimensional increments are relatively large, *Snap* can be very useful. However, in other drawings with large *Limits* and small drawing increment lengths or with complex geometry of irregular interval lengths, *Snap* may not be useful and can be turned *Off*. (See Chapter 6 for details on the *Snap* command.)

The accuracy of the drawing and the size of the *Limits* should be considered when setting the *Snap* value. On one hand, to achieve accuracy and detail, you want the *Snap* to be as small of a dimensional increment as would be used in the drawing. On the other hand, depending on the size of the *Limits*, the *Snap* value should be large enough to make interactive selection (PICKing) fast and easy. As a starting point for determining an appropriate *Snap* value, the default *Snap* value can be multiplied by the "drawing scale factor."

4. Set *Grid*

The *Grid* value setting is usually set equal to, or proportionally larger than, that of the *Snap* value. *Grid* should be set to a proportion that is <u>easily visible</u>. Setting the value to a proportion of *Snap* gives visual indication of the *Snap* increment. For example, a *Grid* value of **1X**, **2X**, or **5X** would give visual display of every 1, 2, or 5 *Snap* increments, respectively. If you are not using *Snap* because only extremely small or irregular interval lengths are needed, you may want to turn *Grid* off. (See Chapter 6 for details on the *Grid* command.)

5. Set the *LTSCALE*

A change in *Limits* (then *Zoom All*) affects the display of non-continuous (hidden, dashed, dotted, etc.) lines. The *LTSCALE* variable controls the spacing of non-continuous lines. The "drawing scale factor" can be used to determine the *LTSCALE* setting. For example, if the default *Limits* (based on sheet size) have been changed by a factor of 2, set the *LTSCALE* to 2. If you prefer a *LTSCALE* setting of other than 1 for a drawing in the default *Limits*, multiply that value by the drawing scale factor (2 in this example).

American National Standards Institute (ANSI) requires that <u>hidden lines be plotted with 1/8"</u> <u>dashes</u>. An AutoCAD drawing plotted full size (1 unit=1") with the default *LTSCALE* value of 1 plots the *Hidden* linetype with 1/4" dashes. Therefore, an <u>*LTSCALE* of .5</u> is more appropriate for a drawing plotted full size. Multiply this value by the drawing scale factor when plotting to scale. If individual lines need to be adjusted for linetype scale, use *CELTSCALE* or *Ddchprop* when the drawing is nearly complete. (See Chapter 12 for details on the *LTSCALE* and *CELTSCALE* variables.)

6. Create *Layers*; Assign *Linetypes* and *Colors*

Using the *Layer* command or the *Layer Control* dialogue box, create the layers that you anticipate needing. Multiple layers can be created with the *New* option. Type in several new names separated by commas. Assign a descriptive name for each layer, indicating its type of geometry, part name, or function. Include a *linetype* designator in the layer name if appropriate; for example, PART1-H and PART1-V indicate hidden and visible line layers for PART1.

Once the *Layers* have been created, assign a *Color* and *Linetype* to each layer. *Colors* can be used to give visual relationships among parts of the drawing. Geometry that is intended to be plotted with different pens (pen size or color) should be drawn in different screen colors. Use the *Linetype* command, *Select Linetype* dialogue, or *Layer Control* dialogue box to load the desired line types. You can load all of the linetypes or load only those that you anticipate using. (See Chapter 12 for details on creating *Layers*, *Linetypes*, and *Colors*.)

7. **Create *Text Styles***

AutoCAD has only one text style as part of the standard prototype drawing (ACAD.DWG). If you desire other *Text Styles*, they are created using the *Style* command or the *Text Style...* option from the *Data* pull-down menu. (See Chapter 19, Inserting and Editing Text.)

If you desire engineering standard text, create a *Text Style* using the ROMANS.SHX font file.

8. **Create Dimension Styles**

If you plan to dimension your drawing, Dimension Styles can be created at this point; however, they are generally created during the dimensioning process. Dimension Styles are names given to groups of dimension variable settings. (See Chapter 29 for information on creating Dimension Styles.)

Although you do not have to create Dimension Styles until you are ready to dimension the geometry, it is helpful to create Dimension Styles as part of a prototype drawing. If you produce similar drawings repeatedly, your dimensioning techniques are probably similar. Much time can be saved by using a prototype drawing with previously created Dimension Styles.

9. **Create a Title Block and Border**

For 2D drawings, it is helpful to insert a title block and border early in the drawing process. This action gives a visual drawing boundary as well as reserves the space occupied by the title block.

Since *Limits* are already set to facilitate drawing full size in the actual *Units*, creating a title block and border which will appear on the final plot in the appropriate size is not difficult. A simple method is to use the drawing scale factor to determine the title block size. Multiply the actual size of the title block and border by the drawing scale factor to determine their dimensions in the drawing.

One common method is to use the *Insert* command to insert a title block and border as a *Block*. If the *Block* is the actual title block and border size, simply use the drawing scale factor as the *X* and *Y* scale factor during the *Insert* command. (See Chapters 21 and 22 for information on *Block* creation and *Insertion*.)

If you are preparing prototype drawings, a title block and border can be included as part of a prototype.

CREATING PROTOTYPE DRAWINGS

Instead of going through the steps for setup each time you begin a new drawing, create one or more "prototype" drawings. A prototype drawing is one which has the initial setup steps (*Units*, *Limits*, *Layers*, *linetypes*, *colors*, etc.) completed and saved, but no geometry has yet been created. Prototype drawings are used as a template or starting point each time you begin a new drawing. AutoCAD actually makes a copy of the prototype you select to begin the drawing. The creation and use of prototype drawings can save hours of preparation.

To make a prototype drawing, begin a *New* drawing using the default prototype drawing (ACAD.DWG), make the initial drawing setups, and use *Saveas* to save the drawing under a different, descriptive name. Then, using DOS commands or *File Utilities*, locate the new drawing in the directory where ACAD.DWG is found (usually in the C:\ACADR13\COMMON\SUPPORT subdirectory), or create another directory for multiple prototype drawings.

The *Create New Drawing* dialogue box (Fig. 13-3) is activated when the *New* command is used. This box allows you to select your new prototype drawing from a pop-up list by selecting the *Prototype...* tile. This action produces the *Prototype Drawing File* dialogue box (Fig. 13-4).

Figure 13-3

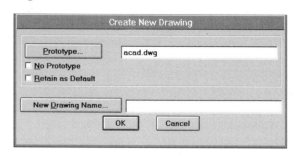

Any drawings (.DWG files) located in the directory where the default drawing (ACAD.DWG) is found are displayed for possible selection as a prototype drawing. Other directories can also be searched for drawings to be used as prototypes.

Several prototype drawings are supplied with AutoCAD in addition to the default ACAD.DWG prototype. The options are given in the following list (see the selections in Fig. 13-4).

Figure 13-4

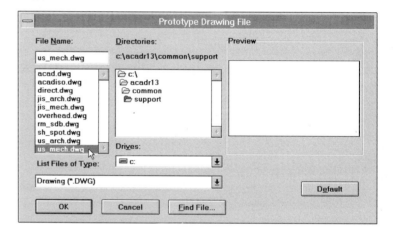

1.	US_ARCH.DWG	96' x 72' (feet) Limits, Architectural units.
2.	US_ MECH.DWG	17 x 11 (inches) Limits, Decimal units.
3.	JIS_ARCH.DWG*	84100 x 59400 (mm) Limits (Model Space), Decimal units.
4.	JIS_MECH.DWG*	420 x 297 (mm) Limits (Model Space), Decimal units.
5.	ACAD.DWG	12 x 9 Limits, Decimal units.
6.	ACADISO.DWG	420 x 297 (mm) Limits, Decimal units.

*JIS is the acronym for Japanese Industrial Standard.

See the Tables of Limits Settings in Chapter 14 for standard plotting scales and intended sheet sizes for the *Limits* settings in these prototypes.

The *Create New Drawing* dialogue box (Fig. 13-3) also allows you to designate a name for a new drawing, if desired. However, if no name is defined, the selected prototype drawing is <u>not</u> overwritten when the *Save* command is used. The new drawing is treated as any other new (blank) drawing. Using *Save* prompts you for a new drawing name.

Multiple prototype drawings can be created, each for a particular situation. For example, you may want to create several prototypes, each having the setup steps completed but with different *Limits* and with the intention to plot each in a different scale or on a different size sheet. Another possibility is to create prototypes with different layering schemes. There are many possibilities, but the specific settings used depend on your applications, typical plotting scales, or your peripheral devices.

R13

Typical drawing steps that can be considered for developing prototype drawings are listed below.

> Set *Units*
> Set *Limits*
> Set *Snap*
> Set *Grid*
> Set *LTSCALE*
> Create *Layers* with color and linetypes assigned
> Create *Text Styles* (see Chapter 19)
> Create Dimension Styles (see Chapter 27)
> Create or *Insert* a standard title block and border

A popular practice is to create a prototype drawing for <u>each sheet size</u> used for plotting. *Limits* are set to the actual sheet size, and other settings and variables (*LTSCALE, DIMSCALE,* text sizes) are set to the actual desired size for the finished full-size plot. Then if you want to create a new drawing and plot on a certain sheet size, start a new drawing using the appropriate prototype.

For laboratories or offices that use only one sheet size, create prototype drawings for <u>each plot scale</u> with the appropriate *Limits, Snap, Grid, Layers, LTSCALE, DIMSCALE,* etc.

You can also create prototypes for different plot scales <u>and</u> different sheet sizes. Make sure you assign appropriate and descriptive names to the prototype drawings.

CHAPTER EXERCISES

For the first three exercises, you will set up several drawings that will be used later for creating geometry. Follow the typical steps for setting up a drawing given in this chapter.

1. A drawing of a gasket is needed. Dimensions are in inches. The drawing will be plotted full size on an 11" x 8.5" sheet. Begin a *New* drawing and assign the name **BARGUIDE**. Follow the steps below.

   A. Set *Units* to *Fractional* and *Precision* to **1/16**.
   B. Set *Limits* to **11 x 8.5**, then *Zoom All*.
   C. Set *Snap* to **1/4** (or **.250**).
   D. Set *Grid* to **1/2** (or **.5**).
   E. Set *LTSCALE* to **.5**.
   F. *Load* the *Center* and *Hidden Linetypes*.
   G. Create the following *layers* and assign the given *Colors* and *Linetypes*:

VISIBLE	*continuous*	*red*
CONSTR	*continuous*	*white*
CENTER	*center*	*green*
HIDDEN	*hidden*	*yellow*
TITLE	*continuous*	*white*
DIM	*continuous*	*cyan*

   H. *Save* the drawing.

2. You are to create a drawing of a wrench. The drawing will be plotted full size on an "A" size sheet, and the dimensions are in millimeters. Begin a *New* drawing and assign the name **WRENCH**. Follow these steps.

    A. Set *Units* to *Decimal* and *Precision* to **0.00**.
    B. Set *Limits* to a metric sheet size, **297** x **210**; then *Zoom All* (scale factor is approximately 25).
    C. Set *Snap* to **1**.
    D. Set *Grid* to **10**.
    E. Set *LTSCALE* to **12.5** (.5 times the scale factor of 25).
    F. *Load* the *Center Linetype*.
    G. Create the following *Layers* and assign the *Colors* and *Linetypes* as shown:

WRENCH	*continuous*	*red*
CONSTR	*continuous*	*white*
CENTER	*center*	*green*
TITLE	*continuous*	*yellow*
DIM	*continuous*	*cyan*

    H. *Save* the drawing.

3. A floorplan of an apartment has been requested. Dimensions are in feet and inches. The drawing will be plotted at 1/2"=1' scale on an 24" x 18" sheet. Begin a *New* drawing and assign the name **APARTMNT**. Continue with the steps below.

    A. Set *Units* to *Architectural* and *Precision* to **1/2**.
    B. Set *Limits* to **48'** x **36'** (576" x 432"); then *Zoom All*.
    C. Set *Snap* to **1** (inch).
    D. Set *Grid* to **12** (inches).
    E. Set *LTSCALE* to **12**.
    F. Create the following *layers* and assign the *Colors*:

FLOORPLN	*red*
CONSTR	*white*
TEXT	*green*
TITLE	*yellow*
DIM	*cyan*

    G. *Save* the drawing.

4. In this exercise, you will create several "generic" prototype drawings that can be used at a later time. Creating the prototypes now will save you time later when you begin new drawings.

    A. Create a prototype drawing for use with decimal dimensions and using standard paper "A" size format. Include the following setups.

        1. Set *Units* to *Decimal* and *Precision* to **0.00**.
        2. Set *Limits* to **11** x **8.5**.
        3. Set *Snap* to **.25**.
        4. Set *Grid* to **1**.
        5. Set *LTSCALE* to **.5**.

6. Create the following *Layers*, assign the *Linetypes* as shown, and assign your choice of *colors*. Create any other layers you think you may need or any assigned by your instructor.

OBJECT	*continuous*
CONSTR	*continuous*
TEXT	*continuous*
TITLE	*continuous*
VPORTS	*continuous*
DIM	*continuous*
HIDDEN	*hidden*
CENTER	*center*
DASHED	*dashed*

7. Use *Saveas* and name the drawing **ASHEET**.

B. Using the drawing in the previous exercise (use *Open* if the drawing is not open), create a prototype for a standard engineering "B" size sheet. Set *Limits* to **17 x 11**. All other settings and layers are OK as they are. Use *Saveas* and assign the name **BSHEET**.

C. *Open* the **ASHEET** drawing (created in exercise A.) and create a prototype for a standard engineering "C" size sheet. Set *Limits* to **22 x 17**. Set *Snap* to **.5**. Keep all the other settings and layers as they are. Use *Saveas* and assign the name **CSHEET**.

D. *Open* the **ASHEET** drawing (created in exercise A.), only in this exercise create a prototype for a standard engineering "D" size sheet. Set *Limits* to **34 x 22**. All other settings and layers do not need to be changed. Use *Saveas* and assign the name **DSHEET**.

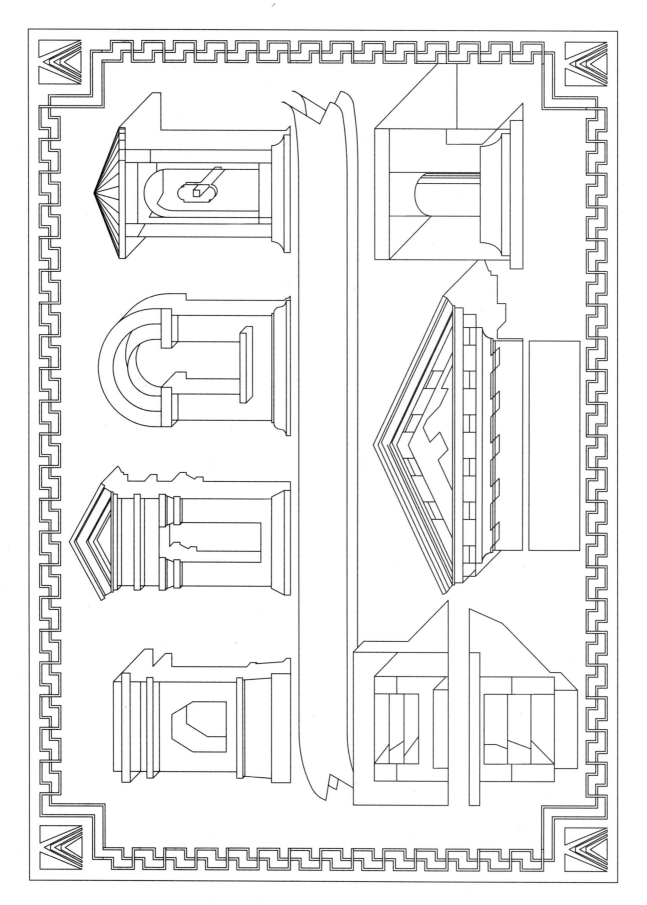

PSSHADOW.DWG Courtesy of Autodesk, Inc.

Chapter 14

PLOTTING

Chapter Objectives

After completing this chapter you should:

1. know the typical steps for plotting;

2. be able to invoke and use the *Plot Configuration* dialogue box;

3. be able to select from available plotting devices and set the paper size and orientation;

4. be able to specify what area of the drawing you want to plot;

5. be able to preview the plot before creating a plotted drawing;

6. be able to specify a scale for plotting a drawing;

7. know how to set up a drawing for plotting to a standard scale on a standard size sheet;

8. be able to use the Tables of Limits Settings to determine *Limits* and scale settings;

9. know that you can output a drawing to a raster file for use with other software programs.

BASICS

Plotting is accomplished from within AutoCAD by invoking the *Plot* command. Using the *Plot* or *Print* command by any command entry method invokes the *Plot Configuration* dialogue box (Fig. 14-1). You have complete control of plotting and printing using the dialogue box.

TYPICAL STEPS TO PLOTTING

Assuming the CAD system has been properly configured so the peripheral devices (plotters and/or printers) are functioning, the typical basic steps to plotting using the *Plot Configuration* dialogue box are listed below.

Figure 14-1

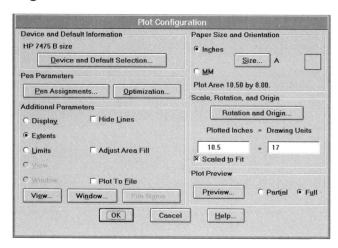

1. Use *Save* to ensure the drawing has been saved in its most recent form before plotting (just in case some problem arises while plotting).

2. Make sure the plotter or printer is turned on, has paper and pens loaded, and is ready to accept the plot information from the computer.

3. Invoke the *Plot Configuration* dialogue box.

4. Check the upper-left corner of the dialogue box to ensure that the intended device has been selected. If not, select the *Device and Default Selection* tile and make the desired choice.

5. Check the upper-right corner of the dialogue box to ensure that the desired paper size has been selected. If not, use the *Size...* tile to do so.

6. Only when necessary, change other options such as *Rotation and Origin* and *Pen Assignments*.

7. Determine and select which area of the drawing to plot: *Display, Extents, Limits, Window,* or *View*.

8. Enter the desired scale for the plot. If no standard scale is needed, toggle *Scaled to Fit* (so the **X** appears in the box).

9. Always *Preview* the plot to ensure that the drawing will be plotted as you expect. Select either a *Full* or *Partial* preview. If the preview does not display the plot as you intended, make the appropriate changes. Otherwise, needless time and media could be wasted.

10. If everything is OK, selecting the *OK* tile causes the drawing to be sent to the plotter for plotting.

USING THE *PLOT* COMMAND

PLOT

PULL-DOWN MENU	SCREEN MENU	TYPE IN	TABLET MENU
File *Print...*	*FILE* *Print:*	*PLOT* *or CTRL+P*	24,W

Invoking *Plot* or *Print* by any method normally invokes the *Plot Configuration* dialogue box (Fig. 14-1). (The *Plot Configuration* dialogue box can be suppressed by setting the *CMDDIA* system variable to **0**. This action displays a text screen instead and allows changing parameters by keyboard entry or plot script.)

Plot Configuration Dialogue Box

Many selections made from the *Plot Configuration* dialogue box allow you to change plotting parameters such as scale, paper size, pen assignments, rotation, and origin of the drawing on the sheet. The latest changes made to plotting options are saved (in the ACAD.CFG file) so they do not have to be re-entered the next time.

Device and Default Selection

Many devices (printers or plotters) can be configured for use with AutoCAD, and all configurations are saved for your selection. For example, you can have both an "A" size and a "D" size plotter as well as a laser printer, any one of which could be used to plot the current file. All devices are first configured through AutoCAD's *Config* command. (See the AutoCAD Installation Guide.)

Selecting the *Device and Default Selection* tile from the *Plot Configuration* dialogue box invokes the *Device and Default Selection* dialogue box Fig. 14-2). Highlighted near the top is displayed the currently selected device along with the other configured choices.

Figure 14-2

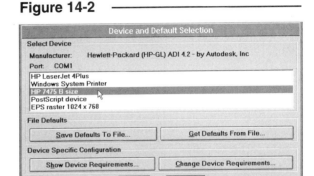

Since multiple devices can be used and there may also be several typical sets of parameters frequently used for each device (scale, pen assignments, etc.), multiple settings of plotting parameters can be saved and retrieved by using the *Save Defaults to File...* and *Get Defaults from File...* tiles in the dialogue box above. The settings can be saved as a .PCP (plotter configuration parameters) file and easily retrieved instead of having to make all of the selections each time you want to change parameters.

Pen Parameters

Selecting the *Pen Assignments* tile produces the dialogue box, enabling you to specify the pens used for plotting based on screen colors (Fig. 14-3). The screen color drives the plotting pen. Select one or several color numbers from the list (Color 1 is selected in the example figure). The *Pen, Ltype, Speed,* and *Width* parameters can then be set on the right side of the dialogue box. Selecting another color updates the values in the *Pen No., Linetype, Speed,* and *Pen Width* columns.

Figure 14-3

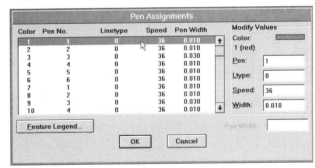

The parameters vary depending on the printer or plotter configured. Generally, multipen plotters and many printer drivers list the number of "pens" available (6 for the example). The *Linetype* column refers to plotter or printer linetypes which are usually set to 0 (continuous), so AutoCAD's supplied drawing linetypes can be used instead (select *Feature Legend* to see what linetypes are available for your device). Pen plotters allow speed adjustment of pen motion (you may want to decrease *Speed* if plotted lines appear "fuzzy"). Many printer drivers provide the capability to vary line width using the *Width* option. You should experiment with possibilities for your printing or plotting device.

Figure 14-4

The *Optimization* tile produces the dialogue box (Fig. 14-4) for specifying up to six levels of pen motion optimization (default levels are automatically set by most device drivers). Optimization is important for enabling pen plotters to draw lines on a sheet in the most efficient order.

Optimizing Pen Motion

☐ No optimization
☒ Adds endpoint swap
☒ Adds pen sorting
☒ Adds limited motion optimization
☒ Adds full motion optimization
☐ Adds elimination of overlapping horizontal or vertical vectors
☐ Adds elimination of overlapping diagonal vectors

OK   Cancel

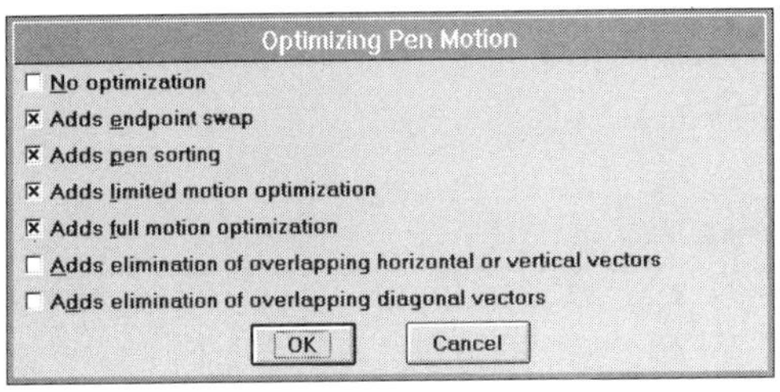

Additional Parameters (What to Plot)

You specify what part of the drawing you want to plot by selecting the desired button from the lower-left corner of the dialogue box (Fig. 14-1). The choices are listed below.

Display

This option plots the current display on the screen. If using viewports, it plots the current viewport display.

Extents

Plotting *Extents* is similar to *Zoom Extents*. This option plots the entire drawing (all objects), disregarding the *Limits*. Use the *Zoom Extents* command in the drawing to make sure the extents have been updated before using this plot option.

Limits

This selection plots the area defined by the *Limits* command (unless plotting a 3D object from other than the plan view).

View

With this option you can plot a view previously saved using the *View* command.

Window

Window allows you to plot any portion of the drawing. You must specify the window by **PICK**ing or supplying coordinates for the lower-left and upper-right corners.

Hide Lines

This option removes hidden lines (edges obscured from view) if you are plotting a 3D surface or solid model.

Adjust Area Fill

Using this option forces AutoCAD to adjust for solid-filled areas (*Plines, Solids*) by pulling the pen inside the filled area by one-half the pen width. Use this for critically accurate plots.

Plot to File

Choosing this option writes the plot to a file instead of making a plot. This action generally creates a .PLT file type for a plotter and .LST for printer. The format of the file depends on the device brand and model that is configured. The plot file can be printed or plotted later <u>without</u> AutoCAD, assuming the correct interpreter for the device is available.

Paper Size and Orientation

Inches or *MM* should be checked to correspond to the units used in the drawing. Assuming the drawing was created using the correct units, a scale for plotting can be calculated without inch to millimeter conversion.

The *Size...* tile invokes the dialogue box shown in Figure 14-5. You can select from the list of available paper sizes handled by the configured device. User sizes within the maximum plot area can also be defined.

Figure 14-5 ————————

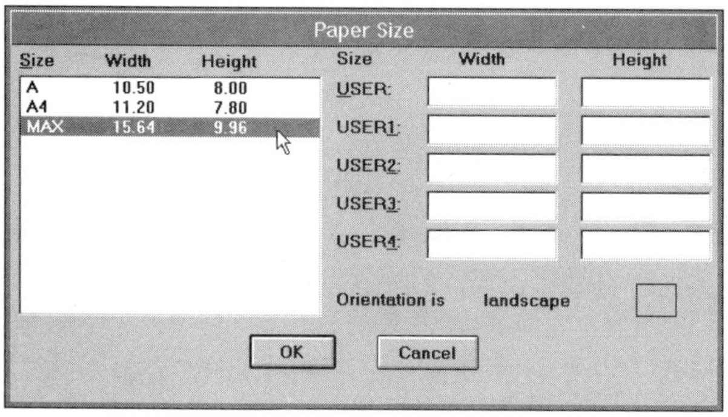

Scale, Rotation, and Origin

Selecting the *Rotation and Origin...* tile invokes the dialogue box shown in Figure 14-6. The drawing can be rotated on the paper in 90 degree intervals. The origin specified indicates the location on the paper from point 0,0 (the plotter or printer's home position) from which the plot will be made. Home position for plotters is the <u>lower-left</u> corner (landscape orientation) and for printers it is the <u>upper-left</u> corner of the paper (portrait orientation).

Figure 14-6 ————————

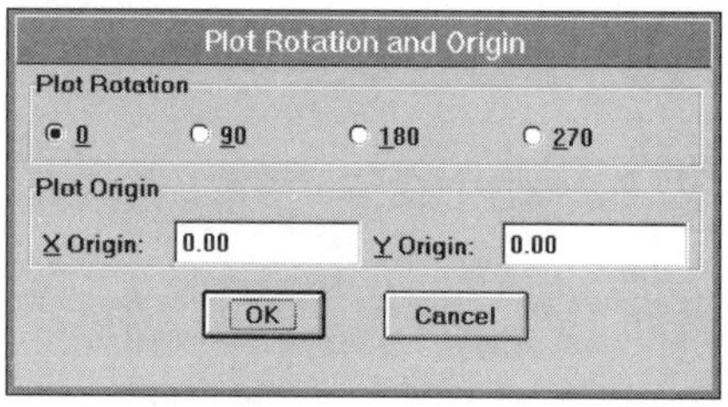

Scaled to Fit **or Plot to Scale**

Near the lower-right corner of the *Plot Configuration* dialogue box (Fig. 14-1) is the area where you designate the plot scale. You have two choices: scale the drawing to automatically fit on the paper or calculate and indicate a specific scale for the drawing to be plotted. By toggling the *Scaled to Fit* box, the drawing is automatically sized to fit on the sheet based on the specified area to plot (*Display, Limits, Extents,* etc.). If you want to plot the drawing to a specific scale, <u>remove the check</u> from the *Scaled to Fit* box and enter the desired ratio in the boxes under *Plotted Inches* (or *Plotted MM*) and *Drawing Units*. Decimals or fractions can be entered. For example, to prepare for a plot of one-half size (1/2"=1"), the following ratios can be entered to achieve a plot at the desired scale: 1=2, 1/2=1, or .5=1. For guidelines on plotting a drawing to scale, see Plotting to Scale in this chapter.

Plot Preview

Selecting the *Partial* tile (Fig. 14-1) displays the effective plotting area as shown in Figure 14-7. Use the *Partial* option of *Plot Preview* to get a quick check showing how the drawing will fit on the sheet. Two rectangles and two sets of dimensions are displayed; the "Paper size" is given and displayed in red and the "Effective area" is given and displayed in blue. The "Effective area" is based on the selection made in the *Additional Parameters* area of the plot dialogue, that is, *Display, Extents, Limits,* etc.

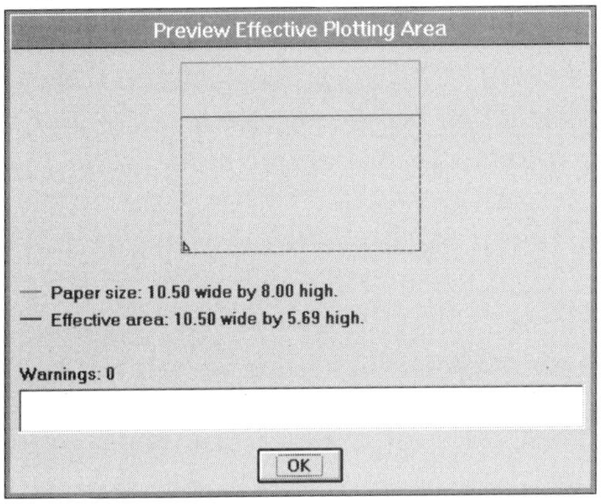

Selecting the *Full* option of *Plot Preview* displays the complete drawing as it will be plotted on the sheet (Fig. 14-8). This function is particularly helpful to ensure the drawing is plotted as you expect. The outer border represents the paper edge. As an additional aid, a *Pan and Zoom* option allows you to check detailed areas of the drawing before making the plot.

Figure 14-7

- Paper size: 10.50 wide by 8.00 high.
- Effective area: 10.50 wide by 5.69 high.

Warnings: 0

Figure 14-8

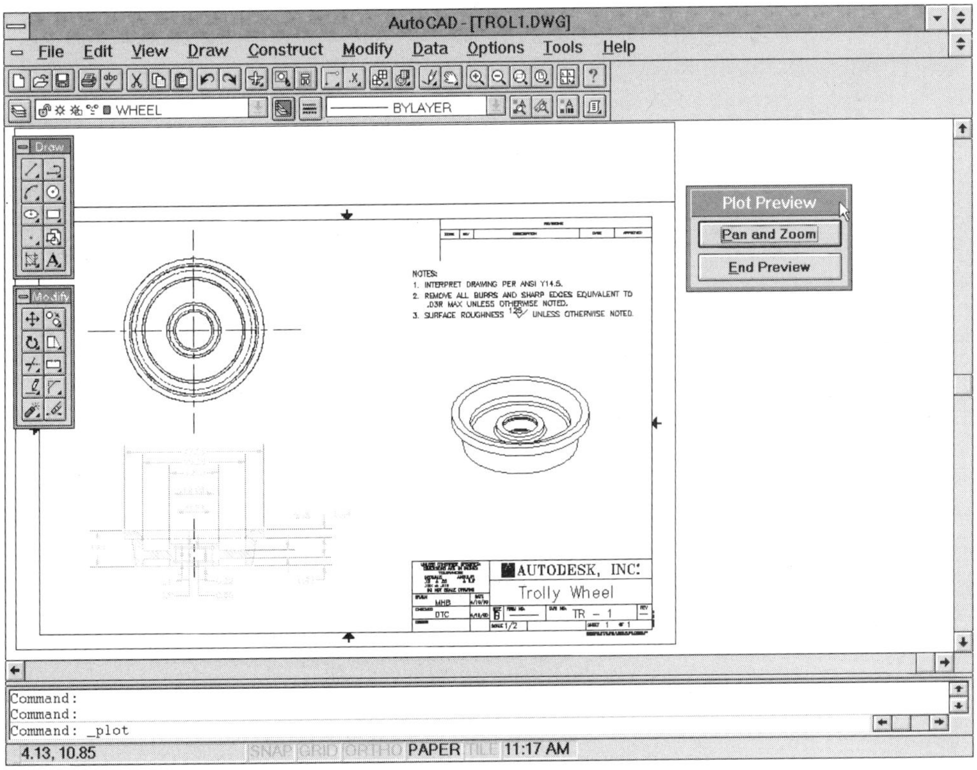

PLOTTING TO SCALE

When you create a <u>manual</u> drawing, a scale is determined before you can begin drawing. The scale is determined by the proportion between the size of the object on the paper and the actual size of the object. You then complete the drawing in that scale so that the actual object is proportionally reduced or enlarged to fit on the paper.

With a <u>CAD</u> drawing you are not restricted to a sheet of paper while drawing, so the geometry is created full size. Set *Limits* to provide an appropriate amount of drawing space; then the geometry can be drawn using the <u>actual dimensions</u> of the object. The resulting drawing on the CAD system is a virtual full-size dimensional replica of the actual object. Not until the CAD drawing is <u>plotted</u> on a fixed size sheet of paper, however, is it <u>scaled</u> to fit on the sheet.

Plotting an AutoCAD drawing to scale usually involves considering the intended sheet size and plot scale when specifying *Limits* during the initial drawing setup. The scale for plotting is based on the proportion of the paper size to the *Limits* (the reciprocal of the "drawing scale factor").

For example, if you want to plot on an 11" x 8.5" sheet, you can set the *Limits* to 22 x 17 (2 x the sheet size). The value of **2** is then the drawing scale factor, and the plot scale (to enter in the *Plot Configuration* dialogue box) is **1/2** or **1=2** (the reciprocal of the drawing scale factor). If, in another case, the calculated drawing scale factor is **4**, then **1/4** or **1=4** would be the plot scale entered to achieve a drawing plotted at 1/4 actual size.

In order to calculate *Limits* and drawing scale factors correctly, you must know the standard paper sizes.

Standard Paper Sizes

<u>Size</u>	<u>Engineering (")</u>	<u>Architectural (")</u>
A	8.5 x 11	9 x 12
B	11 x 17	12 x 18
C	17 x 22	18 x 24
D	22 x 34	24 x 36
E	34 x 44	36 x 48

<u>Size</u>	<u>Metric (mm)</u>
A4	210 x 297
A3	297 x 420
A2	420 x 594
A1	594 x 841
A0	841 x 1189

Guidelines for Plotting to Scale

Plotting to scale preferably begins with the appropriate initial drawing setup. Your choice for *Limits* determines the "drawing scale factor," which in turn is used to determine the plot scale or vice versa. Even though *Limits* can be changed and plot scale calculated at <u>any time</u> in the drawing process, it is usually done in the first few steps. Following are suggested steps for setting up a drawing for plotting to scale.

1. Set *Units* (*Decimal, Architectural, Engineering*, etc.) and *precision* to be used in the drawing.

2. Set *Limits* to a size, allowing geometry creation full size. *Limits* should be <u>set to the sheet size</u> used for plotting <u>times a factor</u>, if necessary, that provides enough area for drawing. This factor (proportion of the new *Limits* to the sheet size) becomes the "<u>drawing scale factor</u>."

$$DSF = \frac{Limits}{sheet\ size}$$

You must also use a scale factor value that will yield a standard drawing scale (1/2"=1", 1/8"=1', 1:50, etc.), instead of a scale that is not a standard (1/3"=1", 3/5"=1', 1:23, etc.). See the Tables of Limit Settings for standard drawing scales.

3. The "drawing scale factor" is used as the scale factor (at least a starting point) for changing all size-related variables (*LTSCALE, DIMSCALE*, Hatch Pattern Scale, etc.). The <u>reciprocal</u> of the drawing scale factor is the plot scale to enter in the *Plot Configuration* dialogue box.

$$Plot\ Scale = \frac{1}{DSF}$$

4. If the drawing is to be created using millimeter dimensions, set *Units* to *Decimal* and use metric values for the sheet size. In this way, the reciprocal of the drawing scale factor is the plot scale, the same as feet and inch drawings. However, multiply the drawing's scale factor by 25.4 (25.4mm = 1") to determine the factor for changing all size-related variables (*LTSCALE, DIMSCALE*, etc.).

$$DSF(mm) = \frac{Limits}{sheet\ size} \times 25.4$$

5. If drawing a border on the sheet, its maximum size cannot exceed the *Plot Area*. The *Plot Area* is given near the upper-right corner of the *Plot Configuration* dialogue box, but the values can be different for different devices. Since plotters or printers do not draw all the way to the edge of the paper, the border should not be drawn outside of the *Plot Area*. Generally, approximately 1/2" offset from each edge of the paper is required. To determine the distance in from the edge of the *Limits* after new *Limits* have been set, multiply 1/2 times the "drawing scale factor." More precisely, calculate the distance based on the *Plot Area* listed for the current device and multiply by the "drawing scale factor."

The **Tables of Limit Settings** (starting on page 187) help to illustrate this point. Sheet sizes are listed in the first column. The next series of columns from left to right indicate incremental changes in *Limits* and proportional changes in Scale Factor.

Simplifying the process of plotting to scale and calculating *Limits* and "drawing scale factor" can be accomplished by preparing prototype drawings. One method is to create a prototype for each sheet size that is used in the lab or office. In this way, the CAD operator begins the session by selecting the prototype drawing representing the sheet size and then multiples <u>those</u> *Limits* by some factor to achieve the desired *Limits* and drawing scale factor. Another method is to create a separate prototype drawing for each scale that you expect to use for plotting. In this way a prototype drawing can be selected with the final *Limits*, drawing scale factor, and plot scale already specified or calculated. This method requires creating a separate prototype for each expected scale <u>and</u> sheet size. (See Chapter 13 for help creating prototype drawings.)

TABLES OF *LIMITS* SETTINGS

Rather than making calculations of *Limits*, drawing scale factor, and plot scale for each drawing, the Tables of Limits Settings on the following pages can be used to make calculating easier. There a four tables, one for each of the following applications:

The tables can be used in either of two ways:

1. *Scale*   Assuming you know the scale you want to use, look along the <u>top</u> row to find the desired <u>scale</u> that you eventually want to plot. Find the desired <u>paper size</u> by looking down the <u>left</u> column. The intersection of the row and column should yield the *Limits* settings to use to achieve the desired plot scale.

2. *Limits*   Calculate how much space (minimum *Limits*) you require to create the drawing actual size. Look down the left column of the appropriate table to find the <u>paper size</u> you want to use for plotting. Look along that row to find the next larger <u>*Limits*</u> settings than your required area. The <u>scale</u> to use for the plot is located on top of that column.

MECHANICAL TABLE OF *LIMITS* SETTINGS
(X axis x Y axis)

Paper Size (Inches)	Drawing Scale Factor 1 / Scale 1"=1" / Plot 1=1	1.33 / 3/4" = 1" / 3 = 4	2 / 1/2" = 1" / 1 = 2	2.67 / 3/8" = 1" / 3 = 8	4 / 1/4" = 1" / 1 = 4	5.33 / 3/16" = 1" / 3 = 16	8 / 1/8" = 1" / 1 = 8
A 11 x 8.5 In	11.0 x 8.5	14.4 x 11.3	22.0 x 17.0	29.3 x 22.7	44.0 x 34.0	58.7 x 45.3	88.0 x 68.0
B 17 x 11 In	17.0 x 11.0	22.7 x 14.7	34.0 x 22.0	45.3 x 29.3	68.0 x 44.0	90.7 x 58.7	136.0 x 88.0
C 22 x 17 In	22.0 x 17.0	29.3 x 22.7	44.0 x 34.0	58.7 x 45.3	88.0 x 68.0	117.0 x 90.7	176.0 x 136.0
D 34 x 22 In	34.0 x 22.0	45.3 x 29.3	68.0 x 44.0	90.7 x 58.7	136.0 x 88.0	181.0 x 117.0	272.0 x 176.0
E 44 x 34 In	44.0 x 34.0	58.7 x 45.3	88.0 x 68.0	117.0 x 90.7	176.0 x 136.0	235.0 x 181.0	352.0 x 272.0

ARCHITECTURAL TABLE OF *LIMITS* SETTINGS
(X axis x Y axis)

Paper Size (Inches)	Drawing Scale Factor 12 / Scale 1" = 1' / Plot 1 = 12	16 / 3/4" = 1' / 1 = 16	24 / 1/2" = 1' / 1 = 24	32 / 3/8" = 1' / 1 = 32	48 / 1/4" = 1' / 1 = 48	96 / 1/8" = 1' / 1 = 96
A 12 x 9 Ft	12 x 9	16.3 x 12	24 x 18	32 x 24	48 x 36	96 x 72
In	144 x 108	192 x 144	288 x 216	384 x 288	576 x 432	1152 x 864
B 18 x 12 Ft	18 x 12	24 x 16	36 x 24	48 x 32	72 x 48	144 x 96
In	216 x 144	288 x 192	432 x 288	576 x 384	864 x 576	1728 x 1152
C 24 x 18 Ft	24 x 18	32 x 24	48 x 36	64 x 48	96 x 72	192 x 144
In	288 x 216	384 x 288	576 x 432	768 x 576	1152 x 864	2304 x 1728
D 36 x 24 Ft	36 x 24	48 x 32	72 x 48	96 x 64	144 x 96	288 x 192
In	432 x 288	576 x 384	864 x 576	1152 x 768	1728 x 1152	3456 x 2304
E 48 x 36 Ft	48 x 36	64 x 48	96 x 72	128 x 96	192 x 144	384 x 288
In	576 x 432	768 x 576	1152 x 864	1536 x 1152	2304 x 1728	4608 x 3465

METRIC TABLE OF *LIMITS* SETTINGS
FOR METRIC SHEET SIZES
(X axis x Y axis)

Paper Size (mm)	Drawing Scale Factor 25.4 / Scale 1:1 / Plot 1 = 1	50.8 / 1:2 / 1 = 2	127 / 1:5 / 1 = 5	254 / 1:10 / 1 = 10	508 / 1:20 / 1 = 20	1270 / 1:50 / 1 = 50	2540 / 1:100 / 1 = 100
A4 297 x 210 mm	297 x 210	594 x 420	1485 x 1050	2970 x 2100	5940 x 4200	14,850 x 10,500	29,700 x 21,000
m	.297 x .210	.594 x .420	1.485 x 1.050	2.97 x 2.10	5.94 x 4.20	14.85 x 10.50	29.70 x 21.00
A3 420 x 297 mm	420 x 297	840 x 594	2100 x 1485	4200 x 2970	8400 x 5940	21,000 x 14,850	42,000 x 29,700
m	.420 x .297	.840 x .594	2.100 x 1.485	4.20 x 2.97	8.40 x 5.94	21.00 x 14.85	42.00 x 29.70
A2 594 x 420 mm	594 x 420	1188 x 840	2970 x 2100	5940 x 4200	11,880 x 8400	29,700 x 21,000	59,400 x 42,000
m	.594 x .420	1.188 x .840	2.970 x 2.100	5.94 x 4.20	11.88 x 8.40	29.70 x 21.00	59.40 x 42.00
A1 841 x 594 mm	841 x 594	1682 x 1188	4205 x 2970	8410 x 5940	16,820 x 11,880	42,050 x 29,700	84,100 x 59,400
m	.841 x .594	1.682 x 1.188	4.205 x 2.970	8.41 x 5.94	16.82 x 11.88	42.05 x 29.70	84.10 x 59.40
A0 1189 x 841 mm	1189 x 841	2378 x 1682	5945 x 4205	11,890 x 8410	23,780 x 16,820	59,450 x 42,050	118,900 x 84,100
m	1.189 x .841	2.378 x 1.682	5.945 x 4.205	11.89 x 8.41	23.78 x 16.82	59.45 x 42.05	118.9 x 84.10

METRIC TABLE OF *LIMITS* SETTINGS
FOR ENGINEERING (8.5 x 11 Format) SHEET SIZES
(X axis x Y axis)

Paper Size (mm)	Drawing Scale Factor 25.4 / Scale 1:1 / Plot 1 = 1	50.8 / 1:2 / 1 = 2	127 / 1:5 / 1 = 5	254 / 1:10 / 1 = 10	508 / 1:20 / 1 = 20	1270 / 1:50 / 1 = 50	2540 / 1:100 / 1 = 100
A 279.4 x 215.9 mm / m	279.4 x 215.9 / 0.2794 x 0.2159	558.8 x 431.8 / 0.5588 x 0.4318	1397 x 1079.5 / 1.397 x 1.0795	2794 x 2159 / 2.794 x 2.159	5588 x 4318 / 5.588 x 4.318	13970 x 10795 / 13.97 x 10.795	27940 x 21590 / 27.94 x 21.59
B 431.8 x 279.4 mm / m	431.8 x 279.4 / 0.4318 x 0.2794	863.6 x 558.8 / 0.8636 x 0.5588	2159 x 1397 / 2.159 x 1.397	4318 x 2794 / 4.318 x 2.794	8636 x 5588 / 8.636 x 5.588	21590 x 13970 / 21.59 x 13.97	43180 x 27940 / 43.18 x 27.94
C 558.8 x 431.8 mm / m	558.8 x 431.8 / 0.5588 x 0.4318	1117.6 x 863.6 / 1.1176 x 0.8636	2794 x 2159 / 2.794 x 2.159	5588 x 4318 / 5.588 x 4.318	11176 x 8636 / 11.176 x 86.36	27940 x 21590 / 27.94 x 21.59	55880 x 43180 / 55.88 x 43.18
D 863.6 x 558.8 mm / m	863.6 x 558.8 / 0.8636 x 0.5588	1727.2 x 1117.6 / 1.7272 x 1.1176	4318 x 2794 / 4.318 x 2.794	8636 x 5588 / 8.636 x 5.588	17272 x 11176 / 17.272 x 11.176	43180 x 27940 / 43.18 x 27.94	86360 x 55880 / 86.36 x 55.88
E 1117.6 x 863.6 mm / m	1117.6 x 863.6 / 1.1176 x 0.8636	2235.2 x 1727.2 / 2.2352 x 1.7272	5588 x 4318 / 5.588 x 4.318	11176 x 8636 / 11.176 x 8.636	22352 x 17272 / 22.352 x 17.272	55880 x 43180 / 55.88 x 43.18	111760 x 86360 / 111.76 x 86.36

CIVIL TABLE OF *LIMITS* SETTINGS
(For Engineering Units)
(X axis x Y axis)

Paper Size (Inches)		Drawing Scale Factor 120 Scale 1" = 10' Plot 1 = 120	240 1" = 20' 1 = 240	360 1" = 30' 1 = 360	480 1" = 40' 1 = 480	600 1" = 50' 1 = 600
A. 11 x 8.5	In	1320 x 1020	2640 x 2040	3960 x 3060	5280 x 4080	6600 x 5100
	Ft	110 x 85	170 x 110	330 x 255	440 x 340	550 x 425
B. 17 x 11	In	2040 x 1320	4080 x 2640	6120 x 3960	8160 x 5280	10,200 x 6600
	Ft	170 x 110	340 x 220	510 x 330	680 x 440	850 x 550
C. 22 x 17	In	2640 x 2040	5280 x 4080	7920 x 6120	10,560 x 8160	13,200 x 10,200
	Ft	220 x 170	440 x 340	660 x 510	880 x 680	1100 x 85
D. 34 x 22	In	4080 x 2640	8160 x 5280	12,240 x 7920	16,320 x 10,560	20,400 x 13,200
	Ft	340 x 220	680 x 440	1020 x 660	1360 x 880	1700 x 1100
E. 44 x 34	In	5280 x 4080	10,560 x 8160	15,840 x 12,240	21,120 x 16,320	26,400 x 20,400
	Ft	440 x 340	880 x 680	1320 x 1020	1760 x 1360	2200 x 1700

Examples for Plotting to Scale

Following are several hypothetical examples of drawings that can be created using the Guidelines for Plotting to Scale. As you read the examples, try to follow the logic and check the Tables of Limits Settings.

A. A one-view drawing of a mechanical part that is 40" in length is to be drawn requiring an area of approximately 40" x 30", and the drawing is to be plotted on an 8.5" x 11" sheet. The prototype drawing *Limits* are preset to 0,0 and 11,8.5. (AutoCAD's default *Limits* are set to 0,0 and 12,9, which represents an uncut sheet size. Prototype *Limits* of 11 x 8.5 are more practical in this case.) The expected plot scale is 1/4"=1". The following steps are used to calculate the new *Limits*.

1. *Units* are set to *decimal*. Each unit represents 1.00 inches.
2. Multiplying the *Limits* of 11 x 8.5 by a factor of **4**, the new *Limits* should be set to **44 x 34**, allowing adequate space for the drawing. The "drawing scale factor" is **4**.
3. All size-related variable default values (*LTSCALE, DIMSCALE*, etc.) are multiplied by **4**. The plot scale is entered in the *Plot Configuration* dialogue box (*Plotted inches = Drawing units*) as **1=4**, **1/4=1** or **.25=1** to achieve a plotted drawing of 1/4"=1".

B. A floorplan of a residence will occupy 60' x 40'. The drawing is to be plotted on a "D" size architectural sheet (24" x 36"). No prepared prototype drawing exists, so the standard AutoCAD default drawing (12 x 9) *Limits* are used. The expected plot scale is 1/2"=1'.

1. *Units* are set to *Architectural*. Each unit represents 1".
2. The floorplan size is converted to inches (60' x 40' = 720" x 480"). The sheet size of 36" x 24" (or 3' x 2') is multiplied by **24** to arrive at *Limits* of **864" x 576"** (72' x 48'), allowing adequate area for the floor plan. The *Limits* are changed to those values.
3. All default values of size-related variables (*LTSCALE, DIMSCALE,* etc.) are multiplied by **24**, the drawing scale factor. The plot scale is entered in the *Plot Configuration* dialogue box (*Plotted inches = Drawing units*) as **1=24**, **1/2=12**, (12 units = 1') or **1/24=1** to achieve a drawing of 1/2"=1' scale.

C. A roadway cloverleaf is to be laid out to fit in an acquired plot of land measuring 1500' x 1000'. The drawing will be plotted on "D" size engineering sheet (34" x 22"). A prototype drawing with *Limits* set equal to the sheet size is used. The expected plot scale is 1"=50'.

1. *Units* are set to *Engineering* (feet and decimal inches). Each unit represents 1.00".
2. The sheet size of 34" x 22" (or 2.833' x 1.833') is multiplied by **600** to arrive at *Limits* of **20400" x 13200"** (1700' x 1100'), allowing enough drawing area for the site. The *Limits* are changed to **1700' x 1100'**.
3. All default values of size-related variables (*LTSCALE, DIMSCALE*, etc.) are multiplied by **600**, the drawing scale factor. The plot scale is entered in the *Plot Configuration* dialogue box (*Plotted inches = Drawing units*) as **1=600** to achieve a drawing of 1"=50' scale.

NOTE: Many civil engineering firms use one unit in AutoCAD to represent one foot. This simplifies the problem of using decimal feet (10 parts/foot rather than 12 parts/foot); however, problems occur if architectural layouts are inserted or otherwise combined with civil work.

D. Three views of a small machine part are to be drawn and dimensioned in millimeters. An area of 480mm x 360mm is needed for the views and dimensions. The part is to be plotted on an A4 size sheet. The expected plot scale is 1:2.

1. *Units* are set to *decimal*. Each unit represents 1.00 millimeters.
2. Setting the *Limits* exactly to the sheet size (297 x 210) would not allow enough area for the drawing. The sheet size is multiplied by a factor of **2** to yield *Limits* of **594 x 420** providing the necessary 480 x 360 area.
3. The plot scale entered in the *Plot Configuration* dialogue box (*Plotted inches = Drawing units*) is **1=2** or **1/2=1** to make a finished plot of 1:2 scale. Since this drawing is metric, the "drawing scale factor" for changing all size-related variable default values (*LTSCALE, DIMSCALE*, etc.) is multiplied by 25.4, or 2 x 25.4 = approximately **50**.

Raster Output Files

There are several ways that you can create a raster file from the AutoCAD image on the screen. Raster files describe an image by mapping rows and columns of dots and defining the color of each dot in the matrix. (AutoCAD drawing files and plot files define a vector file—a description of lines, arcs, and circles, etc., defined by the coordinates of the endpoints, radii, center points, and so on.) Often it is helpful to convert AutoCAD drawing files or other screen images to raster files because numerous graphics, publishing, and word processing software programs accept and manipulate standard raster formats.

Raster file output can be generated from AutoCAD in three ways:

1. Using the *Export* command (see *Export*, Chapter 2)
2. Using the *Config* command to configure a raster output converter as a "plotter" (see below)
3. Using the *Saveimg* command to save the drawing, entire screen area, or rendering (see Chapter 41, Rendering)

Using a Configured Raster File Converter as a "Plotter"

Using the *Config* command (see AutoCAD Installation Guide for options and details of the *Config* command), you can specify that you want to keep a raster file converter as one of your configured plotting devices. From the list of available plotters, select this option:

   14. Raster file export ADI 4.2 - by Autodesk, Inc

Selecting option 14 displays the following screens.

   Supported models:

      1. 320 x 200   (CGA/MCGA Colour)
      2. 640 x 200   (CGA Monochrome)
      3. 640 x 350   (EGA)
      4. 640 x 400
      5. 640 x 480   (VGA)
      6. 720 x 540
      7. 800 x 600
      8. 1024 x 768
      9. 1152 x 900   (Sun standard)
      10. 1600 x 1280 (Sun hi-res)
      11. User-defined

   Enter selection, 1 to 11 <1>:

You can export the drawing in any of the following raster file formats. Please select the format you prefer.

1. GIF (CompuServe Graphics Interchange Format)
2. X Window dump (xwd compatible)
3. Jef Poskanzer's Portable Bitmap Toolkit Formats
4. Microsoft Windows Device-independent Bitmap (.BMP)
5. TrueVision TGA Format
6. Z-Soft PCX Format
7. Sun Rasterfile
8. Flexible Image Transfer System (FITS)
9. Encapsulated PostScript (Adobe-2.0 EPSF-2.0)
10. TIFF (Tag Image File Format)
11. FAX Image (Group 3 Encoding)
12. Amiga IFF / ILBM Format

Enter selection, 1 to 12 <1>:

Saving your changes adds the file converter (with the name you specify) to your list of configured devices that you can choose from in the *Plot Control* dialogue box under *Device and Default Selection* (see Fig. 14-2, last entry in the list).

CHAPTER EXERCISES

1. *Open* the **GASKETA** drawing that you created in Chapter 9 Exercises. What are the drawing *Limits*?

   A. *Plot* the drawing *Extents* on an 11" x 8.5" sheet. Select the *Scale to Fit* box.
   B. Next, *Plot* the drawing *Limits* on the same size sheet. *Scale to Fit.*
   C. Now, *Plot* the drawing *Limits* as before but plot the drawing at **1=1**. Measure the drawing and compare the accuracy with the dimensions given in the exercise in Chapter 9.
   D. Compare the three plots. What are the differences and why did they occur? (When you finish, there is no need to *Save* the changes.)

2. This exercise requires facilities for plotting an engineering "C" size sheet. *Open* drawing **CH12EX3**. Check to ensure the *Limits* are set at **22 x 17**. *Plot* the *Limits* at **1=1**. Measure the plot for accuracy by comparing with the dimensions given for the exercise in Chapter 12. To refresh your memory, this exercise involved adjusting the *LTSCALE* factor. Does the *LTSCALE* in the drawing yield hidden line dashes of 1/8" (for the long lines) on the plot? If not, make the *LTSCALE* adjustment and plot again.

3. For this exercise, you will use a previously created prototype drawing to set up a drawing for plotting to scale. (The drawing will be used in later chapters for creating geometry.) If you know the final plot scale and sheet size, you can plan for the plot during the drawing setup. The *Limits* and other scale-related factors for plotting can be set at this phase. Follow the steps below.

   A drawing of a hammer is needed. The overall dimensions of the hammer are 12 1/2" x about 5". The drawing will be plotted on an 11" x 8.5" sheet. *Open* the prototype **ASHEET** and assign the name **HAMMER**. Follow these steps.

   A. Set *Units* to *Fractional* and *Precision* to **1/16**.
   B. Set *Snap* to **1/8** (or .125).

    C. Set *Grid* to **1/2** (or .5).

    D. Since the geometry will not fit within *Limits* of 11 x 8.5, plotting at full size (1=1) will not be possible. In order to make a plot to a standard scale and show the geometry at the largest possible size on an 11" x 8.5" sheet, consult the Mechanical Table of Limits Settings to determine *Limits* settings for the drawing and a scale for plotting. Find the values for setting *Limits* for a plot at **3/4=1** scale. Set *Limits* appropriately; then *Zoom All*.

    E. An *LTSCALE* of .5 (previously set) creates hidden lines with the 1/8" standard dashes when plotted at 1=1. Therefore, multiply the *LTSCALE* of .5 times the scale factor indicated in the table.

    F. *Save* the drawing.

4. Create a new prototype for architectural applications to plot at 1/8"=1' scale on a "D" size sheet. Open the prototype **DSHEET** and assign the name **D-8-AR**. Set *Units* to *Architectural*. Use the Architectural Table of Limits Settings to determine and set the new *Limits* for a "D" size sheet to plot at **1/8"=1'**. Multiply the existing *LTSCALE* (.5) times the scale factor shown. Turn *Snap* and *Grid* off. *Save* the drawing.

5. Create a new prototype for metric applications to plot at 1:2 scale (1/2 size) on an "A" size sheet. Open the prototype **ASHEET** and assign the name **A-2-M**. Use the Metric Table of Limit Settings to determine and set the new *Limits* for an "A" size sheet to plot at **1=2**. Multiply the existing *LTSCALE*, *Snap*, and *Grid* times the scale factor shown. *Save* the drawing.

6. Create a new prototype for civil engineering applications to plot at 1"=20' scale on a "C" size sheet. Open the prototype **CSHEET** and assign the name **C-20-CV**. Set *Units* to *Engineering*. Use the Civil Table of Limits Settings to determine and set the new *Limits* for a "C" size sheet to plot at **1"=20'**. Multiply the existing *LTSCALE* (.5) times the scale factor shown. Turn *Snap* and *Grid* Off. *Save* the drawing.

7. *Open* the **MANFCELL** drawing from Chapter 10. Check to make sure that the *Limit* settings are at **0,0** and **40',30'**. Make two plots of this drawing on your plotter, according to the instructions.

    A. Make one plot of the drawing using a standard architectural scale. The scale you use is your choice and should be based on the sheet sizes available, as well as the existing geometry size. *Plot* the drawing *Limits*. You may have to alter the *Limits* in order to plot the *Limits* to a standard scale. Use the Architectural Table of Limits settings for guidance.

    B. Make one plot of the drawing using a standard civil engineering scale. Again, the choice of scale is yours and should be based on your available sheet sizes as well as the existing geometry. *Plot* the drawing *Limits*. You may have to alter the *Limits* for this plot also in order to plot the *Limits* to a standard scale. Use the Civil Table of Limits Settings for guidance.

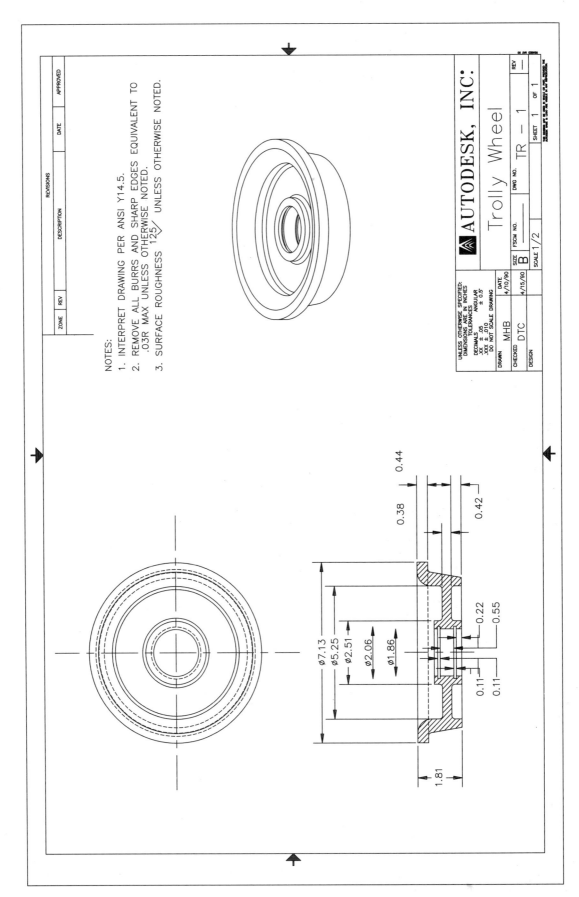

NOTES:
1. INTERPRET DRAWING PER ANSI Y14.5.
2. REMOVE ALL BURRS AND SHARP EDGES EQUIVALENT TO .03R MAX UNLESS OTHERWISE NOTED.
3. SURFACE ROUGHNESS 125 UNLESS OTHERWISE NOTED.

REVISIONS			
ZONE	REV	DESCRIPTION	DATE	APPROVED

AUTODESK, INC:

Trolly Wheel

UNLESS OTHERWISE SPECIFIED: DIMENSIONS ARE IN INCHES				REV
TOLERANCES		FSCM NO.	DWG NO.	—
DECIMALS ANGULAR			TR - 1	
.XX ± .05 ± 0.5°		SIZE B		
.XXX ± .010				SHEET 1 OF 1
DO NOT SCALE DRAWING		SCALE 1/2		

DRAWN	MHB	DATE 4/10/90
CHECKED	DTC	4/15/90
DESIGN		

FSCM NO. ____

0.44
0.38
0.42
0.22
0.55
0.11
0.11
Ø7.13
Ø5.25
Ø2.51
Ø2.06
Ø1.86
1.81

TROL1.DWG Courtesy of Autodesk, Inc.

Chapter 15

DRAW COMMANDS II

Chapter Objectives

After completing this chapter you should:

1. be able to create *Plines* using all of the options;

2. be able to create *Polygons* by the *Circumscribe*, *Inscribe*, and *Edge* methods;

3. be able to create *Ellipses* using the *Axis End* method, the *Center* method, and the *Arc* method;

4. be able to create *Rectangles* by PICKing two corners;

5. be able to create construction lines using the *Xline* and *Ray* commands;

6. be able to use *Donut* to create circles with width;

7. be able to use the *Solid* command to create a filled 2D shape with three or four straight edges;

8. be able to use the *Sketch* command to create "freehand" sketch lines and to use the *SKPOLY* variable to create *Sketch* lines combined into one *Polyline* object;

9. be able to create *Spline* curves passing exactly through the selected points;

10. be able to draw multiple parallel lines with *Mline* and to create multi-line styles with *Mstyle*.

BASICS

Remember that *Draw* commands create AutoCAD objects. The draw commands addressed in this chapter create more complex objects than those discussed in Chapter 8, Draw Commands I. The draw commands covered previously (*Line, Circle, Arc*) were obviously composed of one object, whereas, many of the shapes created by the following commands <u>appear</u> to be composed of several objects, but each shape is actually treated by AutoCAD as <u>one object</u>.

    Pline, Polygon, Ellipse, Rectangle, Xline, Ray, Donut, Solid, Sketch, Spline, and *Mline.*

COMMANDS

PLINE or
POLYLINE

PULL-DOWN MENU	SCREEN MENU	TYPE IN	TABLET MENU
Draw *Polyline*	*DRAW1* *Pline:*	*PLINE* *or PL*	*10,K*

A *Polyline* (or *Pline*) has special features that make this object more versatile than a *Line*. There are three features that are most noticeable when first using *Pline*s:

1. A *Pline* can have a specified *width*, whereas, a *Line* has no width.
2. Several *Pline* segments created with one *Pline* command are treated by AutoCAD as <u>one</u> object, whereas, individual line segments created with one use of the *Line* command are individual objects.
3. A *Pline* can contain arc segments.

Figure 15-1 illustrates *Pline* vs. *Line* and *Arc* comparisons.

The *Pline* command begins with the same prompt as *Line*; however, <u>after</u> the "From point" is established, the *Pline* options are accessible.

Figure 15-1 —————

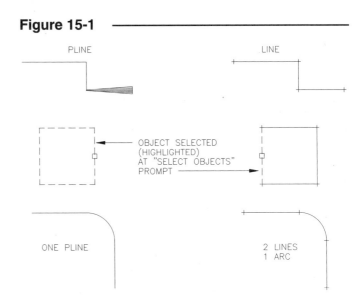

Command: **pline**
From point: **PICK** or (**coordinates**)
Arc/Close/Halfwidth/Length/Undo/Width/ <Endpoint of Line>: **PICK** or (**coordinates**) or (**letter**)

The options and descriptions follow.

Figure 15-2

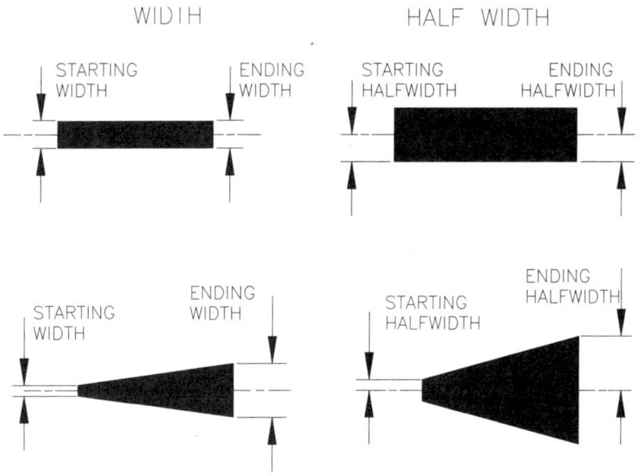

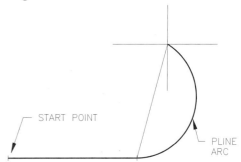

Width

You can use this option to specify starting and ending widths. Width is measured perpendicular to the centerline of the *Pline* segment (Fig. 15-2). *Plines* can be tapered by specifying different starting and ending widths.

Halfwidth

This option allows specifying half of the *Pline* width. *Plines* can be tapered by specifying different starting and ending widths (Fig. 15-2).

Arc

This option (by default) creates an arc segment in a manner similar to the *Arc Continuous* method (see *Arc Contin* in Chapter 8) (Fig. 15-3). Any of several other methods are possible (see Polygon Arc Segments).

Figure 15-3

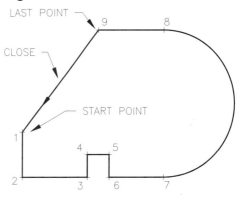

Close

The *Close* option creates the closing segment connecting the first and last points specified with the current *Pline* command as shown in Figure 15-4.

This option can also be used to close a group of connected *Pline* segments into one continuous *Pline*. (A *Pline* closed by PICKing points has a specific start and end point.) A *Pline* *Closed* by this method has special properties if you use *Pedit* for *Pline* editing or if you use the *Fillet* command with the *Pline* option (see *Pedit* Chapter 16 and *Fillet* Chapter 17).

Figure 15-4

Length

Length draws a *Pline* segment at the same angle as, and connected to, the previous segment and uses a length that you specify. If the previous segment was an arc, *Length* makes the current segment tangent to the ending direction (Fig. 15-5).

Undo

Using this option will *Undo* the last *Pline* segment. It can be used repeatedly to undo multiple segments.

Figure 15-5

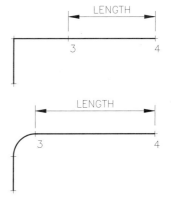

Polyline Arc Segments

When the *Arc* option of *Pline* is selected, the prompt changes to provide the various methods for construction of arcs:

Angle/CEnter/CLose/Direction/Halfwidth/Line/Radius/Second pt/Undo/Width/<Endpoint of Arc>:

Angle

You can draw an arc segment by specifying the included angle (a negative value indicates a clockwise direction for arc generation).

CEnter

This option allows you to specify a specific center point for the arc segment.

CLose

This option closes the *Pline* group with an arc segment.

Direction

Direction allows you to specify an explicit starting direction rather than using the ending direction of the previous segment as a default.

Line

This switches back to the line options of the *Pline* command.

Radius

You can specify an arc radius using this option.

Second pt

Using this option allows specification of a 3-point arc.

Because a shape created with one *Pline* command is <u>one object</u>, manipulation of the shape is generally easier than with several objects. Editing *Plines* is accomplished by using the *Pedit* command. As an alternative, *Plines* can be "broken" back down into individual objects with *Explode*.

Drawing and editing *Plines* can be somewhat involved. As an alternative, you can draw a shape as you would normally with *Line, Circle, Arc, Trim,* etc., and then <u>convert</u> the shape to one *Pline* object using *Pedit*. (See Chapter 16 for details.)

POLYGON

PULL-DOWN MENU	SCREEN MENU	TYPE IN	TABLET MENU
Draw *Polygon >*	*DRAW1* *Polygon:*	*POLYGON*	*9,N*

The *Polygon* command creates a regular polygon (all angles are equal and all sides have equal length). A *Polygon* object appears to be several individual objects but, like a *Pline*, is actually <u>one</u> object. In fact, AutoCAD uses *Pline* to create a *Polygon*. There are two basic options for creating *Polygons*: You can specify an *Edge* (length of one side) or specify the size of an imaginary circle for the *Polygon* to *Inscribe* or *Circumscribe*.

Inscribe/Circumscribe
The command sequence for this default method follows:

> Command: **polygon**
> Number of sides: (Enter a value for the number of sides.)
> Edge/<Center of polygon>: **PICK** or (**coordinates**)
> Inscribed in circle/Circumscribed about circle: *I* or *C*
> Radius of circle: **PICK** or (**value**) or (**coordinates**)

The orientation of the *Polygon* and the imaginary circle are shown in Figure 15-6. A hexagon (6 sides) is used in the example. Note that the *Inscribed* option allows control of one-half of the distance <u>across the corners</u>, and the *circumscribed* option allows control of one-half of the distance <u>across the flats</u>.

Using *ORTHO ON* with specification of the *radius of circle* forces the *Polygon* to a 90 degree orientation.

Figure 15-6

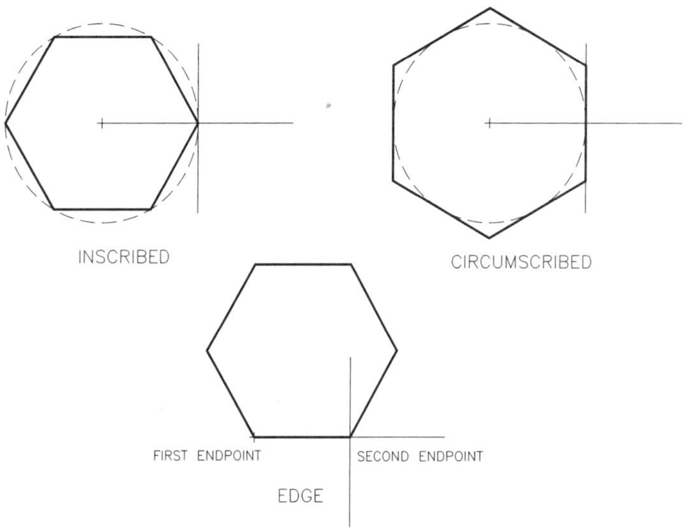

INSCRIBED
CIRCUMSCRIBED
FIRST ENDPOINT   SECOND ENDPOINT
EDGE

Edge
The *Edge* option only requires you to indicate the number of sides desired and to specify the two endpoints of one edge (Fig. 15-6).

> Command: **polygon**
> Number of sides: (**value**) (Enter a value for the number of sides.)
> Edge/<Center of polygon>: *E* (Invokes the edge option.)
> First endpoint of edge: **PICK** or (**coordinates**) (Interactively select or enter coordinates in any format.)
> Second endpoint of edge: **PICK** or (**coordinates**) (Interactively select or enter coordinates in any format.)

Because *Polygons* are created as *Plines*, *Pedit* can be used to change the line width or edit the shape in some way (see *Pedit*, Chapter 16). *Polygons* can also be *Exploded* into individual objects similar to the way other *Plines* can be broken down into component objects (see *Explode*, Chapter 16).

ELLIPSE

PULL-DOWN MENU	SCREEN MENU	TYPE IN	TABLET MENU
Draw *Ellipse >*	*DRAW1* *Ellipse:*	*ELLIPSE*	*10,N*

An *Ellipse* is one object. AutoCAD *Ellipses* are (by default) NURBS curves (see *Spline*). There are three methods of creating *Ellipses* in AutoCAD: (1) specify one <u>axis</u> and the <u>end</u> of the second, (2) specify the <u>center</u> and the ends of each axis, and (3) create an elliptical <u>arc</u>. Each option also permits supplying a rotation angle rather than the second axis length.

R13

Command: **ellipse**
Arc/Center/<Axis endpoint 1>: **PICK** or (**coordinates**) (This is the first endpoint of either the major or minor ellipse.)
Axis endpoint 2: **PICK** or (**coordinates**) (Select a point for the other axis endpoint.)
<Other axis distance>/Rotation: **PICK** or (**coordinates**) (This distance is measured perpendicularly from the established axis.)

Axis End

This default option requires PICKing three points as indicated in the command sequence above (Fig. 15-7).

Figure 15-7

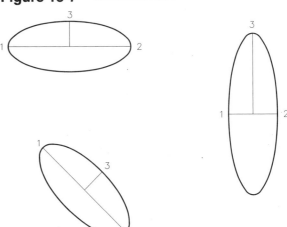

Rotation

If the *Rotation* option is used with the *Axis End* method, the following syntax is used:

<Other axis distance>/Rotation: **R**
Rotation around major axis: **PICK** or (**value**)

The specified angle is the number of degrees the shape is rotated <u>from the circular position</u> (Fig. 15-8).

Figure 15-8

ROTATION = 0   ROTATION = 45   ROTATION = 7

Center

With many practical applications, the center point of the ellipse is known, and therefore the *Center* option should be used (Fig. 15-9).

Command: **ellipse**
Arc/Center/<Axis endpoint 1>: **C**
Center of ellipse: **PICK** or (**coordinates**)
Axis endpoint: **PICK** or (**coordinates**)
<Other axis distance>/Rotation: **PICK** or (**coordinates**) (This distance is measured perpendicularly from the established axis.)

Figure 15-9

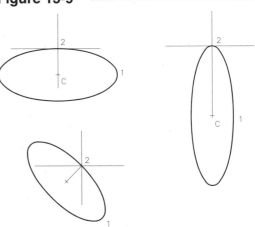

The *Rotation* option appears and can be invoked after specifying the *Center* and first *Axis endpoint*.

Arc

Use this option to construct an elliptical arc (partial ellipse). The procedure is identical to the *Center* option with the addition of specifying the start- and endpoints for the arc (Fig. 15-10).

Command: **ellipse**
Arc/Center/<Axis endpoint 1>: **a**
<Axis endpoint 1>/Center: **PICK** or (**coordinates**)
Axis endpoint 2: **PICK** or (**coordinates**)
<Other axis distance>/Rotation: **PICK** or (**coordinates**)
Parameter/<start angle>: **PICK** or (**angular value**)
Parameter/Included/<end angle>: **PICK** or (**angular value**)
Command:

Figure 15-10

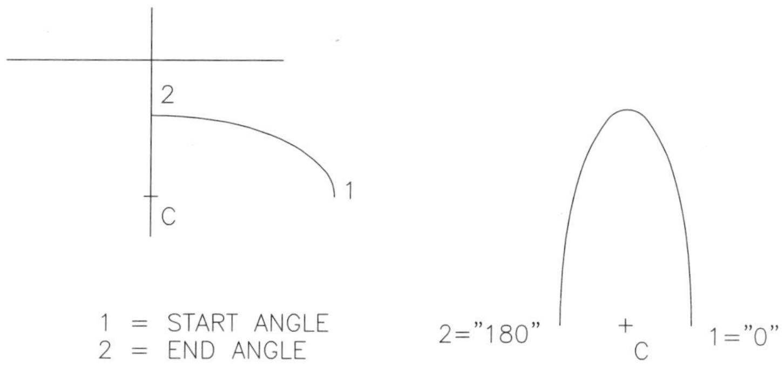

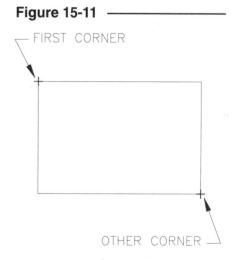

1 = START ANGLE
2 = END ANGLE

2="180"   +   1="0"
              C

The *Parameter* option allows you to specify the start- and endpoint parameters based on the parametric vector equation: $p(u)=c+a*\cos(u)+b*\sin(u)$, where c is the center of the ellipse and a and b are the major and minor axes (see *AutoCAD Command Reference*).

RECTANG

PULL-DOWN MENU	SCREEN MENU	TYPE IN	TABLET MENU
Draw *Polygon >* *Rectangle*	*DRAW1* *Rectang:*	*RECTANG*	---

The *Rectang* command only requires the specification of two diagonal corners for construction of a rectangle, identical to making a selection window (Fig. 15-11). The corners can be PICKed or coordinates can be entered. The rectangle can be any proportion, but the sides are always horizontal and vertical. The completed rectangle is one AutoCAD object, not four separate objects. *Rectangle* uses the *Pline* command to construct the shape; therefore, the *Rectangle* is drawn with the current *Pline width*.

Command: **rectang**
First corner: **PICK** or (**coordinates**)
Other corner: **PICK** or (**coordinates**)
Command:

Figure 15-11

FIRST CORNER

OTHER CORNER

XLINE

	PULL-DOWN MENU	SCREEN MENU	TYPE IN	TABLET MENU
	Draw *Construction Line*	DRAW1 *Xline:*	XLINE	*10,L*

When you draft with pencil and paper, light "construction" lines are used to lay out a drawing. These construction lines are not intended to be part of the finished object lines, but are helpful for preliminary layout such as locating intersections, center points, and projecting between views.

AutoCAD Release 13 introduces two methods of drawing construction lines—*Xline* and *Ray*. An *Xline* is a line with infinite length, therefore having no endpoints. A *Ray* has one "anchored" endpoint and the other end extends to infinity. Even though these lines extend to infinity, they do not affect the drawing *Limits* or *Extents* or change the display or plot area in any way. An *Xline* has no endpoints (*ENDpoint Osnap* cannot be used) but does have a <u>root</u>, which is the theoretical <u>midpoint</u> (*MIDpoint Osnap* can be used). If *Trim* or *Break* is used with *Xlines* or *Rays*, such that two endpoints are created, the construction lines become *Line* objects. *Xlines* and *Rays* are drawn on the current layer and assume the current line-type and color (object-specific or *BYLAYER*).

There are many ways that you can create *Xlines* as shown by the options appearing at the command prompt.

> Command: **xline**
> Hor/Ver/Ang/Bisect/Offset/<From point:>

From point
The default option only requires that you specify two points to construct the *Xline* (Fig. 15-12). The first point becomes the root and anchors the line for the next point specification. The second point, or "Through point," can be PICKed at any location and can pass through any point (*Osnaps* can be used). If horizontal or vertical *Xlines* are needed, this option can be used in conjunction with *ORTHO*.

Figure 15-12

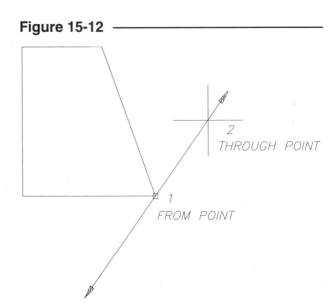

Hor

This option creates a horizontal construction line. You only specify one point, the "Through point" (root) (Fig. 15-13).

Figure 15-13

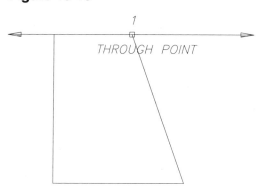

Ver

Ver creates a vertical construction line. You only specify one point, the "Through point" (root) (Fig. 15-14).

Figure 15-14

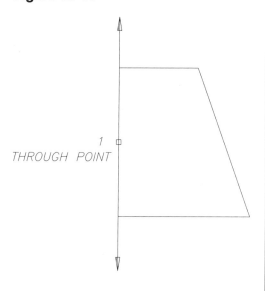

Ang

The *Ang* option provides two ways to specify the desired angle. You can (1) *Enter an angle* or (2) select a *Reference* line (*Line, Xline, Ray,* or *Pline*) as the starting angle, then specify an angle from the selected line (in a counter-clockwise direction) for the *Xline* to be drawn (Fig. 15-15).

Figure 15-15

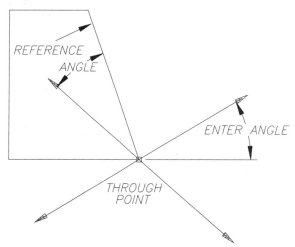

Bisect

This option draws the *Xline* at an angle between two selected points. First, select the angle vertex, then two points to define the angle (Fig. 15-16).

Figure 15-16 ───────────────

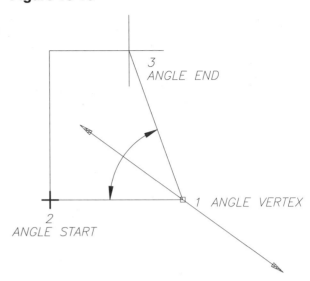

Offset

Offset creates an *Xline* parallel to another line. You can (1) specify a *Distance* from the selected line or (2) PICK a point to create the *Xline Through*. With the *Distance* option, enter the distance, select a line (*Line, Xline, Ray,* or *Pline*); and specify which side to create the offset *Xline*.

Using the *Through* option, select a line (*Line, Xline, Ray,* or *Pline*); then specify a point for the *Xline* to pass through. In each case, the anchor point of the *Xline* is the "root." (See *Offset*, Chapter 17, Construct Commands II.)

Figure 15-17 ───────────────

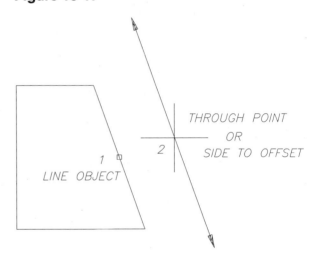

RAY

PULL-DOWN MENU	SCREEN MENU	TYPE IN	TABLET MENU
Draw *Ray*	*DRAW1* *Ray:*	*RAY*	*9,L*

A *Ray* is also a construction line (see *Xline*), but it extends to infinity in only <u>one direction</u> and has one "anchored" endpoint. Like an *Xline*, a *Ray* extends past the drawing area but does not affect the drawing *Limits* or *Extents*. The construction process for a *Ray* is simpler than for an *Xline*, only requiring you to establish a "From point" (endpoint) and a "Through point" (Fig 15-18). Multiple *Rays* can be created in one command.

Figure 15-18 ───────────────

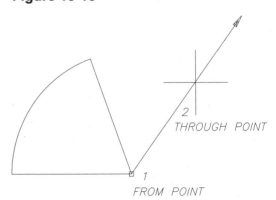

```
Command: ray
From point:
Through point: PICK or (coordinates)
Through point: PICK or (coordinates)
Through point: Enter to complete the command
Command:
```

Rays are especially helpful for construction of geometry about a central reference point or construction of angular features. In each case, the geometry is usually constructed in only one direction from the center or vertex. If horizontal or vertical *Rays* are needed, just toggle on *ORTHO*. *Endpoint* and other appropriate *Osnaps* can be used with *Rays*, but not the *Midpoint* option.

DONUT or DOUGHNUT

PULL-DOWN MENU	SCREEN MENU	TYPE IN	TABLET MENU
Draw *Circle >* *Donut*	*DRAW1* *Donut:*	*DONUT or* *DOUGHNUT*	9,O

A *Donut* is a circle with width (Fig. 15-19). Invoking the command allows changing the inside and outside diameters and creating multiple *Donuts*.

Figure 15-19

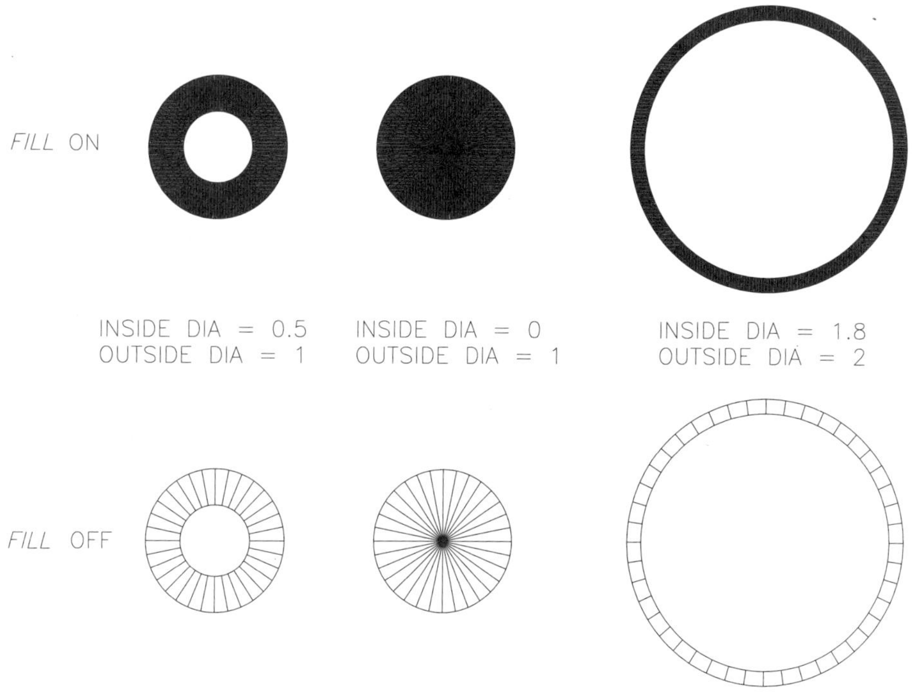

FILL ON

INSIDE DIA = 0.5   INSIDE DIA = 0   INSIDE DIA = 1.8
OUTSIDE DIA = 1   OUTSIDE DIA = 1   OUTSIDE DIA = 2

FILL OFF

```
Command: donut
Inside diameter <current>: (value) or Enter
Outside diameter <current>: (value) or Enter
Center of doughnut: PICK or (coordinates)
Center of doughnut: PICK or (coordinates) or Enter
```

Donuts are actually solid filled circular *Plines* with width. The solid fill for *Donuts*, *Plines*, and other "solid" objects can be turned off with the *Fill* command.

SOLID

PULL-DOWN MENU	SCREEN MENU	TYPE IN	TABLET MENU
Draw *2D Solid*	DRAW1 *Solid:*	SOLID	---

The *Solid* command creates a 2D shape that is <u>filled solid</u> with the current color (object or *BYLAYER*). The shape is <u>not</u> a 3D solid. Each 2D solid has either <u>three or four straight edges</u>. The construction process is relatively simple, but the order of PICKing corners is critical. In order to construct a square or rectangle, draw a bow-tie configuration (Fig. 15-20). Several *Solids* can be connected to produce more complex shapes.

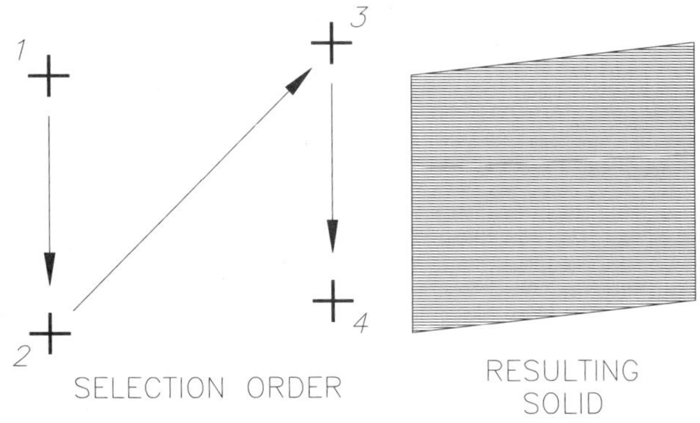

A *Solid* object is useful when you need shapes filled with solid color; for example, three-sided *Solids* can be used for large arrowheads. Keep in mind that solid filled areas may cause problems for some output devices such as plotters with felt pens and thin paper. As an alternative to using *Solid*, enclosed areas can be filled with hatch patterns (see *Bhatch*, Chapter 25).

Figure 15-20 ————————

SELECTION ORDER   RESULTING SOLID

SKETCH

PULL-DOWN MENU	SCREEN MENU	TYPE IN	TABLET MENU
Draw *Sketch*	DRAW1 *Sketch:*	SKETCH	---

The *Sketch* command is unlike other draw commands. *Sketch* quickly creates many short line segments (individual objects) by following the motions of the cursor. *Sketch* is used to give the appearance of a freehand line, as used in Figure 15-21 for the tree and bushes. You do not specify individual endpoints,

Figure 15-21 ————————————————————

but rather draw a "freehand line" by placing the "pen" down, moving the cursor, and then picking up the "pen." This action creates a large number of short *Line* segments. CAUTION: *Sketch* can increase the drawing file size greatly due to the relatively large number of line segment endpoints required to define the *Sketch* "line."

>   Command: *sketch*
>   Record increment <0.1000>: (**value**) or **Enter** (Enter a value to specify the segment increment length or press Enter to accept the default increment.)
>   Sketch. Pen eXit Quit Record Erase Connect. (**letter**) (Enter "p" or press button #1 to put the pen down and begin drawing or enter another letter for another option. After drawing a sketch line, enter "p" or press button #1 again to pick up the pen.)

It is important to specify an *increment* length for the short line segments that are created. This *increment* controls the "resolution" of the *Sketch* line (Fig. 15-22).

Too large of an *increment* makes the straight line segments apparent, while too small of an *increment* unnecessarily increases file size. The default *increment* is 0.1 (appropriate for default *Limits* of 12 x 9) and should be changed proportionally with a change in *Limits*. Generally, multiply the default *increment* of 0.1 times the "drawing scale factor."

Another important rule to consider whenever using *Sketch* is to turn *SNAP Off* and *ORTHO Off*, unless a "stair-step" effect is desired.

Figure 15-22

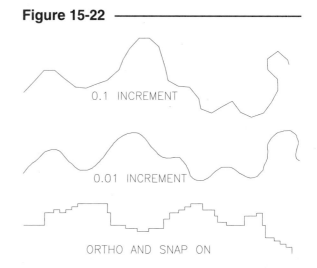

Sketch Options

Options of the *Sketch* command can be activated either by entering the corresponding letter(s) shown in uppercase at the *Sketch* command prompt or by pressing the desired mouse or puck button. For example, putting the "pen" up or down can be done by entering *P* at the command line or by pressing button #1. The options of *Sketch* are as follows.

Pen	Lifts and lowers the pen. Position the cursor at the desired location to begin the line. Lower the pen and draw. Raise the pen when finished with the line.
Record	Records all temporary lines sketched so far without changing the pen position. After recording, the lines cannot be *Erased* with the *Erase* option of *Sketch* (although the normal *Erase* command can be used).
eXit	Records all temporary lines entered and returns to the Command: prompt.
Quit	Discards all temporary lines and returns to the Command: prompt.
Erase	Allows selective erasing of temporary lines (before recording). To erase, move backwards from last sketch line toward the first. Press "p" to indicate the end of an erased area. This method works easily for relatively straight sections. To erase complex sketch lines, *eXit* and use the normal *Erase* command with window, crossing, or pickbox object selection.
Connect	Allows connection to the end of the last temporary sketch line (before recording). Move to the last sketch line and the pen is automatically lowered.
(period)	Draws a straight line (using *Line*) from the last sketched line to the cursor. After adding the straight lines, the pen returns to the up position.

Several options are illustrated in Figure 15-23. The *Pen* option lifts the pen up and down. A *period* (.) causes a straight line segment to be drawn from the last segment to the cursor location. *Erase* is accomplished by entering *E* and making a reverse motion.

As an alternative to the *erase* option of *Sketch*, the *Erase* command can be used to erase all or part of the *Sketch* lines. Using a *Window* or *Crossing Window* is suggested to make selection of all the objects easier.

Figure 15-23 ───────

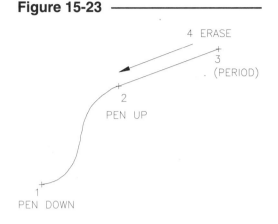

The *SKPOLY* Variable

The *SKPOLY* system variable controls whether AutoCAD creates connected *Sketch* line segments as one *Pline* (one object) or as multiple *Line* segments (separate objects). *SKPOLY* affects <u>newly created</u> *Sketch* lines only.

SKPOLY=0   This setting generates *Sketch* segments as individual *Line* objects. This is the <u>default</u> setting.

SKPOLY=1   This setting generates connected *Sketch* segments as <u>one *Pline* object</u>.

Using editing commands with *Sketch* lines can normally be tedious (when *SKPOLY* is set to the default value of 0). In this case, editing *Sketch* lines usually requires *Zooming* in since the line segments are relatively small. However, changing *SKPOLY* to 1 simplifies operations such as using *Erase* or *Trim*. For example, *Sketch* lines are often used to draw break lines (Fig. 15-25) or to represent broken sections of mechanical parts, in which case use of *Trim* is helpful. If you expect to use *Trim* or other editing commands with *Sketch* lines, change *SKPOLY* to 1 before creating the *Sketch* lines.

Figure 15-24 ───────

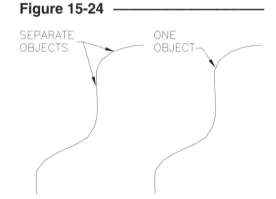

Figure 15-25 ───────

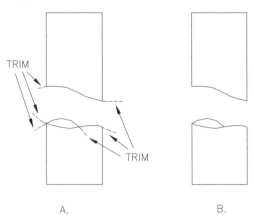

SPLINE

PULL-DOWN MENU	SCREEN MENU	TYPE IN	TABLET MENU
Draw *Spline*	*DRAW1* *Spline:*	*SPLINE*	*9,K*

The *Spline* command creates a NURBS (Non-Uniform Rational Bezier Spline) spline curve. The non-uniform feature allows irregular spacing of selected points to achieve sharp corners, for example. A *Spline* can also be used to create regular (rational) shapes such as arcs, circles, and ellipses. Irregular shapes can be combined with regular curves, all in one spline curve definition.

Spline is the newer and more functional version of a *Spline*-fit *Pline*. The main difference between a *Spline*-fit *Pline* and a *Spline* is that a *Spline* curve passes through the points selected, while the points selected for construction of a *Spline*-fit *Pline* only have a "pull" on the curve. Therefore, *Splines* are more suited to accurate design because the curve passes exactly through the points used to define the curve (data points).

The construction process involves specifying points that the curve will pass through and determining tangent directions for the two ends (for non-closed *Splines*) (Figs. 15-26, 15-27).

The *Close* option allows creation of closed *Splines* (these can be regular curves if the selected points are symmetrically arranged) (Fig. 15-28).

Command: **spline**
Object/<Enter first point>: **PICK** or (**coordinates**)
Enter point: **PICK** or (**coordinates**)
Close/Fit Tolerance/<Enter point>: **PICK** or (**coordinates**)
Close/Fit Tolerance/<Enter point>: **PICK** or (**coordinates**)
Close/Fit Tolerance/<Enter point>: **Enter**
Enter start tangent: **PICK** or **Enter** (Select direction for tangent or Enter for default tangent.)
Enter end tangent: **PICK** or **Enter** (Select direction for tangent.)
Command:

The *Object* option allows you to convert *Spline*-fit *Plines* into NURBS *Splines*. Only *Spline*-fit *Plines* can be converted.

Command: **spline**
Object/<Enter first point>: **o**
Select objects to convert to splines.
Select objects: **PICK**
Select objects: **Enter**
Command:

A *Fit Tolerance* applied to the *Spline* "loosens" the fit of the curve. A tolerance of 0 (default) causes the *Spline* to pass through the data points. Entering a positive value allows the curve to fall away from the points to form a smoother curve (Fig. 15-29).

Close/Fit Tolerance/<Enter point>: **F**
Enter Fit tolerance <0.0000>: (Enter a positive value.)

Figure 15-26

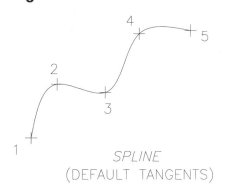

SPLINE
(DEFAULT TANGENTS)

Figure 15-27

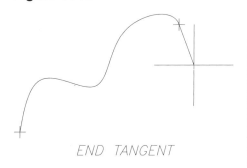

END TANGENT

Figure 15-28

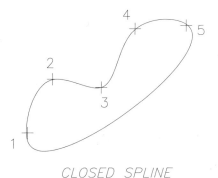

CLOSED SPLINE

Figure 15-29

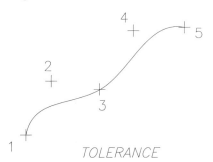

TOLERANCE

MLINE

PULL-DOWN MENU	SCREEN MENU	TYPE IN	TABLET MENU
Draw *Multiline*	DRAW1 Mline:	*MLINE*	9,J

A feature introduced with AutoCAD Release 13 is the multiline command *Mline*. A multiline is a set of <u>parallel lines</u> that behave as <u>one object</u>. The individual lines in the set are called line <u>elements</u> and are defined to your specifications. The set can contain up to 16 individual lines, each having its own offset, linetype, or color.

Mlines are useful for creating drawings composed of many parallel lines. An architectural floor plan, for example, contains many parallel lines representing walls. Instead of constructing the parallel lines individually (symbolizing the wall thickness), only <u>one</u> *Mline* can be drawn to depict the wall. The thickness and other details of the wall are dictated by the definition of the *Mline*.

Mline is the command to <u>draw</u> multilines. To <u>define</u> the individual line elements of a logical set (offset, linetype, color), use the *Mlstyle* command. An *Mlstyle* (multiline style) is a particular combination of defined line elements. Each *Mlstyle* can be saved in an external file with a .MLN filetype. In this way, multilines can be used in different drawings without having to redefine the set. See *Mlstyle* next.

The *Mline* command operates similar to the *Line* command, asking you to specify points.

```
Command: mline
Justification = Top, Scale = 1.00, Style = STANDARD
Justification/Scale/STyle/<From point>: PICK or (coordinates)
<To point>: PICK or (coordinates)
Undo/<To point>: PICK or (coordinates)
Close/Undo/<To point>: PICK or (coordinates)
Close/Undo/<To point>: Enter
Command:
```

Mline provides these three options for drawing multilines:

Justification

Justification of a multiline determines how the multiline is drawn between the points you specify. The choices are *Top*, *Zero*, and *Bottom* (Fig. 15-30). *Top* aligns the top of the set of line elements along the points you PICK as you draw. A *Zero* setting uses the center of the set of line elements as the PICK point, and *Bottom* aligns the bottom line element between PICK points.

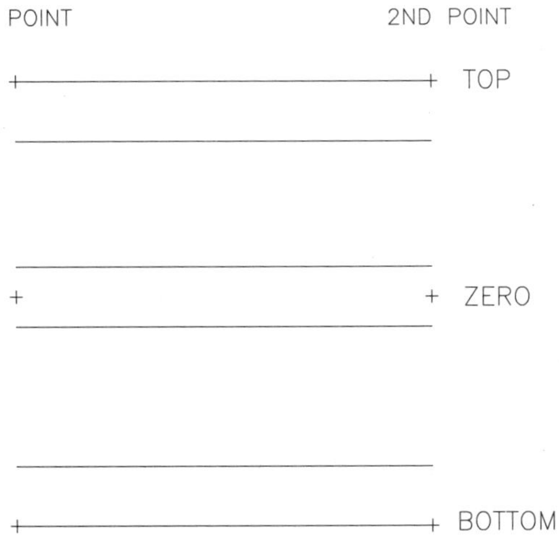

NOTE: The *Justification* methods are defined for drawing from <u>left to right</u> (positive X direction). In other words, using the *Top* justification, the top of the multiline (as it is defined with *Mlstyle*) is between PICK points when you draw from left to right. PICKing points from right to left draws the *Mline* upside-down (as defined in the *Mlstyle* dialogue box).

Figure 15-30

1ST POINT   2ND POINT

TOP

ZERO

BOTTOM

Scale

The *Scale* option controls the overall <u>width</u> of the multiline. The value you specify for the scale factor increases or decreases the defined multiline width proportionately. In Figure 15-31, a scale factor of 2.0 provides a multiple line pattern that is twice as wide as the *Mlstyle* definition; a scale of 3.0 provides a pattern three times the width.

Figure 15-31

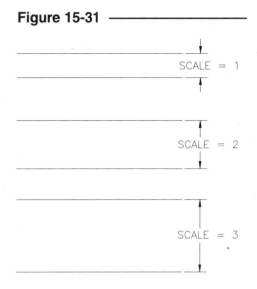

You can also enter negative scale values or a value of 0. A negative scale value flips the order of the multiple line pattern (Fig. 15-32). A value of 0 collapses the multiline into a single line. The utility of the *Scale* option allows you to vary a multiline set proportionally without the need for a complete new multiline definition.

Figure 15-32

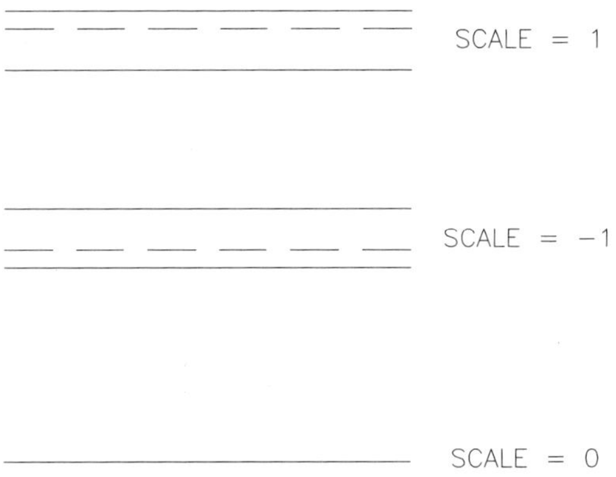

SCALE = 1

SCALE = −1

SCALE = 0

Style

The *Style* option enables you to load different multiline styles provided they have been previously created. Some examples of multiline styles are shown in Figure 15-33. Only one multiline *Style* called STANDARD is provided by AutoCAD. The STANDARD multiline style has two parallel lines defined at one unit width.

Using the *Style* option of the *Mline* command provides only the command line format for setting a current style. Instead, you can use the *Mlstyle* dialogue box to select a current multiline style by a more visible method.

Figure 15-33

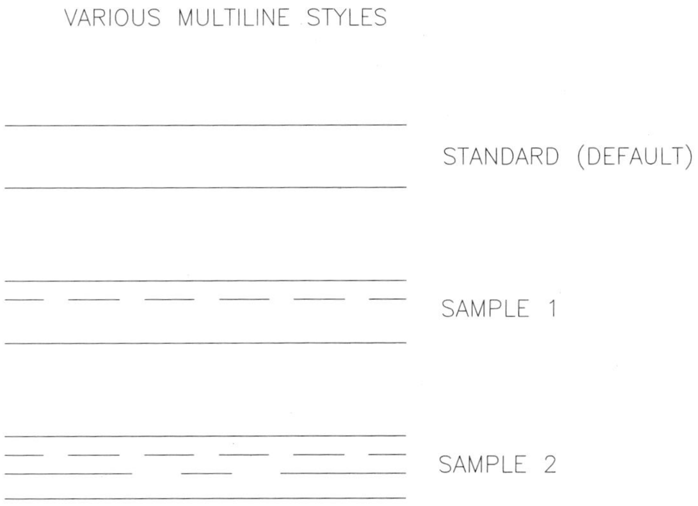

VARIOUS MULTILINE STYLES

STANDARD (DEFAULT)

SAMPLE 1

SAMPLE 2

MLSTYLE

PULL-DOWN MENU	SCREEN MENU	TYPE IN	TABLET MENU
Data Multiline Style...	DATA Mlstyle:	MLSTYLE	---

The *Mline* command draws multilines, whereas, the *Mlstyle* controls the configuration of the multilines that are drawn. Use the *Mlstyle* command to <u>create new</u> multiline definitions or to <u>load, select, and edit</u> previously created multiline styles. Using the *Mlstyle* command by any method invokes the *Multiline Styles* dialogue box (Fig. 15-34). The areas of the three main dialogue boxes are described next. Creating a new multiline style requires several steps that should follow a specific sequence. The Steps for Creating New Multiline Styles and Steps for Editing Multiline Styles are listed after the sections describing the areas of the *Multiline Styles* and nested dialogue boxes.

The *Multiline Styles* Dialogue Box
Element Properties... and *Multiline Properties...*
These two tiles produce dialogue boxes for defining new or changing existing multiline styles. When creating a new style, use these boxes first to define the line elements and their properties before *Naming*, *Adding*, and *Saving* the style. Features of these two dialogue boxes are described later.

Current
This pop-down list provides you with the names of the currently loaded multiline styles. The image tile in the center of the dialogue box provides a representation of the selected *Current* multiline style definition. Therefore, you can select names in the pop-down list to browse through the loaded multiline styles. The *STyle* option of the *Mline* command serves the same purpose, but operates only in command line format and requires you to know the specific *Mlstyle* name and definition.

Name
When you create new multiline styles, use the *Name* edit box to enter the name of the style you have created. The *Mlstyle* should be *Named* <u>after</u> assigning *Element Properties* and *Multiline Properties*. Short names are desirable since a *Description* of the multiline configuration can be entered in the edit box just below *Name*.

Figure 15-34 ——————

Description
The *Description* edit box is an optional feature that allows you to provide a description for a new or existing multiline style definition. The description can contain up to 256 characters.

Load...
The *Load* tile invokes the *Load Multiline Styles* dialogue box so that you can select an existing multiline definition from an external file (Fig. 15-35). The default multiline definition file is ACAD.MLN, which contains the STANDARD multiline style. This file can be appended or a new .MLN file can be created. An .MLN file can contain <u>more than one</u> multiline style.

Figure 15-35 ——————

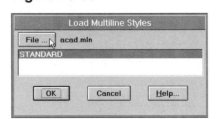

Save...

Selecting the *Save* button invokes the typical save file dialogue box (titled *Save Multiline File*) so that you can save a multiline definition to an external file. Two or more multiline styles can be saved to one external file. Use any descriptive filename and an .MLN file extension is automatically appended. Saving a multiline style to an external file allows you to use the multiline definition in other drawings without having to recreate it.

Add

Once you have defined or edited a new style using the *Element Properties* and *Multiline Properties* dialogue boxes, use the *Add* tile. The *Add* tile adds the new multiline definition to the current multiline style pop-down list. Several multiline styles can be created in this manner.

NOTE: New and edited styles require a new *Name* before using *Add*. You must choose the *OK* button in order to save new multiline definitions to the drawing file.

Rename

The *Rename* tile allows you to rename the current multiline style. First, select the style to be renamed so it appears in both the *Current* and *Name* boxes. Next, change the name in the *Name* box and select *Rename*. The new name should appear in both boxes.

The *Element Properties* Dialogue Box

The *Element Properties...* button (in the *Multiline Styles* dialogue box) invokes the *Element Properties* dialogue box (Fig. 15-36). This dialogue box provides controls for you to define the offset (spacing), linetype, and color properties of individual line elements of a new or existing multiline style.

The *Elements:* list displays the <u>current</u> settings for the multiline style. Each line entry in a style has an offset, color, and linetype associated with it. A multiline definition can have as many as 16 individual line elements defining it. Select (highlight) any element in the list before changing its properties with the options below.

Figure 15-36 ⎯⎯⎯⎯⎯⎯⎯

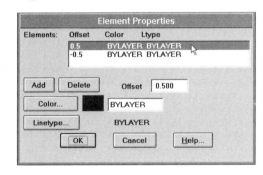

Add

New line elements are added to the list by selecting the *Add* button; then the *Offset*, *Color*, and *Linetype* properties can be assigned.

Delete

The current line element (the highlighted entry in the *Elements:* list) is deleted by selecting the *Delete* button.

Color

Selecting this tile produces the standard *Select Color* dialogue box. *BYLAYER* and *BYBLOCK* settings are valid. Any color selected is assigned to the highlighted line element in the list.

Linetype

Use this to assign a linetype to the highlighted line element. The standard *Select Linetype* dialogue box appears. Linetypes can be *Loaded* from this device.

Offset

Enter a value in the *Offset* edit box for each line element. The offset value is the distance measured perpendicular from the theoretical zero (center) position along the axis of the *Mline*.

The *Multiline Properties* Dialogue Box

Figure 15-37

The *Multiline Properties* dialogue box (Fig. 15-37) is also nested and invoked through the *Multiline Styles* dialogue box. The options here enable you to control end capping, fill, and joint display properties of the multiline style. This device controls features of the <u>multiline style as a whole</u>, whereas the *Element properties* dialogue treats the <u>individual</u> line element properties.

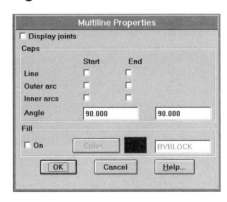

When multiline properties are assigned in this dialogue box, the changes are reflected in the image tile upon returning to the *Multiline Styles* dialogue box. You can cycle back and forth between these two boxes to "see" the changes as you make them. Figure 15-38 illustrates some examples of the options described below.

Figure 15-38

Display Joints

When several segments of an *Mline* are drawn, AutoCAD automatically miters the "joints" so the segments connect with sharp, even corners. The "joint" is the bisector of the angle created by two adjoining segments. The *Display Joints* checkbox toggles on and off this miter line running across all the line elements.

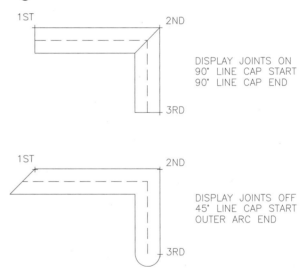

Line

The *Line* checkboxes create <u>straight</u> line caps across either or both of the Start or End segments of the multiline. The *Line* caps are drawn across all line elements.

Outer Arcs

This option creates an arc connecting and tangent to the two outermost line elements. You can control both the Start and End segments.

Inner Arcs

The inner arc option creates an arc between interior line segments. This option works with four or more line elements. In the case of five or more uneven line elements, the middle line is not capped.

Angle

The angle option controls the angle of start and end lines or arcs. Valid values range from 10 to 170 degrees.

Fill

The *Fill* toggle turns off or on the background fill of a multiline. The "X" must appear in the box before the *Color* tile is enabled. Selecting *Color* produces the standard *Select Color* dialogue box. The image tile does not display the multiline fill, but fill appears in the drawing.

Steps for Creating New Multiline Styles

1. Use the *Mlstyle* command to invoke the *Multiline Styles* dialogue box.

2. Use the *Element Properties* dialogue box to define the line elements' offset, linetype, and color properties.

3. Define the multiline end capping, fill, and joint display properties using the *Multiline Properties* dialogue box.

4 Returning to the *Multiline Styles* dialogue box, assign a *Name* to the new style.

5. Use the *Add* button to include the new style to the list of potential current styles and make it the current style.

6. Select *OK* to exit the *Multiline Styles* dialogue box and begin drawing *Mlines* with the new style.

7. If you want to use the new style with other drawings, use *Save* in the *Multiline Styles* dialogue box to save the style to an external .MLN file.

Steps for Editing Existing Multiline Styles

1. Use the *Mlstyle* command to invoke the *Multiline Styles* dialogue box.

2. *Load* the desired multiline style from an external file or select it from the *Current* list. The style name must appear in the *Name* box.

3. If you want to edit the line elements' offset, linetype, and color properties, use the *Element Properties* dialogue box.

4. If you want to edit the multiline end capping, fill, and joint display properties, use the *Multiline Properties* dialogue box.

5. You must assign a <u>new *Name*</u> to the changed style in the *Multiline Styles* dialogue box by editing the old name. You cannot use the same name. An "Invalid name" message appears if you attempt to *Add* using the old name.

6. Then you must *Add* the new (edited) style to the list of potential current styles and make it the current style.

7. Select *OK* to exit the *Multiline Styles* dialogue box and begin drawing *Mlines* with the new style.

8. If you want to use the new (edited) style with other drawings, use *Save* in the *Multiline Styles* dialogue box to save the style to an external .MLN file.

Multiline Styles **Example**

Because the process of creating and editing multiline styles is somewhat involved, here is an
example that you can follow to create a new multiline style. The specifications for two multilines are
given in Figure 15-39. Follow these steps to create
SAMPLE1.

Figure 15-39

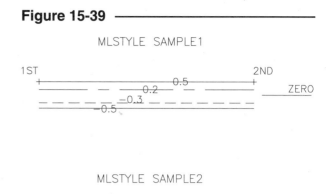

1. Invoke the *Multiline Styles* dialogue box by
    any menu or icon or by typing *Mlstyle*.

2. Select the *Element Properties...* tile to invoke the
    Element Properties dialogue box.

3. Select the *Add* button twice. Four line entries
    should appear in the *Elements:* list box. The two new entries have a 0.0 offset.

4. Highlight one of the new entries and change its offset by entering 0.2 in the *Offset* edit box. Next,
    change the linetype by selecting the *Linetype...* button and choosing the *Center* linetype. (If the *Center*
    linetype is not listed, you should *Load* it.)

5. Highlight the other new entry and change its *Offset* to -0.3. Next, change its *Linetype* to *Hidden*.

6. Select the *OK* button to return to the *Multiline Styles* dialogue box. At this point, enter the name
    SAMPLE1 in the *Name* edit box. Choose the *Add* button to save the new line definition and make it
    current. Last, choose the *OK* button to save the multiline style to the drawing database.

7. Use *Mline* to draw several segments and to test your new multiline style.

8. Use *Mlstyle* again and enter *Multiline Properties* to create *Line* end caps and a *Color Fill* to the style.
    Don't forget to change the name (to SAMPLE1-FILL, for example) and *Add* it to the list.

Now try to create SAMPLE2 multiline style on your own (see Fig. 15-39).

Editing Multilines

Because a multiline is treated as one object and its complex configuration is defined by the multiline
style, traditional editing commands such as *Trim* and *Extend*, etc., cannot be used for typical editing
functions. Instead, a special set of editing functions are designed for *Mlines*. The *Mledit* (multiline edit)
command provides the editing functions for existing multilines and is discussed in Chapter 16. Your
usefulness for *Mlines* is limited until you can edit them with *Mledit*.

POINT FILTERS

DOS PULL-DOWN	WIN PULL-DOWN	SCREEN MENU	TYPE IN	TABLET MENU
Assist *Point Filters...*	*Edit* *Point Filters...*	SERVICE	*. (period)(letters)*	---

A point filter is not a command. A point filter is a method of substituting a known coordinate value into
a command, usually a draw command. For example, when a command prompts you to PICK a point or
enter coordinate values, you can use a point filter to apply an existing object's coordinates for the

command. In fact, you normally use a point filter to utilize only one or two of the existing object's X, Y, or Z values. You can define or "build" the needed X and Y coordinates by using the X coordinate of one known point and Y coordinate of another. *OSNAP*s can be used in conjunction with point filters to snap to an existing object.

Point filters can be accessed by all of the methods shown in the command table on page 218. If you are using AutoCAD for Windows, point filters are also available in a "flyout" fashion from the Standard toolbar (Fig. 15-40).

Figure 15-40 ⎯

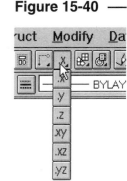

You can use a point filter whenever you are prompted for a point, such as the *Line* "From point:" or "to point:" prompts or the *Circle* "3P/2P/TTR/ <Center point:>" prompt. Specify a point filter by entering a period (.) followed by the letter X, Y, or Z, or a combination of two of the letters. The following examples are valid point filters.

    .X
    .Y
    .Z
    .XY
    .XZ
    .YZ

For example, assume you want to draw a *Line* (Fig. 15-41, highlighted line above) and begin the line at the same X value of an existing line (lower line) so the two lines' endpoints align vertically. When prompted for the "From point:," use an .X point filter to locate and "filter" the existing line's endpoint. The command syntax would read like this:

Figure 15-41 ⎯⎯⎯⎯⎯⎯⎯⎯⎯⎯⎯⎯⎯⎯⎯⎯⎯⎯⎯

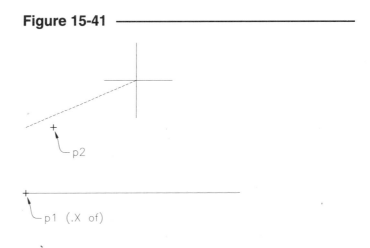

    Command: *line*
    From point: *.X* (type or select .X)
    of

After entering the point filter, AutoCAD responds with "of." Next, PICK the existing line's endpoint (Fig 15-41, p1). AutoCAD filters the X component of the selected point (p1) and passes the value to the *Line* command. AutoCAD responds with:

    (need YZ): **PICK** (PICK to define the Y and Z components)

You must still provide AutoCAD with the Y and Z values. Another point can be PICKed as shown in the figure (p2). To specify the "From point:" of the *Line*, the Y and Z values from the second point (p2) are used, but the X component is the same as that of the first line (p1).

For accuracy, *OSNAP*s should be used. In the previous procedure, the *ENDpoint* should be used to PICK the existing line's endpoint (p1). Enter or select the desired *OSNAP* mode <u>after</u> entering the point filter as shown in this sequence and as illustrated in Figure 15-42.

Figure 15-42

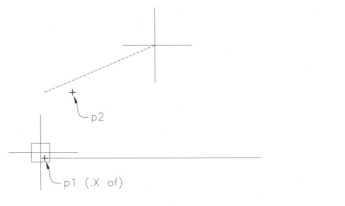

> Command: **line**
> From point: **.X** (type or select .X)
> of **end** (enter *OSNAP* mode)
> of **PICK** (p1)
> (need YZ): **PICK** (p2)
> to point:

The same strategy can be used to designate the other endpoint of the line. For the "to point:," enter an .X point filter at the prompt and use *ENDpoint* to select the other end of the existing line (Fig. 15-43, p3).

Figure 15-43

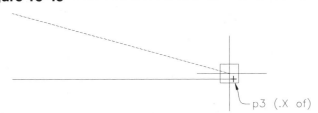

PICK another point (Fig. 15-44, p4) to specify the Y and Z coordinates. The resulting line has the same X coordinates for both of its endpoints as the existing line. The command sequence for the procedure in Figures 15-43 and 15-44 is as follows.

Figure 15-44

> to point: **.X** (type or select .X)
> of **end** (enter *OSNAP* mode and
> press Enter)
> of **PICK** (p3)
> (need YZ): **PICK** (p4)
> to point: **Enter**
> Command:

It is possible to specify a point by filtering one existing object's X coordinate and another object's Y coordinate. The following example illustrates filtering the X component at the *MIDpoint* of one existing line and the Y component at the *MIDpoint* of another existing line.

Figure 15-45

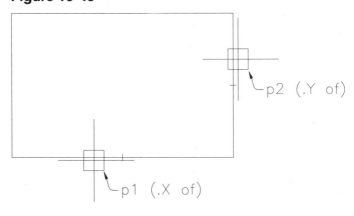

Assume you want to draw a *Circle* with its center located at the center of an existing rectangle (Fig.15-45). The coordinate for the <u>center of the rectangle</u> has an X component equal to that of the midpoint of a horizontal (bottom or top) line and a Y component equal to the midpoint of a vertical (side) line. The command syntax for the operation in Figure 15-45 is as follows.

Command: *circle*
3P/2P/TTR/<Center point>: *.x*
of *mid*
of **PICK** (p1)
(need YZ): *mid*
of **PICK** (p2)
Diameter/<Radius>: **1**
Command:

The resulting *Circle* has its center located at the X value of the horizontal lines and at the Y value of the vertical lines (Fig. 15-46).

For 2D drawings such as those in the previous examples, only .X and .Y point filters need to be used. The .X and .Y filters can be specified in either order. Other examples of practical 2D applications for point filters are given in Chapter 24, Using Point Filters for Alignment.

Many applications in 3D drawings require X, Y and Z coordinate specification. In addition to the .X, .Y, and .Z filters, the .XY, .XZ, and .YZ filters are useful. Chapter 35, Wireframe Modeling, introduces these concepts.

Figure 15-46

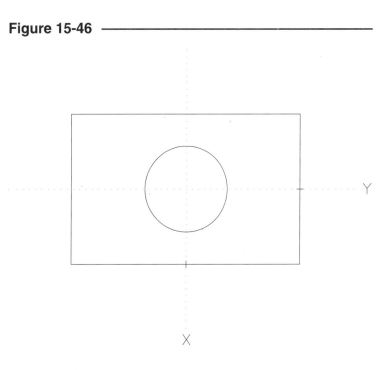

CHAPTER EXERCISES

1. *Pline*

    A. *Open* the **ASHEET** drawing. Draw a border measuring **10 x 7.5** units (starting at coordinate **.5,.5**). Construct the border from a *Pline* of **.02** *width*. Also construct a title block using a *Pline* of **.02** *width* for the outside edges and *Lines* for the inside edges. Provide space in the title block for the following text items: name of company or school, name of drafter or designer, name of checker or instructor, name or number of project or part, date of completion, and scale.

    The title block design can be one of your own, or you can refer to your engineering graphics or architectural drawing reference book for standard title block examples and dimensions. *Saveas* and assign the name **A-BORDER**.

    B. *Open* drawing **BSHEET** and construct a title block and border as in exercise 1A. Allow a **.75** unit margin from the *Limits* on all sides. Use a *Pline* width of **.03**. *Saveas* and assign the name **B-BORDER**.

    C. *Open* drawing **CSHEET** and construct a title block and border as in the previous exercises; however, this time use a *Pline* width of **.04**. *Saveas* and assign the name **C-BORDER**.

2. *Pline, Polygon*

Create the shape shown in Figure 15-47. Draw the outside shape with <u>one contin-uous</u> *Pline* (with 0.00 width). Use *Polygon* for the hexagon. When finished, *Saveas* **CH15EX2**.

Figure 15-47

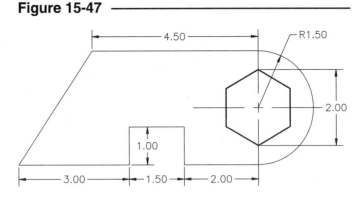

3. *Xline, Ellipse, Rectangle*

Open the **APARTMNT** drawing that you created in Chapter 13. Draw the floorplan of the efficiency apartment on layer FLOORPLAN as shown in Figure 15-48. Use *Saveas* to assign the name **EFF-APT**. Use *Xline* and *Line* to construct the floorplan with 8" width for the exterior walls and 5" for interior walls. Use the *Ellipse* and *Rectangle* commands to design and construct the kitchen sink, tub, wash basin, and toilet. *Save* the drawing but do not exit.

Figure 15-48

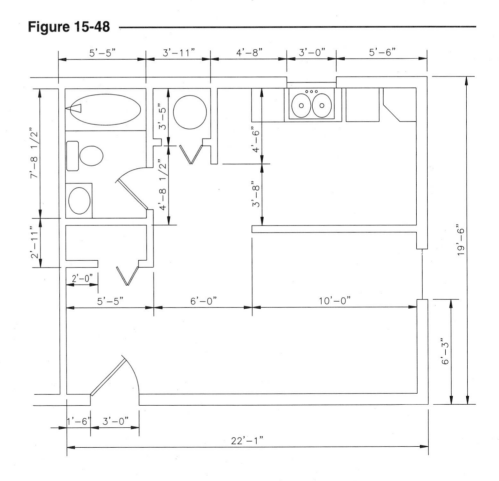

4. *Polygon, Sketch*

Create a plant for the efficiency apartment as shown in Figure 15-49. Locate the plant near the entry. The plant is in a hexagonal pot (use *Polygon*) measuring 18" across the corners. Use *Sketch* to create 2 leaves as shown in figure A. Create a *Polar Array* to develop the other leaves similar to figure B. *Save* the **EFF-APT** drawing.

Figure 15-49 ————————————————

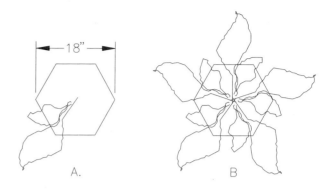

A.   B.

5. *Open* the drawing that you set up in Chapter 13 named **WRENCH**. Complete the construction of the Wrench shown in Figure 15-50. Center the drawing within the *Limits*. Use *Line*, *Circle*, *Arc*, *Ellipse*, and *Polygon* to create the shape, and use *Sketch* for "break lines." Utilize *Trim*, *Rotate*, and other edit commands where necessary. HINT: Draw the wrench head in an orthogonal position; then rotate the entire shape 15°. *Save* the drawing when completed.

Figure 15-50 ————————————————

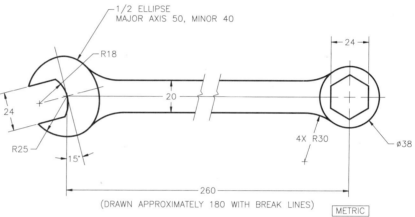

6. *Xline, Spline*

Create the handle shown in Figure 15-51. Construct multiple *Horizontal* and *Vertical* *Xlines* at the given distances on a separate Layer. Construct two *Splines* that make up the handle sides by PICKing the points indicated at the *Xline* intersections. Note the *End Tangent* for one *Spline*. Connect the *Splines* at each end with horizontal *Lines*. *Freeze* the construction (*Xline*) layer. *Save* the drawing as **HANDLE**.

Figure 15-51 ————————————————

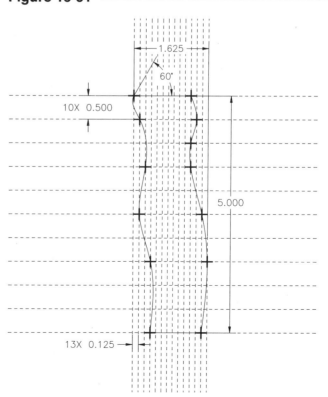

7. *Mline, Mstyle, Sketch*

Figure 15-52 ────────────

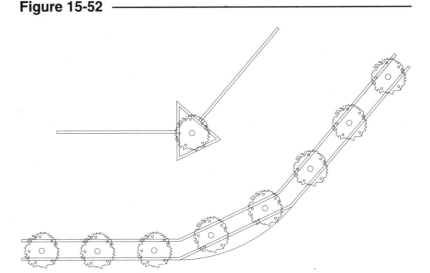

Using the **RET-WALL** drawing that you created in Chapter 8, add the concrete walls, island, and curbs. Use *Mlstyle* to create a multiline style consisting of 2 line elements with *Offsets* of **1** and **-1**. Assign *Start* and *End Caps* at **90** degrees. *Name* the new style **WALL** and *Add* it to the list to make it current. Next, use *Mline* with the *Bottom Justification* and draw one *Mline* along the existing retaining wall centerline. Use *ENDpoint* to snap to the ends of the existing 2 *Lines* and *Arc*. Construct a second *Mline* above that using the following coordinates:

> **60,123**
> **192,123**
> **274,161**
> **372.7,274**

Next, construct the *Closed* triangular island with an *Mline* using *Top Justification*. The coordinates are:

> **192,192**
> **222.58,206.26**
> **192,233**

For the parking curbs, draw two more *Mlines*; each *Mline* snaps to the *MIDpoint* of the island and is **100'** long. The curb on the right has an angle of **49** degrees (use polar coordinate entry). Finally, create trees similar to the ones shown using *Sketch*. Remember to set the *SKPOLY* variable. Create one tree and *Copy* it to the other locations. Spacing between trees is approximately **48'**. *Save* as **RET-WAL2**.

8. **Point Filters**

Figure 15-53 ────────────

A. Begin a *New* drawing named **TABLBASE** from the default ACAD prototype and set the drawing limits to **48** x **32**. Create 2 new *Layers*, named **LEGS** and **TABLE**; then set the **LEGS** layer as *Current*.

B. Use a *Pline* and create the three line segments representing the first leg as shown in Figure 15-53. Begin at the indicated location. (It is not necessary to add the dimensions in your drawing.)

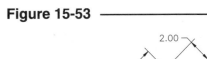

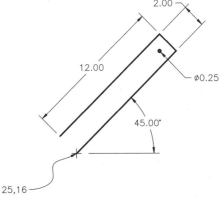

C. Place the first drill hole at the end of the leg using *Circle* with the *Center, Radius* option. Use point filters to indicate the center of the *Circle* by using *ENDPoint* OSNAP to pick as shown (by the "blips") in Figure 15-54.

Figure 15-54 ———

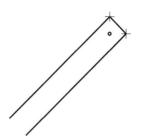

D. Create a *Polar Array* of **4** legs by using the point filters in a similar fashion to indicate the center point of the array. This time use the *ENDPoints* on the bottom of the leg to identify the center point of the *Array* as shown in Figure 15-55.

Figure 15-55 ————————

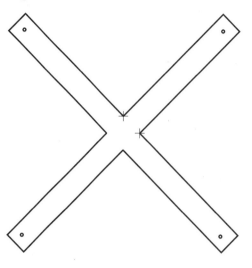

E. Use *Pline* to create a 24" x 24" square table top on the right side of the drawing as shown in Figure 15-56. Use point filters with the *Move* command to move the square's center point to the center point of the array of the 4 legs (HINT: using *.X* and *.Y*, OSNAP to the square's *MIDpoints*).

Figure 15-56 ————————

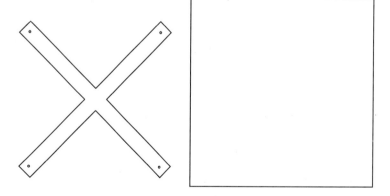

F. Create a smaller square (*Pline*) in the center of the
    table which will act as a support plate for the legs.
    Use point filters on the *MIDpoint* of the legs to get
    the <u>smallest</u> square. There are 4 possible solutions:
    2 are rectangles and 2 are squares, one smaller than
    the other. A hint is given in Figure 15-57. Use *Trim*
    to edit the legs and the support plate to look like
    the Fig. 15-58.

Figure 15-57

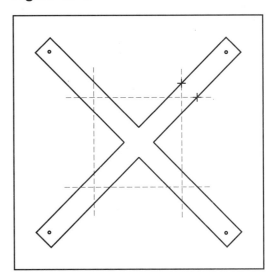

G. Use *Circle* with the *Center, Radius* option to create
    a 4" diameter circle to represent the welded
    support for the center post for this table. Finally,
    add the other 4 drill holes (1/4" diameter) on the
    legs using any method. The table base should
    appear as shown in Figure 15-58. *Save*
    the drawing.

Figure 15-58

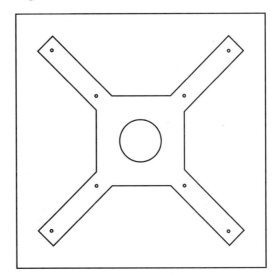

Chapter 16

MODIFY COMMANDS II

Chapter Objectives

After completing this chapter you should:

1. be able to *Stretch* selected objects;

2. be able to *Align* objects with other objects;

3. be able to use *Chprop* to change an object's layer, color, and linetype properties;

4. know how to use *Change* to change points or properties;

5. be able to use *Ddmodify* to modify any type of object;

6. be able to *Explode* a *Pline* or *Polygon* into its component objects and to know that *Explode* can be used with *Blocks* and other composite shapes;

7. be able to use all the *Pedit* options to modify *Plines*;

8. be able to convert *Lines* and *Arcs* to *Plines* using *Pedit*;

9. be able to modify *Splines* with *Splinedit*;

10. be able to edit existing *Mlines* using *Mledit*.

BASICS

This chapter examines commands that are used to modify existing objects. These commands are similar to, but generally more advanced and powerful than, those discussed in Chapter 9, Modify Commands I.

COMMANDS

STRETCH

PULL-DOWN MENU	SCREEN MENU	TYPE IN	TABLET MENU
Modify *Stretch*	*MODIFY* *Stretch:*	*STRETCH*	*17,X*

Objects can be made longer or shorter with *Stretch*. The power of this command lies in the ability to *Stretch* groups of objects while retaining the connectivity of the group (Fig. 16-1). When *Stretched*, *Lines*, and *Plines* become longer or shorter and *Arcs* change radius to become longer or shorter. *Circles* do not stretch; rather, they move if the center is selected within the crossing window.

Figure 16-1

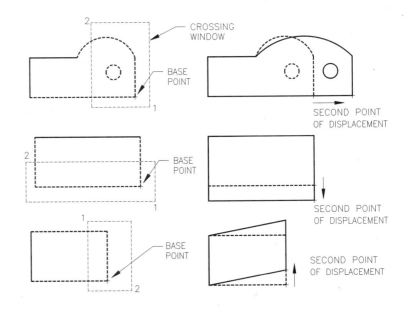

Objects to *Stretch* are not selected by the typical object selection methods but are indicated by a <u>crossing window or crossing polygon only</u>. The *Crossing Window* or *Polygon* should be created so that the objects to *stretch* <u>cross</u> through the window. *Stretch* actually moves the object endpoints that are located within the crossing window.

Following is the command sequence for *Stretch*.

    Command: **stretch**
    Select object(s) to stretch by crossing-window or -polygon...
    Select objects:
    First Corner: **PICK**
    Other Corner: **PICK**
    Select objects: **Enter**
    Base point or displacement: **PICK** or (**coordinates**) (Select a point to use
    as the point to stretch <u>from</u>.)
    Second point of displacement: **PICK** or (**coordinates**) (Select a point to use
    as the point to stretch <u>to</u>.)
    Command:

Stretch can be used to lengthen one object while shortening another. Application of this ability would be repositioning a door or window on a wall (Fig. 16-2).

Figure 16-2

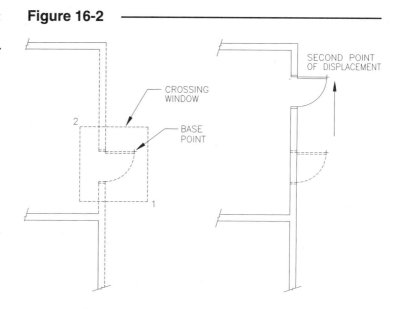

ALIGN

PULL-DOWN MENU	SCREEN MENU	TYPE IN	TABLET MENU
Modify *Align*	*MODIFY* *Align:*	*ALIGN*	*19,Y*

Align provides a means of aligning one shape (an object, a group of objects, a *Block*, a region, or a 3D object) with another shape. The alignment is accomplished by connecting source points (on the shape to be moved) to destination points (on the stationary shape). You can use *OSNAP* modes to select the source and destination points, assuring accurate alignment. Either a 2D or 3D alignment can be accomplished with this command. The command syntax for alignment in a 2D drawing is as follows:

```
Command: align
Select objects: PICK
Select objects: Enter
1st source point: PICK (with OSNAP)
1st destination point: PICK (with OSNAP)
2nd source point: PICK (with OSNAP)
2nd destination point: PICK (with OSNAP)
3rd source point: Enter
<2D> or 3D transformation: Enter
```

This command performs a translation (like *Move*) and a rotation (like *Rotate*) in one motion if needed to align the points as designated (Fig. 16-3).

First, the 1st source point is connected to (actually touches) the 1st destination point (causing a translation). Next, the vector defined by the 1st and 2nd source points is aligned with the vector defined by the 1st and 2nd destination points (causing rotation). If no 3rd destination point is given

Figure 16-3

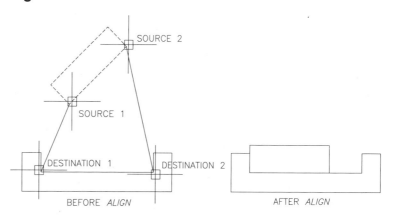

BEFORE *ALIGN*   AFTER *ALIGN*

(needed only for a 3D alignment), a 2D alignment is assumed and is performed on the basis of the two sets of points.

CHPROP

	DOS PULL-DOWN	WIN PULL-DOWN	SCREEN MENU	TYPE IN	TABLET MENU
	Modify Properties...	*Edit Properties...*	*MODIFY DDchpro:*	*CHPROP or DDCHPROP*	*9,V and 10,V*

The *Chprop* (Change Properties) command is a subset of the *Change* command. Typing *Ddchprop* or selecting from the pull-down menu invokes the dialogue box (Fig. 16-4).

After using the icon button or pull-down menu, you must select more than one object (in response to the "Select objects:" prompt) if you want to use the *Change Properties* dialogue box. If only one object is selected, the *Modify* dialogue box appears instead.

Figure 16-4

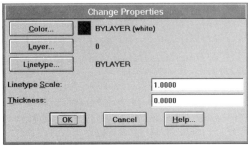

Typing *Chprop* produces the command line format:

```
Command: chprop
Select objects: PICK
Select objects: Enter
Change what property (Color/LAyer/LType/ltScale/Thickness) ?
```

Layer
By changing an object's *Layer*, the object is effectively moved to the designated layer. In doing so, if the object's *Color* and *Linetype* are set to *BYLAYER*, the object assumes the color and linetype of the layer to which it is moved.

Color
It may be desirable in some cases to assign explicit *Color* to an object or objects independently of the layer on which they are drawn. The *Change Properties* command allows changing the color of an existing object from one object color to another or from *BYLAYER* assignment to an object color. An object drawn with an object color can also be changed to *BYLAYER* with this command.

Linetype
An object can assume the *Linetype* assigned *BYLAYER* or can be assigned an object *Linetype*. The *Linetype* option of *Change Properties* is used to change an object's *Linetype* to that of any layer or to any object linetype that has been loaded into the current drawing.

Linetype Scale
An object's linetype scale can be changed with this option, but not the global linetype scale (*Ltscale*). This is the recommended method to alter an object's linetype scale. First, draw all the objects in the current global (across the drawing) *Ltscale*. *Chprop* could then be used with this option to adjust the linetype scale of specific objects. The result would be similar to setting the *Celtscale* before drawing the specific objects. Using *Chprop* to adjust a specific object's linetype scale does not reset the current *Ltscale* or *Celtscale* variables.

Thickness
An object's *Thickness* can be changed by this option. *Thickness* is a three-dimensional quality (Z dimension) assigned to a two-dimensional object (see Chapter 39, Surface Modeling).

CHANGE

PULL-DOWN MENU	SCREEN MENU	TYPE IN	TABLET MENU
Modify *Point*	*MODIFY* *Change:*	*CHANGE*	---

The *Change* command allows changing three options: *Points*, *Properties*, or *Text*.

Point

This option allows changing the endpoint of an object or endpoints of several objects to one new position.

> Command: **change**
> Select objects: **PICK**
> Select objects: **Enter**
> Properties/<Change point>: **PICK** (Select a point to establish as new endpoint of all objects. *OSNAPs* can be used.)

The endpoint(s) of the selected object(s) <u>nearest</u> the new point selected at the "Properties/<Change point>:" prompt is changed to the new point (Fig. 16-5).

Properties

These options are discussed with the previous command. Selecting *Change* with the *Properties* option offers the same possibilities as using the *Chprop* command. The *Elevation* property (a 3D property) of an object can also be changed with *Change* but not with *Chprop*.

> Properties/<Change point>: **p**
> Change what property
> (Color/Elev/LAyer/LType/ltScale/
> Thickness) ?

Figure 16-5

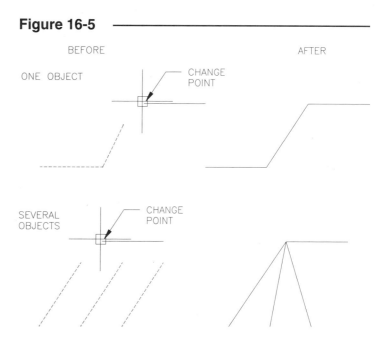

Text

Although the word *Text* does <u>not</u> appear as an option, the *Change* command recognizes text if selected and allows changing the following characteristics of text:

> Text insertion point
> Text style
> Text height
> Text rotation angle
> Textual content

To change text, use the following command syntax:

> Command: **change**
> Select objects: **PICK** (Select one or several lines of existing text.)
> Select objects: **Enter**
> Properties/<Change point>: **Enter**

Enter text insertion point: **PICK** or **Enter** (Pick for a new insertion point or press Enter for no change.)
Text Style: ROMANS (Indicates the style of the selected text.)
New style or RETURN for no change: (**text style name**) or **Enter**
New height <0.2000>: (**value**) or **Enter** (Enter a value for new height or Enter if no change.)
New rotation angle: (**value**) or **Enter** (Enter value for new angle or Enter for no change.)
New text <FILLETS AND ROUNDS .125>: (**new text**) or **Enter** (Enter the new <u>complete line</u> of text or press Enter for no change.)

DDMODIFY

DOS PULL-DOWN	WIN PULL-DOWN	SCREEN MENU	TYPE IN	TABLET MENU
Modify Properties...	*Edit Properties...*	*MODIFY Modify:*	*DDMODIFY*	*9,V and 10,V*

The *Modify* command always invokes a dialogue box. The power of this feature is apparent because the configuration of the dialogue box that appears is <u>specific</u> to the <u>type</u> of object that you select. For example, if you select a *Line*, a dialogue box appears, allowing changes to any properties that a *Line* possesses; or, if you select a *Circle* or some *Text*, a dialogue box appears specific to *Circle* or *Text* properties.

Figure 16-6 displays the dialogue box after selecting a *Line*. Notice the dialogue box title.

Figure 16-6

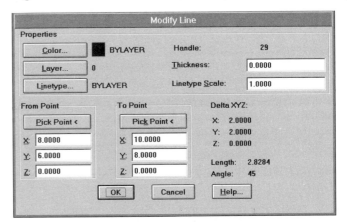

Figure 16-7 displays the dialogue box after a *Spline* selection.

Figure 16-7

The modify dialogue box series provides you with the capabilities of the *Change* command in dialogue box form. <u>All properties that an object possesses</u>, including position in the drawing, can be modified with the respective *Modify* dialogue box.

If using the pull-down menu or icon, PICK only <u>one object</u>. If more than one object is selected, the *Change Properties* dialogue box appears.

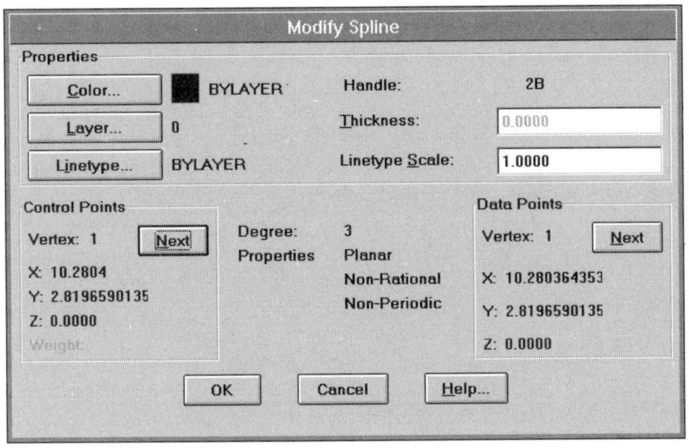

Each *Modify object* dialogue box offers a different set of changeable properties and features, depending on the object selected. Notice that the *Modify Circle* dialogue box (Fig. 16-8) allows changing the radius and coordinates of the center as well as the typical properties (layer, linetype, etc.). Additional information such as diameter, circumference, and area is given.

Figure 16-8

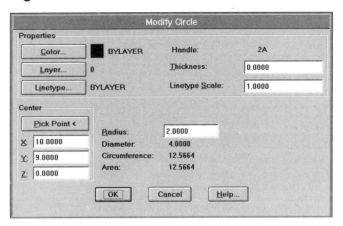

In some cases, the *Modify object* dialogue box enables editing by invoking another dialogue box. If an *Mtext* object is selected, you can select the *Edit Contents...* tile (Fig. 16-9) which produces the same dialogue box that was originally used to create the text.

Figure 16-9

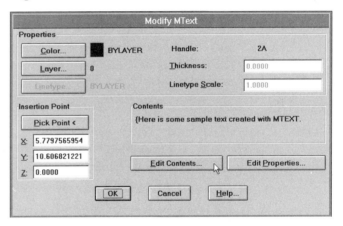

Selecting the *Edit Properties...* tile produces the *Mtext Properties* dialogue box (Fig. 16-10), enabling you to change all properties that text possesses. (See Chapter 19 for information on *Mtext* and other text objects.)

Figure 16-10

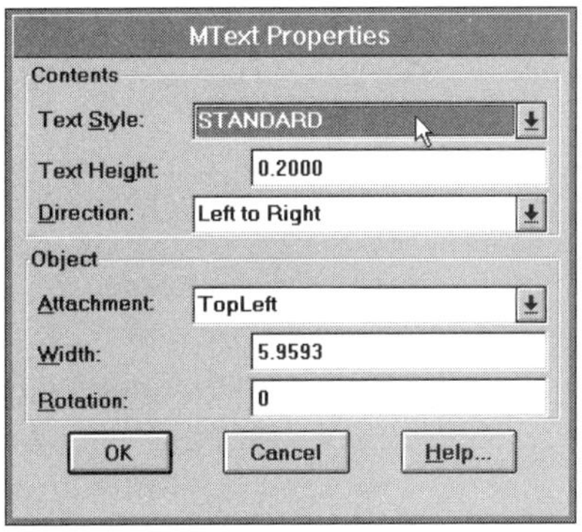

If hatch lines (created with the *Bhatch* command) are selected, the *Modify Associative Hatch* dialogue appears. Selecting the *Hatch Edit...* tile (Fig. 16-11) invokes the *Hatchedit* dialogue box, providing access to all parameters that were used to create the hatched area. (See Chapter 26 for information on hatching.)

Figure 16-11

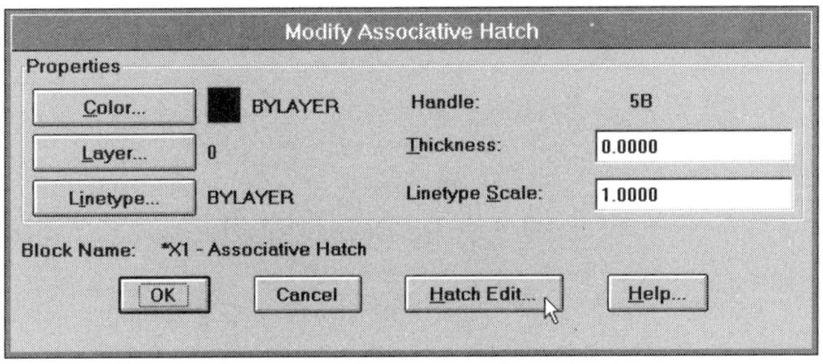

EXPLODE

PULL-DOWN MENU	SCREEN MENU	TYPE IN	TABLET MENU
Modify *Explode*	*MODIFY* *Explode:*	*EXPLODE*	20,W

There are many graphical shapes that can be created in AutoCAD that are made of several elements but are treated as one object, such as *Plines, Polygons, Blocks, Hatch* patterns, and dimensions. The *Explode* command provides you with a means of breaking down or "exploding" the complex shape from one object into its many component segments (Fig. 16-12). Generally, *Explode* is used to allow subsequent editing of one or more of the component objects of a *Pline, Polygon*, or *Block*, etc., which would otherwise be impossible while the complex shape is considered as one object.

Figure 16-12 ——————————

BEFORE EXPLODE   AFTER EXPLODE

1 PLINE SPLINE   16 LINES

1 PLINE   4 LINES

1 POLYGON   6 LINES

1 BLOCK   7 LINES

The *Explode* command has no options and is simple to use. You only need to select the objects to *Explode*.

EACH SHAPE IS ONE OBJECT   EACH SHAPE IS EXPLODED. INTO SEVERAL OBJECTS

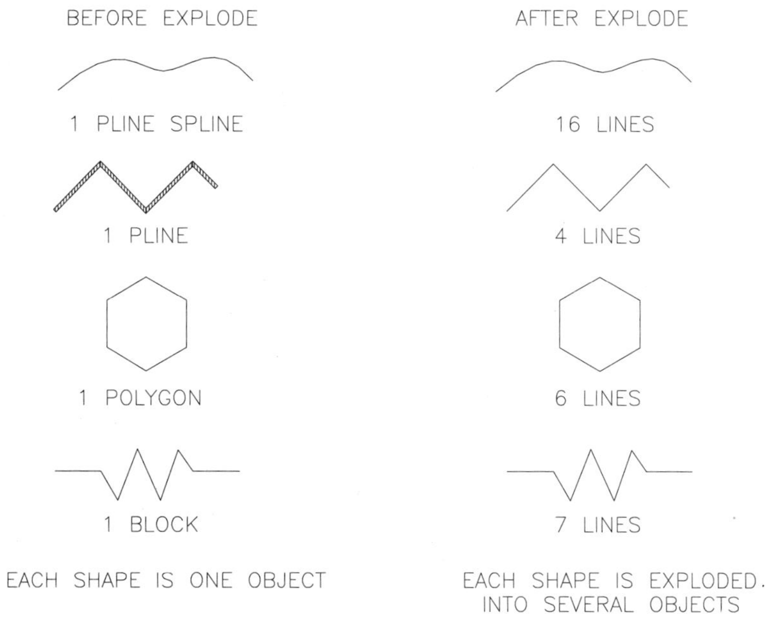

    Command: **explode**
    Select objects: **PICK** (Select one or more *Plines, Blocks*, etc.)
    Select objects: **Enter** (Indicates selection of objects is complete.)
    Command:

When *Plines, Polygons, Blocks*, or hatch patterns are *Exploded*, they are transformed into *Line, Arc*, and *Circle* objects. *Plines* having *width* lose their width information when *Exploded* since *Line, Arc*, and *Circle* objects cannot have width.

PEDIT

PULL-DOWN MENU	SCREEN MENU	TYPE IN	TABLET MENU
Modify *Edit Polyline*	*MODIFY* *Pedit:*	*PEDIT*	19,W

This command provides numerous options for editing *Polylines*. The list of options below exhibits the great flexibility possible with *Polylines*. The first step after invoking *Pedit* is to select the *Pline* to edit.

    Command: **pedit**
    Select polyline: **PICK** (Select the polyline for subsequent editing.)
    Close or Open/Join/Width/Edit vertex/Fit/Spline/Decurve/ Ltype gen/Undo/eXit <X>: (**option**) (Select the desired option from the screen menu or enter the capitalized letter for the desired option.)

Close

Close connects the last segment with the first segment of an existing "open" *Pline*, resulting in a "closed" *Pline* (Fig. 16-13). A closed *Pline* is one continuous object having no specific start or endpoint, as opposed to one closed by PICKing points. This type of closed *Pline* reacts differently to the *Spline* option and to some commands such as *Fillet, Pline* option (Chapter 17).

Open

Open removes the closing segment if the *Close* option was used previously (Fig. 16-13).

Join

This option *Joins,* or connects, any *Plines, Lines,* or *Arcs* that have <u>exact</u> matching endpoints and adds them to the selected *Pline* (Fig. 16-14). Previously *closed Plines* cannot be *Joined.*

Width

Width allows specification of a uniform width for *Pline* segments (Fig. 16-15). Nonuniform width can be specified with the *Edit vertex* option.

Edit vertex

This option is covered in the next section.

Fit

This option converts the *Pline* from straight line segments to arcs. The curve consists of two arcs for each pair of vertices. The resulting curve can be radical if the original *Pline* consists of sharp angles. The resulting curve passes <u>through all</u> vertices (Fig. 16-16).

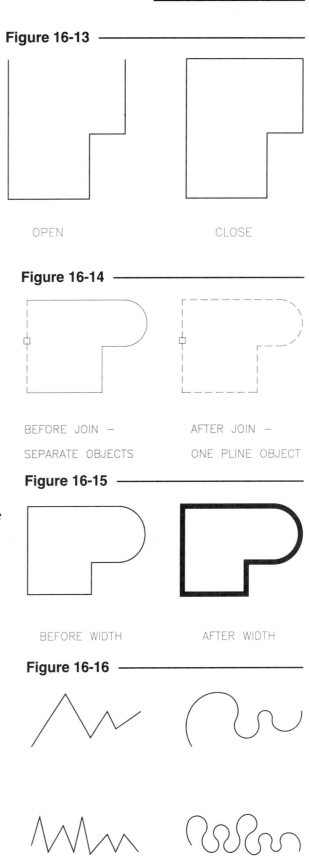

Figure 16-13

OPEN   CLOSE

Figure 16-14

BEFORE JOIN –   AFTER JOIN –

SEPARATE OBJECTS   ONE PLINE OBJECT

Figure 16-15

BEFORE WIDTH   AFTER WIDTH

Figure 16-16

BEFORE FIT   AFTER FIT

Spline

This option converts the *Pline* to a B-spline (Bezier spline). The *Pline* vertices act as "control points" affecting the shape of the curve. The resulting curve passes through <u>only the end</u> vertices. This option produces a less versatile version of the new *Spline* object.

Decurve

Decurve removes the *Spline* or *Fit* curve and returns the *Pline* to its original straight line segments state (Fig. 16-17).

Figure 16-17

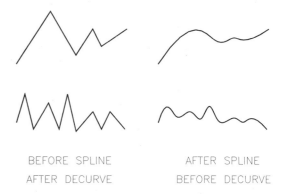

BEFORE SPLINE   AFTER SPLINE
AFTER DECURVE   BEFORE DECURVE

When you use the *Spline* option of *Pedit*, the amount of "pull" can be affected by setting the *SPLINETYPE* system variable to either 5 or 6 <u>before</u> using the *Spline* option. *SPLINETYPE* applies either a quadratic (5=more pull) or cubic (6=less pull) B-spline function (Fig. 16-18).

Figure 16-18

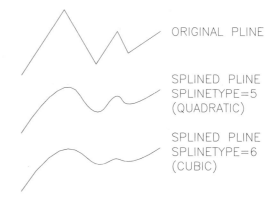

ORIGINAL PLINE

SPLINED PLINE
SPLINETYPE=5
(QUADRATIC)

SPLINED PLINE
SPLINETYPE=6
(CUBIC)

The *SPLINESEGS* system variable controls the number of line segments created when the *Spline* option is used. The variable should be set <u>before</u> using the option to any value (8=default): the higher the value, the more line segments. The actual number of segments in the resulting curve depends on the original number of *Pline* vertices and the value of the *SPLINETYPE* variable (Fig. 16-19).

Figure 16-19

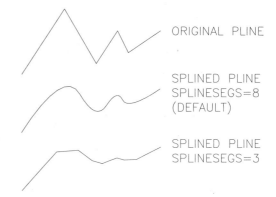

ORIGINAL PLINE

SPLINED PLINE
SPLINESEGS=8
(DEFAULT)

SPLINED PLINE
SPLINESEGS=3

Changing the *SPLFRAME* variable to 1 causes the *Pline* frame (the original straight segments) to be displayed for *Splined* or *Fit Plines*. *Regen* must be used after changing the variable to display the original *Pline* "frame" (Fig. 16-20). The *SPLFRAME* variable can also be set using the *Options* pull-down menu, then *Display >, Spline Frame*.

Figure 16-20

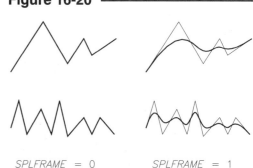

SPLFRAME = 0   SPLFRAME = 1

Ltype gen
This setting controls the generation of non-continuous linetypes for *Plines*. If *Off*, non-continuous linetype dashes start and stop at each vertex, as if the *Pline* segments were individual *Line* segments. For dashed linetypes, each line segment begins and ends with a full dashed segment (Fig. 16-21). If *On*, linetypes are drawn in a consistent pattern, disregarding vertices. In this case, it is possible for a vertex to have a space rather than a dash. Using the *Ltype gen* option <u>retroactively</u> changes *Plines* that have already been drawn. *Ltype gen* affects objects composed of *Plines* such as *Polygons*, *Rectangles*, and *Boundaries*.

Figure 16-21

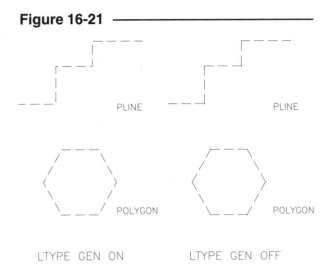

Similarly, the *PLINEGEN* system variable controls how <u>new</u> non-continuous linetypes are drawn for *Plines*. The *Linetype Generation* check from the *Options*, *Linetypes >* pull-down menu sets the *PLINEGEN* variable. A setting of 1 (or a check on the pull-down menu) creates a consistent linetype pattern, disregarding vertices (like *Ltype gen On*). A *PLINEGEN* setting of 0 (no check appearing on the menu) creates linetypes stopping and starting at each vertex (like *Ltype gen Off*). However, *PLINEGEN* is <u>not retroactive</u>—it only affects <u>new</u> *Plines*.

Undo
Undo reverses the most recent *Pedit* operation.

eXit
This option exits the *Pedit* options, keeps the changes, and returns to the Command: prompt.

Vertex Editing

Upon selecting the *Edit Vertex* option from the *Pedit* options list, the group of suboptions is displayed on the screen menu and command line.

> Command: **pedit**
> Select polyline: **PICK** (Select the polyline for subsequent editing.)
> Close or Open/Join/Width/Edit vertex/Fit/Spline/Decurve/Ltype gen/Undo/eXit <X>: **E** (Invokes the Edit vertex suboptions.)
> Next/Previous/Break/Insert/Move/Regen/Straighten/Tangent/ Width/eXit <N>:

Next
AutoCAD places an **X** marker at the first endpoint of the *Pline*. The *Next* and *Previous* options allow you to sequence the marker to the desired vertex (Fig. 16-22).

Previous
See *Next* above.

Figure 16-22

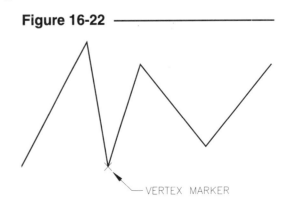

PREVIOUS AND NEXT OPTIONS WILL MOVE THE MARKER TO THE DESIRED VERTEX

Break
This selection causes a break between the marked vertex and the next one selected by the *Next* or *Previous* option prompt (Fig. 16-23):

Next/Previous/Go/eXit <N>:

Selecting *Go* causes the break. An endpoint vertex cannot be selected.

Insert
Insert allows you to insert a new vertex at any location <u>after</u> the vertex that is marked with the **X** (Fig. 16-24).

Move
You are prompted to indicate a new location to *Move* the marked vertex (Fig. 16-25).

Regen
Regen should be used after the *Width* option to display the new changes.

Straighten
You can *Straighten* the *Pline* segments between the current marker and the other marker that you place by one of these options:

Next/Previous/Go/eXit <N>:

Selecting *Go* causes the straightening to occur (Fig. 16-26).

Tangent
Tangent allows you to specify the direction of tangency of the current vertex for use with curve *Fit*ting.

Width
This allows changing the *Width* of the *Pline* segment immediately following the marker, thus achieving a specific width for one segment of the *Pline* (Fig. 16-27). *Width* can be specified with different starting and ending values. *Regen* must then be used to display the changes in width after using this option.

eXit
This option exits from vertex editing, saves changes, and returns to the main *Pedit* prompt.

Figure 16-23

BEFORE BREAK   AFTER BREAK

Figure 16-24

BEFORE INSERT   AFTER INSERT

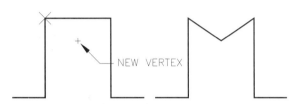

NEW VERTEX

Figure 16-25

BEFORE MOVE   AFTER MOVE

NEW LOCATION

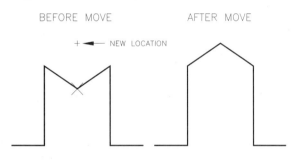

Figure 16-26

BEFORE STRAIGHTEN   AFTER STRAIGHTEN

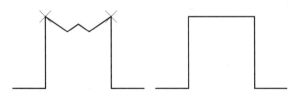

Figure 16-27

BEFORE WIDTH   AFTER WIDTH

Converting *Lines* and *Arcs* to *Plines*

A very important and productive feature of *Pedit* is the ability to convert *Lines* and *Arcs* to *Plines* and closed *Pline* shapes. Potential uses of this option are converting a series of connected *Lines* and *Arcs* to a closed *Pline* for subsequent use with *Offset* or for inquiry of the area (*Area* command) or length (*List* command) of a single shape. The only requirement for conversion of *Lines* and *Arcs* to *Plines* is that the selected objects must have <u>exact</u> matching endpoints.

To accomplish the conversion of objects to *Plines,* simply select a *Line* or *Arc* object and request to turn it into one:

> Command: *pedit*
> Select polyline: **PICK** (Select a *Line* or *Arc*.)
> Object selected is not a Pline
> Do you want to turn it into one? <Y> **Enter** (Instructs AutoCAD to convert the selected object into a *Pline*. Only <u>one</u> object can be selected.)
> Close or Open/Join/Width/Edit vertex/Fit/Spline/Decurve/Ltype gen/Undo/eXit <X>: *J*
> Select objects: **PICK** (Select the object or group of objects to join. Multiple objects can be selected.)
> Select objects: **Enter** (number) segments added to polyline

The resulting conversion is a closed *Polyline* shape.

SPLINEDIT

PULL-DOWN MENU	SCREEN MENU	TYPE IN	TABLET MENU
Modify *Edit Spline*	*MODIFY* *SplinEd:*	*SPLINEDIT*	---

Splinedit is an extremely powerful command for changing the configuration of existing *Splines*. There are multiple methods that you can use to change *Splines*. All of the *Splinedit* methods fall under <u>two sets of options</u>.

The two groups of options that AutoCAD uses to edit *Splines* are based on two sets of points: <u>data points</u> and <u>control points</u>. Data points are the points that were specified when the *Spline* was created—the points that the *Spline* actually <u>passes through</u> (Fig. 16-28). Control points are other points <u>outside of the path</u> of the *Spline* that only have a "<u>pull</u>" effect on the curve (Fig. 16-29).

Figure 16-28 ———

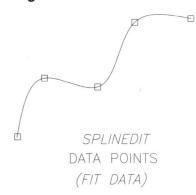

SPLINEDIT
DATA POINTS
(FIT DATA)

Editing *Spline* <u>Data Points</u>

The command prompt displays several levels of options. The top level of options uses the control points method for editing. Select *Fit Data* to use data points for editing. The *Fit Data* methods are <u>recommended</u> for most applications. Since the curve passes directly through the data points, these options offer direct control of the curve path.

> Command: *splinedit*
> Select spline: **PICK**
> Fit Data/Close/Move Vertex/Refine/rEverse/Undo/eXit <X>: *f*
> Add/Close/Delete/Move/Purge/Tangents/toLerance/eXit <X>:
> (option)

Figure 16-29 ———

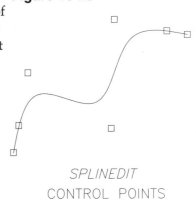

SPLINEDIT
CONTROL POINTS

Add

You can add points to the *Spline*. The *Spline* curve changes to pass through the new points. First, PICK an existing point on the curve. That point and the next one in sequence (in the order of creation) become highlighted. The new point will change the curve between those two highlighted data points (Fig. 16-30).

Figure 16-30

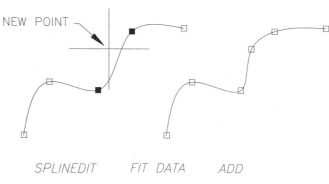

NEW POINT

SPLINEDIT   FIT DATA   ADD

> Select point: **PICK** (Select an existing point on the curve.)
> Enter new point: **PICK** (PICK a new point location.)

Close/Open

The *Close* option only appears if the existing curve is open, and the *Open* prompt only appears if the curve is closed. Selecting either option automatically forces the change. *Close* causes the two ends to become tangent, forming one smooth curve (Fig. 16-31). This <u>tangent continuity</u> is characteristic of *Closed Splines* only. *Splines* that have matching endpoints do not have tangent continuity unless the *Close* option of *Spline* or *Splinedit* is used.

Figure 16-31

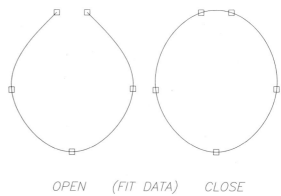

OPEN   (FIT DATA)   CLOSE

Move

You can move any data point to a new location with this option (Fig. 16-32). The beginning endpoint (in the order of creation) becomes highlighted. Type *N* for next or *S* to select the desired data point to move; then PICK the new location.

> Next/Previous/Select Point/eXit/<Enter new location> <N>:

Figure 16-32

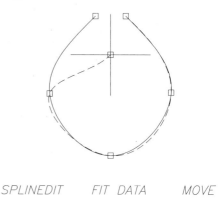

SPLINEDIT   FIT DATA   MOVE

Purge

Purge <u>deletes all data points</u> and renders the *Fit Data* set of options unusable. You are returned to the control point options (top level). To reinstate the points, use *Undo*.

Tangents

You can change the directions for the start and endpoint tangents with this option. This gives the same control that exists with the "Enter start tangent" and "Enter end tangent" prompts of the *Spline* command used when the curves are created (see Fig. 15-27, *Spline, End Tangent*).

toLerance

Use *toLerance* to specify a value, or tolerance, for the curve to "fall." Specifying a tolerance causes the curve to smooth out, or fall, from the data points. The higher the value, the more the curve "loosens." The *toLerance* option of *Splinedit* is identical to the *Fit Tolerance* option available with *Spline* (see Fig. 15-29, *Spline, Tolerance*).

Editing *Spline* <u>Control Points</u>

Use the top level of command options (except *Fit Data*) to edit the *Spline's* control points. These options are similar to those used for editing the data points; however, the results are different since the curve does not pass through the control points.

> Command: **splinedit**
> Select spline: **PICK**
> Fit Data/Close/Move Vertex/Refine/rEverse/Undo/eXit <X>:

Fit Data
Discussed previously.

Close/Open
These options operate similar to the *Fit Data* equivalents; however, the resulting curve falls away from the control points (Fig. 16-33; see also Fig. 16-31, *Fit Data, Close*).

Figure 16-33 ────────────────

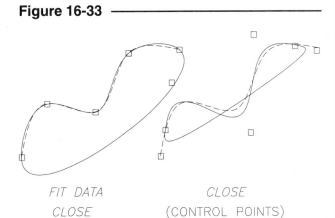

FIT DATA   CLOSE
CLOSE   (CONTROL POINTS)

Move Vertex
Move Vertex allows you to move the location of any control points. This is the control points equivalent to the *Move* option of *Fit Data* (see Fig. 16-32, *Fit Data, Move*). The method of selecting points (*Next/Previous/Select point/eXit/*) is the same as that used for other options.

Refine
Selecting the *Refine* option reveals another level of options.

> Add control point/Elevate Order/Weight/eXit <X>:

Add control points is the control points equivalent to *Fit Data Add* (see Fig. 16-30). At the "Select a point on the Spline" prompt, simply PICK a point near the desired location for the new point to appear. Once the *Refine* option has been used, the *Fit Data* options are not available.

Elevate order allows you to <u>increase the number of control points</u> uniformly along the length of the *Spline*. Enter a value from *n* to 26, where *n* is the current number of points + one. Once a *Spline* is elevated, it cannot be reduced.

Weight is an option that you use to assign a value to the <u>amount of "pull"</u> that a <u>specific control point</u> has on the *Spline* curve. The higher the value, the more "pull," and the closer the curve moves toward the control point. The typical method of selecting points (*Next/Previous/Select point/eXit/*) is used.

rEverse
The *rEverse* option reverses the direction of the *Spline*. The first endpoint (when created) becomes the last endpoint. Reversing the direction may be helpful for selection during the *Move* option.

Grips

Splines can also be edited easily using *Grips* (see Chapter 23). The *Grip* points that appear on the *Spline* are identical to the *Fit Data* points. Editing with *Grips* is a bit more direct and less dependent on the command interface.

MLEDIT

PULL-DOWN MENU	SCREEN MENU	TYPE IN	TABLET MENU
Modify *Edit Multiline...*	*MODIFY* *Mledit:*	*MLEDIT*	---

The *Mledit* command provides tools for editing multilines created with the *Mline* command. Because a multiline is a new type of line object, the typical line editing commands such as *Trim, Extend, Break, Fillet,* and *Chamfer* <u>cannot</u> be used. Instead, the *Mledit* command is required for *Mline* modification and contains several editing functions. These editing functions give you control of multiline intersections.

Invoking the *Mledit* command by any method produces the *Multiline Edit Tools* dialogue box. The dialogue box presents twelve image tiles that you PICK to activate the desired function. <u>Single-clicking</u> on an image tile displays the option name in the lower-left corner of the dialogue box (Fig. 16-34). <u>Double-clicking</u> on an image tile activates that option. The dialogue box then disappears, allowing you to select the desired multiline segments for the editing action.

Figure 16-34 ———————

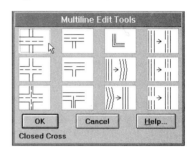

> Command: **mledit** (The *Multiline Edit Tools* dialogue box appears. Select desired option.)
> Select mline: **PICK**
> Select mline(or Undo): **PICK** or **Enter**
> Command:

The *Multiline Edit Tools* dialogue box is organized in columns as follows:

Intersection-Cross	Intersection-Tee	Corner, Vertices	Lines
Closed Cross	Closed Tee	Corner Joint	Cut Single
Open Cross	Open Tee	Vertex Add	Cut All
Merged Cross	Merged Tee	Vertex Delete	Weld

The options are described and illustrated here.

Closed Cross

Use this option to trim one of two intersecting *Mlines*. The <u>first</u> *Mline* PICKed is <u>trimmed</u> to the outer edges of the second. The <u>second</u> *Mline* is "closed." All line elements in the first multiline are trimmed (Fig. 16-35).

Figure 16-35 ———————

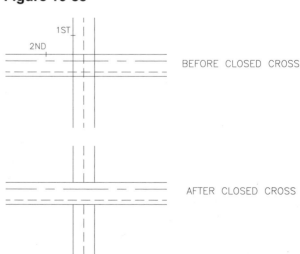

1ST
2ND

BEFORE CLOSED CROSS

AFTER CLOSED CROSS

Open Cross

This option <u>trims both</u> intersecting *Mlines*. Both *Mlines* are "open." <u>All</u> line elements of the <u>first</u> *Mline* PICKed are trimmed to the outer edges of the second. Only the outer line elements of the second multiline are trimmed, while the inner lines continue through the intersection (Fig. 16-36).

Figure 16-36 ――――――――――

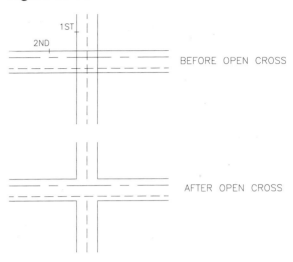

Merged Cross

With this option, the <u>outer</u> line elements of <u>both</u> intersecting *Mlines* are trimmed and the <u>inner line elements merge</u>. The inner line elements merge at the second *Mline's* next set (Fig. 16-37). A full merge (both inner lines continue through) occurs only if the second *Mline* PICKed has no or only one inner line element.

Figure 16-37 ――――――――――

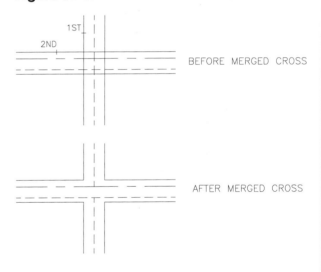

Closed Tee

As indicated by the image tile, a "T" intersection is created rather than a "crossing" intersection. The <u>first</u> *Mline* PICKed is <u>trimmed</u> to the <u>nearest</u> (to the PICK point) outer edge of the second. Only the side of the first *Mline* nearest the PICK point remains. The second *Mline* is not affected (Fig. 16-38).

Figure 16-38 ――――――――――

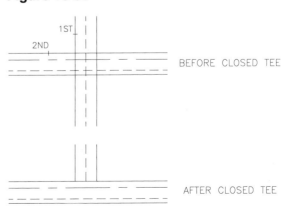

Open Tee

With this "T" intersection, both outer edges of two intersecting *Mlines* are "open." All line elements of the <u>first</u> *Mline* PICKed are <u>trimmed</u> at the outer edges of the second. Only the outer line element of the second is trimmed (Fig. 16-39).

Figure 16-39

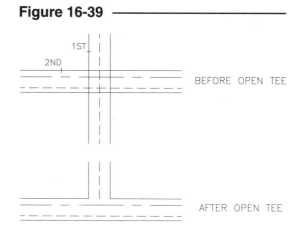

BEFORE OPEN TEE

AFTER OPEN TEE

Merged Tee

This "T" option allows the <u>inner line elements</u> of both intersecting *Mlines merge*. The merge occurs at the second *Mline's* first inner element. Only the side of the first line nearest the PICK point remains (Fig. 16-40).

Figure 16-40

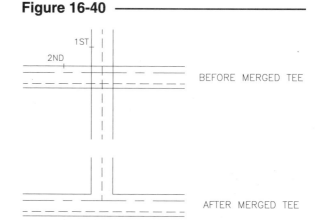

BEFORE MERGED TEE

AFTER MERGED TEE

Corner Joint

This option <u>trims both</u> *Mlines* to create a <u>corner</u>. Only the PICKed sides of the *Mlines* remain and the extending portions of both (if any) are trimmed. All of the inner line elements merge (Fig. 16-41).

Figure 16-41

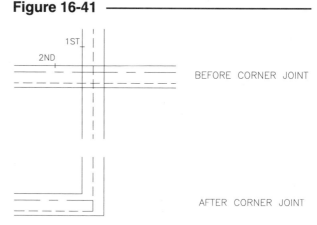

BEFORE CORNER JOINT

AFTER CORNER JOINT

Add Vertex

If you want to add a new corner (vertex) to an existing *Mline*, use this feature. A new vertex is added <u>where you PICK</u> the *Mline*. However, it is not readily apparent that a new vertex exists, nor does the *Mline* visibly change in any way. You must <u>further edit</u> the *Mline* with *Stretch* or grips (see Chapter 23) to create a new "corner" (Fig. 16-42).

Figure 16-42

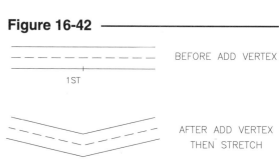

BEFORE ADD VERTEX

AFTER ADD VERTEX
THEN STRETCH

Delete Vertex

Use this feature to remove a corner (vertex) of an *Mline*. The vertex <u>nearest</u> the location you PICK is deleted. The resulting *Mline* contains only one straight segment between the adjacent two vertices. Unlike *Add Vertex*, the *Mline* immediately changes and no further editing is needed to see the effect (Fig. 16-43).

Figure 16-43 ——————————

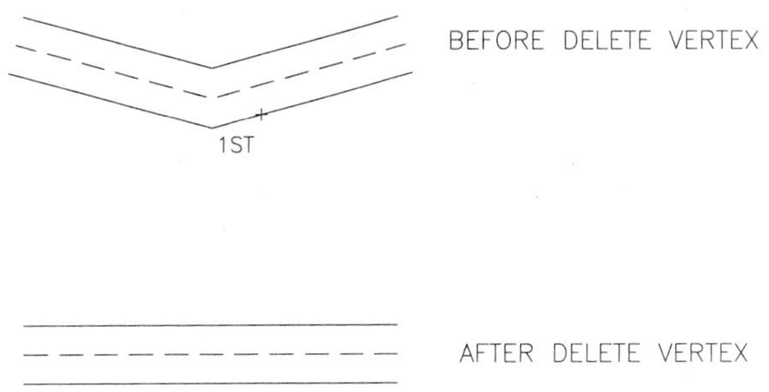

BEFORE DELETE VERTEX

1ST

AFTER DELETE VERTEX

Cut Single

The *Cut* options are used to break (cut) a space in one *Mline*. *Cut Single* <u>breaks any line element</u> that is selected. Similar to *Break 2Points*, the break occurs <u>between the two PICK points</u> (Fig. 16-44). The break points can be on either side of a vertex.

Figure 16-44 ——————————

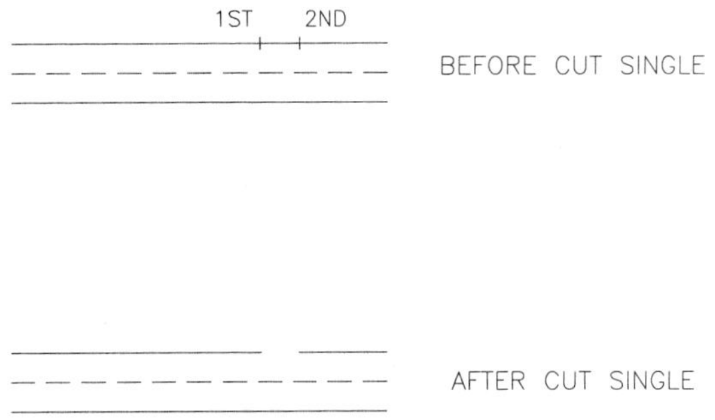

1ST   2ND

BEFORE CUT SINGLE

AFTER CUT SINGLE

Cut All

This *Cut* option <u>breaks all line elements</u> of the selected *Mline*. Any line elements can be selected. The line elements are cut at the PICK points in a direction perpendicular to the axis of the *Mline* (Fig. 16-45). NOTE: Although the *Mline* appears to be cut into two separate *Mlines*, it <u>remains one single object</u>. Using *Stretch* or grips to "move" the *Mline* causes the cut to close again.

Figure 16-45 ——————————

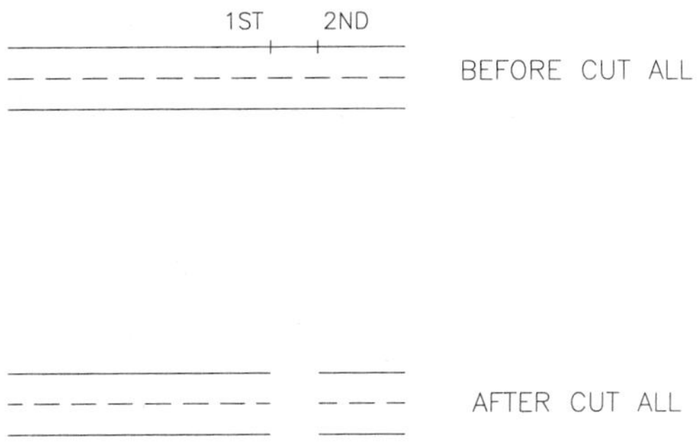

1ST   2ND

BEFORE CUT ALL

AFTER CUT ALL

Weld

This option <u>reverses the action of a *Cut*</u>. The *Mline* is restored to its original continuous configuration. PICK on both sides of the "break" (Fig. 16-46).

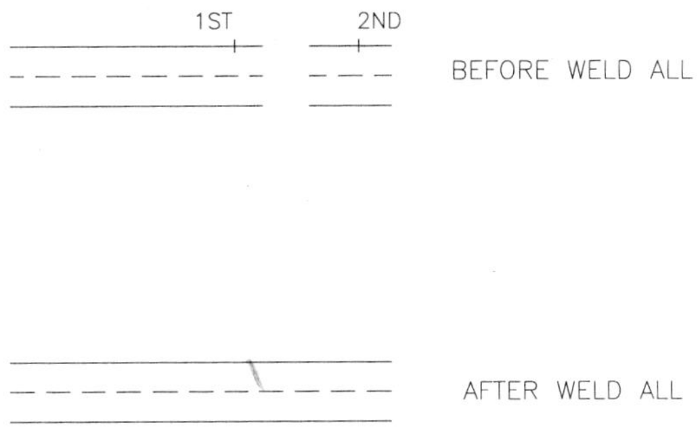

Like other dialogue box-based commands, *Mledit* can also be used in command line format by using the hyphen (-) symbol as a prefix to the command. Key in "-*MLEDIT*" to force the command line interface. The following prompt appears:

Command: **-mledit**
Mline editing option AV/DV/CC/OC/MC/CT/OT/MT/CJ/CS/CA/WA:

Figure 16-46 ——————————

1ST   2ND

BEFORE WELD ALL

AFTER WELD ALL

Entering the acronym activates the related option.

AV   Add Vertex
DV   Delete Vertex
CC   Closed Cross
OC   Open Cross
MC   Merged Cross
CT   Closed Tee
OT   Open Tee
MT   Merged Tee
CJ   Corner Joint
CS   Cut Single
CA   Cut All
WA   Weld All

NOTE: *Mledit* operates only with co-planar *Mlines*

Other Editing Possibilities for *Mlines*
Although it appears that *Mledit* contains the necessary tools to handle all editing possibilities for *Mlines*, that is not necessarily the case. You may experience situations where *Mledit* cannot handle your desired editing request and you have to resort to traditional editing commands. <u>Only</u> in the case that *Mledit* cannot preform as you want, *Explode* the *Mline*, which converts each line element to an individual object. That action allows you to use grips, *Trim*, *Extend*, *Break*, *Fillet*, or *Chamfer* on the individual line elements. Once an *Mline* is *Exploded*, it cannot be converted back to an *Mline*, nor can *Mledit* be used with it.

CHAPTER EXERCISES

1. *Stretch*

   A design change has been requested. *Open* the **SLOT-PLAT** drawing and make the following changes.

   A. The top of the plate (including the slot) must be moved upward. This design change will add 1" to the total height of the Slot Plate. Use *Stretch* to accomplish the change as shown in Figure 16-47. Draw the crossing window as shown.

   B. The notch at the bottom of the plate must be adjusted slightly by relocating it .50 units to the right as shown (highlighted) in Figure 16-48. Draw the crossing window as shown. Use *Saveas* to reassign the name to **SLOTPLT2**.

Figure 16-47 ——————

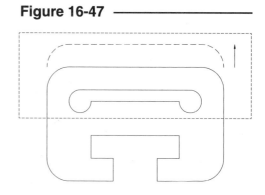

Figure 16-48 ——————

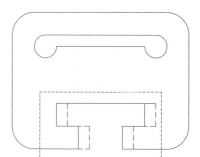

2. *Align*

Figure 16-49

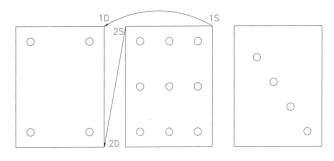

Open the **PLATES** drawing. The three plates are to be stamped at one time on a single sheet of stock measuring 15" x 12". Place the three plates together to achieve the optimum nesting on the sheet stock.

A. Use *Align* to move the plate in the center (with 9 holes). Select the *1st source* and *destination points* (1S, 1D) and *2nd source* and *destination points* (2S, 2D) as shown in Figure 16-49.

B. After the first alignment is complete, use *Align* to move the plate on the right (with 4 diagonal holes). The *source* and *destination points* are indicated in Figure 16-50.

Figure 16-50

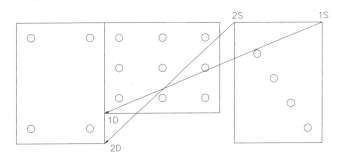

C. Finally, draw the sheet stock outline (15" x 12") using *Line* as shown in Figure 16-51. The plates are ready for production. Use *Saveas* and assign the name **PLATNEST**.

Figure 16-51

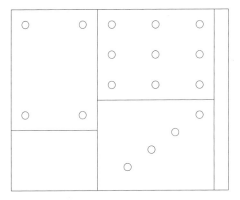

3. *Chprop*

Figure 16-52

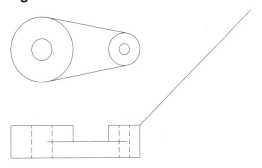

Open the **PIVOTARM** drawing that you worked on in Chapter 9 Exercises. *Load* the *Hidden* and *Center Linetypes*. Make two *New Layers* named **HID** and **CEN** and assign the matching linetypes. Check the *Limits* of the drawing; then calculate and set an appropriate *Ltscale* (usually .5 times the drawing scale factor). Use *Chprop* to change the *Lines* representing the holes in the front view to the **HID** layer as shown in Figure 16-52. *Save* the drawing.

4. *Change*

Figure 16-53 ——————————

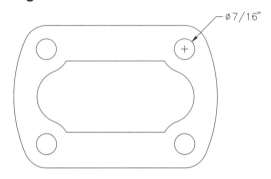

Open **CH8EX3**. *Erase* the *Arc* at the top of the object. *Erase* the *Points* with a window. Invoke the *Change* command. When prompted to *Select objects*, **PICK** all of the inclined *Lines* near the top. When prompted to <Change point>:, enter coordinate **6,8**. The object should appear as that in Figure 16-53. Use *Saveas* and assign the name **CH16EX4**.

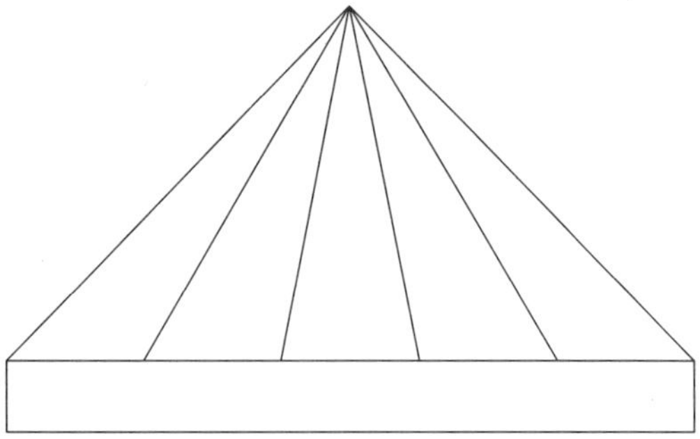

5. *Modify Circle*

Figure 16-54 ——————————

A design change is required for the bolt holes in **GASKETA**. *Open* **GASKETA** and invoke the *Modify* dialogue box. Change each of the four bolt holes to **7/16** diameter. *Save* the drawing.

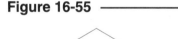

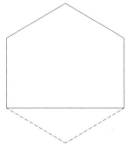

6. *Explode*

Figure 16-55 ——————————

You can quickly create the shape shown (continuous lines) in Figure 16-55 by *Exploding* a *Polygon*. First, start a *New* drawing. Create a **6**-sided *Polygon* with the *Center* at **6,4**. *Circumscribe* the *Polygon* about a **2** unit radius. Next *Explode* the *Polygon* and *Erase* the two *Lines* (highlighted). Draw the bottom *Line* from the two *ENDpoints*.

7. *Pedit*

Figure 16-56 ——————————

Open the **CH15EX2** drawing that you completed in the Chapter 15 Exercises. Use *Pedit* with the *Edit vertex* options to alter the shape as shown in Figure 16-56. For the bottom notch, use *Straighten*. For the top notch, use *Insert*. Use *Saveas* and change the name to **CH16EX7**.

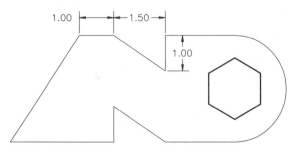

8. *Pline, Pedit*

A. Create a line graph as shown in Figure 16-57 to illustrate the low temperatures for a week. The temperatures are as follows:

X axis	Y axis
Sunday	20
Monday	14
Tuesday	18
Wednesday	26
Thursday	34
Friday	38
Saturday	27

Use equal intervals along each axis. Use a *Pline* for the graph line. *Save* the drawing as **CH16EX8A**. (You will label the graph at a later time.)

B. Use *Pedit* to change the *Pline* to a *Spline*. Note that the graph line is no longer 100% accurate because it does not pass through the original vertices (see Fig. 16-58). Use the *SPLFRAME* variable to display the original "frame" (*Regen* must be used after).

Use the *Modify Object* dialogue box and try the *Cubic* and *Quadratic* options. Which option causes the vertices to have more pull? Find the most accurate option. Set *SPLFRAME* to **0** and *Saveas* **CH16EX8B**.

C. Use *Pedit* to change the curve from *Pline* to *Fit Curve*. Does the graph line pass through the vertices? *Saveas* **CH16EX8C**.

D. *Open* drawing **CH16EX8A**. *Erase* the *Splined Pline* and construct the graph using a *Spline* instead (see 8A for data). *Saveas* **CH16EX8D**. Compare the *Spline* with the variations of *Plines*. Which of the four drawings (A, B, C, or D) is smoothest? Which are most accurate?

E. It was learned that there was a mistake in reporting the temperatures for that week. Thursday's low must be changed to 38 degrees and Friday's to 34 degrees. *Open* **CH16EX8D** (if not already open) and use *Splinedit* to correct the mistake. Use the *Move* option of *Fit Data* so that the exact data points can be altered as shown in Figure 16-60. *Saveas* **CH16EX8E**.

Figure 16-57 ——————

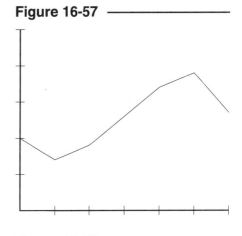

Figure 16-58 ——————

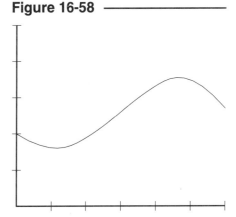

Figure 16-59 ——————

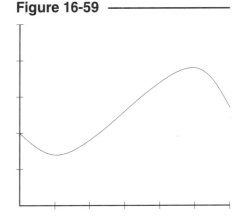

Figure 16-60 ——————

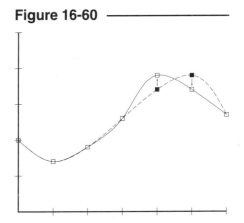

9. **Converting** *Lines*, *Circles*, **and** *Arcs* **to** *Plines*

Use **ASHEET** as a prototype and assign the name **GASKETC**. Change the *Limits* for plotting on a metric A4 sheet at 2:1 (refer to the Metric Table of *Limits* Settings and set *Limits* to 1/2 x *Limits* specified for 1:1 scale). Begin but do not complete the drawing of the Gasket shown in Figure 16-61. First, draw only the <u>inside</u> shape using *Lines* and *Circles* (with *Trim*) or *Arcs*. Then convert the *Lines* and *Arcs* to one closed *Pline* using *Pedit*. Finally, locate and draw the 3 bolt holes. *Save* the drawing. Do not draw the outside shape. The gasket will be completed in Chapter 17 Exercises.

Figure 16-61 ————————

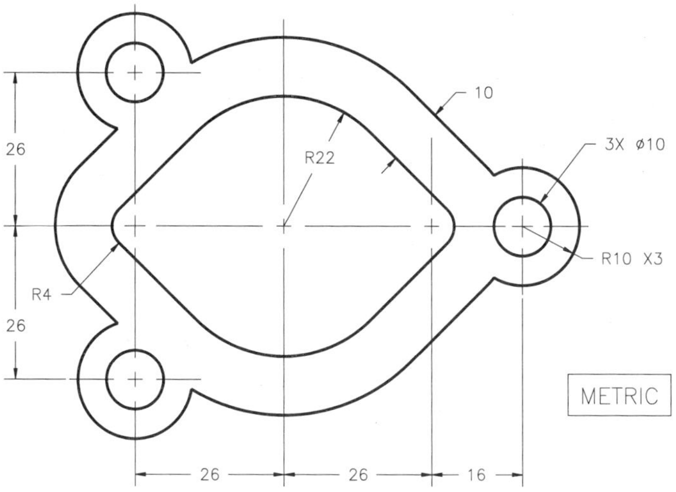

10. *Splinedit*

Open the **HANDLE** drawing that you created in Chapter 15 Exercises. During the testing and analysis process, it was discovered that the shape of the handle should have a more ergonomic design. The finger side (left) should be flatter to accommodate varying sizes of hands, and the thumb side (right) should have more of a protrusion on top to prevent slippage.

First, add more control points uniformly along the length of the left side with *Spinedit*, *Refine*. *Elevate* the *Order* from 4 to **6**, then use *Move Vertex* to align the control points as shown in Figure 16-62.

On the right side of the handle, *Add* two points under the *Fit Data* option to create the protrusion shown in Figure 16-63. You may have to *Reverse* the direction of the *Spline* to add the new points between the two highlighted ones. *SaveAs* **HANDLE2**.

Figure 16-62   **Figure 16-63**

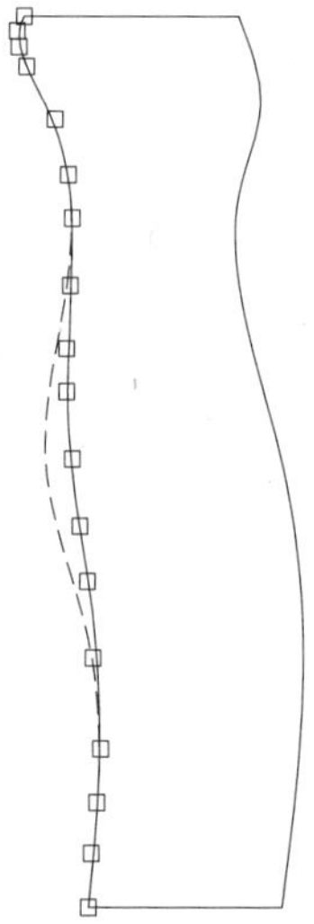

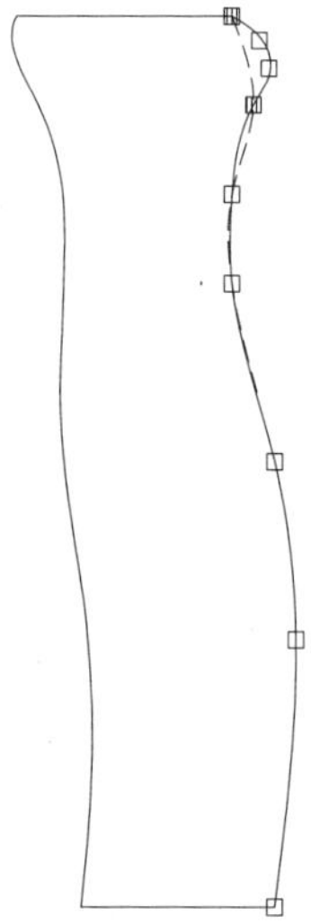

11. *Mline, Mledit, Stretch*

Draw the floor plan of the storage room shown in Figure 16-64. Use *Mline* objects for the walls and *Plines* for the windows and doors. Use *Mledit* to treat the intersections as shown. When your drawing is complete according to the given specifications, use *Stretch* to center the large window along the top wall. Save the drawing as **STORROOM**.

Figure 16-64 ————————

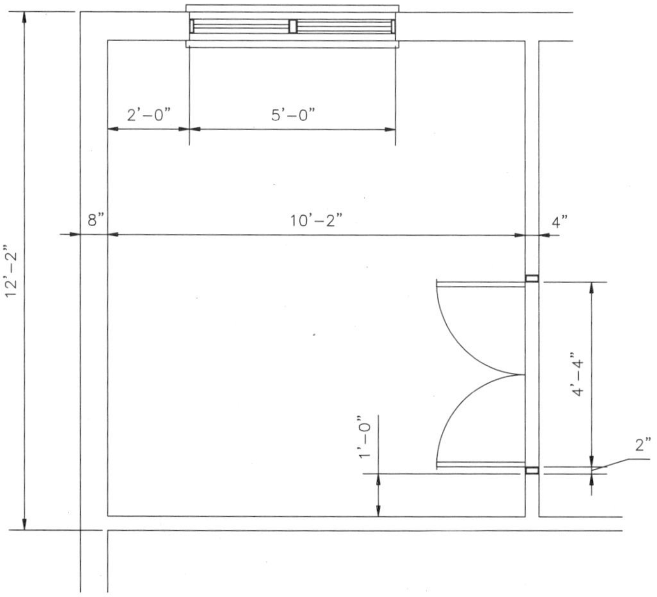

Chapter 17

CONSTRUCT COMMANDS II

Chapter Objectives

After completing this chapter you should:

1. be able to create a *Fillet* between two objects;

2. be able to create a *Chamfer* between two objects;

3. know how to create parallel copies of objects with *Offset*;

4. be able to use *Divide* to add points at equal parts of an object;

5. be able to use *Measure* to add points at specified segment lengths along an object;

6. be able to create a *Boundary* by PICKing inside a closed area;

7. know that objects forming a closed shape can be combined into a *Region* and that composite *Regions* can be created with *Union*, *Subtract*, and *Intersect*.

BASICS

Construct commands <u>use existing</u> objects in some way but also <u>create</u> new objects in the process. The fundamental *Construct* commands were covered in Chapter 10. This chapter deals with another set of somewhat more complex *Construct* commands such as *Fillet, Chamfer, Offset, Divide, Measure, Boundary,* and *Region*. The *Divide* and *Measure* commands are located in the Draw menus, but have been considered Construct commands in AutoCAD releases previous to Release 13.

COMMANDS

FILLET

PULL-DOWN MENU	SCREEN MENU	TYPE IN	TABLET MENU
Construct *Fillet*	*CONSTRCT* *Fillet:*	*FILLET*	*19,X and 20,X*

The *Fillet* command automatically rounds a sharp corner (intersection of two *Lines, Arcs, Circles,* or *Pline* vertices) with a radius. You only specify the radius and select the objects' ends to be *Filleted*. The objects to fillet do <u>not</u> have to completely intersect but can overlap. You can specify whether or not the objects are automatically extended or trimmed as necessary (Fig. 17-1).

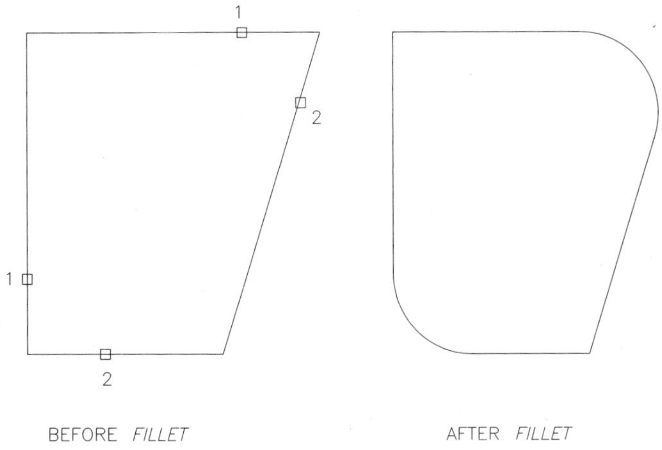

The *Fillet* command must be used first to input the desired *radius* and a second time to select the objects to *Fillet*.

Figure 17-1 ───────────

BEFORE *FILLET*   AFTER *FILLET*

    Command: *fillet*
    (TRIM mode) Current fillet radius=0.000
    Polyline/Radius/Trim/<Select first object>: *r* (Indicates the radius option.)
    Enter fillet radius <0.0000>: (**value**) or **PICK** (Enter a value for the desired fillet radius or select two
    points to interactively specify the radius.)
    Command:

No fillet will be drawn at this time. Repeat the *Fillet* command to select objects to fillet.

    Command: *fillet*
    (TRIM mode) Current fillet radius=0.500
    Polyline/Distances/Trim/<Select first object>: **PICK** (Select one *Line, Arc,* or *Circle* near the point
    where fillet should be created.)
    Select second object: **PICK** (Select second object to fillet near the fillet location.)
    Command:

The fillet is created at the corner selected.

Treatment of *Arcs* and *Circles* with *Fillet* is shown here. Note that the objects to *Fillet* do not have to intersect but can overlap.

Since trimming and extending are done automatically by *Fillet* when necessary, using *Fillet* with a *radius* of *0* has particular usefulness.

Figure 17-2

BEFORE
AFTER
1
2

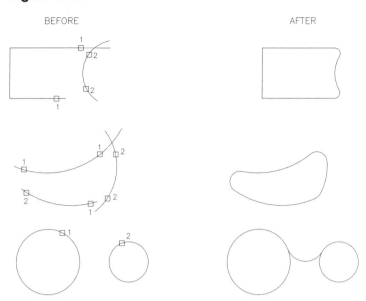

Using *Fillet* with a *0 radius* creates clean, sharp corners even if the original objects overlap or do not intersect (Fig. 17-3).

Figure 17-3

BEFORE
AFTER
1
2

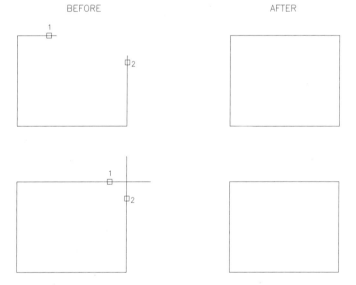

If parallel objects are selected, the *Fillet* is automatically created to the correct radius. Therefore, parallel objects can be filleted at any time <u>without specifying a radius value</u>.

Figure 17-4

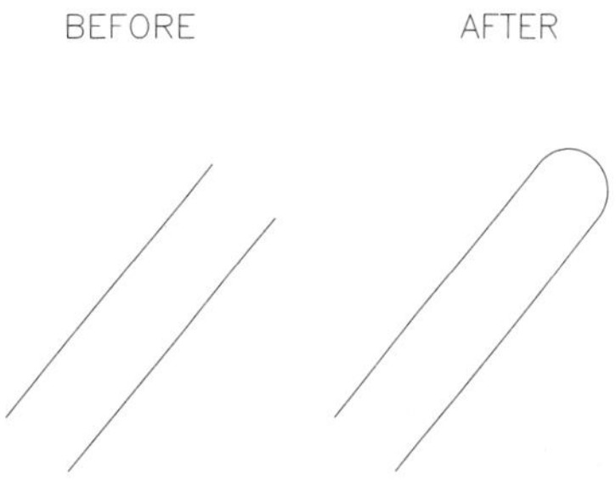

BEFORE
AFTER

R13

Polyline

Fillets can be created on *Polylines* in the same manner as two *Line* objects. Use *Fillet* as you normally would for *Lines*. However, if you want a fillet equal to the specified radius to be added to each vertex of the *Pline* (except the endpoint vertices), use the *Polyline* option; then select anywhere on the *Pline*.

> Command: *fillet*
> Polyline/Distances/<Select first object>: *P*
> (Invokes prompts for the Polyline option.)
> Select 2D polyline: **PICK** (Select the desired polyline.)

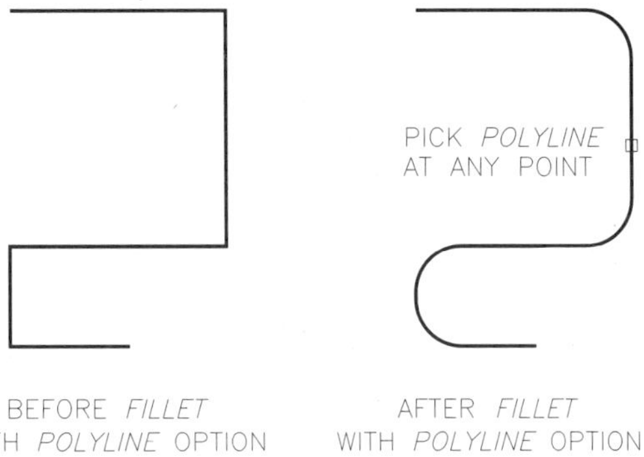

Closed Plines created by the *Close* option of *Pedit* react differently with *Fillet* than *Plines* connected by PICKing matching endpoints. Figure 17-6 illustrates the effect of *Fillet Polyline* on a *Closed Pline* and on a connected *Pline*.

Figure 17-5

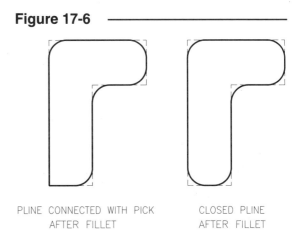

PICK *POLYLINE* AT ANY POINT

BEFORE *FILLET* WITH *POLYLINE* OPTION   AFTER *FILLET* WITH *POLYLINE* OPTION

Figure 17-6

PLINE CONNECTED WITH PICK AFTER FILLET   CLOSED PLINE AFTER FILLET

Trim/Notrim

In the previous figures, the objects are shown having been filleted in the *Trim* mode—that is, with automatically trimmed or extended objects to meet the end of the new fillet radius. The *Notrim* mode creates the fillet without any extending or trimming of the involved objects (Fig. 17-7). Note that the command prompt indicates the current mode (as well as the current radius) when *Fillet* is invoked.

> Command: *fillet*
> (NOTRIM mode) Current fillet radius=2.000
> Polyline/Radius/Trim/<Select first object>:

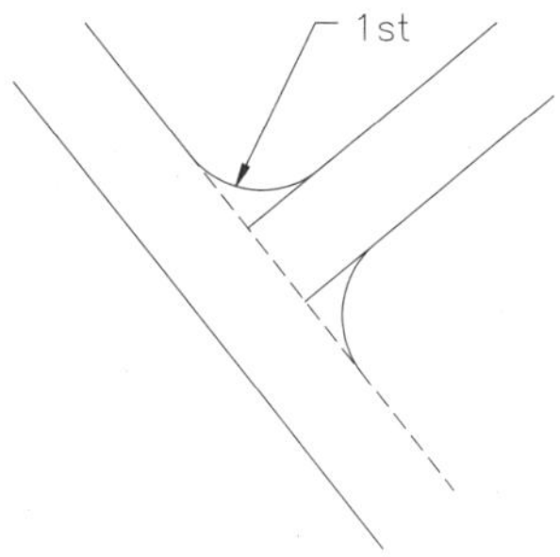

The *Notrim* mode is helpful in situations similar to that in Figure 17-8. In this case, if the intersecting *Lines* were trimmed when the first fillet was created, the longer *Line* (highlighted) would have to be redrawn in order to create the second fillet.

Figure 17-7   **Figure 17-8**

1st

FILLET   NOTRIM

FILLET   NOTRIM

CHAMFER

PULL-DOWN MENU	SCREEN MENU	TYPE IN	TABLET MENU
Construct Chamfer	*CONSTRCT Chamfer:*	*CHAMFER*	*21,X*

Chamfering is a manufacturing process used to replace a sharp corner with an angled surface. In AutoCAD, *Chamfer* is commonly used to change the intersection of two *Lines* or *Plines* by adding an angled line.

R13

The *Chamfer* command is similar to *Fillet*, but rather than rounding with a radius or "fillet," an angled line is automatically drawn at the distances (from the existing corner) that you specify.

Chamfers can be created by <u>two methods</u> in Release 13: *Distance* (specify <u>two distances</u>) or *Angle* (specify a <u>distance and an angle</u>). The current method and the previously specified values are displayed at the Command: prompt along with the options.

    Command: **chamfer**
    (TRIM mode) Current chamfer Dist1 = 0.0000, Dist2 = 0.0000
    Polyline/Distance/Angle/Trim/Method/<Select first line>:

Method
Use this option to indicate which of the two methods you want to use: *Distance* (specify 2 distances) or *Angle* (specify a distance and an angle).

Distance
The *Distance* option is used to specify the two values applied <u>when the *Distance Method* is used</u> to create the chamfer. The values indicate the distances from the corner (intersection of two lines) to each chamfer endpoint (Fig. 17-9). Use the *Chamfer* command once to specify *Distances* and again to draw the chamfer.

Figure 17-9

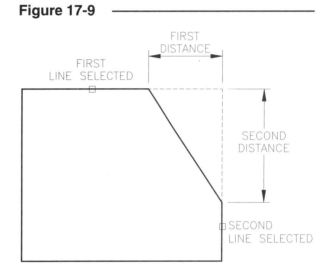

    Command: **chamfer**
    (TRIM mode) Current chamfer Dist1 = 0.0000, Dist2 = 0.0000
    Polyline/Distance/Angle/Trim/Method/<Select first line>: **d** (Indicates the distance option.)
    Enter first chamfer distance <0.0000>: **(value)** or **PICK** (Enter a value for the distance from the existing corner to the endpoint of chamfer on first line or select two points to interactively specify the distance.)
    Enter second chamfer distance <value of first distance>: **Enter**, **(value)** or **PICK** (Press Enter to use same distance as first distance, enter a value, or PICK as before.)
    Command:

Chamfer with distances of 0 reacts like *Fillet* with a radius of 0; that is, overlapping corners can be automatically trimmed and non-intersecting corners can be automatically extended (using *Trim* mode).

Figure 17-10

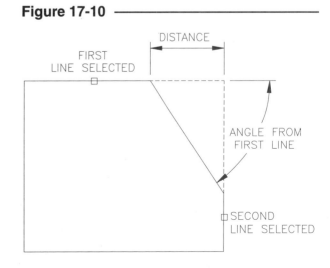

Angle
The *Angle* option allows you to specify the values that are <u>used for the *Angle Method*</u>. The values specify a distance <u>along the first line</u> and an <u>angle from the first line</u> (Fig. 17-10).

Polyline/Distance/Angle/Trim/Method/<Select first line>: **a**
Enter chamfer length on the first line <1.0000>: **(value)**
Enter chamfer angle from the first line <60.0000>: **(value)**

Trim/Notrim

The two lines selected for chamfering do not have to intersect but can overlap or not connect. The *Trim* setting automatically trims or extends the lines selected for the chamfer (Fig. 17-11), while the *Notrim* setting adds the chamfer without changing the length of the selected lines. These two options are the same as those in the *Fillet* command (see *Fillet*).

Figure 17-11 ─────────────────

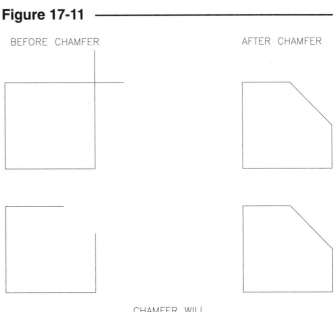

Polyline

The *Polyline* option of *Chamfer* creates chamfers on all vertices of a polyline. All vertices of the *Pline* are chamfered with the supplied distances (Fig. 17-12). The first end of the *Pline* that was <u>drawn</u> takes the first distance. Use *Chamfer* without this option if you want to chamfer only one corner of a *Pline*. This is similar to the same option of *Fillet* (see *Fillet*).

Figure 17-12 ─────────────────

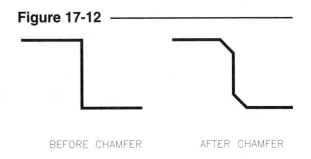

OFFSET

PULL-DOWN MENU	SCREEN MENU	TYPE IN	TABLET MENU
Construct *Offset*	*CONSTRCT* *Offset:*	*OFFSET*	*14,W*

Offset creates a <u>parallel copy</u> of selected objects. Selected objects can be *Lines*, *Arcs*, *Circles*, *Plines*, or other objects. *Offset* is a very useful command that can increase productivity greatly, particularly with *Plines*.

Depending on the object selected, the resulting *Offset* is drawn differently (Fig. 17-13). *Offset* creates a parallel copy of a *Line* equal in length and perpendicular to the original. *Arcs* and *Circles* have a concentric *Offset*. *Offset* closed *Plines* or *Splines* results in a complete parallel shape.

Two options are available with *Offset*: (1) *Offset* a specified *distance* and (2) *Offset through* a specified point (Fig. 17-14).

Distance
The *Distance* option command sequence is as follows:

> Command: *offset*
> Offset distance or Through <Through>: (**value**) or **PICK** (Indicate the distance to offset by entering a value or interactively picking two points.)
> Select objects to offset: **PICK** (Select an object to make a parallel copy of. Only one object can be selected.)
> Side to offset? **PICK** or (**coordinates**) (Select which side of the selected object for offset to be drawn.)
> Select objects to offset: **Enter** (*Offset* can be used repeatedly to offset at the <u>same</u> distance as the previously specified value. Pressing Enter completes command.)
> Command:

Through
The command sequence for *Offset through* is as follows:

> Command: *offset*
> Offset distance or Through <Through>: *T*
> Select objects to offset: **PICK** (Select an object to make a parallel copy of. Only one object can be selected.)
> Through point: **PICK** or (**coordinates**) (Select a point for offset to be drawn through. Coordinates can be entered or point can be selected with or without *OSNAPs*.)
> Select objects to offset: **Enter** (*Offset* can be used repeatedly to specify a <u>different</u> through point. Pressing Enter completes command.)
> Command:

Figure 17-13

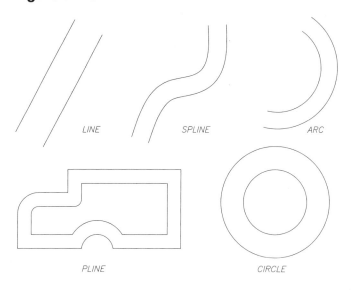

LINE   SPLINE   ARC

PLINE   CIRCLE

Figure 17-14

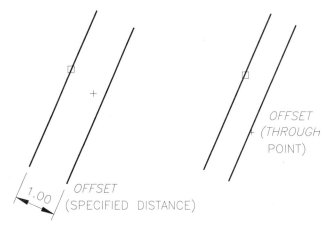

1.00   OFFSET (SPECIFIED DISTANCE)

OFFSET (THROUGH POINT)

OFFSET OPTIONS

Figure 17-15

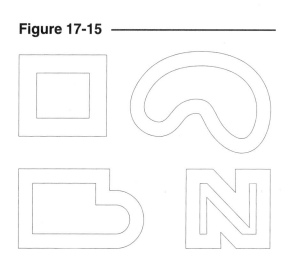

Keep in mind the power of using *Offset* with closed *Pline* or *Spline* shapes (Fig. 17-15). Remember that any closed shape composed of *Lines* and *Arcs* can be converted to one *Pline* object (see *Pedit*, Chapter 16).

DIVIDE

PULL-DOWN MENU	SCREEN MENU	TYPE IN	TABLET MENU
Draw *Point >* *Divide*	DRAW2 *Divide:*	*DIVIDE*	22,W

The *Divide* and *Measure* commands add *Point* objects to existing objects. Both commands are found in the *Draw* menus and toolbars in Release 13, but are considered *Modify* commands in previous releases since they use existing objects and create new ones.

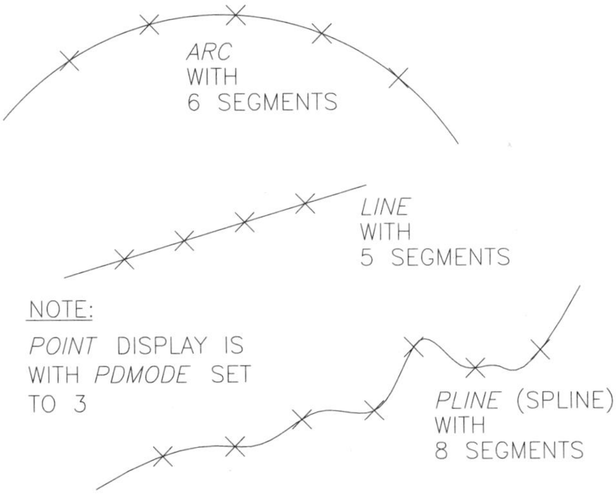

The *Divide* command finds equal intervals along an object such as a *Line*, *Pline*, *Spline*, or *Arc* and adds a *Point* object at each interval. The object being divided is <u>not</u> actually broken into parts—it remains as <u>one</u> object. *Point* objects are automatically added to display the "divisions."

The point objects that are added to the object can be used for subsequent construction by providing a means for *OSNAP*ing to the equally spaced *Node*s.

Figure 17-16

The command sequence for the *Divide* command is as follows:

> Command: **divide**
> Select object to divide: **PICK**
> (Only one object can be selected.)
> <Number of segments>/Block:
> **(value)** (Enter a value for the number of segments.)
> Command:

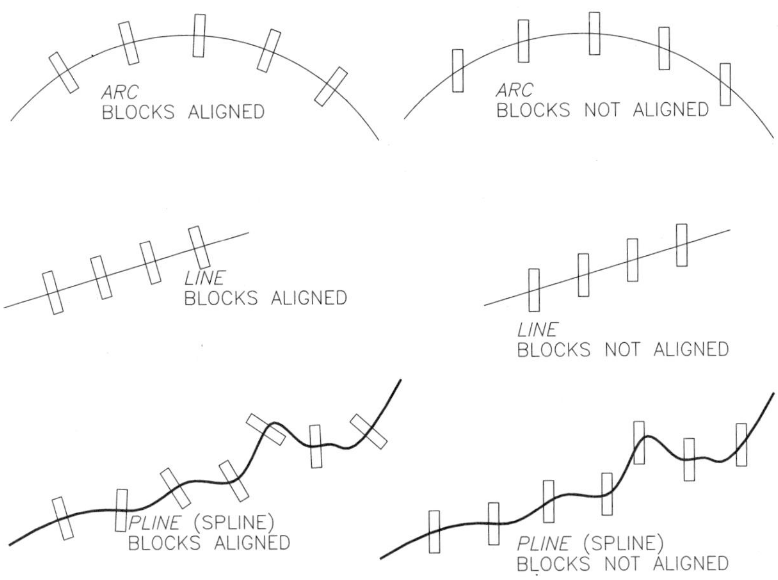

Point objects are added to divide the object selected into the desired number of parts. Therefore, there is <u>one less</u> *Point* added than the number of segments specified.

After using the *Divide* command, the *Point* objects may not be visible

Figure 17-17

unless the point style is changed with the *Point Style...* dialogue box (*Options* pull-down) or by changing the *PDMODE* variable by command line format (see Chapter 8). A *Regen* must be invoked before the new point style will be displayed. Figure 17-16 shows *Points* displayed using a *PDMODE* of 3.

You can request that *Blocks* be inserted rather than *Point* objects along equal divisions of the selected object. Figure 17-17 displays a generic rectangular-shaped block inserted with *Divide*, both aligned and not aligned with a *Line*, *Arc*, and *Pline*. In order to insert a *Block* using the *Divide* command, the name of an <u>existing</u> *Block* must be given. (See Chapter 21, Blocks.)

MEASURE

PULL-DOWN MENU	SCREEN MENU	TYPE IN	TABLET MENU
Draw *Point >* *Measure*	*DRAW2* *Measure:*	*MEASURE*	*22,X*

The *Measure* command is similar to the *Divide* command in that *Point* objects (or *Blocks*) are inserted along the selected object. The *Measure* command, however, allows you to designate the <u>length</u> of segments rather than the <u>number</u> of segments as with the *Divide* command.

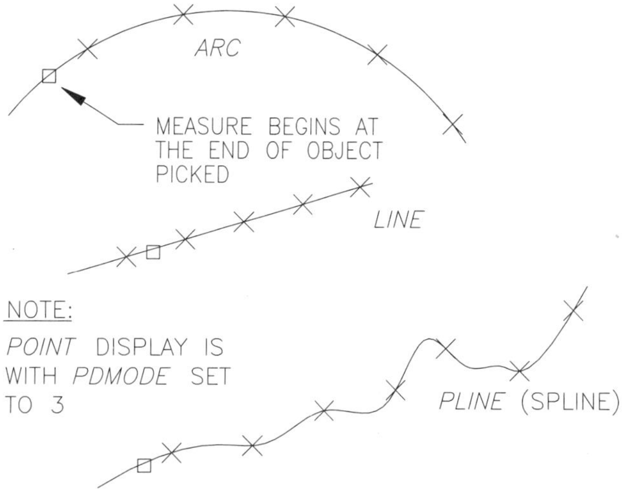

> Command: **measure**
> Select object to measure: **PICK** (Only one object can be selected.)
> <Segments length>/Block: (**value**) (Enter a value for length of one segment.)
> Command:

Point objects are added to the selected object at the designated intervals (lengths). There is one *Point* added for each interval <u>beginning at the end nearest</u> the end used for object selection. The intervals are of equal length except possibly the last segment, which is whatever length is remaining.

You can request that *Blocks* be inserted rather than *Point* objects at the designated intervals of the selected object. Inserting *Blocks* with *Measure* requires that an <u>existing</u> *Block* be used.

Figure 17-18

BOUNDARY

PULL-DOWN MENU	SCREEN MENU	TYPE IN	TABLET MENU
Construct *Bounding Polyline*	*CONSTRCT* *Boundar:*	*BOUNDARY*	---

Boundary finds and draws a boundary from a group of overlapping shapes forming an enclosed area. The shapes can be any AutoCAD objects and can be in any configuration, as long as they form a totally enclosed area. *Boundary* creates either a *Polyline* or *Region* object forming the boundary shape. The resulting *Boundary* does not affect the existing geometry in any way. *Boundary* finds and includes internal closed areas (called islands) such as circles (holes) and traces them as part of the *Boundary*.

To create a *Boundary*, select an internal point in any enclosed area (Fig. 17-19). *Boundary* uses the <u>ray-casting</u> method to find the nearest entity (by default), then traces it around until a complete

Figure 17-19

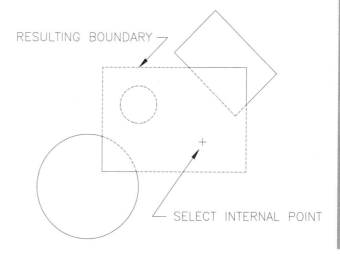

enclosed path is found. The resulting *Boundary* can be used to construct other geometries or can be used to determine the *Area* for the shape (such as a room in a floor plan). The ray-casting method is also used to determine boundaries for sectioning using *Bhatch* (Chapter 26).

Boundary operates in dialogue box mode (Fig. 17-20). After setting the desired options, select the *Pick Points* tile to select the desired internal point (as shown in Fig. 17-19). The options are as follows.

Object Type
Construct either a *Region* or *Polyline* boundary. If islands are found, two or more *Plines* are formed, but only one *Region*.

Define Boundary Set
From Everything on Screen is sufficient for most applications; however, for large drawings you can *Make a New Boundary* set by selecting a smaller set of objects to be considered for ray casting.

Ray-Casting
If *Island Detection* is not selected, you can choose the way AutoCAD defines the boundary. For narrow areas, it may be desirable to use an explicit direction other than *Nearest* (see Ray-Casting, Chapter 26).

Island Detection
This options tells AutoCAD whether or not to include interior enclosed objects in the *Boundary*.

Pick Points
Use this option to PICK an enclosed area in the drawing that is anywhere <u>inside</u> the desired boundary.

Figure 17-20

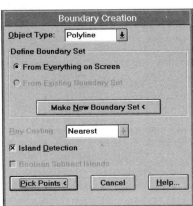

REGION

PULL-DOWN MENU	SCREEN MENU	TYPE IN	TABLET MENU
Construct Region	*CONSTRCT Region:*	*REGION*	8,J

The *Region* command converts one or a set of objects forming a closed shape into one object called a *Region*. This is similar to the way in which a set of objects (*Lines, Arcs, Plines,* etc.) forming a closed shape and having matching endpoints can be converted into a closed *Pline*. A *Region*, however, has special properties.

1. Several *Regions* can be combined with Boolean operations know as *Union, Subtract,* and *Intersect* to form a "composite" *Region*. This process can be repeated until the desired shape is achieved.

2. A *Region* is considered a planar surface. The surface is defined by the edges of the *Region* and no edges can exist within the *Region* perimeter. *Regions* can be used with surface modeling.

In order to create a *Region*, a closed shape must exist. The shape can be composed of one or more objects such as a *Line, Arc, Pline, Circle,* an *Ellipse,* or anything composed of a *Pline* (*Polygon, Rectangle, Boundary*). If more than one object is involved, the endpoints must match (having no gaps or overlaps). Simply invoke the *Region* command and select all objects to be converted to the *Region*.

```
Command: region
Select objects: PICK
Select objects: PICK
Select objects: PICK
Select objects: Enter
1 loop extracted.
1 Region created.
Command:
```

Consider the shape shown in Figure 17-21 composed of four connecting *Lines*. Using *Region* combines the shape into one object, a *Region*. The appearance of the object does not change after the conversion, even though the resuting shape is one object.

Figure 17-21

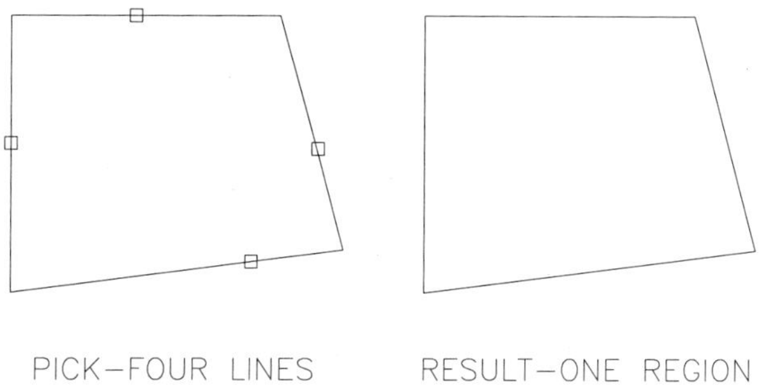

PICK—FOUR LINES   RESULT—ONE REGION

Although the *Region* appears to be no different than a closed *Pline*, it is more powerful because several *Regions* can be combined to form complex shapes (composite *Regions*) using the three Boolean operations explained next. As an example, a set of *Regions* (converted *Circles*) can be combined to form the sprocket with only <u>one</u> *Subtract* operation (Fig. 17-22). Compare the simplicity of this operation to the process of using *Trim* to delete <u>each</u> of the unwanted portions of the small circles.

Figure 17-22

BEFORE
ONE LARGE REGION
ONE SMALL REGION ARRAYED 33 TIMES

AFTER SUBTRACT
ONE COMPOSITE REGION

The Boolean operators, *Union*, *Subtraction*, and *Intersection*, can be used with *Regions* as well as solids. Any number of these commands that are explained next can be used with *Regions* to form complex geometry. To illustrate each of the Boolean commands, consider the shapes shown in Figure 17-23. The *Circle* and the closed *Pline* are <u>first</u> converted to *Regions*; then *Union*, *Subtract*, or *Intersection* can be used.

Figure 17-23

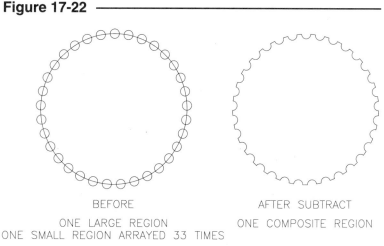

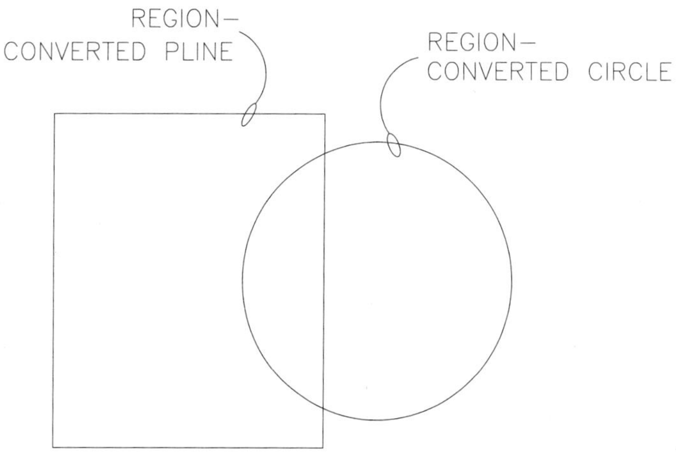

REGION—
CONVERTED PLINE

REGION—
CONVERTED CIRCLE

UNION

PULL-DOWN MENU	SCREEN MENU	TYPE IN	TABLET MENU
Construct *Union*	DRAW2 SOLIDS *Union:*	**UNION**	*13,Y*

Union combines <u>two or more</u> *Regions* (or solids) into <u>one</u> *Region* (or solid). The resulting composite *Region* has the encompassing perimeter and area of the original *Regions*. Invoking *Union* causes AutoCAD to prompt you to select objects. You can select only existing *Regions*.

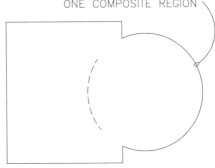

AFTER UNION
ONE COMPOSITE REGION

> Command: **union**
> Select objects: **PICK** (*Region*)
> Select objects: **PICK** (*Region*)
> Select objects: **Enter**
> Command:

The selected *Regions* are combined into one composite *Region* (Fig. 17-24). Any number of Boolean operations can be performed on the *Region(s)*.

Several *Regions* can be selected in response to the "Select objects:" prompt. For example, a composite *Region* such as that in Figure 17-25 can be created with one *Union*.

Figure 17-25 ——————

BEFORE— 10 REGIONS

Two or more *Regions* can be *Unioned* even if they do not overlap. They are simply combined into one object although they still appear as two.

AFTER UNION— ONE REGION

SUBTRACT

PULL-DOWN MENU	SCREEN MENU	TYPE IN	TABLET MENU
Construct *Subtract*	DRAW2 SOLIDS *Subtrac:*	*SUBTRACT*	*14,Y*

Subtract enables you to remove one *Region* (or set of *Regions*) from another. The *Regions* must be created before using *Subtract* (or any Boolean operator). *Subtract* also works with solids (as do the other Boolean operations).

There are two steps to *Subtract*. First, you are prompted to select the *Region* or set of *Regions* to "subtract from" (those that you wish to <u>keep</u>), then to select the *Regions* "to subtract" (those you want to <u>remove</u>). The resulting shape is one composite *Region* comprising the perimeter of the first set minus the second (sometimes called difference).

Command: **subtract**
Select solids and regions to subtract from...
Select objects: **PICK**
Select objects: **Enter**
Select solids and regions to subtract...
Select objects: **PICK**
Select objects: **Enter**
Command:

Figure 17-26

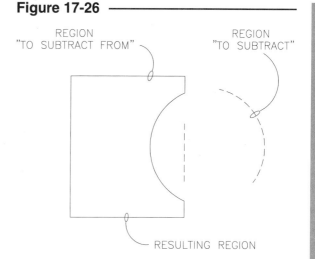

REGION
"TO SUBTRACT FROM"

REGION
"TO SUBTRACT"

RESULTING REGION

Consider the two shapes previously shown in Figure 17-23. The resulting *Region* shown in Figure 17-26 is the result of *Subtracting* the circular *Region* from the rectangular one.

Keep in mind that <u>multiple</u> *Regions* can be selected as the set to keep or as the set to remove. For example, the sprocket illustrated previously (Fig. 17-22) was created by subtracting several circular *Regions* in one operation. Another example is the removal of material to create holes or slots in sheet metal (discussed in Chapter 39, Surfaces).

INTERSECT

PULL-DOWN MENU	SCREEN MENU	TYPE IN	TABLET MENU
Construct *Intersect*	*DRAW2* *SOLIDS* *Intersec:*	*INTERSECT*	*12,Y*

Intersect is the Boolean operator that finds the common area from two or more *Regions*. Consider the rectangular and circular *Regions* previously shown (Fig. 17-23). Using the *Intersect* command and selecting both shapes results in a *Region* comprising only that area that is shared by both shapes (Fig. 17-27).

Command: **intersect**
Select objects: **PICK**
Select objects: **PICK**
Select objects: **Enter**
Command:

If more than two *Regions* are selected, the resulting *Intersection* is composed of only the common area from all shapes (Fig 17-28). If <u>all</u> of the shapes selected do not overlap, a <u>null</u> *Region* is created (all shapes disappear because there is no area that is common to <u>all</u>).

Intersect is a powerful operation when used with solid modeling. Techniques for saving time and file space using Boolean operations such as this are discussed in Chapter 37, Solid Modeling Construction.

Figure 17-27

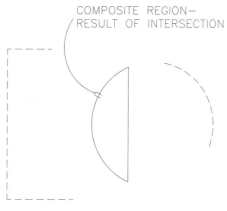

COMPOSITE REGION—
RESULT OF INTERSECTION

Figure 17-28

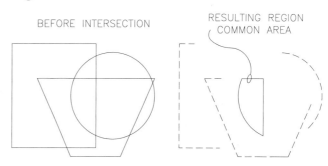

BEFORE INTERSECTION

RESULTING REGION
COMMON AREA

CHAPTER EXERCISES

1. *Fillet*

   Use the **ASHEET** or **A-BORDER** drawing as a prototype and create the "T" Plate shown in Figure 17-29. Use *Fillet* to create all the fillets and rounds as the last step. When finished, *Saveas* **T-PLATE** and plot the drawing at 1=1 scale.

Figure 17-29 ————————————————

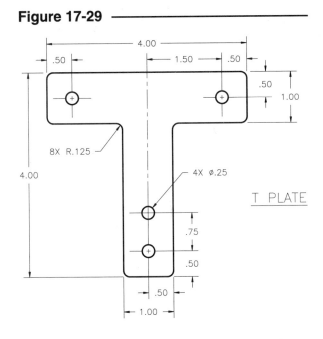

2. *Chamfer*

   Use drawing **A-2-M** as a prototype drawing and assign the name **CBRACKET**. Using the Metric Table of Limits Settings, reset the *Limits* for plotting 1:1. Create the Catch Bracket shown in Figure 17-30. Use *Chamfer* to create the six chamfers. *Save* the drawing and create a plot to scale.

Figure 17-30 ————————————————

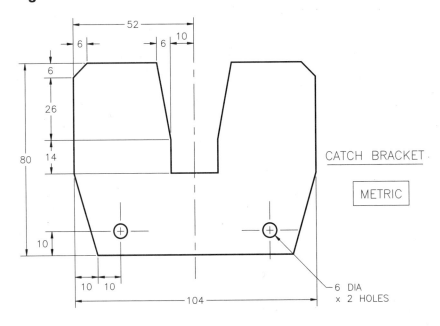

3. *Offset*

Use the **ASHEET** or **A-BORDER** drawing as a prototype and assign the name **SCHEM1**. Create the electrical schematic as shown in Figure 17-31 by drawing *Lines* and *Plines*; then *Offset* as needed. Because this is a schematic, you can create the symbols by approximating the dimensions. *Save* the drawing and create a plot if required.

Figure 17-31 ——————————

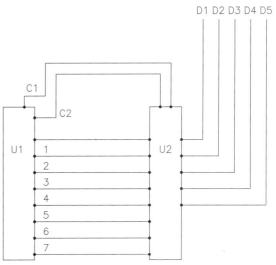

4. *Offset*

Open the **GASKETC** drawing that you began in Chapter 16 Exercises. *Offset* the existing inside shape to create the outside shape (refer to Chapter 16, Exercise 9 for dimensions). Use *Offset* to create concentric circles around the bolt holes. Use *Trim* to complete the gasket. *Save* the drawing and create a plot at 2:1 scale.

5. *Divide, Measure*

Use the **ASHEET** or **A-BORDER** drawing as a prototype and assign the name **BILLMATL**. Create the table in Figure 17-32 to be used as a bill of materials. Draw the bottom *Line* (as dimensioned) and a vertical *Line*. Use *Divide* along the bottom *Line* and *Measure* along the vertical *Line* to locate *Points* as desired. Create *Offsets Through* the *Points* using *NODe OSNAP*. (*ORTHO* and *Trim* may be of help.)

Figure 17-32 ——————————

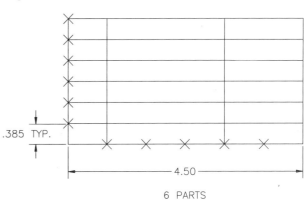

6 PARTS

6. **HAMMER** Drawing

   Open the **HAMMER** drawing that you set up in Chapter 14 Exercises. Create the Hammer shown in Figure 17-33. Make use of *Offset* for determining the center points for *Arc* and *Circle* radii (use the CONSTR layer for construction lines). Use *Fillet* wherever possible. When you finish, *Save* the drawing and create a plot if required.

Figure 17-33 ———

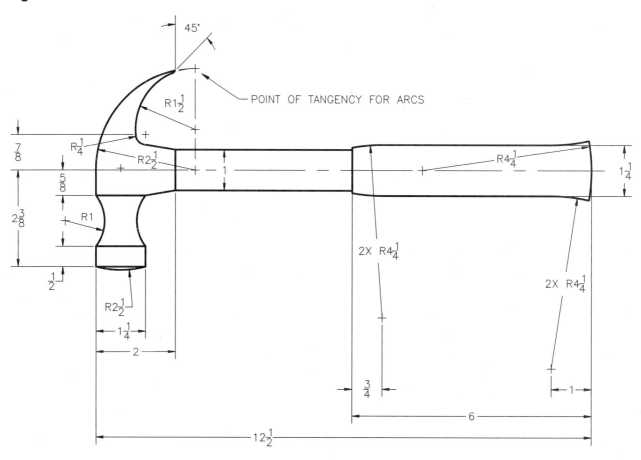

7. *Boundary*

   A. *Open* the **GASKETA** drawing that you modified in Chapter 16 Exercises. Use the *Boundary* command to create a boundary of the <u>outside shape only</u> (no islands). Use *Move Last* to displace the new shape to the right of the existing gasket. Use *SaveAs* and rename the drawing to **GASKT-AR**. Keep this drawing to determine the *Area* of the shape after reading Chapter 18.

   B. *Open* the **PLATNEST** drawing from Chapter 16 Exercises. Create a *Boundary* (with islands) of the plate with four holes arranged diagonally. *Move* the new boundary objects **10** units to the right. Use *SaveAs* to create a file named **PLATN-AR**. The file will be used to determine the *Area* of the plate for calculation of paint application in Chapter 18 Exercises.

8. Create a gear, using regions. Begin a *New* drawing and assign the name **GEAR-REG**.

   A. Set *Limits* at **8 x 6** and *Zoom All*. Create a *Circle* of **1** unit *diameter* with the center at **4,3**. Create a second concentric *Circle* with a *radius* of **1.557**. Create a closed *Pline* by entering the following coordinates:

From point:	**5.571,2.9191**
to point:	**@.17<160**
to point:	**@.0228<94**
to point:	**@.0228<86**
to point:	**@.17<20**
to point:	**c**

      The gear at this stage should look like that in Figure 17-34.

Figure 17-34

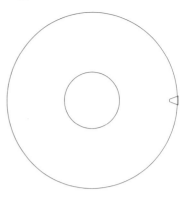

   B. Use the *Region* command to convert each shape to a *Region*.

Figure 17-35

   C. *Array* the small *Region* (tooth) in a *Polar* array about the center of the gear. There are **40** items that are rotated as they are copied. This action should create all the teeth of the gear.

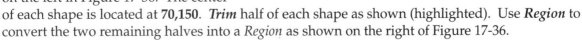

   D. Finally, *Subtract* the small *Circle* and all of the *Plines* (teeth) from the large *Circle*. Use the *Fence* option to select the 40 small *Regions*. The resulting gear should resemble Figure 17-35. *Save* the drawing.

   E. Consider the steps involved if you were to create the gear (as an alternative) by using *Trim* to remove 40 small sections of the large *Circle* and all unwanted parts of the teeth. *Regions* are clearly easier in this case.

9. Create the Wrench using region modeling. Refer to Chapter 15 Exercises for dimensions. Begin a *New* drawing or use a *Prototype* for a metric A4 size sheet. Assign the name **WRNCH-RG**.

Figure 17-36

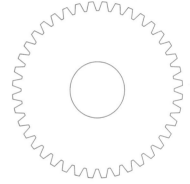

   A. Set *Limits* to **396,280** to prepare the drawing for plotting at 3:4 (the drawing scale factor is 33.87). Set the **GRID** to **10**.

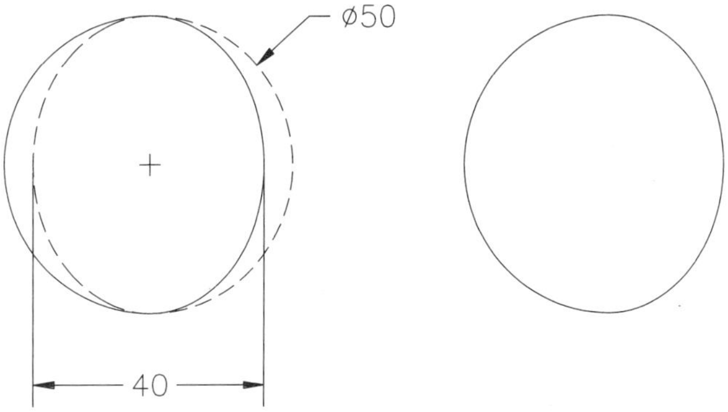

   B. Draw a *Circle* and an *Ellipse* as shown on the left in Figure 17-36. The center of each shape is located at **70,150**. *Trim* half of each shape as shown (highlighted). Use *Region* to convert the two remaining halves into a *Region* as shown on the right of Figure 17-36.

C. Next, create a *Circle* with the center at 120,150 and a diameter as shown in Figure 17-37. Then draw a closed *Pline* in a rectangular shape as shown. The height of the rectangle must be drawn as specified; however, the width of the rectangle can be drawn <u>approximately</u> as shown on the left. Convert each shape to a *Region*; then use *Intersect* to create the region as shown on the right side of the figure.

Figure 17-37

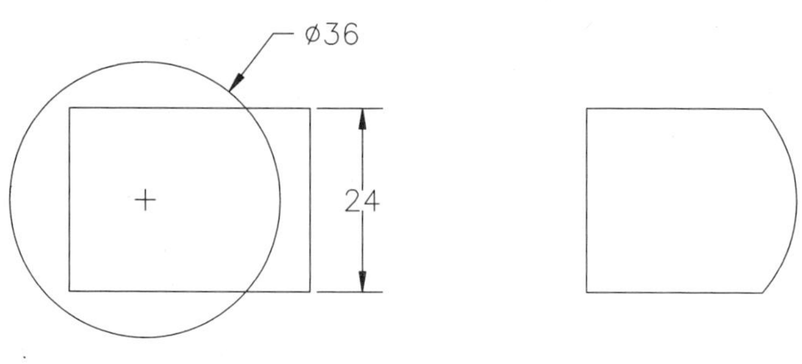

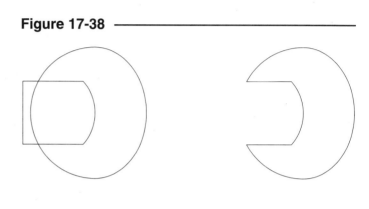

D. *Move* the rectangular-shaped region 68 units to the left to overlap the first region as shown in Figure 17-38. Use *Subtract* to create the composite region on the right representing the head of the wrench.

E. Complete the construction of the wrench in a manner similar to that used in the previous steps. Refer to Chapter 15 Exercises for dimensions of the Wrench. Complete the wrench as one *Region*. *Save* the drawing as **WRNCH-RG**.

Figure 17-38

10. **Retaining Wall**

Open the **RET-WALL** drawing that you created in Chapter 8 Exercises. Annotate the wall with 50 unit stations as shown in Figure 17-39.

HINT: Convert the center line of the retaining wall to a *Pline*; then use the *Measure* command to place *Point* objects at the 50 unit stations. *Offset* the wall on both sides to provide a construction aid in the creation of the perpendicular tick marks. Use *NODe* and *PERpendicular Osnaps*. *Save* the drawing as **RET-WAL3**.

Figure 17-39

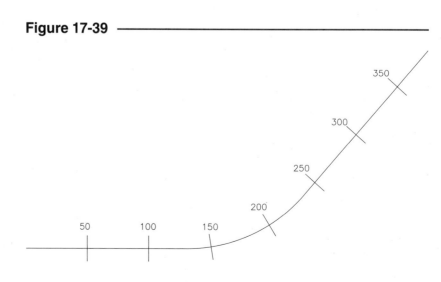

Chapter 18

INQUIRY COMMANDS

Chapter Objectives

After completing this chapter you should:

1. be able to list the *Status* of a drawing;

2. be able to *List* the AutoCAD database information about an object;

3. know how to list the entire database of all objects with *Dblist*;

4. be able to calculate the *Area* of a closed shape with and without "islands";

5. be able to find the *Distance* between two points;

6. be able to report the coordinate value of a selected point using the *ID* command;

7. know how to list the *Time* spent on a drawing or in a session.

BASICS

AutoCAD provides several commands that allow you to find out information about the current drawing status and about specific objects in the drawing. These commands as a group are known as *Inquiry* commands and are grouped together in the menu systems.

Using *Inquiry* commands, you can find out such information as the amount of time spent in the current drawing, the distance between two points, the area of a closed shape, or the database listing of properties for specific objects (coordinates of endpoints, lengths, angles, etc.) as well as other information. The *Inquiry* commands are:

> *Status, List, Dblist, Area, Distance, ID, Time*

COMMANDS

STATUS

PULL-DOWN MENU	SCREEN MENU	TYPE IN	TABLET MENU
Data Status	DATA Status:	STATUS	---

The *Status* command gives many pieces of information related to the current drawing. Typing or **PICK**ing the command from one of the menus causes a text screen to appear similar to the one shown in Figure 18-1.

Figure 18-1

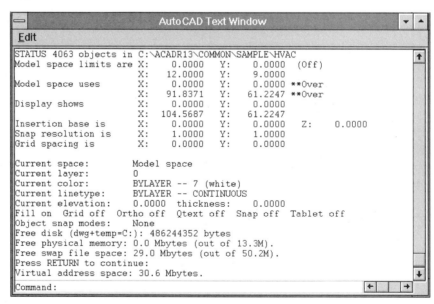

The information items are:

Total number of objects in the current drawing
Model space limits: values set by the *Limits* command in Model Space
Model space uses: area used by the objects (drawing extents)
Display shows: current display or windowed area
Insertion base point: point specified by the *Base* command or default (0,0)
Snap resolution: value specified by the *Snap* command
Grid spacing: value specified by the *Grid* command
Current space: Paper space or Model space
Current layer: name
Current color: current color assignment
Current linetype: current linetype assignment

Current elevation, thickness: 3D properties—current height above the XY plane and Z dimension
ON or OFF status: *FILL, GRID, ORTHO, QTEXT, SNAP, TABLET*
Object Snap Modes: current running *OSNAP* modes
Free disk: space on the current hard disk drive
Free physical memory: amount of free RAM
Free swap file space: amount of free space in the swap (temporary) file
Virtual address space: amount of Windows permanent swap file occupied

LIST

DOS PULL-DOWN	WIN PULL-DOWN	SCREEN MENU	TYPE IN	TABLET MENU
Assist Inquiry > List	*Edit Inquiry > List*	*ASSIST INQUIRY List:*	*LIST*	*2,Q*

The *List* command displays the database list of information in text screen format for one or more specified objects. The information displayed depends on the <u>type</u> of object selected. Invoking the *List* command causes a prompt for you to select objects. AutoCAD then displays the list for the selected objects (see Figures 18-2 and 18-3).

A *List* of a *Line* and an *Arc* is given in Figure 18-2.

For a *Line*, coordinates for the endpoints, line length and angle, current layer, and other information are given.

For an *Arc*, the center coordinate, radius, and start and end angles are given. (The length of an *Arc* can be found in the *Ddmodify* dialogue box when an *Arc* is PICKed.)

The *List* for a *Pline* is shown in Figure 18-3. The location of each vertex is given, as well as the length and area of the entire *Pline*.

Figure 18-2 —————————

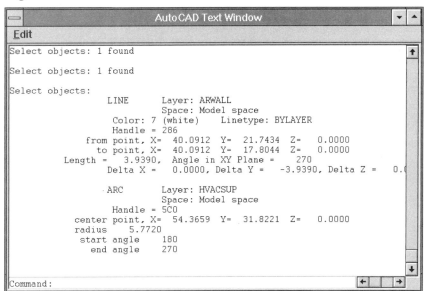

Figure 18-3 —————————

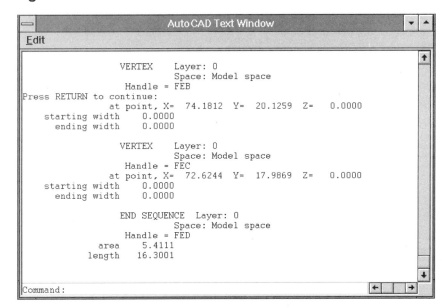

DBLIST

PULL-DOWN MENU	SCREEN MENU	TYPE IN	TABLET MENU
---	---	*DBLIST*	---

The *Dblist* command is similar to the *List* command in that it displays the database listing of objects; however, *Dblist* gives information for <u>every</u> object in the current drawing! This command is generally used when you desire to send the list to a printer or when there are only a few objects in the drawing. If you use this command in a complex drawing, be prepared to page through many screens of information.

AREA

DOS PULL-DOWN	WIN PULL-DOWN	SCREEN MENU	TYPE IN	TABLET MENU
Assist *Inquiry >* *Area*	*Edit* *Inquiry >* *Area*	*ASSIST* *INQUIRY* *Area:*	*AREA*	*1,R*

The *Area* command is helpful for many applications. With this command AutoCAD calculates the area and the perimeter of any enclosed shape in a matter of milliseconds. You specify the area (shape) to consider for calculation by PICKing the *Object* (if it is a closed *Pline, Polygon, Circle, Boundary, Region* or other closed object) or by PICKing points (corners of the outline) to define the shape. The options are given below.

First Point
The command sequence for specifying the area by PICKing points is shown below. This method should only be used for shapes with <u>straight</u> sides.

```
Command: area
<First point>/Object/Add/Subtract: PICK (Locate the first point to designate the shape.)
Next point: PICK (Select the second point to define the shape.)
Next point: PICK (Select the third point.)
Next point: PICK (Continue selecting points until all corners have been selected to completely define
the shape.)
Next point: Enter
Area = nn.nnn  perimeter = nn.nnn
Command:
```

An example of the *Point* method (PICKing points to define the area) is shown here.

Object
If the shape for which you want to find the area and perimeter is a *Circle, Polygon, Ellipse, Boundary, Region,* or closed *Pline,* the *Object* option of the *Area* command can be used. Select the shape with one PICK (since all of these shapes are considered as one object by AutoCAD).

The ability to find the area of a closed *Pline, Region,* or *Boundary* is extremely helpful. Remember that <u>any</u> closed shape, even if it includes *Arcs* and other curves, can be converted to a closed *Pline* with the *Pedit* command (as long as there are no gaps or

Figure 18-4

```
6                              5
(NEXT POINT:)                  (NEXT POINT:)

                3
                (NEXT POINT:)
                                       4
                                       (NEXT POINT:)

1               2
(FIRST POINT:)  (NEXT POINT:)
```

overlaps) or can be used with the *Boundary* command. This method provides you with the ability to easily calculate the area of any shape, curved or straight. In short, convert the shape to a closed *Pline, Region,* or *Boundary* and find the *Area* with the *Object* option.

Add, Subtract

Add and *Subtract* provide you with the means to find the area of a closed shape that has islands, or negative spaces. For example, you may be required to find the surface area of a sheet of material that has several punched holes. In this case, the area of the holes is subtracted from the area defined by the perimeter shape. The *Add* and *Subtract* options are used specifically for that purpose. The following command sequence displays the process of calculating an area and subtracting the area occupied by the holes.

> Command: **area**
> <First point>/Object/Add/Subtract: **a** (Defining the perimeter shape is prefaced by the *Add* option.)
> <First point>/Object/Subtract: **o** (Assuming the perimeter shape is a *Boundary* or closed object.)
> (Add mode) Select object: **PICK** (Select the closed object.)
>
> Area = nn.nnn, Perimeter = nn.nnn
> Total area = nn.nnn
>
> (Add mode) Select object: **Enter** (Indicates completion of the *Add* mode.)
> <First point>/Object/Subtract: **s** (Change to the *Subtract* mode.)
> <First point>/Object/Add: **o** (Assuming the holes are *Circle* objects.)
> (Subtract mode) Select object: **PICK** (Select the first *Circle* to subtract.)
>
> Area = nn.nnn, Perimeter = nn.nnn
> Total area = nn.nnn
>
> (Subtract mode) Select object: **PICK** (Select the second *Circle* to subtract.)
>
> Area = nn.nnn, Perimeter = nn.nnn
> Total area = nn.nnn
>
> (Subtract mode) Select object: **Enter** (Completion of *Subtract* mode.)
> <First point>/Object/Add: **Enter** (Completion of *Area* command.)
> Command:

Make sure that you press Enter between the *Add* and *Subtract* modes.

An example of the last command sequence used to find the area of a shape minus the holes is shown here. Notice that the object selected in the first step is a closed *Pline* shape, including an *Arc*.

Figure 18-5

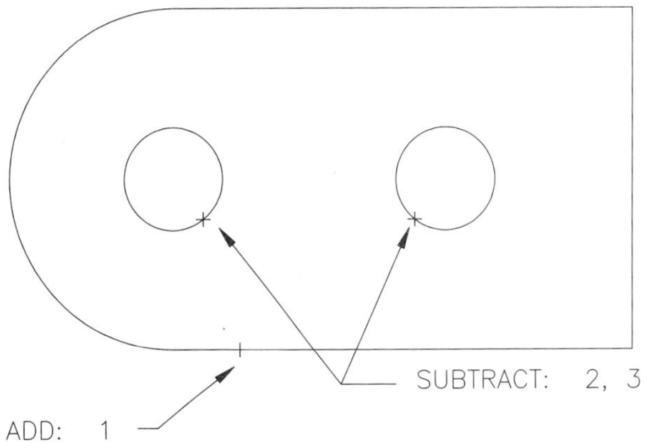

ADD: 1

SUBTRACT: 2, 3

DISTANCE

DOS PULL-DOWN	WIN PULL-DOWN	SCREEN MENU	TYPE IN	TABLET MENU
Assist *Inquiry >* *Distance*	*Edit* *Inquiry >* *Distance*	*ASSIST*	*DIST* *INQUIRY* *Dist:*	*2,R*

The *Distance* command reports the distance between any two points you specify. *OSNAPs* can be used to "snap" to the existing points. This command is helpful in many engineering or architectural applications, such as finding the clearance between two mechanical parts, finding the distance between columns in a building, or finding the size of an opening in a part or doorway. The command is easy to use.

> Command: **dist**
> First point: **PICK** (Use *OSNAPs* if needed.)
> Second point: **PICK**
> Distance = nn.nnn, Angle in XY Plane = nn, Angle from XY Plane = nn
> Delta X = nn.nnn, Delta Y = nn.nnn, Delta Z = nn.nnn

AutoCAD reports the absolute and relative distances as well as the angle of the line between the points.

ID

DOS PULL-DOWN	WIN PULL-DOWN	SCREEN MENU	TYPE IN	TABLET MENU
Assist *Inquiry >* *Locate Point*	*Edit* *Inquiry >* *Locate Point*	*ASSIST* *INQUIRY* *ID:*	*ID*	*1,Q*

The *ID* command reports the coordinate value of any point you select with the cursor. If you require the location associated with a specific object, an *OSNAP* mode (*ENDpoint, MIDpoint, CENter,* etc.) can be used.

> Command: **ID**
> Point: **PICK** or (**coordinate**) (Select a point or enter a coordinate. *OSNAPs* can be used.)
> X = nn.nnn, Y = nn.nnn, Z = nn.nnn
> Command:

NOTE: *ID* also sets AutoCAD's "last point." The last point can be referenced in commands by using the @ (at) symbol with relative rectangular or relative polar coordinates. *ID* creates a "blip" at the location of the coordinates you enter or PICK.

TIME

PULL-DOWN MENU	SCREEN MENU	TYPE IN	TABLET MENU
Data *Time*	*DATA* *Time:*	*TIME*	---

This command is useful for keeping track of the time spent in the current drawing session or total time spent on a particular drawing. Knowing how much time is spent on a drawing can be useful in an office situation for bidding or billing jobs. The *Time* command reports the information shown in Figure 18-6.

The *Total editing time* is automatically kept, starting from when the drawing was first created until the current time. Plotting and printing time is not included in this total, nor is the time spent in a session when changes are discarded.

Display
The *Display* option causes *Time* to repeat the display with the updated times.

ON/OFF/Reset
The *Elapsed timer* is a separate compilation of time controlled by the user. The *Elapsed timer* can be turned *ON* or *OFF* or can be *Reset*.

Time also reports when the next automatic save will be made. The time interval of the Automatic Save feature is controlled by the *SAVETIME* system variable. To set the interval between automatic saves, type *SAVETIME* at the command line and specify a value for time (in minutes). The default interval is 120 minutes.

Figure 18-6

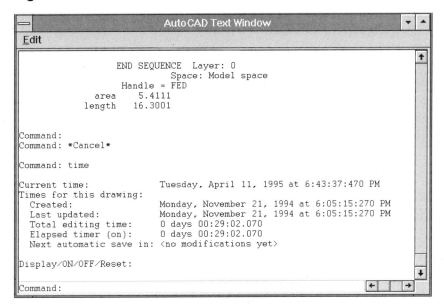

CHAPTER EXERCISES

1. *List*

   A. *Open* the **PLATNEST** drawing from Chapter 16 Exercises. Assume that a laser will be used to cut the plates and holes from the stock, and you must program the coordinates. Use the *List* command to give information on the *Line*s and *Circles* for the one plate with four holes in a diagonal orientation. Determine and write down the coordinates for the 4 corners of the plate and the centers of the 4 holes.

   B. *Open* the **EFF-APT** drawing. Use *List* to determine the area of the inside of the tub. If the tub were filled with 10" of water, what is the volume of water in the tub?

2. *Area*

   A. *Open* the **EFF-APT** drawing. The entry room is to be carpeted at a cost of $10.00 per square yard. Use the *Area* command (with the PICK points option) to determine the cost for carpeting the room.

   B. *Open* the **PLATN-AR** drawing from Chapter 17 Exercises. Using the *Area* command, calculate the wasted material (the two pieces of stock remaining after the 3 plates have been cut or stamped). Use *Boundary* to create objects from the waste areas.

C. The plate with 4 holes arranged diagonally will be painted. Using the *Add* and *Subtract* option of *Area*, calculate the surface area for painting 100 pieces, both sides. Use the *Boundary* on the right (created in Chapter 17) to determine the area. (Remember to press Enter between the *Add* and *Subtract* operations.)

3. *Dist*

A. *Open* the **EFF-APT** drawing. Use the *Dist* command to determine the best location for installing a wall-mounted telephone in the apartment. Where should the telephone be located in order to provide the most equal access from all corners of the apartment? What is the farthest distance that you would have to walk to answer the phone?

B. Using the *Dist* command, determine what length of pipe would be required to connect the kitchen sink drain to the tub drain (only that distance under the floor).

4. **ID**

Open the **PLATNEST** drawing once again. You have now been assigned to program the laser to cut the plate with 4 holes in the corners. Use the **ID** command (with *OSNAPs*) to determine the coordinates for the 4 corners and the hole centers.

5. *Time*

Using the *Time* command, what is the total amount of editing time you spent with the **PLATNEST** drawing? How much time have you spent in this session? How much time until the next automatic save?

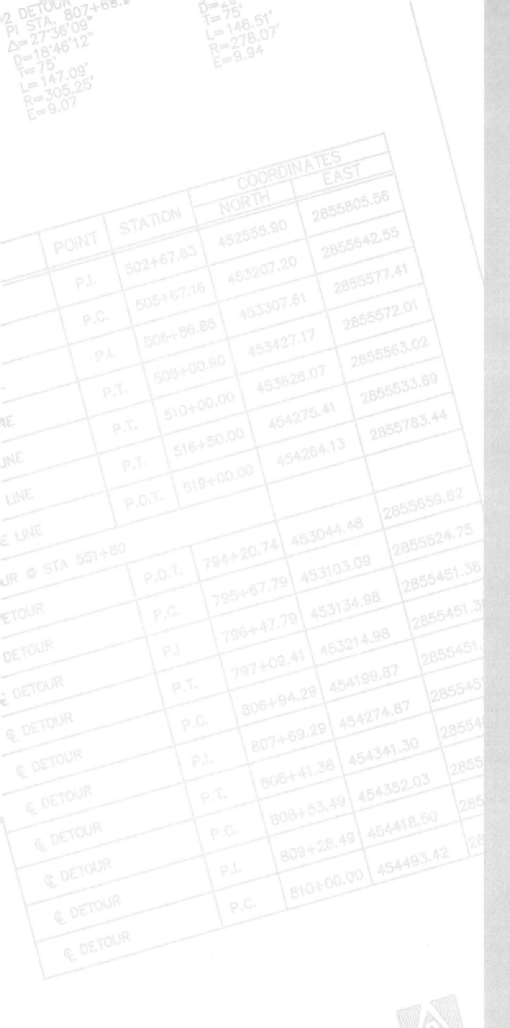

Chapter 19

INSERTING AND EDITING TEXT

Chapter Objectives

After completing this chapter you should:

1. be able to create text in a drawing using *Text*, *Mtext*, and *Dtext*;

2. be able to *Justify* or *Attach* text using each of the methods;

3. be able to <u>create</u> text styles with the *Style* <u>command</u>;

4. be able to <u>select</u> from created text styles with the *Style* <u>option</u> of *Text*, *Mtext*, or *Dtext*;

5. be able to format <u>paragraph</u> text in AutoCAD for DOS or for Windows using *Mtext*;

6. know that *Ddedit* can be used to edit a line of existing text and *Ddmodify* can be used to modify any property of existing text;

7. be able use *Spell* to check spelling and create custom dictionaries;

8. know how features such as *Qtext* (quick text), *TEXTFILL*, and *TEX-TQLTY* can be used to control the appearance of text.

BASICS

The *Dtext*, *Mtext*, and *Text* commands provide you with a means of creating text in an AutoCAD drawing. "Text" in CAD drawings usually refers to sentences, words, or notes created from alphabetical or numerical characters that appear in the drawing. The numeric values that are part of specific dimensions are generally <u>not</u> considered "text," since dimensional values are a component of the dimension created automatically with the use of dimensioning commands.

Text in technical drawings is typically in the form of notes concerning information or descriptions of the objects contained in the drawing. For example, an architectural drawing might have written descriptions of rooms or spaces, special instructions for construction, or notes concerning materials or furnishings (Fig. 19-1). An engineering drawing may contain, in addition to the dimensions, manufacturing notes, bill of materials, schedules, or tables (Fig. 19-2). Technical illustrations may contain part numbers or assembly notes. Title blocks also contain text.

Figure 19-1

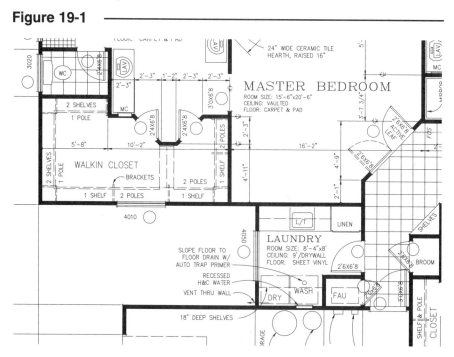

Figure 19-2

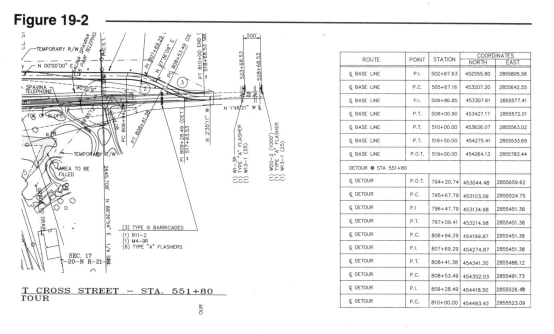

Text in an AutoCAD drawing is treated as an object, just like a *Line* or a *Circle*. Each line can be *Erased, Moved, Rotated,* or otherwise edited as any other graphical object. The letters themselves can be changed individually with special text editing commands. A spell checker is available by using the *Spell* command. Since text is treated as a graphical element, the use of many lines of text in a drawing can slow regeneration time and increase plotting time significantly.

The *Dtext, Mtext,* and *Text* commands perform basically the same function; they create text in a drawing. *Mtext* is the newest and most sophisticated method of text entry. With *Mtext* (multiline text) you can create a paragraph of text that "wraps" within a text boundary (rectangle) that you specify. An *Mtext* paragraph is treated as one AutoCAD object. *Dtext* (dynamic text) displays each character in the drawing as it is typed and allows entry of multiple lines of text. *Text* allows only one line of text and requires an **Enter** or **Return** to display each line of text.

All font files supplied with AutoCAD are located in the ACADR13\COMMON\FONTS directory and have file extensions of .PFA or .PFB (PostScript), .TTF (TrueType), or .SHX (AutoCAD compiled shape files). Any PostScript, TrueType, and .SHX font files are usable with AutoCAD. Additional fonts can be purchased or may already be on your computer (supplied with Windows, word processors, or other software).

Many options for text justification are available. *Justification* is the method of aligning lines of text. For example, if text is right justified, the right ends of the lines of text are aligned.

The form or shape of the individual letters is determined in AutoCAD by the text *style*. Each *style* uses a TrueType, PostScript, or AutoCAD-supplied font. Only one *style*, called *Standard*, has been created as part of the standard default drawing (ACAD.DWG) and uses the TXT.SHX font file.

If any other style of text is desired, it must be created with the *Style* command. When a new *style* is created, it becomes the current one used by the *Dtext, Mtext,* or *Text* command. If several *styles* have been created in a drawing, a particular one can be recalled or made current by using the *style* option of the *Dtext, Mtext,* or *Text* commands.

In summary, the *Style* command allows you to design new styles with your choice of options, such as fonts, width factor, and obliquing angle, whereas, the *style* option of *Dtext, Mtext,* and *Text* allows you to select from existing styles in the drawing that you previously created.

Commands related to using text in an AutoCAD drawing include:

Dtext	Places multiple lines of text in a drawing and allows you to see each letter as it is typed.
Mtext	Places a paragraph of text within a text boundary.
Text	Places text in a drawing one line at a time.
Style	Creates text styles from any font. This command allows you to assign a name for each style.
Ddedit	Invokes a dialogue box for editing text. Allows you to edit individual characters or an entire line of text.
Ddmodify	This is a broad editing command allowing revision of many aspects of text such as height, rotation angle, insertion point, style, or text itself.
Qtext	Short for quick-text, this command temporarily displays a line of text as a box instead of individual characters in order to speed up regeneration time and plot time.
Spell	Checks spelling of existing text in a drawing.

TEXT INSERTION COMMANDS

NOTE: The commands for inserting text are formally named *Dtext, Mtext,* and *Text* (these are the commands used for typing). The menus and icons, however, <u>do not</u> follow that format. The *Mtext* command appears as "**Text**" in the *Draw* pull-down menu, digitizing tablet menu, and icon tool tips (Figs. 19-3 and 19-4). The *Text* command appears as "**Single-line text**" in the pull-down menu and icon tool tips.

Figure 19-3 ——————

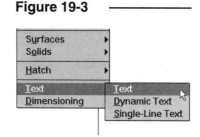

Figure 19-4 ——

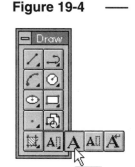

Menu item or Tool Tip (select)		Command name (type)
Text	=	*MTEXT*
Dynamic Text	=	*DTEXT*
Single-Line Text	=	*TEXT*

DTEXT

PULL-DOWN MENU	SCREEN MENU	TYPE IN	TABLET MENU
Draw *Text >* *Dynamic Text*	DRAW2 *Dtext:*	*DTEXT*	---

Dtext (dynamic text) lets you insert text into an AutoCAD drawing. *Dtext* displays each character in the drawing as it is typed. You can enter multiple lines of text without exiting the *Dtext* command. The lines of text do not "wrap." The options are presented below.

    Command: **dtext**
    Justify/Style/<Start point>:

Start Point

The *Start point* for a line of text is the <u>left end</u> of the baseline for the text (Fig. 19-5). *Height* is the distance from the baseline to the top of uppercase letters. Additional lines of text are automatically spaced below and left justified. The *rotation angle* is the angle of the baseline (Fig. 19-6).

The command sequence for this option is:

    Command: **dtext**
    Justify/Style/<Start point>: **PICK** or (**coordinates**)
    Height <0.20>: **Enter** or (**value**)
    Rotation Angle <0>: **Enter** or (**value**)
    Text: (Type the desired line of text and press **Enter**.)
    Text: (Type another line of text and press **Enter**.)
    Text: **Enter**
    Command:

NOTE: When the "Text:" prompt appears, you can also PICK a new location for the next line of text.

Figure 19-5 ————————————

Figure 19-6 ————————————

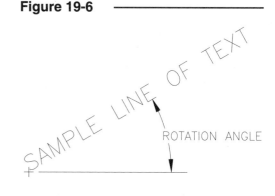

Justify

If you want to use one of the justification methods, invoking this option displays the choices at the prompt.

    Command: **dtext**
    Justify/Style/<Start point>: **J** (Invokes the justification options.)
    Align/Fit/Center/Middle/Right/TL/TC/TR/ML/MC/MR/BL/BC/ BR: (**choice**) (Type capital letters.)

After specifying a justification option, you can enter the desired text in response to the "Text:" prompt. The text is not justified until <u>after</u> you press Enter.

Align

Aligns the line of text between the two points specified (P1, P2). The text height is adjusted automatically (Fig. 19-7).

Fit

Fits (compresses or extends) the line of text between the two points specified (P1, P2). The text height does not change (Fig. 19-7).

Center

Centers the baseline of the first line of text at the specified point. Additional lines of text are centered below the first (Fig 19-8).

Middle

Centers the first line of text both vertically and horizontally about the specified point. Additional lines of text are centered below (Fig. 19-8).

Right

Creates text that is right justified from the specified point (Fig. 19-8).

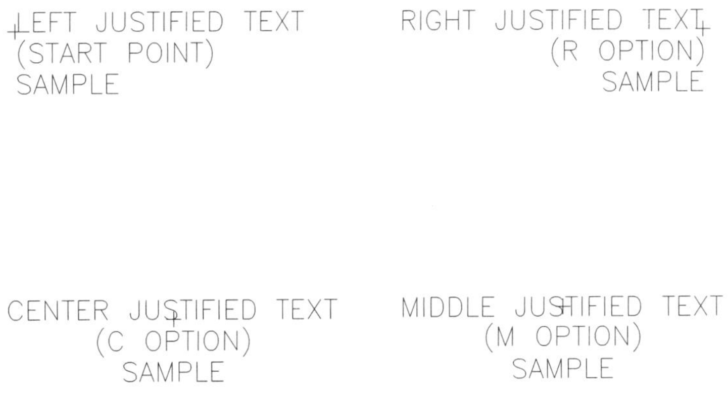

TL

Top Left. Left justifies at the top of the text (Fig. 19-9).

TC

Top Center. Justifies at the center of the top of the line (Fig. 19-9).

TR

Top Right. Right justifies at the top right of the line.

ML

Middle Left. Left justifies at the vertical middle of the line.

Figure 19-7

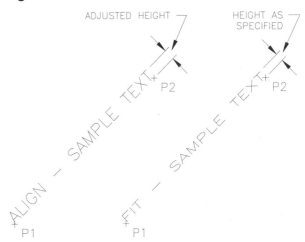

Figure 19-8

LEFT JUSTIFIED TEXT
(START POINT)
SAMPLE

RIGHT JUSTIFIED TEXT
(R OPTION)
SAMPLE

CENTER JUSTIFIED TEXT
(C OPTION)
SAMPLE

MIDDLE JUSTIFIED TEXT
(M OPTION)
SAMPLE

Figure 19-9

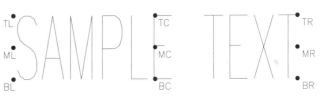

MC

Middle Center. Centers the line of text both vertically and horizontally about the specified point (Fig. 19-9).

MR

Middle Right. Right justifies at the vertical middle of the text.

BL

Bottom Left. Left justifies text at the bottom line of the text (Fig. 19-9).

BC

Bottom Center. Centers the line of text horizontally about the bottom line.

BR

Bottom Right. Right justifies the line of text at the bottom line (Fig. 19-9).

Figure 19-10 illustrates the justification points when both upper- and lowercase letters are used. Notice that when using all uppercase letters, the *MC* and *Middle* points coincide and the *BL, BC, BR* and *Left, Center, Right* points coincide, respectively. If, however, a combination of upper- and lower-case is used, the extenders (for example, on the letter "p") cause a separate "baseline" and "bottom line"; therefore, the *MC* and *Middle* points do not coincide and the *BL, BC, BR* and *Left, Center, Right* options differ.

Figure 19-10

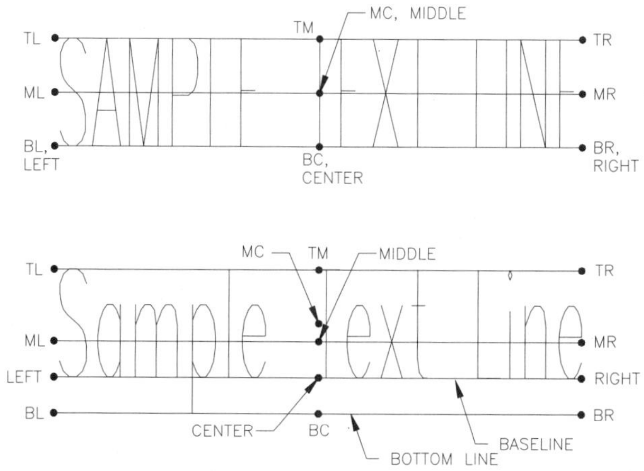

Style (option of *Dtext*, *Mtext*, or *Text*)

The *style* <u>option</u> of the *Dtext*, *Mtext*, or *Text* command allows you to select from the <u>existing</u> text styles which have been previously created as part of the current drawing. The style selected from the list becomes the current style and is used when placing text with *Dtext*, *Mtext*, or *Text*.

Since the only text *style* that is available in the default prototype drawing (ACAD.DWG) is *Standard*, other styles must be created before the *style* option of *Text* is of use. Various text styles are first created with the *Style* <u>command</u> (this topic is discussed later).

Use the *Style* option of *Dtext*, *Mtext*, or *Text* to list existing styles for the drawing. An example listing is shown below.

```
Command: dtext
Justify/Style/<Start point>: s
Style name (or ?) <STANDARD>: ?
Text style(s) to list <*>: Enter

Text styles:

Style name: CTYB        Font files: C:\ACADR13\COMMON\FONTS\CIBT____.PFB
    Height: 0.0000  Width factor: 1.0000  Obliquing angle: 0
    Generation: Normal
```

Style name: RC1   Font files: C:\ACADR13\COMMON\FONTS\ROMANC.SHX
  Height: 0.0000 Width factor: 1.0000 Obliquing angle: 0
  Generation: Normal

Style name: RS1   Font files: C:\ACADR13\COMMON\FONTS\ROMANS.SHX
  Height: 0.0000 Width factor: 1.0000 Obliquing angle: 0
  Generation: Normal

Style name: RS8-I   Font files: C:\ACADR13\COMMON\FONTS\ROMANS.SHX
  Height: 0.0000 Width factor: 0.8000 Obliquing angle: 15
  Generation: Normal

Style name: STANDARD   Font files: txt
  Height: 0.0000 Width factor: 1.0000 Obliquing angle: 0
  Generation: Normal

Current text style: STANDARD
Justify/Style/<Start point>: *Cancel*
Command:

TEXT

PULL-DOWN MENU	SCREEN MENU	TYPE IN	TABLET MENU
Draw *Text >* *Single-Line Text*	---	*TEXT*	---

Text is essentially the same as *Dtext* except that the text is not dynamically displayed one letter at a time as you type, but rather appears in the drawing only after pressing **Enter**. The other difference is that *Dtext* repeatedly displays the "Text:" prompt to allow entering multiple lines of text, whereas, *Text* allows only one line. Otherwise, all the options and capabilities of *Text* are identical to *Dtext*.

Command: **text**
Justify/Style/<Start point>: **PICK**
Height <0.2000>: **Enter** or (**value**)
Rotation angle <0>: **Enter** or (**value**)
Text: **Sample line of text.** (The line of text appears in drawing after pressing Enter.)
Command:

If you want to type another line of text below the previous one with the *Text* command, use *Text* again, but press **Enter** at the first prompt. The *Text* command then responds with the "Text:" prompt, at which time you can enter the next line of text. The new line is automatically spaced below and uses the same height, justification, and other options as the previous line.

MTEXT

PULL-DOWN MENU	SCREEN MENU	TYPE IN	TABLET MENU
Draw *Text >* *Text*	DRAW2 *Mtext:*	*MTEXT*	5,T

A powerful new feature in Release 13 is the command *Mtext*. *Mtext* allows you to create paragraph text defined by a text boundary. This <u>text boundary</u> is a reference rectangle that specifies the insertion point and width of the paragraph. AutoCAD references the created *Mtext* as one object, regardless of the amount of text supplied.

Command: **mtext**
Attach/Rotation/Style/Height/Direction/<Insertion point>: **PICK** or (**option**)
Attach/Rotation/Style/Height/Direction/Width/2Points<Other corner>: **PICK** or (**option**)

When you invoke the *Mtext* command, you supply an "Insertion point" and "Other corner" representing the diagonal corners of the text boundary (like a window). After you PICK the two points defining the text boundary, a text editor appears ready for you to enter the text.

If you are using AutoCAD for DOS, the MS-DOS text editor is automatically invoked when you pick the two corners of the text boundary (Fig. 19-11). Enter the desired text; then use *Exit* from the *File* menu to return to AutoCAD. *Save* your changes. The text is then entered into the drawing at the insertion point of the text boundary.

Figure 19-11

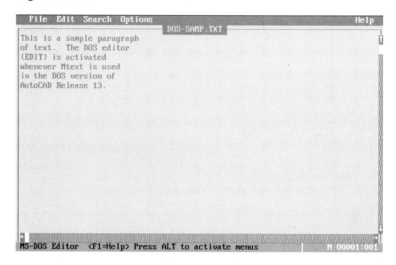

If you are using AutoCAD for Windows, the *Edit Mtext* dialogue box appears. Figure 19-12 depicts the text as it is entered into the dialogue box. PICKing the *OK* tile places the text in the drawing.

No matter which version of AutoCAD Release 13 you are using (Windows or DOS), you can specify a different text editor to use instead of the default editor that appears. DOS users can specify a different text editor using the *MTEXTED* system variable. Windows users can enter a name on the *Misc* page of the *Preferences* dialogue box (Fig. 19-38) or use the *MTEXTED* system variable. Enter "internal" to use the internal Windows text editor.

Figure 19-12

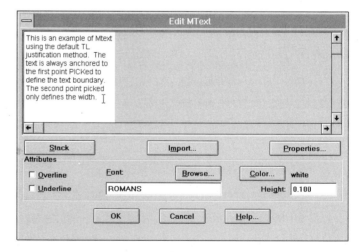

If you are using AutoCAD for Windows, sometimes the *Edit Mtext* dialogue box does not display some fonts. In this case, the *Select Font* dialogue box automatically appears. Specify a substitute font to use in the *Edit Mtext* dialogue box. The dialogue box font does not affect the current *Style*.

Figure 19-13 illustrates the placement of text using the default justification (*Attach*) method, *TL* (*Top Left*).

At first glance, it appears that the text always fits inside the text boundary, such as in the case of using the *TL Attach* option and PICKing the corners as shown in Figure 19-13. Beware!

The text boundary does <u>not</u> necessarily define the outer boundary for the text. Instead, the first point PICKed is the *Mtext* <u>insertion point</u> and the second point determines only the <u>width</u> of the text lines.

The placement of the text with relation to the text boundary is determined by the insertion point and the justification method. <u>The text is always anchored to the first point PICKed</u> (insertion point) no matter where on the text boundary you pick first. For example, if you are using the default *Attach* option (*TL*) and you PICK the bottom right corner <u>first</u> to define the text boundary, the text is anchored to that first point (Fig. 19-14).

Attach

Attach is the justification method. The *Attach* options are *TL, TC, TR, ML, MC, MR, BL, BC,* and *BR*. The *Attach* option determines how the text is justified about the insertion point (first point PICKed).

When you use a justification method for a corner of the paragraph (*TL, TR, BL, BR*), PICK that corner first to establish the insertion point. In that way, you can better define the location of the text in the drawing with the text boundary. For example, using the *BR* option, PICK the <u>bottom right</u> corner of the text boundary <u>first</u> to establish the insertion point, then the upper right (Fig. 19-15).

Figure 19-13 ───────────────

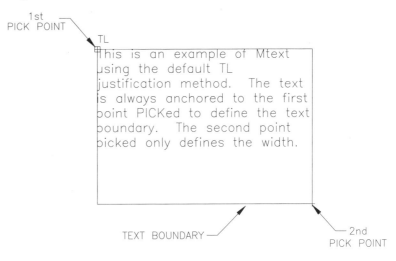

Figure 19-14 ───────────────

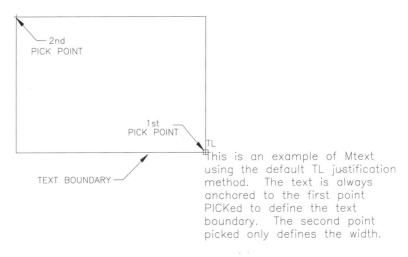

Figure 19-15 ───────────────

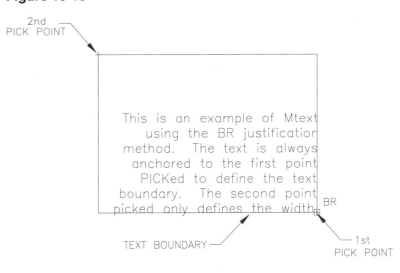

The *Attach* methods are illustrated in Figure 19-16. The illustration shows the relationship among the *Attach* option, the text boundary (as defined by the window that you PICK), and the resulting text paragraph.

Figure 19-16

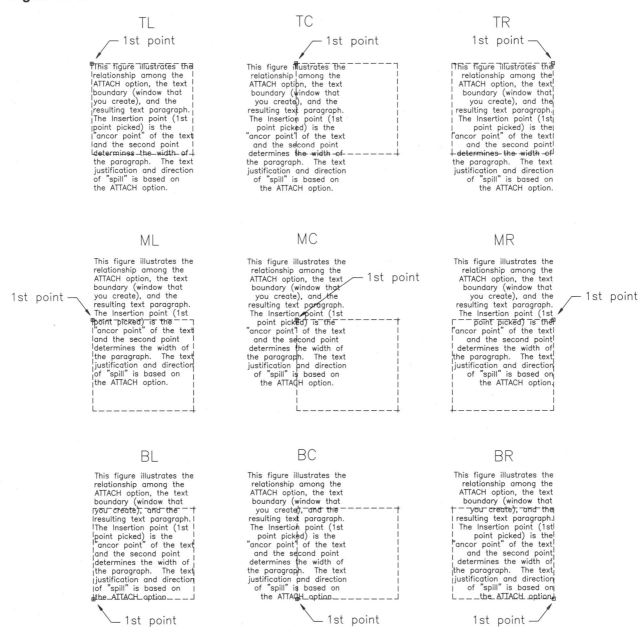

After you have specified the option (*TL, TC, TR, ML, MC, MR, BL, BC, BR*), draw the text boundary by PICKing the *Insertion point* (first point) based on the *Attach* option. The second corner of the boundary defines the width. The height of the boundary is not specified; it depends on the amount of text created. The direction of "spill" is away from the *Insertion point*.

Rotation

The *Rotation* option specifies the rotation angle of the text. A value may be entered or the angle may be specified by PICKing two points. With *Mtext* (as with *Dtext* and *Text*) the text is rotated about the *Insertion* (anchored) point (Fig. 19-17). The illustration shows the rotation of paragraph text created with the *TL* and *TC Attach* options.

Figure 19-17

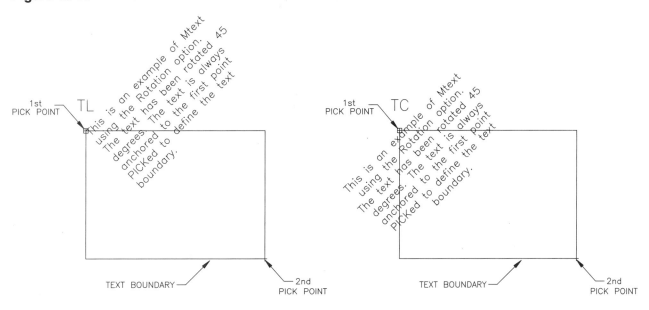

Style

The *Style* option specifies the default text style for *Mtext* (identical to the *Style* option for *Text* or *Dtext*). However, the *Style* of any letter or word of the paragraph text may be modified at a later time using the *Edit Mtext* dialogue box. (See *STYLE* and *DTEXT Style*.)

Height

This option specifies the default height of the uppercase text. A value may be entered or the height may be specified by the distance between two points. Height can also be changed retroactively.

Direction

The direction options for the text are either horizontal (left to right) or vertical (top to bottom).

If *Vertical* is selected, the text paragraph is anchored to the *Insertion* point, but the second point PICKed defines the paragraph <u>height</u>, not the width as with horizontal *Mtext* (Fig. 19-18).

Figure 19-18

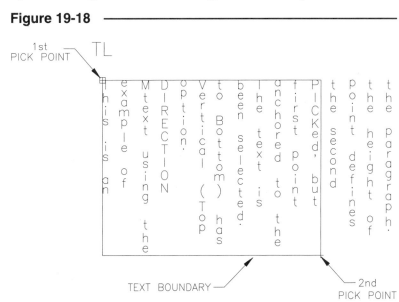

Width/2Points

There are two methods for specifying the width of the text boundary. Enter a value (*Width*) or PICK two points (*2Points*).

Either of these two options can be used as an alternative to specifying the paragraph width with a window (Fig. 19-19).

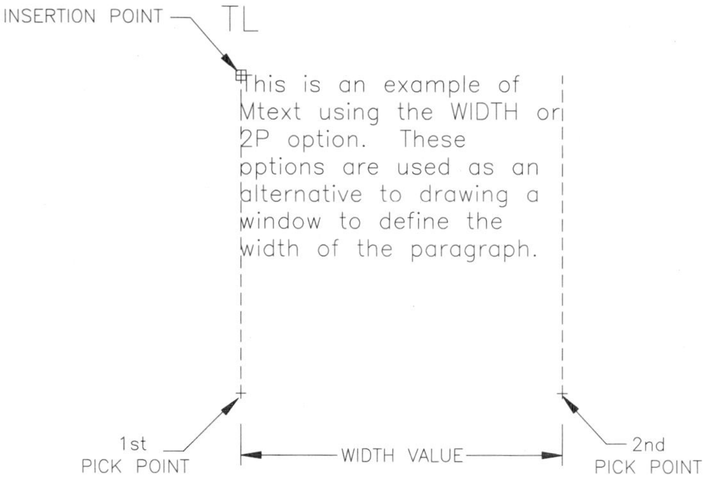

Formatting Paragraph Text (*Mtext*) in AutoCAD for Windows

In AutoCAD for Windows, paragraph text created with *Mtext* can be formatted using the *Edit Mtext* dialogue box when the text is entered, or it can be formatted retroactively using *Ddmodify*, *Ddedit*, or *Mtprop* (these commands are discussed later). Formatting refers to specifying parameters such as overline, underline, color, stacked numbers or fractions, font, height, direction, attachment, and other properties.

Figure 19-19

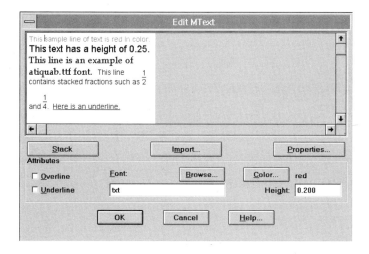

The *Edit Mtext* dialogue box that appears after you specify the text boundary (Fig. 19-20) provides several ways to control the text. You can format all of the text by selecting the options before entering any text (options that you select affect newly entered text). You can format existing text (all text or just a few words or letters) by highlighting it and then selecting the desired options. (Highlight text by holding down the right button while dragging across the desired words or letters.) However, settings made with the *Properties...* option (*Mtext Properties* dialogue box) affect the entire paragraph and may override settings made by other options (such as *Height* and *Font*).

Figure 19-20

Stack

This option stacks words, letters, or numbers (such as fractions) in one line of text. Place a / (slash) or ^ (caret) character between two words, letters, or numbers to be stacked. A / (slash) creates a horizontal line between the stack, such as that needed for fractions, and a ^ (caret) creates the stack without a line. Highlight the words or numbers and then click the *Stack* tile.

Import

This option invokes the *Import Text File* dialogue box. Select any text file that is composed of straight ASCII text. Once the text file is selected, the text is placed in the text boundary.

Properties

This option produces the *Mtext Properties* dialogue box (see *Mtprop* next). Properties set using this feature control the <u>entire paragraph</u>. The *Height* and *Font* options can affect the settings made in the *Edit Mtext* dialogue box. Generally use the *Properties...* to control paragraph-wide formatting and use options in the *Edit Mtext* dialogue box to control settings for selected text.

Attributes

Options in this area allow you to *Underline* or *Overline* selected text, change *Color* or *Height* of selected text, and change the *Font* of selected text. A *Browse* button is provided to help you search for specific font filenames.

Formatting Paragraph Text (*Mtext*) in AutoCAD for DOS

In the DOS version of AutoCAD Release 13, you must enter the formatting codes as you enter the text using the text editor. Text features that can be controlled are underline, overline, height, color, spacing, stacked text, and other options. The following table lists the codes the resulting text.

AutoCAD for DOS Format Codes for Paragraphs

Format code	Purpose	Type this...	To produce this
\O...\o	Turns overline on and off	You have \Omany\o choices	You have $\overline{\text{many}}$ choices
\L...\l	Turns underline on and off	You have \Lmany\l choices	You have <u>many</u> choices
\~	Inserts a nonbreaking space	Keep these\~words together	Keep these words together
\\	Inserts a backslash	slash\\backslash	slash\ backslash
\{...\}	Inserts an opening and closing brace	The \{bracketed\} word	The {bracketed} word
\Cvalue;	Changes to the specified color	Change \C2;these colors	Change these colors
\Filename;	Changes to the specified font file	Change \Ftimes;these fonts	Change these fonts
\Hvalue;	Changes to the specified text height	Change \H2;these sizes	Change these sizes
\S...^...	Stacks the subsequent text at the \ or ^ symbol	1.000\S+0.010^0.000;	$1.000^{+0.010}_{-0.000}$
\Tvalue;	Adjusts the space between characters, from .75 to 4 times	\T2;TRACKING	T R A C K I N G
\Qangle;	Changes obliquing angle	\Q20;OBLIQUE	*OBLIQUE*
\Wvalue;	Change width factor to produce wide text	\W2;Wide	WIDE
\P	Ends paragraph	First paragraph\PSecond paragraph	First paragraph Second paragraph

For example, you may enter the following text in the DOS editor using the *Mtext* command.

```
\C1;This sample line of text is red in color.\P
\C7;\H.25;This text has a height of 0.25.\P
\H.2;\Fromanc;This line is an example of romanc.shx.\P
\Ftxt;This line contains stacked fractions such as \S1^2.
```

The resulting text appears in the AutoCAD for DOS drawing editor (Fig. 19-21).

Figure 19-21

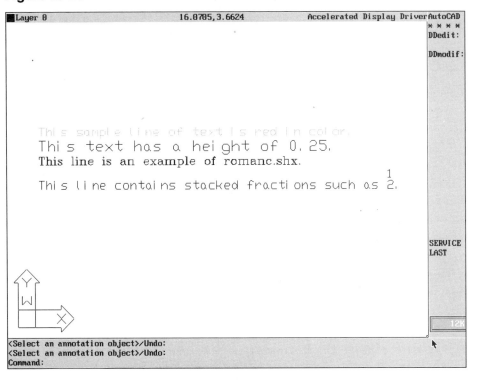

MTPROP

PULL-DOWN MENU	SCREEN MENU	TYPE IN	TABLET MENU
---	---	*MTPROP*	---

This dialogue box (Fig. 19-22) can be invoked by PICKing the *Properties* tile (in the Windows *Edit Mtext* box), by typing *Mtprop,* or by using the *DDmodify* dialogue box. AutoCAD for DOS users must type the command or use *DDmodify* to invoke this dialogue box. The options here are identical to those in the *Mtext* command line format discussed earlier; however, this dialogue box can be used to change properties of paragraphs retroactively.

Figure 19-22

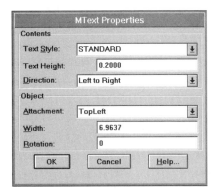

The *Mtprop* dialogue box has options for setting properties of <u>para-graphs</u>. Settings made by this device are retroactive and global for the paragraph. Generally, use this dialogue box first to set proper-ties for the paragraph; then use the *Edit Mtext* dialogue to format specific letters, words, or numbers.

Text Style
This pop-down list produces a list of *Styles* that have been previously created for the drawing. Making a selection assigns the *Style* to the paragraph (except for words or letters that have a specific *Style* assigned using the *Edit Mtext* dialogue box). To create a *Style,* see *Style* next.

Text Height
This setting assigns the text height for the paragraph. This setting overrides a *Height* setting made previ-ously in the *Edit Mtext* dialogue box.

Direction
You can set the direction to *Left to Right* or *Top to Bottom* using this pop-down list (see *Mtext Direction*).

Attachment
This option provides a means to specify the justification and "spill" of the text with respect to the text boundary. Once the text boundary has been specified using the *Mtext* command, it can be changed retroactively using this option (see *Mtext Attach*).

Width
The value in this edit box displays the width that was set previously in the *Mtext* command either by PICKing two corners to define the text boundary or by using the *Width* or *2Points* option. Changing the value resets the paragraph width (see *Mtext*). The width of the text boundary can also be changed retroactively using Grips (see Chapter 23, Grip Editing).

Rotation
Enter a value to change the rotation angle for the paragraph (see *Mtext Rotation*). The entered value represents degrees of rotation from angle zero.

STYLE

PULL-DOWN MENU	SCREEN MENU	TYPE IN	TABLET MENU
Data *Text Style*	*DRAW2* *Style:*	*STYLE*	*4,V*

Text styles can be created by using the *STYLE* command. A text *Style* is created by selecting a font file as a foundation and then specifying several other parameters to define the configuration of the letters. Creating a text style involves specifying the parameters below.

Figure 19-23

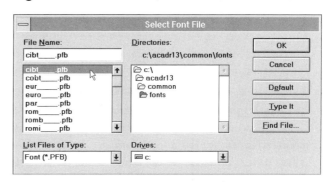

    Command: **style**
    Text style name (or ?) <STANDARD>: (**name**)
    (Assign a name up to 31 characters.)

At this point, the *Select Font File* dialogue box appears (Fig. 19-23). Select any AutoCAD font (.SHX), Postscript font (.PFA or .PFB), or True Type font (.TTF). Font files are normally found in the ACADR13\ COMMON\FONTS subdirectory. Additional fonts may possibly be found elsewhere on your computer hard drive; for example, many TrueType fonts are normally located in the C:\WINDOWS\SYSTEM directory. (For a list of all 76 AutoCAD-supplied Shape, PostScript, and TrueType fonts, including some examples and character maps, see Appendix C of the *AutoCAD User's Guide*.)

    New style. Height <0.0000>: **Enter** or (**value**)
    Width factor <1.0000>: **Enter** or (**value**)
    Obliquing angle <0>: **Enter** or (**value**)
    Backwards? <N> **Enter** or **Y**
    Upside-down? <N> **Enter** or **Y**
    Vertical? <N> **Enter** or **Y**
    (name) is now the current text style.
    Command:

Selecting the font file is the initial step in creating a style. The font file selected then becomes a foundation for "designing" the new style based on your choices for the other parameters. Those parameters are presented in command line format in the following sequence.

Height <0.000>
The height should be 0.000 if you want to be prompted again for height each time the *Dtext*, *Mtext*, or *Text* command is used. In this way, the height is variable for the style each time you insert text. If you want the height to be constant, enter a value other than 0. Then, *Dtext*, *Mtext*, or *Text* will not prompt you for a height since it has already been specified. A specific height assignment also overrides the *DIMTXT* setting (see Chapter 29).

Width factor <1.000>
A *width factor* of 1 keeps the characters proportioned normally. A value less than 1 compresses the width of the text (horizontal dimension) proportionally; a value of greater than 1 extends the text proportionally.

Obliquing angle <0>
An angle of 0 keeps the font file as vertical characters. Entering an angle of 15, for example, would slant the text forward from the existing position, or entering a negative angle would cause a back-slant on a vertically oriented font (Fig. 19-24).

Figure 19-24

Backwards? <Y/N>
Backwards characters can be helpful for special applications, such as those in the printing industry.

Figure 19-25

Upside-down? <Y/N>
Each letter is created upside-down in the order as typed (Fig. 19-25). This is different than entering a rotation angle of 180 in the *Dtext* or *Text* commands. (Turn this book 180 degrees to read the figure.)

Figure 19-26

Vertical? <Y/N>
Vertical letters are shown in Figure 19-26. The normal rotation angle for vertical text when using *Dtext*, *Mtext*, or *Text* is 270.

The new text style that is created automatically becomes the current style inserted when *Dtext*, *Mtext*, *Text*, or dimensioning is used.

Existing text style names can be renamed with the *Rename* command. The existing lines of text in the particular style assume the new text style name.

Since specification of a font file is an initial step in creating a style, it seems logical that different styles could be created using one font file but changing the other parameters. It is possible, and in many cases desirable, to do so. For example, a common practice is to create styles that reference the same font file but have different obliquing angles (often used for lettering on isometric planes). This can be done by using the *Style* command to assign a unique name to each style, or use the same font file for each style, but assign different parameters (obliquing angle, width factor, etc.) to each style. The relationship between fonts, styles, and resulting text is shown in Figure 19-27.

Figure 19-27

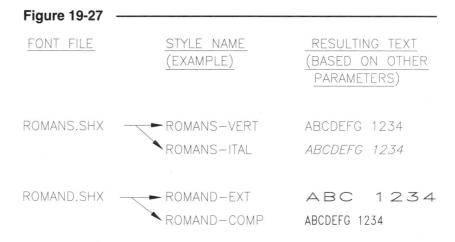

Viewing and Setting the Current Text Styles

In Release 13, creating a text *Style* is difficult since you cannot see what the font files actually look like, even though you must specify a font file to use. There is, however, a way to view the <u>existing</u> styles that are in the current drawing (previously created).

Invoke the *Object Creation Modes* dialogue box (type *Ddemodes*, select from the *Data* pull-down menu, or PICK the icon). From that dialogue box, select the *Text Style* tile. That action produces the *Select Text Style* dialogue box (Fig. 19-28). Selecting a style causes the image window to display the appearance of the style. PICK the *Show All...* tile to view the entire character set (Fig. 19-29). PICKing a choice sets the current *Style*.

Figure 19-28

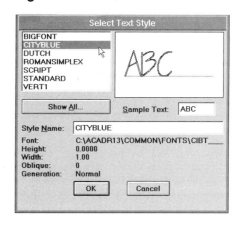

Figure 19-29

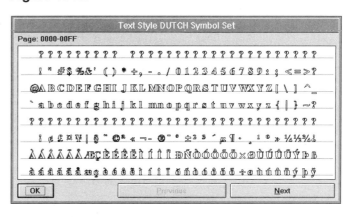

R13

When you create a text *Style*, you cannot see the configuration of characters in a particular font file, at least not in AutoCAD. You can, however, view and load TrueType fonts using the Windows *Control Panel*. Selecting the *Fonts* icon in the *Control Panel* produces the *Fonts* dialogue box (Fig. 19-30). Fonts must be *Added* to Windows <u>before they can be viewed</u>. Use this mechanism to load AutoCAD-supplied fonts (in the C:\ACADR13\COMMON\ FONTS directory) into Windows. Doing so causes the AutoCAD-supplied fonts to be loaded each time Windows is started and allows the fonts to be used in other Windows applications.

Figure 19-30

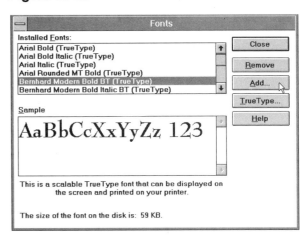

Special Text Characters

Special characters that are often used in drawings can be entered by using the "%%" symbols or by entering the Unicode values for high-ASCII (characters above the 128 range). The %% symbols are used with *Text* and *Dtext* commands, but the Unicode values must be used with *Mtext*. The following codes are typed in response to the "Text:" prompt in the *Dtext* or *Text* command or entered in the *Mtext* text editor. The Unicodes for AutoCAD for Windows are prefaced by a % symbol.

Mtext DOS	*Mtext* Windows	*Text* or *Dtext*	Result	Description
\U+2205	%\U+2205	%%c	ø	diameter (metric)
\U+00b0	%\U+00b0	%%d	°	degrees
		%%o	‾	overscored text
		%%u	___	underscored text
\U+00b1	%\U+00b1	%%p	±	plus or minus
		%%nnn	varies	ASCII text character number
\U+nnnn	%\U+nnnn		varies	Unicode text hexadecimal value

For example, entering "**Chamfer 45%%d**" at the "Text:" prompt draws the following text: **Chamfer 45°**.

Calculating Text Height for Scaled Drawings

To achieve a specific height in a drawing intended to be plotted to scale, multiply the desired text height by the "drawing scale factor." (See Chapter 14, Plotting.) For example, if the drawing scale factor is 48 and the desired text height on the plotted drawing is 1/8", enter **6** (1/8 x 48) in response to the "Height:" prompt of the *Dtext*, *Mtext* or *Text* command.

If *Limits* have already been set, use the following steps to calculate a text height to enter in response to the "Height:" prompt to achieve a specific plotted text height.

1. Determine the sheet size to be used for plotting (for example, 36" x 24").
2. Decide on the text height for the finished plot (for example, .125").
3. Check the *Limits* of the current drawing (for example, 144' x 96' or 1728" x 1152").
4. Divide the *Limits* by the sheet size to determine the drawing scale factor (1728"/36" = 48).
5. Multiply the desired text height by the drawing scale factor (.125 x 48 = 6).

TEXT EDITING COMMANDS

SPELL

PULL-DOWN MENU	SCREEN MENU	TYPE IN	TABLET MENU
Tools *Spelling...*	*TOOLS* *Spell:*	*SPELL*	*4,T*

AutoCAD has an internal spell checker that can be used to check and correct existing text in a drawing after using *Dtext*, *Mtext*, or *Text*. The *Check Spelling* dialogue box has options to *Ignore* the current word or *Change* to the suggested word (Fig. 19-31). The *Ignore All* and *Change All* options treat every occurrence of the highlighted word.

AutoCAD matches the words in the drawing to the words in the current dictionary. If the speller indicates that a word is misspelled but it is a proper name or an acronym you use often, it can be added to the custom dictionary. Choose *Add* if you want to leave a word unchanged but add it to the current custom dictionary. To use the *Add* function, a *Custom dictionary* must be specified in the *Change Dictionaries* dialogue box.

Selecting the *Change Dictionaries...* tile produces the dialogue shown in Figure 19-32. You can select from other *Main Dictionaries* that are provided with your version of AutoCAD. The current main dictionary name is stored in the *DCTMAIN* system variable. AutoCAD for DOS users must use the *DCTMAIN* system variable to change dictionaries.

You can also create a custom dictionary "on the fly" by entering any name in the *Custom dictionary* edit box. A file extension of .CUS should be used with the name. A custom dictionary name must be specified before you can add words. Words can be added by entering the desired word in the *Custom dictionary words* edit box or by using the *Add* tile in the *Check Spelling* dialogue box. Custom dictionaries can be changed during a spell check. The custom dictionary is stored in the *DCTCUST* system variable. AutoCAD for DOS users must use the *DCTCUST* variable to specify the name and can use a text editor to edit the file.

Figure 19-31

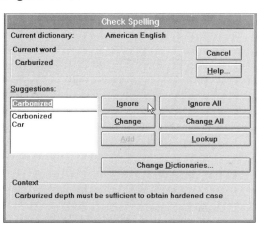

Figure 19-32

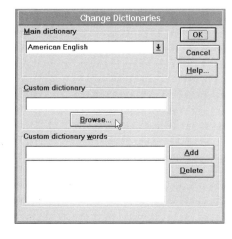

R13

DDEDIT

PULL-DOWN MENU	SCREEN MENU	TYPE IN	TABLET MENU
Modify *Edit Text...*	*MODIFY* *DDedit:*	*DDEDIT*	*5,V*

Ddedit invokes a dialogue box for editing existing text in a drawing. You can edit <u>individual characters</u> or the entire line or paragraph. If the selected text was created by the *Text* or *Dtext* command, the *Edit Text* dialogue appears displaying one line of text (Fig. 19-33). If *Mtext* created the selected text and

Figure 19-33

you are using Windows, the *Edit Mtext* dialogue box appears (the same as that used to create the text). DOS users are presented with the MS-DOS editor for editing the selected *Mtext*.

DDMODIFY

DOS PULL-DOWN	WIN PULL-DOWN	SCREEN MENU	TYPE IN	TABLET MENU
Modify Properties...	*Edit Properties...*	*MODIFY Modify:*	*DDMODIFY*	*9,V and 10,V*

Invoking this command prompts you to select objects and causes the *Modify Text* or *Modify Mtext* dialogue box to appear. As described in Chapter 16, the dialogue box that appears is <u>specific</u> to the type of object that is PICKed— kind of a "smart" dialogue box. If a line of text is PICKed in response to the "Select objects:" prompt, the dialogue box shown in Figure 19-34 appears.

Modify Text allows <u>any</u> kind of editing to text, including an *Upside down*, *Backwards*, *Width factor*, and *Obliquing angle* change.

Figure 19-34

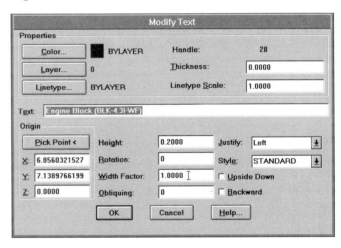

If a paragraph of text (created with *Mtext*) is selected, a similar *Modify Mtext* dialogue box appears (Fig. 19-35). You can *Edit Properties...* (producing the *Mtext Properties* dialogue box) and *Edit Contents* (producing the original *Edit Mtext* box).

Figure 19-35

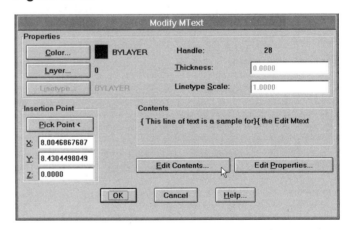

QTEXT

PULL-DOWN MENU	SCREEN MENU	TYPE IN	TABLET MENU
Options Display > Text Frame Only	*OPTIONS DISPLAY Qtext:*	*QTEXT*	*22,Y*

Qtext (quick text) allows you to display a line of text <u>as a box</u> in order to speed up drawing and plotting times. Because lines of text are treated as graphical elements, a drawing with much text can be relatively slower for regenerations and takes considerably more time plotting than the same drawing with little or no text.

When *Qtext* is turned *ON* and the drawing is regenerated, each text line is displayed as a rectangular box (Fig. 19-36). Each box displayed represents one line of text and is approximately equal in size to the associated line of text.

Figure 19-36

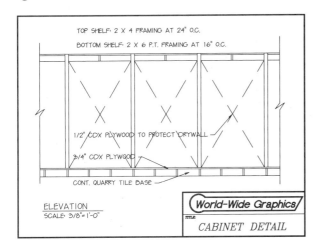
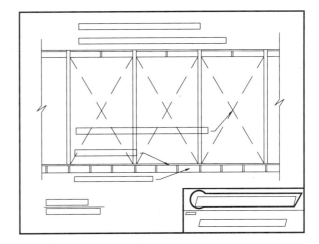

QTEXT OFF   QTEXT ON

For drawings with considerable amounts of text, *Qtext ON* noticeably reduces regeneration time. For check plots (plots made during the drawing or design process used for checking progress), the drawing can be plotted with *Qtext ON*, requiring considerably less plot time. *Qtext* is then turned *OFF* and the drawing must be *Regen*erated to make the final plot.

When *Qtext* is turned *ON*, the text remains in a readable state until a *Regen* is invoked or caused. When *Qtext* is turned *OFF*, the drawing must be regenerated to read the text again.

TEXTQLTY

The *TEXTQLTY* variable (Text Quality) controls the resolution of TrueType and PostScript fonts. The default setting is 50, which is acceptable for almost all applications. The higher the value, the higher the resolution of the characters but the slower the regeneration and plot time. If *TEXTQLTY* is set low, the resolution is low but regeneration and plot times are fast. The difference between a low and a high setting is barely noticeable (visually) unless very large text sizes are used. The variable is global and retroactive. *TEXTQLTY* can be invoked from the *Options, Display >* pull-down menu by selecting *Text Quality*.

TEXTFILL

The *TEXTFILL* variable controls the display of TrueType and Postscript fonts. If *TEXTFILL* is set to 1 (on), these fonts display on the screen and plot with solid-filled characters (Fig. 19-37). If *TEXTFILL* is set to 0 (off), the fonts display as outlined text. The variable controls text display globally and retroactively. A *Regen* should be used after changing the variable to display the new setting.

Figure 19-37

TEXTFILL OFF

TEXTFILL ON

TEXTFILL can be set to 1 (on) using the *Filled Text* option from the *Options, Display* > pull-down menu. The *Outline Text* option sets *TEXTFILL* to 0 (off).

Alternate Fonts and Font Mapping

Fonts in your drawing are specified by the current text style and by individual font formats specified for sections of *Mtext*. Text font files are not stored in the drawing; instead, text objects reference the font files located on the current computer system. Occasionally, a drawing is loaded that references a font file not available on your system. This occurrence is more common with the ability to create text styles using TrueType and Postscript fonts.

By default, AutoCAD substitutes the TXT.SHX for unreferenced fonts. You can use the *FONTALT* system variable to specify a font file that you want to use as an alternate font whenever AutoCAD encounters fonts not located on your system. Typically, .SHX fonts are used as alternates.

You can also set up a <u>font mapping table</u> listing several fonts and substitutes to be used whenever a text object is encountered that references one of the fonts. The current table name is stored in the *FONTMAP* system variable (the default is none, defined by a [.] period). A font mapping table is a plain ASCII file with a .FMP file extension, and it contains one font mapping per line. Each line contains the base font (without the path) followed by a semicolon and the substitute font (with the path).

You can use font mapping to simplify problems that may occur when exchanging drawings with clients. You can also use a font mapping table to substitute fast-drawing .SHX files while drawing and for test plots, then use another table to substitute back the more complex fonts for the final draft. For example, you might want to substitute the Times TrueType font for the ROMANS font and the Arial font for the TXT font. (The second font in each line is the new font that you want to appear in the drawing.)

```
romans;c:\windows\system\times.ttf
txt;c:\windows\system\arial.ttf
```

AutoCAD provides a sample font mapping table called SAMPLE.FMP. The table has 38 substitutions. An excerpt is shown here.

```
bgothl.ttf;txt.shx
bgothm.ttf;txt.shx
compi.ttf;txt.shx
        etc...
swissli.ttf;txt.shx
umath.ttf;txt.shx
vinet.ttf;txt.shx
```

If you are using AutoCAD for Windows, you can specify the font mapping file on the *Misc* page of the *Preferences* dialogue box (Fig. 19-38) or use the *FONTMAP* system variable. AutoCAD for DOS users must use the *FONTMAP* system variable.

Figure 19-38 ———————————————

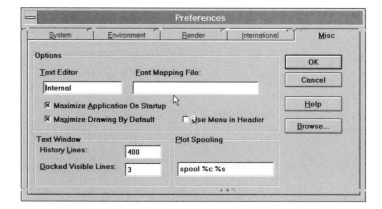

A font mapping table <u>forces</u> the listed substitutions, while an alternate font substitutes the specified font for <u>any</u> font, but <u>only</u> when an unreferenced font is encountered.

Text Attributes

When you want text to be entered into a drawing and associated with some geometry, such as a label for a symbol or number for a part, *Block Attributes* can be used. *Attributes* are text objects attached to *Blocks*. When the *Blocks* are *Inserted* into a drawing, the text *Attributes* are also inserted; however, the content of the text can be entered at the time of the insertion. See Chapter 21, Blocks, and Chapter 22, Block Attributes.

CHAPTER EXERCISES

1. *Dtext*

   Open the **EFF-APT** drawing. Make *Layer* **TEXT** *Current* and use *Dtext* to label the three rooms: **KITCHEN, LIVING ROOM**, and **BATH**. Use the *Standard style* and the *Start point* justification option. When prompted for the *Height:*, enter a value to yield letters of 3/16" on a 1/4"=1' plot (3/16 x the drawing scale factor = text height).

2. *Style, Dtext, Ddedit*

   Open the drawing of the temperature graph you created as **CH16EX8D**. Use *Style* to create two styles based on the *ROMANS* and *ROMANC* font files (accept all defaults). Use *Dtext* with the *Center* justification option to label the days of the week and the temperatures (and degree symbols) with the *ROMANS* style as shown in Figure 19-39. Use a *Height* of **1.6**. Label the axes as shown using the *ROMANC* style. Use *Ddedit* for editing any mistakes. Use *Saveas* and name the drawing **TEMPGRPH**.

Figure 19-39

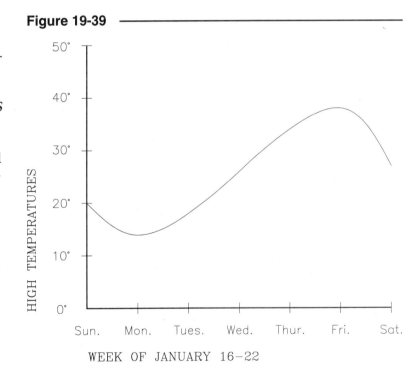

WEEK OF JANUARY 16-22

3. *Style, Dtext*

Open the **BILLMATL** drawing created in the Chapter 17 Exercises. Use *Style* to create a new style using the *ROMANS* font. Use whatever justification methods you need to align the text information (not the titles) as shown in Figure 19-40. Next, type the *Style* command to create a new style that you name as **ROMANS-ITAL**. Use the *Romans* font file and specify a **15** degree *obliquing angle*. Use this style for the **NO., PART NAME,** and **MATERIAL**. *Saveas* **BILLMAT2**.

Figure 19-40 —————

NO.	PART NAME	MATERIAL
1	Base	Cast Iron
2	Centering Screw	N/A
3	Slide Bracket	Mild Steel
4	Swivel Plate	Mild Steel
5	Top Plate	Cast Iron

4. *Edit Text*

Open the **EFF-APT** drawing. Create a new style using the *CIBT____.PFB* font file. Next, invoke the *Ddmodify* command. Use this dialogue box to modify the text style of each of the existing room names to the new style as shown in Figure 19-41. *Saveas* **EFF-APT2**.

Figure 19-41 —————

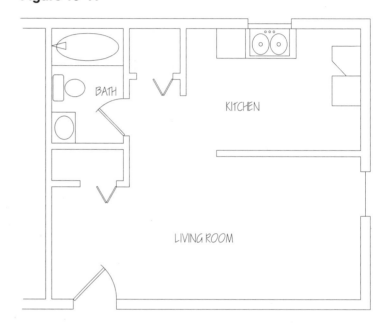

5. *Dtext, Mtext*

Open the **CBRACKET** drawing from Chapter 17 Exercises. Using **ROMANS** font, use *Dtext* to place the part name and METRIC annotation (Fig 19-42). Use a *Height* of **5** and **4,** respectively, and the *Center Justification* option. For the notes, use *Mtext* to create the boundary as shown. Use the default *Attach* method (*TL*) and a *Height* of **3**. Use *Ddedit* or *Ddmodify* if necessary.

Figure 19-42 —————

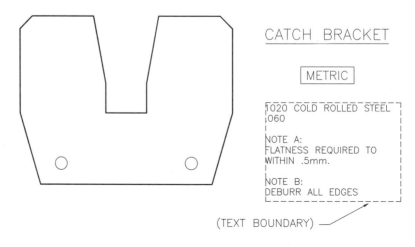

6. *Style*

Create two new styles for each of your prototype drawings: **ASHEET**, **BSHEET**, and **CSHEET**. Use the *ROMANS.SHX* style with the default options for engineering applications or *CIBT____.PFB* for architectural applications. Next, design a style of your choosing to use for larger text as in title blocks or large notes.

7. *Import Text, Ddedit, Ddmodify*

Use a text editor or the DOS editor to create a text file containing words similar to "Temperatures were recorded at Sanderson Field by the National Weather Service." Then *Open* the **TEMPGRPH** drawing and use the *Import* option of *Mtext* to bring the text in the drawing as a note in the graph as shown in Figure 19-43. Use *Ddedit* to edit the text if desired or use *Ddmodify* to change the text style or height.

Figure 19-43

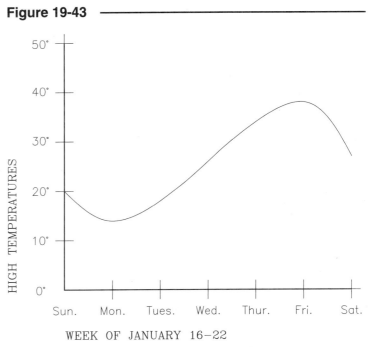

WEEK OF JANUARY 16–22

Temperatures were recorded at Sanderson Field by the National Weather Service.

8. *Create a Title Block*

A. Begin a *New* drawing and assign the name **TBLOCK**. Create the title block as shown in Figure 19-44 or design your own, allowing space for eight text entries. The dimensions are set for an A size sheet. Draw on *Layer* 0. Use a *Pline* with **.02** *width* for the boundary and *Lines* for the interior divisions. (No *Lines* are needed on the right side and bottom because the title block will fit against the border lines.)

Figure 19-44

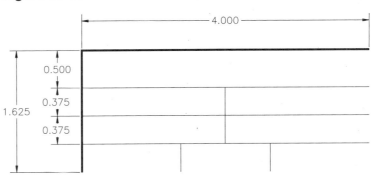

B. Create two text *Styles* using **ROMANS.SHX** and **ROMANC.SHX** font files. Insert text similar to that shown in Figure 19-45. Examples of the fields to create are:

Company or School Name
Part Name or Project Title
Scale
Designer Name
Checker or Instructor Name
Completion Date
Check or Grade Date
Project or Part Number

Figure 19-45

CADD Design Company		
Adjustable Mount	1/2"=1"	
Des.— B.R. Smith	Chk.—JRS	
1/1/96	1/1/96	42B—ADJM

Choose text items relevant to your school or office. *Save* the drawing.

9. *Mtext*

Open the **STORROOM** drawing that you created in Chapter 16 Exercises. Use *Mtext* to create text paragraphs giving specifications as shown in Figure 19-46. Format the text below as shown in the figure. Use **CIBT____.PFB** as the base font file and specify a base *Height* of **3.5"**. Use a *Color* of your choice and **COBT____.PFB** font to emphasize the first line of the Room paragraph. All paragraphs use the *TC Attach* methods except the Contractor Notes paragraph, which is *TL*. Save the drawing as **STORROM2**.

Room:	STORAGE ROOM
	11'-2" x 10'-2"
	Cedar Lined - 2 Walls

Doors:	2 - 2268 DOORS
	Fire Type A
	Andermax

Windows:	2 - 2640 CASEMENT WINDOWS
	Triple Pane Argon Filled
	Andermax

Notes:	Contractor Notes:
	Contractor to verify all dimensions in field. Fill door and window roughouts after door and window placement.

Figure 19-46

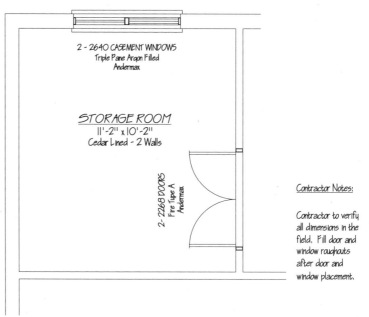

Chapter 20

ADVANCED
SELECTION SETS

Chapter Objectives

After completing this chapter you should:

1. be able to enable or disable Noun/Verb order of editing using the *Object Selection Settings* dialogue box or the *PICKFIRST* system variable;
2. be able to control whether objects are added to or replace the selection set by using the *Object Selection Settings* dialogue box or *PICKADD* variable;
3. know that the pickbox *Auto* window/crossing window feature can be controlled using the *Object Selection Settings* dialogue box or *PICKAUTO* variable;
4. be able to set the preferred window dragging style with the *Object Selection Settings* dialogue box or *PICKDRAG* variable;
5. be able to use *Object Selection Filters* in a complex drawing to find a selection set for future use with an editing command;
6. be able to create named selection sets (Object Groups) with the *Group* command and use options in the *Object Grouping* dialogue box for appropriate applications.

BASICS

When you "Select Objects:", you determine which objects in the drawing are affected by the subsequent editing action by specifying a <u>selection set</u>. You can select the set of objects in several ways. The fundamental methods of object selection (such as PICKing with the pickbox, a *Window*, a *Crossing Window*, etc.) are explained in Chapter 4, Selection Sets. This chapter deals with advanced methods of specifying selection sets and the variables that control your preferences for how selection methods operate. Specifically, this chapter explains:

> Selection Set Variables
> Object Filters
> Object Groups

SELECTION SET VARIABLES

There are four variables that allow you to customize the way you select objects. Keep in mind that selecting objects occurs <u>only for editing</u> commands; therefore, the variables discussed in this chapter affect how you select objects when you <u>edit</u> AutoCAD objects. The variable names and the related action are briefly explained here.

Variable Name	Default Setting	Related Action
PICKFIRST	1	Enables and disables Noun/Verb command syntax. Noun/Verb means *PICK* objects (noun) *FIRST* and then use the edit command (verb).
PICKADD	1	Controls whether objects are *ADD*ed to the selection set when *PICK*ed or replace the selection set when picked. Also controls whether the SHIFT key + #1 button combination removes or adds selected objects to the selection set.
PICKAUTO	1	Enables or disables the *PICK*box *AUTO*matic window/crossing window feature for object selection.
PICKDRAG	0	Enables or disables single *PICK* window *DRAG*ging. When *PICKDRAG* is set to 1, you start the window by pressing the *PICK* button, then draw the window by holding the button down and *DRAG*ging to specify the diagonal corner, and close the window by releasing the button. In other words, windowing is done with one PICK and one release rather than with two PICKs.

Like many system variables, the selection set variables listed above hold an integer value of either 1 or 0. 1 (One) designates a setting of *ON* and 0 designates a setting of *OFF*. System variables that hold an integer value of either 1 or 0 "toggle" a feature *ON* or *OFF*.

Changing the Settings
Settings for the selection set variables can be changed in either of two ways:

1. You can type the variable name at the Command: prompt (just like an AutoCAD command) to change the setting.

2. The *Object Selection Settings* dialogue box (Fig. 20-1) can be PICKed from the *Options* pull-down menu or called by typing *Ddselect*. The four variables listed above can be changed in this dialogue box, but the syntax in the dialogue box is <u>not</u> the same as the variable name. A check in the checkbox by each choice does <u>not</u> necessarily mean a setting of *ON* for the related variable.

When you change any of these four variables, the setting is recorded in the ACAD.CFG file, rather than in the current drawing file as with most variable settings. In this way, the change (which is generally personal preference of the operator) is established at the workstation, not the drawing file.

Figure 20-1 ─────────

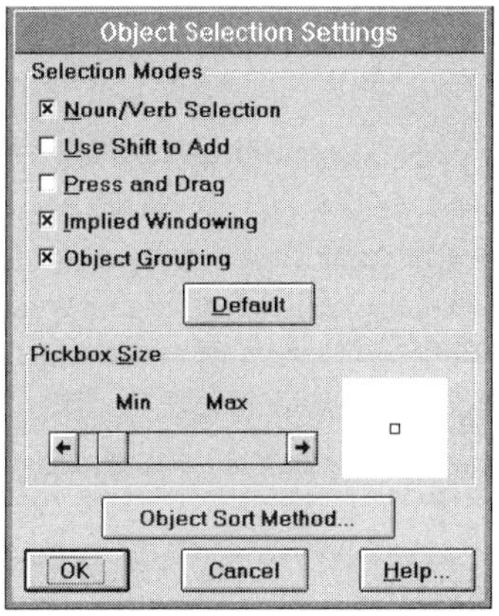

The *Object Selection Settings* dialogue box (Fig. 20-1) displays the default settings for AutoCAD Release 13. Notice the syntax used in the dialogue box does not reflect the variables' names. To avoid confusion, it is suggested that you initially use either the variable names to change the settings in command line format or the dialogue box to change the settings, but not both.

PICKFIRST

NOTE: If the *GRIPS* variable is set to 1, object grips are enabled. Object grips do not hinder your ability to use *PICKFIRST*, but they may distract your attention from the current topic. Setting the *GRIPS* variable to 0 disables object grips. You can type *GRIPS* at the command prompt to change the setting. See Chapter 23 for a full discussion of object grips.

Changing the setting of *PICKFIRST* is easily accomplished in command line mode (typing). However, the *Object Selection Settings* dialogue box can also be used to toggle the setting (Fig. 20-1). The choice is titled *Noun/Verb Selection*, and a check appearing in the box means that *PICKFIRST* is set to 1 (*ON*).

The *PICKFIRST* system variable enables or disables the ability to select objects <u>before</u> using a command. If *PICKFIRST* is set to 1, or *ON*, you can select objects at the Command: prompt <u>before</u> a command is used. *PICKFIRST* means that you PICK the objects FIRST and then invoke the desired command. *PICKFIRST* set to 1 makes the small pickbox appear at the crosshairs when you are not using a command (at the open Command: prompt). *PICKFIRST* set to 1 enables you to select objects with the pickbox, AUto window, or crossing window methods when a command is not in use.

This order of editing is called Noun/Verb; the <u>objects are the nouns</u> and the <u>command is the verb</u>. Noun/Verb editing is preferred by some users because you can decide what objects need to be changed, then decide how (what command) you want to change them. Noun/Verb editing allows AutoCAD to operate like some other CAD systems; that is, the objects are PICKed FIRST and then the command is chosen.

The command syntax for Noun/Verb editing is given next using the *Move* command as an example.

> Command: **PICK** (Use the cursor pickbox or auto window/crossing window to select objects.)
> Command: **PICK** (Continue selecting desired objects.)
> Command: *Move*   (Enter the desired command and AutoCAD responds with the number of objects selected.) 2 found
> Base point or displacement: **PICK** or (**coordinates**)
> Second point of displacement: **PICK** or (**coordinates**)
> Command:

Notice that as soon as the edit command is invoked, AutoCAD reports the number of objects found and uses these as the selection set to act on. You do <u>not</u> get a chance to "Select objects:" within the command. The selection set PICKed <u>immediately</u> before the command is used for the editing action. The command then passes through the "Select objects:" step to the next prompt in the sequence. All editing commands operate the same as with Verb/Noun syntax order with the exception that the "Select objects:" step is bypassed.

Only the pickbox, auto window, and crossing window can be used for object selection with Noun/Verb editing. The other object selection methods (*ALL, Last, Previous, Fence, Window Polygon*, and *Crossing Polygon*) are only available when you are presented with the "Select objects:" prompt.

NOTE: To disable the crosshairs pickbox, *PICKFIRST* and *GRIPS* must be OFF.

PICKADD

The *PICKADD* variable controls whether objects are ADDed to the selection set when they are PICKed or whether selected objects replace the last selection set. This variable is *ON* (set to 1) by default. Most AutoCAD operators work in this mode.

Until you reached this section, it is probable that all PICKing you did was with *PICKADD* set to 1. In other words, every time you selected an object it was added to the selection set. In this way, the selection set is cumulative; that is, each object PICKed is added to the current set. This mode also allows you to use multiple selection methods to build the set. You can PICK with the pickbox, then with a window, then with any other method to continue selecting objects. The "Select objects:" process can only be ended by pressing **Enter.**

With the default option (when *PICKADD* is set to 1 or *ON*), the SHIFT+#1 key combination allows you to deselect, or remove, objects from the current selection set. This has the same result as using the *Remove* option. Deselecting is helpful if you accidentally select objects or if it is easier in some situations to select *ALL* and then deselect (SHIFT+#1) a few objects.

Figure 20-2 ─────────────────────────

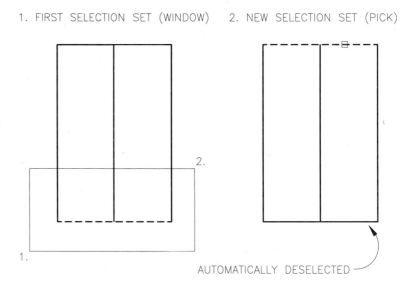

1. FIRST SELECTION SET (WINDOW)   2. NEW SELECTION SET (PICK)

AUTOMATICALLY DESELECTED

When the *PICKADD* variable is set to 0 (*OFF*), objects that you select replace the last selection set. Let's say you select five objects and they become highlighted. If you then select two other objects with a window, they would become highlighted and the other five objects automatically become deselected and unhighlighted. The two new objects would replace the last five to define the new selection set. Figure 20-2 illustrates a similar scenario.

The *PICKADD* variable also controls whether the SHIFT+#1 button combination removes from or adds to the selection set. When *PICKADD* is set to 1 (*ON*), the SHIFT+#1 combination deselects (removes) objects from the selection set. When *PICKADD* is set to 0 (*OFF*), the SHIFT+#1 combination toggles objects in or out of the selection set, depending on the object's current state. In other words (when

PICKADD is *OFF*), if the object is included in the set (highlighted), SHIFT+#1 deselects (unhighlights) it, or if the object is not in the selection set, SHIFT+#1 adds it.

Changing the *PICKADD* variable in the *Object Selection Settings* dialogue box is accomplished by making the desired choice in the checkbox. Changing the setting in this way is confusing because a check by *Use Shift to Add* means that *PICKADD* is *OFF*! Normally, a check means the related variable is *ON*. To avoid confusion, use only one method (typing or dialogue box) to change the setting until you are familiar with it.

It may occur to you that you cannot imagine a practical application for using *PICKADD OFF* and that it makes perfect sense to operate AutoCAD with *PICKADD ON*. This is true for most applications; however, if you use *GRIPS* often, setting *PICKADD* to *OFF* simplifies the process of changing **warm** *Grips* to **cold**. *Grips* are discussed in Chapter 23.

PICKAUTO

The *PICKAUTO* variable controls automatic windowing when the "Select objects:" prompt appears. Automatic windowing (*Implied Windowing*) is the feature that starts the first corner of a window or crossing window when you PICK in an open area. Once the first corner is established, if the cursor is moved to the right, a window is created, and if the cursor is moved to the left, a crossing window is started. See Chapter 4 for details of this feature.

When *PICKAUTO* is set to 1 (or *Implied Windowing* is checked in the dialogue box, Fig. 20-1), the automatic window/crossing is available whenever you select objects. When *PICKAUTO* is set to 0 (or no check appears by *Implied Windowing*), the automatic windowing feature is disabled. However, the *PICK-AUTO* variable is overridden if *GRIPS* are *ON* or if the *PICKFIRST* variable is *ON*. In either of these cases, the crosshairs pickbox and auto windowing are enabled so that objects can be selected at the open Command: prompt.

Auto windowing is a helpful feature and can be used to increase your drawing efficiency. The default setting of *PICKAUTO* is the typical setting for AutoCAD users.

Figure 20-3

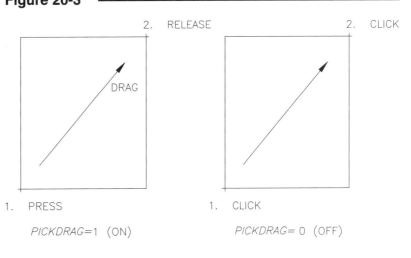

PICKDRAG

This variable controls the method of drawing a selection window. *PICKDRAG* set to 1 or *ON* allows you to draw the window or crossing window by clicking at the first corner, holding down the button, dragging to the other corner, and releasing the button at the other corner (Fig. 20-3). With *PICK-DRAG ON* you can specify diagonal corners of the window with one press and one release rather than with two clicks. Many GUIs (graphical user interfaces) of other software use this method of mouse control.

The default setting of *PICKDRAG* is 0 or *OFF*. This method allows you to create a window by clicking at one corner and again at the other corner. Releases of AutoCAD previous to 12 use this method of window creation exclusively. Most AutoCAD users are accustomed to this style, which accounts for the default setting of *PICKDRAG* to 0 (*OFF*).

OBJECT SELECTION FILTERS

Large and complex AutoCAD drawings require advanced methods of specifying a selection set. For example, consider working with a drawing of a manufacturing plant layout and having to select all of the doors on all floors, or having to select all metal washers of less than 1/2" diameter in a complex mechanical assembly drawing. Rather than spend several minutes PICKing objects, it may be more efficient to use the object filters dialogue box that AutoCAD provides.

The object selection filters feature allows you to specify particular criteria, and AutoCAD will search (filter) the drawing to find objects that match that criteria. You can specify the criteria based on any object type or property. Once AutoCAD finds the objects that match the criteria, that selection set may be used in any editing command requiring the selection of objects. Multiple selection sets can be named

FILTER

DOS PULL-DOWN	WIN PULL-DOWN	SCREEN MENU	TYPE IN	TABLET MENU
Assist *Select Objects* *Selection Filters...*	*Edit* *Select Objects* *Selection Filters...*	*SERVICE* *Filters*	*FILTER*	---

Using the *Filter* command by any method produces the *Object Selection Filters* dialogue box. Figure 20-4 displays the dialogue box when it first appears. The *Select Filter* cluster near the upper right is where you specify the search criteria. After you designate the filters and values, use *Add to List* to cause your choices to appear in the large area at the top of the dialogue box. All filters appearing at the top of the box are applied to the drawing when *Apply* is selected.

Figure 20-4

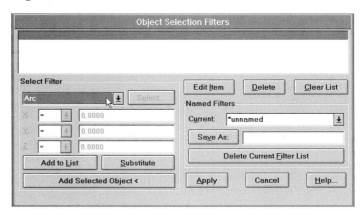

Select Filter (pop-down list)
Activating the pop-down list reveals the possible selection criteria (filters) that you can use, such as *Arc* or *Layer*. You can select one or more of the selection filters shown in the following list. You can also specify a set of values that applies to each filter, for example, *Arcs* with a *radius* of less than 1.00" or *Layers* that begin with "AR."

3Dface	Attribute Tag	Circle Center
Arc	Block Rotation	Circle
Arc Center	Block Position	Circle Radius
Arc Radius	Block	Color
Attribute	Block Name	Dimension
Attribute Position	Body	Dimension Style

Elevation	Normal Vector	Text Style Height
Ellipse	Point Position	Text Position
Ellipse Center	Point	Text Value
Layer	Polyline	Text Rotation
Leader	Ray	Text Style Name
Line	Region	Thickness
Line Start	Shape Position	Tolerance
Line End	Shape Name	Trace
Linetype	Shape	Viewport
Linetype Scale	Solid	Viewport Center
Multiline Style	Solid Body	Xdata
Multiline	Spline	Xline

The listing also provides a series of typical database grouping operators which include AND, OR, XOR, and NOT. For example, you may want to select all *Text* in a drawing but *NOT* the *Text* in a specific text style.

Select

If you select a filter that has multiple values, such as *Layer, Block Name, Text Style Name*, etc., the *Select* button is activated and enables you to select a value from the list (Fig. 20-5). If the *Select* button is grayed out, there are no existing values available.

X

If you select a filter that requires alphanumeric input (numbers or text strings), the X field is used. For example, if you selected *Arc Radius* as a filter, you would select the operator (=, <, >, etc.) from the first pop-down list and key in a numeric value in the edit box (Fig. 20-6). Other examples requiring numeric input are *Circle Radius, Text Rotation*, and *Text Height*.

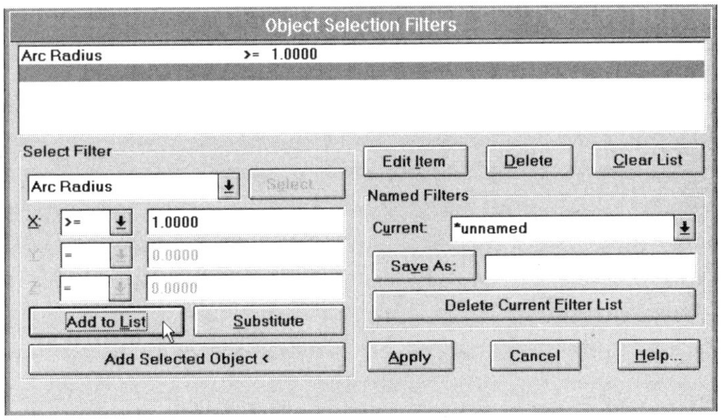

If you select a filter that requires a text string, the string is entered in the X field edit box. Examples are *Attribute Tag* and *Text Value*.

The X field is also used (in conjunction with the Y and Z fields) for filters that require coordinate input in an X,Y,Z format. Example filters include *Arc Center, Block Position, Line Start*, etc.

Figure 20-5 ───────────────

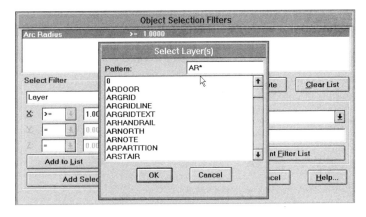

Figure 20-6 ───────────────

Y,Z

These fields are used for coordinate entry of the Y and Z coordinates when needed as one of the criteria for the filter (see X above). Additionally, you may use standard database relational operators such as equal, less than, greater than, etc., to more effectively specify the desired value.

Add to List
Use the *Add to List* button after selecting a filter to force the new selection to appear in the list at the top of the dialogue box.

Substitute
After choosing a value from the *Select* listing or entering values for *X, Y*, and *Z*, *Substitute* replaces the value of the <u>highlighted</u> item in the list (at the top of the dialogue box) with the new choice or value.

Add Selected Object
Use this button to select an object from the drawing that you want to include in the filter list.

Edit Item
Once an item is added to the list, you must use *Edit Item* to change it. First, highlight the item in the filter list (on top); then select *Edit Item*. The filter and values then appear in the *Select Filter* cluster ready for you to specify new values in the *X,Y,Z* fields or you can select a new filter by using the *Select* button.

Delete
This button simply deletes the highlighted item in the filter list.

Clear List
Use *Clear List* to delete all filters in the existing filter list.

Named Filters
The *Named Filters* cluster contains features that enable you to save the current filter configuration to a file for future use with the current drawing. This eliminates the need to rebuild a selection filter used previously.

Current
By default, the current filter list of criteria is *unnamed*, in much the same fashion as the default dimension style. Once a filter list has been saved by name, it appears as a selectable object filter configuration in the pop-down list of named filters.

Save As
Once object filter(s) have been specified and added to the list (on top), you can save the list by name. First, enter a name for the list; then PICK the *Save As* button. The list is automatically set as the current object filter configuration and can be recalled in the future for use in the drawing.

Delete Current Filter List
Deletes the named filter configuration displayed in the *Current* field.

Apply
The *Apply* button applies the current filter list to the current AutoCAD drawing. Using *Apply* causes the dialogue box to disappear and the "Select objects:" prompt to appear. <u>You must specify a selection set (by any method) to be tested against the filter criteria.</u> If you want the filters to apply to the entire drawing (except *Locked* and *Frozen* layers), enter **ALL**. If you only need to search a smaller area of the drawing, PICK objects or use a window or other selection method.

The application of the current filters can be accomplished in two ways:

1. Within a command (transparently)
    At the "Select objects:" prompt, you can invoke *Filter* transparently by selecting from a menu or

typing "*'filter*" (prefaced by an apostrophe). Then set the desired filters, select *Apply*, and specify the selection set to test against the criteria. The resulting (filtered) selection set is used for the current command.

2. At the Command: prompt
   From the Command: prompt (when no command is in use), type or select *Filter*, specify the filter configuration, and then use *Apply*. You are prompted to "Select objects:". Specify *All* or use a selection method to specify the area of the drawing for the filter to be applied against. Press Enter to complete the operation. The filtered selection set is stored in the selection set <u>buffer</u> and can be recalled by using the *Previous* option in response to the next "Select objects:" prompt.

OBJECT GROUPS

Figure 20-7

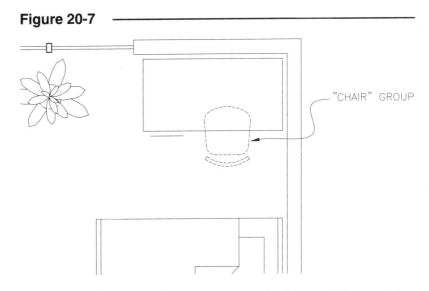

"CHAIR" GROUP

Often, a group of objects that are related in some way in a drawing may require an editing action. For example, all objects representing a chair in a floorplan may need to be selected for *Copying* or changing color or changing to another layer (Fig. 20-7). Or you may have to make several manipulations of all the fasteners in a mechanical drawing or all of the data points in a civil engineering drawing. In complex drawings containing a large number of objects, the process of building such a selection set (with the pickbox, window, or other methods) may take considerable effort. One disadvantage of the traditional selection process in AutoCAD Releases previous to 13 is that selection sets could not be saved and recalled for use at a later time. Release 13 introduces the *Group* command to identify and organize named selection sets.

A <u>Group</u> is a <u>set of objects</u> that has an <u>assigned name</u> and description. The *Group* command allows you to determine the objects you want to include in the group and to assign a name and description. Usually the objects chosen to participate in a group relate to each other in some manner. Objects can be members of more than one group.

Once a group is created, it can be assigned a <u>*Selectable*</u> status. If a group is *Selectable*, the entire group can be automatically selected (highlighted) at any "Select Objects:" prompt by PICKing any individual member, or by typing the word "group" or the letter "G," then giving the group name. For example, if all the objects in a mechanical drawing representing fasteners were assigned to a group named "fasten," the group could be selected during the *Move* command as follows:

```
Command: move
Select objects: g
Enter group name: fasten
18 found
Select objects: Enter
Base point or displacement:
        etc.
```

If the group is assigned a <u>non-selectable</u> status, the group <u>cannot</u> be selected as a whole by any method. Non-selectablility prevents accidentally *Copying* the entire group, for example. If a group is assigned a <u>selectable</u> status, the group can be manipulated as a whole <u>or</u> each member can be edited individually. The Ctrl+A key sequence (or *PICKSTYLE* variable) controls whether PICKing highlights the individual member or the entire group. In other words, you can PICK individual members <u>or</u> an entire selectable group "on the fly" by toggling Ctrl+A.

A group can be thought of as a set of objects that has a level of distinction beyond that of a typical selection set (specified "on the fly" by the pickbox, window, or other method), but not as formal as a *Block*. A *Block* is a group of objects that is combined into <u>one object</u> (using the *Block* command), but individual entities <u>cannot</u> be edited separately. (Blocks are discussed in Chapter 21.) Using groups for effective drawing organization is similar to good layer control; however, with groups you have the versatility to allow members of a group to reside on different layers.

To summarize, using groups involves two basic activities: (1) use the *Group* command to define the objects and assign a name and (2) at any later time, locate (highlight) the group for editing action at the "Select Objects:" prompt by PICKing a member or typing "G" and giving its name.

GROUP

DOS PULL-DOWN	WIN PULL-DOWN	SCREEN MENU	TYPE IN	TABLET MENU
Assist *Group Objects.*	*Edit* *Group Objects.*	SERVICE *Group:*	GROUP	12,V

Invoking the *Group* command by any method produces the *Object Grouping* dialogue box (Fig. 20-8). (The hyphen can be entered as a prefix, such as "-*group*," to present the command line equivalent.) The main purposes of this interface are to <u>create</u> groups and <u>change</u> the properties of existing groups.

The focus of the dialogue box is the *Group Name* list (on top), which gives the list of existing groups and indicates each group's selectable status. If a group is <u>selectable</u>, the entire group can be highlighted by typing the word "group" or letter "G" at the "Select Objects:" prompt, then entering the group name. Alternately, you can PICK one member to highlight the entire group, or use Ctrl+A to PICK only one member. A group that is <u>not selectable</u> cannot be selected as a whole.

Typically, your first activity with the *Object Grouping* dialogue box is to create a new group.

Figure 20-8

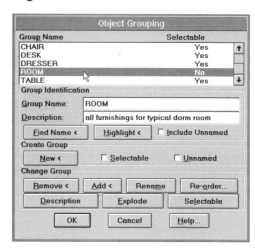

Creating a Named Group

1. Enter the desired name in the *Group Name:* edit box. This must be done as the <u>first</u> step.

2. Enter a unique description for the group in the *Description* edit box. Use up to 64 characters to describe the relationship or characteristic features of the group.

3. Determine if the group is to be selectable or not and indicate so in the *Selectable* check box.

4. Use the *New* button to PICK the desired members (objects) to be included in the group. The dialogue box is temporarily hidden until all desired objects are selected. Once the selection set is chosen (press Enter), the dialogue box reappears with the new group added to the list.

All of the options and details of the *Group Identification* and *Create Group* clusters are explained here.

Group Name:
The *Group Name:* edit box (just below the list) is used to enter the name of a new group that you want to create or to display the name of an existing group selected from the list above that requires changing. When creating a new group, enter the desired name before choosing the set of objects (using the *New* tile).

Description
Including a *Description* for new groups is optional, but this feature is useful in organizing various selection sets in a drawing. A higher level of distinction is added to the groups if a description is included. The description may be up to 64 characters. If a group name is selected from the list, both the group name and description appear in the *Group Identification* cluster.

Find Name

Figure 20-9

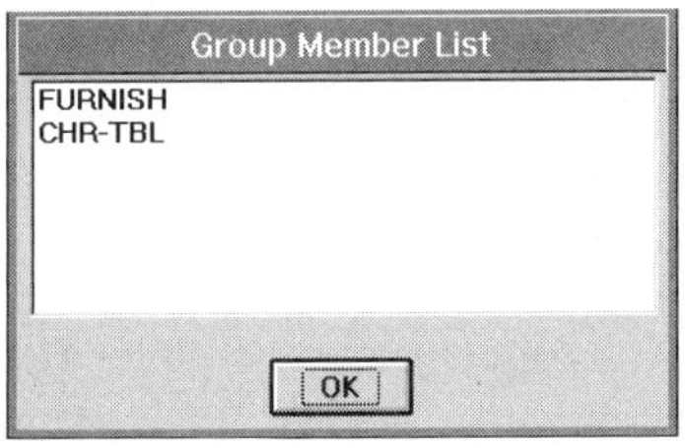

Use this option to find the group name for any object in the drawing. (The name currently appearing in the *Group Name:* edit box does not have an effect on this option.) Using the *Find Name* tile temporarily removes the *Object Grouping* dialogue box and prompts you to "Pick a member of a group." After doing so, AutoCAD responds with the names of the group(s) of which the selected object is a member (Fig. 20-9). If an object is PICKed that is not assigned to a group, AutoCAD responds with "Not a group member." This option can be used immediately upon entering the *Object Grouping* dialogue box, with no other action required.

Highlight
Choosing this tile highlights all members of the group appearing in the *Group Name:* box. The dialogue box temporarily disappears so the drawing can be viewed. Use this to verify which objects are members of the current group.

Include Unnamed

Figure 20-10

When a group is copied (with *Copy*, *Mirror*, etc.), the objects in the new group have a collective relationship like any other group; however, the group is considered an "unnamed group." Toggling the *Include Unnamed* checkbox forces any unnamed groups to be included in the list above (Fig. 20-10). In this way, you can select and manipulate copied groups like any other group, but without having to go through the process to create the group from scratch. The copied group is given a default name such as *A*n*, where *n* is the number of the group created since the beginning of the drawing. You can also create an unnamed group using the *Unnamed* toggle and the *New* tile. An unnamed group can be *Renamed*.

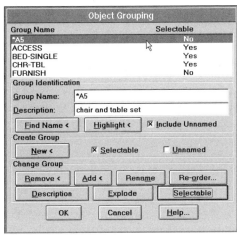

New
The *New* tile in the *Create Group* cluster is used to select the objects that you want to assign as group members. You are returned to the drawing and prompted to "Select objects:". (See Creating a Named Group.)

Selectable
Use this toggle to specify the selectable status for the new group to create. If the "X" appears, the new group is created as a *Selectable* group. A selectable group can be selected as a whole by <u>two methods</u>. When prompted to "Select objects:" during an editing command, you can (1) PICK any individual member of a selectable group or (2) enter "G" and the group name.

When using the PICK method, the Ctrl+A key sequence (or changing the *PICKSTYLE* variable) controls whether an individual member is selected or the entire group. When *PICKSTYLE* is set to 1 or 3, PICKing any member of a <u>selectable</u> group highlights (selects) the entire group. If *PICKSTYLE* is set to 0 or 2, PICKing any member of a selectable group highlights <u>only</u> that member. The Ctrl+A key sequence automatically changes the *PICKSTYLE* variable setting to 0 or 1. Therefore, any member, or the entire group, of a selectable group can be PICKed by toggling Ctrl+A. *PICKSTYLE* has no effect on non-selectable groups.

The *PICKSTYLE* variable can also be changed from the *Object Selection Settings* dialogue box (*Ddselect*). Toggling the "X" in the checkbox sets *PICKSTYLE* to a value of 3 (Fig. 20-11). (A *PICKSTYLE* setting of 2 allows selection of associative hatches only and a setting of 3 allows selection of groups and associative hatches.) The *PICKSTYLE* variable is saved with the drawing file.

Figure 20-11 ——————

For drawings that contain objects that are members of multiple groups, normally the *Selectable* status of the groups (or all but one group) should be toggled off to avoid activating all groups when a member is selected. Groups or group members that are on *Frozen* layers cannot be selected.

Unnamed
If you want to create a group with a default name (*A*n, where *n* is the number of the group created since the beginning of the drawing), use this option. If the "X" appears in the checkbox, you cannot enter a name in the *Group Name* edit box. Use the *New* tile to select the objects to include in the unnamed group. If you keep unnamed groups, toggle *Include Unnamed* on to include these groups in the list. An unnamed group can be *Renamed*.

Typically, you should name groups that you create. When you make a copy of an existing group, assign a new name (with *Rename*) if changes are made to the members. However, if you keep an unnamed group that is an identical copy, a good strategy is to keep the default (*A*n) name as an identifier and add a description like "copy of fasten group." It is suggested that unnamed groups be <u>non-selectable</u> to avoid accidentally selecting the entire group by PICKing one object for a *Copy* or other operation. Remember, you can always change the selectable status when you want to access the entire unnamed group.

Once a group exists, it can be changed in a number of ways. The options for changing a group appear in the *Change Group* cluster of the *Object Grouping* dialogue box.

Changing Properties of a Group

1. Select the group to change from the list on top of the *Object Grouping* dialogue box (Fig. 20-10). Once a group is selected, the name and description appear in the related edit boxes. A group must be selected before the *Change Group* cluster options are enabled.

2. Select the desired option from the choices in the *Change Group* area.

Remove
The *Remove* tile allows you to <u>remove any member</u> of the specified group. The dialogue box disappears temporarily and you are prompted to "Remove objects." If all members of a group are removed, the object group still remains defined in the list box.

Add

Use this option to add new members to the group appearing in the *Group Name:* edit box. The "Select objects:" prompt appears.

Rename

First, select the desired group to rename from the list. Next, type over the existing name in the *Group Name:* edit box and enter the desired new name. Then choose the *Rename* button.

Re-order

See Re-ordering Group Members at the end of this section.

Description

You can change the description for the specified object group with this option. First, select the desired group from the list. Next, edit the contents of the *Description* edit box. Then, select the *Description* tile.

Explode

Use this option to remove a group definition from the drawing. The *Explode* option breaks the current group into its original objects. The group definition is removed from the object group list box; however, the individual group members are not affected in any other way.

Selectable

This option changes the selectable status for a group. Highlight a group name from the list; then choose the *Selectable* tile. The *Yes* or *No* indicator in the Selectable column of the list toggles as you click the tile. See *Selectable* in the discussion of the *Create Group* cluster earlier.

Re-ordering Group Members

When you select objects to be included in new groups, AutoCAD assigns a number to each member. The number corresponds to the sequence that you select the objects. For special applications, the number associated with individual members is critical. For example, a group may be formed to generate a complete tool path where each member of the group represents one motion of the sequence.

The *Re-order* button (in the *Object Grouping* dialogue box) invokes the *Order Group* dialogue box (Fig. 20-12). This dialogue box allows you to change the order of individual group members. To reverse the order, simply select *Reverse Order*. To re-order members of a group to another sequence, use these steps.

1. In the *Order Group* dialogue box, select the group to re-order from the list on top.

2. Select the *Highlight* option to display each group member one at a time. In the small dialogue box that appears, Select *Next* repeatedly to go completely through the current sequence of group members. The sequence begins with 0, so the first object has position 0. Then select OK to return to the *Order Group* dialogue box.

3. In the *Number of Objects* edit box, enter the number of objects that you want to reposition.

4. In the *Remove from Position* edit box, enter the current position of the object to re-order.

Figure 20-12

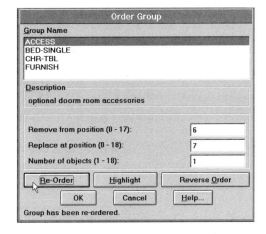

Group has been re-ordered.

5. Enter the new position in the *Replace at Position* edit box.

6. Select *Re-order*.

7. Select *Highlight* again to verify the new order.

Operation of this dialogue box is difficult and is not explained well in the documentation. It is possible to accidentally remove or duplicate members from the group using this device. A more straightforward and stable alternative for re-ordering is to *Explode* the group and make a new group composed of the same members, but PICK the members <u>in the desired order</u>.

Groups Examples

Imagine that you have the task to lay out the facilities for a college dormitory. Using the floor plan provided by the architect, you begin to go through the process of drawing furniture items to be included in a typical room, such as a desk, chair, and accessory furnishings. The drawing may look like that in Figure 20-13.

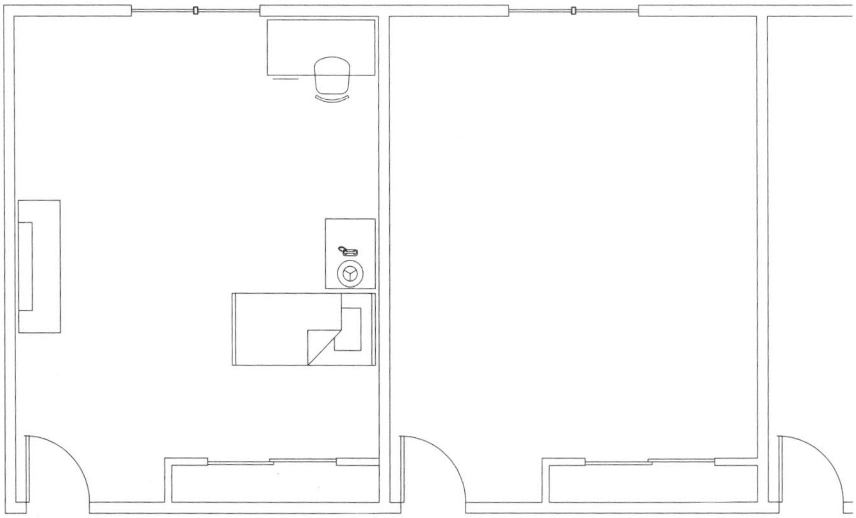

Since each room is to house two students, all objects representing each furniture item must be *Copied*, *Mirrored*, or otherwise manipulated several times to complete the layout for the entire dorm. To *Copy* the chair, for example, by the traditional method (without creating groups), each of the 12 objects (*Lines* and *Arcs*) comprising the chair must be selected <u>each time</u> the chair is manipulated. Instead, combining the individual objects into a group named "CHAIR" would make selection of these items for each operation much easier.

Figure 20-13

To make the CHAIR group, the *Group* command is used to activate the *Object Grouping* dialogue box. The CHAIR group is created by selecting all *Lines* and *Arcs* as members (see previous Figure 20-7). The group is made *Selectable* as shown in Figure 20-14.

Now, any time you want to *Copy* the chair, at the "Select objects:" prompt enter the letter "G" and "CHAIR" to cause the entire group to be highlighted. Alternately, the CHAIR group can be selected by PICKing any *Line* or *Arc* on the chair since the group is selectable.

Figure 20-14

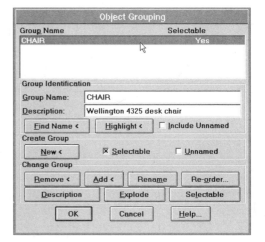

The same procedure is used to combine several objects into a group for each furniture item. The complete suite of groups may appear as shown in the dialogue box shown in Figure 20-15. Toggling on *Include Unnamed* forces the unnamed group to appear in the list. The unnamed group was automatically created when the CHAIR group was copied.

Using the named groups, completing the layout is simplified. Each group (CHAIR, DESK, etc.) is selected and *Copied* to complete the room layout.

The next step in the drawing is to lay out several other rooms. Assuming that other rooms will have the same arrangement of furniture, another group could be made of the entire room layout. (Objects can be members of more than one group.) A group called ROOM is created in the same manner as before, and all objects that are part of furniture items are selected to be members of the group. If the ROOM group is made selectable, all items can be highlighted with one PICK and copied to the other rooms (Fig. 20-16).

After submitting the layout to the client for review, a request is made for you to present alternative room layouts. Going back to the drawing, you discover that each time you select an individual furniture item to manipulate, the entire ROOM group is highlighted. To remedy the situation, the ROOM group is changed to non-selectable with the *GROUP* command. Now the individual furniture items can be selected since the original groups (CHAIR, DESK, BED, etc.) are still *Selectable* (Fig. 20-17).

Figure 20-15

Figure 20-16

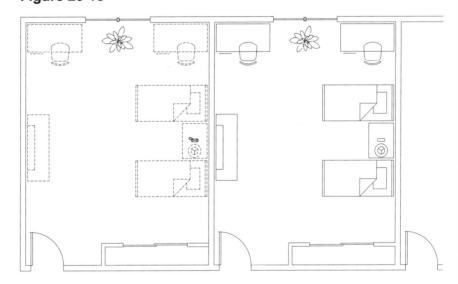

Figure 20-17

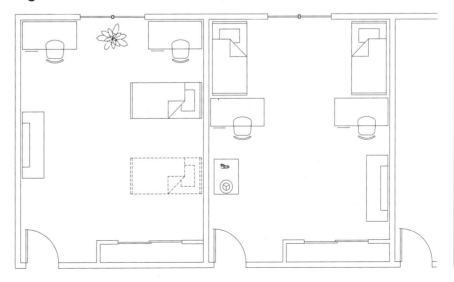

R13

R13

Another, more typical application is the use of *Groups* in conjunction with *Blocks*. A block is a set of objects combined into one object with the *Block* command. A block always behaves as <u>one object</u>. In our dorm room layout, each furniture item could be *Inserted* as a previously defined block. The entire set of blocks (bed, chair, desk, etc.) could be combined into a group called ROOM. In this case, the ROOM group would be set to *Selectable*. This would allow you to select <u>all</u> furniture items as a group by PICKing only one. However, if you wanted to select only <u>one</u> furniture item (Block), use the <u>Ctrl+A</u> key sequence to toggle "<Group off>." With "Group off," individual members of any group (blocks in this case) can be PICKed without having to change the *Selectable* status. See Chapter 21 for more information on *Blocks*.

CHAPTER EXERCISES

1. *PICKFIRST*

Check to ensure that *PICKFIRST* is set to **1** (*ON*). Also make sure *GRIPS* are set to 0 (*OFF*) by typing *GRIPS* at the command prompt or invoking the *Object Selection Settings* dialogue box. For each of the following editing commands you use, make sure you PICK the objects FIRST, then invoke the editing command.

A. *Open* the **PLATES** drawing that you created as an exercise in Chapter 10 (not the PLATNEST drawing). *Erase* 3 of the 4 holes from the plate on the left, leaving only the hole at the lower-left corner (**PICK** the *Circles*; then invoke *Erase*). Create a *Rectangular Array* with **7** rows and **5** columns and **1** unit between each hole (PICK the *Circle* before invoking *Array*). The new plate should have 35 holes as shown in Figure 20-18, plate A.

Figure 20-18

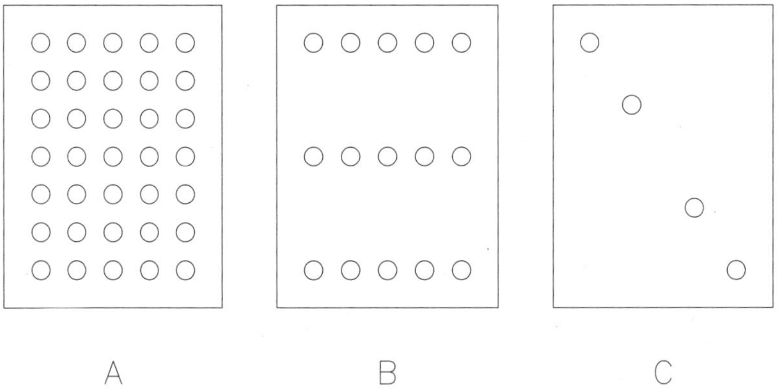

A   B   C

B. For the center plate, **PICK** the 3 holes on the <u>vertical</u> center; then invoke *Copy*. Use the *Multiple* option to create the additional 2 sets of 3 holes on each side of the center column. Your new plate should look like that in Figure 20-18, plate B. Use *Saveas* to assign a new name, **PLATES2**.

C. For the last plate (on the right), **PICK** the two top holes and *Move* them upward. Use the *CENter* of the top hole as the "Basepoint or displacement" and specify a "Second point of displacement" as **1** unit from the top and left edges. Compare your results to Figure 20-18, plate C. *Save* the drawing (as **PLATES2**).

Remember that you can leave the *PICKFIRST* setting *ON* always. This means that you can use both Noun/Verb or Verb/Noun editing at any time. You always have the choice of whether you want to PICK objects first or use the command first.

2. *PICKADD*

Change *PICKADD* to **0** (*OFF*). Remember that if you want to PICK objects and add them to the existing highlighted selection set, hold down the **SHIFT** key; then **PICK**.

A. *Open* the **CH10EX3A** drawing. (The settings for *GRIPS* and *PICKFIRST* have not changed by *Opening* a new drawing.) *Erase* the holes (highlighted *Circles* shown in Figure 20-19) leaving only 4 holes. Use either Noun/Verb or Verb/Noun editing. *Saveas* **FLANGE1**.

B. *Open* drawing **CH10EX3B**. Select all the holes and *Rotate* them **180** degrees to achieve the arrangement shown in Figure 20-20. Any selection method may be used. Try several selection methods to see how *PICKADD* reacts. (The *Fence* option can be used to select all holes without having to use the SHIFT key.) *Saveas* **FLANGE2**. Change the *PICKADD* setting back to **1** (*ON*).

Figure 20-19

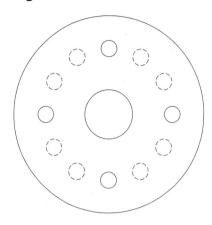

Figure 20-20

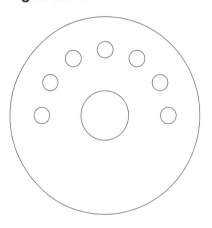

3. *PICKDRAG*

Open the **CH12EX3** drawing. Set *PICKDRAG* to **1** (*ON*). Use *Stretch* to change the front and side views to achieve the new base thickness as indicated in Figure 20-21. (Remember to hold down the PICK button when dragging the mouse or puck.) When finished, *Saveas* **HOLDRCUP**. Change the *PICKDRAG* setting back to **0** (*OFF*).

Figure 20-21

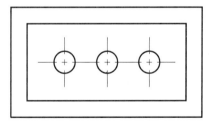

4. **Object Selection Filters**

This exercise involves using object selection filters to change the properties of objects in the drawing. Open the **ASESMP.DWG** from the \ACADR13\COMMON\SAMPLE directory.

A. Notice that all the chairs in the drawing are cyan color. Using *List*, verify that any chair is on the CHAIRS layer. We want to move all of the chairs in the drawing to the FURNITURE layer.

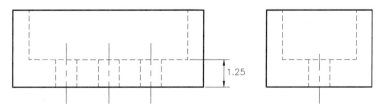

B. At the Command: prompt, invoke the *Object Selection Filters* dialogue box by any method. In the *Select Filter* area, open the pop-down list. Scroll down and choose *Layer*, or type "L" and then choose *Layer*.

C. After the pop-down list closes, choose *Select...* to display the layers available for selection in the current drawing. Choose **CHAIRS**; then choose *OK* and the *Select Layer(s)* dialogue box closes. Select the *Add to List* tile to make "Layer = CHAIRS" appear in the filter criteria list at the top of the dialogue box (Fig. 20-22).

Figure 20-22

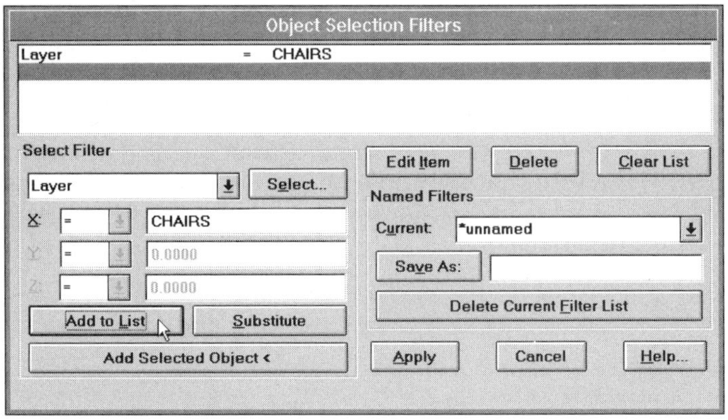

D. Choose *Apply* to apply the filtering criteria to the drawing. When the "Select objects:" prompt appears, type *ALL*; then press **Enter**. From all the objects in the drawing, AutoCAD will filter out those objects that <u>do not</u> meet the filtering criteria and select only those objects that do. When the "Select objects:" prompt returns, press **Enter** to complete the selection process. The new selection set (all of the chairs) is stored in the selection set buffer.

E. Invoke the *Change Properties* command by any method. At the "Select objects:" prompt, type *P* for *Previous* and press **Enter**. AutoCAD uses the 40 chairs stored previously in the buffer as the selection set. Press **Enter** a second time to complete the selection process and the *Change Properties* dialogue box should appear. From the dialogue box, select the *Layer* button. Choose **FURNITURE**, then *OK* to close the *Select Layers* dialogue box and *OK* to close the *Change Properties* dialogue box. All of the chairs in the drawing should change to the color of the FURNITURE layer (green). Use *List* to verify the layer of any chair. Do not save your changes and do not close the drawing.

5. **Object Selection Filters**

Object selection filters enable you to globally select all instances of an object or block for some editing action. In this exercise, we will use the *Erase* command and invoke the *Object Selection Filters* <u>transparently</u> to find and erase all instances of the room tag *Block*.

A. Using the ASESMP drawing again (from exercise 4), invoke the *Erase* command.

B. At the "Select objects:" prompt, invoke the *Object Selection Filters* dialogue box by typing *'FILTER* or selecting from a menu or icon.

C. Choose *Clear List* to start with a new filter criteria list (this action removes "Layer = CHAIRS").

D. In the *Select Filter* area, open the pop-down list and select *Block* from the list. After the pop-down list closes and displays "Block", choose *Add to List*. This will add "Object = Block" to the filter criteria.

E. From the pop-down list, choose *Block Name*; then PICK the *Select...* tile to produce a list of blocks in the drawing. Select **RMTAG** and **RMTAG2**; then choose *OK* for the *Select Layer(s)* dialogue box to close. "RMTAG, RMTAG2" appears in the X= field but not in the filter criteria listing. PICK *Add to List* and you see "Block Name = RMTAG, RMTAG2" in the list at the top of the box (Fig. 20-23).

F. PICK *Apply* to apply the filtering criteria to the drawing. At the "Select objects:" prompt, type *ALL* or make a crossing window around the entire drawing. From all the objects in the drawing, AutoCAD filters out those objects that are NOT the blocks desired and selects only RMTAG and RMTAG2. When the "Select objects:" prompt returns, press **Enter** to complete the selection process. The selection set is used for the *Erase* command, and all of the room tag blocks are erased from the drawing.

Figure 20-23 ——————————

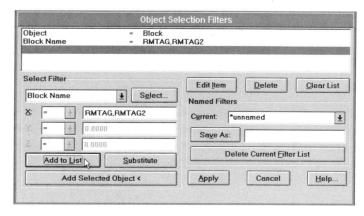

G. Do not save your changes to the ASESMP drawing.

6. **Object Groups**

Figure 20-24 ——————————

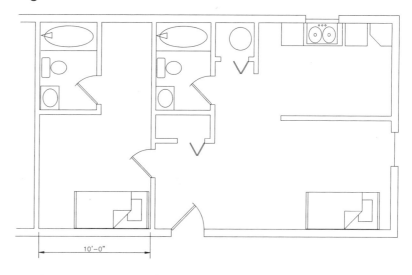

A. *Open* the **EFF-APT2** drawing that you last worked on in Chapter 19 exercises. Create a *Group* for each of the three bathroom fixtures. *Name* one group **WASHBASIN**, give it a *Description*, and include the *Ellipse* and the surrounding *Rectangle* as its members. Make two more groups named **WCLOSET** and **BATHTUB** and select the appropriate members. Next, combine the three fixture groups into one *Group* named **BATHROOM** and give it a description. Then, draw a bed of your own design and combine its members into a *Group* named **SINGLEBED**. Make all five groups *Selectable*. Use *SaveAs* to save and rename the drawing to **2BR-APT**.

B. A small bedroom and bathroom are to be added to the apartment, but a 10' maximum interior span is allowed. One possible design is shown in Figure 20-24. Other more efficient designs are possible. Draw the new walls for the addition, but design the bathroom and bedroom door locations to your personal specifications. Use *Copy* and/or *Mirror* where appropriate. Make the necessary *Trims* and other edits to complete the floorplan.

C. Next, *Copy* or *Mirror* the bathroom fixture groups to the new bathroom. If your design is similar to that in the figure, the BATHROOM group can be copied as a whole. If you need to *Copy* only individual fixtures, take the appropriate action so you don't select the entire BATHROOM group. *Copy* or *Mirror* the **SINGLEBED**. Once completed, activate the *Object Grouping* dialogue box and toggle on *Include Unnamed*. Can you explain what happened? Assign a *Description* to each of the unnamed groups and *Save* the drawing.

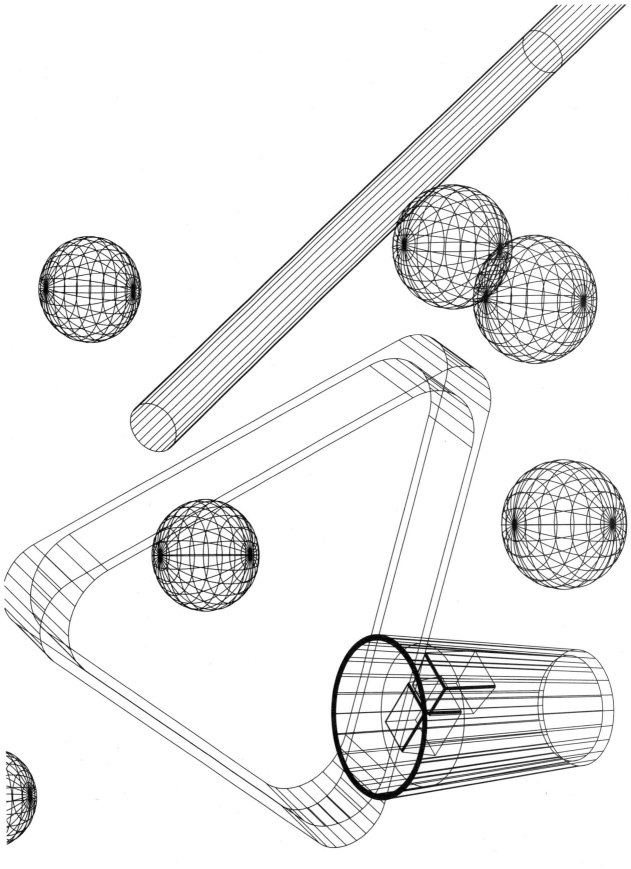

POOL2.DWG

Chapter 21

BLOCKS

Chapter Objectives

After completing this chapter you should:

1. understand the concept of creating and inserting symbols in AutoCAD drawings;

2. be able to use the *Block* command to transform a group of objects into one object that is stored in the current drawing's block definition table;

3. be able to use the *Insert* and *Minsert* commands to bring *Blocks* into drawings;

4. know that *color* and *linetype* of *Blocks* are based on conditions when the *Block* is made;

5. be able to convert *Blocks* to individual objects with *Explode*;

6. be able to use *Wblock* to prepare .DWG files for insertion into other drawings;

7. be able to redefine and globally change previously inserted *Blocks*;

8. be able to define an insertion base point for .DWG files using *Base*.

BASICS

A *Block* is a <u>group</u> of objects that are combined into <u>one</u> object with the *Block* command. The typical application for *Blocks* is in the use of symbols. Many drawings contain symbols, such as doors and windows for architectural drawings, capacitors and resistors for electrical schematics, or pumps and valves for piping and instrumentation drawings. In AutoCAD, symbols are created first by constructing the desired geometry with objects like *Line, Arc, Circle*, etc., then transforming the set of objects comprising the symbol into a *Block*. A description of the objects comprising the *Block* is then stored in the drawing's "block definition table." The *Blocks* can then each be *Insert*ed into a drawing many times and treated as a single object. Text can be attached to *Blocks* (called *Attributes*) and the text can be modified for each *Block* when inserted.

Figure 21-1 compares a shape composed of a set of objects and the same shape after it has been made into a *Block* and *Insert*ed back into the drawing. Notice that the original set of objects is selected (highlighted) individually for editing, whereas, the *Block* is only one object.

Figure 21-1 ————————————————————

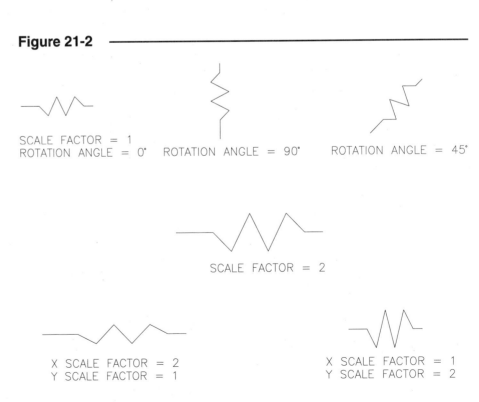

10 OBJECTS   1 OBJECT

Since an inserted *Block* is one object, it uses less file space than a set of objects that is copied with *Copy*. The *Copy* command creates a duplicate set of objects, so that if the original symbol were created with 10 objects, 3 copies would yield a total of 40 objects. If instead the original set of 10 were made into a *Block* and then *Insert*ed 3 times, the total objects would be 13 (the original 10 + 3).

Upon *Insert*ing a *Block*, its scale can be changed and rotational orientation specified without having to use the *Scale* or *Rotate* commands (Fig. 21-2). If a design change is desired in the *Blocks* that have already been *Insert*ed, the original *Block* can be redefined and the previously inserted *Blocks* are automatically updated. *Blocks* can be made to have explicit *Linetype* and *Color*, regardless of the layer they are inserted onto, or they can be made to assume the *Color* and *Linetype* of the layer onto which they are *Insert*ed.

Figure 21-2 ————————————————————

SCALE FACTOR = 1
ROTATION ANGLE = 0°   ROTATION ANGLE = 90°   ROTATION ANGLE = 45°

SCALE FACTOR = 2

X SCALE FACTOR = 2   X SCALE FACTOR = 1
Y SCALE FACTOR = 1   Y SCALE FACTOR = 2

Blocks can be <u>nested</u>; that is, one *Block* can reference another *Block*. Practically, this means that the definition of *Block* "C" can contain *Block* "A" so that when *Block* "C" is inserted, *Block* "A" is also inserted as part of *Block* "C" (Fig. 21-3).

Figure 21-3

BLOCK A

BLOCK B

BLOCK C

BLOCK 'A' NESTED
IN BLOCK 'C'

BLOCK D

BLOCK 'B' AND BLOCK 'C'
NESTED IN BLOCK 'D'

Blocks created within the current drawing can be copied to disk as complete and separate drawing files (.DWG file) by using the *Wblock* command (Write Block). This action allows you to *Insert* the *Blocks* into other drawings. Specifically, when you use the *Insert* command, AutoCAD first searches for the supplied *Block* name in the current drawing's block definition table. If the designated *Block* is not located there, AutoCAD searches the directories for a .DWG file with the designated name.

Commands related to using *Blocks* are:

Block	Creates a *Block* from individual objects
Insert	Inserts a *Block* into a drawing
Ddinsert	Invokes a dialogue box for inserting a *Block*
Minsert	Permits a multiple insert in a rectangular pattern
Explode	Breaks a *Block* into its original set of multiple objects
Wblock	Writes an existing *Block* or a set of objects to a file on disk
Base	Allows specification of an insertion base point
Purge	Deletes uninserted *Blocks* from the block definition table
Rename	Allows renaming *Blocks*

COMMANDS

BLOCK

PULL-DOWN MENU	SCREEN MENU	TYPE IN	TABLET MENU
Construct Block	---	*BLOCK*	*9,W*

After creating the desired *Lines*, *Circles*, *Arcs*, and other objects comprising the geometry for the symbol, the *Block* command is used to transform the set of objects into one object. The command prompt reads as follows:

Command: **Block**
Block name (or ?): (**name**) (Enter a descriptive name for the *Block* up to 31 characters.)
Insertion base point: **PICK** or (**coordinates**)   (Select a point to be used later for insertion.)
Select objects: **PICK**
Select objects: **PICK** (Continue selecting all desired objects.)
Select objects: **Enter**

The *Block* then <u>disappears</u> as it is stored in the current drawing's "block definition table." The *Oops* command can be used to restore the original set of "template" objects (they reappear), but the definition of the *Block* remains in the table.

Using the *?* option of the *Block* command lists the *Blocks* stored in the block definition table. The following command sequence lists the blocks in the ASESMP.DWG.

Command: **block**
Block name (or ?): **?**
Block(s) to list <*>: **Enter**
Defined blocks.
  ADCADD_ZZ
  CB30
  CB36
  CC30
        (etc.)
  DESK2
  DESK3
  DESK4
  DIGITIZE
  DISHWASH
  DOOR
  DOOR2
        (etc.)
  SOFA2
  TABLE1
  TABLE2
  VENDING

User Blocks	External References	Dependent Blocks	Unnamed Blocks
41	0	0	0

Command:

Block Color and *Linetype* Settings

The color and linetype of an inserted *Block* are determined by one of the following settings when the *Block* is created.

1.   When a *Block* is inserted, it is drawn on its original layer with its original *Color* and *Linetype* (when the objects were created), regardless of the layer or *color* and *linetype* settings that are current when the *Block* is inserted (unless conditions 2. or 3. exist).

2.   If a *Block* is created on Layer 0 (Layer 0 is current when the original objects comprising the *Block* are created), then the *Block* assumes the *color* and *linetype* of any layer that is current when it is inserted (Fig 21-4).

3.   If the *Block* is created with the special *BYBLOCK linetype* and *color* setting, the *Block* is inserted with the *Color* and *Linetype* settings that are current during insertion, whether the *BYLAYER* or explicit object *Color* and *Linetype* settings are current.

Figure 21-4

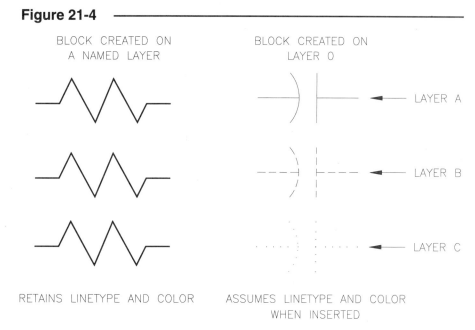

BLOCK CREATED ON
A NAMED LAYER

BLOCK CREATED ON
LAYER 0

◄—— LAYER A

◄—— LAYER B

◄—— LAYER C

RETAINS LINETYPE AND COLOR

ASSUMES LINETYPE AND COLOR
WHEN INSERTED

INSERT

PULL-DOWN MENU	SCREEN MENU	TYPE IN	TABLET MENU
Draw *Insert>* *Block*	*DRAW2* *DDinsert:* *or Insert:*	*INSERT or* *DDINSERT*	*10,W*

Once the *Block* has been created, it is inserted back into the drawing at the desired location(s) with the *Insert* command. *Insert* also allows the *Blocks* to be scaled or rotated upon insertion. The command syntax is given here.

    Command: **insert**
    Block name (or ?): **name** (Type the name of an existing block or .DWG file to insert.)
    Insertion point: **PICK** or (**coordinates**) (Give the desired location of the *Block*.)
    X scale factor <1>/Corner/XYZ: **PICK** or (**value**) (Specifies the size of the *Block* in the X direction.)
    Y scale factor (default=X): (**value**) or **Enter** (Specifies the size in the Y direction.)
    rotation angle: **PICK** or (**value**) (Enter an angle for *Block* rotation.)

Selecting the "*X scale factor*" with the cursor specifies both X and Y factors. The rotation angle can be forced to 90 degree increments by turning *ORTHO* (F8) *On*.

The *Insert* dialogue box can be invoked by using the pull-down menu, icon buttons, or tablet menu or by typing *Ddinsert* (Fig 21-5). Selecting the *Block* tile causes another box to pop up, listing the *Blocks* previously defined in the drawing's block definition table (Fig. 21-6). The desired *Block* is selected from the list. Selecting the *File* tile causes a box

Figure 21-5

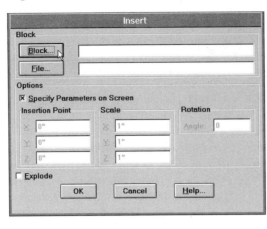

Figure 21-6

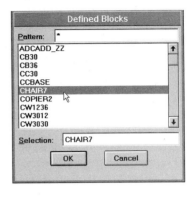

to pop up, allowing selection of any drawing (.DWG files) from any accessible drive and directory for insertion. The *Insert* dialogue box provides explicit value entry of insertion point coordinates, scale, and rotation angle. *Explode* can also be toggled, which would insert the *Block* as multiple objects.

MINSERT

PULL-DOWN MENU	SCREEN MENU	TYPE IN	TABLET MENU
Draw *Insert>* *Multiple Blocks*	DRAW2 *Minsert:*	MINSERT	---

This command allows a <u>multiple insert</u> in a rectangular pattern (Fig. 21-7). *Minsert* is actually a combination of the *Insert* and the *Array Rectangular* commands. The *Blocks* inserted with *Minsert* are associated (the group is treated as one object) and cannot be edited independently (unless *Exploded*).

Examining the command syntax yields the similarity to a *Rectangular Array*.

Figure 21-7

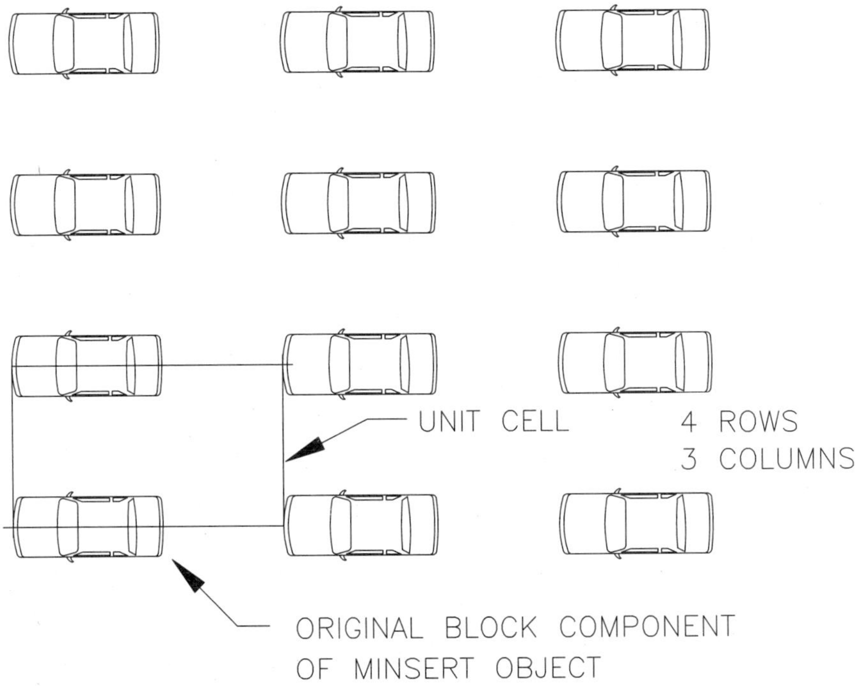

UNIT CELL   4 ROWS
             3 COLUMNS

ORIGINAL BLOCK COMPONENT
OF MINSERT OBJECT

Command: **Minsert**
Block name (or ?): **name**
Insertion point: **PICK** or **(coordinates)**
X scale factor <1>/Corner/XYZ: **(value)** or **PICK**
Y scale factor (default=X): **(value)** or **Enter**
rotation angle: **(value)** or **PICK**
Number of rows (---): **(value)**
Number of columns (|||): **(value)**
Unit cell or distance between rows: **(value)** or **PICK** (Value specifies Y distance from *Block* corner to *Block* corner; PICK allows drawing a unit cell rectangle.)
Distance between columns: **(value)** or **PICK** (Specifies X distance between *Block* corners.)
Command:

EXPLODE

PULL-DOWN MENU	SCREEN MENU	TYPE IN	TABLET MENU
Modify *Explode*	*MODIFY* *Explode:*	*EXPLODE*	*20,W*

Explode breaks a previously inserted *Block* back into its original set of objects (Fig. 21-8), which allows you to edit individual objects comprising the shape. *Blocks* that have been inserted with differing X and Y scale factors or *Blocks* that have been *Minsert*ed can be *Explode*d in Release 13. There are no options for this command.

Figure 21-8

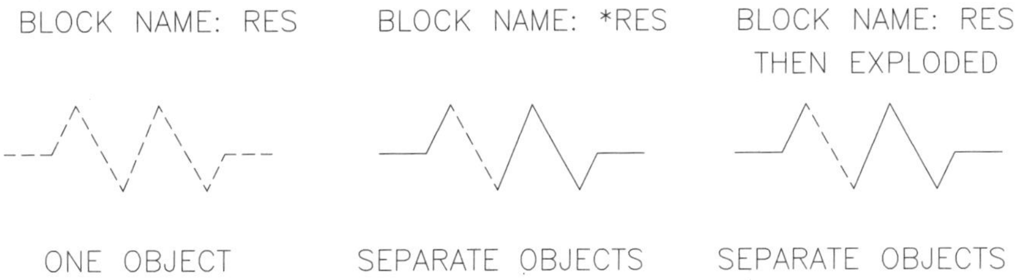

BLOCK NAME: RES

ONE OBJECT

BLOCK NAME: *RES

SEPARATE OBJECTS

BLOCK NAME: RES
THEN EXPLODED

SEPARATE OBJECTS

Command: **explode**
Select objects: **PICK**
Select objects: **Enter**
Command:

Inserting with an * (asterisk) symbol accomplishes the same goal as using *Insert* normally, then *Explode*.

INSERT with *

Using the *Insert* command with the asterisk (*) allows you to insert a *Block*, not as one object, but as the original set of objects comprising the *Block*. In this way, you can edit individual objects in the *Block*, otherwise impossible if the *Block* is only one object (Fig. 21-8).

The normal *Insert* command is used; however, when the desired *Block* name is entered, it is prefaced by the asterisk (*) symbol:

Command: **insert**
Block name (or ?): * **(name)** (Type the * symbol, then the name of an existing block or .DWG file to insert.)
Command:

This action accomplishes the same goal as using *Insert*; then *Explode*.

WBLOCK

	DOS PULL-DOWN	WIN PULL-DOWN	SCREEN MENU	TYPE IN	TABLET MENU
	File *Export >* *Block...*	*File* *Export...* *(*.DWG)...*	**FILE** **EXPORT** *Wblock:*	**WBLOCK**	*8,W*

The *Wblock* command writes a *Block* out to disk as a separate and complete drawing (.DWG) file. The *Block* used for writing to disk can exist in the current drawing's *Block* definition table or can be created by the *Wblock* command. Remember that the *Insert* command inserts *Blocks* (from the current drawing's block definition table) or finds and accepts .DWG files and treats them as *Blocks* upon insertion.

If you are using an existing *Block*, a copy of the *Block* is essentially transformed by the *Wblock* command to create a complete AutoCAD drawing (.DWG) file. The original block definition remains in the current drawing's block definition table. In this way, *Blocks* that were originally intended for insertion into the current drawing can be inserted into other drawings.

If you want to transform a set of objects to be used as a *Block* in other drawings but not in the current one, you can use *Wblock* to transform (a copy of) the objects in the current drawing into a separate .DWG file. This action does not create a *Block* in the current drawing.

As an alternative, if you want to create symbols specifically to be inserted into other drawings, each symbol could be created initially as a separate .DWG file. Figure 21-9 illustrates the relationship among a *Block*, the current drawing, and a *WBlock*.

Figure 21-9

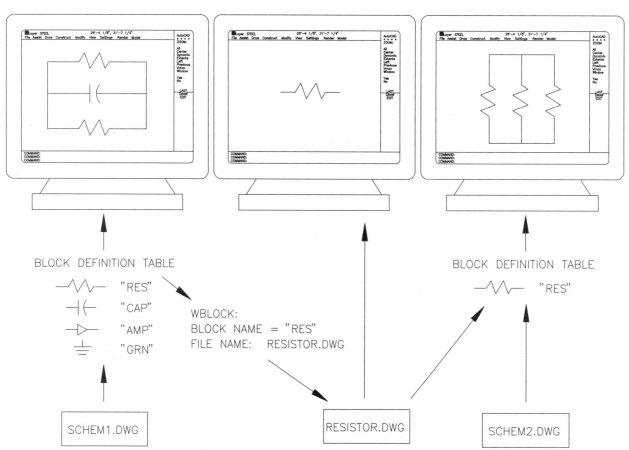

To create *Wblocks* (.DWG files) <u>from existing *Blocks*</u>, follow this command syntax:

Command: **Wblock**
(At this point, the *Create Drawing File* dialogue box appears, prompting you to supply a name for the .DWG file to be created. Typically, a new descriptive name would be typed in the edit box rather than selecting from the existing names.)
Block name: (**name**) (Enter the name of the desired existing *Block*. If the file name given in the previous step is the same as the existing *Block* name, a "=" symbol can be entered at this prompt.)
Command:

A copy of the existing *Block* is then created in the current or selected directory as a *Wblock* (.DWG file).

To create a *Wblock* (.DWG file) to be used as a *Block* in other drawings <u>but not in the current drawing</u>, follow the same steps as before, but when prompted for the "Block name:" press Enter or select *blank* from the screen menu. The next steps are like the *Block* command prompts.

Command: **Wblock**
(The *Create Drawing File* dialogue box appears, prompting you to supply a name for the .DWG file to be created)
Block name: (**Enter**) or (**blank**)
Insertion base point: **PICK** or (**coordinates**) (Pick a point to be used later for insertion.)
Select objects: **PICK**
Select objects: **Enter** (Press Enter to complete selection.)
Command:

An alternative method for creating a *Wblock* is using the *Export Data* dialogue box accessed from the *File* pull-down menu. Make sure you select *Drawing (*.DWG)* as the type of file to export (bottom left of the box, Fig. 21-10). You can create a *Wblock* (.DWG file) from an existing *Block* or from objects that you select from the screen. After specifying the .DWG name you want to create and the dialogue box disappears, you are presented with the same command syntax as above.

Figure 21-10

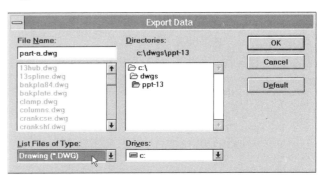

When *Wblocks* are *Inserted*, the *Color* and *Linetype* settings of the *Wblock* are determined by the settings current when the original objects comprising the *Wblock* were created. The three possible settings are the same as those for *Blocks* (see the *Block* command, *Color* and *Linetype* Settings).

When a *Wblock* is *Inserted*, its parent (original) layer is also inserted into the current drawing. *Freezing* <u>either</u> the parent layer or the layer that was current during the insertion causes the *Wblock* to be frozen.

Redefining *Blocks*
If you want to change the configuration of a *Block*, even after it has been inserted, it can be accomplished by redefining the *Block*. In doing so, all of the previous *Block* insertions are automatically and globally

updated (Fig. 21-11). AutoCAD stores two fundamental pieces of information for each *Block* insertion—the insertion point and the *Block* name. The actual block definition is stored in the block definition table. Redefining the *Block* involves changing that definition.

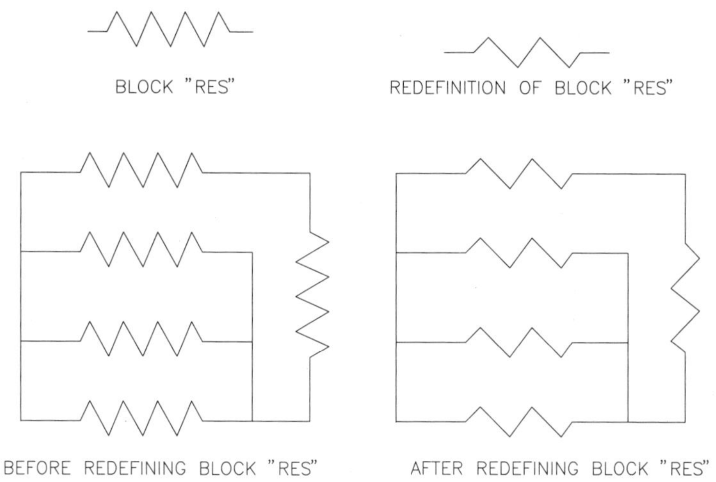

To redefine a *Block*, use the *Block* command. First, draw the new geometry or change the <u>original</u> "template" set of objects. (The change cannot be made using an inserted *Block* unless it is *Exploded* because a *Block* cannot reference itself.) Next, use the *Block* command and select the new or changed geometry. The old *Block* is redefined with the new geometry as long as the <u>original *Block* name</u> is used.

Figure 21-11

BLOCK "RES"

REDEFINITION OF BLOCK "RES"

BEFORE REDEFINING BLOCK "RES"

AFTER REDEFINING BLOCK "RES"

```
Command: block
Block name (or ?): name (Enter the original Block name.)
Block (name) already exists.
Redefine it? <N>: Yes (Answering Y or yes causes the redefinition.)
Insertion base point: PICK or (coordinates) (Select a point to be used later for insertion.)
Select objects: PICK
Select objects: PICK (Continue selecting all desired objects.)
Select objects: Enter
Command:
```

The *Block* is redefined and all insertions of the original *Block* display the new geometry.

The *Block* command can also be used to redefine *Wblocks* that have been inserted. In this case, enter the *Wblock* name (.DWG filename) at the "Block name:" prompt to redefine (actually replace) a previously inserted *Wblock*.

BASE

PULL-DOWN MENU	SCREEN MENU	TYPE IN	TABLET MENU
---	---	*BASE*	---

The *Base* command allows you to specify an "insertion base point" (see the *Block* command) in the current drawing for subsequent insertions. If the *Insert* command is used to bring a .DWG file into another drawing, the insertion base point of the .DWG is 0,0 by default. The *Base* command permits you to specify another location as the insertion base point. The *Base* command is used in the symbol drawing, that is, used in the drawing <u>to be inserted</u>. For example, while creating separate symbol drawings (.DWGs) for subsequent insertion into other drawings, the *Base* command is used to specify an appropriate point on the symbol geometry for the *Insert* command to use as a "handle" other than point 0,0 (see Fig. 21-12).

Figure 21-12

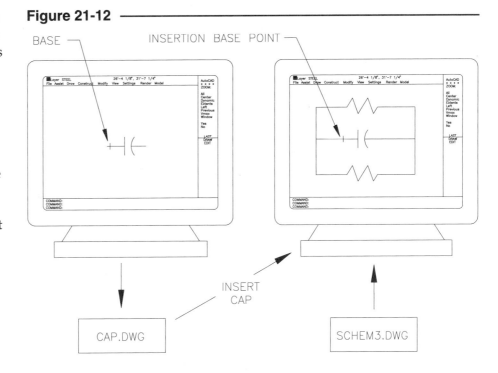

PURGE

Blocks that are part of the current drawing but are not being used (in the block definition table but not *Inserted*) can be *Purged* to minimize file size. See Chapter 30, Miscellanous Commands.

RENAME

Blocks can be *Renamed*.
Use the *Rename* command or type *Ddrename* to invoke the *Rename* dialogue box (see Chapter 30, Miscellanous Commands).

CHAPTER EXERCISES

1. ***Block, Insert.*** In the next several exercises, you will create an office floorplan, then create pieces of furniture as *Blocks* and *Insert* them into the office. All of the block-related commands are used.

   A. Start a *New* drawing and assign the name **OFF-ATT**. Set up the drawing as follows.

1.	*Units*	Architectural	1/2" Precision
2.	*Limits*	48' x 36'	(1/4"=1' scale on an "A" size sheet), drawing scale factor = 48
3.	*Snap*	3	
4.	*Grid*	12	
5.	*Layers*	FLOORPLAN	continuous	colors of your choice, all different
		FURNITURE	continuous	
		ELEC-HDWR	continuous	
		ELEC-LINES	hidden	
		DIM-FLOOR	continuous	
		DIM-ELEC	continuous	
		TEXT	continuous	
		TITLE	continuous	
6.	*Text Style*	City Blueprint	(CITB____.PFB)
7.	*Ltscale*	24	

B.   Create the floorplan shown in Figure 21-13. Center the geometry in the *Limits*. Draw on layer **FLOORPLAN**. Use any method you want for construction (e.g., *Line*, *Pline*, *Xline*, *Mline*, *Offset*, etc.).

Figure 21-13

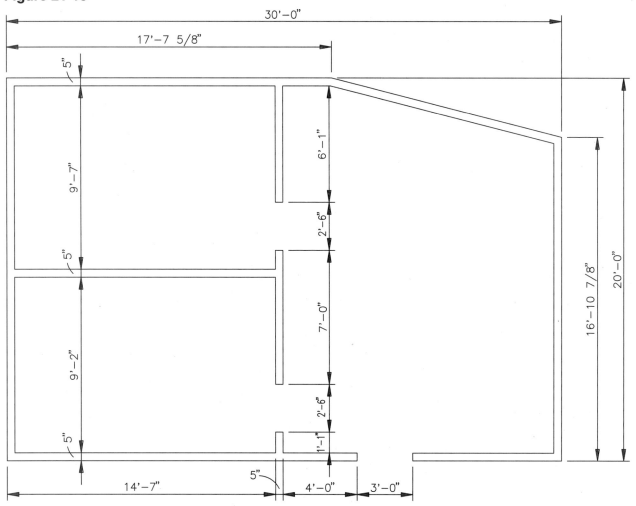

C.   Create the furniture shown in Figure 21-14. Draw on layer **FURNITURE**. Locate the pieces anywhere for now. Do <u>not</u> make each piece a *Block*. *Save* the drawing as **OFF-ATT**.

Now make each piece a *Block*. Use the *name* as indicated and the *insertion base point* as shown by the "blip." Next, use the *Block* command again but with the *?* option to list the block definition table. Use *Saveas* and rename the drawing **OFFICE**.

Figure 21-14

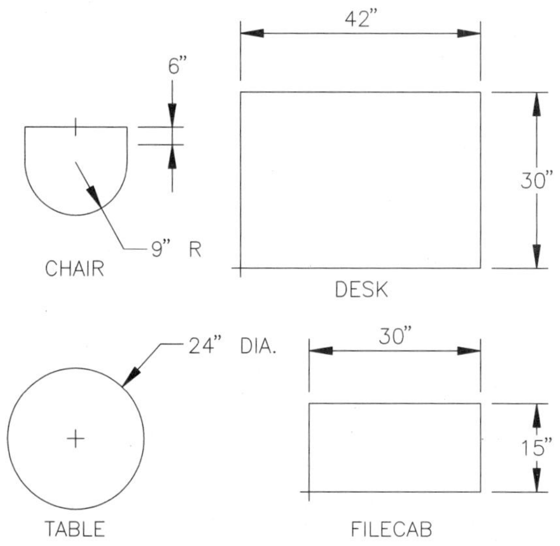

CHAIR

DESK

TABLE

FILECAB

D. Use *Insert* to insert the furniture into the drawing, as shown in Figure 21-15. You may use your own arrangement for the furniture, but *Insert* the same number of each piece as shown.

Save the drawing.

Figure 21-15

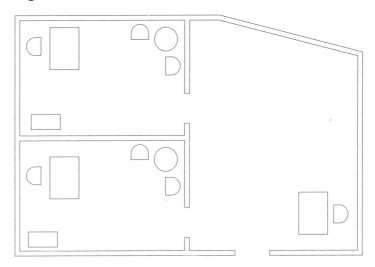

2. **Creating a .DWG file for** *Insertion, Base*

Begin a *New* drawing. Assign the name **CONFTABL**. Create the table as shown in Figure 21-16 on *Layer* 0. Since this drawing is intended for insertion into the **OFFICE** drawing, use the *Base* command to assign an insertion base point at the lower-left corner of the table.

When you are finished, *Save* the drawing.

Figure 21-16

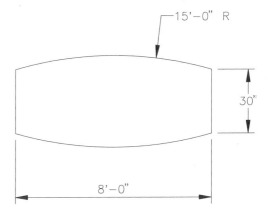

3. *Insert, Explode, Divide*

A. *Open* the **OFFICE** drawing. Ensure that layer **FURNITURE** is current. Use *Insert* to bring the **CONFTABL** drawing in as a *Block* in the placement shown in Figure 21-17.

Notice that the CONF-TABL assumes the line-type and color of the current layer, since it was created on layer **0**.

Figure 21-17

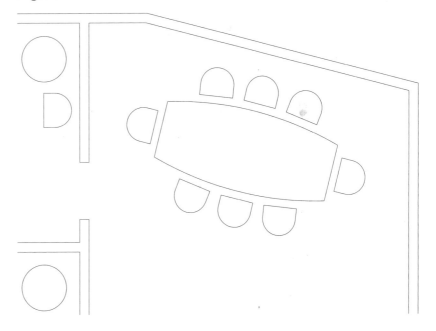

B. *Explode* the CONFTABL. The *Exploded* CONFTABL returns to *Layer* **0**, so use *Chprop* to change it back to *Layer* **FURNITURE**. Then use the *Divide* command (with the *Block* option) to insert the **CHAIR** block as shown in Figure 21-17. Also *Insert* a **CHAIR** at each end of the table. *Save* the drawing.

4. *Wblock, BYBLOCK setting*

Figure 21-18

A. *Open* the **EFF-APT2** drawing you worked on in Chapter 19 Exercises. Use the *Wblock* command to transform the plant into a .DWG file (Fig. 21-18). Use the name **PLANT** and specify the *Insertion base point* at the center. Do not save the EFF-APT2 drawing.

PLANT

B. *Open* the **OFFICE** drawing and *Insert* the **PLANT** into one of the three rooms. The plant probably appears in a different color than the current layer. Why? Check the *Layer* listing to see if any new layers came in with the PLANT block. *Erase* the PLANT block.

C. *Open* the **PLANT** drawing. Change the *Color* and *Linetype* setting of the plant objects to *BYBLOCK*. *Save* the drawing.

D. *Open* the **OFFICE** drawing again and *Insert* the **PLANT** onto the **FURNITURE** layer. It should appear now in the current layer's *color* and *linetype*. *Insert* a **PLANT** into each of the 3 rooms. *Save* the drawing.

5. **Redefining a** *Block*

Figure 21-19

After a successful meeting, the client accepts the proposed office design with one small change. The client requests a slightly larger chair than that specified. *Explode* one of the **CHAIR** blocks. Use the *Scale* command to increase the size <u>slightly</u> or otherwise redesign the chair in some way. Use the *Block* command to redefine the **CHAIR** block. All previous insertions of the CHAIR should reflect the design change. *Save* the drawing. Your design should look similar to that shown in Figure 21-19. *Plot* to a standard scale based on your plotting capabilities.

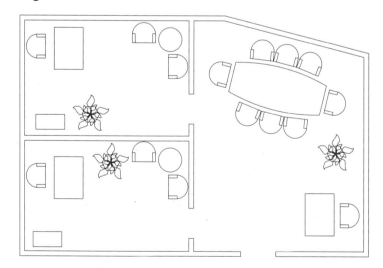

6. Create the process flow diagram shown in Figure 21-20. Create symbols (**Blocks**) for each of the valves and gates. Use the names indicated (for the **Blocks**) and include the text in your drawing. *Save* the drawing as **PFD**.

Figure 21-20

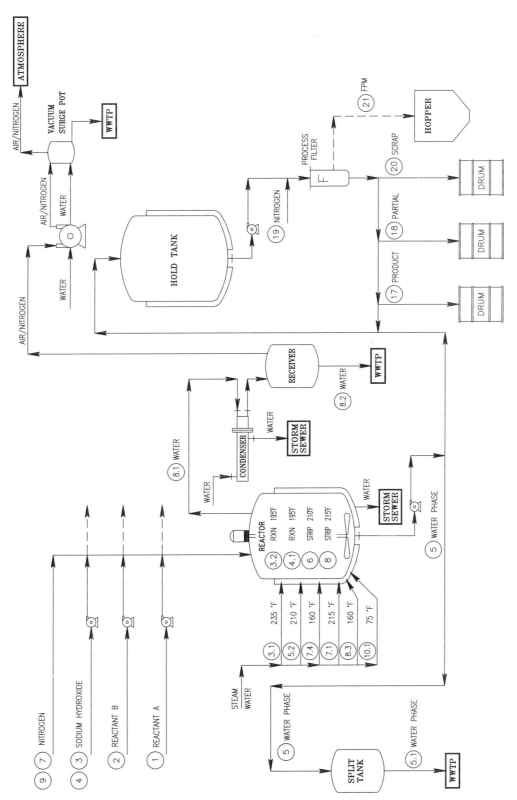

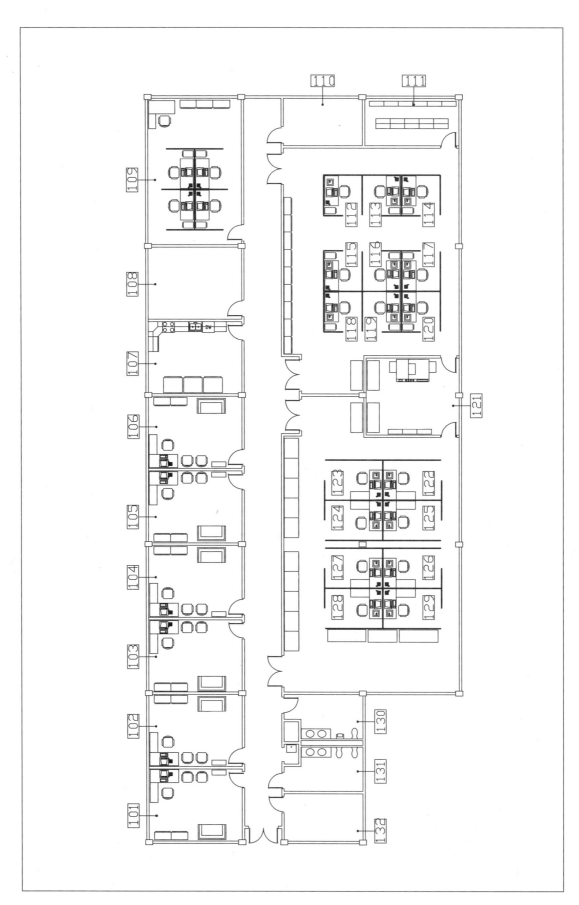

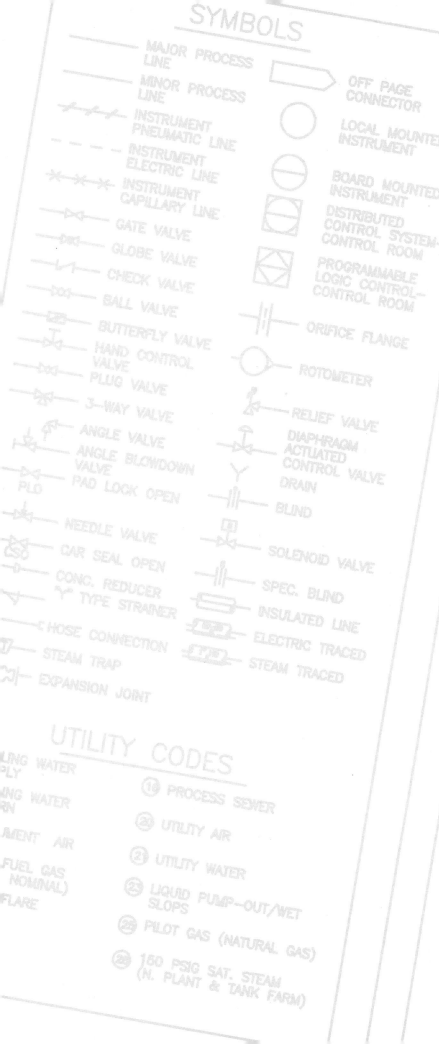

SYMBOLS

MAJOR PROCESS LINE
MINOR PROCESS LINE
INSTRUMENT PNEUMATIC LINE
INSTRUMENT ELECTRIC LINE
INSTRUMENT CAPILLARY LINE
GATE VALVE
GLOBE VALVE
CHECK VALVE
BALL VALVE
BUTTERFLY VALVE
HAND CONTROL VALVE
PLUG VALVE
3-WAY VALVE
ANGLE VALVE
ANGLE BLOWDOWN VALVE
PAD LOCK OPEN
NEEDLE VALVE
CAR SEAL OPEN
CONC. REDUCER
TYPE STRAINER
HOSE CONNECTION
STEAM TRAP
EXPANSION JOINT

OFF PAGE CONNECTOR
LOCAL MOUNTED INSTRUMENT
BOARD MOUNTED INSTRUMENT
DISTRIBUTED CONTROL SYSTEM– CONTROL ROOM
PROGRAMMABLE LOGIC CONTROL– CONTROL ROOM
ORIFICE FLANGE
ROTOMETER
RELIEF VALVE
DIAPHRAGM ACTUATED CONTROL VALVE
DRAIN
BLIND
SOLENOID VALVE
SPEC. BLIND
INSULATED LINE
ELECTRIC TRACED
STEAM TRACED

UTILITY CODES

LING WATER PLY
ING WATER RN
MENT AIR
FUEL GAS NOMINAL)
FLARE

PROCESS SEWER
UTILITY AIR
UTILITY WATER
LIQUID PUMP–OUT/WET SLOPS
PILOT GAS (NATURAL GAS)
160 PSIG SAT. STEAM (N. PLANT & TANK FARM)

Chapter 22

BLOCK ATTRIBUTES

Chapter Objectives

After completing this chapter you should:

1. be able to define block attributes using the *Attdef* command and the *Attribute Definition* dialogue box;

2. be able to specify *Invisible, Constant, Verify,* and *Preset* attribute modes;

3. be able to control the display of attributes in a drawing with *Attdisp*;

4. know how to edit existing attributes with the *Edit Attributes* dialogue box;

5. be able to globally or individually edit attributes using the *Attedit* command;

6. be able to redefine attributes for existing blocks using *Attredef*.

7. be able to create an extract file containing a drawing's attributes in an external text file;

8. know how to create a template file in a text editor for specifying the structure of an extract file.

BASICS

A block <u>attribute</u> is a line of text (numbers or letters) associated with a block. An attribute can be thought of as a label or description for a block. A block can have multiple attributes. The attributes are included with the drawing objects when the block is defined (using the *Block* command). When the block is *Inserted*, its attributes are also *Inserted*.

Since *Blocks* are typically used as symbols in a drawing, attributes are text strings that label or describe each symbol. For example, you can have a series of symbols such as transistors, resistors, capacitors, etc., prepared for creating electrical schematics. The associated attributes can give the related description of each block, such as ohms or wattage values, model number, part number, cost, etc. If your symbols are doors, windows, and fixtures for architectural applications, attached attributes can include size, cost, manufacturer, etc. A mechanical engineer can have a series of blocks representing fasteners with attached attributes to specify fastener type, major diameter, pitch, length, etc. Attributes could even be used to automate the process of entering text into a title block, assuming the title block was *Inserted* as a block or separate .DWG file.

Attributes can add another level of significance to an AutoCAD drawing. Not only can attributes automate the process of placing the text attached to a block, but the inserted attribute information can be <u>extracted</u> from a drawing to form a bill of materials or used for cost analysis, for example. Extracted text can be imported to a database or spreadsheet program for further processing and analysis.

Attributes are created with the *Attdef* (attribute define) command. *Attdef* operates similarly to *Text* or *Dtext*, prompting you for text height, placement, and justification. During attribute definition, parameters can be adjusted that determine how the attributes will appear when they are inserted.

This chapter discusses defining attributes, inserting attributed blocks, displaying and editing attributes in a drawing, and extracting attributes from drawings.

CREATING ATTRIBUTES

Steps for Creating and Inserting Block Attributes

1. Create the objects that will comprise the block. Do not use the *Block* command yet; only draw the geometry.

2. Use the *Attdef* or *Ddattdef* command to create and place the desired text strings associated with the geometry comprising the proposed block.

3. Use the *Block* command to convert the drawing geometry (objects) and the attributes (text) into a named block. When prompted to "*Select objects:*" for the block, select both the drawing objects and the text (attributes). The block and attributes disappear.

4. Use *Insert* to insert the attributed block into the drawing. Edit the text attributes as necessary (if parameters were set as such) during the insertion process.

ATTDEF

PULL-DOWN MENU	SCREEN MENU	TYPE IN	TABLET MENU
Construct Attribute...	*CONSTRCT DDattDef:*	*ATTDEF or DDATTDEF*	*7,W*

Attdef (attribute define) allows you to define attributes for future combination with a block. If you intend to associate the text attributes with drawing objects (*Line, Arc, Circle*, etc.) for the block, it is usually preferred to draw the objects before using *Attdef*. In this way, the text can be located in reference to the drawing objects.

Attdef allows you to create the text and provides justification, height, and rotation options similar to the *Text* and *Dtext* commands. You can also define parameters, called Attribute Modes, specifying how the text will be inserted—*Invisible, Constant, Verify,* or *Preset*.

Figure 22-1 ——————————————

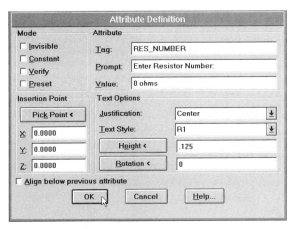

The *Attdef* command differs, depending on the method used to invoke it. If you select from any menus or the icon or type *Ddattdef*, the *Define Attribute* dialogue box appears (Figure 22-1). If you type *Attdef*, the command line format is used. The command line format is presented here first.

```
Command: attdef
Attribute modes — Invisible:N Constant:N Verify:N Preset:N
Enter (ICVP) to change, RETURN when done: Enter or (letter)
Attribute tag: Enter tag, no spaces.
Attribute prompt: Enter desired prompt, spaces allowed.
Default attribute value: Enter desired default text.
Justify/Style/<Start point>: PICK or (option)
Height <0.2000>: Enter, PICK or (value)
Rotation angle <0>: Enter, PICK or (value)
Command:
```

The first option, "attribute modes," is described later. For this example, the default attribute modes have been accepted.

The *Attribute Definition* dialogue box has identical options that are found in the command line format, including justification options. The same entries have been made here to define the first attribute example shown in Figure 22-2.

Figure 22-2 ——————————————

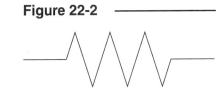

RES_NUMBER

Attribute Tag
This is the descriptor for the <u>type of text</u> to be entered, such as MODEL_NO, PART_NO, NAME, etc. Spaces cannot be used in the Attribute Tag.

Attribute Prompt
The prompt is what words (<u>prompt) you want to appear</u> when the block is *Inserted* and when the actual text (values) must be entered. Spaces and punctuation can be included.

Default Attribute Value
This is the <u>default text</u> that appears with the block when it is *Inserted*. Supply the typical or expected words or numbers.

Justify
Any of the typical text justification methods can be selected using this option. (See Chapter 19, Inserting and Editing Text, if you need help with justification.)

Style
This option allows you to select from existing text *Styles* in the drawing. Otherwise, the attribute is drawn in the current *Style*.

As an example, assume that you are using the *Attdef* or *Ddattdef* command to make attributes attached to a resistor symbol to be *Blocked* (Fig. 22-2). The scenario may appear as follows or as presented in the *Attribute Definition* dialogue box in Figure 22-1.

```
Command: attdef
Attribute modes — Invisible:N Constant:N Verify:N Preset:N
Enter (ICVP) to change, RETURN when done: Enter
Attribute tag: RES_NUMBER
Attribute prompt: Enter Resistor Number:
Default attribute value: 0
Justify/Style/<Start point>: j
Align/Fit/Center/Middle/Right/TL/TC/TR/ML/MC/MR/BL/BC/BR: c
Center point: PICK
Height <0.2000>: .125
Rotation angle <0>: Enter
```

The attribute would then appear at the selected location, as shown in Figure 22-2. Keep in mind that the *Lines* comprising the resistor were created before using *Attdef* or *Ddattdef*. Also remember that the resistor and the attribute are not yet *Blocked*. The *Attribute Tag* <u>only</u> is displayed until the *Block* command is used.

Two other attributes could be created and positioned beneath the first one by pressing **Enter** when prompted for the "<Start point>:" (Command line format) or selecting the "*Align below previous attribute*" checkbox (dialogue box format). The command syntax may read like this.

```
Command: attdef
Attribute modes — Invisible:N Constant:N Verify:N Preset:N
Enter (ICVP) to change, RETURN when done: Enter
Attribute tag: RESISTANCE
Attribute prompt: Enter Resistance:
Default attribute value: 0 ohms
Justify/Style/<Start point>: Enter
Command:

Command: attdef
Attribute modes — Invisible:N Constant:N Verify:N Preset:N
Enter (ICVP) to change, RETURN when done: Enter
Attribute tag: PART_NO
Attribute prompt: Enter Part Number:
Default attribute value: 0-0000
Justify/Style/<Start point>: Enter
Command:
```

The resulting unblocked symbol and three attributes appear as shown in Figure 22-3. Only the *Attribute Tags* are displayed at this point. The *Block* command has not yet been used.

Figure 22-3

RES_NUMBER
RESISTANCE
PART_NO

The *Attributes Modes* define the appearance or the action required when you *Insert* the attributes. The options are as follows.

Invisible
An *Invisible* attribute is not displayed in the drawing after insertion. This option can be used to prevent unnecessary information from cluttering the drawing and slowing regeneration time. The *Attdisp* command can be used later to make these attributes visible.

Constant
This option gives the attribute a fixed value for all insertions of the block. In other words, the attribute always has the same text and cannot be changed. You are not prompted for the value upon insertion.

Verify
This option forces you to verify that the attribute value is correct when the block is inserted.

Preset
This option prevents you from having to enter a value during insertion. The default value is automatically used for the block, although it can be changed later with the *Attedit* command.

The *Attribute Modes* are toggles (Yes or No). In command line format, the options are toggled by entering the appropriate letter, which reverses its current position (Y or N). For example, to create an *Invisible* attribute, type **"I"** at the prompt:

    Command: *attdef*
    Attribute modes — Invisible:N Constant:N Verify:N Preset:N
    Enter (ICVP) to change, RETURN when done: *I*
    Attribute modes — Invisible:Y Constant:N Verify:N Preset:N
    Enter (ICVP) to change, RETURN when done: **Enter**

Note that the second prompt (fourth line) reflects the new position of the previous request.

Alternately, attribute modes could be defined using the *Attribute Definition* dialogue box (Fig. 22-4). The *Mode* cluster of checkboxes (upper-left corner) makes setting attribute modes simpler than in command line format.

Figure 22-4

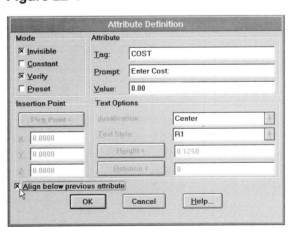

Using our previous example, two additional attributes can be created with specific *Invisible* and *Verify* attribute modes. Either the dialogue box or command line format can be used. The following command syntax shows the creation of an *Invisible* attribute.

    Command: *attdef*
    Attribute modes — Invisible:N Constant:N
    Verify:N Preset:N
    Enter (ICVP) to change, RETURN when done: *I*

Attribute modes — Invisible:Y Constant:N Verify:N Preset:N
Enter (ICVP) to change, RETURN when done: **Enter**
Attribute tag: **MANUFACTURER**
Attribute prompt: **Enter Manufacturer:**
Default attribute value: **Enter**
Justify/Style/<Start point>: **Enter**
Height <0.1250>: **Enter**
Rotation angle <0>: **Enter**
Command:

The first attribute has been defined. Next, a second attribute is defined having *Invisible* and *Verify* parameters. (Figure 22-4 also shows the correct entries for creation of this attribute.)

Command: **attdef**
Attribute modes — Invisible:Y Constant:N Verify:N Preset:N
Enter (ICVP) to change, RETURN when done: **v**
Attribute modes — Invisible:Y Constant:N Verify:Y Preset:N
Enter (ICVP) to change, RETURN when done: **Enter**
Attribute tag: **COST**
Attribute prompt: **Enter Cost:**
Default attribute value: **0.00**
Justify/Style/<Start point>: **Enter**
Command:

Tags for *Invisible* attributes appear as any other attribute tags. The *Values*, however, are invisible when the block is inserted.

Using the *Block* Command to Create an Attributed Block

Next, the *Block* command is used to transform the drawing objects and the text (attributes) into an attributed block. When you are prompted to "Select objects:" in the *Block* command, select the attributes <u>in the order</u> you desire their prompts to appear on insertion. In other words, the first attribute selected during the *Block* command (RES_NUMBER) is the first attribute prompted for editing during the *Insert* command. PICK the attributes <u>one at a time</u> in order. Then PICK the drawing objects (a crossing window can be used). Figure 22-5 shows this sequence.

Figure 22-5

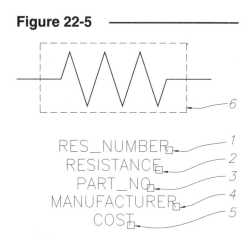

If the attributes are selected with a window, they are inserted in reverse order of creation, so you would be prompted for COST first, MANUFACTURER second, and so on.

Command: **block**
Block name (or ?): **res**
Insertion base point: **PICK**
Select objects: **PICK** (1)
Select objects: **PICK** (2)
Select objects: **PICK** (3)
Select objects: **PICK** (4)
Select objects: **PICK** (5)

Select objects: **PICK** (objects)
Select objects: **Enter**
Command:

As with other blocks, this one disappears after using the *Block* command. Use the *Oops* command to redisplay the original objects if you expect to make further changes. The RES block definition remains in the block definition table.

Inserting **Attributed Blocks**

Use the *Insert* command to bring attributed blocks into your drawing as you would to bring any block into your drawing. After the normal *Insert* command prompts, the attribute prompts (that you defined with *Attdef*) appear. In this step, enter the desired attribute *values* for each block insertion. The prompts appear in dialogue box fashion (*Enter Attributes* dialogue, Fig. 22-7) or in command line format, depending on the setting of the *ATTDIA* variable. (The command line format is the default setting, *ATTDIA*=0. See Appendix A, System Variables.)

The command line format follows.

Command: ***insert***
Block name (or ?): **res**
Insertion point: **PICK**
X scale factor <1> / Corner / XYZ: **Enter**
Y scale factor (default=X): **Enter**
Rotation angle <0>: **Enter**
Enter attribute values
Enter Resistor Number: <0>: **R1**
Enter Resistance: <0 ohms>: **4.7K**
Enter Part Number: <0-0000>: **R-4746**
Enter Manufacturer: **Electro Supply Co.**
Enter Cost <0.00>: **.37**
Verify Attribute values
Enter Cost <.37> : **Enter**
Command:

Figure 22-6

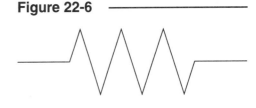

Notice the prompts appearing on insertion are those that you specified as the "Attribute prompt:" with the *Attdef* command or *Ddattdef* dialogue box. The order of the prompts matches the order of selection during the *Block* command. Also note the repeated prompt (*Verify*) for the COST attribute.

Entering the attribute values as indicated above yields the block insertion shown in Figure 22-6. Notice the absence of the last two attribute values (since they are *Invisible*).

Figure 22-7

The *ATTDIA* **Variable**
If the *ATTDIA* system variable is set to a value of 1, the *Enter Attributes* dialogue box (Fig. 22-7) is invoked automatically by the *Insert* command for

Enter Attributes	
Block Name: RES	
Enter Resistor Number:	0
Enter Resistance:	0 ohms
Enter Part Number:	0-0000
Enter Manufacturer:	
Enter Cost	0.00

OK   Cancel   Previous   Next   Help...

entering attribute values. The dialogue box, in that case, would have appeared rather than the command line format for entering attributes. The *Verify* and *Preset* Attribute Mode options have no effect on the dialogue box format of attribute value entry. The dialogue box can hold multiple screens of 10 attributes in each, all connected to 1 block.

The *ATTREQ* Variable

When *Inserting* blocks with attributes, you can force the attribute requests to be suppressed. In other words, you can disable the prompts asking for attribute values when the blocks are *Inserted*. To do this, use the *ATTREQ* (attribute request) system variable. A setting of **1** (the default) turns attribute requesting on, and a value of **0** disables the attribute value prompts.

The attribute prompts can be disabled when you want to *Insert* several blocks but do not want to enter the attribute values right away. The attribute values for each block can be entered at a later time using the *Attedit* or *Ddatte* commands. These attribute editing commands are discussed on the following pages.

DISPLAYING AND EDITING ATTRIBUTES

ATTDISP

PULL-DOWN MENU	SCREEN MENU	TYPE IN	TABLET MENU
Options *Display >* *Attribute Display*	*OPTIONS* *DISPLAY* *AttDisp:*	*ATTDISP*	---

The *Attdisp* (attribute display) command allows you to control the visibility state of all inserted attributes contained in the drawing.

    Command: **attdisp**
    Normal/ON/OFF <current value>: (option)
    Command:

Attdisp has three positions. Changing the state forces a regeneration.

Figure 22-8

ATTDISP

Off   *Normal*   *On*

On
All attributes (normal and *Invisible*) in the drawing are displayed.

Off
No attributes in the drawing are displayed.

R1
4.7K
R-4746

R1
4.7K
R-4746
Electro Supply Co
.37

Normal
Normal attributes are displayed; *Invisible* attributes are not displayed.

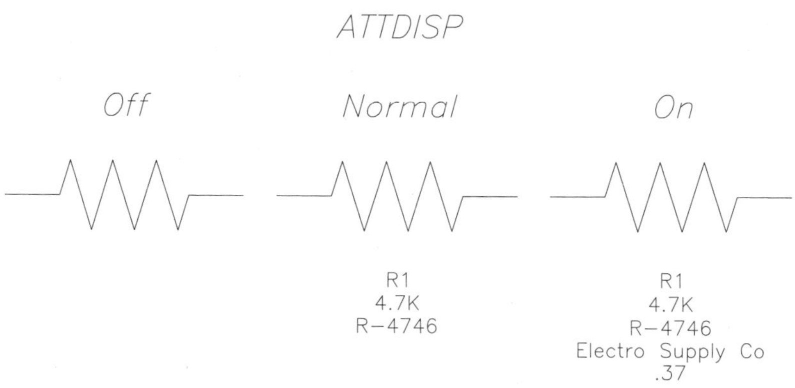

Figure 22-8 illustrates the RES block example with each of the three *Attdisp* options. The last two attributes were defined with *Invisible* modes, but are displayed with the *On* state of *Attdisp*. (Since *Attdisp* affects attributes globally, it is not possible to display the three options at one time in a drawing.)

When attributes are defined using the *Invisible* mode of the *Attdef* command, the attribute values are normally not displayed with the block after *Insertion*. However, the *Attdisp On* option allows you to override the *Invisible* mode. Turning all attributes *Off* with *Attdisp* can be useful for many applications when it is desirable to display or plot only the drawing geometry. The *Attdisp* command changes the *ATTMODE* system variable.

DDATTE

PULL-DOWN MENU	SCREEN MENU	TYPE IN	TABLET MENU
Modify *Attribute* *Edit...*	*MODIFY* *AttEd:*	*DDATTE*	---

The *Ddatte* (Dialogue Attribute Edit) command invokes the *Edit Attributes* dialogue box (Fig. 22-9). This dialogue box allows you to edit attributes of <u>existing</u> blocks in the drawing. The configuration and operation of the box are identical to the *Enter Attributes* dialogue box (Fig. 22-7).

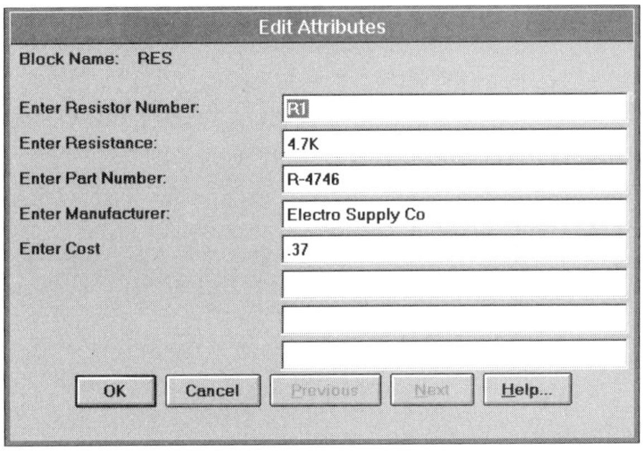

When the *Ddatte* command is entered, AutoCAD requests that you select a block. Any existing attributed block can be selected for attribute editing.

    Command: **ddatte**
    Select block: **PICK**

Figure 22-9

Edit Attributes

Block Name: RES

Enter Resistor Number: R1
Enter Resistance: 4.7K
Enter Part Number: R-4746
Enter Manufacturer: Electro Supply Co
Enter Cost: .37

OK   Cancel   Previous   Next   Help...

At this point, the dialogue box appears. After the desired changes have been made, selecting the *OK* tile updates the selected block with the indicated changes.

MULTIPLE DDATTE

Entering the *Multiple* modifier to this command causes AutoCAD to repeat the *Ddatte* command requesting multiple block selections over and over until you cancel the command with Escape. This variant of the *Ddatte* command must be typed. (See Chapter 30 for other uses of the *Multiple* modifier.)

    Command: **multiple ddatte**
    Select block: **PICK**

This form of the command can be used to query blocks in an existing drawing. For example, instead of using the *Attdisp* command to display the *Invisible* attributes, *Multiple Ddatte* can be used on selected blocks to display the *Invisible* attributes in dialogue box form. Another example is the use of *Attdisp* to turn visibility of <u>all</u> attributes *Off* in a drawing, thus simplifying the drawing appearance and speeding regenerations. The *Multiple Ddatte* command could then be used to query the blocks to display the attributes in dialogue box form.

ATTEDIT

PULL-DOWN MENU	SCREEN MENU	TYPE IN	TABLET MENU
Modify *Attribute* *Edit Globally*	---	*ATTEDIT*	7,X

Attedit (Attribute Edit) is similar to *Ddatte* in that you can edit selected existing attributes. *Attedit*, however, is more powerful in that it allows many options for editing attributes, including editing any properties of selected attributes or global editing of values for all attributes in a drawing.

> Command: **attedit**
> Edit attributes one at a time? <Y>

The following prompts depend on your response to the first prompt.

N (No)

Indicates that you want global editing. (In other words, all attributes are selected.) Attributes can then be further selected by block name, tag, or value. Only attribute <u>values</u> can be edited using this global mode.

Y (Yes)

Allows you to PICK each attribute you want to edit. You can further filter (restrict) the selected set by block name, tag, and value. You can then edit <u>any property or placement</u> of the attribute.

Next, the following prompts appear which allow you to filter, or further restrict, the set of attributes for editing. You can specify the selection set to include only specific block names, tags, or values.

> Block name specification <*>: Enter desired block name(s)
> Attribute tag specification <*>: Enter desired tag(s)
> Attribute value specification <*>: Enter desired value(s)

During this portion of the selection set specification, sets of names, tags, or values can be entered only to filter the set you choose. Commas and wildcard characters can be used (see Chapter 30 for information on using wildcards). Pressing **Enter** accepts the default option of all (*) selected.

Attribute values are <u>case-sensitive</u> (upper- and lowercase letters must be specified exactly). If you have entered null values (for example, if *ATTREQ* was set to **0** during block insertion), you can select all null values to be included in the selection set by using the backslash symbol (\).

The subsequent prompts depend on your previous choice of global or individual editing.

No (Global Editing—Editing Values Only)

> Global edit of attribute values.
> Edit only attributes visible on screen? <Y> **Enter** or (N)

An *N* response indicates all attributes in the selection set to this point can be edited. If your choice is *No*, you are reminded that the drawing will be regenerated after the command, and the next prompt is skipped. If you select *Y*, this prompt appears.

> Select Attributes: **PICK**

Beware! The attributes <u>do not highlight as you select</u> them, but highlight when you press **Enter** to complete the selection. Finally, this prompt appears.

> String to change:
> New string:

At this point, you can enter any string, and AutoCAD searches for it in the selected attributes and replaces all occurrences of the string with the new string. No change is made if the string is not found. The string can be any number of characters and can be embedded within an attribute text. Remember that only the attribute values can be edited with the global mode.

Yes (Individual Editing—Editing Any Property)

After filtering for the block name, attribute tag, and value, AutoCAD prompts:

> Select Attributes: **PICK** (The attributes <u>do not highlight</u> during selection.)
> Value/Position/Height/Angle/Style/Layer/Color/Next <N>:

A marker appears at one of the attributes. Use the *Next* option to move the marker to the attribute you wish to edit. You can then select any other option. After editing the marked attribute, the change is displayed immediately and you can position the marker at another attribute to edit.

The *Value* option invokes this prompt, allowing you to change a specific string.

> Change or Replace? <R>: *c*
> String to change:
> New string:

The *Replace* option responds to this prompt, providing for an entire new value.

> New Attribute value:

You can also change the attribute's *Position, Height, Angle, Style, Layer,* or *Color* by selecting the appropriate option. The prompts are specific and straightforward for these options. There is a surprising amount of flexibility with these options.

Global and Individual Editing Example

Assume that the RES block and a CAP block were inserted several times to create the partial schematic shown in Figure 22-10. The *Attdisp* command is set to *On* to display all the attributes, including the last two for each block, which are normally *Invisible. Attedit* is used to edit the attributes of RES and CAP.

Figure 22-10

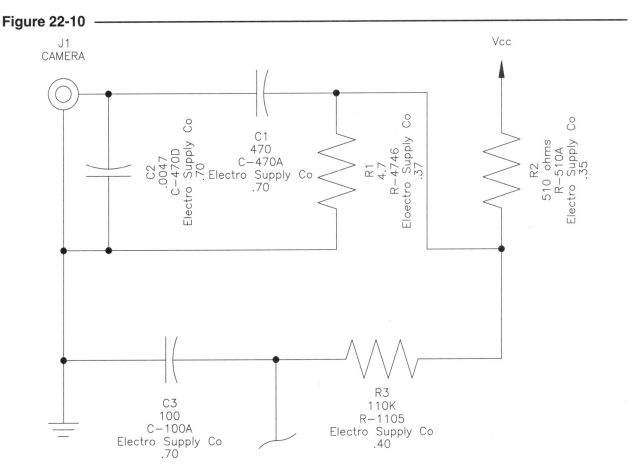

If you wish to change the <u>value</u> of one or several attributes, the global editing mode of *Attedit* would generally be used, since <u>values only</u> can be edited in global mode. For this example, assuming that the supplier changed, the MANUFACTURER attribute for all blocks in the drawing is edited. The command syntax is as follows.

> Command: **attedit**
> Edit attributes one at a time? <Y> **N**
> Global edit of attribute values.
> Edit only attributes visible on screen? <Y> **Enter**
> Block name specification <*>: **Enter**
> Attribute tag specification <*>: **MANUFACTURER**
> Attribute value specification <*>: **Enter**
> Select Attributes: **PICK** (Select specifically the MANUFACTURER attributes.)
> 6 attributes selected.
> String to change: **Electro Supply Co**
> New string: **Sparks R Us**
> Command:

Figure 22-11

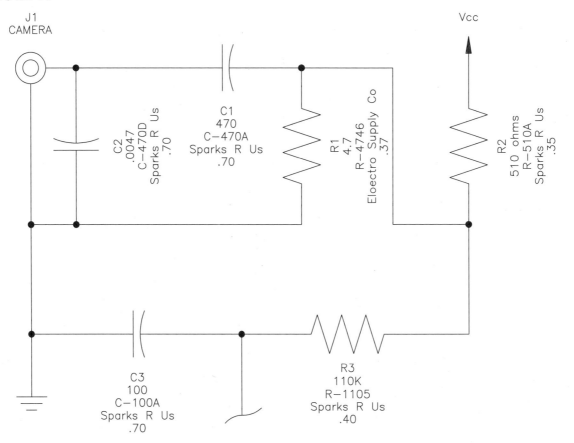

All instances of the "Electro Supply Co" redisplay with the new string. Note that resistor R1 did not change because the string did not match (due to misspelling). *Ddatte* can be used to edit the value of that attribute individually.

The individual editing mode of *Attedit* can be used to change the <u>height</u> of text for the RES_NUMBER and CAP_NUMBER attribute for both the RES and CAP blocks. The command syntax is as follows.

```
Command: attedit
Edit attributes one at a time? <Y> Enter
Block name specification <*>: Enter
Attribute tag specification <*>: Enter
Attribute value specification <*>: Enter
Select Attributes: PICK
6 attributes selected.
Value/Position/Height/Angle/Style/Layer/Color/Next <N>: H
New height <0.1250>: .2
Value/Position/Height/Angle/Style/Layer/Color/Next <N>: Enter
Value/Position/Height/Angle/Style/Layer/Color/Next <N>: H
New height <0.1250>: .2
     etc.
```

The result of the new attribute text height for CAP and RES blocks is shown in Figure 22-12. *Attdisp* has been changed to *Normal* (*Invisible* attributes do not display).

Figure 22-12

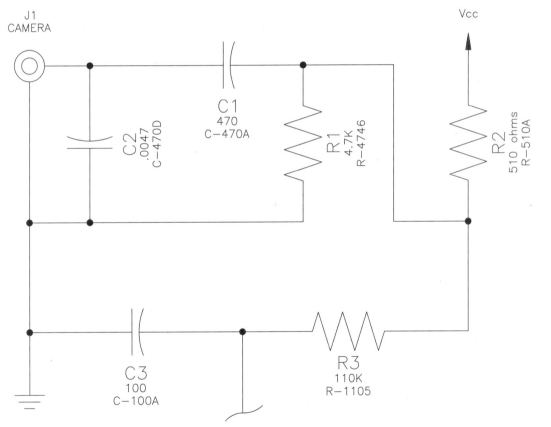

ATTREDEF

PULL-DOWN MENU	SCREEN MENU	TYPE IN	TABLET MENU
Modify Attribute Redefine	---	*ATTREDEF*	---

The *Attredef* command (Attribute redefine) enables you to redefine an attributed block. *Attredef* operates similarly to the method of redefining a block discussed previously in Chapter 21; that is, the old block definition (only with attributes in this case) is replaced with a newer one. To use the *Attredef* feature, the new objects (to be *Blocked*) with attributes defined must be in place <u>before</u> invoking the command.

Creating the new objects and attributes is easily accomplished by *Inserting* the old block, *Exploding* it, then making the desired changes to the attributes and objects. Figure 22-13 illustrates a new RES block definition (in the lower-right corner) before using *Attredef*.

Once the new geometry and attributes have been created, invoke *Attredef*. The command operates only in command line format as follows.

Figure 22-13

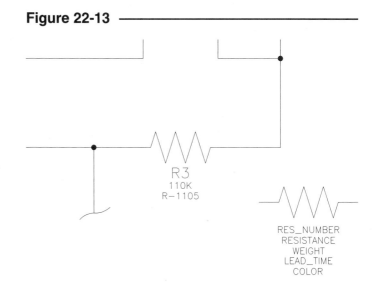

Command: **attredef**
Name of Block you wish to redefine: **RES**
Select objects for new Block...
Select objects: **PICK** attributes in order
Select objects: **PICK** attributes in order
    (etc.)
Select objects: **PICK** objects (geometry)
Select objects: **Enter**
Insertion base point of new Block: **PICK**
Verify attribute values
Verify attribute values
    (etc.)
Command:

The block definition is updated, and all instances of the block automatically and globally change to display the new changes. All attributes that were changed reflect the default values. *Ddatte* can be used later to make the desired corrections to the individual attributes.

Figure 22-14 displays one of the RES blocks after redefining. Notice that the third attribute is invisible as it was before it was *Exploded*. For this attribute, the mode was not changed. The new last attribute, however, was changed to a normal attribute mode and therefore appears after using *Attredef*.

Figure 22-14

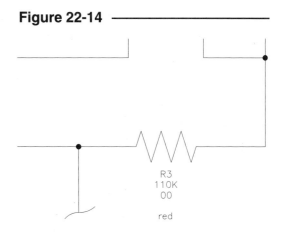

Keep in mind that if you want to specify new attributes after *Exploding* the old block, there are three alternative methods: you can use *Ddedit*, *Ddmodify*, or *Attdef*. *Ddedit*, the dialogue box for editing text, recognizes the text as attributes but allows you to change only the attribute *Tags*. Figure 22-15 illustrates using the *Ddedit* dialogue box for changing the RES_NUMBER tag.

Figure 22-15

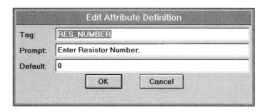

Optionally, the *Ddmodify* dialogue box can be invoked. Not only does *Ddmodify* recognize the text as attributes, but the Tag, Prompt, default Value, and attribute modes can be modified. Figure 22-16 displays this dialogue box for the same operation. Notice all of the possible changes that can be made.

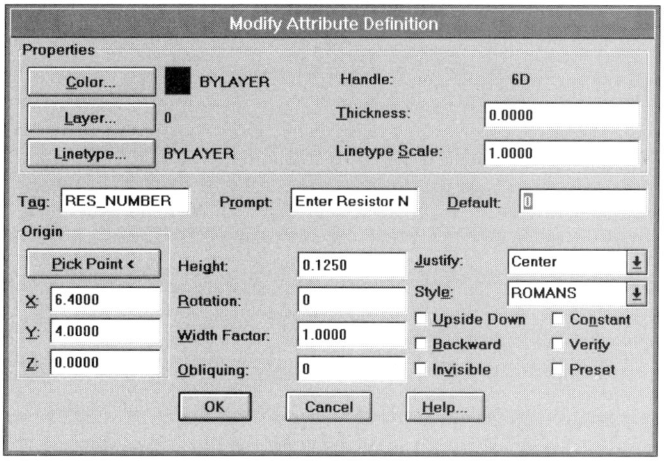

Instead of using *Ddedit* or *Ddmodify* to change <u>existing</u> attributes, new attributes can be created "from scratch" with *Attdef*. Remember that if you want to change the attributes when redefining a block, one of these three operations must take place before using *Attredef*.

Figure 22-16

EXTRACTING ATTRIBUTES

The *Attext* (attribute extract) command and related *Ddattext* (attribute extract dialogue box) allow you to extract a list of the existing blocks and text attributes from the current drawing. In other words, a list of all, or a subset, of the blocks and attributes that are in a drawing can be written to a separate file (extracted) in text form. The resulting text file can be used as a report indicating a variety of information, such as the name, number, location, layer, and scale factor of the blocks, as well as the block attributes. If desired, the extract file can then be imported to a database or spreadsheet package for further analysis or calculations.

Steps for Creating Extract Files

1. In AutoCAD, *Insert* all desired blocks and related attributes into the drawing. *Save* the drawing.

2. With a word processor or text editor, create a <u>template</u> file. The template file specifies what information should be included in the <u>extract</u> file and how the extract file should be structured. (A template file is not required if you specify a *DXF* format for the extract file.)

3. In AutoCAD, use the *Attext* or *Ddattext* command to specify the name of the template file to be used and to create the extract file.

4. Examine the extract file in the text editor or word processor or import the extract file into a database or spreadsheet package.

Creating the Template File (Step 2)

The template file is created in a text editor (such as MS-DOS Editor, Norton Editor®, or Windows Notepad®) or word processor (Microsoft Word® or WordPerfect®) in non-document mode. The template file must be in straight ASCII form (no internal word processing codes). The template file <u>must</u> be given a .TXT file extension.

Each <u>line</u> of the template file specifies a <u>column</u> of information, or field, to be written in the extract file, including the name of the column, the width of the column (number of characters or numerals), and the numerical precision. Each block that matches a line in the template file creates an column in the extract file.

The possible fields that AutoCAD allows you to specify and the format that you must use for each are shown below. Use any of the fields you want when creating the template file. The first two columns below are included in the template file (not the comments in the third column).

BL:LEVEL	Nwww000	(Block nesting level)
BL:NAME	Cwww000	(Block name)
BL:X	Nwwwddd	(X coordinate of Block insertion point)
BL:Y	Nwwwddd	(Y coordinate of Block insertion point)
BL:Z	Nwwwddd	(Z coordinate of Block insertion point)
BL:NUMBER	Nwww000	(Block counter; same for all members of MINSERT)
BL:HANDLE	Cwww000	(Block handle; same for all members of MINSERT)
BL:LAYER	Cwww000	(Block insertion layer name)
BL:ORIENT	Nwwwddd	(Block rotation angle)
BL:XSCALE	Nwwwddd	(X scale factor of Block)
BL:YSCALE	Nwwwddd	(Y scale factor of Block)
BL:ZSCALE	Nwwwddd	(Z scale factor of Block)
BL:XEXTRUDE	Nwwwddd	(X component of Block's extrusion direction)
BL:YEXTRUDE	Nwwwddd	(Y component of Block's extrusion direction)
BL:ZEXTRUDE	Nwwwddd	(Z component of Block's extrusion direction)
BL:SPACE	Cwww000	(Space between fields)
Attribute Tag	Cwww000	(Attribute tag, character)
Attribute Tag	Nwwwddd	(Attribute tag, numeric)

All items in the first column (in Courier font) must be spelled exactly as shown, if used. Use spaces rather than tabs or indents to separate the second column entries. In the second column, the first letter must be **N** or **C**, representing a numerical or character field. The three w's indicate digits that specify the field width (number of characters or numbers). The last three digits (**0** or **d**) specify the number of decimal places you desire for the field (**0** indicates that no decimals can be specified for that field).

The template file can specify any or all of the possible fields in any order, but should be listed in the order you wish the extract file to display. Each template file must include at least one attribute field. If a block contains any of the specified attributes, it is listed in the extract file; otherwise it is skipped. If a block contains some, but not all, of the specified attributes, the blank fields are filled with spaces or zeros.

A sample template file for the schematic drawing example in Figure 22-12 is shown here.

BL:NAME	C004000
BL:X	N005002
BL:Y	N005002
BL:SPACE	C002000
RES_NUMBER	C004000
RESISTANCE	C009000
CAP_NUMBER	C004000
CAPACITANCE	C006000
PART_NO	C007000
MANUFACTURER	C012000
COST	N005002

Creating the Extract File (Step 3)

ATTEXT

DOS PULL-DOWN	WIN PULL-DOWN	SCREEN MENU	TYPE IN	TABLET MENU
File *Export* *Attributes...*	*File* *Export...* **.DXX (DXF* *format only)*	---	*ATTEXT or* *DDATTEXT*	---

Once you have created a template file, you can use the *Attext* command (for command line format) or invoke the *Attribute Extraction* dialogue box by the (DOS) pull-down menu or *Ddattext* command. The command line format syntax is as follows.

> Command: **attext**
> CDF, SDF, or DXF Attribute extract (or Objects)? <C>: **Enter** or (**option**)

Instead of using the *Attext* command, you may prefer to use the *Ddattext* command, which invokes the *Attribute Extraction* dialogue box (Fig. 22-17). This dialogue box serves the same functions as the *Attext* command.

You can use the *Select Objects* option (or the *Objects* option in command line format) if you want to PICK only certain block attributes to be included in the extract file.

The *File Format* specifies the structure of the extract file. You can specify either a *SDF*, *CDF*, or *DXF* format for the extract file.

Figure 22-17 ———————

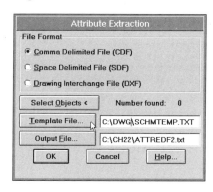

SDF
SDF (Space Delimited Format) uses spaces to separate the fields. The *SDF* format is more readable because it appears in columnar format. Numerical fields are right-justified, whereas character fields are left-justified. Therefore, it may be necessary to include a space field (BL:SPACE or BL:DUMMY) after a numeric field that would otherwise be followed immediately by a character field. This method is used in the example template file shown previously.

CDF
CDF (Comma Delimited Format) uses a character that you specify to separate the fields of the extract file. The default character for *CDF* is a comma (,). Some database packages require a *CDF* format for files to be imported.

DXF
The *DXF* format is a variation of the standard AutoCAD *DXF* (Data Interchange File format); however, it contains only block and attribute information. This format contains more information than the *SDF* and *CDF* files and is generally harder to interpret. *DXF* is a standard format and therefore does <u>not</u> request a template file. (In AutoCAD for Windows, selecting *Export* from the *File* pull-down menu allows you to create a *DXF* format extract file only. The *Attext* or *Ddattext* commands must be typed if you want an *SDF* or *CDF* format extract file.)

After specifying the desired format, you must specify the *Template File* (name of previously created template file) and *Output File* (name of the extract file to create). The default extract file name is the same as the drawing name but with the .TXT extension.

PICKing the *Template File* tile invokes the *Template File* dialogue box (Fig. 22-18). PICKing the *Output File* tile invokes the *Output File* dialogue box (Fig. 22-19). If you use the command line format (*Attext*), the dialogue boxes automatically appear (when *FILEDIA*=1).

The *Template File* dialogue box requests the name of the file you wish to use as a template. This file must have been previously created. The template file must have a .TXT file extension.

Enter the desired name for the extract file in the edit box of the *Extract File* dialogue box. AutoCAD uses the <u>drawing</u> name as the default extract file name and appends the .TXT file extension.

If the *FILEDIA* variable is set to 0 (file dialogue boxes turned off), the dialogue boxes do not appear, and requests for template and extract file names appear in command line format as follows.

Figure 22-18 ────────────────

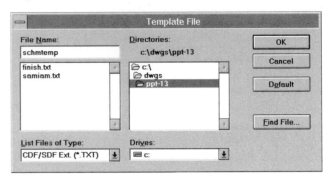

Figure 22-19 ────────────────

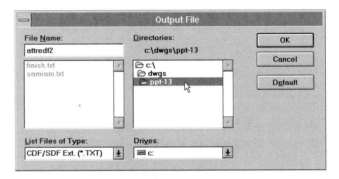

> Template file <default>: Enter name of template file with .TXT extension.
> Extract filename <drawing name>: Enter desired name of extract file.

Finally, AutoCAD then creates the extract file based on the specified parameters, displaying a message similar to the following.

> 6 records in extract file.
> Command:

If you receive an error message, check the format of your template file. An error can occur if, for example, you have a BL:NAME field with a width of 10 characters, but a block in the drawing has a name 12 characters long.

Below is the sample extract file that is created using the electrical schematic drawing and the previous example template file.

Sample Extract File

```
RES   7.25 5.75   R1   4.7                 R-4746 Sparks R Us   0.37
RES  10.00 5.75   R2   510 ohms            R-510A Sparks R Us   0.35
CAP   6.00 7.00              C1   470      C-470A Sparks R Us   0.70
CAP   3.75 5.75              C2   .0047    C-470D Sparks R Us   0.70
CAP   4.50 2.75              C3   100      C-100A Sparks R Us   0.70
RES   8.00 2.75   R3   110K                R-1105 Sparks R Us   0.40
```

This extract file lists the block name, X and Y location of the block resistor number, resistance value, capacitor number, capacitance value, manufacturer, and cost. Compare the resulting extract file with the matching template file shown next. Remember that each <u>line</u> in the template file creates a <u>column</u> in the extract file.

Sample (Matching) Template File

```
BL:NAME          C004000
BL:X             N005002
BL:Y             N005002
BL:SPACE         C002000
RES_NUMBER       C004000
RESISTANCE       C009000
CAP_NUMBER       C004000
CAPACITANCE      C006000
PART_NO          C007000
MANUFACTURER     C012000
COST             N005002
```

The extract file below was created from the template file shown above using the *CDF* option.

```
'RES', 7.25, 5.75,'','R1','4.7K','','','R-4746','Sparks R Us', 0.37
'RES',10.00, 5.75,'','R2','510 ohms','','','R-510A','Sparks R Us', 0.35
'CAP', 6.00, 7.00,'','','','C1','470','C-470A','Sparks R Us', 0.70
'CAP', 3.75, 5.75,'','','','C2','.0047','C-470D','Sparks R Us', 0.70
'CAP', 4.50, 2.75,'','','','C3','100','C-100A','Sparks R Us', 0.70
'RES', 8.00, 2.75,'','R3','110K','','','R-1105','Sparks R Us', 0.40
```

CHAPTER EXERCISES

1. **Create an Attributed Title Block**

    A. Open the **TBLOCK** drawing that you created in Chapter 20, Exercise 8. Because we need to create block attributes, *Erase* the existing text so only the lines remain. (Alternately, you can begin a *New* drawing and follow the instructions for Chapter 20, Exercise 8A. Do not complete 8B.)

    B. *SaveAs* **TBLOCKAT**. Check the drawing to ensure that two 2 text *Styles* exist using *Roman Simplex* and *Roman Complex* font files (if not, create the two *Styles*). Next, define attributes similar to those described below using *Attdef* or *Ddattdef*. Substitute your personalized *Tags*, *Prompts*, and *Values* where appropriate or as assigned (such as your name in place of B. R. Smith).

Tag	Prompt	Value	Mode
COMPANY		CADD Design Co.	const
PROJ_TITLE	Enter Project Title	PROJ-	
SCALE	Enter Scale	1"=1"	
DES_NAME		Des.-B.R.Smith	const
CHK_NAME	Enter Checker Name	Ch.-	
COMP_DATE	Enter Completion Date	1/1/96	
CHK_DATE	Enter Check Date	1/1/96	
PROJ_NO	Enter Project Number	PROJ	verif

The completed attributes should appear similar to those shown in Figure 22-20. *Save* the drawing.

C. Use the **Base** command to assign the **Insertion base point**. **PICK** the lower-right corner (shown in Figure 22-20 by the "blip") as the *Insertion base point*.

Since the entire TBLOCKAT drawing .(DWG file) will be inserted as a block, you do not have to use the *Block* command to define the attributed block. *Save* the drawing (as **TBLOCKAT**).

D. Begin a *New* drawing and use the **ASHEET** drawing as a **Prototype**. Set the **TITLE** layer *current* and draw a border with a **Pline** of **.02** *width*. Set the **ATTDIA** variable to **1** (*On*). Use the *Insert* command to bring the **TBLOCKAT** drawing in as a block. The *Enter Attributes* dialogue box should appear. Enter the attributes to complete the title block similar to that shown in Figure 22-21. Do not *Save* the drawing.

Figure 22-20 ───────────────────

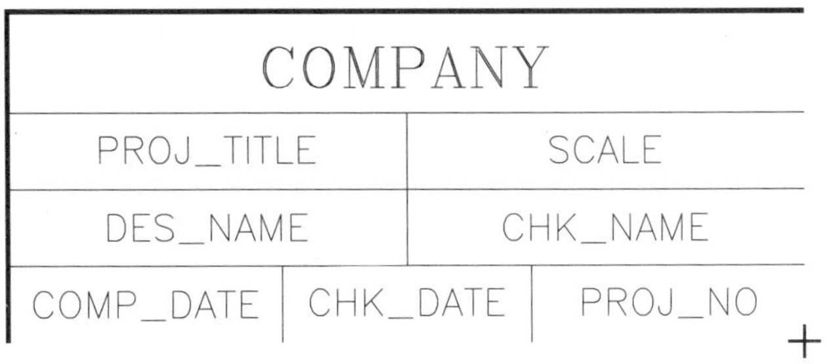

COMPANY		
PROJ_TITLE		SCALE
DES_NAME		CHK_NAME
COMP_DATE	CHK_DATE	PROJ_NO

+

Figure 22-21 ───────────────────

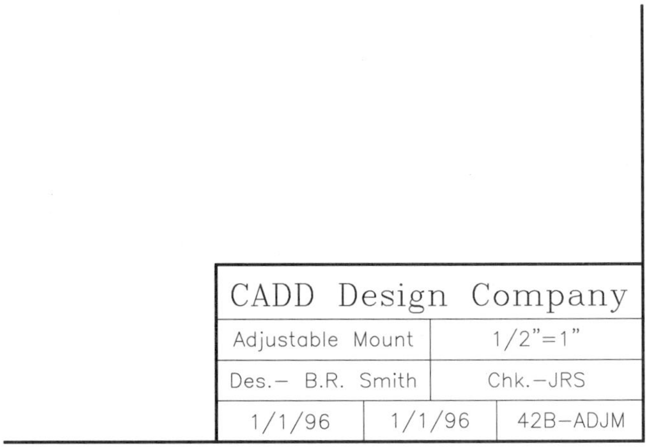

CADD Design Company		
Adjustable Mount		1/2"=1"
Des.— B.R. Smith		Chk.—JRS
1/1/96	1/1/96	42B—ADJM

2. Create Attributed Blocks for the OFF-ATT Drawing

A. *Open* the **OFF-ATT** drawing that you prepared in Chapter 21 Exercises. The drawing should have the office floorplan completed and the geometry drawn for the furniture blocks. The furniture has not yet been transformed to *Blocks*. You are ready to create attributes for the furniture, as shown in Figure 22-22.

Include the information on the next page for the proposed blocks. Use the same *Tag*, *Prompt*, and *Mode* for each proposed block. The *Values* are different, depending on the furniture item.

Figure 22-22 ───────────────────

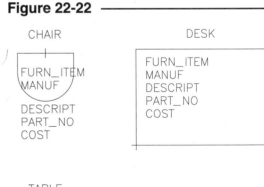

CHAIR

FURN_ITEM
MANUF
DESCRIPT
PART_NO
COST

DESK

FURN_ITEM
MANUF
DESCRIPT
PART_NO
COST

TABLE
FURN_ITEM
MANUF
DESCRIPT
+
PART_NO
COST

FILECAB

FURN_ITEM
MANUF
DESCRIPT
PART_NO
COST

Tag	Prompt	Mode
FURN_ITEM	Enter furniture item	
MANUF	Enter manufacturer	
DESCRIPT	Enter model or size	
PART_NO	Enter part number	Invisible
COST	Enter dealer cost	Invisible

Values

CHAIR	DESK	TABLE	FILE CABINET
WELLTON	KERSEY	KERSEY	STEELMAN
SWIVEL	50" x 30"	ROUND 2'	28 x 3
C-143	KER-29	KER-13	3-28-L
79.99	249.95	42.50	129.99

B. Next, use the **Block** command to make each attributed block. Use the block *names* shown (Figure 22-22). Select the attributes <u>in the order</u> you want them to appear upon insertion; then select the geometry. Use the **Insertion base points** as shown. *Save* the drawing.

C. Set the **ATTDIA** variable to **0** (*Off*). **Insert** the blocks into the office and accept the default values. Create an arrangement similar to that shown in Figure 22-23.

Figure 22-23 ——————————————————

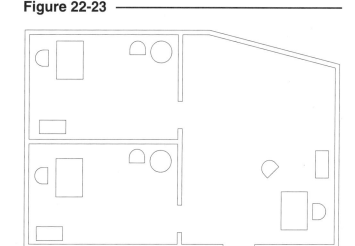

D. Use the **ATTDISP** variable and change the setting to *Off*. Do the attributes disappear?

E. A price change has been reported for all KERSEY furniture items. Your buyer has negotiated an additional 10% off the current dealer cost. Type in the **Multiple Ddatte** command and select each block one at a time to view the attributes. Make the COST changes as necessary. Use *Saveas* and assign the new name **OFF-ATT2**.

F. Change the **ATTDISP** setting back to **Normal**. It would be helpful to increase the **Height** of the FURN_ITEM attribute (CHAIR, TABLE, etc.). Use the **Attedit** command and answer *Yes* to "Edit attributes one at a time?" Enter **FURN_ITEM** in response to "Attribute tag specification" and accept the default for the other two prompts. Select all the FURN_ITEM attributes (no highlighting occurs at this time). Increase the **Height** to **3"** for each. If everything looks correct, *Save* the drawing.

3. **Extract Attributes**

A. A cost analysis of the office design is required to check against the $3,400.00 budget allocated for furnishings. This can be accomplished by extracting the attributes into a report. Use a text editor or word processor (in ASCII or non-document mode) to generate the template file below. (Ensure that you have no extra spaces or lines.) Name the file **OFF-TMPL.TXT**.

```
BL:NAME        C008000
BL:X           N008002
BL:Y           N008002
BL:SPACE       C002000
FUR_ITEM       C014000
MANUF          C012000
COST           N006002
```

B. Use the *Ddattext* command. Select *SDF* format. Specify **OFF-EXT.TXT** for the extract file name. The resulting extract file should appear similar to that below.

```
DESK      165.00   348.00   DESK            KERSEY     224.95
DESK      165.00   228.00   DESK            KERSEY     224.95
DESK      405.00   174.00   DESK            KERSEY     224.95
CHAIR     156.00   327.00   CHAIR           WELLTON     79.99
CHAIR     153.00   204.00   CHAIR           WELLTON     79.99
CHAIR     249.00   336.00   CHAIR           WELLTON     79.99
CHAIR     249.00   216.00   CHAIR           WELLTON     79.99
CHAIR     447.00   153.00   CHAIR           WELLTON     79.99
CHAIR     387.00   189.00   CHAIR           WELLTON     79.99
TABLE     276.00   204.00   TABLE           KERSEY      38.25
TABLE     276.00   327.00   TABLE           KERSEY      38.25
FILECAB   450.00   225.00   FILE CABINET    STEELMAN   129.99
FILECAB   135.00   132.00   FILE CABINET    STEELMAN   129.99
FILECAB   135.00   249.00   FILE CABINET    STEELMAN   129.99
```

C. Total the COST column to acquire the total furnishings cost so far for the job. If you purchase the $880 conference table and 8 more chairs, how much money will be left in the budget to purchase plants and wall decorations?

4. Use *Attredef* to redefine the CHAIR block in the OFF-ATT drawing. Make a *Copy* of one chair and *Explode* it. Change the geometry in some way (add arms to the chair, for example). Use *Ddedit* or *Ddmodify* to change the **COST** attribute. Increase the default cost value by 15%. Then use *Attredef* to define the new block and to redefine all the existing CHAIR blocks. Use *SaveAs* and assign the name **OFF-ATT3**. Finally, create a new extract file and calculate the total cost for the office (the original template file can be used again).

5. Create the electrical schematic illustrated in Figure 22-24. Use *Blocks* for the symbols. The text associated with the symbols should be created as attributes. Use the following block names and tags.

Block Names:　　RES
　　　　　　　　CAP
　　　　　　　　GRD
　　　　　　　　AMP

Attribute Tags:　PART_NUM
　　　　　　　　MANUF_NUM
　　　　　　　　RESISTANCE
　　　　　　　　CAPACITANCE

(Only the RES and CAP blocks have values for resistance or capacitance.) When you are finished with the drawing, create an extract file reporting information for all attribute tags (X and Y coordinate data is not needed). Save the drawing as **SCHEM2**.

Figure 22-24

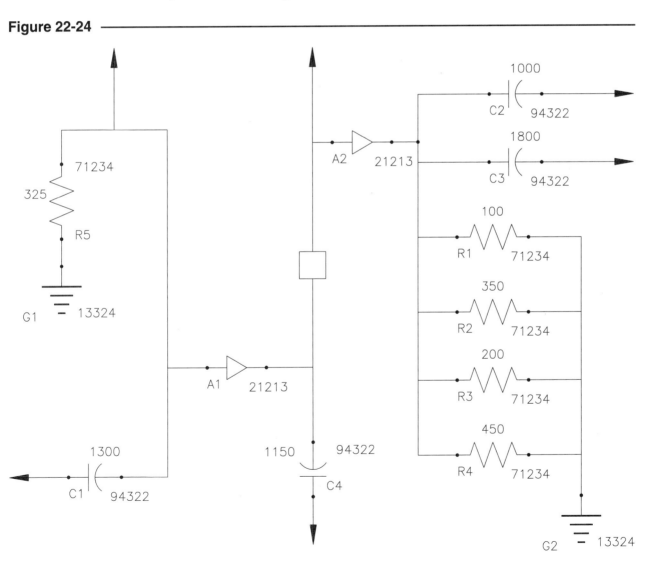

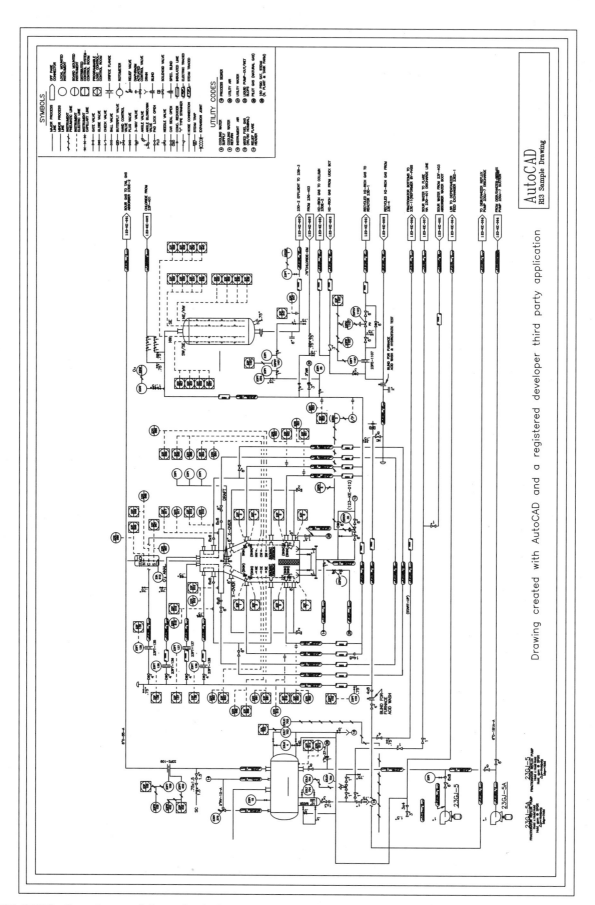

PNID.DWG Courtesy of Autodesk, Inc.

Chapter 23

GRIP EDITING

Chapter Objectives

After completing this chapter you should:

1. be able to use the *GRIPS* variable to enable or disable object grips;

2. be able to activate the grips on any object;

3. be able to make an object's grips warm, hot, or cold;

4. be able to use each of the grip editing options, namely, STRETCH, MOVE, ROTATE, SCALE, and MIRROR;

5. be able to use the Copy and Base suboptions;

6. be able to use the auxiliary grid that is automatically created when the Copy suboption is used;

7. be able to change grip variable settings using the *Grips* dialogue box or the command line format.

BASICS

Grips provide an alternative method of editing AutoCAD objects. The object grips are available for use by setting the *GRIPS* variable to **1**. Object grips are small squares appearing on selected objects at end-points, midpoints, or centers, etc. The object grips are activated (made visible) by **PICK**ing objects with the cursor pickbox only <u>when no commands are in use</u> (at the open Command: prompt). Grips are like small, magnetic *OSNAPs* (*ENDpoint, MIDpoint, CENter, QUAdrant*, etc.) that can be used for snapping one object to another, for example. If the cursor is moved within the small square, it is automatically "snapped" to the grip. Grips can replace the use of *OSNAP* for many applications. The grip option allows you to STRETCH, MOVE, ROTATE, SCALE, MIRROR, or COPY objects without invoking the normal editing commands or *OSNAPs*.

As an example, the endpoint of a *Line* could be "snapped" to the endpoint of an *Arc* (shown in Figure 23-1) by the following steps:

Figure 23-1 ─────────────────

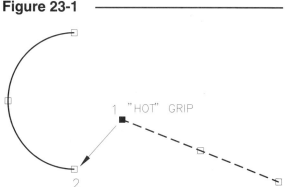

1. Activate the grips by selecting both objects. Selection is done when no commands are in use (during the open Command: prompt).
2. Select the grip at the endpoint of the *Line* (1). The grip turns **hot** (red).
3. The ** STRETCH ** option appears in place of the Command: prompt.
4. STRETCH the *Line* to the endpoint grip on the *Arc* (2). **PICK** when the cursor "snaps" to the grip.
5. The *Line* and the *Arc* should then have connecting endpoints. The Command: prompt reappears. Press Escape twice to cancel (deactivate) the grips.

GRIPS FEATURES

GRIPS

PULL-DOWN MENU	SCREEN MENU	TYPE IN	TABLET MENU
Options *Grips...*	*OPTIONS* *DDgrips:*	*GRIPS or* *DDGRIPS*	---

Grips are enabled or disabled by changing the setting of the system variable, *GRIPS*. A setting of 1 enables or turns *ON* GRIPS and a setting of **0** disables or turns *OFF GRIPS*. This variable can be typed at the Command: prompt, or the *Grips* dialogue box can be invoked from the *Options* pull-down menu, or by typing *Ddgrips* (Fig. 23-2). Using the dialogue box, toggle *Enable Grips* to turn *GRIPS ON*. The default setting in AutoCAD Release 13 for the *GRIPS* variable is **1** (*ON*). (See Grip Settings near the end of the chapter for explanations of the other options in the *Grips* dialogue box.)

Figure 23-2 ─────────────────

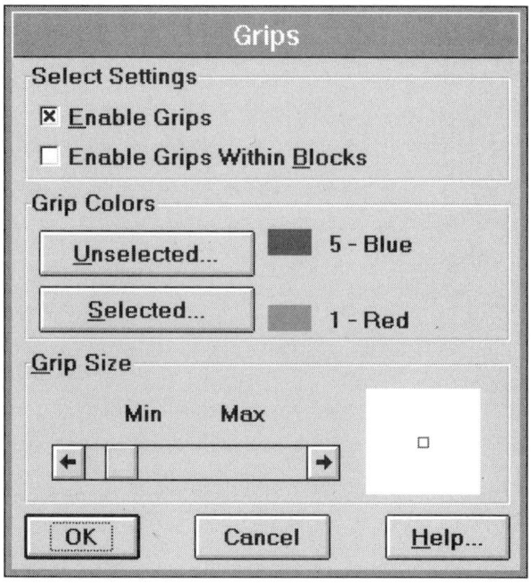

The *GRIPS* variable is saved in the ACAD.CFG file rather than in the current drawing as with most other system variables. Variables saved in the ACAD.CFG file are effective for any drawing session on that <u>particular computer</u>, no matter which drawing is current. The reasoning is that grip-related variables (and selection set-related variables) are a matter of personal preference and therefore should remain constant for a particular CAD station.

When *GRIPS* have been enabled, a small pickbox (3 pixels is the default size) appears at the center of the cursor crosshairs. (The pickbox also appears if the *PICKFIRST* system variable is set to **1**.) This pickbox operates in the same manner as the pickbox appearing during the "Select objects:" prompt. Only the pickbox, *AUto window*, or *AUto crossing window* methods can be used for selecting objects to activate the grips. (These three options are the only options available for Noun/Verb object selection as well.)

Activating Grips on Objects

Figure 23-3

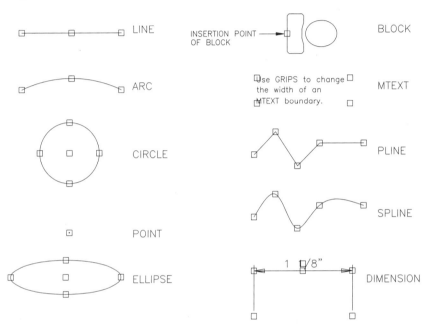

The grips on objects are activated by selecting desired objects with the crosshair pickbox, window, or crossing window. This action is done when no commands are in use (at the open Command: prompt). When an object has been selected, two things happen: the grips appear and the object is highlighted. The grips are the small blue (default color) boxes appearing at the endpoints, midpoint, center, quadrants, vertices, insertion point, or other locations depending on the object type (Fig. 23-3). Highlighting indicates that the object is included in the selection set.

Warm, Hot, and Cold Grips

Figure 23-4

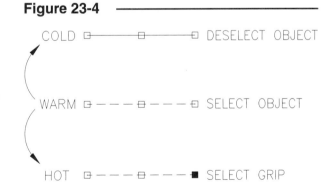

Grips can have three states: **warm, hot,** or **cold** (Fig. 23-4).

A grip is always **warm** first. When an object is selected, it is **warm**—its grips are displayed in blue (default color) and the object is highlighted. The grips can then be made **hot** or **cold**. **Cold** grips are also blue, but the object becomes <u>unhighlighted</u>.

Cold grips are created by <u>deselecting</u> a highlighted <u>object</u> that has **warm** grips. In other words, removing the **warm** grip object from the selection set with SHIFT+#1, or using the *Remove* mode, makes its grips **cold**. A **cold** grip can be used as a point to snap <u>to</u>. A **cold** grip's object is not in the selection set and therefore is not affected by the MOVE, ROTATE, or other editing action. Pressing Escape <u>once</u> changes all **warm** grips to **cold** and clears the selection set. Pressing Escape again deactivates all grips. (In short, press Escape <u>twice</u> to cancel grips entirely.)

A **hot** grip is red (by default) and its object is almost always highlighted. Any grip can be changed to **hot** by selecting the grip itself. A **hot grip is the default base point** used for the editing action such as MOVE, ROTATE, SCALE, or MIRROR, or is the stretch point for STRETCH. When a **hot** grip exists, a new series of prompts appear in place of the Command: prompt that displays the various grip editing options. A grip must be changed to **hot** before the editing options appear. A grip can be transformed from **cold** to **hot,** but the object is not highlighted (included in the selection set). Two or more grips can be made **hot** simultaneously by pressing SHIFT while selecting each grip.

If you have made a *Grip* **hot** and want to deactivate it, possibly to make another *Grip* **hot** instead, press Escape once. This returns the object to a **warm** state. In effect, this is an undo only for the **hot** Grip. Pressing Escape twice makes the *Grips* **cold,** and pressing Escape again cancels all *Grips*.

The three states of grips can be summarized as follows:

Cold	blue grips unhighlighted object	The object is not part of the selection set, but cold grips can be used to "snap" to or used as an alternate base point.
Warm	blue grips highlighted object	The object is included in selection set and is affected by the editing action.
Hot	red grips highlighted object	The base point or control point for the editing action depending on which option is used. The object is included in selection set.

Pressing Escape demotes only the highest grips one level.

Grip State	Press Escape once	Press Escape twice	Press Escape three times
only **cold**	Grips are deactivated		
warm, **cold**	**warm** demoted to **cold**	Grips are deactivated	
hot, warm, cold	**hot** demoted to **warm**	**warm** demoted to **cold**	Grips are deactivated

Grip Editing Options

When a **hot grip** has been activated, the grip editing options are available. The Command: prompt is replaced by the STRETCH, MOVE, ROTATE, SCALE, or MIRROR grip editing options. You can sequentially cycle through the options by pressing the Space bar or Enter. The editing options are displayed in the following figures.

** STRETCH **   **Figure 23-5** ⎯⎯⎯⎯⎯⎯⎯⎯⎯
<Stretch to point>/Base point/Copy/Undo/eXit:

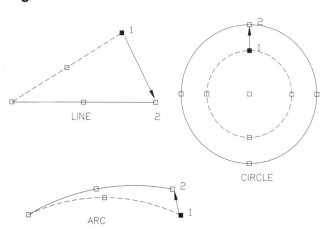

** MOVE **
<Move to point>/Base point/Copy/Undo/eXit:

Figure 23-6

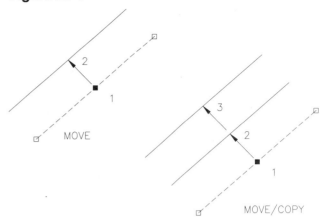

** ROTATE **
<Rotate angle>/Base point/Copy/Undo/Reference/eXit:

Figure 23-7

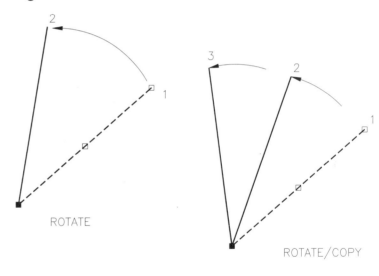

** SCALE **
<Scale factor>/Base point/Copy/Undo/Reference/eXit:

Figure 23-8

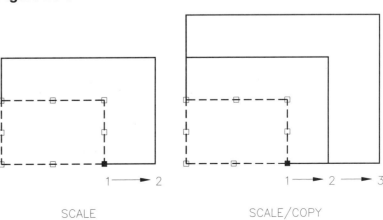

** MIRROR **
<Second point>/Base point/
Copy/Undo/eXit:

Figure 23-9

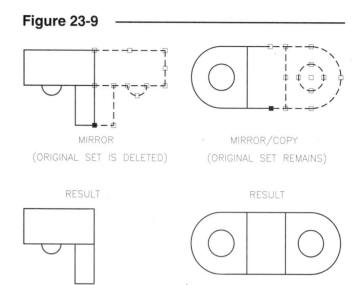

MIRROR
(ORIGINAL SET IS DELETED)

MIRROR/COPY
(ORIGINAL SET REMAINS)

RESULT

RESULT

The *Grip* options are easy to understand and use. Each option operates like the full AutoCAD command by the same name. Generally, the editing option used (except for STRETCH) affects all highlighted objects. The **hot** grip is the base point for each operation. The suboptions, Base and Copy, are explained next.

NOTE: The STRETCH option differs from other options in two ways. First, STRETCH affects <u>only</u> the object that is attached to the **hot** grip, rather than affecting all highlighted objects. Second, STRETCH is not available when a **cold** grip has been changed directly to a **hot** because its object is not in the selection set and therefore cannot be stretched.

Base
The Base suboption appears with all of the main grip editing options (STRETCH, MOVE, etc.). Base allows using any other grip as the base point instead of the **hot** grip. The letter *B* is typed to invoke this suboption.

Copy
Copy is a suboption of every main choice. Activating this suboption by typing the letter *C* invokes a Multiple copy mode, such that whatever set of objects is STRETCHed, MOVEd, ROTATEd, etc., becomes the first of an unlimited number of copies (see the previous five figures). The Multiple mode remains active until eXiting back to the Command: prompt.

Figure 23-10

SHIFT 3

SHIFT 6

2

SHIFT 5

SHIFT 4

1

X

Y

MOVE/COPY

SHIFT: X=Y

SHIFT 4

SHIFT 5

SHIFT 3

2

X

Y

SHIFT 6

SHIFT 7

SHIFT 8

SHIFT 9

MOVE/COPY

SHIFT: X=Y

Undo
The Undo option, invoked by typing the letter *U*, will undo the last Copy or the last Base point selection. Undo <u>only</u> functions after a Base or Copy operation.

Auxiliary Grid
An auxiliary grid is <u>automatically</u> established on creating the first Copy (Fig. 23-10). The grid

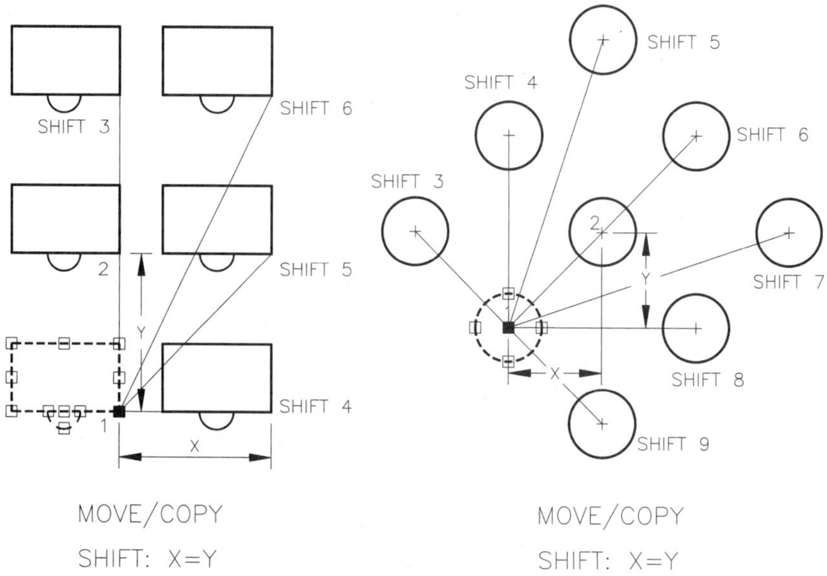

is activated by pressing SHIFT while placing the subsequent copies. The subsequent copies are then "snapped" to the grid in the same manner that *SNAP* functions. The spacing of this auxiliary grid is determined by the location of the first Copy, that is, the X and Y intervals between the base point and the second point.

For example, a "polar array" can be simulated with grips by using ROTATE with the Copy suboption (Fig. 23-11).

Figure 23-11

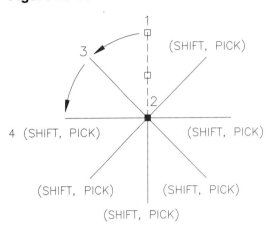

ROTATE/COPY
SHIFT – ANGLES EQUAL

The "array" can be constructed by making one Copy, then using the auxiliary grid to achieve equal angular spacing. The steps for creating a "polar array" are as follows:

1. Select the object(s) to array.

2. Select a grip on the set of objects to use as the center of the array. Cycle to the ROTATE option by pressing the Space bar or Enter. Type *C* and **Enter** to invoke the Copy suboption.

3. Make the first copy at any desired location.

4. After making the first copy, activate the auxiliary angular grid by holding down SHIFT while making the other copies.

5. Cancel the grips or select another command from the menus.

Editing Dimensions

One of the most effective applications of grips is as a dimension editor. Because grips exist at the dimension's extension line origins, arrowhead endpoints, and dimensional value, a dimension can be changed in many ways and still retain its associativity (Fig. 23-12). See Chapter 28, Dimensioning, for further information about dimensions, associativity, and editing dimensions with *Grips*.

Figure 23-12

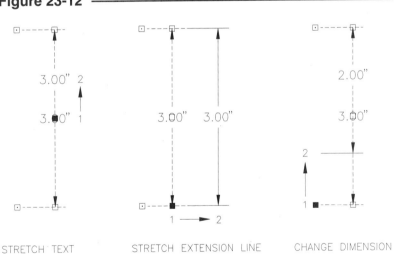

STRETCH TEXT   STRETCH EXTENSION LINE   CHANGE DIMENSION

GUIDELINES FOR USING GRIPS

Although there are many ways to use grips based on the existing objects and the desired application, a general set of guidelines for using grips is given here.

1. Create the objects to edit.

2. Select **warm** and **cold** grips first. This is usually accomplished by selecting <u>all</u> grips first (**warm** state), then <u>deselecting</u> objects to establish the desired **cold** grips.

3. Select the desired **hot** grip(s). The *Grip* options should appear in place of the Command: line.

4. Press Space or Enter to cycle to the desired editing option (STRETCH, MOVE, ROTATE, SCALE, MIRROR).

5. Select the desired suboptions, if any. If the Copy suboption is needed or the Base point needs to be re-specified, do so at this time. Base or Copy can be selected in either order.

6. Make the desired STRETCH, MOVE, ROTATE, SCALE, or MIRROR.

7. Cancel the grips by pressing Escape twice or selecting a command from a menu.

GRIPS SETTINGS

There are several settings available in the *Grips* dialogue box (Fig. 23-13) that control the way grips appear or operate. The settings can also be changed by typing in the related variable name at the command prompt.

Figure 23-13 ⸺⸺

Enable Grips
If an "X" appears in the checkbox, *Grips* are enabled for the workstation. A check sets the *GRIPS* variable to 1 (on). Removing the check disables grips and sets *GRIPS*=0 (off). The default setting is on.

Enable Grips Within Blocks
When no check appears in this box, only one grip at the block's insertion point is visible (Fig. 23-14). This allows you to work with a block as one object. The related variable is *GRIPBLOCK*, with a setting of 0=off. This is the default setting (disabled).

When the box is checked, *GRIP-BLOCK* is set to 1. All grips on all objects contained in the block are visible and functional (Fig. 23-14). This allows you to use any grip on any object within the block. This does <u>not</u> mean that the block is *Exploded*—the block retains its one-object integrity and individual entities in the block cannot be edited independently. This feature only permits you to use the grips on each of the block's components.

Figure 23-14 ⸺⸺⸺⸺⸺⸺⸺⸺⸺⸺⸺⸺⸺⸺⸺⸺

GRIPBLOCK = 0

GRIPBLOCK = 1

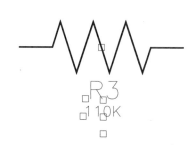

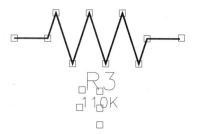

Notice in Figure 23-14 how the insertion point is not accessible when *GRIPBLOCK* is set to 1. Notice also that there are two grips on each of the normal attributes and only one on the *Invisible* attribute and that these grips do not change with the two *GRIPBLOCK* settings.

Grip Colors Unselected
This setting enables you to change the color of **warm** and **cold** grips. PICKing the *Unselected...* tile produces the *Select Color* dialogue box (identical to that used with other color settings). The default setting is blue (ACI number 5). Alternately, the *GRIPCOLOR* variable can be typed and any ACI number from 0 to 255 can be entered.

Grip Colors Selected
The color of **hot** grips can be specified with this option. The *Selected...* tile produces the *Select Color* dialogue box. You can also type *GRIPHOT* and enter any ACI number to make the change. The default color is red (1).

Grip Size
Use the slider bar to interactively increase or decrease the size of the grip "box." The *GRIPSIZE* variable could alternately be used. The default size is 3 pixel square (*GRIPSIZE=3*).

NOTE: All *Grip*-related variable settings are saved in the ACAD.CFG file rather than in the current drawing file. This generally means that changes in these variables remain with the computer, not the drawing being used.

Point Specification Precedence
When you select a point with the input device, AutoCAD uses a point specification precedence to determine which location on the drawing to find. The hierarchy is listed here.

1. Object Snap (*OSNAP*).
2. Explicit coordinate entry (absolute, relative, or polar coordinates).
3. *ORTHO.*
4. Point filters (XY filters).
5. *Grips* auxiliary grid (rectangular and circular).
6. *Grips* (on objects).
7. *SNAP* (F9 grid snap).
8. Digitizing a point location.

Practically, this means that *OSNAP* has priority over any other point selection mode. As far as *Grips* are concerned, *ORTHO* overrides *Grips*, so turn off *ORTHO* if you want to snap to *Grips*. Although *Grips* override *SNAP* (F9), it is suggested that *SNAP be turned Off* while using *Grips* to simplify PICKing.

More Grips
Because *Grips* have such a wide range of editing potential and because different AutoCAD objects react to *Grips* in different ways, discussion of grip editing is integrated into other chapters. For example, dimensions and surface models have special editing capabilities for *Grips*; therefore, those topics are covered in the related chapters.

CHAPTER EXERCISES

1. *Open* the **CH16EX8D** drawing. Use the grips on the existing *Spline* to generate a new graph displaying the temperatures for the following week. **PICK** the *Spline* to activate **warm** grips. Use the **STRETCH** option to stretch the first data point grip to the value indicated below for Sunday's temperature. **Cancel** the grips; then repeat the steps for each data point on the graph. *Save* the drawing as **CH23EX1**.

Figure 23-15 ────────────

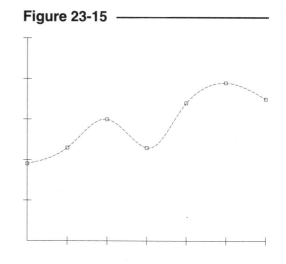

X axis	Y axis
Sunday	29
Monday	32
Tuesday	40
Wednesday	33
Thursday	44
Friday	49
Saturday	45

2. *Open* **CH16EX4** drawing. Activate **grips** on the *Line* to the far right. Make the top grip **hot**. Use the **STRETCH** option to stretch the top grip to the right to create a vertical *Line*. **Cancel** the grips.

Next, activate the **grips** for all the *Lines* (including the vertical one on the right); then make the vertical *Line* grips **cold** as shown in Figure 23-16. **STRETCH** the top of all inclined *Lines* to the top of the vertical *Line* by making the common top grips **hot**, then stretching to the cold **grip** of the vertical *Line*. *Save* the drawing as **CH23EX2**.

Figure 23-16 ────────────

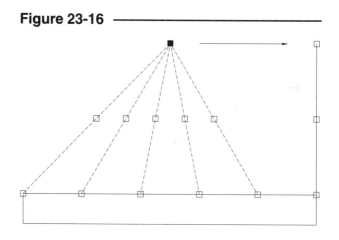

3. This exercise involves all the options of grip editing to create a Space Plate. Begin a *New* drawing or use the **ASHEET** *Prototype* and use *Saveas* to assign the name **SPACEPLT**.

   A. Set the *Snap* value to **.125**. Draw the geometry shown in Figure 23-17 using the *Line* and *Circle* commands.

Figure 23-17 ────────────

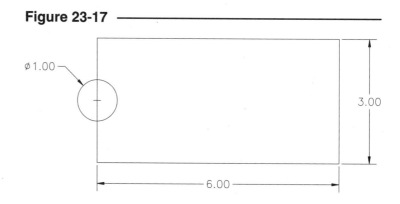

B. Activate the **grips** on the *Circle*. Make the center grip **hot**. Cycle to the **MOVE** option. Enter *C* for the **Copy** option. You should then get the prompt for **MOVE (multiple)**. Make two copies as shown in Figure 23-18. The new *Circles* should be spaced evenly, with the one at the far right in the center of the rectangle. If the spacing is off, use **grips** with the **STRETCH** option to make the correction.

Figure 23-18

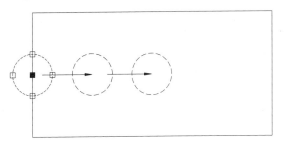

C. Activate the **grips** on the number 2 *Circle* (from the left) to make them **warm**. Also activate the **grips** on the bottom horizontal *Line*, but make them **cold**. Make the center *Circle* grip **hot** and cycle to the **MIRROR** option. Enter *C* for the **Copy** option. (You'll see the **MIRROR (multiple)** prompt.) Then enter *B* to specify a new base point as indicated in Figure 23-19. Turn *On* *ORTHO* and specify the mirror axis as shown to create the new *Circle* (shown in Fig. 23-19 in hidden linetype).

Figure 23-19

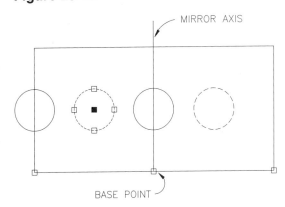

D. Use *Trim* to trim away the outer half of the *Circle* and the interior portion of the vertical *Line* on the left side of the Space Plate. Activate the **grips** on the two vertical *Lines* and the new *Arc*. Make the common grip **hot** (on the *Arc* and *Line* as shown in Fig. 23-20) and **STRETCH** it downward .5 units. (Note how you can affect multiple objects by selecting a common grip.) **Stretch** the upper end of the *Arc* upward .5 units.

Figure 23-20

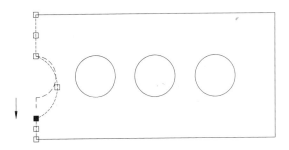

E. *Erase* the *Line* on the right side of the Space Plate. Use the same method that you used in step C to **MIRROR** the *Lines* and *Arc* to the right side of the plate (as shown in Fig. 23-21).

(REMINDER: Make sure that you make the grips on the bottom *Line* **cold**. After you select the **hot** grip, use the **Copy** option <u>and</u> the **Basepoint** option. Use *ORTHO*.)

Figure 23-21

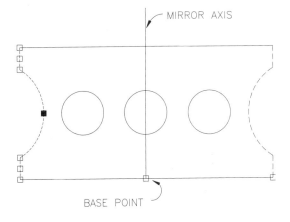

F.   In this step, you will **STRETCH** the top edge upward one unit and the bottom edge downward one unit by selecting <u>multiple</u> **hot** grips.

Select the desired horizontal <u>and</u> attached vertical *Lines*. Hold down SHIFT while selecting <u>each</u> of the endpoint grips, as shown in Figure 23-22. Although they appear **hot**, you must select one of the two again to activate the **STRETCH** option.

Figure 23-22

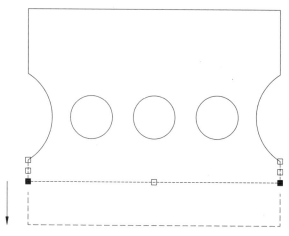

G.   In this step, two more *Circles* are created by the **ROTATE** option (see Figure 23-23). Select the three existing *Circles* to make the grips **warm**. Deselect the center *Circle* so that it will not be copied. PICK the center grip to make it **hot**. Cycle to the **ROTATE** option. Enter *C* for the **Copy** option. Make sure *ORTHO* is *On* and create the new *Circles*.

Figure 23-23

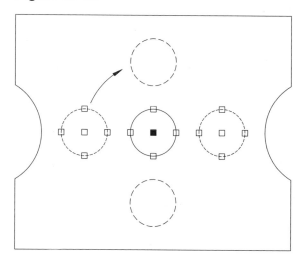

H.   Select the center *Circle* and make the center grip **hot** (Fig. 23-24). Cycle to the **SCALE** option. The scale factor is **1.5**. Since the *Circle* is a 1 unit diameter, it can be interactively scaled (watch the *COORDS* display), or you can enter the value. The drawing is complete. *Save* the drawing as **SPACEPLT**.

Figure 23-24

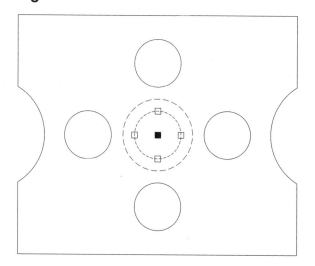

4. *Open* the **STORROM2** drawing from Chapter 19 Exercises. Use the grips to **STRETCH, MOVE,** or **ROTATE** each text paragraph to achieve the results shown in Figure 23-25. *SaveAs* **STORROM3**.

Figure 23-25

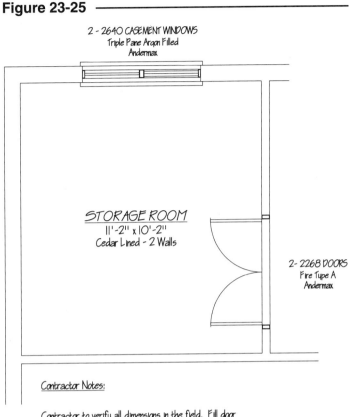

Contractor Notes:

Contractor to verify all dimensions in the field. Fill door and window roughouts after door and window placement.

5. *Open* the **TPLATE** drawing that you created in Chapter 17. An order has arrived for a modified version of the part. The new plate requires two new holes along the top, a 1″ increase in the height, and a .5″ increase from the vertical center to the hole on the left (Fig. 23-26). Use grips to **STRETCH** and **Copy** the necessary components of the existing part. Use *SaveAs* to rename the part to **TPLATEB**.

Figure 23-26

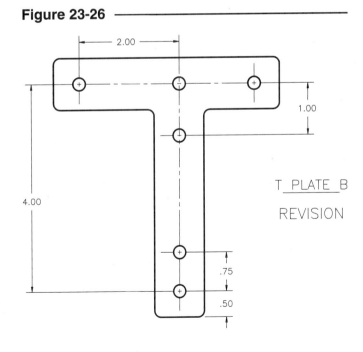

6. *Open* the **OFFICE** drawing that you worked on in Chapter 21 Exercises. Use grips to **STRETCH, MOVE, ROTATE, SCALE, MIRROR,** and **Copy** the furniture *Blocks*. Experiment with each option. Change the *GRIPBLOCK* variable to enable all the grips on the *Blocks* for some of the editing. *Save* any changes that you like.

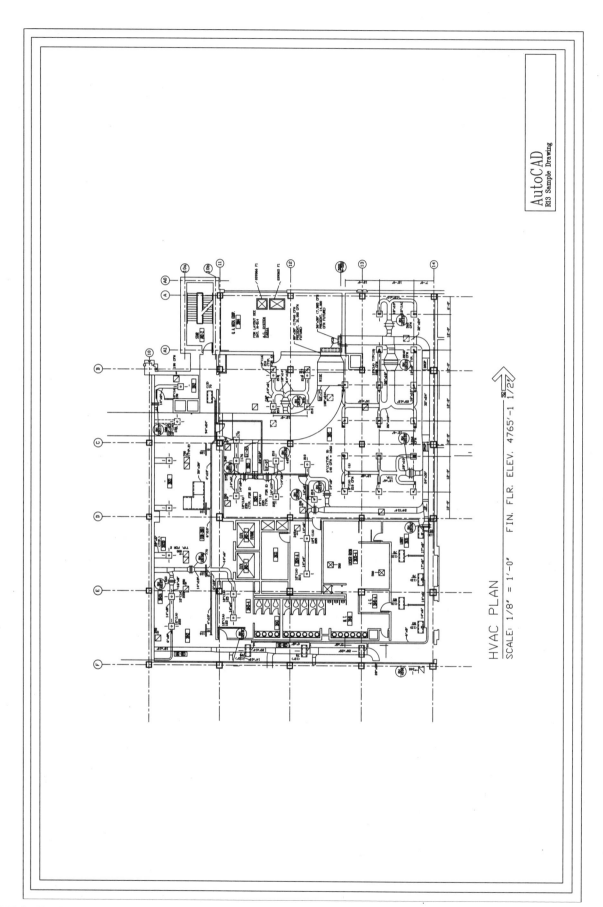

HVAC PLAN
SCALE: 1/8" = 1'-0"   FIN. FLR. ELEV. 4765'-1 1/2"

AutoCAD
R13 Sample Drawing

HVAC.DWG Courtesy of Autodesk, Inc.

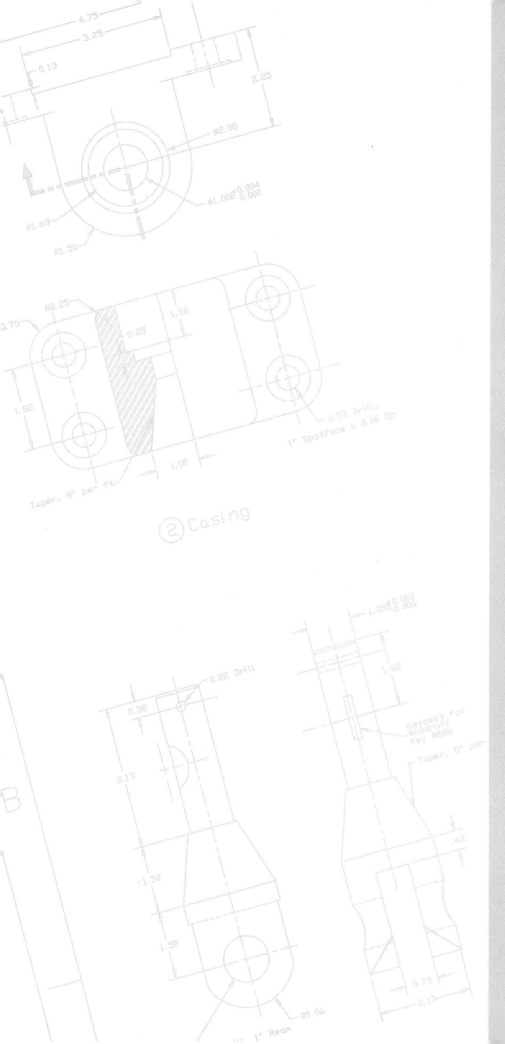

Chapter 24

MULTIVIEW DRAWING

Chapter Objectives

After completing this chapter you should:

1. know how to use the crosshairs for checking alignment of views;

2. be able to draw projection lines using *ORTHO* and *SNAP*;

3. be able to use *Xline* and *Ray* to create construction lines;

4. know how to use *Offset* for construction of views;

5. be able to use point filters for alignment of lines and views;

6. be able to use construction layers for managing construction lines and notes;

7. be able to use linetypes and layers to draw and manage ANSI standard linetypes;

8. know how to create fillets, rounds, and runouts;

9. know the typical guidelines for creating a three-view multiview drawing.

BASICS

Multiview drawings are used to represent 3D objects on 2D media. The standards and conventions related to multiview drawings have been developed over years of using and optimizing a system of representing real objects on paper. Now that our technology has developed to a point that we can create 3D models, some of the methods we use to generate multiview drawings have changed, but the standards and conventions have been retained so that we can continue to have a universally understood method of communication.

This chapter illustrates methods of creating 2D multiview drawings with AutoCAD (without a 3D model) while complying with industry standards. (Creating 2D drawings from 3D models is addressed in Chapter 41.) There are many techniques that can be used to construct multiview drawings with AutoCAD because of its versatility. The methods shown in this chapter are the more common methods because they are derived from traditional manual techniques. Other methods are possible.

PROJECTION AND ALIGNMENT OF VIEWS

Projection theory and conventions of multiview drawing dictate that the views are aligned with each other and oriented in a particular relationship. AutoCAD has particular features, such as horizontal/vertical crosshairs, *SNAP*, *ORTHO*, construction lines (*Xline, Ray*), Object Snap, and point filters, that can be used effectively for facilitating projection and alignment of views.

Using the Crosshairs to Check Alignment of Views

The crosshairs are arranged in a perpendicular fashion and can be used for a "visual" check for alignment of views and object features. For example, Figure 24-1, illustrates the use of the crosshairs to check the alignment of a hole.

In Figure 24-1, the crosshairs are located along the tangents of the circular view of the hole. Following the vertical and horizontal elements of the crosshairs reveals that the hole is located correctly in the top view but appears to be aligned <u>incorrectly</u> in the right side view.

Figure 24-1

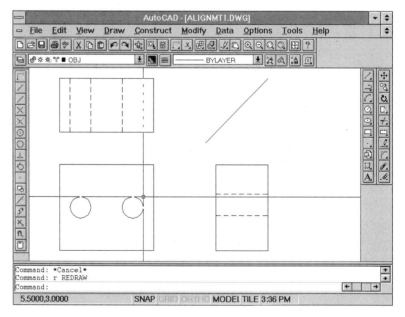

Keep in mind that only in some cases can the crosshairs be used as a "visual" check for alignment. <u>Only</u> in cases where all of the geometry elements are at *SNAP* increments and *SNAP* is *ON* are the crosshairs 100% accurate for inspecting alignment. In Figure 24-2, all dimensions of the object are at 1/8 increments. Since *SNAP* is set to a value of .125 and is *ON*, the crosshairs can be used as a valid alignment check. In this case, both views have <u>correct</u> alignment.

Figure 24-2 ─────────────

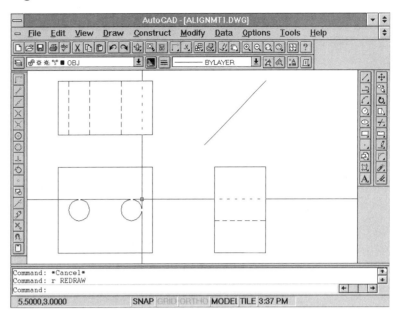

Using *ORTHO* and *OSNAP* to Draw Projection Lines

ORTHO (F8) can be used effectively in concert with *OSNAP* to draw projection lines during construction of multiview drawings. For example, drawing a *Line* interactively with *ORTHO ON* forces the *Line* to be drawn in either a horizontal or vertical direction.

Figure 24-3 simulates this feature while drawing projection *Lines* from the top view over to a 45 degree miter line (intended for transfer of dimensions to the side view). The "From point:" of the *Line* originated from the *ENDpoint* of the *Line* on the top view.

Figure 24-3 ─────────────

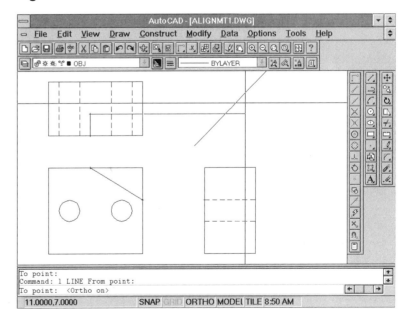

Figure 24-4 illustrates the next step. The vertical projection *Line* is drawn from the *INTersection* of the 45 degree line and the last projection line. *ORTHO* forces the *Line* to the correct vertical alignment with the side view.

Remember that any draw <u>or</u> edit command that requires PICKing is a candidate for *ORTHO* and/or *OSNAP*.

NOTE: *OSNAP* overrides *ORTHO*. If *ORTHO* is *ON* and you are using an *OSNAP* mode to PICK the "to point:" of a *Line*, the *OSNAP* mode has priority; and, therefore, the construction may not result in an orthogonal *Line*.

Figure 24-4

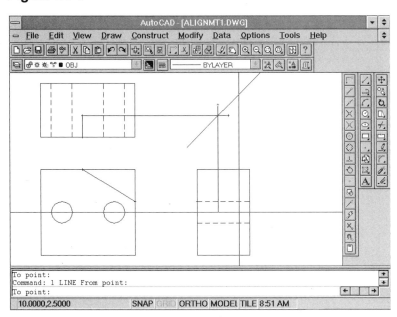

Using *Xline* and *Ray* for Construction Lines

Another strategy for constructing multiview drawings is to make use of the AutoCAD construction line commands *Xline* and *Ray*.

Xlines can be created to "box in" the views and ensure proper alignment. *Ray* is suited for creating the 45 degree miter line for projection between the top and side views. The advantage to using this method is that horizontal and vertical *Xlines* can be created quickly.

These lines can be *Trimmed* to become part of the finished view, or other lines could be drawn "on top of" the construction lines to create the final lines of the views. In either case, <u>construction lines should be drawn on a separate layer</u> so that the layer can be frozen before plotting. If you intend to *Trim* the construction lines so that they become part of the final geometry, draw them originally on the view layers.

Figure 24-5

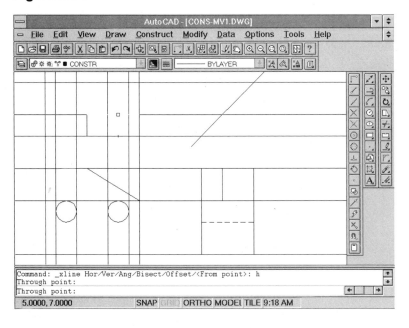

Using *Offset* for Construction of Views

An alternative to using the traditional miter line method for construction of a view by projection, the *Offset* command can be used to transfer distances from one view and to construct another. The *Distance* option of *Offset* provides this alternative.

For example, assume that the side view was completed and you need to construct a top view (Fig. 24-6). First, create a horizontal line as the inner edge of the top view (shown highlighted) by *Offset* or other method. To create the outer edge of the top view (shown in phantom linetype), use *Offset* and PICK points (1) and (2) to specify the *distance*. Select the existing line (3) as the *"Object to Offset:"*, then PICK the *"Side to offset?"* at the current crosshairs position.

Realignment of Views Using *ORTHO* and *SNAP*

Another application of *ORTHO* and *OSNAP* is the use of *Move* to change the location of an entire view.

For example, assume that the views of the multiview in Figure 24-7 are complete and ready for dimensioning; however, there is not enough room between the front and side views. You can invoke the *Move* command, select the entire view with a *window* or other option, and "slide" the entire view outward. *ORTHO* assures the proper alignment. Make sure *SNAP* is *ON* during the *Move* (if *SNAP* was used in the original construction). This action assures that the final position of the view is on a *SNAP* point and that the objects retain their orientation with respect to the *SNAP*.

An alternative to *Moving* the view interactively is use of coordinate specification (absolute, relative rectangular, or relative polar).

Using Point Filters for Alignment

If you want to draw a *Line* so that it ends or begins in alignment with another object or view, X or Y point filters can be used. For example, Figure 24-8 shows the construction of a *Line* in the top view. It is desired to end the *Line* in align-

Figure 24-6

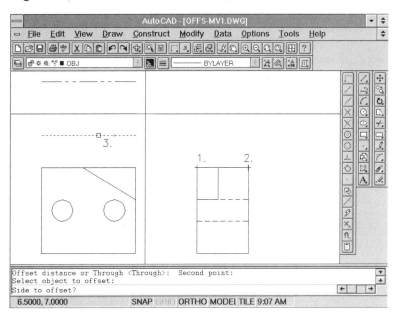

Figure 24-7

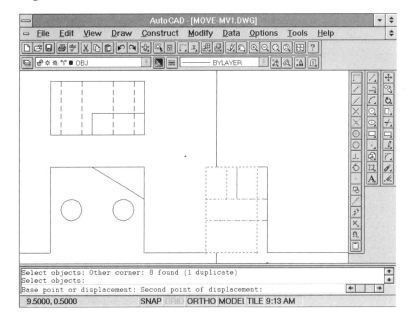

Figure 24-8

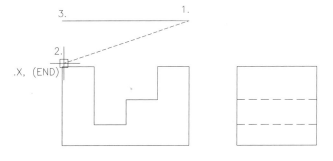

ment with the X position directly above the left side of the front view. An *.X* point filter is used to accomplish this action. *ORTHO* *is On*. The following command syntax is used for the construction.

Figure 24-9

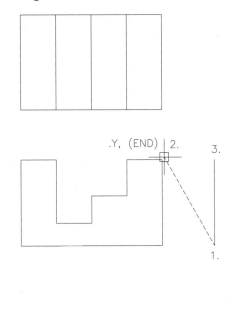

> Command: **line**
> From point: **PICK** (1.)
> To point: **.x** (Type ".X"; then press **Enter**.)
> **of ENDpoint of   PICK** (2.) (AutoCAD uses only the X value of the point selected.)
> (need YZ): **PICK** (anywhere near 3. AutoCAD uses the Y and Z points selected.)
> To point: **Enter**
> Command:

Another possibility is to use a .Y point filter for construction in alignment with the Y value (height) of existing objects (Fig. 24-9). In this case, enter a **.Y** in response to the "to point:" prompt and press Enter. The point you PICK (2) supplies only the Y value. AutoCAD responds with "(need XZ)". PICK again near (3) to supply the X value. Make sure *ORTHO* is *On*.

X and Y point filters can be used anytime AutoCAD requires point selection. For example, alignment of the side view (Fig. 24-10, highlighted) can be corrected by invoking the *Move* command, entering a Y point filter, and selecting the *ENDpoint* of the front view (2) as the second point of displacement. The X coordinate can be supplied by PICKing (3) with *ORTHO On*. The resulting position of the side view is aligned with the front.

Figure 24-10

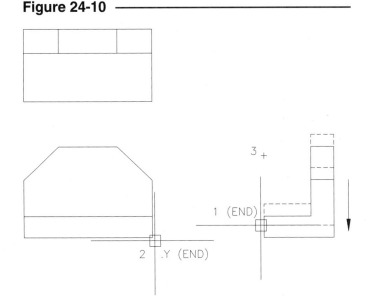

USING CONSTRUCTION LAYERS

The use of layers for isolating construction lines can make drawing and editing faster and easier. The creation of multiview drawings can involve construction lines, reference points, or notes that are not intended for the final plot. Rather than *Erasing* these construction lines, points, or notes before plotting, they can be created on a separate layer and turned *Off* or made *Frozen* before running the final plot. If design changes are required, as they often are, the construction layers can be turned *On*, rather than having to recreate the construction.

There are two strategies for creating construction objects on separate layers.

1. Use Layer 0 for construction lines, reference points, and notes. This method can be used for fast, simple drawings.

2. Create a new layer for construction lines, reference points, and notes. Use this method for more complex drawings or drawings involving use of *Blocks* on Layer 0.

For example, consider the drawing during construction in Figure 24-11. A separate layer has been created for the construction lines, notes, and reference points.

In Figure 24-12, the same drawing is shown ready for making the final plot. Notice that the construction Layer has been *Frozen*.

If you are plotting the *Limits*, and the construction layer has objects outside the *Limits*, the construction layer should be *Frozen*, rather than being turned *Off*, unless only *Xlines* and *Rays* exist on the layer.

Figure 24-11 ——————

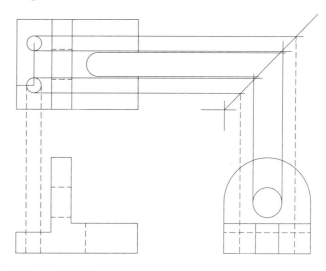

Figure 24-12 ——————

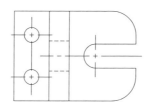

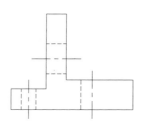

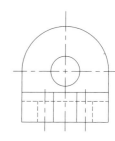

USING LINETYPES

Different types of lines are used to represent different features of a multiview drawing. Linetypes in AutoCAD are accessed by the *Linetype* command or dialogue boxes or by selection in the *Layer Control* dialogue box. *Linetypes* can be changed retroactively by the *Change Properties* or the *Modify* dialogue boxes. *Linetypes* can be assigned to individual objects specifically or to layers (*BYLAYER*). See Chapter 12 for a full discussion on this topic.

AutoCAD complies with the ANSI and ISO standards for linetypes. The principal AutoCAD linetypes used in multiview drawings and the associated names are shown in Figure 24-13.

Figure 24-13 ——————

———————————— CONTINUOUS

— — — — — — — HIDDEN

— — — — — CENTER

——— — — ——— PHANTOM

— — — — — DASHED

Many other linetypes are provided in AutoCAD. Refer to Chapter 12 for the full list and illustration of the linetypes.

Other standard lines are created by AutoCAD automatically. For example, dimension lines can be automatically drawn when using dimensioning commands (Chapter 28), and section lines can be automatically drawn when using the *Hatch* command (Chapter 26).

AutoCAD linetypes do not have a specified thickness, but can be created by either creating *Plines* and specifying *Width* or by plotting with specific width pens. (See Chapter 15 for information on *Plines* and Chapter 14 for information on plotting.)

Drawing Hidden and Center Lines

Although AutoCAD supplies ANSI standard linetypes, the application of those linetypes does not always follow ANSI standards. For example, you do <u>not</u> have control over the placement of the individual dashes of center lines and hidden lines. (You have control of only the endpoints of the lines and the *Ltscale*.) Therefore, the short dashes of center lines may not cross exactly at the circle centers, or the dashes of hidden lines may not always intersect as desired.

Figure 24-14 illustrates a typical application of AutoCAD *Hidden* and *Center* linetypes. Notice that the horizontal center line in the front view does not automatically locate the short dashes correctly, and the hidden lines in the right side view incorrectly intersect the center vertical line.

Figure 24-14 ─────────────

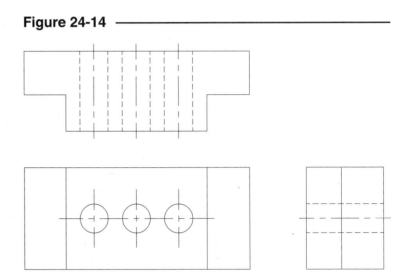

You do, however, have control of the endpoints of the lines. Draw lines with the *Center* linetype such that the endpoints are symmetric about the circle or group of circles. This action assures that the short dash occurs at the center of the circle (if an odd number of dashes are generated). Figure 24-15 illustrates correct and incorrect technique.

You can also control the relative size of noncontinuous linetypes with the *Ltscale* variable. <u>In some cases</u>, the variable can be adjusted to achieve the desired results.

Figure 24-15 ─────────────

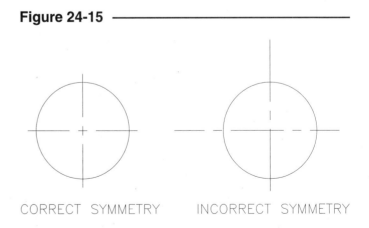

CORRECT SYMMETRY   INCORRECT SYMMETRY

For example, Figure 24-16 demonstrates the use of *Ltscale* to adjust the center line dashes to the correct spacing. Remember that *Ltscale* adjusts linetypes globally (all linetypes across the drawing).

When the *Ltscale* has been optimally adjusted for the drawing globally, use the *Ddmodify* dialogue box to adjust the linetype scale of individual objects. In this way, the drawing lines can originally be created to the global linetype scale without regard to the *Celtscale*. The finished drawing linetype scale can be adjusted with *Ltscale* globally; then only those objects that need further adjusting can be fine-tuned retroactively with *Ddmodify*.

Figure 24-16

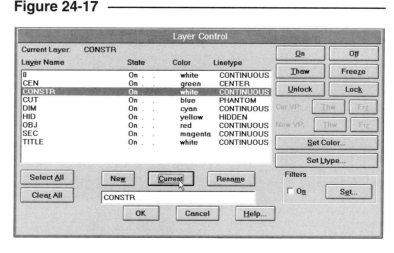

INCORRECT LTSCALE SETTING

CORRECT LTSCALE SETTING

The *Center* command (a dimensioning command) can be used to draw center lines automatically with correct symmetry and spacing (see Chapter 28).

Managing Linetypes and Colors

There are two strategies for assigning linetypes and colors: *BYLAYER* and object-specific assignment. In either case, thoughtful layer utilization for linetypes will make your drawings more flexible and efficient.

BYLAYER Linetypes and Colors

The *BYLAYER* linetype and color settings are recommended when you want the most control over linetype visibility and plotting. This is accomplished by creating layers with the *Layer Control* dialogue box and using *Set Color* and *Set Ltype* for each layer. After you assign *Linetypes* to specific layers, you simply set the layer (with the desired linetype) as the *Current* layer and draw on that layer in order to draw objects in a specific linetype.

A prototype drawing for creating typical multiview drawings could be set up with the layer and linetype assignments similar to that shown in Figure 24-17. Notice the layer names, associated colors, and assigned *Ltypes*.

Using this strategy (*BYLAYER Linetype* and *Color* assignment) gives you flexibility. You can control the linetype visibility by controlling the layer visibility. You can control the associated plotting pen for each linetype (in the *Plot Control* dialogue box) if each linetype is assigned a specific color. You can also retroactively change the linetype and color of an existing object by changing the object's *Layer* property with the *Change Properties* or the *Modify* dialogue box. Objects changed to a different layer assume the *color* and *linetype* of the new layer.

Figure 24-17

Current Layer:	CONSTR		
Layer Name	State	Color	Linetype
0	On . .	white	CONTINUOUS
CEN	On . .	green	CENTER
CONSTR	On . .	white	CONTINUOUS
CUT	On . .	blue	PHANTOM
DIM	On . .	cyan	CONTINUOUS
HID	On . .	yellow	HIDDEN
OBJ	On . .	red	CONTINUOUS
SEC	On . .	magenta	CONTINUOUS
TITLE	On . .	white	CONTINUOUS

Another strategy for multiview drawings involving several parts, such as an assembly, is to create layers for each linetype <u>specific to each part</u>, as shown in Figure 24-18. With this strategy, each part has the complete set of linetypes, but only one color per part in order to distinguish the part from others in the display.

Figure 24-18 ──────────

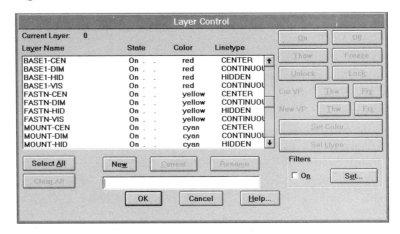

Related layer <u>groups</u> can be selected within the dialogue box using the *Filters* dialogue box. If the *Layer* command is used instead, wildcards can be typed for layer selection. For example, entering "?????-HID" selects all of the layers with hidden lines, or entering "MOUNT*" would select all of the layers associated with the "MOUNT" part.

Object *Linetypes and Colors*
Although this method can be complex, object-specific linetype and color assignment can also be managed easier by skillful utilization of layers. One method is to create one layer for each part or each group of related geometry (Fig. 24-19). The *BYLAYER* color and linetype settings should be left to the defaults. Then object-specific linetype settings can be assigned using the *Linetype* command or *Ddltype* dialogue box, and color settings can be assigned using the *Color* command or *Ddcolor* dialogue box.

Figure 24-19 ──────────

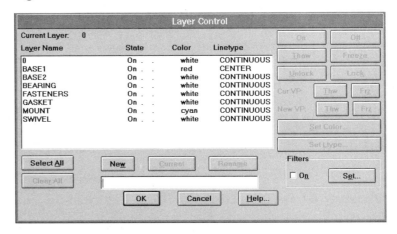

(Colors provide the means for controlling plotted line weights). For assemblies, all lines related to one part would be drawn on one layer. Remember that you can draw everything with one linetype and color setting, then use *Ddchprop* to retroactively set the desired color and linetype for each set of objects. Visibility of parts can be controlled by *Freezing* or *Thawing* part layers. You cannot isolate and control visibility of linetypes or colors by this method.

CREATING FILLETS, ROUNDS, AND RUNOUTS

Many mechanical metal or plastic parts manufactured from a molding process have slightly rounded corners. The otherwise sharp corners are rounded because of limitations in the molding process or for safety. A convex corner is called a <u>round</u> and a concave corner is called a <u>fillet</u>. These fillets and rounds are created easily in AutoCAD by using the *Fillet* command.

The example in Figure 24-20 shows a multiview drawing of a part with sharp corners before the fillets and rounds are drawn.

Figure 24-20

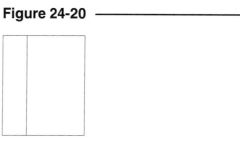

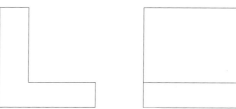

The corners are rounded using the *Fillet* command. First, use *Fillet* to specify the *Radius*. Once the *Radius* is specified, just select the desired lines to *Fillet* near the end to round.

If the *Fillet* is in the middle portion of a *Line* instead of the end, *Extend* can be used to reconnect the part of the *Line* automatically trimmed by *Fillet*, or *Fillet* can be used in the *Notrim* mode.

The finish marks ("V" shaped symbols) indicate machined surfaces. Finished surfaces have sharp corners.

Figure 24-21

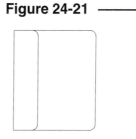

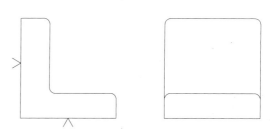

When two filleted edges intersect at less than a 90 degree angle, a <u>runout</u> should be drawn as shown in the top view of the multiview drawing. A runout is a visual representation of the complex fillet that would actually exist on the part.

Figure 24-22

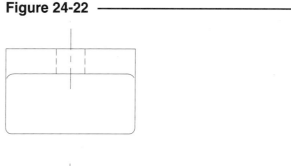

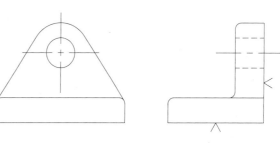

A close-up of the runouts is shown in Figure 24-23. There is no AutoCAD command provided for this specific function. The *3point* option of the *Arc* command can be used to create the runouts, although other options can be used. Alternately, the *Circle TTR* option can be used with *Trim* to achieve the desired effect. As a general rule, use the same radius or slightly larger than that given for the fillets and rounds, but draw it less than 90 degrees.

Figure 24-23

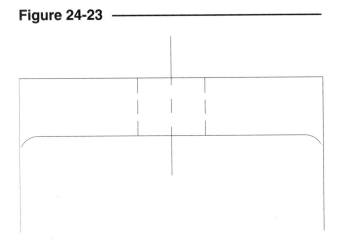

GUIDELINES FOR CREATING A TYPICAL THREE-VIEW DRAWING

Following are some guidelines for creating the three-view drawing in Figure 24-24. This object is used only as an example. The steps or particular construction procedure may vary, depending on the specific object drawn. Dimensions are shown in the figure so you can create the multiview drawing as an exercise.

Figure 24-24

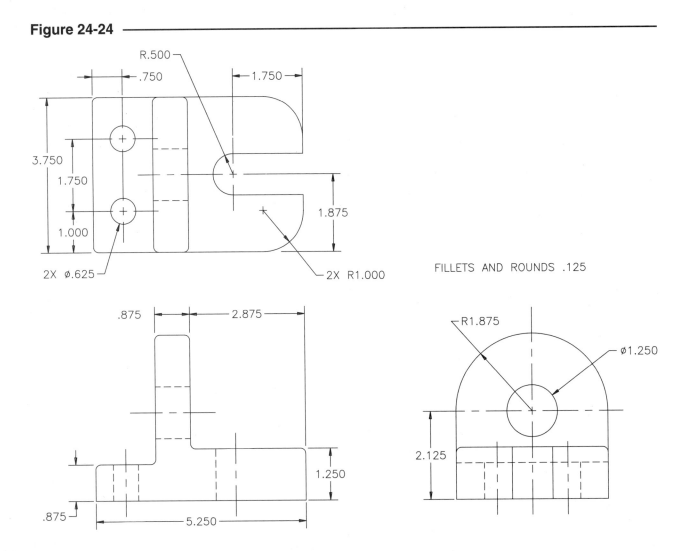

1. Drawing Setup

    Units are set to *Decimal* with 3 places of *Precision*. *Limits* of 22 x 17 are set to allow enough drawing space for both views. The finished drawing can be plotted on a "B" size sheet at a scale of 1"=1" or on an "A" size sheet at a scale of 1/2"=1". *Snap* is set to an increment of .125. *Grid* is set to an increment of .5. *Ltscale* is not changed from the default of 1. Layers are created (OBJ, HID, CEN, DIM, BORDER, and CONSTR) with appropriate *Ltypes* and *Colors* assigned.

2. An outline of each view is "blocked in" by drawing the appropriate *Lines* and *Circles* on the OBJ layer similar to that shown in Figure 24-25. Ensure that *SNAP* is *ON*. *ORTHO* should be turned *ON* when appropriate. Use the crosshairs to ensure that the views align horizontally and vertically. Note that the top edge of the front view was determined by projecting from the *Circle* in the right side view.

Figure 24-25

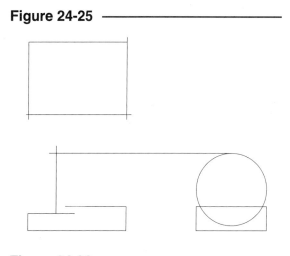

Another method for construction of a multiview drawing is shown in Figure 24-26. This method uses the *Xline* and *Ray* commands to create construction and projection lines. Here all the views are blocked in and some of the object lines have been formed. The construction lines should be kept on a separate layer, except in the case where *Xlines* and *Rays* can be trimmed and converted to the object lines. (The following illustrations do not display this method because of the difficulty in seeing which are object and construction lines.)

Figure 24-26

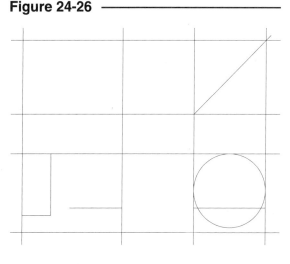

3. This drawing requires some projection between the top and side views (Fig. 24-27). The CONSTR layer is set as *Current*. Two *Lines* are drawn from the inside edges of the two views (using *OSNAP* and *ORTHO* for alignment). A 45 degree miter line is constructed for the projection lines to "make the turn." A *Ray* is suited for this purpose.

Figure 24-27

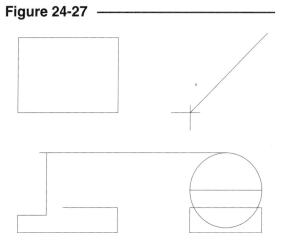

4. Details are added to the front and top views (Fig. 24-28). The projection line from the side view to the front view (previous figure) is *Trimmed*. A *Circle* representing the hole is drawn in the side view and projected up and over to the top view and to the front view. The object lines are drawn on layer OBJ and some projection lines are drawn on layer CONSTR. The horizontal projection lines from the 45 degree miter line are drawn on layer HID awaiting *Trimming*. Alternately, those two projection lines could be drawn on layer CONSTR and changed to the appropriate layer with *Change Properties* after *Trimming*.

Figure 24-28 ────────────

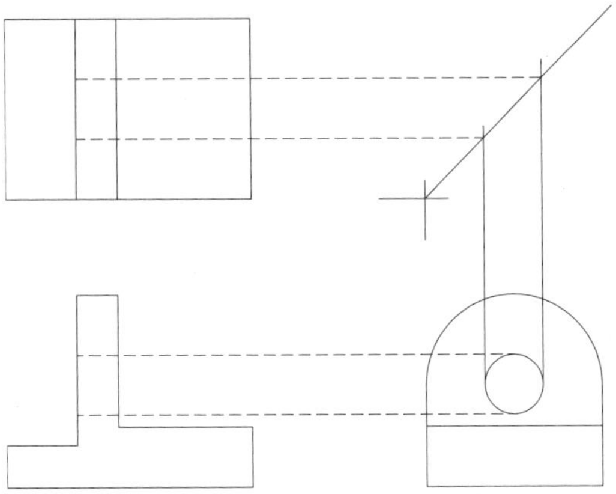

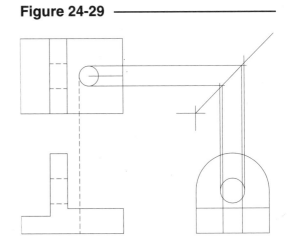

5. The hidden lines used for projection to the top view and front view (previous figure) are *Trimmed*. The slot is created in the top view with a *Circle* and projected to the side and front views. It is usually faster and easier to draw round object features in their circular view first, then project to the other views. Make sure you use the correct layers (OBJ, CONSTR, HID) for the appropriate features. If you do not, *Ddmodify* can be used retroactively.

Figure 24-29 ────────────

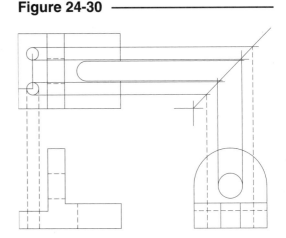

6. The lines shown in the previous figure as projection lines or construction lines for the slot are *Trimmed* or *Erased*. The holes in the top view are drawn on layer OBJ and projected to the other views. The projection lines and hidden lines are drawn on

Figure 24-30 ────────────

their respective layers.

7. *Trim* the appropriate hidden lines. *Freeze* layer
    CONSTR. On layer OBJ, use *Fillet* to create the
    rounded corners in the top view. Draw the correct
    center lines for the holes on layer CEN. The value for
    Ltscale should be adjusted to achieve the optimum
    center line spacing. *Ddmodify* can be used to adjust
    individual object linetype scale.

Figure 24-31

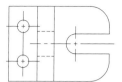

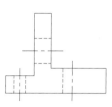 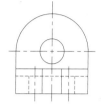

Figure 24-32

8. Fillets and rounds are added using the *Fillet*
    command. The runouts are created by drawing a
    3point Arc and *Trimming* or *Extending* the *Line* ends as
    necessary. Use *Zoom* for this detail work.

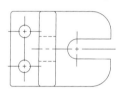

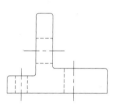 

Figure 24-33

9. Add a border and a title
    block using *Pline*.
    Include the part name,
    company, draftsperson,
    scale, date, and
    drawing file name in
    the title block. The
    drawing is ready for
    dimensioning and man-
    ufacturing notes.

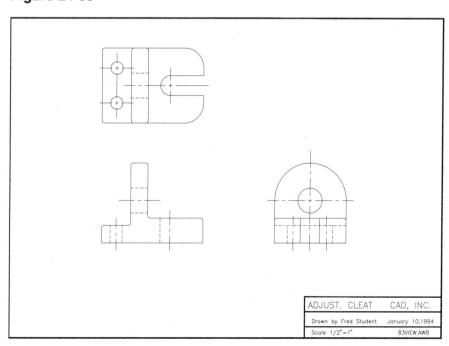

ADJUST. CLEAT   CAD, INC.

Drawn by Fred Student   January 10,1994

Scale 1/2"=1"   83VIEW.AWB

CHAPTER EXERCISES

1. *Open* the **PIVOTARM** drawing that you last edited in Chapter 16 Exercises.

    A. Create the right side view. Use *OSNAP* and *ORTHO* to create *Lines* or *Rays* to the miter line and down to the right side view as shown in Figure 24-34. *Offset* may be used effectively for this purpose instead. Use *Extend, Offset,* or *Ray* to create the projection lines from the front view to the right side view.

Figure 24-34 —————————————

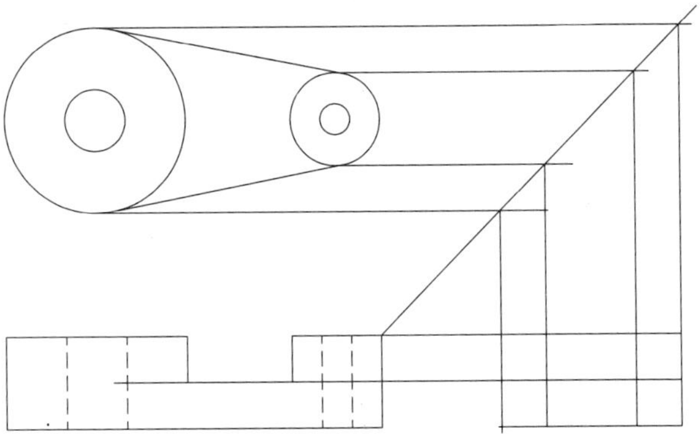

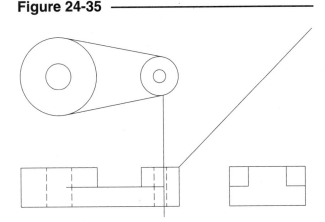

    B. *Trim* or *Erase* the unwanted projection lines, as shown in Figure 24-35. Draw a *Line* or *Ray* from the *ENDpoint* of the diagonal *Line* in the top view down to the front to supply the boundary edge for *Trimming* the horizontal *Line* in the front view as shown.

Figure 24-35 —————————————

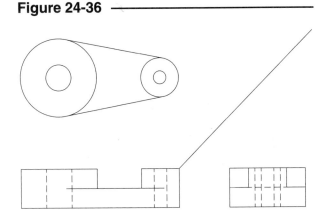

    C. Next, create the hidden lines for the holes by the same fashion as before. Make use of previously created *Layers* for achieving the desired *Linetypes*. Complete the side view by adding the horizontal hidden *Line* in the center of the view.

Figure 24-36 —————————————

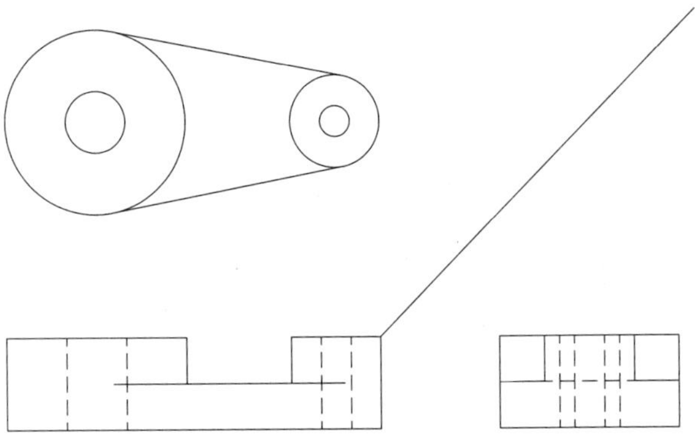

D. Another hole for a set screw must be added to the small end of the Pivot Arm. Construct a *Circle* of **4mm** diameter with its center located **8mm** from the top edge in the side view as shown in Figure 24-37. Project the set screw hole to the other views.

Figure 24-37 ――――――

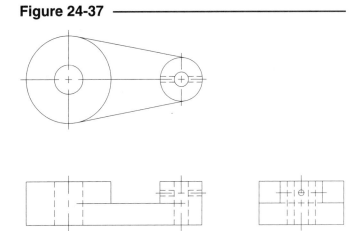

E. Make new layers **CONSTR, OBJ,** and **TITLE** and change objects to the appropriate layers with *Change Properties*. *Freeze* layer **CONSTR**. Add center lines on the **CEN** layer as shown in Figure 24-37. Change the *Ltscale* to **18**. To complete the PIVOTARM drawing, draw a *Pline* border (*width* **.02** x scale factor) and *Insert* the **TBLOCKAT** drawing that you created in Chapter 22 Exercises.

For exercises 2 through 5, construct and plot the multiview drawings as instructed. Use an appropriate *prototype* drawing for each exercise unless instructed otherwise. Use conventional practices for *layers* and *linetypes*. Draw a *Pline* border with the correct *width* and *Insert* your **TBLOCK** or **TBLOCKAT** drawing.

2. Make a two-view multiview drawing of the Clip. *Plot* the drawing full size (**1=1**). Use the **ASHEET** prototype drawing to achieve the desired plot scale. *Save* the drawing as **CLIP**.

Figure 24-38 ――――――

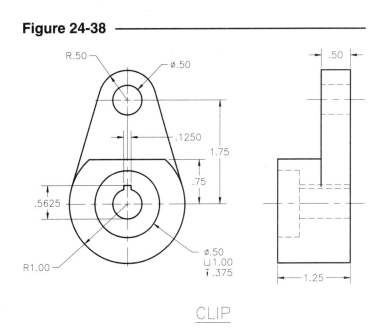

3. Make a three-view multiview drawing of the Bar Guide and *Plot* it **1=1**. Use the **BAR-GUIDE** drawing you set up in Chapter 13 Exercises. Note that a partial *Ellipse* will appear in one of the views.

Figure 24-39

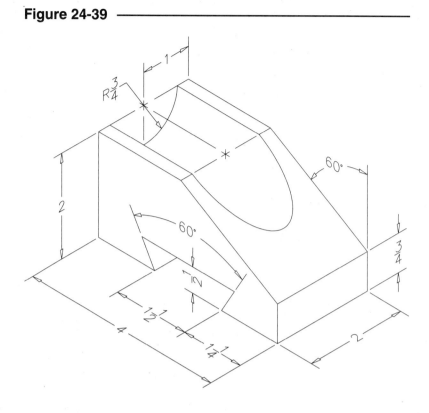

4. Construct a multi-view drawing of the Saddle. Three views are needed. The channel along the bottom of the part intersects with the saddle on top to create a slotted hole visible in the top view. *Plot* the drawing at **1=1**. *Save* as **SADDLE**.

Figure 24-40

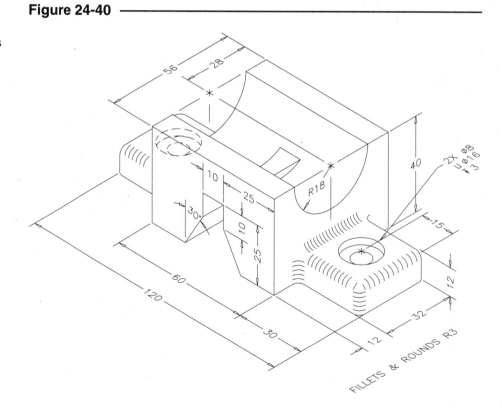

5. Draw a multiview of the Adjustable Mount shown in Figure 24-41. Determine an appropriate prototype drawing to use and scale for plotting based on your plotter capabilities. *Plot* the drawing to an accepted scale. *Save* the drawing as **ADJMOUNT**.

Figure 24-41

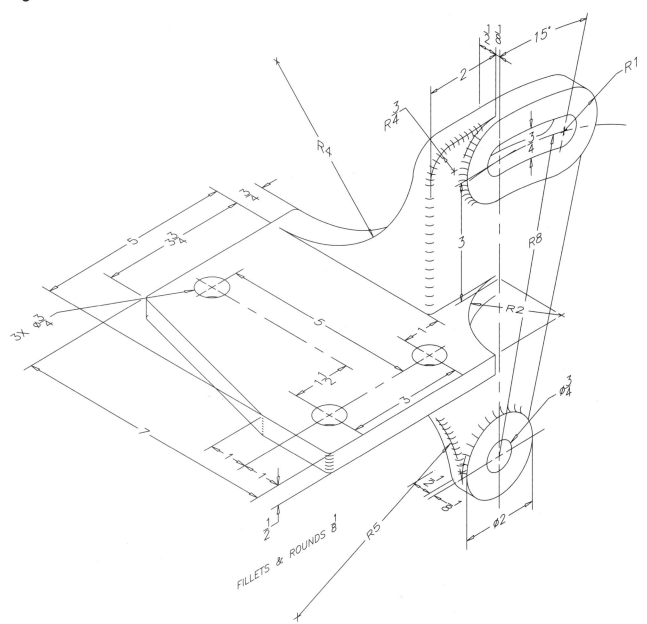

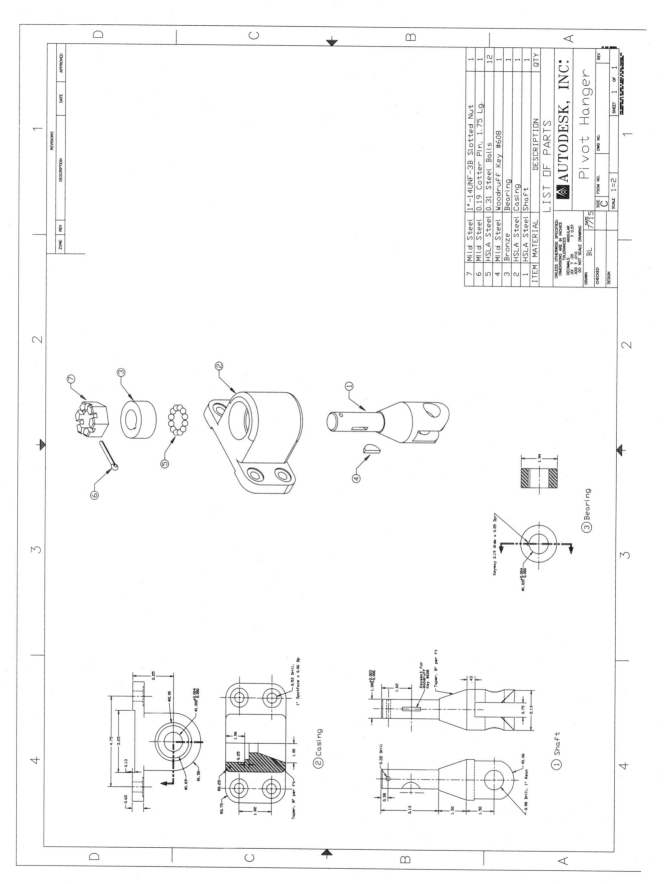

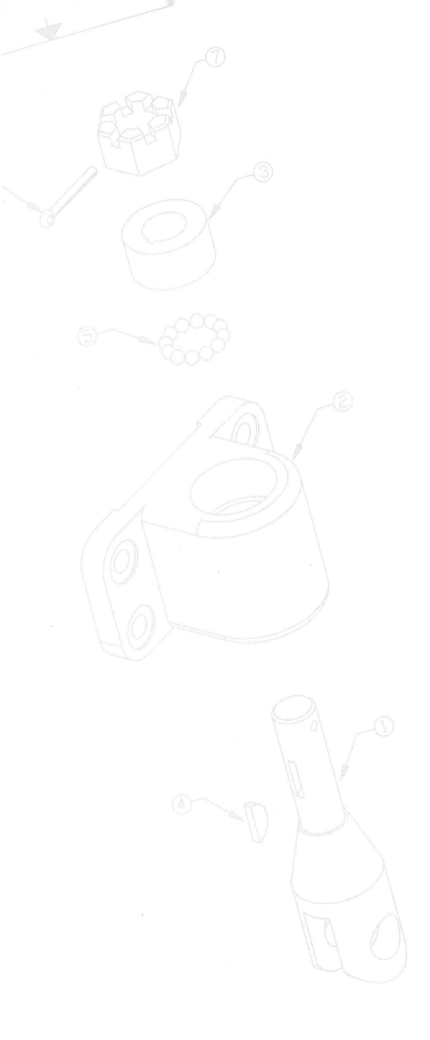

Chapter 25
PICTORIAL DRAWINGS

Chapter Objectives

After completing this chapter you should be able to:

1. activate the *Isometric Style* of *Snap* for creating isometric drawings;

2. draw on the three isometric planes by toggling *Isoplane* using CTRL+E;

3. create isometric ellipses with the *Isocircle* option of *Ellipse*;

4. construct an isometric drawing in AutoCAD;

5. create Oblique Cavalier and Cabinet drawings in AutoCAD.

BASICS

Isometric drawings and oblique drawings are pictorial drawings. Pictorial drawings show three principal faces of the object in one view. A pictorial drawing is a drawing of a 3D object as if you were positioned to see (typically) some of the front, some of the top, and some of the side of the object. All three dimensions of the object (width, height, and depth) are visible in a pictorial drawing.

Multiview drawings differ from pictorial drawings because a multiview only shows two dimensions in each view, so two or more views are needed to see all three dimensions of the object. A pictorial drawing shows all dimensions in the one view. Pictorial drawings depict the object similar to the way you are accustomed to viewing objects in everyday life, that is, seeing all three dimensions. Figure 25-1 and Figure 25-2 show the same object in multiview and in pictorial representation, respectively.

Types of Pictorial Drawings

Pictorial drawings are classified as follows.

1. Axonometric drawings
    a. Isometric drawings
    b. Dimetric drawings
    c. Trimetric drawings

2. Oblique drawings

Axonometric drawings are characterized by how the angle of the edges or axes (axon-) are measured (-metric) with respect to each other.

Isometric drawings are drawn so that each of the axes have equal angular measurement. ("Isometric" means equal measurement.) The isometric axes are always drawn at 120 degree increments (Fig. 25-3). All rectilinear lines on the object (representing horizontal and vertical edges—not inclined or oblique) are drawn on the isometric axes.

A 3D object seen "in isometric" is thought of as being oriented so that each of three perpendicular faces (such as the top, front, and side) are seen equally. In other words, the angles formed between the line of sight and each of the principal faces are equal.

Figure 25-1 ——————————

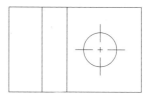

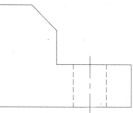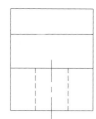

Figure 25-2 ——————————

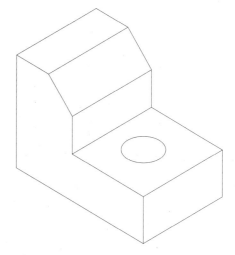

Figure 25-3 ——————————

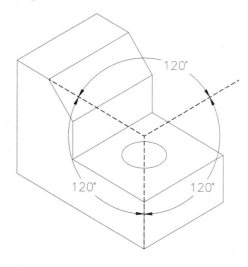

Dimetric drawings are constructed so that the angle of two of the three axes are equal. There are many possibilities for dimetric axes. A common orientation for dimetric drawings is shown in Figure 25-4. For 3D objects seen from a dimetric viewpoint, the angles formed between the line of sight and each of two principal faces are equal.

Figure 25-4

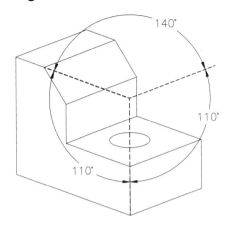

Trimetric drawings have three unequal angles between the axes. Numerous possibilities exist. A common orientation for trimetric drawings is shown in Figure 25-5.

Oblique drawings are characterized by a vertical axis and horizontal axis for the two dimensions of the front face and a third (receding) axis of either 30, 45, or 60 degrees (Fig. 25-6). Oblique drawings depict the true size and shape of the front face, but add the depth to what would otherwise be a typical 2D view. This technique simplifies construction of drawings for objects that have contours in the profile view (front face) but relatively few features along the depth. Viewing a 3D object from an oblique viewpoint is not possible.

Figure 25-5

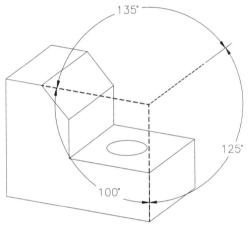

This chapter will explain the construction of isometric and oblique drawings in AutoCAD.

Pictorial Drawings Are 2D Drawings

Isometric, Dimetric, Trimetric, and Oblique drawings are <u>2D drawings</u>, whether created with AutoCAD or otherwise. Pictorial drawing was invented before the existence of CAD and therefore was intended to simulate a 3D object on a 2D plane (the plane of the paper). If AutoCAD is used to create the pictorial, the geometry lies on a 2D plane—the XY plane. All coordinates defining objects have X and Y values with a Z value of 0. When the *Isometric* style of *Snap* is activated, an isometrically structured *SNAP* and *GRID* appear on the XY plane.

Figure 25-6

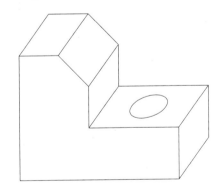

Figure 25-7 illustrates the 2D nature of an isometric drawing created in AutoCAD. Isometric lines are created on the XY plane. The *Isometric SNAP* and *GRID* are also on the 2D plane. (The *Vpoint* command was used to give other than a *Plan* view of the drawing in this figure.)

Although pictorial drawings are based on the theory of projecting 3D objects onto 2D planes, it is physically possible to achieve an axonometric (isometric, dimetric, or trimetric) viewpoint of a 3D object using a 3D CAD system. In AutoCAD, the *Vpoint* command is used to specify the observer's position in 3D space with respect to a 3D model. Chapter 34 discusses the specific commands and values needed to attain axonometric viewpoints of a 3D model.

Figure 25-7

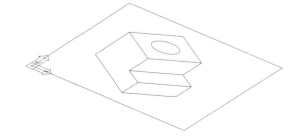

ISOMETRIC DRAWING IN AutoCAD

AutoCAD provides the capability to construct isometric drawings. An isometric *SNAP* and *GRID* are available, as well as a utility for creation of isometrically correct ellipses. Isometric lines are created with the *Line* command. There are no special options of *Line* for isometric drawing, but isometric *SNAP* and *GRID* can be used to force *Lines* to an isometric orientation. Begin creating an isometric drawing in AutoCAD by activating the *Isometric Style* option of the *Snap* command. This action can be done using any of the options listed in the following command table.

SNAP

PULL-DOWN MENU	SCREEN MENU	TYPE IN	TABLET MENU
Options *Drawing Aids...*	*OPTIONS* *DDrmode:*	*SNAP or* *DDRMODES*	21,V

Command: **snap**
Snap spacing or ON/OFF/Aspect/Rotate/Style <1.0000>: **s**
Standard/Isometric <S>: **I**
Vertical spacing <1.0000>: **Enter**
Command:

Alternately, toggling the indicated checkbox in the lower-right corner of the *Drawing Aids* dialogue box activates the Isometric *SNAP* and *GRID* (Fig. 25-8).

Figure 25-9 illustrates the effect of setting the Isometric *SNAP* and *GRID*. Notice the new position of the crosshairs.

Using <u>CTRL+E</u> (pressing the CTRL key and the letter E simultaneously) toggles the crosshairs to one of three possible *Isoplanes* (AutoCAD's term for the three faces of the isometric pictorial). If *ORTHO* is *ON*, only <u>isometric</u> lines are drawn; that is, you can only draw *Lines* aligned with the isometric axes. *Lines* can be drawn on only two axes for each isoplane. CTRL+E allows drawing on the two axes aligned with another face of the object. *ORTHO* is *OFF* in order to draw inclined or oblique lines (not on the isometric axis). The functions of *GRID* (F7) and *SNAP* (F9) remain unchanged.

With *SNAP ON*, toggle *COORDS* (F6) several times and examine the read-out as you move the cursor. The <u>absolute coordinate format is of</u>

Figure 25-8 ———————

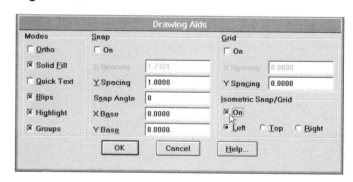

Figure 25-9 ———————

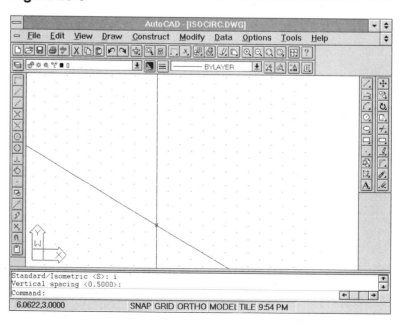

no particular assistance while drawing in isometric because of the configuration of the *GRID*. The relative polar format, however, is very helpful. Use relative polar format for *COORDS* while drawing in isometric (see Fig. 25-10).

The effects of changing the *Isoplane* are shown in the following figures. Press CTRL+E to change *Isoplane*.

With *ORTHO ON*, drawing a *Line* is limited to the two axes of the current *Isoplane*. Only one side of a cube, for example, can be drawn on the current *Isoplane*. Watch *COORDS* (in a polar format) to give the length of the current *Line* as you draw (lower left corner of the screen).

Toggling CTRL+E switches the crosshairs and the effect of *ORTHO* to another *Isoplane*. One other side of a cube can be constructed on this *Isoplane* (Fig. 25-11).

Toggling CTRL+E again forces the crosshairs and the effect of *ORTHO* to the third *Isoplane*. The third side of the cube can be constructed.

Isometric Ellipses

Isometric ellipses are easily drawn in AutoCAD by using the *Isocircle* option of the *Ellipse* command. This option only appears when the isometric *SNAP* is *ON*.

Figure 25-10

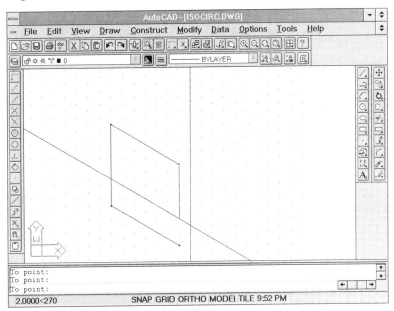

Figure 25-11

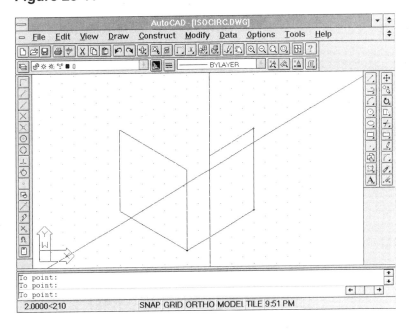

ELLIPSE

PULL-DOWN MENU	SCREEN MENU	TYPE IN	TABLET MENU
Draw *Ellipse >* *Axis, End*	*DRAW1:* *Ellipse:*	*ELLIPSE,* *I*	*10,N*

Although the *Isocircle* option does not appear in the pull-down or digitizing tablet menus, it can be invoked as an option of the *Ellipse* command. You must type "I" to use the *Isocircle* option. The command syntax is as follows.

Command: *ellipse*
<Axis endpoint 1>/Center/Isocircle: *I*
Center of circle: **PICK** or (**coordinates**)
<Circle radius>/Diameter: **PICK** or (**coordinates**)

After selecting the center point of the *Isocircle*, the isometrically correct ellipse appears on the screen on the current *Isoplane*. Use CTRL+E to toggle the ellipse to the correct orientation. When defining the radius interactively, use *ORTHO* to force the rubberband line to an isometric axis (Fig. 25-12).

Since isometric angles are equal, all isometric ellipses have the same proportion (major to minor axis). The only differences in isometric ellipses are the size and the orientation (*Isoplane*).

Figure 25-12 ————————————————

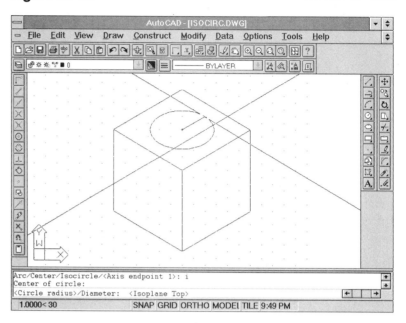

Figure 25-13 shows three ellipses correctly oriented on their respective faces. Use CTRL+E to toggle the correct *Isoplane* orientation: *Isoplane Top*, *Isoplane Left*, or *Isoplane Right*.

When defining the radius or diameter of an ellipse, it should always be measured in an isometric direction. In other words, an isometric ellipse is always measured on the two isometric axes (or center lines) parallel with the plane of the ellipse.

If you define the radius or diameter interactively, use *ORTHO ON*. If you enter a value, AutoCAD automatically applies the value to the correct isometric axes.

Figure 25-13 ————————————————

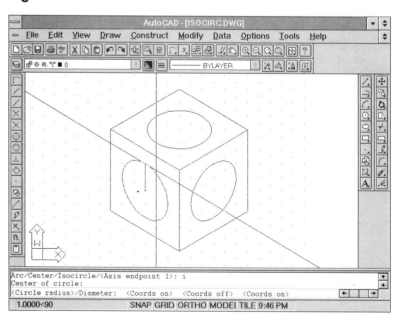

Creating an Isometric Drawing

In this exercise, the object in Figure 25-14 is drawn in isometric.

The initial steps to create an isometric drawing begin with the typical setup (see Chapter 6, Drawing Setup).

1. Set the desired *Units*.

2. Set appropriate *Limits*.

3. Set the *Isometric Style* of *Snap* and specify an appropriate value for spacing.

Figure 25-14

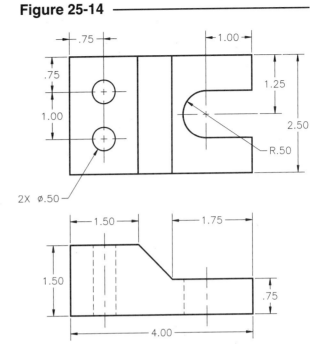

4. The next step involves creating an isometric framework of the desired object. In other words, draw an isometric box equal to the overall dimensions of the object. Using the dimensions given in Figure 25-14, create the encompassing isometric box with the *Line* command (Fig. 25-15).

Use *ORTHO* to force isometric *Lines*. Watch the *COORDS* display (in a relative polar format) to give the current lengths as you draw.

Figure 25-15

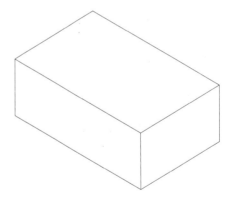

5. Add the lines defining the lower surface. Define the needed edge of the upper isometric surface as shown.

Figure 25-16

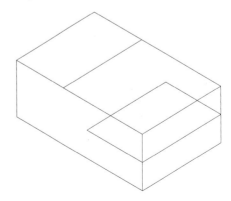

6. The <u>inclined</u> edges of the inclined surface can only be drawn (with *Line*) when *ORTHO* is *OFF*. <u>Inclined</u> lines in isometric cannot be drawn by transferring the lengths of the lines, but only by defining the <u>ends</u> of the inclined lines on <u>isometric</u> lines, then connecting the endpoints. Next, *Trim* or *Erase* the necessary *Lines*.

Figure 25-17 ———

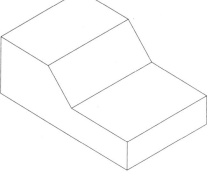

7. Draw the slot by constructing an *Ellipse* with the *Isocircle* option. Draw the two *Lines* connecting the circle to the right edge. *Trim* the unwanted part of the *Ellipse* (highlighted) using the *Lines* as cutting edges.

Figure 25-18 ———

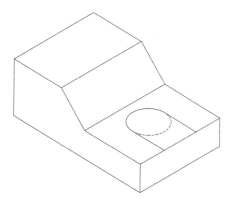

8. *Copy* the far *Line* and the *Ellipse* down to the bottom surface. Add two vertical *Lines* at the end of the slot.

Figure 25-19 ———

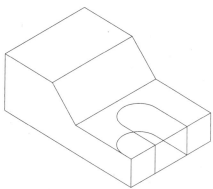

9. Use *Trim* to remove the part of the *Ellipse* that would normally be hidden from view. *Trim* the *Lines* along the right edge at the opening of the slot.

Figure 25-20 ———

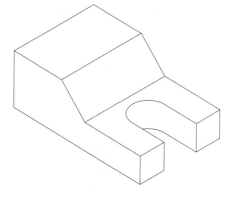

10. Add the two holes on the top with *Ellipse, Isocircle* option. Use *ORTHO ON* when defining the radius. *Copy* can also be used to create the second *Ellipse* from the first.

Figure 25-21

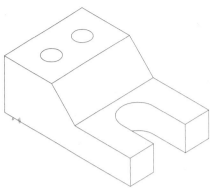

Dimensioning Isometric Drawings in AutoCAD

Refer to Chapter 28, Dimensioning, for details on how to dimension isometric drawings.

OBLIQUE DRAWING IN AutoCAD

Figure 25-22

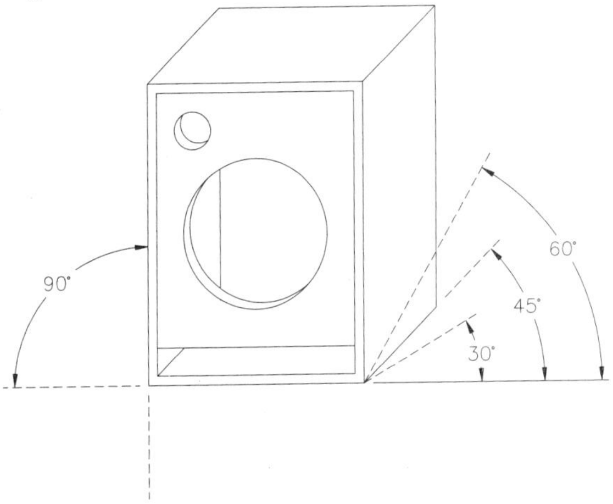

Oblique drawings are characterized by having two axes at a 90 degree orientation. Typically, you should locate the <u>front face</u> of the object along these two axes. Since the object's characteristic shape is seen in the front view, an oblique drawing allows you to create all shapes parallel to the front face true size and shape as you would in a multiview drawing. Circles on or parallel to the front face can be drawn as circles. The third axis, the receding axis, can be drawn at a choice of angles, 30, 45, or 60 degrees, depending on whether you want to show more of the top or the side of the object.

Figure 25-22 illustrates the axes orientation of an oblique drawing, including the choice of angles for the receding axis.

Another option allowed with oblique drawings is the measurement used for the receding axis. Using the full depth of the object along the receding axis is called <u>Cavalier</u> oblique drawing. This method depicts the object (a cube with a hole in this case) as having an elongated depth (Fig. 25-23).

Figure 25-23

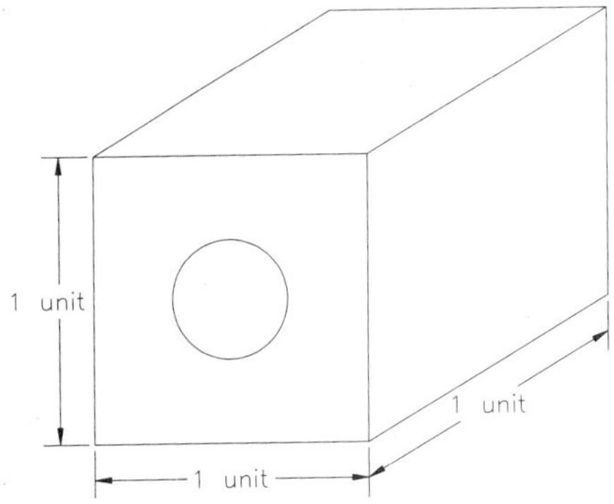

Using 1/2 or 3/4 of the true depth along the receding axis gives a more realistic pictorial representation of the object. This is called a <u>Cabinet</u> oblique (Fig. 25-24).

There are no functions or commands in AutoCAD that are intended specifically for oblique drawing. However, *SNAP* and *GRID* can be aligned with the receding axis using the *Rotate* option of the *Snap* command to simplify the construction of edges of the object along that axis. The steps for creating a typical oblique drawing are given next.

Figure 25-24

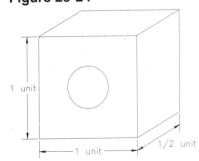

The object in Figure 25-25 is used for the example. From the dimensions given in the multiview, create a cabinet oblique with the receding axis at 45 degrees.

Figure 25-25

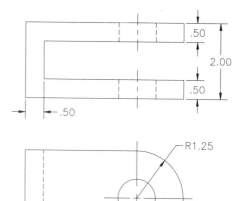

1. Create the characteristic shape of the front face of the object as shown in the front view.

Figure 25-26

2. Use *Copy* with the *Multiple* option to copy the front face back on the receding axis. Polar coordinates can be entered as the "second point of displacement." For example, the first *Copy* should be located at **@.25<45** relative to the "Base point." (Remember to calculate 1/2 of the actual depth.) As an alternative, a *Line* can be drawn at 45 degrees and *Divided* to place *Points* at .25 increments. *Multiple Copies* of the front face can be OSNAPed with the *NODe* option.

Figure 25-27

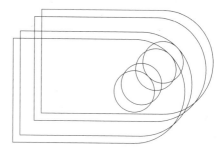

3. Draw the *Line* representing the edge on the upper left of the object along the receding axis. Use *ENDpoint OSNAP* to connect the *Lines*. Make a *Copy* of the *Line* or draw another *Line* .5 units to the right. Drop a vertical *Line* from the *INTersection* as shown.

Figure 25-28

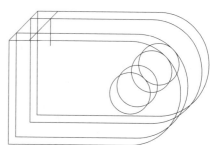

4. Use *Trim* and *Erase* to remove the unwanted parts of the *Lines* and *Circles* (those edges that are normally obscured).

Figure 25-29

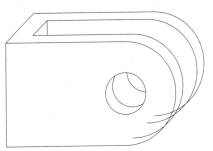

5. *Zoom* with a *window* to the lower right corner of the drawing. Draw a *Line TANgent* to the edges of the arcs to define the limiting elements along the receding axis. *Trim* the unwanted segments of the arcs.

Figure 25-30

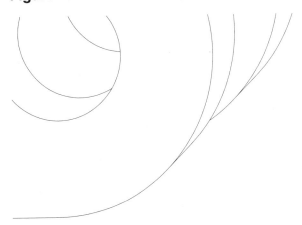

The resulting cabinet oblique drawing should appear like that in Figure 25-31.

Figure 25-31

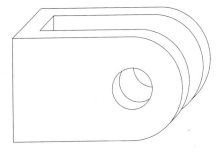

CHAPTER EXERCISES

Isometric Drawing

For exercises 1, 2, and 3 create isometric drawings as instructed. To begin, use an appropriate prototype drawing and draw a *Pline* border and insert the **TBLOCKAT**.

1. Create an isometric drawing of the cylinder shown in Figure 25-32. *Save* the drawing as **CYLINDER** and *Plot* so the drawing is *Scaled to Fit* on an "A" size sheet.

Figure 25-32 ─────────────────

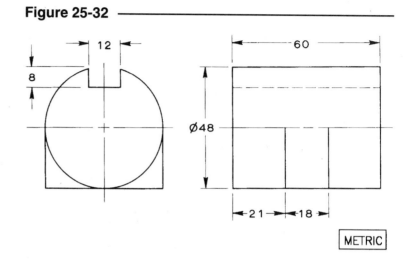

2. Make an isometric drawing of the Corner Brace shown in Figure 25-33. *Save* the drawing as **CRNBRACE**. *Plot* at **1=1** scale on an "A" size sheet.

Figure 25-33 ─────────────────

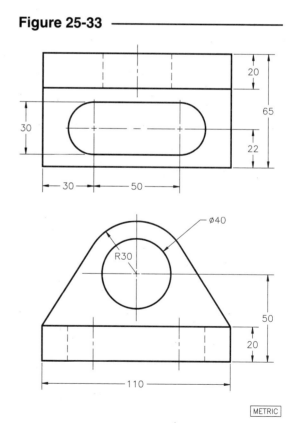

3. Draw the Support Bracket (Fig. 25-34) in isometric. The drawing can be *Plotted* at **1=1** scale on an "A" size sheet. *Save* the drawing and assign the name **SBRACKET**.

Figure 25-34 ──────────────

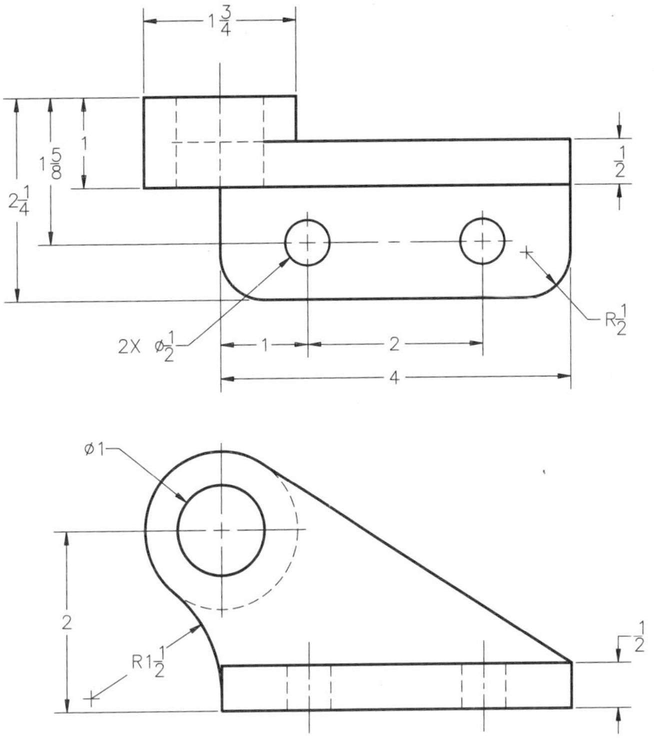

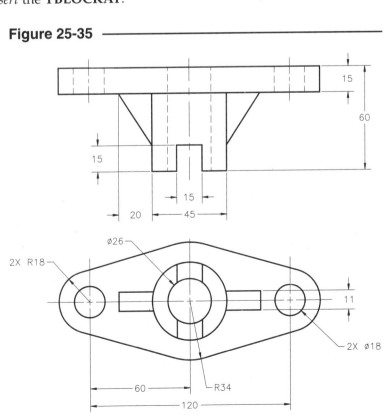

Oblique Drawing

For exercises 4 and 5, create oblique drawings as instructed. To begin, use an appropriate prototype drawing and draw a *Pline* border and *Insert* the **TBLOCKAT**.

4. Make an oblique cabinet projection of the Bearing shown in Figure 25-35. Construct all dimensions on the receding axis 1/2 of the actual length. Select the optimum angle for the receding axis to be able to view the 15 x 15 slot. *Plot* at **1=1** scale on an "A" size sheet. *Save* the drawing as **BEARING**.

Figure 25-35 ──────────────

5. Construct a cavalier oblique drawing of the Pulley showing the circular view true size and shape. The illustration in Figure 25-36 gives only the side view. All vertical dimensions in the figure are diameters. *Save* the drawing as **PULLEY** and make a *Plot* on an "A" size sheet at **1=1**.

Figure 25-36

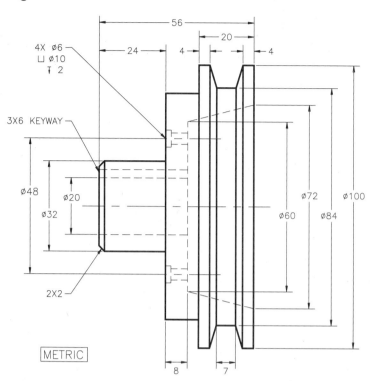

Chapter 26
SECTION VIEWS

Chapter Objectives

After completing this chapter you should:

1. be able to use the *Bhatch* command to select associative hatch patterns;

2. be able to specify a *Scale* and *Angle* for hatch lines;

3. know how to define a boundary for hatching using the *Pick Points* (ray-casting) and *Select objects* methods;

4. be able to *Preview* the hatch and make necessary adjustments, then *Apply* the hatch pattern;

5. be able to use *Hatch* to create non-associative hatch lines and discard the boundary;

6. know how to use *Hatchedit* to modify parameters of existing hatch patterns in the drawing.

7. be able to create a cutting plane line for a section view.

BASICS

A section view is a view of the interior of an object after it has been imaginarily cut open to reveal the object's inner details. A section view is only one of two or more views of a multiview drawing describing the object. For example, a multiview drawing of a machine part may contain three views, one of which is a section view.

Hatch lines (also known as section lines) are drawn in the section view to indicate the solid material that has been cut through. Each combination of section lines is called a hatch <u>pattern</u>, and each pattern is used to represent a specific material. In full and half section views, hidden lines are omitted since the inside of the object is visible.

ANSI (American National Standards Institute) and ISO (International Standards Organization) have published standard configurations for section lines, and AutoCAD Release 13 supports those standards. However, since the first shipping of Release 13, ANSI no longer specifies section line pattern standards.

A cutting plane line is drawn in an adjacent view to the section view to indicate the plane that imaginarily cuts through the object. Arrows on each end of the cutting plane line indicate the line of sight for the section view. ANSI dictates that a thick dashed or phantom line be used as the standard cutting plane line.

This chapter discusses the AutoCAD methods used to draw hatch lines for section views and related cutting plane lines. The *Bhatch* (boundary hatch) command allows you to select an enclosed area and select the hatch pattern and the parameters for the appearance of the hatch pattern; then AutoCAD automatically draws the hatch (section) lines. Existing hatch lines in the drawing can be modified using *Hatchedit*. Cutting plane lines are created in AutoCAD by using a dashed linetype. The line itself should be created with the *Pline* command to achieve line width.

DEFINING AND EDITING HATCH PATTERNS AND HATCH BOUNDARIES

A hatch pattern is composed of many lines that have a particular linetype, spacing, and angle. Many standard hatch patterns are provided by AutoCAD for your selection. Rather than having to draw each section line individually, you are required only to specify the area to be hatched and AutoCAD fills the designated area with the selected hatch pattern. An AutoCAD hatch pattern is inserted as <u>one object</u>. For example, you can *Erase* the inserted hatch pattern by selecting only one line in the pattern, and the entire pattern in the area is *Erased*.

Figure 26-1 ————————————

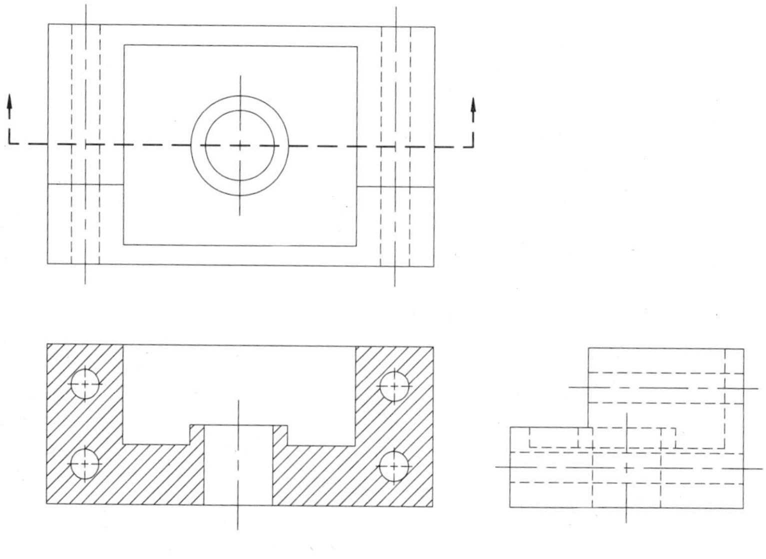

In a typical section view (Fig. 26-1), the hatch pattern completely fills the area representing the material that has been cut through. With the *Bhatch* command you can define the boundary of an area to be hatched simply by pointing inside of an enclosed area.

Both the *Hatch* and the *Bhatch* commands fill a specified area with a selected hatch pattern. *Hatch* requires that you select <u>each object</u> defining the boundary, whereas the *Bhatch* command finds the boundary automatically (by ray-casting) when you point inside it. Additionally, *Hatch* operates in command line format, whereas *Bhatch* operates in dialogue box fashion. For these reasons, *Bhatch* is superior to *Hatch* and is recommended in most cases for drawing section views.

Hatch patterns created with *Bhatch* are <u>associative</u>. Associative hatch patterns are associated to the boundary geometry such that when the shape of the boundary changes (by *Stretch, Scale, Rotate, Move, Ddmodify,* Grips, etc.), the hatch pattern automatically reforms itself to conform to the new shape (Fig. 26-2). For example, if a design change required a larger diameter for a hole, *Ddmodify* could be used to change the diameter of the hole, and the surrounding section lines would automatically adapt to the new diameter.

Figure 26-2

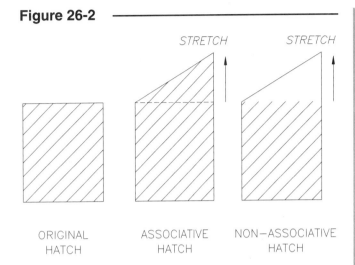

Once the hatch patterns have been drawn, any feature of the existing hatch pattern (created with *Bhatch*) can be changed retroactively using *Hatchedit*. The *Hatchedit* dialogue box gives access to the same options that were used to create the hatch (in the *Boundary Hatch* dialogue box). Changing the scale, angle, or pattern of any existing section view in the drawing is a simple process.

Steps for Creating a Section View Using the *Bhatch* Command

1. Create the view that contains the area to be hatched using typical draw commands such as *Line, Arc, Circle, Pline,* etc. If you intend to have text inside the area to be hatched, add the text before hatching.

2. Invoke the *Bhatch* command. The *Boundary Hatch* dialogue box appears (Fig. 26-3).

3. Specify the *Pattern Type* to use. Select the desired pattern by clicking on the image tile until the desired pattern appears, or select from the *Pattern* pop-down list.

4. Specify the *Scale* and *Angle* in the dialogue box.

5. Define the area to be hatched by PICKing an internal point (AutoCAD automatically traces the boundary) or by individually selecting the objects.

6. *Preview* the hatch to make sure everything is as expected. Adjust hatching parameters as necessary and *Preview* again.

7. *Apply* the hatch. The hatch pattern is automatically drawn and becomes an associated object in the drawing.

8. If other areas are to be hatched, additional internal points or objects can be selected to define the new area for hatching. The parameters previously used are again applied to the new hatch area by default. You may want to *Inherit Properties* from a previously applied hatch.

9. Draw a cutting plane line in a view adjacent to the section view. The *Pline* command with a *Dashed* or *Phantom* linetype is used. Arrows at the ends of the cutting plane line indicate the line of sight for the section view.

10. If any aspect of the hatch lines needs to be edited at a later time, *Hatchedit* can be used to change those properties. If the hatch boundary is changed by *Stretch, Rotate, Scale, Move, Ddmodify,* etc., the hatched area will conform to the new boundary.

The *Bhatch* and *Hatchedit* commands with all dialogue boxes and options are explained in detail on the following pages.

BHATCH

PULL-DOWN MENU	SCREEN MENU	TYPE IN	TABLET MENU
Draw *Hatch >* *Hatch...*	*CONSTRCT* *Bhatch:*	*BHATCH*	*16,W*

Bhatch allows you to create hatch lines for a section view (or for other purposes) by simply PICKing inside a closed boundary. A closed boundary refers to an area completely enclosed by objects. *Bhatch* locates the closed boundary automatically by creating a <u>temporary *Pline*</u> that follows the outline found by the ray-casting technique, fills the area with hatch lines, and then deletes the boundary (default option) after hatching is completed. *Bhatch* ignores all objects or parts of objects that are not part of the boundary.

Any method of invoking *Bhatch* yields the *Boundary Hatch* dialogue box (Fig. 26-3). Typically, the first step in the *Boundary Hatch* dialogue box is the selection of a hatch pattern.

Figure 26-3

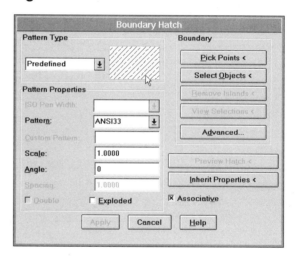

Boundary Hatch Dialogue Box Options

Pattern Type
This option allows you to specify the type of the hatch pattern: *Predefined, User-defined,* or *Custom.* Use *Predefined* for standard hatch pattern styles that AutoCAD provides (in the ACAD.PAT file).

Predefined
There are <u>two ways to select</u> from the *Predefined* patterns: you can use the *Pattern* pop-down list (see below) or you can PICK the image tile displaying a sample of the pattern. Clicking in the tile causes the display to sequence through the possible selections.

User-defined
To define a simple hatch pattern "on the fly," select the *User-defined* tile. This causes the *Pattern* and *Scale* options to be disabled and the *Angle, Spacing,* and *Double* options to be enabled. Creating a *User-defined* pattern is easy. Specify the *Angle* of the lines, the *Spacing* between lines, and optionally create *Double* (perpendicular) lines. All *User-defined* patterns have continuous lines.

Custom
Custom patterns are previously created user-defined patterns stored in other than the ACAD.PAT file. Custom patterns can contain continuous, dashed and dotted line combinations. See AutoCAD Customization Guide for information on creating and saving custom hatch patterns.

Pattern Properties
This cluster is used to specify the type of hatch pattern to be drawn and the parameters that govern its appearance.

ISO Pen Width
You must select an ISO hatch pattern for this tile to be enabled. Selecting an *ISO Pen Width* from the pop-down list automatically sets the scale and enters the value in the *Scale* edit box. See *Scale*.

Pattern...
Selecting the *Pattern* pop-down list (Fig. 26-4) displays the name of each predefined pattern. Making a selection sets that as the current pattern and causes the pattern to display in the window above. Using the up and down arrow keys causes the name and display (in the image tile) to sequence.

The list of AutoCAD predefined patterns is shown below. The patterns are defined and stored in the ACAD.PAT file.

Figure 26-4 ───────────

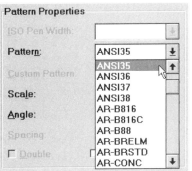

Pattern Type	Description
ANGLE	- Angle steel
ANSI31	- ANSI Iron, Brick, Stone masonry
ANSI32	- ANSI Steel
ANSI33	- ANSI Bronze, Brass, Copper
ANSI34	- ANSI Plastic, Rubber
ANSI35	- ANSI Fire brick, Refractory material
ANSI36	- ANSI Marble, Slate, Glass
ANSI37	- ANSI Lead, Zinc, Magnesium, Sound/Heat/Elec Insulation
ANSI38	- ANSI Aluminum
AR-B816	- 8x16 Block elevation stretcher bond
AR-B816C	- 8x16 Block elevation stretcher bond with mortar joints
AR-B88	- 8x8 Block elevation stretcher bond
AR-BRELM	- Standard brick elevation english bond with mortar joints
AR-BRSTD	- Standard brick elevation stretcher bond
AR-CONC	- Random dot and stone pattern
AR-HBONE	- Standard brick herringbone pattern @ 45 degrees
AR-PARQ1	- 2x12 Parquet flooring: pattern of 12x12
AR-RROOF	- Roof shingle texture
AR-RSHKE	- Roof wood shake texture
AR-SAND	- Random dot pattern
BOX	- Box steel
BRASS	- Brass material
BRICK	- Brick or masonry-type surface

BRSTONE	- Brick and stone
CLAY	- Clay material
CORK	- Cork material
CROSS	- A series of crosses
DASH	- Dashed lines
DOLMIT	- Geological rock layering
DOTS	- A series of dots
EARTH	- Earth or ground (subterranean)
ESCHER	- Escher pattern
FLEX	- Flexible material
GRASS	- Grass area
GRATE	- Grated area
HEX	- Hexagons
HONEY	- Honeycomb pattern
HOUND	- Houndstooth check
INSUL	- Insulation material
LINE	- Parallel horizontal lines
MUDST	- Mud and sand
NET	- Horizontal / vertical grid
NET3	- Network pattern 0-60-120
PLAST	- Plastic material
PLASTI	- Plastic material
SACNCR	- Concrete
SQUARE	- Small aligned squares
STARS	- Star of David
STEEL	- Steel material
SWAMP	- Swampy area
TRANS	- Heat transfer material
TRIANG	- Equilateral triangles
ZIGZAG	- Staircase effect
ACAD_ISO02W100	- dashed line
ACAD_ISO03W100	- dashed space line
ACAD_ISO04W100	- long dashed dotted line
ACAD_ISO05W100	- long dashed double dotted line
ACAD_ISO06W100	- long dashed triplicate dotted line
ACAD_ISO07W100	- dotted line
ACAD_ISO08W100	- long dashed short dashed line
ACAD_ISO09W100	- long dashed double-short-dashed line
ACAD_ISO10W100	- dashed dotted line
ACAD_ISO11W100	- double-dashed dotted line
ACAD_ISO12W100	- dashed double-dotted line
ACAD_ISO13W100	- double-dashed double-dotted line
ACAD_ISO14W100	- dashed triplicate-dotted line
ACAD_ISO15W100	- double-dashed triplicate-dotted line

Figure 26-5 displays each of the AutoCAD hatch patterns defined in the ACAD.PAT file. Note that the patterns are not shown to scale.

Figure 26-5

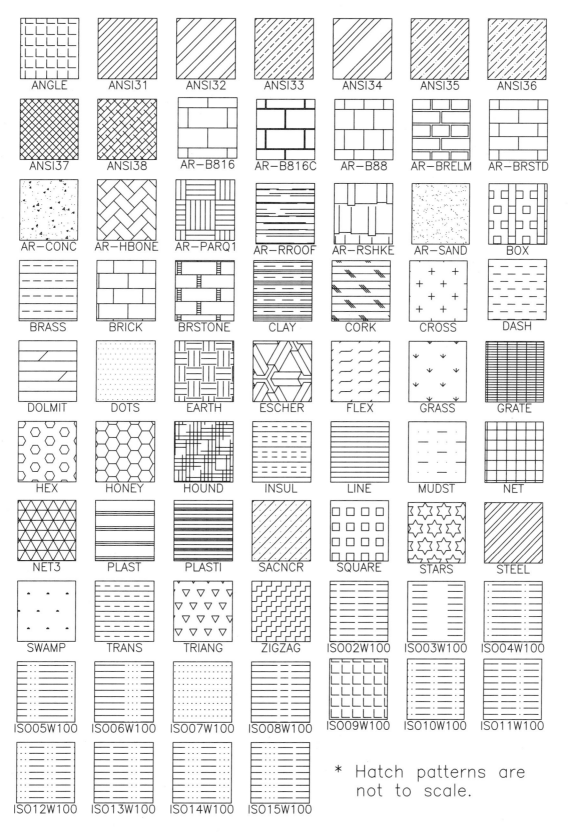

* Hatch patterns are not to scale.

Since hatch patterns have their own linetype, the *Continuous* linetype or a layer with the *Continuous* line-type <u>should be current</u> when hatching. After selecting a pattern, specify the desired *Scale* and *Angle* of the pattern.

Scale
The value entered in this edit box is a scale factor that is applied to the existing selected pattern. Normally, this scale factor should be changed proportionally with changes in the drawing *Limits*. Like many other scale factors (*LTSCALE, DIMSCALE*), AutoCAD defaults are set to a value of 1, which is appropriate for the default *Limits* of 12 x 9. If you have calculated the drawing scale factor, it can be applied here (see Chapter 13). In the example, *Limits* are set to 22 x 17, so a *Scale* of 1.8 is used. The *Scale* value is stored in the *HPSCALE* system variable.

ISO hatch patterns are intended for use with metric drawings; therefore, the scale (spacing between hatch lines) is much greater than for inch drawings. Because *Limits* values for metric sheet sizes are greater than for inch-based drawings (25.4 times greater than comparable inch drawings), the ISO hatch pattern scales are automatically compensated. If you want to use an ISO pattern with inch-based draw-ings, calculate a hatch pattern scale based on the drawing scale factor and multiply by .039 (1/25.4).

Angle
The *Angle* specification determines the angle (slant) of the hatch lines. The default angle of 0 represents whatever angle is displayed in the pattern's image tile. Any value entered deflects the existing pattern by the specified value (in degrees). The value entered in this box is held in the *HPANG* system variable.

Spacing
This option is enabled only if *User-defined* pattern is specified. Enter a value for the distance between lines.

Double
Only for a *User-defined* pattern, check this box to have a second set of lines drawn at 90 degrees to the original set.

Exploded
Bhatch normally draws a hatch pattern as one object, similar to a *Block*. Checking this box causes the hatch patterns to be pre-exploded when inserted. (This is similar to *Inserting* a *Block* with an asterisk [*] prefixing the *Block* name.) Exploded hatch patterns allow you to edit the hatch lines individually. Exploded hatch patterns are non-associative.

Boundary—Selecting the Hatch Area
Once the hatch pattern and options have been selected, you must indicate to AutoCAD what area(s) should be hatched. Either the *Pick Points* method, *Select Objects* method, or a combination of both can be used to accomplish this.

Pick Points <
This tile should be selected if you want AutoCAD to automatically determine the boundaries for hatch-ing using the <u>ray-casting</u> technique. You only need to select a point <u>inside</u> the area you want to hatch. The point selected must be inside a <u>completely closed shape</u>. When the *Pick Points* tile is selected, AutoCAD gives the following prompts.

    Select internal point: **PICK**
    Selecting everything...
    Selecting everything visible...

Analyzing the selected data...
Analyzing the internal islands...
Select internal point: **PICK** another area or **Enter**

When an internal point is PICKed, AutoCAD traces and highlights the boundary. The interior area is then analyzed for islands to be included in the hatch boundary. Multiple boundaries can be designated by selecting multiple internal points. Type *U* to undo the last one, if necessary.

For the example section view, only one internal point is selected, as shown in Figure 26-6. From that point, AutoCAD casts rays in four directions to find the nearest object, then traces along the objects in a counter-clockwise direction until a closed boundary is found. Next, the "islands" are recognized. The location of the point selected is usually not critical. However, the point must be PICKed inside the expected boundary. If there are any gaps in the area, a complete boundary cannot be formed and a boundary error message appears (Fig. 26-7).

Figure 26-6

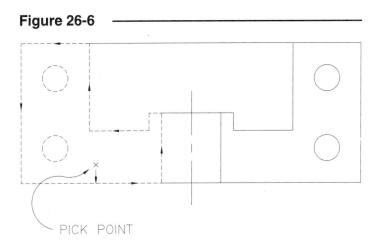

PICK POINT

Figure 26-7

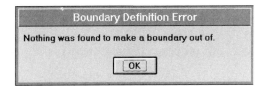

Select Objects<
Alternately, you can designate the boundary with the *Select Objects* method. Using the *Select Objects* method, you specify the boundary objects rather than letting AutoCAD locate a boundary using ray-casting. With the *Select Objects* method, no temporary *Pline* boundary is created as with the *Pick Points* (ray-casting) method. Therefore, the selected objects must form a closed shape with no gaps or overlaps. If gaps exist (Fig. 26-8) or if the objects extend past the desired hatch area (Fig. 26-9), AutoCAD cannot interpret the intended hatch area correctly, and problems will occur.

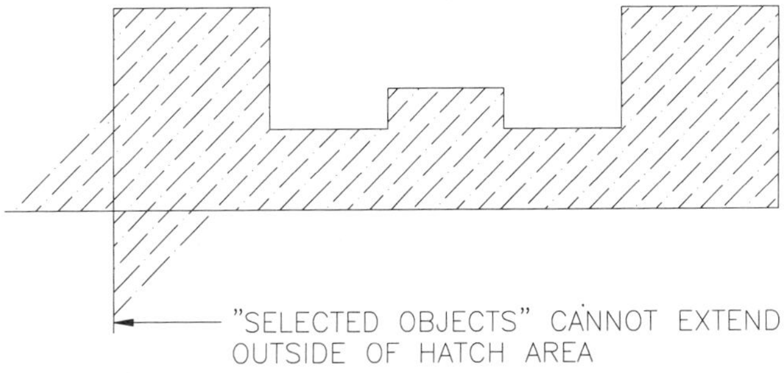

The *Select Objects* option can operate nicely in conjunction with the *Pick Points* method. For example, assume that you used *Pick Points* to determine the boundary (with islands) and then used the *Remove Islands* feature to remove interior objects (such as circular "holes") from the hatch boundary set. If you later decided to include those islands, you could use *Select Objects* to bring those islands back into the boundary set.

Figure 26-8

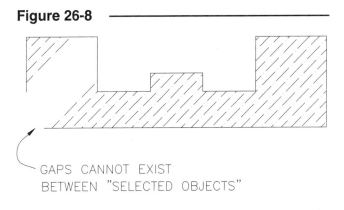

GAPS CANNOT EXIST
BETWEEN "SELECTED OBJECTS"

Figure 26-9

"SELECTED OBJECTS" CANNOT EXTEND
OUTSIDE OF HATCH AREA

Remove Islands <
PICKing this tile allows you to select specific islands to remove from those AutoCAD has found (by ray-casting) within the outer boundary. If hatch lines have been drawn, be careful to *Zoom* in close enough to select the desired boundary and not the hatch pattern.

View Selections <
Clicking the *View Selections* tile causes AutoCAD to highlight all selected boundaries. This can be used as a check to ensure the desired areas are selected.

Advanced...
This tile invokes the *Advanced Options* dialogue box (see *Advanced Options* Dialogue Box).

Preview Hatch <
You should always use the *Preview Hatch* option after specifying the hatch parameters and selecting boundaries, but before you *Apply* the hatch. This option allows you to temporarily look at the hatch pattern in your drawing with the current settings applied and allows you to adjust the settings, if necessary, before using *Apply*. After viewing the drawing, pressing the *Continue* tile redisplays the *Boundary Hatch* dialogue box, allowing you to make adjustments.

Inherit Properties <
This option allows you to select a hatch pattern from one existing in the drawing. The dialogue box disappears and the "Select hatch objects:" prompt appears. PICKing a previously drawn hatch pattern resets all the parameters in the *Boundary Hatch* dialogue box for subsequent application to another hatch area.

Associative
This checkbox toggles (on or off) the associative property for newly applied hatch patterns. Associative hatch patterns automatically update by conforming to the new boundary shape when the boundary is changed (see Fig. 26-2). A non-associative hatch pattern is static even when the boundary changes.

Apply
This is typically the <u>last step</u> to the hatching process with *Bhatch*. Selecting *Apply* causes AutoCAD to create the hatch using all the parameters specified in the *Boundary Hatch* dialogue box and return to the Command: prompt for further drawing and editing.

Advanced Options Dialogue Box

Figure 26-10

Object Type
Bhatch creates *Polyline* or *Region* boundaries. This option is enabled only when the *Retain Boundaries* box is checked (Fig. 26-10).

Define Boundary Set
By default, AutoCAD examines <u>all objects in the drawing</u> when determining the boundaries by the ray-casting method. (The *From Everything on Screen* box is checked by default when you begin the *Bhatch* command.) For complex drawings, examining all objects can take some time. In that case, you may want to specify a smaller boundary set for AutoCAD to consider. Clicking the *Make New Boundary Set* tile clears the dialogue boxes and permits you to select objects or select a smaller window to define the new set.

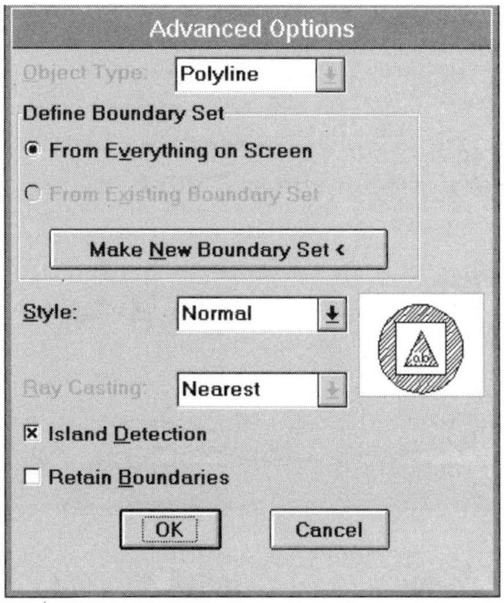

Style

This section allows you to specify how the hatch pattern is drawn when the area inside the defined boundary contains text or closed areas (islands). Select the text from the list or PICK the icons displayed in the window. These options are applicable <u>only</u> when interior objects (islands) have been included in the selection set (considered for hatching). Otherwise, if only the outer shape is included in the selection set, the results are identical to the *Ignore* option.

Normal

This should be used for most applications of *Bhatch*. Text or closed shapes within the outer border are considered in such cases. Hatching will begin at the outer boundary and move inward alternating between applying and not applying the pattern as interior shapes or text are encountered (Fig. 26-11).

Figure 26-11 ————————————

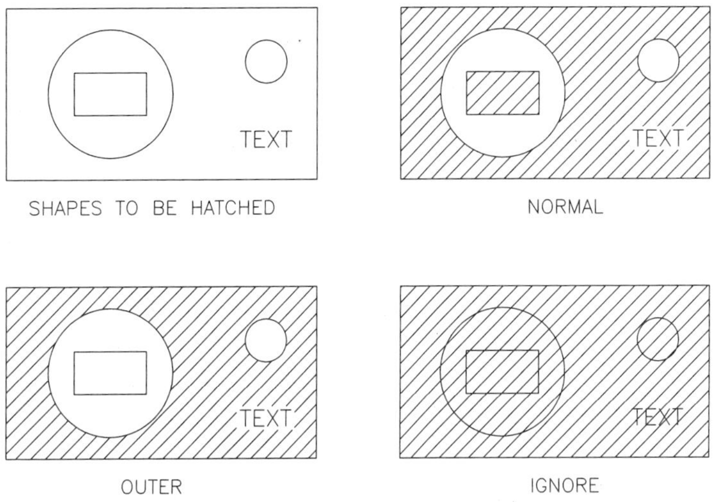

Outer

This option causes AutoCAD to hatch only the outer closed shape. Hatching is turned off for all interior closed shapes (Fig. 26-11).

Ignore

Ignore draws the hatch pattern from the outer boundary inward ignoring any interior shapes. The resulting hatch pattern is drawn through the interior shapes (Fig. 26-11).

Ray-Casting

<u>When *Island Detection* is turned off</u>, you can determine the ray-casting <u>direction</u> used. The default ray-casting option (when using the *Pick Points* method) is *Nearest*, meaning that AutoCAD locates the nearest object to the selected point by casting "rays" in four directions. When you PICK a point, the nearest object found might not be the boundary you intended, but may instead be an island (Fig. 26-12). Since *Island Detection* is off, AutoCAD gives an error message of "Point is outside of boundary." You can select a new point or change to a specific X or Y direction for ray-casting by clicking the pop-down list. The options are *Nearest*, +*X*, -*X*, +*Y*, and -*Y*.

Figure 26-12 ————————————

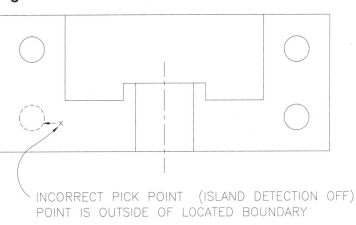

INCORRECT PICK POINT   (ISLAND DETECTION OFF)
POINT IS OUTSIDE OF LOCATED BOUNDARY

Island Detection

Removing the check in this box causes AutoCAD to trace the outer boundary only and ignore any internal closed areas (islands) when the hatch pattern is applied.

Retain Boundaries

When AutoCAD uses the ray-casting method to locate a boundary for hatching, a temporary *Pline* is created for hatching, then discarded after the hatching process. Checking this box forces AutoCAD to <u>keep</u> the boundary. When the box is checked, *Bhatch* creates two objects—the hatch pattern and the boundary object. (You can specify whether you want to create a *Pline* or a *Region* boundary in the *Object Type* pop-down list.) Using this option and erasing the hatch pattern accomplishes the same results as using the *Boundary* command.

Figure 26-13

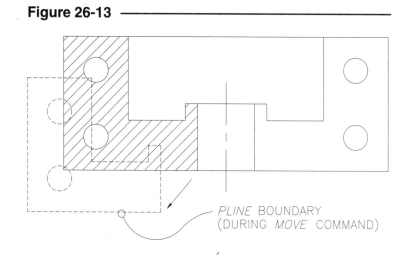

PLINE BOUNDARY
(DURING *MOVE* COMMAND)

After using *Bhatch*, the *Pline* or *Region* can be used for other purposes. To test this function, complete a *Bhatch* with the *Retain Boundaries* box checked; then use *Move* (make sure you select the boundary) to reveal the new boundary object.

HATCH

PULL-DOWN MENU	SCREEN MENU	TYPE IN	TABLET MENU
—	—	*HATCH*	—

Hatch must be typed at the keyboard since it is not available from the menus. *Hatch* operates in a command line format with many of the options available in the *Bhatch* dialogue box. However, *Hatch* creates a <u>non-associative</u> hatch pattern and <u>does not use the ray-casting</u> method ("select internal point:") to create a boundary. Generally, *Bhatch* would be used instead of *Hatch* except for special cases.

You can use *Hatch* to find a boundary from existing objects. The objects must form a complete closed shape, just as with *Bhatch*. The shape can be composed of <u>one</u> closed object such as a *Pline, Polygon, Spline, Circle*, etc., or composed of <u>several</u> objects forming a closed area such as *Lines* and *Arcs*, etc. For example, the shape in Figure 26-14 can be hatched correctly with *Hatch*, whether it is composed of one object (*Pline, Region*, etc.) or several objects (*Lines, Arc*, etc.).

Figure 26-14

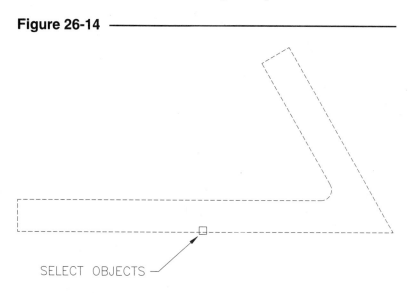

SELECT OBJECTS

If you select several objects to define the boundary, the objects must comprise <u>only the boundary shape</u> and not extend past the desired boundary. If objects extend past the desired boundary (Fig. 26-15) or if there are gaps, the resulting hatch will be <u>incorrect</u> as shown in Figures 26-8 and 26-9.

Figure 26-15

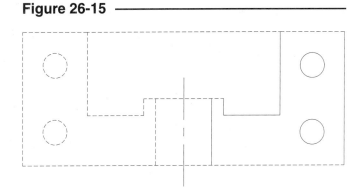

```
Command: hatch
Pattern (? or name/U,style) <ANSI31>: (style or pattern name)
Scale for pattern <1.0000>: (value) or Enter
Angle for pattern <0>: (value) or Enter
Select hatch boundaries or RETURN for direct hatch option
Select objects: PICK
Select objects: Enter
Command:
```

Direct Hatch

With the *Direct Hatch* method of *Hatch*, you <u>specify points</u> to define the boundary, <u>not objects</u>. The significance of this method is that you can create a hatch pattern without using existing objects as the boundary. In addition, you can select whether you want to <u>retain or discard the boundary</u> after the pattern is applied (Fig. 26-16).

Figure 26-16

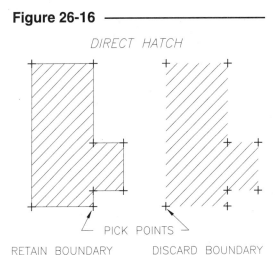

DIRECT HATCH

PICK POINTS

RETAIN BOUNDARY   DISCARD BOUNDARY

```
Command: hatch
Pattern (? or name/U,style) <ANSI31>: (pattern name, style) or Enter
Scale for pattern <1.0000>: (value) or Enter
Angle for pattern <0>: (value) or Enter
Select hatch boundaries or RETURN for direct hatch option
Select objects: Enter
Retain polyline? <N> Y or Enter
From point: PICK or (coordinates)
Arc/Close/Length/Undo/<Next point>: PICK or (coordinates)
Arc/Close/Length/Undo/<Next point>: PICK or (coordinates)
Arc/Close/Length/Undo/<Next point>: PICK or (coordinates)
Arc/Close/Length/Undo/<Next point>: c
From point or RETURN to apply hatch: Enter
Command:
```

R13

For special cases when you do not want a hatch area boundary to appear in the drawing (Fig. 26-17), you can use the *Direct Hatch* method to specify a hatch area, then discard the boundary *Pline*.

Figure 26-17

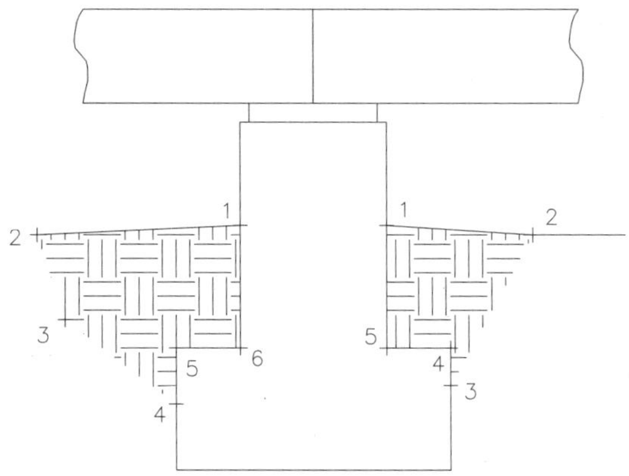

HATCHEDIT

PULL-DOWN MENU	SCREEN MENU	TYPE IN	TABLET MENU
Modify *Edit Hatch...*	*MODIFY* *HatchEd:*	*HATCHEDIT*	*17,W*

Hatchedit allows you to modify an <u>existing associative</u> hatch pattern in the drawing. This feature of AutoCAD makes the hatching process more flexible because you can hatch several areas to quickly create a "rough" drawing, then retroactively fine-tune the hatching parameters when the drawing nears completion with *Hatchedit*.

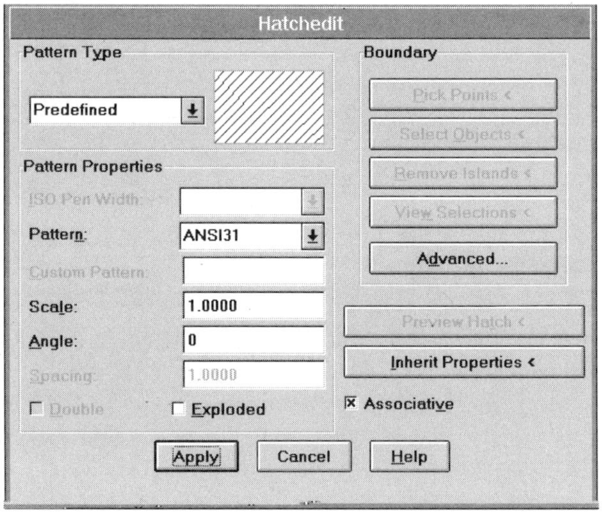

Invoking the *Hatchedit* command by any method produces the *Hatchedit* dialogue box (Fig. 26-18). The dialogue box provides options for changing the *Pattern, Scale, Angle,* and *Style* properties of the existing hatch. You can also change the hatch to non-associative and *Exploded*.

Apparent in Figure 26-18, the *Hatchedit* dialogue box is essentially the same as the *Boundary Hatch* dialogue box with some of the options disabled. For an explanation of the options that are available with *Hatchedit*, see *Boundary Hatch* earlier in this chapter.

Figure 26-18

DRAWING CUTTING PLANE LINES

Most section views (full, half, and offset sections) require a cutting plane line to indicate the plane on which the object is cut. The cutting plane line is drawn in a view <u>adjacent</u> to the section view because the line indicates the plane of the cut from its edge view. (In the section view, the cutting plane is perpendicular to the line of sight, therefore, not visible as a line.)

Standards provide two optional line types for cutting plane lines. In AutoCAD, the two linetypes are *Dashed* and *Phantom,* as shown in Figure 26-19. Arrows at the ends of the cutting plane line indicate the <u>line-of-sight</u> for the section view.

Figure 26-19

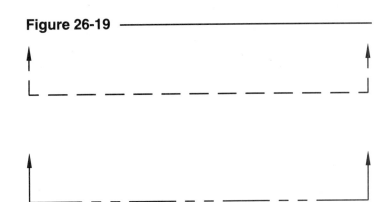

Cutting plane lines should be drawn or plotted in a <u>heavy</u> line weight. This is accomplished in AutoCAD by using the *Pline* command to draw the cutting plane line having width assigned using the *Width* option. For potting full size, a width of .02 for small plots (8.5 x 11, or 17 x 22) to .03 for large plots is recommended. Keep in mind that appearance of the *Pline Width* is affected by the drawing plot scale, and, therefore, *Width* should be increased or decreased by that proportion. For example, if you changed the *Limits*, multiply .02 times the drawing scale factor. (See Chapter 13 for information on drawing scale factor.)

Figure 26-20

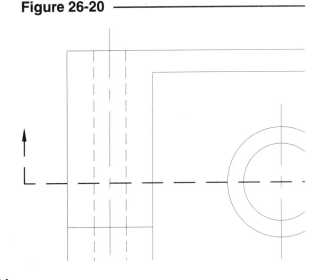

For the example section view, a cutting plane line is created in the top view to indicate the plane on which the object is cut and the line of sight for the section view (Fig. 26-21). (The cutting plane could be drawn in the side view, but the top would be much clearer.) First, a *New* layer named CUT is created and the *Dashed linetype* is assigned to the layer. The layer is *Set* as the *Current* layer. Next, construct a *Pline* with the desired *Width* to represent the cutting plane line.

Figure 26-21

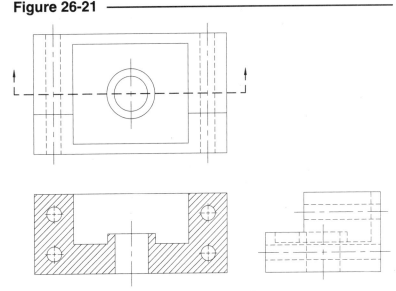

The resulting cutting plane line appears as shown in Figure 26-21 but without the arrow heads. The horizontal center line for the hole (top view) was *Erased* before creating the cutting plane line.

The last step is to add arrowheads to the ends of the cutting plane line. This can be accomplished by either using the *Solid* command to draw a filled triangle or drawing a dimension *Leader*. Since you only want the arrowhead to show, draw the leader line "on top of" the *Pline* and as short as possible. The *Leader* can be *Scaled* or *Rotated* if necessary, then *Copied* to the other end of the cutting plane line. See Chapter 28, Dimensioning, for details on the *Leader* command.

The resulting multiview drawing with section view is complete and ready for dimensioning, drawing a border, and inserting a title block (Fig. 26-21).

CHAPTER EXERCISES

For the following exercises, create the section views as instructed. Use an appropriate prototype drawing for each unless instructed otherwise. Include a border and title block for each drawing.

1. *Open* the **SADDLE** drawing that you created in Chapter 24. Convert the front view to a full section. *Save* the drawing as **SADL-SEC**. *Plot* the drawing at **1=1** scale.

2. Make a multiview drawing of the Bearing shown in Figure 26-22. Convert the front view to a full section view. Add the necessary cutting plane line in the top view. *Save* the drawing as **BEAR-SEC**. Make a *Plot* at full size.

Figure 26-22

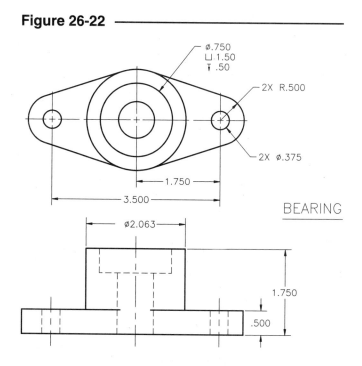

BEARING

3. Create a multiview drawing of the Clip shown in Figure 26-23. Include a side view as a full section view. You can use the **CLIP** drawing you created in Chapter 24 and convert the side view to a section view. Add the necessary cutting plane line in the front view. *Plot* the finished drawing at **1=1** scale and *Saveas* **CLIP-SEC**.

Figure 26-23

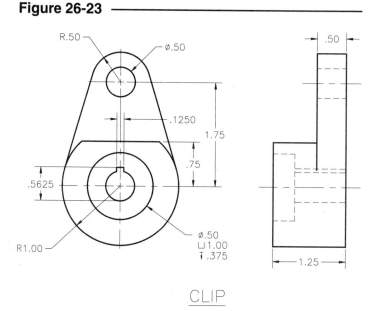

CLIP

4. Create a multiview drawing, including two full sections of the Stop Block as shown in Figure 26-24. Section B-B' should replace the side view shown in the figure. *Save* the drawing as **SPBK-SEC**. *Plot* the drawing at **1=2** scale.

Figure 26-24

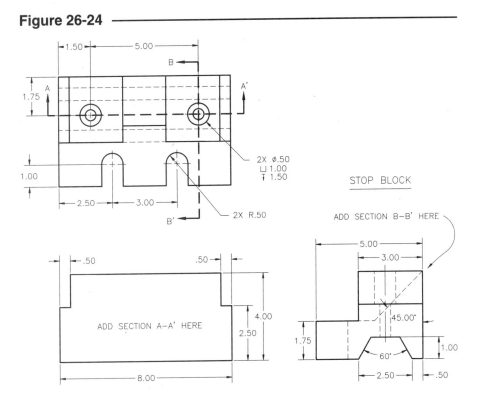

5. Make a multiview drawing, including a half section of the Pulley. All vertical dimensions are diameters. Two views (including the half section) are sufficient to describe the part. Add the necessary cutting plane line. *Save* the drawing as **PUL-SEC** and make a *Plot* at **1=1** scale.

Figure 26-25

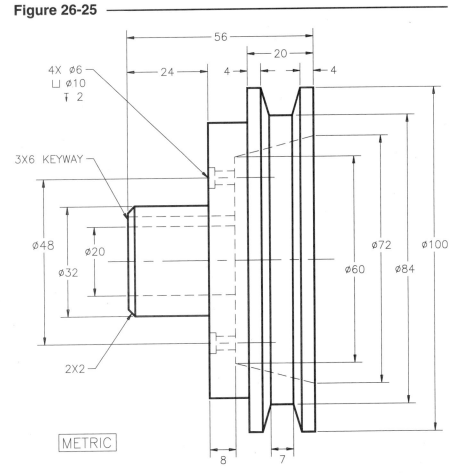

6. Draw the Grade Beam foundation detail in Figure 26-26. Do not include the dimensions in your drawing. Use the **Bhatch** command to hatch the concrete slab with **AR-CONC** hatch pattern. Use *Sketch* to draw the grade line and *Hatch* with the **EARTH** hatch pattern.   *Save* the drawing as **GRADBEAM**.

Figure 26-26

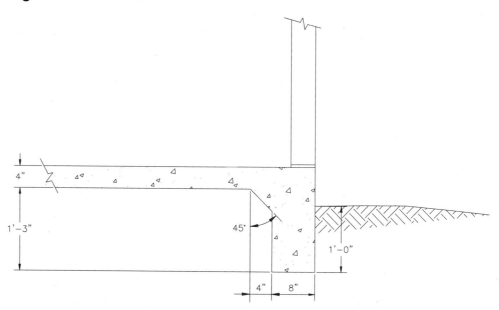

Chapter 27

AUXILIARY VIEWS

Chapter Objectives

After completing this chapter you should:

1. be able to use the *Rotate* option of *Snap* to change the angle of the *SNAP*, *GRID*, and *ORTHO*;

2. know how to use the *Offset* command to create parallel line copies;

3. be able to use *Xline* and *Ray* to create construction lines for auxiliary views.

BASICS

AutoCAD provides no features explicitly for the creation of auxiliary views in a 2D drawing. No new commands are discussed in this chapter. There are, however, three particular features that have been discussed earlier that can assist you in construction of auxiliary views. Those features are the *SNAP* rotation, the *Offset* command, and the *Xline* and *Ray* commands.

An auxiliary view is a supplementary view among a series of multiviews. The auxiliary view is drawn in addition to the typical views that are mutually perpendicular (top, front, side). An auxiliary view is one that is normal (the line-of-sight is perpendicular) to an inclined surface of the object. Therefore, the auxiliary view is constructed by projecting in a 90 degree direction from the edge view of an inclined surface in order to show the true size and shape of the inclined surface. The edge view of the inclined surface could be at any angle (depending on the object), so lines are typically drawn parallel and perpendicular relative to that edge view. Hence, the *SNAP* rotation feature, the *Offset* command, and the *Xline* and *Ray* commands can provide assistance in this task.

Figure 27-1

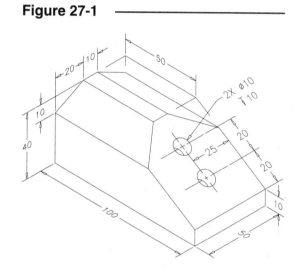

An example mechanical part used for the application of these AutoCAD features related to auxiliary view construction is shown in Figure 27-1. As you can see, there is an inclined surface that contains two drilled holes. To describe this object adequately, an auxiliary view should be created to show the true size and shape of the inclined surface.

This chapter explains the construction of a partial auxiliary view for the example object in Figure 27-1.

CONSTRUCTING AN AUXILIARY VIEW

Setting Up the Principal Views

To begin this drawing, the typical steps are followed for drawing setup (Chapter 13). Because the dimensions are in millimeters, *Limits* should be set accordingly. For example, to provide enough space to draw the views full size and to plot full size on an A4 sheet, *Limits* of 297 x 210 are specified.

In preparation for the auxiliary view, the principal views are "blocked in," as shown in Figure 27-2. The purpose of this step is to ensure that the desired views fit and are optimally spaced within the allocated

Figure 27-2

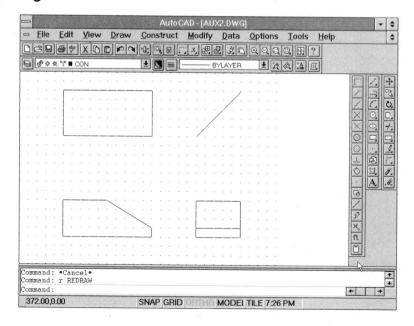

Limits. If there is too little or too much room, adjustments can be made to the *Limits.* Notice that space has been allotted between the views for a partial auxiliary view to be projected from the front view.

Before additional construction on the principal views is undertaken, initial steps in the construction of the partial auxiliary view should be performed. The projection of the auxiliary view requires drawing lines perpendicular and parallel to the inclined surface. One or more of the three alternatives (explained next) can be used.

Using *Snap Rotate*

One possibility to construct an auxiliary view is to use the *Snap* command with the *Rotate* option. This action permits you to rotate the *SNAP* to any angle about a specified base point. The *GRID* automatically follows the *SNAP*. Turning *ORTHO ON* forces *Lines* to be drawn orthogonally with respect to the rotated *SNAP* and *GRID*.

Figure 27-3 displays the *SNAP* and *GRID* after rotation. The command syntax is given below.

Figure 27-3

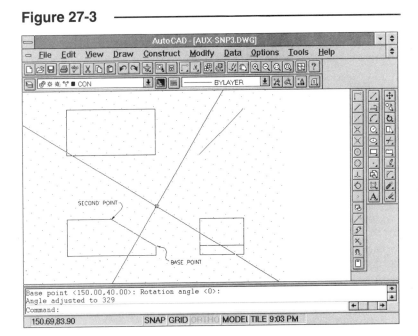

Command: **snap**
Snap spacing or ON/OFF/Aspect/Rotate/Style <current>: **r**
Base point <0.00,0.00>: **PICK** or (**coordinates**) (Starts a rubberband line.)
Rotation angle <0>: **PICK** or (**value**) (PICK to specify the second point to define the angle.
See Fig. 27-3.)
Command:

PICK (or specify coordinates for) the endpoint of the *Line* representing the inclined surface as the Base point. At the "Rotation angle:" prompt, a value can be entered or another point (the other end of the inclined *Line*) can be PICKed. Use *OSNAP* when PICKing the *END*points. If you want to enter a value but don't know what angle to rotate to, use *List* to display the angle of the inclined *Line*. The *GRID* and *SNAP* should align with the inclined plane as shown in Figure 27-3.

After rotating the *SNAP* and *GRID*, the partial auxiliary view can be "blocked in," as displayed in Figure 27-4. Begin by projecting *Lines* up from and perpendicular to the inclined surface. (Make sure *ORTHO* is *ON*.) Next, two *Lines* representing the depth of the view should be constructed parallel to the inclined surface and perpendicular to the previous two projection lines. The depth dimension of the object in the auxiliary view is equal to the depth dimension in the top or right view. *Trim* as necessary.

Locate the centers of the holes in the auxiliary view and construct two *Circles*. It is generally preferred to construct circular shapes in the view in which they appear as circles, then project to the other views. That is particularly true for this type of auxiliary since the other views contain ellipses. The centers can be located by projection from the front view or by *Offsetting Lines* from the view outline.

Next, project lines from the *Circles* and their centers back to the inclined surface. Use of a hidden line layer can be helpful here. While the *SNAP* and *GRID* are rotated, construct the *Lines* representing the bottom of the holes in the front view. (Alternately, *Offset* could be used to copy the inclined edge down to the hole bottoms; then *Trim* the unwanted portions of the *Lines*.)

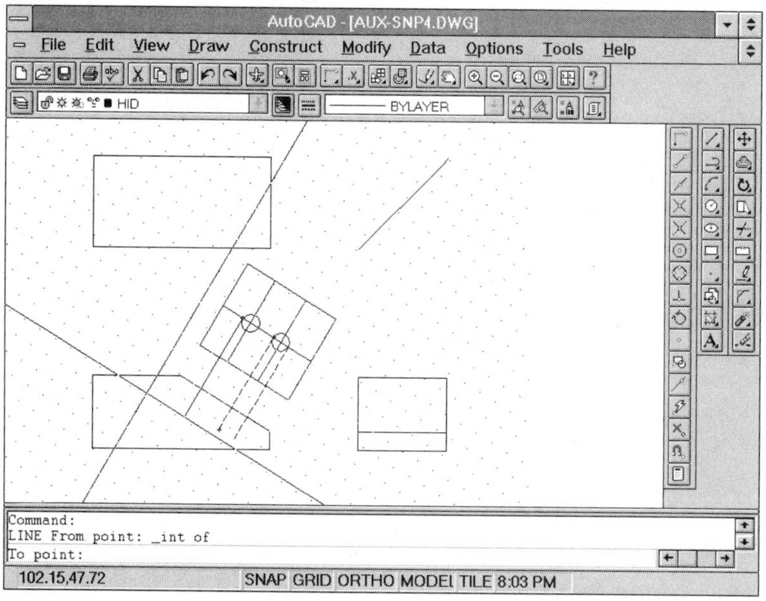

Rotating *SNAP* Back to the Original Position
Before details can be added to the other views, the *SNAP* and *GRID* should be rotated back to the original position. It is very important to rotate back using the <u>same base point</u>. Fortunately, AutoCAD remembers the original base point so you can accept the default for the prompt. Next, enter a value of **0** when rotating back to the original position. (When using the *Snap Rotate* option, the value entered for the angle of rotation is absolute, not relative to the current position. For example, if the *Snap* was rotated to 45 degrees, rotate back to 0 degrees, not -45.)

Figure 27-4

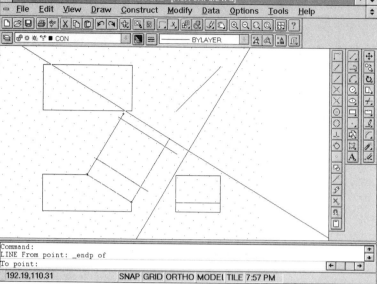

Figure 27-5

Command: **snap**
Snap spacing or ON/OFF/Aspect/Rotate/Style <2.00>: **r**
Base point <150.00,40.00>: **Enter**   (AutoCAD remembers the previous base point.)
Rotation angle <329>: **0**
Command:

Construction of multiview drawings with auxiliaries typically involves repeated rotation of the *SNAP* and *GRID* to the angle of the inclined surface and back again as needed.

With the *SNAP* and *GRID* in the original position, details can be added to the other views as shown in Figure 27-6. Since the two circles appear as ellipses in the top and right side views, project lines from the circles' centers and limiting elements on the inclined surface. Locate centers for the two *Ellipses* to be drawn in the top and right side views.

Figure 27-6

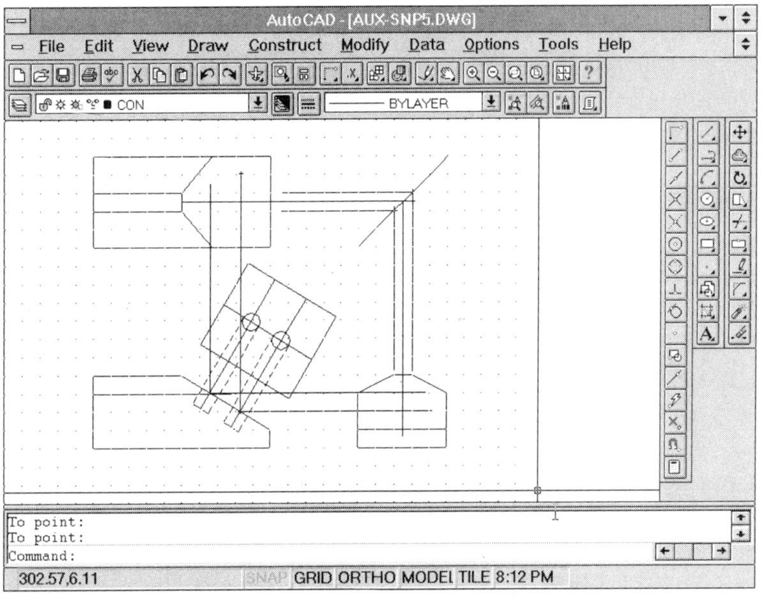

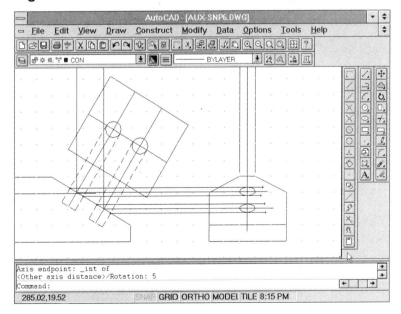

Use the *Ellipse* command to construct the ellipses in the top and right side views. Using the *Center* option of *Ellipse*, specify the center by PICKing with the *INTersection OSNAP* mode. *OSNAP* to the appropriate construction line *INTersection* for the first axis endpoint. For the second axis endpoint (as shown), use the actual circle diameter, since that dimension is not foreshortened.

Figure 27-7

The remaining steps for completing the drawing involve finalizing the perimeter shape of the partial auxiliary view and *Copying* the *Ellipses* to the bottom of the hole positions. The *SNAP* and *GRID* should be rotated back to project the new edges found in the front view (Fig. 27-8).

At this point, the multiview drawing with auxiliary view is ready for center lines, dimensioning, and construction or insertion of a border and title block.

Figure 27-8

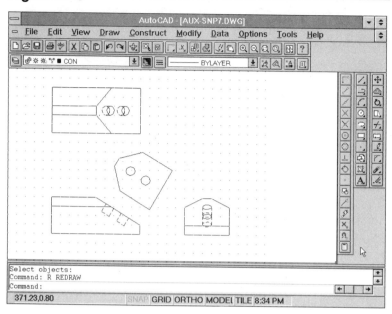

Using the *Offset* Command

Another possibility, and an alternative to the *SNAP* rotation, is to use *Offset* to make parallel *Lines*. This command can be particularly useful for construction of the "blocked in" partial auxiliary view because it is not necessary to rotate the *SNAP* and *GRID*.

Invoke the *Offset* command and specify a distance. The first distance is arbitrary. Specify an appropriate value between the front view inclined plane and the nearest edge of the auxiliary view (20 for the example). *Offset* the new *Line* at a distance of 50 (for the example) or PICK two points (equal to the depth of the view).

Note that the *Offset* lines have equal length to the original and therefore do not require additional editing (Fig. 27-9).

Figure 27-9

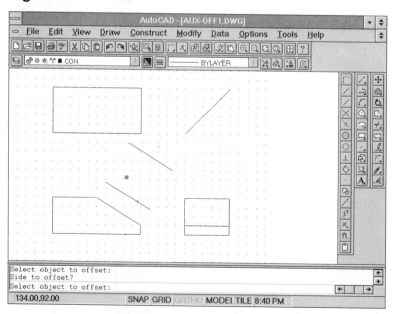

Next, two *Lines* would be drawn between *ENDpoints* of the existing offset lines to complete the rectangle. *Offset* could be used again to construct additional lines to facilitate the construction of the two circles in the partial auxiliary view (Fig 27-10).

From this point forward, the construction process would be similar to the example given previously (Figs. 27-5 through 27-8). Even though *Offset* does not require that the *SNAP* be *Rotated*, the complete construction of the auxiliary view could be simplified by using the rotated *SNAP* and *GRID* in conjunction with *Offset*.

Figure 27-10

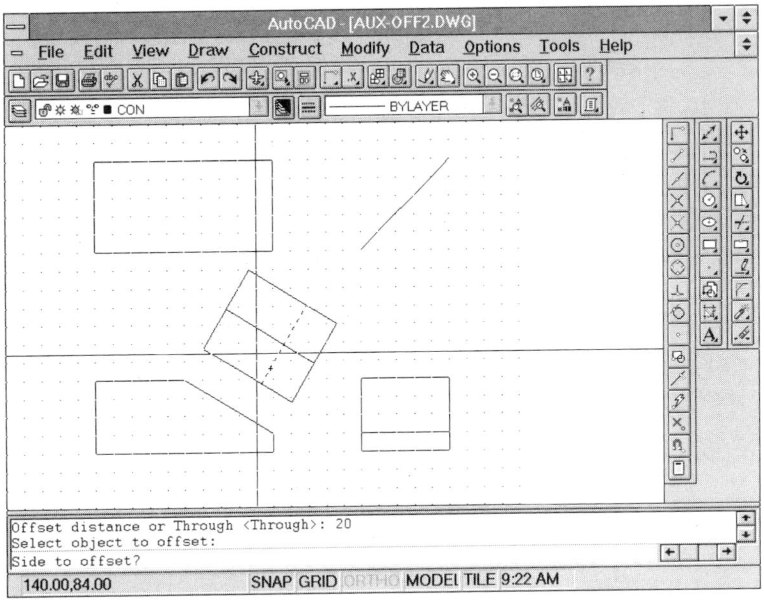

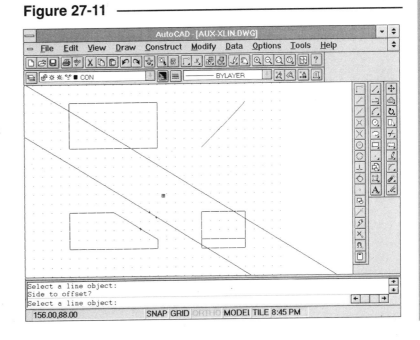

Using the *Xline* and *Ray* Commands

As a third alternative for construction of auxiliary views, the *Xline* and *Ray* commands could be used to create construction lines. This *Xline* command offers several options shown below.

> Command: **Xline**
> Hor/Ver/Ang/Bisect/Offset/<From point:>

The *Ang* option can be used to create a construction line at a specified angle. In this case, the angle specified would be that of the inclined plane or perpendicular to the inclined plane. The *Offset* option works well for drawing construction lines parallel to the inclined plane, especially in the case where the angle of the plane is not known.

Figure 27-11 illustrates the use of *Xline Offset* to create construction lines for the partial auxiliary view. The *Offset* option operates similarly to the *Offset* command described previously. Remember that an *Xline* extends to infinity but can be *Trimmed*, in which case it is converted to *Ray* (*Trim* once) or to a *Line* (*Trim* twice). See Chapter 15 for more information on the *Xline* command.

Figure 27-11

The *Ray* command also creates construction lines; however, the *Ray* has one anchored point and the other end extends to infinity.

Command: **Ray**
From point: **PICK** or (**coordinates**)
To point: **PICK** or (**coordinates**)

Rays are helpful for auxiliary view construction when you want to create projection lines perpendicular to the inclined plane. In Figure 27-12, two *Rays* are constructed from the *END*points of the inclined plane and *PER*pendicular to the existing *Xlines*. Using *Xlines* and *Rays* in conjunction is an <u>excellent method</u> for "blocking in" the view.

There are two strategies for creating drawings using *Xlines* and *Rays*. First, these construction lines can be created on a separate layer and set up as a framework for the object lines. The object lines would then be drawn "on top of" the construction lines using *Osnaps*, but would be drawn on the object layer. The con-

Figure 27-12

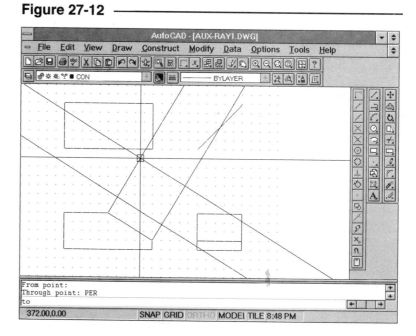

struction layer would be *Frozen* for plotting. The other strategy is to create the construction lines on the object layer. Through a series of *Trims* and other modifications, the *Xlines* and *Rays* are transformed to the finished object lines.

Now that you are aware of several methods for constructing auxiliary views, use any one method or a combination of methods for your drawings. No matter which methods are used, the final lines that are needed for the finished auxiliary view should be the same. It is up to you to use the methods that are the most appropriate for the particular application, or are the easiest and quickest for you personally.

Constructing Full Auxiliary Views

The construction of a full auxiliary view begins with the partial view. After initial construction of the partial view, begin the construction of the full auxiliary by projecting the other edges and features of the object (other than the inclined plane) to the existing auxiliary view.

The procedure for constructing full auxiliary views in AutoCAD is essentially the same as that for partial auxiliary views. Use of the *Offset, Xline,* and *Ray* commands and *SNAP* and *GRID* rotation should be used as illustrated for the partial auxiliary view example. Because a full auxiliary view is projected at the same angle as a partial, the same rotation angle and base point would be used for the *SNAP*.

CHAPTER EXERCISES

For the following exercises, create the multiview drawing, including the partial or full auxiliary view as indicated. Use the appropriate prototype drawing based on the given dimensions and indicated plot scale.

1. Make a multiview drawing with a partial auxiliary view of the example used in this chapter. Refer to Figure 27-1 for dimensions. *Save* the drawing as **CH27EX1**. *Plot* on an "A" size sheet at **1=1** scale.

2. Recreate the views given in Figure 27-13 and add a partial auxiliary view. *Save* the drawing as **CH27EX2** and *Plot* on an "A" size sheet at **2=1** scale.

Figure 27-13

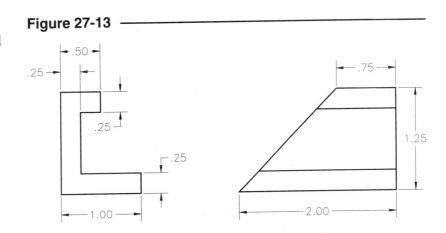

3. Recreate the views shown in Figure 27-14 and add a partial auxiliary view. *Save* the drawing as **CH27EX3**. Make a *Plot* on an "A" size sheet at **1=1** scale.

Figure 27-14

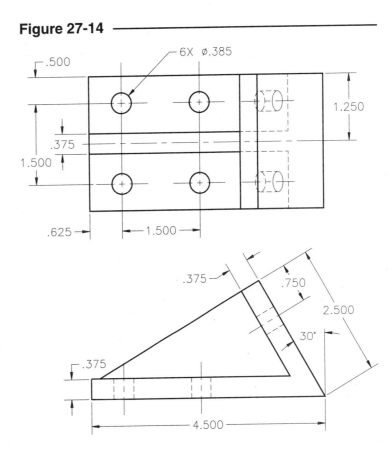

4. Make a multiview drawing of the given views in Figure 27-15. Add a full auxiliary view. *Save* the drawing as **CH27EX4**. *Plot* the drawing at an appropriate scale on an "A" size sheet.

Figure 27-15

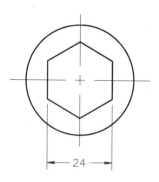

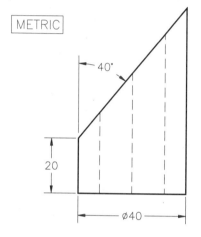

5. Draw the front, top, and a partial auxiliary view of the Holder. Make a *Plot* full size. Save the drawing as **HOLDER**.

Figure 27-16

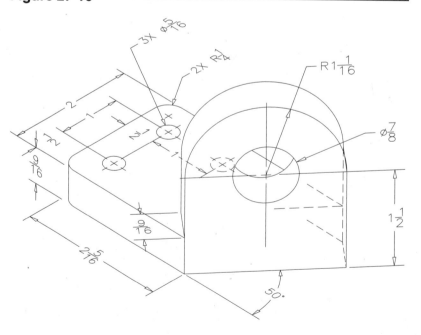

6. Draw three principal views and a full auxiliary view of the V-block shown in Figure 27-17. *Save* the drawing as **VBLOCK**. *Plot* to an accepted scale.

Figure 27-17

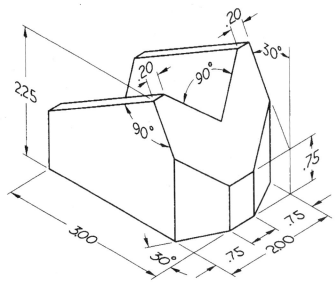

7. Draw two principal views and a partial auxiliary of the Angle Brace. *Save* as **ANGLBRAC**. Make a plot to an accepted scale on an "A" or "B" size sheet.

Figure 27-18

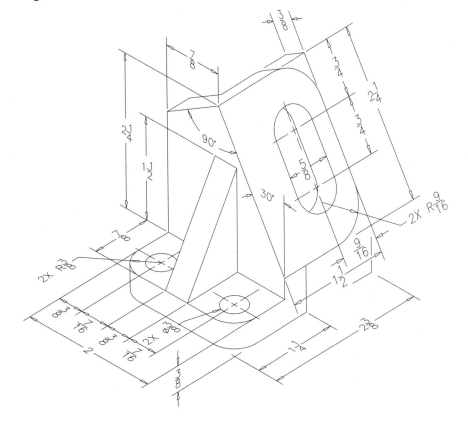

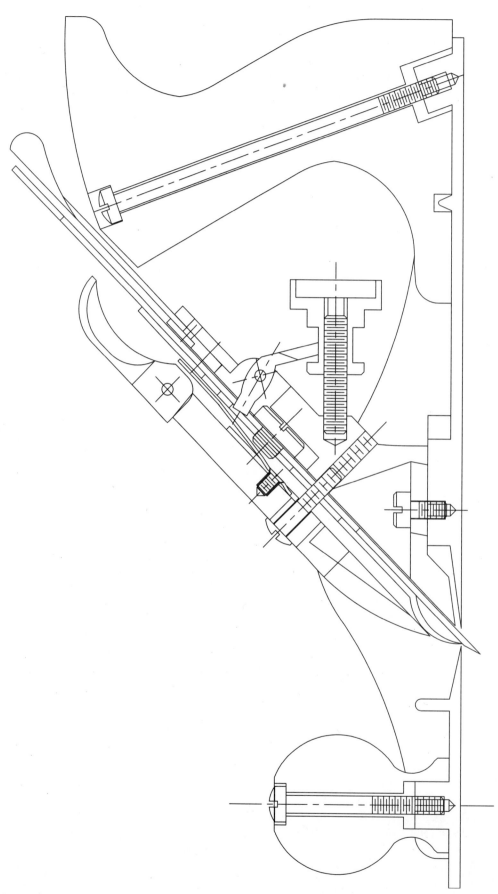

JAKPLANE.DWG Courtesy of Autodesk, Inc.

Chapter 28
DIMENSIONING

Chapter Objectives

After completing this chapter you should:

1. be able to create linear dimensions with *Dimlinear*;

2. be able to append *Dimcontinue* and *Dimbaseline* dimensions to existing dimensions;

3. be able to create *Angular*, *Diameter*, and *Radius* dimensions;

4. know how to affix notes to drawings with *Leaders*;

5. know that *Dimordinate* can be used to specify Xdatum and Ydatum dimensions;

6. be able to create and apply Geometric Dimensioning and Tolerancing symbols using the *Tolerance* command and dialogue boxes;

7. know the possible methods for editing associative dimensions and dimensioning text;

8. know how to dimension isometric drawings.

BASICS

As you know, drawings created with CAD systems should be constructed with the same dimensions and units as the real-world objects they represent. The importance of this practice is evident when you begin applying dimensions to the drawing geometry in AutoCAD. The features of the object that you specify for dimensioning are automatically measured, and those values are used for the dimensioning text. If the geometry has been drawn accurately, the dimensions will be created correctly.

The main features of a dimension are:

Figure 28-1

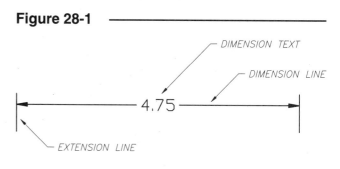

1. Dimension line
2. Extension lines
3. Dimension text (usually a numeric value)
4. Arrowheads or tick marks

AutoCAD dimensioning is <u>semi-automatic</u>. When you invoke a command to create a linear dimension, AutoCAD only requires that you PICK an object or specify the extension line origins (where you want the extension lines to begin) and PICK the location of the dimension line (distance from the object). AutoCAD then measures the feature and draws the extension lines, dimension line, arrowheads, and dimension text.

For linear dimensioning commands, there are <u>two ways</u> to specify placement for a dimension in AutoCAD: you can PICK the <u>object</u> to be dimensioned or you can PICK the two <u>extension line origins</u>. The simplest method is to select the object because it requires only one PICK (Fig. 28-2).

Figure 28-2

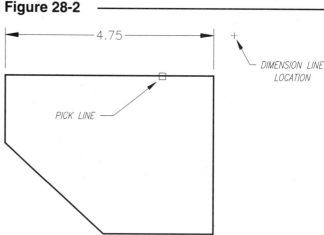

```
Command: dimlinear
First extension line origin or RETURN to
select: Enter
Select object to dimension: PICK
```

The other method is to PICK the extension line origins (Fig. 28-3). *Osnaps* should be used to PICK the object (endpoints in this case) so that the dimension is <u>associated</u> with the object.

Figure 28-3

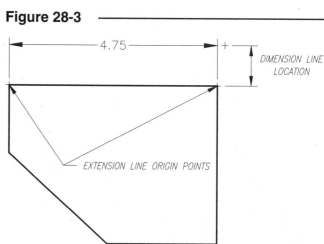

```
Command: dimlinear
First extension line origin or RETURN to
select: PICK
Second extension line origin: PICK
```

Once the dimension is attached to the object, you specify how far you want the dimension to be placed from the object (called the "Dimension line location").

Dimensioning in AutoCAD is <u>associative</u> (by default). Because the extension line origins are "associated" with the geometry, the dimension text automatically updates if the geometry is *Stretched, Rotated, Scaled,* or likewise edited using grips.

Because dimensioning is semi-automatic, <u>dimensioning variables</u> are used to control the way dimensions are created. Dimensioning variables can be used to control features such as text or arrow size, direction of the leader arrow for radial or diametrical dimensions, format of the text, and many other possible options. Groups of variable settings can be named and saved as <u>Dimension Styles</u>. Dimensioning variables and dimension styles are discussed in Chapter 29.

The dimension commands can be invoked by the typical methods. The bottom of the *Draw* pull-down menu contains the dimensioning commands (Fig. 28-4). AutoCAD for Windows users can summon the dimensioning toolbar, which provides an efficient means of inputting commands (Fig. 28-5).

Figure 28-4 ———————————————————————

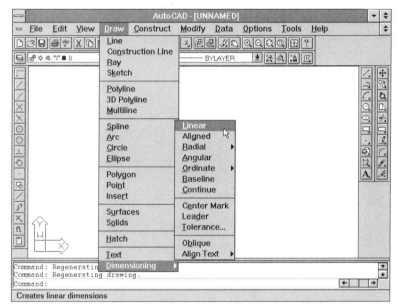

Figure 28-5 ———————————

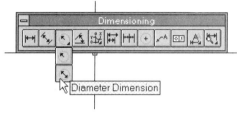

DIMENSION DRAWING COMMANDS

DIMLINEAR

PULL-DOWN MENU	SCREEN MENU	TYPE IN	TABLET MENU
Draw *Dimensioning >* *Linear*	*DRAWDIM* *Linear:*	*DIMLINEAR* *or DIMLIN*	*4,X and 5,X*

Dimlinear creates a <u>horizontal, vertical, or rotated</u> dimension. If the object selected is a horizontal line (or the extension line origins are horizontally oriented), the resulting dimension is a horizontal dimension. This situation is displayed in the previous illustrations (Figs. 28-2 and 28-3), or if the selected object or extension line origins are vertically oriented, the resulting dimension is vertical (Fig. 28-6).

Figure 28-6 ——————————————

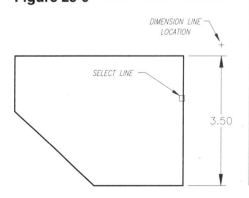

When you dimension an inclined object (or if the selected extension line origins are diagonally oriented), a vertical <u>or</u> horizontal dimension can be made, depending on where you drag the dimension line in relation to the object. If the "Dimension line location" is more to the side, a vertical dimension is created (Fig. 28-7), or if you drag farther up or down, a horizontal dimension results (Fig 28-8).

If you select the extension line origins, it is very important to PICK the <u>object's endpoints</u> if the dimensions are to be truly associative (associated with the geometry). *OSNAP* should be used to find the object's *ENDpoint*, *INTersection*, etc., unless that part of the geometry is located at a *SNAP* point.

Figure 28-7

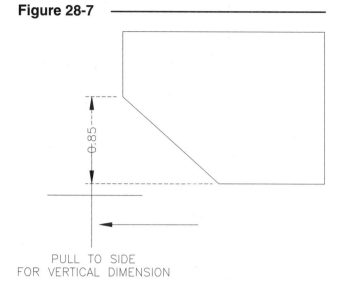

PULL TO SIDE
FOR VERTICAL DIMENSION

Command: **dimlinear**
First extension line origin or RETURN to select: **endp of** PICK
Second extension line origin: **endp of** PICK
Dimension line location (Text/Angle/Horizontal/Vertical/Rotated): **PICK** (where you want the dimension line placed)
Command:

When you pick the location for the dimension line, AutoCAD automatically measures the object and inserts the correct numerical value. The other options are explained next.

Figure 28-8

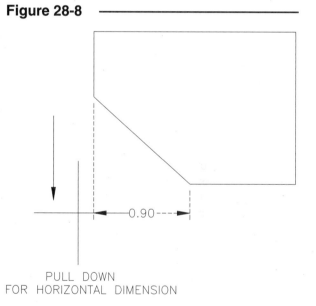

PULL DOWN
FOR HORIZONTAL DIMENSION

Rotated
If you want the dimension line to be drawn at an angle instead of vertical or horizontal, use this option. Selecting an inclined line, as in the previous two illustrations, would normally create a horizontal or vertical dimension. The *Rotated* option allows you to enter an <u>angular value</u> for the dimension line to be drawn. For example, selecting the diagonal line and specifying the appropriate angle would create the dimension shown in Figure 28-9. This object, however, could be more easily dimensioned with the *Dimaligned* command (see *Dimaligned*).

Figure 28-9

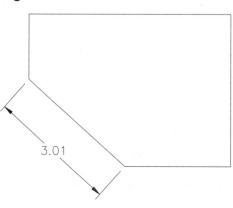

A *Rotated* dimension should be used when the geometry has "steps" or any time the desired dimension line angle is different than the dimensioned feature (when you need extension lines of different lengths). Figure 28-10 illustrates the result of using a *Rotated* dimension to give the correct dimension line angle and extension line origins for the given object. In this case, the extension line origins were explicitly PICKed. The feature of *Rotated* that makes it unique is that you specify the <u>angle</u> that the dimension line will be drawn.

Figure 28-10

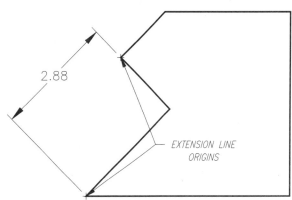

Text

This option allows you to change the existing, or insert additional, text to the AutoCAD-supplied numerical value. The text is entered by the *Edit Mtext* dialogue box (AutoCAD for Windows) or the command line (AutoCAD for DOS). The less-than and greater-than symbols (< >) represent the AutoCAD-supplied dimensional value. Place text or numbers inside the symbols if you want to override the correct measurement (not advised) or place text outside the symbols if you want to add annotation to the numerical value. For example, entering the letters "mm" after the symbols (Fig. 28-11) would create a dimensional value, as shown in Figure 28-12. Notice that the options normally available in the *Edit Mtext* dialogue box are usable, such as *Stacked* fractions, text *Style,* and other *Properties.*

Figure 28-11

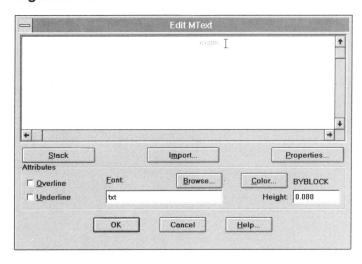

NOTE: Changing the AutoCAD-measured value should be discouraged. If the geometry is drawn accurately, the dimensional value is correct. If you specify other dimension text, the text value is <u>not</u> updated in the event of *Stretching, Rotating,* or otherwise editing the associative dimension.

Figure 28-12

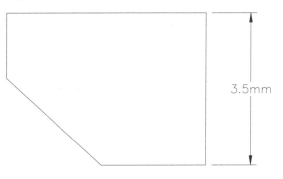

Angle

This creates text drawn at the angle you specify. Use this for special cases when the text must be drawn to a specific angle other than horizontal. (It is also possible to make the text automatically align with the angle of the dimension line using the *Dimension Styles* dialogue box. See Chapter 29).

Horizontal

Use the *Horizontal* option when you want to force a horizontal dimension for an inclined line and the desired placement of the dimension line would otherwise cause a vertical dimension.

Vertical

This option forces a *Vertical* dimension for any case.

DIMALIGNED

PULL-DOWN MENU	SCREEN MENU	TYPE IN	TABLET MENU
Draw Dimensioning > Aligned	DRAWDIM Aligned:	DIMALIGNED or DIMALI	5,Y

An *Aligned* dimension is aligned with (at the same angle as) the selected object or the extension line origins. For example, when *Aligned* is used to dimension the angled object shown in Figure 28-13, the resulting dimension aligns with the *Line*. This holds true for either option—PICKing the object or the extension line origins. If a *Circle* is PICKed, the dimension line is aligned with the selected point on the *Circle* and its center.

Figure 28-13 ——————

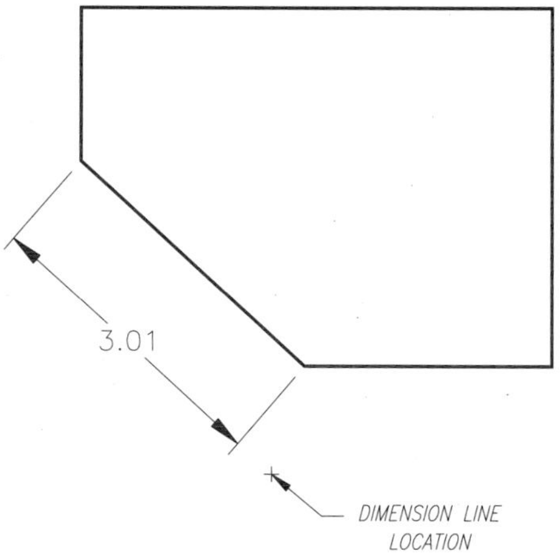

The command syntax for the *Aligned* command accepting the defaults is:

    Command: **dimaligned**
    First extension line origin or RETURN to select: **PICK**
    Second extension line origin: **PICK**
    Dimension line location (Text/Angle): **PICK**
    Command:

The two options (*Text/Angle*) operate similar to those for *Dimlinear*.

Text
You can change the AutoCAD-supplied numerical value or add other annotation to the value. *Text* uses the *Edit Mtext* dialogue box (Windows) or command line (DOS) interface for text entry.

Angle
Enter a value for the angle that the text will be drawn.

The typical application for *Aligned* is for dimensioning an angled but <u>straight</u> feature of an object, as shown in Figure 28-13. *Aligned* should not be used to dimension an object feature that contains "steps," as shown in Figure 28-10. *Aligned* always draws <u>extension lines of equal length</u>.

DIMBASELINE

PULL-DOWN MENU	SCREEN MENU	TYPE IN	TABLET MENU
Draw Dimensioning > Baseline	DRAWDIM Baselin:	DIMBASELINE or DIMBASE	2,X

Dimbaseline allows you to create a dimension that uses an extension line origin from a previously created dimension. Successive *Dimbaseline* dimensions can be used to create the style of dimensioning shown in Figure 28-14.

A baseline dimension must be connected to an existing dimension. If *Dimbaseline* is invoked immediately after another dimensioning command, you are required only to specify the second extension line origin since AutoCAD knows to use the <u>previous</u> dimension's <u>first</u> extension line origin.

Figure 28-14 ——————

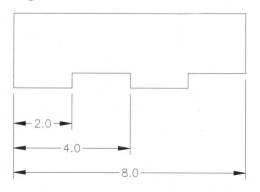

Command: *dimbaseline*
Second extension line origin or RETURN to select: **PICK**
Second extension line origin or RETURN to select: **Enter**
Select base dimension: **Enter**
Command:

The previous dimension's first extension line is used also for the baseline dimension (Fig. 28-15). Therefore, you only specify the second extension line origin. Note that you are not required to specify the dimension line location. AutoCAD spaces the new dimension line automatically, based on the setting of the dimension line increment variable (Chapter 29).

Figure 28-15

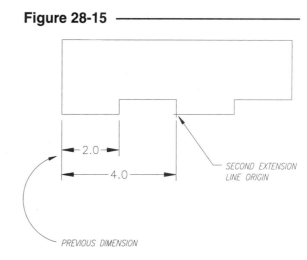

If you wish to create a *Dimbaseline* dimension using a dimension other than the one created immediately preceding, use the "Return to select" option (Fig. 28-16).

Figure 28-16

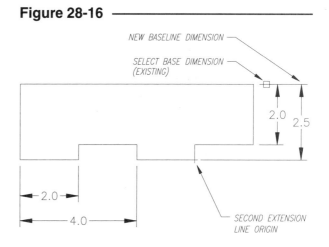

Command: *dimbaseline*
Second extension line origin or RETURN to select: **Enter**
Select base dimension: **PICK** (Select the existing extension line to be used.)
Second extension line origin or RETURN to select: **PICK** (Select the second extension line origin.)
Select base dimension: **Enter**
Command:

The extension line selected as the base dimension becomes the first extension line for the new *Dimbaseline* dimension.

In Release 13, *Dimbaseline* can be used with rotated, aligned, angular, and ordinate dimensions.

DIMCONTINUE

PULL-DOWN MENU	SCREEN MENU	TYPE IN	TABLET MENU
Draw Dimensioning > Continue	*DRAWDIM Continu:*	*DIMCONTINUE or DIMCONT*	*3,X*

Dimcontinue dimensions continue in a line from a previously created dimension. *Dimcontinue* dimension lines are attached to, and drawn the same distance from, the object as an existing dimension.

Dimcontinue is similar to *Dimbaseline* except that an existing dimension's <u>second</u> extension line is used to begin the new dimension. In other words, the new dimension is connected to the <u>second</u> extension line, rather than to the <u>first</u>, as with a *Dimbaseline* dimension (Fig. 28-17).

The command syntax is as follows:

> Command: **dimcontinue**
> Second extension line origin or RETURN to select:
> **PICK**
> Second extension line origin or RETURN to select:
> **Enter**
> Select continued dimension: **Enter**
> Command:

Assuming a dimension was just drawn, *Dimcontinue* could be used to place the next dimension, as shown in Figure 28-18.

If you want to create a *Dimcontinue* dimension and attach it to an extension line other than the previous dimension's second extension line, you can "RETURN to select." This option allows you to continue from any existing dimension by selecting it.

In Release 13, *Dimcontinue* can be used with rotated, aligned, angular, and ordinate dimensions.

Figure 28-17

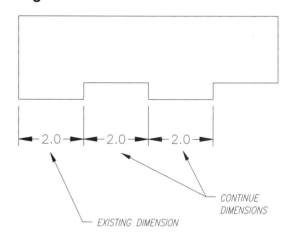

Figure 28-18

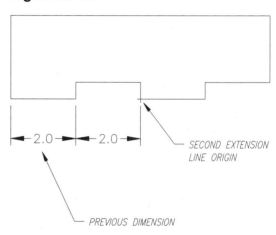

DIMDIAMETER

PULL-DOWN MENU	SCREEN MENU	TYPE IN	TABLET MENU
Draw Dimensioning > Radial > Diameter	*DRAWDIM Diametr:*	*DIMDIAMETER or DIMDIA*	*2,Y*

The *Dimdiameter* command creates a diametrical dimension by selecting any *Circle*. Diametrical dimensions should be used for full 360 degree *Circles* and can be used for *Arcs* of more than 180 degrees.

> Command: **dimdiameter**
> Select arc or circle: **PICK**
> Dimension line location (Text/Angle): **PICK**
> Command:

You can PICK the circle at any location. AutoCAD allows you to adjust the position of the dimension line to any angle (Fig. 28-19). Dimension lines for diametrical or radial dimensions should be drawn to a regular angle, such as 30, 45, or 60 degrees, never vertical or horizontal.

Figure 28-19

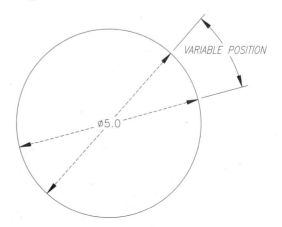

The default variable settings for diameter dimensions create a dimension, as shown in Figure 28-19. This is the accepted ANSI standard for dimensioning large *Circles* or when sufficient room exists for text and arrows inside the circle. Dimensioning variables should be changed from the defaults to force the dimension line and text outside of the circle for dimensioning small circles.

A typical diametrical dimension appears as the example in Figure 28-20. According to ANSI standards, a diameter dimension line and arrow should point inward (toward the center) for holes or small circles where the dimension line and text do not fit within the *Circle*. To create a *Dimdiameter* dimension with the arrow pointing inward, the variables that control these features should be set to *User Defined* and *Arrows Only Fit* in the *Format* dimension style dialogue box (see Chapter 29).

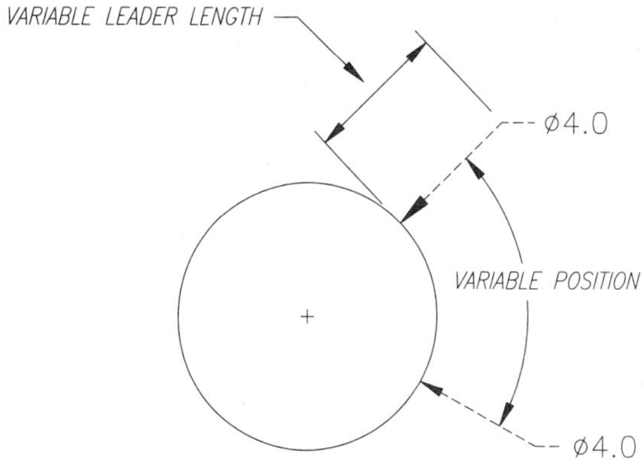

Notice that the *Diameter* command creates center marks at the *Circle's* center. Center marks can also be drawn by the *Dimcenter* command (discussed later in this chapter). AutoCAD uses the center and the point selected on the *Circle* to maintain its associativity.

Figure 28-20 ─────────────

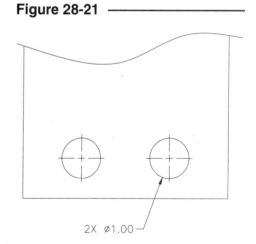

Text
The *Text* option can be used to modify or add annotation to the default value. Notice in these figures that AutoCAD automatically created the phi symbol (Ø) placed before the dimension value. This symbol is the latest standard used to represent diameters. If you prefer to add a prefix before, or a suffix after, the dimension value, it can be accomplished with the *Text* option. This operates as described for the *Text* option of *Dimlinear*. Remember that the < > symbols represent the AutoCAD-measured value so the additional text should be inserted on either side of the symbols. Inserting a prefix by this method <u>does not override</u> the phi symbol (Ø) (Fig. 28-21). A prefix or suffix can alternately be added to the measured value by using the *Dimension Styles* dialogue box and entering text or values in the *Prefix* or *Suffix* edit box. Entering a *Prefix* by that method, however, <u>overrides</u> the phi symbol (see Chapter 29, Dimensioning Variables and Dimension Styles).

Figure 28-21 ─────────────

Angle
With this option, you can specify an angle (other than the default) for the text to be drawn by entering a value.

DIMRADIUS

PULL-DOWN MENU	SCREEN MENU	TYPE IN	TABLET MENU
Draw *Dimensioning >* *Radial >* *Radius*	*DIMDRAW* *Radius:*	*DIMRADIUS* *or DIMRAD*	*1,Y*

Dimradius is used to create a dimension for an arc of anything less than half of a circle. ANSI standards dictate that a *Radius* dimension line should point outward (from the arc's center), unless there is insufficient room, in which case the line can be drawn on the outside pointing inward, as with a leader. The text can be located inside an arc (if sufficient room exists) or is forced outside of small *Arcs* on a leader.

Command: ***dimradius***
Select arc or circle: **PICK**
Dimension line location (Text/Angle): **PICK**
Command:

Figure 28-22

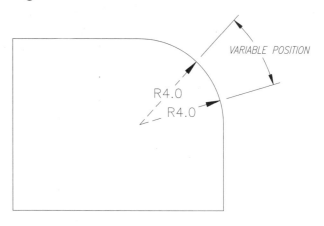

Assuming the defaults, a *Dimradius* dimension should appear, as shown in Figure 28-22. Placement of the dimension line is variable. Dimension lines for arcs and circles should be positioned at a regular angle such as 30, 45, or 60 degrees, never vertical or horizontal.

Notice that the *Dimradius* command does not automatically create center marks at the *Arc's* center when the text is drawn inside. Center marks can be created using the *Center* command (discussed next).

Figure 28-23

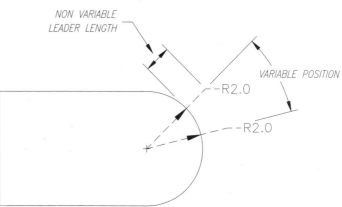

If sufficient room exists (as with large *Arcs*), the dimension is drawn with the text inside, as shown in the previous figure. For smaller arcs, AutoCAD automatically forces the text outside of the *Arc* (Fig. 28-23). In this case, the leader length is not variable, but the position of the dimension line is variable. No changes have to be made to the default Dimension Style (called STANDARD) for this to occur.

Radial dimensions can be created so that the leader length <u>is variable</u> by setting the appropriate dimension variable. In the *Format* dialogue box, select the *User Defined* checkbox to enable dynamic dragging of the radial text and leader length to your liking. (See Chapter 29.)

Figure 28-24

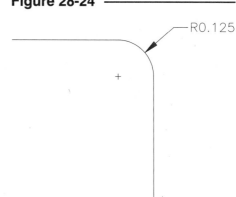

For a very small radius, such as that shown in Figure 28-24, there is insufficient room for the dimension line and text to fit inside the *Arc*. In this case, AutoCAD automatically forces the text outside with the leader pointing inward toward the center. Once again, no changes have to be made to the default settings for this to occur.

Text
The *Text* option can be used to modify or add annotation to the default value. AutoCAD automatically inserts the letter "R" before the numerical text whenever a *Dimradius* dimension is created. This is the correct notation for radius dimensions. The *Text* option calls the *Edit Mtext* dialogue box (Windows) or uses command line format (DOS) for entering text. Remember that AutoCAD uses the < > symbols to represent the AutoCAD-supplied value. Entering text inside the < > symbols overrides the measured value. Entering text before the symbols adds a prefix <u>without overriding the "R" designation</u>. Alternately, text can be added by using the *Prefix* and *Suffix* options of the *Dimension Styles* dialogue box series; however, a *Prefix* entered in the edit box <u>replaces</u> the letter "R." (See Chapter 29.)

Angle
With this option, you can specify an angle (other than the default) for the <u>text</u> to be drawn by entering a value.

DIMCENTER

PULL-DOWN MENU	SCREEN MENU	TYPE IN	TABLET MENU
Draw Dimensioning > Center Mark	*DRAWDIM Center:*	*DIMCENTER or DIMCEN*	*1,W*

R13

The *Dimcenter* command draws a center mark on any selected *Arc* or *Circle*. As shown earlier, the *Dimdiameter* command and the *Dimradius* command sometimes create the center marks automatically.

The command only requires you to select the desired *Circle* or *Arc* to acquire the center marks.

Command: **dimcenter**
Select arc or circle: **PICK**
Command:

No matter if the center mark is created by the *Center* command or by the *Diameter* or *Radius* commands, the center mark can be either a small cross or complete center lines extending past the *Circle* or *Arc*. The type of center mark drawn is controlled by the *Mark* or *Line* setting in the *Geometry* dialogue box from the *Dimension Style* series (Fig 28-25). (See Chapter 29.)

When dimensioning, short center marks should be used for *Arcs* of less than 180 degrees, and full center lines should be drawn for *Circles* and for *Arcs* of 180 degrees or more (Fig. 28-26).

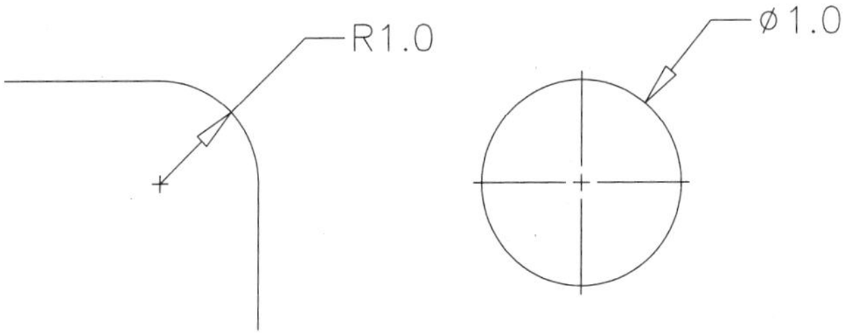

NOTE: Since the center marks created with the *Dimcenter* command are <u>not</u> associative, they may be *Trimmed*, *Erased*, or otherwise edited, as shown in Figure 28-27. The center marks created with the *Dimradius* or *Dimdiameter* commands <u>are</u> associative and cannot be edited.

The lines comprising the center marks created with *Dimcenter* can be *Erased* or otherwise edited. In the case of a 180 degree *Arc*, two center mark lines can be shortened using *Break,* and one line can be *Erased* to achieve center lines as shown in Figure 28-27.

Figure 28-25 ————————————

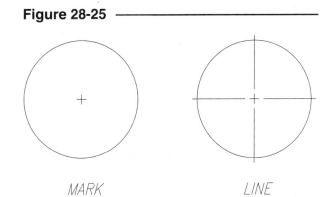

MARK   LINE

Figure 28-26 ————————————

Figure 28-27 ————————————

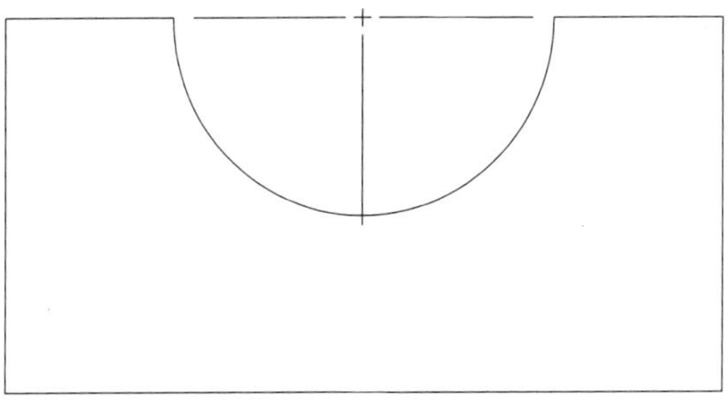

DIMANGULAR

PULL-DOWN MENU	SCREEN MENU	TYPE IN	TABLET MENU
Draw Dimensioning > Angular	*DRAWDIM Angular:*	*DIMANGULAR or DIMANG*	*3,Y*

R13

The *Dimangular* command provides many possible methods of creating an angular dimension.

A typical angular dimension is created between two *Lines* that form an angle (of other than 90 degrees). The dimension line for an angular dimension is radiused with its center at the vertex of the angle (Figure 28-28). A *Dimangular* dimension automatically adds the degree symbol (°) to the dimension text. The dimension text format is controlled by the current settings for *Units* in the *Dimension Style* dialogue box.

AutoCAD automates the process of creating this type of dimension by offering options within the command syntax. The default options create a dimension, as shown here.

Figure 28-28

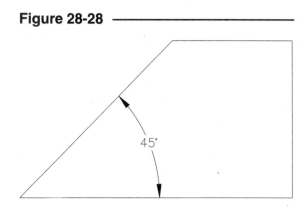

> Command: **dimangular**
> Select arc, circle, line, or RETURN: **PICK** the first line.
> Second line: **PICK** the second line.
> Dimension arc line location (Text/Angle): **PICK** (the desired location of the radiused dimension line).
> Command:

Dimangular dimensioning offers some very useful and easy-to-use options for placing the desired dimension line and text location.

At the "Dimension arc line location (Text/Angle):" prompt, you can move the cursor around the vertex to dynamically display possible placements available for the dimension. The dimension can be placed in any of four positions as well as any distance from the vertex (Figure 28-29). Extension lines are automatically created as needed.

The *Dimangular* command offers other options, including dimensioning angles for *Arcs*, *Circles*, or allowing selection of any three points.

Figure 28-29

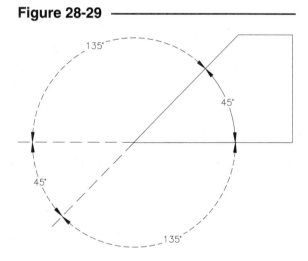

If you select an *Arc* in response to the "Select arc, circle, line, or RETURN:" prompt, AutoCAD uses the *Arc's* center as the vertex and the *Arc* endpoints to generate the extension lines. You can select either angle of the *Arc* to dimension (Figure 28-30).

Figure 28-30

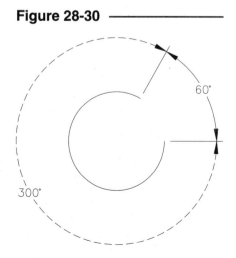

If you select a *Circle*, AutoCAD uses the PICK point as the first extension line origin. The second extension line origin does not have to be on the *Circle*, as shown in Figure 28-31.

Figure 28-31

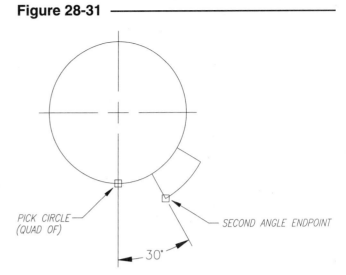

If you press **Enter** in response to the "Select arc, circle, line, or RETURN:" prompt, AutoCAD responds with the following:

```
Angle vertex: PICK
First angle endpoint: PICK
Second angle endpoint: PICK
```

This option allows you to apply an *Angular* dimension to a variety of shapes.

PICK CIRCLE
(QUAD OF)

SECOND ANGLE ENDPOINT

30°

LEADER

PULL-DOWN MENU	SCREEN MENU	TYPE IN	TABLET MENU
Draw Dimensioning > Leader	*DRAWDIM Leader:*	*LEADER or LEAD*	*1,X*

The *Leader* command allows you to create an associative leader similar to that created with the *Diameter* command. The *Leader* command is intended to give dimensional notes such as the manufacturing or construction specifications shown here.

```
Command: leader
From point: PICK
To point: PICK
To point (Format/Annotation/Undo)<Annotation>:
CASE HARDEN
<Mtext>: Enter
Command:
```

At the "From point:" prompt, select the desired location for the arrow. You should use *SNAP* or an *OSNAP* option (such as *NEArest*, in this case) to ensure the arrow touches the desired object.

A short horizontal line segment called the "hook line" is automatically added to the last line segment drawn if the leader line is 15 degrees or more from horizontal. Note that command syntax for the *Leader* in Figure 28-32 indicates only one line segment was PICKed. A *Leader* can have as many segments as you desire (Fig. 28-33).

If you do not enter text at the "Annotation:" prompt, another series of options are available.

Figure 28-32

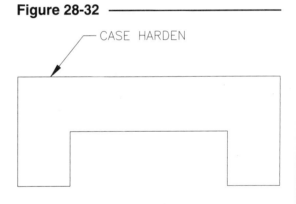

CASE HARDEN

Figure 28-33

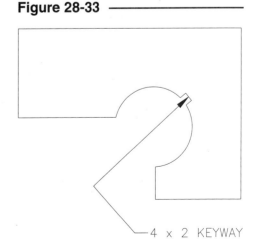

4 x 2 KEYWAY

R13

```
Command: leader
From point: PICK
To point: PICK
To point (Format/Annotation/Undo)<Annotation>: Enter or (option) or (text)
Annotation (or return for options): Enter or (text)
Tolerance/Copy/Block/None/<Mtext>: Enter or (option)
Command:
```

All of the options for *Leader* are given here.

Format
This option produces another list of choices.

Spline/STraight/Arrow/None/<Exit>:

Spline/STraight
You can draw either a *Spline* or straight version of the leader line with these options. The resulting *Spline* leader line has the characteristics of a normal *Spline*. An example of a *Splined* leader is shown in Figure 28-34.

Figure 28-34 ⎯⎯⎯⎯⎯⎯⎯⎯⎯⎯⎯⎯

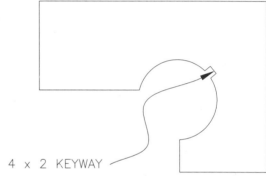

4 x 2 KEYWAY

Arrow/None
This option draws the leader line with or without an arrowhead at the start point.

Annotation
This option prompts for text to insert at the end of the *Leader* line.

Mtext
The *Edit Mtext* dialogue box or MS-DOS editor appears with this option (depending on your version of AutoCAD). Text can be entered into paragraph form using the *Mtext* text boundary mechanism (see *Mtext*, Chapter 19).

Tolerance
This option produces a feature control frame using the *Geometric Tolerances* dialogue boxes (see *Tolerance*).

Copy
You can copy existing *Text, Dtext,* or *Mtext* objects from the drawing to be placed at the end of the *Leader* line. The copied object is associated with the *Leader* line.

Block
An existing *Block* of your selection can be placed at the end of the *Leader* line. The same prompts as the *Insert* command are used.

None
Using this option draws the *Leader* line with no annotation.

Undo
This option undoes the last vertex point of the *Leader* line.

Since a *Leader* is associative, it is affected by the current dimension style settings. You can control the *Leader's* arrowhead type, scale, color, etc., with the related dimensioning variables (see Chapter 29).

R13

DIMORDINATE

PULL-DOWN MENU	SCREEN MENU	TYPE IN	TABLET MENU
Draw Dimensioning > Ordinate >	DRAWDIM Ordinat:	DIMORDINATE or DIMORD	4,Y

Ordinate dimensioning is a specialized method of dimensioning used in the manufacturing of flat components such as those in the sheet metal industry. Because the thickness (depth) of the parts is uniform, only the width and height dimensions are specified as Xdatum and Ydatum dimensions.

Dimordinate dimensions give an Xdatum or a Ydatum distance between object "features" and a reference point on the geometry treated as the origin, usually the lower-left corner of the part. This method of dimensioning is relatively simple to create and easy to understand. Each dimension is composed only of one leader line and the aligned numerical value.

Figure 28-35 ─────────────────

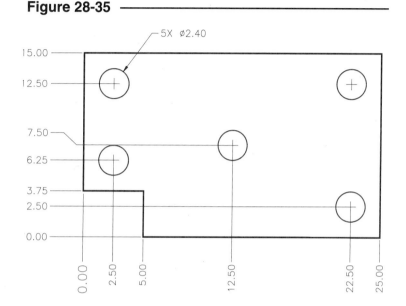

To create ordinate dimensions in AutoCAD, the *UCS* command should be used first to establish a new 0,0 point. *UCS*, which stands for User Coordinate System, allows you to establish a new coordinate system with the origin and the orientation of the axes anywhere in 3D space (see Chapters 33 and 35 for complete details). In this case, we need only to change the location of the origin and leave the orientation of the axes as is. Type **UCS** and use the *Origin* option to PICK a new origin as shown (Fig. 28-36).

When you create a *Dimordinate* dimension, AutoCAD only requires you to (1) PICK the object "Feature" and then (2) specify the

Figure 28-36 ─────────────────

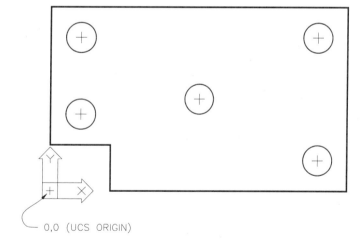

"Leader endpoint:". The dimension text is automatically aligned with the leader line.

It is not necessary in most cases to indicate whether you are creating an Xdatum or a Ydatum. Using the default option of *Dimordinate*, AutoCAD makes the determination based on the direction of the leader you specify (step 2). If the leader is <u>perpendicular</u> (or almost perpendicular) to the X axis, an Xdatum is created. If the leader is (almost) <u>perpendicular</u> to the Y axis, a Ydatum is created. The command syntax for a *Dimordinate* dimension is this.

```
Command: dimord
Select Feature: PICK
Leader endpoint (Xdatum/Ydatum/Text): PICK
Command:
```

A *Dimordinate* dimension is created in Figure 28-37 by PICKing the object feature and the leader endpoint. That's all there is to it. The dimension is a Ydatum; yet AutoCAD automatically makes that determination, since the leader is perpendicular to the Y axis. It is a good practice to turn *ORTHO ON* in order to ensure the leader lines are drawn horizontally or vertically.

Figure 28-37

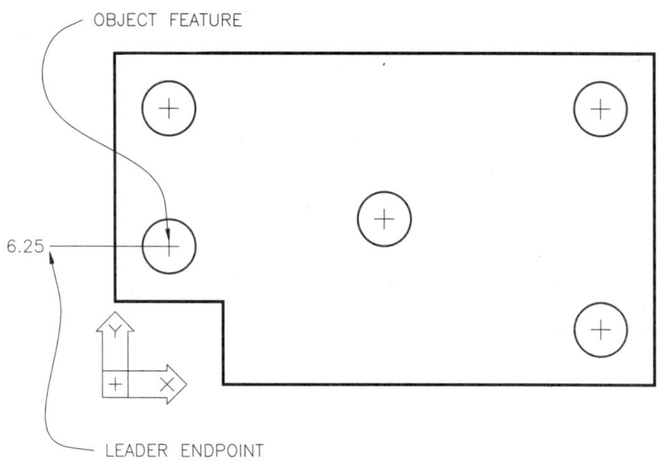

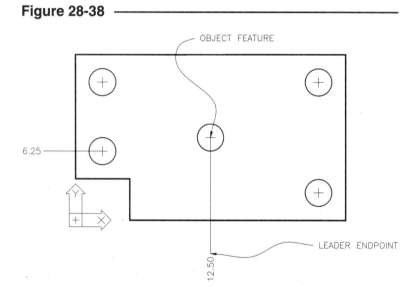

An Xdatum *Dimordinate* dimension is created in the same manner. Just PICK the object feature and the other end of the leader line (Figure 28-38). The leader is perpendicular to the X axis; therefore, an Xdatum dimension is created.

Figure 28-38

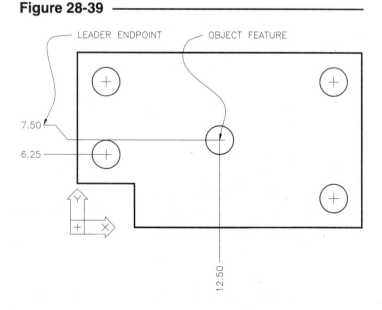

The leader line does not have to be purely horizontal or vertical. In some cases, where the dimension text is crowded, it is desirable to place the end of the leader so that sufficient room is provided for the dimension text. In other words, draw the leader line at an angle. (*ORTHO* must be turned *Off* to specify an offset leader line.) AutoCAD automatically creates an offset in the leader as shown in the 7.50 Ydatum dimension in Figure 28-39. As long as the leader is more perpendicular to the X axis, an X datum is drawn and vice versa.

Figure 28-39

Xdatum/Ydatum

The *Xdatum* and *Ydatum* options are used to specify one of these dimensions explicitly. This is necessary in case the leader line that you specify is more perpendicular to the <u>other</u> axis that you want to measure along. The command syntax would be as follows:

```
Command: dimord
Select Feature: PICK
Leader endpoint (Xdatum/Ydatum/Text): X
Leader endpoint: PICK
Command:
```

Text

The *Text* option operates similarly to the same option of other dimensioning commands. Invoking *Text* produces the *Mtext* dialogue box. Any text placed inside the < > characters overrides the AutoCAD-measure dimensional value. Any additional text entered on either side of the < > symbols is treated as a prefix or suffix to the measured value. All other options in the *Mtext* dialogue box are usable for ordinate dimensions.

TOLERANCE

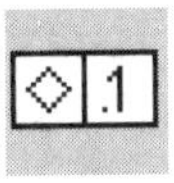

PULL-DOWN MENU	SCREEN MENU	TYPE IN	TABLET MENU
Draw Dimensioning > Tolerance...	*DRAWDIM Toleran:*	*TOLERANCE or TOL*	*1,V*

Geometric dimensioning and tolerancing (GDT) has become an essential component of detail drawings of manufactured parts. Standard symbols are used to define the geometric aspects of the parts and how the parts function in relation to other parts of an assembly. The *Tolerance* command in AutoCAD Release 13 produces a series of dialogue boxes for you to create the symbols, values, and feature control frames needed to dimension a drawing with GDT. Invoking the *Tolerance* command produces the *Symbol* dialogue box (Fig. 28-42) and the *Geometric Tolerance* dialogue box. These dialogue boxes can also be accessed by the *Leader* command. Unlike general dimensioning in AutoCAD, geometric dimensioning is <u>not associative</u>; however, you can use *Ddedit* to edit the components of an existing feature control frame.

Some common examples of geometric dimensioning may be a control of the flatness of a surface, the parallelism of one surface relative to another, or the positioning of a group of holes to the outside surfaces of the part. Most of the conditions are controls that cannot be stated with the other AutoCAD dimensioning commands.

This book does not provide instruction on how to use geometric dimensioning, rather how to use AutoCAD Release 13 to apply the symbology. The ASME Y14.5M - 1994 Dimensioning and Tolerancing standard is the authority on the topic in the United States. The symbol application presented in AutoCAD Release 13 is actually based on the 1982 release of the Y14.5 standard. Some of the symbols in the 1994 version are modified from the 1982 standard.

The dimensioning symbols are placed in a feature control frame (FCF). This frame is composed of a minimum of two sections and a maximum of three different sections (Fig. 28-40).

Figure 28-40

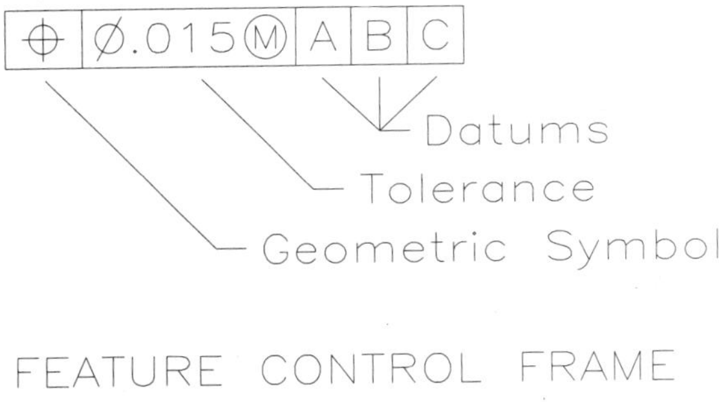

⊕ | ⌀.015Ⓜ | A | B | C

Datums
Tolerance
Geometric Symbol

FEATURE CONTROL FRAME

The first section of the FCF houses one of 14 possible geometric characteristic symbols (Fig. 28-41).

The second section of the FCF contains the tolerance information. The third section includes any datum references.

In AutoCAD Release 13, the *Tolerance* command allows you to specify the values and symbols needed for a feature control frame. The lines comprising the frame itself are automatically generated. Invoking *Tolerance* by any method produces the *Symbol* dialogue box (Fig. 28-42).

Here you select the geometric characteristic symbol to use for the new feature control frame. If you want to specify a *Datum Identifier* only and do not need to select a symbol, click *OK* to bypass this step.

Once the symbol has been selected, the *Geometric Tolerance* dialogue box appears for you to specify the tolerance values and datums. The areas of the *Geometric Tolerance* dialogue box are explained here.

Sym
This image tile displays the symbol previously selected from the *Symbol* dialogue box. If you want to change the symbol, click on the image tile to return to the *Symbol* dialogue box for another selection.

Tolerance 1
This area is used to specify the first tolerance value in the feature control frame. This value specifies the amount of allowable deviation for the geometric feature. The three sections in this cluster are:

Dia
If a cylindrical tolerance zone is specified, a diameter symbol can be placed before the value by clicking in this area.

Value
Enter the tolerance value in this edit box.

MC
A material condition symbol can be placed after the value by choosing this tile. The *Material Condition* dialogue box appears for your selection (Fig. 28-44).

M	Maximum material condition
L	Least material condition
S	Regardless of feature size

Once you select a material condition or cancel, the *Geometric Tolerance* dialogue box reappears.

Figure 28-41 ───────────

—	Straightness	∩	Profile of a Line
▱	Flatness	◠	Profile of a Surface
○	Circularity	↗	Circular Runout
⌀	Cylindricity	↗↗	Total Runout
//	Parallelism	⊕	Position
⊥	Perpendicularity	◎	Concentricity
∠	Angularity	═	Symmetry

GEOMETRIC CHARACTERISTIC SYMBOLS

Figure 28-42 ───────────

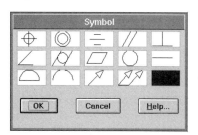

Figure 28-43 ───────────────────────

Figure 28-44 ───────────

Tolerance 2
Using this section creates a second tolerance area in the feature control frame. GDT standards, however, require only one tolerance area. The options in this section are identical to *Tolerance 1*.

Datum 1
This section allows you to specify the primary datum reference for the current feature control frame. A datum is the exact (theoretical) geometric feature that the current feature references to establish its tolerance zone.

> *Datum*
> Enter the primary datum letter (A, B, C, etc.) for the FCF in this edit box.

> *MC*
> Choosing the *MC* tile allows you to specify a material condition modifier for the datum using the *Material Condition* dialogue box (Fig. 28-44).

Datum 2
This section is used if you need to create a second datum reference in the feature control frame. The options are identical to those for *Datum 1*.

Datum 3
Use this section if you need to specify a third datum reference for the current feature control frame.

Height
The edit box allows entry of a value for a projected tolerance zone in the feature control frame. A projected tolerance zone specifies a permissible cylindrical tolerance that is projected above the surface of the part. The axis of the control feature must remain within the stated tolerance.

Projected Tolerance Zone
Click this section to insert a projected tolerance zone symbol (a circled "P") after the value.

Datum Identifier
This option creates a datum feature symbol. The edit box allows entry of the value (letter) indicating the datum. A hyphen should be included on each side of the datum letter, such as "-A-".

After using the dialogue boxes and specifying the necessary values and symbols, AutoCAD prompts for you to PICK a location on the drawing for the feature control symbol or datum identifier.

    Enter tolerance location: **PICK**

The feature control symbol or datum identifier is drawn as specified.

Editing Feature Control Frames
The AutoCAD-generated feature control frames are not associative and can be *Erased*, *Moved*, or otherwise edited without consequence to the related geometry objects. Feature control frames created with *Tolerance* are treated as one object; therefore, editing an individual component of a feature control frame is not possible unless *Ddedit* is used.

Ddedit is normally used to edit text, but if an existing feature control frame is selected in response to the "<Select an annotation object>/undo:" prompt, the *Geometric Tolerance* dialogue box appears. The edit boxes in this dialogue box contain the values and symbols from the selected FCF. Making the appropriate changes updates the selected FCF. (See Chapter 19 for detailed information on *Ddedit*.)

Basic Dimensions

Basic dimensions are often required in drawings using GDT. Basic dimensions in AutoCAD are created by using the *Dimension Styles* dialogue box (or by entering a negative value in the *DIMGAP* variable). The procedure is explained briefly in the following example (application 5) and discussed further in Chapter 29, Dimension Styles and Dimension Variables.

GDT-Related Dimension Variables

Some aspects of how AutoCAD draws the GDT symbols can be controlled using dimension variables and dimension styles (discussed fully in Chapter 29). These variables are:

DIMCLRE	Controls the color of the FCF
DIMCLRT	Controls the color of the tolerance text
DIMGAP	Controls the gap between the FCF and the text, and controls the existance of a basic dimension box
DIMTXT	Controls the size of the tolerance text
DIMTSTSTY	Controls the style of the tolerance text

Geometric Dimensioning and Tolerancing Example

There are six different geometric dimensioning and tolerancing examples shown on the SPACER drawing in Figure 28-45. Each example is indicated on the drawing and in the following text by a number, 1 through 6. The purpose of the examples is to explain how to use the geometric dimensioning features of AutoCAD Release 13. In each example, any method shown in the *Tolerance* command table can be used to invoke the command and dialogue boxes.

Figure 28-45

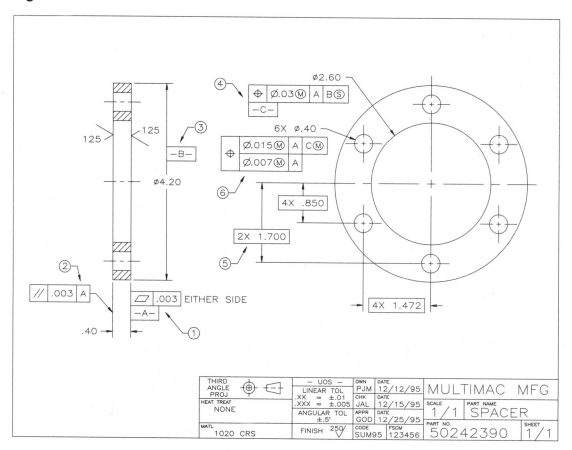

1. Flatness Application

The first specification applied is flatness. In addition to one of the surfaces being controlled for flatness, it is also identified as a datum surface. Both of these conditions are applied in the same application.

> Command: **tolerance** (The *Symbol* dialogue box appears.)
> PICK the *flatness* symbol, then the **OK** button. (The *Geometric Tolerance* dialogue box appears, Fig. 28-46.)
> PICK the *Tolerance 1 Value* box and type ".003" as a tolerance.
> PICK the *Datum Identifier* box and type "-A-".
> PICK the **OK** button. (The *Geometric Tolerance* dialogue box disappears.)
> Enter tolerance location: **PICK** (PICK a point on the right extension line where you want the middle of the left vertical line of the flatness part of the FCF to be attached, Fig. 28-47.)
> Command:

Figure 28-46

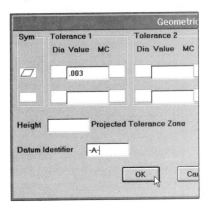

Because either side of the SPACER can be chosen for the flatness specification, the note "EITHER SIDE" is entered next to the FCF in Figure 28-45.

Figure 28-47

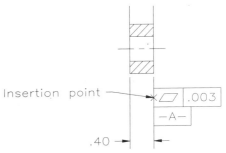

2. Parallelism Application

The second application is a parallelism specification to the opposite side of the part. This control is applied using a *Leader*.

> Command: **leader**
> From point: **PICK** (PICK a point on the left extension line, Fig. 28-45.)
> To point: **PICK** (PICK a location on the middle of the right vertical line of the FCF.)
> To point (Format/Annotation/Undo)<Annotation>: **Enter**
> Annotation (or RETURN for options): **Enter**
> Tolerance/Copy/Block/None/<Mtext>: **T** (The *Symbol* dialogue box appears.)
> PICK the *parallelism* symbol, then **OK** to activate the *Geometric Tolerance* dialogue box.
> PICK the *Tolerance 1 Value* box and type ".003" as a tolerance.
> PICK the *Datum 1 Datum* box and type "A".
> PICK the **OK** button. (The *Geometric Tolerance* dialogue box clears and the parallelism FCF is placed to the left of the leader.)
> Command:

If the leader had projected to the right of the controlled surface, the FCF would be placed on the right of the leader.

3. Datum Application

The third application is the B datum on the 4.20 diameter. This datum is used later in the position specification.

> Command: **tolerance** (The *Symbol* dialogue box appears.)
> PICK the **OK** button. (The *Geometric Tolerance* dialogue box appears.)
> PICK the *Datum Identifier* box and type "-B-". (The *Geometric Tolerance* dialogue box clears.)
> Enter tolerance location: **PICK** (PICK a point on the dimension line of the 4.20 diameter.)
> Command:

4.   Position Application

The fourth application is a position specification of the 2.60 diameter hole. It is identified as a C datum because it will be used in the position specification of the six mounting holes. This specification creates a relationship between inside and outside diameters and a perpendicularity requirement to datum A.

Command: **tolerance** (The *Symbol* dialogue box appears.)
PICK the *position* symbol, then the *OK* button to produce the *Geometric Tolerance* dialogue box.
PICK the *Tolerance 1 Dia* box. (This places a diameter symbol in front of the tolerance.)
PICK the *Tolerance 1 Value* box and type ".03" as a tolerance.
PICK the *Tolerance 1 MC* box. (The *Material Condition* dialogue box appears.)
PICK the circled *M* and the *OK* button.
PICK the *Datum 1 Datum* box and type "A".
PICK the *Datum 2 Datum* box and type "B".
PICK the *Datum 2 MC* box to produce the *Material Condition* dialogue box.
PICK the circled *S* and then the *OK* button.
PICK the *Datum Identifier* box and type "-C-".
PICK the *OK* button to return to the drawing.
Enter tolerance location: **PICK** (PICK a point that places the FCF below the 2.60 diameter [Fig. 28-45].)
Command:

If you need to move the FCF with *Move* or grips, select any part of the FCF or its contents since it is treated as one object.

5.   Basic Dimension Application

The fifth application concerns basic dimensions. Position uses basic (theoretically exact) location dimensions to locate holes because the tolerances are stated in the FCF. Before applying these dimensions, the *Dimension Style* must be changed.   (See Chapter 29 for a complete discussion of Dimension Styles).

Command: **ddim** (Or use any method to invoke the *Dimension Styles* dialogue box.)
PICK the *Annotation* button. (The *Annotation* dialogue box appears.)
PICK the *Tolerance Methods* pop-down list.
PICK *Basic*, then the *OK* button.
PICK the *OK* button in the *Dimension Styles* dialogue box.
Command: **dimlinear** (Use the *dimlinear* command to apply each of the three linear basic dimensions shown in Figure 28-45.)

6.   Composite Position Application

The sixth application is the composite position specification. A composite specification consists of two separate lines but only one geometric symbol. To achieve this result requires entering data on the top and bottom lines in the *Geometric Tolerance* dialogue box.

Command: **tolerance**
PICK the *position* symbol, then the *OK* button in the *Symbol* dialogue box.
PICK the *Tolerance 1 Dia* box in the *Geometric Tolerance* dialogue box.
PICK the *Tolerance 1 Value* box and enter ".015" as a tolerance.
PICK the *Tolerance 1 MC* box. (The *Material Condition* dialogue box appears.)
PICK the circled *M* and then *OK*.
PICK the *Datum 1 Datum* box and type "A".
PICK the *Datum 2 Datum* box and type "C".
PICK the *Datum 2 MC* box. (The *Material Condition* dialogue box appears.)
PICK the circled *M* and then the *OK* button.

PICK the *Sym* box under the position symbol to produce the *Symbol* dialogue box.
PICK the *position* symbol, then the *OK* button.
PICK the *Tolerance 1 Dia* box on the second line.
PICK the *Tolerance 1 Value* box on the second line and type ".007" as a tolerance.
PICK the *Tolerance 1 MC* box on the second line. (The *Material Condition* dialogue box appears.)
PICK the circled *M* and the *OK* button.
PICK the *Datum 1 Datum* box and type "A".
PICK the *OK* button. (The *Geometric Tolerance* dialogue box clears.)
Enter tolerance location: **PICK** (PICK a point that places the FCF below the .40 diameter, Fig. 28-45.)
Command:

Datum Targets

The COVER drawing (Fig. 28-48) uses datum targets to locate the part in 3D space. AutoCAD Release 13 does not provide any commands to apply datum targets. The best way to apply these symbols is to use *Blocks* and attributes. The target circle diameter is 3.5 times the letter height. The dividing line is always drawn horizontally through the center of the circle.

Figure 28-48

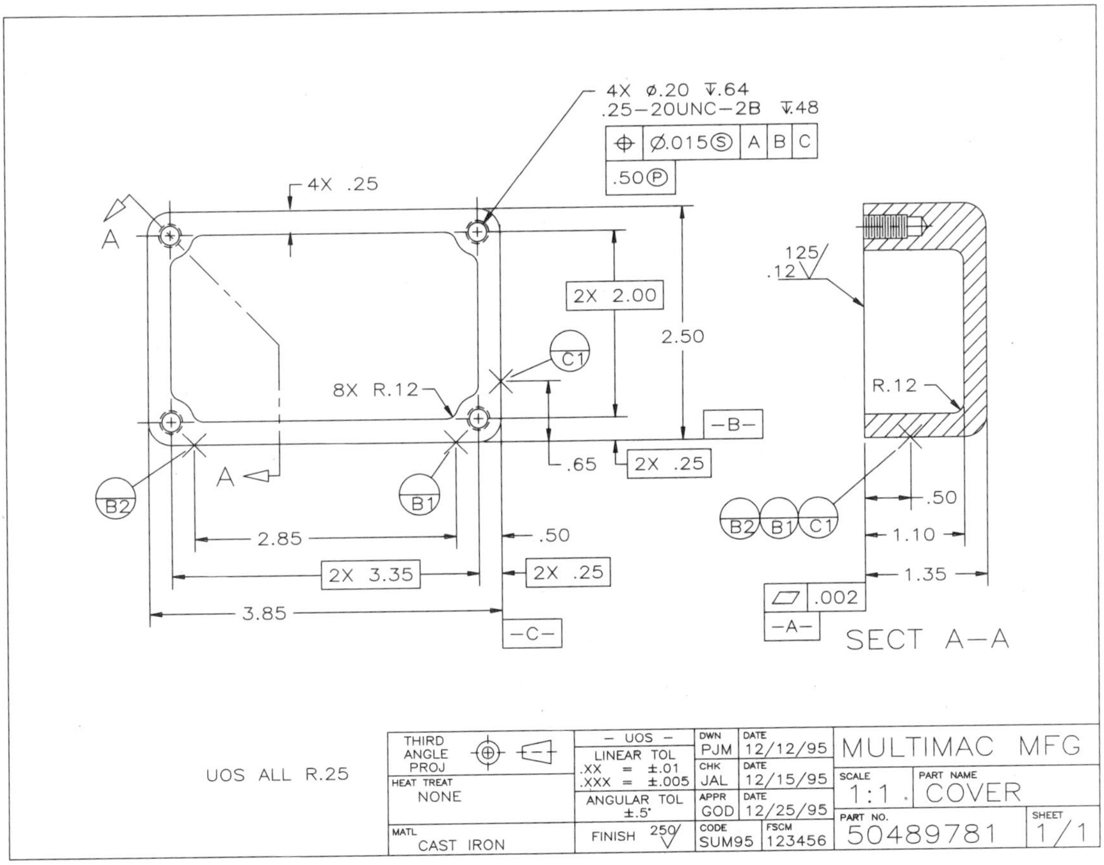

Projected Tolerance Zone Application

The COVER drawing also uses a projected tolerance with the position specification. A projected tolerance zone is used primarily with internally threaded holes and dowel holes. In this case, the concern is not the position and orientation of the threaded hole, rather the position and orientation of the fastener inserted into the hole—specifically the shank of the fastener; therefore, the tolerance zone projects above the surface of the part and not within the part. This condition is especially important when the hole allowance is small.

Command: **tolerance**
PICK the *position* tile and *OK* in the *Symbol* dialogue box.
PICK the *Height* box in the *Geometric Tolerance* dialogue box and enter ".50".
PICK the *Projected Tolerance Zone* box. A circled *P* appears.
PICK the *OK* button in the *Geometric Tolerance* box.
Enter tolerance location: **PICK** (PICK a point that places the FCF below the .20 diameter, Fig. 28-48.)
Command:

This section has presented only the mechanics of GDT symbol application in AutoCAD Release 13. Geometric dimensioning and tolerancing can be a complicated and detailed subject to learn. There are many different combination possibilities that may appear in a feature control frame. However, for any one feature, there are very few possibilities. Knowing which of the possibilities is best comes from a fundamental knowledge of GDT. Knowledge of GDT increases your understanding of design, tooling, manufacturing, and inspection concepts and processes.

DIM

In AutoCAD releases previous to Release 13, dimensioning commands had to be entered at the "Dim:" prompt and could not be entered at the "Command:" prompt. The "Dim:" prompt puts AutoCAD in the dimensioning mode so earlier release dimensioning commands can be used. This convention can also be used in Release 13. The *DIM* command must be typed in Release 13 to produce the "Dim:" prompt. Enter *E* or *Exit* or press Escape to exit the dimensioning mode and return to the "Command:" prompt. The syntax is as follows.

Command: **dim**
Dim:

Release 12 and previous dimensioning command names do not have the "dim" prefix; therefore, using the "Dim:" prompt for them is required. Almost all of the Release 12 commands have the same name as the Release 13 version, but without the "dim" prefix. For example, *Dimdiameter* is "*Diameter*" in Release 12. In Release 13, you can enter these older dimensioning command names (without the "dim" prefix) at the "Dim:" prompt, for example:

Command: **dim**
Dim: **diameter**

With the exception of a few dimensioning commands, the Release 12 dimensioning commands are the same as the Release 13 versions without the "dim" prefix. There are, however, several other older commands that can be used in Release 13 at the "Dim:" prompt.

UNDO or U
Erases the last dimension objects or dimension variable setting.

UPDATE
Performs the same action as *Dimstyle, Apply*.

STYLE
Changes the current <u>text</u> style.

HORIZONTAL
Performs the same action as *Dimlinear, Horizontal*.

VERTICAL

Performs the same action as *Dimlinear, Vertical.*

ROTATED

Performs the same action as *Dimlinear, Rotate.*

Another use for the "Dim:" prompt is for the *Viewport* option of *DIMLFAC*, which is not available by any other method (see *DIMLFAC*, Chapter 32).

EDITING DIMENSIONS

Associative Dimensions

AutoCAD creates associative dimensions by default. Associative dimensions contain "definition points" that define points in the dimensions such as extension line origins, placement of dimension line, the selected points of *Circles* and *Arcs*, and the centers of those *Circles* and *Arcs*. If the geometry is modified by certain editing commands (more specifically, if the definition points are changed), the dimension components, including the numerical value, automatically update. When you create the first associative dimension, AutoCAD automatically creates a new layer called DEFPOINTS that contains all the definition points. The layer should be kept in a *Frozen* state. If you alter the points on this layer, existing dimensions lose their associativity and you eliminate the possibility of automatic editing.

All of the dimensioning commands are associative by default, and the resulting dimensions would be affected by the editing commands listed below. The *DIMASO* variable can be changed to make new dimensions unassociative if you desire (see Chapter 29). The commands that affect associative dimensions are *Extend, Mirror, Rotate, Scale, Stretch, Trim* (linear dimensions only), *Array* (if rotated in a *Polar* array), and grip editing options.

These commands cause the changed dimension to adjust to the changed angle or length. For example, if you use *Stretch* to change some geometry with associative dimensions, the numerical values and extension lines automatically update as the related geometry changes (Fig. 28-49). Remember to use a <u>crossing window</u> for selection with *Stretch* and to include the extension line <u>origin</u> (definition point) in the selection set.

Figure 28-49

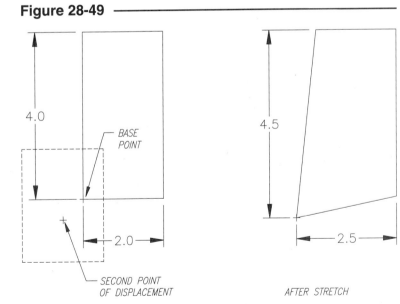

Grip Editing Dimensions

Grips can be used effectively for editing dimensions. Any of the grip options (STRETCH, MOVE, ROTATE, SCALE, and MIRROR) are applicable. Depending on the type of dimension (linear, radial, angular, etc.), grips appear at several locations on the dimension when you activate the grips by selecting the dimension at the Command: prompt. Associative dimensions offer the most powerful editing possibilities, although non-associative dimension components can also be edited with grips. There are many ways in which grips can be used to alter the measured value and configuration of dimensions. Some possibilities are discussed and illustrated next.

Figure 28-50 shows the grips for each type of associative dimension. Linear dimensions (horizontal, vertical, and rotated) and aligned and angular dimensions have grips at each extension line origin, the dimension line position, and a grip at the text. A diameter dimension has grips defining two points on the diameter as well as one defining the leader length. The radius dimension has center and radius grips as well as a leader grip.

With dimension grips, a wide variety of editing options are possible. Any of the grips can be PICKed to make them **hot** grips. All grip options are valid methods for editing dimensions.

Figure 28-50

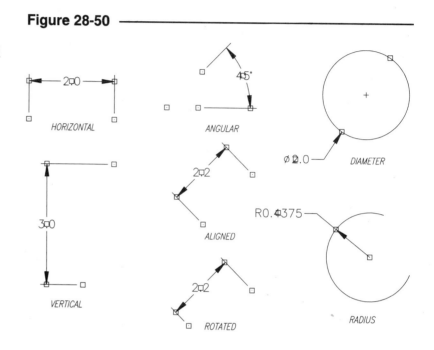

For example (Fig. 28-51), a horizontal dimension value can be increased by stretching an extension line origin grip in a horizontal direction. A vertical direction movement changes the length of the extension line. The dimension line placement is changed by stretching its grips. The dimension text can be stretched to any position by manipulating its grip.

Figure 28-51

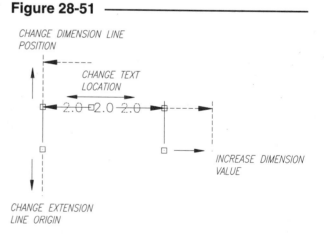

An angular dimension can be increased by stretching the extension line origin grip. The numerical value automatically updates.

Figure 28-52

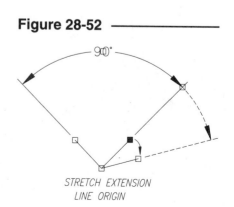

Stretching a rotated dimension's extension line origin allows changing the length of the dimension as well as the length of the extension line. An aligned dimension's extension line origin grip also allows you to change the aligned <u>angle</u> of the dimension.

Figure 28-53

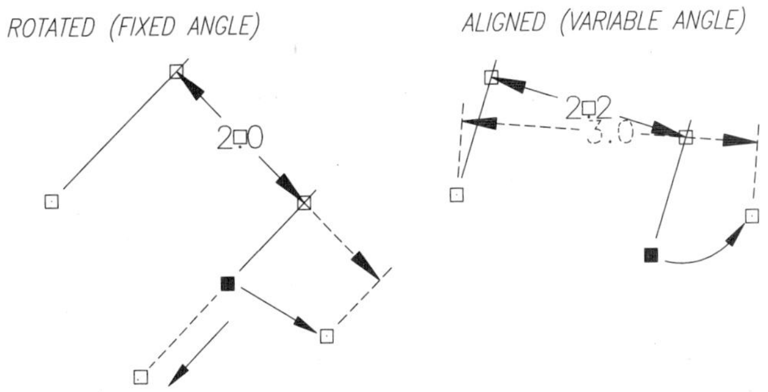

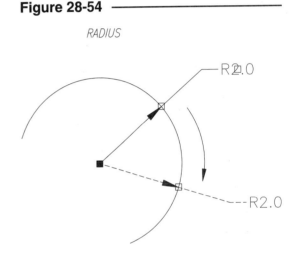

Rotating the <u>center</u> grip of a radius dimension (with the ROTATE option) allows you to reposition the location of the dimension around the *Arc*. Note that the text remains in its original horizontal orientation.

Many other possibilities exist for editing dimensions using grips. Experiment on your own to discover some of the possibilities that are not shown here.

Figure 28-54

RADIUS

Exploding Associative Dimensions

Associative dimensions are treated as one object. If *Erase* is used with an associative dimension, the entire dimension (dimension line, extension lines, arrows, and text) is selected and *Erased*.

Explode can be used to break an associative dimension into its component parts. The individual components can then be edited. For example, after *Exploding*, an extension line can be *Erased* or text can be *Moved*.

There are two main drawbacks to *Exploding* associative dimensions. First, the associative property is lost. Editing commands or *Grips* cannot be used to change the entire dimension, but affect only the component objects. More importantly, Dimension Styles cannot be used with unassociative dimensions. Secondly, the dimension is *Exploded* onto Layer 0 and loses its *color* and *linetype* properties. This can include additional work to reestablish the desired layer, *color*, and *linetype*.

Dimension Editing Commands

Several commands are provided to facilitate easy editing of existing dimensions in a drawing. Most of these commands are intended to allow variations in the appearance of dimension <u>text</u>. These editing commands operate <u>only</u> with <u>associative</u> dimensions.

R13

DIMTEDIT

PULL-DOWN MENU	SCREEN MENU	TYPE IN	TABLET MENU
Draw *Dimensioning >* *Align Text >*	*MOD DIM* *DimTedt:*	*DIMTEDIT* *or DIMTED*	*3,W to 5,W*

Dimtedit (text edit) allows you to change the position or orientation of the text for a single associative dimension. To move the position of text, this command syntax is used.

Figure 28-55

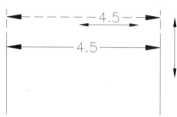

Command: **Dimtedit**
Select dimension: **PICK**
Enter text location (Left/Right/Home/Angle): **PICK**

At the "Enter text location" prompt, drag the text to the desired location. The selected text and dimension line can be changed to any position, while the text and dimension line retain their associativity.

Angle *or* Rotate

The *Angle* option works with any *Horizontal, Vertical, Aligned, Rotated, Radius,* or *Diameter* dimensions. You are prompted for the new <u>text</u> angle (Figs. 28-56).

Figure 28-56

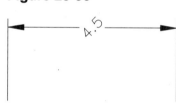

Command: **dimtedit**
Select dimension: **PICK**
Enter text location (Left/Right/Home/Angle): **a**
Enter text angle: **45**
Command:

Home

The text can be restored to its original (default) rotation angle with the *Home* option. The text retains its right/left position.

Figure 28-57

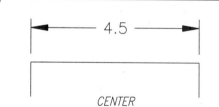

CENTER

Right/Left

The *Right* and *Left* options automatically justify the dimension text at the extreme right and left ends, respectively, of the dimension line. The arrow and a short section of the dimension line, however, remain between the text and closest extension line (Fig. 28-57).

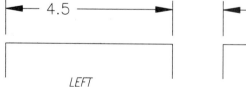

LEFT

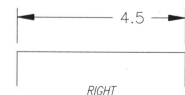

RIGHT

Center

The *Center* option brings the text to the center of the dimension line without losing the rotation angle (Fig. 28-57)

DIMEDIT

PULL-DOWN MENU	SCREEN MENU	TYPE IN	TABLET MENU
Draw *Dimensioning >* *Oblique, Align text >*	*MOD DIM* *DimEdit:*	*DIMEDIT* *or DIMED*	---

The *Dimedit* command allows you to change the angle of the extension lines to an obliquing angle and provides several ways to edit dimension text. Two of the text editing options (*Home, Rotate*) duplicate those of the *Dimtedit* command. Another feature (*New*) allows you to change the text value and annotation.

> Command: **dimedit**
> Dimension Edit (Home/New/Rotate/Oblique) <Home>:

Home
This option moves the dimension text back to its original angular orientation angle without changing the left/right position. *Home* is a duplicate of the *Dimtedit* option of the same name.

New
You can change the text value and annotation of existing text. The same mechanism appears when you create the dimension and use the *Text* option—that is, the *Edit Mtext* dialogue box appears (Windows) or the command line format prompt appears (DOS). Remember that AutoCAD draws the dimension value in place of the < > characters. Add a prefix before these characters or a suffix after. Entering text to replace the < > characters (erase them) causes your new text to appear instead of the AutoCAD-supplied value.

Placing text or numbers <u>inside</u> the symbols overrides the correct measurement and creates static, non-associative text. The original AutoCAD-measured value <u>can be restored</u>, however, using the *New* option. Simply invoke *Dimedit* and *New*, but do not enter any value in the *Edit Mtext* dialogue box (Windows) or at the Command: line prompt (DOS). After selecting the desired dimension, the AutoCAD-measured value is restored.

Rotate
AutoCAD prompts for an angle to rotate the text. Enter an absolute angle (relative to angle 0). This option is identical to the *Angle* option of *Dimtedit*.

Oblique
This option is unique to *Dimedit*. Entering an angle at the prompt affects the extension lines. Enter an absolute angle.

> Enter obliquing angle (RETURN for none):

Normally, the extension lines are perpendicular to the dimension lines. In some cases, it is desirable to set an obliquing angle for the extension lines, such as when dimensions are crowded and hard to read (Fig. 28-58) or for dimensioning isometric drawings (see Dimensioning Isometric Drawings).

Figure 28-58

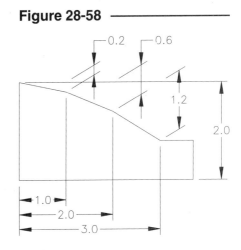

DDMODIFY

DOS PULL-DOWN	WIN PULL-DOWN	SCREEN MENU	TYPE IN	TABLET MENU
Modify Properties...	*Edit Properties...*	MODIFY *Modify...*	DDMODIFY	*9,V and 10,V*

Figure 28-59

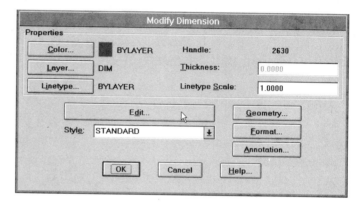

The *Ddmodify* command (discussed in Chapter 16) can be used effectively for a wide range of dimension editing purposes. Selecting a dimension at the "Select objects:" prompt produces the *Modify Dimension* dialogue box (Fig. 28-59). This dialogue box provides access to the *Edit Mtext, Geometry, Format*, and *Annotation* dialogue boxes.

If you want to change the dimension text content, select the *Edit...* tile. The *Edit Mtext* dialogue box appears and provides you with the same options that are available whenever the dialogue box appears (such as with *Dimedit New* or the *Text* option of dimension creation commands). Use this to change any aspect of the text including *Font, Height, Color, Style,* etc.

If you want to change other aspects of the dimension object, such as the appearance of the dimension lines, extension lines, how the text value is displayed, etc., select the *Geometry, Format,* or *Annotation* tiles. This action produces a series of dialogue boxes that change <u>dimension variables</u>. Keep in mind that when you use this interface for changing dimension variables, the change creates a <u>dimension style override</u> and applies the change to the selected dimension object. For information on dimension variables, dimension styles, and dimension style overrides, read Chapter 29, Dimension Styles and Dimension Variables.

Customizing Dimensioning Text

As discussed earlier, you can specify dimensioning text other than what AutoCAD measures and supplies as the default text, using the *Text* option of the individual dimension creation commands. In addition, the text can be modified at a later time using the *Ddmodify* command or the *New* option of *Dimedit*, both of which provide access to the *Edit Mtext* dialogue box (*Dimedit* in AutoCAD for DOS uses the command line format).

The less-than and greater-than symbols (< >) represent the AutoCAD-supplied dimensional value. Placing text or numbers <u>inside</u> the symbols overrides the correct measurement (not advised) and creates static text. Text placed inside the < > symbols is not associative and is <u>not</u> updated in the event of *Stretching, Rotating,* or otherwise editing the associative dimension. The original text can only be retrieved using the *New* option of *Dimedit*.

Text placed outside of the < > symbols, however, acts only as a prefix/suffix to the measured value. In the case of a diameter or radius dimension, AutoCAD automatically inserts a diameter symbol (Ø) or radius designator (R) before the dimension value. Inserting a prefix with the *Edit Mtext* dialogue box <u>does not override</u> the AutoCAD symbols; however, entering a *Prefix* or *Suffix* using the *Dimension Styles* dialogue box <u>overrides</u> the symbols. This feature is important in correct ANSI standard dimensioning for entering the number of times a feature occurs. For example, one of two holes having the same diameter would be dimensioned "2X Ø1.00" (see Figure 28-21).

You can also enter special characters by using the Unicode values or "%%" symbols. The following codes can be entered <u>outside</u> the < > symbols (in the *Edit Mtext* dialogue box or command line prompt) for *Dimedit New, Edit Mtext,* or the *Text* option of dimensioning commands.

Mtext DOS	*Edit Mtext* Windows	*Mtext* Either	Result	Description
\U+2205	%\U+2205	%%c	ø	diameter (metric)
\U+00b0	%\U+00b0	%%d	°	degrees
		%%o	⎯⎯	overscored text
		%%u	___	underscored text
\U+00b1	%\U+00b1	%%p	±	plus or minus
		%%nnn	varies	ASCII text character number
\U+nnnn	%\U+nnnn		varies	Unicode text hexadecimal value

DIMENSIONING ISOMETRIC DRAWINGS

Dimensioning Isometric drawings in AutoCAD is accomplished using *Dimaligned* dimensions and then adjusting the angle of the extension lines with the *Oblique* option of *Dimedit*. The technique follows two basic steps.

Figure 28-60 ⎯⎯⎯⎯⎯⎯⎯⎯⎯

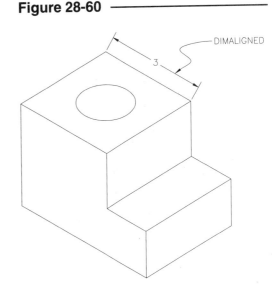

1. Use *Dimaligned* or the *Vertical* option of *Dimlinear* to place a dimension along one edge of the isometric face. Isometric dimensions should be drawn on the isometric axes lines (vertical or at a 30° rotation from horizontal) (Fig. 28-60).

2. Use the *Oblique* dimensioning option of *Dimedit* and select the dimension just created. When prompted to "Enter obliquing angle," enter the desired value (**30** in this case) or PICK two points designating the desired angle. The extension lines should change to the designated angle. In AutoCAD, the possible obliquing angles for isometric dimensions are **30, 150, 210,** or **330**.

Figure 28-61 ⎯⎯⎯⎯⎯⎯⎯⎯⎯

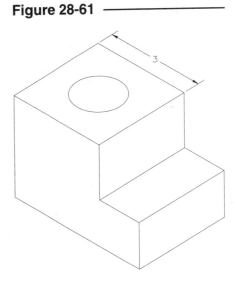

Place isometric dimensions so that they align with the face of the particular feature. Dimensioning the object in the previous illustrations would continue as follows.

Create a *Dimlinear, vertical* dimension along a vertical edge.

Figure 28-62

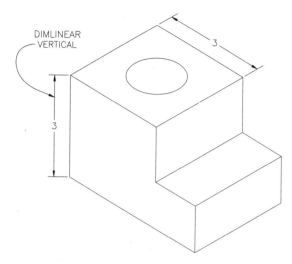

Use *Dimedit, Oblique* to force the dimension to an isometric axis orientation. Enter a value of **150** or PICK two points in response to the "Enter obliquing angle:" prompt.

Figure 28-63

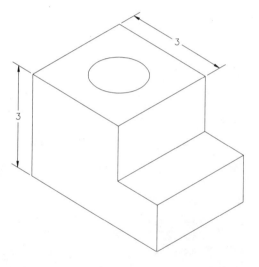

For isometric dimensioning, the extension line origin points <u>must</u> be aligned with the isometric axes. If not, the dimension is not properly oriented. This is important when dimensioning an isometric ellipse (such as this case) or an inclined or oblique edge. Construct center lines for the ellipse on the isometric axes. Next, construct an *Aligned* dimension and *OSNAP* the extension line origins to the center lines. Finally, use *Dimedit Oblique* to reorient the angle of the extension lines.

Figure 28-64

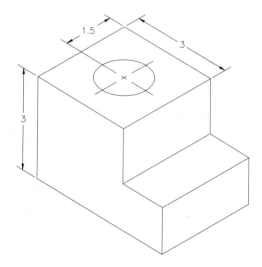

Using the same technique, other appropriate *Dimlinear vertical* or *Aligned* dimensions are placed and reoriented with *Oblique*. Use a *Leader* to dimension a diameter of an *Isocircle*, since *Dimdiameter* cannot be used for an ellipse.

Figure 28-65

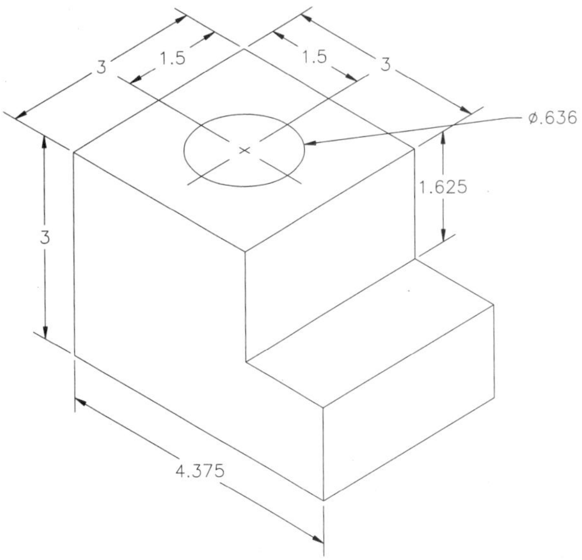

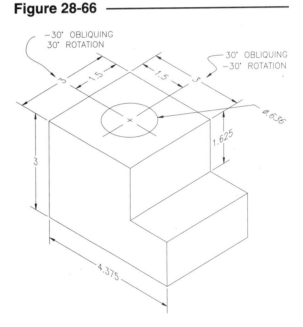

The dimensioning text can be treated two ways. (1) For quick and simple isometric dimensioning, <u>unidirectional</u> dimensioning (all values read from the bottom) is preferred since there is no automatic method for drawing the numerical values in an isometric plane (Fig. 28-65). (2) As a better alternative, text *Styles* could be created with the correct obliquing angles (30 and -30 degrees). The text must also be rotated to the correct angle using the *Rotate* option of the dimension commands or by using *Dimedit Rotate* (Fig. 28-66). Optionally, *Dimension Styles* could be created with the correct variables set for text style and rotation angle for dimensioning on each isoplane.

Figure 28-66

CHAPTER EXERCISES

Only four exercises are offered in this chapter to give you a start with the dimensioning commands. Many other dimensioning exercises are given at the end of Chapter 29, Dimension Styles and Dimension Variables. Since most dimensioning practices in AutoCAD require the use of dimensioning variables and dimension styles, that information should be discussed before you can begin dimensioning effectively.

The units that AutoCAD uses for the dimensioning values are based on the *Units* and *Precision* settings in the *Annotation* dialogue box accessed through the *Dimension Styles* dialogue box. You can dimension these drawings using the default settings, or if you are adventurous, you can change the *Units* and *Precision* settings for each drawing to match the dimensions shown in the figures. (Type *DDIM*, select *Annotation...*, then *Units*.)

Other dimensioning features may appear different than those in the figures because of the variables set in the AutoCAD default STANDARD dimension style. For example, the default settings for diameter and radius dimensions may draw the text and dimension lines differently than you desire. After reading Chapter 29, those features in your exercises can be changed retroactively by changing the dimension style.

1. **Open** the **PLATES** drawing that you created in Chapter 10 Exercises. **Erase** the plate on the right. Use **Move** to move the remaining two plates apart, allowing 5 units between. Create a **New** layer called **DIM** and make it **Current**. Create a **Text Style** using **Romans** font. Dimension the two plates, as shown in Figure 28-67. **Save** the drawing as **PLATES-D**.

Figure 28-67

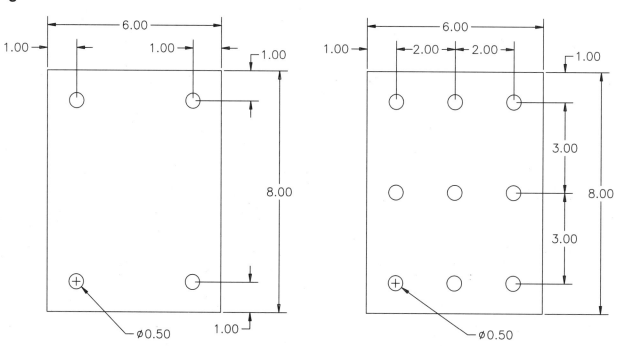

2. **Open** the **CH16EX7** drawing. Create a **New** layer called **DIM** and make it **Current**. Create a **Text Style** using **Romans** font. Dimension the part, as shown in Figure 28-68. **Save** the drawing as **CH28EX2**. Draw a **Pline** border of .02 **width** and **Insert TBLOCK** or **TBLOCKAT**. **Plot** on an "A" size sheet using **Scale to Fit**.

Figure 28-68

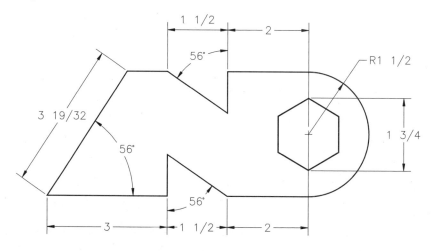

3. *Open* the **GASKETA** drawing that you created in Chapter 9 Exercises. Create a *New* layer called **DIM** and make it *Current*. Create a *Text Style* using *Romans* font. Dimension the part as shown in Figure 28-69. *Save* the drawing as **GASKETD**.

   Draw a *Pline* border with .02 *width* and *Insert* **TBLOCK** or **TBLOCKAT** with an **8/11** scale factor. *Plot* the drawing *Scaled to Fit* on an "A" size sheet.

Figure 28-69 ───────────────────

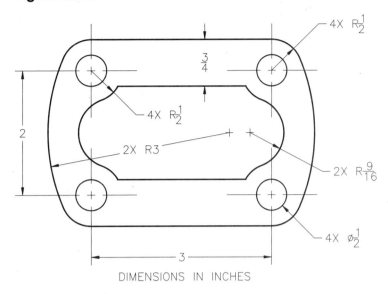

DIMENSIONS IN INCHES

4. *Open* the **BARGUIDE** multiview drawing that you created in Chapter 24 Exercises. Create the dimensions on the **DIM** layer. Keep in mind that you have more possibilities for placement of dimensions than are shown in the pictorial in Fig. 28-70.

Figure 28-70 ───────────────────

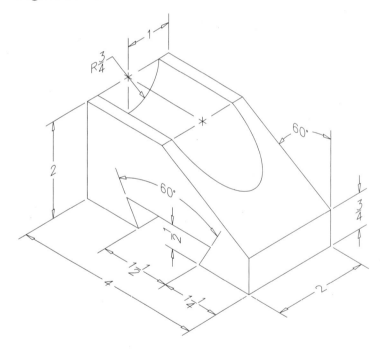

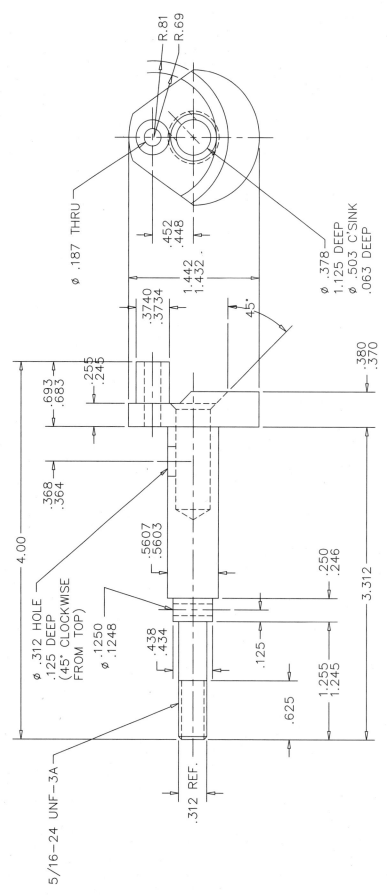

R.81
R.69

Ø .187 THRU

.452
.448

1.442
1.432

Ø .378
1.125 DEEP
Ø .503 C'SINK
.063 DEEP

.3740
.3734

45°

.255
.245

.380
.370

.693
.683

.368
.364

.5607
.5603

.250
.246

4.00

3.312

Ø .312 HOLE
.125 DEEP
(45° CLOCKWISE
FROM TOP)

Ø .1250
.1248

.438
.434

.125

1.255
1.245

.625

5/16—24 UNF—3A

.312 REF.

Chapter 29
DIMENSION STYLES AND DIMENSION VARIABLES
Chapter Objectives

After completing this chapter you should:

1. be able to *Save* and restore dimension styles with the *Dimension Styles* dialogue box or in command line format with the *Dimstyle* command;

2. know how to create dimension style families and specify variables for each child;

3. know how to create and apply dimension style overrides by either command line or dialogue box methods;

4. be able to control dimension variable settings using the *Geometry, Format,* and *Annotation* dialogue boxes;

5. be able to use this chapter as a reference for specifying settings using formal dimension variable names in command line format;

6. be able to modify dimensions using *Dimstyle Apply* and *Dimoverride*;

7. know the guidelines for dimensioning.

BASICS

Dimension Variables

Since a large part of AutoCAD's dimensioning capabilities are automatic, some method must be provided for you to control the way dimensions are drawn. A set of <u>dimension variables</u> allows you to affect the way dimensions are drawn by controlling sizes, distances, appearance of extension and dimension lines, and dimension text formats.

An example of a dimension variable is *DIMSCALE* (if typed) or *Overall Scaling* (if selected from a dialogue box, Fig 29-1). This variable controls the overall size of the dimension features (such as text, arrowheads, gaps, etc.). Changing the value from 1.00 to 1.50, for example, makes all of the size-related features of the drawn dimension 1.5 times as large as the default size of 1.00 (Fig. 29-2). Other examples of features controlled by dimension variables are arrowhead type, orientation of the text, text style, units and precision, suppression of extension lines, fit of text and arrows (inside or outside of extension lines), direction of leaders for radii and diameters (pointing in or out), etc. The dimension variable changes that you make affect the <u>appearance</u> of the dimensions that you create.

Figure 29-1 ─────

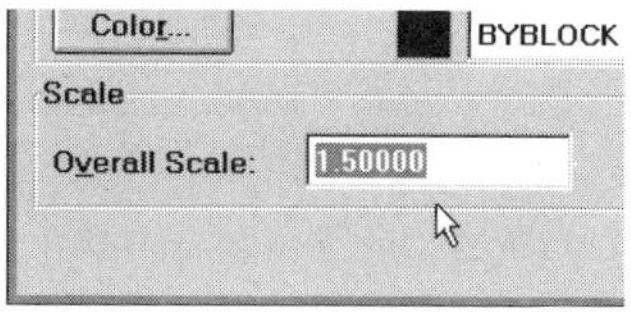

Figure 29-2 ─────────

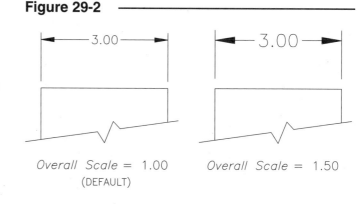

Overall Scale = 1.00
(DEFAULT)   *Overall Scale = 1.50*

There are two basic ways to control dimensioning variables:

1. use the *Dimension Styles* dialogue box series (Fig. 29-3);

2. type the dimension variable name in command line format.

The dialogue boxes employ "user friendly" terminology and selection, while the command line format uses the formal dimension variable names.

Changes to dimension variables are usually made <u>before</u> you create the affected dimensions. Dimension variable changes are <u>not automatically retroactive</u>, in contrast to *LTSCALE*, for example, which can be continually modified to adjust the spacing of existing non-continuous lines. Changes to dimensioning variables only affect <u>newly created</u> dimensions unless those changes are *Saved* to an existing *Dimension Style* that was in effect when previous dimensions were created. Generally, dimensioning variables should be set <u>before</u> creating the desired dimensions.

Figure 29-3 ──────────────

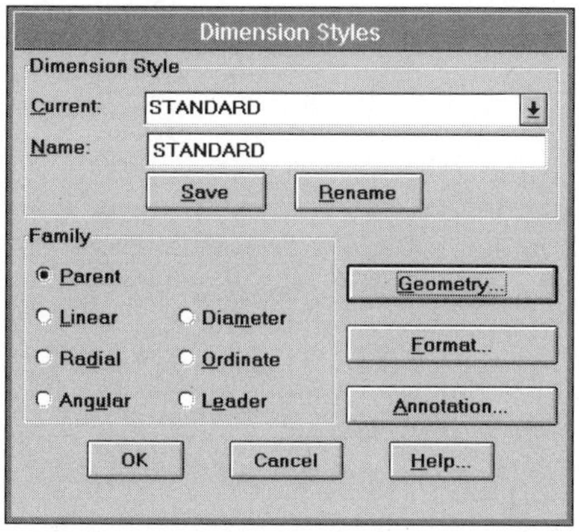

Dimension Styles

All associative dimensions are part of a <u>dimension style</u>. The default (and the only supplied) dimension style is named STANDARD (Fig. 29-3). Logically, this dimension style has all of the default dimension variable settings for creating a dimension with the typical size and appearance. Similar to layers, you can create, name, and specify settings for any number of dimension styles. Each dimension style contains the dimension variable settings that you select. <u>A dimension style is a group of dimension variable settings that has been saved under a name you assign</u>. When you select a dimension style from the

Current: list (or *Restore* a *Dimstyle*), AutoCAD remembers and resets that <u>particular combination of dimension variable settings</u>.

Imagine dimensioning a complex drawing <u>without</u> having dimension styles (Fig. 29-4). In order to create a dimension using limit dimensioning (as shown in the diameter dimension), for example, you would change the desired variable settings, then "draw" the dimension. To draw another dimension without extension lines (as shown in the interior slot), you would have to reset the previous variables and make changes to other variables in order to place the special dimensions as you prefer. This same process would be repeated each time you want to create a new type of dimension. If you needed to add another dimension with the limits, you would have to reset the same variables as before.

Figure 29-4 ───────

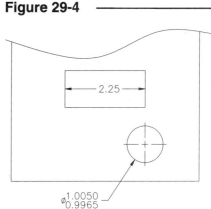

To simplify this process, you can create and save a dimension style for each particular "style" of dimension. Each time you want to draw a particular style of dimension, select the style name from the list and begin drawing. A dimension style could contain all the default settings plus only one or two dimension variable changes or a large number of variable changes.

NOTE: When you make dimension variable changes that you want to keep, make sure you save them to an existing or new style name (by PICKing the *Save* tile).

Another advantage of using dimension styles is that <u>existing</u> dimensions in the drawing can be globally modified by making a change and saving it to the dimension style(s). Knowing that all dimensions are part of a dimension style, making a change in the variable settings using the *Geometry...*, *Format...*, or *Annotation...*dialogue boxes and *Saving* that change results in an <u>automatic update</u> for all existing dimensions drawn with that style.

Dimension Style Families

In the previous chapter, you learned about the various <u>classifications</u> of dimensions, such as linear, angular, radial, diameter, ordinate, and leader. You may want the appearance of each of these classifications of dimensions to vary: for example, all radius dimensions to appear with the dimension line pointing out and all diameter dimensions to appear with the dimension line inside pointing in. It is logical to assume that a new dimension style would have to be created for each variation. However, a new dimension style name is not necessary for each classification of dimension. AutoCAD provides <u>dimension style families</u> for the purpose of providing variations within each named dimension style.

The dimension style <u>names</u> that you create are assigned to a dimension style <u>family</u>. Each dimension style family has a <u>parent</u> and six <u>children</u>. The children are <u>linear, angular, diameter, radial, ordinate, and leader</u>. If the *Parent* button is selected in the *Dimension Styles* dialogue box (Fig 29-3) when a variable change is made, the variable setting affects the entire family. If any one of the buttons for the children (*Linear, Angular, Radial*, etc.) is selected when saving a variable, the variable affects only that child (classification of dimension) (Fig. 29-6, next page). When a dimension is drawn, AutoCAD knows what classification of dimension is created and applies the selected variables to that child.

AutoCAD refers to these children as $0, $2, $3, $4, $6, and $7, respectively, as appended suffixes to the parent name. These suffix codes may seem trivial because the user does not need to be concerned about them, since AutoCAD automatically applies the appropriate style to the given dimension type.

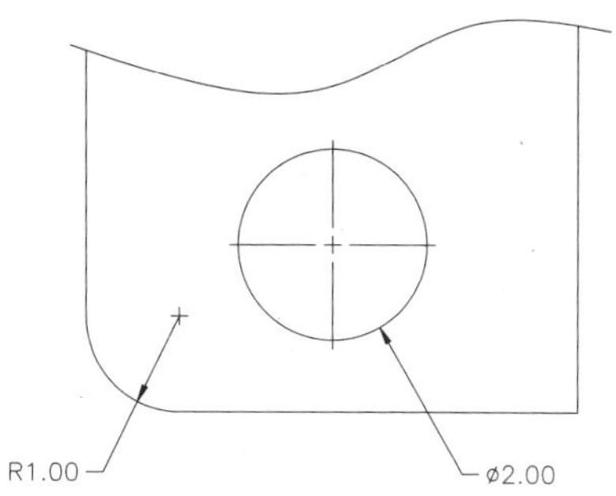

As an example, you may want to force the dimension line and text outside of circles for the diameter dimensions for the DETAILS dimension style family (Fig. 29-6). First, click on the *Diameter* radio button. Second, make the necessary variable change (in the *Fit* section of the *Annotation* dialogue box—explained later). Third, save the change to the dimension style by selecting *Save* in the *Dimension Styles* dialogue box (Fig 29-6). When the dimension is drawn, the dimension line and arrow should appear as shown (Fig. 29-5). Listing the dimension (use the *List* command) reports the style name for that dimension as DETAILS$3.

Figure 29-5

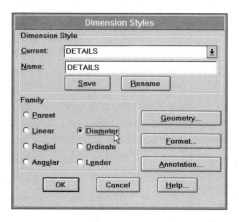

R1.00   ⌀2.00

In summary, a dimension style family is simply a set of dimension variables related by name. Variations within the family are allowed, in that each child (classification of dimension) can possess its own subset of variables. Therefore, each child inherits all the variables of the parent in addition to any others that may be assigned individually.

Dimension Style Overrides

When you make the variable change and <u>do not *Save*</u> it to the current dimension style, AutoCAD remembers the setting nevertheless. The change is appended to the <u>current</u> style as a <u>dimension style override</u>. This is particularly helpful if you need a special feature on one or two dimensions but do not want to update the dimension style (and all existing dimensions of the style) with the new change.

A dimension style override is created by <u>changing a variable setting but not saving it</u> to the current dimension style. You can create an override by using the *Dimension Styles* dialogue box series to set a variable and exiting without using *Save* or by changing a variable setting by command line format. (If you type the name of a dimension variable and change a value at the command prompt "on the fly," the current dimension style is used as a base style.) When an override is made, a new style name is created with a "+" placed as a prefix and the new style is set current. Each new dimension created with the new modified style applies the overridden variables. If you list one of these dimensions (using *List*), the new style name and the overridden variables are displayed. Dimension style overrides <u>can only be saved to the *Parent* style</u> and cannot be created for an individual child.

DIMENSION STYLES

DDIM

PULL-DOWN MENU	SCREEN MENU	TYPE IN	TABLET MENU
Data *Dimension Style...*	*DATA* *DDim:*	*DDIM*	*4,V and 5,V*

The *Ddim* command produces the *Dimension Styles* dialogue box (Fig. 29-6). This is the primary interface for creating new dimension styles and making existing dimension styles current. This dialogue box also provides access to the three boxes that enable you to change dimension variables. The radio buttons are used to select a classification of dimension (child) for applying variable changes. (Please read the previous sections of this chapter for an introduction to these concepts.) The available options are explained next.

Figure 29-6

Current:

Select the desired <u>existing</u> style from the pop-down list to set it as the current style. The dimension style appearing in the box is the current style that is used for drawing subsequent dimensions. Additionally, the current style is the template used for any operations within the *Dimension Style* dialogue box series, such as (1) creating a new style, (2) making modifications to the current style by changing dimension variables, then using *Save*, or (3) renaming the style. A name appearing with a "+" (plus) symbol before the name, "+STANDARD," for example, means that a variable has been changed but not yet *Saved* to the dimension style (see Dimension Overrides).

Name:

Enter a name in the box to be used for creating a new style or renaming an existing style. The name appearing in the *Current:* box is the template for the new style or renamed style.

Save

Select this tile after creating a new style or making the desired variable changes to the current style. Changing a variable setting and exiting the dialogue box without saving creates a dimension style override.

Rename

Select this option to replace the old style name (appearing in the *Current:* box) with the new name (appearing in the *Name:* box). Begin this operation by entering the desired new name in the *Name:* box.

Geometry...

This tile produces the *Geometry* dialogue box (explained in detail in the following section). The *Geometry* box enables you to make dimension variable changes that affect the appearance of <u>arrowheads</u>, <u>dimension lines</u>, and <u>extension lines</u>.

Format...

This tile produces the *Format* dialogue box (explained in detail in the following section). You can make variable changes related to <u>location and orientation of dimension text</u> in the *Format* box.

Annotation...

The *Annotation* dialogue box is the interface for dimension variables controlling the <u>content of the dimension text</u>.

Family

Use this section to specify the classification of dimension that you want to affect using the variable controls in the *Geometry, Format,* and *Annotation* boxes. Select the desired family member <u>first</u>; then make the desired adjustments. The family members are:

Parent

Select this button to create a dimension style family or to make familywide dimension variable changes.

Linear, Angular, Radial, Diameter, Ordinate, and Leader

Select the desired classification (child) for subsequent dimension variable changes.

Creating a New Dimension Style Family Using the *Dimension Styles* Dialogue Box

1. Select the *Parent* button in the *Dimension Styles* dialogue box (see Fig. 29-6).

2. Select the desired dimension style name from the *Current:* list to use as a template. Whatever style appears in this edit box is used as a template. The new style will contain all of the variable settings of the template plus any changes you make and *Save*. Usually, the STANDARD style is used as a template.

3. Type over or modify the name in the *Name:* edit box to assign the new name.

4. Change the desired dimension variables from the *Geometry...*, *Format...*, or *Annotation...* dialogue boxes (discussed in detail later). Familywide variables such as *Overall Scale* are set at this stage. Select the *OK* tile in each of these boxes to keep your changes.

5. After returning to the *Dimension Styles* dialogue box, PICK *Save* to assign the variable changes to the new dimension style family. The new style becomes current. Then select the *OK* tile. *Cancel* cancels the creation of the new dimension style.

NOTE: Do not change the STANDARD style or you lose your ability to easily restore all of the default settings. Generally, make dimension styles with new names using STANDARD as a <u>template</u>.

Setting Dimension Variables for a Child Using the *Dimension Styles* Dialogue Box

1. Select the desired <u>existing</u> dimension style family name from the *Current:* list (see Fig. 29-6).

2. Select the desired classification of dimension (child) such as *Linear*, *Angular*, *Radial*, etc.

3. Change the desired dimension variables from the *Geometry...*, *Format...*, or *Annotation...* dialogue boxes (discussed in detail later). Select the *OK* tile in each of these boxes to keep your changes.

4. After returning to the *Dimension Styles* dialogue box, PICK *Save* to assign the variable changes to the dimension style family. Then select the *OK* tile.

Restoring a Dimension Style Using the *Dimension Styles* Dialogue Box

1. Select the desired style name from the *Current:* list. The style should then appear in the *Name:* edit box. Select the *OK* tile.

2. The selected dimension style becomes the current style and remains so until another is made current. Any dimensions created while the style is current contain the features dictated by the style's variable settings.

Modifying a Dimension Style and Updating Existing Dimensions

1. Select the desired style name from the *Current:* list in the *Dimension Styles* dialogue box.

2. Change the desired dimension variables from the *Geometry...*, *Format...*, or *Annotation...* dialogue boxes. Select the *OK* tile in each of these boxes to keep your changes. When you select the *Save* tile in the main dialogue box, the current dimension style is updated.

3. As you exit the dialogue box, you will notice some activity in the Drawing Editor. All dimensions originally created with that style are <u>automatically</u> updated with the new variables.

DIMSTYLE

PULL-DOWN MENU	SCREEN MENU	TYPE IN	TABLET MENU
---	*DRAWDIM* *Dimstyl:*	*DIMSTYLE* *or DIMSTY*	---

The *Dimstyle* command is the command line format equivalent to the *Dimension Style* dialogue box. Operations that are performed by the dialogue box can also be accomplished with the *Dimstyle* command. The *Apply* option offers one other important feature that is <u>not</u> available in the dialogue box.

```
Command: dimstyle
dimension style: STANDARD
Dimension Style Edit (Save/Restore/STatus/Variables/Apply/?) <Restore>:
```

Save
Use this option to <u>create a new</u> dimension style. The new style assumes all of the current dimension variable settings comprised of those from the current style, plus any other variables changed by command line format (overrides). The new dimension style becomes the current style.

```
Dimension Style Edit (Save/Restore/STatus/Variables/Apply/?) <Restore>: s
?/Name for new dimension style:
```

Restore
This option prompts for an existing dimension style name to restore. The restored style becomes the current style. You can use the "RETURN to select:" option to PICK a dimension object that references the style you want to restore.

STatus
Status gives the <u>current settings</u> for all dimension variables. The displayed list comprises the settings of the current dimension style and any overrides. All 58 dimension variables are listed.

```
Dimension Style Edit (Save/Restore/STatus/Variables/Apply/?) <Restore>: st
```

```
DIMALT   Off           Alternate units selected
DIMALTD  2             Alternate unit decimal places
DIMALTF  25.4000       Alternate unit scale factor
DIMALTTD 2             Alternate tolerance decimal places
etc.
```

Variables
You can use this option to <u>list</u> the dimension variable settings for <u>any existing dimension style</u>. You cannot modify the settings.

```
Dimension Style Edit (Save/Restore/STatus/Variables/Apply/?) <Restore>: v
?/Enter dimension style name or RETURN to select dimension:
```

Enter the name of any style or use "RETURN to select:" to PICK a dimension object that references the desired style. A list of all variables and settings appears.

~stylename
This variation can be entered in response to the *Variables* option. Entering a dimension style name preceded by the tilde symbol (~) displays the <u>differences between the current style and the (~)named style</u>.

R13

For example, assume that you wanted to display the <u>differences</u> between STANDARD and the current dimension style (LIMITS-1, for example). Use *Variables* with the ~ symbol. (The ~ symbol is used as a wildcard to mean "all but.")

```
Command: dimstyle
dimension style: LIMITS-1
Dimension Style Edit (Save/Restore/STatus/Variables/Apply/?) <Restore>: v
?/Enter dimension style name or RETURN to select dimension: ~standard
Differences between STANDARD and current settings:
```

	STANDARD	Current Setting
DIMLIM	Off	On
DIMTFAC	1.0000	0.7000
DIMTM	0.0000	0.1000
DIMTP	0.0000	0.0500

```
?/Enter dimension style name or RETURN to select dimension: *Cancel*
Command:
```

This option is very useful for keeping track of your dimension styles and their variable settings.

Apply
Use *Apply* to <u>update dimension objects</u> that you PICK with the current variable settings. The current variable settings can contain those of the current dimension style plus any overrides. The selected object loses its reference to its original style and is "adopted" by the applied dimension style family.

```
Dimension Style Edit (Save/Restore/STatus/Variables/Apply/?) <Restore>: a
Select objects:
```

This is a useful tool for <u>changing an existing dimension object from one style to another</u>. Simply make the desired dimension style current; then use *Apply* and select the dimension objects to change to that style.

DIMENSION VARIABLES

Now that you understand how to create and use dimension styles and dimension style families, let's explore the dimension variables. There are <u>two methods</u> that can be used to set dimension variables: the *Dimension Styles* dialogue box series and command line format. First, we will examine the *Geometry, Format,* and *Annotation* dialogue boxes (accessible through the *Dimension Styles* dialogue box). These dialogue boxes contain an interface for setting the dimension variables. Dimension variables can alternately be set by typing the formal name of the variable and changing the desired value (discussed after this section on dialogue boxes). However, the dialogue boxes offer a more understandable terminology, buttons, check boxes, lists, and several image tiles that automatically change the variables when you click on the image.

Changing Dimension Variables Using the Dialogue Boxes
In this section, the three main dialogue boxes for changing variables are explained. The headings for the paragraphs below include the <u>option</u> title in the dialogue box and the related dimension <u>variable</u> name in parentheses.

Geometry...

Choosing the *Geometry...* button in the *Dimension Styles* dialogue box (Fig. 29-6) opens the *Geometry* dialogue box (Fig. 29-7). Use this box to change variables that control the <u>appearance of arrowheads, dimension lines, and extension lines</u>. The *Geometry* dialogue box contains five specific areas explained in the following sections:

Figure 29-7

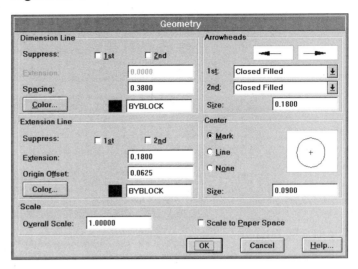

Overall Scale (DIMSCALE)

The *Overall Scale* value globally affects the scale of <u>all size-related features</u> of dimension objects, such as arrowheads, text height, extension line gaps (from the object), and extensions (past dimension lines), etc. All other size-related values (variables) appearing in the dialogue box series are <u>multiplied by the *Overall Scale*</u>. Therefore, to keep all features proportional, change this one setting rather than each of the others individually.

Although this area is located at the bottom of the box, it is probably the most important option. Because the *Overall Scale* should be set as a familywide variable, enter this value as the <u>first step</u> in creating a dimension style. Select *Parent* family member before making this setting.

Figure 29-8

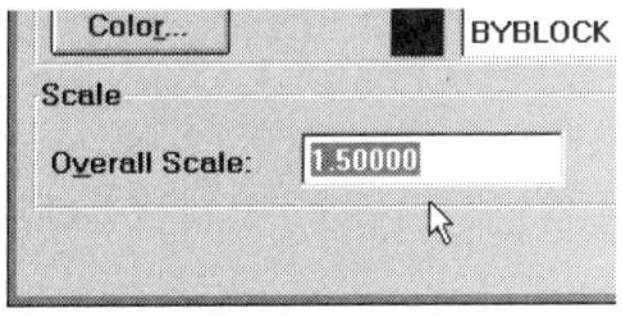

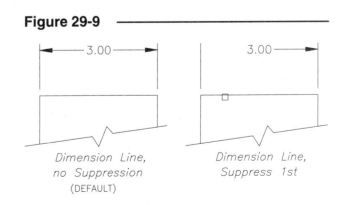

Changes in this variable should be based on the *Limits* and plot scale. You can use the "drawing scale factor" to determine this value. (See Drawing Scale Factor, Chapter 13.) The *Overall Scale* value is stored in the *DIMSCALE* variable.

Scale to Paper Space

Checking this box forces dimensions to appear in the same size for all viewports (Paper Space viewports created with *Mview*). Toggling this on sets *DIMSCALE* to 0. See Chapter 32 for detailed information on this subject.

Dimension Line

Suppress 1st, 2nd (DIMSD1, DIMSD2)

This area allows you to suppress (not draw) the *1st* or *2nd* dimension line, or both (Fig. 29-9). The <u>first</u> dimension line would be on the "First extension line origin" side or nearest the end of object PICKed in response to "Select object to dimension." These toggles change the *DIMSD1* and *DIMSD2* dimension variables.

Figure 29-9

3.00

3.00

Dimension Line,
no Suppression
(DEFAULT)

Dimension Line,
Suppress 1st

R13

Extension (**DIMDLE**)

The *Extension* edit box is disabled unless the *Oblique* arrowhead type is selected (in the *Arrowheads* section). The *Extension* value controls the length of dimension line that extends past the dimension line for *Oblique* "arrows" (Fig. 29-10).

Figure 29-10 ────────────

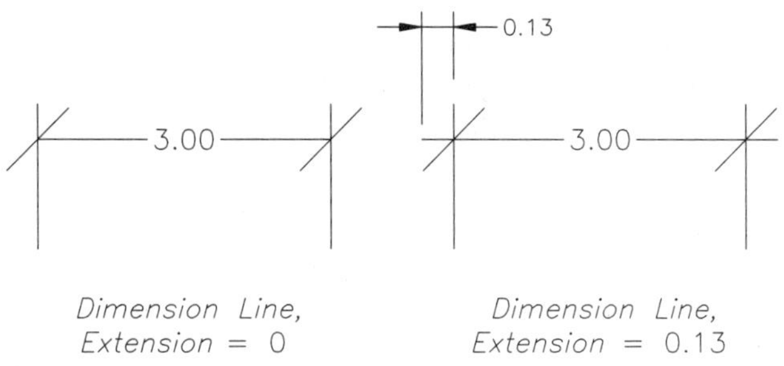

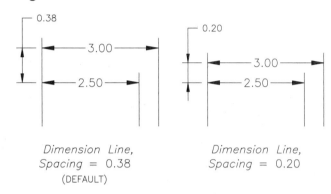

Dimension Line,
Extension = 0

Dimension Line,
Extension = 0.13

Spacing (**DIMDLI**)

The *Spacing* edit box reflects the value that AutoCAD uses in baseline dimensioning to "stack" the dimension line above or below the previous one (Fig. 29-11). This value is held in the *DIMDLI* variable.

Figure 29-11 ────────────

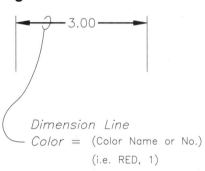

Dimension Line,
Spacing = 0.38
(DEFAULT)

Dimension Line,
Spacing = 0.20

Color (**DIMCLRD**)

The *Color* button allows you to choose the color for the dimension line (Fig. 29-12). Assigning a specific color to the dimension lines, extension lines, and dimension text enables you to plot these features with different line widths or colors (pen assignments are made in the *Plot Control* dialogue box). This feature corresponds to the *DIMCLRD* variable.

Figure 29-12 ────────────

Dimension Line
Color = (Color Name or No.)
(i.e. RED, 1)

Extension Line

Suppress 1st, 2nd (**DIMSE1, DIMSE2**)

This area is similar to the *Dimension Line* area and can be easily confused with it, so be careful! This area allows you to suppress the *1st* or *2nd* extension line or both (Fig. 29-13). These options correspond to the *DIMSE1* and *DIMSE2* dimension variables.

Figure 29-13 ────────────

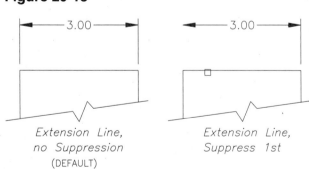

Extension Line,
no Suppression
(DEFAULT)

Extension Line,
Suppress 1st

Extension (DIMEXE)

The *Extension* edit box reflects the value that AutoCAD uses to set the distance for the extension line to extend beyond the dimension line (Fig. 29-14). This value is held in the *DIMEXE* variable. Generally, this value does not require changing since it is automatically multiplied by the *Overall Scale*.

Figure 29-14

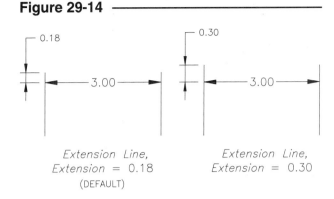

Extension Line,
Extension = 0.18
(DEFAULT)

Extension Line,
Extension = 0.30

Origin Offset (DIMEXO)

The *Origin Offset* value specifies the distance between the origin points and the extension lines (Fig. 29-15). This offset distance allows you to PICK the object corners, yet the extension lines maintain the required gap from the object. This value rarely requires input since it is affected by *Overall Scale*. The value is stored in the *DIMEXO* variable.

Figure 29-15

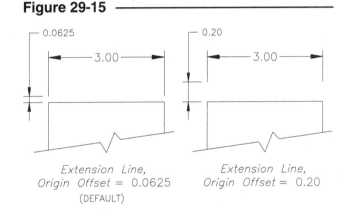

Extension Line,
Origin Offset = 0.0625
(DEFAULT)

Extension Line,
Origin Offset = 0.20

Color (DIMCLRE)

The *Color* button allows you to choose the color for the extension lines (Fig. 29-16). This feature corresponds to the *DIMCLRE* variable.

Figure 29-16

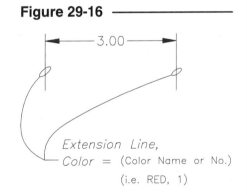

Extension Line,
Color = (Color Name or No.)
(i.e. RED, 1)

Arrowheads
1st, 2nd (DIMBLK, DIMBLK1, DIMBLK2)

This area contains two pop-down lists of various arrowhead types, including dots and ticks. Each list corresponds to the *1st* or *2nd* arrowhead created in the drawn dimension. The image tiles display each arrowhead type selected. Click in the first image tile to change both arrowheads, or click in each to change them individually (Fig. 29-17). The variables affected are *DIMBLK*, *DIMBLK1*, *DIMBLK2*, and *DIMSAH* (see Dimension Variables Table for details).

Figure 29-17

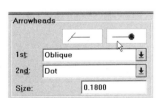

Size **(DIMASZ)**

The size of the arrow can be specified in the *Size* edit box (Fig. 29-18). The *DIMASZ* variable holds the value. Remember that *Size* is multiplied by *Overall Scale*.

Figure 29-18

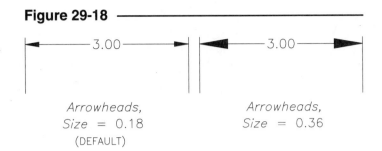

Arrowheads,
Size = 0.18
(DEFAULT)

Arrowheads,
Size = 0.36

Center

Mark, Line, None **(DIMCEN)**

The radio buttons determine how center marks are drawn when the dimension commands *Dimcenter, Dimdiameter,* or *Dimradius* are used (Fig. 29-19). The image tile displays the *Mark, Line,* or *None* radio button feature specified. This area actually controls the value of <u>one</u> dimension variable, *DIMCEN* (by using a 0, positive, or negative value) (see Fig. 29-20).

Figure 29-19

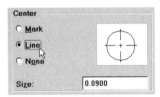

Size **(DIMCEN)**

The *Size* edit box controls the size of the short dashes and extensions past the arc or circle. The value is stored in the *DIMCEN* variable (Fig. 29-20). Only positive values can be (and need to be) entered in the <u>dialogue box</u>.

Figure 29-20

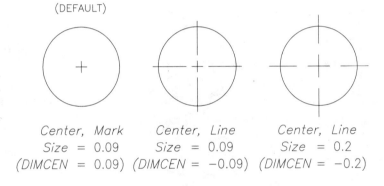

(DEFAULT)

Center, Mark
Size = 0.09
(DIMCEN = 0.09)

Center, Line
Size = 0.09
(DIMCEN = −0.09)

Center, Line
Size = 0.2
(DIMCEN = −0.2)

Format...

The *Format* dialogue box (Fig. 29-21) provides control of the <u>location and orientation of the text with respect to the dimension line</u>.

Figure 29-21

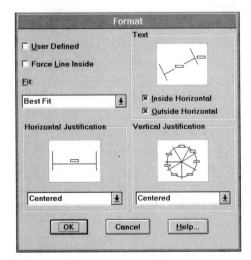

User Defined (DIMUPT)

Checking the *User Defined* box enables you to select the insertion point of the dimension text when dimensions are drawn. It is useful to toggle this on for the *Diameter* family member so that text can be dynamically dragged outside of the circle (Fig. 29-22). Checking this box disables the *Horizontal Justification* options. The value for this switch is stored in the *DIMUPT* dimension variable.

Figure 29-22

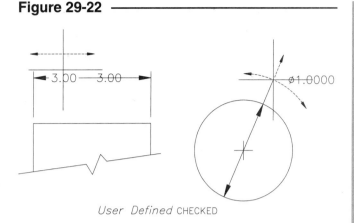

User Defined CHECKED

Force Line Inside (DIMTOFL)

The *Force Line Inside* toggle sets the value of *DIMTOFL* on or off. When this variable is on, a dimension line is drawn between the extension lines when the arrows are drawn outside the extension lines (Fig. 29-23).

Figure 29-23

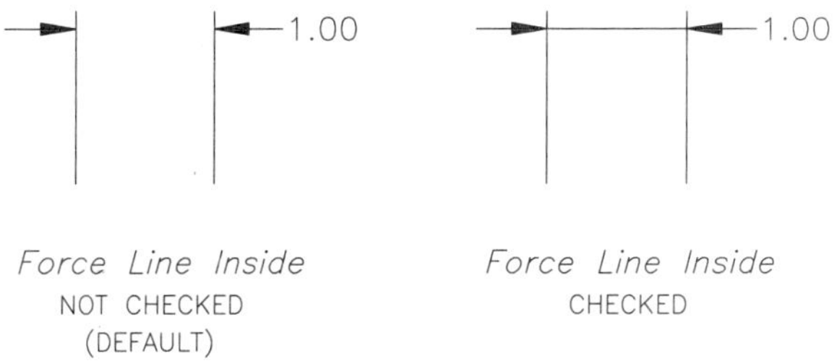

Force Line Inside
NOT CHECKED
(DEFAULT)

Force Line Inside
CHECKED

Fit: (DIMFIT)

The *Fit* pop-down list determines how text and arrows are treated <u>only in the case that there is insufficient room</u> between the extension lines for the text, arrows, and dimension lines. In most cases, when space permits all features to fit inside, the *Fit* setting has no effect on the placement. If there is absolutely not enough room for text or arrows, all options behave similarly—text and arrows are placed outside. The five *Fit* options set the value of the dimension variable *DIMFIT* to 0 through 4.

The *Text and Arrows* option <u>keeps the text and arrows together</u> always. If space does not permit both features to fit between the extension lines, it places the text and arrows outside the extension lines (Fig. 29-24). (*DIMFIT* = 0.)

Figure 29-24

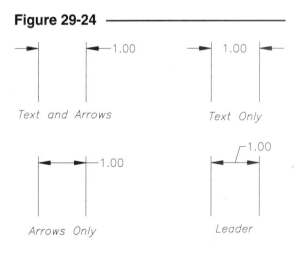

Text and Arrows

Text Only

Arrows Only

Leader

The *Text Only* option keeps the <u>text between the extension lines</u> and the arrows on the outside. If the text absolutely cannot fit, it is placed outside the extension lines (Fig. 29-24). (*DIMFIT* is set to 1.)

The *Arrows Only* option places the text on the outside and the <u>arrows on the inside</u> unless the arrows cannot fit, in which case they are placed on the outside as well (Fig. 29-24). (*DIMFIT* is set to 2.)

The *Best Fit* option behaves similarly to *Text Only*, except that in the case that the text cannot fit, the text is placed outside the extension lines and the arrows are placed inside. However, if the arrows cannot fit either, both text and arrows are placed outside the extension lines. This is the default setting for the STANDARD style. (*DIMFIT* = 3.)

The *Leader* option enables the creation of leaders. If text cannot fit between the extension lines, then leaders to the text are created automatically (Fig. 29-24). (*DIMFIT* is set to 4.)

Text–Inside/Outside Horizontal (DIMTIH, DIMTOH)

The *Text* section in the upper right of the dialogue box sets the <u>orientation of the dimension text to horizontal or aligned</u> (with the dimension line). The setting can be selected from the pop-down list or by <u>clicking on the image tile</u> (Fig. 29-25). The results of the changes are obvious by the configuration in the image tile. Your choice sets the value for variables *DIMTIH* and *DIMTOH*.

Figure 29-25 —

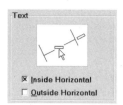

Horizontal Justification (DIMJUST)

The *Horizontal Justification* section determines the <u>horizontal location of the text with respect to the dimension line</u>. Change the setting with the pop-down list or by clicking the image tile. The choice sets the value for *DIMJUST*.

Figure 29-26 —

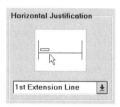

Vertical Justification (DIMTAD, DIMTIH)

The *Vertical Justification* section operates similarly to the *Horizontal Justification* feature. Changes can be made through selection from the pop-down list or by clicking on the image tile. The possible orientation options are displayed in the image tile. The selections modify the values of the *DIMTAD* (four possible settings) and *DIMTIH* variables together; therefore, eight different images are possible. Experiment with these settings and examine the changes to the image tile.

Figure 29-27 —

Annotation...

The *Annotation* dialogue box (Fig. 29-28) controls the <u>format of the annotation (text) of a dimension</u>. You can vary the AutoCAD-supplied numerical value that is drawn in the dimension in several ways. Features such as the text style and height, prefix and/or suffix, alternate units (for inch and metric notation), and several variations of tolerance and limit dimensions are possible. These features are displayed in the dialogue box in four separate areas.

Figure 29-28 ———————————

Annotation	
Primary Units	**Alternate Units**
Units...	☐ Enable Units Units...
Prefix:	Prefix:
Suffix:	Suffix:
1.00	[25.4]
Tolerance	**Text**
Method: None	Style: STANDARD
Upper Value: 0.0000	Height: 0.1800
Lower Value: 0.0000	Gap: 0.0900
Justification: Middle	Color... BYBLOCK
Height: 1.0000	Round Off: 0.0000
	OK Cancel Help...

Primary Units (DIMUNIT)

The *Primary Units* section (top left) controls the display of units, precision, and prefix and/or suffix. Selecting the *Units* tile summons the *Primary Units* dialogue (Fig. 29-29). You can select the *Unit* type from the pop-down list (Fig. 29-30). These are the same unit types available with the *Units* and *Ddunits* command (*Decimal, Scientific, Engineering, Architectural,* and *Fractional*) with the addition of *Architectural (stacked)* and *Fractional (stacked)* (available with Release 13 version c2 or later). Remember that your selection affects the <u>units drawn in dimension objects, not the global drawing units</u>. Examples of the resulting dimension objects for the two fractional and two architectural unit choices are shown in Figure 29-31. The choice for *Primary Units* is stored in the *DIMUNIT* variable. This pop-down list is disabled for an *Angular* family member.

Figure 29-29 ————

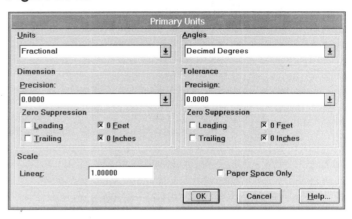

Figure 29-30 ————

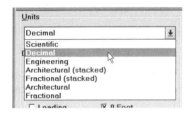

Figure 29-31 ————————————

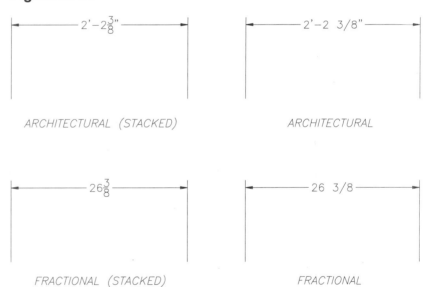

Dimension, Precision (DIMDEC)

The *Precision* pop-down list in the *Dimension* section specifies the number of places for decimal dimensions or denominator for fractional dimensions. This setting does not alter the drawing units precision. This value is stored in the *DIMDEC* variable.

Dimension, Zero Suppression (DIMZIN)

The *Zero Suppression* section controls how zeros are drawn in a dimension when they occur. A check in one of these boxes means that zeros are <u>not drawn for that case</u>. This sets the value for *DIMZIN*.

Angles (DIMAUNIT)

The *Angles* section sets the unit type for angular dimensions from a pop-down list, including *Decimal degrees, Deg/Min/Sec, Grads, Radians,* and *Surveyor* (units). This list is only enabled for *Parent* and *Angular* family members. The variable used for the angular units is *DIMAUNIT*.

Tolerance (DIMTDEC, DIMTZIN)

Use the *Tolerance* cluster area of the *Primary Units* dialogue box to set values when drawing tolerance dimensions (see *Tolerance*). The *Precision* and *Zero Suppression* operate identically to the *Dimension* section. The affected variables are *DIMTDEC* and *DIMTZIN*.

Scale, Linear (DIMLFAC)

The value appearing in the *Linear Scale* section of the *Primary Units* dialogue box is a <u>multiplier</u> for the AutoCAD-measured numerical value. The default is 1. Entering a 2 would cause AutoCAD to draw a value two times the actual measured value (Fig. 29-32). This feature is used when a drawing is created in some scale other than the actual size, such as in an enlarged detail created in the same drawing as the full view. For example, if you wanted to make a detail (enlarged view) of a portion of a part, create

Figure 29-32

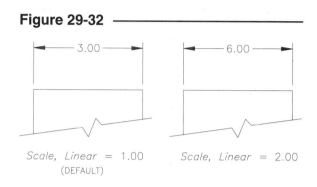

the detail two times the actual size, enter .5 in the *Linear Scale* edit box, dimension the detail, and AutoCAD will display the actual part measurements rather than the actual measured value of the enlarged AutoCAD objects. This value is stored in the *DIMLFAC* variable.

NOTE: The image tile in the *Primary Units* section of the *Annotation* dialogue box does <u>not</u> display the units and precision selected. It only displays the options selected from the *Tolerance* section below.

Alternate Units (DIMALTx)

You can specify that AutoCAD draws <u>alternate units</u> (a <u>second set</u> of numerical values) when placing a dimension (Fig. 29-33). In the *Annotation* dialogue box (Fig. 29-28), the *Enable Units* toggle can be checked to enable the *Units...* button of the *Alternate Units* cluster. The *Alternate Units* dialogue box features are nearly the same as *Primary Units* with the exception of the *Linear Scale*. The value appearing in this field is a multiplier for the AutoCAD-measured value. Note that *Linear Scale* in the *Aternate Units* dialogue box is set to 25.4, the inch-to-milimeter conversion factor (Fig. 29-34). In many industries, both inch units and metric units are required for all dimensions.

Figure 29-33

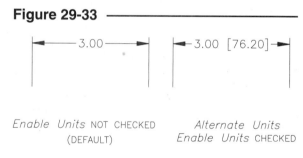

Figure 29-34

Because the alternate unit options parallel the primary unit options, a parallel set of variables is used to store the related values. The variable names are *DIMALTU* for alternate units, *DIMALTD* for alternate units decimal places, *DIMALTF* for alternate linear scale, *DIMALTZ* for alternate units zero suppression, *DIMALTTZ* for alternate units tolerance zero suppression, and *DIMALTTD* for alternate units tolerance decimal places. *DIMALT* stores the on/off toggle for enabling alternate units.

Prefix/Suffix (DIMPOST, DIMAPOST)

In both the *Primary Units* and *Alternate Units* sections of the *Annotation* dialogue box (Fig. 29-28), the *Prefix* and *Suffix* edit box holds any text that you want to add to the AutoCAD-supplied dimensional value. For example, entering the string " mm" or a " TYP." in the *Suffix* edit box would produce text as shown in Figure 29-35. (In such a case, don't forget the space between the numerical value and the suffix.) The string is stored in the variable *DIMPOST* and in *DIMAPOST* for alternate units prefix/suffix.

Figure 29-35

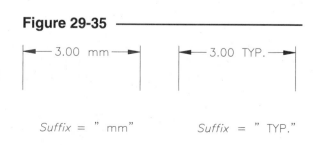

If you use the *Prefix* box to enter letters or values, any AutoCAD-supplied symbols (for radius and diameter dimensions) are overridden (not drawn). For example, if you want to specify that a specific hole appears twice, you should indicate by designating a "2X" before the diameter dimension. However, doing so by this method overrides the phi (Ø) symbol that AutoCAD inserts before the value. Instead, use the *Text* option within the dimensioning command, or use *Dimedit* to add a prefix to an existing dimension having an AutoCAD-supplied symbol (see Figure 28-21 and related text, and *Dimedit*).

Tolerance

Figure 29-36

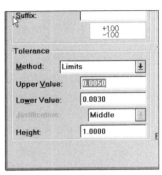

Method (*DIMTOL, DIMLIM, DIMGAP*)

The *Tolerance Method* displays a pop-down list with five types: *None*, *Symmetrical*, *Deviation*, *Limits*, and *Basic*. Each format is displayed in the image tile <u>above</u> this section (actually in the *Primary Units* section) (Fig. 29-36). You can click in the image tile above to cycle through the formats. The four possibilities (other than *None*) are illustrated in Figure 29-37. The *Symmetrical* and *Deviation* methods create plus/minus dimensions and turn on the *DIMTOL* variable. The *Limits* method creates limit dimensions and turns the *DIMLIM* variable on. The *Basic* method creates a basic dimension by drawing a box around the dimensional value, which is accomplished by changing the *DIMGAP* to a negative value.

Upper Value/Lower Value (*DIMTP, DIMTM*)

An *Upper Value* and *Lower Value* can be entered in the edit boxes for the *Deviation* and *Limits* method types. In these cases, the *Upper Value* (*DIMTP*—DIM Tolerance Plus) is added to the measured dimension and the *Lower Value* (*DIMTP*—DIM Tolerance Minus) is subtracted (Fig. 29-37). An *Upper Value* only is needed for *Symmetrical* and is applied as both the plus and minus value.

Figure 29-37

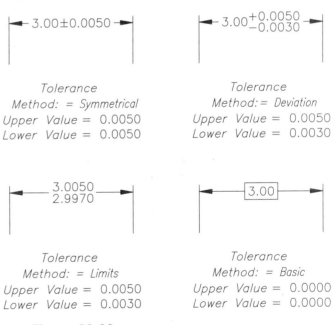

Height (*DIMTFAC*)

The height of the <u>tolerance text</u> is controlled with the *Height* edit box value. The entered value is a <u>proportion</u> of the primary dimension value height. For example, a value of .75 would draw the tolerance text at 75% of the primary text height (Fig. 29-38). The *Tolerance Height* value is <u>not reflected in the image tile above</u>. The setting affects the *Symmetrical*, *Deviation*, and *Limits* tolerance methods. The value is stored in the *DIMTFAC* (Text FACtor) variable.

Figure 29-38

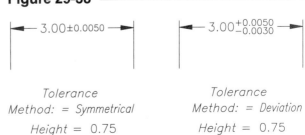

Justification (DIMTOLJ)

Justification places the tolerance dimension values with either a top, middle, or bottom alignment with the primary dimension value. The result <u>is displayed</u> in the image tile. The *Justification* feature is enabled only for *Symmetrical* and *Deviation* dimension methods (Fig. 29-39).

Figure 29-39

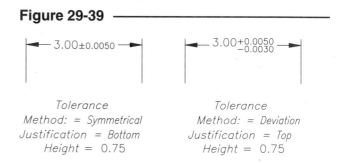

Text

Style (DIMTXSTY)

The *Text* cluster controls the text *Style, Height,* and *Color* of the dimension text. The text styles are chosen from a pop-down list of <u>existing</u> styles. The advantage is different dimension styles can have different text styles. The text style used for dimensions remains constant (as defined by the dimension style) and does not change when other text styles in the drawing are made current (as defined by *Style, Dtext, Text,* or *Mtext*). The *DIMTXSTY* variable holds the text style name for the dimension style.

Figure 29-40

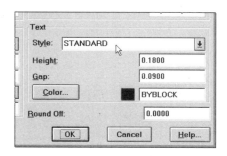

Height (DIMTXT)

This value specifies the <u>primary text height</u>; however, this value is multiplied by the *Overall Scale* (*DIMSCALE*) to determine the actual drawn text height. Change *Height* if you want to increase or decrease only the text height (Fig. 29-41). Change instead the *Overall Scale* to change all size-related features (arrows, gaps, text, etc.) proportionally. The value is stored in *DIMTXT*.

Figure 29-41

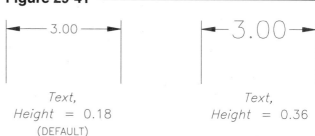

Gap (DIMGAP)

The *Gap* edit box sets the distance between the dimension text and its dimension line (Fig. 29-42). The "gap" is actually an invisible box around the text. Changing the *DIMGAP* variable to a negative value makes the box visible and is used for creating a *Basic* dimension (see *Tolerance, Method*).

Figure 29-42

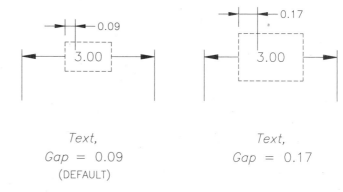

Color (DIMCLRT)

Select this edit box to activate the standard *Select Color* dialogue box. The color choice is assigned to the dimension text only (Fig. 29-43). This is useful for printing or plotting the dimension text in a darker color or wider pen.

Figure 29-43

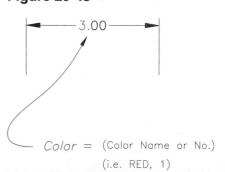

Round Off (DIMRND)

The *Round Off* edit box rounds the primary dimension value to the decimal place (or fraction) specified (Fig. 29-44). Normally, AutoCAD values are kept to 14 significant places but are rounded to the place dictated by the dimension *Primary Units, Precision* (*DIMDEC*). Use this feature to round up or down appropriately to the specified decimal or fraction.

Figure 29-44

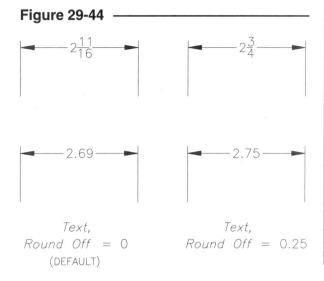

Changing Dimension Variables Using Command Line Format

(VARIABLE NAME)	PULL-DOWN MENU	SCREEN MENU	TYPE IN	TABLET MENU
	---	---	*(VARIABLE NAME)*	---

As an alternative to setting dimension variables through the *Geometry, Format,* and *Annotation* dialogue boxes, you can type the dimensioning variable name at the Command: prompt. There is a noticeable difference in the two methods—the dialogue boxes use <u>different nomenclature</u> than the formal dimensioning variable names used in command line format; that is, the dialogue boxes use descriptive terms that, if selected, make the appropriate change to the dimensioning variable. The formal dimensioning variable names accessed by command line format, however, all begin with the letters *DIM*, are limited to eight characters, and are only accessible by typing.

Another important but subtle difference in the two methods is the act of saving dimension variable settings to a dimension style. Remember that all drawn dimensions are part of a dimension style, whether it is STANDARD or some user-created style. The act of saving variable changes made through the *Dimension Styles* dialogue boxes is accomplished by selecting the *Save* tile upon exiting. When you change dimension variables by command line format, the changes become <u>overrides</u> until you use the *Save* option of the *Dimstyle* command or *Dimension Styles* dialogue box. When a variable change is made, it becomes an <u>override that is applied to the current dimension style</u> and affects only the newly drawn dimensions. Variable changes must be *Saved* to become a permanent part of the style and to retroactively affect all dimensions created with that style.

In order to access and change a variable's setting by name, simply type the variable name at the Command: prompt. For dimension variables that require distances, you can enter the distance (in any format accepted by the current *Units* settings) or you can designate by (PICKing) two points.

For example, to change the value of the *DIMSCALE* to **.5**, this command syntax is used.

```
Command: dimscale
New value for dimscale <1.0000>: .5
Command:
```

Dimension Variables Table

This table is a summary of the dimensioning variables. Each variable has a brief description, the type of variable it is, and its <u>default setting</u> (taken from the *AutoCAD Command Reference*, Appendix A, System Variables, p. 669). Remember that the dimension variables and the current settings can be listed using the *STatus* and *Variables* options of the *Dimstyle* command.

Variable	Characteristics	Description
DIMALT	Type: Switch Saved in: Drawing Initial value: Off	When turned on, enables alternate units dimensioning. See also *DIMALTD, DIMALTF, DIMALTZ (DIMALTTZ, DIMALTTD)*, and *DIMAPOST*.
DIMALTD	Type: Integer Saved in: Drawing Initial value: 2	Controls alternate units decimal places. If *DIMALT* is enabled, *DIMALTD* governs the number of decimal places displayed in the alternate measurement.
DIMALTF	Type: Real Saved in: Drawing Initial value: 25.4000	Controls alternate units scale factor. If *DIMALT* is enabled, *DIMALTF* multiplies linear dimensions by a factor to produce a value in an alternate system of measurement.
DIMALTTD	Type: Integer Saved in: Drawing Initial value: 2	Sets the number of decimal places for the tolerance values of an alternate units dimension. *DIMALTTD* sets this value when entered on the command line or set in the Alternate Units section of the Annotation dialog box.
DIMALTTZ	Type: Integer Saved in: Drawing Initial value: 0	Toggles suppression of zeros for tolerance values. *DIMALTTZ* sets this value when entered on the command line or set in the Alternate Units section of the Annotation dialog box.
DIMALTU	Type: Integer Saved in: Drawing Initial value: 2	Sets the units format for alternate units of all dimension style family members except angular. 1 Scientific 2 Decimal 3 Engineering 4 Architectural 5 Fractional *DIMALTU* sets this value when entered on the command line or set in the Alternate Units section of the Annotation dialog box.
DIMALTZ	Type: Integer Saved in: Drawing Initial value: 0	Toggles suppression of zeros for alternate unit dimension values. 0 Turns off suppression of zeros. 1 Turns on suppression of zeros. *DIMALTZ* sets this value when entered on the command line or set in the Alternate Units section of the Annotation dialog box.

Variable	Characteristics	Description
DIMAPOST	Type: String Saved in: Drawing Initial value: ""	Specifies a text prefix or suffix (or both) to the alternate dimension measurement for all types of dimensions except angular. For instance, if the current Units mode is Architectural, *DIMALT* is enabled, *DIMALTF* is 25.4, *DIMALTD* is 2, and *DIMAPOST* is set to "mm," a distance of 10 units would be edited as 10"[254.00mm]. To disable an established prefix or suffix (or both), set it to a single period (.).
DIMASO	Type: Switch Saved in: Drawing Initial value: On	Controls the creation of associative dimension objects. Off No association between the dimension and points on the object. The lines, arcs, arrowheads, and text of a dimension are drawn as separate objects. On Creates an association between the dimension and definition points located on a feature of the object, such as an intersection of two lines. If the feature is moved, so must the definition point be. The elements are formed into a single object associated with the geometry used to define it. The *DIMASO* value is not stored in a dimension style.
DIMASZ	Type: Real Saved in: Drawing Initial value: 0.1800	Controls the size of dimension line and leader line arrowheads. Also controls the size of hook lines. Multiples of the arrowhead size determine whether dimension lines and text are to fit between the extension lines. Also used to scale arrowhead blocks if set to *DIMBLK*. *DIMASZ* has no effect when *DIMTSZ* is other than zero.
DIMAUNIT	Type: Integer Saved in: Drawing Initial value: 0	Sets the angle format for angular dimension. 0 Decimal degrees 1 Degrees/minutes/seconds 2 Gradians 3 Radians 4 Surveyor's units *DIMAUNIT* sets this value when entered on the command line or set from the Primary Units section of the Annotation dialog box.
DIMBLK	Type: String Saved in: Drawing Initial value: ""	Sets the name of a block to be drawn instead of the normal arrowhead at the ends of the dimension line or leader line. To disable an established block name, set it to a single period (.).
DIMBLK1	Type: String Saved in: Drawing Initial value: ""	If *DIMSAH* is on, *DIMBLK1* specifies user-defined arrowhead blocks for the first end of the dimension line. This variable contains the name of a previously defined block. To disable an established block name, set it to a single period (.).

R13

Variable	Characteristics	Description
DIMBLK2	Type: String Saved in: Drawing Initial value: ""	If *DIMSAH* is on, *DIMBLK2* specifies user-defined arrowhead blocks for the second end of the dimension line. This variable contains the name of a previously defined block. To disable an established block name, set it to a single period (.).
DIMCEN	Type: Real Saved in: Drawing Initial value: 0.0900	Controls drawing of circle or arc center marks and center lines by the *DIMCENTER, DIMDIAMETER,* and *DIMRADIUS* dimensioning commands. 0 No center marks or lines are drawn. <0 Center lines are drawn. >0 Center marks are drawn. The absolute value specifies the size of the mark portion of the center line. *DIMRADIUS* and *DIMDIAMETER* draw the center mark or line only if the dimension line is placed outside the circle or arc.
DIMCLRD	Type: Integer Saved in: Drawing Initial value: 0	Assigns colors to dimension lines, arrowheads, and dimension leader lines. Also controls the color of leader lines created with the *LEADER* command. The color can be any valid color number or special color label *BYBLOCK* or *BYLAYER*. Using the *SETVAR* command, supply the color number. Integer equivalents for *BYBLOCK* and *BYLAYER* are 0 and 256, respectively. From the Command prompt, set the color values by entering *DIMCLRD* and then a standard color name or *BYBLOCK* or *BYLAYER*.
DIMCLRE	Type: Integer Saved in: Drawing Initial value: 0	Assigns colors to dimension extension lines. The color can be any valid color number or the special color label *BYBLOCK* or *BYLAYER*. See *DIMCLRD*.
DIMCLRT	Type: Integer Saved in: Drawing Initial value: 0	Assigns colors to dimension text. The color can be any valid color number or the special color label *BYBLOCK* or *BYLAYER*. See *DIMCLRD*.
DIMDEC	Type: Integer Saved in: Drawing Initial value: 4	Sets the number of decimal places for the tolerance values of a primary units dimension. *DIMDEC* stores this value when entered on the commend line or set in the Primary Units section of the Annotation dialog box.
DIMDLE	Type: Real Saved in: Drawing Initial value: 0.0000	Extends the dimension line beyond the extension line when oblique strokes are drawn instead of arrowheads.
DIMDLI	Type: Real Saved in: Drawing Initial value: 0.3800	Controls the dimension line spacing for baseline dimensions. Each baseline dimension is offset by this amount, if necessary, to avoid drawing over the previous dimension.
DIMEXE	Type: Real Saved in: Drawing Initial value: 0.1800	Determines how far to extend the extension line beyond the dimension line.

Variable	Characteristics	Description
DIMEXO	Type: Real Saved in: Drawing Initial value: 0.0625	Determines how far extension lines are offset from origin points. If you point directly at the corners of an object to be dimensioned, the extension lines stop just short of the object.
DIMFIT	Type: Integer Saved in: Drawing Initial value: 3	Controls the placement of text and arrowheads inside or outside extension lines based on the available space between the extension lines. 0 Places text and arrowheads between the extension lines if space is available. Otherwise places both text and arrowheads outside extension lines. 1 If space is available, places text and arrowheads between the extension lines. When enough space is available for text, places text between the extension lines and arrowheads outside them. When not enough space is available for text, places both text and arrowheads outside extension lines. 2 If space is available, places text and arrowheads between the extension lines. When space is available for the text only, AutoCAD places the text between the extension lines and the arrowheads outside. When space is available for the arrowheads only, AutoCAD places them between the extension lines and the text outside. When no space is available for either text or arrowheads, AutoCAD places them both outside the extension lines. 3 Places whatever best fits between the extension lines. 4 Creates leader lines when there is not enough space for text between extension lines. Horizontal justification controls whether the text is drawn to the right or the left of the leader. For more information, see *DIMJUST*.
DIMGAP	Type: Real Saved in: Drawing Initial value: 0.0900	Sets the distance around the dimension text when you break the dimension line to accommodate dimension text. Also sets the gap between annotation and a hook line created with the *LEADER* command. A negative *DIMGAP* value creates basic dimensioning-dimension text with a box around its full extents. AutoCAD also used *DIMGAP* as the minimum length for pieces of the dimension line. When calculating the default position for the dimension text, it positions the text inside the extension lines only if doing so breaks the dimension lines into two segments at least as long as *DIMGAP*. Text placed above or below the dimension line is moved inside if there is room for the arrowheads, dimension text, and a margin between them at least as large as *DIMGAP*: 2 * (*DIMASZ* + *DIMGAP*).

R13

Variable	Characteristics	Description
DIMJUST	Type: Integer Saved in: Drawing Initial value: 0	Controls horizontal dimension text position. 0 Center-justifies the text between the extension lines. 1 Positions the text next to the first extension line. 2 Positions the text next to the second extension line. 3 Positions the text above and aligned with the first extension line. 4 Positions the text above and aligned with the second extension line.
DIMLFAC	Type: Real Saved in: Drawing Initial value: 1.0000	Sets a global scale factor for linear dimensioning measurements. All linear distances measured by dimensioning (including radii, diameters, and coordinates) are multiplied by the DIMLFAC setting before being converted to dimension text. DIMLFAC has no effect on angular dimensions, and it is not applied to the values held in DIMTM, DIMTP, or DIMRND. If you are creating a dimension in paper space and DIMLFAC is nonzero, AutoCAD multiplies the distance measured by the absolute value of DIMLFAC. In model space, negative values are ignored, and the value 1.0 is used instead. AutoCAD computes a value for DIMLFAC if you try to change DIMLFAC from the Dim prompt while in paper space and you select the Viewport option. Dim: **dimlfac** Current value <1.0000> New value (Viewport): **v** Select viewport to set scale: AutoCAD calculates the scaling of model space to paper space and assigns the negative of this value to DIMLFAC.
DIMLIM	Type: Switch Saved in: Drawing Initial value: Off	When turned on, generates dimension limits as the default text. Setting DIMLIM on forces DIMTOL to be off.
DIMPOST	Type: String Saved in: Drawing Initial value: ""	Specifies a text prefix or suffix (or both) to the dimension measurement. For example, to establish a suffix for millimeters, set DIMPOST to mm; a distance of 19.2 units would be displayed as 19.2mm. If tolerances are enabled, the suffix is applied to the tolerances as well as to the main dimension. To separate DIMPOST values into prefix and suffix parts of the dimension text, use the <> mechanism; this allows AutoCAD to use the DIMPOST values as text. Use this mechanism for angular dimension.
DIMRND	Type: Real Saved in: Drawing Initial value: 0.0000	Rounds all dimensioning distances to the specified value. For instance, if DIMRND is set to 0.25, all distances round to the nearest 0.25 unit. If you set DIMRND to 1.0, all distances round to the nearest integer. Note that the number of digits edited after the decimal point depends on the precision set by DIMDEC. DIMRND does not apply to angular dimensions.

Variable	Characteristics	Description
DIMSAH	Type: Switch Saved in: Drawing Initial value: Off	Controls use of user-defined arrowhead blocks at the ends of the dimension line. Off Normal arrowheads or user-defined arrowhead blocks set by *DIMBLK* are used. On User-defined arrowhead blocks are used. *DIMBLK1* and *DIMBLK2* specify different user-defined arrowhead blocks for each end of the dimension line.
DIMSCALE	Type: Real Saved in: Drawing Initial value: 1.0000	Sets the overall scale factor applied to dimensioning variables that specify sizes, distances, or offsets. It is not applied to tolerances or to measured lengths, coordinates, or angles. Also affects the scale of leader objects created with the *LEADER* command. 0.0 AutoCAD computes a reasonable default value based on the scaling between the current model space viewport and paper space. If you are in paper space, or in model space and not using the paper space feature, the scale factor is 1.0. >0 AutoCAD computes a scale factor that leads text sizes, arrowhead sizes, and other scaled distances to plot at their face values.
DIMSD1	Type: Switch Saved in: Drawing Initial value: Off	When turned on, suppresses drawing of the first dimension line.
DIMSD2	Type: Switch Saved in: Drawing Initial value: Off	When turned on, suppresses drawing of the second dimension line.
DIMSE1	Type: Switch Saved in: Drawing Initial value: Off	When turned on, suppresses drawing of the first extension line.
DIMSE2	Type: Switch Saved in: Drawing Initial value: Off	When turned on, suppresses drawing of the second extension line.
DIMSHO	Type: Switch Saved in: Drawing Initial value: On	When turned on, controls redefinition of dimension objects while dragging. Associative dimensions recompute dynamically as they are dragged. Radius or diameter leader length input uses dynamic dragging and ignores *DIMSHO*. On some computers, dynamic dragging can be very slow, so you can set *DIMSHO* to off to drag the original image instead. The *DIMSHO* value is not stored in a dimension style.
DIMSOXD	Type: Switch Saved in: Drawing Initial value: Off	When turned on, suppresses drawing of dimension lines outside the extension lines. If the dimension lines would be outside the extension lines and *DIMTIX* is on, setting *DIMSOXD* to on suppresses the dimension line. If *DIMTIX* is off, *DIMSOXD* has no effect.

R13

Variable	Characteristics	Description
DIMSTYLE	(Read-only) Type: String Saved in: Drawing	Sets the current dimension style by name. To change the dimension style, use *DDIM* or the *DIMSTYLE* dimensioning command.
DIMTAD	Type: Integer Saved in: Drawing Initial value: 0	Controls vertical position of text in relation to the dimension line. 0 Centers the dimension text between the extension lines. 1 Places the dimension text above the dimension line except when the dimension line is not horizontal and text inside the extension lines is forced horizontal (*DIMTIH* = 1). The distance from the dimension line to the baseline of the lowest line of text is the current *DIMGAP* value. 2 Places the dimension text on the side of the dimension line farthest away from the defining points. 3 Places the dimension text to conform to a JIS representation.
DIMTDEC	Type: Integer Saved in: Drawing Initial value: 4	Sets the number of decimal places for the tolerance values for a primary units dimension.
DIMTFAC	Type: Real Saved in: Drawing Initial value: 1.0000	Specifies a scale factor for text height of tolerance values relative to the dimension text height as set by *DIMTXT*. $DIMTFAC = \dfrac{\text{Tolerance Height}}{\text{Text Height}}$ For example, if *DIMTFAC* is set to 1.0, the text height of tolerances is the same as the dimension text. If *DIMTFAC* is set to 0.75, the text height of tolerances is three-quarters the size of dimension text. Use *DIMTFAC* for plus and minus tolerance strings when *DIMTOL* is on and *DIMTM* is not equal to *DIMTP* or when *DIMLIM* is on.
DIMTIH	Type: Switch Saved in: Drawing Initial value: On	Controls the position of dimension text inside the extension lines for all dimension types except ordinate dimensions. Off Aligns text with the dimension line. On Draw text horizontally.
DIMTIX	Type: Switch Saved in: Drawing Initial value: Off	Draw text between extension lines. Off The result varies with the type of dimension. For linear and angular dimensions, AutoCAD places text inside the extension lines if there is sufficient room. For radius and diameter dimensions, setting *DIMTIX* off forces the text outside the circle or arc. On Draw dimension text between the extension lines even if AutocAD would ordinarily place it outside those lines.

Variable	Characteristics	Description
DIMTM	Type: Real Saved in: Drawing Initial value: 0.0000	When *DIMTOL* or *DIMLIM* is on, sets the minimum (or lower) tolerance limit for dimension text. AutoCAD accepts signed values for *DIMTM*. If *DIMTOL* is on and *DIMTP* and *DIMTM* are set to the same value, AutoCAD draws a ± symbol followed by the tolerance value. If *DIMTM* and *DIMTP* values differ, the upper tolerance is drawn above the lower, and a plus sign is added to the *DIMTP* value if it is positive. For *DIMTM*, AutoCAD uses the negative of the value you enter (adding a minus sign if you specify a positive number and a plus sign if you specify a negative number). No sign is added to a value of zero.
DIMTOFL	Type: Switch Saved in: Drawing Initial value: Off	When turned on, draws a dimension line between the extension lines, even when the text is placed outside the extension lines. For radius and diameter dimensions (while *DIMTIX* is off), draws a dimension line and arrowheads inside the circle or arc and places the text and leader outside.
DIMTOH	Type: Switch Saved in: Drawing Initial value: On	When turned on, controls the position of dimension text outside the extension lines. 0 Aligns text with the dimension line. 1 Draw text horizontally.
DIMTOL	Type: Switch Saved in: Drawing Initial value: Off	When turned on, appends dimension tolerances to dimension text. Setting *DIMTOL* on forces *DIMLIM* off.
DIMTOLJ	Type: Integer Saved in: Drawing Initial value: 1	Sets the vertical justification for tolerance values relative to the nominal dimension text. 0 Bottom 1 Middle 2 Top
DIMTP	Type: Real Saved in: Drawing Initial value: 0.0000	When *DIMTOL* or *DIMLIM* is on, sets the maximum (or upper) tolerance limit for dimension text. AutoCAD accepts signed values for *DIMTP*. If *DIMTOL* is on and *DIMTP* and *DIMTM* are set to the same value, AutoCAD draws a ± symbol followed by the tolerance value. If *DIMTM* and *DIMTP* values differ, the upper tolerance is drawn above the lower and a plus sign is added to the *DIMTP* value if it is positive.
DIMTSZ	Type: Real Saved in: Drawing Initial value: 0.0000	Specifies the size of oblique strokes drawn instead of arrowheads for linear, radius, and diameter dimension. 0 Draws arrows. >0 Draws oblique strokes instead of arrows. Size of oblique strokes is determined by this value multiplied by the *DIMSCALE* value. Also determines if dimension lines and text fit between extension lines.

R13

Variable	Characteristics	Description
DIMTVP	Type: Real Saved in: Drawing Initial value: 0.0000	Adjusts the vertical position of dimension text above or below the dimension line. AutoCAD uses the *DIMTVP* value when *DIMTAD* is off. The magnitude of the vertical offset of text is the product of the text height and *DIMTVP*. Setting *DIMTVP* to 1.0 is equivalent to setting *DIMTAD* to on. AutoCAD splits the dimension line to accommodate the text only if the absolute value of *DIMTVP* is less than 0.7.
DIMTXSTY	Type: String Saved in: Drawing Initial value: "STANDARD"	Specifies the text style of the dimension.
DIMTXT	Type: Real Saved in: Drawing Initial value: 0.1800	Specifies the height of dimension text, unless the current text style has a fixed height.
DIMTZIN	Type: Integer Saved in: Drawing Initial value: 0	Toggles suppression of zeros for tolerance values. *DIMZIN* stores this value when entered on the command line or set in the Primary Units section of the Annotation dialog box.
DIMUNIT	Type: Integer Saved in: Drawing Initial value: 2	Sets the units format for all dimension style family members except angular. 1 Scientific 2 Decimal 3 Engineering 4 Architectural 5 Fractional
DIMUPT	Type: Switch Saved in: Drawing Initial value: Off	Controls cursor functionality for User Positioned Text. 0 Cursor controls only the dimension line location. 1 Cursor controls the text position as well as the dimension line location.
DIMZIN	Type: Integer Saved in: Drawing Initial value: 0	Controls the suppression of the inches portion of a feet-and-inches dimension when the distance is an integral number of feet, or the feet portion when the distance is less than one foot. 0 Suppresses zero feet and precisely zero inches 1 Includes zero feet and precisely zero inches 2 Includes zero feet and suppresses zero inches 3 Includes zero inches and suppresses zero feet *DIMZIN* stores this value when entered on the command line or set in the Primary Units section of the Annotation dialog box.

R13

R13

DIMOVERRIDE	PULL-DOWN MENU	SCREEN MENU	TYPE IN	TABLET MENU
	---	MOD DIM *Overrid:*	*DIMOVERRIDE* *or DIMOVER*	---

Dimoverrride grants you a great deal of control to <u>edit existing dimensions</u>. The abilities enabled by *Dimoverride* are <u>unique</u> in that no other dimensioning commands or options allow you to retroactively modify dimensions in such a way.

Dimoverride enables you to <u>make variable changes</u> to dimensions that exist in your drawing <u>without changing the dimension style</u> that the dimension references (was created under). For example, using *Dimoverride,* you can make a variable change and select existing dimension objects to apply the change. The existing dimension does not lose its reference to the parent dimension style nor is the dimension style changed in any way. In effect, you can <u>override the dimension styles for selected dimension objects</u>. There are two steps: set the desired variable and select dimension objects to alter.

```
Command: dimoverride
Dimension variable to override (or Clear to remove overrides): (variable name)
Current value <current value> New value: (value)
Dimension variable to override: (variable name) or Enter
Select objects: PICK
Select objects: PICK or Enter
Command:
```

The *Dimoverride* feature differs from creating overrides in two ways: <u>overrides</u> (variable changes that are made but not *Saved*) (1) are <u>appended</u> to the *Parent* dimension style and (2) are applied to <u>newly created</u> dimensions only and are not retroactive. In contrast, *Dimoverride* affects only the selected existing dimensions and does not change the parent dimension style.

Dimoverride is useful as a "back door" approach to dimensioning. Once dimensions have been created, you may want to make a few modifications, but you do not want the changes to affect dimension styles (resulting in an update to all existing dimensions that reference the dimension styles). *Dimoverride* offers that capability. You can even make one variable change to affect all dimensions globally without having to change all the dimension styles. For example, you may be required to make a test plot of the drawing in a different scale than originally intended, necessitating a new global *Dimscale*. Use *Dimoverride* to make the change for the plot.

```
Command: dimoverride
Dimension variable to override (or Clear to remove overrides): dimscale
Current value <1.0000> New value: .5
Dimension variable to override: Enter
Select objects: (window entire drawing) Other corner: 128 found
Select objects: Enter
Command:
```

This action results in having all the existing dimensions reflect the new *DIMSCALE*. No other dimension variables or any dimension styles are affected. After making the plot to the desired plot scale, *Dimoverride* can be used again with the *Clear* option to set *DIMSCALE* back to the original value.

Clear

The *Clear* option removes the overrides from the <u>selected dimension objects</u>. It does not remove overrides from the current dimension style.

```
Command: dimoverride
Dimension variable to override (or Clear to remove overrides): c
Select objects: PICK
Select objects: Enter
Command:
```

The dimension then displays the variable settings as specified by the dimension style it references without any overrides (as if the dimension were originally created without the overrides). Using *Clear* does not remove the overrides that are appended to the dimension style so that if another dimension is drawn, the overrides apply.

Dimoverride is a very powerful and useful tool because it provides capabilities that are not available by any other method. You should experiment with it now so you can use it later to simplify otherwise difficult dimension editing situations.

GUIDELINES FOR DIMENSIONING IN AutoCAD

Listed in this section are some guidelines to use for dimensioning a drawing using dimensioning variables and dimension styles. Although there are other strategies for dimensioning, two strategies are offered here as a framework so you can develop an organized approach to dimensioning.

In almost every case, dimensioning is one of the last steps in creating a drawing, since the geometry must exist in order to dimension it. You may need to review the steps for drawing setup, including the concept of "drawing scale factor" (Chapter 13).

Strategy 1. Dimensioning a Single Drawing

This method assumes that the fundamental steps have been taken to set up the drawing and create the geometry. Assume this has been accomplished:

Drawing setup is completed: *Units, Limits, Snap, Grid, Ltscale, Layers*, border, and title block.
The drawing geometry (objects comprising the subject of the drawing) has been created.

Now you are ready to dimension the drawing subject (of the multiview drawing, pictorial drawing, floorplan, or whatever type of drawing).

1. Create a *Layer* (named DIM, or similar) for dimensioning if one has not already been created. Set *Continuous* linetype and appropriate color. Make it the *current* layer.

2. Set the *Overall Scale (DIMSCALE)* based on drawing *Limits* and expected plotting size.

   <u>For plotted dimension text of 3/16":</u>

   Multiply *Overall Scale (DIMSCALE)* times the "drawing scale factor." The default *Overall Scale* is set to 1, which creates dimensioning text of approximately 3/16" (default *Text Height:* or DIMTXT =.18) when plotted full size. All other size-related dimensioning variables' defaults are set appropriately.

<u>For plotted dimension text of 1/8":</u>

Multiply *Overall Scale* times the "drawing scale factor," <u>times .7</u>. Since the *Overall Scale* times the scale factor produces dimensioning text of .18, then .18 x .7 = .126 or approximately 1/8". (See Optional Method for Fixed Dimension Text Height.)

3. Before changing any other variables, save a new dimension style family (select *Parent*) named "TEMPLATE" or other descriptive name. Since the TEMPLATE dimension style has the default settings (except the new *Overall Scale*), it should be used as a template when you create most new dimension styles. The *Overall Scale* is already set appropriately for new dimension styles in the drawing. If you use the *Dimension Styles* dialogue box to do this, remember that you must select the *Save* tile and exit the dialogue box in order to save the dimension style. The STANDARD style can be restored if you need to reset all the initial variable defaults.

4. Create all the relatively simple dimensions first. These are dimensions that are easy and fast and require <u>no other dimension variable changes</u>. Begin with linear dimensions; then progress to the other types of dimensions.

5. Create the special dimensions next. These are dimensions that require variable changes. Create appropriate dimension styles by changing the necessary variables; then *Save* each set of variables (relating to a particular style of dimension) to an appropriate dimension style name. Specify dimension variables for the classification of dimension (children) in each dimension style when appropriate. The dimension styles can be created "on the fly" or as a group before dimensioning. Use TEMPLATE as your base dimension style when appropriate.

   For the few dimensions that require variable settings that are unique for that style, you can create dimension variable overrides. Change the desired variable(s), but do not *Save* to the style so the other dimensions in the style are not affected.

6. When all of the dimensions are in place, make the final adjustments. Four methods can be used:

   a. Use *Dimstyle Apply* to apply (update) selected variables with the current settings. This means setting the required styles and/or overrides, then *Apply*ing them to selected dimensions. You can also change a dimension from one style to another with *Apply*.

   b. Use *Ddmodify* to select and edit individual dimension objects. The *Modify Dimension* dialogue box that appears allows you to edit the selected dimension object or the dimension text (see Chapter 28, Editing Dimensions). This dialogue box provides access to the *Geometry, Format*, and *Annotation* dialogue boxes (normally accessed through the *Dimension Styles* dialogue box). Making a change to a dimension in this manner (using the *Geometry, Format*, and *Annotation* dialogue boxes) creates a dimension override that is appended to the dimension style and applies it to the selected dimension. This results in the same action as creating a dimension override by another method and applying it to a selected dimension using *Dimstyle Apply*.

   c. To make changes to the dimension <u>text content</u> only, use either the *Ddmodify* dialogue box (*Edit...* button), *Dimtedit*, or *Dimedit*.

   d. Use *Dimoverride* to make changes to selected dimensions without affecting the parent dimension style in any way. You can change the variable <u>and</u> select the dimension objects in this one command. Use *Dimoverride* to make necessary global updates to all dimensions, such as a change in *Overall Scale*.

R13

Strategy 2. Creating Dimension Styles as Part of Prototype Drawings

1. Begin a *New* drawing or *Open* an existing *Prototype*. Assign a descriptive name.

2. Create a DIM *Layer* for dimensioning with *continuous* linetype and appropriate color (if one has not already been created).

3. Set the *Overall Scale* accounting for the drawing *Limits* and expected plotting size. Use the guidelines given in Strategy 1, step 2.

4. Before changing any other variables, save a dimension style named "TEMPLATE." This should be used as a template when you create most new dimension styles. The *Overall Scale* is already set appropriately for new dimension styles in the drawing.

5. Create the appropriate dimension styles for expected drawing geometry. Use TEMPLATE dimension style as a base style when appropriate.

6. *Save* and *Exit* the newly created prototype drawing.

7. Use this prototype in the future for creating new drawings. Restore the desired dimension styles to create the appropriate dimensions.

Using a prototype drawing with prepared dimension styles is a preferred alternative to repeatedly creating the same dimension styles for each new drawing.

Optional Method for Fixed Dimension Text Height in Prototype Drawings

To summarize Strategy 1, step 2., the default *Overall Scale* (DIMSCALE =1) times the default *Text Height* (DIMTXT =.18) produces dimensioning text of approximately 3/16" when plotted to 1=1. To create 1/8" text, multiply *Overall Scale* times .7 (.18 x .7 = .126). As an alternative to this method, try the following.

For 1/8" dimensions, for example, multiply the initial values of the size-related variables by .7, namely:

Text Height	(DIMTXT)	.18 x .7 = .126
Arrow Size	(DIMASZ)	.18 x .7 = .126
Extension Line Extension	(DIMEXE)	.18 x .7 = .126
Dimension Line Spacing	(DIMDLI)	.38 x .7 = .266
Text Gap	(DIMGAP)	.09 x .7 = .063

Save these settings in your prototype drawing(s). When you are ready to dimension, simply multiply *Overall Scale* (1) times the "drawing scale factor."

Although this method may seem complex, the drawing setup for individual drawings is simplified. For example, assume your prototype drawing contained preset *Limits* to the paper size, say 11 x 8.5. In addition, the previously mentioned dimension variables were set to produce 1/8" (or whatever) dimensions when plotted full size. Other variables such as *LTSCALE* could be appropriately set. Then, when you wish to plot a drawing to 1=1, everything is preset. If you wish to plot to 1=2, simply multiply all the size-related variables (*Limits, Overall Scale, Ltscale*, etc.) times 2!

CHAPTER EXERCISES

For each of the following exercises, use the existing drawings, as instructed. Create dimensions on the DIM (or other appropriate) layer. Follow the Guidelines for Dimensioning given in the chapter, including setting an appropriate *Overall Scale* based on the drawing scale factor. Use dimension variables and create and use dimension styles when needed.

1. **Dimensioning a Multiview**

   Open the **SADDLE** drawing that you created in Chapter 24 Exercises. Set the appropriate dimensional *Units* and *Precision*. Add the dimensions as shown. Because the illustration in Figure 29-45 is in isometric, placement of the dimensions can be improved for your multiview. Use optimum placement for the dimensions. *Save* the drawing as **SADDL-DM** and make a *Plot* to scale.

Figure 29-45

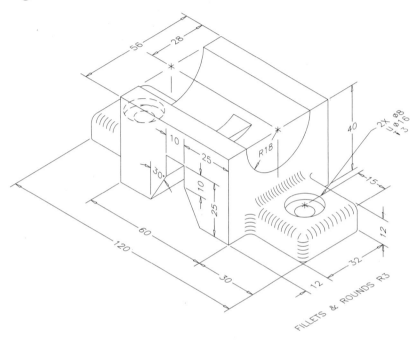

2. **Architectural Dimensioning**

   Open the **OFFICE** drawing that you completed in Chapter 21. Dimension the floorplan as shown in Figure 21-13. Add *Text* to name the rooms. *Save* the drawing as **OFF-DIM** and make a *Plot* to an accepted scale and sheet size based on your plotter capabilities.

Figure 29-46

3. **Dimensioning an Auxiliary**

   Open the **ANGLBRAC** drawing that you created in Chapter 25. Dimension as shown in Figure 29-46, but convert the dimensions to *Decimal*. Use the Guidelines for Dimensioning. Dimension the slot width as a *Limit* dimension— .6248/.6255. *Save* the drawing as **ANGL-DIM** and *Plot* to an accepted scale.

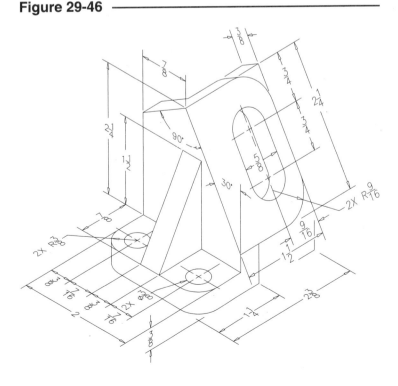

4. **Isometric Dimensioning**

    Dimension the Support Bracket that you
    created as an isometric drawing named
    SBRACKET in the Chapter 25 Exercises.
    Convert the dimensions to *Decimal*. All
    of the dimensions shown in Figure 29-47
    should appear on your drawing in the
    optimum placement. *Save* the drawing as
    SBRCK-DM and *Plot* to **1=1** on and "A"
    size sheet.

    Figure 29-47 ──────────────────

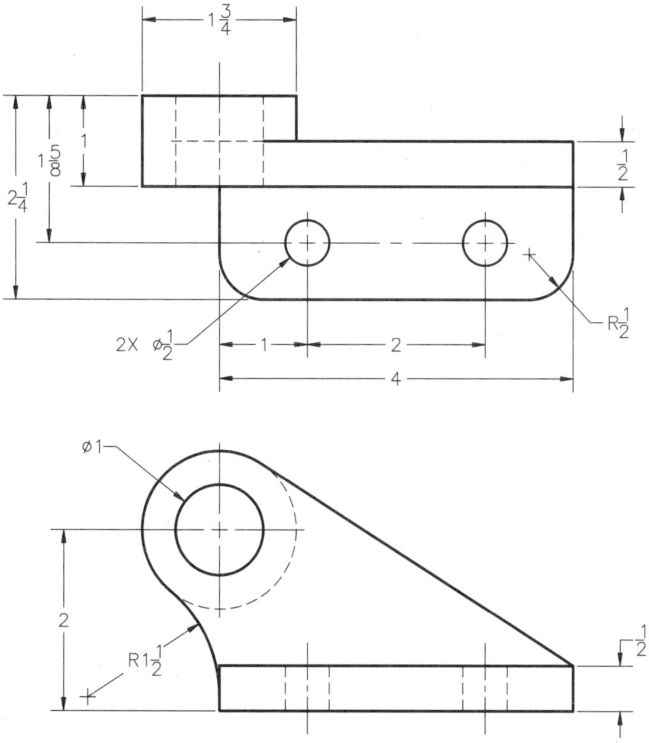

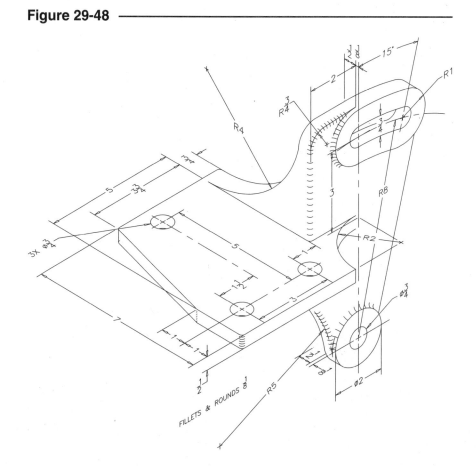

5. **Dimensioning a Multiview**

    Open the **ADJMOUNT**
    drawing that you com-
    pleted in Chapter 24.
    Add the dimensions
    shown in Figure 29-48.
    Set appropriate dimen-
    sional *Units* and
    Precision. Calculate and
    set an appropriate *DIM-
    SCALE*. Use the
    Guidelines for
    Dimensioning given in
    this chapter. Save the
    drawing as **ADJM-DIM**
    and make a *Plot* to an
    accepted scale.

    Figure 29-48 ──────────────────

6. **Geometric Dimensioning and Tolerancing**

This exercise involves Flatness, Profile of a Surface, and Position applications. *Open* the dimensioned **ANGL-DIM** drawing you worked on in Exercise 3 and add the following geometric dimensions:

A. **Flatness** specification of **.002** to the bottom surface.

B. **Profile of a Surface** specification of **.005** to the angled surface relative to the bottom surface and the right side surface of the 1/4 dimension. The 30° angle must be *Basic*.

C. **Position** specification of **.01** for the two mounting holes relative to the bottom surface and two other surfaces that are perpendicular to the bottom. Remember, the location dimensions must be *Basic* dimensions.

Use *Saveas* to save and name the drawing **ANGL-TOL**.

7. **Geometric Dimensioning and Tolerancing**

This exercise involves a Cylindricity and Runout application. Draw the IDLER shown in Figure 29-49. Apply a **Cylindricity** specification of **.002** to the small diameter and a **Circular Runout** specification of **.007** to the large diameter relative to the small diameter as shown. The P730 neck has a .07 radius and **30°** angle. *Save* the drawing as **IDLERDIM**.

Figure 29-49 ────────────────────────────

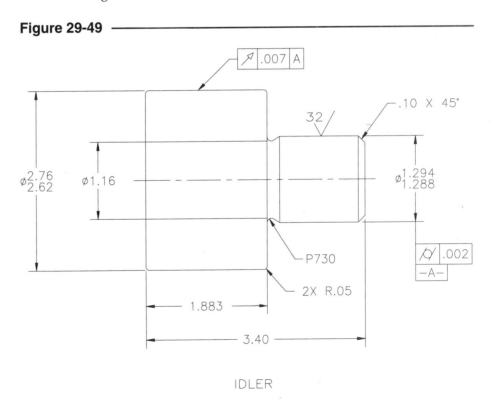

IDLER

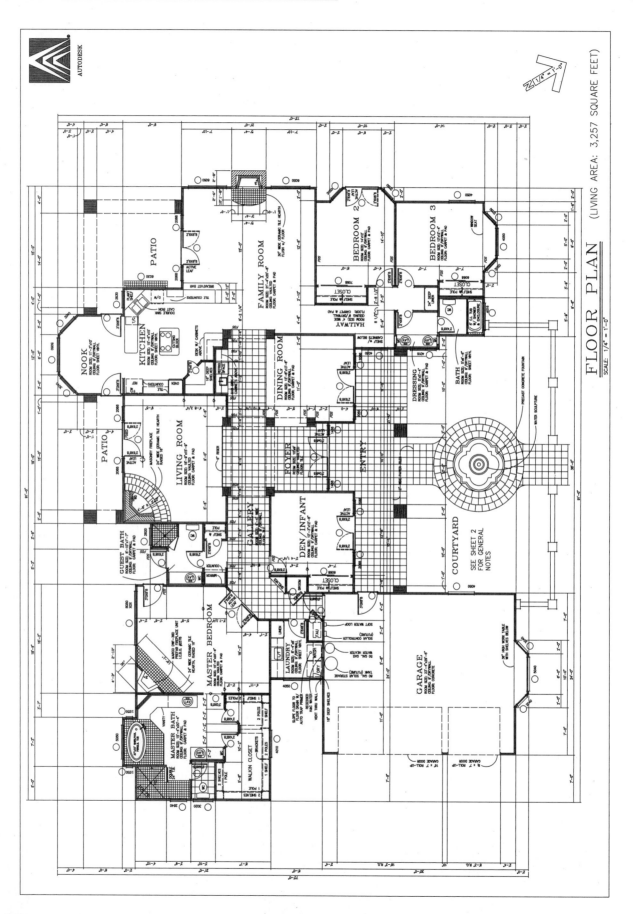

FLOOR PLAN (LIVING AREA: 3,257 SQUARE FEET)

SCALE: 1/4" = 1'-0"

Chapter 30
MISCELLANEOUS COMMANDS AND FEATURES

Chapter Objectives

After completing this chapter you should:

1. be able to manage named objects and files using wildcards, *Rename*, *Purge*, and *MAXSORT*;

2. know when the display commands *Regenall*, *Redrawall*, *Regenauto*, *Fill*, *BLIPMODE*, and *DRAGMODE* are useful;

3. be able to create and view slides with *Mslide* and *Vslide*;

4. know how to create and run a *Script* for viewing slide shows;

5. know how to use the *Multiple* modifier to automatically repeat commands;

6. be able to reinitialize devices and I/O ports using *Reinit* and be able to check the current drawing for errors using *Audit*;

7. be able to control the display of dialogue boxes with the *FILEDIA* and *CMDDIA* system variables;

8. know how to use *Cal* to invoke the geometry calculator for computing arithmetic expressions, locating points, and creating and editing geometry.

BASICS

This chapter discusses several unrelated groups of commands and features that are helpful for intermediate-level AutoCAD users. The following commands, variables, and features are covered in this chapter.

Managing Named Objects
    Wildcards
    Rename, Ddrename
    Purge
    MAXSORT

Miscellaneous Display Commands and Variables
    Redrawall
    Regenall
    Regenauto
    Fill
    DRAGMODE
    BLIPMODE

Using Slides and Scripts
    Mslide
    Vslide
    Creating and Using Scripts
    Creating a Slide Show
    Script

Miscellaneous Commands and Features
    Multiple Modifier
    Reinit
    Audit
    FILEDIA
    CMDDIA

The Geometry Calculator
    Cal
    Calculator Functions and Examples

MANAGING NAMED OBJECTS

There are objects that AutoCAD keeps in a drawing file other than those we know as graphical entities (*Line, Circle, Arc*, etc.) called <u>Named Objects</u>. The named objects are:

Blocks
Dimension Styles
Layers
Linetypes
Text Styles
User Coordinate Systems
Views
Viewport configurations

Wildcard characters, the *Rename* command, and the *Purge* command can be used to access or alter named objects.

Using Wildcards

Whenever AutoCAD prompts for a list of names, such as file names, system variables, *Block* names, *Layer* names, or other named objects, any of the wildcards in the following wildcard list can be used to access those names. These wildcards help you specify a select group of named objects from a long list without having to repeatedly type or enter the complete spelling for <u>each</u> name in the list.

For example, the asterisk (*) is a common wildcard that is used to represent any alphanumeric string (group of letters or numbers). You may choose to specify a list of layers all beginning with the letters "DIM" and ending with any string. Using the *Layer* command and entering "DIM*" in response to the *?* option yields a list of only the layer names beginning with DIM.

Commands that Accept Wildcards

There are several AutoCAD commands that prompt you for a name or list of names or display a list of names to match your specification. Any command that has a ? option provides a list. Wildcards can be used with any of these commands.

Attedit
Block
Dimstyle
Insert
Layer
Linetype
Load
Rename
Setvar
Style
UCS
View
Vplayer
Xref

Valid Wildcards that Can Be Used in AutoCAD

The following list defines valid wildcard characters that can be used in AutoCAD.

Character	Definition
# (pound)	Matches any numeric digit
@ (at)	Matches any alpha character
. (period)	Matches any nonalphanumeric character
* (asterisk)	Matches any string, including the null string. It can be used anywhere in the search pattern—at the beginning, middle, or end of the string
? (question mark)	Matches any single character
~ (tilde)	Matches anything but the pattern
[...]	Matches any one of the characters enclosed
[~...]	Matches any character not enclosed
- (hyphen)	Used with brackets to specify a range for a one character
' (reverse quote)	Escapes special characters (reads next character literally)

Below are listed one or more examples for each application of wildcard patterns.

Pattern	Will match or include . . .	But not . . .
ABC	Only ABC	
~ABC	Anything but ABC	
A?C	Any 3-character sequence beginning with A and ending with C	AC, ABCD, AXXC, or XABC
AB?	ABA, AB3, ABZ, etc.	AB, ABCE, or XAB
?BC	ABC, 3BC, XBC, etc.	AB, ABCD, BC, or XXBC
A*C	AAC, AC, ABC, AX3C, etc.	XA or ABCD
A*	Anything starting with A	XAAA
*AB	Anything ending with AB	ABX
AB	AB anywhere in string	AXB
~*AB*	All strings without AB	AB, ABX, XAB, or XABX
'*AB	*AB	AB, XAB, or *ABC
[AB]C	AC or BC	ABC or XAC
[~AB]C	XC or YC	AC, BC, or XXC
[A-J]C	AC, BC, JC, etc.	ABC, AJC, or MC
[~A-J]C	Any character not in the range A-J, followed by C	AC, BC, or JC

Wildcard Examples

For example, assume that you have a drawing of a two-story residential floorplan with the following *Layers* and related settings.

Layer name	State	Color	Linetype
0	On	7 (white)	CONTINUOUS
1-ELEC-DIM	On	7 (white)	CONTINUOUS
1-ELEC-LAY	On	7 (white)	CONTINUOUS
1-ELEC-TXT	On	7 (white)	CONTINUOUS
1-FLPN-DIM	On	7 (white)	CONTINUOUS
1-FLPN-LAY	On	7 (white)	CONTINUOUS
1-FLPN-TXT	On	7 (white)	CONTINUOUS
1-HVAC-DIM	On	7 (white)	CONTINUOUS
1-HVAC-LAY	On	7 (white)	CONTINUOUS
1-HVAC-TXT	On	7 (white)	CONTINUOUS
2-ELEC-DIM	On	7 (white)	CONTINUOUS
2-ELEC-LAY	On	7 (white)	CONTINUOUS
2-ELEC-TXT	On	7 (white)	CONTINUOUS
2-FLPN-DIM	On	7 (white)	CONTINUOUS
2-FLPN-LAY	On	7 (white)	CONTINUOUS

Layer name	State	Color	Linetype
2-FLPN-TXT	On	7 (white)	CONTINUOUS
2-HVAC-DIM	On	7 (white)	CONTINUOUS
2-HVAC-LAY	On	7 (white)	CONTINUOUS
2-HVAC-TXT	On	7 (white)	CONTINUOUS

If you wanted to turn *Off* all the layers related to the second floor (names beginning with "2"), you can use the asterisk (*) wildcard as follows:

```
Command: Layer
?/Make/Set/New/ON/OFF/Color/Ltype/Freeze/Thaw/LOck/Unlock: off
Layer name(s) to turn Off: 2*
?/Make/Set/New/ON/OFF/Color/Ltype/Freeze/Thaw/LOck/Unlock: ?
Layer name(s) to list <*>:
```

Layer name	State	Color	Linetype
0	On	7 (white)	CONTINUOUS
1-ELEC-DIM	On	7 (white)	CONTINUOUS
1-ELEC-LAY	On	7 (white)	CONTINUOUS
1-ELEC-TXT	On	7 (white)	CONTINUOUS
1-FLPN-DIM	On	7 (white)	CONTINUOUS
1-FLPN-LAY	On	7 (white)	CONTINUOUS
1-FLPN-TXT	On	7 (white)	CONTINUOUS
1-HVAC-DIM	On	7 (white)	CONTINUOUS
1-HVAC-LAY	On	7 (white)	CONTINUOUS
1-HVAC-TXT	On	7 (white)	CONTINUOUS
2-ELEC-DIM	Off	7 (white)	CONTINUOUS
2-ELEC-LAY	Off	7 (white)	CONTINUOUS
2-ELEC-TXT	Off	7 (white)	CONTINUOUS
2-FLPN-DIM	Off	7 (white)	CONTINUOUS
2-FLPN-LAY	Off	7 (white)	CONTINUOUS
2-FLPN-TXT	Off	7 (white)	CONTINUOUS
2-HVAC-DIM	Off	7 (white)	CONTINUOUS
2-HVAC-LAY	Off	7 (white)	CONTINUOUS
2-HVAC-TXT	Off	7 (white)	CONTINUOUS

You may want to *Freeze* all layers (both floors) related to the electrical layout (having ELEC in the layer name). (Assume all the layers are *On* again.) You could use the question mark (?) to represent any floor number and an asterisk (*) for any string after ELEC as follows.

```
Command: Layer
?/Make/Set/New/ON/OFF/Color/Ltype/Freeze/Thaw/LOck/Unlock: fr
Layer name(s) to Freeze: ?-elec*
?/Make/Set/New/ON/OFF/Color/Ltype/Freeze/Thaw/LOck/Unlock: ?
Layer name(s) to list <*>:
```

Layer name	State	Color	Linetype
0	On	7 (white)	CONTINUOUS
1-ELEC-DIM	Frozen	7 (white)	CONTINUOUS
1-ELEC-LAY	Frozen	7 (white)	CONTINUOUS
1-ELEC-TXT	Frozen	7 (white)	CONTINUOUS
1-FLPN-DIM	On	7 (white)	CONTINUOUS

1-FLPN-LAY	On	7 (white)	CONTINUOUS
1-FLPN-TXT	On	7 (white)	CONTINUOUS
1-HVAC-DIM	On	7 (white)	CONTINUOUS
1-HVAC-LAY	On	7 (white)	CONTINUOUS
1-HVAC-TXT	On	7 (white)	CONTINUOUS
2-ELEC-DIM	Frozen	7 (white)	CONTINUOUS
2-ELEC-LAY	Frozen	7 (white)	CONTINUOUS
2-ELEC-TXT	Frozen	7 (white)	CONTINUOUS
2-FLPN-DIM	On	7 (white)	CONTINUOUS
2-FLPN-LAY	On	7 (white)	CONTINUOUS
2-FLPN-TXT	On	7 (white)	CONTINUOUS
2-HVAC-DIM	On	7 (white)	CONTINUOUS
2-HVAC-LAY	On	7 (white)	CONTINUOUS
2-HVAC-TXT	On	7 (white)	CONTINUOUS

You may want to use only the layout layers (names ending with LAY) and *Freeze* all the other layers. (Assume all layers are *On* and *Thawed*.) The tilde (~) character can be used to match anything but the pattern given. The tilde (~) character is translated as "anything except."

Command: **layer**
?/Make/Set/New/ON/OFF/Color/Ltype/Freeze/Thaw/LOck/Unlock: **fr**
Layer name(s) to Freeze: **~*lay**
?/Make/Set/New/ON/OFF/Color/Ltype/Freeze/Thaw/LOck/Unlock: **?**
Layer name(s) to list <*>:

Layer name	State	Color	Linetype
0	On	7 (white)	CONTINUOUS
1-ELEC-DIM	Frozen	7 (white)	CONTINUOUS
1-ELEC-LAY	On	7 (white)	CONTINUOUS
1-ELEC-TXT	Frozen	7 (white)	CONTINUOUS
1-FLPN-DIM	Frozen	7 (white)	CONTINUOUS
1-FLPN-LAY	On	7 (white)	CONTINUOUS
1-FLPN-TXT	Frozen	7 (white)	CONTINUOUS
1-HVAC-DIM	Frozen	7 (white)	CONTINUOUS
1-HVAC-LAY	On	7 (white)	CONTINUOUS
1-HVAC-TXT	Frozen	7 (white)	CONTINUOUS
2-ELEC-DIM	Frozen	7 (white)	CONTINUOUS
2-ELEC-LAY	On	7 (white)	CONTINUOUS
2-ELEC-TXT	Frozen	7 (white)	CONTINUOUS
2-FLPN-DIM	Frozen	7 (white)	CONTINUOUS
2-FLPN-LAY	On	7 (white)	CONTINUOUS
2-FLPN-TXT	Frozen	7 (white)	CONTINUOUS
2-HVAC-DIM	Frozen	7 (white)	CONTINUOUS
2-HVAC-LAY	On	7 (white)	CONTINUOUS
2-HVAC-TXT	Frozen	7 (white)	CONTINUOUS

Remember that wildcards can be used with many AutoCAD commands. For example, you may want to load a certain set of *Linetypes*, perhaps all the HIDDEN variations. The following sequence could be used:

Command: **linetype**
?/Create/Load/Set: **l**
Linetype(s) to load: **hid***

Linetype HIDDEN loaded.
Linetype HIDDEN2 loaded.
Linetype HIDDENX2 loaded.

Or you may want to load all of the linetypes except the "X2" variations. This syntax could be used:

Command: **linetype**
?/Create/Load/Set: **1**
Linetype(s) to load: **~*x2**

Linetype BORDER loaded.
Linetype BORDER2 loaded.
Linetype CENTER loaded.
Linetype CENTER2 loaded.
Linetype DASHDOT loaded.
Linetype DASHDOT2 loaded.
Linetype DASHED loaded.
Linetype DASHED2 loaded.
etc.

RENAME

PULL-DOWN MENU	SCREEN MENU	TYPE IN	TABLET MENU
Data *Rename...*	*DATA* *Rename:*	*RENAME or* *DDRENAME*	---

The *Rename* and *Ddrename* commands allow you to rename <u>any named object</u> that is part of the current drawing. *Rename* does not have the same function as the *Rename File* option of the *File Utilities*, which only renames file names. *Rename* and the related dialogue box accessed by the *Ddrename* command allow you to rename the named objects listed at the beginning of this chapter: namely, Blocks, Dimension Styles, Layers, Linetypes, Text Styles, User Coordinate Systems, Views, and Viewport configurations.

The *Rename* command can be used to rename objects one at a time. For example, the command sequence might be as follows:

Command: **rename**
Block/Dimstyle/LAyer/LType/Style/Ucs/VIew/VPort: **la** (use the *Layer* option)
Old layer name: **dim-sec**
New layer name: **d-sec**
Command:

Wildcard characters are not allowed with the *Rename* command, only with the dialogue box.

Optionally, if you prefer to use the dialogue box, you can type *Ddrename* or select *Rename* from the menus to access the dialogue box.

Selecting from the *Named Objects* list displays the related objects that exist in the current drawing. To rename an object, select or type the old name so it appears in the *Old Name* edit box. Specify the new name in the *Rename To:* edit box (Fig. 30-1). You must then PICK the *Rename To:* tile and the new name will appear in the list. Then select the *OK* tile to confirm.

Figure 30-1

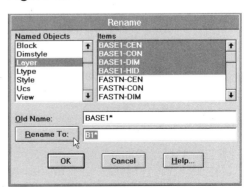

The *Rename* dialogue box can be used with wildcard characters to specify a list of named objects for renaming. For example, if you desired to rename all the "BASE1*" layers so that the characters "BASE" were replaced with only the letter "B", the following sequence would be used.

1. In the *Old Name* edit box, enter "BASE1*" and press Enter. All of the layers beginning with "BASE1" are highlighted.

2. In the *Rename To:* edit box, enter "B1*." Next, PICK the *Rename To:* tile. Finally, PICK the *OK* tile to confirm the change.

PURGE

PULL-DOWN MENU	SCREEN MENU	TYPE IN	TABLET MENU
Data *Purge >*	*DATA* *Purge*	*PURGE*	---

Purge allows you to selectively delete any named object that is not referenced in the drawing. In other words, if the drawing has any named objects defined but not appearing in the drawing, they can be deleted with *Purge*. Examples of unreferenced named objects are:

> *Blocks* that have been defined but not *Inserted*.
> *Layers* that exist without objects residing on the layers.
> *Dimension Styles* that have been defined, yet no dimensions are created in the style.
> *Linetypes* that were loaded but not used.
> *Shapes* that were loaded but not used.
> *Text Styles* that have been defined, yet no text has been created in the *Style*.
> (*APpids* are ADS and AutoLISP application IDs used by programmers).
> *MLine Styles* that have been defined but do not appear in the drawing.
> *Views* that are saved but not being used.

Since these named objects occupy a small amount of space in the drawing, using *Purge* to delete unused named objects reduces the file size. This is helpful when drawings are created using prototype drawings that contain many unused named objects or when other drawings are inserted that contain many unused *Layers* or *Blocks*, etc. The command options are listed here.

Command: **purge**
Purge unused Blocks/Dimstyles/LAyers/LTypes/SHapes/STyles/APpids/Mlinestyles/All:

You can select one type of object to be *Purged,* or select *All* to have all named objects listed. (*View* does not appear as an option, but *Views* are prompted for deletion if the *All* option is used.) AutoCAD lists all named objects matching the type selected. For example, if you specified *LAyers* to purge, AutoCAD responds with a list of <u>unused</u> layers that may look something like this:

> Purge layer HID? <N>
> Purge layer CON? <N>
> Purge layer CEN? <N>
> Purge layer HIGH? <N>
> Purge layer TEXT? <N>
> Purge layer DOT? <N>
> Purge layer DEFPOINTS? <N>
> Purge layer DIM? <N>
> Command:

Answering with a "Y" causes the deletion of the named object. The other named object options operate similarly.

Purge can be used at <u>any time</u> in a drawing session in Release 13. In releases of AutoCAD previous to Release 13, *Purge* must be invoked <u>before</u> any objects are created or edited (before the database has been changed) in a particular drawing session. Usually, this means the drawing should be *Saved* (or *Exited*); then *Purge* should be invoked immediately (or after *Opening* the drawing again).

MAXSORT

The *MAXSORT* system variable controls the maximum number of named objects or files that are alphabetically sorted when a list is produced in a dialogue box or command line listing. The default setting is 200, meaning that a maximum of 200 items are sorted. If the list contains more than the number specified in *MAXSORT*, no sorting is done.

If *MAXSORT* is set to 0, no alphabetical sorting is done and the list is displayed in the order that the items were created. It may be helpful in some cases to set *MAXSORT* to 0 if you want items to be displayed in the order they were created. For example, if *MAXSORT* is set to 0, the display of layers may appear, as shown in Figure 30-2. Change the variable by typing "maxsort" at the Command: prompt or by using the *Setvar* command.

Figure 30-2

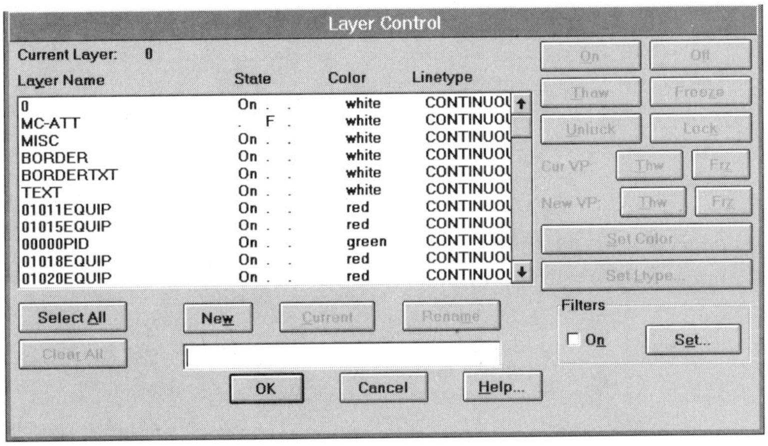

Keep in mind that display of <u>external files</u> in AutoCAD for Windows (or when using some DOS utilities) may appear in alphabetical order, even though *MAXSORT* is set to 0. The Windows sorting (or other DOS utilities) overrides the *MAXSORT* setting for external files only, but should not affect named objects (internal). The setting for *MAXSORT* is saved in the configuration file (ACAD.CFG).

MISCELLANEOUS DISPLAY COMMANDS

This section explains display commands that are used occasionally for special purposes. Knowledge and proper use of these commands can speed drawing time and control display features to your preferences.

REDRAWALL

PULL-DOWN MENU	SCREEN MENU	TYPE IN	TABLET MENU
View *Redraw All*	*VIEW* *RedrwAl:*	*REDRAWALL*	*11, Q and 11, R*

As you know, the *Redraw* command cleans up the screen of all "blips" and redraws objects that have been partly removed by *Erasing* other objects. The *Redraw* command redraws the entire screen if you are not using viewports or redraws <u>only the current viewport</u> if you are using viewports.

The *Redrawall* command redraws the screen for <u>all viewports</u>. Viewports are separate areas of the screen that can be controlled to display a particular part or view of the geometry. Viewports are of two types: paper space (floating) viewports created with the *Mview* command and tiled viewports created with the *Vports* command (see Chapter 32).

REGENALL

PULL-DOWN MENU	SCREEN MENU	TYPE IN	TABLET MENU
---	---	*REGENALL*	*11,K*

In most cases, when changes are made to a drawing that affect the appearance of the objects on the screen, the drawing is automatically regenerated. In a few cases, when changes are made to system variables, such as a new *PDMODE* (*Point* type), the *Regen* or *Regenall* command should be used to display the effect of the new setting.

The *Regen* command causes a regeneration of the entire drawing; however, if you are using viewports, *Regen* will only redraw the <u>current viewport</u>. The *Regenall* command should be used if you are using viewports (paper space or tiled viewports) and want to regenerate <u>all viewports</u>. (See Chapter 32 for information on using paper space and tiled viewports.)

REGENAUTO

PULL-DOWN MENU	SCREEN MENU	TYPE IN	TABLET MENU
---	*OPTIONS* *Rengenmo:*	*REGENAUTO*	---

When changes are made to a drawing that affect the appearance of the objects on the screen, the drawing is generally regenerated automatically. A regeneration can be somewhat time-consuming if you are working on an extremely complex drawing or are using a relatively slow computer. In some cases, you may be performing several operations that cause regenerations between intermediate steps that you feel are unnecessary.

Regenauto allows you to control whether automatic regenerations are performed. *Regenauto* is *On* by default, but for special situations you may want to turn the automatic regenerations *Off* temporarily. The setting of *Regenauto* is stored in the *REGENMODE* variable (1=*On* and 0=*Off*). If *Regenauto* is *Off* and a regeneration is needed, AutoCAD prompts:

    About to regen—proceed? <Y>

If you prompt with a *No* response, the regeneration will be aborted.

BLIPMODE

PULL-DOWN MENU	SCREEN MENU	TYPE IN	TABLET MENU
Options *Drawing Aids...* *Blips*	*OPTIONS* *DDrmode:* *Blips*	*BLIPMODE*	---

"Blips" are the small markers that appear on the screen whenever you PICK a point. The blips are automatically erased upon a *Redraw* or *Regen*.

The *BLIPMODE* system variable allows you to control the generation of the temporary marker blips. The *BLIPMODE* is *On* by default. When *BLIPMODE* is *Off*, no marker blips appear. The command format is this:

    Command: **blipmode**
    ON/OFF <ON>: (option)

The setting is saved with the drawing file in the *BLIPMODE* system variable. The variable can also be accessed using the *Setvar* command (see Appendix A).

DRAGMODE

PULL-DOWN MENU	SCREEN MENU	TYPE IN	TABLET MENU
---	OPTIONS *Dragmod:*	*DRAGMODE*	---

AutoCAD dynamically displays some objects such as *Circles, Blocks, Polygons,* etc., as you draw or insert them. This dynamic feature is called "dragging." If you are using a slow computer, or for certain operations, you may wish to turn dragging off.

The *DRAGMODE* system variable provides three positions for the dynamic dragging feature. The command format is as follows:

Command: **dragmode**
ON/OFF/Auto <Auto>: (option)

By default, *DRAGMODE* is set to *Auto.* In this position, dragging is automatically displayed whenever possible, based on the ability of the command in use to support it. Commands that support this feature issue a request for dragging when the command is used. This request is automatically filled when *DRAGMODE* is in the *Auto* position.

When *DRAGMODE* is *On,* you must enter "*drag*" at the command prompt when the request is issued if you want to enable dragging. If *DRAGMODE* is *Off,* dragging is not displayed and all requests are automatically ignored. The *DRAGMODE* variable setting is stored with the current drawing file.

FILL

PULL-DOWN MENU	SCREEN MENU	TYPE IN	TABLET MENU
Options *Drawing Modes...* *Solid Fill*	OPTIONS *DDrmode:* *Solid Fill*	*FILL*	---

The *Fill* command controls the display of objects that are filled with solid color. Commands that create solid filled objects are *Donut, Solid,* and *Pline* (with *width*). *Fill* can be toggled *On* or *Off* to display or plot the objects with or without solid color. The command format produces this prompt:

Command: **fill**
ON/OFF <On>: (option)
Command:

Figure 30-3 displays several objects with *Fill On* and *Off.* The default position for the *Fill* command is *On.* If *Fill* is changed, the drawing must be regenerated to display the effects of the change. The setting for *Fill* is stored in the *FILLMODE* system variable.

Since solid filling may be time-consuming to regenerate a drawing with many wide *Plines, Donuts,* and *Solids,* it may be useful to turn *Fill Off* temporarily. *Fill Off* would be <u>especially</u> helpful for speeding up test plots.

Figure 30-3

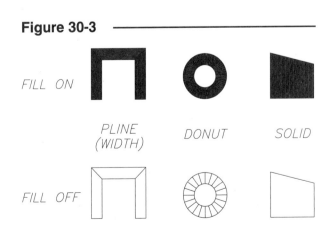

FILL ON

FILL OFF

PLINE (WIDTH)　　DONUT　　SOLID

USING SLIDES AND SCRIPTS

A slide is a "snapshot" of an AutoCAD drawing that can be made and saved to a file using the *Mslide* command. The resulting slide file contains only one image with no other drawing information. Slide files can later be viewed in AutoCAD using the *Vslide* command. A prepared series of slides can be presented at a later time, much like a slide show. This section also explains how to create a self-running slide show from your slide files by creating and running a *Script*.

MSLIDE

PULL-DOWN MENU	SCREEN MENU	TYPE IN	TABLET MENU
Tools *Slide >* *Save...*	*TOOLS* *Mslide:*	*MSLIDE*	---

Mslide is short for "make slide." A slide is a "screen capture" of the current AutoCAD display. The image that is saved is composed of the objects that appear in the drawing editor when the *Mslide* command is issued (excluding the menus, tool bars, grid, crosshairs, and command line). If tiled or floating viewports are active, the current viewport's image is captured. When a slide is made, the resulting image is saved as a file in the directory of your choice with an extension of .SLD.

Mslide is simple to use. Assume that you are working on a drawing—for example, Figure 30-4—and want to take a "snapshot" of the image using *Mslide*. Invoke the command by any method.

> Command: **mslide** (The *Create Slide File* dialogue box appears. Assign a name and directory.)
> Command:

When the *Create Slide File* dialogue box appears (Fig. 30-5), assign a name and directory for the slide. (If the *FILEDIA* variable is set to 0, the command line format is activated instead of the dialogue box.) Only the file name is required because AutoCAD automatically assigns the .SLD file extension. The drawing image is saved without the grid, crosshairs, menus, toolbars, etc. Only the drawing image is saved in the .SLD; no other drawing information is saved. Therefore, an .SLD file is much smaller (file size in bytes) than the corresponding .DWG file. Use the *Vslide* command to view the slide again.

Figure 30-4 —————————

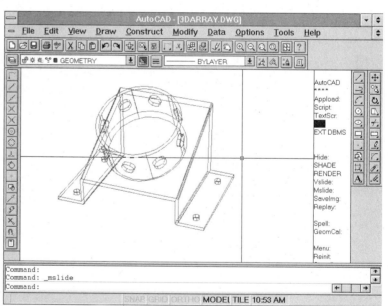

Figure 30-5 —————————

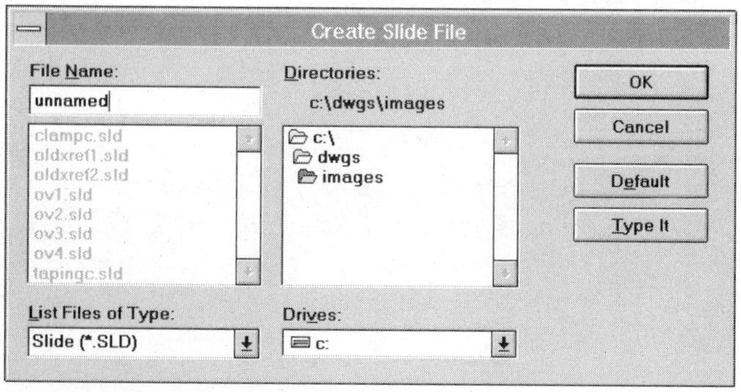

AutoCAD .SLD files are proprietary, meaning the file format was developed by AutoCAD to be used in AutoCAD. The .SLD file format is not widely used like a .TIF, .GIF, .PCX, etc., but can be viewed or converted by some software. Slide files are also a convenient format for saving an image created with the AutoCAD *Shade* command (see Chapter 34, 3D Viewing and Display).

VSLIDE

PULL-DOWN MENU	SCREEN MENU	TYPE IN	TABLET MENU
Tools *Slide >* *View...*	*TOOLS* *Vslide:*	*VSLIDE*	---

Vslide is short for "view slide." Use this command to view previously made AutoCAD slide (.SLD) files. Assuming previously created slide files are accessible, invoke *Vslide* by any method.

Command: **vslide** (The *Select Slide File* dialogue box appears. Select the desired directory and slide name.)
Command:

When the *Select Slide File* dialogue appears (Fig. 30-6), enter or select the desired directory and slide name. The selected slide then appears in the drawing editor (if viewports are active, it appears in the current viewport). Using the slide from the previous example (see *Mslide*), the slide image is "projected" in the drawing editor (Fig 30-7).

A slide file may be viewed during any AutoCAD session. If a drawing is in progress, the slide file is projected on top of the current drawing, much like a photographic slide is displayed on a projection screen or wall. Because a slide file contains only a description of the display, the slide file image cannot be edited. You cannot use *Pan* or *Zoom* to modify the display of the slide. In fact, any AutoCAD display command issued (*Redraw*, *Pan*, *Zoom*, etc.) will cause the slide to disappear and act upon the current drawing, not the slide. After a slide has been viewed, use *Redraw* to refresh the current drawing before using draw or edit commands. Because .SLD files are generally much smaller and contain less information than .DWG files, viewing a slide is much faster than loading a drawing.

Slide files are helpful for keeping a visual record of drawings, since the .SLD file is much smaller and faster loading than the corresponding .DWG file. The most common use for a series of slides is giving a presentation or a demonstration. Using prepared slides to present a complex drawing is much faster and more reliable than using *Pan* and *Zoom*. A script file (*.SCR) file can be created to "run" a series of slide files—a scripted slide show (see Creating and Using Scripts).

Figure 30-6

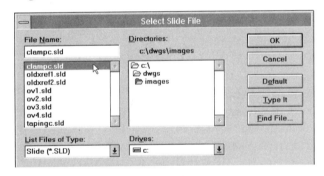

Figure 30-7

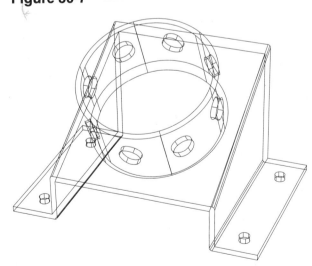

Creating and Using Scripts

Scripts are text files that contain AutoCAD commands. Similar to a batch routine written in DOS, a script file contains a user-specified listing of the desired AutoCAD commands. To run a script, use the *Script* command. AutoCAD reads and operates each command and option in the sequence it is listed in the script file. A script file contains essentially the same text that you would enter at the command line during a drawing session. When a script is executed, each line of the script is echoed at the command line.

Script files can be used for a number of purposes. If you want to give a presentation, you can create a self-running display of a series of slides by creating a script file. For this purpose, the script file repeats the *Vslide* command and the slide names. Since a script can contain any AutoCAD commands, you could make scripts to execute a series of frequently used commands—like a macro (this topic is discussed in Chapter 42, Customization). You could even recreate an entire drawing by listing every command used to create the drawing in the script file.

There are three basic steps to creating and running a script:

1. In AutoCAD, determine the commands, options, and responses that you want to include in the script file. This can involve a "practice run" to determine each step. You may have to write down each command, option, and response. The *Logfileon* and *Logfileoff* commands can help with this process (see Chapter 42).

    If you are creating a slide show, the slides must be created first. A practice run of the show using *Vslide* can be helpful to ensure you know the correct slide sequence.

2. Use a text editor such as DOS Edit, Windows Notepad, or other program that can save an ASCII text file. Include all the desired commands. Save the file as an .SCR file extension.

3   In AutoCAD, use the *Script* command to locate, load, and run the script.

Creating a Slide Show

Assume that you have created the slides and know the sequence that you want to display them. You are ready to create the script file. Use any text editor or word processor that can create text files in ASCII format (without internal word processing codes). The script file should be saved using any descriptive file name, but should have a .SCR file extension.

Begin the script file (in your text editor) by entering the *Vslide* command. When the *Vslide* command is issued in AutoCAD, the "Slide file:" prompt appears. Therefore, your next line of text (in the script file) should be the name of the desired slide file (SLIDE1, for example) without the .SLD extension. Upper- or lowercase letters can be used. For example, the script file at this point might look like this:

```
VSLIDE
SLIDE1
```

Each line or space in a script file is equivalent to one AutoCAD command, option, or response by the user. In other words, place a space or begin a new line for each time you would press Enter in AutoCAD. The file would be translated as:

```
Command: VSLIDE Enter
Slide file: SLIDE1 Enter
```

You probably want to allow the slide to stay visible for a specific amount of time—for example, 5 seconds—then move on to the next slide. You may also want the slide show to be self-repeating automatically for use during presentations or an open house. A few script-controlling commands are given here that will enable you to more effectively present the slide show.

DELAY With the *Delay* command, you can enter the number of milliseconds you wish to have the current slide displayed. For example, a 5 second display of the slide would be accomplished by entering "*Delay 5000.*" When entering the delay time, consider that the slide will remain displayed while the next *Vslide* command is issued, as well as during the time that it takes your system to retrieve and display the next slide.

RSCRIPT Typically entered as the last line of a script file, this command loops to the first line of the script and repeats the script indefinitely (until you interrupt with Backspace or Escape). Make sure you include an <u>extra space or line</u> after the *Rscript* line (to act as an Enter).

RESUME This command cannot be used in the script file, but must be typed at the keyboard during a script execution. You can interrupt a script, then type *Resume* to pick up with the script again. See *Script* next for details on using *Resume*.

An example script file is given here for displaying two slides (SLIDE1 and SLIDE2), then the drawing in the background, then repeating the show.

```
VSLIDE
SLIDE1
DELAY 2000
VSLIDE
SLIDE2
DELAY 500
REDRAW
DELAY 1000
RSCRIPT
```

In the script above, SLIDE1 displays for 2 seconds, SLIDE2 displays for .5 seconds, the *Redraw* causes the drawing (in the background) to appear and display for 1 second, and then the entire script repeats.

The drive and directory location of the slide files is significant. The slide files should be located in the path designated by the PATH= statement (in the AUTOEXEC.BAT file) or in the environment (set by the ACADR13.BAT file). Otherwise, the path should be given in the script file before each slide name as shown below.

```
VSLIDE
C:\DWGS\IMAGES\SLIDE1
DELAY 2000
VSLIDE
C:\DWGS\IMAGES\SLIDE2
DELAY 500
REDRAW
DELAY 1000
RSCRIPT
```

Once the script is created and saved as an .SCR file, return to AutoCAD and test it by using the *Script* command.

SCRIPT

PULL-DOWN MENU	SCREEN MENU	TYPE IN	TABLET MENU
Tools *Run Script...*	*TOOLS* *Script:*	*SCRIPT*	---

The *Script* command allows you to locate, load, and run a script file. Invoking the *Script* command produces the *Select Script File* dialogue box (Fig. 30-8).

> Command: **script** (The *Select Script File* dialogue box appears. Select the desired directory and script name.)
> Command:

In the dialogue box, the desired directory and file can be selected. Notice the default file extension of .SCR. (If the *FILEDIA* variable is set to 0, the dialogue box does not appear and the "Script file:" prompt appears at the Command line instead.)

Figure 30-8

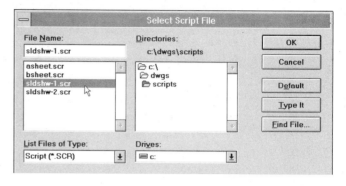

When the file is selected, the script executes. There is nothing more to do at this point other than watch the script (or begin your verbal presentation). If you are giving a verbal presentation, here are some other ideas.

1. Text slides can be created as an introduction, conclusion, and topic or section heading. Just use the *Mtext*, *Dtext*, or *Text* command to create the desired text screen in AutoCAD; then create a slide with *Mslide*.

2. To temporarily interrupt the script and view a particular slide, press the Backspace or Escape key. This enables you to discuss one slide indefinitely or stop to answer questions. Typing *Resume* causes the script to pick up again from the stopping point.

   Remember that any AutoCAD drawing can be in the background while the slide show is projected over the drawing. The Backspace-*Resume* feature allows you to cut from the slides and return to the drawing for editing, *Pans*, or *Zooms*, then return to the slide show. You may want to have a drawing loaded in the background (an entire view of the drawing, for example) and show slides "on top" (close-ups, etc.).

NOTE: The *FILEDIA* variable does not have to be set to 0 before running a slide show script. Even though the *Vslide* command normally invokes a dialogue box, the command line format is automatically activated when using *Vslide* from a script. With scripts using other commands that activate dialogue boxes, it may be helpful to set *FILEDIA* to 0.

MISCELLANEOUS COMMANDS AND VARIABLES

This section contains information on a group of unrelated intermediate-level commands and variables. The commands and variables are explained in this section are:

Reinit, Audit, Multiple, FILDIA, and *CMDDIA*

REINIT

PULL-DOWN MENU	SCREEN MENU	TYPE IN	TABLET MENU
Tools *Reinitialize...*	*TOOLS* *Reinit:*	*REINIT*	---

Many software programs require you to exit and restart the program in order for reinitialization to be performed. AutoCAD provides the *Reinit* command to prevent having to exit AutoCAD to accomplish this task.

The *Reinit* command reinitializes the input/output ports of the computer (to the digitizer and plotter); reinitializes the communications link to the peripheral devices, such as the digitizer and monitor; and reinitializes the AutoCAD Program Parameters (ACAD.PGP) file. Reinitialization may be necessary if you physically switch the port cable from the plotter to the printer and back or if a peripheral device loses power temporarily. Occasionally, the monitor may lose alignment or color synchronization and have to be reinitialized. If you edit the ACAD.PGP file, it must be reinitialized before you can use the new changes in AutoCAD (see Chapter 42 for information on the ACAD.PGP file).

Invoking the *Reinit* command causes the *Re-initialization* dialogue box to appear (Fig. 30-9). You may check one or several of the boxes. PICKing the *OK* tile causes an immediate reinitialization.

Figure 30-9

If you are using AutoCAD for Windows and have configured the digitizer as the "Current System Pointing Device," AutoCAD uses the Windows mouse driver; therefore, the "Digitizer" checkbox is disabled. If your pointing device is disabled and you need to use this dialogue box, use TAB to move to the desired options, the space bar to check the boxes, and Enter to execute an *OK*.

MULTIPLE

PULL-DOWN MENU	SCREEN MENU	TYPE IN	TABLET MENU
---	---	*MULTIPLE*	---

Multiple is not a command, but rather a <u>command modifier</u> (or adjective) since it is used in conjunction with another command. Entering "*multiple*" at the Command: prompt <u>as a prefix</u> to almost any command causes the command to automatically repeat until you stop the sequence with Escape. For example, if you wanted to use the *Insert* command repetitively, you enter the following.

    Command: **multiple insert**

The *insert* command would repeat until you stop it with Escape. This is helpful for inserting multiple *Blocks*.

The multiple modifier repeats only the command, not the command options. For example, if you wanted to repeatedly use *Circle* with the *Tangent, Tangent, Radius* option, the *TTR* would have to be entered each time the *Circle* command was automatically repeated.

AUDIT

PULL-DOWN MENU	SCREEN MENU	TYPE IN	TABLET MENU
File *Management* *Audit*	*FILE* *MANAGE* *Audit:*	*AUDIT*	---

The *Audit* command is AutoCAD's diagnostic utility for checking drawing files and correcting errors. *Audit* will examine the current drawing. You can decide whether or not AutoCAD should fix any errors if they are found. The command may yield a display something like this.

```
Command: audit
Fix any errors detected? <N> y
10      Blocks audited
15      Blocks audited
Pass 1 100      objects audited
Pass 1 200      objects audited
Pass 1 282      objects audited
Pass 2 100      objects audited
Pass 2 200      objects audited
Pass 2 282      objects audited
Pass 3 100      objects audited
Pass 3 200      objects audited
Pass 3 282      objects audited
Total errors found 0 fixed 0
Command:
```

If errors are detected and you requested them to be fixed, the last line of the report indicates the number of errors found and the number fixed. If *Audit* cannot fix the errors, try the *Recover* command (see Chapter 2).

You can create an ASCII report file by changing the *AUDITCTL* system variable to 1. In this case, when the *Audit* command is used, AutoCAD automatically writes the report out to disk in the current directory using the current drawing file name and an .ADT file extension. The default setting for *AUDITCTL* is 0 (off).

FILEDIA

This system variable enables and disables FILE-related DIAlogue boxes. File-related dialog boxes are those that are used for reading or writing files. For example, when you request to *Open* a file, the *Select File* dialog box appears (Fig. 30-10).

Figure 30-10 ────────────

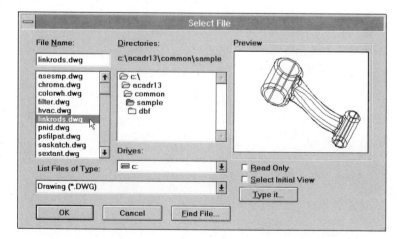

The settings for *FILEDIA* are as follows:

FILEDIA = 1   File dialogue boxes appear when a file command is invoked (default setting)

FILEDIA = 0   File dialogue boxes are disabled and command prompts are used

The *FILEDIA* variable can be set to 0 to present the command line prompt shown below instead of the *Select File* dialogue box.

Command: **open**
Enter name of drawing:

If file dialogue boxes are disabled, they can be invoked at the command line by entering a tilde (~) symbol as a prefix to the command. For example, when *FILEDIA* is set to 0, invoking the *Open* command by any method produces the command prompt; however, typing "~open" produces the *Select File* dialogue box.

Disabling the dialogue boxes can be helpful for running a script file. Since dialogue boxes require user input with a pointing device, some scripts require the command line interface to be used instead of dialogue boxes.

The *FILEDIA* variable setting is saved in the configuration file (ACAD.CFG).

CMDDIA

The *CMDDIA* variable controls the display of dialogue boxes for the *Plot* command and for external databases. For example, if *CMDDIA* is set to 0, the *Plot Configuration* dialogue box does not appear when the *Plot* command is used, but the command prompts appear instead.

Command: **plot**
What to plot — Display, Extents, Limits, View, or Window <D>:
Device Name: HP LaserJet 4 Plus/4M Plus
Output Port: LPT1:
Driver Version: 3.16

Use the Control Panel to make permanent changes to
a printer's configuration.

Plot device is System Printer ADI 4.2 - by Autodesk, Inc
Description: Windows System Printer
Plot optimization level = 0
Plot will NOT be written to a selected file
Sizes are in Inches and the style is landscape
Plot origin is at (0.00,0.00)
Plotting area is 7.93 wide by 10.49 high (MAX size)
Plot is rotated 90 degrees
Area fill will NOT be adjusted for pen width
Hidden lines will NOT be removed
Plot will be scaled to fit available area

Do you want to change anything? (No/Yes/File/Save) <N>:
Effective plotting area: 7.00 wide by 10.49 high
Plot complete.
Command:

Using the command line interface is helpful for plotting from a script file since user input with a pointing device (required for dialogue boxes) is not possible in a script. Script files can be written for batch plotting. The *CMDDIA* variable is saved in the configuration file (ACAD.CFG).

ATTDIA

The *ATTDIA* variable controls the display of the *Enter Attributes* dialogue box. The default setting is 0 (off). Ensure the setting is off if you are using a script to enter attributes. The variable is saved in the drawing file. (See Chapter 22, Block Attributes, for more information.)

THE GEOMETRY CALCULATOR

The geometry calculator can be used as a standard 10-key calculator and can also be used to calculate the location of points in a drawing. It can be used transparently (within a command) to calculate and pass values to the current command. The real power of the geometry calculator is the ability to be used with existing geometry utilizing *OSNAPs*. The geometry calculator is an ADS application that was introduced with Release 12.

The geometric calculator provides the following capabilities:

1. It can be used as a standard calculator to return values for arithmetic expressions.

2. The calculator can be used transparently to compute numbers, distances, angles, and vector directions as input for a command.

3. The calculator can be used transparently to pass coordinate data to the current command. This feature simplifies creating new geometry and editing existing geometry by enabling you to locate points that are not easily accessible by other means.

4. *OSNAPs* can be used in the expressions to further enhance your ability to use existing geometry (coordinates) in calculations.

5. Built-in functions are available as shortcuts for using *OSNAPs*, creating geometry, and making mathematical calculations and conversions.

6. The calculator can be used as a programmable calculator because of its ability to store variables and interact with AutoLISP defined functions and expressions.

CAL

PULL-DOWN MENU	SCREEN MENU	TYPE IN	TABLET MENU
Tools *Calculator*	*TOOLS* *GeomCal:*	*CAL*	*2,P*

The calculator prompts you for the entry of an "expression." The calculator uses the command line interface as shown in this example (divide 12 by 5).

```
Command: cal
Initializing...>> Expression: 12/5
2.4
Command:
```

The expression can contain arithmetic expressions, vector points, coordinates, and variables. When you enter the expression, the geometry calculator recognizes the following standard operation priorities:

1. Expressions in parentheses are considered first, beginning with the innermost.
2. Exponents are calculated first, any multiplication or division is calculated next, and addition or subtraction is calculated last.
3. Operators of equal precedence (for example, several multiplications) are taken from left to right.

These expressions can be applied to existing geometry using standard *OSNAP* functions or used in any AutoCAD command where points, vectors, and numbers are expected. The calculator supports many of the standard numeric functions found on typical scientific calculators.

Numeric Operators

Operator	Operation
()	group expressions
^	exponentiation
*,/	multiplication and division
+,-	addition and subtraction

A few examples of simple mathematical expressions using numeric operators are given here.

(5+6)*2	=	22
2^2*(14/2)	=	28
((6/2)-1)*PI	=	6.28319

Format for Feet and Inches
The default unit of measure for distances is one inch; however, feet and inches can be entered as follows:

feet'-inches" or *feet'inches"*

Expressions using feet and inch notation convert to real numbers as in the following examples.

3'	evaluates to	3*12=36.0
3.75'	evaluates to	3*12+ 9= 45.0
4'-5"	evaluates to	4*12+ 5= 53.0
6.5'3"	evaluates to	6*12+ 6+ 3=81.0

Format for Angles
The default unit of measure for angles is decimal degrees and is entered like this:

*deg**d**min'sec"*

Enter a number followed by an **r** to designate radians or **g** to designate grads. Examples are as follows.

45d15'22"
0d15'22"
1.55r
21g

Points and Vectors

Both points and vectors can be used in expressions. A point or vector is a set of real numbers enclosed in brackets [ ]. You can omit from your input string coordinates with a value of zero and the comma(s) immediately preceding the right bracket. Some examples of this syntax are shown below:

[2,5,8]	=	2,5,8
[1,2]	=	1,2,0
[,,4]	=	0,0,4
[ ]	=	0,0,0

A point defines a location in space. A vector defines a direction in space. You can add a vector to a point to obtain another point. (In the examples later in this chapter, the notation p1,p2 is used to designate points and v1,v2 is used to designate vectors.)

Point Formats

The calculator also supports the standard input format for rectangular, polar, relative, and other input.

Coordinate entry method	Format
Relative rectangular	[@X,Y,Z}
Relative polar	[@dist<angle]
Relative cylindrical	[@dist<angle,Z]
Relative spherical	[@dist<angle<angle]
WCS (overrides UCS)	use the * (asterisk) prefix inside brackets: [*X,Y,Z]

Standard Numeric Functions

The geometric calculator supports these standard numeric functions.

Function	Description
sin(*angle*)	Sine of the angle.
cos(*angle*)	Cosine of the angle.
tang(*angle*)	Tangent of the angle.
asin(*real*)	Arcsine of the number. The number must be between -1 and 1.
acos(*real*)	Arccosine of the number. The number must be between -1 and 1.
atan(*real*)	Arctangent of the number.
In(*real*)	Natural log of the number.
log(*real*)	Base-10 log of the number.
exp(*real*)	Natural exponent of the number.
exp10(*real*)	Base-10 exponent of the number.
sqr(*real*)	Square of a number.
sqrt(*real*)	Square root of a number. The number must be non-negative.
abs(*real*)	Absolute value of the number.
round(*real*)	Number rounded to the nearest integer.
trunc(*real*)	Integer potion of the number.

Function	Description
r2d(*angle*)	Angles in radians converted to degrees. For example, r2d(pi) converts the constant pi to 180 degrees.
d2r(*angle*)	Angles in degrees converted to radians. For example, d2r (180) converts 180 degrees to radians and returns the value of the constant pi.
pi	The constant pi.

OSNAP Modes

You can include *OSNAP* modes as part of an arithmetic expression. When CAL encounters an *OSNAP* mode, the aperature appears and you are prompted to "Select entity for (*OPTION*) snap:". The selected *OSNAP* point coordinate values are passed to the expression for evaluation. To use *OSNAP* modes, enter the three-character name in the expression.

CAL *OSNAP* Mode	AutoCAD *OSNAP* Mode
END	ENDPOINT
INS	INSERT
INT	INTERSECTION
MID	MIDPOINT
CEN	CENTER
NEA	NEAREST
NOD	NODE
QUA	QUADRANT
PER	PERPENDICULAR
TAN	TANGENT

Built-in Functions

The Geometry Calculator has a number of "built-in" functions that provide a variety of utilities to be used for conversions and inquiries of existing geometry.

Function	Description
abs(v)	Calculates the length of vector v, a non-negative real number.
abs([1,2,4])	Calculates the length of vector [1,2,4].
ang(p)	Angle between the X axis and vector p.
ang(p1, p2)	Angle between the X axis and line (p1, p2).
ang(apex, p1, p2)	Angle between the lines (apex, p1) and (apex, p2) projected onto the XY plane.
ang(apex, p1, p2, p)	Angle between the lines (apex, p1) and (apex, p2).
cvunit(1,inch,cm)	Converts the value 1 from inches to centimeters.

Function	Description
cur	Sets the value of the variable *LASTPOINT*.
cur(p)	Pick a point using the graphics cursor with a rubberband line from point p.
dist(p1, p2)	Distance between points p1 and p2.
dpl(p, p1, p2)	Distance between point p and the line (p1, p2).
dpp(p, p1, p2, p3)	Distance between point p and the plane defined by p1, p2& p3.
ill(p1, p2, p3, p4)	Intersection of lines (p1, p2) and (p3, p4).
ilp(p1,p2,p3,p4,p5)	Intersection of line (p1, p2) and plane defined by p3, p4& p5.
nor	Unit vector normal to a circle, arc or arc polyline segment.
nor(v)	Unit vector in the XY plane and normal to the vector v.
nor(p1, p2)	Unit vector in the XY plane and normal to the line (p1, p2).
nor(p1, p2, p3)	Unit vector normal to plane defined by p1, p2 & p3.
pld(pl, p2, units)	Point on the line (p1, p2) that is drawing units away from the point p1.
plt(p1, p2, t)	Point on line (p1, p2) that is t segments from p1. A segment = distance from p1 to p2.
rad	Radius of the selected object.
rot(p, origin, ang)	Rotates point p through angle ang using a line parallel to the Z axis passing through origin as the axis of rotation.
rot(p1, p2, ang)	Rotates point p through angle ang using line (p1, p2) as the axis of rotation.
u2w(p1)	Converts point p1 expressed in WCS to the current UCS.
vec(p1, p2)	Vector from point p1 to point p2.
vec1(p1, p2)	Unit vector from point p1 to point p2.
w2u(p1)	Converts point p1 expressed in WCS to the current UCS.

Shortcut Functions

In addition to computing numbers and points, you can use the calculator to create and edit geometry in your drawing. This is one of the most powerful features of *CAL*. The following table lists the geometric functions supported by the calculator. Using these shortcuts prevents you from having to enter the three-letter *OSNAP* mode and parentheses in the expression.

Function	Shortcut for	Description
dee	dist(end, end)	Distance between two endpoints.
ille	ill(end, end, end, end)	Intersection of two lines defined by four endpoints.
mee	(end+end)/2	Midpoint between two endpoints.
nee	nor(end, end)	Unit vector in the XY plane and normal to two endpoints.
vee	vec(end, end)	Vector from two endpoints.
vee1	vec1(end, end)	Unit vector from two endpoints.

Point Filter Functions

You can use these fuctions to filter the X,Y, and Z components of a point or vector coordinate.

Function	Description
xyof(*p1*)	X and Y components of a point. The Z component is set to 0.0.
xzof(*p1*)	X and Z components of a point. The Y component is set to 0.0.
yzof(*p1*)	Y and Z components of a point. The X component is set to 0.0.
xof(*p1*)	X component of a point. The Y and Z components are set to 0.0.
yof(*p1*)	Y component of a point. The X and Z components are set to 0.0.
zof(*p1*)	Z component of a point. The X and Y components are set to 0.0.
rxof(*p1*)	X component of a point.
ryof(*p1*)	Y component of a point.
rzof(*p1*)	Z component of a point.

Geometry Calculator Examples

Point, Vector, and *OSNAPs* Example

Figure 30-11

The following example places the beginning of a *Line* [1,-.5] units over from the selected *QUAdrant* of a *Circle*, then adds two more calculated vectors to create a wedge (Fig. 30-11). Don't forget to enter an apostrophe (') to use *Cal* transparently if you are typing the command.

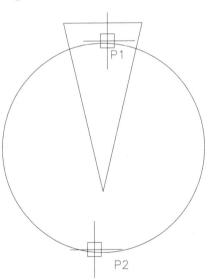

```
Command: Line
From point: 'cal
>>Expression: qua+[-1,.5]
>>Select entity for QUA snap: PICK
(PICK the top quadrant on the circle, P1.)
```

To continue with the line from the previous sequence, a vector is added to a current point to obtain the next point on the line.

```
To point: 'cal
>> Expression: cur+[,1.5]
>> Enter a point: qua
of PICK  (PICK the bottom quadrant of the circle, P2.)
```

To finish the wedge, the next point of the vector is placed in the same fashion as the first point.

```
To point: 'cal
>> Expression: qua+[1,.5]
>> Select entity for QUA snap: PICK  (PICK the top quadrant of the circle, P1 again.)
To point: c  (To close the wedge shape.)
```

Numeric Functions and Built-in Functions Example

The following example displays the use of numeric functions and built-in functions in finding the circumference and area of a *Circle* (no figure).

To find the circumference of a *Circle*, first create the variable (R1) which collects the circle radius. Entering any variable name (R1 in this case) followed by an equal (=) sign stores the value or point to an AutoLISP variable.

```
Command: 'cal
>> Expression: R1=rad
>> Select circle, arc or polyline segment for RAD function: PICK   (PICK anywhere on a Circle.)
2.58261
```

The value is stored to variable R1. Then enter the radius in a numeric function to determine the circumference.

```
Command: 'cal
>> Expression: 2*pi*R1
16.227
```

Now use the radius variable (R1) in a numeric function format to determine the area of a circle.

```
Command: 'cal
>> Expression: pi*sqr(R1)
20.9541
```

OSNAP Examples

In the following example, the calculator returns the point (Fig. 30-12, point A) halfway between the center of the circle and the endpoint of the object.

Figure 30-12

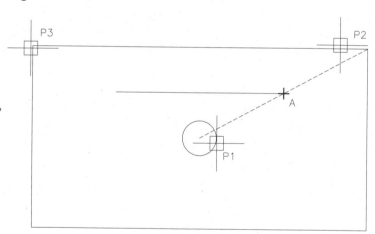

```
Command: Line
From point: 'cal
>> Expression: (cen+end)/2
>> Select entity for CEN snap: PICK
(PICK any point on the circle, P1).
>> Select entity for END snap: PICK
(PICK the upper-right corner of the
rectangle, P2.)
```

AutoCAD finds the point halfway between the selected points (A) and passes the coordinate to the *Line* command as the "From point:". Do the same to determine the "To point:" of the *Line*.

```
To point: 'cal
>> Expression: (cen+end)/2
>> Select entity for CEN snap: PICK   (PICK the circle, P1 again.)
>> Select entity for END snap: PICK   (PICK the upper-left corner of the rectangle, P3.)
To point: Enter
```

The *Line* is drawn with its endpoints halfway between the *OSNAP*s.

This example uses *END* and *CEN* to calculate the centroid (Fig. 30-13, point B) defined by 3 points (2 end-points and the center of a circle).

Figure 30-13

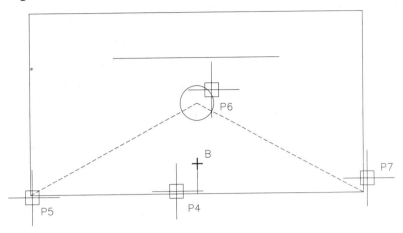

> Command: **Line**
> From point: **mid**
> of **PICK** (PICK the bottom horizontal line of the rectangle, P4.)
> To point: **'cal**
> \>> Expression:
> **(end+cen+end)/3**
> \>> Select entity for END snap:
> **PICK** (PICK the lower-left corner of the rectangle, P5.)
> \>> Select entity for CEN snap: **PICK** (PICK the circle, P6.)
> \>> Select entity for END snap: **PICK** (PICK the lower-right corner of the rectangle, P7.)
> To point: **Enter**

For the next drawing example, *Cal* prompts for an object, then returns a point that is 1 unit to the left of the selected object's midpoint. In the second sequence, the point is placed 1 unit to the right of the selected object's midpoint.

Figure 30-14

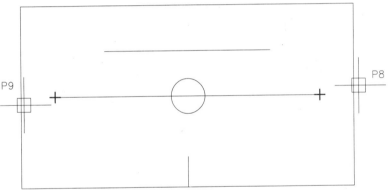

> Command: **Line**
> From point: **'cal**
> \>> Expression: **mid+[-1,]**
> \>> Select entity for MID snap:
> **PICK** (PICK the right vertical line of the rectangle, P8.)
>
> To point: **'cal**
> \>> Expression: **mid+[1,]**
> \>> Select entity for MID snap: **PICK** (PICK the left vertical line of the rectangle, P9.)
> To point: **Enter**
> Command:

Shortcut Function Examples
The calculator shortcut functions are used to add text and circles to the previous drawing. In the first example, middle justified text is placed at the intersection of two lines defined by endpoints (*ille*) (Fig. 30-15).

Figure 30-15

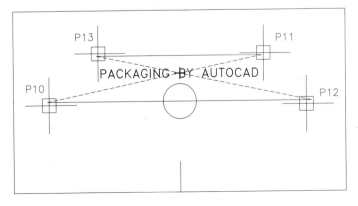

Command: *dtext*
Justify/Style/<Start point>: *j*
Align/Fit/Center/Middle/Right/TL/TC/TR/ML/MC/MR/BL/BC/BR: *m*
Middle point: `**'cal**
>> Expression: **ille**
>> Select one endpoint for ILLE:First line: **PICK** (PICK the left end of the long horizontal line, P10.)
>> Select another endpoint for ILLE:First line: **PICK** (PICK the right end of the short horizontal line, P11.)
>> Select one endpoint for ILLE:Second line: **PICK** (PICK the right end of the long horizontal line, P12.)
>> Select another endpoint for ILLE:Second line: **PICK** (PICK the left end of the short horizontal line, P13.)
Height <0.2000>: **Enter**
Rotation angle <0>: **Enter**
Text: **PACKAGING BY AUTOCAD**
Text: **Enter**

Use another built-in function to return the midpoint between two endpoints (*mee*) for the center of a circle (Fig. 30-16).

Command: *Circle*
3P/2P/TTR/<Center point>: **'CAL**
>> Expression: *mee*
>> Select one endpoint for MEE: **PICK** (PICK the left end of the long horizontal line, P14.)>> Select another endpoint for MEE: **PICK** (PICK the left end of the short horizontal line, P15.)
Diameter/<Radius> <0.5000>: **.25**

Figure 30-16

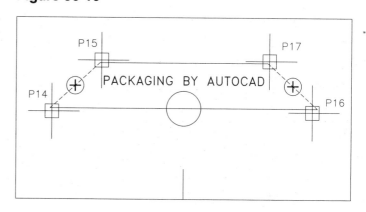

Command: CIRCLE 3P/2P/TTR/<Center point>: **'CAL**
>> Expression: **mee**
>> Select one endpoint for MEE: **PICK** (PICK the right end of the long horizontal line, P16.)
>> Select another endpoint for MEE: **PICK** (PICK the right end of the short horizontal line, P17.)
Diameter/<Radius> <0.2500>: **Enter**
Command:

The Geometry Calculator has tremendous power, but it can only be beneficial if you know how and when to use it. Review the function tables (particularly the Built-in and Shortcut Functions) and practice with the expressions. Many of the functions can save drawing time and allow you to construct and edit more efficiently than by other methods.

CHAPTER EXERCISES

1. **Wildcards**

    In this exercise, you will use wildcards to manage layers for a complex drawing. *Open* the AutoCAD **HVAC** drawing that is located in the \COMMON\SAMPLE directory. Use the *Layer Control* dialogue box to view the layers. Examine the layer names; then *Cancel*.

A. Type the *Layer* command. *Freeze* all of the layers whose names begin with the letters **AR**. (Hint: enter **AR*** at the Layer name(s) to Freeze: prompt.) Do you notice the change in the drawing? Use the *Layer Control* dialogue box or list the layers using the *?* option to view the *State* of the layers.

B. *Thaw* all layers (use the asterisk *). Now *Freeze* all of the layers <u>except</u> the architectural layers (those beginning with **AR**). (Hint: enter **~AR*** at the "Layer name(s) to Freeze:" prompt.) Do only the walls appear in the drawing now? Examine the list of layers and their *State*. *Thaw* all layers again.

C. Next, *Freeze* all of the layers except the grid layers (layers that have a "GRID" string). (Hint: enter **~*GRID*** at the "Layer name(s) to Freeze:" prompt.) Do only the grids appear in the drawing now? Examine the list of layers and their *State*. *(Layer 0 cannot be Frozen because it is the Current layer.)* *Thaw* all layers again and do <u>not</u> *Save* changes.

2. *Rename*

Open the **OFF-ATT2** drawing that you last worked on in Chapter 22. Enter *Ddrename* (or select *Rename* from a menu) to produce the *Rename* dialogue box. *Rename* the *Blocks* as follows:

New Name	Old Name
DSK	**DESK**
CHR	**CHAIR**
TBL	**TABLE**
FLC	**FILECAB**

Next, use the *Rename* dialogue box again to rename the *Layers* as indicated below.

New Name	Old Name
FLOORPLN-DIM	**DIM-FLOOR**
ELEC-DIM	**DIM-ELEC**

Use the *Rename* dialogue box again to change the *Text Style* name as follows.

New Name	Old Name
ARCH-FONT	**CITY BLUEPRINT**

Save the drawing and *Exit* AutoCAD.

3. *Purge*

While in DOS or with the Windows File Manager, find the directory and check the file size of OFF-ATT2.DWG. Now, *Open* **OFF-ATT2** and use *Purge*. Answer *Yes* to *Purge* any unreferenced named objects. *Exit* AutoCAD and *Save Changes*. Check the file size again. Is the file size slightly smaller?

4. *Multiple* modifier

Open the **OFF-ATT2** drawing again and prepare to *Insert* several more furniture *Blocks* into the office. Type *Multiple* at the Command: prompt, then a space, then *Insert* and return. Proceed to *Insert* the *Blocks*. Notice that you do not have to repeatedly enter the *Insert* command. Now try the *Multiple* modifier with the *Line* command. Remember this for use with other repetitive commands. (Do not *Save* the drawing.)

5. *Audit*

   With the OFF-ATT2 drawing open, use the *Audit* command to report any errors. If errors exist, use *Audit* again to fix the errors.

6. *BLIPMODE, DRAGMODE*

   A. Begin a *New* drawing using your **ASHEET** prototype. Turn *BLIPMODE Off*. Experiment with this setting by drawing a few *Lines* and *Circles*. Use *Erase*. Notice that you do not have to *Redraw* as often as you did when *BLIPMODE* was *On*.

   B. Now change the setting of **DRAGMODE** to *Off*. Draw a few *Circles*, a *Polygon*, an *Ellipse*, and then **dimension** your figures. Do you prefer *DRAGMODE On* or *Off*?

   C. Since the *BLIPMODE* and *DRAGMODE* system variables are saved with the drawing file, you can make the settings in the prototype drawings so they will preset to your preference when you begin a *New* drawing (if you prefer other than the default settings). If you prefer *BLIP-MODE* or *DRAGMODE Off*, *Exit* the **ASHEET** and *Discard Changes*. Use *Open* to open each of the prototype drawings (**ASHEET**, **BSHEET**, and **CSHEET**), change the desired setting, and *Save*.

7. *Fill, Regen*

   Open the **SASKATCH** sample drawing (from the \COMMON\SAMPLE directory). Once the drawing has loaded, type *Regen* and check the length of time it takes for the regeneration to complete (use your stopwatch or "count" the seconds). Now turn *Fill Off*. Also turn *Qtext On*. Make another *Regen* as before and check the time. Is there any improvement?

   Imagine the time required for plotting this drawing using a pen plotter. *Fill* and *Qtext* can be set to save time for test plots. If you have a pen plotter, make a plot of the drawing with *Fill* and *Qtext* set in each position. How many minutes are saved with *Qtext on* and *Fill off*? (Do <u>not</u> *Save* the changes to SASKATCH).

8. *Mslide, Vslide*

   A. *Open* your choice of the following sample drawings: **ASESMP**, **HVAC**, **PNID**, or **STRUCTUR**. (Assuming C:\ACADR13 is where AutoCAD is loaded on your computer, the drawings are located in the C:\ACADR13\COMMON\SAMPLE directory.) Make eight to ten slides of the drawing, showing several detailed areas (using *Zoom* and *Pan*, etc.) and at least one slide showing the entire drawing. Experiment with *Freezing* layers and include several slides with some layers frozen. Assign descriptive names for the slides so you can determine the subject of each slide by its name. Strive to describe as much as possible about the drawing in the limited number of slides.

   B. When the slides of the drawing are complete, prepare at least two text slides to use as informative material such as an introduction, conclusion, or topic headings (make the text in one or more separate drawings; then use *Mslide*).

   C Finally, use *Vslide* to view your slides and determine the optimum sequence to describe the drawing. Write down the order of the slides that you choose.

9. *Script*

Use **DOS Edit, Windows Notepad**, or other text editor to create a script file to run your slide show. Include appropriate *delays* to allow viewing time or time for you to verbally describe the slides. Make the script self-repeating. Name the script **XXXSHOW** (where XXX represents your initials). In AutoCAD, use *Script* to run the show to "de-bug" it and optimize the delays.

10. **Geometry Calculator**

A. This exercise utilizes several *Cal* functions. Begin by drawing the shape shown in Figure 30-17 using a *Pline*. Do not draw the dimensions. *Save* the drawing as **CAL-EX**.

Figure 30-17

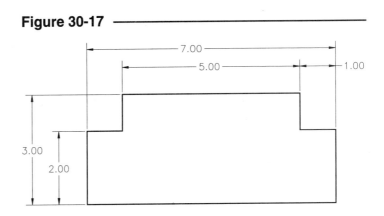

B. Draw the *Circle* in the center of the *Pline* shape with a **.5** unit *radius* (Fig. 30-18). The center of the *Circle* is located halfway between the *MIDpoints* of the top and bottom horizontal line segments. Use the *Calculator* transparently to place the *Center* of the *Circle*.

Figure 30-18

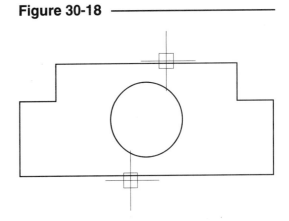

Hint: Command: **circle**
CIRCLE 3P/2P/TTR/<Center point>: **'cal**
> Expression: **(mid+mid)/2**

C. Draw the small *Circle* (Fig. 30-19) with a **.1** *radius*. Its *Center* is located **.25** units to the right and **.25** units up from the lower-left corner of the *Pline* shape. Use *Cal* transparently to place the *Circle*.

Figure 30-19

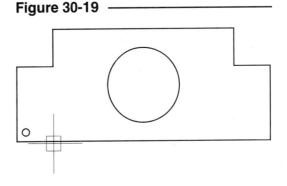

Hint: Command: **circle**
3P/2P/TTR/<Center point>: **'cal**
>> Expression: **end+[.25,.25]**

D. Create the *Circle* in the upper-right corner
    (Fig. 30-20, P1). It has a *Radius* of **1.5** times
    the existing small *Circle*. Store the existing
    small circle radius to a variable named **R1**.
    Then create the new *Circle* with the *Center*
    located **.5** units to the left and down from the
    upper-right corner.

Figure 30-20

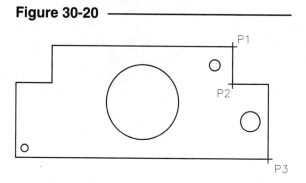

Hint 1: >> Expression: `R1=rad`
Hint 2: >> Expression: `end+[-.5,-.5]`

E. The last *Circle* (on the far right) is located midway between two endpoints (P2 and P3). It has a
    radius of **1.8** times the size of the last circle that you created. Use a shortcut function and vari-
    able (if necessary) to create the *Circle*. *Save* the drawing.

Chapter 31
XREFERENCES

Chapter Objectives

After completing this chapter you should:

1. know the difference between an *Xrefed* drawing and an *Inserted* drawing;
2. be able to *Attach* an externally referenced drawing to the current drawing;
3. understand that an *Overlay* drawing cannot be nested;
4. be able to *Reload* an *Xrefed* drawing while in a drawing session;
5. be able to *Detach* an externally referenced drawing;
6. know the naming scheme for dependent objects (*Blocks, Layers, Text Styles,* etc.);
7. be able to *Bind* an entire *Xrefed* drawing and *Xbind* individual named objects;
8. be able to use the *VISRETAIN* variable to retain dependent layer visibility settings;
9. know how to control the creation of *Xref* log files (.XLG) with the *XREFCTL* variable;
10. know several techniques for managing externally referenced drawing files.

BASICS

AutoCAD's Xreference (external reference) feature enables you to view another drawing from within the current drawing. The externally referenced drawing (Xref) is visible in the same screen as the current drawing; however, you cannot draw in or edit the Xref drawing.

Similar to the *Insert* command's ability to bring another drawing into the current drawing as a *Block*, the *Xref* command can bring any drawing (or *WBlock*) into the current drawing but not as a permanent part of the current drawing. Comparisons between an *Inserted* drawing and an *Xrefed* drawing are outlined below.

INSERT	XREF
Any drawing can be *Inserted* as a *Block*.	Any drawing can be *Xrefed*.
The drawing comes in as a *Block*.	The drawing comes in as an *Xref*.
The *Block* drawing is a permanent part of the current drawing.	The *Xref* is not permanent, only "attached" or "overlayed."
The current drawing file size increases approximately equal to the *Block* drawing size.	The current drawing increases only by a small amount (enough to store the *Xref* name and path).
The *Inserted Block* drawing is static. It never changes.	Each time the current drawing is opened, it loads the most current version of the *Xref* drawing.
If the original drawing that was used as the *Block* is changed, the *Inserted Block* does not change because it is not linked to the original drawing.	If the original *Xref* drawing is changed, the changes are automatically reflected when the current drawing is *Opened*.
Objects of the *Inserted* drawing cannot be changed in the current drawing unless *Exploded*.	The *Xref* cannot be changed in the current drawing. Changes are typically made in the original drawing.
The current drawing can contain multiple *Block*s.	The current drawing can contain multiple *Xrefs*.
A *Block* drawing cannot be converted to an *Xref*.	An *Xref* can be converted to a *Block*. The *Bind* option makes it a *Block*—a permanent part of the current drawing.
A *Block* is *Inserted* on the current layer.	An *Xref* drawing's layers are also *Xrefed* and visibility of its layers can be controlled independently.
Only the drawing geometry of a *Block* is *Inserted*.	Any "named objects" of an *Xref* can be referenced in the current drawing if *Xbind* is used.
Blocks can be nested.	An *Attached Xref* can be nested.
Any *Block* that is referenced by another *Block* is "nested."	An *Overlay Xref* cannot be nested.
A "circular" reference is not allowed with *Blocks* (X references Y and Y references X) because nested *Blocks* are also referenced.	An *Overlay Xref* can be used to prevent nesting and allow circular references.

As you can see, an *Xrefed* drawing has similarities and differences to an *Inserted* drawing. The following figures illustrate both the differences and similarities between an *Xrefed* drawing and an *Inserted* one.

Figure 31-1

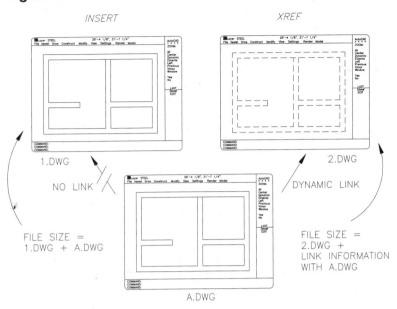

The relationship between the current (parent) drawing and a drawing that has been *Inserted* and one that has been *Xreferenced* is illustrated here (Fig. 31-1). The *Inserted* drawing becomes a permanent part of the current drawing. No link exists between the parent drawing and the original *Inserted* drawing. In contrast, the *Xrefed* drawing is <u>not</u> a permanent part of the parent drawing but is a dynamic one-way link between the two drawings. In this way, when the original *Xrefed* drawing is edited, the changes are reflected in the parent drawing (if a *Reload* is invoked or when the parent drawing is *Opened* next). The file size of the parent drawing for the *Inserted* case is the sum of both the drawings whereas the file size of the parent drawing for the *Xref* case is only the original size plus the link information.

Some of the <u>similarities</u> between *Xreferenced* drawings and *Inserted* drawings are shown in the following figures.

Figure 31-2

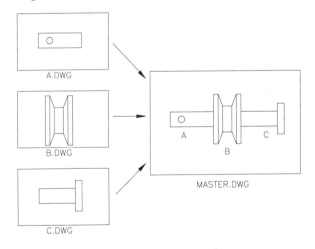

Any number of drawings can be *Xrefed* or *Inserted* into the current drawing (Fig. 31-2). For example, component parts can be *Xrefed* to compile an assembly drawing.

The current drawing can contain nested *Xrefs*. This feature is also similar to *Blocks*. For example, the OFFICE drawing can *Xref* a TABLE drawing and the TABLE drawing can *Xref* a CHAIR drawing. Therefore, the CHAIR drawing is considered a "nested" *Xref* in the OFFICE drawing (Fig. 31-3).

Figure 31-3

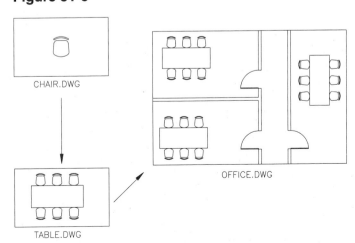

One of the main features and purposes of an *Xref* drawing is that it <u>cannot be edited</u>. Even though an *Xrefed* drawing's named objects (layers, linetypes, text styles, etc.) are attached, you cannot draw or edit on any of its layers. You do, however, have complete control over the <u>visibility</u> of the *Xref* drawing's layers. The *State* of the layers (*On, Off, Freeze,* and *Thaw*) of the *Xref* drawing can be controlled like any layers in the parent drawing.

The named objects (*Layers, Text Styles, Blocks, Views,* etc.) that may be part of an *Xref* drawing become <u>dependent</u> objects when they are *Xrefed* to the parent drawing. These dependent objects cannot be renamed, changed, or used in the parent drawing. They can, however, be converted individually (permanently attached) to the parent drawing with the *Xbind* command.

Xref drawings have many applications. *Xrefs* are particularly useful in a networked office or laboratory environment. For example, several people may be working on one project, each person constructing individual components of a project. The components may be mechanical parts of an assembly, or electrical, plumbing, and HVAC layouts for a construction project, or several areas of a plant layout. In any case, each person can *Xref* another person's drawing as an external reference without fear of the original drawing being edited.

As an example of the usefulness of *Xrefs*, a project coordinator could *Open* a new drawing, *Xref* all components of an assembly, analyze the relationships among components, and plot the compilation of the components (Fig. 31-2). The master drawing may not even contain any objects other than *Xrefs*, yet each time it is *Opened*, it would contain the most up-to-date component drawings.

In another application, an entire team can access (*Xref, Attach*) the same master layout, such as a floor plan, assembly drawing, or topographic map. Figure 31-4 represents a mechanical design team working on an automobile assembly and all accessing the master body drawing. Each team member "sees" the master drawing, but cannot change it. If any changes are made to the original master drawing, all team members see the updates whenever they *Reload* the Xref or *Open* their drawing.

Figure 31-4

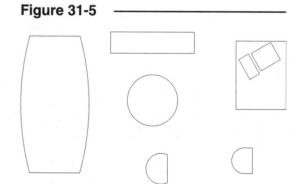

The simplicity of using Xreferences is that one command, *Xref*, controls almost all of the external referencing features. Several options permit you to create, sever, or change the link between the parent drawing and the *Xref* drawing.

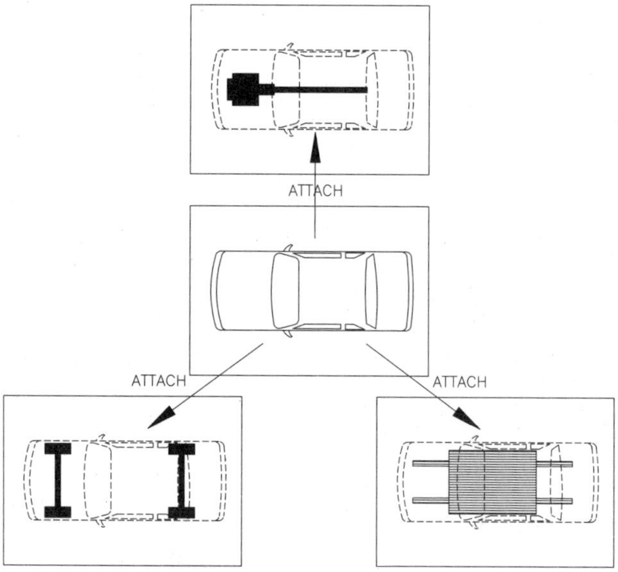

An *Xref* Example

Assume that you are an interior designer in an architectural firm. The project drawings are stored on a local network so all team members have access to all drawings related to a particular project. Your job is to design the interior layout comprised of chairs, tables, desks, and file cabinets for an office complex. You use a prototype drawing named INTERIOR.DWG for all of your office interiors. It is a blank drawing that contains only block definitions (not yet *Inserted*) of each chair, desk, etc., as shown in Figure 31-5. The *Block* definitions are: CHAIR, CONCHAIR, DESK, TABLE, FILECAB, and CONTABLE.

Figure 31-5

An architect on the team has almost completed the floorplan for the project. You use the *Attach* option of the *Xref* command to "see" the architect's floorplan drawing, OFFICEX.DWG. The *Xrefed* drawing is visible; however, it cannot be altered. The visibility of the individual dependent layers can be controlled with the *Layer* command or *Layer Control* dialogue box. For example, layers showing the HVAC, electrical layout, and other details are *Frozen* to yield only the floor plan layer needed for the interior layout (Fig. 31-6).

Figure 31-6

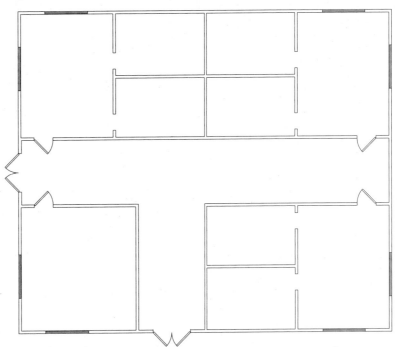

Next, you draw objects in the current drawing, or in this case *Insert* the office furniture *Block*s that are defined in the current drawing (INTERIOR.DWG). The resulting drawing would display a complete layout of the office floorplan plus the *Inserted* furniture—as if it were one drawing (see Figure 31-7). You *Save* your drawing and go home for the evening.

Figure 31-7

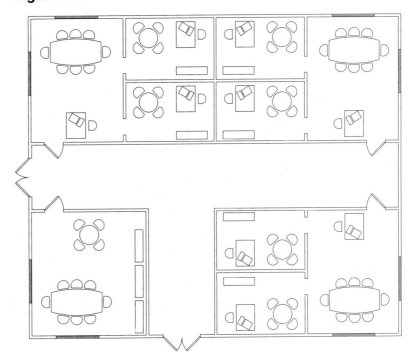

That evening, the architect makes a change to the floorplan. He works on the original OFFICEX drawing that you *Xrefed*. The individual office entry doors in the halls are moved to be more centrally located. The new layout appears in Figure 31-8.

Figure 31-8

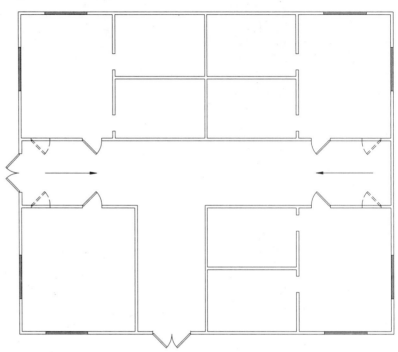

The next day, you *Open* the INTERIOR drawing. The automatic loading of the OFFICEX drawing displays the latest version of the office floorplan with the design changes. The appropriate changes to the interior drawing must be made, such as relocating the furniture by the hall doors (Fig. 31-9). When all parts of the office complex are completed, the INTERIOR (parent) drawing could be plotted to show the office floorplan and the interior layout. The resulting plot would include objects in the parent drawing and the visible *Xref* drawing layers.

Figure 31-9

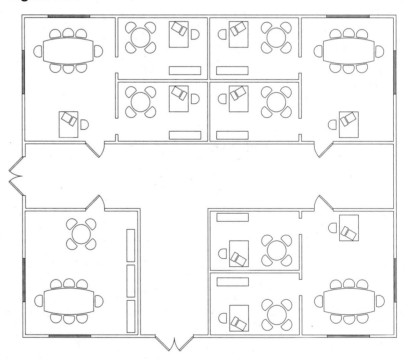

AutoCAD's ability to externally reference drawings makes team projects much more flexible and efficient. If the *Xref* capability did not exist, the OFFICEX drawing would have to be *Inserted* as a *Block*, and design changes made later to the OFFICEX drawing would not be apparent. The original OFFICEX *Block* would have to be *Erased*, *Purged*, and the new drawing *Inserted*.

XREF AND RELATED COMMANDS AND VARIABLES

The *Xref* command, its options, and related commands are located in the *File* pull-down menu (Fig. 31-10). If you are using AutoCAD for Windows, an *External Reference* tool bar can be activated by using the *Toolbar* command or selecting it from the *Tools* pull-down menu (Fig. 31-11).

Figure 31-10

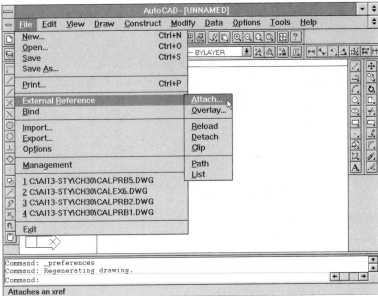

Figure 31-11

	PULL-DOWN MENU	SCREEN MENU	TYPE IN	TABLET MENU
XREF	*File* *External Reference >*	*FILE* *Xref:*	*XREF*	*8,X to 10,X*

The *Xref* command provides you with control of externally referenced drawings. The options allow you to *Attach, Overlay, Detach, Reload, Bind,* and reset the *Path* for an Xref.

Command: **xref**
?/Bind/Detach/Path/Reload/Overlay/<Attach>:

Attach

 This (the default) option attaches one drawing to another by making the Xref drawing visible in the "parent" drawing. Even though the Xref drawing is visible, it cannot be edited from within the parent drawing. *Attach* creates a one-way link between two drawings (Fig. 31-12).

Figure 31-12

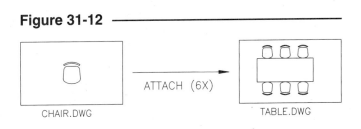

To use *Attach, Open* the "parent" drawing, invoke *Xref,* and select the name of the drawing you want to attach. You must specify the insertion point, scale factors, and rotation angle.

Command: **xref**
?/Bind/Detach/Path/Reload/
Overlay/<Attach>: **Enter** (The *Select file to attach* dialogue box appears, Fig. 31-13.)
Attach Xref CHAIR: CHAIR.DWG
CHAIR loaded.
Insertion point: **PICK** or
(**coordinates**)
X scale factor <1> / Corner / XYZ:
Enter or (**value**) or (**option**)
Y scale factor (default=X): **Enter** or
(**value**)
Rotation angle <0>: **Enter** or (**value**)
Command:

Figure 31-13 ————————————————

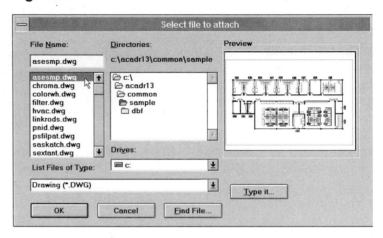

This action causes the specified drawing to appear in the current drawing similar to the way a drawing appears when it is *Inserted* as a *Block*. Notice the similarity of the last four prompts to the *Insert* command. The "X scale factor:", "Y scale factor:", and "Rotation angle:" prompts operate identically to the *Insert* command. Similar to the action of *Insert*, the base point of the *Xref* drawing is its 0,0 point unless a different base point has been previously defined with the *Base* command.

Each time the current drawing is *Opened*, the *Attached* drawing is loaded as an *Xref*. More than one reference drawing can be *Attached* to the current drawing. A single reference drawing can be *Attached* to any number of insertion points in the current drawing. The dependent objects in the reference drawing (*Layers*, *Blocks*, *Text styles*, etc.) are assigned new names, "external drawing|old name" (See Dependent Objects and Names).

Overlay

An *Xref Overlay* is similar to an *Attached Xref* with one main difference—an *Overlay* cannot be nested. In other words, if you *Attach* a drawing that (itself) has an *Overlay*, the *Overlay* does not appear in your drawing. On the other hand, if the first drawing is *Attached*, it appears when the parent drawing is *Attached* to another drawing (Fig. 31-14). The command syntax for *Overlay* is identical to *Attach*.

Figure 31-14 ————————————————

The *Overlay* option enables "circular" Xrefs to occur by preventing unwanted nested Xrefs. This is helpful in a networking environment where many drawings Xref other drawings. For example, assume drawing B has drawing A as an *Overlay*. As you work on drawing C, you *Xref* and view only drawing B without drawing B's overlays—namely drawing A. This occurs because drawing A is an *Overlay* to B, not *Attached*. If all drawings are *Overlays*, no nesting occurs (Fig. 31-15).

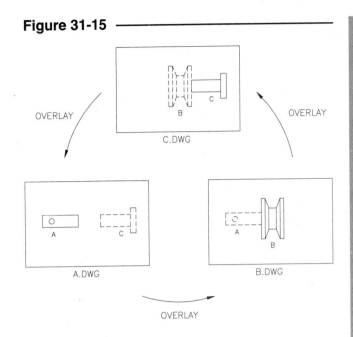

Figure 31-15

The overlay concept is particularly useful in a concurrent engineering project where all team members must access each other's work simultaneously. In the case of a design team working on an automobile assembly, each team member can *Attach* the master body drawing and also *Overlay* the individual subassembly drawings (Fig. 31-16). *Overlay* enables each member to *Xref* all drawings without bringing in each drawing's nested Xreferences.

One limitation of *Overlay* is that (*Block*) attributes are not visible in an *Overlay* Xref. An *Attached* Xref displays attribute information, but the information cannot be changed in the parent drawing.

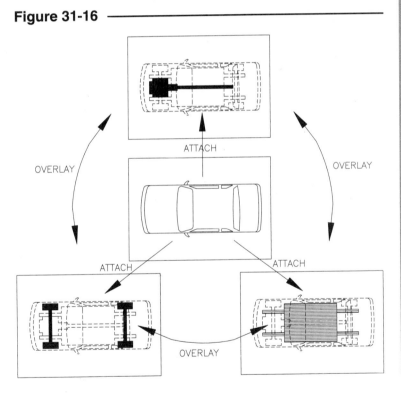

Figure 31-16

Detach

Detach severs the link between the parent drawing and the Xref. Using this option causes the *Xrefed* drawing to "drop" from view immediately. When the parent drawing is *Opened*, the previously *Attached* drawing is <u>no longer</u> loaded as an Xref.

? (list)

 This option lists all existing external references in the current drawing. An example is shown here:

```
Command: xref
?/Bind/Detach/Path/Reload/Overlay/<Attach>: ?
Xref(s) to list <*>: Enter
```

Xref name	Path	Xref type
GASKET	C:\DWGS\MECH\GASKET.DWG	Attach
BOLT	C:\DWGS\MECH\BOLT.DWG	Attach
PLATES	C:\DWGS\MECH\PLATES.DWG	Overlay

```
Total Xref(s): 3
Command:
```

Path

You can respecify the directory location of the external drawing using the *Path* option. This is necessary if an *Xrefed* drawing has been relocated to another drive or directory on the computer hard drive or network drives. For example, if the PLATES drawing (that your parent drawing referenced) was relocated to another drive and directory, use the *Path* option to specify the new location. The command syntax follows. Using the *Path* option forces a reload.

```
Command: xref
?/Bind/Detach/Path/Reload/Overlay/<Attach>: path
Edit path for which xref(s): PLATES
    Scanning...
Xref name: PLATES
Old path: C:\DWGS\MECH\PLATES.DWG
New path: x:\dwgs\job496\plates.dwg (Enter new path.)
Reload Xref PLATES: x:\dwgs\job496\plates.dwg
PLATES loaded. Regenerating drawing.
Command:
```

When you archive (back up) drawings, remember also to back up the drives and directories where the Xref drawings are located. One possible file management technique is to create a directory especially for all Xrefs. In a networking environment, access rights to Xref directories must be granted.

An alternative to using the *Path* option is using the ACAD environment to specify the location of Xrefs. The directories specified by the ACAD environment (as set by the ACADR13.BAT file or ACADENV.INI file) are searched when a drawing with an Xref is loaded. Therefore, the *Path* option is used as an individual Xref location designator, while the ACAD environment is used as a general search path for all Xrefs.

Reload

This option forces a *Reload* of the external drawing at any time while the current drawing is in the drawing editor. This ensures that the current drawing contains the <u>most recent version</u> of the external drawing. In a networking environment, you cannot *Attach, Bind,* or *Reload* an external drawing which is in an editing session because the external drawing is locked (a .DWK file exists).

Bind

The *Bind* option <u>converts</u> the <u>*Xref*</u> drawing to a <u>*Block*</u> in the current drawing, then terminates the external reference partnership. The original *Xrefed* drawing is not affected. The names of the dependent objects in the external drawing are changed to avoid possible conflicts in the case that the parent and Xref drawing have dependent objects with the same name (see Dependent Objects and Names). If you want to only bind selected named objects, use the *Xbind* command.

Bind all

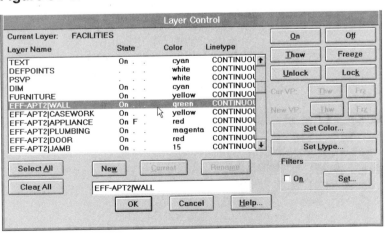

Although "Bind all" is not an option listed in the command syntax, you can bind all Xrefs by selecting the icon, selecting the option from the menus, or by entering an asterisk (*) at the "Xref(s) to bind:" prompt. This action converts every *Xref* in the drawing into a *Block*. If you are planning to send a copy of a drawing that contains Xrefs to a client or vendor, this option is useful for combining the parent and all the component drawings into one file. *Bind all* is often performed at the completion of a project.

Dependent Objects and Names

The <u>named objects</u> that have been created as part of a drawing become <u>dependent objects</u> when the drawing is *Xrefed*. The named objects of an Xref drawing are listed here:

*Block*s
Dimension Styles
Linetypes
Layers
Text Styles
User Coordinate Systems
Views
Viewport Configurations

These dependent objects <u>cannot</u> be renamed or changed in the parent drawing. Dependent text or dimension styles cannot be used in the parent drawing. You cannot draw on dependent layers; you can only control the visibility of the dependent layers. You <u>can</u>, however, *Bind* the entire Xref and the dependent named objects, or you can bind individual dependent objects with the *Xbind* command. *Xbind* converts an individual dependent object into a permanent part of the parent drawing. (See *Xbind*.)

When an Xref contains named objects, the names of the dependent objects are changed (in the parent drawing). A new naming scheme is necessary because conflicts would occur if the Xref drawing and the parent drawing both contained *Layers* or *Blocks*, etc., with the same names, as would happen if both drawings used the same prototype. When a drawing is *Attached*, its original object names are prefixed by the drawing name and separated by a pipe (|) symbol. For example, if a drawing named EFF-APT2.DWG is *Xrefed* and it contains a WALL layer, it is be renamed (in the parent drawing) to EFF-APT2|WALL. Likewise, if the Xref drawing contains the block named TUB, it is renamed in the parent drawing to EFF-APT2|TUB. In the parent drawing, the *Layer Control* dialogue box displays the original layers as well as the dependent layers (prefixed with "EFF-APT2|") (Fig. 31-17).

Figure 31-17

Likewise, listing the *Blocks* yields a display showing both the original *Blocks* in the parent drawing and the dependent *Blocks* from EFF-APT2 drawing. Note that the Xref is also listed. The same naming scheme operates with all named objects—*Dimstyles, Text styles, Views*, etc.

```
Command: block
Block name (or ?): ?
Block(s) to list <*>: Enter
Defined blocks.
 BED
 CHAIR
 DESK
 TABLE
 EFF-APT2                 Xref: resolved
 EFF-APT2|RANGE           Xdep: EFF-APT2
 EFF-APT2|REFRIG          Xdep: EFF-APT2
 EFF-APT2|TUB             Xdep: EFF-APT2
 EFF-APT2|TOILET          Xdep: EFF-APT2
 EFF-APT2|TOWLRACK        Xdep: EFF-APT2
 EFF-APT2|SINK            Xdep: EFF-APT2

 User        External       Dependent      Unnamed
 Blocks      References     Blocks         Blocks
 4           1             6              0

Command:
```

Notice the blocks from the dependent drawing (originally named RANGE and REFRIG, etc.) are prefixed with EFF-APT2|.

If you want to bind the Xref drawing using the *Bind* option, the link is severed and the Xref drawing becomes a *Block* in the parent drawing. Or if you want to bind only <u>individual</u> named objects, the *Xbind* command could be used. In either case, the dependent objects are renamed. The pipe (|) character is replaced with three characters: a "$", a number, and another "$". For example, layer EFF-APT2|WALL is renamed to EFF-APT2$1$WALL. Since the layers become a permanent part of the parent drawing, the *Rename* command could then be used to change the names if desired.

XBIND

PULL-DOWN MENU	SCREEN MENU	TYPE IN	TABLET MENU
File *Bind >*	**FILE** *Xbind*	*XBIND*	---

The *Xbind* command is a separate command; it is not an option of the *Xref* command as are most other Xreference controls. *Xbind* is similar to *Bind*, except that *Xbind* binds an <u>individual</u> dependent object, whereas *Bind* converts the <u>entire</u> *Xref* drawing to a *Block*. Any of the listed dependent named objects (see Dependent Objects and Names) that exist in a drawing can be converted to a permanent and usable part of the current drawing with *Xbind*. In effect, *Xbind* makes a copy of the named object since the original named object is not removed from the dependent drawing.

The *Xbind* options can be accessed by command line format or by selecting the appropriate option from the menus or (Windows) icons. The options are:

Block

 Select this option to *Xbind* a *Block* from the *Xrefed* drawing. The *Block* can then be inserted into the current drawing and has no link to the original Xref drawing.

Dimension Style

 This option allows you to make a dependent Dimension Style a permanent part of the current drawing. Dimensions can be created in the current drawing that reference the new Dimension Style.

Layer

 Any dependent layer can be brought into the current drawing with this option. The geometry that resides on that layer does <u>not</u> become part of the current drawing, only the layer name and its properties. *Xbinding* a layer also *Xbinds* the layer's color and linetype.

Linetype

 A linetype from an Xrefed drawing can be bound to the current drawing using this option. This action has the same effect as loading the linetype.

Text Style

 If a text style exists in an Xrefed drawing that you want to use in the current drawing, use this option to bring it into the current drawing. New text can be created or existing text can be modified to reference the new text style.

As an example, if you want to *Xbind* the TUB *Block* from the EFF-APT2 drawing, the command syntax would be as follows:

```
Command: xbind
Block/Dimstyle/LAyer/LType/Style: b
Dependent Block name(s): EFF-APT2 | TUB
    Scanning...
1 Block(s) bound.
Command:
```

The name given in response to the "Dependent (option) Name(s):" must be the <u>full name</u> as it appears in the current (parent) drawing, <u>including</u> the dependent drawing name prefix and pipe (|) character. The name of the object (*Block, Layer,* etc.) which was the subject of the *Xbind* is changed using the same naming scheme as used with the *Bind* option of *Xref*. The pipe (|) character is changed to n. In the example, the *Block* name would be changed to EFF-APT2$1$TUB. The listing of *Blocks* in the INTERIOR drawing (using *Block*, ?) yields the following list:

```
Command: block
Block name (or ?): ?
Block(s) to list <*>: Enter
Defined blocks.
  BED
  CHAIR
  DESK
  TABLE
```

EFF-APT2	Xref: resolved
EFF-APT2$1$TUB	
EFF-APT2|RANGE	Xdep: EFF-APT2
EFF-APT2|REFRIG	Xdep: EFF-APT2
EFF-APT2|TOILET	Xdep: EFF-APT2
EFF-APT2|TOWLRACK	Xdep: EFF-APT2
EFF-APT2|SINK	Xdep: EFF-APT2

User Blocks	External References	Dependent Blocks	Unnamed Blocks
5	1	5	0

Command:

The name(s) of permanent *Block*s could subsequently be changed with the *Rename* command, if desired.

When the *Block* is bound, it can be *Inserted* like any normal *Block*. *Xbinding* other dependent objects makes them a permanent part of the current drawing and available to be used in the drawing.

VISRETAIN

This variable controls dependent layer *State*. Remember that you cannot draw or edit on a dependent layer; however, you can change the layer's *State* (*On, Off, Freeze, Thaw*) with the *Layer* command, *Layer Control* dialogue box, or layer pop-down list (Windows only). The setting of *VISRETAIN* determines if the visibility settings that have been made are retained when the Xref is reloaded.

When *VISRETAIN* is set to 1 in the parent drawing, all the global layer settings (*Freeze, Thaw,* and *On, Off*) are <u>retained</u> for the Xreferenced dependent layers. When you *Save* the drawing, the visibility for dependent layers is saved with the <u>current</u> (parent) drawing, regardless of whether the visibility has changed in the externally referenced drawing itself. In other words, if *VISRETAIN=1* in the parent drawing, the *Layer State* settings for dependent layers are saved. If *VISRETAIN* is set to 0, then dependent layer visibility is determined by the settings in the <u>external</u> drawing.

XREFCTL

AutoCAD has a tracking mechanism for the Xref activity for a particular drawing. It is an external ASCII log file which is maintained on each drawing and contains information on external references. Creation of the log file is controlled with the *XREFCTL* variable.

If *XREFCTL* is set to 1, a log file registers each *Attach, Overlay, Bind, Detach,* and *Reload* of each external reference for the current drawing. This file has the same name as the current drawing and a file extension ".XLG". The log file is always placed in the same directory as the current drawing. Whenever the drawing is *Opened* again and the *Xref* command is used, the activity is appended to an existing log. XLG files have <u>no direct connection</u> to the drawing and can be deleted if desired without consequences to the related drawing file.

If *XREFCTL* is set to 0 (the default), no log file is created or appended. The *XREFCTL* variable is saved in the ACAD.CFG file.

An example .XLG file is shown here. This file lists the activity from the previous example when the OFFICEX drawing was *Xrefed* to the INTERIOR drawing.

```
==============================
Drawing: C:\DWGS\INTERIOR
Date/Time: 10/05/95 16:03:51
Operation: Attach Xref
==============================

Attach Xref OFFICEX: officex

    Update Block symbol table:
     Appending symbol: OFFICEX|DOOR
     Appending symbol: OFFICEX|WINDOW
    Block update complete.

    Update Ltype symbol table:
     Appending symbol: OFFICEX|BORDER
     Appending symbol: OFFICEX|BORDER2
     Appending symbol: OFFICEX|BORDERX2
     Appending symbol: OFFICEX|CENTER
     Appending symbol: OFFICEX|CENTER2
     Appending symbol: OFFICEX|CENTERX2
     Appending symbol: OFFICEX|DASHDOT
     Appending symbol: OFFICEX|DASHDOT2
     Appending symbol: OFFICEX|DASHDOTX2
     Appending symbol: OFFICEX|DASHED
     Appending symbol: OFFICEX|DASHED2
     Appending symbol: OFFICEX|DASHEDX2
     Appending symbol: OFFICEX|DIVIDE
     Appending symbol: OFFICEX|DIVIDE2
     Appending symbol: OFFICEX|DIVIDEX2
     Appending symbol: OFFICEX|DOT
     Appending symbol: OFFICEX|DOT2
     Appending symbol: OFFICEX|DOTX2
     Appending symbol: OFFICEX|HIDDEN
     Appending symbol: OFFICEX|HIDDEN2
     Appending symbol: OFFICEX|HIDDENX2
     Appending symbol: OFFICEX|PHANTOM
     Appending symbol: OFFICEX|PHANTOM2
     Appending symbol: OFFICEX|PHANTOMX2
    Ltype update complete.

    Update Layer symbol table:
     Appending symbol: OFFICEX|FLOORPLAN
     Appending symbol: OFFICEX|FACILITIES
     Appending symbol: OFFICEX|ELECTRICAL
     Appending symbol: OFFICEX|TEXT
     Appending symbol: DEFPOINTS
     Appending symbol: OFFICEX|PSVP
     Appending symbol: OFFICEX|TBLCK
    Layer update complete.

    Update Style symbol table:
     Appending symbol: OFFICEX|STANDARD
     Appending symbol: OFFICEX|ROMANS
     Appending symbol: OFFICEX|COMPLEX
```

Appending symbol: OFFICEX|SIMPLEX
Style update complete.

Update Appid symbol table:
Appid update complete.

Update Dimstyle symbol table:
 Appending symbol: OFFICEX|ST1
 Appending symbol: OFFICEX|ST2
Dimstyle update complete.
OFFICEX loaded.

Managing *Xref* Drawings

Because of the external reference feature, the contents of a drawing can be stored in multiple drawing files and directories. In other words, if a drawing has Xrefs, the drawing is actually composed of several drawings, each possibly located in a different directory. This means that special procedures to handle drawings linked in external reference partnerships should be considered when drawings are to be backed up or sent to clients. Three possible solutions to consider are listed here:

1. Modify the current drawing's path to the external reference drawing so they are both stored in the same directory; then archive them together.

2. Archive the directory of the external reference drawing along with the drawing which references it. Tape backups can do this automatically. The DOS XCOPY command can help with this.

3. Make the external reference drawing a permanent part of the current drawing with the *Bind All* option of the *Xref* command prior to archiving. This option is preferred when a finished drawing set is sent to a client.

XREFCLIP

Xrefclip is a special external reference application for Paper Space viewports. This command is discussed in Chapter 32, Tiled Viewports and Paper Space Viewports.

CHAPTER EXERCISES

1. *Xref Attach*

   Use the **SLOTPLT2** drawing that you modified last (with *Stretch*) in Chapter 16 Exercises. The Slot Plate is to be manufactured by a stamping process. Your job is to nest as many pieces as possible within the largest stock sheet size of 30" x 20" that the press will handle.

   A. *Open* the SLOTPLT2 drawing and use the *Base* command to specify a base point at the plate's lower-left corner. *Save* the drawing.

B. Begin a *New* drawing using the **DSHEET** prototype and assign the name **SLOTNEST**. Draw the boundary of the stock sheet (30" x 20"). *Xref Attach* the **SLOTPLT2** into the sheet drawing multiple times as shown in Figure 31-18 to determine the optimum nesting pattern for the Slot Plate and to minimize wasted material. The Slot Plate can be rotated to any angle but cannot be scaled. Can you fit 12 pieces within the sheet stock? *Save* the drawing.

Figure 31-18 ─────────

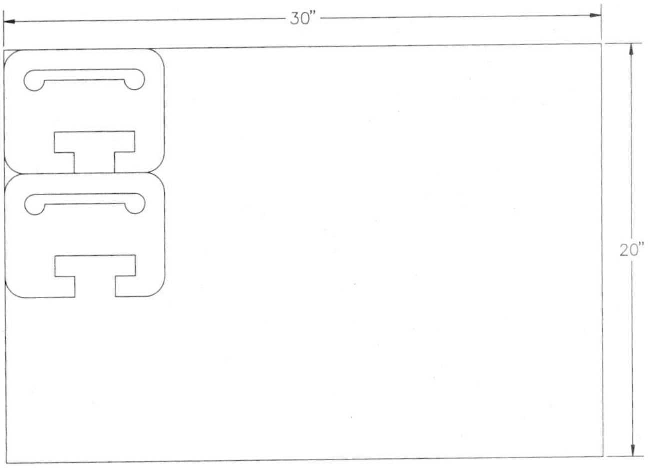

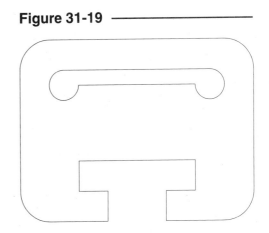

C. In the final test of the piece, it was determined that a symmetrical orientation of the "T" slot in the bottom would allow for a simplified assembly. *Open* the **SLOTPLT2** drawing and use *Stretch* to center the "T" slot about the vertical axis as shown in Figure 31-19. *Save* the new change.

Figure 31-19 ─────────

D. *Open* the **SLOTNEST** drawing. Is the design change reflected in the nested pieces?

2. *Attach, Detach, Xbind, VISRETAIN*

As the interior design consultant for an architectural firm, you are required to place furniture in an efficiency apartment. You can use some of the furniture drawings (*Blocks*) that you specified for a previous job, the office drawing, and *Insert* them into the apartment along with some new *Blocks* that you create.

A. Use the **CSHEET** as a *prototype* and set *Architectural Units* and set *Limits* of **48' x 36'**. (Scale factor is 24 and plot scale is 1/2"=1' or 1=24). Assign the name **INTERIOR**. *Xref* the **OFFICE** drawing that you created in Chapter 21 Exercises. Examine the layers (using the *Layer Control* dialogue box) and list (?) the *Blocks*. *Freeze* the **TEXT** layer. Use *Xbind* to bring the **CHAIR**, **DESK**, and **TABLE** *Blocks* and the **FURNITURE** *Layer* into the INTERIOR drawing. *Detach* the **OFFICE** drawing. Then *Rename* the new *Blocks* and the new *Layer* to the original names (without the **OFFICE0** prefix). In the INTERIOR drawing, create a new *Block* called **BED**. Use measurements for a queen size (60" x 80"). *Save* the INTERIOR drawing.

B. *Xref* the **EFF-APT2** drawing (from Chapter 30 Exercises) into the INTERIOR.DWG. Change the *Layer* visibility to turn *Off* the **EFF-APT2 | TEXT** layer. *Insert* the furniture *Blocks* into the apartment on *Layer* **FURNITURE**. Lay out the apartment as you choose; however, your design should include at least one insertion of each of the furniture *Blocks* as shown in Figure 31-20. When you are finished with the design, *Save* the INTERIOR drawing.

Figure 31-20 ————————————

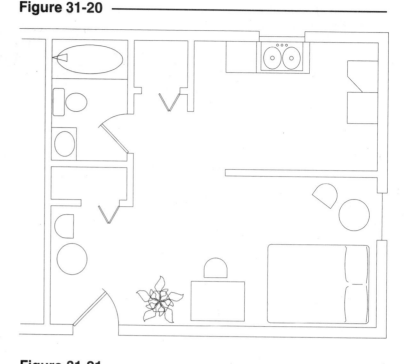

C. Assuming you are now the architect, a design change is requested by the client. In order to meet the fire code, the entry doorway must be moved farther from the end of the hall within the row of several apartments. *Open* the **EFF-APT2** drawing and use *Stretch* to relocate the entrance **8'** to the right as shown in Figure 31-21. *Save* the EFF- APT2 drawing.

Figure 31-21 ————————————

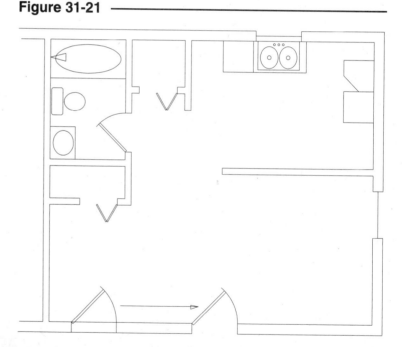

D. Next (as the interior design consultant), *Open* the **INTERIOR** drawing. Notice that the design change made by the architect is reflected in your INTERIOR drawing. Does the text appear in the drawing? *Freeze* the **TEXT** layer again, but this time change the *VISRETAIN* variable to **1**. Make the necessary alterations to the interior layout to accommodate the new entry location. *Save* the INTERIOR drawing.

3. *Xref Attach*

As project manager for a mechanical engineering team, you are responsible for coordinating an assembly composed of 5 parts. The parts are being designed by several people on the team. You are to create a new drawing and *Xref* each part, check for correct construction and assembly of the parts, and make the final plot.

A. The first step is to create two new parts (as <u>separate</u> drawings) named **SLEEVE** and **SHAFT**, as shown in Figure 31-22. Use appropriate drawing setup and layering techniques. In each case, draw the two views on <u>separate layers</u> (so that appearance of each view can be controlled by layer visibility). Use the *Base* command to specify an insertion point at the right end of the rectangular views at the center line.

Figure 31-22 ————————————————

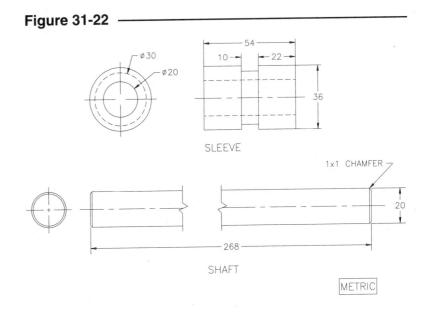

B. You will eventually *Xref* the drawings **SHAFT, SLEEVE, PUL-SEC** (from Chapter 26 Exercises), **SADDLE** (from Chapter 24 Exercises), and **BOLT** (from Chapter 10 Exercises) to achieve the assembly as shown in Figure 31-23. Before creating the assembly, *Open* each of the drawings and use *Chprop* to move the desired view (with all related geometry, no dimensions) to a new layer. You may also want to set a *Base* point for each drawing.

Figure 31-23 ————————————————

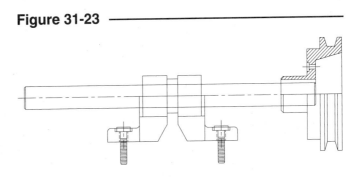

C. Finally, begin a *New* drawing (or use a *Prototype*) and assign the name **ASSY**. Set appropriate *Limits*. Make a *Layer* called **XREF** and set it *Current*. *Xref* the drawings to complete the assembly. The **BOLT** drawing must be scaled to acquire a diameter of **6mm**. Use the *Layer Control* dialogue box to achieve the desired visibility for the *Xrefs*. Set *VISRETAIN* to **1**. Make a *Plot* to scale. *Save* the **ASSY** drawing.

4. *Xref Overlay*

A. Assume you are now the project coordinator/checker for the assembly. (If it is possible in your lab or office, exchange the SHAFT drawings [by diskette or by network] with another person so that you can perform this step for each other.) Begin a *New* drawing and make a *Layer* called **CHECK**. Next, *Xref Overlay* the **SHAFT** drawing (of your partner). On the CHECK layer, insert some *text* by any method and a dimension similar to that shown in Figure 31-24. *Save* the CHECK drawing. (When completed, exchange the CHECK and SHAFT drawings back.)

Figure 31-24 ————————————————————————————————

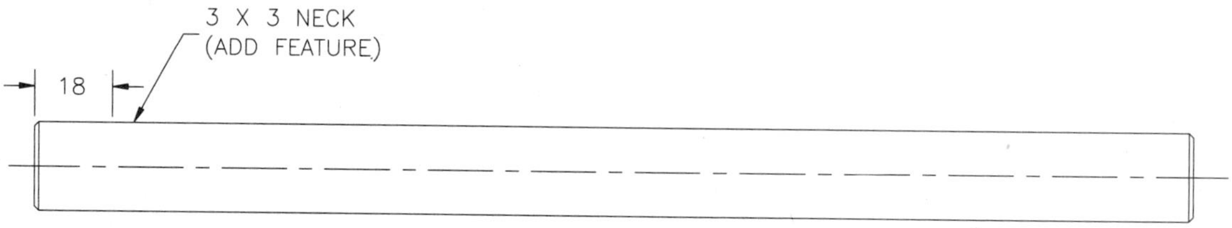

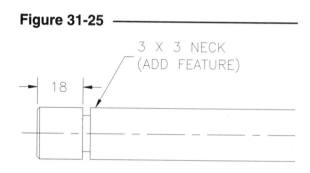

B. *Open* the **SHAFT** drawing. In order to see the notes from the checker, *Xref Overlay* the **CHECK** drawing. The instructions for the change in design should appear. (Notice that the *Overlay* option allows a circular *Xref* since SHAFT references CHECK and CHECK references SHAFT.) Make the changes by adding the 3 x 3 NECK to the geometry (Fig. 31-25). *Save* the **SHAFT** drawing (with the *Overlay*).

Figure 31-25 ————————————————

C. Now *Open* the **ASSY** drawing. The most recent *Xrefs* are automatically loaded, so the design change should appear (Fig. 31-26). Why don't the checker notes (from CHECK drawing) appear? Finally, *Save* the drawing and make another plot.

Figure 31-26 ————————————————————————————————

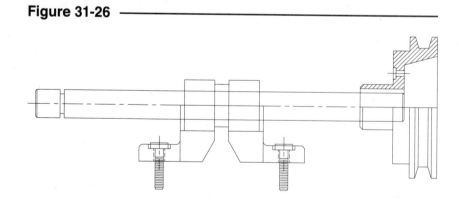

Chapter 32

TILED VIEWPORTS AND PAPER SPACE VIEWPORTS

Chapter Objectives

After completing this chapter you should:

1. know the difference between tiled viewports and paper space viewports and the purpose of the *TILEMODE* variable;

2. be able to create, *Save*, and *Restore* tiled viewport configurations using the *Vports* command and *Tiled Viewport Layout* dialogue box;

3. be able to use the options of *Mview* to create viewports in paper space;

4. be able to use paper space to display multiple viewports of one drawing and to display viewports of several *Xrefed* drawings;

5. be able to use *Vplayer* or the *Layer Control* dialogue box to control viewport-specific layer visibility;

6. be able to use *Mvsetup* for viewport creation and title block insertion in paper space.

BASICS

There are two types of viewports in AutoCAD, <u>tiled</u> viewports and <u>paper space</u> (or floating) viewports. Tiled viewports are simple to use and easy to understand. Paper space viewports are used mainly for special plotting applications and are more complex.

Tiled viewports divide the screen into several areas that fit together with no space between, like <u>tiles</u>. Tiled viewports are created by the *Vports* command. Each tiled viewport can show a different area of the drawing by using display commands—especially helpful for 3D models. *Vports* divides the <u>screen</u> into multiple sections, allowing you to view different parts of a drawing on one screen. Tiled viewports can make construction and editing of complex drawings more efficient than repeatedly using display commands to view detailed areas. Tiled viewports were introduced with AutoCAD Release 10.

Paper space (floating) viewports are used for plotting several views of a drawing, or several drawings, on one sheet. Paper space viewports are used to set up a sheet of paper for plotting. The *Mview* command is used to create viewports in paper space. *Mview* allows several viewports to exist on the screen, but the viewports can be any size and rectangular proportion, unlike tiled viewports. Paper space viewports are generally used when the drawing is complete and ready to prepare a plot. Paper space viewports were introduced with AutoCAD Release 11.

AutoCAD allows you to work on your drawing in two separate spaces—model space and paper space. The space that you have been drawing in up to this time is called model space. The Drawing Editor begins a drawing in model space by default. The model geometry objects (that represent the subject of the drawing) are almost always drawn in model space. Paper space is normally used to set up the configuration of the plotting sheet.

Another fundamental difference between tiled viewports and paper space viewports is the space in which these viewports exist. Tiled viewports exist only when model space is active; therefore, they are sometimes referred to as "model space viewports" or "tiled model space." Paper space viewports do not exist in the same space as the model geometry. In order to create or use paper space viewports, paper space must first be activated. Release 13 of AutoCAD refers to viewports created in paper space as "floating viewports."

Figure 32-1

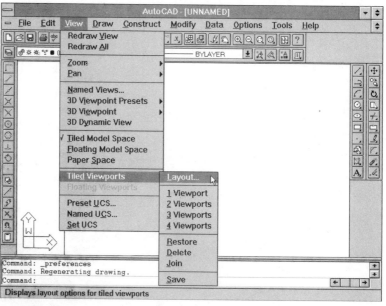

Although both tiled viewports and paper space viewports can be used in one drawing, they <u>cannot be used at the same time</u>. Therefore, the *TILEMODE* variable controls which type of viewport can be enabled at a specific point in time. Moreover, *TILEMODE* effectively controls which space is active— model space or paper space.

Commands related to creating and activating tiled and floating viewports are located in the *View* pull-down menu (Fig. 32-1). If you are using AutoCAD for Windows, three icon tools fly out from the Standard toolbar that control the setting of the *TILEMODE* variable and the active state of model space and paper space (Fig. 32-2).

Figure 32-2

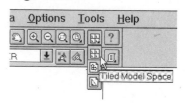

TILEMODE

PULL-DOWN MENU	SCREEN MENU	TYPE IN	TABLET MENU
View *Tiled Model Space, or* *Paper Space*	*VIEW* *Tilemod:*	*TILEMODE*	3,R

When paper space viewports were introduced with Release 11, a new system variable called *TILEMODE* was also introduced. Since only <u>one</u> type of viewport can be used at a time, the *TILEMODE* system variable is used to enable one or the other type of viewports. More importantly, *TILEMODE* is a toggle that switches between using only model space or using paper space.

When *TILEMODE* is set to 1 (*TILEMODE* is *On*), only tiled viewports in model space can be used. The viewports themselves must be created with the *Vports* command. The variable can be typed, or you can select *Tiled Model Space* from the *View* pull-down menu, or PICK the icon tool (with four small "tiles"). In AutoCAD for Windows, *TILEMODE* can also be toggled by double-clicking the word "TILE" on the Status Line. *TILEMODE On* is the default setting for the AutoCAD prototype drawing ACAD.DWG; so normally, model space is active and only tiled viewports can be used.

If *TILEMODE* is set to 0 (*TILEMODE* is *Off*), paper space is enabled and paper space-style viewports are available. Viewports in paper space must be created with the *Mview* command. Change *TILEMODE* to *Off* by typing the variable, selecting *Paper Space* from the *View* pull-down menu, or PICKing the icon tool (that looks like a drafting triangle). Therefore, setting *TILEMODE* to 0 disables display of model space and tiled viewports and automatically enables paper space.

Whether or not viewports of any kind have been created with either the *Vports* or the *Mview* commands, the setting of *TILEMODE* displays the following.

TILEMODE setting	Resulting display
1	model space only—tiled (*Vports*) viewports can be used
0	paper space—paper space (*Mview*) viewports can be used

Switching the *TILEMODE* setting does not affect any objects you have drawn. The setting may affect the visibility of objects in the display.

This chapter discusses both tiled viewports and paper space viewports. Tiled viewports are discussed first because they are easier to use and understand.

TILED VIEWPORTS

All controls for tiled viewports are included in the *Vports* command. Tiled viewports are useful for displaying several views of one or more 2D drawings simultaneously on the screen. Using tiled viewports for displaying several views of a 3D drawing is discussed in Chapter 34.

VPORTS

PULL-DOWN MENU	SCREEN MENU	TYPE IN	TABLET MENU
View *Tiled Viewports*	*VIEW* *Vports: or* *TileVpt:*	*VPORTS*	5,R

The *Vports* command allows <u>tiled</u> viewports to be created on the screen. *Vports* divides the screen into several areas. *Vports* (tiled viewports) are available only when the *TILEMODE* variable is set to **1**. Tiled *Vports* affect <u>only the screen display</u>. The viewport configuration <u>cannot be plotted</u>. If the *Plot* command is used, only the <u>current</u> viewport display is plotted.

Figure 32-3 displays the AutoCAD drawing editor after the *Vports* command was used to divide the screen into tiled viewports. Tiled viewports always fit together like tiles with no space between. The shape and location of the viewports are not flexible as with paper space viewports.

Figure 32-3

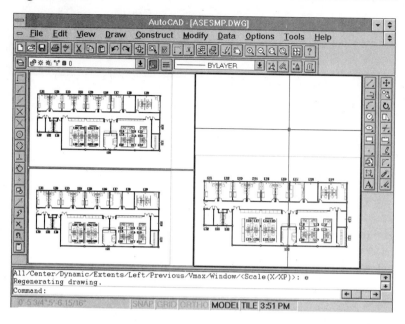

The *View* pull-down menu (Fig. 32-1) can be used to display the *Tiled Viewport Layout* dialogue box (Fig. 32-4). This option in the pull-down menu is enabled only if *TILEMODE*=1. The dialogue box allows you to PICK the image tile representing the layout that you want.

Figure 32-4

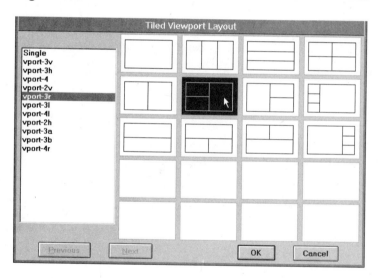

After you select the desired layout, the previous display appears in <u>each</u> of the viewports. For example, if a full view of office layout was displayed when you use the *Vports* command or the related dialogue box, the resulting display in <u>each</u> viewport would be the same full view of the office (Fig. 32-3). It is up to you then to use viewing commands (*Zoom*, *Pan*, etc.) in the active viewport to specify what areas of the drawing you want to see in each viewport. There is no automatic viewpoint configuration option with *Vports*.

A popular arrangement of view-points for construction and editing of 2D drawings is a combination of an overall view and one or two *Zoomed* views (Fig. 32-5). You cannot draw or project from one viewport to another. Keep in mind that there is only <u>one model</u> (drawing), but several views of it on the screen. Notice that the active or current viewport displays the crosshairs, while moving the point-ing device to another viewport dis-plays only the pointer (small arrow) in that viewport.

A viewport is made active by PICKing in it. Any display com-mands (*Zoom, Vpoint, Redraw,* etc.) and drawing aids (*SNAP, GRID,*

Figure 32-5

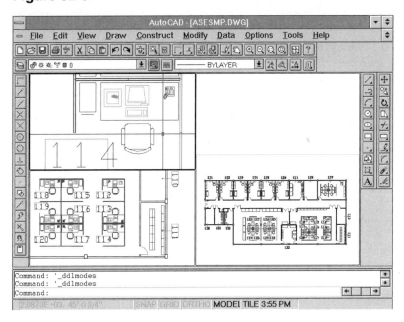

ORTHO) used affect only the <u>current viewport</u>. Draw and edit commands that affect the model are potentially apparent in all viewports (for every display of the affected part of the model). *Redrawall* and *Regenall* can be used to redraw and regenerate all viewports.

You can begin a drawing command in one viewport and finish in another. In other words, you can toggle viewports within a command. For example, you can use the *Line* command to PICK the "From point:" in one viewport, then make another viewport current to PICK the "to point:".

Using the command line format, the syntax for *Vports* is as follows:

```
Command: vports
Save/Restore/Delete/Join/SIngle/?/2/<3>/4: Enter or (option)
Horizontal/Vertical/Above/Below/Left/<Right>: Enter or (option)
Regenerating drawing.
Command:
```

Save
Allows you to assign a name and save the current viewport configuration. A viewport configuration is the particular arrangement of viewports and the display settings (*Zoom, Pan,* etc.) in each viewport. Up to 31 characters can be used when assigning a name. The configuration can be *Restored* at a later time.

Restore
Redisplays a previously *Saved* viewport configuration. AutoCAD prompts for the assigned name.

Delete
Deletes a named viewport configuration. AutoCAD prompts for the assigned name.

Join

This option allows you to combine (join) two adjacent viewports. The viewports to join must share a common edge the full length of each viewport. For example, if four equal viewports were displayed, two adjacent viewports could be joined to produce a total of three viewports. You must select a *dominant* viewport. The *dominant* viewport determines the display to be used for the new viewport.

SIngle

Changes back to a single screen display using the current viewport's display.

?

Displays the identification numbers and screen positions of named (saved) and active viewport configurations. The screen positions are relative to the lower-left corner of the screen (0,0) and the upper-right (1,1).

2, 3, 4

Use these options to create 2, 3, or 4 viewports. You can choose the configuration. The possibilities are illustrated if you use the *Tiled Viewport Layout* dialogue box.

The *Vports* command can be used most effectively when constructing and editing drawings, whereas, paper space viewports are generally used when the model is complete and ready to prepare a plot. (See Chapter 34 for more information on tiled viewports.)

PAPER SPACE (FLOATING) VIEWPORTS

The two spaces that AutoCAD provides are model space and paper space. When you start AutoCAD and begin a drawing, model space is active by default. Objects that represent the subject of the drawing (model geometry) are normally drawn in model space. Dimensioning is also performed in model space because it is associative—directly associated to the model geometry. The model geometry is usually completed before using paper space.

Paper space represents the <u>paper that you plot or print on</u>. When you enter paper space for the first time, you see a blank "sheet." In order to see any model geometry, viewports in paper space must be created with *Mview* (like cutting rectangular holes) so you can "see" into model space. Any number or size of rectangular shaped viewports can be created in paper space. Since there is only <u>one model space</u> in a drawing, you see the same model space geometry in each viewport. You can, however, control which

layers are *Frozen* and *Thawed* and the scale of the geometry displayed <u>in each viewport</u>. Since paper space represents the actual paper used for plotting, plot from paper space at a scale of 1=1.

Consider this brief example to explain the basics of using paper space. In order to keep this example simple, only one viewport is created to set up a drawing for plotting.

First, the part geometry is created in model space as usual (Fig. 32-6). Associative dimensions are also created in model space. This step is the same method that you would have normally used to create a drawing.

Figure 32-6

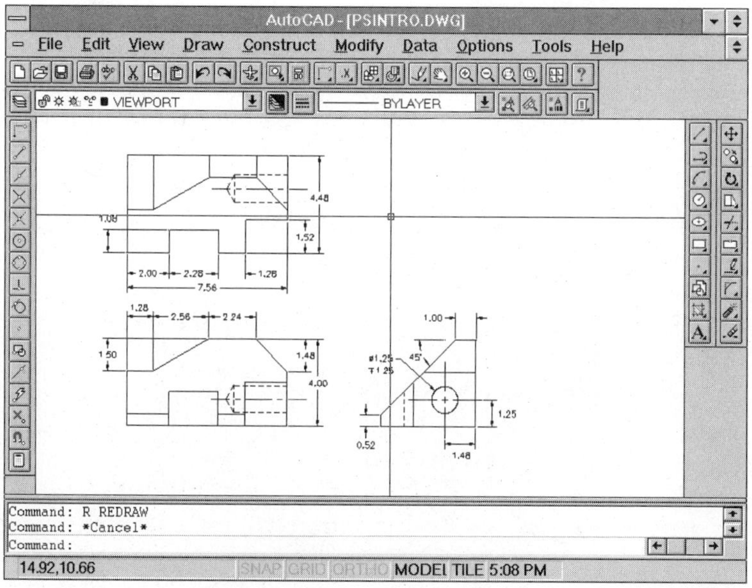

When the part geometry is complete, enable paper space. To do this, change the setting of the *TILEMODE* variable to 0. (See the previous *TILEMODE* command table for several possible methods of toggling the *TILEMODE* variable.)

By setting the *TILEMODE* variable to 0, you are automatically switched to paper space. When you enable paper space for the first time in a drawing, a "blank sheet" appears. The *Limits* command is used to set the paper space *Limits* to the sheet size intended for plotting. Objects such as a title block and border are created <u>in paper space</u> (Fig. 32-7). Normally, only objects that are <u>annotations</u> for the drawing (tile blocks, tables, border, company logo, etc.) are drawn in paper space.

A viewport must be created in the "paper" with the *Mview* command in order for you to "look" into model space. All of the model geometry in the drawing initially appears in the viewport. At this point, there is no specific scale relation between paper space units and the size of the geometry in the viewport (Fig. 32-8).

You can control the scale of model space to paper space and what part of model space geometry you see in a viewport. Two methods are used to control the geometry that is visible in a particular viewport.

Figure 32-7

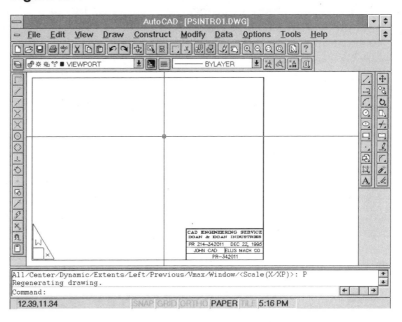

Figure 32-8

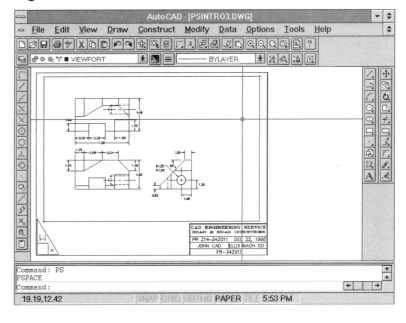

1. **Display commands**
   The *Zoom, Pan, View, Vpoint* and other display commands allow you to specify the part of model space you want to see in a viewport. There is even a *Zoom XP* option used to <u>scale</u> the geometry in model space units "times paper space" units. *Zoom XP* is the method used to define the <u>scale</u> of model geometry for the final plot.

2. **Viewport-specific layer visibility control**
   You can control what <u>layers</u> are visible in specific viewports. This function is often used for displaying different model space geometry in separate viewports. The *Vplayer* (Viewport layer) command or the *Cur VP* and *New VP* buttons in the *Layer Control* dialogue box are used for this purpose.

For example, the *Zoom* command could be used in model space to display a detail of the model geometry in a viewport. In this case, the model geometry is scaled to 3/4 size by using *Zoom 3/4XP*.

While in a drawing session with paper space enabled, the *Mspace* (Model Space) and *Pspace* (Paper Space) commands allow you to switch between paper space (outside a viewport) and floating model space (inside a viewport) so you can draw or edit in either space. Commands that are used will affect the objects or display of the current space. An object <u>cannot be in both spaces</u>. You can, however, draw in paper space and <u>*OSNAP* to objects in model space</u>. When drawing is completed, activate paper space and plot at 1=1 since paper space *Limits* are set to the <u>actual paper size</u>.

Figure 32-9

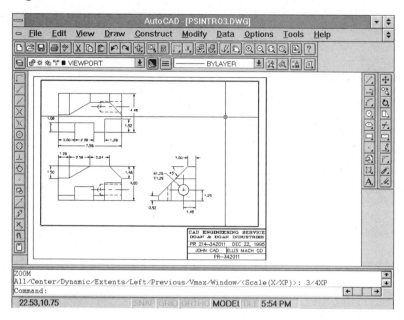

Reasons for Using Paper Space

Paper space is intended to be an aid to plotting. Since paper space represents a sheet of paper, it provides you with a means of preparing specific plotting sheet configurations.

In the previous example, paper space was used with the typical 2D drawing by creating the model geometry as usual but using paper space for the border, title block, tables, or other annotations. If you are creating a typical 2D drawing, you don't have to use paper space and probably shouldn't use paper space. The typical methods for creating drawings and plots all in model space are still valid and should be used except for special cases.

Paper space should be used if you want to prepare plots with <u>multiple views</u> or <u>multiple drawings</u> as listed here.

1. Use paper space to plot several views of the same drawing on one sheet, possibly in different scales, such as a main view and a detail. (Alternately, model space only can be used to accomplish the same result by using the *DIMLFAC* variable for dimensioning, for example, an enlarged detail.)

2. Use paper space to plot several drawings on one sheet. This action is accomplished by using *Xref* to bring several drawings into model space and by using layer visibility control to display individual drawings in separate viewports.

3. Use paper space to plot different views (e.g., top, front, side) of a 3D model on one sheet.

Basic concepts, commands, related system variables, and examples of the applications above are given later in the chapter. Chapter 41 discusses 3D applications.

Guidelines for Using Paper Space

Although there are other alternatives, the typical steps using paper space to set up a drawing for plotting are listed here.

1. Create the part geometry in model space. Associative dimensions are also created in model space.

2. Switch to paper space by changing *TILEMODE* to 0 by any method.

3. Set up paper space using the following steps.

   A. Set *Limits* in paper space equal to the sheet size used for plotting. (Paper space has its own *Limits, Snap*, and *Grid* settings.)
   B. *Zoom All* in paper space.
   C. Set the desired *Snap* and *Grid* for paper space.
   D. Make a layer named BORDER or TITLE and *Set* that layer as current.
   E. Draw, *Insert*, or *Xref* a border and a title block.

4. Make viewports in paper space.

   A. Make a layer named VIEWPORT (or other descriptive name) and set it as the *Current* layer (it can be turned *Off* later if you do not want the viewport objects to appear in the plot).
   B. Use the *Mview* command to make viewports. Each viewport contains a view of model space geometry.

5. Control the display of model space graphics in each viewport. Complete these steps for each viewport.

   A. Use the *Mspace* (*MS* or *Floating Model Space*) command to "go into" model space (in the viewport). Move the crosshairs and PICK to activate the desired viewport.
   B. Use *Zoom XP* to scale the display of the model units to paper space units. This action dictates the plot scale for the model space graphics. The *Zoom XP* factor is the same as the plot scale factor that would otherwise be used (reciprocal of the "drawing scale factor"). For example: *Zoom Center .5XP* or *Zoom Left 1/2XP* would scale the model geometry at 1/2 times paper space units.
   C. Use the *Vplayer* command or the *Cur VP* and *New VP* buttons in the *Layer Control* dialogue box to control the layer visibility for each viewport.

6. Plot from paper space at a scale of 1=1.

   A. Use the *Pspace* (*PS*) command to switch to paper space.
   B. If desired, turn *Off* the VIEWPORT layer so the viewport borders do not plot.
   C. Plot the drawing from paper space at a plot scale of 1=1 since paper space is set to the actual paper size. The paper space geometry will plot full size, and the resulting model space geometry will be plotted to the same <u>scale</u> as the *Zoom XP* factor.

PAPER SPACE COMMANDS AND VARIABLES

MVIEW

PULL-DOWN MENU	SCREEN MENU	TYPE IN	TABLET MENU
View *Floating Viewports >*	*VIEW* *Mview:*	*MVIEW*	*3,P to 5,Q*

Mview provides several options for creating paper space viewport objects (sometimes called "floating viewports"). *Mview* must be used in paper space (*TILEMODE=0*), so if you have switched to model space, invoking *Mview* (by typing or screen menu) automatically and temporarily switches back to paper space. The *Floating Viewports* option in the *View* pull-down menu is enabled only when *TILEMODE*=0. There is no limit to the number of paper space viewports that can be created in a drawing. The command syntax to create one viewport (the default option) is as follows:

> Command: **mview**
> ON/OFF/Hideplot/Fit/2/3/4/Restore/<First Point>: **PICK** or (**coordinates**)
> Other corner: **PICK** or (**coordinates**)
> Regenerating drawing.
> Command:

This action creates one rectangular viewport between the diagonal corners specified. The other options are described here briefly.

ON

On turns on the display of model space geometry in the selected viewport. Select the desired viewport to turn on.

OFF

Turn off the display of model space geometry in the selected viewport with this option. Select the desired viewport to turn off.

Hideplot

Hideplot causes hidden line removal in the selected viewport during a <u>plot</u>. This is used for 3D surface or solid models. Select the desired viewport.

Fit

Fit creates a new viewport and fits it to the size of the current display. If you are *Zoomed* in paper space, the resulting viewport is the size of the *Zoomed* area. The new viewport becomes the current viewport.

Restore

Use this option to create new viewports in the same relative pattern as a named tiled viewport configuration (see Tiled Viewports).

2/3/4

These options create a number of viewports within a rectangular area that you specify. The *2* option allows you to arrange 2 viewports either *Vertically* or *Horizontally*. The *4* option automatically divides the specified area into 4 equal viewports. Figure 32-10 displays the possible configurations using the *3* option. Using this option yields the following prompt:

> Horizontal/Vertical/Above/Below/Left/<Right>:

After making the desired selection, AutoCAD prompts: "Fit/<First Point>:". The *Fit* option automatically fills the current display with the specified number of viewport configurations (similar to the *Fit* option described earlier).

Figure 32-10

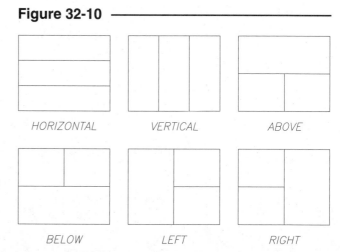

HORIZONTAL   VERTICAL   ABOVE

BELOW   LEFT   RIGHT

Paper space viewports created with *Mview* are treated by AutoCAD as <u>objects</u>. Like other objects, *Mview* viewports can be affected by most editing commands. For example, you could use *Mview* to create one viewport, then use *Copy* or *Array* to create other viewports. You could edit the size of viewports with *Stretch* or *Scale*. Additionally, you can use *Move* (Fig. 32-11) to relocate the position of viewports. Delete a viewport using *Erase*. You must be in paper space to PICK the viewport objects (borders). The viewports created by *Mview* or other editing methods are always rectangular and have a vertical and horizontal orientation (they cannot be *Rotated*).

Figure 32-11

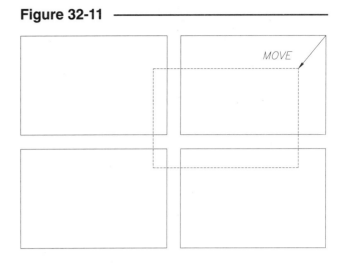

Floating viewports can also overlap (Fig. 32-11). This feature makes it possible for geometry appearing in different viewports to occupy the same area on the screen or on a plot.

NOTE: Avoid creating one viewport completely within another's border because visibility and selection problems may result.

Model Space, Paper Space, and Floating Model Space

Previously, it was stated that there are two spaces: paper space and model space. The *TILE-MODE* variable controls which of these two spaces is active. However, if paper space is enabled (*TILEMODE*=0) and viewports in paper space have been created, there are three possible spaces: model space, paper space, and floating model space. <u>Floating model space is model space inside a paper space viewport</u>. The *Pspace* and *Mspace* commands control whether the crosshairs are outside or inside a viewport (when *TILEMODE*=0) (Fig. 32-12).

Figure 32-12

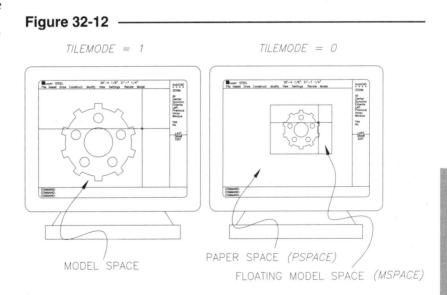

In releases of AutoCAD previous to Release 13, the correct combination of *TILEMODE*, *Pspace*, and *Mspace* had to be used to work in one of the three spaces. In Release 13, the term "Floating Model Space" is used to avoid the confusion. Additionally, making an icon selection or pull-down menu selection (*Paper Space* or *Floating Model Space*) automatically toggles the correct *TILEMODE* setting and invokes the *Pspace* or *Mspace* command. If you prefer to type, *TILEMODE* must be set independently.

PSPACE

PULL-DOWN MENU	SCREEN MENU	TYPE IN	TABLET MENU
View *Paper Space*	*VIEW* *Pspace:*	*PSPACE* *or PS*	*13, V*

The *Pspace* command switches from model space (inside a viewport) to paper space (outside a viewport). The crosshairs are displayed <u>across the entire screen</u> when in paper space (see Fig. 32-8), while the crosshairs only appear inside the current viewport if the *Mspace* command is used (see Fig. 32-9). If you type this command or select it from the screen menu, paper space must be enabled by setting *TILEMODE* to 0. If *TILEMODE* is set to 1, the following message appears:

Command: **pspace**
** Command not allowed unless TILEMODE is set to 0 **
Command:

Selecting the command from the pull-down menu or icon tool also automatically sets *TILEMODE* to 0 so paper space is enabled. Therefore, it is possible to use the menu selection or icon to go from *TILEMODE*=1 directly to paper space.

MSPACE

PULL-DOWN MENU	SCREEN MENU	TYPE IN	TABLET MENU
View *Floating Model Space*	*VIEW* *Mspace:*	*MSPACE* *or MS*	*14,V*

The *Mspace* command switches from paper space to model space <u>inside a viewport</u>. If floating viewports exist in the drawing when you use the command, you are switched to the last active viewport. The crosshairs appear only <u>in</u> that viewport. The current viewport displays a heavy border. You can switch to another viewport (make another current) by PICKing in it.

If you select this command from the pull-down menu or icon tools, *TILEMODE* is automatically set to 0. If no viewports exist, the *Mview* command is automatically invoked. If you type the command or use the screen menu, *TILEMODE* must previoulsy be set to 0, there must be at least one paper space viewport, and it must be *On* (not turned *Off* by the *Mview* command) or AutoCAD issues a message and cancels the command.

VPLAYER

PULL-DOWN MENU	SCREEN MENU	TYPE IN	TABLET MENU
Data *Viewport Layer Controls*	*DATA* *VPlayer:*	*VPLAYER*	---

The *Vplayer* (Viewport Layer) command provides options for control of the layers you want to see in each viewport (viewport-specific layer visibility control). With *Vplayer* you can specify the *State* (*Freeze/Thaw* and *Off/On*) of the drawing layers in any existing or new viewport. You do <u>not</u> have to make the desired viewport current before using *Vplayer*.

The *Layer* command allows you to *Freeze/Thaw* layers <u>globally</u>, whereas, *Vplayer* allows you to *Freeze/Thaw* layers that are <u>viewport-specific</u>. The *TILEMODE* variable must be set to 0 for the *Vplayer* command to operate, and a layer's global (*Layer*) settings must be *On* and *Thawed* to be affected by the *Vplayer* settings.

For example, you may have two paper space viewports set up, such as in Figure 32-13. In order to control the visibility of the DIM (dimensioning) layer for a specific viewport, the command syntax shown below would be used. In this case, the DIM layer is *Frozen* in the right viewport.

Figure 32-13

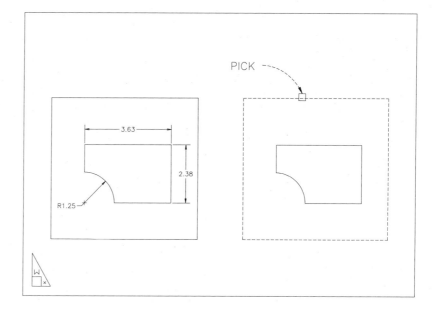

Notice in the command sequence below that if floating model space is active, AutoCAD automatically switches to paper space to allow you to make the selection (viewport objects can only be PICKed from paper space).

```
Command: vplayer
?/Freeze/Thaw/Reset/Newfrz/Vpvisdflt: freeze
Layer(s) to Freeze: dim
All/Select/<Current>: S  (Use the Select option.)
Switching to Paper space.
Select objects: PICK  (Select the desired viewport object. See Figure 32-13.)
Select objects: Enter
Switching to Model space.
?/Freeze/Thaw/Reset/Newfrz/Vpvisdflt: Enter
Regenerating drawing.
Command:
```

The *Vplayer Current* option automatically selects the current viewport. The **All** option automatically selects all viewports. Note that the *Select* option switches to paper space so that the viewport objects (borders) can be selected. The *Freeze* or *Thaw* does not take place until the command is completed and the drawing is automatically regenerated. All of the options are explained briefly here.

?
This option lists the frozen layers in the current viewport or a selected viewport. AutoCAD automatically switches to paper space if you are in model space to allow you to select the viewport object.

Freeze
This option controls the visibility of specified layers in the current or selected viewports. You are prompted for layer(s) to *Freeze*, then to select which viewports for the *Freeze* to affect.

Thaw
This option turns the visibility control back to the global settings of *On/Off/Freeze/Thaw* in the *Layer* command. The procedure for specification of layers and viewports is identical to the *Freeze* option procedure.

Reset
Reset returns the layer visibility status to the default if one was specified with *Vpvisdflt*, which is described next. You are prompted for "Layer(s) to Reset" and viewports to select by "All/Select/<Current>:".

Newfrz

This option <u>creates new layers</u>. The new layers are frozen in all viewports. This is a shortcut when you want to create a new layer that is visible only in the current viewport. Use *Newfrz* to create the new layer, then use *Vplayer Thaw* to make it visible only in that (or other selected) viewport(s). You are prompted for "New viewport frozen layer name(s):". You may enter one name or several separated by commas.

Vpvisdflt

This option allows you to set up <u>layer visibility</u> for <u>new</u> viewports. This is handy when you want to create new viewports, but do not want any of the <u>existing</u> layers to be visible in the new viewports. This option is particularly helpful for *Xrefs*. For example, suppose you created a viewport and *Xrefed* a drawing "into" the viewport. Before creating new viewports and *Xrefing* other drawings "into" them, use *Vpvisdflt* to set the default layer visibility to *Off* for the <u>existing</u> *Xrefed* layers in new viewports. (See the following application example.) You are prompted for a list of layers and whether they should be *Thawed* or *Frozen*.

Layer Control **Dialogue Box**

As an alternative to the *Vplayer* command, the *Layer Control* dialogue box (Figure 32-14) can be used to *Freeze/Thaw* current or new viewports. The *Cur VP* and *New VP* tiles on the right side of the dialogue box control viewport-specific layer visibility.

The *Cur VP* and *New VP* tiles in the *Layer Control* dialogue box are grayed out when *TILEMODE* is set to 1. If paper space is enabled (*TILEMODE*=0) and a viewport is active (the crosshairs are in a viewport), the *Layer Control* dialogue box that appears gives the *State* of layers <u>specific</u> to the <u>current viewport</u>. In other words, the *State* column may display <u>different</u> information, depending on which viewport is current, when you invoke the *Layer Control* dialogue box. If you are in paper space (the crosshairs are in paper space), the *Freeze/Thaw* tiles affect the selected layer's *State* globally, but not in individual viewports. The tiles perform the following functions.

Cur VP

This tile sets the *Freeze/Thaw* state for the highlighted layer(s) in the current viewport.

New VP

Use this tile to set the *Freeze/Thaw* state for the selected layer(s) in new viewports (any viewports that are subsequently created).

For example, the *Cur VP* tile could be used to *Freeze* the MOUNT-DIM and BASE1-DIM layers. The procedure in this case is to switch to model space (*MS*), make the right viewport active, and then invoke the *Layer Control* dialogue box. In the dialogue box (Figure 32-14), select the desired layers (*-DIM) and select the *Frz* tile for the *Cur VP*. The letter "C" appears in the *State* column to indicate the MOUNT-DIM and BASE1-DIM layers are *Frozen* in the current viewport. Note also that the BASE1* layers have been *Frozen* for new layers indicated by the letter "N".

Figure 32-14 ⎯⎯⎯⎯⎯⎯⎯⎯⎯⎯⎯⎯⎯⎯⎯⎯

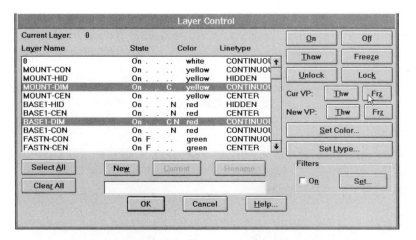

The *Layer Control* dialogue box is helpful for listing the viewport-specific layer visibility, but only for the <u>current</u> viewport. Keep in mind that the dialogue box requires that the <u>specific</u> viewport be current, whereas the *Vplayer* command provides viewport-specific layer visibility control for <u>any</u> viewport, current or otherwise.

If you are using AutoCAD for Windows, the layer pop-down list is a handy tool for setting viewport-specific layer visibility "on the fly" (Fig. 32-15). The third column of icons from the right is used for <u>current</u> <u>viewport *Freeze/Thaw*</u>. Notice in the figure all of the BASE1-* layers are *Frozen* for the current viewport while all other layers are *Thawed* (and *On*) for the current viewport. Keep in mind that this list allows changing settings for the current viewport only, one layer at a time. For working with large numbers of layers and multiple viewports, the *Layer Control* dialogue box and the *Vplayer* command are more efficient.

Figure 32-15

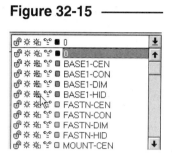

ZOOM XP Factors

Paper space objects such as title block and border should correspond to the paper on a 1=1 scale. Paper space is intended to represent the plotting sheet. *Limits* in <u>paper space</u> should be set to the exact paper size, and the finished drawing is plotted <u>from paper space</u> to a scale of 1=1. The model space geometry, however, should be true scale in real-world units, and *Limits* in <u>model space</u> are generally set to accommodate that geometry.

When model space geometry appears in a viewport in paper space, the size of the <u>displayed</u> geometry can be controlled so that it appears and plots in the correct scale. This action is accomplished with the *XP* option of the *Zoom* command. *XP* means "times paper space." Thus, model space geometry is *Zoomed* to some factor "times paper space."

Since paper space is set to the actual size of the paper, the *Zoom XP* factor that should be used for a viewport is <u>equivalent to the plot scale</u> that would otherwise be used for plotting that geometry in model space. The *Zoom XP* factor is the reciprocal of the "drawing scale factor" (Chapter 13). *Zoom XP* <u>only</u> while you are "in" the desired model space viewport. Fractions or decimals are accepted.

For example, if the model space geometry would normally be plotted at 1/2"=1" or 1:2, the *Zoom* factor would be .5*XP* or 1/2*XP*. If a drawing would normally be plotted at 1/4"=1', the *Zoom* factor would be 1/48*XP*. Other examples are given below.

1:5	*Zoom* .2*XP* or 1/5 XP
1:10	*Zoom* .1*XP* or 1/10XP
1:20	*Zoom* .05*XP* or 1/20XP
1/2"=1"	*Zoom* 1/2*XP*
3/8"=1"	*Zoom* 3/8*XP*
1/4"=1"	*Zoom* 1/4*XP*
1/8"=1"	*Zoom* 1/8*XP*
3"=1'	*Zoom* 1/4*XP*
1"=1'	*Zoom* 1/12*XP*
3/4'=1'	*Zoom* 1/16*XP*
1/2"=1'	*Zoom* 1/24*XP*
3/8"=1'	*Zoom* 1/32*XP*
1/4"=1'	*Zoom* 1/48*XP*
1/8"=1'	*Zoom* 1/96*XP*

Refer to the Tables of Limits Settings, Chapter 14, for other plot scale factors.

Dimensioning in Floating Viewports Using *Scale to Paper Space* (**DIMSCALE**)

The option in the *Dimension Styles, Geometry* dialogue box (*DIMSCALE* variable) has a special meaning when you dimension in paper space. As you know, this variable allows you to control the size of the dimensioning features (arrows, text, etc.). *Scale to Paper Space* (*DIMSCALE*) can be set to ensure that dimensions appearing in <u>different</u> viewports of different *Zoom XP* factors have the <u>same</u> text sizes, arrow sizes, etc.

If the *Scale to Paper Space* option is checked (or *DIMSCALE* is set to 0), AutoCAD computes a value based on the scaling between the <u>current viewport</u> and paper space. In other words, a *DIMSCALE* of 0 leads to dimension text sizes, arrow sizes, and other scaled distances to plot at their original face values by counteracting the effects of the viewport's *Zoom* factor. If you are in paper space, AutoCAD uses a scale factor of 1.0.

For example, assume that you have completed the model geometry for a part with associative dimensions in model space as you would normally. Next, enable paper space and create two viewports to display two views, as shown in Figure 32-16. *Zoom XP* factors have been applied to model geometry in each viewport as follows:

Left-	*Zoom 1XP*
Right-	*Zoom 2XP*

Notice how the dimension sizes are displayed according to the *Zoom XP* values.

In order to force the dimensions to appear the same size in each viewport, switch to paper space and check *Scale to Paper Space* (or set *DIMSCALE* to 0). This forces the viewport-specific *DIMSCALE* to be divided by the *Zoom* factor.

Next, switch to floating model space, activate the desired viewport, and use the *Dimstyle* command with the *Apply* option and select the three existing dimensions, as shown in Figure 32-17. Notice that dimensions appearing in both viewports can only be displayed in one size (there is only one model space geometry).

Figure 32-16 ────────────

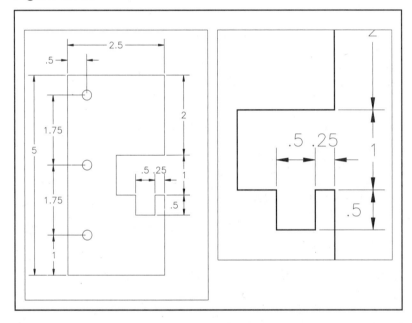

Figure 32-17 ────────────

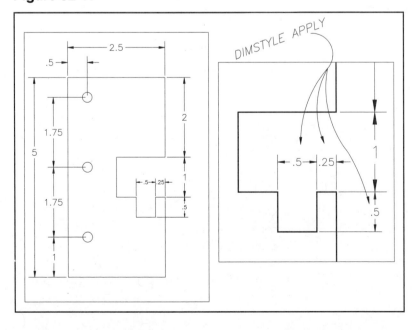

An alternative is to create dimensions on separate layers for each viewport (or use *Change Properties* to change layers for existing dimensions). In this way you can have viewport-specific layer visibility for dimensions and avoid the problem of having dimensions appearing in both viewports (Fig. 32-18).

Figure 32-18

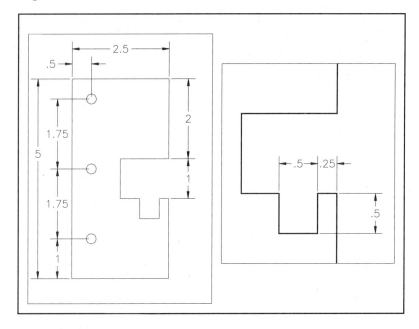

Dimensioning in Paper Space Using *DIMLFAC*

Even though part geometry should be dimensioned in model space (so the dimensions are associated with the model), you can place dimensions in paper space for particular situations. The *DIMLFAC* variable has special meaning when placing <u>dimensions in paper space</u> related to geometry in model space. If you set *DIMLFAC* to a negative value equal to the *Zoom* factor of the desired viewport, AutoCAD generates a measured length (dimension text value) relative to the model space units instead of paper space units. This is done automatically if you use the *Viewport* option of *DIMLFAC*, as described below. If you are creating a dimension in model space, negative values are ignored and the value of 1.0 is used instead.

AutoCAD computes a value of *DIMLFAC* for you if you change *DIMLFAC* from the "Dim:" prompt while in paper space and you select the *Viewport* option. You <u>must be in paper space</u> and invoke *DIMLFAC* from the Dim: prompt (not the Command: prompt) to enable the *Viewport* option.

> Command: **dim**
> Dim: **dimlfac**
> Current value <1.0000> New value (Viewport): **v**
> Select viewport to set scale: **PICK** the desired viewport object.
> Dimlfac set to *-nnn.nn*
> Dim:

AutoCAD calculates the scaling of model space to paper space (*Zoom XP* factor) and assigns the negative of this value to *DIMLFAC*. Setting the *DIMLFAC* variable with the *Viewport* option causes the measured value to be calculated relative to the model space geometry rather than indicating the actual paper space measurement.

For example, suppose an additional dimension is required for the detailed view and you need to create the dimension in paper space since there is insufficient room in the viewport. First, switch to paper space; then create the associative dimension in paper space (see Fig. 32-19 above the right viewport). *OSNAP* can be used to snap to the model space geometry.

When dimensioning in paper space using the <u>default</u> *DIMLFAC* setting, the dimensional value as measured by AutoCAD appears in <u>paper space units</u> as in Figure 32-19. Obviously, this is an <u>incorrect</u> value for the model space geometry.

DIMLFAC should be set for paper space using the *Viewport* option (at the Dim: prompt). Select the viewport object (border). Create the dimension again, or use *Dimstyle Apply* to update an existing dimension to the new *DIMLFAC* setting. The resulting dimension is displayed relative to model space units as shown in Figure 32-20.

The VIEWPORT layer can be *Frozen* with the *Layer Control* dialogue box to prepare the drawing for plotting, as shown in Figure 32-20.

Figure 32-19

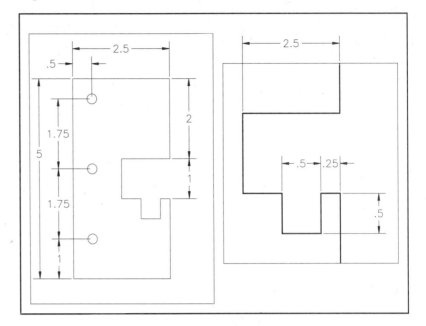

Figure 32-20

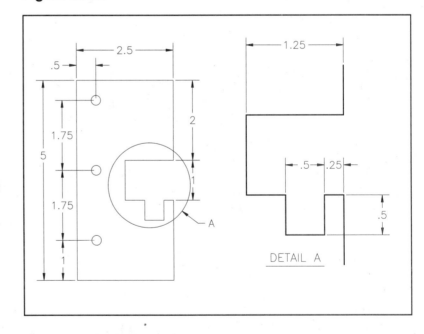

PSLTSCALE

PULL-DOWN MENU	SCREEN MENU	TYPE IN	TABLET MENU
Options *Linetypes >* *Paper Space Linetype Scale*	*OPTIONS* *Psltscl:*	*PSLTSCALE*	---

LTSCALE controls linetype scaling <u>globally</u> for the drawing, whereas the *PSLTSCALE* variable controls the linetype scaling for non-continuous lines only in <u>paper space</u>. A *PSLTSCALE* setting of 1 (the default setting) displays all non-continuous lines relative to paper space units so that all lines in both spaces and in different viewports appear the same regardless of viewport *Zoom* values. *LTSCALE* can still be used to change linetype scaling globally regardless of the *PSLTSCALE* setting.

If *PSLTSCALE* is set to 0, linetype spacing is controlled by the *LTSCALE* variable and based on the drawing units in the space the objects are created in (paper or model). In other words, if *PSLTSCALE* is 0, the linetypes appear different lengths if the units in paper and model spaces are scaled differently or if different viewports are scaled differently as in Figure 32-21.

If *PSLTSCALE* is changed, a *Regenall* must be used to display the effects of the new setting.

Figure 32-21

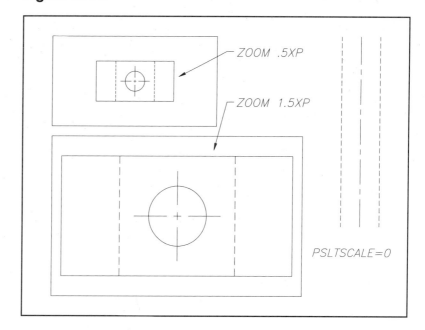

If *PSLTSCALE* is set to 1 (and *TILE-MODE* is 0), the linetype scales for both spaces are <u>scaled to paper space units</u> so that all dashed lines <u>appear equal</u>. The model geometry in viewports can have different *Zoom XP* factors, yet the linetypes display the same (as shown in Figure 32-22).

Figure 32-22

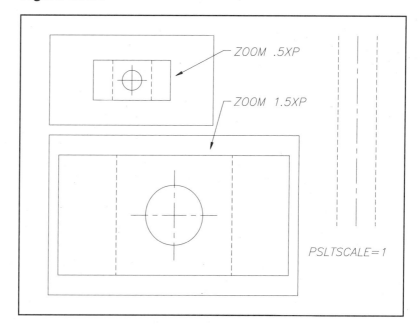

XREFCLIP

PULL-DOWN MENU	SCREEN MENU	TYPE IN	TABLET MENU
File *External Reference* *Clip*	---	*XREFCLIP*	---

Xrefclip is a special external reference application for paper space viewports. *Xrefclip* is an automated routine that inserts a drawing as an *Attached Xref* in a paper space viewport. During the process, you can assign a new layer name for the Xref to be inserted onto, determine the scale factor, and draw a window around ("clip") the portion of the Xref drawing that you want to appear in the viewport. Using this automated process is more efficient than completing each of the necessary commands individually because viewport-specific layer visibility is set automatically rather than having to use *Vplayer* or the *Layer Control* dialogue box. This command is especially helpful for inserting multiple Xrefs, each into a specific paper space viewport.

For example, assume you wanted to set up a drawing for plotting, but wanted to include both the HUB drawing and the PLATE drawing on the sheet. *Xrefclip* could be used to insert both drawings and set the correct viewport-specific layer visibility as follows:

> Command: **xrefclip**
> Initializing...
> Enable paper space? <Y>: **Enter**
> Entering Paper space.
> Regenerating drawing.
> Xref name: **hub** (Specify name of desired Xref drawing.)
> Clip onto what layer? **xhub** (Enter a <u>new</u> layer name for Xref to be inserted.)
> First corner of clip box: **PICK** (The drawing temporarily appears. PICK to specify first corner of drawing to be clipped.)
> Other corner: **PICK** (PICK the other corner.)
> Enter the ratio of paper space units to model space units...
> Number of paper space units <1.0>: **1** (The ratio of this and the next entry specify the <u>reciprocal</u> of the *Zoom XP* factor.)
> Number of model space units <1.0>: **.75** (In this case, the display equals *Zoom .75XP*.)
> Insertion point for clip: **PICK** (Specify insertion point.)
> Command:

The Xref drawing is inserted to your specifications (Fig. 32-23). The name you assign as the new layer is the insertion layer. AutoCAD automatically creates a new layer for the viewport object by appending "-VP" to the name you provide (see the layer pop-down list, Fig. 32-23). The viewport layer can be frozen to make the viewport border disappear.

When specifying the values for "Number of paper space units" and "Number of model space units," enter the values in the <u>opposite</u> order that you would expect. In other words, enter the <u>reciprocal</u> of the *Zoom XP* factor. (See Examples of Using Paper Space Viewports.)

Figure 32-23

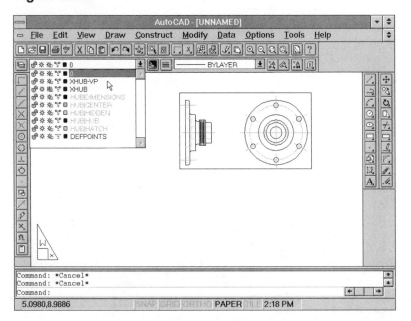

Figure 32-24

The same steps are followed to insert the PLATE drawing as an Xref. The advantage of using this utility is the automatic layer settings. Examining the *Layer Control* dialogue box reveals that the XHUB and XPLATE layers are *Frozen* for New viewports (note the "N" designation in the *State* column, Fig. 32-24). This ensures that objects from the HUB drawing do not appear in the PLATE viewport, and vice versa.

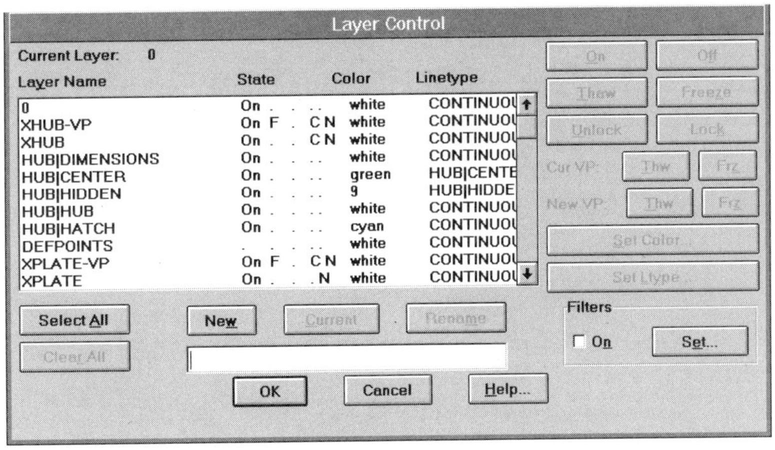

EXAMPLES OF USING PAPER SPACE VIEWPORTS

Remember that the reasons for using paper space viewports are listed near the beginning of the section on Paper Space Viewports. Following are examples of the first two applications listed: using paper space viewports to display two views of one drawing and using paper space to display several Xrefed drawings on one sheet. Applications of paper space for 3D drawings are discussed in Chapter 41.

1. Viewports for Different Views of One Drawing

In this case, a full view of the part is displayed in one viewport and a detail of the part is displayed in a different scale in a second viewport.

1. Create the part geometry in model space.

Begin AutoCAD and create the part geometry as you normally would (model space is enabled by default when you enter the Drawing Editor). Associative dimensions are placed on the part in model space (Fig. 32-25).

Figure 32-25

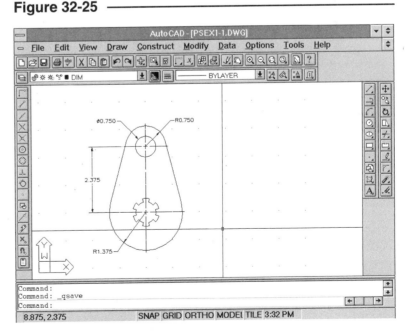

2.   Switch to paper space by changing *TILEMODE* to 0.

When *TILEMODE* is set to **0**, you are automatically switched from model space to paper space. To remind you that paper space is enabled, the letter **P** appears on the status line (DOS), or the word "TILE" is grayed out and "PAPER" appears (Windows). The coordinate system icon (in the lower-left corner of the Drawing Editor) changes to a drafting triangle (Fig. 32-26).

Figure 32-26

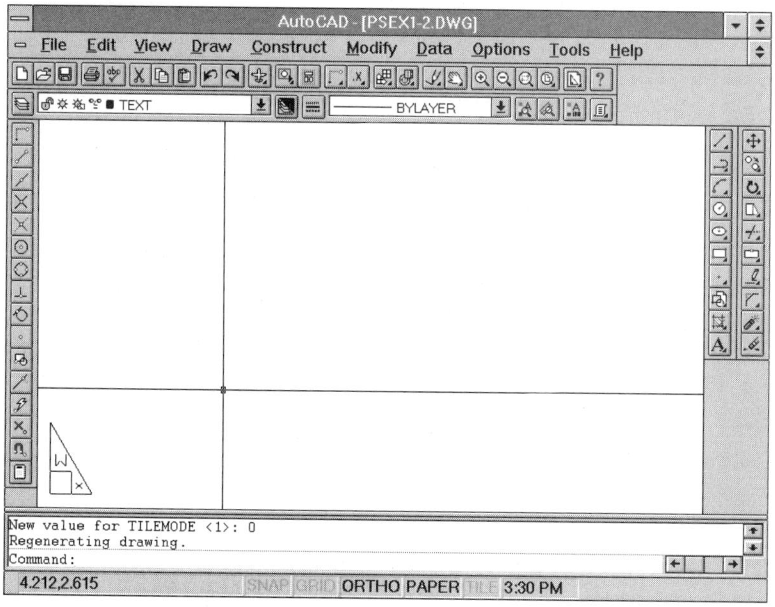

3.   Set up paper space to mimic the plot sheet.

Paper space can have *Limits*, *Snap*, and *Grid* settings independent of those settings in model space. Set paper space *Limits* <u>equal to the paper size</u>. *Snap* and *Grid* spacing can be set to an appropriate value.

Make a new layer called BORDER or TITLE for the title block and border. Draw, *Insert*, or *Xref* the title block and border on the new layer (Fig. 32-27).

Figure 32-27

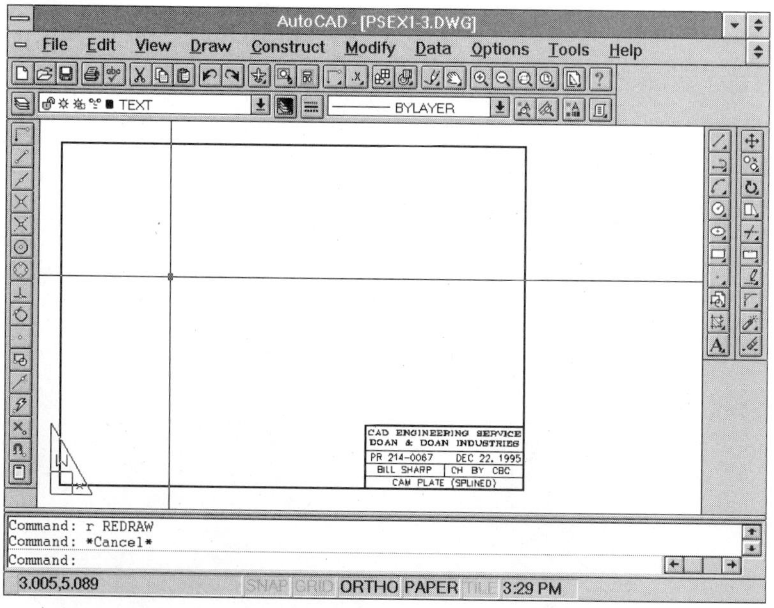

4. Make viewports in paper space.

Make a layer named VIEWPORT and set it as the *Current* layer. Next, draw viewport objects with the *Mview* command <u>while in paper space</u> in order to see part geometry created in model space. Paper space viewports are windows into model space, hence the term "floating model space" (Fig. 32-28).

Paper space viewports created with *Mview* are actually <u>objects</u> drawn on the current layer. Because they are objects, they are affected by *Move, Copy, Array, Scale,* and *Erase* and can overlap one another. Subsequent viewports can be created by *Copying* or *Arraying* existing viewports or by using the *Mview* command. You can use *Mview* to make 2, 3, or 4 viewports or to *Fit* multiple viewports into a window (see *Mview*).

When several paper space viewports exist, you see the same display of model space in each floating viewport by default. Remember that there is <u>only one model space</u>, so you will see it in each viewport (see Figure 32-29). You can, however, control the part of model space you wish to see in each viewport by using display or layer commands.

A second viewport is created by the *Mview* command or other commands (like *Copy* and *Stretch,* for example). The new viewport is also a window into model space (Fig. 32-29). By default, the display is the same geometry as in the first viewport.

Figure 32-28

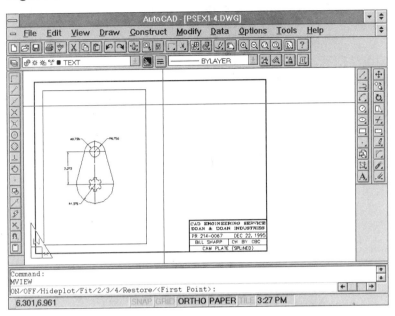

Figure 32-29

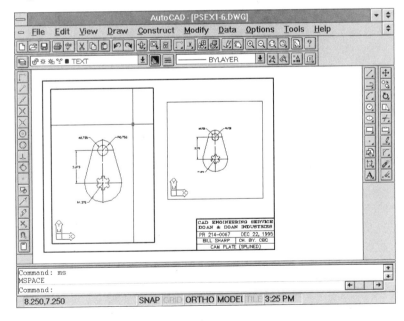

You can switch between drawing in paper space and model space by using *Pspace* (*PS*) and *Mspace* (*MS*) commands. The letter "P" is displayed on the status line (DOS) when in paper space or the words "PAPER" or "MODEL" appear (Windows). If you are in floating model space, the crosshairs are only visible <u>within</u> the viewport, as shown in Figure 32-29. When in paper space, the crosshairs extend <u>completely across</u> the screen, as shown in Figure 32-28. The current viewport is highlighted by a thick border. You can make a different viewport current by PICKing a point inside it.

5. Control the display of model space graphics in each viewport with display commands and layer visibility controls.

Use the *Mspace* (*MS*) command to activate model space. Move the crosshairs and PICK to activate the desired viewport. Use *Zoom XP* to scale the display of the model units to paper space units. In this case, *Zoom 1XP* would be used to scale the model geometry in the left viewport to 1 times paper space units. The geometry in the right viewport is scaled to 2 times paper space units by using *Zoom 2XP* (Fig. 32-30).

Figure 32-30 —————————————

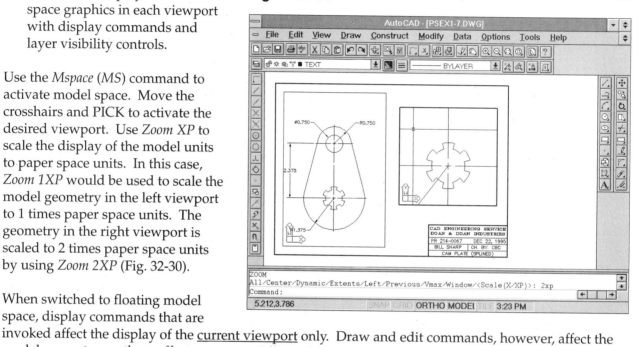

When switched to floating model space, display commands that are invoked affect the display of the <u>current viewport</u> only. Draw and edit commands, however, affect the <u>model geometry</u>, so these effects are potentially visible in <u>all viewports</u>.

Next, set the viewport-specific layer visibility. Use the *Vplayer* command or the *Cur VP* and *New VP* options in the *Layer Control* dialogue box to control which layers are visible in which viewports. The desired layer(s) can be *Frozen* or *Thawed* for each viewport. For example, the dimension layer could be frozen for the right viewport only to yield a display as shown in Figure 32-31.

Figure 32-31 —————————————

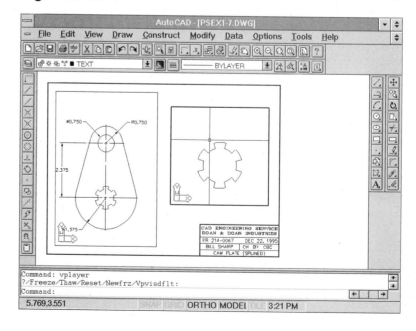

6. Make the final adjustments in paper space and plot at a scale of 1=1.

Use the *Pspace (PS)* command to switch to paper space. Annotations can be added to the drawing in paper space (such as the "Detail A" notes) (Fig. 32-32).

Figure 32-32

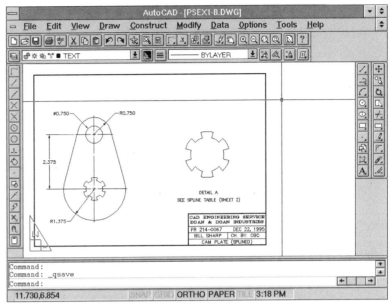

Because the viewports are on a separate layer, you can control the display of the rectangular viewport borders (objects) by controlling the layer's visibility. Turning the VIEWPORT layer (or whatever name is assigned) *Off* prevents the viewport objects from displaying. This is useful when the drawing is ready for plotting.

Plot the drawing from paper space at a plot scale of 1=1. Since paper space is set to the actual paper size, the paper space geometry plots full size, and the model space geometry plots at the scale determined by the *Zoom XP* factor.

2. Viewports for *Xrefed* Drawings

In the following example, multiple viewports are created. The drawing also contains several *Xrefs*, each *Xref* appearing in a separate viewport. Viewport-specific layer visibility control is important for this application to ensure that <u>only one *Xref*</u> is displayed in <u>each viewport</u>. This example describes a typical procedure. Slightly different applications may require different procedures. Two alternate methods are outlined: (A) using *Xrefclip* and (B) using *Mview* and typical viewport-specific layer visibility control.

A. Using *XREFCLIP*

First, a *New* drawing is begun and *Units* are set to *Architectural*. Paper space is enabled immediately by setting *TILEMODE* to 0, then setting *Limits* in paper space equal to a "D" size sheet (36 x 24). After performing a *Zoom All*, the TITLE layer is created. Next, a *Pline* border is drawn and a title block is drawn, *Inserted*, or *Xrefed* on layer TITLE. The drawing at this point should appear like that in Figure 32-33.

Figure 32-33

The *Xrefclip* command is used to Xref the first drawing—a door detail named DOOR.DWG. Using *Xrefclip*, the drawing name is specified, the corners of the drawing are "clipped," and the scale is given as follows:

```
Command: xrefclip
Initializing...
Xref name: door
Clip onto what layer? xdoor
First corner of clip box: PICK
Other corner: PICK
Enter the ratio of paper space units to model space units...
Number of paper space units <1.0>: 16
Number of model space units <1.0>: 1
Insertion point for clip:  PICK
Command:
```

The layer name specified must be a <u>new</u> layer, and it is used as the <u>current</u> layer for the Xref. Another layer is automatically created with a "-VP" suffix for the viewport *object* so that the viewport border can be *Frozen* at a later time (see *Xrefclip*).

In order to make the drawing appear in the viewport and plot to the correct scale, the ratio of paper space to model space is entered next. Enter values in the <u>opposite</u> sequence to the prompts "paper space units" and "model space units." Although this description is confusing, enter the <u>reciprocal</u> of the *Zoom XP* or plot scale factor. The original door drawing was created full size and would normally be plotted on a "D" size sheet at a scale of 3/4"=1'. Since paper space is set to the actual paper size, the drawing is scaled proportionally by using a *Zoom* factor of *1/16XP*. (3/4"=12" is equal to 1/16.)

When the corners for the "clip box" are PICKed, there is no way to make a window larger than the drawing, so the viewport may slightly clip the desired view. The <u>viewport object</u> can be *Scaled* to a factor of 1.2, for example, to achieve the desired viewport size. *Pan* can be used to center the door in the viewport if necessary, or *Zoom XP* could be used at a later time to change the size of the part geometry in the viewport, if needed. The resulting drawing appears in Figure 32-34.

Figure 32-34

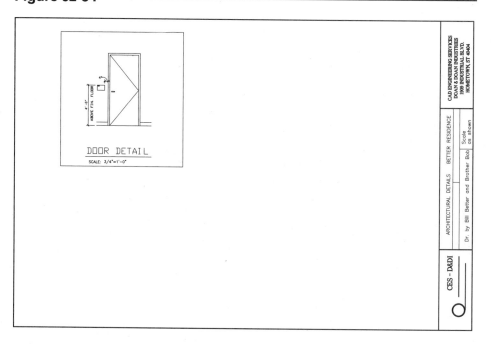

Another detail drawing, WALL, is inserted as an Xref using *Xrefclip* as before. The intended plot scale for the WALL drawing is 3"=1', so the values entered for "paper space units" and "model space units" are 32 and 1. The drawing should be plotted to a scale of 1/32 or scaled in the viewport by using a *Zoom* factor of 1/32XP (3/8"=12" is equal to 1/32). The drawing, at this point, appears as that in Figure 32-35.

Note that only one drawing appears in each viewport. The *Xrefclip* command automatically sets each Xref layer to be *Frozen* for new viewports and visible only in the respective viewport.

Figure 32-35

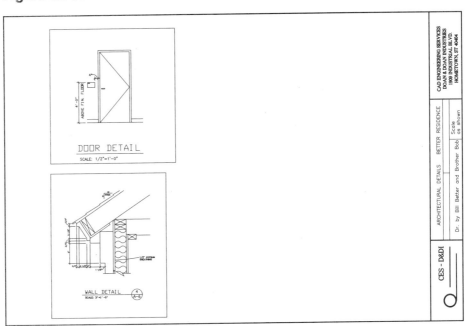

Finally, the *Xrefclip* command is used again to bring in the wall section drawing named SECTION. The same procedure as before is followed. The intended plot scale is 3/4"=1', so values of 16 and 1 are entered (3/4=12 equals 1/16). The drawing appears as that in Figure 32-36.

Figure 32-36

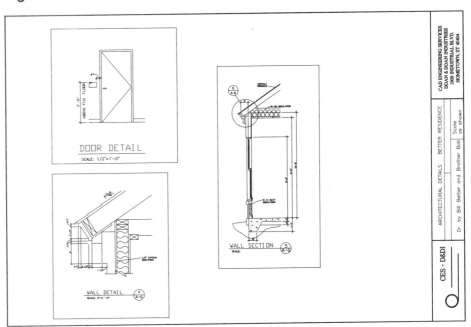

If desired, the viewport objects can be moved with the *Move* command to create a more equally distributed layout. The crosshairs must be in paper space to select the viewport borders.

Lastly, the layers containing the viewport objects (XDOOR-VP, XWALL-VP, and XSECTION-VP) are *Frozen* so the viewport borders do not appear.

NOTE: In order to retain all of the viewport-specific visibility settings for the layers, <u>*VISRETAIN* must be set to 1</u>. If *VISRETAIN* is not changed from the default of 0, all viewport-specific layer visibility settings will be lost, including those automatically made by *Xrefclip*. If *VISRETAIN*=0 and the drawing is *Opened* again, all Xrefed drawings will appear in all viewports.

The resulting drawing, as shown in Figure 32-37, is ready for plotting.

Figure 32-37

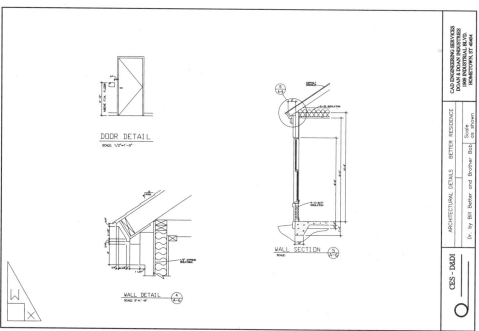

B. Using *MVIEW* and the *Layer Control* Dialogue Box

An alternative method is given here for completing the same drawing as before (Fig. 32-37). This method is more involved because *Xrefclip* is not used to make viewports, *Xref* the drawings, create the layers, and set the visibility for the layers. This method is given as an aid for situations when it is not practical to use *Xrefclip*.

First, a *New* drawing is begun and *Units* are set to *Architectural*. Paper space is enabled immediately by setting *TILEMODE* to 0, then setting *Limits* in paper space equal to a "D" size sheet (36 x 24). After doing a *Zoom All*, the XREF, VIEWPORT, and TITLE layers are created. These layers are necessary since *Xrefclip* is not used to automatically create the layers needed for visibility control of the viewport objects and the Xref information that is attached. Next, a *Pline* border is drawn and a title block is drawn, *Inserted*, or *Xrefed* on layer TITLE.

Then the VIEWPORT layer is set as the current layer, and *Mview* is used to create a viewport. The drawing, at this point, should appear similar to that in Figure 32-33, but with one empty viewport.

The *MS* (*Mspace*) command is used to activate model space so the *Xrefed* drawings will come into model space. The current layer is then set to XREF. The *Xref* command with the *Attach* option is used to bring in the first drawing—the DOOR.DWG. Accepting all the defaults, the drawing may not appear until *Zoom Extents* is used to make the geometry visible in the viewport.

In order to make the drawing appear in the viewport and plot to the correct scale, a *Zoom XP* factor should be used. The original door drawing was created full size and would normally be plotted on a "D" size sheet at a scale of 3/4"=1'. Since paper space is set to the actual paper size, the drawing is scaled proportionally by using a *Zoom* factor of *1/16XP* as before. *Pan* is used to center the door in the viewport. The resulting drawing would be the same as in Figure 32-34.

Before creating another viewport, *PS* is used to activate paper space and the current layer is set to VIEW-PORT. A second viewport is created with the *Mview* or *Copy* command. The current layer is set again to XREF and model space is activated with *MS*. Another detail drawing, WALL, is *Attached* with *Xref*. The intended plot scale for the WALL drawing is 3"=1', accomplished by using *Zoom 1/4XP*. The drawing, at this point, appears similar to Figure 32-38.

Figure 32-38

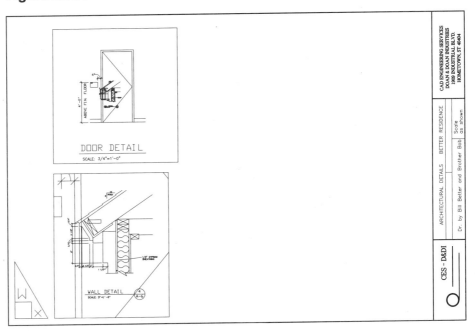

Note that <u>both drawings appear in each viewport</u> (Fig. 32-38). They have each been *Xrefed* into model space, and there is only one model space (this is apparent if *TILE-MODE* is changed to 1). Viewport-specific layer control must be exercised to display only one *Xref* per viewport. Using the *Layer Control* dialogue box, the visibility of dependent layers can be controlled for each viewport. With the bottom viewport active (WALL detail), all the DOOR drawing layers are selected and frozen for the <u>current</u>

Figure 32-39

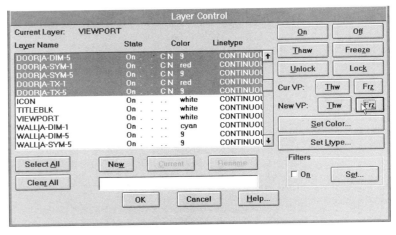

viewport, and <u>new</u> viewports by PICKing the *Frz* tile for *Cur VP* and for *New VP*, as shown in Figure 32-39. Confirming the dialogue box (PICK *OK*) regenerates the new display.

Next, visibility for the top viewport must be specified. The top viewport is made active and the dialogue box invoked again. Remember that the *Layer Control* dialogue box displays settings specific to the <u>active</u> viewport. All of the WALL drawing dependent layers are set to *Frz* for the *Cur VP* and for *New VP*. The correct layer visibility appears like that in Figure 32-35. The dependent WALL and DOOR layers do not appear in any new viewports.

Alternatively, the *Vplayer* command could be used to accomplish the viewport-specific layer visibility. (See the alternate method at the end of this section.)

Next, paper space is activated (with *PS*) and the current layer is set to VIEWPORT. One more viewport is created with *Mview*. The WALL* and DOOR* layers do not appear in the new viewport because of the previous action to *Frz, New VP*. Model space is activated and the right viewport is made current. Layer XREF is set current. *Xref* is used to *Attach* the SECTION detail drawing. It is *Zoomed* to *1/16XP* to achieve a scale of 3/4"=1'.

Now, even though the DOOR and WALL layers appear only in the appropriate viewports, all of the SECTION dependent layers appear in all viewports. The *Vplayer* command can be used to control layer visibility as an alternative to the *Layer Control* dialogue box. *Vplayer* can be used to set a default visibility setting for specific layers with the *Freeze* option. *Vplayer* can be invoked from paper space or model space. The asterisk (*) is used to specify all SECTION layers, as shown in the following command sequence:

```
Command: vplayer
?/Freeze/Thaw/Reset/Newfrz/Vpvisdflt: f
Layer(s) to Freeze: SECTION*
All/Select/<Current>: s  (use the Select option)
Select objects: PICK  (top viewport object)
Select objects: PICK  (bottom viewport object)
Select objects: Enter
?/Freeze/Thaw/Reset/Newfrz/Vpvisdflt: Enter
Regenerating drawing.
Command:
```

Lastly, the VIEWPORT layer is *Frozen* so the viewport borders do not appear. The resulting drawing, as shown in Figure 32-37, is ready for plotting.

Alternate Layer Visibility Control Method

As an alternative method of layer control for the previous example, the *Vpvisdflt* option of *Vplayer* can be used to set the default visibility settings for new viewports. The procedure is as follows:

1. Create the first viewport and *Xref* the DOOR drawing as before.

2. Invoke the *Vplayer* command with the *Vpvisdflt* option as follows:

```
Command: vplayer
?/Freeze/Thaw/Reset/Newfrz/Vpvisdflt: v
Layer name(s) to change default viewport visibility: DOOR*
Change default viewport visibility to Frozen/<Thawed>: f
?/Freeze/Thaw/Reset/Newfrz/Vpvisdflt: Enter
Command:
```

The DOOR layers are frozen for any <u>new</u> viewports that are created.

3. Create the second viewport and *Xref* the WALL drawing as before.

4. Invoke *Vplayer* and use the *Vpvisdflt* option to freeze the WALL* layers for <u>new</u> viewports.

5. Invoke *Vplayer* and use the *Freeze* option to freeze the WALL* layers for the first viewport.

6. Continue this sequence for the last viewport.

USING *MVSETUP* AND PAPER SPACE FOR 2D DRAWINGS

Mvsetup is an AutoLISP program supplied with AutoCAD that enables you to automatically create, scale, and align paper space viewports and insert title blocks for 2D or 3D model geometry. Several ANSI (American National Standards Institute) and ISO (International Standards Organization) title blocks and borders are available for insertion.

Mvsetup can be used when *TILEMODE* is On or Off. If you choose to use *Mvsetup* when *TILEMODE* is On, AutoCAD draws a "bounding box" border and ends the command. However, using *Mvsetup* in conjunction with paper space (with *TILEMODE* Off) displays the power of this routine. This section describes the use of *Mvsetup* with paper space for 2D drawings. A popular application for *Mvsetup* is displaying 3D objects in a typical multiview-type viewport configuration. *Mvsetup* is discussed for that purpose in Chapter 41.

MVSETUP

PULL-DOWN MENU	SCREEN MENU	TYPE IN	TABLET MENU
View Floating Viewports > MV Setup	---	MVSETUP	---

The *Mvsetup* (multiview setup) command is actually an AutoLISP routine that is accessible, either through the *View* pull-down menu or by typing *Mvsetup*. One application of *Mvsetup* with paper space (*TILEMODE* is 0) is for the setup of paper space viewports and insertion of title blocks for 2D drawings.

Mvsetup can be used with *TILEMODE* at either setting (1 or 0); however, *TILEMODE* must be set to 0 for the *Floating Viewports* option on the *View* pull-down menu to be enabled. If paper space has not been enabled (*TILEMODE* = 1), *Mvsetup* asks if you want to enable it. For *TILEMODE* set to 0, the command syntax is listed here. The options are explained here:

```
Command: mvsetup
Initializing...
Align/Create/Scale viewports/Options/Title block/Undo:
```

Create
Using this option displays the following prompt:

```
Delete objects/Undo/<Create viewports>:
```

Create viewports

Available Mview viewport layout options:

0.   None
1.   Single
2.   Std. Engineering
3.   Array of Viewports

1. Single
This option prompts for a first and other point to define the viewport.

2. Std. Engineering
This option is for 3D drawings and is discussed in Chapter 41.

3. Array of Viewports
Selecting this option prompts for a bounding box and a number of viewports along the X and Y axes. You can also specify a distance between viewports. The resulting viewports are of equal size.

Delete objects
Use *Delete objects* to delete existing <u>viewports</u>.

Undo
Undoes the previous *Mvsetup* operation (without exiting *Mvsetup*).

Options
Options is used for <u>title block and border insertion options</u>. Using this displays the following prompt:

Set Layer/LImits/Units/Xref:

Set Layer
This selection allows you to specify a layer on which to insert a title block and border. The layer can be existing or you can name a new one.

Limits
If desired, this option resets the *Limits* after inserting the title block and border to the drawing extents defined by the border.

Units
You may specify inch or millimeter units for use in paper space.

Xref
This option is used to specify if the title block and border are to be *Attached* as an Xref or *Inserted* as a Block.

Title block
Choosing this option displays the prompt: Delete objects/Origin/Undo/<Insert title block>:

Delete Objects
This option allows you to delete (erase) objects from paper space without having to leave the *Mvsetup* routine. It operates like the *Erase* command.

Origin
You can relocate the plotter origin point for the sheet with this option. You are prompted to PICK a point.

Undo
Undoes the last *Mvsetup* operation (without exiting *Mvsetup*).

Insert title block
Provides the following options and title blocks with borders for insertion.

Available title block options:

0:	None
1:	ISO A4 Size(mm)
2:	ISO A3 Size(mm)
3:	ISO A2 Size(mm)
4:	ISO A1 Size(mm)
5:	ISO A0 Size(mm)
6:	ANSI-V Size(in) (Vertical A size)
7:	ANSI-A Size(in)
8:	ANSI-B Size(in)
9:	ANSI-C Size(in)
10:	ANSI-D Size(in)
11:	ANSI-E Size(in)
12:	Arch/Engineering (24 x 36in)
13:	Generic D size Sheet (24 x 36in)

Add/Delete/Redisplay/<Number of entry to load>:

Entering a number causes the appropriate size border and title block to be created. Custom borders can be created and inserted instead of the AutoCAD-supplied ones by using the *Add* option. The *Add* option allows you to add title block options to the list shown above. *Delete* will delete options from the list.

Typical Steps for Using *Mvsetup* (with Paper Space) for 2D Drawings
The typical steps for using *Mvsetup* for this application are as follows:

1. Create the 2D drawing in model space.

2. Load *Mvsetup* and use *Options* to set the preferences for title block insertion and to specify the units to be used.

3. Use *Title block* to *Insert* or *Xref* one of many AutoCAD-supplied or user-supplied borders and title blocks.

4. Use the *Create* option to make one or an array of paper space viewports. (The *"Std. Engineering"* option is intended for 3D drawings.)

5. Use *Scale viewports* to set the scale factor (*Zoom XP* factor) for the geometry displayed in the viewports.

Using *Mvsetup* to Create a Single Viewport in Paper Space

Following is a simple example of using *Mvsetup* to create a paper space viewport and insert a title and border for a completed 2D drawing. Assume that you have just completed the drawing shown in Figure 32-40. The geometry and dimensions are created in model space.

Normally, the next step is to set *TILEMODE* to 0, which enables paper space. Invoke *Mvsetup*. (Typing *Mvsetup* automatically enables paper space; however, *TILEMODE* must be set to 0 for the pull-down menu *MV Setup* option to be enabled.) From the first prompt, select *Options*. Use *Set Layer* to define an existing layer or create a new layer (named TITLE or similar descriptive name) for title block and border insertion.

Figure 32-40 ———————————

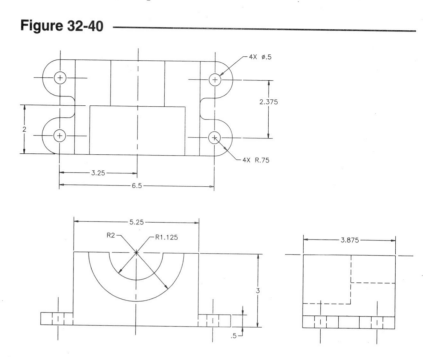

The *Limits* option can be used to automatically set paper space *Limits* equal to the paper space extents after the border and title block are inserted (the drawing *Extents* is equal to the border size). Also use the *Xref* option to specify whether the title block and border are to be *Inserted* or *Xrefed*. Next, use the *Title block* option and then *Insert title block*. Since this drawing is intended to be plotted on a "B" size sheet, for this example, option 8. *ANSI-B size* is selected. The resulting title block appears in paper space (Fig. 32-41).

Figure 32-41 ———————————

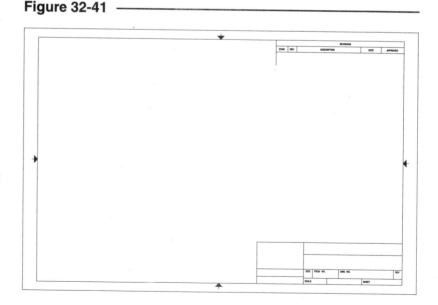

Next, layer VIEWPORT (or other descriptive name) must be created and made current for the viewport objects. To make the viewports, the *Create* option of the *Mvsetup* command is invoked; then *Create viewports* is selected. From the list of available viewport layouts, *1. Single* is designated. PICK the "First point" and the "Other corner" to define the viewport size. By default, the model geometry is displayed in the viewport at maximum size (AutoCAD causes a *Zoom Extents*) (Fig. 32-42).

Figure 32-42 ————————

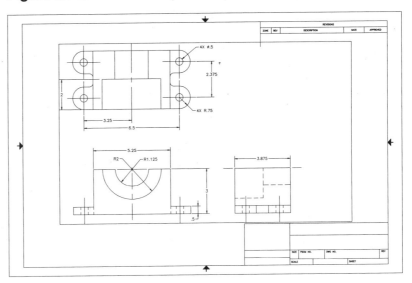

In order to display the model geometry to scale, the *Scale viewports* option from the main prompt is selected. AutoCAD requires you to enter the ratio of "paper space units" to "model space units." This ratio is the *Zoom XP* factor; for example, 1 paper space unit to 2 model space units equals *Zoom 1/2XP*. (This is correct but opposite to the *Xrefclip* sequence. *Mvsetup* responds correctly to the values entered for "paper space units" and "model space units," whereas *Xrefclip* responds incorrectly [Release 13 c2].)

The resulting drawing should appear as shown in Figure 32-43. Enter the desired text into the title block. If desired, *Freeze* the VIEW-PORT layer. The drawing is ready for plotting.

Figure 32-43 ————————

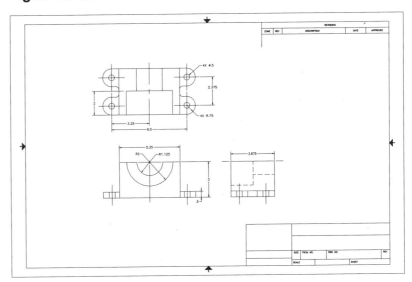

The *Mvsetup* command is an AutoLISP program that can be used to automate the process of setting up paper space viewports. *Mvsetup* can save time and effort compared to the previous methods discussed in which the steps are not as automated. See Chapter 41 for using *Mvsetup* and other methods to create 2D (paper space) drawings from 3D models.

CHAPTER EXERCISES

1. *Vports* **(Tiled Viewports)**

    Open the **ASESMP** drawing. If AutoCAD is installed on your computer at C:\ACADR13, then the sample drawing is located in C:\ACADR13\COMMON\SAMPLE directory.

    A. Invoke *Tiled Viewports* by the pull-down menu; then select *Layout....* When the *Tiled Viewport Layout* dialogue box appears, choose the *vport-3r* (or image tile just left of center). The resulting viewport configuration should appear as Figure 32-3.

    B. Using *Zoom* and *Pan* in the individual viewports, produce a display with an overall view on the right and two detailed views on the left (similar to that shown in Figure 32-5).

    C. Type the *Vports* command. Use the *Save* option to save the viewport configuration as **3R**. Use *Vports* again and change the display to a *Single* screen. Now use *SaveAs* to save the drawing as **ASESMP-2** and <u>reset the path to your working directory</u>.

    D. *Open* **ASESMP-2**. Use the *?* option of *Vports*; then *Restore* **3R** to ensure the viewport configuration was saved as expected. Invoke a *Single* viewport again. Finally, use *Vports* or the *Tiled Viewport Layout* dialogue box to create another viewport configuration of your choosing. *Save* the viewport configuration and assign an appropriate name. *Save* the **ASESMP-2** drawing.

2. *TILEMODE, Mview*

    In this exercise, you will enable paper space, draw a border and insert a title block, and show a drawing in viewport.

    A. *Open* the **ASSY2** drawing that you created in the Chapter 31 Exercises (make sure all of the Xrefed drawings are also located in your working directory). Use *Xref* with the *Bind* option to bind all of the Xrefed drawings. Use *SaveAs* to save and name the drawing as **ASSY2-PS**.

    B. Set *TILEMODE* to **0**. Set *Limits* in paper space to the paper size that you intend to plot on. Set paper space *Snap* and *Grid* to an appropriate size (**.250"** or **6mm**). Make a *New Layer* named **TITLE** and set it as the *Current* layer. Draw a border and draw, *Insert*, or *Xref* a title block (in paper space).

    C. Make a *New Layer* called **VIEWPORT** or **VPORT** and set it as *Current*. Next, use *Mview* to create one viewport. Make the viewport as large as possible while staying within the confines of the title block and border. Type *MS* to activate model space in the viewport, and use *Zoom XP* to scale the model geometry times paper space (remember that the geometry is in millimeter units). Enter the scale in the title block (scale=XP factor).

D. Turn *Off* the **VIEWPORT** layer and *Save* the drawing (as ASSY2-PS). *Plot* the drawing <u>from paper space</u> at **1=1**. Your drawing should appear as Figure 32-44.

Figure 32-44

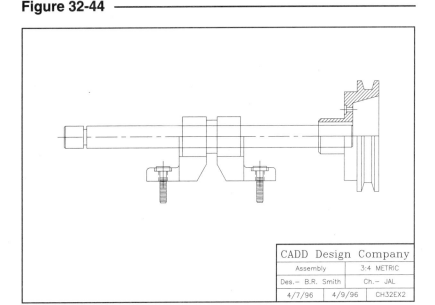

CADD Design Company	
Assembly	3:4 METRIC
Des.– B.R. Smith	Ch.– JAL
4/7/96	4/9/96	CH32EX2

3. *TILEMODE, Mview, DIMSCALE*

In this exercise, you will use paper space with 3 viewports to show an overall view of a drawing and two details in different scales. *DIMSCALE* (*Overall Scaling*) will be set to 0 (*Scale to Paper Space*) to produce dimension features appearing equal in size.

A. *Open* the **EFF-APT2** drawing that you worked on in Chapter 31 Exercises. *Erase* the plant. Create a text *Style* using *Roman Simplex* font. Create dimensions for the interior of each room on the **DIM** layer. *Zoom* in, and on another *New Layer* named **DIM2** give the dimensions for the wash basin in the Bath and the counter for the Kitchen sink.

B. Change *TILEMODE* to **0**. Set *Limits* to the paper size for plotting. Set appropriate *Snap* and *Grid* increments. Set *Layer* **TITLE** *Current*. Draw, *Insert*, or *Xref* a border and title block.

C. Make a *New Layer* named **VIEWPORT** and set it as the *Current* layer. Use *Mview* to make one viewport on the right, occupying approximately 2/3 of the page. Use *Mview* again to make two smaller viewports in the remaining space on the left.

D. Activate the large viewport (in *MS*) and *Zoom XP* to achieve the largest possible display of the apartment to an <u>accepted scale</u>. In the top-left viewport, use display controls (including *Zoom XP*) to produce a scaled detail of the Bath. Produce a <u>scaled</u> detail of the kitchen sink in the lower-left viewport.

E. Use the *Layer Control* dialogue box to *Freeze* layer **DIM2** in the large viewport and *Freeze* layer **DIM** in the two small viewports. Change to *PS*. Set *DIMSCALE* to 0 (*Overall Scaling* checkbox will be set to *Scale to Paper Space*). Return to *MS* and use *Dimstyle Apply* to update the dimensions in the small viewports so that the dimensions appear the same size in all viewports.

F. Return to paper space and turn *Off Layer* **VIEWPORT**. Use *Text* (in paper space) to label the detail views and give the scale for each. *Save* the drawing as **EFF-APT3** and *Plot* from paper space at **1=1**. The final plot should look similar to Figure 32-45.

Figure 32-45

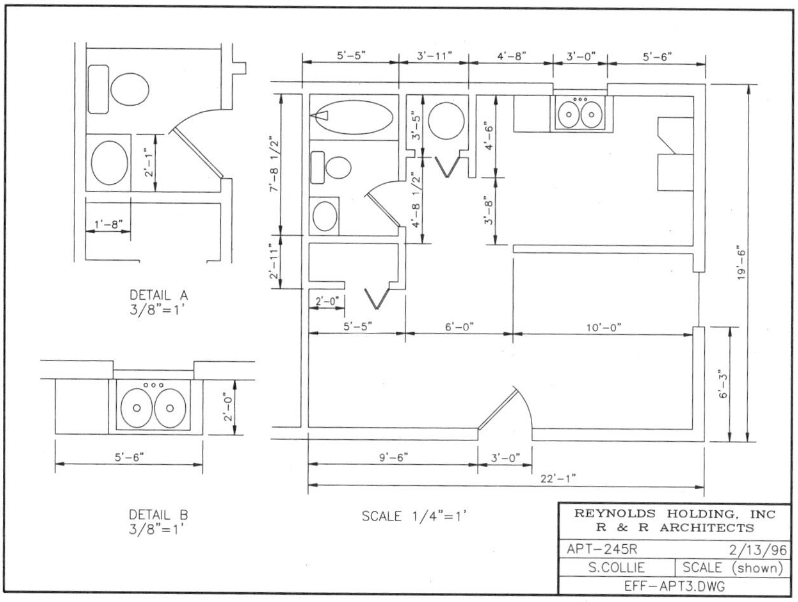

4. *TILEMODE, Mview, Xref*, **Viewport-Specific Layer Visibility**

In this exercise, you will create three paper space viewports and display three *Xrefed* drawings, one in each viewport. Viewport-specific layer visibility control will be exercised to produce the desired display.

A. Begin a *New* drawing using a *Prototype* to correspond to the sheet size you intend to plot on. Create *New Layers* named **TITLE**, **XREF**, and **VIEWPORT**. Set *TILEMODE* to **0** and prepare paper space with *Limits, Snap, Grid*, a border, and title block. On the **VIEWPORT** layer, use *Mview* to create a viewport occupying about 1/2 of the page on the right side.

B. Make the **XREF** layer *Current*. Change to *MS*. In the viewport, *Xref* **GASKETD** drawing. Use *Zoom* with an *XP* value to scale it to paper space. Use the *Layer Control* dialogue box to *Freeze* the **GASKETD | DIM** layer and to *Freeze* all **GASKETD*** layers for *New VP*.

C. Option 1.   Change to *PS* and create two more viewports on *Layer* **VIEWPORT** equal in size to the first. Set *Layer* **XREF** *Current* and *Xref* the **GASKETB** and the **GASKETC** drawings. Change to *MS* and use the *Layer Control* dialogue box or *Vplayer* to constrain only one gasket to appear in each viewport.

Option 2.   Change to *PS* and create one more viewport on *Layer* **VIEWPORT** equal in size to the first. Set *Layer* **XREF** *Current* and *Xref* only the **GASKETB** drawing. Change to *MS* and use the *Layer Control* dialogue box or *Vplayer* to set the **GASKETB** visibility for the existing and new viewports. Repeat these steps for **GASKETC**.

D. Use *Zoom XP* values to produce a scaled view of each new gasket. Change to *PS* and *Freeze* layer **VIEWPORT**. Use *Text* to label the gaskets. *Plot* the drawing to scale. Your plot should look similar to Figure 32-46. *Save* the drawing as **GASKETS**.

Figure 32-46

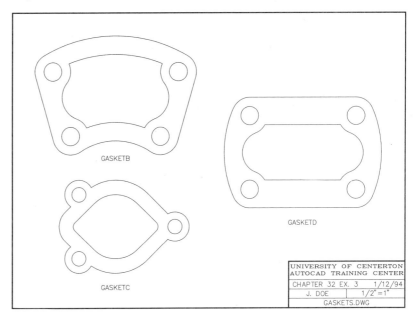

5. *Xrefclip*

In this exercise, *Xrefclip* is used to create a drawing similar to the previous exercise.

A. Begin a *New* drawing using a *Prototype* to correspond to the sheet size you intend to plot on. Create only one *New Layer* named **TITLE**. Since *Xrefclip* is to be used, the other necessary layers are automatically created. Set *TILEMODE* to **0** and prepare paper space with *Limits*, *Snap*, *Grid*, a border, and title block. *Save* the drawing as **GASKETS2**.

B. Use the *Xrefclip* command to make the first viewport and Xref the **GASKETD** drawing. Enter the appropriate ratio of paper space to model space (reciprocal of the *Zoom XP* value used in the previous exercise). Specify the new layer to create as **GASD**. After the drawing has been inserted, *Scale* the viewport to a factor of **1.2**, if necessary. Finally, use the *Layer Control* dialogue box to view the layers and verify that the **GASD** and **GASD-VP** layers have been created. Notice the viewport-specific visibility settings that are automatically set.

C. Use the same method to Xref the **GASKETB** and the **GASKETC** drawings, similar to the arrangement in the previous exercise. Use the appropriate scale ratios. Assign layer names of **GASB** and **GASC**. Clip the viewports as before and *Scale* the viewports up if necessary. Use the *Layer Control* dialogue box to view the settings.

D. In paper space, *Freeze* layers ***-VP**. Use *Text* to label the gaskets. *Plot* the drawing to scale. Your plot should look similar to the previous plot. *Save* the drawing as **GASKETS2**.

E. Which of the two methods (*Xrefclip* or *Mview*, *Layer*, etc.) do you prefer, and why?

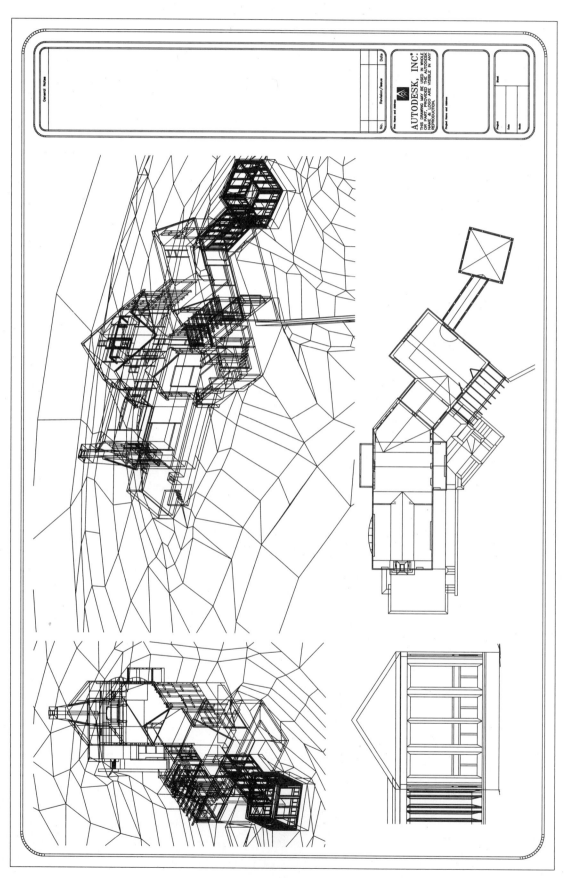

SITE-3D2.DWG Courtesy of Autodesk, Inc.

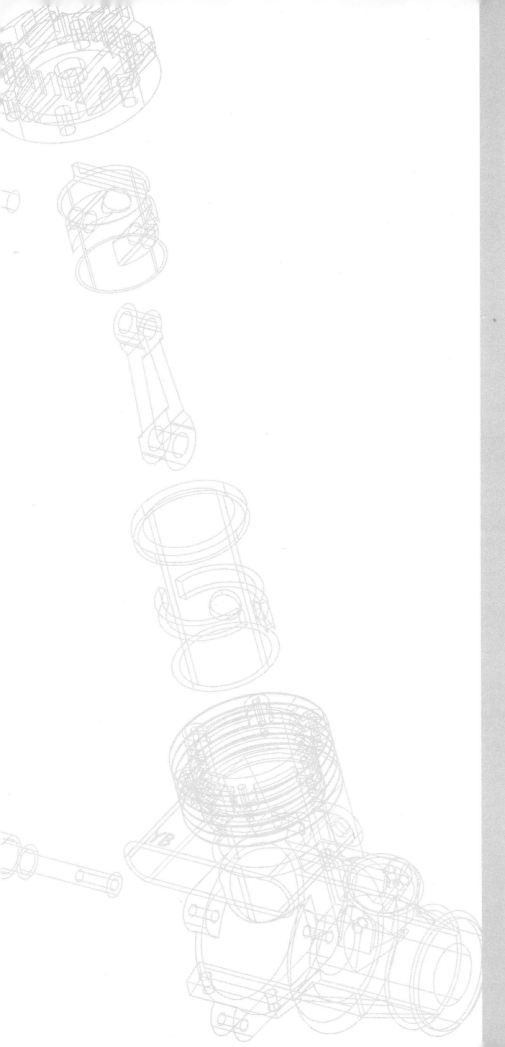

Chapter 33

3D MODELING BASICS

Chapter Objectives

After completing this chapter you should:

1. know the characteristics of wireframe, surface, and solid models;

2. know the five formats for 3D coordinate entry;

3. understand the orientation of the World Coordinate System (WCS);

4. be able to use the right-hand rule for orientation of the X, Y, and Z axes and for determining positive and negative rotation about an axis;

5. be able to control the appearance and positioning of the Coordinate System Icon with the *Ucsicon* command.

3D MODELING TYPES

There are three basic types of 3D (three-dimensional) models created by CAD systems used to represent actual objects. They are:

1. Wireframe models
2. Surface models
3. Solid models

These three types of 3D models range from a simple description to a very complete description of an actual object. The different types of models require different construction techniques, although many concepts of 3D modeling are the same for creating any type of model on any type of CAD system.

Wireframe Models

"Wireframe" is a good descriptor of this type of modeling. A wireframe model of a cube is like a model constructed of 12 coat-hanger wires. Each wire represents an <u>edge</u> of the actual object. The <u>surfaces</u> of the object are <u>not</u> defined; only the boundaries of surfaces are represented by edges. No wires exist where edges do not exist. The model is see-through since it has no surfaces to obscure the back edges. A wireframe model has complete dimensional information but contains no volume. Examples of wireframe models are shown in Figures 33-1 and 33-2.

Wireframe models are relatively easy and quick to construct; however, they are not very useful for visualization purposes because of their "transparency." For example, does Figure 33-1 display the cube as if you are looking towards a top-front edge or looking toward a bottom-back edge? Wireframe models tend to have an optical illusion effect, allowing you to visualize the object from two opposite directions unless another visual clue such as perspective is given.

With AutoCAD a wireframe model is constructed by creating 2D objects in 3D space. The *Line, Circle, Arc,* and other 2D draw and edit commands are used to create the "wires," but 3D coordinates must be specified. The cube in Figure 33-1 was created with 12 *Line* segments. AutoCAD provides all the necessary tools to easily construct, edit, and view wireframe models.

Figure 33-1 ———

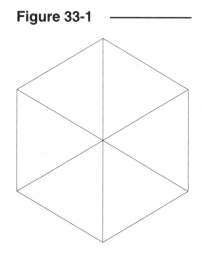

Figure 33-2 ———

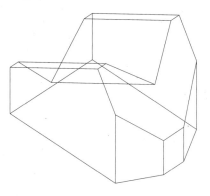

A wireframe model offers many advantages over a 2D engineering drawing. Wireframe models are useful in industry for providing computerized replicas of actual objects. A wireframe model is dimensionally complete and accurate for all three dimensions. Visualization of a wireframe is generally better than a 2D drawing because the model can be viewed from any position or a perspective can be easily attained. The 3D database can be used to test and analyze the object <u>three dimensionally</u>. The sheet metal industry, for example, uses wireframe models to calculate flat patterns complete with bending allowances. A wireframe model can also be used as a foundation for construction of a surface model. Because a wireframe describes edges but not surfaces, wireframe modeling is appropriate to describe objects with planar or single-curved surfaces, but not compound curved surfaces.

Surface Models

Surface models provide a better description of an object than a wireframe, principally because the surfaces as well as the edges are defined. A surface model of a cube is like a cardboard box—all the surfaces and edges are defined, but there is nothing inside. Therefore, a surface model has volume but no mass. A surface model provides an excellent visual representation of an actual 3D object because the front surfaces obscure the back surfaces and edges from view. Figure 33-3 shows a surface model of a cube, and Figure 33-4 displays a surface model of a somewhat more complex shape. Notice that a surface model leaves no question as to which side of the object you are viewing.

Surface models require a relatively tedious construction process. Each surface must be constructed individually. Each surface must be created in, or moved to, the correct orientation with respect to the other surfaces of the object. In AutoCAD, a surface is constructed by defining its edges. Often, wireframe models are used as a framework to build and attach surfaces. The complexity of the construction process of a surface is related to the number and shapes of its edges. AutoCAD Release 13 is not a complete surface modeler. The tools provided allow construction of simple planar and single curved surfaces, but there are few capabilities for construction of double-curved or other complex surfaces. No NURBS (Non-Uniform Rational B-Splines) surfacing capabilities exist in Release 13, although these capabilities are available in another Autodesk product called AutoSurf™.

Most CAD systems, including AutoCAD, can display surface and solid models in both wireframe and "hidden" representation. Figure 33-4 shows the object "hidden" (with the *Hide* command). Figure 33-5 displays the same object in "wireframe" (the default) representation. Surface modeling systems use wireframe representation during the construction and editing process to speed computing time. The user activates the "hidden" representation after completing the model to enhance visibility. A reasonable amount of computing time is required to calculate the surface model "visibility." That is, the process required to determine which surfaces would obscure other surfaces for every position of the model would require noticeable computing time, so wireframe display is used during the model construction process.

Figure 33-3

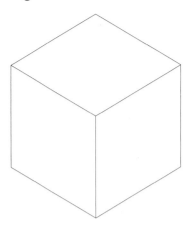

Figure 33-4

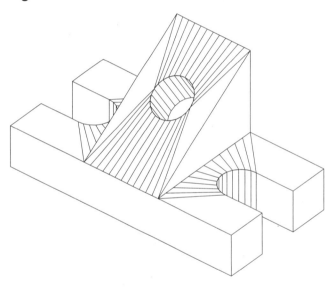

Figure 33-5

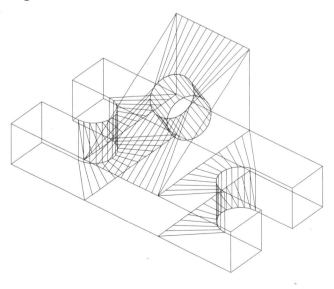

Solid Models

Solid modeling is the most complete and descriptive type of 3D modeling. A solid model is a complete computerized replica of the actual object. A solid model contains the complete surface and edge definition, as well as description of the interior features of the object. If a solid model is cut in half (sectioned), the interior features become visible. Since a solid model is "solid," it can be assigned material characteristics and is considered to have mass. Because solid models have volume and mass, most solid modeling systems include capabilities to automatically calculate volumetric and mass properties.

Figure 33-6 ———————————————————————

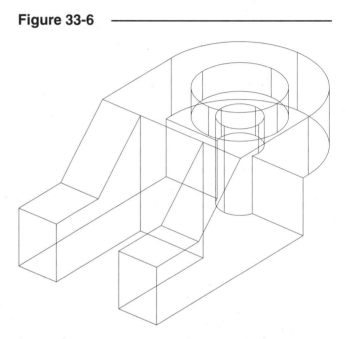

Solid model construction techniques are generally much simpler (and much more fun) than those of surface models. AutoCAD's solid modeler, called ACIS, is a <u>hybrid</u> modeler. That is, ACIS is a combination CSG (Constructive Solid Geometry) and B-Rep (Boundary Representation) modeler. CSG is characterized by its simple and straight-forward construction techniques of combining primitive shapes (boxes, cylinders, wedges, etc.) utilizing Boolean operations (*Union*, *Subtract*, and *Intersect*, etc.). Boundary Representation modeling defines a model in terms of its edges and surfaces (boundaries) and determines the solid model based on which side of the surfaces the model lies. The user interface and construction techniques used in ACIS (primitive shapes combined by Boolean operations) are CSG-based, whereas the B-Rep capabilities are invoked automatically to display models in mesh representation and are transparent to the user. Figure 33-6 displays a solid model constructed of simple primitive shapes combined by Boolean operations.

Figure 33-7 ———————————————————————

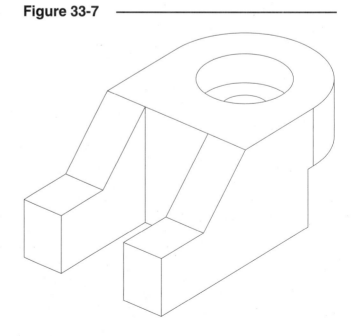

The CSG modeling techniques offer you the advantage of complete and relatively simple editing. CSG construction typically begins by specifying dimensions for simple primitive shapes such as boxes or cylinders, then combining the primitives using Boolean operations to create a "composite" solid. Other primitives and/or composite solids can be combined by the same process. Several repetitions of this process can be continued until the desired solid model is finally achieved. CSG construction techniques are discussed in detail in Chapter 37.

Solid models, like surface models, are capable of either wireframe or "hidden" display. Generally, wireframe display is used during construction (Fig. 33-6), and hidden representation is used to display the finished model (Fig. 33-7).

3D COORDINATE ENTRY

When creating a model in three-dimensional drawing space, the concept of the X and Y coordinate system, which is used for two-dimensional drawing, must be expanded to include the third dimension, Z, which is measured from the origin in a direction perpendicular to the plane defined by X and Y. Remember that two-dimensional CAD systems use X and Y coordinate values to define and store the location of drawing elements such as *Lines* and *Circles*. Likewise, a three-dimensional CAD system keeps a database of X, Y, and Z coordinate values to define locations and sizes of two- and three-dimensional elements. For example, a *Line* is a two-dimensional object, yet the location of its endpoints in three-dimensional space must be specified and stored in the database using X, Y, and Z coordinates (Fig. 33-8). The X, Y, and Z coordinates are always defined in that order, delineated by commas. The AutoCAD Coordinate Display (*COORDS*), however, only displays X and Y values, even though a three-dimensional model can be displayed in the Drawing Editor.

Figure 33-8

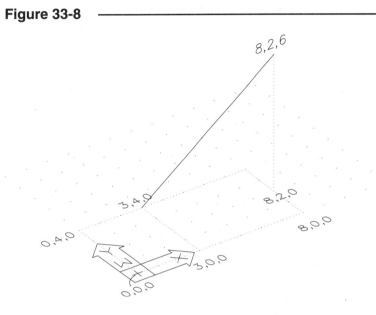

The icon that appears in the lower-left corner of the AutoCAD Drawing Editor is called the Coordinate System Icon (Fig. 33-9). The Coordinate System Icon displays the directions for the X and the Y axes and the orientation of the XY plane and can be made to locate itself at the origin, 0,0. The X coordinate values increase going to the right along the X axis, and the Y values increase going upward along the Y axis.

Figure 33-9

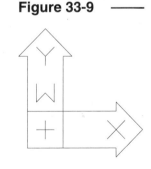

The Z axis is not indicated by the Coordinate System Icon, but is assumed to be in a direction <u>perpendicular</u> to the XY plane. In other words, in the default orientation (when you begin a new drawing), the XY plane is <u>parallel</u> with the screen and the Z axis is <u>perpendicular</u> to, and out of, the screen (Fig. 33-10).

Figure 33-10

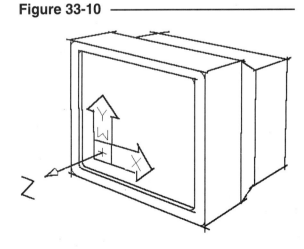

3D Coordinate Entry Formats

Because construction in three dimensions requires the definition of X, Y, <u>and</u> Z values, the methods of coordinate entry used for 2D construction must be expanded to include the Z value. The four methods of command entry used for 2D construction are valid for 3D coordinates with the addition of a Z value specification. Relative polar coordinate specification (@dist<angle) is expanded to form two other coordinate entry methods available explicitly for 3D coordinate entry. The five methods of coordinate entry for 3D construction follow:

1. **Interactive coordinates**   **PICK**   Use the cursor to select points on the screen. *OSNAP* or point filters must be used to select a point in 3D space; otherwise, points selected are <u>on the XY plane</u>.

2. **Absolute coordinates**   **X,Y,Z**   Enter explicit X, Y, and Z values relative to point 0,0.

3. **Relative rectangular coordinates**   **@X,Y,Z**   Enter explicit X, Y, and Z values relative to the last point.

4. **Cylindrical coordinates (relative)**   **@dist<angle,Z**   Enter a distance value, an angle in the XY plane value, and a Z value, all relative to the last point.

5. **Spherical coordinates (relative)**   **@dist<angle<angle**   Enter a distance value, an angle <u>in</u> the XY plane value, and an angle <u>from</u> the XY plane value, all relative to the last point.

Cylindrical and spherical coordinates can be given <u>without</u> the @ symbol, in which case the location specified is relative to point 0,0,0 (the origin). This method is useful if you are creating geometry centered around the origin. Otherwise, the @ symbol is used to establish points in space relative to the last point.

Examples of each of the five 3D coordinate entry methods are illustrated in the following section. In the illustrations, the orientation of the observer has been changed from the default plan view in order to enable the visibility of the three dimensions.

Interactive Coordinate Specification
Figure 33-11 illustrates using the <u>interactive</u> method to PICK a location in 3D space. *OSNAP* <u>must</u> be used in order to PICK in 3D space. Any point PICKed with the input device without *OSNAP* will result in a location <u>on the XY plane</u>. In this example, the *ENDpoint OSNAP* mode is used to establish the "to point:" of a second *Line* by snapping to the end of an existing vertical *Line* at 8,2,6.

Figure 33-11

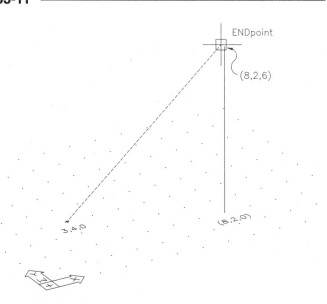

```
Command: Line
From point: 3,4,0
to point: ENDpoint of PICK
```

Absolute Coordinates

Figure 33-12 illustrates the <u>absolute</u> coordinate entry to draw the *Line*. The endpoints of the *Line* are given as explicit X,Y,Z coordinates.

Figure 33-12

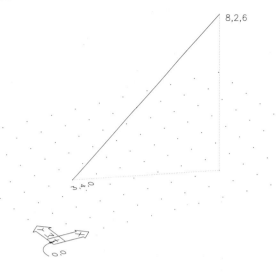

```
Command: Line
From point: 3,4,0
To point: 8,2,6
Command:
```

Relative Rectangular Coordinates

Relative rectangular coordinate entry is displayed in Figure 33-13. The "From point:" of the *Line* is given in absolute coordinates, and the "to point:" end of the *Line* is given as X,Y,Z values <u>relative</u> to the last point.

Figure 33-13

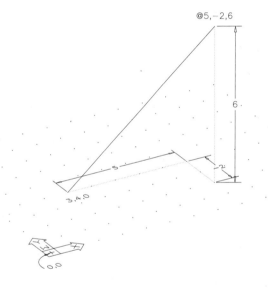

```
Command: Line
From point: 3,4,0
to point: @5,-2,6
Command:
```

Cylindrical Coordinates (Relative)

Cylindrical and spherical coordinates are an extension of polar coordinates with a provision for the third dimension. Relative cylindrical coordinates give the distance <u>in</u> the XY plane, angle <u>in</u> the XY plane, and Z dimension and can be relative to the last point by prefixing the @ symbol. The *Line* in Figure 33-14 is drawn with absolute and relative cylindrical coordinates. (The *Line* established is approximately the same *Line* as in the previous figures.)

Figure 33-14

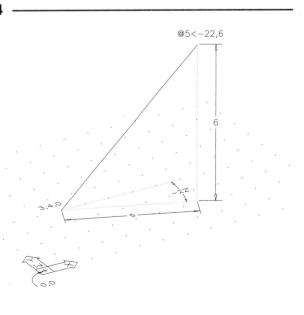

```
Command: Line
From point: 3,4,0
to point: @5<-22,6
Command:
```

Spherical Coordinates (Relative)

Spherical coordinates are also an extension of polar coordinates with a provision for specifying the third dimension in angular format. Spherical coordinates specify a distance, an angle <u>in</u> the XY plane, and an angle <u>from</u> the XY plane and can be relative to the last point by prefixing the @ symbol. The distance specified is a <u>3D distance</u>, not a distance in the XY plane. Figure 33-15 illustrates the creation of approximately the same line as in the previous figures using absolute and relative spherical coordinates.

Figure 33-15

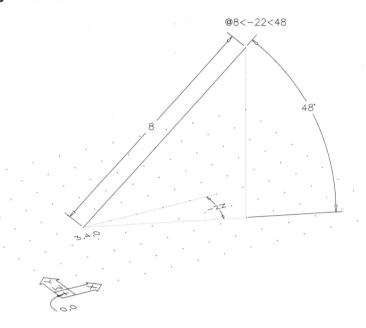

```
Command: Line
From point: 3,4,0
to point: @8<-22<48
Command:
```

Point Filters

Point filters are used to filter X and/or Y and/or Z coordinate values from a location PICKed with the pointing device. Point filtering makes it possible to build an X,Y,Z coordinate specification from a combination of point(s) selected on the screen and point(s) entered at the keyboard. A .XY (read "point XY") filter would extract, or filter, the X and Y coordinate value from the location PICKed and then prompt you to enter a Z value. Valid point filters are listed below. (See also Point Filters, Chapter 15.)

.X	Filters (finds) the X component of the location PICKed with the pointing device.
.Y	Filters the Y component of the location PICKed.
.Z	Filters the Z component of the location PICKed.
.XY	Filters the X and Y components of the location PICKed.
.XZ	Filters the X and Z components of the location PICKed.
.YZ	Filters the Y and Z components of the location PICKed.

The .XY filter is the most commonly used point filter for 3D construction and editing. Because 3D construction often begins on the XY plane of the current coordinate system, elements in Z space are easily constructed by selecting existing points on the XY plane using .XY filters and then entering the Z component of the desired 3D coordinate specification by keyboard. For example, in order to draw a line in Z space two units above an existing line on the XY plane, the .XY filter can be used in combination with *ENDpoint OSNAP* to supply the XY component for the new line. See Figure 33-16 for an illustration of the following command sequence:

```
Command: Line
From point: .XY of
END of PICK (Select one ENDpoint of the existing line on the XY plane.)
(need Z) 2
to point: .XY of
END of PICK (Select the other ENDpoint of the existing line.)
(need Z) 2
Command:
```

Typing **.XY** and pressing **Enter** cause AutoCAD to respond with "of" similar to the way "of" appears after typing an *OSNAP* mode. When a location is specified using an .XY filter, AutoCAD responds with "(need Z)" and, likewise, when other filters are used, AutoCAD prompts for the missing component(s).

Figure 33-16

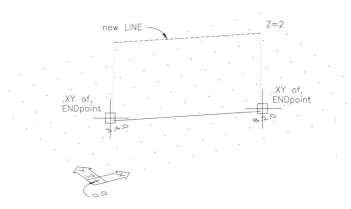

COORDINATE SYSTEMS

In AutoCAD two kinds of coordinate systems can exist, the World Coordinate System (WCS) and one or more User Coordinate Systems (UCS). The World Coordinate System always exists in any drawing and cannot be deleted. The user can also create and save multiple User Coordinate Systems to make construction of a particular 3D geometry easier. Only one coordinate system can be active at any one time, either the WCS or one of the user-created UCSs.

The World Coordinate System (WCS) and WCS Icon

The World Coordinate System (WCS) is the default coordinate system in AutoCAD for defining the position of drawing objects in 2D or 3D space. The WCS is always available and cannot be erased or removed, but is deactivated temporarily when utilizing another coordinate system created by the user (UCS). The icon that appears (by default) at the lower-left corner of the Drawing Editor (Fig. 33-9) indicates the orientation of the WCS. The coordinate system icon indicates only X and Y directions, so Z is

assumed to be perpendicular to the XY plane. The icon, whose appearance (*ON, OFF*) is controlled by the *Ucsicon* command, appears for the WCS and for any UCS. However, the letter "W" appears in the icon slightly above the origin only when the WCS is active.

Figure 33-17

The orientation of the WCS with respect to Earth may be different among CAD systems. In AutoCAD the WCS has an architectural orientation such that the XY plane is a horizontal plane with respect to Earth, making Z the height dimension. A 2D drawing (X and Y coordinates only) is thought of as being viewed from above, sometimes called a plan view. Therefore, in a 3D AutoCAD drawing, X is the width dimension, Y is the depth dimension, and Z is height. This default orientation is like viewing a floorplan—from above (Fig. 33-17).

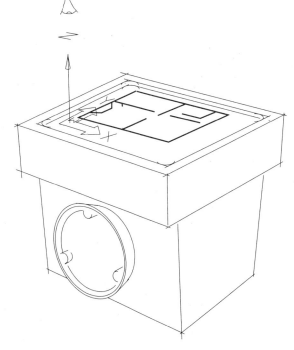

Some CAD systems that have a mechanical engineering orientation align their World Coordinate Systems such that the XY plane is a vertical plane intended for drawing a front view. In other words, some mechanical engineering CAD systems define X as the width dimension, Y as height, and Z as depth.

User Coordinate Systems (UCS) and Icons

There are no User Coordinate Systems that exist as part of the AutoCAD default prototype drawing (ACAD.DWG) as it comes "out of the box." UCSs are created to suit the 3D model when and where they are needed.

Creating geometry is relatively simple when only having to deal with X and Y coordinates, such as in creating a 2D drawing or when creating simple 3D geometry with uniform Z dimensions. However, 3D models containing complex shapes on planes not parallel with the XY plane are good candidates for UCSs (Fig. 33-18).

Figure 33-18 ⎯⎯⎯⎯⎯⎯⎯⎯⎯⎯⎯⎯⎯⎯⎯⎯

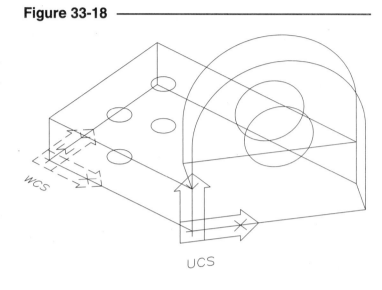

A User Coordinate System is thought of as a construction plane created to simplify creation of geometry on a specific plane or surface of the object. The user creates the UCS, aligning its XY plane with a surface of the object, such as along an inclined plane, with the UCS origin typically at a corner or center of the surface.

The user can then create geometry aligned with that plane by defining only X and Y coordinate values of the current UCS (Fig. 33-19). The *SNAP* and *GRID* automatically align with the current coordinate system, providing *SNAP* points and enhancing visualization of the construction plane. Practically speaking, it is easier in some cases to specify only X and Y coordinates with respect to a specific plane on the object rather than calculating X, Y, and Z values with respect to the World Coordinate System.

Figure 33-19 ⎯⎯⎯⎯⎯⎯⎯⎯⎯⎯⎯⎯⎯⎯⎯⎯

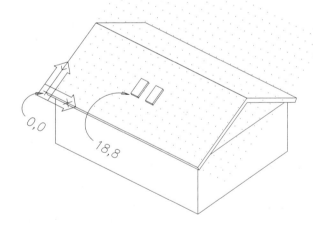

User Coordinate Systems can be created by any of several options of the *UCS* command. Once a UCS has been created, it becomes the current coordinate system. Only one coordinate system can be active; therefore, it is suggested that UCSs be saved (by using the *Save* option of *UCS*) for possible future geometry creation or editing.

When a UCS is created, the icon at the lower-left corner of the screen can be made to automatically align itself with the UCS along with *SNAP* and *GRID*. The letter "W," however, only appears on the icon when the WCS is active (when the WCS is the current coordinate system). When creating 3D geometry, it is recommended that the *ORigin* option of the *Ucsicon* command be used to place the icon always at the origin of the current UCS, rather than in the lower-left corner of the screen. Since the origin of the UCS is typically specified as a corner or center of the construction plane, aligning the Coordinate System Icon with the current origin aids your visualization of the UCS orientation. The Coordinate Display (*COORDS*) in the Status Line always displays only the X and Y values of the current coordinate system, whether it is WCS or UCS.

THE RIGHT-HAND RULE

AutoCAD complies with the right-hand rule for defining the orientation of the X, Y, and Z axes. The right-hand rule states that if your right hand is held partially open, the thumb, first, and middle fingers define positive X, Y, and Z directions, respectively, and positive rotation about any axis is like screwing in a light bulb.

More precisely, if the thumb and first two fingers are held out to be mutually perpendicular, the thumb points in the positive X direction, the first finger points in the positive Y direction, and the middle finger points in the positive Z direction (Fig. 33-20).

In this position, looking toward your hand from the tip of your middle finger is like the default AutoCAD viewing orientation—positive X is to the right, positive Y is up, and positive Z is toward you.

Figure 33-20 ——————————————

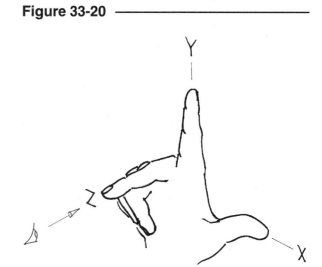

Positive rotation about any axis is <u>counterclockwise looking toward the origin</u>. For example, when you view your right hand, positive rotation about the X axis is as if you look down your thumb toward the hand (origin) and twist your hand counterclockwise (Fig. 33-21).

Figure 33-21 ——————————————

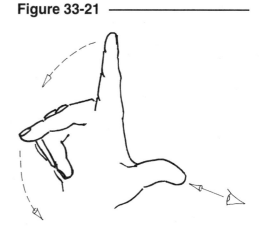

Figure 33-22 shows the Coordinate System Icon in a +90 degree rotation about the X axis (like the previous figure). This orientation is typical for setting up a <u>front</u> view UCS for drawing on a plane parallel with the front surface of an object.

Figure 33-22 ———————

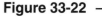

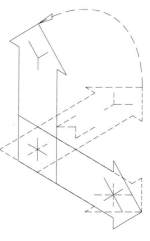

Positive rotation about the Y axis would be as if looking down your first finger toward the hand (origin) and twisting counterclockwise (Fig. 33-23).

Figure 33-23

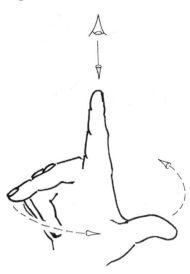

Figure 33-24 illustrates the Coordinate System Icon with a +90 degree rotation about the Y axis (like the previous figure). To avoid confusion in relating this figure to Figure 33-23, consider that the icon is oriented on the XY plane as a horizontal plane in its original (highlighted) position, whereas Figure 33-23 shows the hand in an upright position. (Compare Figures 33-17 and 33-10.)

Figure 33-24

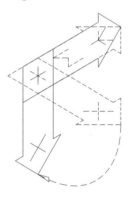

Positive rotation about the Z axis would be as if looking toward your hand from the end of your middle finger and twisting counterclockwise (Fig. 33-25).

Figure 33-25

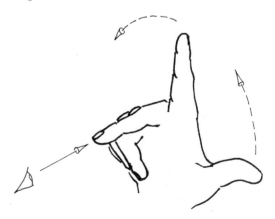

Figure 33-26 shows the Coordinate System Icon with a +90 degree rotation about the Z axis. Again notice the orientation of the icon is horizontal, whereas the hand (Fig. 33-25) is upright.

Figure 33-26

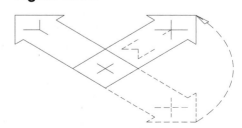

UCS ICON CONTROL

UCSICON

PULL-DOWN MENU	SCREEN MENU	TYPE IN	TABLET MENU
Options *UCS* *Icon or Icon Origin*	*OPTIONS* *UCSicon:*	*UCSICON*	---

The *Ucsicon* command controls the appearance and positioning of the Coordinate System Icon. In order to aid your visualization of the current UCS or the WCS, it is <u>highly</u> recommended that the Coordinate System Icon be turned *ON* and positioned at the *ORigin*.

> Command: **ucsicon**
> ON/OFF/All/Noorigin/ORigin<ON>: **on**
> Command:

This option causes the Coordinate System Icon to appear (Fig. 33-27).

The *Ucsicon* command must be invoked again to use the *ORigin* option.

> Command: **ucsicon**
> ON/OFF/All/Noorigin/ORigin<ON>: **or**
> Command:

Figure 33-27 —————————————

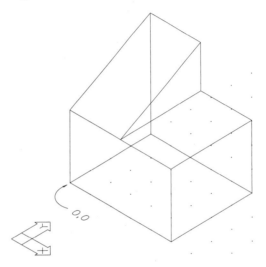

This setting causes the icon to move to the origin of the current coordinate system (Fig. 33-28).

The icon does not always appear at the origin after using some viewing commands like *Vpoint*. This is because *Vpoint* causes a *Zoom Extents*, forcing the geometry against the border of the graphics screen (or viewport) area, which prevents the icon from aligning with the origin. In order to cause the icon to appear at the origin, try using *Zoom* with a **.9X** magnification factor. This action usually brings the geometry slightly in from the border and allows the icon to align itself with the origin.

Figure 33-28 —————————————

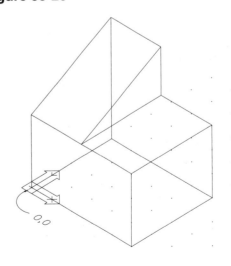

Options of the *Ucsicon* command are:

ON   Turns the Coordinate System Icon on.

OFF   Turns the Coordinate System Icon off.

All   Causes the *Ucsicon* settings to be effective for all viewports.

Noorigin   Causes the icon to appear always in the lower-left corner of the screen, not at the origin.

ORigin   Forces the placement and orientation of the icon to align with the origin of the current coordinate system.

Now that you know the basics of 3D modeling, you will develop your skills in viewing and displaying 3D models (Chapter 34, 3D Viewing and Display). It is imperative that you are able to view objects from different viewpoints in 3D space before you learn to construct them.

CHAPTER EXERCISES

1.   What are the three types of 3D models?

2.   What characterizes each of the three types of 3D models?

3.   What kind of modeling techniques does AutoCAD's solid modeling system use?

4.   What are the five formats for 3D coordinate specification?

5.   Examine the 3D geometry shown in Figure 33-29. Specify the designated coordinates in the specified formats below.

Figure 33-29

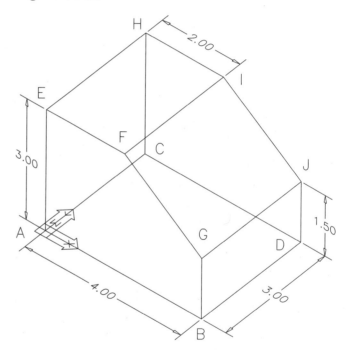

   A.   Give the coordinate of corner D in absolute format.

   B.   Give the coordinate of corner F in absolute format.

   C.   Give the coordinate of corner H in absolute format.

   D.   Give the coordinate of corner J in absolute format.

   E.   What are the coordinates of the line that define edge F-I?

   F.   What are the coordinates of the line that define edge J-I?

   G.   Assume point E is the "last point." Give the coordinates of point I in relative rectangular format.

   H.   Point I is now the last point. Give the coordinates of point J in relative rectangular format.

   I.   Point J is now the last point. Give the coordinates of point A in relative rectangular format.

   J.   What are the coordinates of corner G in cylindrical format (from the origin)?

   K.   If E is the "last point," what are the coordinates of corner C in relative cylindrical format?

Chapter 34

3D VIEWING AND DISPLAY

Chapter Objectives

After completing this chapter you should:

1. be able to recognize a 3D model in wireframe, perspective, *Hide*, *Shade*, and *Render* display representations;
2. be able to use the *3D Viewpoint Presets* to quickly attain the desired view;
3. be able to use *Vpoint* to view a 3D model from various viewpoints;
4. be able to use the *Vector*, *Axes*, and *Rotate* options of *Vpoint*;
5. be able to use *Dview* to specify a *TArget* and *CAmera* point and to generate a perspective with the *Distance* option;
6. be able to use the *PAn*, *Zoom*, *TWist*, *CLip*, and *Hide* options of *Dview*;
7. be able to create several configurations of tiled viewports with the *Vports* command;
8. know how to suppress "hidden lines" of a solid or surface model with the *Hide* command;
9. know how to *Shade* a solid model using four *SHADEDGE* options.

AutoCAD'S 3D VIEWING AND DISPLAY CAPABILITIES

Viewing Commands

These commands allow you to change the direction from which you view a 3D model or otherwise affect the view of the 3D model.

Vpoint   *Vpoint* allows you to change your viewpoint of a 3D model. The object remains stationary while the viewpoint of the observer changes. Three options are provided: *Vector, Axes,* and *Rotate*. There are many useful *3D Viewpoint Presets* available in Release 13.

Plan   The *Plan* command automatically gives the observer a plan (top) view of the object. The plan view can be with respect to the WCS (World Coordinate System) or an existing UCS (User Coordinate System).

Dview   This command allows you to dynamically (interactively) rotate the viewpoint of the observer about 3D objects. *Dview* also allows generation of perspective views.

Zoom   Although *Zoom* operates in 3D just as in 2D, the *Zoom Previous* option restores the previous 3D viewpoint.

View   The *View* command can be used with 3D viewing to *Save* and *Restore* 3D viewpoints.

Vports   The *Vports* command creates tiled viewports. *Vports* does not actually change the viewpoint of the model, but divides the screen into several viewports and allows you to display several viewpoints or sizes of the model on one screen.

Display Commands

In most CAD systems, <u>surface and solid models are shown in a wireframe display</u> during the construction and editing process. It would take too much time for the CAD system to calculate which surfaces obscure other surfaces every time a change is made to the model or viewpoint. Once the model is completed and the desired viewpoint has been attained, these commands can change the appearance of a 3D surface or solid model from the default wireframe representation by displaying the surfaces.

Hide   This command removes normally "hidden" edges and surfaces from a solid or surface model, making it appear as an opaque rather than a transparent object.

Shade   The *Shade* command fills the surfaces with the object's color and calculates light reflection by applying gradient shading (variable gray values) to the surfaces.

Render   *Render* allows you to create and place lights in 3D space, adjust the light intensity, and assign materials (color and reflective qualities) to the surfaces. This is the most sophisticated of the visualization capabilities offered in AutoCAD.

When using the viewing commands *Vpoint, Dview,* and *Plan,* it is important to imagine that the <u>observer moves about the object</u>, rather than imagining that the object rotates. The object and the coordinate system (and icon) always remain <u>stationary</u> and always keep the same orientation with respect to Earth. Since the observer moves and not the geometry, the objects' coordinate values retain their integrity, whereas if the geometry rotated within the coordinate system, all coordinate values of the objects would have to change as the object rotated. The *Vpoint, Dview,* and *Plan* commands change only the viewpoint of the <u>observer</u>.

Figure 34-1

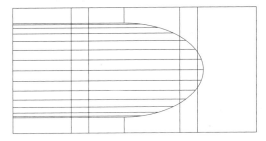

Plan

Figure 34-2

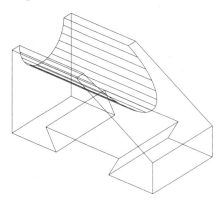

Vpoint (wireframe representation)

Figure 34-3

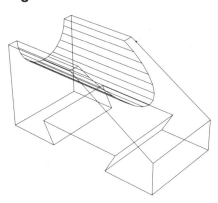

Dview, Distance (perspective)

Figure 34-4

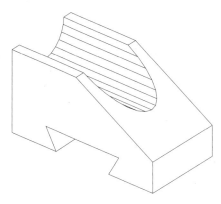

Hide (surface or solid model)

Figure 34-5

Shade (surface or solid model)

Figure 34-6

Render (surface or solid model)

As the 3D viewing commands are discussed, it would be helpful if you opened a 3D drawing that could be used to practice the viewing commands. *Open* the **SEXTANT** drawing located in the ACADR13\COMMON\SAMPLE directory. When the drawing comes up, it is displayed in a paper space viewport. Type *TILEMODE* and change the value to 1. This action causes a display of model space only. Remember to turn *On* the *Ucsicon* and force it to the origin.

3D VIEWING COMMANDS

3D VIEWPOINT PRESETS

PULL-DOWN MENU	SCREEN MENU	TYPE IN	TABLET MENU
View *3D Viewpoint Presets >*	*VIEW* *Vpoint:*	---	---

AutoCAD Release 13 introduced the *3D Viewpoint Presets,* which really speed up the process of attaining common views of 3D objects. All of these options actually use the *Vpoint* command and automatically enter in coordinate values. The other options of *Vpoint* can be used for other particular viewing angles (see *Vpoint* next). These options can be selected from the DOS or Windows *View* pull-down menus (Fig. 34-7).

Figure 34-7

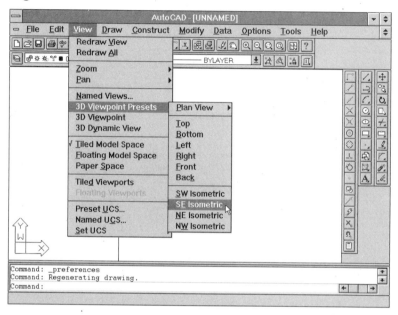

If you are using AutoCAD for Windows, the options are accessible from the Standard toolbar (Fig. 34-8). If you prefer a separate toolbar, one can be invoked from the toolbar list and made to float or dock.

Each of the *3D Viewpoint Presets* options is described next. The SEXTANT drawing is displayed for several viewpoints (the *Hide* command was used in these figures for clarity). It is important to remember that for each view, imagine you are viewing the object from the indicated position in space. The object does not rotate.

Figure 34-8

Top

The object is viewed from the top (Fig 34-9). Selecting this option shows the XY plane from above (the default orientation when you begin a *New* drawing). Notice the position of the WCS icon. This orientation should be used periodically during construction of a 3D model to check for proper alignment of parts.

Figure 34-9

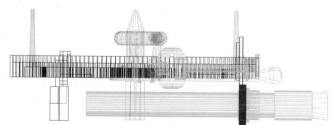

Bottom

This option displays the object as if you are looking up at it from the bottom. AutoCAD uses the *Vpoint* command and automatically enters in coordinates to show this view. The coordinate system icon appears backwards when viewed from the bottom.

Left

This is looking at the object from the left side. Again the *Vpoint* command is used by AutoCAD to give this view.

Right

Imagine looking at the object from the right side (Fig. 34-10). This view is used often as one of the primary views for mechanical part drawing. The coordinate system icon does not appear in this view, but a "broken pencil" is displayed instead (meaning that it is not a good idea to draw on the XY plane from this view).

Figure 34-10

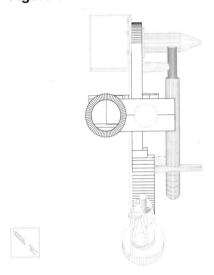

Front

Selecting this option displays the object from the front view. This is a common view that can be used often during the construction process. The front view is usually the "profile" view for mechanical parts (Fig. 34-11).

Figure 34-11

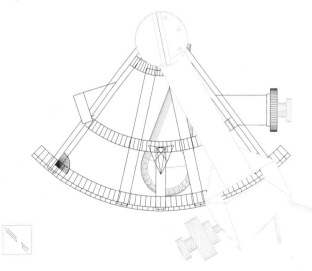

Back

Back displays the object as if the observer is behind the object. Remember that the object does not rotate; the observer moves.

SW Isometric

Isometric views are used more than the "orthographic" views (front, top, right, etc.) for constructing a 3D model. Isometric viewpoints give more information about the model because you can see three dimensions instead of only two dimensions (as in the previously discussed views).

SE Isometric

The southeast isometric is generally the first choice for displaying 3D geometry. If the object is constructed with its base on the XY plane so that X is width, Y is depth, and Z equals height, this orientation shows the front, top, and right sides of the object. Try to use this viewpoint as your principal mode of viewing during construction. Note the orientation of the WCS icon (Fig. 34-12).

NE Isometric

The northeast isometric shows the right side, top, and back (if the object is oriented in the manner described earlier).

NW Isometric

This viewpoint allows the observer to look at the left side, top, and back of the 3D object (Fig. 34-13).

NOTE: The *3D Viewpoint Presets* always display the object (or orient the observer) with respect to the World Coordinate System. For example, the *Top* option always shows the plan view of the WCS XY plane. Even if another coordinate system (UCS) is active, AutoCAD temporarily switches back to the WCS to attain the selected viewpoint.

Figure 34-12

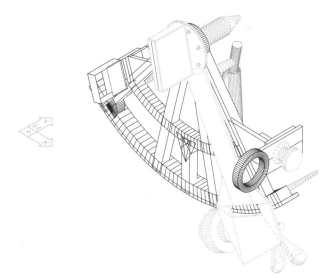

Figure 34-13

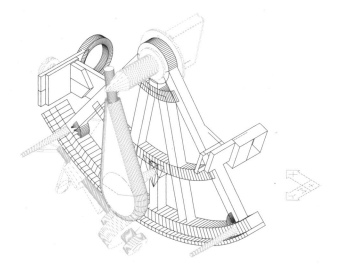

VPOINT

PULL-DOWN MENU	SCREEN MENU	TYPE IN	TABLET MENU
View *3D Viewpoint*	*VIEW* *Vpoint:*	*VPOINT*	*1,K*

The *3D Viewpoint Presets* options actually use the *Vpoint* command to generate the typical views of a 3D object. In some cases, it is necessary to display a 3D object from a direction other than the typical *Vpoints* attained through the presets. For example, an object with 45 degree angled planes or with regular proportions would present a visually confusing description if a perfect isometric view were given (some lines in the view would overlap and angles would align). Instead, a viewpoint slightly off of a pure isometric would show the angled surfaces and regular proportions more clearly. In cases such as these, one of the three options of the *Vpoint* command should be used. The three options are: *Rotate*, *Vector*, and *Axes* (or *Tripod*).

The *Vpoint* command displays a parallel projection rather than a perspective projection. In a parallel projection, all visual rays from the observer to the object are parallel as if the observer were (theoretically) an infinite distance from the object. The resulting display shows all parallel edges of the object as being parallel in the display. This projection differs from a perspective projection, where parts of the object that are farther from the observer appear smaller and parallel edges converge to a point.

Rotate

The name of this option is somewhat misleading because the object is not rotated. The *Rotate* option prompts for two angles in the WCS (by default) which specify a vector indicating the direction of viewing. The two angles are (1) the angle in the XY plane and (2) the angle from the XY plane. The observer is positioned along the vector looking toward the origin.

```
Command: Vpoint
Rotate <View point><0,0,1>: R
Enter angle in XY plane from X axis <270>: 315
Enter angle from XY plane <90>: 35
Command:
```

The first angle is the angle <u>in</u> the XY plane at which the observer is positioned looking toward the origin. This angle is just like specifying an angle in 2D. The second angle is the angle that the observer is positioned <u>up or down from</u> the XY plane. The two angles are given with respect to the WCS (Fig. 34-14).

Angles of **315** and **35** specified in response to the *Rotate* option display an almost <u>perfect isometric</u> viewing angle. An isometric drawing often displays some of the top, front, and right sides of the object. For some regularly proportioned objects, perfect isometric viewing angles can cause visualization difficulties, while a slightly different angle can display the object more clearly. Figure 34-15 and Figure 34-16 display a cube from an almost perfect isometric viewing angle (**315** and **35**) and from a slightly different viewing angle (**310** and **40**), respectively.

Figure 34-14

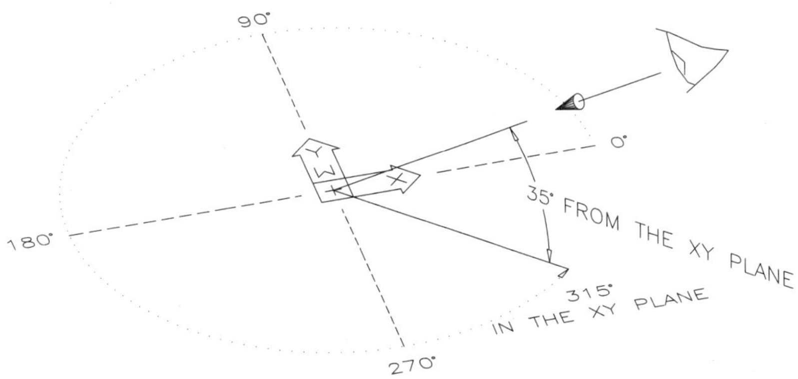

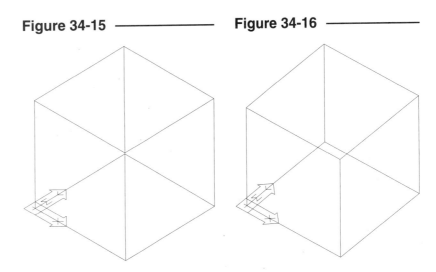

Figure 34-15   **Figure 34-16**

The *Vpoint Rotate* option can be used to display 3D objects from a front, top, or side view. *Rotate* angles for common views are:

Top	270, 90
Front	270, 0
Right side	0,0
Southeast isometric	315, 35.27
Southwest isometric	225, 35.27

Vector

Another option of the *Vpoint* command is to enter X,Y,Z coordinate values. The coordinate values indicate the position in 3D space at which the observer is located. The coordinate values do not specify an absolute position, but rather specify a <u>vector</u> passing through the coordinate position and the origin. In other words, the observer is located at <u>any point along the vector looking toward the origin</u>.

Because the *Vpoint* command generates a parallel projection and since parallel projection does not consider a distance (which is only considered in perspective projection), the magnitude of the coordinate <u>values</u> is of no importance, only the relationship among the values. Values of 1,-1,1 would generate the same display as 2,-2,2.

The command syntax for specifying a perfect isometric viewing angle is as follows:

```
Command: vpoint
Rotate <View point><0,0,1>: 1,-1,1
Command:
```

Coordinates of 1,-1,1 generate a display from a perfect isometric viewing angle.

Figure 34-17 illustrates positioning the observer in space, using coordinates of 1,-1,1. Using *Vpoint* coordinates of 1,-1,1 generates an isometric display similar to *Rotate* angles of 315, 35, or *SE Isometric*.

Figure 34-17 ————————————————————

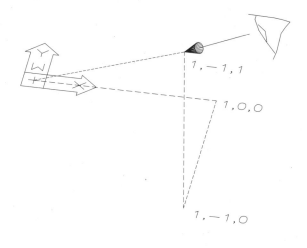

Other typical views of an object can be easily achieved by entering coordinates at the *Vpoint* command. Consider the following coordinate values and the resulting displays:

Coordinates	Display
0,0,1	Top
0,-1,0	Front
1,0,0	Right side
1,-1,1	Southeast isometric
-1,-1,1	Southwest isometric

Axes or Tripod

This option displays a three-pole axes system which rotates dynamically on the screen as the cursor is moved within a "globe." The axes represent the X, Y, and Z axes of the WCS. When you PICK the desired viewing position, the geometry is displayed in that orientation. Because the viewing direction is specified by PICKing a point, it is difficult to specify an exact viewpoint.

The *Axes* option does not appear on the command line as one of the possible *Vpoint* methods. This option must be invoked by pressing Enter at the "Rotate<Viewpoint> <(coordinates)>:" prompt, or by selecting *Axes* or *Tripod* from one of the menus. When the *Axes* method is invoked, the current drawing temporarily disappears and a three-pole axes system appears at the center of the screen. The axes are dynamically rotated by moving the cursor (a small cross) in a small "globe" at the upper right of the screen (Fig. 34-18).

Figure 34-18

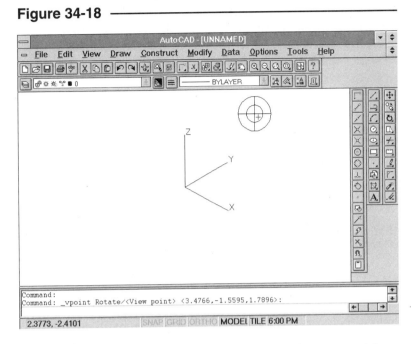

The three-pole axes indicate the orientation of the X, Y, and Z axes for the new *Vpoint*. The center of the "globe" represents the North Pole, so moving the cursor to that location generates a plan, or top, view. The small circle of the globe represents the Equator, so moving the cursor to any location on the Equator generates an elevation view (front, side, back, etc.). The outside circle represents the South Pole, so locating the cursor there shows a bottom view. When you PICK, the axes disappear and the current drawing is displayed from the new viewpoint. The command format for using the *Axes* method is as follows:

```
Command: Vpoint
Rotate <Viewpoint><(current coordinates)>: Enter (axes appear)
PICK (Select desired cursor location.)
Regenerating drawing.  (Current drawing appears showing the new viewpoint.)
```

Using the *Axes* method of *Vpoint* is quick and easy. Because no exact *Vpoint* can be given, it is difficult to achieve the exact *Vpoint* twice. Therefore, if you are working with a complex drawing that requires a <u>specific</u> viewpoint of a 3D model, use another option of *Vpoint* or save the desired *Vpoint* as a named *View*.

Using *Zoom .9X* with *Vpoint*

In the SEXTANT drawing (Figs. 34-9, 34-12, and 34-13), the Coordinate System Icon was previously turned *ON* and forced to appear at the *ORigin*. This action was accomplished by the *Ucsicon* command (see *Ucsicon*, Chapter 33). The icon does not <u>always</u> appear at the origin after using the *Vpoint* command. This is because *Vpoint* causes a *Zoom Extents*, forcing the geometry against the border of the graphics screen area. This sometimes prevents the icon from aligning with the origin since the origin can also be against the border of the graphics screen area. In order to cause the icon to appear at the origin, try using *Zoom* with a .9X magnification factor. This action usually brings the geometry slightly away from the border and allows the icon to "pop" into place at the origin.

Isometric, Dimetric, and Trimetric Viewpoints

Assuming your 3D model is at least partially complete, an <u>axonometric-type</u> of viewpoint can be achieved. This is done by using the *Vpoint* command or the *3D Viewpoint Presets*.

In Chapter 25, Pictorial Drawings, the three types of axonometric drawings (isometric, dimetric, and trimetric) are discussed and illustrated. Keep in mind that a true axonometric drawing is a 2D drawing made to show three sides of an object. This section discusses viewing 3D drawings (wireframe, surface, or solid models) from viewpoints that simulate isometric, dimetric, or trimetric views.

Isometric *Viewpoints*

An isometric view is characterized by having equal angles between all three axes. To achieve an isometric-type of a viewpoint, use the *3D Viewpoint Presets,* as discussed earlier. Alternately, the *Vpoint* command can be used with either the *Rotate* or *Vector* option. Those settings are as follows:

> *Rotate*
>
> Any combination of **45, 135, 225,** or **315** entered as the "angle in the XY plane" and either **35.27** or **-35.27** as the "angle from the XY plane" yield an isometric-type *Vpoint.*

> *Vector*
>
> In response to "Viewpoint <0,0,1>:" enter any combination of positive or negative **1**'s (ones) as coordinate entry to yield some type of an isometric *Vpoint.*

Dimetric *Viewpoints*

A dimetric view is characterized by having equal angles between two of the three axes. A dimetric-type of a viewpoint can be attained most easily by using the *Rotate* option of *Vpoint*. Although there are many possible viewing angles technically considered dimetric, the correct settings for a typical dimetric viewing angle (Fig. 34-19) are as follows:

Figure 34-19

> *Rotate*
>
> In response to the prompts "Enter angle in XY plane from X axis" and "Enter angle from XY plane", enter values of **315** and **15.54**, respectively.

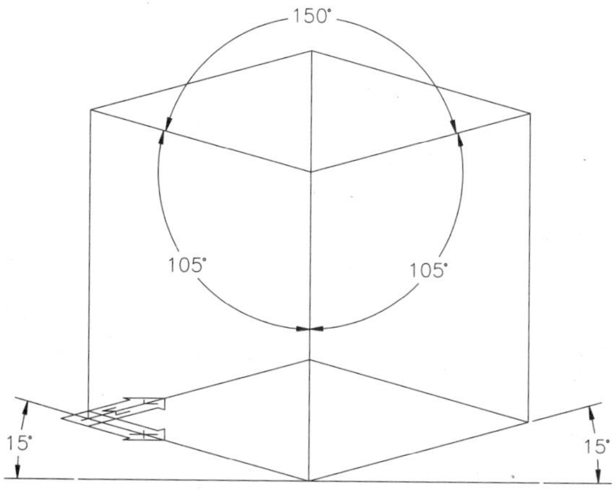

A wireframe model of a cube in dimetric appears in Figure 34-19. This typical dimetric-type orientation has two axes at 15 degrees from horizontal.

You can enter **45, 135, 225,** or **315** as the "angle in the XY plane from the X axis." This assures that two of the three angles between axes are equal. Any value can be entered as the "angle from the XY plane." Technically, this creates a dimetric view.

Trimetric *Viewpoints*

The definition of a trimetric drawing requires that the angles between the axes be underline. Therefore, any viewpoint other that an isometric or dimetric falls into this category. However, a typical combination of angles can be approximated by entering the following values with the *Rotate* option of the *Vpoint* command.

Figure 34-20

> Angle in the XY plane from the X axis: **294.55**
> Angle from the XY plane: **22.7**

These entries result in the viewpoint shown in Figure 34-20. The resulting angles between two of the axes and horizontal are 10 and 40 degrees.

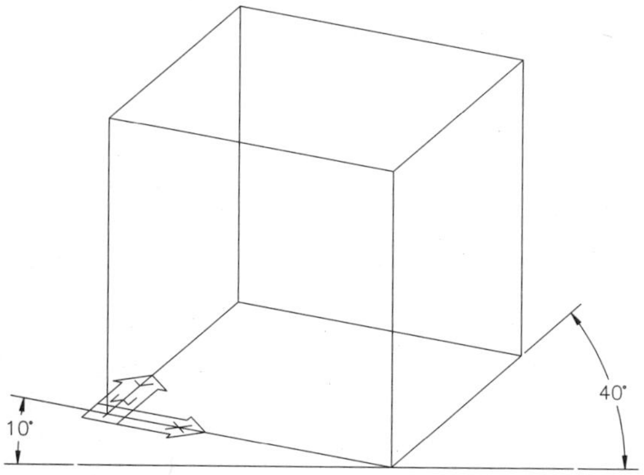

DDVPOINT

PULL-DOWN MENU	SCREEN MENU	TYPE IN	TABLET MENU
---	*VIEW* *Vpoint:* *Ddvpoint:*	*DDVPOINT*	---

The *Ddvpoint* command produces the *Viewpoint Presets* dialogue box (Fig. 34-21). This tool is an interface for attaining viewpoints that could otherwise be attained with the *3D Viewpoint Presets* or the *Vpoint* command.

Ddvpoint serves the same function as the *Rotate* option of *Vpoint*. You can specify angles *From: X Axis* and *From: XY Plane*. Angular values can be entered in the edit boxes, or you can PICK anywhere in the image tiles to specify the angles. PICKing in the enclosed boxes results in a regular angle (e.g., 45, 90, or 10, 30) while PICKing near the sundial-like "hands" results in irregular angles (see pointer in Fig. 34-21). The *Set to Plan View* tile produces a plan view.

Figure 34-21 ——————

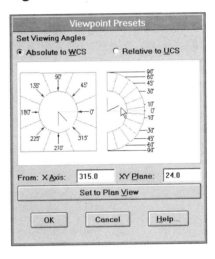

The *3D Viewpoint Presets* are newer and faster for producing standard views and are suggested for most cases. There is one option, however, that *Ddvpoint* offers that is not available by other means. The *Relative to UCS* radio button calculates the viewing angles with respect to the current UCS rather than the WCS. Normally, the viewing angles should be absolute to WCS, but certain situations may require this alternative. Viewing angles relative to the current UCS can produce some surprising viewpoints if you are not completely secure with the model and observer orientation in 3D space.

NOTE: When you use this tool, ensure that the *Absolute to WCS* radio button is checked unless you are sure the specified angles should be applied relative to the current UCS.

PLAN

PULL-DOWN MENU	SCREEN MENU	TYPE IN	TABLET MENU
View *3D Viewpoint Presets >* *Plan View >*	*VIEW* *Plan:*	*PLAN*	2,K

This command is useful to quickly display a plan view of any UCS.

    Command: **plan**
    <Current UCS>/Ucs/World: (**letter**) or **Enter**

Responding by pressing Enter causes AutoCAD to display the plan (top) view of the current UCS. Typing *W* causes the display to show the plan view of the World Coordinate System. The *World* option does <u>not</u> cause the WCS to become the active coordinate system, but only displays its plan view. Invoking the *UCS* option displays the following prompt:

    ?/Name of UCS:

The *?* displays a list of existing UCSs. Entering the name of an existing UCS displays a plan view of that UCS.

ZOOM

The *Zoom* command can be used effectively with 3D models just as with 2D drawings. There are, however, two options of *Zoom* that are particularly applicable to 3D work: *Previous* and *<magnification factor>*.

Previous

This option of *Zoom* restores the previous display. When you are using *3D Viewpoint Presets*, *Vpoint*, *Dview*, and *Plan* for viewing a 3D model, *Zoom Previous* will display the previous viewpoint.

<magnification factor>

When a *Vpoint* is specified, AutoCAD automatically causes a *Zoom Extents* which leaves the 3D model against the borders of the screen. If you are using the *Ucsicon* with the *ORigin* option, invoking a *Zoom .9X* or *.8X* usually allows room for the icon to "pop" back to the origin position.

VIEW

The *View* command can also be used effectively for 3D modeling. When a desirable viewpoint is achieved by the *Vpoint* or *Dview* commands, the viewpoint can be saved with the *Save* option of *View*. *Restoring* the *View* is often easier than using *Vpoint* or *Dview* again.

DVIEW

PULL-DOWN MENU	SCREEN MENU	TYPE IN	TABLET MENU
View *3D Dynamic View*	*VIEW* *Dview:*	DVIEW	*3,J and 3,K*

Dview (Dynamic View) has many capabilities for displaying a 3D model. It can be used like *Vpoint* to specify different viewpoints of an object. *Dview* can be used to change the *TArget* (point to look *at*) and the *CAmera* (point to view *from*) as well as to *Zoom*, *PAn*, and establish clipping planes. *Dview* is commonly used to generate <u>perspective projections</u> of the current drawing.

Because *Dview* dynamically displays rotation or other movement of objects on the screen, you are first given the chance to select objects for this action. If your 3D drawing is large and complex, select only the "framework" of the set of objects; otherwise, select all objects for dynamic action. If too many objects are selected, the dynamic motion is slow and difficult to see.

As an alternative, if a null selection set is used (**Enter** is pressed in response to the "Select objects:" prompt), the DVIEWBLOCK house appears, which is used temporarily for dynamic movement (Fig. 34-22).

Figure 34-22

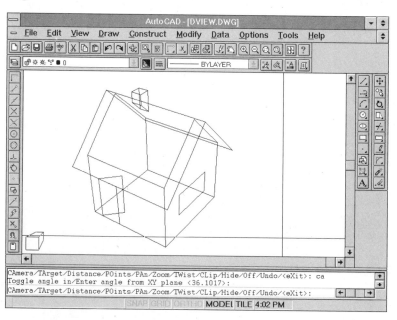

When the dynamic action of the command is completed, the entire 3D object reappears on the screen in the new position. The command syntax for *Dview* is:

Command: **dview**
Select objects: **PICK** or **Enter** (Select objects or press Enter for the DVIEWBLOCK house.)
Select objects: **Enter** (Completes the selection process.)
CAmera/TArget/Distance/POints/PAn/Zoom/TWist/CLip/Hide/Off/ Undo/<eXit>: (**option**)

The *Dview* options are given here in the best order for understanding related concepts.

eXit

This option should be used to save the resulting *Dview* display after using any of the other options to generate the desired view or perspective of the 3D model. *Dview* must be exited before any other AutoCAD commands can be used. Using the *Dview eXit* option saves the current display and returns to the Command: prompt. Remember to enter an *X*, not an *E*.

CAmera

CAmera allows you to specify a point representing the <u>observer's location</u>, like the *Vpoint* command, only *Dview CAmera* is <u>dynamic</u>. Although it appears that the object is being dynamically rotated, imagine that the <u>observer</u> is changing position. When you PICK the desired position, AutoCAD records a coordinate value representing the *CAmera* position. (The *CAmera* position can be specified by entering coordinate values when using the *POints* option rather than the *CAmera* option.)

When the *CAmera* option is selected, the selected objects appear to rotate with movement of the crosshairs. If the crosshairs are positioned at the center of the screen, the objects are viewed from the positive X axis on the XY plane (like *Vpoint Rotate* angles 0, 0). Moving the crosshairs to the upper left displays the objects from a viewing angle similar to a SE Isometric viewpoint (or enter angles of 35, 315) (Fig. 34-23). Vertical cursor movement allows you to view from above or below, and horizontal cursor movement allows you to view from side to side. Since *Dview* displays a wireframe image, it may be difficult to see which "side" of the object you are viewing. The Coordinate System Icon reappears only after PICKing a *CAmera* position.

Figure 34-23

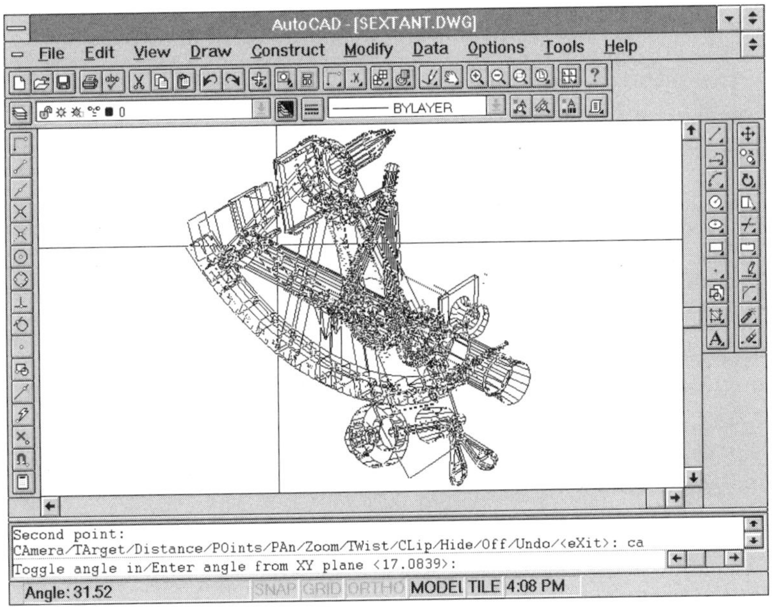

Rather than PICKing a *CAmera* position interactively, you can specify angles in the XY plane and from the XY plane. This method is like the *Vpoint* command, except the angles are given in the <u>reverse order</u>; first specify the angle <u>from</u> the XY plane, then the angle <u>in</u> the XY plane.

Command: **dview**
Select objects: **PICK** or **Enter** (Select objects or press Enter for the DVIEWBLOCK house.)
Select objects: **Enter** (Completes the selection process.)
CAmera/TArget/Distance/POints/PAn/Zoom/TWist/CLip/Hide/Off/ Undo/<eXit>: **ca**
Toggle angle in/Enter angle from XY plane<0.00>: (**value**) or **PICK**
Toggle angle from/Enter angle in XY plane from XY axis<0.00>: (**value**)

TArget

The *TArget* is the point that the *CAmera* (observer position) is focused on (looking toward). For comparison, when using the *Vpoint* command, the observer always looks toward the <u>origin</u>. A default *TArget* is automatically calculated by AutoCAD approximately at the <u>center of the selected geometry</u>. The *TArget* option allows you to specify any position to focus on. This is accomplished with the *TArget* option either interactively or by specifying angles.

Selecting a *TArget* position can also be accomplished by specifying angles <u>from</u> the XY plane and <u>in</u> the XY plane. The current *TArget* angles are always <u>opposite</u> the current *CAmera* angles. Another method for specifying the *TArget* is the *POints* option (see *POints*).

If you use the interactive method, use caution. It is not reasonable to interactively PICK a point in 3D space on a 2D screen. Therefore, <u>use OSNAPs</u> whenever PICKing a the *TArget* position. The *TArget* option is useful for viewing specific areas of a large 3D model such as an architectural plan. For example, the *CAmera* (observer) can be stationed in the middle of a room, and a separate display of each end of the room can be generated by *OSNAPing* to two *TArget*s, one at each end of the room (Fig. 34-24 and 34-25).

Figure 34-24 ——————————

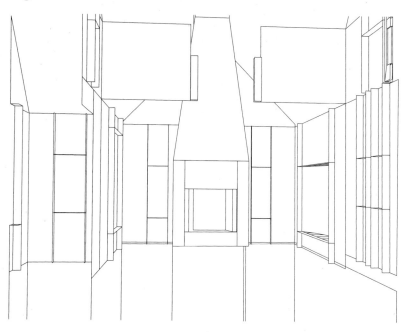

Figure 34-25 ——————————

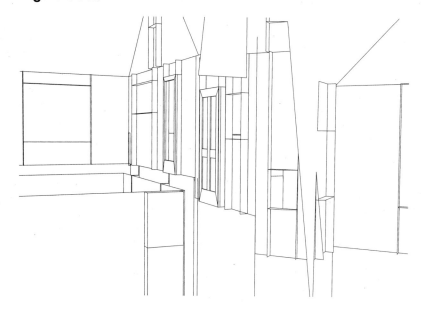

POints

Another method for specifying the *TArget* and/or the *CAmera* is the *POints* option. This option allows specification of the *CAmera* and/or *TArget* points <u>either</u> by specifying coordinate values or by interactive selection. Either use *OSNAPs* to interactively PICK a *CAmera/TArget*, or enter coordinate values to designate an <u>exact</u> *CAmera/TArget* position (assuming you are familiar with the coordinate geometry of the 3D model). The *POints* option can also be used to list the current *TArget* coordinates established automatically by AutoCAD (unless you previously specified a *TArget*).

```
CAmera/TArget/Distance/POints/PAn/Zoom/TWist/CLip/Hide/Off/ Undo/<eXit>: po
Enter target point<(current coordinates)>: (coordinates) or (PICK)
Enter camera point<(current coordinates)>: (coordinates) or (PICK)
```

Distance

The distance option of *Dview* generates <u>perspective</u> projections. *Distance* takes into account the distance that the *CAmera* is from the *TArget*, whereas all other *Dview* options (and *Vpoint* options) use a vector between the *CAmera* and *TArget* to generate <u>parallel</u> projections.

Distance is used to adjust the <u>amount</u> of perspective, not the <u>size</u> of the display. Disregard the size of the display as you use *Distance*. The size of the display can be adjusted <u>later</u> with the *Zoom* option of *Dview*.

Distance uses a slide bar along the top of the screen to allow you to interactively adjust the amount of perspective (distance) for the display. The default value (1X on the slide bar) represents the previously specified distance between the *CAmera* and *TArget* points (Fig. 34-26).

A default distance of 1 is used unless you previously specified the points in response to the *Vpoint* command or entered values in response to the *POints* option of *Dview*. Otherwise, the default distance is usually too small, and the slide bar must be adjusted to a greater value. The *Distance* option can be used repeatedly, or a value entered, in order to generate a distance greater than 16X.

Figure 34-26 ─────────────

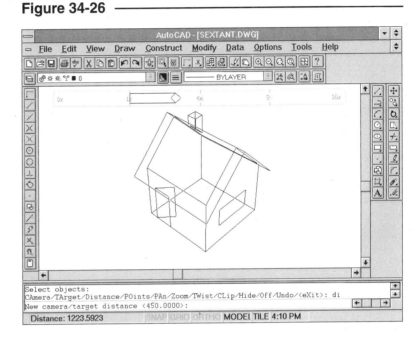

Practice using *Dview Distance* with the SEXTANT drawing to generate a perspective.

Zoom

The *Zoom* option of *Dview* changes the size of the 3D objects with respect to the screen display. <u>Zoom does not affect the amount of perspective</u>. The *Zoom* option should be used after the *Distance* option to adjust the size of the geometry so that it is visible and appropriately sized on the screen. *Distance* often makes the geometry too large or too small so that it must be adjusted with *Zoom*.

Zoom allows you to use the slider bar for interactive adjustment or to enter a camera lens size at the keyboard. The "lens length" represents that of a 35mm camera, with 50mm being the default length (zoom factor of 1X). The *COORDS* display (on the Status Line) dynamically lists the lens length as the slider bar is moved.

    CAmera/TArget/Distance/POints/PAn/Zoom/TWist/CLip/Hide/Off/ Undo/<eXit>: **z**
    Adjust lens length<50.000mm>: **PICK** or (**value**) (Use slider bar or enter a value.)
    CAmera/TArget/Distance/POints/PAn/Zoom/TWist/CLip/Hide/Off/ Undo/<eXit>:

PAn

The *PAn* option of *Dview* operates similarly to the full *PAN* command. *Dview PAn*, however, is <u>dynamic</u> and fully 3D. As you use *Dview PAn*, you can watch the 3D model as it is moved and see the 3D features of the object adjust in real-time as your viewpoint of the object changes. *Dview PAn* allows panning both vertically and horizontally. The command syntax is similar to the full *PAN* command.

    CAmera/TArget/Distance/POints/PAn/Zoom/TWist/CLip/Hide/Off/ Undo/<eXit>: *pa*
    Displacement base point: **PICK** or (**coordinates**) (Usually, *PAn* is used interactively.)
    Second point of displacement: move and **PICK**
    CAmera/TArget/Distance/POints/PAn/Zoom/TWist/CLip/Hide/Off/ Undo/<eXit>:

PAn is generally used to center the geometry on the screen after *Distance* and *Zoom* are used. The three *Dview* options, *Distance, Zoom,* and *PAn,* can be used as a related group of commands to generate perspective projections and to size and center the 3D model appropriately on the screen.

Off

Once a perspective projection of a drawing has been generated (*Dview Distance* used), draw and edit commands <u>cannot</u> be used. Perspective drawings in AutoCAD are intended for display and output only. The drawing <u>can</u> be plotted and rendered, and slides can be made while perspective is in effect. When the perspective mode is active, a small icon representing a perspective box is displayed in the lower-left corner of the screen (see Fig. 34-22).

The *Off* option of *Dview* turns off <u>perspective</u> mode only and allows further editing and drawing with the existing geometry. When *Off* is used, a parallel projection of the geometry is generated, but all other changes to the display of the geometry made with *Dview* remain in effect. Figure 34-27 shows the SEXTANT drawing in parallel projection (*Off* used).

Figure 34-27

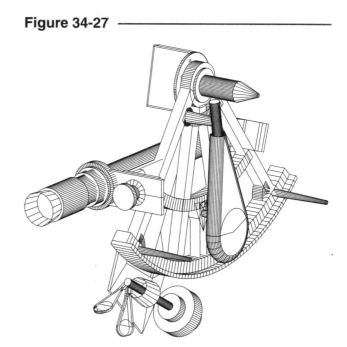

Figure 34-28 shows the SEXTANT in perspective mode (*Distance* used). There is <u>no</u> *On* option of *Dview*; therefore, in order to change back to perspective mode, you must use the *Distance* option again. Fortunately, AutoCAD remembers the previous *Distance* setting, so accepting the defaults generates the previous perspective.

Figure 34-28

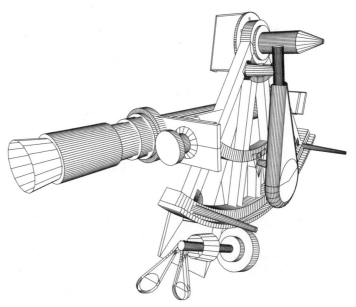

TWist

TWist is used to rotate the 3D geometry on the screen. The 3D model twists (rotates) about the line of sight (between *CAmera* point and *TArget* point). *TWist* operates interactively so you can see the position of the 3D model as you move the cursor. As an alternative, an angle can be entered at the keyboard. The *TWist* angle is measured counterclockwise starting at the 0 degree angle in X positive direction. *TWist* is typically used to tilt the 3D model for a particular effect. The *COORDS* display (on the Status Line) lists the current twist angle interactively. Figure 34-29 displays the SEXTANT drawing during a *TWist*.

Figure 34-29

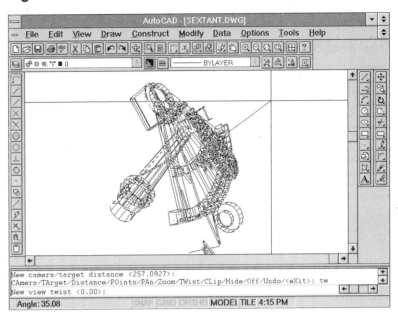

CAmera/TArget/Distance/POints/PAn/Zoom/TWist/CLip/Hide/Off/ Undo/<eXit>: *tw*
New view twist<0.000>: move and **PICK** or (**value**)
CAmera/TArget/Distance/POints/PAn/Zoom/TWist/CLip/Hide/Off/ Undo/<eXit>:

CLip

In many applications, it is desirable to display only a part of a 3D model. For example, an architect may want to display a view of a room in a house but not include the roof in the display.

The *CLip* option of *Dview* is used to establish a *Front* or *Back* clipping plane in a 3D model. Any geometry <u>behind</u> a *Back* clipping plane or any geometry in <u>front</u> of a *Front* clipping plane is <u>not</u> displayed. In the architectural example, a *Front* clipping plane could be established just below the roof of the model. Everything in front of (between the *CAmera* and) the clipping plane would not be included in the resulting display. A view of the room's interior would then be visible from above without being obscured by the roof. Likewise, a *Back* clipping plane could be established in a model to eliminate portions of the model that can distract the viewer's attention from the focus of the display.

The *Front* and *Back* clipping planes are like invisible walls <u>perpendicular to the line of sight</u> between the *CAmera* and the *TArget*. Like the other options of *Dview*, *CLip* is dynamic and uses slider bars, so you can move clipping planes dynamically forward and backward. As an alternative, you can enter a distance from the *TArget* (for *Back* clipping planes) or from the *CAmera* (for *Front* clipping planes). Clipping planes can be used in a parallel or perspective projection. The command syntax for creating a *Front* clipping plane is as follows:

CAmera/TArget/Distance/POints/PAn/Zoom/TWist/CLip/Hide/Off/ Undo/<eXit>: *cl*
Front/Back/<Off>: *f*
Eye/On/Off<Distance from target><1.0000>: move and **PICK** or (**value**)

Establishing a clipping plane distance automatically turns it
On. Off can be used to disable an established clipping plane.
Figure 34-30 displays the SEXTANT drawing in hidden repre-
sentation with a front clipping plane established.

Figure 34-30

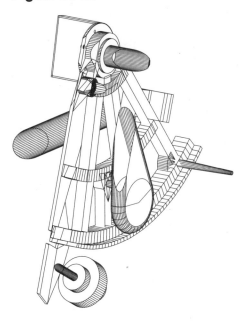

Hide

The *Hide* option of *Dview* removes hidden lines from a surface or solid model for the current screen
display. *Hide* causes all edges and surfaces that would normally be obscured by other surfaces or edges
to be removed so that the model appears solid rather than "see through." There are no options of *Hide*.
Hide remains active only for the current display. If another option of *Dview* is used, or if *Dview* is exited,
hidden lines reappear. Figures 34-31 and 34-32 display the SEXTANT drawing before and after *Hide* has
been performed.

Figure 34-31 ——————————————————   **Figure 34-32** ——————————————————

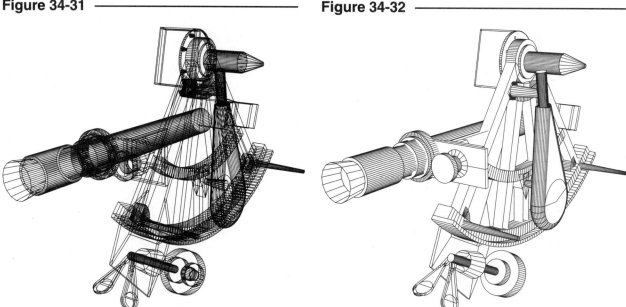

Undo

Undo reverses the effect of the last *Dview* option. Multiple *Undo*s can be performed to step backward through the *Dview* operations.

Saving *Dview* Images

Many *Dview* options such as *Distance*, *Hide*, and *Clip* are intended to be used for display of a 3D model, not necessarily to enhance drawing and editing capabilities. As a matter of fact, you cannot draw in any of these modes. When these *Dview* options are used to generate the desired view of the object, you can plot the display or "save" the image by using *Mslide* or *Render* and *Saveimg* (see Chapter 40).

VPORTS

PULL-DOWN MENU	SCREEN MENU	TYPE IN	TABLET MENU
View *Tiled Viewports >*	*VIEW* *Vports:*	*VPORTS*	*3,R and 5,R*

The *Vports* command allows <u>tiled</u> viewports to be created on the screen. *Vports* allows the screen to be divided into several areas. Tiled viewports are different than paper space viewports. (See Chapter 32, Tiled Viewports and Paper Space Viewports.)

Vports (tiled viewports) are available only when the *TILEMODE* variable is set to **1**. Tiled *Vports* affect <u>only the screen display</u>. The viewport configuration <u>cannot be plotted</u>. If the *Plot* command is used, only the <u>current</u> viewport display is plotted. Figure 34-33 displays the AutoCAD drawing editor after the *Vports* command was used to divide the screen into tiled viewports.

After you select the desired layout, the previous display appears in <u>each</u> of the viewports. For example, if a front view of the 3D model is displayed when you use the *Vports* command or the related dialogue box, the resulting display in each of the viewports would be the front view (see Fig. 34-33). It is

Figure 34-33

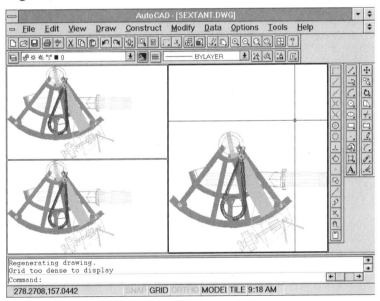

up to you then to use viewing commands (*Vpoint*, *Dview*, *Plan*, *Zoom*, etc.) to specify what viewpoints or areas of the model you want to see in each viewport. There is no automatic viewpoint configuration option with *Vports*.

A popular arrangement of viewpoints for construction and editing of 3D models is a combination of principal views (top, front, side, etc.) and an isometric or other pictorial type of viewpoint (Fig. 34-34). You can use *Zoom* with magnification factors to size the model in each viewport and use *PAn* to "align" the views. There is, however, <u>no automatic method</u> of alignment of views to achieve a true orthogonal projection. You cannot draw or project from one viewport to another.

A viewport is made active by PICKing a point in it. Any <u>display</u> commands (*Zoom*, *Vpoint*, *Redraw*, etc.) and drawing aids (*SNAP, GRID, ORTHO*) used affect only the <u>current viewport</u>. <u>Draw and edit</u> commands that affect the model are potentially apparent in *all* <u>viewports</u> (for every display of the affected part of the model). *Redrawall* and *Regenall* can be used to redraw and regenerate all viewports (See Chapter 32.).

The *Vports* command can be used most effectively when constructing and editing 3D geometry, whereas paper space viewports are generally used when the model is complete and ready to prepare a plot. *Vports* is typi-

Figure 34-34

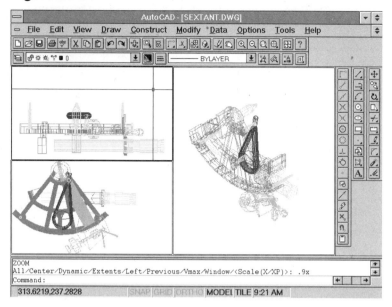

cally used to display a different <u>*Vpoint*</u> of the 3D model in each viewport, as in Figure 34-34. In this way, you can create 3D geometry and view the construction from different *Vpoint*s in order to enhance your visibility in all three dimensions.

3D DISPLAY COMMANDS

Commands that are used for changing the appearance of a surface or solid model in AutoCAD are *Hide*, *Shade*, and *Render*. By default, surface and solid models are shown in wireframe representation in order to speed computing time during construction. As you know, wireframe representation can somewhat hinder your visualization of a model because it presents the model as transparent. To display surfaces and solid models as opaque and to remove the normally obscured edges, *Hide*, *Shade*, or *Render* can be used.

Wireframe models are not affected by these commands since they do not contain surfaces. Wireframe models can only be displayed in wireframe representation.

HIDE

PULL-DOWN MENU	SCREEN MENU	TYPE IN	TABLET MENU
Tools *Hide*	*TOOLS* *Hide:*	*HIDE*	*1,N*

The *Hide* command suppresses the hidden lines (lines that would normally be obscured from view by opaque surfaces) for the current display or viewport.

Command: **hide**

There are no options for the command. The current display may go blank for a period of time depending on the complexity of the model(s); then the new display with hidden lines removed temporarily appears.

The hidden line display is only maintained for the <u>current display</u>. Once a regeneration occurs, the model is displayed in wireframe representation again. You <u>cannot *Plot*</u> the display generated by *Hide*. Instead, use the *Hide Lines* option of the *Plot Configuration* dialogue box (or *Hideplot* option of *Mview* for paper space viewports).

Figure 34-35 displays the SEXTANT model in the default wireframe representation, and Figure 34-36 illustrates the use of *Hide* with the same drawing.

Figure 34-35 ————————————————

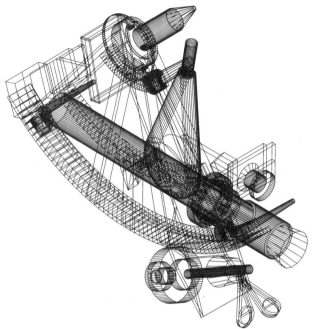

Figure 34-36 ————————————————

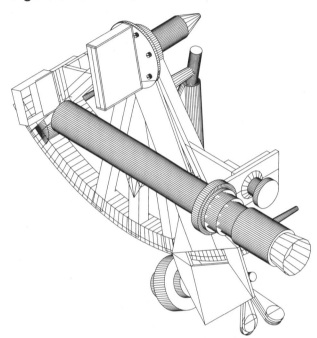

SHADE

PULL-DOWN MENU	SCREEN MENU	TYPE IN	TABLET MENU
Tools *Shade >*	*TOOLS* *SHADE* *Shade:*	*SHADE*	*2,O*

The *Shade* command allows you to shade a surface or solid model in a full-screen display or in the current viewport. A shaded image is present only for the duration of the current display (until a *Regen*) and <u>cannot be plotted</u>. The image can be saved using the *Mslide* command. You can think of the shaded display as being projected in front of the current drawing. You cannot draw or edit the drawing while a shaded image is displayed. If you want to view or edit the original drawing again, use *Regen*.

Shade automatically positions one light in space and sets a default intensity. The light location is always over your right shoulder. Several options allow you to fill the model surfaces and/or edges with the object color.

Two system variables control how the shade appears: *SHADEDGE* and *SHADEDIF*. *SHADEDGE* controls how the surfaces and edges are shaded. The only lighting control is a percentage of diffuse and ambient light adjusted by *SHADEDIF*. Any changes made to the variables are displayed on the <u>next</u> use of the *Shade* command.

If you select *Shade* from the *Tools* pull-down menu, the *SHADEDGE* options appear on a cascading menu (Fig 34-37) and prevent you from having to change the variable setting by other means. By contrast, if you type the *Shade* command, the *SHADEDGE* variable must be previously set. The four possible settings are given next (with the integer values used for typing).

Figure 34-37 ————————————

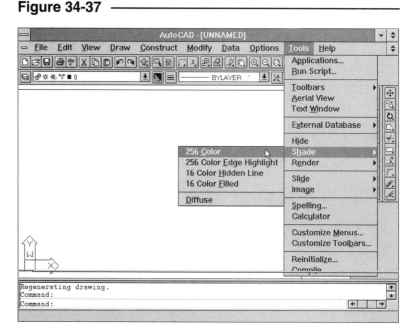

256 Color, (0)

The object surfaces are shaded in gradient values of the object color (Fig. 34-38). The object's visible edges are not highlighted. This option requires 256 color display capabilities of the monitor and video card. (Keep in mind that these figures have been converted to gray scale.)

Figure 34-38 ————————————

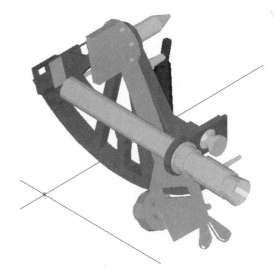

256 Color Edge Highlight, (1)
This option shades the surfaces in gradient values of the object color and highlights the visible edges in the background color (Fig. 34-39). This option also requires a 256 color display.

Figure 34-39

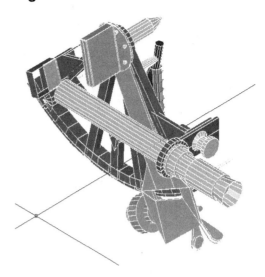

16 Color Hidden Line, (2)
This option simulates hidden line removal. The resulting display is similar to using the *Hide* command. All surfaces are painted in the background color, and the visible edges display the object color (Fig. 34-40). This display works well for monitors with only 16 colors or for monochrome displays.

Figure 34-40

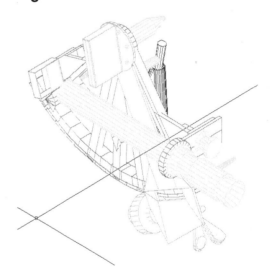

16 Color Filled, (3)
The surfaces are filled solid with the object's color <u>without</u> gradient shading. The visible edges are drawn in the background color (Fig. 34-41). This display also works well for display capabilities of 16 colors and for monochrome displays.

Figure 34-41

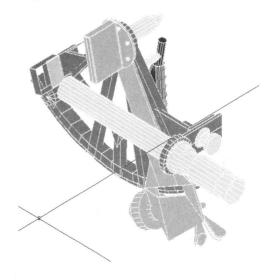

SHADEDIF

When you use 256 color shading, *SHADEDIF* can be used to control the contrast of those values. Two kinds of lights are used with *Shade:* ambient and diffuse. The *SHADEDIF* variable controls the amount of diffuse (reflected) lighting versus the ambient (overall) light. The default setting of 70 specifies 70% diffuse and 30% ambient light. The higher the *SHADEDIF* setting, the greater the reflected light and the greater the contrast of surfaces on the object. The lower the *SHADEDIF* setting, the lower the contrast and the more all surfaces are lighted equally.

RENDER

PULL-DOWN MENU	SCREEN MENU	TYPE IN	TABLET MENU
Tools *Render >* *Render*	*TOOLS* *RENDER* *Render:*	*RENDER*	*1,L*

AutoCAD has sophisticated capabilities for generating a photo-realistic surface or solid object. With these capabilities, you can place lights in 3D space, assign light intensity and color, and attach material finishes to objects in the model. *Render* is the command that causes the current rendering parameters to be applied and generates the rendered display. Although much time and effort can be spent adjusting parameters, *Render* can be used anytime to generate a display using the default parameters. (See Chapter 40, Rendering).

CHAPTER EXERCISES

1. In this exercise, you will use an AutoCAD sample drawing to practice with *3D Viewpoint Presets*. **Open** the **LINKRODS** drawing from the **SAMPLE** directory. (If AutoCAD is installed in the C:\ACADR13 directory, then the sample drawings are found in C:\ACADR13\COMMON\SAMPLE.)

    A. Use any method to generate a *Top* view. *Zoom* with a magnification factor of *.9X*. Examine the view and notice the orientation of the coordinate system icon.

    B. Produce a *Front* view. *Zoom .9X*. Notice the new icon. Remember that you cannot see the XY plane, so it is not a good idea to draw on that plane from this *Vpoint*.

    C. Generate a *Right* view. *Zoom .9X*.

    D. Produce a *Top* view again. Next, view the LINKROD from the *SE Isometric* viewpoint. Notice the position of the WCS Icon.

    E. Finally, generate both a *SW Isometric* and a *NW Isometric*. In each case, examine the WCS icon to orient your viewing direction.

    F. Experiment and practice more if you want. Do <u>not</u> save the drawing.

2. *Open* the **SEXTANT** drawing from the **SAMPLE** directory. When the drawing appears, change **TILEMODE** to **1** (you can type *Tilemode*, then change the setting to 1).

   A. Generate a *SW Isometric* viewpoint. Turn *On* the *Ucsicon* and examine its position. Next, use the *ORigin* option of *Ucsicon*, and examine the new placement. (If the icon does not locate itself at the origin, *Zoom* out until it does.)

   B. Generate a *SE Isometric* viewpoint; then *Pan* to the right until the coordinate system icon appears at the origin.

   C. View the SEXTANT from the *Front*. Next, generate a *Top* view and *Zoom* at *.9X*. Notice the icon.

   D. Now generate the viewpoint that looks into the eyepiece.

   E. Use *Vpoint* with the *Axes* (or *Tripod*) option to view the SEXTANT looking from the southeast direction and from slightly above. (HINT: PICK the lower-right quadrant inside the small circle.) Use *Vpoint* with the *Axes* option to view the SEXTANT looking from the southwest and slightly above. View the SEXTANT again from the back side (PICK on the "equator" at the top of the small circle).

   F. Do <u>not</u> save the drawing.

3. *Open* a *New* drawing to practice with *Dview*. You do not have to assign a name. Immediately invoke the *Dview* command. When prompted to "Select objects:", press **Enter**. The DVIEWBLOCK house should appear as you view from above.

   A. Use the *Zoom* option of *Dview* to make the house smaller by moving the slider bar or entering a scale factor of *.5*. Now use the *CAmera* option. Place the crosshairs slightly to the upper left of center of the screen and PICK. Use the *Hide* option of *Dview* to remove hidden edges.

   B. Next, invoke the *Distance* option. Since the default distance is so small, you can enter a value of **35** or use *Distance* with the slider bar to the maximum position twice. Note the perspective generation. To compare to a parallel projection, use the *Off* option. To turn the perspective on again, use the *Distance* option and accept the default value.

   C. Now use the *CLip* option and set up a *Front* clipping plane. Slide the plane into the house slowly until the roof begins to disappear, then **PICK**. Turn the front clipping plane *Off*; then use a *Back* clipping plane in the same manner. Finally, turn the back clipping plane *Off*.

   D. Use the *TWist* option. *TWist* the house around approximately 90 degrees. Use *TWist* again to bring the house to its normal position.

   E. Experiment more if you like. Do <u>not</u> *Save* the drawing.

4. **Open** the **SEXTANT** drawing. Generate a display similar to that in Figure 34-32. Use *Dview* with the *CAmera*, *Distance*, *Zoom*, *PAn*, and *Hide* options. If you want to save the drawing, make sure you use *SaveAs* to rename the drawing to **SEXTANT2** and to save it <u>in your working directory</u>.

5. **Open** the **LINKRODS** drawing again.

A. Generate a *Top* view. Use *Vports* or the *Tiled Viewports Layout* dialogue box to generate 3 viewports with the large vertical viewport on the *right*. The LINKRODS should appear in a top view in all viewports.

B. Use the *Vpoint* command or *3D Viewpoint Presets* to create a specific *Vpoint* for each viewport, as given below and shown in Figure 34-42. *Zoom* at a *.9X* magnification factor in the top and front viewports.

Upper left	*Top* view
Lower left	*Front* view
Right	*SE Isometric*

Figure 34-42

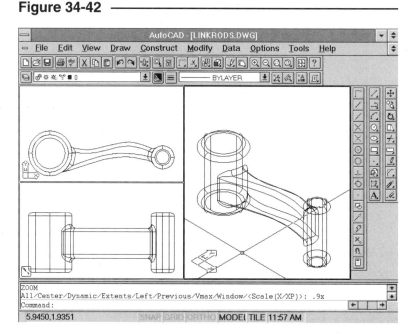

6. **Open** the **SEXTANT** drawing again. Change the *TILEMODE* setting to *1*.

A. Use the *Hide* command to remove hidden edges.

B. *Shade* the sextant with each of the *SHADEDGE* options:

256 Color
256 Color Edge Highlight
16 Color Hidden Line
16 Color Filled

C. Next, use *Vports* or the *Tiled Viewports Layout* dialogue box to generate 2 *Vertical* viewports. *Zoom Extents*; then *Zoom* at *.9X* in each viewport. In the left viewport, use *Hide*, and in the right *Shade* the sextant with the most realistic option. The drawing should look similar to that in Figure 34-43.

Figure 34-43

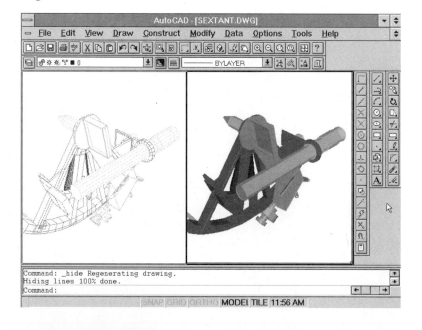

7. In this exercise, you will create a simple solid model that you can use for practicing creation of User Coordinate Systems in Chapter 35. You will also get an introduction to some of the solid modeling construction techniques discussed in Chapter 37.

A. Begin a *New* drawing and name it *SOLID1*. Turn *On* the *Ucsicon* and force it to appear at the *ORigin*.

B. Type *Box* to create a solid box. When the prompts appear, use **0,0,0** as the "Corner of box." Next, use the *Length* option and give dimensions for the Length, Width, and Height as **5, 4,** and **3**. A rectangle should appear. Change your viewpoint to *SE Isometric* to view the box. *Zoom* with a magnification factor of *.6X.*

Figure 34-44 ———————————

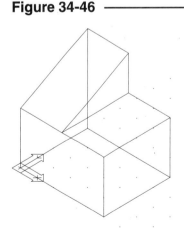

C. Type the *Wedge* command. When the prompts appear, use **0,0,0** as the "Corner of wedge." Again use the *Length* option and give the dimensions of **4, 2.5,** and **2** for *Length, Width,* and *Height*. Your solid model should appear as that in Figure 34-44.

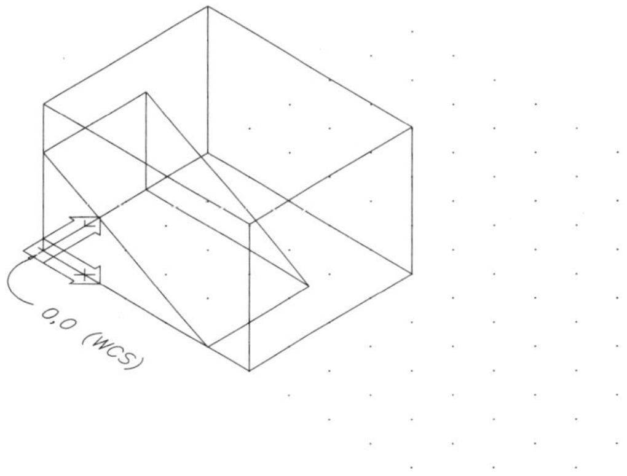

D. Use *Rotate* and select <u>only the wedge</u>. Use **0,0** as the "Base point" and enter **-90** as the "Rotation angle." The model should appear as Figure 34-45.

Figure 34-45 ———————————

E. Now use *Move* and select the wedge for moving. Use **0,0** as the "Base point" and enter **0,4,3** as the "Second point of displacement."

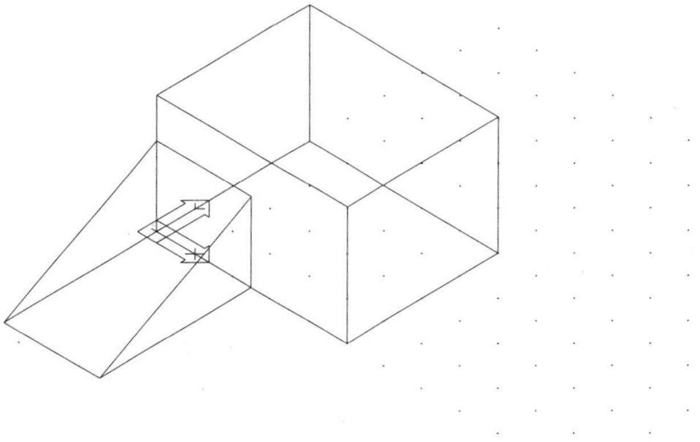

F. Finally, type *Union*. When prompted to "Select objects," PICK <u>both</u> the wedge and the box. The finished solid model should look like Figure 34-46. *Save* the drawing.

Figure 34-46 ———————————

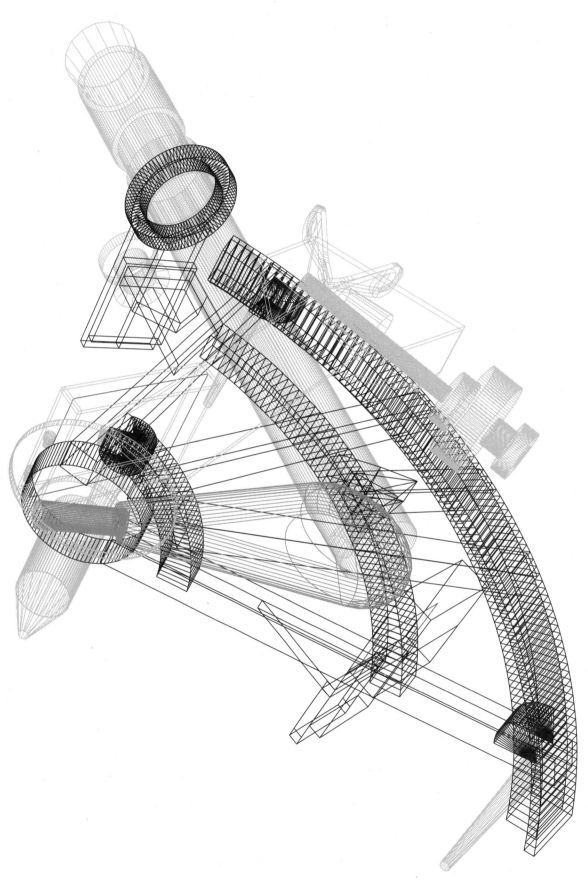

SEXTANT.DWG Courtesy of Autodesk, Inc.

Chapter 35

USER COORDINATE SYSTEMS

Chapter Objectives

After completing this chapter you should:

1. know how to create, *Save*, *Restore*, and *Delete* User Coordinate Systems;

2. be able to create UCSs by the *Origin*, *Zaxis*, *3point*, *Object*, *View*, *X*, *Y*, or *Z* methods;

3. know how to create UCSs using the *UCS Orientation* dialogue box;

4. be able to use the *UCSFOL-LOW* variable to automatically display a plan view of new UCSs.

BASICS

There are no User Coordinate Systems that exist as part of the AutoCAD default prototype drawing (ACAD.DWG) as it comes "out of the box." UCSs are created to simplify construction of the 3D model when and where they are needed.

When you create a multiview or other 2D drawing, creating geometry is relatively simple since you only have to deal with X and Y coordinates. However, when you create 3D models, you usually have to consider the Z coordinates, which makes the construction process more complex. Constructing some geometries in 3D can be very difficult, especially when the objects have shapes on planes not parallel with, or perpendicular to, the XY plane or not aligned with the WCS (World Coordinate System).

UCSs are created when needed to simplify the construction process of a 3D object. For example, imagine specifying the coordinates for the centers of the cylindrical shapes in Figure 35-1, using only world coordinates. Instead, if a UCS were created on the face of the object containing the cylinders (the inclined plane), the construction process would be much simpler. To draw on the new UCS, only the X and Y coordinates (of the UCS) would be needed to specify the centers, since anything drawn on that plane has a Z value of 0. The Coordinate Display (*COORDS*) in the Status Line always displays only the X and Y values of the <u>current</u> coordinate system, whether it is the WCS or a UCS.

Figure 35-1

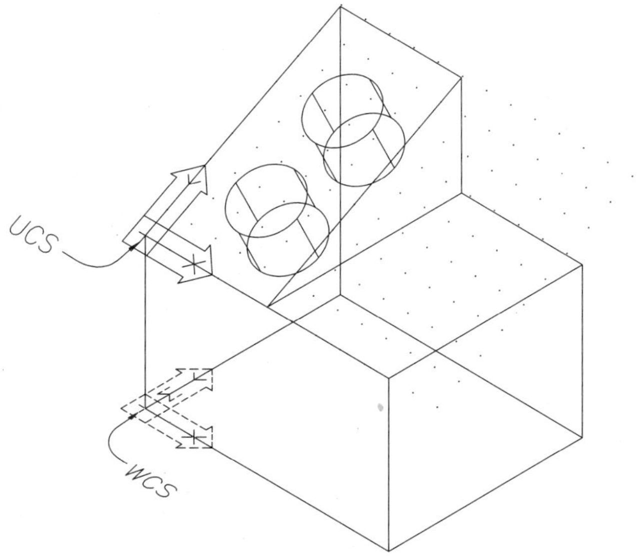

Generally, you would create a UCS aligning its XY plane with a surface of the object, such as along an inclined plane, with the UCS origin typically at a corner or center of the surface. Any coordinates that you specify (in any format) are assumed to be user coordinates (coordinates that lie in or align with the current UCS). Even when you PICK points interactively, they fall on the XY plane of the current UCS. The *SNAP* and *GRID* automatically align with the current coordinate system XY plane, providing *SNAP* points and enhancing your visualization of the construction plane.

UCS COMMANDS AND VARIABLES

User Coordinate Systems are created by using any of several options of the *UCS* command. Once a UCS has been created, it becomes the current coordinate system. <u>Only one coordinate system can be active</u>. If you switch among several UCS's and the WCS, you should save the UCSs when you create them (by using the *Save* option of *UCS*) and restore them at a later time (using the *Restore* option).

When creating 3D models, it is recommended that the <u>*ORigin*</u> option of the <u>*Ucsicon*</u> command <u>be used</u> to place the icon always at the origin of the current UCS, rather than in the lower-left corner of the screen. Since the origin of the UCS is typically specified as a corner or center of the construction plane, aligning the Coordinate System Icon with the current origin aids the user's visualization of the UCS orientation.

UCS

PULL-DOWN MENU	SCREEN MENU	TYPE IN	TABLET MENU
View *Set UCS >*	*VIEW* *UCS:*	*UCS*	*4,J or 4,K*

The *UCS* command allows you to create, save, restore, and delete UCSs. There are many possibilities for creating UCS's to align with any geometry.

Command: **ucs**
Origin/ZAxis/3point/Object/View/X/Y/Z/Previous/Save/Restore /Delete/?<World>: (**letter**) (Enter
capitalized letters of desired option.)

The *UCS* command options are available through the *View* pull-down menu. This location of the *UCS* command, however, is misleading in that <u>UCSs have no association with views or viewpoints.</u> Creating or restoring a UCS <u>does not</u> change the view (unless the *UCSFOLLOW* variable is *On*), and <u>changing a viewpoint never changes the UCS.</u>

Figure 35-2

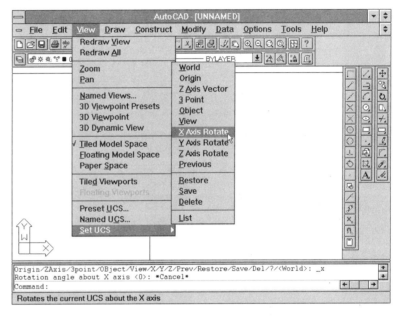

If you are using AutoCAD for Windows, the *UCS* group is available on the Standard toolbar (Fig. 35-3). If you prefer, a separate *UCS* toolbar can be brought on the screen and made to float or dock.

When you create UCSs, AutoCAD prompts for points. These points can be entered as coordinate values at the keyboard, or points on existing geometry can be PICKed. *OSNAP*s should be used to PICK points in 3D space. Understanding the right-hand rule is imperative when creating UCSs.

(If you completed the SOLID1 drawing from Chapter 34, Exercise 7, *Open* the drawing and try the *UCS* options as you read along through this chapter.)

Figure 35-3

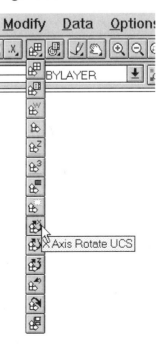

Origin

This option defines a new UCS by specifying a new X,Y,Z location for the origin. The <u>orientation</u> of the UCS (direction of X,Y,Z axes) remains the same; only the location of the origin changes. AutoCAD prompts:

Origin point<0,0,0>:

Coordinates may be specified in any format or PICKed (use *OSNAPs* in 3D space).

Figure 35-4

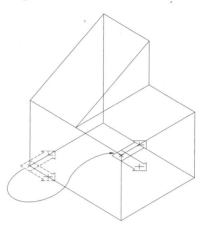

ZAxis

You can define a new UCS by specifying an <u>origin</u> and a direction for the <u>Z axis</u>. Only the two points are needed. The X <u>or</u> Y axis generally remains parallel with the current UCS XY plane, depending on how the Z axis is tilted. AutoCAD prompts:

Origin point <0,0,0>:
Point on positive portion of the Z axis <default>:

Figure 35-5

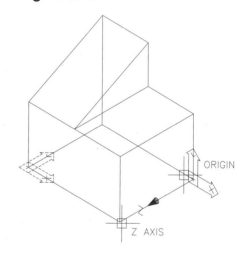

3point

The new UCS is defined by (1) the <u>origin</u>, (2) a point on the <u>X axis</u> (positive direction), and (3) a point on the <u>Y axis</u> (positive direction) or <u>XY plane</u> (positive Y). This is the most universal of all the UCS options (works for most cases). It helps if you have geometry established that can be PICKed with *OSNAP* to establish the points. The prompts are:

Origin point <0,0,0>:
Point on positive portion of the X axis <default>:
Point on positive-Y portion of the UCS XY plane <default>:

Figure 35-6

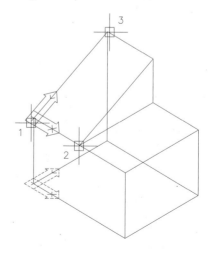

Object

This option creates a new UCS aligned with the selected object. The orientation of the new UCS is based on the type of object selected and the XY plane that was current when the object was created. This option is intended for use primarily with <u>wireframe</u> or <u>surface</u> model objects.

AutoCAD prompts:

Figure 35-7

> Select object to align UCS:

The following list gives the orientation of the UCS using the *Object* option for each type of object.

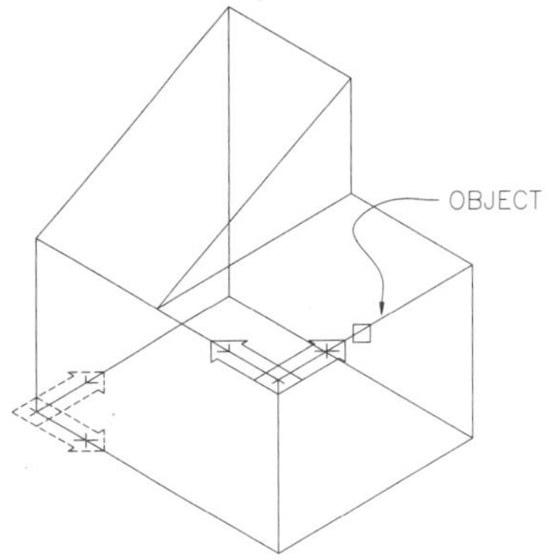

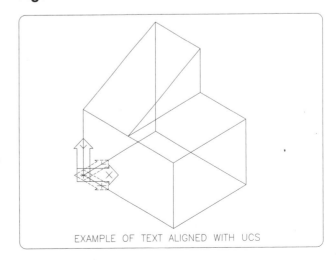

Object	Orientation of New UCS
Line	The end nearest the point PICKed becomes the new UCS origin. The new X axis aligns with the *Line*. The XY plane keeps the same orientation as the previous UCS.
Circle	The center becomes the new UCS origin with the X axis passing through the PICK point.
Arc	The center becomes the new UCS origin. The X axis passes through the endpoint of the *Arc* that is closest to the pick point.
Point	The new UCS origin is at the *Point*. The X axis is derived by an arbitrary but consistent "arbitrary axis algorithm." (See the *AutoCAD Customization Manual*.)
2D *Pline*	The *Pline* start point is the new UCS origin with the X axis extending from the start point to the next vertex.
Solid	The first point of the *Solid* determines the new UCS origin. The new X axis lies along the line between the first two points.
Dimension	The new UCS origin is the middle point of the dimension text. The direction of the new X axis is parallel to the X axis of the UCS that was current when the dimension was drawn.
3Dface	The new UCS origin is the first point of the *3Dface*, the X axis aligns with the first two points, and the Y positive side is on that of the first and fourth points. (See Chapter 39, Surface Modeling, *3Dface*.)
Text, Insertion, or Attribute	The new UCS origin is the insertion point of the object, while the new X axis is defined by the rotation of the object around its extrusion direction. Thus, the object you PICK to establish a new UCS will have a rotation angle of 0 in the new UCS.

View

Figure 35-8

This *UCS* option creates a UCS parallel with the screen (perpendicular to the viewing angle). The UCS <u>origin</u> remains unchanged. This option is handy if you wish to use the current viewpoint and include a border, title, or other annotation. There are no options or prompts.

EXAMPLE OF TEXT ALIGNED WITH UCS

X   Y   Z

Each of these options rotates the UCS about the indicated axis according to the right-hand rule. The command prompt is:

Rotation angle about *n* axis:

Figure 35-9

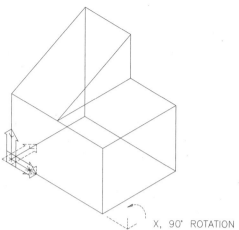

X, 90° ROTATION

The angle can be entered by PICKing two points or by entering a value. This option can be repeated or combined with other options to achieve the desired location of the UCS. It is imperative that the right-hand rule is followed when rotating the UCS about an axis (see Chapter 33).

Previous

Use this option to restore the previous UCS. AutoCAD remembers the ten previous UCSs used. *Previous* can be used repeatedly to step back through the UCSs.

Save

Invoking this option prompts for a name for saving the current UCS. Up to 31 characters can be used in the name. Entering a name causes AutoCAD to save the current UCS. The *?* option and the *Dducs* command list all previously saved UCSs.

Restore

Any *Saved* UCS can be restored with this option. The *Restored* UCS becomes the <u>current</u> UCS. The *?* option and the *Dducs* command list the previously saved UCSs.

Delete

You can remove a *Saved* UCS with this option. Entering the name of an existing UCS causes AutoCAD to delete it.

?

This option lists the origin and X, Y, and Z axes for any saved UCS you specify.

World

Using this option makes the WCS (World Coordinate System) the current coordinate system.

It is important to remember that changing to another UCS does <u>not</u> change the display (unless *UCSFOLLOW* is activated). Only <u>one</u> coordinate system (WCS or a UCS) can be current at a time. If you are using viewports, several *Viewpoints* can be displayed, but only <u>one</u> UCS can be current and it appears in all viewports.

DDUCSP

PULL-DOWN MENU	SCREEN MENU	TYPE IN	TABLET MENU
View *Preset UCS...*	*VIEW* *DDucsp:*	*DDUCSP*	*5,K*

If you prefer to do things a bit more automatically, the *Dducsp* command (UCS Presets) lets you set up new UCSs simply by selecting an image tile in the *UCS Orientation* dialogue box (Fig. 35-10). These options result in the same functions accomplished by the *UCS* command.

The images displayed in this dialogue box are somewhat misleading. The selections <u>do not necessarily reposition the UCS on the face of the object</u> indicated in the images, but <u>rotate the coordinate system to the new orientation</u>.

Figure 35-10 ————————

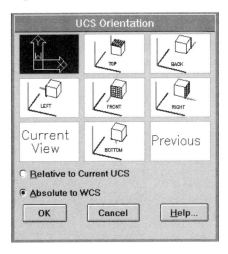

For example, if the current coordinate system were the WCS, selecting the *Right* option would rotate the UCS to the correct orientation <u>keeping the same origin</u>, but would not move the UCS to the right-most face of the object (Fig. 35-11).

Figure 35-11 ——————————————————

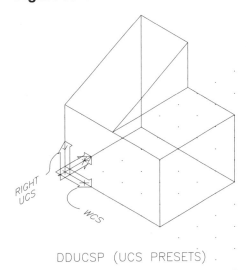

DDUCSP (UCS PRESETS)

NOTE: Always check the settings of the two buttons near the bottom of the dialogue box. <u>Generally, UCSs are established *Absolute to the WCS*</u>. Be careful when creating a UCS *Relative to the Current UCS*— you may get some unexpected results.

DDUCS

PULL-DOWN MENU	SCREEN MENU	TYPE IN	TABLET MENU
View *Named UCS...*	VIEW DDucs:	*DDUCS*	5, J

The *Dducs* command invokes the *UCS Control* dialogue box (Fig. 35-12). By using this tool, named UCS's (those that have been previously *Saved*) can be made the current UCS by highlighting the desired name from the list and checking the *Current* tile. This performs the same action as *UCS, Restore*. Named UCS's can also be *Renamed*, *Deleted*, or *Listed* from this dialogue box.

Figure 35-12 ────────────

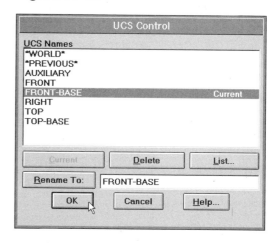

UCSFOLLOW

PULL-DOWN MENU	SCREEN MENU	TYPE IN	TABLET MENU
Options *UCS >* *Follow*	OPTIONS UCSfoll:	*UCSFOLLOW*	---

The *UCSFOLLOW* system variable, if set to 1 (*On*), causes the <u>plan view</u> of a UCS to be displayed automatically <u>when a UCS is made current</u>. The default setting for *UCSFOLLOW* is 0 (*Off*). *UCSFOLLOW* can be set separately for each viewport.

For example, consider the case shown in Figure 35-13. Two tiled viewports (*Vports*) are being used, and the *UCSFOLLOW* variable is turned *On* for the <u>left</u> viewport only. Notice that a UCS created on the inclined surface is current. The left viewport shows the plan view of this UCS automatically, while the right viewport shows the model in the same orientation no matter what coordinate system is current. If the WCS were made active, the right viewport would keep the same viewpoint, while the left would automatically show a plan view when the change was made.

Figure 35-13 ────────────

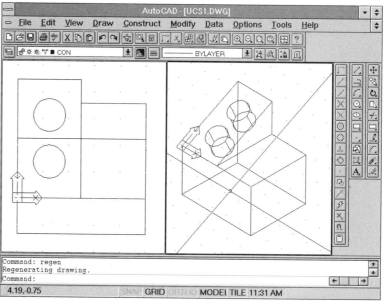

NOTE: When *UCSFOLLOW* is set to 1, the display does not change <u>until</u> a new UCS is created or restored.

UCSFOLLOW is the only variable or command that directly links a change in UCS to an automatic change in viewpoint. Normally, changing to a different current UCS does not change the display, except in this case (when *UCSFOLLOW* is set to 1). On the other hand, making a change in viewpoint <u>never</u> causes a change in UCS.

3D Basics and Wireframe, Surface, and Solid Modeling

Now that you understand the basics of 3D modeling, you are ready to progress to construction and editing of wireframe, surface, and solid models. Almost all the topics discussed in Chapters 33, 34, and 35 are applicable to <u>all types</u> of 3D modeling.

In terms of a complete and accurate description of an actual object, the three types of models range from wireframe to surface to solid. The next several chapters, however, present the modeling types in a different order: wireframe models, solid models, and surface models. This is a logical order from simple to complex with respect to command functions and construction and editing complexity. That is to say, wireframe construction and editing is the simplest, and surface construction and editing is the most tedious and complex.

CHAPTER EXERCISES

1. Using the model in Figure 35-14, assume a UCS was created by rotating about the X axis 90 degrees from the existing orientation (World Coordinate System).

   A. What are the absolute coordinates of corner F?

   B. What are the absolute coordinates of corner H?

   C. What are the absolute coordinates of corner J?

2. Using the model in Figure 35-14, assume a UCS was created by rotating about the X axis 90 degrees from the existing orientation (WCS) and then rotating 90 degrees about the (new) Y.

   A. What are the absolute coordinates of corner F?

   B. What are the absolute coordinates of corner H?

   C. What are the absolute coordinates of corner J?

Figure 35-14 ─────────────

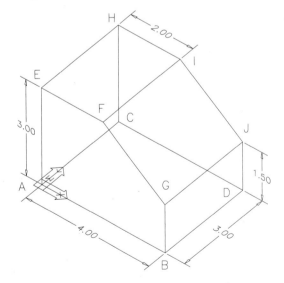

3.   *Open* the **SOLID1** drawing that you created in Chapter 34, Exercise 7. View the object from a *SE Isometric Vpoint*. Make sure that the *UCSicon* is *On* and set to the *ORigin*.

Figure 35-15

A.   Create a *UCS* with a vertical XY plane on the front surface of the model as shown in Figure 35-15. *Save* the UCS as **FRONT**.

B.   Change the coordinate system back to the *World*. Now, create a *UCS* with the XY plane on the top horizontal surface and with the orientation as shown in Figure 35-15 as TOP1. *Save* the UCS as **TOP1**.

C.   Change the coordinate system back to the *World*. Next, create the *UCS* shown in the figure as TOP2. *Save* the UCS under the name **TOP2**.

D.   Activate the *WCS* again. Create and *Save* the **RIGHT** UCS.

E.   Use *SaveAs* and change the drawing name to **SOLIDUCS**.

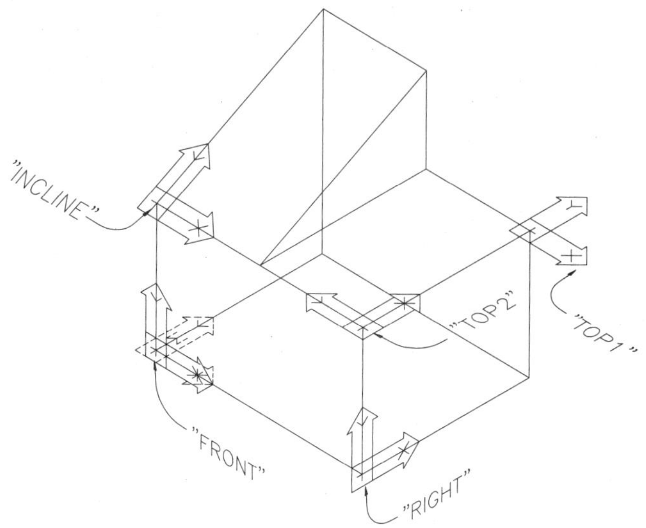

4.   Using the same drawing, make the *WCS* the active coordinate system. In this exercise, you will create a model and screen display like that in Figure 35-13.

A.   Create **2** *Vertical* tiled viewports. Use *Zoom* in each viewport if needed to display the model at an appropriate size. Make sure the *UCSicon* appears at the origin. Activate the <u>left</u> viewport. Set *UCSFOLLOW On* in that viewport only. (The change in display will not occur until the next change in UCS setting.)

B.   Use the right viewport to create the **INCLINE UCS**, as shown in Figure 35-15. *Regenall* to display the new viewpoint.

C.   In either viewport create two cylinders as follows: Type *cylinder*; specify **1.25,1** as the *center*, **.5** as the *radius*, and **-1** (negative 1) as the *height*. The new cylinder should appear in both viewports.

D.   Use *Copy* to create the second cylinder. Specify the existing center as the "Basepoint, of displacement." To specify the basepoint, you can enter coordinates of **1.25,1** or **PICK** the center with *Osnap*. Make the copy **1.5** units above the original (in a Y direction). Again, you can PICK interactively or use relative coordinates to specify the second point of displacement.

E.   Use *SaveAs* and assign the name **SOLID2**.

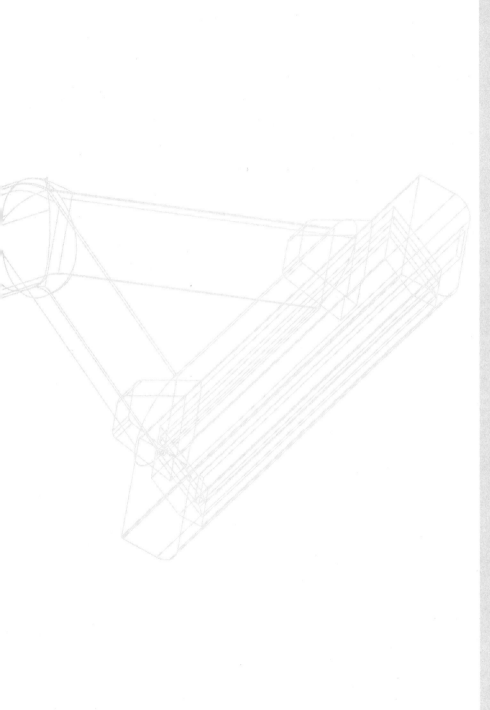

Chapter 36
WIREFRAME MODELING

Chapter Objectives

After completing this chapter you should:

1. understand how common 2D draw and edit commands are used to create 3D wireframe models;

2. gain experience in specification of 3D coordinates;

3. gain experience with 3D viewing commands;

4. be able to apply point filters to 3D model construction;

5. gain fundamental experience with creating, *Saving*, and *Restoring* User Coordinate Systems;

6. be able to create, *Save*, and *Restore* tiled viewport configurations;

7. be able to manipulate the Coordinate System Icon.

BASICS

Wireframe models are created in AutoCAD by using common draw commands that create 2D objects. When draw commands are used with X ,Y, and Z coordinate specification, geometry is created in 3D space. A true wireframe model is simply a combination of 2D elements in 3D space.

A *Line*, for example, can be drawn in 3D space by specifying 3D coordinates in response to the "From point:" and "to point:" prompts (Fig. 36-1).

> Command: *line*
> From point: **3,2,0**
> to point: **8,2,6**
> Command:

The same procedure of entering 3D coordinate values can be applied to other draw commands such as *Arc, Circle,* etc. These 2D objects are combined in 3D space to create wireframe models. There are no draw commands that are used <u>specifically</u> for creating 3D wireframe geometry (with the exception of *3Dpoly*). It is the use of 3D viewing and display, User Coordinate Systems (UCS), and 3D coordinate entry that are the principal features of AutoCAD, along with the usual 2D object creation commands, that allow you to create wireframe models. Specification of 3D coordinate values (Chapter 33), 3D display and viewing (Chapter 34), and the use of UCSs (Chapter 35) aid in creating wireframe models as well as surface and solid models. The *3Dpoly* command is discussed at the end of this chapter.

Figure 36-1

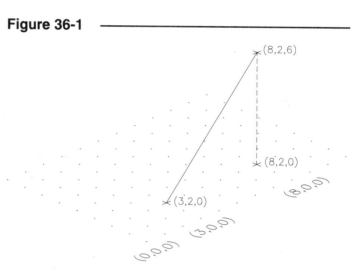

WIREFRAME MODELING TUTORIAL

Because you are experienced in 2D geometry creation, it is efficient to apply your experience, combined with the concepts already given in the previous three chapters, to create a wireframe model in order to learn fundamental modeling techniques. Using the tutorial in this chapter, you create the wireframe model of the Stop Plate shown in Figure 36-2 in a step-by-step fashion. The Wireframe Modeling Tutorial employs the following fundamental modeling techniques:

> 3D coordinate entry
> Point filters
> *Vports*
> An introduction to User Coordinate Systems
> *Ucsicon* manipulation

Figure 36-2

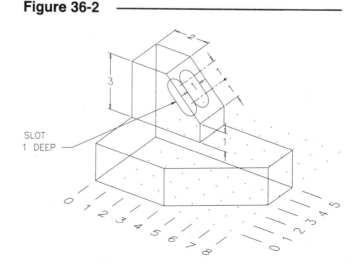

It is suggested that you follow along and work on your computer as you read through the pages of this tutorial. The Wireframe Modeling Tutorial has 22 steps. The steps give written instructions with illustrations.

Additional hints, such as explicit coordinate values and menus that can be used to access the commands, are given on pages immediately following the tutorial (titled Hints). Try to complete the wireframe modeling tutorial without looking at the hints given on the following pages. Refer to Hints only if you need assistance.

1. Set up your drawing.

   A. Start AutoCAD. Begin a *New* drawing and name the drawing **WIREFRAM**.
   B. Examine the figure on the previous page showing the completed wireframe model. Notice that all of the dimensions are to the nearest unit. For this exercise, assume generic units.
   C. Keep the default *Decimal Units*. Set *Units Precision* **.00** (two places to the right of the decimal).
   D. Keep the default *Limits* (assuming they are already set to 0,0 and 12,9 or close to those values). It appears from Figure 36-2 that the drawing space needed is a minimum of 8 units by 5 units on the XY plane.
   E. Turn on the *SNAP*.
   F. Turn on the *GRID*.
   G. Make a layer named **MODEL**. Set it as the *Current* layer. Set a *Color,* if desired.

2. Draw the base of the part on the XY plane.

   Figure 36-3

   A. Use *Line*. Begin at the origin (0,0,0) and draw the shape of the base of the Stop Plate. (It is a good practice to begin construction of any 3D model at 0,0,0.) Use *SNAP* as you draw and watch the *COORDS* display. See Figure 36-3.
   B. Change your *Vpoint* with the *Rotate* option. Specify angles of **305, 30**. Next, *Zoom .9X*.
   C. Turn the *Ucsicon ON* and force it to the *ORigin*. See Figure 36-4 to see if you have the correct *Vpoint*.

3. Begin drawing the lines bounding the top "surface" of the base by using absolute coordinates and .XY filters.

   Figure 36-4

   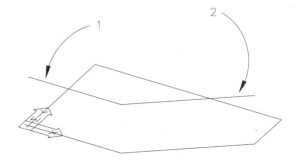

   A. Draw the first two *Lines,* as shown in Figure 36-4, by entering <u>absolute</u> coordinates. You cannot PICK points interactively (without *OSNAP*) since it results in selections only <u>on the XY plane</u> of the current coordinate system. Do not exit the *Line* command when you finish.

B. Draw *Lines* 3 and 4 using **.XY** point filters (Figure 36-5). Do not exit the *Line* command.
C. Complete the shape defining the top surface (*Line* 5) by using the **Close** option. The completed shape should look like Figure 36-5.

Figure 36-5

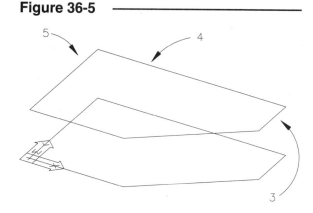

4. There is an easier way to construct the top "surface"; that is, use *Copy* to create the top "surface" from the bottom "surface."

A. *Erase* the 5 lines defining the top shape.
B. Use *Copy* and select the 5 lines defining the bottom shape. You can PICK **0,0,0** as the "Base Point." The "second point of displacement" can be specified by entering absolute coordinates or relative coordinates or by using an .XY filter. Compare your results with Figure 36-5.

5. Check your work and *Save* it to disk.

A. Use **Plan** to see if all of the *Lines* defining the top shape appear to be aligned with those on the bottom. The correct results at this point should look like Figure 36-3 since the top shape is directly above the bottom.
B. Use **Zoom Previous** to display the previous view (same as *Vpoint, Rotate,* 305,30.)
C. If you have errors, correct them. You can use *Undo* or *Erase* the incorrect *Lines* and redraw them. See Hints for further assistance. You may have to use *OSNAP* or enter absolute coordinates to begin a new *Line* at an existing *END*point.
D. *Save* your drawing. Since you already defined a name, *Qsave* is automatically invoked when you use *Save*.

6. Draw the vertical *Lines* between the base and top "surfaces" using the following methods.

Figure 36-6

A. Enter absolute coordinates (X, Y, and Z values) to draw the first two vertical *Lines* shown in Figure 36-6 (1, 2).
B. Use another method (interactive coordinate entry) to draw the remaining three *Lines* (3, 4, 5). You have learned that if you PICK a point, with or without *SNAP*, the selected point is on the XY plane of the current coordinate system. *OSNAP*, however, allows you to PICK points in 3D space. Begin each of the three *Lines* ("From point:") by using *SNAP* and picking the appropriate point on the XY plane. The second point of each *Line* ("to point:") can only be specified by using *OSNAP* (use **END**point).

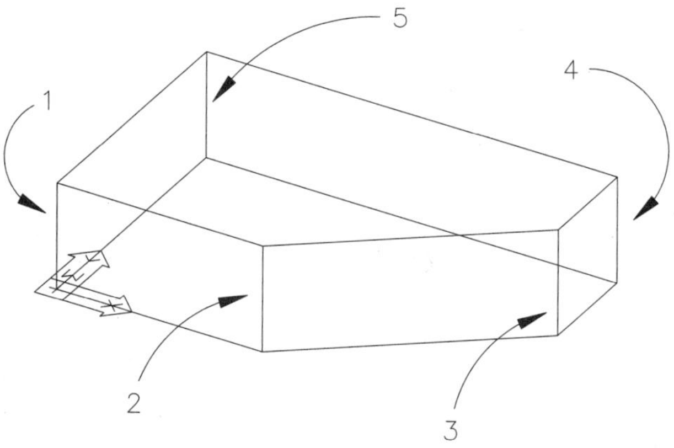

C. Once again, there is an easier method. *Erase* four lines and <u>leave one</u>. You can use *Copy* with the *Multiple* option to copy the one vertical *Line* around to the other positions. Make sure you select the *Multiple* option. In response to the "Base point or displacement:" prompt, select the base of the remaining *Line* (on the XY plane) with *SNAP ON*. In response to "second point of displacement:" make the multiple copies.

D. Use a *Plan* view to check your work. *Zoom Previous*. Correct your work, if necessary.

7. Draw two *Lines* defining a vertical plane. Often in the process of beginning a 3D model (when geometry has not yet been created in some positions), it may be necessary to use absolute coordinates. This is one of those cases.

A. Use absolute coordinates to draw the two *Lines* shown in Figure 36-7. Refer to Figure 36-2 for the dimensions.

B. *Zoom Extents* and then *Zoom .9X* so that the coordinate system icon appears at the origin. Your screen should look like Figure 36-7.

Figure 36-7 ———————————————

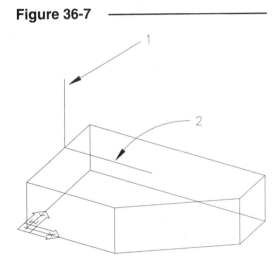

8. Rather than drawing the next objects by defining absolute coordinates, you can establish a vertical construction plane and just PICK points with *SNAP* and *GRID* on the construction plane.

A. This can be done by creating a new UCS (User Coordinate System). Invoke the *UCS* command by typing *UCS* or by selecting it from the menus. Use the *3point* option and select the line *ENDpoints* in the order indicated (Figure 36-8) to define the origin, point on X axis, and point on Y axis.

Figure 36-8 ———————————————

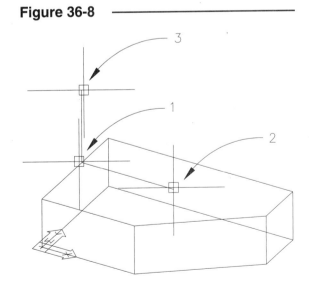

B. The Coordinate System Icon should appear in the position shown in Figure 36-9. Notice that the *GRID* and *SNAP* have followed the new UCS. Move the cursor and note the orientation of the crosshairs. You can now draw on this vertical construction plane simply by PICKing points on the XY plane of the new UCS!

If your UCS does not appear like that in the figure, *UNDO* and try again.

Figure 36-9

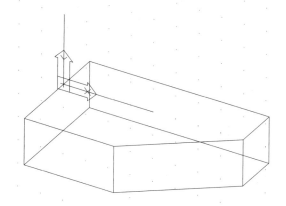

C. Draw the *Lines* to complete the geometry on the XY plane of the UCS. Refer to Figure 36-2 for the dimensions. The Stop Plate should look like that in Figure 36-10.

Figure 36-10

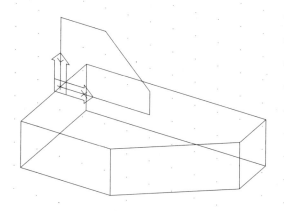

9. Check your work; save the drawing and the newly created UCS.

A. View your drawing from a plan view of the UCS. Invoke *Plan* and accept the default option "*<current UCS>*." If your work appears to be correct, use *Zoom Previous*.

B. Save your new UCS. Invoke the *UCS* command as before. Use the *Save* option and assign the name **FRONT**.

10. Create a second vertical surface behind the first with *Copy* (Fig. 36-11). You can give coordinates relative to the (new) current UCS.

Figure 36-11

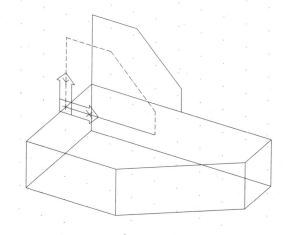

A. Invoke *Copy*. Select the four lines (highlighted) comprising the vertical plane (on the current UCS). Do <u>not</u> select the bottom line defining the plane. Specify **0,0** as the "Base point:" and give either absolute or relative coordinates (with respect to the current UCS) as the "second point of displacement." Note that the direction to *Copy* is <u>negative</u> Z.

B. Alternately, using *Copy* with *OSNAP* would be valid here since you can PICK (with *OSNAP*) the back corner.

11. Draw the horizontal lines between the two vertical "surfaces" using one of several possible methods.

A. Use the **Line** command to connect the two vertical surfaces with four horizontal edges as shown in Figure 36-12. With *SNAP* on, you can **PICK** points on the XY plane of the UCS. Use *OSNAP* to **PICK** the **ENDpoints** of the lines on the back vertical plane.

B. As another possibility, you could draw only one **Line** by the previous method and **Copy** it with the **Multiple** option to the other three locations. In this case, **PICK** the "Base point" on the XY plane (with *SNAP ON*). Specifying the "second point(s) of displacement" is easily done (also at *SNAP* points).

Figure 36-12 ——————————

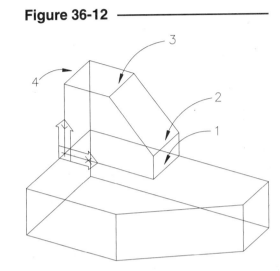

12. A wireframe model uses 2D objects to define the bounding edges of "surfaces." There should be no objects that do not fulfill this purpose. If you examine Figure 36-13, you notice two lines that should be removed (highlighted). These lines do not define edges since they each exist between coplanar "surfaces." Remove these lines with *Trim*.

Figure 36-13 ——————————

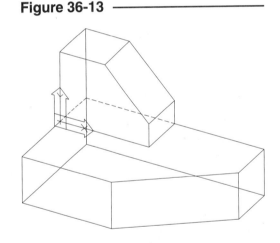

Trimming 2D objects in 3D space requires special attention. You have two choices for using *Trim* in this case: *Projmode = None* or *View*. You can use the *View* option of *Projmode* (to trim any objects that appear to intersect from the current view) or you must select the vertical *Line* as a cutting edge (because with the *None* option of *Projmode*, you cannot select a cutting edge that is perpendicular to the XY plane of the current coordinate system). In other words, when *Projmode=None*, you can only select the vertical *Line* as the cutting edge, but when *Projmode=View*, either the vertical or horizontal *Line* can be used as the cutting edge.

A. Use *Trim* and select either *Line* (highlighted, Fig. 36-14) as the *cutting edge*. Change the **Projmode** to **View** and *Trim* the indicated **Line**s. Use *Trim* again to trim the other indicated horizontal *Line* (previous figure).

B. Change back to the WCS. Invoke **UCS**; make the **World** coordinate system current.

Figure 36-14 ——————————

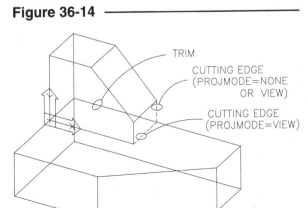

13. Check your work and *Save* your drawing.

Figure 36-15

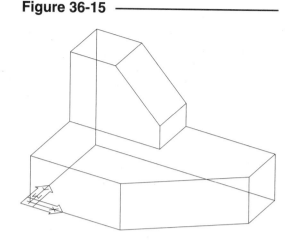

    A. Make sure your wireframe model looks like that in Figure 36-15.
    B. Use *Save* to secure your drawing.

14. It may be wise to examine your model from other viewpoints. As an additional check of your work and as a review of 3D viewing, follow these steps.

    A. Invoke *UCS* and *Restore* the UCS you saved called **FRONT**. Now use *Plan* with the *Current UCS* option. This view represents a front view and should allow you to visualize the alignment of the two vertical planes constructed in the last several steps.
    B. Next, use *UCS* and restore the **World** Coordinate System. Then use *Plan* again with the *Current UCS* option. Check your model from this viewing angle.
    C. Finally, use *Vpoint Rotate* and enter angles of **305** and **30**. This should return to your original viewpoint.

15. Instead of constantly changing *Vpoints*, it would be convenient to have several *Vpoints* of your model visible on the screen <u>at one time</u>. This can be done with the *Vports* (Viewports) command. In order to enhance visualization of your model for the following constructions, divide your screen into four sections or viewports with *Vports* and then set a different *Vpoint* in each viewport.

    A. The first step is to type *Vports* or select from the *View* pull-down menu *Tiled Viewports >, Layout...*. Specify **4** (four) viewports. Your screen should appear as that in Figure 36-16. Move your cursor around in the viewports. The crosshairs only appear in the <u>current</u> viewport. Only <u>one</u> viewport can be current at a time. Any change you make to the model appears in all viewports. You cannot draw <u>between</u> viewports; however, you can begin a draw or edit command in one viewport and finish in another. Experiment by drawing and *Erasing* a *Line*.

Figure 36-16

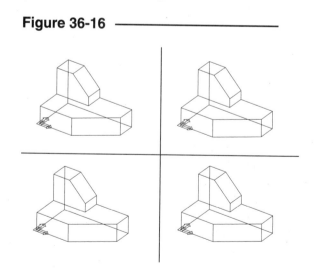

    B. Now configure the upper-left viewport with a top view. Make the upper-left viewport the current viewport. To produce a top view, use the *Plan* command. Next, use *Zoom* with a **.9X** magnification factor to bring the edges of the model slightly away from the viewport borders.

C. Now make the lower-left viewport current. In order to configure this for a front view, use the **3D Viewpoint Presets** with the **Front** option. Next, **Zoom .9x** in this viewport. Use the **Ucsicon** command with the **All** option to make the icon appear at the origin for all viewports. Check your results with Figure 36-17.

Figure 36-17 ——————————

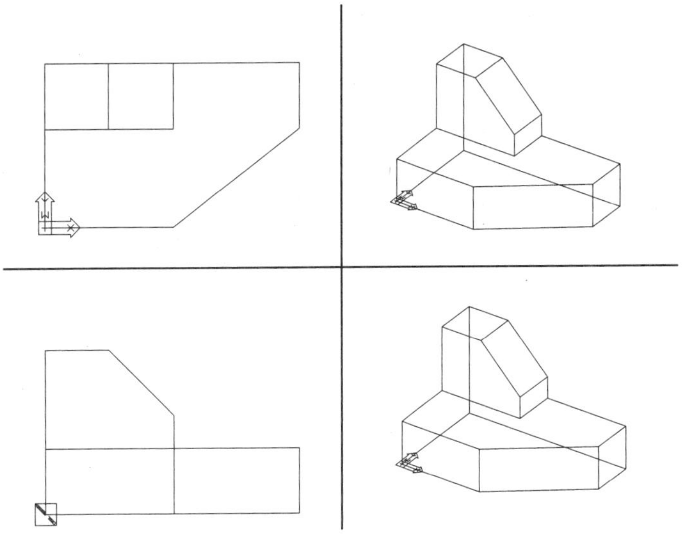

Note that by using viewports you can achieve multiple views of the model; however, only <u>one coordinate system</u> can be current at a time. The Coordinate System icon appears in all viewports, indicating the current coordinate system orientation. The *Ucsicon* *ORigin* and *All* settings force the icons to appear at the origin in all viewports. Since the XY plane of the coordinate system is not visible in the lower-left viewport, a different symbol appears in place of the Coordinate System Icon. This icon, a broken pencil, indicates that it is not a good idea to draw from the viewpoint because you cannot see the XY plane.

16. In the next construction, add the milled slot in the inclined surface of the Stop Plate. Because the slot is represented by geometry parallel with the inclined surface, a UCS should be created on the surface to facilitate the construction.

Figure 36-18 ——————————

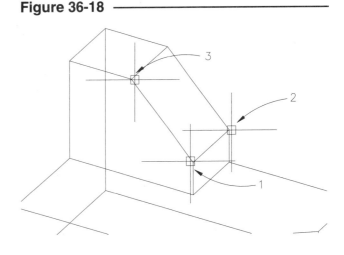

A. Make the lower-right viewport current. Use the **UCS 3point** option. Select the three points indicated in Figure 36-18 for (1) the "Origin," (2) "Point on the positive X axis," and (3) "Point on the positive Y axis portion on the XY plane." Make sure you *OSNAP* with the **ENDpoint** option.

B. The icon should move to the new UCS origin. Its orientation should appear as that in Figure 36-19. Notice that the new coordinate system is current in all viewports.

Figure 36-19 ——————————

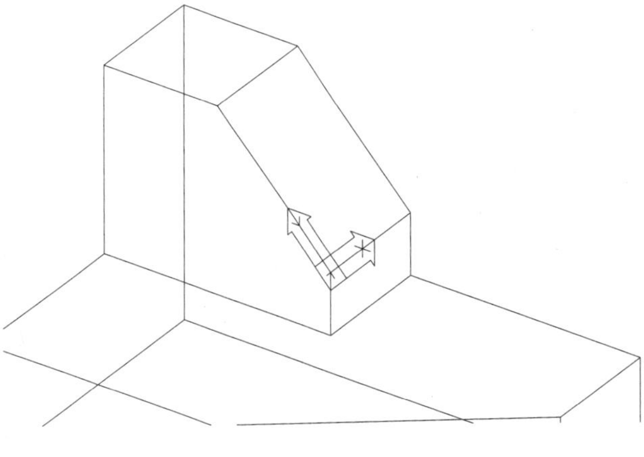

C. Save this new UCS by using the **UCS** command with the *Save* option. Assign the name **AUX** (short for auxiliary view).

(Remember to check the Hints <u>if</u> you have trouble.)

17. To enhance your visualization of the inclined surface, change your viewpoint for the lower-right viewport.

Figure 36-20 ———————

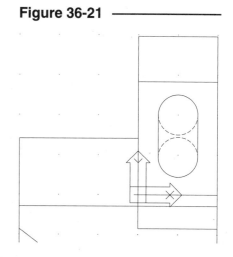

   A. Make sure that the lower-right viewport is current. Use the **Plan** command and accept the default *<Current UCS>*. This action should yield a view normal to the inclined surface—an auxiliary view.
   B. It would also be helpful to **Zoom** in with a window to only the inclined surface. Do so. Your results (for that viewport) should look like Figure 36-20.

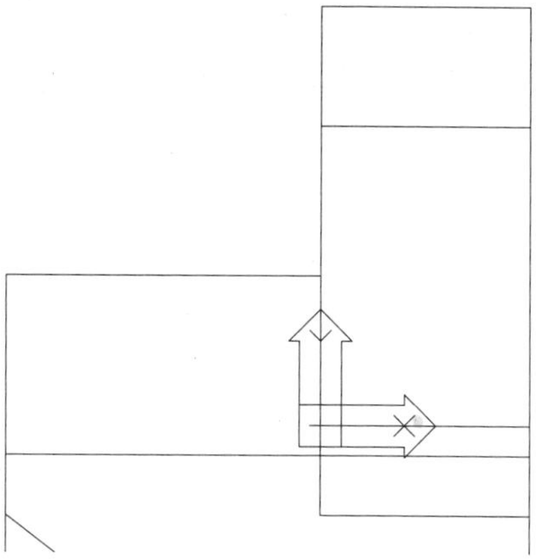

18. The next several steps guide you through the construction of the slot. Refer to Figure 36-2 for the dimensions of the slot.

   A. Turn on the *SNAP* and *GRID* for the viewport.

   Figure 36-21 ———————

   B. Draw two **Circles** with a .5 radius. The center of the lower circle is at coordinate **1,1** (of the UCS). The other circle center is one unit above.
   C. Draw two vertical **Lines** connecting the circles. Use *TANgent* or *QUAdrant OSNAP*.
   D. Use **Trim** to remove the inner halves of the *Circles* (highlighted). Notice that changes made in one viewport are reflected in the other viewports.

19. The slot has a depth of 1 unit. Create the bottom of the slot by *Copy*ing the shape created on the top "surface."

   A. With the current UCS, the direction of the *Copy* is in a <u>negative</u> Z direction. Use **Copy** and select the two *Arcs* and two *Lines* comprising the slot. Use the *CENter* of an *Arc* or the origin of the UCS as the "base point." The "second point of displacement" can be specified using absolute or relative coordinates.

   Figure 36-22 ———————

   B. Check to ensure that the copy has been made correctly. Compare your work to that in Figure 36-22. No other lines are needed to define the slot. The "surface" on the inside of the slot has a smooth transition from curved to straight, so no additional edges (represented by lines) exist.

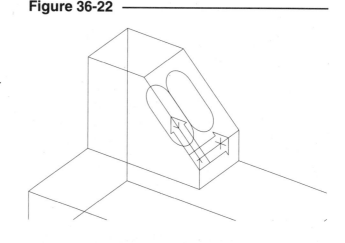

20. The geometry defining the Stop Plate is complete at this point. There are no other edges needed to define the "surfaces." However, you may be called on to make a design change to this part in the future. Before you change your display back to a *Single* viewport and save your work, it is helpful to *Save* the viewport configuration so that it can be recalled in a future session. Unless you save the current viewport configuration, you have to respecify the *Vpoints* for each viewport.

   A. Use the *Vports* command and the *Save* option (not the *SAVE* command). You can specify any name for the viewport configuration. A descriptive name for this configuration is **FTIA** (short for Front, Top, Isometric, and Auxiliary). Using this convention tells you how many viewports (by the number of letters in the name) and the viewpoints of each viewport when searching through a list of named viewports.

   B. When changing back to a single viewport, the <u>current</u> viewport becomes the single viewport. Make the upper-right viewport (isometric-type viewpoint) current. Invoke the *Vports* command and the *SIngle* option. The resulting screen should display only the isometric-type viewpoint (like Figure 36-23). If needed, the viewport configuration can be recalled in the future by using the *Restore* option of *Vports*.

Figure 36-23

   C. Before saving your drawing, you should make the WCS current by using the *UCS* command. Notice that changing display options (like *Vpoint* or *Vports*) has no effect on the UCS. UCS controls are independent from display controls (unless the *UCSFOLLOW* variable is set to 1).

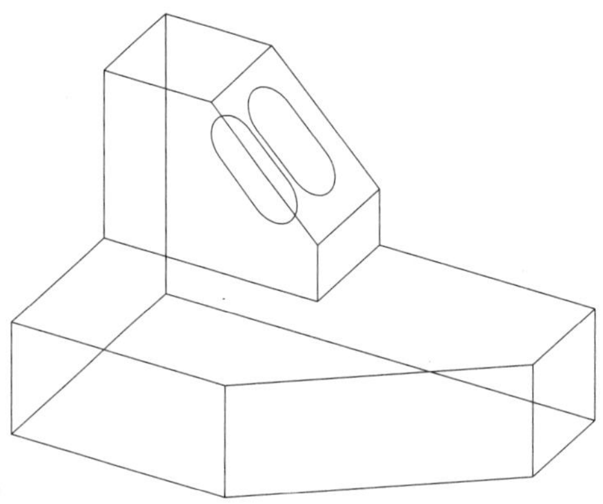

21. *Save* your drawing. Use this drawing for practicing with display commands covered in the previous chapters, 3D Viewing and Display and User Coordinate Systems. The Stop Plate is especially good for practicing with *Dview*.

22. When you are finished experimenting with display and view commands, *Exit* AutoCAD and do not save your changes.

Hints

H1.   A. Start AutoCAD by the method you normally use at your computer workstation. Select the *File* pull-down menu, *New...*.
     B. (no help needed)
     C. *Data* pull-down menu, *Units...*.
     D. (no help needed)
     E. Press **F9**. Make sure the word **SNAP** appears on the Status Line.
     F. Press **F7**. The *GRID* should be visible.
     G. *Data* pull-down menu, *Layer...*, type **MODEL** in the edit box, select *New*, then *Current* and *OK*.

H2.   A. *Draw* pull-down menu, *Line*. Make sure *SNAP* is *ON*. The *COORDS* display helps you keep track of the line lengths as you draw. You may have to press **F6** until *COORDS* displays a cursor tracking or polar display.
     B. Type *Vpoint*. Type *r*. Enter **305** for the first angle and **30** for the second. Type **Z** (for *Zoom*). Enter **.9X**
     C. *Options* pull-down, *UCS >*; then check *Icon*. Do it again for the *Icon Origin* option.

H3.   A. Line 1   From point: **0,0,2**
                     to point: **4,0,2**
           Line 2   to point: **8,3,2**
                     to point: do not press **Enter** yet

       B. If you happened to exit the *Line* command, you can use *Line* again and attach to the last end-point by entering an "@" in response to the "From point:" prompt. If that does not work, use *OSNAP* **END**point to locate the end of the last *Line*.

<u>Using point filters:</u> At the "to point:" prompt, type **.XY** and press **Enter**. AutoCAD responds with "of." **PICK** a point on the XY plane <u>directly below</u> the desired location for the *Line* end (Fig 36-24). AutoCAD responds with "(need Z)." Enter a value of **2**. The resulting *Line* end coordinate has the X and Y values of the

Figure 36-24 ─────────

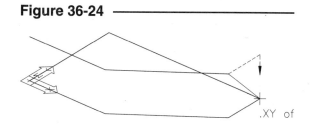

.XY of

point you PICKed and the Z value of 2. In other words, since you can only PICK points on the XY plane, using the .XY point filter locates only the X and Y coordinates of the selected point and allows you to specify the Z coordinate separately.

       C. Enter the letter **C** in response to the "to point:" prompt. AutoCAD *closes* the first and last *Line* segments created in one use of the *Line* command. If you used the *Line* command two or more times to complete the shape defining the top "surface," this option does not work. In that case, use absolute coordinates, .XY filters, or *OSNAP* **END**point to connect to the final endpoint.

H4.   A. Type **E** for *Erase* or use the ***Modify*** pull-down, ***Erase***.
       B. Type **CP** for *Copy* or use the ***Construct*** pull-down, ***Copy***. Select the 5 *Lines* in response to "Select objects:." PICK or enter **0,0,0** as the "Base point or displacement." Enter either **0,0,2** (absolute coordinates) or **@0,0,2** (relative coordinates) in response to "second point of displacement:."

H5.   A. Type ***Plan*** and then the **W** option or select ***View*** pull-down, ***3D Viewpoint Presets >, Plan View >, World***.
       B. Type **Z** for *Zoom* and type **P** for *Previous*.
       C. If you have mistakes, correct them by first *Erasing* the incorrect *Lines*. Begin redrawing at the last correct *Line* **END**point. You have to use absolute coordinates, .XY filters, or *OSNAP* **END**point to attach the new *Line* to the old.
       D. Type ***Save*** or select ***File*** pull-down, ***Save***.

H6.   A. Line 1   From point: **0,0,0**
                     to point: **0,0,2**
           Line 2   From point: **4,0,0**
                     to point: **4,0,2**
       B. Line 3   From point:
                     PICK point a.
                     to point:
                     ENDpoint of, **PICK** point b.

Figure 36-25 ─────────

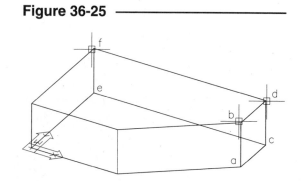

Line 4   From point:
          PICK point c.
          to point:
          *END*point of, **PICK** point d.
Line 5   From point:
          PICK point e.
          to point:
          *END*point of, **PICK** point f.

   C. Type *E* for *Erase*. *Erase* the last four vertical lines, leaving the first. Type *CP* for *Copy*. Select the remaining vertical line. At the next prompt, type *M* for *Multiple*. When asked for the "Base Point:," select the bottom of the line (on the XY plane). At the "second point of displacement:" prompt, pick the other locations for the new lines.

   D. *View* pull-down, *3D Viewpoint Presets >*, *Plan View >*, *World*. Examine your work. Type *Z* for *Zoom*. Type *P* for *Previous*.

H7.   A. Line 1   From point: **0,3,2**
                    to point: **0,3,5**
            Line 2   From point: **0,3,2**
                    to point: **4,3,2**

   B. Type *Z*. Type *E* for *Extents*. Press *Enter* to invoke the last command (*Zoom*). Type **.9X**.

H8.   A. Type *UCS*. Type *3* for *3point*. When prompted for the first point ("Origin"), invoke the cursor (*OSNAP*) menu and select *ENDpoint*. **PICK** point 1 (Fig. 36-8). When prompted for the second point ("Point on positive portion of the X-axis"), again use *ENDpoint* and **PICK** point 2. Repeat for the third point ("Point on positive Y portion of the UCS XY plane").

   B. If you have trouble establishing this UCS, you can type the letter *U* to undo one step. Repeat until the icon is returned to the origin of the WCS orientation. If that does not work for you, type *UCS* and use the *World* option. Repeat the steps given in the previous instructions. Make sure you use *OSNAP* correctly to **PICK** the indicated *ENDpoint*s.

   C. When constructing the *Lines* representing the vertical plane, ensure that *SNAP* (F9) and *GRID* (F7) are *ON*. Notice how you can only **PICK** points on the XY plane of the UCS with the cursor. This makes drawing objects on the plane very easy. Use the *Line* command to draw the remaining edges defining the vertical "surface."

H9.   A. *View* pull-down menu, *3D Viewpoint Presets >*, *Plan View >*, *Current*. Check your work. Then type *Z*, then *P*. Correct your work if necessary.

   B. Type *UCS*. Type *S* for the *Save* option. Enter the name **FRONT**.

H10.   A. Type *CP* or select *Copy* from the *Construct* pull-down menu. Select the indicated four *Lines* (Figure 36-11). For the basepoint, enter or **PICK 0,0**. For the second point of displacement, enter **0,0,-2**.

Figure 36-26

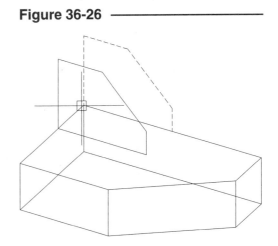

   B. Alternately, perform the same sequence except, when prompted for the "second point of displacement:," select *ENDpoint* from the *OSNAP* menu and **PICK** the corner indicated in Figure 36-26.

H11. A. Type *L* for *Line*. At the "From point:" prompt **PICK** point (a) on the UCS XY plane (Fig. 36-27). You should be able to *SNAP* to the point. At the "to point:" prompt, select the *ENDpoint OSNAP* option and **PICK** point (b). Repeat the steps for the other 3 *Lines*.

Figure 36-27

B. Alternately, draw only the first *Line* (line 1, Figure 36-12). Type *CP* for *Copy*. Select the first *Line*. Type *M* for *Multiple*. At the "Base point:" prompt, **PICK** point (a) (Fig. 36-27). Since this point is on the XY plane, PICK (with *SNAP ON*). For the second points of displacement, **PICK** the other corners of the vertical surface on the XY plane (with *SNAP ON*).

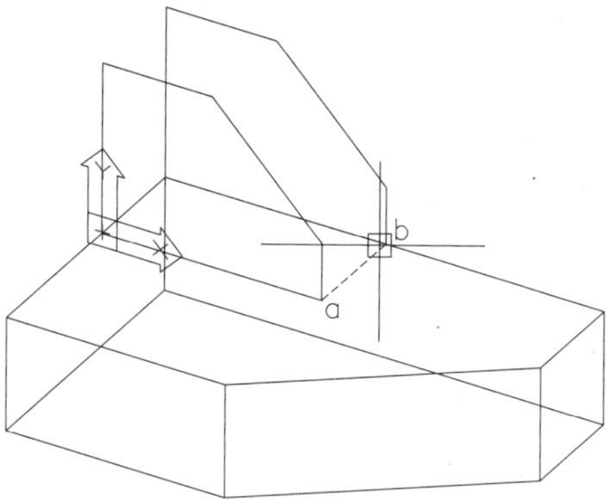

H12. A. *Modify* pull-down, **Trim.** Select either the vertical or horizontal *Line* (as indicated in Figure 36-14) as the cutting edge. Change *Projmode* to *View*. Complete the trim operation. With *Projmode* now set to *View*, **Trim** the other *Line* indicated (Fig. 35-13).

B. Type *UCS*, then *W* for *World*. The WCS icon should appear at the origin (Fig. 36-15).

H13. A. If your wireframe model is not correct, make the necessary changes before the next step.

B. *File* pull-down, **Save.**

H14. A. *View* pull-down, *Named UCS....* In the *UCS Control* dialogue box, select **FRONT**. **PICK** the *Current* tile, then *OK*. Make sure you PICK <u>*Current*</u>. Then, from the *View* pull-down, select *3D Viewpoint Presets >*, *Plan View >*, *Current*. Examine your figure from this viewpoint.

B. Invoke the *UCS Control* dialogue box again and set *World* as *Current*. Next, use the *View* pull-down menu again to see a *Plan View* of the *World* coordinate system.

C. Type *Vpoint*, then *R* for the *Rotate* option. Enter **305** for the "angle in the XY plane from the X axis." Enter **30** for the "angle from the XY plane."

H15. A. No help needed for creating viewports. To experiment with creating and erasing *Lines*, invoke the **Line** command and **PICK** points in the current viewport (wherever the crosshairs appear). Now, use *Line* again and **PICK** only the "From point:." Move your cursor to another viewport and make it current (**PICK**). **PICK** the "to point:" in the new viewport. Notice that you can change the current viewport <u>within</u> a command to facilitate using the same draw command (or edit command) in multiple viewports. *Erase* the experimental *Lines*.

B. **PICK** the top-left viewport to make it current. Viewing commands that you use affect only the current viewport. Select (*View* pull-down), *3D Viewpoint Presets >*, *Plan View >*, *World*. Type *Z* for *Zoom*, then *.9X*.

C. **PICK** the lower-left viewport. Select *3D Viewpoint Presets*, *Front*. Next, type *Z*, then *.9X*. Type *Ucsicon*, then *A* for the *All* option.

H16.   A. **PICK** the lower-right viewport. Type *UCS*, then **3**. When prompted for the "Origin," select *ENDpoint* from the *OSNAP* menu and **PICK** point 1 (see Figure 36-18). Use *ENDpoint OSNAP* to select the other two points.

      B. No help needed.

      C. Select the *View* pull-down menu, *Named UCS...*. When the *UCS Control* dialogue appears, **PICK** the current UCS "***No Name***." In the edit box, type over the *No Name* with the name **AUX**. **PICK** *OK*.

H17.   A. **PICK** the lower-right viewport. Select *View* pull-down, *3D Viewpoint Presets >*, *Plan View >*, *Current*.

      B. Type *Z*. Make a window around the entire inclined surface.

H18.   A. Check to see if *SNAP* and *GRID* are *ON*. If not, press **F9** (*SNAP*) or **F7** (*GRID*).

      B. Select the *Draw* pull-down menu, then *Circle >* with the *Center, Radius* option. For the center, **PICK** point **1,1** (watch the *COORDS* display). Enter a value of **.5** for the radius. Repeat this for the second *Circle*, but the center is at **1,2**.

      C. Type *L* for *Line*. At the "From point:" prompt, select the *QUAdrant OSNAP* mode and **PICK** point (a) (Fig. 36-28). At the "to point:" prompt, use *QUAdrant* again and **PICK** point (b).

      D. *Modify* pull-down, *Trim*. Select the two *Lines* as *Cutting edges* and *Trim* the inner halves of the circles, as shown in Figure 36-21.

Figure 36-28 ──────────────

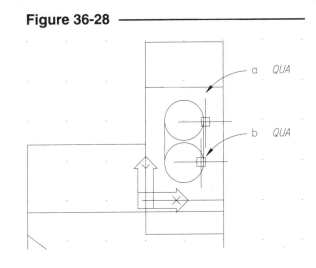

H19.   A. Type *CP*. Select the two arcs and two lines comprising the slot. At the "Base point or displacement:" prompt, Enter **0,0,0**. At the "second point of displacement:" prompt, enter **0,0,-1**.

      B. No help needed.

H20.   A. Type *Vports*, then *S* for *Save*. At the "Name for new viewport configuration prompt," enter **FTIA**.

      B. **PICK** the upper right viewport. Type *Vports*. Type *SI* for the *Single* option. Activate *Vports* again. Type *?* to display a list of viewports. The name FTIA should appear. Type *Vports* again. This time type *R* for *Restore*. Give the name **TFIA**. Finally, type *U* to undo the last action.

      C. Select the *View* pull-down menu and then *UCS >*, *Named UCS...*. **PICK** *World* from the list and make it *Current*.

H21.   *File* pull-down, *Save*.

H22.   *File* pull-down, *Exit* AutoCAD.

COMMANDS

The draw and edit commands that operate for 2D drawings are used to create 3D elements by entering X,Y,Z values, or by using UCSs. *Pline* cannot be used with 3D coordinate entry. Instead, the *3Dpoly* command is used especially for creating 3D polylines.

3DPOLY

PULL-DOWN MENU	SCREEN MENU	TYPE IN	TABLET MENU
Draw *3D Polyline*	DRAW1 *3Dpoly:*	3DPOLY	10,P

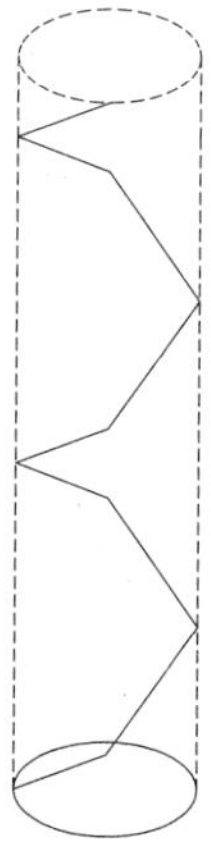

A line created by *3Dpoly* is a *Pline* with 3D coordinates. The *Pline* command only allows 2D coordinate entry, whereas the *3Dpoly* command allows you to create <u>straight</u> poly-line segments in 3D space by specifying 3D coordinates. A *3Dpoly* line has the "single object" characteristic of normal *Plines*; that is, several *3Dpoly* line segments created with one *3Dpoly* command are treated as one object by AutoCAD. A *3Dpoly* line can be used for creating 3D B-splines using the *Spline curve* option of the *Pedit* command.

Figure 36-29

```
Command: 3dpoly
From point: PICK or (X,Y,Z coordinates)
Close/Undo/<Endpoint of line>: PICK or (X,Y,Z coordinates) or
(option)
```

If you PICK points or specify coordinate values, AutoCAD simply connects the points with straight polyline segments in 3D space. For example, *3Dpoly* could be used to draw line segments in a spiral fashion by specifying coordinates or PICKing points (Fig. 36-29).

Close
This option closes the last point to the first point entered in the command sequence.

Undo
This option deletes the last segment and allows you to specify another point for the new segment.

A *3Dpoly* does <u>not</u> have the other features or options of a *Pline* such as *Arc* segments and line *Width*.

Special options of *Pedit* can be used with *3Dpoly* lines to *Close, Edit Vertex, Spine curve,* or *Decurve* the *3Dpoly*. You can also use grips to edit the *3Dpoly*. Although some applications may require a helix, *3Dpoly* and *Pedit* <u>cannot</u> be used in conjunction to do this. The *Spine curve* option of the *Pedit* command converts the *3Dpoly* to a Polyline version of a B-Spline, not a true NURBS spline. A *Spline* fit *Polyline* does not pass through the vertices that were specified when the *Pline* or *3DPoly* was created. The *Spline* command, however, <u>can</u> be used to specify points in 3D to create a true helix (Fig. 36-30).

Figure 36-30

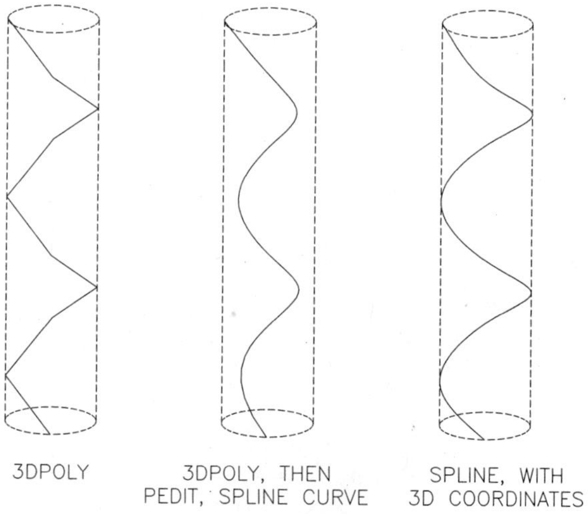

| 3DPOLY | 3DPOLY, THEN
PEDIT, SPLINE CURVE | SPLINE, WITH
3D COORDINATES |

Lines and *Arcs* cannot be converted to *3Dpoly* lines using *Pedit*. You can, however, convert *Lines* and *Arcs* to *Plines* if they lie on the XY plane of the current UCS. Spline-fit *Plines* and *3Dpoly* lines can be converted to NURBS splines with the *Object* option of the *Spline* command, but the conversion does not realign the new *Spline* to pass through the original vertices.

CHAPTER EXERCISES

1–4. Introduction to Wireframes

Create a wireframe model of each of the objects in Figures 36-31 through 36-34. Use each dimension marker in the figure to equal one unit in AutoCAD. Begin with the lower-left corner of the model located at 0,0,0. Assign the names **WFEX1**, **WFEX2**, **WFEX3**, and **WFEX4**.

Figure 36-31 ————————————

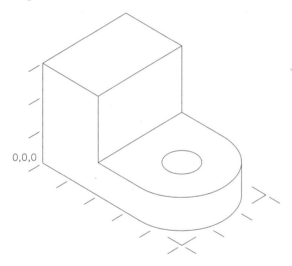

0,0,0

Figure 36-32 ————————————

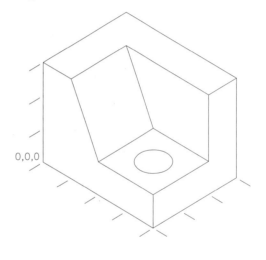

0,0,0

Figure 36-33 ————————————————

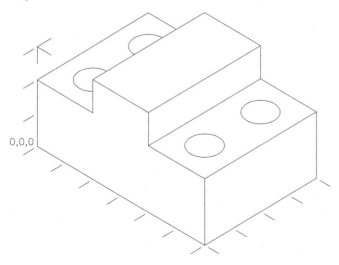

0,0,0

Figure 36-34 ————————————

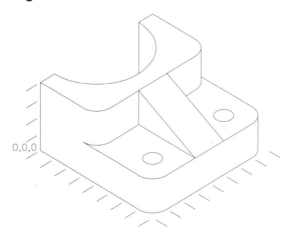

0,0,0

5. Create a wireframe model of the Corner Brace shown in Figure 36-35. *Save* the drawing as **CBRAC-WF**.

Figure 36-35

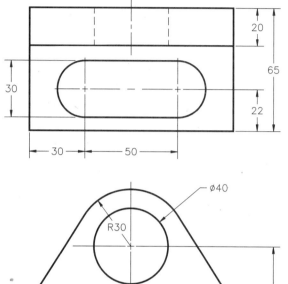

METRIC

6. Make a wireframe model of the V-block (Figure 36-36). *Save* as **VBLCK-WF**.

Figure 36-36

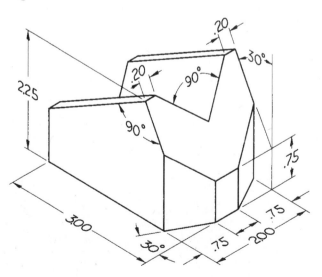

7. Make a wireframe model of the Bar Guide (Figure 36-37). *Save* as **BGUID-WF**.

Figure 36-37 ——————————————————————

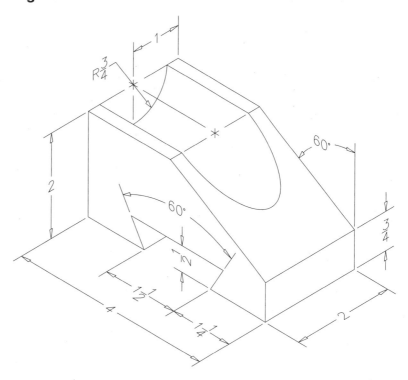

8. Make a wireframe model of the Angle Brace (Figure 36-38). *Save* as **ANGLB-WF**.

Figure 36-38 ——————————————————————

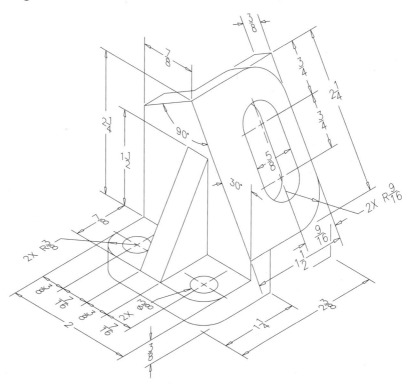

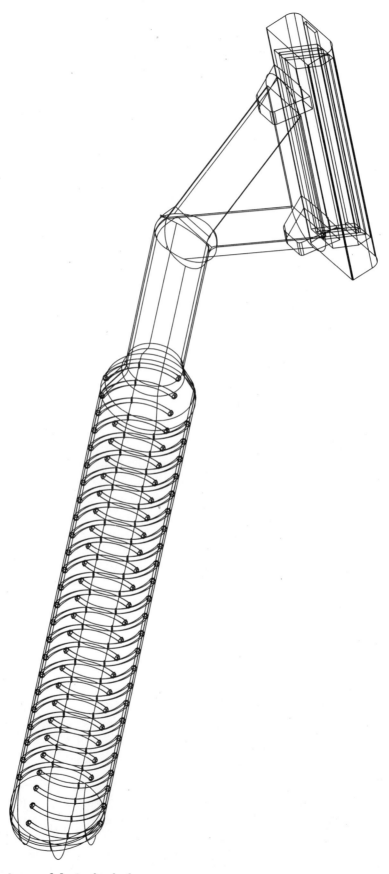

SHAVE.DWG Courtesy of Autodesk, Inc.

Chapter 37
SOLID MODELING CONSTRUCTION

Chapter Objectives

After completing this chapter you should:

1. be able to create solid model primitives using the following commands: *Box, Wedge, Cone, Cylinder, Torus,* and *Sphere*;

2. be able to create swept solids from existing 2D shapes using the *Extrude* and *Revolve* commands;

3. be able to *Move* objects in 3D space;

4. know how to assemble a solid to another solid in 3D space using *Align*;

5. be able to rotate a solid about any axis in 3D space with *Rotate3D*;

6. be able to mirror a solid about any axis in 3D space with *Mirror3D*;

7. be able to create rectangular and circular copies with *3Darray*;

8. be able to combine multiple primitives into one composite solid using *Union, Subtract,* and *Intersect*;

9. know how to create beveled edges and rounded corners using *Chamfer* and *Fillet*.

BASICS

The ACIS solid modeler is included in AutoCAD Release 13. With the ACIS modeler, you can create complex 3D parts and assemblies using Boolean operations to combine simple shapes, called *primitives*. This modeling technique is often referred to as CSG or Constructive Solid Geometry modeling. ACIS also provides a method for analyzing and sectioning the geometry of the models (Chapter 38).

The techniques used with ACIS for construction of many solid models follow three general steps:

1. Construct simple 3D <u>primitive</u> solids, or create 2D shapes and convert them to 3D solids by extruding or revolving.

2. Create the primitives <u>in location</u> relative to the associated primitives, or <u>move</u> the primitives into the desired location relative to the associated primitives.

3. Use <u>Boolean operations</u> (such as *Union*, *Subtract*, or *Intersect*) to combine the primitives to form a <u>composite solid</u>.

A solid model is an informationally complete representation of the shape of a physical object. Solid modeling differs from wireframe or surface modeling in two fundamental ways: (1) the information is more complete in a solid model and (2) the method of construction of the model itself is relatively easy to construct and edit.

The ACIS solid modeler is called a <u>hybrid modeler</u> because it maintains two principal types of data describing a model—geometric spatial data and topographic data. The geometric spatial data is a description of the model in terms of its construction. The construction is accomplished by creating regular geometric 3D shapes such as boxes, cones, wedges, cylinders, etc. (primitive solids), and combining them using union, subtract, and intersect (Boolean operations) to form composite solids. The topological data, or <u>boundary representation</u> (B-rep), is responsible for the display capabilities necessary for meshing, hiding, and rendering and is unnoticeable to the user. AutoCAD keeps a B-rep file with the model even though CSG techniques are used to create the solids.

CONSTRUCTIVE SOLID GEOMETRY TECHNIQUES

AutoCAD uses Constructive Solid Geometry (CSG) techniques for construction of solid models. CSG is characterized by solid primitives combined by Boolean operations to form composite solids. The CSG technique is a relatively fast and intuitive way of modeling that imitates the manufacturing process.

Primitives

Solid primitives are the basic building blocks that make up more complex solid models. The ACIS primitives commands are:

BOX	Creates a solid box or cube
CONE	Creates a solid cone with a circular or elliptical base
CYLINDER	Creates a solid cylinder with a circular or elliptical base
EXTRUDE	Creates a solid by extruding (adding a Z dimension to) a closed 2D object (*Pline, Circle, Region*)
REVOLVE	Creates a solid by revolving a shape about an axis
SHPERE	Creates a solid sphere
TORUS	Creates a solid torus
WEDGE	Creates a solid wedge

Primitives can be created by entering the command name or by selecting from the menus or icons.

Boolean Operations

Primitives are combined to create complex solids by using Boolean operations. The ACIS Boolean operators are listed below. An illustration and detailed description are given for each of the commands.

UNION   Unions (joins) selected solids.

SUBTRACT   Subtracts one set of solids from another.

INTERSECT   Creates a solid of intersection (common volume) from the selected solids.

Primitives are created at the desired location, or are moved into the desired location, before using a Boolean operator. In other words, two or more primitives can occupy the same space (or part of the same space), yet are separate solids. When a Boolean operation is performed, the solids are combined or altered in some way to create one solid. AutoCAD takes care of deleting or adding the necessary geometry and displays the new composite solid complete with the correct configuration and lines of intersection.

Figure 37-1

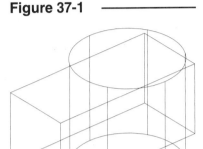

Consider the two solids shown in Figure 37-1. When solids are created, they can occupy the same physical space. A Boolean operation is used to combine the solids into a composite solid and it interprets the resulting utilization of space.

UNION

Union creates a union of the two solids into one composite solid (Fig. 37-2). The lines of intersection between the two shapes are calculated and displayed by AutoCAD . (The solid is displayed in the figure after performing a *Hide*.)

Figure 37-2

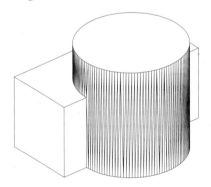

SUBTRACT

Subtract removes one or more solids from another solid. ACIS calculates the resulting composite solid. The term "difference" is sometimes used rather than "subtract." In Figure 37-3, the cylinder has been subtracted from the box.

Figure 37-3

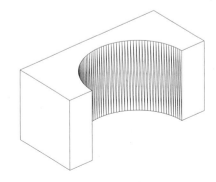

INTERSECT

Intersect calculates the intersection between two or more solids. When *Intersect* is used with *Regions* (2D surfaces), it determines the shared <u>area</u>. Used with solids, as in Figure 37-4, *Intersect* creates a solid comprised of the shared <u>volume</u> of the cylinder and the box. In other words, the result of *Intersect* is a solid that has only the volume which is part of both (or all) of the selected solids.

Figure 37-4 —

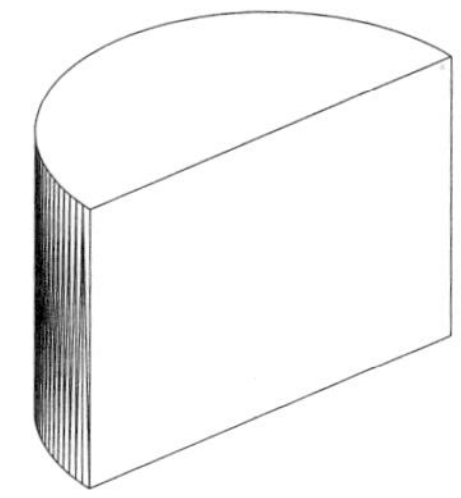

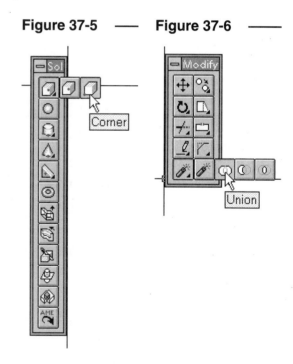

SOLID PRIMITIVES COMMANDS

This section explains the commands that allow you to create primitives used for construction of composite solid models. The commands allow you to specify the dimensions and the orientation of the solids. Once primitives are created, they are combined with other solids using Boolean operations to form composite solids.

NOTE: If you use a pointing device to PICK points, use *OSNAP* when possible to PICK points in 3D space. If you do not use *OSNAP*, the selected points are located on the current XY construction plane, so the true points may not be obvious. It is recommended that you use *OSNAP* or enter values.

The solid modeling commands are located in groups. The commands for the creation of solid primitives are located in a group in the *Draw* menus under *Solids*. For creation of solid primitives in AutoCAD for Windows, you may want to bring the Solids toolbar to the screen. This toolbar is of the floating/docked variety (Fig. 37-5). Commands used for moving solids are found in the *Construct* menus and in the Modify toolbar. Boolean operations are a bit hard to find (a good candidate for menu customization). Booleans are in the *Construct* pull-down, *DRAW2* screen menu, and the Modify toolbar (Fig. 37-6).

Figure 37-5 —— **Figure 37-6** ——

NOTE: When you begin to construct a solid model, <u>create the primitives at location 0,0,0</u> (or some other <u>known point</u>) rather than PICKing points anywhere in space. It is very helpful to know where the primitives are located in 3D space so they can be moved or rotated in the correct orientation with respect to other primitives when they are assembled to composite solids.

BOX

PULL-DOWN MENU	SCREEN MENU	TYPE IN	TABLET MENU
Draw *Solids >* *Box >*	*DRAW2* *SOLIDS* *Box:*	BOX	7,M

Box creates a solid box primitive to your dimensional specifications. You can specify dimensions of the box by PICKing or by entering values. The box can be defined by (1) giving the corners of the base, then height, (2) by locating the center and height, or (3) by giving each of the three dimensions. The base of the box is oriented parallel to the current XY plane.

Command: **box**
Center/<Corner of box><0,0,0>: **PICK** or (**coordinates**) or (**letter**) or **Enter**

Options for the *Box* command are listed as follows:

Corner of box

Pressing **Enter** begins the corner of a box at 0,0,0 of the current coordinate system. In this case, the box can be moved into its desired location later. As an alternative, a coordinate position can be entered or **PICK**ed as the starting corner of the box. AutoCAD responds with:

Cube/Length/<Other corner>:

The other corner can be PICKed or specified by coordinates. The *Cube* option requires only one dimension to define the cube.

Length
The *Length* option prompts you for the three dimensions of the box in the order of X, Y, and Z. (NOTE: The *Length* option prompts for the box *Length*, *Width*, and *Height*. AutoCAD really means *Width*, *Depth*, and *Height*, since the term "Length" actually refers to <u>any</u> generic measurement.)

Figure 37-7 shows a box created at 0,0,0 with width, depth, and height dimensions of 5, 4, and 3.

Figure 37-7

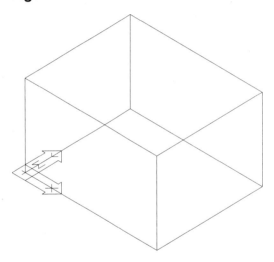

Center

With this option, you first locate the center of the box, then specify the three dimensions of the box. AutoCAD prompts:

Center of box: **PICK** or (**coordinates**)

Specify the center location. AutoCAD responds with:

Cube/Length/<corner of box>:

The resulting solid box is centered about the specified point (0,0,0 for the example, Figure 37-8).

Figure 37-8

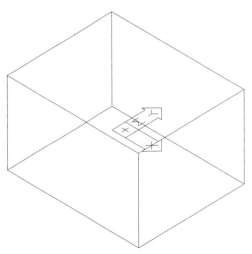

Figure 37-9 illustrates a *Box* created with the *Center* option using *OSNAP* to snap to the *CENter* of the top of the cylinder. Note that the center of the box is the <u>volumetric</u> center, not the center of the base.

Figure 37-9 —————

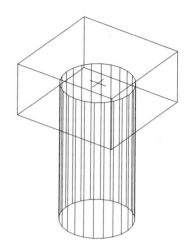

CONE

PULL-DOWN MENU	SCREEN MENU	TYPE IN	TABLET MENU
Draw *Solids >* *Cone >*	DRAW2 SOLIDS *Cone:*	CONE	7,J

Cone creates a right circular or elliptical solid cone ("right" means the axis forms a right angle with the base). You can specify the center location, radius (or diameter), and height. By default, the orientation of the cylinder is determined by the current UCS so that the base lies on the XY plane and height is perpendicular (in a Z direction). Alternately, the orientation can be defined by using the *Apex* option.

Center Point

Using the defaults (center at 0,0,0, PICK a radius, enter a value for height), the cone is generated in the orientation shown in Figure 37-10.

Figure 37-10 —————

 The cone here may differ in detail (number of contour lines), depending on the current setting of the *ISOLINES* variable. The default prompts are shown as follows:

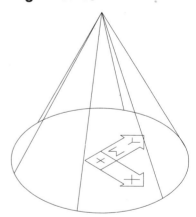

```
Command:  cone
Elliptical/<Center point><0,0,0>: PICK or (coordinates)
Diameter/<Radius>: PICK or (coordinates)
Apex/<Height>: PICK or (value)
Command:
```

Invoking the *Apex* option (after *Center point* of the base and *Radius* or *Diameter* have been specified) displays the following prompt:

Figure 37-11 —————

```
Apex: PICK or (coordinates)
```

Locating a point for the apex defines the height and orientation of the cone (Fig. 37-11). The axis of the cone is aligned with the line between the specified center point and the *Apex* point, and the height is equal to the distance between the two points.

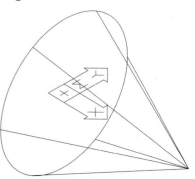

The solid model in Figure 37-12 was created with a *Cone* and a *Cylinder*. The cylinder was created first, then the cone was created using the *Apex* option of *Cone*. The orientation of the *Cone* was generated by PICKing the *CENter* of one end of the cylinder for the "Center point" of the base of the cone and the *CENter* of the cylinder's other end for the *Apex*. *Union* created the composite model.

Figure 37-12

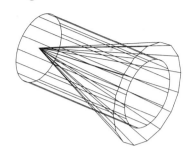
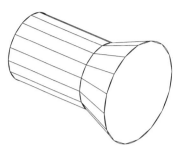

Elliptical

This option draws a cone with an elliptical base (Fig. 37-13). You specify two axis endpoints to define the elliptical base. An elliptical cone can be created using the *Center, Apex,* or *Height* options.

Figure 37-13

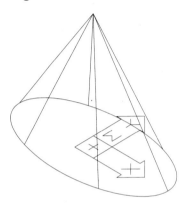

Elliptical/<center point> <0,0,0>: **e**
Center/<Axis endpoint>: **c**
Center of ellipse <0,0,0>: **PICK** or **(coordinates)**
Axis endpoint: **PICK** or **(coordinates)**
Other axis distance: **PICK** or **(coordinates)**
Apex/<Height>:

CYLINDER

PULL-DOWN MENU	SCREEN MENU	TYPE IN	TABLET MENU
Draw *Solids >* *Cylinder >*	*DRAW2* *SOLIDS* *Cylindr:*	*CYLINDER*	*7,L*

Cylinder creates a cylinder with an elliptical or circular base with a center location, diameter, and height you specify. Default orientation of the cylinder is determined by the current UCS, such that the circular plane is coplanar with the XY plane and height is in a Z direction. However, the orientation can be defined otherwise by the *Center of other end* option.

Center Point

Figure 37-14

The default options create a cylinder in the orientation shown in Figure 37-14.

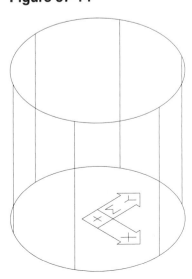

Command: *cylinder*
Elliptical/<Center point><0,0,0>: **PICK** or **(coordinates)** or
Enter
Diameter/<Radius>: **PICK** or **(coordinates)**
Center other end/<Height>: **Pick** or **(coordinates)**

Elliptical

This option draws a cylinder with an elliptical base (Fig. 37-15). Specify two axis endpoints to define the elliptical base. An elliptical cylinder can be created using the *Center, Center other end,* or *Height* options.

Elliptical/<center point> <0,0,0>: **e**
Center/<Axis endpoint>: **c**
Center of ellipse <0,0,0>: **PICK** or **(coordinates)**
Axis endpoint: **PICK** or **(coordinates)**
Other axis distance: **PICK** or **(coordinates)**
Center other end/<Height>:

Figure 37-15

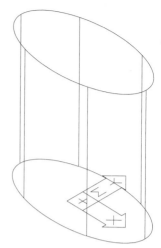

The ***Center other end*** option of *Cylinder* is similar to *Cone Apex* option in that the height and orientation are defined by the *Center point* and the *Center other end*. In Figure 37-16, a hole is created in the *Box* by using *Center other end* option and *OSNAP*ing to the diagonal lines' *MID*points, then *Subtract*ing the *Cylinder* from the *Box*.

Figure 37-16

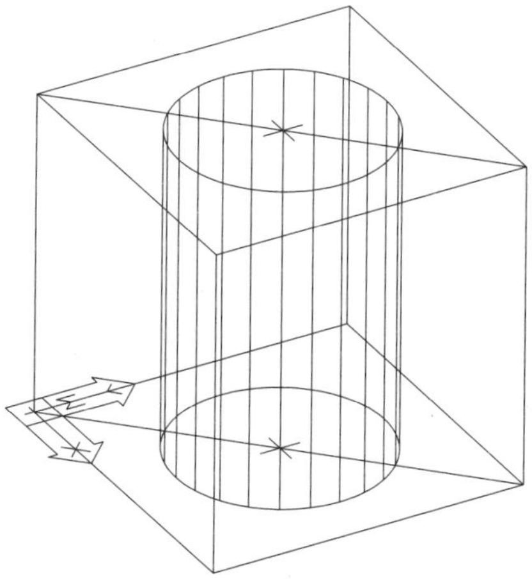

WEDGE

PULL-DOWN MENU	SCREEN MENU	TYPE IN	TABLET MENU
Draw *Solids >* *Wedge >*	DRAW2 SOLIDS: *Wedge:*	WEDGE	7,N

Corner of Wedge

Wedge creates a wedge solid primitive. By default, the base of the wedge is parallel with the current UCS XY plane, and the <u>slope of the wedge is along the X axis</u>.

Command: **wedge**
Center/<Corner of wedge><0,0,0>: **PICK** or **(coordinates)**
Cube/Length/<other corner>: **PICK** or **(coordinates)**

Figure 37-17

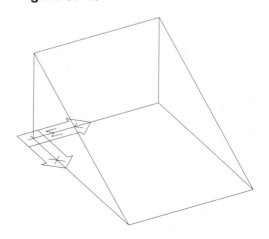

Accepting all the defaults, a *Wedge* can be created as shown in Figure 37-17, with the slope along the X axis.

Invoking the **Length** option prompts you for the *Length, Width,* and *Depth.* AutoCAD really means width (X dimension), depth (Y dimension), and height (Z dimension).

Center

The point you specify as the center is actually in the center of an imaginary box, half of which is occupied by the wedge. Therefore, the center point is actually at the <u>center of the sloping side of the wedge</u> (Fig. 37-18).

Figure 37-18 —————

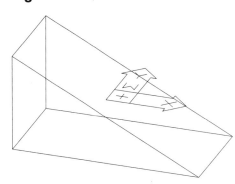

SPHERE

PULL-DOWN MENU	SCREEN MENU	TYPE IN	TABLET MENU
Draw *Solids >* *Sphere*	*DRAW2* *SOLIDS* *Sphere:*	*SPHERE*	*7,K*

Sphere allows you to create a solid sphere by defining its center point and radius or diameter.

Figure 37-19 —————

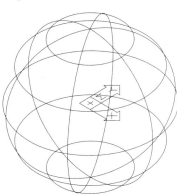

```
Command: sphere
<Center point><0,0,0>: PICK or (coordinates)
Diameter/<radius>: PICK or (coordinates)
Command:
```

Creating a *Sphere* with the default options would yield a sphere similar to that in Figure 37-19.

TORUS

PULL-DOWN MENU	SCREEN MENU	TYPE IN	TABLET MENU
Draw *Solids >* *Torus*	*DRAW2* *SOLIDS* *Torus:*	*TORUS*	*7,O*

Torus creates a torus (donut shaped) solid primitive using the dimensions you specify. Two dimensions are needed: (1) the radius or diameter of the tube and (2) the radius or diameter from the axis of the torus to the center of the tube. AutoCAD prompts:

```
Command: torus
<Center of torus><0,0,0>: PICK or (coordinates) or Enter
Diameter/<radius> of torus: PICK or (coordinates)
Diameter/<radius> of tube: PICK or (coordinates)
Command:
```

Figure 37-20 shows a *Torus* created using the default orientation with the axis of the tube aligned with the Z axis of the UCS and the center of the torus at 0,0,0. (*Hide* was used for this display.)

Figure 37-20 ——————

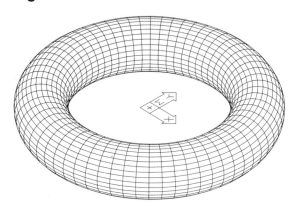

A self-intersecting torus is allowed with the *Torus* command. A self-intersecting torus is created by specifying a torus radius less than the tube radius. Figure 37-21 illustrates a torus with a torus radius of 3 and a tube radius of 4.

Figure 37-21 ——————

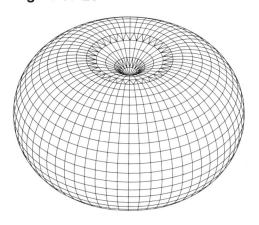

EXTRUDE

PULL-DOWN MENU	SCREEN MENU	TYPE IN	TABLET MENU
Draw *Solids >* *Extrude*	*DRAW2* *SOLIDS* *Extrude:*	*EXTRUDE*	*8,K*

Extrude (like *Revolve*) is a "sweeping operation." Sweeping operations use existing 2D objects to create a solid.

Extrude means to add a Z (height dimension) to an otherwise 2D shape. This command extrudes an existing closed 2D shape such as a *Circle, Polygon, Ellipse, Pline, Spline,* or *Region*. Only closed 2D shapes can be extruded in Release 13. The closed 2D shape cannot be self-intersecting (crossing over itself).

There are two methods for determining the direction of extruding: perpendicular to the shape and along a *Path*. With the default method, the selected 2D shape is extruded perpendicular to the plane of the shape regardless of the current UCS orientation. Using the *Path* method, you can extrude the existing closed 2D shape along any existing path determined by a *Line, Arc, Spline,* or *Pline*.

The versatility of this command lies in the fact that any closed shape that can be created by (or converted to) a *Pline, Spline, Region,* etc., no matter how complex, can be transformed into a solid and can be extruded perpendicularly or along a *Path*. *Extrude* can simplify the creation of many solids that may otherwise take much more time and effort using typical primitives and Boolean operations. Create the closed 2D shape first; then invoke *Extrude*.

```
Command: extrude
Select objects: PICK
Path/<Height of Extrusion>: (value)
Extrusion taper angle <0>: (value) or Enter
Command:
```

Figure 37-22 shows a *Pline* before and after using *Extrude*.

Figure 37-22

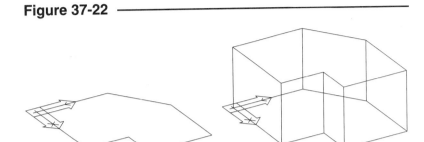

A taper angle can be specified for the extrusion. The resulting solid has sides extruded inward at the specified angle (Fig. 37-23). This is helpful for developing parts for molds that require a slight draft angle to facilitate easy removal of the part from the mold.

Figure 37-23

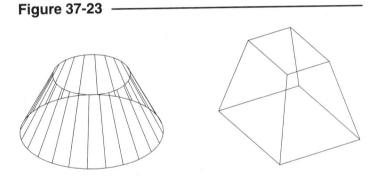

Many complex shapes based on closed 2D *Splines* or *Plines* can be transformed to solids using *Extrude* (Fig. 37-24).

Figure 37-24

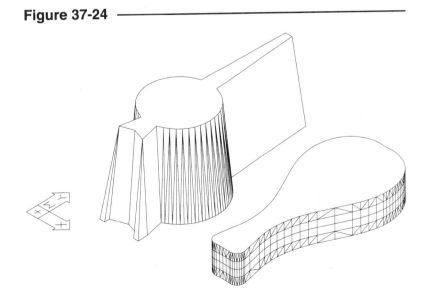

The *Path* option allows you to sweep the 2D shape along an existing line or curve called a "path." The *Path* can be composed of a *Line, Arc, Ellipse, Pline,* or *Spline* (or can be different shapes converted to a *Pline*). This path must lie in a plane. Figure 37-25 shows a closed *Pline* extruded along a *Pline* path and a curved *Spline* path.

Figure 37-25

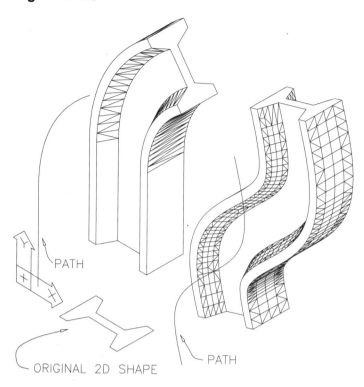

```
Command: extrude
Select objects: PICK
Path/<Height of Extrusion>: path
Select path: PICK
Command:
```

The path cannot lie in the same plane as the 2D shape to be extruded, since the plane of the 2D shape is always extruded perpendicular along the path. If one of the endpoints of the path is not located on the plane of the 2D shape, AutoCAD will automatically move the path to the center of the profile temporarily. Notice how the original 2D shape was extruded perpendicularly to the path (Fig. 37-26).

Revolve creates a swept solid. *Revolve* creates a solid by revolving a 2D shape about a selected axis. The

Figure 37-26

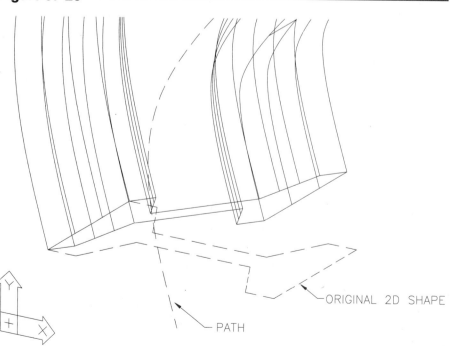

REVOLVE

PULL-DOWN MENU	SCREEN MENU	TYPE IN	TABLET MENU
Draw *Solids >* *Revolve*	DRAW2 SOLIDS: *Revolve:*	REVOLVE	8,L

Revolve creates a swept solid. *Revolve* creates a solid by revolving a 2D shape about a selected axis. The 2D shape to revolve can be a *Pline, Polygon, Circle, Ellipse, Spline*, or a *Region* object. Only one object at a time can be revolved. *Splines* or *Plines* selected for revolving must be closed. The command syntax for *Revolve* (accepting the defaults) is:

```
Command: revolve
Select objects: PICK
Select objects: Enter (Indicates completion of selection process.)
Axis of revolution - Object/X/Y/<Start point of axis>: PICK
End point of axis: PICK
Angle of revolution <full circle>: (value) or Enter
Command:
```

Figure 37-27 illustrates a possibility for an existing *Pline* shape and the resulting *revolved* shape generated through a full circle.

Because *Revolve* acts on an existing object, the 2D shape intended for revolution should be created in the desired orientation. There are multiple options for selecting an axis of revolution.

Object
A *Line* or single segment *Pline* can be selected for an axis. The positive axis direction is from the closest endpoint PICKed to the farthest.

X or Y
Uses the positive *X* or *Y* axis of the current UCS as the positive axis direction.

Figure 37-27

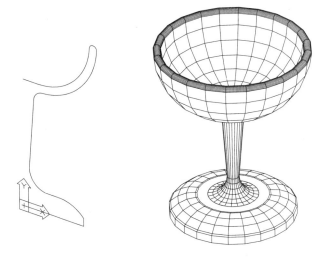

Start point of axis
Defines two points in the drawing to use as an axis (length is irrelevant). Select any two points in 3D space. The two points do <u>not</u> have to be coplanar with the 2D shape.

If the *Object* or *Start point* options are used, the selected object or the two indicated points do <u>not</u> have to be coplanar with the 2D shape. The axis of revolution used is <u>always on the plane of the 2D shape</u> to revolve and is aligned with the direction of the object or selected points.

Figure 37-28 demonstrates a possible use of the *Object* option of *Revolve*. In this case, a *Pline* square is revolved about a *Line* object. Note that the *Line* used for the axis is <u>not</u> on the same plane as the *Pline*. *Revolve* uses an axis <u>on the plane</u> of the revolved shape aligned with the direction of the selected axis. In this case, the endpoints of the *Line* are 0,-1,-1 and 0,1,1 so the shape is actually revolved about the Y axis.

Figure 37-28 ───────────

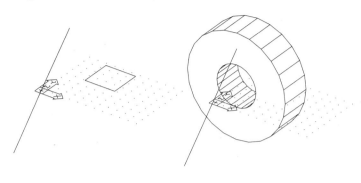

After defining the axis of revolution, *Revolve* requests the number of degrees for the object to be revolved. Any angle can be entered.

Figure 37-29 ───────────

Another possibility for revolving a 2D shape is shown in Figure 37-29. The shape is generated through 270 degrees.

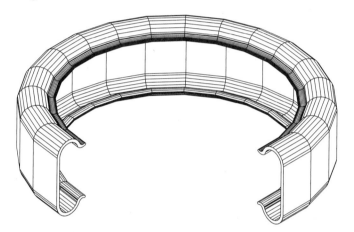

COMMANDS FOR MOVING SOLIDS

When you create the desired primitives, Boolean operations are used to construct the composite solids. However, the primitives must be in the correct position and orientation with respect to each other before Boolean operations can be performed. You can either create the primitives in the desired position during construction (by using UCSs) or move the primitives into position after their creation. Several methods that allow you to move solid primitives are explained in this section.

When constructing 3D geometry, it is critical that the objects are located in space at some <u>known</u> position. Do <u>not</u> create primitives at any convenient place in the drawing; know the position. The location is important when you begin the process of moving primitives to assemble 3D composite solids. Of course, *OSNAPs* can be used, but sometimes it is necessary to use coordinate values in absolute, rectangular, or polar format. A good practice is to <u>create primitives at the final location</u> if possible (use UCSs when needed) or <u>create the primitives at 0,0,0</u>, then <u>move</u> them preceding the Boolean operations.

MOVE

PULL-DOWN MENU	SCREEN MENU	TYPE IN	TABLET MENU
Modify *Move*	*MODIFY* *Move:*	*MOVE*	15,W

The *Move* command that you use for moving 2D objects in 2D drawings can also be used to move 3D primitives. Generally, *Move* is used to change the position of an object in one plane (translation), which is typical of 2D drawings. *Move* can also be used to move an ACIS primitive in 3D space <u>if</u> *OSNAPs* or 3D coordinates are used.

Move operates in 3D just as you used it in 2D. Previously, you used *Move* only for repositioning objects in the XY plane, so it was only necessary to PICK or use X and Y coordinates. Using *Move* in 3D space requires entering X, Y, and Z values or using *OSNAPs*.

For example, to create the composite solid used in the figures in Chapter 35, a *Wedge* primitive was *Moved* into position on top of the *Box*. The *Wedge* was created at 0,0,0, then rotated. Figure 37-30 illustrates the movement using absolute coordinates described in the syntax below:

Figure 37-30

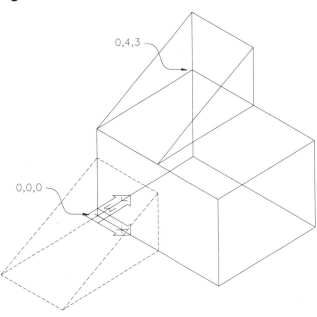

```
Command: move
Select objects: PICK
Select objects: Enter
<Base point of displacement>/Multiple:
0,0,0
Second point of displacement: 0,4,3
Command:
```

Alternately, you can use *OSNAPs* to select geometry in 3D space. Figure 37-31 illustrates the same *Move* operation using *ENDpoint* *OSNAPs* instead of entering coordinates.

Figure 37-31

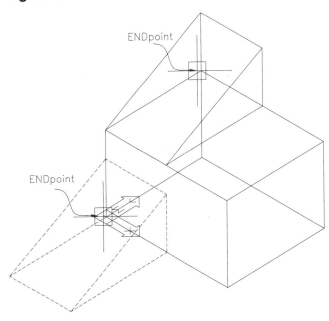

ALIGN

PULL-DOWN MENU	SCREEN MENU	TYPE IN	TABLET MENU
Modify *Align*	*MODIFY* *Align:*	*ALIGN*	19,Y

Align is an ADS application that is loaded automatically when typing or selecting this command from the menus. *Align* is discussed in Chapter 16 but only in terms of 2D alignment.

Align is, however, a very powerful 3D command because it automatically performs 3D <u>translation and rotation</u> if needed. *Align* is more intuitive and in many situations is easier to use than *Move*. All you have to do is select the points on two 3D objects that you want to align (connect).

Align provides a means of aligning one shape (an object, a group of objects, a block, a region, or a 3D solid) with another shape. The alignment is accomplished by connecting source points (on the shape to be moved) to destination points (on the stationary shape). You can use *OSNAP* modes to select the source and destination points, assuring accurate alignment. Either a 2D or 3D alignment can be accomplished with this command. The command syntax for 3D alignment is as follows:

```
Command: align
Select objects: PICK (Select object to move.)
Select objects: Enter
1st source point: PICK (use OSNAP)
1st destination point: PICK (use OSNAP)
2nd source point: PICK (use OSNAP)
2nd destination point: PICK (use OSNAP)
3rd source point: PICK (use OSNAP)
3rd destination point: PICK (use OSNAP)
```

After the source and destination points have been designated, lines connecting those points temporarily remain until *Align* performs the action (Fig. 37-32).

Align performs a translation (like *Move*) and two rotations (like *Rotate*), each in separate planes to align the points as designated. The motion automatically performed by *Align* is actually done in three steps.

Initially, the first source point is connected to the first destination point (translation). These two points are the only set that physically <u>touch</u>.

Figure 37-32 ———————————————

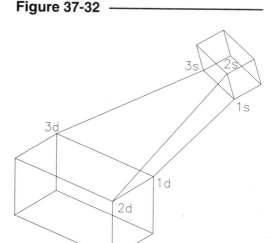

Next, the vector defined by the first and second source points is aligned with the vector defined by the first and second destination points. The length of the segments between the first and second points on each object is of no consequence because AutoCAD only considers the <u>vector direction</u>. This second motion is a rotation along one axis.

Figure 37-33 ———————————————

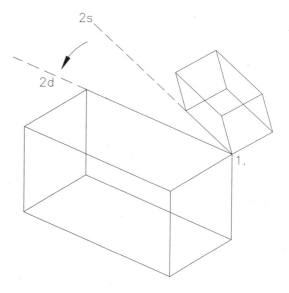

Finally, the third set of points are aligned similarly. This third motion is a rotation along the other axis, completing the alignment.

Figure 37-34

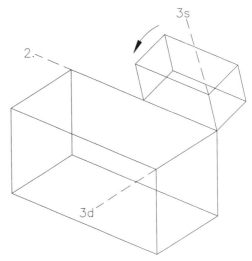

In some cases, such as when cylindrical objects are aligned, only two sets of points have to be specified. For example, if aligning a shaft with a hole (Fig. 37-35), the first set of points (source and destination) specify the attachment of the base of the shaft with the bottom of the hole (use *CENter OSNAPs*). The second set of points specify the alignment of the axes of the two cylindrical shapes. A third set of points is <u>not</u> required because the radial alignment between the two objects is not important. When only two sets of points are specified, AutoCAD asks if a 2D or 3D alignment is desired. The command syntax is as follows.

Figure 37-35

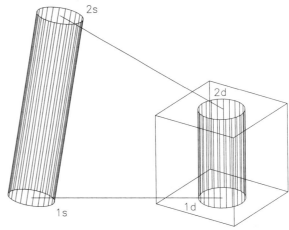

```
Command: align
Select objects: PICK
Select objects: Enter
1st source point: cen of PICK
1st destination point: cen of PICK
2nd source point: cen of PICK
2nd destination point: cen of PICK
3rd source point: Enter
<2d> or 3d transformation: 3
Command:
```

ROTATE3D

PULL-DOWN MENU	SCREEN MENU	TYPE IN	TABLET MENU
Construct *3D Rotate*	*CONSTRCT* *Rotat3D:*	*ROTATE3D*	*20,Y*

Rotate3D is very useful for any type of 3D modeling, particularly with CSG, where primitives must be moved, rotated, or otherwise aligned with other primitives before Boolean operations can be performed.

Rotate3D allows you to rotate a 3D object about any axis in 3D space. Many alternatives are available for defining the desired rotational axis. Following is the command sequence for rotating a 3D object using the default (*2points*) option.

> Command: `rotate3d`
> Select objects: `PICK`
> Select objects: `Enter` (Indicates completion of selection process.)
> Axis by Object/Last/View/Xaxis/Yaxis/Zaxis/<2points>: `PICK` or (`coordinates`) (Select the first point to define the rotational axis.)
> 2nd point on axis: `PICK` or (`coordinates`) (Select the second point to define rotational axis.)
> <Rotation angle>/Reference: `PICK` or (`value`) (Select two points to define the rotation angle or enter a value. If two points are PICKed, the angle between the points in the XY plane of the current UCS determine the angle of rotation.)

The options are explained next.

2points

The power of *Rotate3D* (over *Rotate*) is that any points or objects in <u>3D space</u> can be used to define the axis for rotation. When using the default (*2points* option), remember you can use *OSNAP* to select points on existing 3D objects. Figure 37-36 illustrates the *2points* option used to select two points with *OSNAP* on the solid object selected for rotating.

Figure 37-36

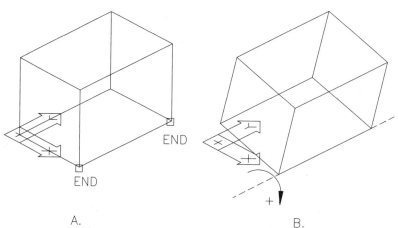

A.

B.

Object

This option allows you to rotate about a selected 2D object. You can select a *Line*, *Circle*, *Arc*, or 2D *Pline* segment. The rotational axis is aligned with the selected *Line* or *Pline* segment. Positive rotation is determined by the right-hand rule and the "arbitrary axis algorithm." When selecting *Arc* or *Circle* objects, the rotational axis is perpendicular to the plane of the *Arc* or *Circle* passing through the center. You <u>cannot</u> select the edge of a Release 13 solid object with this option.

Last

This option allows you to rotate about the axis used for the last rotation.

Figure 37-37

View

The *View* option allows you to pick a point on the screen and rotates the selected object(s) about an axis perpendicular to the screen and passing through the selected point (Fig. 37-37).

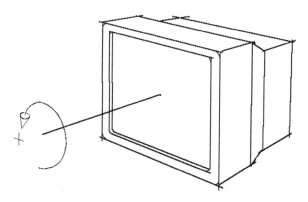

Xaxis

With this option, you can rotate the selected objects about the X axis of the current UCS or any axis parallel to the X axis of the current UCS. You are prompted to pick a point on the X axis. The point selected defines an axis for rotation parallel to the current X axis passing through the selected point. You can use *OSNAP* to select points on existing 3D objects (Fig. 37-38). The current X axis can be used if the point you select is on the X axis.

Figure 37-38

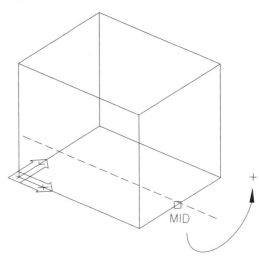

Yaxis

This option allows you to use the Y axis of the current UCS or any axis parallel to the Y axis of the current UCS as the axis of rotation. The point you select defines a rotational axis parallel to the current Y axis passing through the point. *OSNAP* can be used to snap to existing geometry (Fig. 37-39).

Figure 37-39

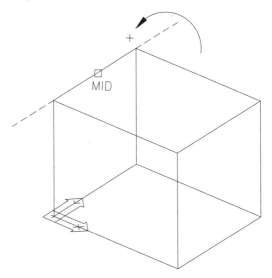

Zaxis

With this option, you can use the Z axis of the current UCS or any axis parallel to the Z axis of the current UCS as the axis of rotation. The point you select defines a rotational axis parallel to the current Z axis passing through the point. Figure 37-40 indicates the use of the *MIDpoint OSNAP* to establish a vertical (parallel to Z) rotational axis.

Figure 37-40

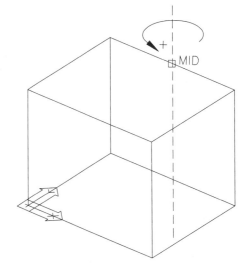

Reference

After you have specified the axis for rotation, you must specify the rotation angle. You are presented with the following prompt.

> <Rotation angle>/Reference: **r** (Indicates the *Reference* option.)
> Reference angle: **PICK** or (**value**) (PICK two points; *OSNAPs* can be used. You can enter a value.)
> New angle: **PICK** or (**value**) (Specify the new angle by either method.)

The angle you specify for the reference (relative) is used instead of angle 0 (absolute) for the starting position. You can enter either a value or PICK two points to specify the angle. You then specify a new angle. The *Reference* angle you select is rotated to the absolute angle position you specify as the "New angle."

Figure 37-41 illustrates how *ENDpoint OSNAPs* are used to select a *Reference* angle. The "New angle" is specified as **90**. AutoCAD rotates the reference angle to the 90 degree position.

Figure 37-41 ─────────────

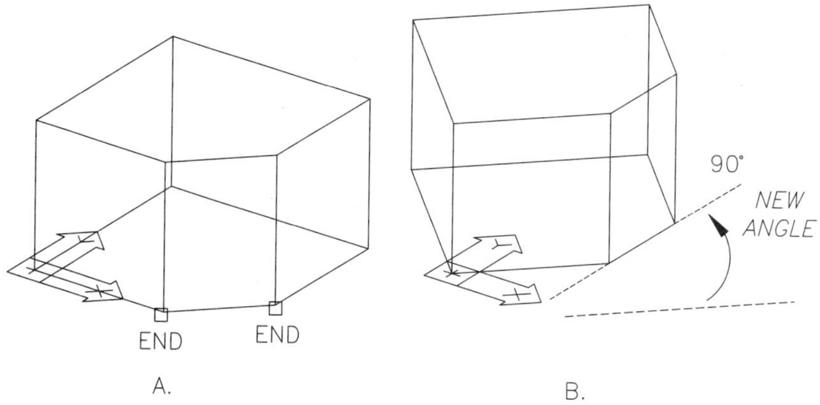

MIRROR3D

PULL-DOWN MENU	SCREEN MENU	TYPE IN	TABLET MENU
Construct *3D Mirror*	*CONSTRCT* *Mirro3D:*	*MIRROR3D*	*21,Y*

Mirror3D operates similar to the 2D version of the command *Mirror* in that mirrored replicas of selected objects are created. With *Mirror* (2D) the selected objects are mirrored about an axis. The axis is defined by a vector lying in the XY plane. With *Mirror3D*, selected objects are mirrored about a <u>plane</u>. *Mirror3D* provides multiple options for specifying the plane to mirror about.

> Command: **mirror3d**
> Select objects: **PICK** (Select one or multiple objects to mirror.)
> Select objects: **Enter** (Indicate completion of the selection process.)
> Plane by Object/Last/Zaxis/View/XY/YZ/ZX/<3points>: **PICK** or (**letters**) (PICK points for the default option or enter a letter(s) to designate option.)

The options are listed and explained next. A phantom icon is shown <u>only</u> in the following figures to aid your visualization of the mirroring plane.

3points

The *3points* option mirrors selected objects about the plane you specify by selecting three points to define the plane. You can PICK points (with or without *OSNAP*) or give coordinates. *MIDpoint OSNAP* is used to define the 3 points in Figure 37-42 (A) to achieve the result in (B).

Figure 37-42 ─────────────

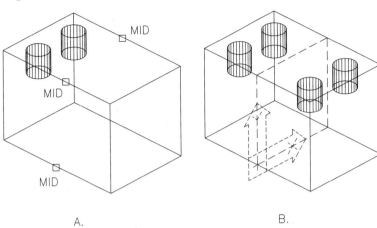

A.

B.

Object

Using this option establishes a mirroring plane with the plane of a 2D object. Selecting an *Arc* or *Circle* automatically mirrors selected objects using the plane in which the *Arc* or *Circle* lies. The plane defined by a *Pline* segment is the XY plane of the *Pline* when the *Pline* segment was created. Using a *Line* object or edge of an ACIS solid is not allowed because neither defines a plane. Figure 37-43 shows a box mirrored about the plane defined by the *Circle* object. Using *Subtract* produces the result shown in (B).

Figure 37-43 ─────────────

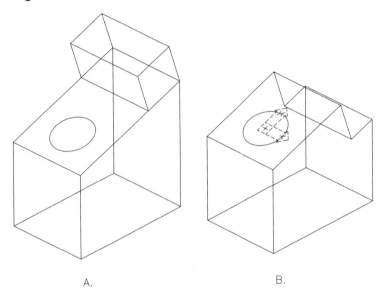

A.

B.

Last

Selecting this option uses the plane that was last used for mirroring.

Zaxis

With this option, the mirror plane is the <u>XY</u> plane perpendicular to a Z vector you specify. The first point you specify on the Z axis establishes the location of the XY plane origin (a point through which the plane passes). The second point establishes the Z axis and the orientation of the XY plane (perpendicular to the Z axis). Figure 37-44 illustrates this concept. Note that this option only requires two PICK points.

Figure 37-44 ─────────────

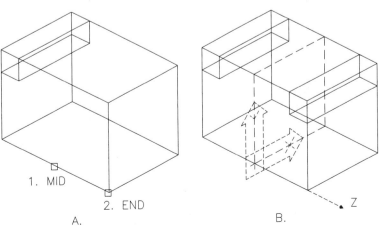

A.

B.

View

The *View* option of *Rotate3D* uses a mirroring plane <u>parallel</u> with the screen and perpendicular to your line of sight based on your current viewpoint. You are required to select a point on the plane. Accepting the default (0,0,0) establishes the mirroring plane passing through the current origin. Any other point can be selected. You must change *Vpoint* to "see" the mirrored objects (Fig. 37-45).

Figure 37-45

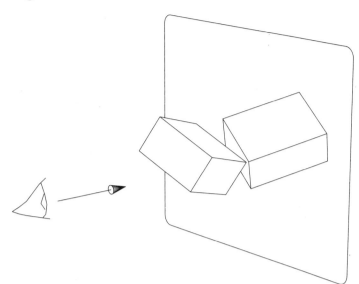

XY

This option situates a mirroring plane parallel with the current XY plane. You can specify a point through which the mirroring plane passes. Figure 37-46 represents a plane established by selecting the *CENter* of an existing solid.

Figure 37-46

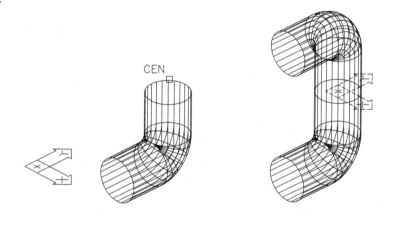

A.   B.

YZ

Using the *YZ* option constructs a plane to mirror about that is parallel with the current YZ plane. Any point can be selected through which the plane will pass (Fig. 37-47).

Figure 37-47

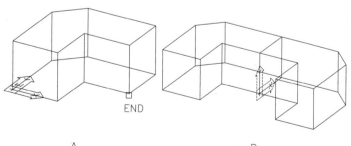

A.   B.

ZX

This option uses a plane parallel with the current ZX plane for mirroring. Figure 37-48 shows a point selected on the *MIDpoint* of an existing edge to mirror two holes.

Figure 37-48

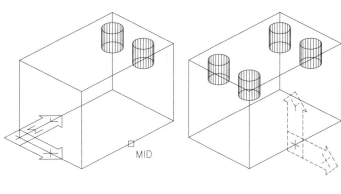

A.   B.

3DARRAY

PULL-DOWN MENU	SCREEN MENU	TYPE IN	TABLET MENU
Construct *3D Array*	*CONSTRCT* *3Darray:*	*3DARRAY*	---

Rectangular

With this option of *3Darray*, you create a 3D array specifying three dimensions—the number of and distance between rows (along the Y axis), the number/distance of columns (along the X axis), and the number/distance of levels (along the Z axis). Technically, the result is an array in a <u>prism</u> configuration <u>rather than a rectangle</u>.

```
Command: 3darray
Initializing...  3DARRAY loaded.
Select objects: PICK
Select objects: Enter
Rectangular or Polar array (R/P): r
Number of rows (---) <1>: (value)
Number of columns (|||) <1>: (value)
Number of levels (...) <1>: (value)
Distance between rows (---): PICK or (value)
Distance between columns (|||): PICK or (value)
Distance between levels (...): PICK or (value)
Command:
```

The selection set can be one or more objects. The entire set is treated as one object for arraying. All values entered must be positive.

Figures 37-49 and 37-50 illustrate creating a *Rectangular 3Darray* of a cylinder with 3 rows, 4 columns, and 2 levels.

Figure 37-49

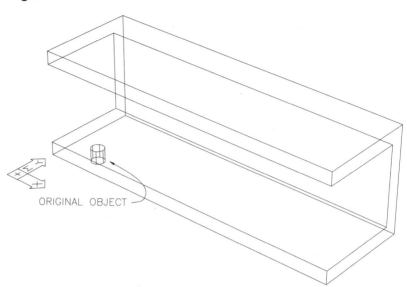

ORIGINAL OBJECT

The cylinders are *Subtracted* from the extrusion to form the finished part.

Figure 37-50

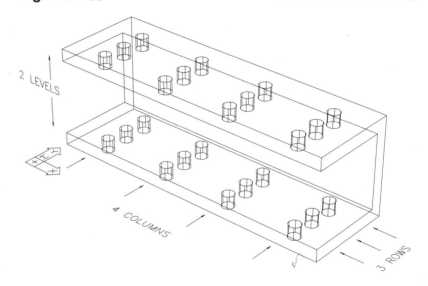

2 LEVELS

4 COLUMNS

3 ROWS

Polar

Similar to a *Polar Array* (2D), this option creates an array of selected objects in a <u>circular</u> fashion. The only difference in the 3D version is that an array is created about an <u>axis of rotation</u> (3D) rather than a point (2D). Specification of an axis of rotation requires two points in 3D space.

```
Command: 3darray
Select objects: PICK
Select objects: Enter
Rectangular or Polar array (R/P): p
Number of items: 8
Angle to fill <360>: Enter or (value)
Rotate objects as they are copied? <Y>: Enter or N
Center point of array: PICK or (coordinates)
Second point on axis of rotation: PICK or (coordinates)
Command:
```

In Figures 37-51 and 37-52, a *3Darray* is created to form a series of holes from a cylinder. The axis of rotation is the center axis of the large cylinder specified by PICKing the *CENter* of the top and bottom circles.

Figure 37-51

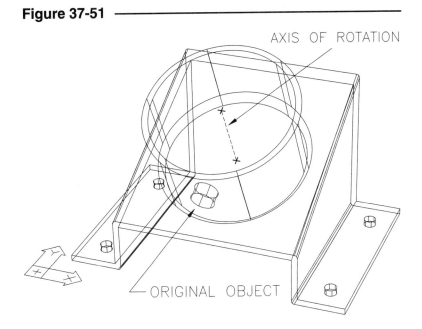

After the eight items are arrayed, the small cylinders are subtracted from the large cylinder to create the holes.

Figure 37-52

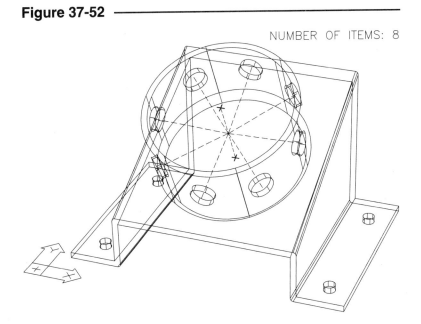

BOOLEAN OPERATION COMMANDS

Once the individual 3D primitives have been created and moved into place, you are ready to put together the parts. The primitives can be "assembled" or combined by Boolean operations to create composite solids. The Boolean operations found in AutoCAD are listed in this section: *Union*, *Subtract*, and *Intersect*.

UNION

PULL-DOWN MENU	SCREEN MENU	TYPE IN	TABLET MENU
Construct Union	DRAW2 SOLIDS Union:	UNION	13,Y

Union joins selected primitives or composite solids to form one composite solid. Usually, the selected solids occupy portions of the same space, yet are separate solids. *Union* creates one solid comprised of the total encompassing volume of the selected solids. (You can union solids even if the solids do not overlap.) All lines of intersections (surface boundaries) are calculated and displayed by AutoCAD. Multiple solid objects can be unioned with one *Union* command.

    Command: solunion
    Select objects: PICK (Select two or more solids.)
    Select objects: Enter (Indicate completion of the selection process.)
    Command:

Two solid boxes are combined into one composite solid with *Union* (Fig 37-53). The original two solids (A) occupy the same physical space. The resulting union (B) consists of the total contained volume. The new lines of intersection are automatically calculated and displayed. *Hide* was used to enhance visualization in (B).

Figure 37-53
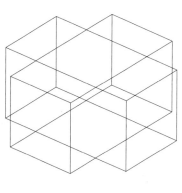
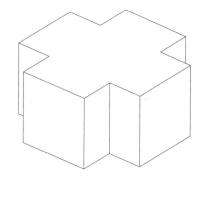

A.   B.

Because the volume occupied by any one of the primitives is included in the resulting composite solid, any redundant volumes are immaterial. The two primitives in Figure 37-54 (A) yield the same enclosed volume as the composite solid (B).

Figure 37-54
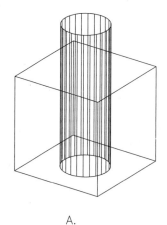
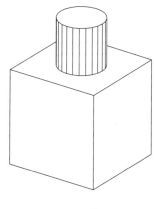

A.   B.

Multiple objects can be selected in response to the *Union* "Select objects:" prompt. It is not necessary, nor is it efficient, to use several successive Boolean operations if one or two can accomplish the same result.

Two primitives that have coincident faces (touching sides) can be joined with *Union*. Several "blocks" can be put together to form a composite solid.

Figure 37-55 illustrates how several primitives having coincident faces (A) can be combined into a composite solid (B). <u>Only one *Union* is required</u> to yield the composite solid.

Figure 37-55

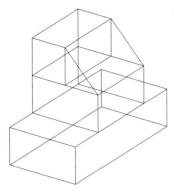 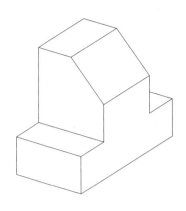

A. B.

SUBTRACT

PULL-DOWN MENU	SCREEN MENU	TYPE IN	TABLET MENU
Construct *Subtract*	*DRAW2* *SOLIDS* *Subtrac:*	*SUBTRACT*	*14,Y*

R13

Subtract takes the difference of one set of solids from another. *Subtract* operates with *Regions* as well as solids. When using solids, *Subtract* subtracts the <u>volume</u> of one set of solids from another set of solids. Either set can contain only one or several solids. *Subtract* requires that you first select the set of solids that will remain (the "source objects"), then select the set you want to subtract from the first.

```
Command: subtract
Select solids and regions to subtract from...
Select objects: PICK
Select objects: Enter
Select solids and regions to subtract...
Select objects: PICK
Select objects: Enter
Command:
```

The entire volume of the solid or set of solids that is subtracted is completely removed, leaving the remaining volume of the source set.

To create a box with a hole, a cylinder is located in the same 3D space as the box (see Figure 37-56). *Subtract* is used to subtract the entire volume of the cylinder from the box. Note that the cylinder can have any height, as long as it is at least equal in height to the box.

Because you can select more than one object for the objects "to subtract from" and the objects "to subtract," many possible construction techniques are possible.

Figure 37-56

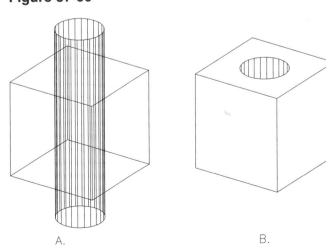

A. B.

If you select multiple solids in response to the select objects "to subtract from" prompt, they are <u>automatically</u> unioned. This is known as an <u>*n*-way Boolean</u> operation. Using *Subtract* in this manner is very efficient and fast.

Figure 37-57 illustrates an *n*-way Boolean. The two boxes (A) are selected in response to the objects "to subtract from" prompt. The cylinder is selected as the objects "to subtract...". *Subtract* joins the source objects (identical to a *Union*) and subtracts the cylinder. The resulting composite solid is shown in (B).

Figure 37-57

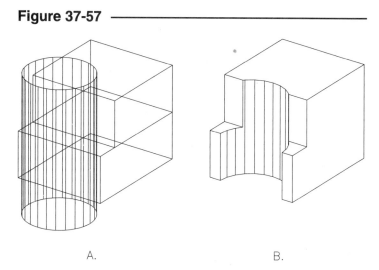

A.   B.

INTERSECT

PULL-DOWN MENU	SCREEN MENU	TYPE IN	TABLET MENU
Construct Intersection	*DRAW2 SOLIDS: Intersec:*	*INTERSECT*	*12,Y*

Intersect creates composite solids by calculating the intersection of two or more solids. The intersection is the common volume <u>shared</u> by the selected objects. Only the 3D space that is <u>part of all</u> of the selected objects is included in the resulting composite solid. *Intersect* requires only that you select the solids from which the intersection is to be calculated.

Command: **intersect**
Select objects: **PICK** (Select all desired solids.)
Select objects: **Enter** (Indicates completion of the selection process.)
Command:

An example of *Intersect* is shown in Figure 37-58. The cylinder and the box share common 3D space (A). The result of the *Intersect* is a composite solid that represents that common space (B).

Figure 37-58

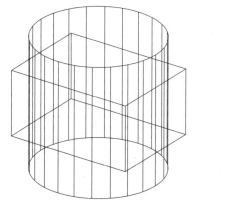
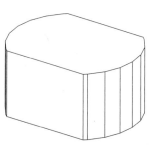

A.   B.

Intersect can be very effective when used in conjunction with *Extrude*. A technique known as <u>reverse drafting</u> can be used to create composite solids that may otherwise require several primitives and several Boolean operations. Consider the composite solid shown in Figure 37-55 A. Using *Union*, the composite shape requires four primitives.

A more efficient technique than unioning several box primitives is to create two *Pline* shapes on vertical planes (Fig. 37-59). Each *Pline* shape represents the outline of the desired shape from its respective view: in this case, the front and side views. The *Pline* shapes are intended to be extruded to occupy the same space. It is apparent from this illustration why this technique is called reverse drafting.

Figure 37-59

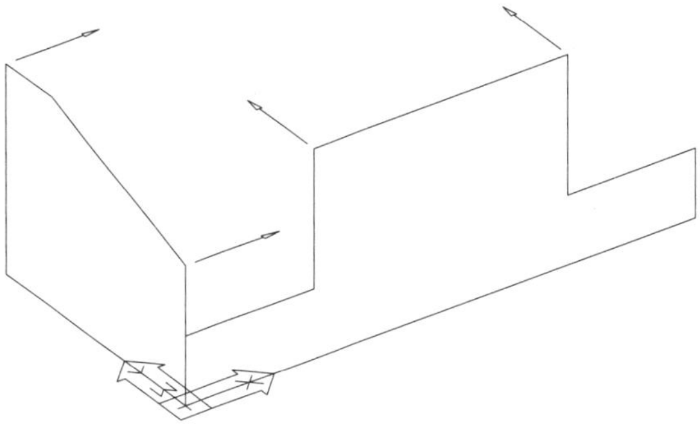

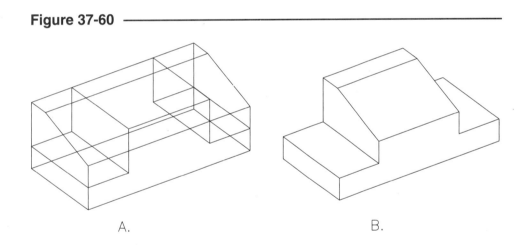

The two *Pline* "views" are extruded with *Extrude* to comprise the total volume of the desired solid (Fig. 37-60 A). Finally, *Intersect* is used to calculate the common volume and create the composite solid (B.).

Figure 37-60

A.   B.

CHAMFER

PULL-DOWN MENU	SCREEN MENU	TYPE IN	TABLET MENU
Construct *Chamfer*	*CONSTRCT* *Chamfer:*	*CHAMFER*	21,X

R13

Chamfering is a machining operation that bevels a sharp corner. *Chamfer* chamfers selected edges of an AutoCAD solid as well as 2D objects. Technically, *Chamfer* (used with a solid) is a Boolean operation because it creates a wedge primitive and then adds to, or subtracts from, the selected solid.

When you select a solid, *Chamfer* recognizes the object as a solid and <u>switches to the solid version of prompts and options</u>. Therefore, all of the 2D options are not available for use with a solid, <u>only the "distances" method</u>. When using *Chamfer*, you must both select the "base surface" and indicate which edge(s) on that surface you wish to chamfer.

```
Command: chamfer
(TRIM mode) Current chamfer Length = 0.5000, Angle = 30.0000
Polyline/Distance/Angle/Trim/Method/<Select first line>: PICK  (Select solid)
Select base surface: PICK  (Select any edge of the desired solid face)
Next/<OK>: N or Enter
Enter base surface distance <1.0000>: Enter  or  (value)
Enter other surface distance <0.5000>: Enter  or  (value)
Loop/<Select edge>: PICK  (Select edge to be chamfered)
Loop/<Select edge>: Enter
Command:
```

When AutoCAD prompts to select the "base surface," only an edge can be selected since the solids are displayed in wireframe. When you select an edge, AutoCAD highlights one of the two surfaces connected to the selected edge. Therefore, you must use the "Next/<OK>:" option to indicate which of the two surfaces you want to chamfer (Fig. 37-61 A). The two distances are applied to the object, as shown in Figure 37-61 B.

Figure 37-61 ──────────────────────────────

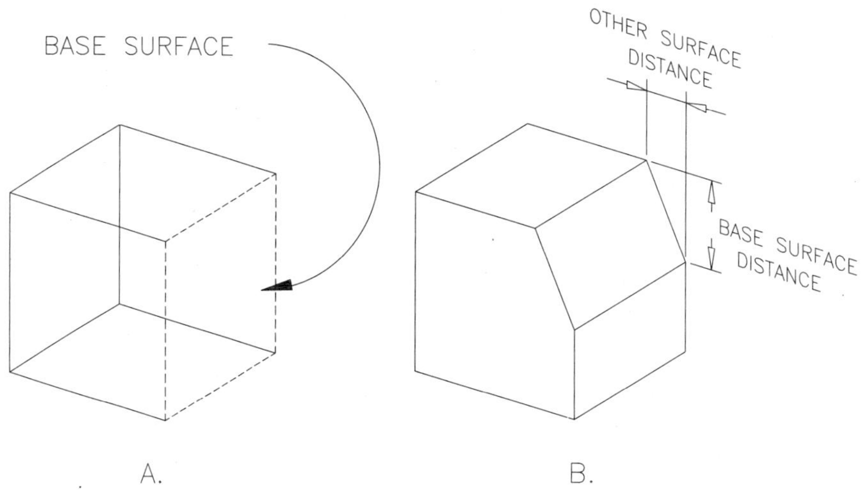

BASE SURFACE

OTHER SURFACE DISTANCE

BASE SURFACE DISTANCE

A.   B.

You can chamfer multiple edges of the selected "base surface" simply by PICKing them at the "<Select Edge>:" prompt (Fig. 37-62). If the base surface is adjacent to cylindrical edges, the bevel follows the curved shape.

Figure 37-62 ──────────────────────────────

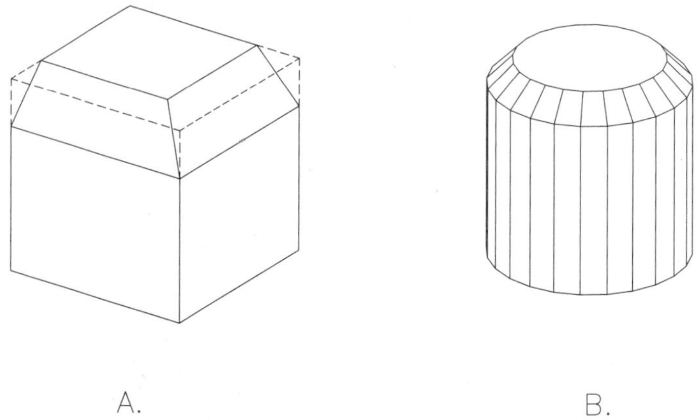

A.   B.

Loop

The *Loop* option chamfers the entire perimeter of the base surface. Simply PICK any edge on the base surface.

Loop/<Select edge>: *1*
Edge/<Select edge loop>: **PICK**
Edge/<Select edge loop>: **Enter**
Command:

Edge

The *Edge* option switches back to the "Select edge" method.

Figure 37-63

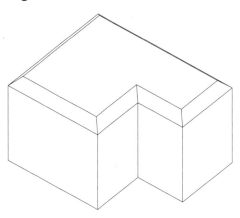

FILLET

PULL-DOWN MENU	SCREEN MENU	TYPE IN	TABLET MENU
Construct Fillet	CONSTRCT Fillet:	FILLET	20,X

Fillet creates fillets (concave corners) or rounds (convex corners) on selected solids, just as with 2D objects. Technically, *Fillet* creates a rounded primitive and automatically performs the Boolean needed to add or subtract it from the selected solids.

When using *Fillet* with a solid, the command <u>switches</u> to a special group of prompts and options for 3D filleting, and the <u>2D options become invalid</u>. After selecting the solid, you must specify the desired radius and then select the edges to fillet. When selecting edges to fillet, the edges must be PICKed individually. Figure 37-64 depicts concave and convex fillets created with *Fillet*. The selected edges are highlighted.

Figure 37-64

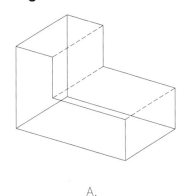

A.

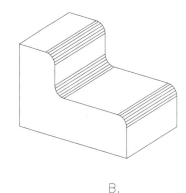

B.

Command: *fillet*
(TRIM mode) Current fillet radius = 0.5000
Polyline/Radius/Trim/<Select first object>: **PICK** (Select solid)
Chain/Radius/<Select edge>: Enter radius: **(value)**
Chain/Radius/<Select edge>: **PICK**
Chain/Radius/<Select edge>: **PICK**
Chain/Radius/<Select edge>: **Enter**
n edges selected for fillet.
Command:

Curved surfaces can be treated with *Fillet,* as shown in Figure 37-65. If you want to fillet intersecting concave or convex edges, *Fillet* handles your request, providing you specify all edges in <u>one</u> use of the command. Figure 37-65 shows the selected edges (highlighted) and the resulting solid. Make sure you select <u>all</u> edges together (in one *Fillet* command).

Figure 37-65

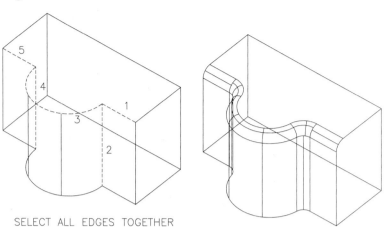

SELECT ALL EDGES TOGETHER

Chain

The *Chain* option allows you to fillet a series of connecting edges. Select the edges to form the chain (Fig. 37-66). If the chain is obvious (only one direct path), you can PICK only the ending edges, and AutoCAD will find the most direct path (series of connected edges).

Figure 37-66

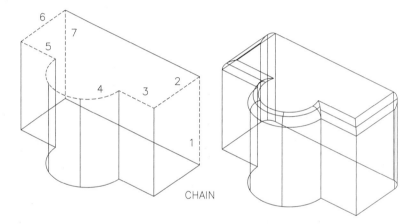

CHAIN

```
Chain/Radius/<Select edge>: c
Edge/Radius/<Select edge
chain>: PICK
```

Edge

This option cycles back to the "<Select edge>:" prompt.

Radius

This method returns to the "Enter radius:" prompt.

DESIGN EFFICIENCY

Now that you know the complete sequence for creating composite solid models, you can work toward improving design efficiency. The typical construction sequence is: (1) create primitives, (2) ensure the primitives are in place by using UCSs, or any of several move and rotate options, and (3) combine the primitives into a composite solid using Boolean operations. The typical step-by-step, "building-block" strategy, however, may not lead to the most efficient design. In order to minimize computation and construction time, you should <u>minimize the number of Boolean operations</u> and, if possible, the <u>number of primitives</u> you use.

For any composite solid, there are usually several strategies that could be used to construct the geometry. You should plan your designs ahead of time, striving to minimize primitives and Boolean operations.

For example, consider the procedure shown in Figure 37-55. As discussed, it is more efficient to accomplish all unions with one *Union*, rather than each union as a separate step. Even better, create a closed *Pline* shape of the profile; then use *Extrude*. Figure 37-57 is another example of design efficiency based on using an *n*-way Boolean. Multiple solids can be unioned automatically by selecting them at the select objects "to subtract from" prompt of *Subtract*. Also consider the strategy of reverse drafting, as shown in Figure 37-59. Using *Extrude* in concert with *Intersect* can minimize design complexity and time.

In order to create efficient designs and minimize Boolean operations and primitives, keep these strategies in mind:

- Execute as many subtractions, unions, or intersections as possible within one *Subtract*, *Union*, or *Intersect* command.

- Use *n*-way Booleans with *Subtract*. Combine solids (union) automatically by selecting <u>multiple</u> objects "to subtract from," and then select "objects to subtract."

- Make use of *Plines* or regions for complex profile geometry; then *Extrude* the profile shape. This is almost always more efficient for complex curved profile creation than using multiple Boolean operations.

- Make use of reverse drafting by extruding the "view" profiles (*Plines* or *Regions*) with *Extrude*, then finding the common volume with *Intersect*.

CHAPTER EXERCISES

1. What are the typical three steps for creating composite solids?

2. Why is ACIS called a hybrid modeler?

3. Consider the two solids in Figure 37-67. They are two extruded hexagons that are overlapping (occupying the same 3D space).

    A. Sketch the resulting composite solid if you performed a *Union* on the two solids.

    B. Sketch the resulting composite solid if you performed an *Intersect* on the two solids.

    C. Sketch the resulting composite solid if you performed a *Subtract* on the two solids.

Figure 37-67

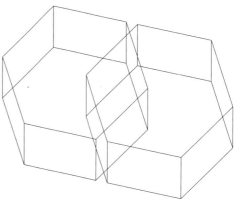

For the following exercises, use a *Prototype* drawing or begin a *New* drawing. Turn *On* the *Ucsicon* and set it to the *Origin*. Set the *Vpoint* with the *Rotate* option to angles of **310, 30**.

4. Open a drawing and assign the name **CH37EX4**.

    Figure 37-68 ─────────

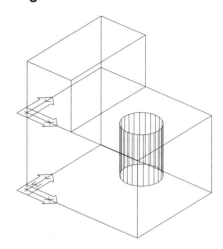

A. Create a *box* with the lower-left corner at **0,0,0**. The *Lengths* are **5**, **4**, and **3**.

B. Create a second *box* at a new UCS as shown in Figure 37-68 (use the *ORigin* option). The *box* dimensions are **2 x 4 x 2**.

C. Create a *Cylinder*. Use the same UCS as in the previous step. The *cylinder Center* is at **3.5,2** (of the *UCS*), the *Diameter* is **1.5**, and the *Height* is **-2**.

D. *Save* the drawing.

E. Perform a *Union* to combine the two boxes. Next, use *Subtract* to subtract the cylinder to create a hole. The resulting composite solid should look like that in Figure 37-69. *Save* the drawing.

    Figure 37-69 ─────────

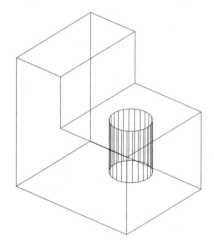

5. Open a drawing and assign the name **CH37EX5**.

    Figure 37-70 ─────────

A. Create a *Wedge* at point **0,0,0** with the *Lengths* of **5, 4, 3**.

B. Create a *3point UCS* option with an orientation indicated in Figure 37-70. Create a *Cone* with the *Center* at **2,3** (of the UCS) and a *Diameter* of **2** and a *Height* of **-4**.

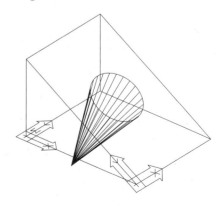

C. *Subtract* the cone from the wedge. The resulting composite solid should resemble Figure 37-71. *Save* the drawing.

Figure 37-71 ———————

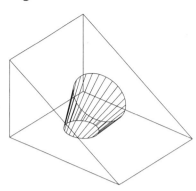

6. Open a drawing and assign the name **CH37EX6**. Display a *Plan* view.

Figure 37-72 ————————————————

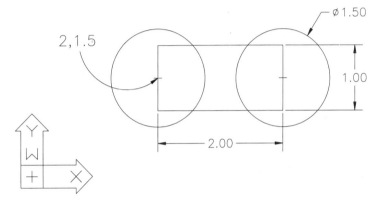

A. Create 2 *Circles* as shown in Figure 37-72, with dimensions and locations as specified. Use *Pline* to construct the rectangular shape. Combine the 3 shapes into a *Region* by using the *Region* and *Union* commands <u>or</u> converting the <u>outside</u> shape into a *Pline* using *Trim* and *Pedit*.

B. Change the display to an isometric-type *Vpoint*. *Extrude* the *Region* or *Pline* with a *Height* of **3** (no *taper angle*).

C. Create a *Box* with the lower-left corner at **0,0**. The *Lengths* of the box are **6, 3, 3**.

D. *Subtract* the extruded shape from the box. Your composite solid should look like that in Figure 37-73. *Save* the drawing.

Figure 37-73 ———————

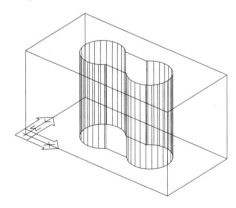

7.   Open a drawing and assign the name **CH37EX7**.
     Display a *Plan* view.

     A. Create a closed *Pline* shape symmetrical
         about the X axis with the locational and
         dimensional specifications given in Fig-
         ure 37-74.

     B. Change to an isometric-type *Vpoint*. Use
         Revolve to generate a complete circular
         shape from the closed *Pline*. Revolve about
         the **Y** axis.

     C. Create a *Torus* with the *Center* at **0,0**. The
         Radius of torus is **3** and the *Radius of tube* is
         .5. The two shapes should intersect.

     D. Use *Hide* to generate a display like Figure 37-75.

     E. Create a *Cylinder* with the *Center* at **0,0,0**, a *Radius* of **3**, and
         a *Height* of **8**.

     F. Use *Rotate3D* to rotate the vertically oriented shape **90**
         degrees about the X axis (the *Pline* shape that was previously
         converted to a solid—not the torus). Next, move the shape
         up (positive Z) **6** units with *Move*.

     G. Move the torus up **4** units with *Move*.

     H. The solid primitives should appear as those in Figure 37-76. (*Hide*
         has been used for the figure.)

Figure 37-74 ————————————

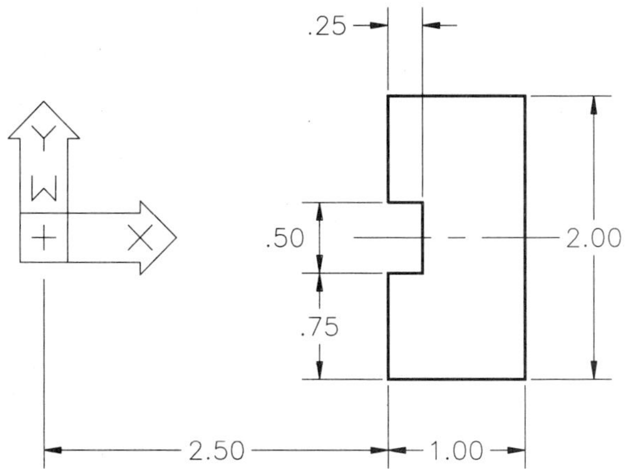

Figure 37-75 ————————

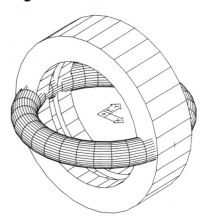

Figure 37-76 ————————

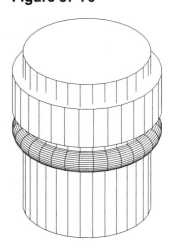

I. Use *Subtract* to subtract both revolved shapes from the cylinder. Use *Hide*. The solid should resemble that in Figure 37-77. *Save* the drawing.

Figure 37-77

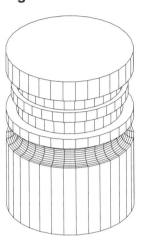

8. Begin a *New* drawing or use a *Prototype*. Assign the name **FAUCET**.

A. Draw 3 closed *Pline* shapes, as shown in Figure 37-78. Assume symmetry about the longitudinal axis. Use the WCS and create 2 new *UCS*s for the geometry. Use *3point Arcs* for the "front" profile.

Figure 37-78

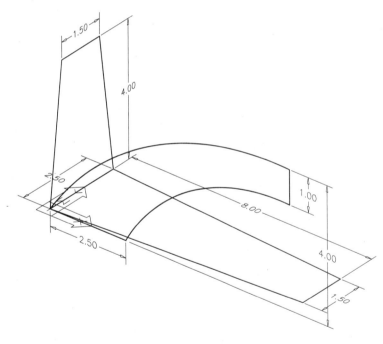

B. *Extrude* each of the 3 profiles into the same space. Make sure you specify the correct positive or negative *Height* value.

Figure 37-79

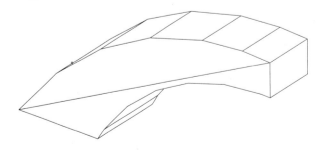

C. Finally, use *Intersect* to create the composite solid of the Faucet. *Save* the drawing.

D. (Optional) Create a nozzle extending down from the small end. Then create a channel for the water to flow (through the inside) and subtract it from the faucet.

9. Construct a solid model of the Bar Guide in Figure 37-80. Strive for the most efficient design. It is possible to construct this object with one *Extrude* and one *Subtract*. Save the model as **BGUID-SL**.

Figure 37-80

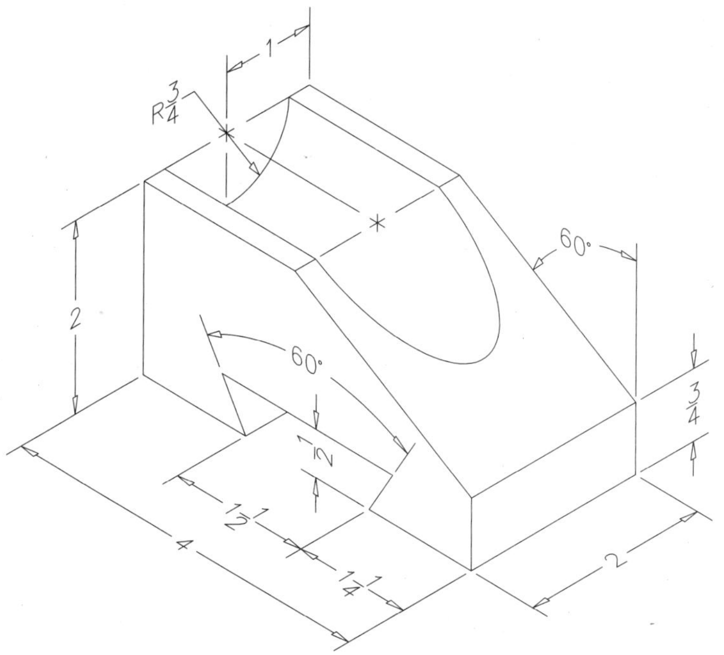

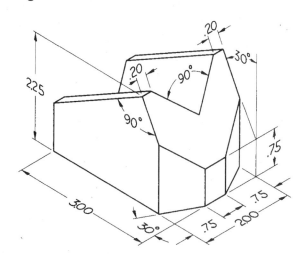

10. Make a solid model of the V-block shown in Figure 37-81. There are several strategies that could be used for construction of this object. Strive for the most efficient design. Plan your approach by sketching a few possibilities. Save the model as **VBLOK-SL**.

Figure 37-81

11. Construct a composite solid model of the Support Bracket using efficient techniques. Save the model as **SUPBK-SL**.

Figure 37-82

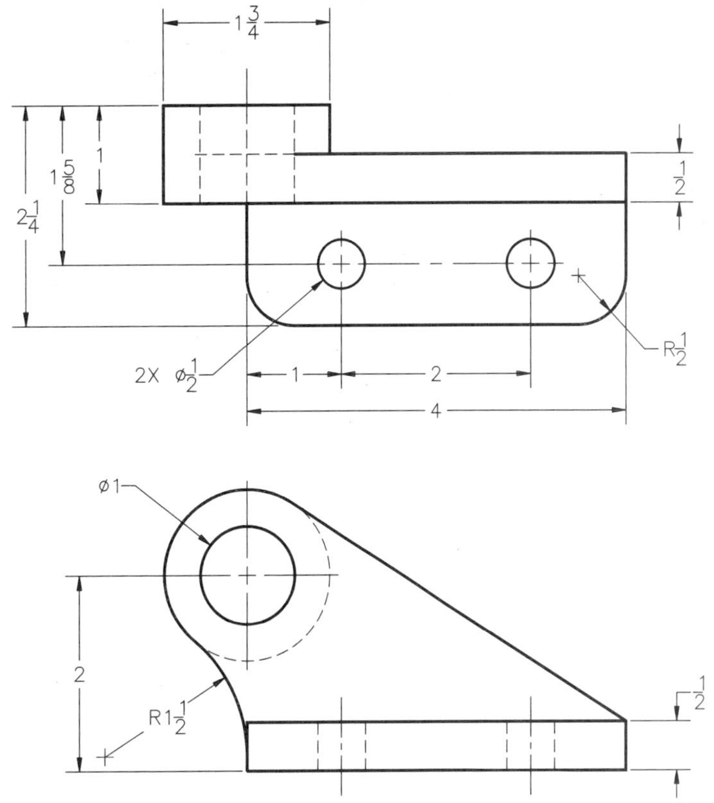

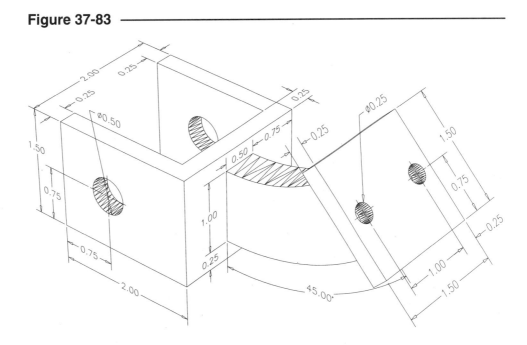

12. Construct the Swivel shown in Figure 37-83. The center arm requires *Extruding* the 1.00 x 0.50 rectangular shape along an arc path through 45 degrees. Save the drawing as **SWIVEL**.

Figure 37-83

13. Construct a solid model of the Angle Brace shown in Figure 37-84. Use efficient design techniques. Save the drawing as **AGLBR-SL**.

Figure 37-84

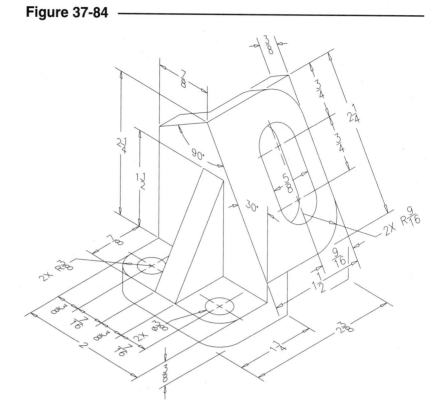

14. Construct a solid model of the Saddle shown in Figure 37-85. An efficient design can be utilized by creating **Pline** profiles of the top "view" and the front "view," as shown in Figure 37-86. Use **Extrude** and **Intersect** to produce a composite solid. Additional Boolean operations are required to complete the part. The finished model should look like Figure 37-87 (with *Hide* performed). Save the drawing as **SADL-SL**.

Figure 37-85

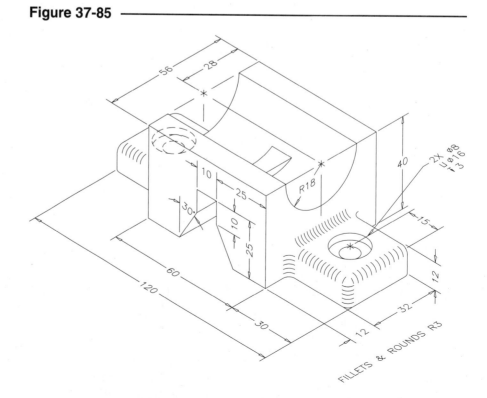

Figure 37-86 —————————————————

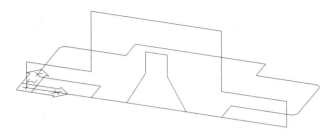

Figure 37-87 —————————————————

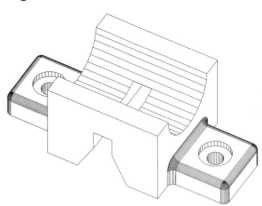

15. Construct a solid model of a bicycle handle bar. Create a center line (Fig. 37-88) as a *Path* to extrude a *Circle* through. Three mutually perpendicular coordinate systems are required: the **WORLD**, the **SIDE**, and the **FRONT**. The center line path consists of three separate *Plines*. First, create the 370 length *Pline* with 60 radii arcs on each end on the WCS. Then create the drop portion of the bars using the SIDE *UCS*. Create <u>three</u> *Circles* using the FRONT *UCS*, and extrude one along each *Path*.

Figure 37-88 —————————————————

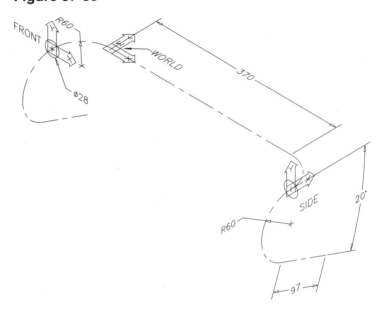

Plot the bar and *Hide Lines* as shown in Figure 37-89. *Save* the drawing as **DROPBAR**.

Figure 37-89 —————————————————

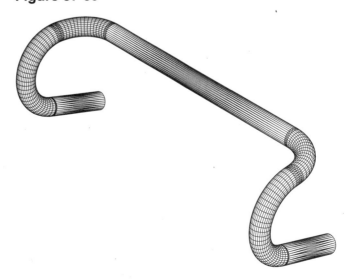

16. Create a solid model of the Pulley. All vertical dimensions are diameters. Orientation of primitives is critical in the construction of this model. Try creating the circular shapes on the XY plane (circular axis aligns with Z axis of the WCS). After the construction, use *Rotate3D* to align the circular axis of the composite solid with the Y axis of the WCS. *Save* the drawing as **PULLY-SL**.

Figure 37-90

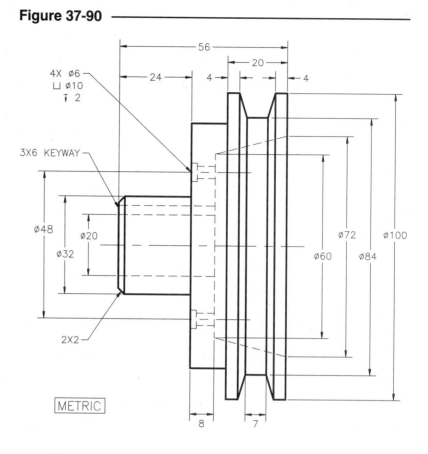

17. Create a composite solid model of the Adjustable Mount (Fig. 37-91). Use *Move* and other methods to move and align the primitives. Use of efficient design techniques is extremely important with a model of this complexity. Assign the name **ADJMT-SL**.

Figure 37-91

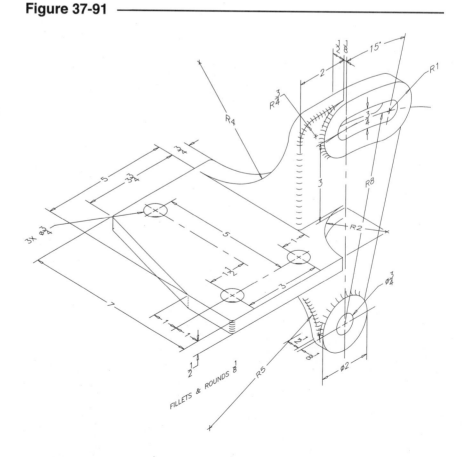

Chapter 38
MISCELLANEOUS SOLIDS FEATURES

Chapter Objectives

After completing this chapter you should be able to:

1. use the *ISOLINES*, *DISPSILH*, and *FACETRES* variables to control the display of tessellation lines, silhouette lines, and mesh density for solid models;

2. calculate mass properties of a solid model using *Massprop*;

3. determine if *Interference* exists between two or more solids and create a solid equal in volume to the interference;

4. create a 2D section view for a solid model using *Section* and *Bhatch*;

5. use *Slice* to cut a solid model at any desired cutting plane and retain one or both halves;

6. convert AME (Release 2 or 2.1) solid models to AutoCAD Release 13 ACIS solid models with *AMECONVERT*;

7. use *STLOUT* to create a file suitable for use with rapid prototyping apparatus.

BASICS

Several topics are discussed in this chapter related to solid modeling capabilities for AutoCAD Release 13 ACIS models. The topics are categorized in the following sections:

> Solid Modeling Display Variables
> Analyzing Solid Models
> Creating Sections from Solids
> Converting Solids

SOLID MODELING DISPLAY VARIABLES

AutoCAD solid models are displayed in wireframe representation by default. Wireframe representation requires less computation time and less complex file structure, so your drawing time can be spent more efficiently. When you use *Hide* or *Shade*, the solid models are automatically meshed before they are displayed with hidden lines removed or as a shaded image. This meshed version of the model is apparent when you use *Hide* on cylindrical or curved surfaces.

There are three variables that control the display for wireframe and meshed solids. The *ISOLINES* variable controls the number of tessellation lines that are used to visually define cylindrical surfaces for wireframes. The *DISPSILH* variable can be toggled on or off to display silhouette lines for wireframe displays. *FACETRES* is the variable that controls the density of the mesh apparent with *Hide*. The variables are accessed by typing the names at the Command: prompt.

Figure 38-1 ──────────────

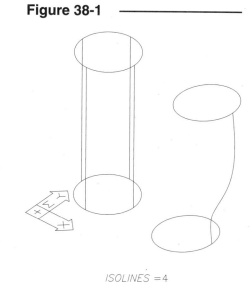

ISOLINES = 4

ISOLINES

This variable sets the <u>number of tessellation lines</u> that appear on a curved surface when shown in <u>wireframe</u> representation. The default setting for *ISOLINES* is 4 (Fig. 38-1). A solid of extrusion shows fewer tessellation lines (the current *ISOLINES* setting less 4) to speed regeneration time.

A higher setting gives better visualization of the curved surfaces, but takes more computing time (Fig. 38-2). After changing the *ISOLINES* setting, *Regen* the drawing to see the new display.

NOTE: In an isometric view attained by the *3D Viewpoint Presets*, the 4 lines (like Fig. 38-1) appear to overlap—they align when viewed from any perfect isometric angle.

Figure 38-2 ──────────────

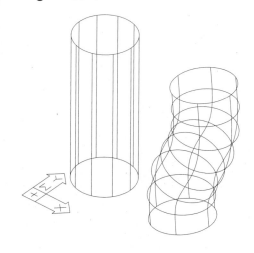

ISOLINES = 10

DISPSILH

This variable can be turned on to display the limiting element contour lines, or silhouette, of curved shapes for a wireframe display (Fig. 38-3). The default setting is 0 (off). Since the silhouette lines are <u>viewpoint dependent</u>, significant computing time is taken to generate the display. You should <u>not</u> leave *DISPSILH* on 1 during construction.

DISPSILH has a special function when used with *Hide*. When *DISPSILH* has the default setting of 0 and a *Hide* is performed, the solids appear opaque but display the mesh lines (Fig. 38-4). If *DISPSILH* is set to 1 before *Hide* is performed, the solids appear opaque but do <u>not</u> display the mesh lines (Fig. 38-5).

Figure 38-3

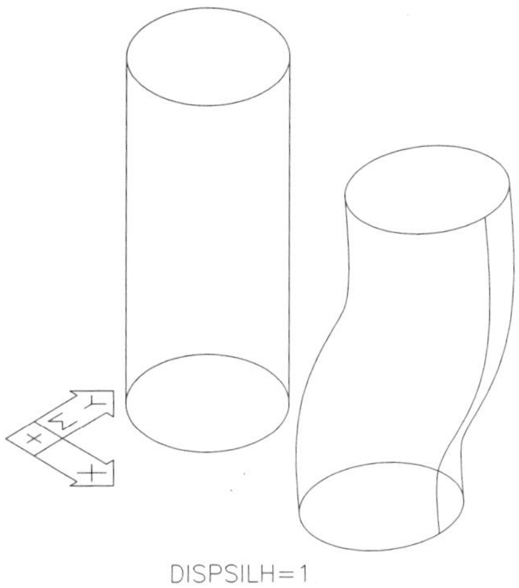

DISPSILH=1
ISOLINES=0

Figure 38-4

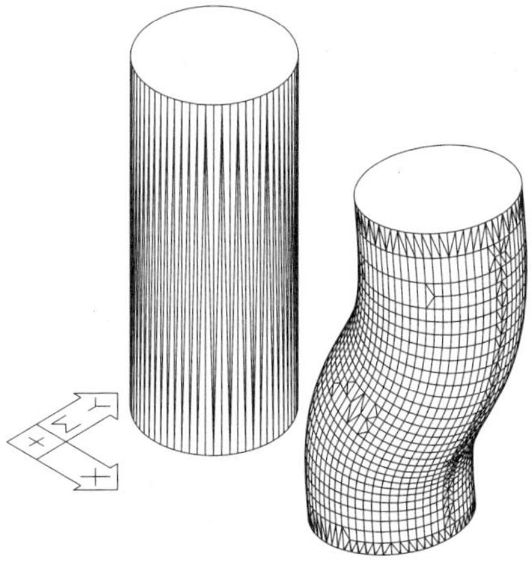

DISPSILH=0
THEN HIDE

Figure 38-5

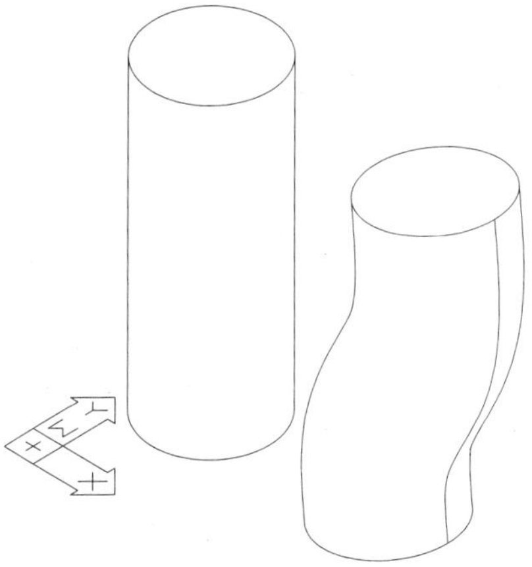

DISPSILH=1
THEN HIDE

FACETRES

FACETRES controls the <u>density of the mesh</u> that is automatically created when a <u>*Hide* or a *Shade*</u> is performed. The default setting is .5, as shown in Figure 38-6. Decreasing the value produces a coarser mesh (Fig. 38-7), while increasing the value produces a finer mesh. The higher the value, the more computation time involved to generate the display or plot. The density of the mesh is actually a factor of both the *FACETRES* setting and the *VIEWRES* setting. Increasing *VIEWRES* also makes the mesh more dense. *FACETRES* can be set to any value between .01 and 10.

Figure 38-6

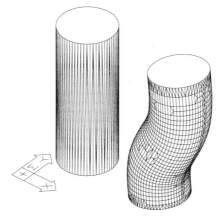

FACETRES =0.5

Figure 38-7

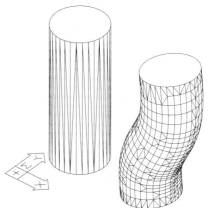

FACETRES =0.2

R13

ANALYZING SOLID MODELS

Two commands in AutoCAD allow you to inquire about and analyze the solid geometry. *Massprop* calculates a variety of properties for the selected ACIS solid model. AutoCAD does the calculation and lists the information in screen or text window format. The data can be saved to a file for future exportation to a report document or analysis package. The *Interfere* command finds the interference of two or more solids and highlights the overlapping features so you can make necessary alterations.

MASSPROP

DOS PULL-DOWN	WIN PULL-DOWN	SCREEN MENU	TYPE IN	TABLET MENU
Assist Inquiry > Mass Properties	*Edit Inquiry > Mass Properties*	*ASSIST INQUIRY: MassPro:*	*MASSPROP*	*1,P*

Since solid models define a complete description of the geometry, they are ideal for mass properties analysis. The *Massprop* command automatically computes a variety of mass properties.

Mass properties are useful for a variety of applications. The data generated by the *Massprop* command can be saved to an .MPR file for future exportation in order to develop bills of material, stress analysis, kinematics studies, and dynamics analysis.

Applying the *Massprop* command to a solid model produces a text screen displaying the following list of calculations (Fig. 38-8).

Figure 38-8

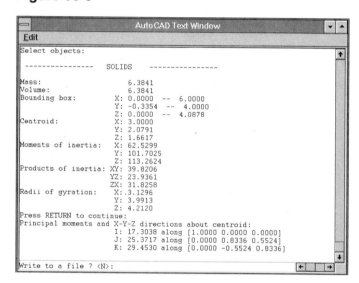

Mass	Mass is a measure of the weight of a solid. Mass is also considered a measure of a solid's resistance to linear acceleration (overcoming inertia).
Volume	This value specifies the amount of space occupied by the solid.
Bounding Box	These lengths specify the extreme width, depth, and height of the selected solid.
Centroid	This is the center of mass. The solid theoretically can be balanced when supported only at this point. The centroid is also considered the geometrical center.
Moments of Inertia	Moments convey how the mass is distributed around the X, Y, and Z axes of the current coordinate system. These values are a measure of a solid's resistance to <u>angular</u> acceleration (mass is a measure of a solid's resistance to <u>linear</u> acceleration). Moments of inertia are helpful for stress computations.
Products of Inertia	These values specify the solid's resistance to <u>angular</u> acceleration with respect to two axes at a time (XY, YZ, or ZX). Products of inertia are also useful for stress analysis.

Radii of Gyration

If the object were a concentrated solid mass without holes or other features, the radii of gyration represent these theoretical dimensions (radius about each axis) such that the same moments of inertia would be computed.

Principal Moments and X, Y, Z Directions

In structural mechanics, it is sometimes important to determine the orientation of the axes about which the moments of inertia are at a maximum. When the moments of inertia about centroidal axes become a maximum, the products of inertia become zero. These particular axes are called the principal axes, and the corresponding moments of inertia with respect to these axes are the principal moments (about the centroid).

INTERFERE

PULL-DOWN MENU	SCREEN MENU	TYPE IN	TABLET MENU
Draw *Solids >* *Interference*	DRAW2 *SOLIDS* Intrfer:	*INTERFERE*	---

In AutoCAD, unlike real life, it is possible to create two solids that occupy the same physical space. *Interfere* checks solids to determine whether or not they interfere (occupy the same space). If there is interference, *Interfere* reports the overlap and allows you to create a new solid from the interfering volume, if you desire. Normally, you specify two sets of solids for AutoCAD to check against each other.

```
Command: Interfere
Select the first set of solids...
Select objects: PICK
Select objects: Enter
1 solid selected.
Select the second set of solids...
Select objects: PICK
Select objects: Enter
1 solid selected.
Comparing 1 solid against 1 solid.
Interfering solids (first  set): 1
              (second set): 1
Interfering pairs:          1
Create interference solids? <N>: y
Command:
```

If you answer "yes" to the last prompt, a new solid is created equal to the exact size and volume of the interference. The original solids are not changed in any way. If no interference is found, AutoCAD reports "Solids do not interfere."

For example, consider the two solids shown in Figure 38-9. (The parts are displayed in wireframe representation.) The two shapes fit together as an assembly. The locating pin on the part on the right should fit in the hole in the left part.

Figure 38-9

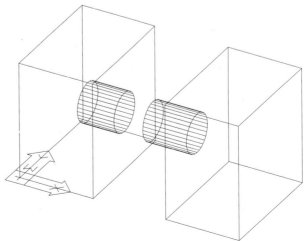

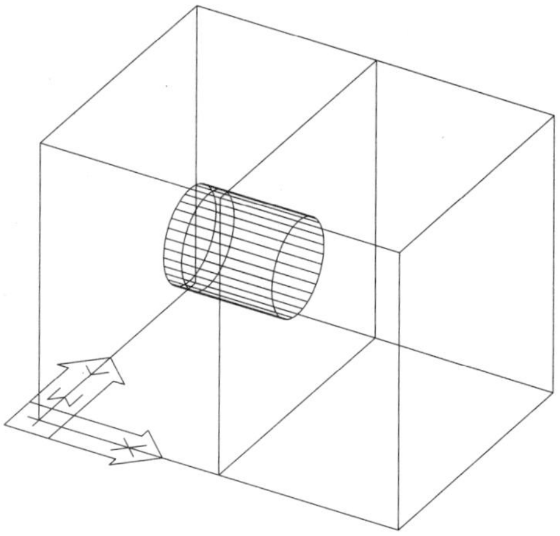

Sliding the parts together until the two vertical faces meet produces the assembly shown in Figure 38-10. There appears to be some inconsistency in the assembly of the hole and the pin. Either the pin extends beyond the hole (interference) or the hole is deeper than necessary (no interference). Using *Interfere*, you can find an overlap and create a solid is created by answering "yes" to "Create interference solids?" Use *Move* with the *Last* selection option to view and analyze the solid of interference.

Figure 38-10 ——————————

You can compare <u>more than two</u> solids against each other with *Interfere*. This is accomplished by selecting <u>all desired solids at the first prompt</u> and none at the second.

    Select the first set of solids... **PICK**
    Select the second set of solids... **Enter**

AutoCAD then compares all solids in the first set against each other. If more than one interference is found, AutoCAD highlights intersecting solids, one pair at a time.

CREATING SECTIONS FROM SOLIDS

Two AutoCAD commands are intended to create sections from solid models. *Section* is a drafting feature that creates a 2D "section view." The cross section is determined by specifying a cutting plane. A cross section view is automatically created based on the solid geometry that intersects the cutting plane. The original solid is not affected by the action of *Section*. *Slice* actually cuts the solid at the specified cutting plane. *Slice* therefore creates two solids from the original one and offers the possibility to retain both halves or only one. Many options are available for placement of the cutting plane.

SECTION

PULL-DOWN MENU	SCREEN MENU	TYPE IN	TABLET MENU
Draw *Solids >* *Section*	DRAW2 *SOLIDS* *Section:*	*SECTION*	16,Y

Section creates a 2D cross section of a solid or set of solids. The cross section created by *Solsect* is considered a traditional 2D section view. The cross section is defined by a cutting plane, and the resulting section is determined by any solid material that passes through the cutting plane. The cutting plane can be specified by a variety of methods. The options for establishing the cutting plane are listed in the command prompt.

    Command: *section*
    Select objects: **PICK**
    Select objects: **Enter**
    Sectioning plane by Entity/Last/Zaxis/View/XY/YZ/ZX /<3points>:

For example, assume a cross section is desired for the geometry shown in Figure 38-11. To create the section, you must define the cutting plane.

Figure 38-11

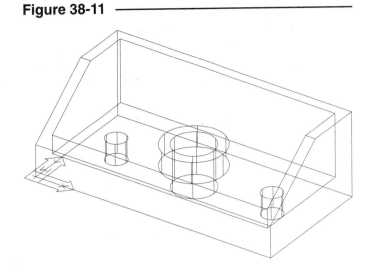

For this case, the *ZX* option is used and the requested point is defined to establish the position of the plane, as shown in Figure 38-12. The cross section will be created on this plane.

Once the cutting plane is established, a cross section is automatically created by *Section*. The resulting geometry is a *Region* created on the <u>current</u> layer.

Figure 38-12

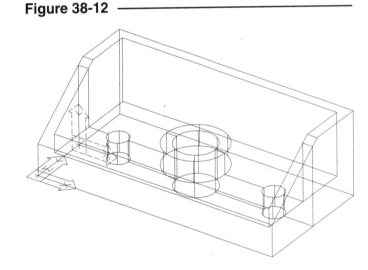

If needed, the *Region* and hatch lines can be *Moved* and used for a 2D section view. *Bhatch* can be used to apply hatch lines to the *Region* after using *Section*. However, to apply hatch lines to the four areas in Figure 38-13, the (one) *Region* must be *Exploded* into separate *Regions*, and each *Exploded* a second time to break the *Regions* into *Lines* that *Bhatch* can interpret as boundaries. Additional lines must be added to make a complete section view.

Figure 38-13

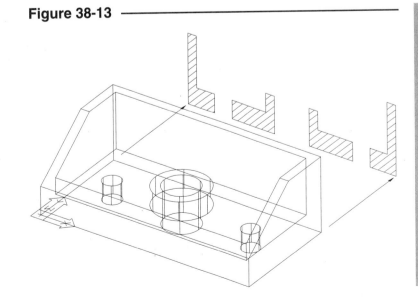

R13

SLICE

PULL-DOWN MENU	SCREEN MENU	TYPE IN	TABLET MENU
Draw *Solids* *Slice*	*DRAW2* *SOLIDS* *Slice:*	*SLICE*	*17,Y*

Slice creates a true solid section. *Slice* cuts an ACIS solid or set of solids on a specified cutting plane. The original solid is converted to two solids. You have the option to keep both halves or only the half that you specify. Examine the following command syntax:

```
Command: slice
Select objects: PICK
Select objects: Enter
Slicing plane by Object/Last/Zaxis/View/XY/YZ/ZX/<3points>: (option)
Point on XY plane <0,0,0>: PICK
Both sides/<Point on desired side of the plane>: PICK
Command:
```

Entering *B* at the "Both sides/<Point on desired side of plane>:" prompt retains the solids on both sides of the cutting plane. Otherwise, you can pick a point on either side of the plane to specify which half to keep.

For example, using the solid model shown previously in Figure 38-11, you can use *Slice* to create a new sectioned solid shown here. The *ZX* method is used to define the cutting plane midway through the solid. Next, the new solid to retain was specified by PICKing a point on that geometry. The resulting sectioned solid is shown in Figure 38-14. Note that the solid on the near side of the cutting plane was not retained.

Figure 38-14 ————————————————

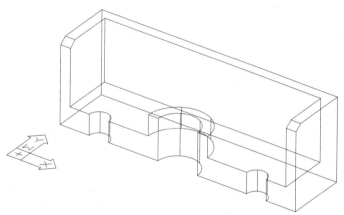

CONVERTING SOLIDS

AutoCAD Release 13 provides several utilities for converting solids to and from other file formats. Older AutoCAD solid models created with AME can be converted to a Release 13 ACIS model with some success. Other file utilities allow you to import and export .SAT files and to create files for use with stereolithography apparatus.

AMECONVERT

PULL-DOWN MENU	SCREEN MENU	TYPE IN	TABLET MENU
Draw *Solids* *AME Convert*	*DRAW2* *SOLIDS* *AMEconv:*	*AMECONVERT*	---

Ameconvert is a conversion utility to convert older solid models (created with AME Release 2 or 2.1) to AutoCAD Release 13 ACIS solid models. The command is simple to use; however, the conversion may change the model slightly. If the selected solids to convert are not AME Release 2 or 2.1, AutoCAD ignores the request.

The newer Release 13 solid modeler, ACIS, creates solids of higher accuracy than the older AME modeler. Because of this new accuracy, objects that are converted may change in appearance and form. For example, two shapes that were originally considered sufficiently close and combined by Boolean operations in the old modeler may be interpreted as slightly offset in the ACIS modeler. This can occur for converted features such as fillets, chamfers, and through holes. Occasionally, a solid created in the older AME model is converted into two or more solids in Release 13 ACIS modeler.

Solids that are converted to Release 13 ACIS solids can be edited using Release 13 solids commands. Converted solids that do not convert as expected can usually be edited in Release 13 to produce an equivalent, but more accurate, solid.

STLOUT

DOS PULL-DOWN	WIN PULL-DOWN	SCREEN MENU	TYPE IN	TABLET MENU
File *Export >* *Stereolithography*	*File* *Export >* **.STL*	*FILE* *EXPORT* *STLout:*	*STLOUT*	---

The *Stlout* command converts an ACIS solid model to a file suitable for use with rapid prototyping apparatus. Use *Stlout* if you want to use an ACIS solid to create a prototype part using stereo lithography or sintering technology. This technology reads the CAD data and creates a part by using a laser to solidify microthin layers of plastic or wax polymer or powder. A complex 3D prototype can be created from a CAD drawing in a matter of hours.

Stlout writes an ASCII or binary .STL file from an ACIS solid model. The model must reside entirely within the positive X,Y,Z octant of the WCS (all part geometry coordinates must be positive).

```
Command: stlout
Select a single solid for STL output:
Select objects: PICK
Create a binary STL file ? <Y>: Enter Y or N to create an ASCII file.
Command:
```

AutoCAD displays the *Create .STL File* dialogue box for you to designate a name and path for the file to create.

When you design parts with AutoCAD to be generated by stereolithography apparatus, it is a good idea to create the profile view (that which contains the most complex geometry) parallel to the XY plane. In this way, the aliasing (stair-step effect) on angled or curved surfaces, caused by incremental passes of the laser, is minimized.

ACISIN

DOS PULL-DOWN	WIN PULL-DOWN	SCREEN MENU	TYPE IN	TABLET MENU
AssistFile *Import >* *SAT...*	*File* *Import >* *ACIS (*.SAT)*	*FILE* *IMPORT* *SATin:*	*ACISIN*	---

The *Acisin* command imports an ACIS solid model stored in a .SAT (ASCII) file format. This utility can be used to import .SAT files describing a solid model created by AutoCAD Release 13 or other CAD systems that create ACIS solid models. The *Select ACIS File* dialogue box appears, allowing you to select the desired file. AutoCAD reads the file and builds the model in the current drawing.

ACISOUT

DOS PULL-DOWN	WIN PULL-DOWN	SCREEN MENU	TYPE IN	TABLET MENU
File *Export >* *SAT...*	*File* *Export >* *ACIS (*.SAT)*	FILE EXPORT ACISout:	ACISOUT	---

This utility is used to export an ACIS solid model to a .SAT (ASCII) file format that can later be read by AutoCAD Release 13 or other CAD systems utilizing the ACIS modeler. The *Create ACIS File* dialogue box is used to define the desired name and path for the file to be created.

CHAPTER EXERCISES

1. *Open* the **SADL-SL** drawing that you created in Chapter 37 Exercises. Calculate *Mass Properties* for the Saddle. Write the report out to a file named **SADL-SL.MPR**. Use a text editor or the DOS TYPE command to examine the file.

2. *Open* the **SADL-SL** drawing again. Use *Slice* to cut the model in half longitudinally. Use an appropriate method to establish the "slicing plane" in order to achieve the resulting model, as shown in Figure 38-15. Use *Saveas* and assign the name **SADL-CUT**.

Figure 38-15 ────────────

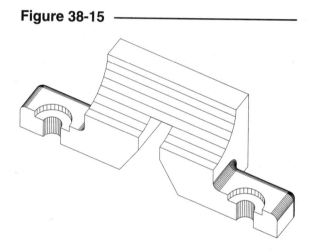

3. *Open* the **PULLY-SL** drawing that you created in Chapter 37 Exercises.

    Make a *New Layer* named **SECTION** and set it *Current*. Then use the *Section* command to create a full section "view" of the pulley. Establish a vertical cutting plane through the center of the model. Remove the section view object (*Region*) with the *Move* command, translating **100** units in the **X** direction. The model and the new section view should appear as in Figure 38-16 (*Hide* was performed on the Pulley to enhance visualization). Complete the view by establishing a *UCS* at the section view, then adding the *Bhatch,* as shown in Figure 38-16. Finally, create the necessary *Lines* to complete the view. *Saveas* **PULLY-SC**.

Figure 38-16 ────────────

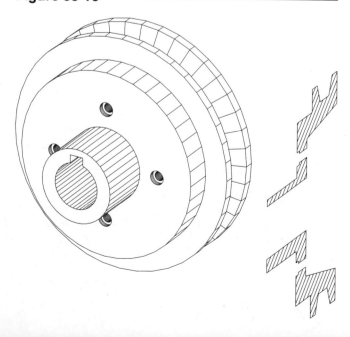

4. *Open* the **SADL-SL** drawing that you created in the Chapter 37 Exercises. Change the *ISOLINES* setting to display **10** tessellation lines. Use the *Hide* command to create a meshed hidden display. Change the *FACETRES* setting to display a coarser mesh and use *Hide* again. Make a plot of the model with the coarse mesh and with hidden lines (check the *Hide Lines* box in the *Plot Configuration* dialogue box).

Next, change the *FACETRES* setting to display a fine mesh. Use *Hide* to reveal the change. Make a plot of the model with *Hide Lines* checked to display the fine mesh. Then set the *DISPSILH* variable to **1** and make another plot with lines hidden. What is the difference in the last two plots? *Save* the **SADL-SL** file with the new settings.

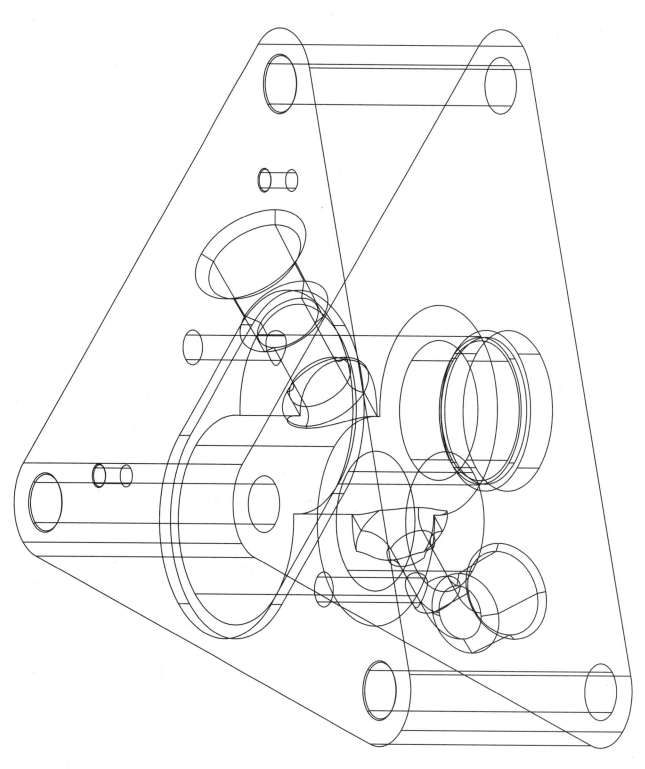

PUMPSOL.DWG Courtesy of Autodesk, Inc.

Chapter 39

SURFACE MODELING

Chapter Objectives

After completing this chapter you should:

1. be able to create planar surfaces bounded by straight edges using *3Dface*;

2. be able to edit *3Dfaces* with Grips and create invisible edges between *3Dfaces* using *Edge*;

3. be able to create meshed surfaces bounded by straight sides using *3Dmesh*;

4. be able to create geometrically defined meshed surfaces using *Rulesurf, Tabsurf, Revsurf,* and *Edgesurf*;

5. be able to edit polygon meshes (*3Dmesh, Rulesurf, Tabsurf, Revsurf,* and *Edgesurf*) using *Pedit, Explode,* and Grips;

6. be able to create *Regions* for use with surface models;

7. be able to use surface modeling primitives (*3D Objects*) to aid in construction of complex surface models;

8. be able to use *Thickness* and *Elevation* to create surfaces from 2D draw commands.

BASICS

A surface model is more sophisticated than a wireframe model because it contains the description of surfaces as well as the description of edges. Surface models can contain descriptions of complex curves, whereas, surfaces on a wireframe are assumed to be planar or single curved. Surface models are superior to wireframe models in that they provide better visualization cues. The surface information describes how the surfaces appear and gives the model a "solid" look, since surfaces that are nearer to the observer naturally obscure the surfaces and edges that are behind.

Generally, surface models do not describe physical objects as completely and as accurately as solid models. A surface model can be compared to a cardboard box—it has surfaces but is hollow inside. If a surface model is sectioned (cut in half), there is only air inside, whereas a solid model can be sectioned to reveal its interior features. Therefore, surface models have volume, whereas solid models have volume and mass. Curved surfaces are defined by discrete meshes composed of straight edges; therefore, small "gaps" may exist where a curved surface is adjacent to a planar surface.

Surface modeling is similar to wireframe and solid modeling in that 3D coordinate values must be used to create and edit the geometry. However, the construction and editing process of surface modeling is complex and somewhat tedious compared to wireframe and solid modeling. Each surface must be defined by describing the edges that bound the surface. Each surface must be constructed individually in location or moved into location with respect to other surfaces that comprise the 3D model.

Surface modeling is the type of 3D modeling that is best suited for efficiently defining complex curved shapes such as automobile bodies, aircraft fuselages, and ship hulls. Thus, surface modeling is a necessity for 3D modeling in many industries.

The surface modeling capabilities of AutoCAD Release 13 provide solutions for only a small portion of the possible applications. AutoCAD Release 13 does not utilize NURBS (Non-Uniform Rational B-Spline) surfacing techniques, which is the current preferred surface modeling technology. NURBS technology is utilized, however, in Autodesk's AutoSurf™ product line.

The categories of surfaces and commands that AutoCAD Release 13 provides to create surface models are as follows:

Surfaces with straight edges (usually planar)

3Dface	A surface defined by 3 or 4 straight edges

Meshed surfaces (polygon meshes)

3Dmesh	A planar, curved, or complex surface defined by a mesh
Pface	A surface with any number of vertices and faces

Geometrically defined meshed surfaces (polygon meshes)

Edgesurf	A surface defined by "patching" together 4 straight or curved edges
Rulesurf	A surface created between 2 straight or curved edges
Revsurf	A surface revolved from any 2D shape about an axis
Tabsurf	A surface created by sweeping a 2D shape in the direction specified by a vector

Surface model primitives

3D Objects...	A menu of complete 3D primitive surface models (box, cone, wedge, sphere, etc.) is available. These simple 3D shapes can be used as a basis for construction of more complex shapes.

Thickness, Solid

AutoCAD's early methods for creation of planar "extrusions" of 2D shapes are discussed briefly.

Regions can be used to simplify construction of complex planar surfaces for use with surface models. The region modeler utilizes Boolean operations, which makes creation of surfaces with holes and/or complex outlines relatively easy.

A visualization enhancement for surfaces is provided by the *Hide* command. Normally, during construction, surfaces are displayed by default (like solids) in <u>wireframe</u> representation. *Hide* causes a regeneration of the display showing surfaces as <u>opaque</u>, therefore obscuring other surfaces or objects behind them.

The surface modeling commands can be accessed easily from the *Draw* pull-down menu (Fig. 39-1). If you are using AutoCAD for Windows, a Surfaces toolbar can be activated to provide quick access to these commands (Fig. 39-2).

The surfacing commands are discussed first in this chapter. Then, application of the surfacing commands to create a complete 3D model is discussed.

Figure 39-1

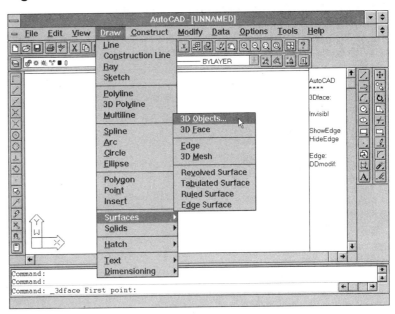

Figure 39-2

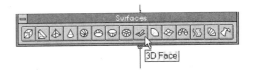

SURFACES WITH STRAIGHT EDGES

3DFACE

PULL-DOWN MENU	SCREEN MENU	TYPE IN	TABLET MENU
Draw *Surfaces >* *3D Face*	*DRAW2* *SURFACES* *3Dface:*	*3DFACE*	*9,P*

3Dface creates a surface bounded by three or four straight edges. The three- or four-sided surface can be connected to other *3Dfaces* within the same *3Dface* command sequence, similar to the way several *Line* segments created in one command sequence are connected. Beware, there is <u>no *Undo* option</u> for *3Dface*. The command sequence is:

Command: ***3dface***
First Point: **PICK** or (**coordinates**)
Second point: **PICK** or (**coordinates**)
Third point: **PICK** or (**coordinates**)
Fourth point: **PICK** or (**coordinates**)
Third point: **PICK** or (**coordinates**)
Fourth point: **PICK** or (**coordinates**)
Third point: **Enter** (Indicates completion of the *3Dface* sequence.)

After completing four points, AutoCAD connects the next point ("Third point:") to the previous fourth point. The next fourth point is connected to the previous third point, and so on. Figure 39-3 shows the sequence for attaching several *3Dface* segments in one command sequence.

In the example, each edge of the *3Dface* is <u>coplanar</u>, as is the entire sequence of *3Dfaces* (the Z value of every point on each edge is 0). The edges must be <u>straight</u>, but not necessarily coplanar. Entering specific coordinate values, using point filters, or using *OSNAP* in 3D space allows you to create geometry with *3Dface* that is not on a plane. The following command sequence creates a *3Dface* as a complex curve by entering a different Z value for the fourth point (Fig. 39-4).

> Command: **3dface**
> First Point: **PICK**
> Second point: **PICK**
> Third point: **PICK**
> Fourth point: **.XY**
> of **PICK**
> (need Z): **2**
> Third point: **Enter**
> Command:

Although it is possible to use *3Dface* to create complex curved surfaces, the surface curve is not visible as it would be if a mesh were used. A *3Dmesh* provides superior visibility and flexibility and is recommended for such a surface.

Figure 39-5 displays a possibility for creating nonplanar geometry in one command sequence. .XY filters can be used to PICK points, or absolute X,Y,Z values can be entered.

Figure 39-3

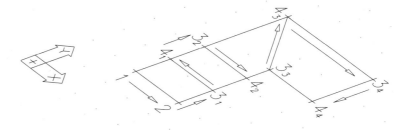

Figure 39-4

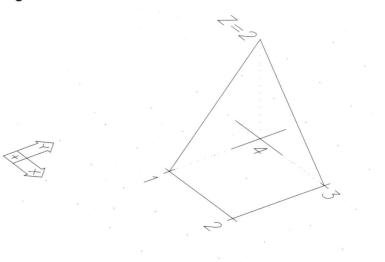

Figure 39-5

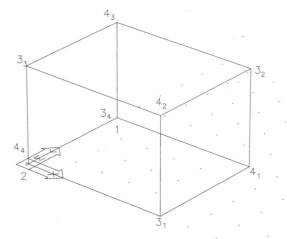

The lines between *3Dface* segments in Figure 39-3 are visible even though the segments are coplanar. AutoCAD provides two methods for making invisible edges. The first method requires that you enter the letter *"I"* immediately before the <u>first</u> of the two points that define an invisible edge. For the shape shown in Figure 39-6, enter the letter *"I"* <u>before</u> points 3_1, 3_2, and 3_3. The second, and much easier, method for defining invisible edges of *3Dfaces* is to use the *Edge* command.

EDGE

PULL-DOWN MENU	SCREEN MENU	TYPE IN	TABLET MENU
Draw *Surfaces >* *Edge:*	*DRAW2* *SURFACES* *Edge:*	*EDGE*	---

The first method for creating invisible edges described above takes careful planning. The same action shown in Figure 39-6 can be accomplished much more easily and <u>retroactively</u> by this second method. AutoCAD provides the *Edge* command to create invisible edges after construction of the *3Dface*. The command prompt is:

> Command: **edge**
> Display<select edge>: **PICK**

Selecting edges converts visible edges to invisible edges. <u>Any</u> edges on the *3Dface* can be made invisible by this method. The *Display* option causes selected invisible edges to become visible again.

Figure 39-6

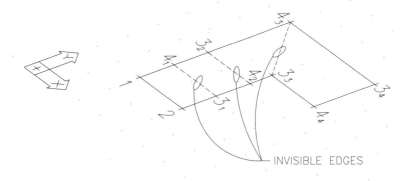

INVISIBLE EDGES

Applications of *3Dface*

3Dface is used to construct 3D surface models by creating individual (planar) faces or connected faces. For relatively simple models, the faces are placed in space as they are constructed. A construction strategy to use for more complex models is to first construct a wireframe model and then attach surfaces (*3Dfaces* or other surfaces) to the wireframe. The wireframe geometry can be constructed on a separate layer; then the layer can be turned off after the surfacing is complete.

Figure 39-7

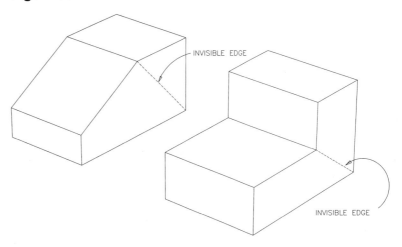

INVISIBLE EDGE

INVISIBLE EDGE

Figures 39-7 and 39-8 show some applications of *3Dface* for construction of surface models. Remember, *3Dface* can be used <u>only</u> for construction of surfaces with straight edges.

The edges made invisible by *Edge* are displayed in these figures in a hidden linetype. *Hide* has also been used to enhance visualization. You may want to use *Hide* periodically to enhance the visibility of surfaces.

Figure 39-8

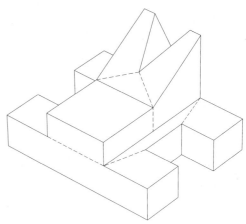

Editing *3Dfaces*

Grips can be used to edit *3Dfaces*. Each *3Dface* has three or four grips (one for each corner). Activating grips (PICKing the *3Dface* at the open Command: prompt), makes the individual *3Dface* surface become highlighted and display its **warm** grips. If you then make one of the three or four grips **hot**, all of the normal grip editing options are available, i.e., STRETCH, MOVE, ROTATE, SCALE, and MIRROR. The single activated *3Dface* surface can then be edited. MOVE, for example, could be used to move the single activated surface to another location.

Figure 39-9

The STRETCH option, however, is generally the most useful grip editing option, since all of the other options change the entire surface. The STRETCH option allows you to change one (or more) corner(s) of the *3Dface* rather than the entire surface, as with the other options. For example, Figure 39-9 shows six *3Dfaces* connected to form a box. One corner of the box could be relocated by activating the grips on two of the *3Dfaces*. Two grips (common to one intersection) can be made **hot** simultaneously by holding down SHIFT while PICKing the **hot** grip. When the STRETCH option appears at the command line, stretch the common **hot** grips to the new location, as shown (highlighted) in the figure.

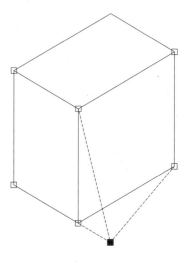

Explode or *Pedit* <u>cannot</u> be used to edit *3Dfaces*.

CREATING MESHED SURFACES

Figure 39-10

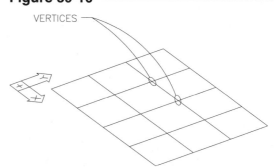

Meshes are versatile methods for generating a surface. *Ai_mesh* can be used to create a simple planar surface bounded by <u>four</u> straight edges (Fig. 39-10), or *3Dmesh* can be used to create a complex surface defining an irregular shape bounded by <u>four</u> sides (Fig. 39-11). The surface created with *Ai_mesh* or *3Dmesh* differs from a *3Dface* because the surface is defined by a "mesh." A mesh is a series of vertices (sometimes called nodes) arranged in rows and columns connected by lines. *Pedit* or grips can be used to edit the resulting mesh (see *Editing Polygon Meshes*, this chapter).

Figure 39-11

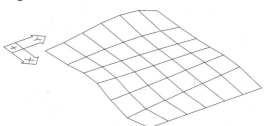

AI_MESH

PULL-DOWN MENU	SCREEN MENU	TYPE IN	TABLET MENU
Draw *Surfaces >* *3D Objects...* *Mesh:*	*DRAW2* *SURFACES* *Mesh:*	*AI_MESH*	---

Ai_mesh can be used to create a simple planar surface bounded by <u>four</u> straight edges (Fig. 39-10). Using this command causes:

> Command: **ai_mesh**
> First corner: **PICK** or (**coordinates**)
> Second corner: **PICK** or (**coordinates**)
> Third corner: **PICK** or (**coordinates**)
> Fourth corner: **PICK** or (**coordinates**)
> Mesh *M* size: (**value**) (Enter a value for the number of vertices in the *M* direction.)
> Mesh *N* size: (**value**) (Enter a value for the number of vertices in the *N* direction.)
> Command:

First, specify the four corners of the mesh. The number of vertices along each side is defined by the *M* size and the *N* size. The *M* direction is <u>perpendicular</u> to the first side specified, and the *N* direction is <u>perpendicular</u> to the second side specified (Fig. 39-12).

The values specified for the *M* size and *N* size <u>include</u> the vertices along the edges of the surface. The *M* and *N* sizes are the numbers of rows and columns of vertices (density of the mesh).

Ai_mesh can quickly generate a complex curved surface with straight edges by specifying nonplanar coordinates for the corners. The following command sequence is used to generate the surface shown in Figure 39-13.

> Command: **ai_mesh**
> First corner: **1,1,0**
> Second corner: **5,1,0**
> Third corner: **5,5,0**
> Fourth corner: **1,5,2**
> Mesh *M* size: **4**
> Mesh *N* size: **6**
> Command:

Ai_mesh visually defines the curvature of a surface better than *3Dface* because of the mesh lines.

Figure 39-14 illustrates an application for a nonplanar *Ai_mesh*.

Figure 39-12

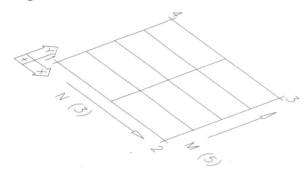

Figure 39-13

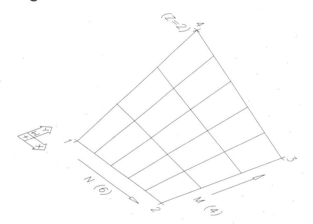

Figure 39-14

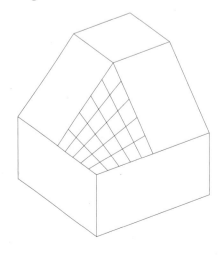

3DMESH

PULL-DOWN MENU	SCREEN MENU	TYPE IN	TABLET MENU
Draw *Surfaces >* *3D Mesh*	*DRAW2* *SURFACES* *3Dmesh:*	3DMESH	---

3Dmesh is a versatile tool for generating a complex surface. It is used to create a complex surface defining an irregular shape bounded by <u>four</u> sides (Fig. 39-11). *Pedit* or grips can be used to edit the *3Dmesh* retroactively.

3Dmesh prompts for coordinate values for the placement of <u>each</u> vertex, allowing you to create a variety of shapes. A numbering scheme is used to label each vertex. The first vertex in the <u>first</u> row in the M direction is labeled *0,0*, the second in the first row is labeled *0,1*, and so on. The first vertex in the <u>second</u> row is labeled *1,0*, the second in that row is *1,1*, and so on.

Since each vertex can be given explicit coordinates, a surface can be created to define any shape. An example is shown in Figure 39-15. This command is useful for developing geographical topographies. The command syntax for this method of defining a *3Dmesh* is as follows:

Command: **3dmesh**
M size: (**value**) (Enter a value for the
number of vertices in the *M* direction.)
N size: (**value**) (Enter a value for the number
of vertices in the *N* direction.)
Vertex (0,0): **PICK** or (**coordinates**)
Vertex (0,1): **PICK** or (**coordinates**)
Vertex (0,2): **PICK** or (**coordinates**)
(continues sequence for all vertices in the row)
Vertex (1,0): **PICK** or (**coordinates**)
Vertex (1,1): **PICK** or (**coordinates**)
Vertex (1,2): **PICK** or (**coordinates**)
(continues sequence for all vertices in the row)
Vertex (2,0): **PICK** or (**coordinates**)
Vertex (2,1): **PICK** or (**coordinates**)
Vertex (2,2): **PICK** or (**coordinates**)
(continues sequence for all vertices in the row)
(sequence continues for all rows)
Command:

Figure 39-15 ─────────────────

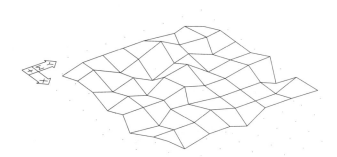

Obviously, using *3Dmesh* is very tedious. For complex shapes such as topographical maps, an AutoLISP program can be written to read coordinate data from an external file to generate the mesh.

PFACE

PULL-DOWN MENU	SCREEN MENU	TYPE IN	TABLET MENU
---	*DRAW2* *SURFACES* *Pface:*	PFACE	---

The *Pface* (polyface mesh) command can be used to create a polygon mesh of virtually any topology. *Pface* is the most versatile of any of the 3D mesh commands. It allows creation of any shape, any number of vertices, and even objects that are not physically connected, yet are considered as the same object.

The *Pface* command, however, is designed primarily for use by applications that run with AutoCAD and for use by other software developers. *Pedit* cannot be used to edit *Pface*s.

The procedure for creation of geometry with *Pface* is somewhat like the previous procedure for *3Dmesh*. There are two basic steps to *Pface*. AutoCAD first prompts for the coordinate location for each vertex. Any number of vertices can be defined.

> Command: **Pface**
> Vertex 1: **(coordinates)**
> Vertex 2: **(coordinates)**
> (The sequence continues until pressing **Enter**.)

Secondly, AutoCAD prompts for the vertices to be assigned to each face. A face can be attached to any set of vertices.

> Face 1, vertex 1: **(number)** (Enter number of vertex for face to be attached.)
> Face 1, vertex 2: **(number)** (Press **Enter** to complete face.)
> Face 2, vertex 1: **(number)**
> Face 2, vertex 2: **(number)** (Press **Enter** twice to complete command.)
> Command:

Specifying a *Pface* mesh of any size can be tedious. The geometrically defined mesh commands (*Rulesurf, Tabsurf, Revsurf,* and *Edgesurf*) are more convenient to use for most applications.

CREATING GEOMETRICALLY DEFINED MESHES

Geometrically defined meshes are meshed surfaces that are created by "attaching" a surface to existing geometry. In other words, geometrically defined meshed surfaces <u>require existing geometry</u> to define them. *Edgesurf, Rulesurf, Tabsurf,* and *Revsurf* are the commands that create these meshes. The geometry used may differ for the application, but always consists of either two or four objects (*Lines, Circles, Arcs,* or *Plines*).

Controlling the Mesh Density

Geometrically defined mesh commands (*Edgesurf, Rulesurf, Revsurf,* and *Tabsurf*) do not prompt the user for the number of vertices in the *M* and *N* direction. Instead, the number of vertices is determined by the settings of the *SURFTAB1* and *SURFTAB2* variables. The number of vertices includes the endpoints of the edge.

> Command: **surftab1**
> New value for SURFTAB1 <6>: **(value)**
> Command:

SURFTAB1 and *SURFTAB2* must be set <u>before</u> using *Edgesurf, Rulesurf, Revsurf,* and *Tabsurf*. These variables are <u>not</u> retroactive for previously created surface meshes.

The individual surfaces (1 by 1 meshes between vertices) created by geometrically defined meshes are composed of a series of <u>straight</u> edges connecting the vertices. These edges do not curve, but only change direction between vertices to approximate curved edges. The higher the settings of *SURFTAB1* and *SURFTAB2,* the more closely these straight edges match the defining curved edges.

Note that the defining edges of geometrically defined mesh <u>do not become part</u> of the surface; they remain as separate objects. Therefore, you can construct surface models by utilizing existing wireframe model objects as the defining edges. If the wireframe model is on a separate layer, that layer can be *Frozen* after constructing the surfaces to reveal only the surfaces.

EDGESURF

PULL-DOWN MENU	SCREEN MENU	TYPE IN	TABLET MENU
Draw *Surfaces >* *Edge Surface*	*DRAW2* *SURFACES* *Edgsurf:*	*EDGESURF*	8,O

An *Edgesurf* is a meshed surface generated between <u>four existing</u> edges. The four edges can be of any shape as long as they have connecting end points (no gaps, no overlaps). The four edges can be *Lines*, *Arcs*, or *Plines*. The four edges can be selected in any order. The surface that is generated between the edges is sometimes called a Coon's surface patch. *Edgesurf* interpolates the edges and generates a smooth transitional mesh, or patch, between the four shapes.

The command syntax is as follows:

```
Command: edgesurf
Select edge 1: PICK
Select edge 2: PICK
Select edge 3: PICK
Select edge 4: PICK
Command:
```

Figure 39-16 displays an *Edgesurf* generated from four planar edges. Settings for *SURFTAB1* and *SURFTAB2* are *6* and *8*.

The relation of *SURFTAB1* and *SURFTAB2* for any *Edgesurf* are given here:

SURFTAB1	1st edge picked
SURFTAB2	2nd edge picked

Edges used to define an *Edgesurf* may be <u>nonplanar</u>, resulting in a smooth, nonplanar surface, as displayed in Figure 39-17. Remember, the edges may be any *Pline* shape in 3D space. Use *Hide* to enhance your visibility of nonplanar surfaces.

Figure 39-16 ————————————————

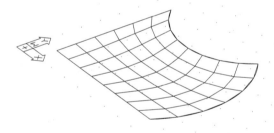

Figure 39-17 ————————————————

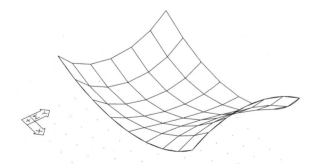

RULESURF

PULL-DOWN MENU	SCREEN MENU	TYPE IN	TABLET MENU
Draw *Surfaces >* *Ruled Surface*	*DRAW2* *SURFACES* *Rulsurf:*	*RULESURF*	*8,M*

A *Rulesurf* is a polygon meshed surface created between <u>two edges</u>. The edges can be *Lines, Arcs,* or *Plines.* The command syntax only asks for the two "defining curves." The two defining edges must <u>both</u> be open or closed.

Figure 39-18 displays two planar *Rulesurfs*.

Figure 39-18 ————————————

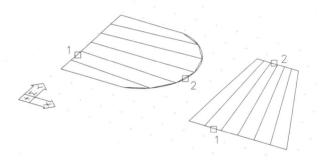

Figure 39-19 displays possibilities for creating *Rulesurfs* between two edges that are nonplanar.

The command syntax for *Rulesurf* is as follows:

    Command: **rulesurf**
    Select first defining curve: **PICK**
    Select second defining curve: **PICK**
    Command:

Figure 39-19 ————————————

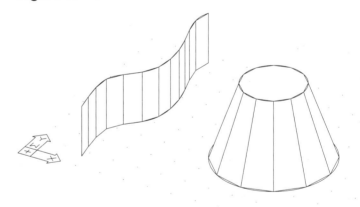

A cylinder can be created with *Rulesurf* by utilizing two *Circles* lying on different planes as the defining curves. A cone can be created by creating a *Rulesurf* between a *Circle* and a *Point* (Fig. 39-20), or a complex shape can be created using two identical closed *Pline* shapes (Fig. 39-20).

Figure 39-20 ————————————

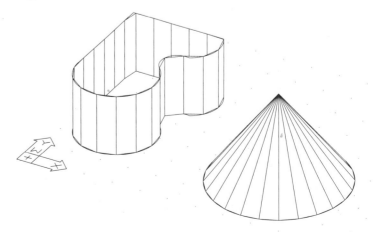

For open defining edges (not *Circles* or closed *Plines*), the *Rulesurf* is generated connecting the two <u>selected</u> ends of the defining edges. Figure 39-21 illustrates the two possibilities for generating a *Rulesurf* between the same two straight nonplanar *Lines* based on the endpoints selected.

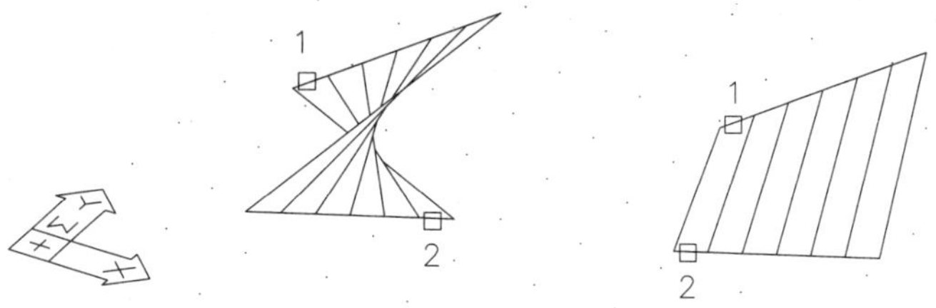

Since the curve is stretched between only two edges, the number of vertices along the *defining curve* is determined only by the value previously specified for *SURFTAB1*.

Figure 39-21

| SURFTAB1 | defining curve |
| SURFTAB2 | not used |

TABSURF

PULL-DOWN MENU	SCREEN MENU	TYPE IN	TABLET MENU
Draw *Surfaces >* *Tabulated Surface*	DRAW2 SURFACES *Tabsurf:*	*TABSURF*	8,P

A *Tabsurf* is generated by an existing *path curve* and a *direction vector*. The *curve path* (generatrix) is extruded in the direction of, and equal in length to, the *direction vector* (directrix) to create a swept surface. The path curve can be a *Line, Arc, Circle, 2D Polyline,* or *3D Polyline*. The direction vector can be a *Line* or an open 2D *Pline*. If a curved *Pline* is used, the surface is generated in a direction connecting the two end vertices of the *Pline*.

A *Circle* can be swept with *Tabsurf* to generate a cylinder (Fig. 39-22). The *Tabsurf* has only N direction; therefore, the current setting of *SURFTAB1* controls the number of vertices along the *path curve*.

The relation of *SURFTAB1* and *SURFTAB2* for *Tabsurf* are:

| SURFTAB1 | Path curve |
| SURFTAB2 | not used |

The *Tabsurf* is generated in the direction <u>opposite</u> the end of the direction vector that is selected. This is evident in both Figures 39-22 and 39-23.

The command sequence is:

    Command: **tabsurf**
    Select path curve: **PICK**
    Select direction vector: **PICK**

Figure 39-22

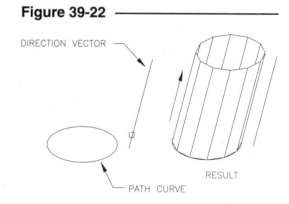

Figure 39-23

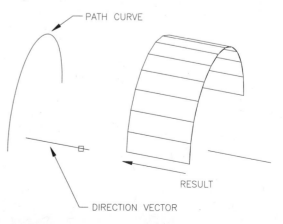

REVSURF

PULL-DOWN MENU	SCREEN MENU	TYPE IN	TABLET MENU
Draw *Surfaces >* *Revolved Surface*	*DRAW2* *SURFACES* *Revsurf:*	*REVSURF*	*8,N*

This command creates a surface of revolution by revolving an existing *path curve* around an *axis*. The path curve can be a *Line, Arc, Circle,* 2D, or 3D *Pline*. The *axis* can be a *Line* or open *Pline*. If a curved *Pline* is used as the *axis*, only the endpoint vertices are considered for the axis of revolution.

```
Command: revsurf
Select path curve: PICK
Select axis of revolution: PICK
Start angle<0>: PICK or (value)
Included angle (+=ccw, -=cw)<Full circle>: PICK or (value)
Command:
```

The structure of the command allows many variations. The *path curve* can be open or closed. The *axis* can be in any plane. The *start angle* and *included angle* allow for complete (closed) or partial (open) revolutions of the surface in any orientation. Figures 39-24 and 39-25 show possible *Revsurfs* created with *path curves* generated through 360 degrees.

The wine glass was created with an open *path curve* generated through 360 degrees (Fig. 39-24).

The number of vertices in the direction of revolution is controlled by the setting of *SURFTAB2*. The *SURFTAB1* setting controls the number of vertices along the length of the *path curve*.

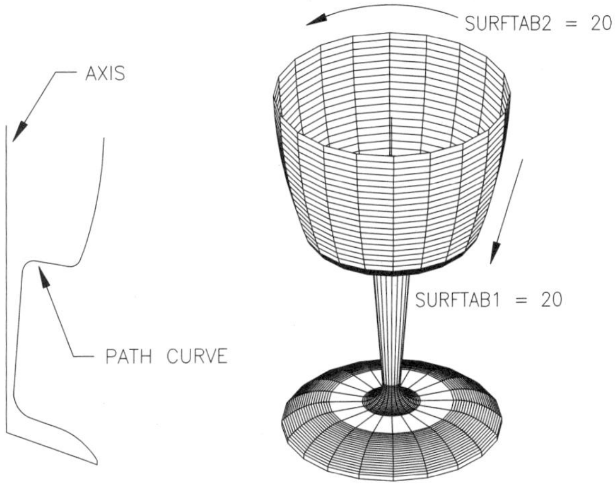

The relation of *SURFTAB1* and *SURFTAB2* for *Revsurf* is given here:

SURFTAB1   *Axis of revolution*
SURFTAB2   *Path curve*

A torus can be created by using a closed *path curve* generated through 360 degrees (Fig. 39-25). In this case, the surface begins at the *path curve*, is revolved all the way around the axis, and closes on itself.

When generating a curve path through <u>less than</u> 360 degrees, you must specify the included angle. Entering a positive angle specifies a counterclockwise direction of revolution, and a negative angle specification causes a clockwise revolution. As an alternative, you can pick different points on the *axis of revolution*. The end of the line PICKed represents the end nearest the origin for positive rotation using the Right-Hand Rule.

Figure 39-24

Figure 39-25

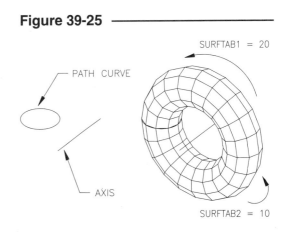

Figure 39-26 displays a *Revsurf* generated through 90 degrees. The end of the *axis of revolution* PICKed specifies the direction of positive rotation.

Figure 39-26 ————————————————

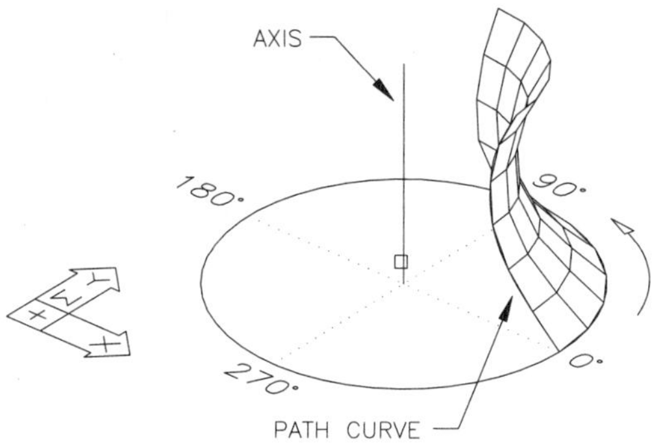

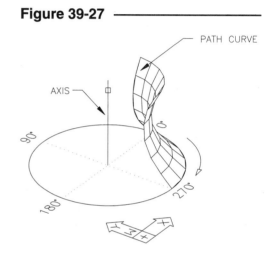

Figure 39-27 displays a *Revsurf* generated in a negative revolution direction, accomplished by specifying a negative angle or by PICKing a point specifying an inverted origin (of the Right-Hand Rule) for rotation.

Figure 39-27 ————————————————

EDITING POLYGON MESHES

There are several ways that existing AutoCAD polygon meshed surfaces (*3Dmesh, Rulesurf, Tabsurf, Revsurf,* and *Edgesurf*) can be changed. The use of *Pedit, Grips,* and *Explode* each provide special capabilities.

PEDIT with Polygon Meshes

One of the options of *Pedit* is *Edit vertex*, which allows editing of individual vertices of a *Pline*. Vertex editing can also be accomplished with *3Dmesh*es, *Revsurfs, Edgesurfs, Tabsurfs,* and *Rulesurfs*. *Pedit* does <u>not</u> allow editing of *3Dfaces*. See Chapter 16 for information on using *Pedit* with 2D objects.

```
Command: Pedit
Select Polyline: PICK (Select the surface.)
Edit vertex/Smooth surface/Desmooth/Mclose/Nclose/Undo /eXit<X>:
```

Each *Pedit* option for editing Polygon Meshes is explained and illustrated here.

Edit Vertex

Invoking this option causes the display of another set of options at the command prompt which allows you to locate the vertex that you wish to edit.

```
Vertex(0,0).Next/Previous/Left/Right/Up/Down/Move/ REgen/eXit<N>:
```

Pressing Enter locates the marker (X) at the next vertex. Selecting *Left/Right* or *Up/Down* controls the direction of the movement in the *N* and *M* directions (as specified by *SURFTAB1* and *SURFTAB2* when the surfaces were created) (Fig. 39-28).

Figure 39-28

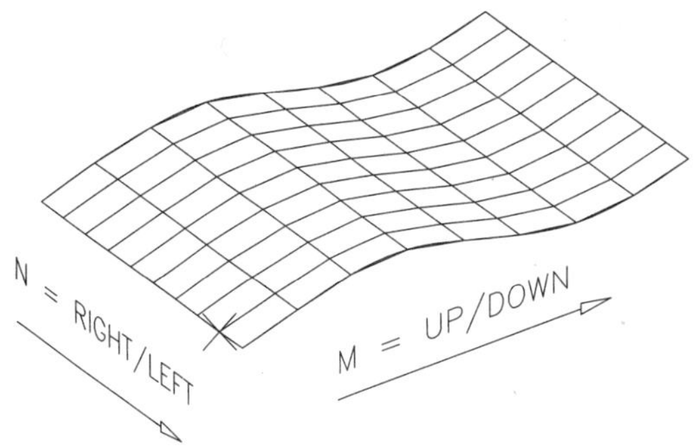

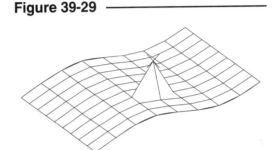

Once the vertex has been located, use the *Move* option to move the vertex to any location in 3D space (Fig. 39-29).

Figure 39-29

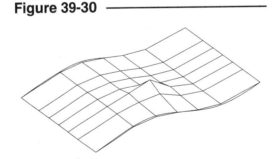

Smooth surface
Invoking this option causes the surface to be smoothed using the current setting of *SURFTYPE* (described later) (Fig. 39-30).

Figure 39-30

Desmooth
The *Desmooth* option reverses the effect of *Smooth*.

Mclose/Nclose
The *Mclose* and *Nclose* options cause the surface to close in either the *M* or *N* directions. The last and first set of vertices automatically connect. Figure 39-31 displays a half-cylindrical surface closed with *Nclose*.

Figure 39-31

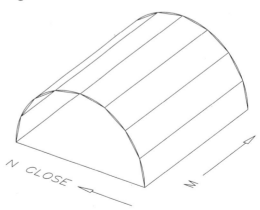

Undo
Undo reverses the last operation with *Pedit*.

eXit
This option is used to keep the editing changes, exit the *Pedit* command, and return to the Command: prompt.

Variables Affecting Polygon Meshes

SURFTYPE

This variable affects the degree of smoothing of a surface when using the *Smooth* option of *Pedit*. The command prompt syntax is shown here:

Command: *Surftype*
New value for Surftype<6>: (**value**)

The values allowed are **5**, **6**, and **8**. The options are illustrated in the following figures.

Original polygon mesh (Fig. 39-32)

SURFTYPE=5
Quadratic B-spline surface (Fig. 39-33)

SURFTYPE=6
Cubic B-Spline surface (Fig. 39-34)

SURFTYPE=8
Bezier surface (Fig. 39-35)

Figure 39-32

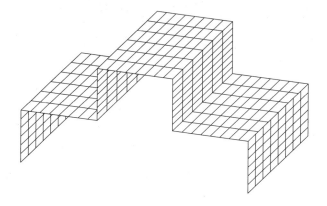

Figure 39-33

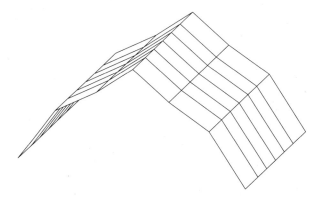

Figure 39-34

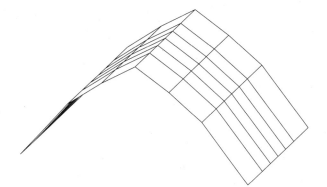

Figure 39-35

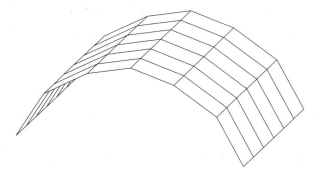

SPLFRAME

PULL-DOWN MENU	SCREEN MENU	TYPE IN	TABLET MENU
Options *Display >* *Spline Frame*	*OPTIONS* *DISPLAY* *SplFram:*	*SPLFRAME*	---

The *SPLFRAME* (spline frame) variable causes the original polygon mesh to be displayed along with the smoothed version of the surface. The values allowed are **0** for off and **1** for on. *SPLFRAME* can also be used with 2D polylines when using the *Spline* option.

SPLFRAME is set to **1** in Figure 39-36 to display the original polygon mesh.

Figure 39-36 ————————

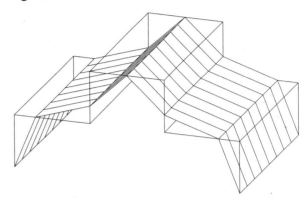

Editing Polygon Meshes with Grips

Grips can be used to edit the individual vertices of a polygon mesh (*3Dmesh, Edgesurf, Rulesurf, Tabsurf,* and *Revsurf*). Normally, the STRETCH option of grip editing would be used to stretch (move) the location of a single vertex grip. The other grip editing options (MOVE, SCALE, ROTATE, MIRROR) affect the entire polygon mesh. Selecting the mesh at the open Command: prompt activates all of the grips (one for each vertex) and makes them **warm**. Selecting one of the individual grips again makes that one **hot** and able to be relocated with the STRETCH option.

For example, a *3Dmesh* could be generated to define a surface with a rough texture, such as a chipped stone (Fig. 39-37).

Grip editing STRETCH option could be used to relocate individual vertices of the mesh. The result is a surface with a rough or bumpy surface (Fig. 39-38).

Although the concept is simple, some care should be taken to assure that the individual vertices are moved in the desired plane. Since grip editing is interactive, any points PICKed are moved to the <u>current XY plane</u>. Careful use of UCSs can ensure that the vertices are STRETCHed in the desired XY plane.

Figure 39-37 ————————

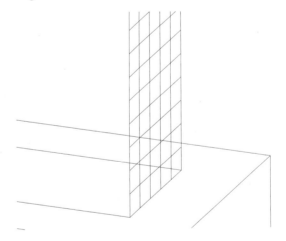

Figure 39-38 ————————

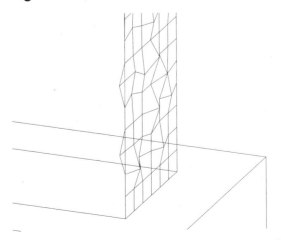

Editing Polygon Meshes with *Explode*

The *Explode* command can be used to allow editing *3Dmesh*es, geometrically defined meshes (*Edgesurf, Revsurf,* etc.), 3D primitives (*3D Objects...*), and *Regions.*

When used with other AutoCAD objects, *Explode* will "break down" the object group into a lower level of objects; for example, a *Pline* can be broken into its individual segments with *Explode.* Likewise, *Explode* will "break down" a 3D polygon mesh, for example, into individual 1 by 1 meshes (in effect, *3Dfaces*). *Explode* will affect any polygon meshes (*3Dmesh, Edgesurf, Revsurf, Tabsurf, Rulesurf*). *Explode* converts a polygon mesh into its individual 1 by 1 meshes (*3Dfaces*) (Fig. 39-39).

Figure 39-39 ─────────

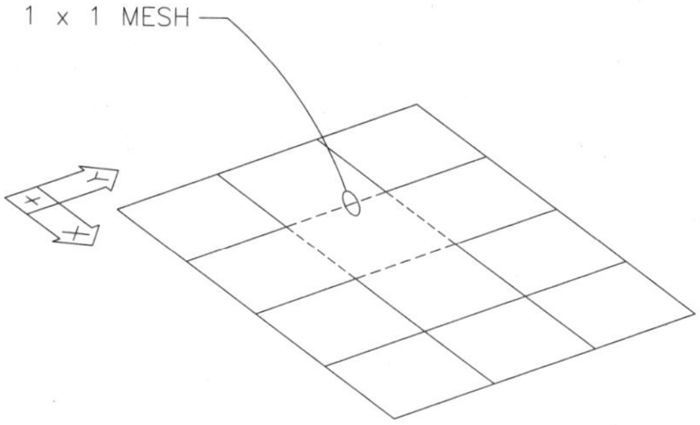

1 x 1 MESH ─

CONSTRUCTION TECHNIQUES FOR POLYGON MESHES AND *3DFACES*

Surfaces are created individually and combined to form a complete surface model. The surfaces can be created and moved into place in order to "assemble" the complete model, or surfaces can be created in place to form the finished model. Because polygon meshes require existing geometry to define the surfaces, the construction technique generally used is:

1. Construct a wireframe model (or partial wireframe) defining the edges of the surfaces on a separate layer.
2. Attach polygon mesh and other surfaces to the wireframe using another layer.

The creation of UCSs greatly assists in constructing 3D elements in 3D space during construction of the wireframe and surfaces. The sequence in the creation of a complete surface model is given here as a sample surface modeling strategy.

Surface Model Example 1

Consider the object in Figure 39-40. To create a surface model of this object, first create a partial wireframe.

Figure 39-40 ─────────

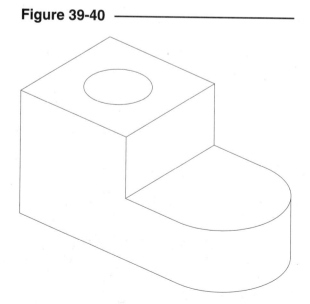

1. Create part of a wireframe model using *Line* and *Circle* elements. Create the wireframe on a separate layer. Begin the geometry at the origin. Use *Vpoint* to enable visualization of three dimensions (Fig. 39-41).

Figure 39-41 ——————————

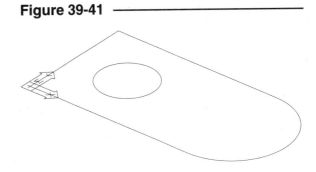

2. *Copy* the usable objects to the top plane by specifying a Z dimension at the "second point of displacement" prompt (Fig. 39-42).

Figure 39-42 ——————————

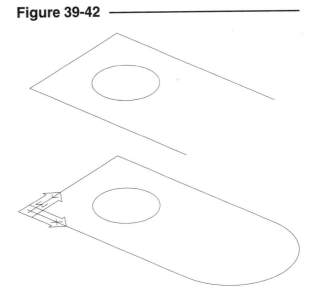

3. Create a UCS on this new plane using the *Origin* option. *OSNAP* the *Origin* to the existing geometry. Draw the connecting *Line* and *Trim* the extensions (Fig. 39-43).

Figure 39-43 ——————————

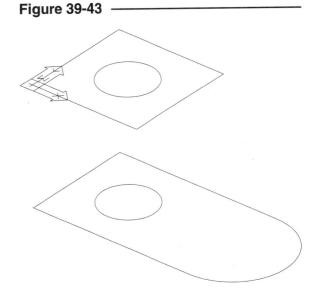

4. *Copy* the *Arc* and two attached *Lines* specifying a Z dimension for the "second point of displacement." *Copy* the *Line* drawn last (on the top plane) specifying a negative Z dimension. *Trim* the extending *Line* ends. A new *UCS* is not necessary on this plane (Fig. 39-44).

    This is not a complete wireframe, but it includes all the edges that are necessary to begin attaching surfaces.

Figure 39-44

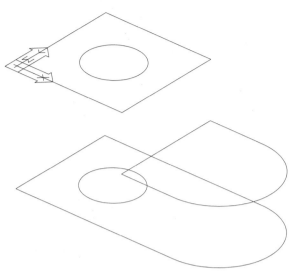

5. On a new layer, a 2-segment *3Dface* is created by PICKing the *ENDpoints* of the wireframe objects in the order indicated. Remember that *3Dface* segments connect at the 3rd and 4th points (Fig. 39-45). (*Hide* is used in this figure to provide visibility of the *3Dface*.)

Figure 39-45

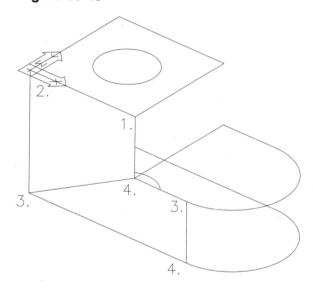

6. The *3Dface* is *Copied* to the opposite side of the model. A vertical *3Dface* is created between the top and the intermediate plane (Fig. 39-46). Another vertical *3Dface* is created on the back (not visible). (*Hide* is used again in this figure. Notice how the *Circle* is treated.)

Figure 39-46

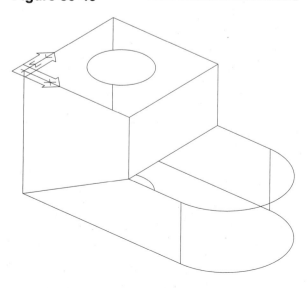

7. *Rulesurf* is used to create the rounded surface shown between the two *Arcs* (Fig. 39-47). The *SURFTAB1* and *SURFTAB2* variables were previously set to 12.

Figure 39-47

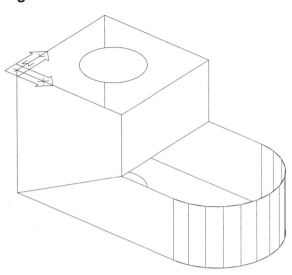

8. Next, a *Rulesurf* is used to create the cylindrical hole surface between the *Circles* on the top and bottom planes. The wireframe layer was *Frozen* before *Hide* was used for this figure (Fig. 39- 48).

Figure 39-48

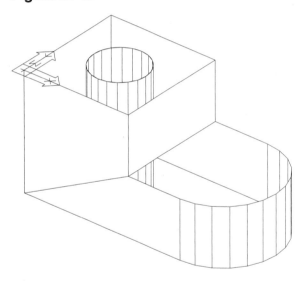

9. The surface connecting the *Arc* and three *Lines* is created by *Edgesurf* (Fig. 39-49).

10. The only remaining surfaces to create are the top and bottom. <u>There is no</u> polygon mesh, *3Dface*, or *3Dmesh* that can be generated to create a simple surface configuration such as that on top—a surface with a hole! It must be accomplished by creating several adjoining surfaces.

Figure 39-49

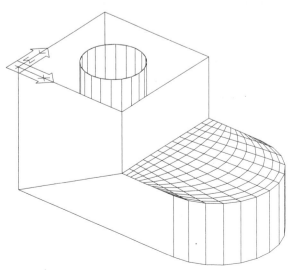

There are several possible methods for construction of a surface with a hole. (The top surface has been isolated here for simplicity.) Probably the simplest method is shown here (Fig. 39-50). First, the *Circle* must be <u>replaced</u> by two 180 degree *Arcs*. Next a *Rulesurf* is created between one *Arc* and one edge as shown.

Figure 39-50

11. The top plane is completed by creating another *Rulesurf* and two triangular *3Dfaces* adjoining the *Rulesurfs* (Fig. 39-51). (Wireframe elements are <u>not</u> required for the *3Dface*.)

Figure 39-51

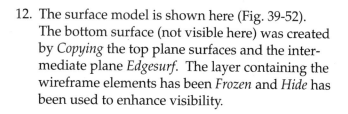

12. The surface model is shown here (Fig. 39-52). The bottom surface (not visible here) was created by *Copying* the top plane surfaces and the intermediate plane *Edgesurf*. The layer containing the wireframe elements has been *Frozen* and *Hide* has been used to enhance visibility.

Figure 39-52

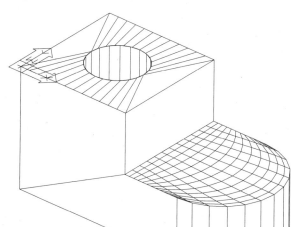

13. The mesh lines shown in Figure 39-53 are not visible when a *Render* is performed. This figure illustrates the completed model after using *Render*. *Shade* also provides options to display or to hide the edge and mesh lines.

Figure 39-53

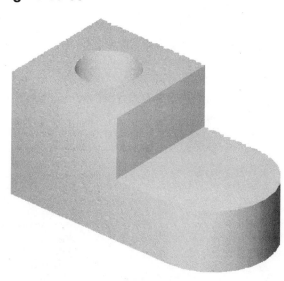

Limitations of Polygon Meshes and *3Dface*

From the previous example of the creation of a relatively simple 3D surface model, you can imagine how construction of some shapes with *3Dface* or polygon meshes can be somewhat involved. The particular characteristics of a surface that cause some difficulty in creation are the surfaces that embody many edges or that have holes, slots, or other "islands." Examine the surfaces shown in Figure 39-54. Although some of these shapes are fairly common, the construction techniques using *3Dfaces* and polygon meshes could be very involved.

3Dface and polygon meshes would <u>not</u> be an efficient construction technique to use in the creation of shapes such as these. Another AutoCAD feature, Region Modeling, can be used to easily create such shapes. Region models can be combined with *3Dfaces*, polygon meshes, and other surfacing techniques to create surface models.

Figure 39-54 ────────────

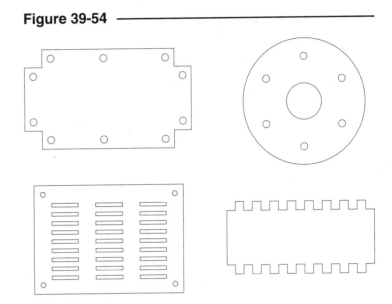

REGION MODELING APPLICATIONS

Region modeling is sometimes defined in the AutoCAD documentation as "2D solid modeling," <u>not</u> "surface modeling." This is because region modeling applies solid modeling techniques, namely, Boolean operations, to 2D closed objects. Practically, however, *Regions* can be considered surfaces.

A region is created by applying the *Region* command to <u>closed</u> 2D objects such as *Plines, Circles, Ellipses,* and *Polygons* (see Chapter 17). *Regions* are always <u>planar</u>. <u>Composite</u> regions can be constructed by combining multiple *Regions* using Boolean operations. AutoCAD allows you to utilize the Boolean operations *Union, Subtract,* and *Intersect* with *Regions* to create planar surfaces with holes and complex shapes. These surfaces can then be combined with other surfaces (regions, *3Dfaces,* or polygon meshes) on other planes to create complex surface models.

Region modeling solves the problem of creating relatively simple surfaces that are not easily accomplished with the polygon mesh commands such as *3Dmesh, Rulesurf, Revsurf, Tabsurf,* and *Edgesurf.* Region modeling makes creation of surfaces with islands (holes) especially easy.

For example, consider the creation of a rectangular surface with a circular hole. This problem is addressed in the previous Surface Model Example 1 (Fig. 39-51). Using the polygon mesh commands, this relatively simple surface requires four *Lines,* two *Arcs* as a wireframe structure, then two *Rulesurfs* and two *3Dfaces* to complete the surface.

With the Region Modeler, the same surface can be created by using *Subtract* with a circular *Region* (create a *Circle*; then use *Region*) and a rectangular *Region* (draw a closed rectangle with *Line*, *Pline*, or *Rectangle*; then use *Region*) (Fig 39-55).

Consider the surfaces shown in Figure 39-54. Imagine the amount of work involved in creating the surfaces using commands such as *3Dface*, *3Dmesh*, *Rulesurf*, *Revsurf*, *Tabsurf*, and *Edgesurf*. Next, consider the work involved to create these shapes as regions. Surfaces such as these are very common for mechanical applications for surface models.

Figure 39-55 ─────────

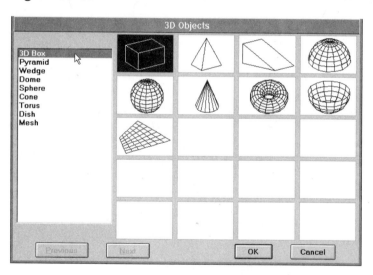

SURFACE MODELING PRIMITIVES

3D Objects...

PULL-DOWN MENU	SCREEN MENU	TYPE IN	TABLET MENU
Draw *Surfaces >* *3D Objects...*	*DRAW2* *SURFACES* *(choice)*	*AI_(choice)*	---

This command allows you to create 3D surface <u>primitives</u>. A primitive is a simple 3D geometric shape such as a *box, cone, dish, dome, mesh, pyramid, sphere, torus,* or *wedge* (the mesh is discussed earlier). These primitives are pre-created shapes composed of *3Dfaces* or polygon meshes. The primitives in the *3D Objects* icon menu are surface models (Figure 39-56).

Surface primitives can be created by selecting the image tiles in the *3D Objects* dialogue box, by selecting from the *SUR-FACES* screen menu, or by typing the object name prefaced by "AI_"; for example "AI_BOX" summons the prompts for constructing a box.

Figure 39-56 ─────────

AutoCAD prompts you for the dimensions of the primitive. Depending on the type of primitive chosen, the prompts differ. The prompts for a *box* are given here:

```
Command: ai_box
Corner of box: PICK or (value)
Length: PICK or (value)
Cube<Width>: PICK or (value)
Height: PICK or (value)
Rotation angle about Z axis: PICK or (value)
Command:
```

These primitives are composed of AutoCAD surfaces. The 3D primitives (*3D Objects*) are provided to simplify the process of creating complex surface models. Generally, the primitives have to be edited and combined with other surfaces to build the complex model you need for a particular application. In this case, editing commands (*Pedit, Explode,* Grip editing, etc.) discussed in this chapter can be used along with other surfacing capabilities (*3Dmesh, 3Dface, Revsurf, Edgesurf, Region,* etc.). The editing methods differ depending on the type of surface. *Pedit, Explode,* and Grips can be used with any polygon mesh (*torus, sphere, dome, dish, cone*). *Pedit* <u>cannot</u> be used with *3Dfaces* (*box, wedge, pyramid*); however, *Explode* and Grip editing can be used. See Editing Polygon Meshes and Editing *3Dfaces* in this chapter.

For example, the *Box* can be *exploded* into its individual *3Dfaces*. Figure 39-57 exhibits the box in its original form. Figure 39-58 illustrates the *box* after it has been *Exploded* and the top *3Dface* removed to reveal the inside. (*Hide* has been performed in these figures to enhance visualization.)

Figure 39-57 ——————————

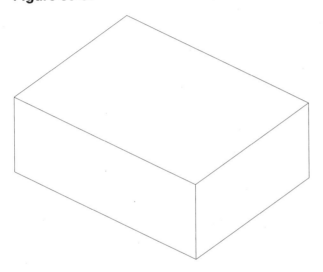

Figure 39-58 ——————————

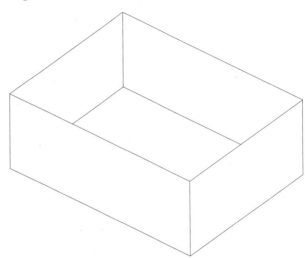

Surface Model Example 2

The following example is given as a sample of surface model construction strategy utilizing *3D Objects* combined with *3Dfaces* and polygon meshes.

In this example, the object in Figure 39-59 is constructed from 3D Primitives (*3D Objects*), edited, and combined with other surfaces.

Figure 39-59 ——————————

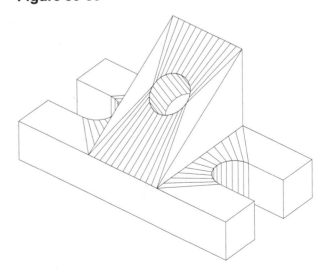

1. The drawing is set up by creating a layer for the surface model and setting the *Ucsicon ON* and at the *Origin*. The construction begins by selecting a *3D Box* from the *3D Objects* dialogue box.

Figure 39-60

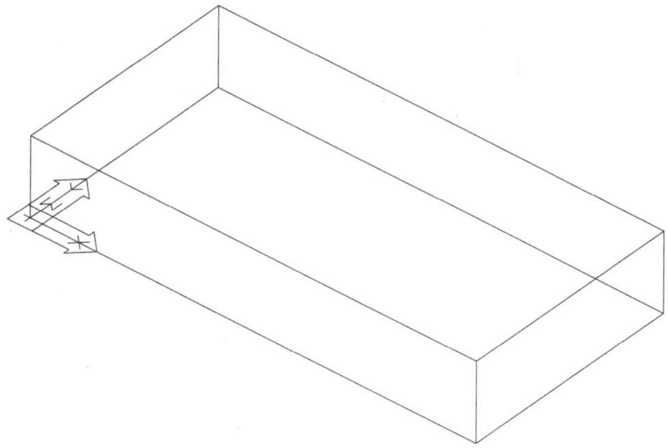

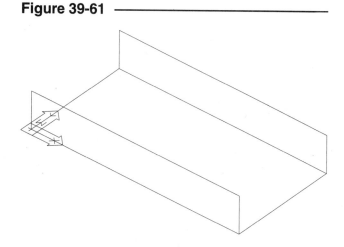

2. The *3D Box* is *Exploded* and the top and side faces are *Erased* (Fig. 39-61).

Figure 39-61

3. A *UCS* is created with the *Origin* option with its location (using *OSNAP*) on the top plane.

Figure 39-62

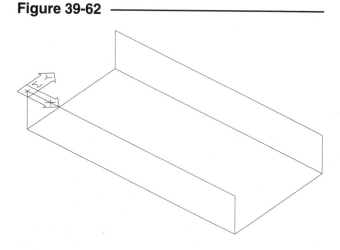

4. A new *Layer* is created for a wireframe. Wireframe elements (*Line, Arc*) are added to prepare for creating *3Dfaces* and polygon meshes (Fig. 39-63).

Figure 39-63

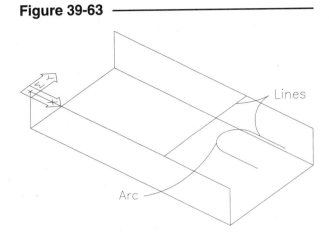

5. *SURFTAB1* and *SURFTAB2* are set to 12. *Rulesurf* and *3Dface* are used to create part of the top surface. (*Hide* is used in this figure to define the surfaces.)

Figure 39-64

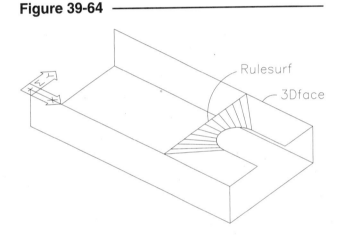

6. The bottom surface (part of the original *3D Box*) is erased. The new surfaces and wireframe elements are *copied* to the bottom plane (Fig. 39-65).

Figure 39-65

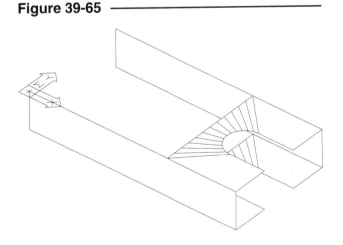

7. A *Rulesurf* and four *3Dfaces* are created, connecting the top and bottom surfaces. Use of layers is critical but somewhat laborious at this point. Only the wireframe elements can be selected as the defining edges for *Rulesurf*; therefore, turning the surface model layer *off* is helpful to allow selection of the wireframe elements. Alternately, press Ctrl while PICKing to cycle the selection of only the wireframe element. .

Figure 39-66

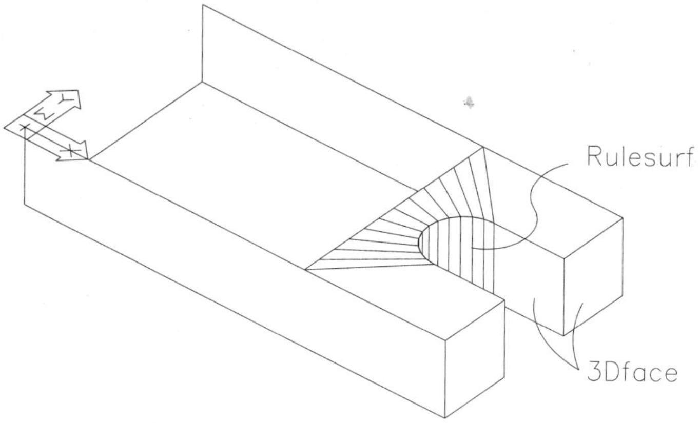

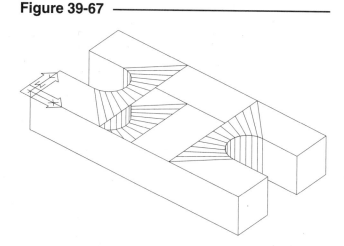

8. Next, the eleven surfaces are mirrored to the other side (Fig. 39-67). *Mirror3D* is used with the YZ option and PICKing the *MIDpoint* of the long surface across the front as the "point on YZ plane." A *3Dface* is created to fill the opening on the bottom surface.

Figure 39-67

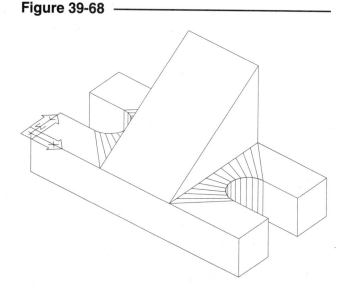

9. The *3D Objects* dialogue box is used again to select a *Wedge*. The *Wedge* is placed in the center of the top surface.

Figure 39-68

10. *Explode* breaks the *Wedge* into its individual *3Dfaces*. The inclined plane is *Erased* (Fig. 39-69).

Figure 39-69

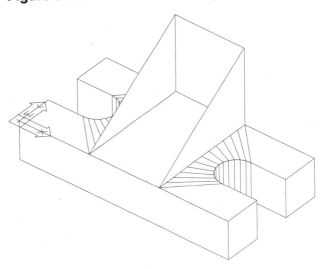

11. A new *UCS* is created to enable the construction of a new inclined surface with the hole. The *3point* option would be effective in this case.

Figure 39-70

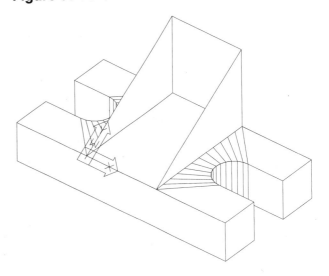

12. Wireframe elements (four *Arcs* and two *Lines*) are created on the wireframe layer as a foundation for construction of the new inclined surface and hole (Fig. 39-71).

Figure 39-71

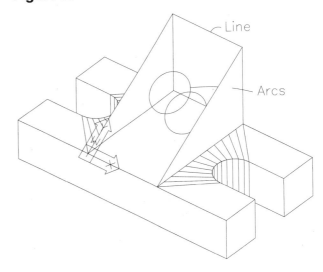

13. An inclined surface and hole are created on the surface model layer by applying the technique used in Surface Model Example 1 (or *Region* can be used). (Wireframe elements are not required for *3Dfaces*.)

Figure 39-72

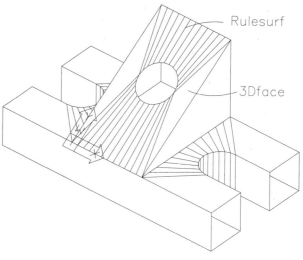

Rulesurf

3Dface

14. The model is completed by using *Rulesurf* to create the hole surface (sides), and a *Circle* establishes the bottom of the hole. Keep in mind that the *Rulesurf* must be defined by the original *Arcs*, not by the previous *Rulesurf* of the inclined plane (Fig. 39-73).

Figure 39-73

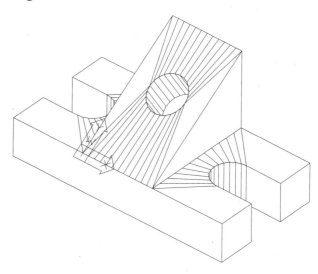

15. Figure 39-74 illustrates the completed surface model after performing a *Render*.

Figure 39-74

USING *THICKNESS* AND *ELEVATION*

THICKNESS and *ELEVATION*

PULL-DOWN MENU	SCREEN MENU	TYPE IN	TABLET MENU
Data *Object Creation...*	---	*THICKNESS or* *ELEVATION*	9,Y

Thickness and *Elevation* were introduced with Version 2.1 (1985) as AutoCAD's first capability for creating 3D objects. *Thickness* and *Elevation* are still useful for creating simple surfaces. <u>Any</u> 2D object (*Line*, *Circle*, *Arc*, *Pline*, etc.) can be assigned a *Thickness* or *Elevation* property. *Thickness* and *Elevation* are usually assigned before using a 2D command; however, they can also be changed later using *Change* or *Ddmodify*.

Thickness is a value representing a <u>Z dimension</u> for a 2D object. The new object is created using the typical draw command (*Line*, *Circle*, or *Arc*, etc.), but the resulting object has a uniform Z dimension as assigned. For example, a two unit high cylinder can be created by setting *Thickness* to 2 and then using the *Circle* command (Fig. 39-75).

Figure 39-75

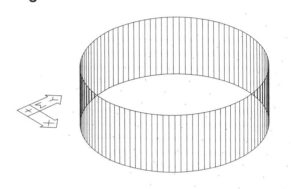

Thickness is <u>always perpendicular</u> to the XY plane of the object. Until later versions of AutoCAD, this posed a major limitation with the use of *Thickness*. This limited cylinders, for example, to having a vertical orientation <u>only</u>; no cylinders could be created with a horizontal orientation. The term "2 ½-D" was used to describe this capability of CAD packages during this phase of development.

Today, with the ability to create User Coordinate Systems (UCS), *Thickness* can be used to create surfaces in any orientation. Therefore, the effectiveness of *Thickness* and *Elevation* commands is increased. Figure 39-76 displays a cylinder oriented horizontally, achieved by creating a UCS having a vertical XY plane and a horizontal Z dimension. UCSs can be created to achieve any orientation for using *Thickness*.

Figure 39-76

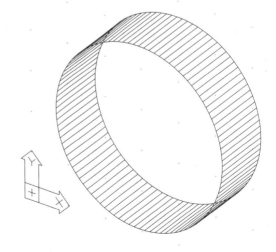

With a *Thickness* set to a value greater than **0**, commands normally used to create 2D objects can be used to create 3D surfaces having a uniform Z dimension perpendicular to the current XY plane. Figure 39-77 shows a *Line*, *Arc*, and *Point* possessing *Thickness* property. Note that a *Point* object with *Thickness* creates a line perpendicular to the current XY plane.

Figure 39-77

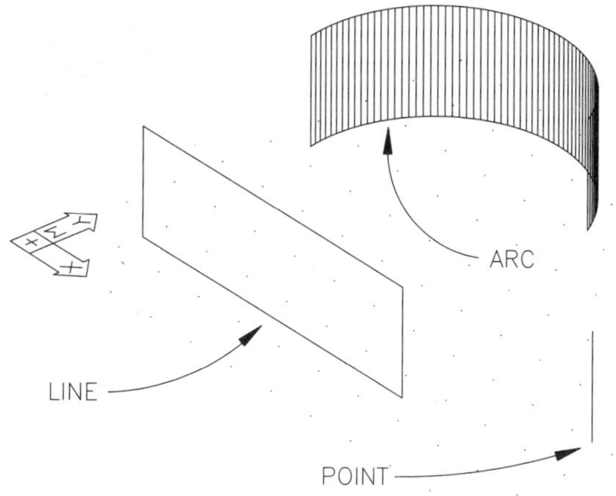

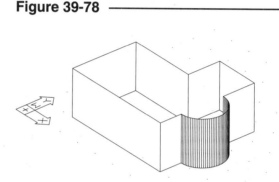

The ability to create *Plines* with *Thickness* offers many possibilities for developing complex surface models (Fig. 39-78). (Keep in mind that 2D shapes created with *Line* and *Arc* objects can be converted to *Plines* with *Pedit*.)

Figure 39-78

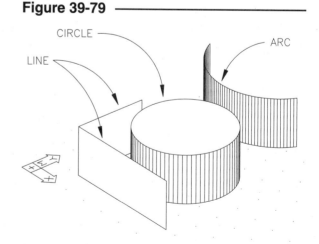

Using the *Hide* command with surfaces created with *Thickness* enhances your visibility. Figures 39-78 and 39-79 show examples of *Hide*. Notice that *Circles* created with *Thickness* have a "top." Other closed shapes created with *Line* or *Pline* do <u>not</u> have a "top."

Assigning a value for *Thickness* causes all subsequently created objects to have the assigned *Thickness* property. *Thickness* must be set back to **0** to create normal 2D objects.

Elevation controls the Z dimension of the "base plane" for subsequently created objects. Normally, unless an explicit Z value is given, 2D objects (with or without *Thickness*) are created on the XY plane or at an *Elevation* of **0**. Changing the value of the *Elevation* changes the "base plane," or the elevation, of the construction plane for newly created objects.

Figure 39-79

Figure 39-80 displays the same objects as in the previous figure except the *Circle* has an *Elevation* of **2** (level with the top edges of the other objects). It may be necessary to use *Hide* or several *Vpoints* to "see" the relationship of objects with different *Elevations*.

Like *Thickness, Elevation* should be set back to 0 to create geometry normally on the XY plane.

Figure 39-80

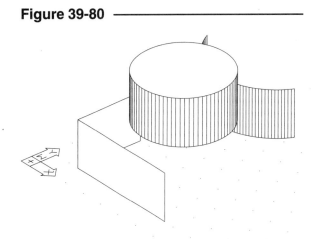

Changing *Thickness* and *Elevation*

Because *Thickness* and *Elevation* are properties that 2D objects may possess (like *Color* and *Linetype*), they can be changed or assigned <u>retroactively</u>. *Elevation* can only be changed retroactively using the *Change* command with the *Properties* option (see Chapter 16). *Thickness* can be changed using the *Modify* dialogue box.

DDMODIFY

Using the *Ddmodify* command (see Chapter 16) produces a dialogue box providing the ability to change the *Thickness* of <u>existing</u> objects (Fig. 39-81).

As an alternative to setting *Thickness* before creating surfaces, the 2D geometry can first be created and then changed to 3D surfaces by using this dialogue box to retroactively set *Thickness*.

Figure 39-81

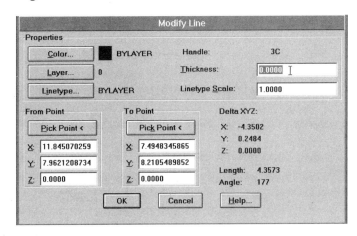

Figure 39-82 displays 2D *Pline* shapes. The *Modify* dialogue box can be used to change the *Thickness* of the shape to create a 3D surface model.

Figure 39-82

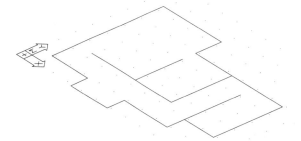

Figure 39-83 shows the same *Pline* shapes as in the previous figure after the *Thickness* property was changed to generate the 3D surface model.

If you want to change an object's *Elevation*, the *Change* command can be used. The command syntax is as follows:

Figure 39-83

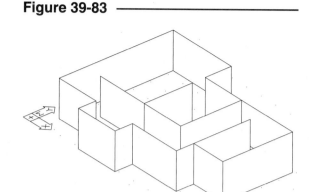

```
Command: change
Select objects: PICK
Select objects: Enter
Properties/<Change point>: p
Change what property
(Color/Elev/LAyer/LType/ltScale/Thickness) ? e
New elevation <0.0000>: (value)
Change what property (Color/Elev/LAyer/LType/ltScale/Thickness) ? Enter
Command:
```

CHAPTER EXERCISES

1-3. Create a surface model of each of the objects in Figures 39-84 through 39-86. These are the same objects you worked with in Chapter 36, Wireframe Modeling. You can use each of the Chapter 36 Exercises wireframes (**WFEX1**, **WFEX2**, and **WFEX3**) as a "skeleton" on which to attach surfaces. Make sure you create a *New Layer* for the surfaces. Use each dimension marker in the figure to equal one unit in AutoCAD. Locate the lower-left corner of the model at coordinate **0,0,0**. Assign the names **SURFEX1**, **SURFEX2**, and **SURFEX3**. Make a plot of each model with hidden lines removed.

Figure 39-84

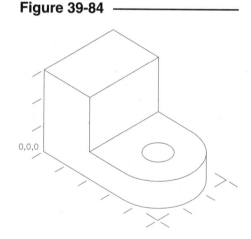

Figure 39-85

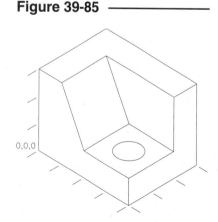

Figure 39-86

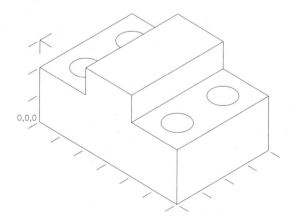

4. *Open* the **WFEX4** drawing that you created in Chapter 36 Exercises. *Saveas* **SURFEX4**. For this exercise, create a surface model using a combination of regions and polygon meshes. Use the existing wireframe geometry. Convert the *Lines, Arcs,* and *Circles* representing <u>planar</u> surfaces to closed *Plines*, then to regions. Use polygon meshes for the curved surfaces. *Save* the drawing. Generate a pictorial *Vpoint* and align a *UCS* with the *View*. *Plot* the drawing with hidden lines removed.

Figure 39-87

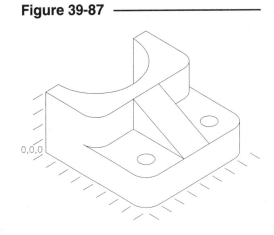

5. Create a surface model of the Bar Guide shown in Figure 39-88. You may want to use the **BGUID-WF** drawing that you created in Chapter 36 Exercises as a wireframe foundation. Make a *New Layer* for the surface model. Align a *UCS* with the *View* and create a title block and border. *Plot* the model with hidden lines removed. *Save* the surface model as **BGD-SURF**.

Figure 39-88

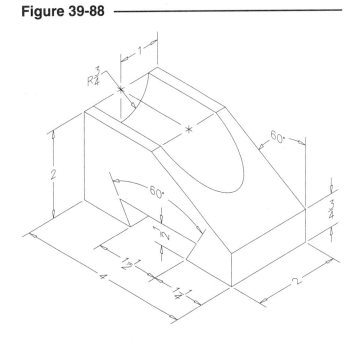

6. Create a surface model of the Saddle in Figure 39-89. There is no previously created wireframe model, so you must begin a *New* drawing or use a *Prototype*. The fillets and rounds should be created using *Rulesurf* or *Tabsurf*. *Revsurf* must be used to create the complex fillets and rounds at the corners. Align a *UCS* with the *View* and create a title block and border. Plot the drawing with hidden lines removed. *Save* the drawing as **SDL-SURF**.

Figure 39-89

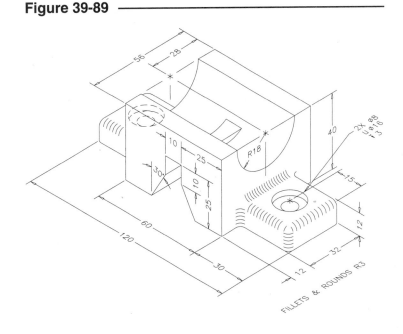

7. Begin a *New* drawing (or use a *Prototype*) for the Pulley shown in Figure 39-90. This is the same object that you worked on in Chapter 26 Exercises. As a reminder, the vertical dimensions are diameters. Use *Revsurf* to create the curved (cylindrical) surfaces. Use *Regions* to create the vertical circular faces that would appear on the front and back (the surfaces containing the 4 counterbored holes or the keyway). Display the completed surface model from a pictorial *Vpoint*. Align a *UCS* with the *View* and create a border and title block. *Save* the drawing as **PUL-SURF**. *Plot* the model with the *Hide Lines* option.

Figure 39-90

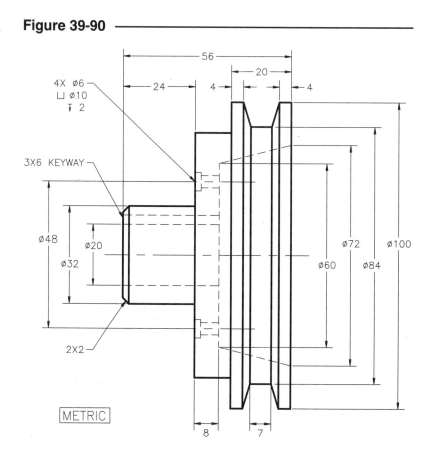

Chapter 40

RENDERING

Chapter Objectives

After completing this chapter you should:

1. know the typical steps for rendering a surface or solid model using Render;

2. understand and be able to create and set parameters for the four types of lighting: *Ambient Light*, *Point Light*, *Distant Light*, and *Spotlight*;

3. be able to select *Materials* from the *Materials Library*, *Import* them into the drawing, and *Attach* them to objects, colors, or layers;

4. be able to create *New* and *Modify* existing material properties of *Color*, *Ambient*, *Reflection*, and *Roughness*;

5. know how to use *Rpref* to specify parameters for rendering;

6. be able to create a rendering using the *Render* command;

7. be able to use *Saveimg* to save and *Replay* to replay rendered images.

BASICS

AutoCAD provides the ability to enhance the visualization of a <u>surface</u> or a <u>solid</u> model with the *Hide, Shade,* and *Render* commands. Because the default representation for surface and solid models is wireframe representation, it is difficult for the viewer to sense the three-dimensional properties of the model in this mode. *Hide, Shade,* and *Render* change the appearance of a model from wireframe to "solid." *Hide* calculates which surfaces obscure others and displays only the visible ones, and *Shade* adds the object color to the model. *Render* adds another level of realism to surface and solid models by giving you control of lights, colors, and materials.

Shade (discussed in Chapter 34, 3D Viewing and Display) is a simple and quick method that uses a default light location and fills the surfaces of the 3D model with the object color. You have control of only two variables, *SHADEDIF* and *SHADEDGE,* that affect the results of the shaded model.

Render, on the other hand, involves the use of *Light* sources and the application of surface *Materials* for the 3D model. You control the type, intensity, color, and positioning of lights in 3D space. Render also provides a variety of materials for attachment to objects, colors, or layers, and allows you to adjust the properties of the material.

Render is intended to be used as a visualization tool for 3D models. Visualization of a design before it has been constructed or manufactured can be of significant value. Presentation of a model with light sources and materials can reveal aspects of a design that may otherwise be possible only after construction or manufacturing. For example, a rendered architectural setting may give the designer and client previews of color, lighting, or spacial relationships. Or a rendered model may allow the engineer to preview the functional relationship of mechanical parts in a manner otherwise impossible with wireframe representation. Thus, this "realistic" presentation, made possible by *Render,* can shorten the design feedback cycle and improve communication between designers, engineers, architects, contractors, and clients.

With AutoCAD Render, you can render to a viewport or to the whole screen as a separate rendering display. The *Render* command uses the *Lights* and *Materials* you assign and calculates the display based on the parameters that you specify. If no *Lights* or *Materials* are created for the drawing, a default light and material are used to render the current viewport. If you have created several *Lights, Materials,* and *Views,* you can use the *Scene* command to specify a particular named *View* and a combination of *Lights.* No light sources in Render cast shadows.

The rendered screen image created with the *Render* command can be saved as a TIFF, TGA, and/or a GIF file and replayed at a later time. The *Rendering Preferences* dialogue box provides control for format and quality of the rendered image.

Figure 40-1

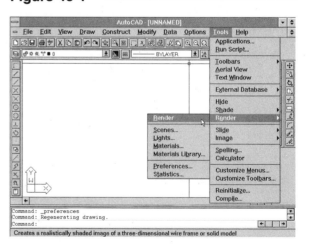

Rendering commands can be accessed by typing or selecting from the *Tools* screen menu and pull-down menu (Fig. 40-1). If you are using AutoCAD for Windows, a Render toolbar is available (Fig. 40-2). Optionally, five rendering commands can be selected from the digitizing menu.

Figure 40-2

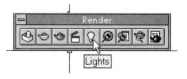

Typical Steps for Using Render

Although a rendering of a 3D surface or solid model can be created easily using default settings, the following steps are normally taken to create a rendering with the desired effect.

1. As with using *Shade*, you must first create or open an existing 3D model. Both surface and solid models can be rendered.

2. Use *Vpoint* or *Dview* to specify the desired viewing position. Perspective generations (created with *Dview Distance*) are allowed. If you want to create several renderings from different viewpoints, use the *Save* option of *View* to save each display to a named view so it can be *Restored* at a later time.

3. Use the *Lights* dialogue box series to create one or more lights. Parameters such as light type, intensity, color, and location (position in space) can be specified.

4. Use the *Materials* dialogue box series to select the desired material(s) for the object(s). The material properties such as specification of color and reflective qualities can be adjusted. You can *Preview* the material as you adjust the parameters.

5. If you have created several *Views*, *Materials*, and *Lights*, use the *Scenes* dialogue box to select the specific combination of *Lights* and the desired *View* for the rendered scene.

6. Specify the desired format and quality for the rendering by the *Rendering Preferences* dialogue box. Several options are available for the rendering.

7. Use the *Render* command to create the rendered image on the screen.

8. Because rendering normally involves a process of continual adjustment to *Light* and *Material* parameters, any or all of steps 2 through 7 can be repeated to make the desired adjustments. Don't expect to achieve exactly what you want the first time.

9. When the final adjustments have been made, use the *Rendering Preferences* dialogue box to create a *Phong* render to achieve the highest quality image.

10. Use the *Render* command again to calculate the rendered display or hard copy. Usually, you should render to the screen until you have just the image you want; then save to a file or hard copy, if desired.

11. If you rendered to the screen, you can then save the rendered image to a .TIF, .GIF, or .TGA file using the *Save Image* dialogue box.

Now that you know the general procedure for creating a rendered image, the lighting and material concepts and commands are presented next. Examples of the dialogue boxes used to achieve the desired effects are included in the following information.

CREATING LIGHTS FOR THE MODEL

AutoCAD recognizes four types of light: *Ambient Light*, *Point Light*, *Distant Light,* and *Spotlight*. *Point Lights*, *Distant Lights,* and *Spotlights* can be positioned anywhere in space and adjusted for color and intensity. *Distant Lights* and *Spotlights* can be set to shine in a specific direction, whereas *Point Lights* shine in all directions. *Ambient Light* has no location and affects all surfaces equally. *Ambient Light* can only be controlled for color and intensity. No lights cast shadows. All light passes unobstructed through surfaces.

Ambient Light

Ambient Light is the overall lighting of surfaces. Each surface is illuminated with an equal amount of ambient light, regardless of the surface's position. Thus, you cannot distinguish the adjoining faces of a box or curvature of a sphere when this is the only type of light in the model. Figure 40-3 illustrates the rendering of a box and sphere with <u>only</u> ambient light.

Adjusting ambient light would be like using a dimmer switch to darken or lighten a room except that the light has no source or direction. Ambient light is the most unrealistic type of light, but it is needed to display "background" surfaces that may not be illuminated by point or distant lights. You do not create or position an *Ambient Light* in the model; it is ever-present unless its intensity has been set to zero.

Figure 40-3

Distant Light

A *Distant Light* shines in one direction and has parallel rays. It is used to simulate sunlight. Because *Distant Light* represents the sun, you specify only a direction vector, not a light location. The vector determines the direction of the parallel beams of light which extend to infinity. Similar to sunlight, the light intensity does not fall off (grow dimmer) for surfaces farther away from the "source." Illumination of a surface is determined only by the angle between the surface and the light beams—surfaces that are perpendicular to the beams are more brightly illuminated.

Figure 40-4 illustrates a box and sphere illuminated by <u>only</u> one *Distant Light*

Figure 40-4

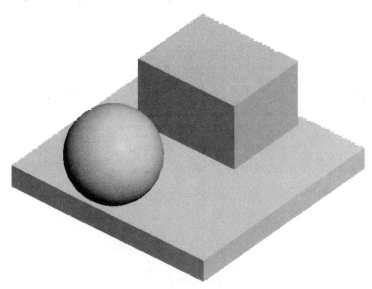

shining from above and to the right. Notice how each surface is illuminated differently because of the angle of the surface to the direction vector, yet each individual flat surface is illuminated evenly across the entire surface.

Point Light

A *Point Light* is inserted at the location you specify, but no direction vector is needed since this light shines in all directions. Point light would be typical of the light emitted from a light bulb. Point light falls off (grows dimmer) as the distance between the light source and surfaces increases, so surfaces close to the light are brighter than those at a distance. The box in Figure 40-5 is illuminated by <u>only</u> one *Point Light* above and to the right side. Notice how the light falls off the farther the surfaces are from the light source.

Figure 40-5

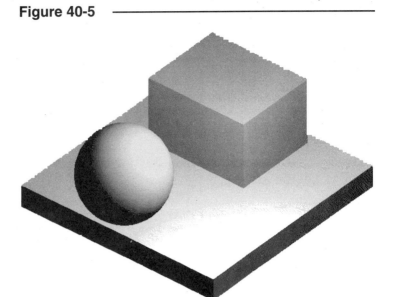

Spotlight

Spotlights have characteristics much like a spotlight used for stage lighting. You can specify the light's *Location* in space as well as the point that it shines toward (*Target*). Like point lights, the light falls off as the illuminated surfaces become farther from the light *Location*. Similar to stage spotlights, the beams of light from the source (*Location*) to the *Target* form a "cone" of light. Figure 40-6 shows the box and sphere illuminated by a *Spotlight* shining from directly above the objects. Notice the circular illuminated area formed by the cone of light. The angle of a *Spotlight's* cone of light can be adjusted for full illumination and for light fall-off.

Figure 40-6

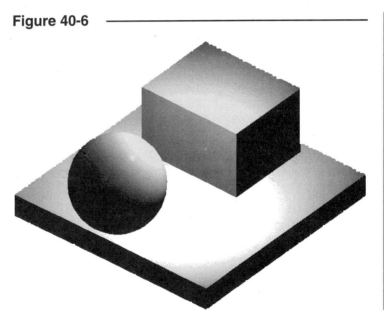

R13

For *Point Lights*, *Distant Lights*, and *Spotlights*, the brightness of a rendered surface depends on the following parameters:

1. The *Intensity* of the light can be specified. The higher the *Intensity*, the brighter the rendered surfaces appear.

2. The *Color* of the light can be specified. The lighter the *Color*, the brighter the rendered surfaces appear.

3. The angle between the light source and the surface affects the brightness of the surface. A surface that shines the brightest is one in which the light is shining perpendicular to the surface. The more angled the surface is from perpendicular, the darker it appears.

4. The distance between the light and the surface affects brightness (*Point Lights* and *Spotlights* only).

For dramatic effects, only one light might be used; however, for most renderings several lights or a combination of types of lights is used. Typically, a mix of *Ambient Light* and one or two other lights is used. Figure 40-7 illustrates the box and sphere illuminated by a combination of *Point, Distant*, and *Ambient* lighting.

Now that you understand the types of lights and the effects of each type on a rendered object, examine the commands that let you insert and control the lights.

Figure 40-7

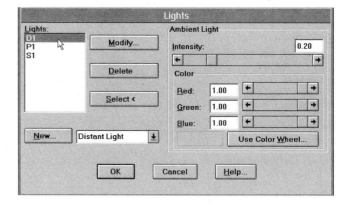

LIGHT

PULL-DOWN MENU	SCREEN MENU	TYPE IN	TABLET MENU
Tools *Render >* *Lights...*	*TOOLS* *RENDER* *Lights:*	*LIGHT*	*2,M*

When you invoke the *Light* command by any method, the *Lights* dialogue box appears, as shown in Figure 40-8.

New...
To create a new light, select the type of light (*Distant Light, Point Light,* or *Spotlight*) from the pop-down list and PICK the *New* tile. The appropriate dialogue box for the type of light appears and allows you to set the light's parameters. The light types and related dialogue boxes are discussed later.

Figure 40-8

Lights:
The *Lights:* section in the upper-left corner displays any existing (previously created) lights. Using the related buttons beside the list, you can *Modify..., Delete,* or *Select* (from the drawing) an existing light. Modifying a light offers the <u>same dialogue box</u> and options used to create a new light.

Ambient Light
The *Ambient Light* section (upper right) is where the percentage of ambient light is set by using the slider bar or by entering a value in the edit box. The setting is <u>global</u> and affects all surfaces equally. Generally a percentage of .30 is a good starting value.

You can determine the *Color* of light that is emitted by the ambient source by using the slider bars in the *Lights* dialogue box (Fig. 40-8) or by PICKing the *Use Color Wheel...* button. The **Color** dialogue box appears (Fig. 40-9).

The *Color* Dialogue Box

All lights can be assigned a color using this dialogue box (Fig. 40-9). The selected color is the color that the light emits. Although each <u>object</u> in the model can have a color (determined by the object's assigned material), the light color casts a hue on the object's surfaces. Normally, white or bright colors are used for lights. Light color can be assigned by four systems described below. The current color adjustments are displayed in the color swatch titled *Color Selected*.

Figure 40-9

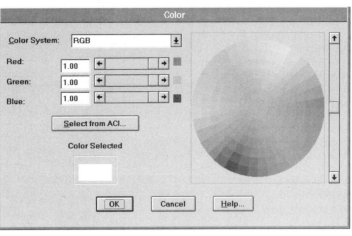

1. **Color wheel**
   The desired color can be PICKed from the selections in the wheel. The value (gray scale) of the entire set of colors in the wheel can be changed by using the slider bar on the right: up for lighter colors, down for darker.

2. *RGB*
   Make sure *RGB* is selected from the *Color System:* pop-down list. This is the same method available in the *Lights* dialogue box. The *RGB* system determines the color by the amount of *Red, Green,* and *Blue* components. Values for each can be entered into the edit boxes or changed using the slider bars. View the *Color Selected* box to see the changes. Pure red, green, or blue hues can be achieved by moving <u>only</u> that color to the right. Moving all of the *Red, Green,* and *Blue* color bars to the left produces black, and moving all to the right produces white.

3. *HLS*
   You must select *HLS* from the *Color System* pop-down edit box. The slider bars adjust the *Hue, Lightness,* and *Saturation* visible in the small boxes. The mix of *HLS* appears in the *Color Selected* swatch.

   Hue   Controls the color (red, blue, yellow, etc.).

   Lightness Controls the value (white to black). White is all the way to the right, or a value of 1.0, and black is to the left, or 0.

   Saturation Controls the purity of the color (mix of *Hue* and *Lightness*). Pure color is to the right, or a value of 1.0, and pure gray scale is to the left, or 0.

   A pure hue is achieved by a *Lightness* of .5 and *Saturation* of 1.

4. *Select from ACI...*
   Selecting this option invokes the 256-color ACI (AutoCAD Color Index) palette (Fig. 40-10). Select the desired color from the palette or enter the name or number in the edit box. If your monitor or video card only supports 16 colors, you can only select from the *Standard Colors* and *Gray Shades*.

Figure 40-10

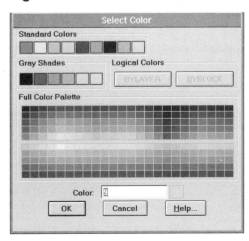

Creating New, and Modifying Existing, Lights

To insert new lights in your drawing, select the type of light (*Point Light*, *Distant Light*, or *Spotlight*) from the pop-down list in the *Lights* dialogue box (Fig. 40-8); then pick the *New...* button. A different dialogue box titled *New (type) Light* appears, depending on your light choice.

If you want to modify an existing light, select the light name from the *Lights:* list (in the *Lights* dialogue box) and PICK the *Modify...* button. The dialogue box that appears is titled *Modify (type) Light* but is otherwise identical to the dialogue box used to create the new light (*New (type) Light*).

New Point Light and *Modify Point Light* Dialogue Boxes

Light Name
When creating a new light, assign a name for the light in the *Light Name:* edit box as a first step (Fig. 40-11). In this example, "P1" is assigned as the name for a new point light. Existing light names can be renamed by changing the name in the edit box and selecting *OK*.

Intensity
Intensity is a value that specifies the brightness of the light; the higher the value, the brighter the light. The intensity can be set with the slider bar or by entering a value in the edit box. The resulting brightness of a surface illuminated by a *Point* light is based on several variables such as intensity, color, attenuation, distance to the surface, and angle between the surface and the light beams.

Figure 40-11 ————————————————

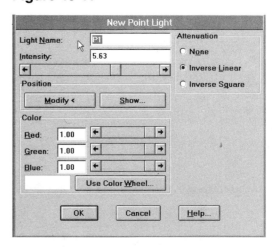

Position
When a light is created, AutoCAD automatically assigns a default location for the light based on the existing geometry. Selecting the *Show* tile displays the default *Location* of the light (Figure 40-12). The *Location* is the coordinate position of the light in 3D space (*Target* is enabled only for *Spotlights*). You can change the position by selecting the *Modify* tile, then entering the desired coordinates, or PICKing a new location (use *OSNAP* to PICK in 3D space).

Figure 40-12 ————————————————

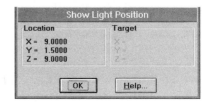

Color
The color of a *Point* light (as any other light type) can be assigned using the RGB slider bars or selecting the *Use Color Wheel...* button (see previous explanation in *Color* Dialogue Box).

Attenuation
Point Lights possess a fall-off quality similar to actual lighting. That is, the farther the light beams travel from the source (*Location*), the dimmer the light becomes. *Point Light Attenuation* has three options.

None
This option forces the light emitted from a point light to keep full intensity no matter how far the rendered surfaces are from the source. This is similar to a *Distant Light*.

Inverse Linear
This option sets an inverse linear relation between the distance and the illumination. The brightness of a rendered surface is inversely proportional to the distance from the source. Put another way, there is a 1 to 1 relationship between distance and darkness. Generally, *Inverse Linear* attenuation is the easiest to work with and appears realistic for most AutoCAD renderings.

Inverse Square
This is the greatest degree of light fall-off. The amount of light reaching a surface is inversely proportional to the square of the distance. In other words, if the rendered surfaces are 2, 3, and 4 units from the light source, the illumination for each will be $1/2^2$, $1/3^2$, and $1/4^2$ ($1/4$, $1/9$, and $1/16$) as strong. This option simulates the physical law explaining light fall-off in actuality.

New Distant Light and *Modify Distant Light* Dialogue Boxes

Distant Light simulates sunlight. With distant lights, parallel beams of light illuminate the solid or surface objects. Distance lights have no location or target, only a direction vector. Distance light has no attenuation, so the beams of light maintain the same intensity regardless of the location of the surfaces. The direction vector is specified by using either the *Azimuth* and *Altitude* or *Light Source Vector* sections of the *Distant Light* dialogue box (Fig. 40-13). The model is assumed to be oriented in space with the XY plane of the WCS representing horizontal (Earth's surface), and north is a positive Y direction.

Figure 40-13

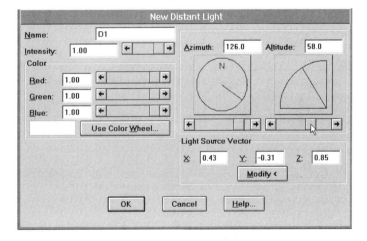

Azimuth
Azimuth is the bearing in degrees from north in a clockwise direction; for example, due east is 90 degrees. PICK in the image tile, use the slider bars, or enter a value in the edit box to make your selection.

Altitude
Altitude is the slope of the direction vector specified in degrees from horizontal; for example, 90 degrees specifies a light source from directly above (high noon), or 20 to 30 degrees simulates sunlight in the early morning or late afternoon. PICK in the image tile, use the slider bars, or enter a value in the edit box to make your selection.

Light Source Vector
An alternative to the *Azimuth* and *Altitude* method, the *Light Source Vector* edit boxes specify the location of a "source" related to 0,0,0 of the WCS. You can enter values in the edit boxes.

Name, **Intensity**, **and** *Color*
The *Name*, *Intensity*, and *Color* sections in the dialogue boxes operate identically to the same sections in the other dialogue boxes (see previous discussion).

New Spotlight and *Modify Spotlight* Dialogue Boxes

A *Spotlight* has characteristics similar to a spotlight used for stage lighting. Because you can specify a *Location* and a *Target* for the *Spotlight*, any surface or area of a surface or solid model can be illuminated from any direction. In addition, the angle of the "cone" of light (formed as the light beams travel from the source) can be adjusted. Spotlights also possess attenuation, color, and intensity. All options are available from the *New Spotlight* (Fig. 40-14) and *Modify Spotlight* dialogue boxes.

Figure 40-14

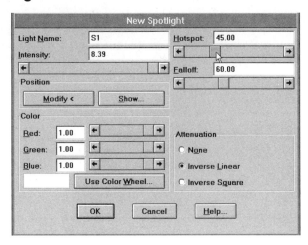

Hotspot and *Falloff*

These two sections determine characteristics of the cone of light emitted from a *Spotlight*. The *Hotspot* is the area of the model that receives full illumination (Fig. 40-15). The size of this area is determined by the angular value entered in the edit box or appearing there as a result of moving the slider bars. The light begins to fall off just outside the *Hotspot* until approaching no illumination at the *Falloff* cone. The area outside the *Falloff* cone receives no illumination. The *Falloff* angle must be equal to or greater than the *Hotspot* angle.

Position

You can indicate the *Location* and *Target* for the *Spotlight* in this cluster. A default *Location* and *Target* are calculated by AutoCAD for you when you create the light and those coordinates can be viewed by selecting the *Show...* tile (see Fig. 40-12). To specify another *Location* and *Target*, select *Modify <*. Enter coordinate values or PICK points (use *OSNAP* when PICKing in 3D space).

Light Name, Intensity, Color, Attenuation

These options operate identically to the same options appearing in the *Distant* and *Point Light* dialogue boxes. See *Distant Light* Dialogue Boxes and *Point Light* Dialogue Boxes.

Light Icons

For any light, an icon representing the light type and position appears in the drawing at the light *Location* (Fig. 40-16 and 40-17). These icons are actually *Block* insertions that appear in the drawing but not in renderings. The light icons are inserted on layer ASHADE, which is automatically created by AutoCAD when you place the first light. This layer can be *Frozen* to prevent the icons from appearing in drawings or plots.

Figure 40-15

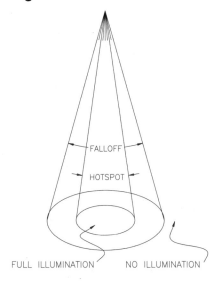

Figure 40-16

DISTANT   POINT   SPOT

Figure 40-17

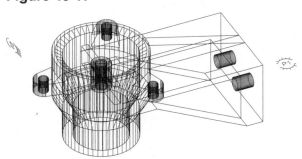

You can use the *Move* command to reposition the lights; however, it is recommended that you use the *Location* and *Target* options in the light dialogue boxes. Changing a *Distance Light* location with *Move* also moves the *Target* position. A light can be deleted by *Erasing* its icon or by using the *Delete* option in the *Lights* dialogue box.

USING MATERIALS IN THE MODEL

When the lights have been inserted and adjusted for position, color, attenuation, and intensity, you are ready to select *Materials* and attach them to the model. Because the default prototype drawing has no materials loaded, one or more materials must be selected from the *Material Library*. Once the desired materials have been imported into the drawing, you must attach them to components of the model. Different materials can be attached to different components of the model. A material can be attached to an object, layer, or ACI (AutoCAD Color Index number). If a material is attached to a layer or ACI, every object on the layer or having the ACI assumes the material. Materials can be modified to have a particular color or reflective quality.

MATLIB

PULL-DOWN MENU	SCREEN MENU	TYPE IN	TABLET MENU
Tools *Render >* *Material Library...*	*TOOLS* *RENDER* *MatLib:*	*MATLIB*	---

The *Matlib* command summons the dialogue box that provides access to the AutoCAD-supplied materials (Fig. 40-18). The names in the *Library List:* (right side) represent the choices from the RENDER.MLI file. A material is brought into the drawing by highlighting it and selecting the *Import* button. The selected material(s) then appear in the *Materials List* (left side) representing all of the materials currently in the drawing and ready for attachment to the model components. Importing materials increases file size, so import only those that are needed. This dialogue box can also be summoned from the *Materials* dialogue box (see next).

Figure 40-18

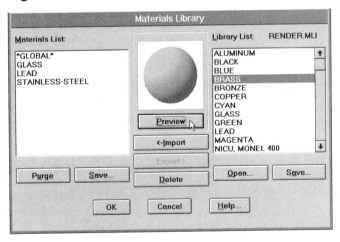

Preview
You can highlight <u>one material at a time</u> (from either list) and select the *Preview* button to see how the material appears attached to the sphere.

Import
Import brings material descriptions into the drawing from the RENDER.MLI or other .MLI files. If you try to import a name that exists in the drawing, the *Reconcile Imported Material Names* dialogue box appears. After materials are imported, select *OK*; then use the *Rmat* command (*Materials* dialogue box) to attach materials to objects, layers, or ACI numbers.

Export

Use this button to add selected materials from the *Materials List* to the *Library List*. This is useful when you have created a new material or modified an existing material and want to save it in the material library for use in other drawings.

Delete

This option deletes selected materials from the *Materials List* or the *Library List*. Deleting materials from the *Library List* does not delete them from the RENDER.MLI file.

Purge (Materials List:)

Use this button to purge all unattached materials from the material list. Unattached materials are those that have been imported but have not been attached to objects, layers, or ACI numbers using the *Rmat* command (*Materials* dialogue box).

Save (Materials List:)

The materials listed on this side can be saved to a .MLI file for use in other drawings. Assign the desired file name to save in the *Library File* dialogue box that appears.

Open (Library List:)

Material library (.MLI) files other than the default RENDER.MLI can be opened for material selection and used in the current drawing. Other .MLI files could be those you have created or those supplied with other software. AutoVision .MLI files can be used with AutoCAD; however, AutoCAD displays only *Color*, *Ambient*, *Reflection*, and *Roughness* characteristics.

Save (Library List:)

The materials listed in the library list can be saved to a .MLI file for use in other drawings. If you have created new or modified existing materials, they can be saved in the RENDER or other .MLI file. Assign the desired file name to save in the subsequent *Library File* dialogue box.

RMAT

PULL-DOWN MENU	SCREEN MENU	TYPE IN	TABLET MENU
Tools *Render >* *Materials...*	*TOOLS* *RENDER* *Mater'l:*	*RMAT*	*1M*

After materials have been imported from the materials library (see *Matlib*), this dialogue box is used to attach selected materials to AutoCAD objects, layers, or ACI numbers. You can also gain access to the tools for creating new, and modifying existing, materials from this dialogue box (Fig. 40-19).

Figure 40-19

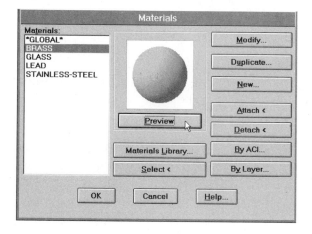

Materials

This list represents the materials that are available for attachment. The list includes the materials imported previously using the *Materials Library* dialogue box and a material named *GLOBAL*, which is the default material for objects with no material attached.

Preview

Use this button to see how the selected material (one at a time) appears on the sphere.

Materials Library...

This button invokes the *Materials Library* dialogue box for importation of other materials (see *Matlib*).

Select <

This option temporarily removes the dialogue box to allow selection of an object. When an object is selected, the *Materials Library* dialogue box reappears with the material name and attachment method used displayed at the bottom of the dialogue box.

Attach <

Use this button to attach the highlighted material from the *Materials:* list to an object. The dialogue box is temporarily removed to allow selection of an object. When the *Render* command is used, the object is rendered with the attached material.

Detach

The *Detach* option allows you to unattach an assigned material by selecting an object.

By ACI...

You can attach a material to an *ACI* (AutoCAD Color Index number) using this button. With this method of attachment, every object in the drawing that has the selected color number displays the attached material when the *Render* command is used. The *Attach by AutoCAD Color Index* dialogue box appears (Fig. 40-20).

To attach a material, you must select <u>both</u> the desired material from the list on the left and the desired color or number from the list on the right. Then PICK the *Attach* button and the material name appears next to the color in the *Select ACI:* list (see Fig. 40-20). If you want to *Detach* a material from a color number, select the choice from the *Select ACI:* list only; then PICK *Detach*.

Figure 40-20

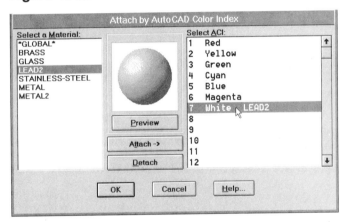

By Layer...

The *Attach by Layer* dialogue box (not shown) operates identically to the *Attach by AutoCAD Color Index* dialogue box. To attach a material, select <u>both</u> the desired material and the desired layer; then PICK *Attach*. Attached materials appear in the list with the layer name.

Modify...

Select a material from the list and choose the *Modify...* button to produce the *Modify Standard Material* dialogue box. See Creating New and Modifying Existing Materials.

Duplicate...

If you want to create a new material but use an existing material as a starting point, choose this method. The highlighted name from the *Materials List:* is used as a template. The *New Standard Material* dialogue box appears. See Creating New and Modifying Existing Materials.

New...

This button produces the *New Standard Material* dialogue box and enables you to create a new material "from scratch." See Creating New and Modifying Existing Materials.

CREATING NEW, AND MODIFYING EXISTING, MATERIALS

Render allows you to control four attributes that define a material: *Color, Ambient, Reflection,* and *Roughness*. For each attribute, the *Value* (intensity) and *Color* can be adjusted. These adjustments are made in the *Modify Standard Color* and *New Standard Color* dialogue boxes (Fig. 40-25). The attributes are defined here.

Color	*Color* is the global color of the material. The color (hue) and the value (intensity) can be adjusted. Technically, *Color* represents the light that is reflected in a diffuse manner. Diffuse light reflection affects all surfaces equally, not accounting for highlights (highlights are controlled by the *Reflection* attribute). Setting a low *Color* value makes the surfaces appear dark and dull (Fig 40-21, left sphere). Increasing the *Color* value makes the surface reflect more light; therefore, the assigned color appears brighter (right sphere).

Figure 40-21

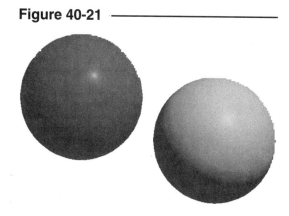

Ambient	Ambient light is background light that illuminates all surfaces. Because most of the surfaces are illuminated by *Point Lights, Distant Lights,* and *Spotlights,* adjusting the *Ambient* attribute controls the color and intensity of material "in the shadows." A low *Ambient* setting makes surfaces in the "shadows" appear dark (Fig. 40-22, left sphere), while a high *Ambient* setting increases the <u>overall lighting</u> and makes the "shadows" brighter (right sphere).

Figure 40-22

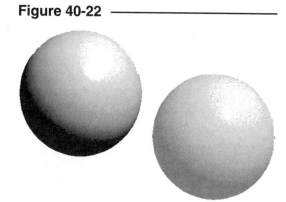

Reflection	This attribute controls the light that is reflected from *Point Lights, Distant Lights,* and *Spotlights. Reflection* accounts for the highlights on an object (technically called specular reflection). Controlling the value of *Reflection* increases or decreases the amount of reflected light. Use a low *Reflection* value to make the surfaces appear flat or matte, like blotting paper or soft material (Fig. 40-23, left sphere). Use a high *Reflection* value to increase light contrast on surfaces from *Point Lights, Distant Lights,* and *Spotlights* (right sphere).

Figure 40-23

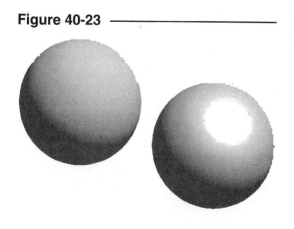

Roughness

Roughness is a function of *Reflection*—if *Reflection* value is 0, *Roughness* has no effect. *Roughness* does not affect the amount of highlight, only the <u>size</u> of the highlight. A smaller *Roughness* value produces a small shiny spot on a sphere. Use a small *Roughness* value to produce a hard, shiny material (Fig. 40-24, left sphere). If a surface has a high *Roughness* value, its reflection is spread in a less perfect, larger cone. The larger the *Roughness* value, the larger the cone of reflection and the larger the highlight (right sphere).

Figure 40-24

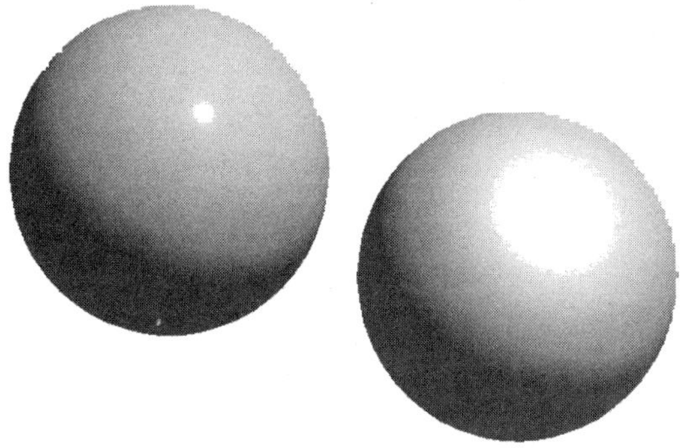

To make adjustments to the material's attributes, select either *Modify...*, *Duplicate...*, or *New...* from the *Materials* dialogue box (Fig. 40-19). In any case, the resulting dialogue box is the same; however, the title of the dialogue box differs. For example, if you selected *Modify...*, the *Modify Standard Material* title is used (Fig. 40-25); otherwise, the *New Standard Material* title is used. Options in the dialogue box are described here.

Figure 40-25

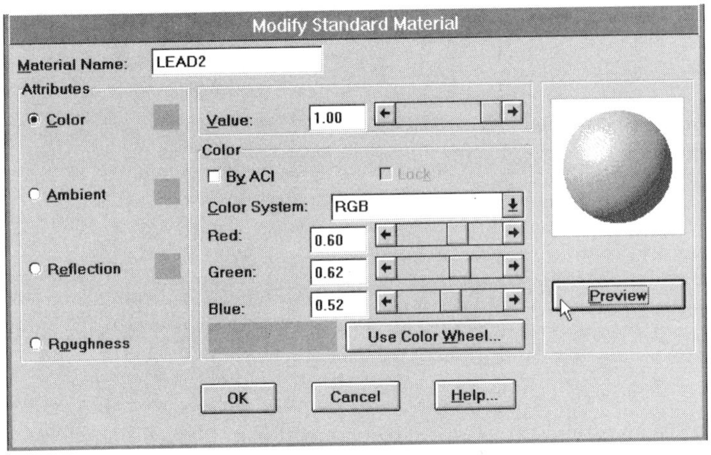

Material Name:
If you are modifying an existing material, the name appears here. You can rename an existing material, but it does not create a duplicate material. (Choose the *Duplicate...* button in the *Materials* dialogue box to keep the original material and create a new one.)

Attributes
Only one of these radio buttons can be depressed. The selected *Color, Ambient, Reflection,* or *Roughness* button determines the attribute to be adjusted in the *Value* and *Color* clusters.

Value
The magnitude of the selected attribute is adjusted by using the slider bar or entering a value in the edit box.

Color
This cluster enables you to set the color for each material attribute four ways: *RGB* system, *HLS* system, *Color Wheel,* and *ACI* pallet. These methods are identical to those used for setting light colors explained previously (see Creating Lights for the Model).

By ACI
If *By ACI* is checked in the *Color* cluster, the material color is set to match the object's drawing color (assigned *BYLAYER* or as an object-specific setting). In this case, the color is fixed to the object's drawing color and cannot be changed. Removing the "X" in the checkbox enables the other options and allows you to set color by one of the four color systems.

Lock

This is a useful checkbox to use if you want the *Ambient* and *Reflection* attribute colors to remain the same as the main *Color*. In this way, you can make adjustments to the attribute *Values* while ensuring that all reflection colors are not changed.

USING *SCENES*

When the *Lights* have been inserted and *Materials* have been attached and adjusted, you can use the *Render* command to calculate the rendered view and display it in the viewport or in the rendering screen (whichever is configured). If no *Scene* has been specified, AutoCAD uses the current view, and all lights in the rendering. However, you can choose to use *Scene* to specify a particular view or lighting combination. *Scenes* are helpful if you want to create several renderings of a model using different viewpoints and different light combinations.

SCENE

PULL-DOWN MENU	SCREEN MENU	TYPE IN	TABLET MENU
Tools *Render >* *Scenes...*	*TOOLS* *RENDER* *Scenes:*	*SCENE*	2,L

If you want to render objects from one of several named *Views* or use different light combinations for a viewpoint, you can use the *Scene* command to select the *View* and *Light* combinations for each render. You can save particular *Views* and lighting configurations to a *Scene* with a name that you assign. This action allows you to create multiple renderings without having to recreate the configuration each time. *Scenes* do not have icons that are inserted into the drawing like *Light* icons.

Invoking the *Scene* command by any method displays the *Scenes* dialogue box (Fig. 40-26). Selecting the **NONE** entry renders the current viewpoint and uses all lights inserted in the drawing. If no lights are inserted, AutoCAD uses one from over the shoulder like the one used for *Shade*.

Figure 40-26

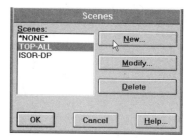

New...

Selecting the *New...* option allows you to create a new *Scene* for the drawing and produces the *New Scene* dialogue box (Fig. 40-27).

Modify...

This option produces the *Modify Scene* dialogue box where you can modify existing *Scenes*. This dialogue box is the same as the *New Scene* dialogue.

Delete

Delete removes the highlighted scene from the drawing.

Figure 40-27

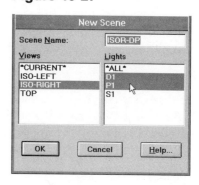

Creating New, and Modifying Existing, Scenes

The *New Scene* and the *Modify Scene* dialogue boxes allow you to select from a list of existing named *Views* and inserted *Lights*. First, assign the desired name for the scene by entering it in the edit box in the upper right (Fig. 40-27). The name is limited to eight characters.

The *Views* column lists all previously created views. The **CURRENT** view can be selected if no *Views* have been previously assigned. You can only have <u>one *View*</u> in a *Scene*. Selecting an existing view makes it the current view for the drawing as well as that used for the subsequent *Render*.

You can also select *Lights* from the list to be included for the rendering of the scene. Any number of lights can be selected for a scene. Highlighted lights are included in the scene. Selecting a non-highlighted light adds it to the scene. There is no limit to the number of *Scenes* that can be created.

SPECIFYING RENDERING PREFERENCES

Before creating the first rendering using the *Render* command, rendering preferences should be set in the *Rendering Preferences* dialogue box.

RPREF

PULL-DOWN MENU	SCREEN MENU	TYPE IN	TABLET MENU
Tools *Render >* *Preferences...*	*TOOLS* *RENDER* *Prefer:*	*RPREF*	*1,O*

The *Rpref* command invokes the *Rendering Preferences* dialogue box (Fig. 40-28). This box lets you specify options that are used when you render the view or scene. It is a good habit to determine or check the settings in this dialogue box immediately before using the *Render* command. Since rendering takes time, taking a minute to make sure the desired options are set beforehand can save wasted rendering time.

Figure 40-28

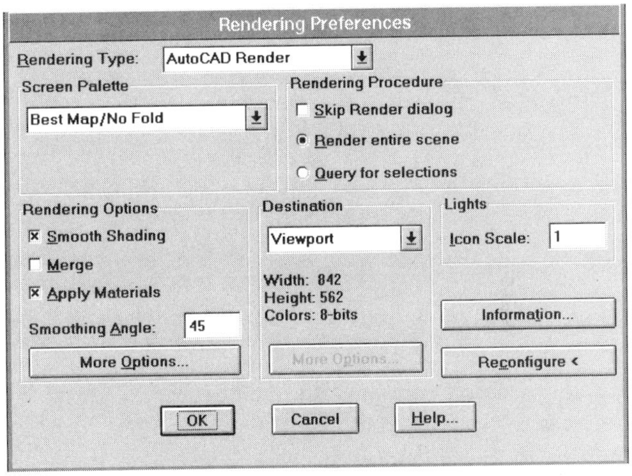

Rendering Preferences **Dialogue Box**

Rendering Type
This pop-down lists *AutoCAD Render* and other rendering options that can be installed, such as AutoVision.

Screen Palette
These options control how colors are mapped if Render is configured to render in 256 colors to a viewport; otherwise, the options are grayed out.

Best Map/No Fold
This option uses the best color map available for your system for the rendering viewport and for drawing vectors in other viewports and does not fold the AutoCAD vector colors into colors 1-8. The vectors in other viewports may change colors somewhat after rendering (called color flashing).

Best Map/Fold
This option uses the best color map available for your system. When you render in a viewport, this setting folds the colors in the non-rendered viewports to the standard eight colors. There is no color flashing in the non-rendering viewports.

Fixed ACADMap
This option uses the AutoCAD 256-color map for both renderings and drawing vectors. The non-rendered viewports retain their original colors.

Rendering Procedure

Skip Render Dialogue
Normally, the *Render* dialogue box appears when you use the *Render* command. Checking this box skips this procedure. The *Render* dialogue box (Fig. 40-30) is almost identical to the *Rendering Preferences* dialogue box, except this option is not included.

Render Entire Scene
When you render, AutoCAD automatically selects everything for the render if this button is selected.

Query for Selections
When you render, you are prompted to specify a selection set to render if this button is selected.

Rendering Options

Smooth Shading
If *Smooth Shading* is checked, Render automatically smoothes out the multifaceted appearance of polygon meshes. With *Smooth Shading* off, the mesh edges appear in the final rendering. If an edge defines a corner of greater than 45 degrees, it is not affected by *Smooth Shading*.

Merge
This option is only available with *Full Render* and for 24-bit color devices (16 million colors). *Merge* allows you to merge a smaller rendered object with the rendering in the framebuffer (previously rendered screen). In other words, first render a scene or *Replay* an existing rendering to fill the framebuffer; then turn on *Merge* and render a smaller object or area. *Merge* combines the most recent rendering (foreground) with the contents of the framebuffer (background). This is helpful if you want to re-render a small part of the previous rendering or combine a new image with an existing saved rendering.

Apply Materials
This option applies your materials when the rendering is calculated. If *Apply Materials* is not checked, Render uses the color, ambient, and reflection settings for the default *GLOBAL* material for the rendering.

Smoothing Angle
This value determines the angle at which smoothing is applied. For any angles on the object less than the value specified, AutoCAD renders as if no edge exists (see *Smooth Shading*).

More Options...
Selecting this tile produces a dialogue box with advanced options. See *AutoCAD Rendering Options Dialogue Box* at the end of this section (Fig. 40-29).

Destination

Viewport
If this option is checked, Render calculates the rendering and displays it in the Drawing Editor. If you are using tiled or paper space viewports, the rendering is in the current viewport.

Rendering Window (AutoCAD for Windows Only)
If you are using AutoCAD for Windows, selecting this option creates the render in a separate window, not in the Drawing Editor. (AutoCAD for DOS users can use *Rconfig* to configure for rendering to a separate rendering window.)

File
If this option is checked, the rendering is calculated and written to the file, but is not displayed. You can specify the type of file to render to by selecting *More Options...* in this cluster, which produces the *File Output Configuration* dialogue box. See *File Output Configuration* Dialogue Box in Saving and Replaying Renderings.

Lights

Icon Scale
Enter a value to scale the *Light* icons that are inserted into the drawing. Any value larger than 0 is valid.

Information
This tile produces an informational dialogue box giving your current configuration and Render version.

Reconfigure
This option allows you to reconfigure the display and hard copy devices for Render. This action can also be performed by using the *Rconfig* command. See *Rconfig*.

AutoCAD Rendering Options **Dialogue Box**
The *Rendering Options* dialogue box (Fig. 40-29) appears when you select *More Options...* in the *Rendering Options* section of the *Rendering Preferences* dialogue box.

Figure 40-29

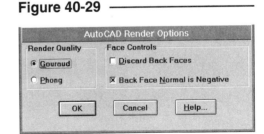

Render Quality

Gouraud
This method calculates light intensity at each <u>vertex</u> and interpolates the intensities between vertices. As a result, a sphere, for example, may have a diamond-shaped highlight.

Phong
This creates the most realistic type of rendering with higher-quality highlights. Phong calculates light intensity at each pixel.

Face Controls

Discard Back Faces
This setting prevents Render from reading the back faces of surfaces when rendering, which can save considerable time calculating the rendering (see *Back Face Normal is Negative*).

Back Face NormalIs Negative
Checking this setting reverses which faces Render considers as back faces. Normally, a positive normal vector points outward from the interior of the object toward the viewer. When constructing surfaces such as a *3Dface*, specifying vertices in a counterclockwise direction creates a positive normal vector toward the observer. Turning off this setting reverses the direction AutoCAD considers back faces. If surfaces in a surface model rendering are black and *Discard Back Faces* is checked, reverse this setting or turn off *Discard Back Faces*.

CREATING THE RENDERING

Finally, after inserting *Lights*, attaching *Materials*, and setting the *Rendering Preferences*, you are ready to create the rendering. Using the *Render* command is the easiest step in creating a rendering because Render does the work.

RENDER

PULL-DOWN MENU	SCREEN MENU	TYPE IN	TABLET MENU
Tools *Render >* *Render...*	*TOOLS* *RENDER* *Render:*	*RENDER*	*1,L*

Using this command causes Render to calculate and display the rendered scene to the configured device. The rendering is generated according to the settings in the *Rendering Preferences* or *Render* dialogue box. Render uses the *Lights* and *View* selected in the *Scene* dialogue. If no *Scene* has been created, the current view is rendered with all *Lights*.

After issuing the *Render* command, the *Render* dialogue box appears (Fig. 40-30) unless the *Skip Render Dialogue* option is checked in the *Rendering Preferences* dialogue box. This dialogue box offers the same options as the *Rendering Preferences* dialogue box.

There are no options or any other action that is required of you except to wait for the rendering to be displayed (or written to the hard copy device). Rendering can take considerable time, depending on the complexity of the scene, your computer system capabilities, and the settings in the *Rendering Preferences* dialogue box.

Figure 40-30

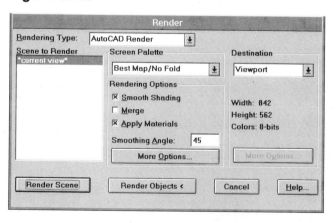

If you specified that Render make a hard copy (in the *Rendering Preferences* dialogue box), the rendering is calculated and written to the specified file or device but is not displayed on the screen (see Saving and Replaying Renderings and *Rconfig*). Alternately, if the *Viewport* or *Rendering Window* is the selected *Destination* and you decide to save the rendered screen display after creating the rendering, you can use *Saveimg* (see *Saveimg*).

Canceling the Rendering Process
You can stop the rendering by pressing Esc (or Ctrl+C in AutoCAD for DOS).

Rendering Example
The Intake Housing is used here as an example for inserting *Lights*, creating a *Material*, and creating a rendering (refer to Typical Steps for Using Render).

After the geometry is completed, *Dview* or *Vpoint* is used to provide an appropriate viewing orientation for the rendering (Fig. 40-31). If desired, the viewpoint can be saved to a named *View* to be used later for defining *Scenes*.

Figure 40-31

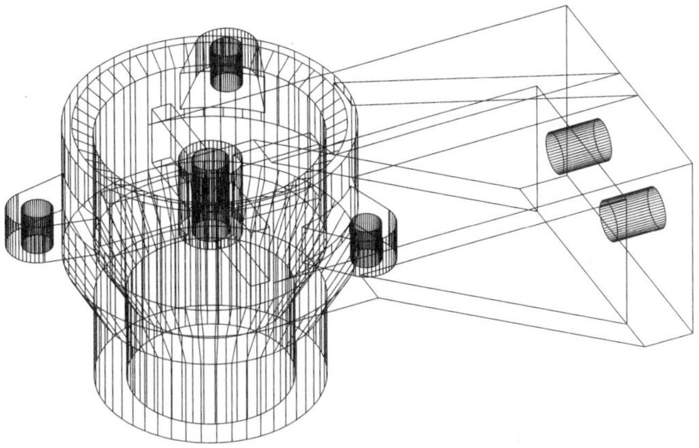

Next, the *Lights* dialogue box series is used to insert a light in the drawing. For this example, the first light is a *Point Light* positioned to the upper right. Setting the *Point Light* color to a cool color (very light shade of purple or blue) can be used to reinforce the appearance of metallic surfaces. Generating a *Render* displays the results of the light position and intensity. You can make several adjustments to position and intensity settings, then generate renderings until the desired effect is obtained (Fig. 40-32).

Figure 40-32

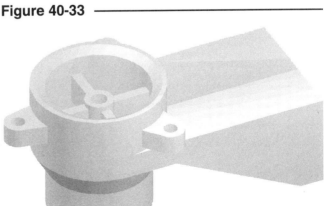

This light position in Figure 40-32 illuminates the front, top, and right sides of the Intake Housing. Notice how the point light illumination falls off along the top surface. Since only one light is used, the top and right side surfaces appear very bright, while the back of the cylinder has no light.

A rendering with only one point light can create drastic contrast from one side of the model to the other. Therefore, a second *Light* is inserted into the drawing to provide more even and realistic illumination over the surfaces of the model. This second light is a *Distant* light positioned on the left side and having a *Target* location at the base of the cylindrical element.

Figure 40-33

A *Render* reveals the initial settings (Fig. 40-33). The new light compensates for the previously dark left side of the model; however, with both lights, the model has a bright, washed-out effect. *Intensity* for the lights is adjusted to provide slightly less illumination. Make several *Intensity, Location,* and *Color* adjustments, if necessary, to achieve the desired effects. A useful technique is to use a slightly different color for the two lights; for example, with the *Distant Light,* use a warm tone (light yellow).

Figure 40-34

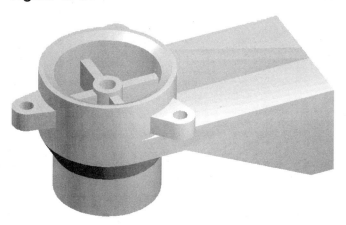

With the desired lighting set, the *Material* should then be considered. The model at this stage appears to have the surface properties of a matte material. The surfaces seem to reflect light evenly like a soft material.

In order for the observer to perceive the model as a hard metal such as machined cast iron, a *Material* is selected and attached. *Steel* or *NICU, Monel 400* can be used to simulate the actual material of the part. The material can be modified to achieve particular reflective qualities if desired. A low *Ambient* setting and a high *Color* value intensify the contrast of the light reflection between surfaces and amplify the cylindrical shape. A high *Reflection* value, coupled with low *Roughness,* creates the highlights generated by hard, shiny, metallic surfaces.

The resulting rendering is evenly illuminated, yet has enough contrast and highlighting to yield a realistic and interesting image (Fig. 40-34).

SAVING, PRINTING, AND REPLAYING RENDERINGS

Renderings can be saved to files in a number of ways. If you have used the Render command and want to save the image to a file, use *Saveimg.* If you want to render directly to a file, the *File* option of the *Destination* cluster of the *Rendering Preferences* dialogue box can be checked. Alternately, you can configure to render to a hard copy device. If you are using AutoCAD for Windows, you can send the rendering directly to the printer. To replay an image from a file, use *Replay.*

SAVEIMG

PULL-DOWN MENU	SCREEN MENU	TYPE IN	TABLET MENU
Tools *Image >* *Save...*	*TOOLS* *Saveimg:*	*SAVEIMG*	---

The *Saveimg* command allows you to save the rendered image in the rendering screen or viewport to a GIF, TIFF, or TGA file format. The image can be displayed at a later time with the *Replay* command. No matter how long it took for Render to calculate and display the original rendering, when it is saved to a GIF, TIFF, or TGA file, it can be *Replayed* in a matter of seconds.

The *Saveimg* command can also save the <u>drawing screen</u> (for any drawing, not only renderings) with or without the menus and the command line to the raster file type you specify. This can be useful if you want to import the screen image to a word processor to include in a document.

If you want to create a rendering and save it to a file directly (without first rendering to the screen), you can select *File* as the *Destination* in the *Rendering Preferences* dialogue box (see Rendering to a File, next). You can also render to a hard copy device if one is configured. Depending on the configured device, many file formats are available (see *Rconfig*).

The *Saveimg* command invoked by any method produces the *Save Image* dialogue box, where you can select the file format and the portion of the image you want to save. There are two forms of the dialogue box based on your current configuration—set to render either to a viewport (Fig. 40-35) or to a separate rendering window (Fig. 40-36).

Figure 40-35 ————

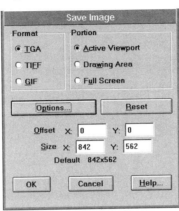

Figure 40-36 ————

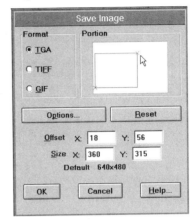

Format

TGA
This is the Truevision v2.0 format (.TGA file extension). It is a 32-bit format (16 million colors). A partial image can be saved with the *Size* and *Offset* options.

TIFF
Also a 32-bit format, this option is a Tagged Image File Format (.TIF file extension). A partial image can be saved with the *Size* and *Offset* options.

GIF
This is the CompuServe image format (.GIF file extension). The *Size* and *Offset* options let you save a portion of the image.

Options
Depending on the type of file (TIF and TGA only), file compression is available.

Offset
This option sets the lower-left corner for the image to save. The X and Y values are in screen pixels.

Size
This option sets the upper-right corner for the image in pixels.

Reset
This option resets the *Offset* and *Size* values to the full-screen defaults.

Portion
The *Portion* option lets you save part of the image. The methods of determining the portion you want to save differ based on the current configuration, either set to render to a viewport (Fig. 40-35) or set to render to a separate rendering screen or window (Fig. 40-36).

Render to a Viewport

Active Viewport   Saves the image in the active viewport only (when multiple viewports are used).

Drawing Area   Saves the display in the drawing area without menus or command line.

Full Screen   Saves the drawing area, menus, and command line.

Render to a separate window

The image tile selector allows you to PICK the lower left and upper right corners of the image to save, or you can enter X,Y values in the *Offset* and *Size* edit boxes.

Saving a Rendered Image to a File

If your choice for *Destination* is *File*, you can render directly to the selected file format without rendering to the screen. In this case, when *Render* is invoked, the screen display keeps its previous drawing or image and the calculated rendering is written to the designated file.

When *File* is selected as the *Destination* in either the *Render* dialogue box (see *Render,* Fig. 40-30) or in the *Rendering Preferences* dialogue box (see *Rpref,* Fig. 40-28), you can choose the file format for the rendering to be written by selecting *More Options...* button. The *File Output Configuration* dialogue box appears (Fig. 40-37).

Figure 40-37

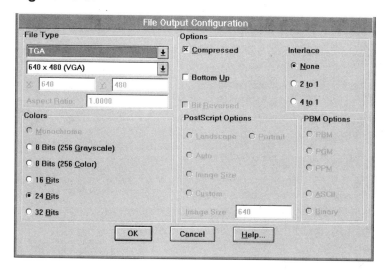

File Type

This specifies the type of output file and rendering resolution. Supported types are: GIF, X11, BMP, TGA, PCX, SUN, FITS, TIFF, FAX, EPS, IFF, and PBM. Screen resolution is the number of pixels displayed and is a function of the configured display driver.

Aspect Ratio

This sets the aspect ratio (ratio of horizontal/vertical).

Colors

There are several options for the number of colors based on the file type.

Options

Compression turns on file compression if supported by the selected file type. *Bottom Up* starts the scan lines from the bottom left instead of the top left.

Interlace

None turns off interlacing. Checking *2 to 1* or *4 to 1* sets those interlacing modes on.

PostScript Options and PMB Options

These options are only available if *PostScript* or *PBM* are selected as a file type.

Saving a Rendering to a Bitmap (BMP) File in AutoCAD for DOS

Any time you are using AutoCAD Release 13 for DOS, you can create a .BMP file of the drawing screen or rendering window by pressing the Print Screen key on the keyboard. This is a feature of the Vibrant Graphics driver written for the DOS version of AutoCAD Release 13. Capturing the pixel map (bitmap) of the screen is sometimes called making a "screen capture." When Print Screen is pressed, a file name of VIBSCRN.BMP is automatically assigned to the first screen capture (bitmap file) created, VIB0001.BMP is assigned to the second, VIB0002.BMP to the third, and so on. These .BMP images <u>cannot</u> be replayed using the *Replay* command, but can be read by many other graphics, paint, or viewing programs.

The image that is created includes the entire screen since there is no mechanism for cropping the image as it is written. However, if you are using AutoCAD for DOS and want to "capture" a bitmap of just a rendered image, first, configure to render to a separate rendering screen using the *Rconfig* command (see *Rconfig*). Next, create the rendering as you normally would with *Render*. When the image is displayed in the rendering screen, press Print Screen to capture the rendering.

Rendering and Printing from a Rendering Window in AutoCAD for Windows

If you are using AutoCAD for Windows and you have selected *Render Window* as the *Destination* in either the *Render* dialogue box (see *Render*, Fig. 40-30) or in the *Rendering Preferences* dialogue box (see *Rpref*, Fig. 40-28), your renderings will appear in a separate window (Fig. 40-38). You can toggle between the rendering window and AutoCAD using the Windows Task List or the Alt+Tab key sequence.

Figure 40-38

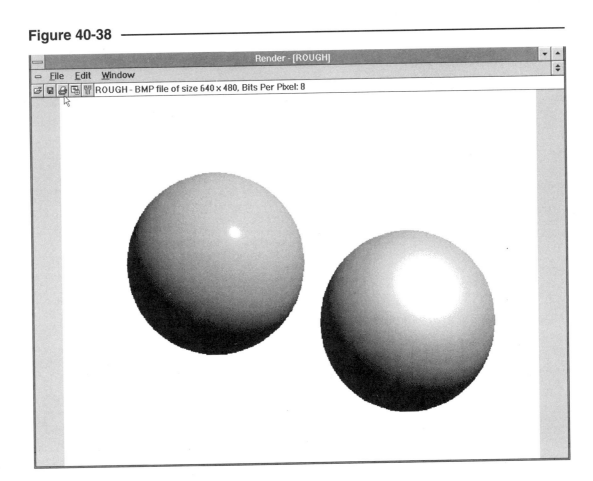

There are several options here that are not available by other means. For example, several options for printing a rendered image are available by selecting either the print icon or *Print* from the *File* pull-down menu. If you have configured AutoCAD to use the configured Windows printer, the *Print* dialogue box appears (Fig. 40-39).

Printing is allowed across several pages by using the *Tile Pages* slider bars. You can also drag the position squares at the corners of the image to change or reproportion the size or reposition the image on the selected sheet(s).

Figure 40-39

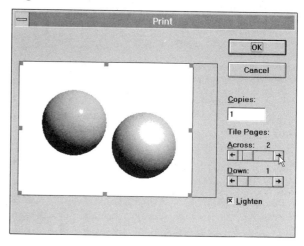

Selecting the options icon or *Option* from the *File* pull-down menu produces the *Windows Render Options* dialogue box (Fig. 40-40). Here you can change the resolution (*Size in Pixels*) and *Color Depth* of the bitmap image.

Figure 40-40

REPLAY

PULL-DOWN MENU	SCREEN MENU	TYPE IN	TABLET MENU
Tools *Image >* *View...*	*TOOLS* *Replay:*	*REPLAY*	---

The *Replay* command opens the *Replay* dialogue box (Fig. 40-41) where you specify the file you want to replay. You can replay any TIFF, GIF, or TGA files. Enter the desired file format to replay in the *List Files of Type:* or *Pattern:* edit box to make the existing files appear in the files list. After you select the file to replay, the *Image Specifications* dialogue box (Fig. 40-42) appears.

Figure 40-41

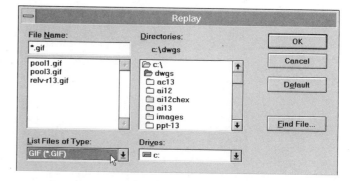

In the *Image Specifications* dialogue box (Fig. 40-42), you can specify that the entire image or a portion of the image be displayed. You can also offset the image in the screen area.

The *Image* area of the dialogue box displays the full image size (listed below in the *Image Size* edit boxes). You can display the full image or PICK the lower-left and upper-right corners in this box to define a portion of the image to display. Optionally, you can enter the lower left corner X,Y values (in pixels) in the *Image Offset* edit box and the image size (in pixels) in the *Image Size* edit box.

The *Screen* image box allows you to PICK the location on the screen for the image to be replayed. Just PICK a location in this image tile to specify the new location for the <u>center</u> of the image. Alternately, the lower-left corner position can be specified by entering X,Y values (in pixels) in the *Screen Offset* edit boxes. When AutoCAD displays the image, the size is limited to the size (in pixels) of the window in which it is displayed.

Figure 40-42

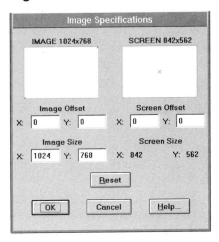

RENDERUNLOAD

When you first use any rendering command in an AutoCAD session, the AutoCAD Render application loads into memory. This may cause a slow-down in performance if you have a system with limited memory. The *Renderunload* command must be typed at the command prompt. There are no options.

    Command: **renderunload**
    Command:

After issuing the command, some memory in your computer is freed. Rendering commands are still available as before, but when you issue a rendering command again, Render will have to reload. *Renderunload* should be used if you are finished rendering but want to continue working in AutoCAD.

R13

RCONFIG

PULL-DOWN MENU	SCREEN MENU	TYPE IN	TABLET MENU
Tools *Render >* *Preferences...* *Reconfigure*	*TOOLS* *RENDER* *Config:*	*RCONFIG*	---

When you use a Render command for the first time after installation, you must configure the type of display driver and hard copy device you want to use. The *Rconfig* command allows you to <u>re</u>configure your Render setup during a rendering session. The *Rconfig* command appears differently if you are using AutoCAD for Windows or AutoCAD for DOS.

AutoCAD for DOS

When you invoke *Rconfig*, AutoCAD displays the current configuration for the display driver and hard copy device, which may look something like the following text display.

Command: **rconfig**
copyrights, etc., displayed

Configuration menu

0. Exit to drawing editor
1. Show current configuration

2. Configure rendering device
3. Configure hard copy rendering device

Enter selection <0>:

Configuring the Rendering Device

Configuring the rendering device (select 2.) displays a prompt similar to the following:

Your current Rendering display is:
 AutoCAD's configured P386 ADI combined display/rendering driver
Do you want to select a different one? <N>

If you want to configure a new display driver, you should first read the section on configuring AutoCAD in the AutoCAD Installation Guide for DOS, as well as the documentation that is supplied with your monitor and video card.

The rendering device possibilities are limited by your monitor capabilities and video card. The capabilities usually range from 640 x 480 pixels (horizontal x vertical picture elements or "dots") with 16 colors to 1280 x 1024 pixels with 16 million colors or higher. If you have a typical SVGA (Super VGA) high resolution monitor and matching video card, your display should be capable of 1024 x 768 pixels and 256 colors or 65,000 colors. Generally, the pixel resolution is based on your monitor capabilities, while the number of colors can be increased by adding RAM on the video card.

Depending on your monitor and video card capabilities, you may be able to use the currently configured display driver, but you can reconfigure Render to render to a viewport or to a separate rendering screen. This is accomplished by selecting option **2** from the Render configuration menu. Depending on your current driver, the syntax would be something like the following:

Select mode to run display/rendering combined driver:

1. Render to display viewport.
2. Render to rendering screen.

Choosing option 1 causes renderings to be displayed in the Drawing Editor. If you are using tiled or paper space viewports, the rendering is generated in the current viewport.

Choosing option 2 causes renderings to display in a separate, full-screen window. After viewing a rendering, press F1 to return to the Drawing Editor.

Configuring the Hardcopy Rendering Device

If you have a printer manufacturer-supplied protected mode device driver, you can configure your printer to accept and print rendered images. For example, some Hewlett-Packard HPGL/2 devices can be configured to use the *Hprender* command (at the AutoCAD command prompt) to configure and print AutoCAD renderings. Third-party driver files (.EXP) must be copied into the AutoCAD device driver directory and the *RHPADI* environment variable set to define the driver location. See the AutoCAD Installation Guide for DOS.

AutoCAD for Windows

When you use *Rconfig* in AutoCAD for Windows, the choices are different than those for AutoCAD for DOS.

Command: **rconfig**

Configuration menu

0. Exit to drawing editor
1. Show current configuration

2. Configure rendering device
3. Configure Render Window

Enter selection <0>:

All selections in AutoCAD for Windows are automatic. Because AutoCAD for Windows uses the system printer and shares the system video driver, using *Rconfig* is automatic for the AutoCAD-supplied drivers at the time of this writing. You can specify whether you want to render to a *Viewport* or *Rendering Window* using the *Render* dialogue box or *Rendering Preferences* dialogue box.

MISCELLANEOUS RENDERING TIPS

When you prepare the models for rendering, consider these factors.

Drawing Outward-Facing Surfaces for Surface Models

AutoCAD uses the "normal" on each face to determine which is a front face and which is a back face. A normal is a vector that is perpendicular to each polygon face on your model and points outward from the surface. If you draw the face (such as a 3Dface) by PICKing counterclockwise, the normals point outward; if you draw the face clockwise, the normals point inward. You should draw all faces consistently. Mixing methods produces unexpected rendering results. AutoCAD calculates all the normals in the drawing during rendering.

If all surface model faces are drawn consistently, all normals should point outward from (or inward toward) the model. If problems still result in rendering, you can select *Back Face Normal Is Negative* in the *Rendering Preferences* dialogue box (see *Rpref*).

If all faces are created consistently, you can save time in the rendering process by turning on *Discard Back Faces* in the *Rendering Preferences* dialogue box. This action discards the faces with normals pointing away from your viewpoint because they wouldn't be visible from that viewpoint. The time saved is proportional to the number of faces discarded and the total number of faces.

VIEWRES and *FACETRES*

The value you set with the *VIEWRES* command controls the accuracy of the display of circles, arcs, and ellipses. To increase performance while you draw, set to a low value for *VIEWRES*. However, to make sure you get a good-quality rendering, raise the value before rendering drawings that contain arcs or circles. (See Solid Modeling Display Variables, Chapter 38.)

The *FACETRES* system variable controls the smoothness of meshed solids as well as the smoothness of shaded and rendered curved solids. It is linked to the value set by the *VIEWRES* command: when *FACETRES* is set to 1, there is a one-to-one correspondence between the viewing resolution of circles, arcs, and ellipses, and the tessellation of solid objects. When *FACETRES* is set to two, the tessellation will be twice that set by *VIEWRES*, and so on. When you raise and lower the value of *VIEWRES*, objects affected by both *VIEWRES* and *FACETRES* are affected. When you raise and lower the value of *FACETRES*, only solid objects are affected.

Setting the Rendering Background Color in AutoCAD for Windows

You can set the AutoCAD viewport background color in the AutoCAD Window Colors dialogue box (see Chapter 1). Rendering to a viewport always renders against the background color you set for the AutoCAD graphics screen. The Windows Render window background color matches the AutoCAD background color.

AutoVision

If you are interested in more advanced rendering features, you may investigate Autodesk's advanced rendering product called AutoVision. This product runs inside AutoCAD and operates much like Render, but includes other advanced features.

The main feature of AutoVision is raytracing. Raytracing is the process of tracing rays of light from the source as they are obscured by surfaces (causing shadows) or bounce from surfaces (causing reflections). Shadows and reflections add the qualities necessary to create a photo-realistic rendering. AutoVision also provides a wide variety of materials and includes some basic animation utilities.

An example of an AutoVision rendering is shown in Figure 40-43. Notice the shadows and reflections from the two light sources.

Figure 40-43

CHAPTER EXERCISES

1. *Open* the **PULLY-SL** drawing that you created in Chapter 37 Exercises. Refer to the "Typical Steps for Using Render" in this chapter to create a rendering. As an aid, follow these brief suggestions.

   Create a *Vpoint* showing the best view of the Pulley. Create a *Distant Light* located to the left side and slightly above the Pulley. Create a *Point Light* located to the right side and above. Define and *Attach* a *Material* representing Steel. Modify the material to have high *Reflective* and low *Roughness* values. Perform several *Gouraud Renders* and adjust the *Light* positions and intensity until you find the desired results. Experiment also with the *Material* properties. When you have the best settings, perform a *Phong Render*. Finally use *Saveimg* to save the rendering as **PULLY-FR.GIF**. Use *Replay* to ensure the image is saved. *Save* the drawing.

Figure 40-44

2. *Open* the **SADL-SL** model that you created in Chapter 37 Exercises. For this rendering, use *Dview* to generate a useful viewpoint and a small amount of perspective (*Distance*). Set up two lights—a cool-colored *Distant Light* to the left and above, and a warm-colored *Point Light* to the right and nearer to the *Camera* location. *Attach* a *Material* to represent metal. *Modify* the material to have a high *Reflective* value and a low *Roughness* value.

Create several *Gouraud Renderings* to adjust the light intensities. The *Point Light* should provide slightly more light (at the near end of the model), and the *Distant Light* should provide slightly less (on the far side). The varying light intensities with the color effects give the proper impression of distance. Also make necessary adjustments to the *Material* parameters. When you have a good combination, compare your image to Figure 40-45 and create a *Phong Render*. Save the rendering to a .GIF file with the file name **SADL-1**. *Save* the drawing.

Figure 40-45

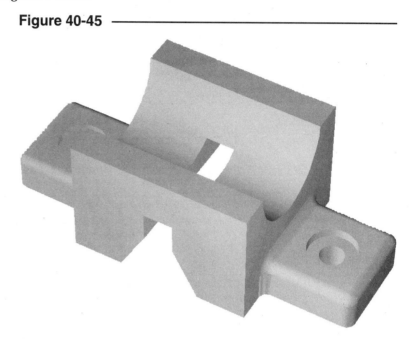

3. *Open* the **PULLY-SL** drawing again. Save the existing *Viewpoint* (from the previous rendering, problem 1) to a named *View*. Create another *Vpoint* to show the back of the part. Try to show several of the through holes in the view. Save the new *Vpoint* to a named *View*. Create one more *Light* with a *Location* of your choosing. In order to create the new rendering, create a *Scene* by selecting the new *View*, the new *Light*, and one of the *Lights* previously created for the first rendering. Experiment to see which of the original two lights gives the best results. Adjust the light *Intensities* and *Colors* if necessary. When you have your best rendering, use *Saving* and name the rendering **PULLY-BK.GIF**.

4. *Open* **SADL-SL** again. Make a solid *Box* with *Length* **500**, *Width* **500**, and *Height* **-20**. Position the box, if necessary (with *Move*), to be directly below and centered about the saddle. This should serve as a base or "table top" for the saddle to rest on and provide a background for the *Spotlight* you are about to create. *Attach* the *Material* named *White* to the "table." Now, insert a *Spotlight* overhead and slightly to the right of the Saddle. Make the *Spotlight Target* at the center of the Saddle geometry. Assign a warm color to the *Spotlight*. Adjust the *Intensity* of the *Point* light down so that the *Spotlight* provides the primary illumination from this viewing direction. Perform a *Gouraud Rendering* to test the angles of the *Hotspot* and *Falloff*. Make adjustments to those values so the Saddle is fully illuminated but the light falls off completely before reaching the "table edges." Perform several *Renderings* to test and adjust the lighting parameters. Any of several parameters can be adjusted—*Intensities*, *Colors*, and light *Locations*. Create several renderings and use *Saving* to assign the names **SADL-2**, **SADL-3**, and so on. Use *Replay* to compare and determine the best renderings.

5. *Open* the **ADJMT-SL** or other solid or surface model that you would like to render. There are several good possibilities with the AutoCAD sample drawings (in the SAMPLE subdirectory). Achieving skill with Render requires time and experimentation. Experiment with different *Lights*, *Materials*, and *Scenes*. Have fun.

Chapter 41

CREATING 2D DRAWINGS FROM 3D MODELS

Chapter Objectives

After completing this chapter you should:

1. know what features are offered in AutoCAD Release 12, AutoCAD Release 13, and AutoCAD Designer for creating 2D drawings from 3D models;

2. know the suggested procedure for using the *Standard Engineering* option of *Mvsetup*;

3. be able to use *Mvsetup* to create viewports showing the standard engineering "views" of an existing 3D model;

4. be able to create hidden lines for a 2D drawing converted from a 3D wireframe;

5. be able to create dimensions with correct visibility settings for each viewport in a drawing with paper space viewports.

BASICS

This chapter discusses the use of AutoCAD features and Autodesk products that assist in the creation of a 2D drawing from a 3D model. The only feature of AutoCAD Release 13 available for this purpose is *Mvsetup*. Other products for the purpose of creating 2D drawings from 3D models are briefly discussed next.

AutoCAD Release 13

Mvsetup is an AutoLISP routine that can be invoked by selecting from the pull-down menus or by typing at the command prompt. It operates with <u>any type</u> of 3D model. This routine automatically sets up paper space viewports. It also has a series of options that allow alternate arrangements for the viewports. If you use the *Standard Engineering* option, *Mvsetup* creates the viewports and automatically places the 3D model correctly with a top, front, right side, and isometric viewpoints. Although the viewports are set up and the 3D geometry is arranged for you, other operations are required to create a 2D drawing complete with hidden lines and dimensions with correct visibility within viewports.

AutoCAD Release 12

AutoCAD Release 12 provides several features for converting 3D models to 2D drawings. As of Release 13 Version c3, these features have not yet been converted from the Release 12 AME solid modeler to operate with the Release 13 ACIS modeler. The features of AutoCAD Release 12 for creating 2D drawings from 3D models that are <u>not</u> available with Release 13 are listed here.

Project is an AutoLISP program that projects a <u>wireframe</u> model onto a 2D plane. The resulting projected geometry can be converted to *Blocks* or *Wblocks* and *Inserted* to create the principal views of an engineering drawing. Additional editing work is required to convert the projected geometry to conventional views with hidden and visible lines.

The *Solprof* command creates a profile of AME <u>solid</u> models. The profiled geometry can be used as a wireframe or projected onto a 2D plane. *Solprof* creates new layers for the profile geometry, complete with correct visible and hidden lines. *Solprof* can be used in conjunction with *Mvsetup* to create standard engineering views.

SOLVIEW is far more automated and powerful than the other features listed. This program is the best alternative for creating 2D drawings from AME solid models. Since *SOLVIEW* is an ADS application, it must be loaded before it can be used. *SOLVIEW* provides two commands that are entered at the command prompt, *Solview* and *Soldraw*. *Solview* is similar to *Mvsetup* in that it automatically sets up the views in paper space viewports (*Solview* or *Mvsetup* will operate for any type of 3D model). It is more powerful than *Mvsetup*, however, because you can select which views you want, including section and auxiliary views, and the placement you want for the views. *Solview* also creates layers for use with *Soldraw*. The *Soldraw* command projects the geometry (of AME solid models only) onto a 2D plane and automatically uses the newly created layering scheme for creating the 2D geometry. Dimensions can be created as an additional "manual" step on layers provided by *Solview*, complete with correct viewport-specific visibility.

AutoCAD Designer

Since the introduction of AutoCAD Release 12, Autodesk has presented AutoCAD Designer. AutoCAD Designer is a separate software package that runs in conjunction with (and requires) AutoCAD. This product is intended particularly for mechanical applications and includes capabilities for constructing 3D models and 2D drawings.

AutoCAD Designer is a parametric-based solid modeler, meaning that parametric relationships rather than dimensional values can be specified for geometric features. In this way, when you change a dimension, the related features also change. The model construction method is features-based rather than Boolean-based. With features modeling, typical manufacturing operation terms are used to create geometry. For example, you may use the *Hole* command instead of creating a *Cylinder* and *Subtracting* it. In addition, Designer automatically creates a 2D drawing with dimensions from the 3D model. The 2D and 3D geometries are bi-directionally linked so that if you make a (dimensional) change to one, the other is automatically updated.

USING *MVSETUP* FOR STANDARD ENGINEERING DRAWINGS

Mvsetup is the one feature in AutoCAD Release 13 that aids in the creation of 2D drawings from 3D models. Because this text covers AutoCAD Release 13 specifically, *Mvsetup* is the sole topic discussed in detail in this chapter.

Mvsetup is an AutoLISP program that assists you in setting up paper space viewports. The *Standard Engineering* option can be used to set up a 3D model in viewports, each viewport having a different standard view. The fundamental concepts and details of all other options of *Mvsetup* are discussed in Chapter 32, Tiled and Paper Space Viewports. Refer to Chapter 32 if you need more information on *Mvsetup* or guidelines for using paper space viewports, since only the *Standard Engineering* option of *Mvsetup* is discussed in this chapter.

MVSETUP

PULL-DOWN MENU	SCREEN MENU	TYPE IN	TABLET MENU
View *Floating Viewports >* *MV Setup*	---	*MVSETUP*	---

This section discusses the use of *Mvsetup* using the *Standard Engineering* option—the options for creating engineering drawings from 3D models. This option of *Mvsetup* operates with any type of 3D model. It automatically creates four viewports and displays the model from four *Vpoints* (front, top, side, and isometric views).

The *Mvsetup* (Multiview setup) command is actually an AutoLISP routine that is accessible either through the *View* pull-down menu (Fig. 41-1) or by typing *Mvsetup*. For the application of *Mvsetup* for creating standard engineering paper space viewports, the sequence is given here.

Figure 41-1

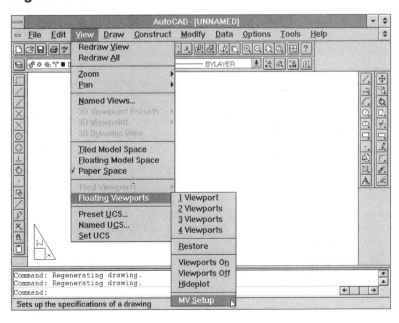

Typical Steps for Using the *Standard Engineering* Option of *Mvsetup*

1. Create the 3D part geometry in model space.

2. Create a layer for viewports and a layer for the title block (named VPORTS and TITLE, for example). Set the viewports layer current.

3. Invoke *Mvsetup* and use *Options* to set the *Mvsetup* preferences.

4. Use *Title block* to *Insert* or *Xref* one of many AutoCAD-supplied or user-supplied borders and title blocks.

5. Use the *Create* option to make the paper space viewports. Select the *Standard Engineering* option from the list.

6. Use *Scale viewports* to set the scale factor (*Zoom XP* factor) for the model geometry displayed in the viewports.

7. The model geometry that appears in each viewport must then be aligned with the display in adjacent viewports using the *Align* option.

8. From this point, other AutoCAD commands must be used to create dimensions for the views or to convert some lines to "invisible" lines.

Mvsetup Example

To illustrate these steps, the Adjustable Slide (solid model) is used as an example.

1. Create the 3D part geometry in model space. The Adjustable Slide is shown here as it exists in model space. It is shown from an isometric-type *Vpoint* in wireframe representation in order to reveal the internal features.

2. Create a VPORTS layer for viewports and a TITLE layer for the title block. Set the VPORTS layer current.

3. Invoke *Mvsetup* and use *Options* to set the *Mvsetup* preferences. For the example, the *Layer* option is used to specify the layer for the title block. Additionally, the *Limits* option is used to automatically set paper space *Limits* equal to the border extents.

Figure 41-2

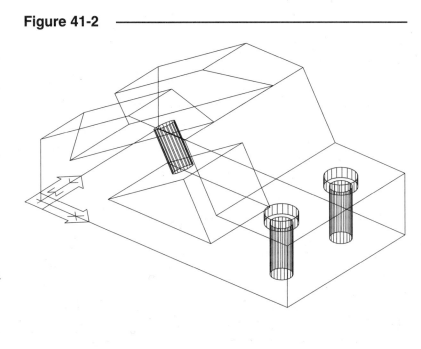

Command: ***mvsetup***
Enable Paper/Modelspace? <Y>: **Enter**
Regenerating drawing.
Align/Create/Scale viewports/Options/Title block/Undo: ***o***
Set Layer/LImits/Units/Xref: ***L***
Layer name for title block or . for current layer: **title**
Set Layer/LImits/Units/Xref: ***Li***
Set drawing limits? <N>: ***y***
Set Layer/LImits/Units/Xref: **Enter**
Align/Create/Scale viewports/Options/Title block/Undo:

4. The *Title* block option is used to insert a title block and border in paper space.

    Align/Create/Scale viewports/Options/Title block/Undo: ***t***
    Delete objects/Origin/Undo/<Insert title block>: **Enter**
    Available title block options:
    0:     None
    1:     ISO A4 Size(mm)
    2:     ISO A3 Size(mm)
    (13 Title block options are displayed here. See Chapter 32 for details on this option.)
    Add/Delete/Redisplay/<Number of entry to load>: ***8***
    Create a drawing named ansi-b.dwg? <Y>: ***n***
    Align/Create/Scale viewports/Options/Title block/Undo:

The previously selected options produce a title block and border appearing in paper space, as shown in Figure 41-3. The 3D model is not visible because viewports have not yet been created.

Figure 41-3 ————————————————————————————————

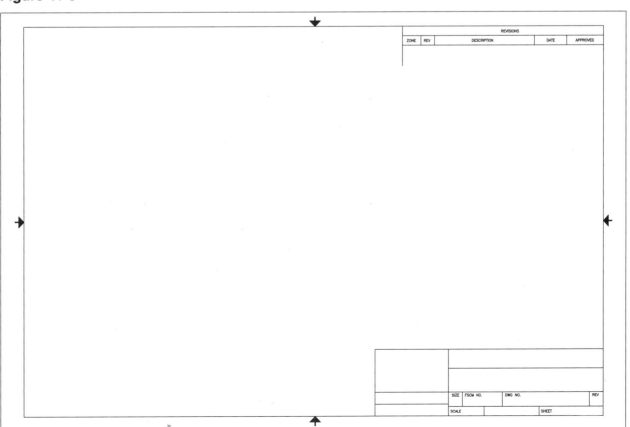

5. Use the *Create* option of *Mvsetup* to create the desired viewport configuration.

> Align/Create/Scale viewports/Options/Title block/Undo: *c*
> Delete objects/Undo/<Create viewports>: **Enter**
> Available Mview viewport layout options:
> > 0:   None
> > 1:   Single
> > 2:   Std. Engineering
> > 3:   Array of Viewports
> Redisplay/<Number of entry to load>: **2**
> Bounding area for viewports. First point: **PICK**
> Other point: **PICK**
> Distance between viewports in X. <0.0>: **Enter**
> Distance between viewports in Y. <0.0>: **Enter**

Select the "2: *Std. Engineering*" option. PICK two corners to define the bounding area for the four new viewports. The action produces four new viewports and automatically defines a *Vpoint* for each viewport. The resulting drawing displays the standard engineering front, top, and right side views of the 3D model in addition to an isometric-type view, as shown in Figure 41-4.

Figure 41-4

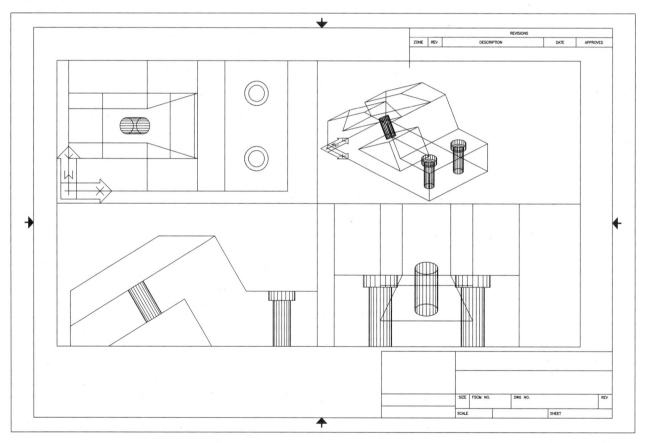

6. Notice in Figure 41-4 that the geometry in each viewport is displayed at its maximum size, as if a *Zoom Extents* were used. The *Scale viewports* option is used to set a scale for the geometry in each viewport.

> Align/Create/Scale viewports/Options/Title block/Undo: **s**
> Select the viewports to scale:
> Select objects: **PICK** the <u>viewport objects</u>
> Select objects: **Enter**
> Set zoom scale factors for viewports. Interactively/<Uniform>: **u**
> Enter the ratio of paper space units to model space units...
> Number of paper space units. <1.0>: **Enter** or (**value**)
> Number of model space units. <1.0>: **Enter** or (**value**)
> Align/Create/Scale viewports/Options/Title block/Undo:

Make sure you select the viewport objects (borders) at the "Select viewports to scale" prompt. The *Uniform* option ensures that the 3D model will be scaled to the same proportion in each viewport. The ratio of paper space units to model space units is like a *Zoom XP* factor; for example, a ratio of 1 paper space unit to 2 model space units is equivalent to a *Zoom 1/2XP*.

The above action produces the scaling of the 3D model space units relative to paper space units, as shown in Figure 41-5.

Figure 41-5

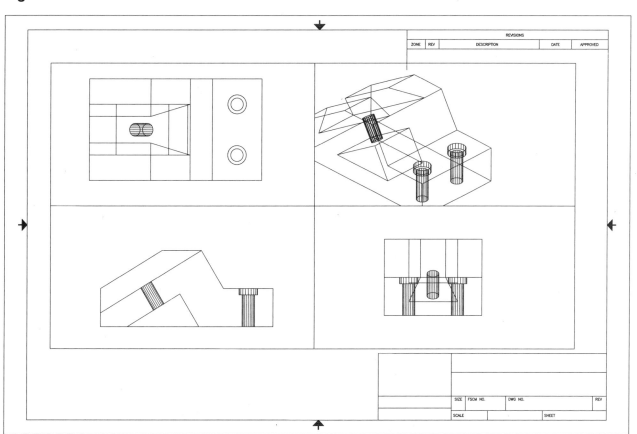

There is still one major problem in the resulting drawing. The views are not orthogonally aligned exactly as they should be. Examine the front and the right side view (Fig. 41-5) and notice that they do not align horizontally.

7.   Use the *Align* option of *Mvsetup* to orthogonally align the views. In this case, the right side view is aligned with the front using the *Horizontal* option, and the top is aligned with the front view using the *Vertical* option.

> Align/Create/Scale viewports/Options/Title block/Undo: ***a***
> Angled/Horizontal/Vertical alignment/Rotate view/Undo? ***h***
> Basepoint: ***ENDp*** of   **PICK**
> Other point: ***ENDp*** of   **PICK**
> Angled/Horizontal/Vertical alignment/Rotate view/Undo? ***v***
> Basepoint: ***ENDp*** of **PICK**
> Other point: ***ENDp*** of **PICK**
> Angled/Horizontal/Vertical alignment/Rotate view/Undo?
> Align/Create/Scale viewports/Options/Title block/Undo:

Since the front view is used in this case for aligning the other views <u>to it</u>, the front view establishes the "Basepoint." Select the bottom right edge of the front view as the "Basepoint" as shown (Fig. 41-6). Notice that it is important to use an *OSNAP* option for the PICK. When prompted for the "Other point," the right side viewport must be activated before PICKing its geometry. The "Other point" is a bottom edge on the right side view.

The *Vertical* option is used to select model geometry for alignment of the top view to the front. The resulting drawing appears as shown in Figure 41-6.

Figure 41-6

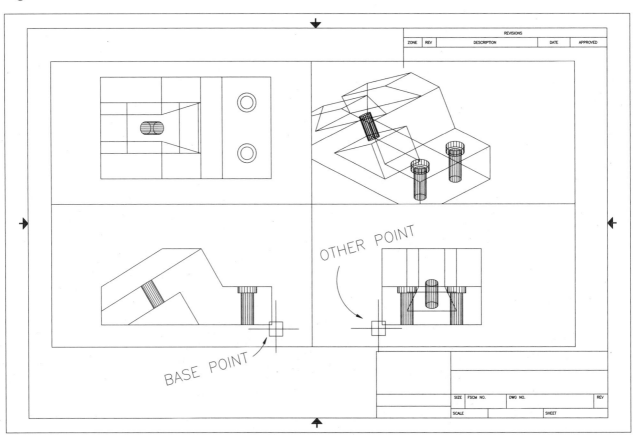

An additional step is required for this example in order to display the isometric view completely within the viewport. *Zoom Center* and *Zoom XP* can be used to locate and size the model appropriately.

Finally, the VPORTS layer created for inserting the viewports can be turned *Off* or *Frozen* to display the views without the viewport borders, as shown in Figure 41-7.

This is as far as *Mvsetup* goes. As you notice, the result is not a complete conventional multiview drawing because there are no dimensions nor are there hidden lines representing the invisible edges of the object. Since the views are actually different *Vpoints* of a 3D model, hidden lines are not possible for solid models using *Mvsetup*, but hidden lines can be created for wireframe models.

Figure 41-7

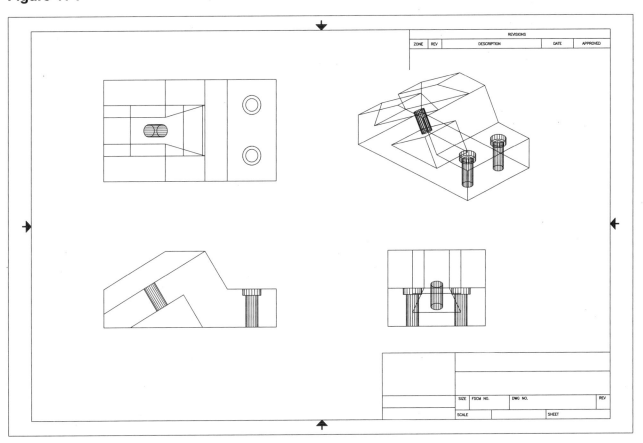

Creating Hidden Lines from a 3D Model

If a complete 2D drawing is to be constructed from the 3D model, some lines from the model must be converted to "invisible" lines. It is not possible to convert edges of a solid or surface model to a hidden linetype, but edges of a wireframe model can be converted. Because a wireframe model is composed of simple objects such as *Line*, *Arc*, *Circle*, etc., these objects can easily be changed to a hidden linetype or to a layer with a hidden linetype assigned. Probably the simplest way to create the "invisible" lines is to use *Ddmodify*, select the desired objects, and change them to a layer having a hidden linetype assigned.

Better yet, it is desirable to create a separate hidden layer for each view (viewport). In this way, you have control over each view's hidden-layer visibility. For example, you may want to turn off just the isometric viewport's hidden lines or change that layer's linetype to continuous. Creating separate layers for each viewport's hidden linetypes may take more effort but affords you the most flexibility for displaying the drawing. Refer to Chapter 32, Tiled and Paper Space Viewports, for more information on viewport-specific layer visibility.

Creating Dimensions for a 3D Model

If you use *Mvsetup* or any other method of creating 2D "views" of a 3D model in paper space viewports, dimensions can be created for each view. This is accomplished by creating the dimensions for each view on a separate layer and making each dimensioning layer visible only in the appropriate view (viewport). For example, assume you have used *Mvsetup* to create the top, front, and right side views of a model. The strategy for dimensioning is as follows:

1. Create three new layers: DIM-TOP, DIM-FRONT, and DIM-SIDE.

2. If not existing, create and save three UCSs named TOP, FRONT, and SIDE, each with its XY plane parallel to the matching view.

3. Starting with the front viewpoint, make the FRONT UCS active and make layer DIM-FRONT the current layer. Create the dimensions for the front view on this UCS and layer.

4. Make layer DIM-FRONT frozen for all <u>other</u> viewports so the dimensions for the front view appear only in the front viewport.

5. Moving to the TOP viewport, set its matching UCS and layer current. Create the dimensions for the view. Make layer DIM-TOP frozen for all other viewports.

6. Do the same for the remaining side view.

Don't forget any other procedures necessary for a complete 2D drawing, such as turning off the viewport layer, insertion of title block and border, etc.

CHAPTER EXERCISES

1. **Using *Mvsetup* With a Solid Model**

    A. *Open* the **BGUID-SL** drawing that you created in Chapter 37 Exercises. Use *Saveas* to assign a new name, **BGUD-MVS**. Create two new *Layers* named **VPORTS** and **TITLE**. Make **VPORTS** the *Current* layer. Use *Mvsetup* with the following *Options*: *Layer*, *Limits*, and *Title*. Insert the *B-size* sheet title block. Then use the *Create* option for *Standard Engineering* set up. *Scale* the geometry in each viewport *Uniformly* to a factor of **1**. The drawing should look like Figure 41-8. *Save* the drawing.

    B. Note that the "views" do not line up correctly in Figure 41-8. Use the *Align* option of *Mvsetup* for both *Vertical* and *Horizontal* alignment. Use *Zoom* to *Center* and size the isometric view properly. The completed drawing should look like Figure 41-9. *Save* the drawing and make a *Plot* to scale.

Figure 41-8

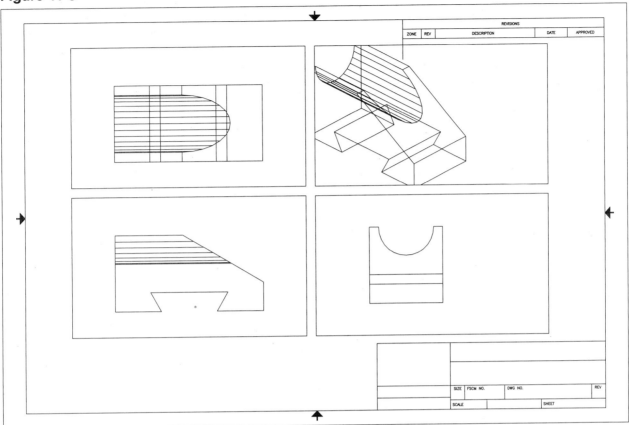

Figure 41-9

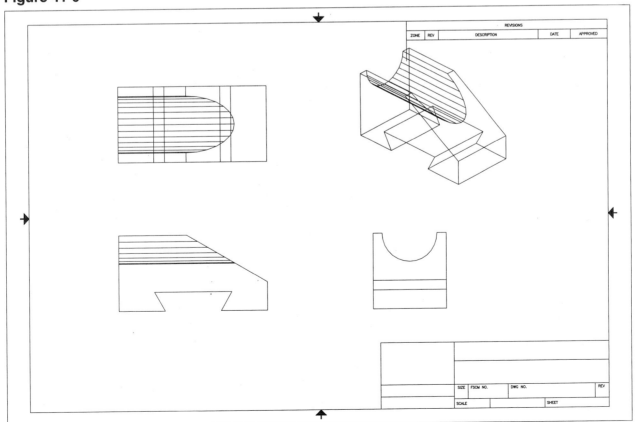

2. **Using *Mvsetup* With a Wireframe Model**

    A. *Open* the **BGUID-WF** drawing that you created in Chapter 36 Exercises. Use *Saveas* to assign a new name, **BGUD-MV2**. Make a *Layer* for the viewports and one for the title block. Set the viewports layer *Current*. Use *Mvsetup* with the same procedure as in the previous exercise, step A.

    B. Use the *Align* option of *Mvsetup* for both *Vertical* and *Horizontal* alignment. Use *Zoom* to *Center* and size the isometric view properly. *Save* the drawing.

    C. Convert the necessary lines to "invisible" lines by creating four new *Layer*s for hidden lines, one for each viewport. Assign the *Hidden* linetype to each new layer. Use the *Cur VP Frz* and *New VP Frz* options to assign the correct viewport-specific layer visibility. Using *Ddmodify*, change the appropriate lines to the matching layers.

Figure 41-10

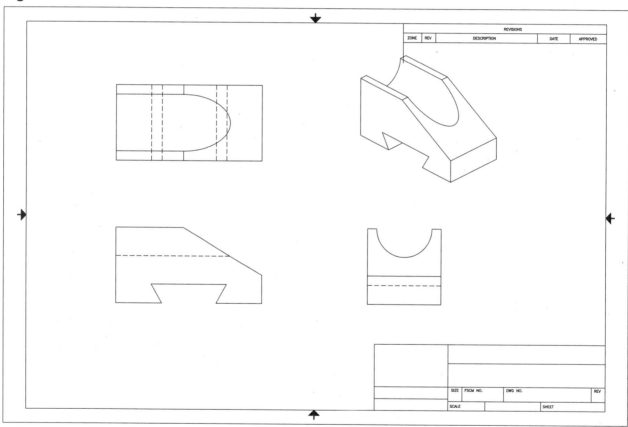

    D. *Freeze* the invisible edges of the wireframe model in the isometric viewport. Save the drawing.

3. **Creating Dimensions for the New 2D Drawing**

    Open the **BGUD-MV2** drawing if not already open. Use *Saveas* to save the drawing as **BGUD-MV3**. Create dimensions for the views. Follow the steps given in the chapter to create the appropriate UCSs, create the layers, and draw the dimensions. Don't forget to set the correct visibility settings for each **DIM** layer. *Save* the drawing and *Plot* to scale.

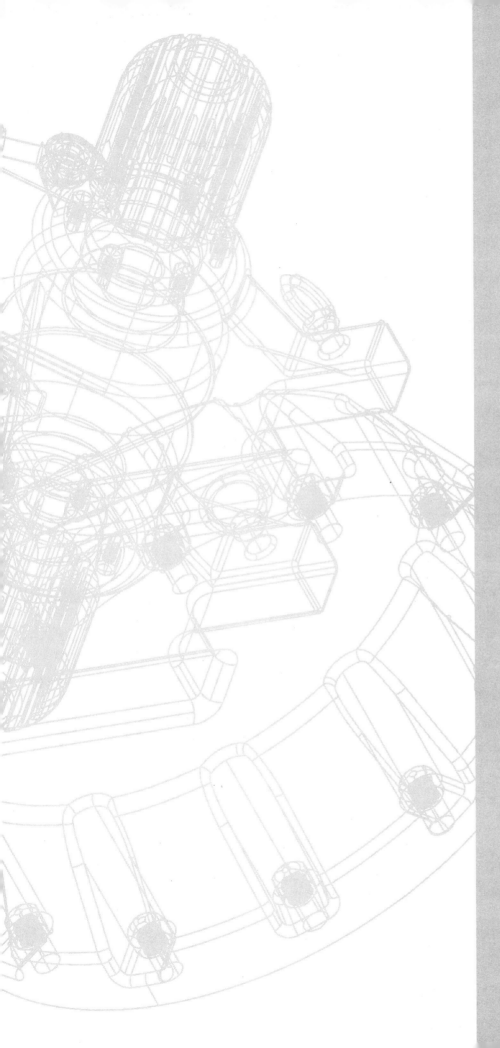

Chapter 42

CUSTOMIZATION

Chapter Objectives

After completing this chapter you should:

1. be able to customize the AutoCAD for Windows existing toolbars and create new toolbars;

2. be able to create new, and modify existing, tool button icons and assign them to perform special tasks;

3. be able to create your own simple and complex linetypes;

4. be able to customize the ACAD.PGP file to create your own command aliases;

5. be able to create script files for accomplishing repetitive tasks automatically;

6. know that AutoCAD menu files can be customized to include your own features in the pull-down menus, screen menus, and pointing-device button menus.

BASICS

This chapter is offered as an introduction to customizing AutoCAD. Autodesk has written AutoCAD with an "open" architecture that allows you to customize the way the program operates to suit your particular needs. You have the ability to change any of the menus and toolbars as well as create new linetypes. You can also write programs in AutoLISP, a variation of the LISP programming language, to further customize AutoCAD. Programs written in C can also be used by AutoCAD through the ADS utility.

This chapter is intended to give you a start with AutoCAD customization. There are many topics too involved or advanced to discuss in one chapter, such as AutoLISP and ADS and menu customization. Many books are available on these subjects. Most of the customization features not found in this chapter, as well as technical details of topics discussed in this chapter, can be found in the AutoCAD Customization Guide document supplied with the software.

The topics that are best for beginning your customization experience are introduced in this chapter. They are:

> Customizing the AutoCAD for Windows toolbars and icon buttons
> Creating your own simple and complex linetypes
> Customizing the ACAD.PGP file and creating command aliases
> Creating script files to use for automated activities

CUSTOMIZING THE AUTOCAD FOR WINDOWS TOOLBARS

In the DOS and Windows versions of AutoCAD, you have the ability to create customized screen and pull-down menus. By doing so, you can create a menu that contains your most frequently used commands or even create new menu selections that invoke "new" commands: that is, choices that activate a command, particular command option, system variable, or series of commands not previously offered in the menus.

AutoCAD Release 13 for Windows provides an interface for you to customize toolbars. By creating new toolbar groups and new tool "buttons," you can attain many of the same capabilities as with menu customization. With the toolbars, button, and flyout dialogue boxes, you can accomplish these actions:

> Modify existing toolbar groups
> Create new toolbar groups
> Modify existing tool buttons
> Create new tool buttons

First, you should gain experience with modifying existing and creating new toolbars, then try creating new icon buttons.

Modifying Existing, and Creating New, Toolbar Groups

In AutoCAD Release 13 for Windows, you can modify existing toolbars or create your own toolbar by placing the tools you want into a group. For example, you can make a new toolbar that contains your most frequently used solid modeling commands <u>and</u> the Boolean tools, thus allowing you to turn off the Solids and Modify toolbar. The *Tbconfig* command provides access to a series of dialogue boxes that allow you to specify which tools to include in an existing or new toolbar. This section explains the options of the *Toolbars* and related dialogue boxes and suggests steps for modifying and creating toolbars.

TBCONFIG	DOS PULL-DOWN	WIN PULL-DOWN	SCREEN MENU	TYPE IN	TABLET MENU
	---	*Tools, Customize Tools*	---	*TBCONFIG*	---

Using the *Tbconfig* command produces the *Toolbars* dialogue box (Fig. 42-1). You can access the *Toolbars* dialogue box by the methods shown in the command table above or by right-clicking on any tool. The options are presented below.

Toolbars

This list gives the existing toolbar names. If you want to modify an existing toolbar group, select the name of the toolbar.

Close

The *Close* option closes the *Toolbars* dialogue box. If you have edited an existing toolbar or created a new one, AutoCAD automatically compiles the menu structure so that the toolbar can be used immediately.

New

New opens the *New Toolbar* dialogue box and allows you to create a new toolbar (Fig. 42-2). Enter the name, or title, of the new toolbar you want to create in the *Name* edit box. Once a name has been entered, choose *OK* to have the new toolbar appear in the drawing and the name added to the *Toolbars* dialogue box list. When a new toolbar is created, a small box with a title bar but no tools in it appears near the top of the AutoCAD window.

Delete

The *Delete* option deletes the toolbar name currently highlighted in the list. You are prompted for a confirmation for the delete, at which point you can choose *Yes* or *No*.

Customize

This option produces the *Customize Toolbars* dialogue box (Fig 42-3). Here, you choose the tools (buttons) to be added to or removed from any toolbar that is displayed in the Drawing Editor. To add a tool to an open toolbar, simply drag the tool from the current category and drop it into the toolbar. Remove an existing tool from a toolbar by dragging it from the toolbar and releasing it in the graphics area of the Drawing Editor. The toolbar must be visible in order to add or remove a tool. If the toolbar is "hidden," use the *Properties* option to display the toolbar.

Figure 42-1

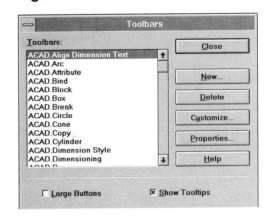

Figure 42-2

Figure 42-3

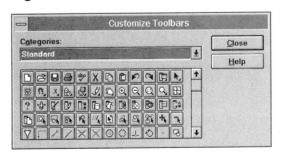

R13

To locate the tools you want to work with, use the *Categories* pop-down list to select the group of tools you need. There are 13 categories that contain all the tools found in the Release 13 toolbars. The available categories are:

Object Properties   Render
Standards   External Database
Surfaces   External Reference
Solids   Dimensioning
Draw   Miscellaneous
Modify   Custom
Attribute

After selecting the category, choose a tool and "drag and drop" it into a toolbar. Choose *Close* to close the *Customize Toolbars* dialogue box when you are finished editing a toolbar. When you choose *Close* from the *Toolbars* dialogue box, AutoCAD compiles the menu structure so that you can use the edited toolbar.

Figure 42-4

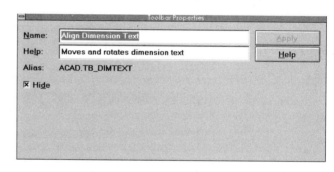

Properties

The *Toolbar Properties* dialogue box (Fig. 42-4) appears with this selection and allows you to specify the name and help message for a toolbar. The *Name* edit box allows you to specify a name for a new toolbar or edit an existing toolbar name. The *Help* field enables you to type information about the toolbar that appears when accessed from the *Help* command. If a toolbar is not visible in the Drawing Editor, it is considered "hidden" or closed. The *Hide* toggle controls toolbar visibility. The *Alias* is automatically created by AutoCAD when a toolbar is made and cannot be edited from this dialogue box. Select *Apply* to apply the changes you have made. To close the *Toolbar Properties* dialogue box, choose the small close bar (once, not a double-click) in the upper-left corner of the dialogue box.

Help

The *Help* option opens the AutoCAD Help program, which gives help regarding the *TBCONFIG* command.

Large Buttons

This option doubles the number of pixels (from 16 x 16 to 32 x 32) used to display the tool buttons. Users with difficulty seeing the icons or who use a very high-resolution display should find the use of *Large Buttons* less straining on the eyes.

Show Tooltips

A "tooltip" is the small text string displayed in a yellow box when you rest the pointer on a tool button. This toggle enables you to turn on or off the display of tooltips.

Steps for Modifying an Existing Toolbar

1. If it is not already visible in the Drawing Editor, display the tool bar group that you want to modify by using the *Toolbars* option of the *Tools* pull-down menu or typing the *Toolbar* command.

2. Invoke the *Toolbars* dialogue box by any method (see previous *TBCONFIG* command table).

3. Choose the *Customize* button to open the *Customize Toolbars* dialogue box.

4. When the *Customize Toolbars* dialogue box is open, you can:

   A. Remove any tool from a visible toolbar by dragging it out of the toolbar group and dropping it into the graphics area of the Drawing Editor.

   B. Move any tool from one group to another by dragging and dropping.

   C. Add a tool from the *Customize Toolbars* dialogue box to a visible toolbar group. See Step 5.

5. To add a tool to a visible group (without removing it from another group), select the desired tool's group from the *Categories* drop-down list. This displays the available tool icons in the toolbar group ("category"). Drag the desired tool(s) from the dialogue box and drop into the desired visible toolbar group. In Figure 42-5, the Boolean tools (*Union, Subtract, Intersect*) are being added to the Solids toolbar group.

Figure 42-5

6. *Close* the *Customize Toolbars* dialogue box; then *Close* the *Toolbars* dialogue box. AutoCAD automatically compiles the ACAD.MNR and ACAD.MNS menu files. This enables the modified toolbars to be used immediately.

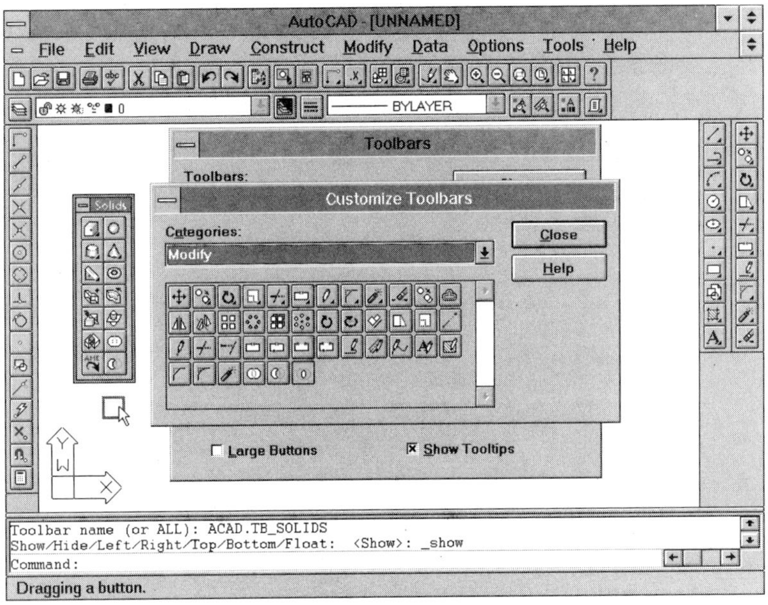

Steps for Creating a New Toolbar Group

1. Invoke the *Toolbars* dialogue box by any method.

2. Choose *New* to open the *New Toolbar* dialogue box. In the *Toolbar Name* field, enter the new name, for example, "My Toolbar". PICK the *OK* button. When the dialogue box closes, your new toolbar name (ACAD.My Toolbar) is highlighted in the toolbar listing. The new empty toolbar appears near the top of the AutoCAD drawing window.

3. Drag the new toolbar down into an open drawing area; then choose *Customize* from the *Toolbars* dialogue box. From the *Customize* dialogue box, drag and drop any tool icons onto the new toolbar (Fig. 42-6). Use the *Categories*: list to highlight toolbar groups and display any tool icon that you need. (The tooltip does not appear on tools in the *Customize* dialogue box, only on tools that have been placed in a toolbar.)

4. *Close* the *Customize Toolbars* dialogue box; then *Close* the *Toolbars* dialogue box. AutoCAD automatically compiles the ACAD.MNR and ACAD.MNS menu files.

Figure 42-6

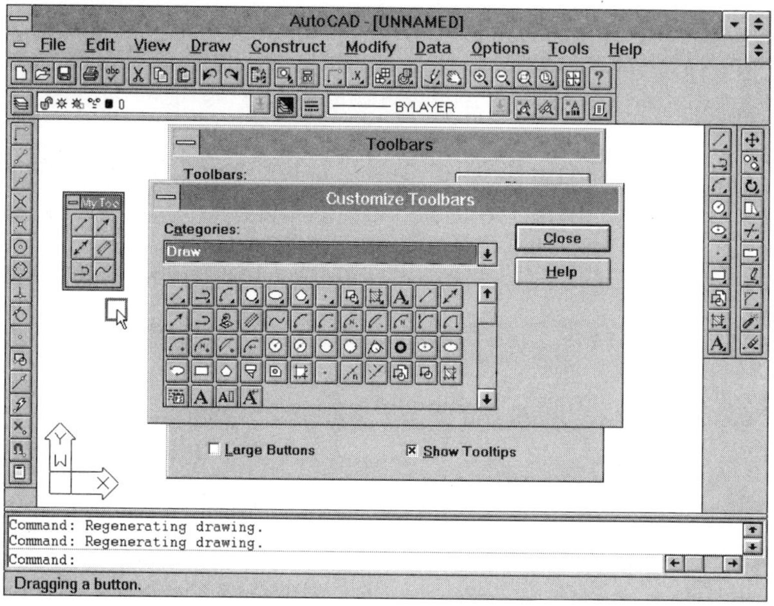

5. If you want to customize the help message for your new toolbar, open the *Toolbars* dialogue box and highlight the new toolbar name from the *Toolbars:* list. Select the *Properties* button to produce the *Toolbar Properties* dialogue box where the *Help* edit box is available. After entering the desired help massage, select *Apply*; then *Close* all the dialogue boxes.

Note: If you are dragging a tool from a category in the *Customize Toolbars* dialogue box and release the tool in the graphics area prior to dropping it into an existing toolbar, a new toolbar is created with the name "Toolbar*n*" where *n* is a number. To close the toolbar, pick the toolbar's close bar in the upper left corner. Delete it from the *Toolbars* dialogue box listing by scrolling down to "ACAD.Toolbar*n*", then select the *Delete* button. *Close* the *Customize Toolbars* dialogue box.

Customizing Existing, and Creating New, Buttons

Not only can you modify existing, and create new, toolbar groups in AutoCAD Release 13, you can customize individual buttons. Existing buttons can be modified and new buttons can be created. You can modify or create the image that appears on the icon and assign the command(s) that are activated when you PICK the button. The *Button Properties* dialogue box provides the interface for "drawing" the button image and assigning the associated command.

The *Button Properties* dialogue box (Fig. 42-7) is invoked by double right-clicking on any tool button visible in the Drawing Editor. Alternately, you can open the *Customize Toolbars* dialogue box, then right-click (once) on any visible tool button. The areas of the *Button Properties* dialogue box are described as follows:

Figure 42-7

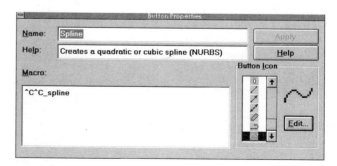

Name

This edit box defines the name of the button which also serves as the "tool tip" string that appears when the pointer rests on the button.

Help

This field contains the "help string" that appears at the bottom of the screen over the status bar when the pointer rests on the button.

Macro

Enter any command, command and option, series of commands, system variable changes, etc., in this edit box. Similar to menu customization, all commands, options, or system variables must contain the exact spelling as you would enter at the command prompt. Spaces in the string are treated as Returns (pressing the Enter key).

Button Icon

Use this area and slider bar to select any of the AutoCAD-supplied icons for editing.

Edit

Selecting this button produces the *Button Editor* (Fig. 42-8). The *Button Editor* is like a miniature "paint" program that you can use to modify existing, or create new, button images. From the top of the editor, select a pencil for sketching, a line drawing instrument, a circle and ellipse drawing instrument, or an eraser. The color pallet appears on the right. Activate the *Grid* to "see" the pixels. You can *Clear* the entire button face, *Open* an existing button (.BMP file), or *Undo* the last drawing sequence. The drawing procedure is quite simple and fun. Use *Save* to save your work to a .BMP file before you *Close* the editor, or you can *Close* without saving. Use *Saveas* to rename the button image to a .BMP file. After you *Close*, select *Apply* from the *Button Properties* dialogue box to force the selected tool (that you originally selected from the Drawing editor) to assume the new button face.

Figure 42-8

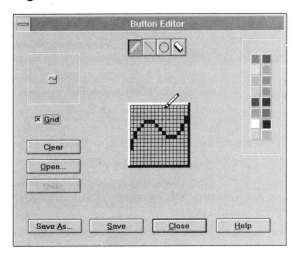

Steps for Changing Existing, and Creating New, Buttons

Changing Existing Buttons

1. Double right-click (click twice quickly) on any existing tool button (except a flyout button) visible in the Drawing Editor. The *Toolbars* and the *Button Properties* dialogue boxes appear.

    Alternate Method: Invoke the *Toolbars* dialogue box by any method. Then right-click (once) on any existing tool button visible in the Drawing Editor. The *Button Properties* dialogue box appears.

2. If it is necessary to change the appearance of the icon, select *Edit...* to produce the *Button Editor*. Make the necessary changes, *Save* the changes, and select *Apply* to have the new icon appear on the button in the Drawing Editor.

3. Make any desired changes in the *Name:* and *Help:* edit boxes.

4. Enter the new action desired for the button in the *Macro:* area. You can alter the existing action or delete the existing action and create a new series of commands or variable changes. Select *Apply*.

5. Close the *Button Properties* dialogue box; then *Close* the *Toolbars* dialogue box. AutoCAD automatically compiles the ACAD.MNR and ACAD.MNS menu files.

Creating New Buttons

1. If you want the new button(s) to reside in a new toolbar group, create the new toolbar group first (see Steps for Creating a New Toolbar Group). If you want the new button to reside in an existing group, make sure the toolbar is visible in the Drawing Editor.

2. Invoke the *Toolbars* dialogue box by any method. Then select the *Customize* tile to make the *Customize Toolbars* dialogue box appear.

3. In the *Customize Toolbars* dialogue box, select *Custom* from the *Categories* pop-down list. Drag and drop the empty button (not the flyout button) into the desired toolbar (into the Drawing Editor). *Close* the *Customize Toolbars* dialogue box.

4. Right-click (once) on the new empty button (in the Drawing Editor). The *Button Properties* dialogue box appears.

5. Select *Edit...* to produce the *Button Editor*. Design the new button, *Save* the changes, and *Close* the *Button Editor*.

6. Make the desired entries in the *Name:* and *Help:* edit boxes.

7. Enter the new action desired for the button in the *Macro:* area. Select *Apply* to have the new icon appear on the button in the Drawing Editor.

8. Close the *Button Properties* dialogue box, and then *Close* the *Toolbars* dialogue box. AutoCAD automatically compiles the ACAD.MNR and ACAD.MNS menu files.

An Example Custom Toolbar Group and Buttons

Assume you work for a civil engineering firm and utilize *Point* objects often in your work. You decide to create a new toolbar group to change the display of the *Point* objects with <u>one</u> PICK rather than accessing the *Point Style* dialogue box from the *Data* pull-down menu, PICKing the desired style, PICKing the OK button, and invoking a *Regen* (five PICKs required). To create a custom toolbar, you must create new button icons, assign the buttons to set the *PDMODE* system variable to the appropriate value, and then invoke a *Regen*.

Figure 42-9 illustrates the custom toolbar group under construction. The new toolbar group (in the Drawing Editor, left side) is titled *PDmodes*. Only three buttons have been created at this time, with one under construction for changing the *Point* style to a circle with a cross (*PDMODE* 34). The other two buttons change *PDMODE* to values of 2 and 3.

Note the contents of the *Button Properties* dialogue box (Fig. 42-9). The *Button Editor* (*Edit...*) was used previously to create the new icon (circle and two crossing lines). The *Name:* edit box contains the "tool tip" text (note the pointer on the left resting on the button). The *Help:*

Figure 42-9

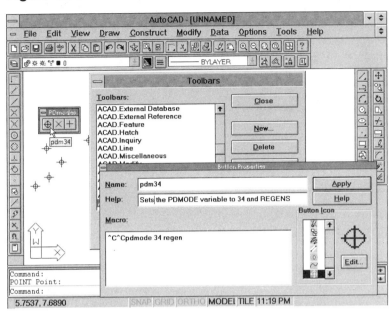

edit box contains the "help string" that appears at the Status Line (not shown during construction). The *Macro:* area contains two *Cancels* (^C^C), the *PDMODE* system variable call, a space to force a Return (like pressing Enter), the desired value (34), another space (Return), and the *Regen* command.

When this toolbar group is complete, selecting any one of the buttons causes the *Point* objects in the drawing to immediately display the new point style.

Using the *Flyout Properties* Dialogue Box

Flyout tools have a small right triangle in the lower-right corner and cause several related buttons to "fly out." If you right-click on a flyout tool while the *Toolbars* dialogue box is open (or double right-click anytime on a flyout tool), the *Flyout Properties* dialogue box appears (Fig. 42-10).

The *Flyout Properties* dialogue box allows you to assign existing flyout groups to a new button. To illustrate, assume you created a new toolbar group with draw commands such as *Line, Arc, Pline, Circle, Ray, Xline, Spline*, etc. Using the methods described previously, you give each command a separate button, or, put another way, one button exists in the toolbar for each command. In order to keep the toolbar group as small as possible, you could instead assign the *Line* flyout group (including *Line, Ray*, and *Xline*) to one button in the toolbar using the *Flyout Properties* dialogue box. The options in the *Flyout Properties* dialogue box are these:

Figure 42-10

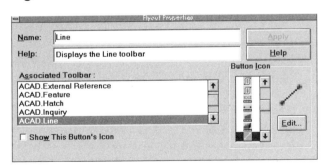

Name:
Enter the string for the "tool tip" that appears when the pointer rests on the button.

Help:
Enter the "help string" that appears on the Status Line when the pointer rests on the button.

Associated Toolbar:
Select the existing flyout group (from the list) that you want to "fly out" when the button is selected.

Edit...
Selecting this produces the *Button Editor*. (See Customizing Existing, and Creating New, Buttons.)

Show This Button's Icon
If you have made your own icon for the flyout group using the *Button Editor*, checking this box forces your icon to display on the button. If this is not checked, the icon normally used for that group is displayed.

Apply
This applies the icon and entries of the other fields. You must *Apply*, then close the *Flyout Properties* dialogue box and the *Toolbars* dialogue box to use the new flyouts properly.

Steps for Assigning an Existing Flyout Group to a New Button

1. Make sure the toolbar (to attach the flyouts) is visible in the Drawing Editor.

2. Invoke the *Toolbars* dialogue box by any method. Then select the *Customize* tile to make the *Customize Toolbars* dialogue box appear.

3. In the *Customize Toolbars* dialogue box, select *Custom* from the *Categories* pop-down list. Drag and drop the flyout button into the desired toolbar (into the Drawing Editor). *Close* the *Customize Toolbars* dialogue box.

4. Right-click (once) on the new empty flyout button (in the Drawing Editor). The *Flyout Properties* dialogue box appears.

5. Select *Edit...* to produce the *Button Editor*. Design the new button, *Save* the changes, and *Close* the *Button Editor*.

6. Make the desired entries in the *Name:* and *Help:* edit boxes.

7. Select the desired flyout group to attach to the button from the *Associated Toolbar* list. Check the *Show This Button's Icon* box to use your new icon. Select *Apply* to have the new icon appear on the button in the Drawing Editor.

8. Close the *Flyout Properties* dialogue box, and then *Close* the *Toolbars* dialogue box. AutoCAD automatically compiles the ACAD.MNR and ACAD.MNS menu files.

An Example New Flyout Group

Using the *PDMODES* toolbar group from the previous example, assume you wanted to add the *Point* creation command flyout group (*Point, Divide, Measure*) to the toolbar group. First, the *Toolbars* and *Customize Toolbars* dialogue boxes are invoked, and the empty flyout button is dropped into the PDmodes toolbar group (steps 1., 2., and 3.).

Next, the *Flyout Properties* dialogue box is produced by right-clicking on the new flyout button. A new icon is created (the letter "P") to designate the purpose of the button (Fig. 42-11). After assigning the *ACAD.Point* flyouts to the button, entering the *Name* and *Help* text strings, and checking *Show This Button's Icon*, select *Apply*.

Figure 42-11 ─────────

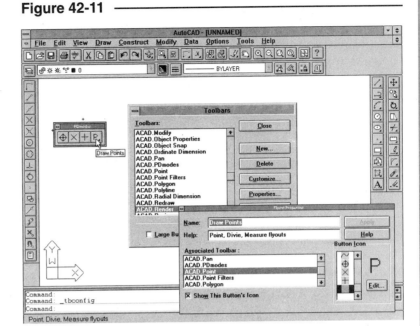

The resulting *Point* flyout group appears whenever the new icon is selected (Fig. 42-12).

Figure 42-12 ·

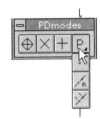

CREATING CUSTOM LINETYPES

AutoCAD has a wide variety of linetype definitions from which you can choose (Chapter 12, Layers, Linetypes, and Colors). These definitions are stored in an ASCII file called ACAD.LIN. These are called simple linetypes. Some complex linetypes are also provided by AutoCAD and are in the LTYPESHP.LIN file. Complex linetypes include text or graphical shapes within the definition of the linetype pattern. However, you are not limited to these linetype definitions. New linetypes can be easily created that contain the line spacing, text, and shapes that you need.

Linetypes are created by using a text editor or word processor to describe the components of the linetype. The DOS Editor or the Windows Notepad are sufficient text editors that create ASCII files (only alphanumeric characters without word processing codes) and can be used for this purpose. New linetype definitions are stored in ASCII files that you name and assign with an .LIN file extension. The file names should indicate the nature of the linetype definitions. For example, ELECT.LIN can include linetype definitions for electrical layouts, or CIVIL.LIN can contain linetype definitions for the civil engineering discipline. This scheme promotes better file maintenance than appending custom linetypes to the ACAD.LIN file.

Creating Simple Linetypes

A linetype definition is created by typing the necessary characters using a text editor and saving as an .LIN file. Examine the basic components of a simple linetype definition below. Each element of the linetype definition is separated by a comma (with no spaces). A linetype definition includes the following items:

1. The <u>name</u> of the linetype with a prefix of *

2. A <u>description</u> of the linetype (either text or symbols)

3. The <u>alignment</u> field

4. Numerical <u>distances</u> for dashes, dots, and spaces

5. The <u>shape</u> or <u>text</u> creation elements (contained in square brackets [ ])

A Simple Linetype Example

An example of creating a line that looks like line definition "EXAMPLE1"in the figure is the following:

```
*example1,a sample linetype ____  . .  _____ . __
A,1.0,-0.25,0,-0.1,0,-0.25,1.5,-0.25,0,-0.25,0.5,-0.5
```

The above definition can be analyzed as follows:

1. The name of the linetype is "EXAMPLE1."

2. A description of the linetype is a "sample" of the linetype that you create with the keyboard characters: ____ . . _____ . __ (Note that this "graphical" description is created using the underscore and period characters.)

3. A   This is the alignment field.

4. 1.0   A positive value designates a line segment. This segment has a 1 unit length.

5. -0.25   A negative value denotes a gap or blank space. This gap has a length of 0.25.

6. 0   A value of 0 creates a dot.

7. repeat of the previous elements.

Figure 42-13 shows the "EXAMPLE1" linetype defined above.

Figure 42-13 ───────────────────────────────────────

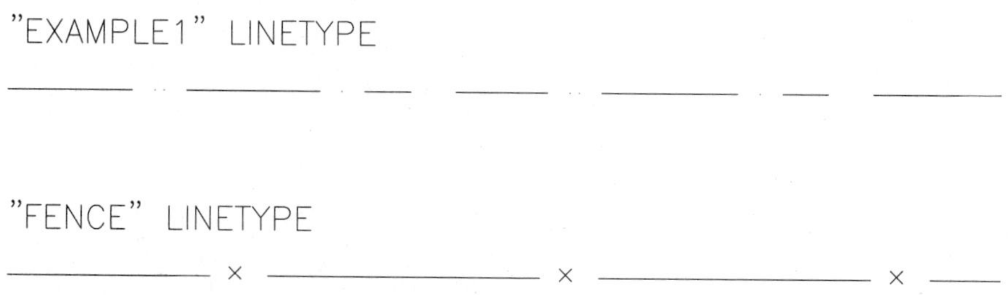

"EXAMPLE1" LINETYPE

───── · · ─────── · ─ ──── ───── ───── ──── ─────

"FENCE" LINETYPE

──────── × ──────────── × ────────── × ────

Creating a Complex Linetype

In a complex linetype, two additional fields are possible in the definition and are placed in brackets [ ]. These fields are the Shape field and the String field. Each field has the following form:

Shapes: [shape description, shape file, scale, rotation, Xoffset, Yoffset]
Strings: ["text string," text style name, scale, rotation, Xoffset, Yoffset]

For linetypes containing shapes, the shape description and the compiled file name (.SHX) are provided in the first two places of the field. In comparison, a linetype containing a text string has the text string in quotes (" ") and the defined text style name in its first two places. If the text style does not exist, the current text style is used. The last four places of a string and shape fields are the same. They are described as follows:

Scale	S=*value*	This is the scale factor by which the height of the text or shape definition is multiplied.
Rotation	R=*value* or A=*value*	A rotation angle for the text or shape is given here. The "A" designator is for an absolute rotational value, regardless of the the angle of the current line segment. The "R" designator is to specify a rotational value relative to the angle of the current line segment.
Xoffset	X= *value*	You can specify an X offset value from the end of the last element with this value.
Yoffset	Y=*value*	Specify a Y offset value from the end of the last element with this value.

Complex Linetype Examples

```
*PL,Property Line ----PL----PL----
A,0.5,-0.5,[PLSYM,SYMBOLS.SHX,S=1.5,R=0,X=-0.1,Y=-0.1],-0.5,0.5,1

*Fence,Fence line ----x----x----x----
A,1.5,-0.25,["x",STANDARD,S=0.2,R=0.0,X=0.05,Y=-0.1],-0.4,1.5
```

See Figure 42-13 for a sample of the "Fence" linetype defined above. For more examples of simple and complex linetypes, use the DOS editor or the Windows Notepad to open the ACAD.LIN and LTYPE-SHP.LIN files. It is suggested that you make <u>new</u> files when you create your first linetypes rather than appending to the ACAD.LIN or the LTYPESHP.LIN files.

CUSTOMIZING THE ACAD.PGP FILE

The ACAD.PGP (AutoCAD Program Parameter) file is an ASCII text file that provides two main features. It provides a link between AutoCAD and other DOS programs by specifying what external programs can be accessed from within AutoCAD, and it defines command aliases—the one- or two-letter shortcuts for commands. In short, the ACAD.PGP file defines what commands can be typed at the AutoCAD Command: prompt that are not native to AutoCAD.

Because the ACAD.PGP file is an ASCII file, you can edit the file to add your own command aliases and to define which external commands you want to use from within AutoCAD. Use any text editor, such as DOS EDIT, to view and modify the file. The AutoCAD Release 13 ACAD.PGP file follows:

```
; acad.pgp - External Command and Command Alias definitions
; External Command format:
;     <Command name>,[<DOS request>],<Memory
reserve>,[*]<Prompt>,<Return code>

; Examples of External Commands for DOS

CATALOG,DIR /W,0,File specification: ,0
DEL,DEL,         0,File to delete: ,4
DIR,DIR,         0,File specification: ,0
EDIT,EDIT,       0,File to edit: ,4
SH,,             0,*OS Command: ,4
SHELL,,          0,*OS Command: ,4
TYPE,TYPE,       0,File to list: ,0

; Command alias format:
;     <Alias>,*<Full command name>

; Sample aliases for AutoCAD Commands
; These examples reflect the most frequently used commands.
; Each alias uses a small amount of memory, so don't go
; overboard on systems with tight memory.

A,        *ARC
C,        *CIRCLE
CP,       *COPY
DV,       *DVIEW
E,        *ERASE
L,        *LINE
LA,       *LAYER
LT,       *LINETYPE
M,        *MOVE
MS,       *MSPACE
P,        *PAN
PS,       *PSPACE
PL,       *PLINE
R,        *REDRAW
T,        *MTEXT
Z,        *ZOOM


3DLINE, *LINE

; Give Windows an AV command like DOS has
AV,       *DSVIEWER
; Menu says "Exit", so make an alias
EXIT,     *QUIT

; easy access to _PKSER (serial number) system variable
SERIAL, *_PKSER
```

```
; Dimensioning Commands.
DIMALI,  *DIMALIGNED
DIMANG,  *DIMANGULAR
DIMBASE,*DIMBASELINE
DIMCONT,*DIMCONTINUE
DIMDIA,  *DIMDIAMETER
DIMED,   *DIMEDIT
DIMTED,  *DIMTEDIT
DIMLIN,  *DIMLINEAR
DIMORD,  *DIMORDINATE
DIMRAD,  *DIMRADIUS
DIMSTY,  *DIMSTYLE
DIMOVER, *DIMOVERRIDE
LEAD,    *LEADER
TOL,     *TOLERANCE
```

The top section of the file (first 10 lines) specifies the external commands that can be used from within AutoCAD. The rest of the file defines the command aliases that can be used in AutoCAD.

Specifying External Commands

The External Commands section of the ACAD.PGP file determines what DOS commands or other programs can be accessed from within AutoCAD by typing the command at the AutoCAD Command: prompt. This is an important feature for users of AutoCAD on the DOS platform. However, the built-in multi-tasking capabilities of Microsoft Windows make this feature less significant for Windows users. This feature is extremely useful for increasing the DOS user's productivity.

By examining this section of the file, you can see that the following DOS commands are already usable from within AutoCAD.

```
CATALOG,DIR /W,0,File specification: ,0
DEL,DEL,      0,File to delete: ,4
DIR,DIR,      0,File specification: ,0
EDIT,EDIT,    0,File to edit: ,4
SH,,          0,*OS Command: ,4
SHELL,,       0,*OS Command: ,4
TYPE,TYPE,    0,File to list: ,0
```

For example, type DIR from the Command: prompt to list the contents of the current directory. Also note the *Shell* command is defined here (see Chapter 2 for information on using *Shell*).

Note that EDIT, the Microsoft DOS text editor, can be activated by typing EDIT at the command line. In this case, EDIT appears while AutoCAD runs "in the background," similar to the action of using *Mtext* in AutoCAD for DOS. This in itself makes customizing ACAD.PGP possible from within AutoCAD.

NOTE: If you edit ACAD.PGP while AutoCAD is running, use the *Reinit* command after editing to reinitialize ACAD.PGP to make the new changes usable (see Chapter 30 for information on *Reinit*).

If you use another text editor—Norton Editor, for example—you can change the ACAD.PGP file to allow "NE" to be typed at the command prompt. Do this by changing this:

```
EDIT,EDIT,     0,File to edit: ,4
```

to this:

```
    NE,NE,              0,File to edit: ,4
```

Ensure you follow the format guidelines specified in the first line of the section:

```
; External Command format:
;    <Command name>,[<DOS request>],<Memory reserve>,[*]<Prompt>,
<Return code>
```

You should also use spaces (press the space bar) instead of tabs in the ACAD.PGP file.

Defining Command Aliases

Autodesk provides only 16 command aliases for the draw and editing commands, in addition to many dimensioning commands. You can add more aliases, delete the defined aliases that you don't use, or alter the aliases that AutoCAD provides. The draw and edit command aliases defined are:

```
    A,        *ARC
    C,        *CIRCLE
    CP,       *COPY
    DV,       *DVIEW
    E,        *ERASE
    L,        *LINE
    LA,       *LAYER
    LT,       *LINETYPE
    M,        *MOVE
    MS,       *MSPACE
    P,        *PAN
    PS,       *PSPACE
    PL,       *PLINE
    R,        *REDRAW
    T,        *MTEXT
    Z,        *ZOOM
```

You probably use some other commands often, and creating an alias for them could increase your productivity. For example, TR may be defined for the *Trim* command, EX for *Extend*, and LN for *Lengthen*. To do this, follow the format specified at the beginning of the aliases section (give the alias and a comma, space over, and then give the AutoCAD command prefaced by an asterisk). Your new aliases would appear like this in the list:

```
    TR,       *TRIM
    EX,       *EXTEND
    LN,       *LENGTHEN
```

You may want to modify some of the defined aliases. For example, you could change the alias C to mean *Copy* rather than *Circle*. An alternative to *Circle* could be CI.

You can make comments anywhere in the ACAD.PGP by typing a semicolon (;) at the beginning of the line. This is helpful for making note of the changes that you have made.

One last suggestion: make a copy of the ACAD.PGP on diskette or in another directory before you begin experimenting, just in case.

CREATING SCRIPT FILES

A script file is an ASCII text file that contains a series of AutoCAD commands to be performed in succession. A script file is an external file that you create with a text editor and assign an .SCR extension. The script file is composed of commands in the sequence that you would normally use just as if you entered the commands at the AutoCAD command prompt. The *Script* command is used to tell AutoCAD to run the specified script file. When AutoCAD "runs" a script file, each command in the file is executed in the order that it is listed.

Script files have many uses, such as presenting a slide show, creating drawing geometry, or invoking a series of AutoCAD commands you use often—like a "macro." Script files are commonly used for repetitive tasks such as setting up a drawing. In fact, script "macros" may be incorporated directly into a menu file, thereby eliminating the need for an external .SCR file. However, in this chapter, only independent script files are addressed.

Chapter 30 discusses the *Script* command and the steps for creating scripts to present slide shows. A script for viewing slides uses the *Vslide* and *Delay* commands repetitively. If you are not familiar with the procedure for creating and running a script for this fundamental application, please review Using Slides and Scripts in Chapter 30.

Scripts for Drawing Setups

As you become familiar with AutoCAD, you realize there are several steps which are repeated each time you set up a new drawing. For example, several commands are used and variables are set to prepare the drawing for geometry construction and for eventual plotting. Drawing setup is a good candidate for script application. Script files can be created to perform those repetitive drawing setup steps for you. Although an interactive LISP routine would provide a more efficient and powerful method for this task, creating a script is relatively simple and does not require much knowledge or effort beyond that of the AutoCAD commands that would typically be used. Keep in mind that prototype drawings that have many of the initial settings can be used as an alternative to creating a script for drawing setup. However, one advantage of a script (in general) is that it can be executed in any drawing and at any time during the drawing process.

For example, assume that you often set up drawings for plotting at a 1/4" = 1'-0" scale on a 24" x 36" sheet of paper. This involves setting *Limits, Grid, Snap, LTSCALE, DIMSCALE,* and *Scaling* an existing title block and border. Instead of executing each of these operations each time "manually," create a script to automate the process. Here are the steps.

1. Open your text editor from within AutoCAD or before starting AutoCAD. Creating scripts while AutoCAD is running is the most efficient method for writing and "debugging" scripts. In AutoCAD for DOS, use EDIT (or other text editor specified in the ACAD.PGP) to open your text editor. If you are using AutoCAD for Windows, press Alt+Tab to access the Program Manager and activate Notepad. Alternately, use *Shell* to shell out of AutoCAD and run your text editor.

2. Create the ASCII text file with the commands that you would normally use for setting up the drawing. Remember (from Chapter 30) that a space or a new line in the script is read as a Return (pressing the Enter key) while the script executes in AutoCAD. The script file may be written like this:

```
LIMITS 0,0 1728,1152
GRID 48
SNAP 12
LTSCALE 48
SCALE ALL  0,0 48
DIMSCALE 48
DIMSTYLE SAVE STANDARD Y
```

3. Save the file with an .SCR extension. A good name for this file is SETUP48.SCR. Consider locating the file in a directory in the AutoCAD environment (such as in the ACADR13\COMMON\SUPPORT directory) or in a location with other scripts.

4. Return to AutoCAD and use the *Script* command to test the script. Don't expect the script to operate the first time if this is your first experience writing scripts. It is common to have "bugs" in the script. For example, an extra space in the file can cause the script to get out of the intended sequence. An extra space in the script is hard to locate (since it is not visible), particularly using DOS EDIT. A good text editor allows the cursor to move only to places occupied by a character (including a space) and should be used for script writing.

Examining the commands in SETUP48.SCR, first, set the *Limits* using inch values. *Scale All* is used to scale the existing border and title block. The "DIMSTYLE SAVE STANDARD Y" line saves the *DIMSCALE* setting to the STANDARD dimension style. (If a dimension style other than STANDARD exists, the new *DIMSCALE* setting should be incorporated also into these dimension styles.) Keep in mind that scripts operate as if the commands were entered at the command prompt, not as you might operate using dialogue boxes.

Many other possibilities exist for drawing setup scripts. For example, you could set *Units* (command) and the *DIMUNITS* variable. You may want to create a script for each plot scale and sheet size. It depends on your particular applications, hence the term "customization."

Possible applications for scripts are numerous. In addition to drawing setups, scripts can be used for geometry creation. It is possible to write scripts to create particular geometry "in real time" as the script executes. For example, repetitively drawn shapes could be created by scripts as an alternative to inserting *Blocks*. This idea is not generally used, but it may have advantages for certain applications. There are endless possibilities for script applications. Generally, anytime you find yourself performing the same tasks or series of commands repetitively, remember that a script can automate that process.

Special Script Commands

Creating scripts is a very straightforward procedure because the script file contains the AutoCAD commands that you would normally use at the command prompt for the particular operation. There are a few commands that are intended for use specifically with scripts and other commands that can be used as an aid to create or run script files. Those commands are listed next. Many of these commands are discussed in detail in Using Slides and Scripts, Chapter 30.

SCRIPT   Use this command in AutoCAD to instruct AutoCAD to load and execute a script. The *Select Script File* dialogue box appears, prompting you for the desired script file (see Chapter 30).

DELAY   Include this command in a script file to force a delay (specified in milliseconds) until the next command in the script is executed. *Delay* is commonly used in script files that display slide shows (see Chapter 30).

RSCRIPT   *Rscript* is short for "Repeat script." This command can be entered as the last line of a script file to make the script repeat until interrupted. *Rscript* is helpful for self-running slide shows (see Chapter 30).

RESUME   If you want to interrupt a script with the Break or backspace key, type *Resume* to resume the script from the point at which it was interrupted. This command has no purpose in the script file itself, but is intended to be typed at the keyboard (see Chapter 30).

LOGFILEON/   These commands are used to turn on and off the log file creation utility in
LOGFILEOFF   AutoCAD. When *Logfileon* is used, the conversation that appears at the command prompt (command history) is written to an external text file until *Logfileoff* is used (explained next in this chapter).

LOGFILEON/LOGFILEOFF

DOS PULL-DOWN	WIN PULL-DOWN	SCREEN MENU	TYPE IN	TABLET MENU
---	*Options* *Preferences...* *Environment* *Log File*	---	*LOGFILEON* *LOGFILEOFF*	---

Logfileon and *Logfileoff* are used to turn on and off the creation of the AutoCAD log file. The log file is a text file that contains the command history—the text that appears at the command line. When *Logfileon* is invoked, nothing appears to happen; however, any commands, prompts, or other text that appear at the command prompt from that time on are copied and written to the AutoCAD log file. Use *Logfileoff* to close the log file and discontinue recording the command history.

If the log file is on, AutoCAD continues to write to the log file, and each AutoCAD session in the log is separated by a dashed line. If you turn *Logfileoff* and *Logfileon* again, the new session is appended to the existing file. The default log file name is ACAD.LOG. The name and path of the file can be changed in the AutoCAD for Windows *Preferences* dialogue box.

The ACAD.LOG file is an ASCII text file that can be edited. The file has no direct link to AutoCAD and can be deleted without consequence to AutoCAD operation. The log file cannot be accessed externally until *Logfileoff* is used or AutoCAD is exited.

A sample log file is shown here:

```
[ AutoCAD - Sun Sep 10 16:32:56 1995 ]————————————————————

Command: _line From point:
To point:
To point:
To point:
Command: _circle 3P/2P/TTR/<Center point>: Diameter/<Radius>:
Command: _copy
Select objects: 1 found
Select objects: 1 found
Select objects: 1 found
Select objects:
<Base point or displacement>/Multiple: Second point of displacement:
Command: _trim
Select cutting edges: (Projmode = UCS, Edgemode = No extend)
Select objects: 1 found
```

```
Select objects: 1 found
Select objects:
<Select object to trim>/Project/Edge/Undo:
<Select object to trim>/Project/Edge/Undo:
<Select object to trim>/Project/Edge/Undo:
Command: _qsave Current drawing name set to C:\DWGS\TESTLOG.
Command: logfileoff
```

The log file is especially helpful when you are writing scripts. When you create a script file, the commands and options listed in the file must be typed in the exact sequence that would occur if you were actually using AutoCAD. In order to write the script correctly, you have three choices: (1) remember every command and prompt exactly as it would occur in AutoCAD; (2) go through a "dry run" in AutoCAD and write down every step; (3) turn *Logfileon*; then execute a "dry run" to have all the steps and resulting text recorded.

In other words, turn *Logfileon* to create a rough script file. Then turn *Logfileoff*, open the ACAD.LOG, and edit out the AutoCAD prompts such as "Command:" and "Select objects:," etc. Finally, save the file to the desired name with an .SCR extension.

CUSTOMIZING MENU FILES

One of the special features in AutoCAD is the ability to customize the menu system. Autodesk enables you to change the menu system by providing the primary menu, ACAD.MNU, as an ASCII text file. You can use a word processor or text editor to change the entries in the ACAD.MNU file to include your own combinations of commands, command options, and system variable settings. The menu file is organized in sections; each section controls a separate function, such as the pointing device buttons, the pull-down menus, the screen menu, the digitizing tablet menu, and the toolbars.

The ability to modify the existing menu file and to create new menu files gives you a surprising amount of power to control the way AutoCAD operates. However, customizing the menus requires knowledge of the menu organization and special codes (characters) that are understood by AutoCAD for performing specific tasks. Although specific knowledge is required for customizing the AutoCAD menus, it is easy to begin learning menu operation by making small changes to the existing menus or creating simple menus "from scratch."

Customizing dialogue boxes is generally considered a separate topic because dialogue box design uses DCL (Dialogue Control Language) and dialogue box operation utilizes AutoLISP.

Because of the relative complexity of menu customization and the amount of material required to discuss menu customization completely, this topic is not included in this text. Refer to Chapter 5 of the AutoCAD Customization Guide, Custom Menus, for more information on this powerful AutoCAD feature.

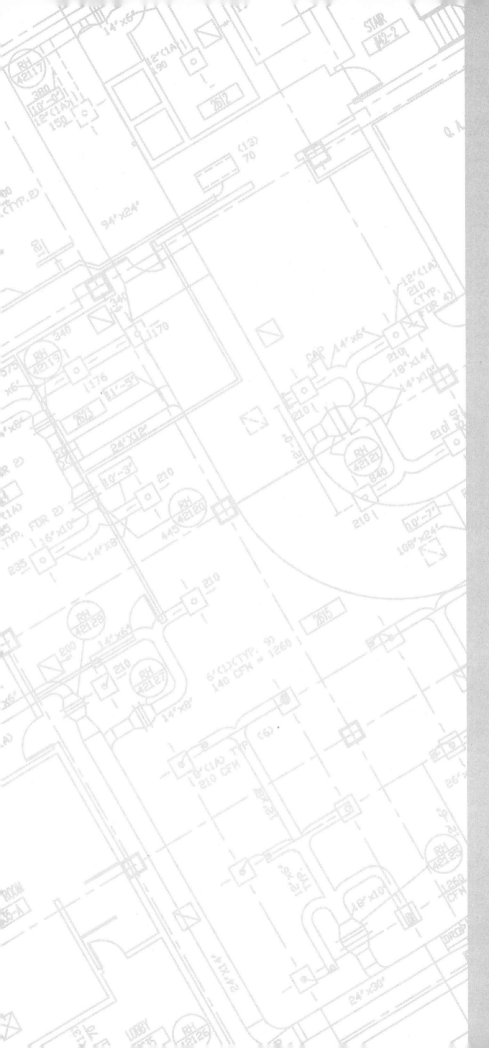

Appendices
CONTENTS

SYSTEM VARIABLES

This complete list of AutoCAD system variables is reprinted from the AutoCAD Command Reference for Release 13. These variables can be examined and changed (unless they are read-only) at the Command: prompt by typing the variable name or by using the *Setvar* command. Most of the system variables are saved in the drawing itself, while others are saved in the AutoCAD general configuration file, ACAD.CFG.

Variable name	Type	Saved in	Initial Value	Meaning
ACADPREFIX	String		-	The directory path, if any, specified by the ACAD environment variable with path separators appended if necessary (read-only).
ACADVER	String		-	This is the AutoCAD version number, which can have values like "12" or "12a" (read-only). Note that this differs from the DXF file $ACADVER header variable, which contains the drawing database level number.
AFLAGS	Integer		0	Attribute flags bit-code for ATTDEF command (sum of the following): 0 = No Attribute mode selected 1 = Invisible 2 = Constant 4 = Verify 8 = Preset
ANGBASE	Real	Drawing	0.0000	Angle 0 direction (with respect to the current UCS).
ANGDIR	Integer	Drawing	0	1 = clockwise angles, 0 = counterclockwise (with respect to the current UCS).
APERTURE	Integer	Config	10	Object snap target height, in pixels (default value = 10).
AREA	Real		-	Last area computed by AREA, LIST, or DBLIST (read-only).
ATTDIA	Integer	Drawing	0	1 causes the Insert command to use a dialogue box for entry of Attribute values; 0 to issue prompts.
ATTMODE	Integer	Drawing	1	Attribute display mode (0 = off, 1 = normal, 2 = on).
ATTREQ	Integer	Drawing	1	0 assumes defaults for the values of all Attributes during Insert of Blocks; 1 enables prompts (or dialogue box) for Attribute values, as selected by ATTDIA.
AUDITCTL	Integer	Config	1	Controls whether an .adt log file (audit report file) is created: 0 = Disables (or prevents) the writing of .adt log files 1 = Enables the writing of .adt log files by the AUDIT Zcommand.

Variable name	Type	Saved in	Initial Value	Meaning
AUNITS	Integer	Drawing	0	Angular units mode (0 = decimal degrees, 1 = degrees/minutes/seconds, 2 = grads, 3 = radians, 4 = surveyor's units).
AUPREC	Integer	Drawing	0	Angular units decimal places.
BACKZ	Real	Drawing	-	Back clipping plane offset from the target plane for the current viewport, in drawing units. Meaningful only if the Back clipping bit in VIEWMODE is on. The distance of the back clipping plane from the camera point can be found by subtracting BACKZ from the camera-to-target distance (read-only).
BLIPMODE	Integer	Drawing	1	Marker blips on if 1, off if 0.
CDATE	Real		-	Calendar date/time (read-only) (special format).
CECOLOR	String	Drawing	BYLAYER	Sets the color for new entities.
CELTSCALE	Real	Drawing	1.0000	Sets the current global linetype scale for objects.
CELTYPE	String	Drawing	BYLAYER	Sets the linetype for new entities.
CHAMFERA	Real	Drawing	0.0000	Sets the first chamfer distance.
CHAMFERB	Real	Drawing	0.0000	Sets the second chamfer distance.
CHAMFERC	Real	Drawing	0.0000	Sets the chamfer length.
CHAMFERD	Real	Drawing	0.0000	Sets the chamfer angle.
CHAMMODE	Integer	Not saved	0	Sets the input method by which AutoCAD creates chamfers. 0 = Requires two chamfer distances. 1 = Requires one chamfer length and an angle.
CIRCLERAD	Real		0.0000	Sets the default circle radius. To specify no default, enter 0 (zero).
CLAYER	String	Drawing	0	Sets the current layer.
CMDACTIVE	Integer			Bit-code that indicates whether an ordinary command, transparent command, script, or dialogue box is active (read-only). It is the sum of the following: 1 = Ordinary command is active 2 = Ordinary command and a transparent command are active 4 = Script is active 8 = Dialogue box is active
CMDDIA	Integer	Config	1	1 = Use dialogue boxes for PLOT command. 0 = Don't use dialogue boxes for PLOT command.

R13

R13

R13

Variable name	Type	Saved in	Initial Value	Meaning
CMDECHO	Integer		1	When the AutoLISP (command) function is used, prompts and input are echoed if this variable is 1, but not if it is 0.
CMDNAMES	String		-	Displays in English the name of the command (and transparent command) that is currently active. For example: LINE'ZOOM indicates that the ZOOM command is being used transparently during the LINE command
CMLJUST	Integer	Config	0	Specifies multiline justification. 0 = Top 1 = Middle 2 = Bottom
CMLSCALE	Real	Config	1.0000	Controls the overall width of a multiline. A scale factor of 2.0 produces a multiline that is twice as wide as the style definition. A zero scale factor collapses the multiline into a single line. A negative scale factor flips the order of the offset lines (that is, the smallest or most negative is placed on top when the multiline is drawn from left to right).
CMLSTYLE	String	Config	""	Sets the name of the multiline style that AutoCAD uses to draw the multiline.
COORDS	Integer	Drawing	1	If 0, coordinate display is updated on point picks only. If 1, display of absolute coordinates is continuously updated. If 2, distance and angle from last point are displayed when a distance or angle is requested.
CVPORT	Integer	Drawing	2	The identification number of the current viewport.
DATE	Real		-	Julian date/time (read-only) (special format)
DBMOD	Integer		-	Bit-code that indicates the drawing modification status (read-only). It is the sum of the following: 1 = Entity database modified 2 = Symbol table modified 4 = Database variable modified 8 = Window modified 16 = View modified
DCTCUST	String	Config	""	Displays the current custom spelling dictionary path and file name.

R13

Variable name	Type	Saved in	Initial Value	Meaning
DCTMAIN	String	Config	""	Displays the current main spelling dictionary file name. The full path is not shown because this file is expected to reside in the *\support* directory. You can specify a default main spelling dictionary using the SETVAR command. Contact Autodesk for available dictionaries.
DELOBJ	Integer	Drawing	1	Controls whether objects used to create other objects are retained or deleted from the drawing database. 0 Objects are deleted. 1 Objects are retained.
DIASTAT	Integer		-	Dialogue box exit status. If 0, the most recent dialogue box was exited via "CANCEL." If 1, the most recent dialogue box was exited via "OK" (read-only).
DIMxxx	Assorted	Drawing	-	All the dimensioning variables are also accessible as system variables. (See Ch. 29.)
DISPSILH	Integer	Drawing	0	Controls the display of silhouette curves of body objects in wireframe mode. 0 = Off 1 = On
DISTANCE	Real		-	Distance computed by DIST command (read-only)
DONUTID	Real		0.5000	Default donut inside diameter. Can be zero.
DONUTOD	Real		1.0000	Default donut outside diameter. Must be nonzero. If DONUTID is larger than DONUTOD, the two values are swapped by the next command.
DRAGMODE	Integer	Drawing	2	0 = no dragging, 1 = on if requested, 2 = auto
DRAGP1	Integer	Config	10	Regen-drag input sampling rate
DRAGP2	Integer	Config	25	Fast-drag input sampling rate
DWGCODEPAGE	String	Drawing	-	Drawing code page. This variable is set to the system code page when a new drawing is created, but, otherwise, AutoCAD doesn't maintain it. It should reflect the code page of the drawing, and you can set it to any of the values used by the SYSCODEPAGE system variable or "undefined." It is saved in the header.

Variable name	Type	Saved in	Initial Value	Meaning
DWGNAME	String		-	Drawing name as entered by the user. If the drawing hasn't been named yet, DWGNAME reports that it is "unnamed." If the user specified a drive/directory prefix, it is included as well (read-only).
DWGPREFIX	String		-	Drive/directory prefix for drawing (read-only).
DWGTITLED	Integer		-	Bit-code that indicates whether the current drawing has been named (read-only): 0 = The drawing hasn't been named. 1 = The drawing has been named.
DWGWRITE	Integer		1	Controls the initial state of the read-only toggle in the OPEN command's "Open Drawing" standard file dialogue box: 0 = Opens the drawing for reading only. 1 = Opens the drawing for reading and writing.
EDGEMODE	Integer	Not saved	0	Controls how the TRIM and EXTEND commands determine cutting and boundary edges. 0 = Uses the selected edge without an extension. 1 = Extends or trims the object to an imaginary extension of the cutting or boundary object.
ELEVATION	Real	Drawing	0.0000	Current 3D elevation, relative to the current UCS for the current space
EXPERT	Integer		0	Controls the issuance of certain "Are you sure?" prompts, as indicated next: 0 = Issues all prompts normally. 1 = Suppresses "About to regen, proceed?" and "Really want to turn the current layer off?" 2 = Suppresses the preceding prompts and BLOCK's "Block already defined. Redefine it?" and SAVE/WBLOCK's "A drawing with this name already exists. Overwrite it?" 3 = Suppresses the preceding prompts and those issued by LINETYPE if you try to load a linetype that's already loaded or create a new linetype in a file that already defines it. 4 = Suppresses the preceding prompts and those issued by "UCS SAVE" and "VPORTS Save" if the name you supply already exists. 5 = Suppresses the preceding prompts and those issued by "DIM SAVE" and "DIM OVERRIDE" if the dimension style name you supply already exists (the entries are redefined). When a prompt is suppressed

Variable name	Type	Saved in	Initial Value	Meaning
				by EXPERT, the operation in question is performed as though you had responded Y to the prompt. In the future, values greater than 5 may be used to suppress additional safety prompts. The setting of EXPERT can affect scripts, menu macros, AutoLISP, and the command functions.
EXPLMODE	Integer	Drawing	1	Controls whether the EXPLODE command supports non-uniformly scaled (NUS) blocks. 0 = Does not explode NUS blocks. 1 = Explodes NUS blocks.
EXTMAX	3D point	Drawing	-	Upper-right point of drawing extents. Expands outward as new objects are drawn; shrinks only by ZOOM All or ZOOM Extents. Reported in World coordinates for the current space (read-only).
EXTMIN	3D point	Drawing	-	Lower-left point of drawing extents. Expands outward as new objects are drawn; shrinks only by ZOOM All or ZOOM Extents. Reported in World coordinates for the current space (read-only).
FACETRES	Real	Drawing	0.5	Further adjusts the smoothness of shaded and hidden line-removed objects. Valid values are from 0.01 to 10.0.
FFLIMIT	Integer	Config	0	Limits the number of PostScript and TrueType fonts in memory. Valid values are from 0 to 100. If set to 0, there is no limit.
FILEDIA	Integer	Config	1	1 = Use file dialogue boxes, if possible. 0 = don't use file dialogue boxes unless requested via ~ (tilde).
FILLETRAD	Real	Drawing	0.0000	Fillet radius.
FILLMODE	Integer	Drawing	1	Fill mode on if 1, off if 0.
FONTALT	String	Config	""	Specifies the alternate font to be used when the specified font file cannot be located. If an alternate font is not specified, AutoCAD displays a warning.
FONTMAP	String	Config	""	Specifies the font mapping file to be used when the specified font cannot be located. A font mapping file contains one font mapping per line where the original font and the substitute font are separated by a semicolon (;). For example, to substitute romans with the Times TrueType font, you would have a line in your mapping file that reads: **romans;c:\windows\system\times.ttf**

R13

R13

R13

Variable name	Type	Saved in	Initial Value	Meaning
FRONTZ	Real	Drawing	-	Front clipping plane offset from the target plane for the current viewport, in drawing units. Meaningful only if the front clipping bit in VIEWMODE is On and the Front clip not at eye bit is also On. The distance of the front clipping plane from the camera point can be found by subtracting FRONTZ from the camera-to-target distance (read-only).
GRIDMODE	Integer	Drawing	0	1 = grid on for current viewport; 0 = grid off.
GRIDUNIT	2D point	Drawing	0.000, 0.0000	Grid spacing for current viewport, X and Y.
GRIPBLOCK	Integer	Config	0	Controls the assignment of grips in blocks: 0 = Assigns grip only to the insertion point of the block. 1 = Assigns grips to entities within the block.
GRIPCOLOR	Integer	Config	5	Color of nonselected grips; drawn as a box outline.
GRIPHOT	Integer (1-255)	Config	1	Color of selected grips; drawn as a filled box.
GRIPS	Integer	Config	1	Allows the use of selection set grips for the Stretch, Move, Rotate, Scale, and Mirror modes: 0 = Disables grips. 1 = Enables grips. To adjust the size of the grips, use the GRIPSIZE variable. To adjust the effective pick area used by the graphics cursor when you snap to a grip, use the GRIPSIZE system variable.
GRIPSIZE	Integer (1-255)	Config	3	The size in pixels of the box drawn to display the grip.
HANDLES	Integer	Drawing	-	If 0, entity handles are disabled. If 1, handles are on (read-only).
HIGHLIGHT	Integer		1	Object selection highlighting on if 1, off if 0. HIGHLIGHT does not affect objects selected with grips.
HPANG	Real		0.0000	Default hatch pattern angle.
HPBOUND	Real	Drawing	1	Controls the object type created by the BHATCH and BOUNDARY commands. 0 = Creates a polyline. 1 = Creates a region.
HPDOUBLE	Integer		0	Default hatch pattern doubling for "U" user-defined patterns: 0 = Disables doubling 1 = Enables doubling

Variable name	Type	Saved in	Initial Value	Meaning
HPNAME	String		""	Default hatch pattern name. Up to 34 characters, no spaces allowed. Returns "" if there is no default. Enter . (period) to set no default.
HPSCALE	Real		1.0000	Default hatch pattern scale factor. Must be nonzero.
HPSPACE	Real		1.0000	Default hatch pattern line spacing for "U" user-defined simple patterns. Must be nonzero.
INSBASE	3D point	Drawing	0,0,0	Insertion base point (set by BASE command) expressed in UCS coordinates for the current space.
INSNAME	String		""	Default block name for DDINSERT or INSERT. The name must conform to symbol naming conventions. Returns "" if there is no default. Enter . (period) to set no default.
ISOLINES	Integer	Drawing	4	Specifies the number of isolines per surface on objects. Valid integer values are from 0 to 2047.
LASTANGLE	Real		-	The end angle of the last arc entered, relative to the XY plane of the current UCS for the current space (read-only).
LASTPOINT	3D point		0,0,0	The last point entered, expressed in UCS coordinates for the current space. Referenced by @ during keyboard entry.
LENSLENGTH	Real	Drawing	-	Length of the lens (in millimeters) used in perspective viewing, for the current viewport (read-only).
LIMCHECK	Integer	Drawing	0	Limits checking for the current space. On if 1, off if 0.
LIMMAX	2D point	Drawing	12.0000, 9.0000	Upper-right drawing limits for the current space, expressed in World coordinates
LIMMIN	2D point	Drawing	0.0000, 0.0000	Lower-left drawing limits for the current space, expressed in World coordinates
LOCALE	String	Not saved	"en"	Displays the ISO language code of the current AutoCAD version you're running (read-only).
LOGINNAME	String		-	Displays the user's name as configured or input when AutoCAD is loaded (read-only).
LTSCALE	Real	Drawing	1.0000	Global linetype scale factor.

R13

R13

Variable name	Type	Saved in	Initial Value	Meaning
LUNITS	Integer	Drawing	2	Linear units mode (1 = scientific, 2 = decimal, 3 = engineering, 4 = architectural, 5 = fractional).
LUPREC	Integer	Drawing	4	Linear units decimal places or denominator
MAXACTVP	Integer		16	Maximum number of viewports to regenerate at one time
MAXSORT	Integer	Config	200	Maximum number of symbol/file names to be sorted by listing commands. If the total number of items exceeds this number, then none of the items are sorted.
MENUCTL	Integer	Config	1	Controls the page switching of the screen menu: 0 = Screen menu doesn't switch pages in response to keyboard command entry. 1 = Screen menu switches pages in response to keyboard command entry.
MENUECHO	Integer		0	Menu echo/prompt control bits (sum of the following): 1 = Suppresses echo of menu items (^P in a menu item toggles echoing). 2 = Suppresses printing of system prompts during menu. 4 = Disables ^P toggle of menu echoing. 8 = Debugging aid for DIESEL macros. Prints input/output strings.
MENUNAME	String	Drawing	-	The name of the currently loaded menu file. Includes a drive/path prefix if you entered it (read-only).
MIRRTEXT	Integer	Drawing	1	MIRROR command reflects text if nonzero; retains text direction if 0.
MODEMACRO	String		""	Allows you to display a text string in the status line, such as the name of the current drawing, time/date stamp, or special modes. You can use MODEMACRO to display a simple string of text, or use special text strings written in the DIESEL macro language to have AutoCAD evaluate the macro from time to time and base the status line on user-selected conditions. See the *AutoCAD Customization Guide* for details.
MTEXTED	String	Config	""	Sets the name of the program to use for editing mtext objects.
OFFSETDIST	Real		-1.0000	Sets the default distance. If you enter a negative value, it defaults to Through mode.

Variable name	Type	Saved in	Initial Value	Meaning
ORTHOMODE	Integer	Drawing	0	Ortho mode on if 1, off if 0.
OSMODE	Integer	Drawing	0	Sets object snap modes using the following bit codes. To specify more than one osnap, enter the sum of their values. For example, entering 3 specifies the Endpoint (1) and Midpoint (2) osnaps. 0 = None 1 = Endpoint 2 = Midpoint 4 = Center 8 = Node 16 = Quadrant 32 = Intersection 64 = Insertion 128 = Perpendicular 256 = Tangent 512 = Nearest 1024 = Quick
PDMODE	Integer	Drawing	0	Point entity display mode.
PDSIZE	Real	Drawing	0.0000	Point entity display size.
PELLIPSE	Integer	Drawing	0	Controls the ellipse type created with ELLIPSE. 0 = Creates a true ellipse object. 1 = Creates a polyline representation of an ellipse.
PERIMETER	Real		-	Perimeter computed by AREA, LIST, or DBLIST (read-only).
PFACEVMAX	Integer		-	Maximum number of vertices per face (read-only)
PICKADD	Integer	Config	1	Controls additive selection of entities: 0 = Disables PICKADD. The most recently selected entities, either by an individual pick or windowing, become the selection set. Previously selected entities are removed from the selection set. You can add more entities to the selection set, however, by holding down the Shift key while selecting. 1 = Enables PICKADD. Each entity you select, either individually or by windowing, is added to the current selection set. To remove entities from the selection set, hold down the Shift key while selecting.

R13

Variable name	Type	Saved in	Initial Value	Meaning
PICKAUTO	Integer	Config	1	Controls automatic windowing when the Select objects: prompt appears: 0 = Disables PICKAUTO. 1 = Allows you to draw a selection window (both window and crossing window) automatically at the Select objects: prompt.
PICKBOX	Integer	Config	3	Object selection target height, in pixels.
PICKDRAG	Integer	Config	0	Controls the method of drawing a selection window: 0 = You draw the selection window by clicking the mouse at one corner and then at the other corner. 1 = You draw the selection window by clicking at one corner, holding down the mouse button, dragging, and releasing the mouse button at the other corner.
PICKFIRST	Integer	Config	1	Controls the method of entity selection so that you can select objects first, and then use an edit/inquiry command: 0 = Disables PICKFIRST. 1 = Enables PICKFIRST.
PICKSTYLE	Integer	Drawing	3	Controls group selection and associative hatch selection. 0 = No group selection or associative hatch selection 1 = Group selection. 2 = Associative hatch selection. 3 = Group selection and associative hatch selection.
PLATFORM	String		-	Read-only message that indicates which version of AutoCAD is in use. This is a string such as one of the following: Microsoft Windows 386 DOS Extender Apple Macintosh Sun4/SPARCstation DECstation Silicon Graphics Iris Indigo
PLINEGEN	Integer	Drawing	0	Sets the linetype pattern generation around the vertices of a 2D Polyline. When set to 1, PLINEGEN causes the linetype to be generated in a continuous pattern around the vertices of the Polyline. When set to 0, Polylines are generated with the linetype to start and end with a dash at each vertex. PLINEGEN doesn't apply to Polylines with tapered segments.

R13

Variable name	Type	Saved in	Initial Value	Meaning
PLINEWID	Real	Drawing	0.0000	Default polyline width. It can be zero.
PLOTID	String	Config	""	Changes the default plotter, based on its assigned description.
PLOTROTMODE	Integer	Drawing	1	Controls the orientation of plots. 0 = Rotates the effective plotting area so that the corner with the Rotation icon aligns with the paper at the lower left for 0, top left for 90, top right for 180, and lower right for 270. 1 = Aligns the lower-left corner of the effective plotting area with the lower-left corner of the paper.
PLOTTER	Integer	Config	0	Changes the default plotter, based on its assigned integer (0-maximum configured). You can create up to 29 configurations.
POLYSIDES	Integer		4	Default number of sides for the POLYGON command. The range is 3-1024.
POPUPS	Integer		-	1 = if the currently configured display driver supports dialogue boxes, the menu bar, pull-down menus, and icon menus. 0 if these features are not available (read-only).
PROJMODE	Integer	Config	1	Sets the current Projection mode for Trim or Extend operations. 0 = True 3D mode (no projection). 1 = Project to the XY plane of the current UCS. 2 = Project to the current view plane.
PSLTSCALE	Integer	Drawing	1	Controls paper space linetype scaling: 0 = No special linetype scaling. 1 = Viewport scaling governs linetype scaling.
PSPROLOG	String	Config	""	Assigns a name for a prologue section to be read from the acad.psf file when using the PSOUT command. See the AutoCAD Customization Guide for details.
PSQUALITY	Integer	Config	75	Controls the rendering quality of PostScript images and whether they are drawn as filled objects or as outlines. A zero setting disables PostScript image generation, and a nonzero setting enables PostScript generation. Positive setting: Sets the number of pixels per AutoCAD drawing unit for the PostScript resolution. Negative setting: Still sets the number of pixels per drawing unit, but uses the absolute value. Causes AutoCAD to show the PostScript paths as outlines and doesn't fill them.

R13

R13

R13

Variable name	Type	Saved in	Initial Value	Meaning
QTEXTMODE	Integer	Drawing	0	Quick text mode on if 1, off if 0
RASTERPREVIEW	Integer	Drawing	0	Controls whether drawing preview images are saved with the drawing and sets the format type. 0 = BMP only 1 = BMP and WMF 2 = WMF only 3 = No preview image created
REGENMODE	Integer	Drawing	1	REGENAUTO on if 1, off if 0
RE-INIT	Integer		0	Reinitializes the I/O ports, digitizer, display, plotter, and *acad.pgp* file using the following bit codes. To specify more than one reinitialization, enter the sum of their values, for example, 3, to specify both digitizer port (1) and plotter port (2) reinitialization: 1 = Digitizer port reinitialization 2 = Plotter port reinitialization 4 = Digitizer reinitialization 8 = Display reinitialization 16 = PGP file reinitialization (reload)
RIASPECT	Real	Not saved	0.0000	Changes the image aspect ratio for imported raster images. GIF and TIFF images specify the pixel aspect ratio to prevent circles from displaying as ellipses when images are transported to differently shaped displays. The ratio stored in RIASPECT overrides any specification in the GIF and TIFF file you import. PCX files contain no aspect ratio. A useful RIASPECT setting is 0.8333, which is the ratio for importing VGA or MCGA images in 320 x 200 mode.
RIBACKG	Integer	Not saved	0	Specifies the background color number for imported raster images. Areas of the image equal to the background are not converted to solid objects in the block. If you have a different screen background, set RIBACKG to the AutoCAD color number corresponding to your screen background. For example, if you use a white screen background, specify **ribackg 7**. Use RIBACKG to reduce the size of the imported image by setting the background color as the color that makes up most of your raster image.

R13

Variable name	Type	Saved in	Initial Value	Meaning
RIEDGE	Integer	Not saved	0	Controls the edge detection feature: 0 = Disables edge detection. 1-255 = Sets the threshold for RIEDGE detection. GIFIN, PCXIN, and TIFFIN use the value for detecting features in the drawing. To trace over an imported raster image, use RIEDGE to locate the edges of the features of the image and include only these edges in the drawing. To import an image for viewing and not for tracing edges, set RIBACKG to 0. If you're importing an image for a monochrome display, use RIEDGE or the brightness threshold setting RITHRESH.
RIGAMUT	Integer	Not saved	256	Controls the number of colors GIFIN, PCXIN, and TIFFIN use when they import a color image. If you're using a display with less than 256 colors, setting RIGAMUT restricts the colors used by these commands. Common settings for RIGAMUT are 8 and 16.
RIGREY	Integer	Not saved	0	Imports an image as a gray-scale image: 0 = Disables gray-scale image importing. >0 = Converts each pixel in the image to a gray-scale value. Because AutoCAD has relatively few gray shades, importing an image using RIGREY reduces the size of the imported image in the drawing database while preserving essential details. Using the edge detection variable, RIEDGE achieves similar effects. The gray-scale value is based on the human eye response function defined for NTSC television (the YIQ color system).
RITHRESH	Integer	Not saved	0	Controls importing an image based on luminance (brightness): 0 = Turns off RITHRESH. >0 = Rasterin uses a brightness threshold filter, so only pixels with a luminance value greater than the RITHRESH value are included in the drawing. The default value is 0, which turns off the brightness threshold feature. If you have an image with a dark, "noisy" background and a light foreground, you can use RITHRESH to drop out the background and import just the brighter foreground material.

R13

Variable name	Type	Saved in	Initial Value	Meaning
SAVEFILE	String	Config	-	Current auto-save filename (read-only).
SAVENAME	String		-	The filename you save the drawing to (read-only).
SAVETIME	Integer	Config	120	Automatic save interval, in minutes (or 0 to disable automatic saves). The SAVETIME timer starts as soon as you make a change to a drawing and is reset and restarts by a manual SAVE, SAVEAS, or QSAVE. The current drawing is saved to *auto.sv$*.
SCREENBOXES	Integer	Config	-	The number of boxes in the screen menu area of the graphics area. If the screen menu is disabled (configured off), SCREENBOXES is zero. On platforms that permit the AutoCAD graphics window to be resized or the screen menu to be reconfigured during an editing session, the value of this variable might change during the editing session (read-only).
SCREENMODE	Integer	Config	-	A (read-only) bit code indicating the graphics/text state of the AutoCAD display. It is the sum of the following bit values: 0 = Text screen is displayed. 1 = Graphics mode is displayed. 2 = Dual-screen display configuration.
SCREENSIZE	2D point		-	Current viewport size in pixels, X and Y (read-only).
SHADEDGE	Integer	Drawing	3	0 = Faces shaded, edges not highlighted. 1 = Faces shaded, edges drawn in background color. 2 = Faces not filled, edges in entity color. 3 = Faces in entity color, edges in background color.
SHADEDIF	Integer	Drawing	70	Ratio of diffuse reflective light to ambient light (in percent of diffuse reflective light).
SHPNAME	String		""	Default shape name. Must conform to symbol naming conventions. If no default is set, it returns a "". Enter . (period) to set no default.
SKETCHINC	Real	Drawing	0.1000	SKETCH record increment.
SKPOLY	Integer	Drawing	0	SKETCH generates lines if 0, Polylines if 1.
SNAPANG	Real	Drawing	0	Snap/grid rotation angle (UCS-relative) for the current viewport.
SNAPBASE	2D point	Drawing	0.0000, 0.0000	Snap/grid origin point for the current viewport (in UCS X,Y coordinates).

Variable name	Type	Saved in	Initial Value	Meaning
SNAPISOPAIR	Integer	Drawing	0	Current isometric plane (0 = left, 1 = top, 2 = right) for the current viewport.
SNAPMODE	Integer	Drawing	0	1 = snap on for current viewport; 0 = snap off.
SNAPSTYL	Integer	Drawing	0	Snap style for current viewport (0 = standard, 1 = isometric).
SNAPUNIT	2D point	Drawing	1.0000, 1.0000	Snap spacing for current viewport, X and Y.
SORTENTS	Integer	Config	96	Controls the display of entity sort order operations using the following codes. To select more than one, enter the sum of their codes; for example, enter 3 to specify codes 1 and 2. The default, 96, specifies sort operations for plotting and PostScript output: 0 = Displays SORTENTS. 1 = Sort for object selection. 2 = Sort for object snap. 4 = Sort for redraws. 8 = Sort for MSLIDE slide creation. 16 = Sort for REGENs. 32 = Sort for plotting. 64 = Sort for PostScript output.
SLPFRAME	Integer	Drawing	0	If = 1: • The control polygon for spline fit Polylines is to be displayed. • Only the defining mesh of a surface fit polygon mesh is displayed (the fit surface is not displayed). • Invisible edges of 3D Faces are displayed If = 0: • Does not display the control polygon for spline fit Polylines. • Displays the fit surface of a polygon mesh, not the defining mesh. • Does not display the invisible edges of 3D Faces.
SPLINESEGS	Integer	Drawing	8	The number of line segments to be generated for each spline patch.
SPLINETYPE	Integer	Drawing	6	Type of spline curve to be generated by PEDIT Spline. The valid values are: 5 = quadratic B-spline 6 = cubic B-spline.
SURFTAB1	Integer	Drawing	6	Number of tabulations to be generated for RULESURF and TABSURF. Also mesh density in the M direction for REVSURF and EDGESURF.

Variable name	Type	Saved in	Initial Value	Meaning
SURFTAB2	Integer	Drawing	6	Mesh density in the N direction for REVSURF and EDGESURF.
SURFTYPE	Integer	Drawing	6	Type of surface fitting to be performed by PEDIT Smooth. The valid values are: 5 = Quadratic B-spline surface. 6 = Cubic B-spline surface. 8 = Bezier surface.
SURFU	Integer	Drawing	6	Surface density in the M direction
SURFV	Integer	Drawing	6	Surface density in the N direction
SYSCODEPAGE	String	Drawing	-	Indicates the system code page specified in *acad.xmf* (read-only). Codes are as follows: ascii dos932 dos437 iso8859-1 dos850 iso8859-2 dos852 iso8859-3 dos855 iso8859-4 dos857 iso8859-5 dos860 iso8859-6 dos861 iso8859-7 dos863 iso8859-8 dos864 iso8859-9 dos865 mac-roman dos869
TABMODE	Integer		0	Controls the use of tablet mode: 0 = Disables tablet mode. 1 = Enables tablet mode.
TARGET	3D point	Drawing	-	Location (in UCS coordinates) of the target (look-at) point for the current viewport (read-only).
TDCREATE	Real	Drawing	-	Time and date of drawing creation (read-only).
TDINDWG	Real	Drawing	-	Total editing time (read-only).
TDUPDATE	Real	Drawing	-	Time and date of last update/save (read-only).
TDSRTIMER	Real	Drawing	-	User elapsed timer (read-only).
TEMPPREFIX	String		-	This variable contains the directory name (if any) configured for placement of temporary files with a path separator appended, if necessary (read-only).

Variable name	Type	Saved in	Initial Value	Meaning
TEXTEVAL	Integer		0	If = 0, all responses to prompts for text strings and attribute values are taken literally. If = 1, text starting with "(" or "!" is evaluated as an AutoLISP expression, as for nontextual input. Note: The DTEXT command takes all input literally, regardless of the setting of TEXTEVAL.
TEXTFILL	Integer	Drawing	1	Controls the filling of Bitstream, TrueType, and Adobe Type 1 fonts. 0 = Displays text as outlines. 1 = Displays text as filled images.
TEXTQLTY	Real	Drawing	50	Sets the resolution of Bitstream, TrueType, and Adobe Type 1 fonts. Lower values decrease resolution and increase display and plotting speed. Higher values increase resolution and decrease display and plotting speed. Valid values are 0 to 100.0.
TEXTSIZE	Real	Drawing	0.2000	The default height for new Text entities drawn with the current text style (meaningless if the style has a fixed height).
TEXTSTYLE	String	Drawing	Standard	Contains the name of the current text style.
THICKNESS	Real	Drawing	0.0000	Current 3D thickness.
TILEMODE	Integer	Drawing	1	1 = Release 10 compatibility mode (uses VPORTS). 0 = Enables paper space and Viewport entities (uses MVIEW).
TOOLTIPS	Integer	Config	1	Controls the display of ToolTips. (Windows only) 0 = Turns off display of ToolTips. 1 = Turns on display of ToolTips.
TRACEWID	Real	Drawing	0.0500	Default trace width.
TREEDEPTH	Integer	Drawing	3020	A 4-digit (maximum) code that specifies the number of times the tree-structured spatial index may divide into branches, hence affecting the speed in which AutoCAD searches the database before completing an action. The first two digits refer to the depth of the model space nodes, and the second two digits refer to the depth of paper space nodes. Use a positive setting for 3D drawings and a negative setting for 2D drawings.

R13

R13

R13

Variable name	Type	Saved in	Initial Value	Meaning
TREEMAX	Integer	Config	10000000	Limits memory consumption during drawing regeneration by limiting the maximum number of nodes in the spatial index (oct-tree). The value for TREEMAX is stored in the AutoCAD configuration file. By imposing a fixed limit with TREEMAX, you can load drawings created on systems with more memory than your system and with a larger TREEDEPTH than your system can handle. These drawings, if left unchecked, have an oct-tree large enough to eventually consume more memory than is available to your computer. TREEMAX also provides a safeguard against experimentation with inappropriately high TREEDEPTH values.
TRIMMODE	Integer	Not saved	1	Controls whether AutoCAD trims selected edges for chamfers and fillets. 0 = Leaves selected edges intact. 1 = Trims selected edges to the endpoints of chamfer lines and fillet arcs.
UCSFOLLOW	Integer	Drawing	0	If = 1, any UCS change causes an automatic change to plan view of the new UCS (in the current viewport). If = 0, a UCS change doesn't affect the view. The setting of UCSFOLLOW is maintained separately for both spaces and can be accessed in either space, but the setting is ignored while in paper space (it is always treated as if set to 0).
UCSICON	Integer	Drawing	1	The coordinate system icon bit-code for the current viewport (sum of the following): 1 = On—icon display enabled 2 = Origin—if icon display is enabled, the icon floats to the UCS origin if possible
UCSNAME	String	Drawing	-	Name of the current coordinate system for the current space. Returns a null string if the current UCS is unnamed (read-only).
UCSORG	3D point	Drawing	-	The origin point of the current coordinate system for the current space. This value is always returned in World coordinates (read-only).
UCSXDIR	3D point	Drawing	-	The X-direction of the current UCS for the current space (read-only).
UCSYDIR	3D point	Drawing	-	The Y-direction of the current UCS for the current space (read-only).

Variable name	Type	Saved in	Initial Value	Meaning
UNDOCTL	Integer		-	A (read-only) code indicating the state of the UNDO feature. It is the sum of the following values: 1 = Set if UNDO is enabled. 2 = Set if only one command can be undone. 4 = Set if Auto-group mode is enabled. 8 = Set if a group is currently active.
UNDOMARKS	Integer		-	The (read-only) number of marks that have been placed in the UNDO control stream by the UNDO command's Mark option. The Mark and Back options are unavailable if a group is currently active.
UNITMODE	Integer	Drawing	0	0 = Displays fractional, feet and inches, and surveyor's angles as previously set. 1 = Displays fractional, feet and inches, and surveyor's angles in input format.
VIEWCTR	2D point	Drawing	-	Center of view in current viewport, expressed in UCS coordinates (read-only).
VIEWDIR	3D vector	Drawing	-	The current viewport's viewing direction expressed in UCS coordinates. This describes the camera point as a 3D offset from the TARGET point (read-only).
VIEWMODE	Integer	Drawing	-	Viewing mode bit-code for the current viewport (read-only). The value is the sum of the following: 1 = Perspective view active. 2 = Front clipping on. 4 = Back clipping on. 8 = UCS follow mode on. 16 = Front clip not at eye. If On, the front clip distance (FRONTZ) determines the front clipping plane. If Off, FRONTZ is ignored and the front clipping plane is set to pass through the camera point (i.e., vectors behind the camera are not displayed). This flag is ignored if the front clipping bit (2) is off.
VIEWSIZE	Real	Drawing	-	Height of view in current viewport, expressed in drawing units (read-only).
VIEWTWIST	Real	Drawing	-	View twist angle for the current viewport (read-only).

Variable name	Type	Saved in	Initial Value	Meaning
VISRETAIN	Integer	Drawing	0	If = 0, the current drawing's On/Off, Freeze/Thaw, color, and linetype settings for Xref-dependent layers take precedence over the layer settings in the Xref drawing. If = 1, On/Off, Freeze/Thaw, color, and linetype settings in the Xref drawing take precedence over the xref layer definition in the current drawing.
VSMAX	3D point		-	The upper-right corner of the current viewport's virtual screen, expressed in UCS coordinates (read-only).
VSMIN	3D point		-	The lower-left corner of the current viewport's virtual screen, expressed in UCS coordinates (read-only).
WORLDUCS	Integer		-	If = 1, the current UCS is the same as the World Coordinate System. If = 0, it is not (read-only).
WORLDVIEW	Integer	Drawing	1	DVIEW and VPOINT command input is relative to the current UCS. If this variable is set to 1, the current UCS is changed to the WCS for the duration of a DVIEW or VPOINT command.
XREFCTL	Integer	Config	0	Controls whether .*xlg* files (external reference log files) are written: 0 = Xref log (.*xlg*) files not written. 1 = Xref log (.*xlg*) files written.

CAD References for *Engineering Graphics Communication*, Bertoline, et al.

NA=Not Applicable—capabilities not provided in AutoCAD or not discussed.

CAD References for *Technical Graphics Communication*, Bertoline, et al.

NA=Not Applicable—capabilities not provided in
AutoCAD or not discussed.

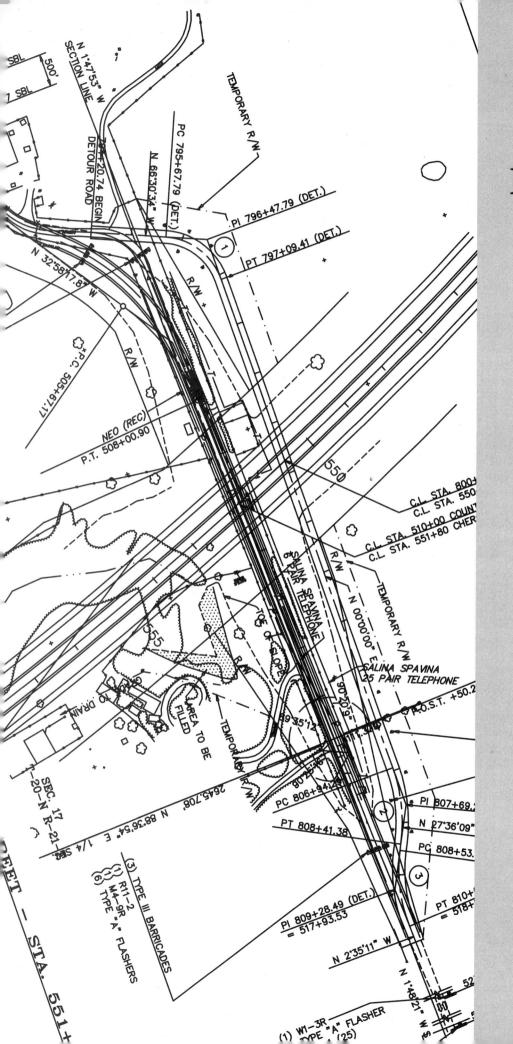

Index